the Developing Child

twelfth edition

Helen Bee

•

Denise Boyd

Houston Community College

Allyn & Bacon

Boston   New York   San Francisco
Mexico City   Montreal   Toronto   London   Madrid   Munich   Paris
Hong Kong   Singapore   Tokyo   Cape Town   Sydney

This book is dedicated to my two favorite growing children,
Mackenzie and Madeleine.

Senior Acquisitions Editor:	Stephen Frail
Series Editorial Assistant:	Kat Motter
Senior Developmental Editor:	Christina Lembo
Marketing Manager:	Brandy Dawson
Production Editor:	Patrick Cash-Peterson
Editorial Production Service:	Lifland et al., Bookmakers
Manufacturing Buyer:	JoAnne Sweeney
Electronic Composition:	Modern Graphics, Inc.
Interior Design:	Glenna Collett, Jean Hammond, and Joyce Weston
Photo Researcher:	Sarah Evertson
Cover Designer:	Kristina Mose-Libon

Library of Congress Cataloging-in-Publication Data

Bee, Helen L.,
    The developing child / Helen Bee, Denise Boyd. — 12th ed.
       p. cm.
    ISBN 978-0-205-68593-6
    1. Child psychology—Textbooks. 2. Child development—Textbooks. I. Boyd, Denise Roberts. II. Title.

    BF721.B336 2010
    155.4—dc22

2008052504

10 9 8 7 6 5 4 3 2 1 Q-WC-V 13 12 11 10 09

Allyn & Bacon
is an imprint of

www.pearsonhighered.com

ISBN-10: 0-205-68593-5

ISBN-13: 978-0-205-68593-6

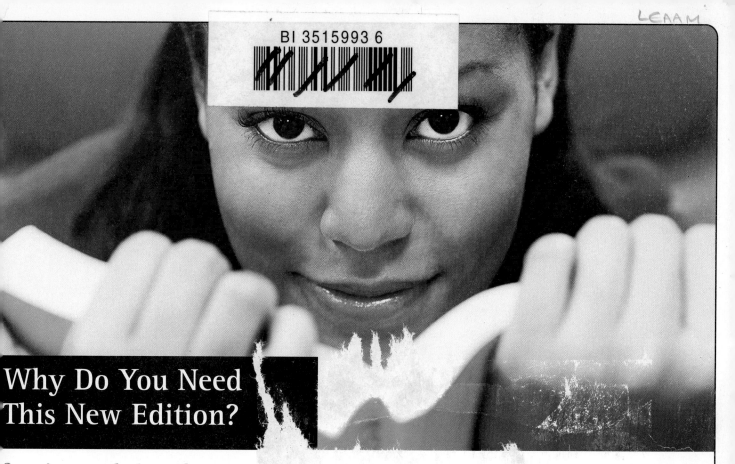

Why Do You Need This New Edition?

If you're wondering why you should buy this new edition of *The Developing Child,* here are 4 good reasons!

1 A new learning system helps you ORGANIZE and RETAIN chapter material as you read. Each chapter is structured around *numbered Learning Objectives,* which clearly identify the key concepts covered in each section and help you organize and retain the material as you proceed through the chapter. You'll find these Learning Objectives in an outline on the first page of each chapter, in the margins next to each sub-heading, and in the Summary section at the end of each chapter so you can structure your review.

2 PRACTICE TESTS in MYDEVELOPMENTLAB (www.mydevelopmentlab.com) help you prepare for exams. Go online to test your knowledge of chapter content and to obtain an individually tailored study plan identifying which concepts you've mastered and which need a more thorough review.

3 Chapter-opening vignettes and boxes include a number of NEW TOPICS that relate text material to real people and real situations. *Topics that are new to this edition* include semi-identical twins, a water-skiing toddler, the Lost Boys of Sudan, pediatric bipolar disorder, suggested ways to help children who are afraid to go to school, and possible solutions for parents who can't get their children to go to bed at night.

4 An UPDATED VISUAL PROGRAM helps to make concepts and theories more approachable and understandable. The text's photos, tables, and figures, a number of which are *new or revised in this edition,* illustrate key concepts in clear, accessible ways. Also, new videos and simulations, including MyVirtualChild, are available within MyDevelopmentLab to further enhance and reinforce your learning experience.

PEARSON
Longman

Brief Contents

Contents

Part 4   **The Thinking Child**

Chapter 8   The Development of Language   203

Features

To the Student

Hello, and welcome to the study of a fascinating subject—children and their development. Welcome, too, to the adventure of science. From the very first edition of this book, one of Helen Bee's goals has been to convey a sense of excitement about scientific inquiry. We hope that each of you gains some feeling for the way psychologists think, the kinds of questions they ask, and the ways they go about trying to answer those questions. We also want you to gain some sense of the theoretical and intellectual ferment that is part of any science. Think of psychology as a kind of detective story: Psychologists discover clues after hard, often painstaking work; they make guesses or hypotheses; and then they search for new clues to check on those hypotheses.

Of course, we also want you to come away from reading this book with a firm foundation of knowledge in the field. Although there is much that developmental psychologists do not yet know or understand, a great many facts and observations have accumulated. These facts and observations will be of help to you professionally if you are planning (or are already in) a career that involves working with children, such as teaching, nursing, social work, medicine, or psychology; the information will also be useful to you as a parent, now or in the future. We hope you enjoy the reading as much as we have enjoyed the writing.

How to Work with This Textbook

To get the most out of any textbook, you should think of yourself as working with it so that you can understand and remember the information in it, rather than reading it as you would a magazine, a newspaper article, or a novel. To work with your textbook most effectively, take advantage of its structural and pedagogical features.

Learning Objectives Before you read each chapter, read over the Learning Objectives at its beginning. Each of these Learning Objectives is paired with one of the subsections of the chapter, so these questions provide an outline for the material you should know by the end of the chapter. More information will stick in your mind if you have an idea of what to expect.

Vignettes The story at the beginning of each chapter will engage your interest in the major topics and themes.

Headings and Subheadings Think of the headings and their subheadings as a way of dividing the information that follows them into categories. The information in each major section and subsection is linked to the heading and subheading under which it is found. Each of the Learning Objectives listed at the beginning of the chapter is repeated next

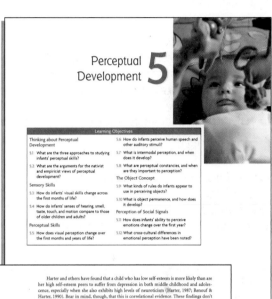

poverty explains the higher rates of infant death among Native Americans and African Americans, the two groups with the highest rates of poverty. However, infant mortality rates among Hispanic American groups suggest that the link between poverty and infant mortality is not so straightforward. The infant mortality rate among Mexican American babies is 5.8 per 1,000, and the mortality rate for infants of Cuban, South, and Central American ancestry is only 5.5 per 1,000 (MacDorman & Atkinson, 1999). These groups are almost as likely to be poor as African Americans and Native Americans. In contrast, Puerto Rican families are not likely to be poorer than other Hispanic American families, but the mortality rate is 7.9 per 1,000 among their infants. Similarly, rates of early prenatal care—defined as consulting a doctor or midwife during the first trimester of pregnancy—are nearly identical for African American women and Hispanic American women (National Center for Health Statistics [NCHS], 2007). Consequently, access to prenatal care cannot explain differences in infant mortality across these groups (see Figure 3.5).

Interestingly, mortality rates among the babies of immigrants of all racial and ethnic groups are lower than those among babies of U.S.-born mothers. This finding also challenges the poverty explanation for racial and ethnic group differences in infant mortality, because immigrant women are more likely to be poor and less likely to receive prenatal care than women born in the United States (MacDorman & Atkinson, 1999). Many researchers suggest that lower rates of tobacco and alcohol use among women born outside the United States may be an important factor.

Think Critically

- How would you go about raising public awareness of the advantages of breastfeeding, the importance of early immunizations, and the developmental risks associated with ear infections?
- Generate your own hypothesis to explain group differences in infant mortality. What kind of information would you need to test your hypothesis?

Conduct Your Own Research

You can find out more about women's childbearing-related worries by carrying out what researchers call a *free-response* study. Simply ask several women, both pregnant and nonpregnant if you can, to express their concerns in their own words. Write down what they say. When you have collected a number of responses, analyze them for common themes.

Summary

BIRTH

3.1 What decisions must parents make about the birth process in industrialized societies?
- Parents must decide whether to use pain-relieving drugs during delivery, whether their baby should be born in a hospital or other setting, and whether the father should be present for the delivery. Most drugs given to a woman during delivery pass through to the infant's bloodstream and have short-term effects on infant responsiveness. In uncomplicated, low-risk pregnancies, delivery at home or in a birth center may be as safe as hospital delivery. The presence of the father during delivery has a variety of positive consequences, including reducing the mother's experience of pain, but being present for the birth does not appear to affect the father's attachment to the infant.

3.2 What are the events and risks associated with each stage of the birth process?
- The normal birth process has three stages: dilation and effacement, delivery, and placental delivery. Several types of problems may occur at birth, including reduced oxygen supply to the infant (anoxia). Slightly more than one-quarter of all deliveries in the United States today are by cesarean section. Newborns are typically assessed using the Apgar score, which is a rating on five dimensions. Most parents show intense interest in the new baby's features, especially the eyes.

3.3 What are some of the possible consequences of low birth weight?
- Infants born weighing less than 2,500 grams are designated as low birth weight (LBW); those below 1,500 grams are very low birth weight (VLBW); those below 1,000 grams are extremely low birth weight (ELBW). The lower the weight, the greater the risk of neonatal death or of significant lasting problems, such as low IQ score or learning disabilities.

BEHAVIOR IN EARLY INFANCY

3.4 What reflexes and behavioral states are exhibited by infants?
- Infants have a wide range of reflexes. Some, such as the sucking reflex, are essential for life. Other primitive reflexes are present in the newborn but disappear in the first year. Cycles of sleeping, waking, and crying are present from the beginning.

3.5 What kinds of motor, sensory, and perceptual abilities do newborns have?
- Motor skills are only rudimentary at birth. Perceptual skills include the ability to focus both eyes; visually track slowly moving objects; discriminate the mother by sight, smell, and sound; and respond to smells, tastes, and touch.

3.6 What types of learning do infants exhibit?
- Within the first few weeks of life, babies are able to learn through association of stimuli (classical conditioning), from pleasant and unpleasant consequences (operant conditioning), from categorization of stimuli (schematic learning), and from repeated exposure to stimuli (habituation).

3.7 How do newborns differ in temperament, and what skills do they bring to social interactions?
- Babies differ from one another on several dimensions, including vigor of response, general activity rate, restlessness, irritability, and cuddliness. Thomas and Chess identified three temperamental categories: easy, difficult, and slow-to-warm-up. Infants develop the ability to express a range of emotions, such as pleasure and distress, over the first year.

HEALTH AND WELLNESS IN EARLY INFANCY

3.8 What are the infant's nutritional, health-care, and immunization needs?
- Breast milk or formula supplies all of an infant's nutritional needs until 6 months of age. Babies require periodic check-ups to track their growth and development. They also need to be immunized against a variety of diseases.

3.9 What kinds of illnesses typically occur in infancy?
- Common illnesses of childhood include diarrhea, upper respiratory infections, and ear infections. In the developing world, diarrhea is the leading cause of infant death. In the industrialized world, ear infections are the most serious of these illnesses, although they are rarely fatal. All forms of upper respiratory illness are more common among children in day care than among those reared at home.

3.10 What factors contribute to infant mortality?
- In the United States and other industrialized countries, most infant deaths in the first weeks are due to congenital anomalies or low birth weight; after the first weeks, sudden infant death syndrome (SIDS) is the most common cause of death in the first year. African American, Native Hawaiian, and Native American infants display higher rates of infant mortality than White Americans and other ethnic groups in the United States. Poverty may be a factor, but other groups with similar rates of poverty, such as Hispanic Americans, have lower infant mortality rates than African Americans, Native Hawaiians, and Native Americans.

Key Terms

adaptive reflexes (p. 68)
anoxia (p. 63)
Babinski reflex (p. 68)
cephalocaudal (p. 73)
cesarean section (c-section) (p. 64)
colic (p. 72)
difficult child (p. 76)
dilation (p. 62)
dynamic systems theory (p. 69)
easy child (p. 76)
effacement (p. 62)
extremely low birth weight (ELBW) (p. 66)

habituation (p. 75)
learning (p. 74)
low birth weight (LBW) (p. 66)
Moro reflex (p. 68)
otitis media (OM) (p. 80)
perception (p. 73)
preterm infant (p. 66)
primitive reflexes (p. 68)
proximodistal (p. 73)
reflexes (p. 68)
respiratory distress syndrome (p. 67)
rooting reflex (p. 68)
schematic learning (p. 75)

sensation (p. 73)
slow-to-warm-up child (p. 76)
small-for-date infant (p. 67)
states of consciousness (p. 70)
sudden infant death syndrome (SIDS) (p. 81)
temperament (p. 76)
very low birth weight (VLBW) (p. 66)

to its corresponding subheading, to help you keep in mind the big picture. Thinking of the material in this way creates a kind of information network in your mind that will make it easier to recall the material when you are tested. Structuring your notes to correspond to these headings and Learning Objectives will help even more. To have the best chance of creating the information network, stop reading between major sections, reflect back on what you have read, and review your written notes.

Margin Glossary Key terms are defined in the margins. As you come to each boldfaced term in the text, stop and read its definition in the margin. Then go back and reread the sentence that introduced the key term. Reading over the key terms in the margins just before you take an exam can also be a helpful review strategy if you have thoroughly studied the material in which the terms are introduced.

Think Critically Questions Think Critically questions encourage you to relate material in the book to your own experiences. They can also help you remember the text because linking new information to things you already know is a highly effective memory strategy.

Conduct Your Own Research Each chapter ends with a feature that encourages you to replicate the findings of a developmental study in an informal way or find out more about a specific topic.

Summary Looking over the chapter summary can also help you assess how much information you remember. The summaries are organized by the same Learning Objective questions presented at the beginning of the chapter.

Key Terms Key terms are listed alphabetically at the end of each chapter in addition to being defined in the margins. When you finish a chapter, try to recall the definition of each term. A page number is listed for each term, so you can easily look back if you can't remember a definition.

At this point, the task of understanding and remembering the information in a developmental psychology textbook may seem overwhelming. However, when you finish reading this book, you will have a better understanding of both yourself and other people. So, the benefit you will derive from all your hard work will be well worth it.

Denise Boyd

To the Instructor

One of the greatest challenges in updating a text is being open to new theories and concepts and willing to rethink and reorganize whole chapters, rather than sticking reflexively (or defensively) to old rubrics. Revising also sometimes includes eliminating favorite examples that are out of date and searching for new metaphors that will speak to current students. Perhaps hardest of all, one must cut as well as add material. Over many editions, the changes accumulate; if you were to compare this edition to the first edition, published in 1975, you would find almost no common sentences, let alone common paragraphs. Still, my goal was to retain most of the threads running from the first through the eleventh editions that made Helen Bee's approach to development unique. In particular, four central goals have guided the writing of *The Developing Child*:

- To actively engage the student in as many ways as possible.
- To find that difficult but essential balance among theory, research, and practical application.
- To present the most current thinking and research.
- To maintain a strong emphasis on culture.

New to the Twelfth Edition

The Twelfth Edition presents updated information about the theories and research presented in the previous edition, as well as additions to most chapters. The following list highlights some of the more significant changes to each chapter.

Chapter 1
- A new section called "Three Kinds of Change" discusses normative age-graded, normative history-graded, and nonnormative changes.
- A new table summarizes the various research methods covered in the chapter.
- The new *Developmental Science in the Real World* box is titled "Helping Children Who Are Afraid to Go to School."

Chapter 2
- A new chapter-opening vignette on *semi-identical twins* examines what happens when twins receive identical genes from their mother and different genes from their father.
- Topics on which discussion has been updated include genomic imprinting, fetal brain development, HIV/AIDS, prescription/over-the-counter drugs, maternal weight-consciousness during pregnancy, and how maternal age impacts fetal development.
- Several new images highlight insights into prenatal development gained via the use of new technologies, including a three-dimensional sonogram of fetal yawning, a graph showing correlations between fetal brain development and fetal behavior, and an MRI of a fetal brain.

Chapter 3
- New topics covered include Esther Thelen's dynamic systems theory of infant reflex and motor development and ethnic differences in early prenatal care.

Chapter 4

- A new chapter-opening vignette on a waterskiing toddler examines how maturational and experiential elements work together to influence development.
- New topics covered include the prefrontal cortex, stabilization of the growth curve, transgendered teens, and the impact of handedness on development.
- Topics on which coverage has been expanded and updated include STDs, the influence of diet on secular trends in age at menarche and secondary sex characteristic development, and excessive weight gain in childhood.
- Two new tables show which drugs adolescents abuse and the environmental factors associated with poverty and health.
- The new *Developmental Science in the Real World* box is titled "A Good Night's Sleep for Kids (and Parents, Too!)."

Chapter 5

- A new chapter-opening vignette on one child's interpretation of the Pledge of Allegiance examines the intricacies of perceptual development.

Chapter 6

- A new chapter-opening vignette examines what happens when children at different ages—and different Piagetian stages—play a board game together.
- New topics covered include figurative and operative schemes; centration and decentration; relational complexity, seriation, and transitivity; response inhibition; and memory strategies.

Chapter 7

- New topics covered include creativity, the relationship between family characteristics and IQ scores, data on IQ scores of "virtual" twins, and information on group IQ tests.
- New figures compare correlations of IQ scores of people of different degrees of biological relations and show correlations of identical and fraternal twins from birth to adulthood.

Chapter 8

- The new *Thinking about Research* box is titled "Sign Language and Gestures in Children Who Are Deaf."
- Coverage of the different methods of reading instruction (i.e., systematic and explicit phonics, whole language, and the balanced approach) has been expanded.

Chapter 9

- The new *Developmental Science in the Real World* box is titled "Temperamental Surgency in the Toddler Classroom."
- The new *Thinking about Research* box is titled "Locus of Control and Adolescent Health."
- New coverage of Bandura's theory of reciprocal determinism is accompanied by a new figure.

Chapter 10

- The new *Thinking about Research* box is titled "Gender Differences in Temperament: Real or Imagined?"
- A new figure illustrates the changes in sex-role rigidity/flexibility across age.

Chapter 11

- A new chapter-opening vignette discusses the intellectual and psychosocial resilience of the Lost Boys of Sudan.

- There is a new discussion of homosexual teenage romantic relationships.
- The concept of internal working models has been integrated into the discussion of attachment theory.

Chapter 12
- The discussion of Eisenberg's model of prosocial reasoning has been updated.

Chapter 13
- The two sections on family dynamics and interaction—"Other Aspects of Family Dynamics" and "Dimensions of Family Interaction"—have been integrated for a stronger, more focused presentation of the material.
- New topics covered include Belsky's model of family interaction, mirror neurons, and blended and extended families.

Chapter 14
- Revised and updated sections include those on nonparental care; television, video games, computers, and electronic multitasking; and child poverty.
- The developmental and academic approaches are included in new coverage of early childhood education.

Chapter 15
- A new chapter-opening vignette examines how eating disorders and other nonnormative changes can impact development.
- The new *Thinking about Research* box is titled "Pediatric Bipolar Disorder."
- New content includes a section on how theoretical perspectives explain atypical development, coverage of oppositional defiant disorder, and new tables on ADHD and categories of mental retardation.
- The section on developmental psychopathology has been revised and updated.

Epilogue
- Coverage of brain development has been added to the milestones tables.

Pedagogy

The Twelfth Edition of *The Developing Child* includes several important pedagogical features.

Learning Objectives   Learning Objectives, each paired with one of the subsections of the chapter, are introduced on the first page of the chapter. The Learning Objectives reappear in the margin next to the corresponding chapter subsection and again in the end-of-chapter summary. The Learning Objectives help students organize and retain the material as they read the textbook by informing them of the key information they are expected to take away from that section of the chapter. The Learning Objectives help you, the instructor, assess student learning outcomes because they are tied to the test items in the accompanying *Test Bank*.

Vignettes   Each chapter begins with a compelling vignette, which engages readers' interest in the chapter's topic.

Margin Glossary   All boldfaced terms in the text are defined in the margin as well as in a glossary at the end of the book.

Think Critically Questions   The critical thinking questions at the end of the chapter encourage students to relate information in the text to their own personal experiences.

Conduct Your Own Research   Each chapter ends with a feature that gives readers instructions for either replicating the findings of a developmental study in an informal way or finding out more about a specific topic.

Summary   Summaries are organized by major chapter heading and include bulleted entries summarizing the information that follows each subheading.

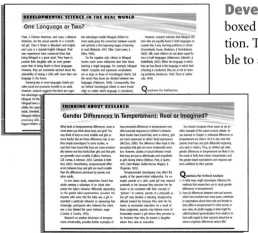

Developmental Science in the Real World   Every chapter includes a boxed discussion of the application of scientific knowledge to a practical question. The intent of these discussions is to show students not only that it is possible to study applied questions with scientific methods but also that all the theory and research they are reading about has some relevance to their own lives. To facilitate this goal, each *Developmental Science in the Real World* box begins with a brief vignette about a parenting issue and ends with questions for reflection, which encourage readers to apply the ideas in the box to that issue.

Thinking about Research   Every chapter includes a boxed discussion of a particularly important study or series of studies. Each *Thinking about Research* box ends with two questions for critical analysis, which encourage readers to critically evaluate the findings presented in the box.

Teaching and Learning Package

Print Test Bank and MyTest Computerized Test Bank (Print Test Bank ISBN: 0-205-68827-6)   Richard Cavasina of California University of Pennsylvania has provided an extensively updated Test Bank containing over 1500 thoroughly reviewed questions, including multiple choice, completion (fill in the blank), and critical essays. Test items have also been written to test student comprehension of select multimedia assets found within MyDevelopmentLab, for instructors who wish to make MyDevelopmentLab a central component of their course. Every test item is correlated with the Learning Objectives introduced in the textbook. All questions are accompanied by the correct answer, a page reference, a difficulty ranking, and a question-type designation. The *Test Bank* is also available in Pearson MyTest (www.pearsonmytest.com), a powerful assessment generation program that helps instructors easily create and print quizzes and exams. Questions and tests can be authored on-line, allowing instructors ultimate flexibility and the ability to efficiently manage assessments anytime, anywhere.

Instructor's Manual with CD-ROM (ISBN: 0-205-68826-8)   The *Instructor's Manual*, prepared by Amanda Nolen of the University of Arkansas at Little Rock, is a wonderful tool for classroom preparation and management. A brand new "easy-to-find" format includes detailed cross-references to features in the *Instructor's Manual* as well as to other print and media supplements and outside teaching resources. The *Instructor's Manual* is both comprehensive and extensive. Each chapter includes the following resources:

- An At-a-Glance Grid, with detailed pedagogical information, references to both print and media supplements for each concept, and a chapter overview.

- An Integrated Teaching Outline, with summaries of key concepts.

- Teaching objectives, which correlate with the Grade Aid with Practice Tests learning objectives.

- List of key terms.

- Lecture material, including outlines and suggested discussion topics, with references to pertinent activities in the *Instructor's Manual* and videos from the Allyn & Bacon video library.

- Updated classroom activities and demonstrations.
- An updated list of video, media, print, and Web resources.
- Discussion of the CD-ROM *Development: Journey through Childhood and Adolescence*, including pertinent discussion questions and a full table of contents.

The appendix includes a compilation of handouts and video offerings.

PowerPoint™ Presentation   Andrew R. Getzfeld of New York University has prepared a PowerPoint presentation that is an exciting interactive tool for use in the classroom. Each chapter includes the following:

- Key points covered in the textbook.
- Images from the textbook, with demonstrations.

The PowerPoint files are available on our Instructor's Resource Center for your convenience (www.pearsonhighered.com/IRC). Please contact your Pearson representative if you do not have access to the Instructor's Resource Center.

Transparencies for Child Development (ISBN: 0-205-40747-1)   Approximately 125 full-color acetates allow instructors to enhance classroom lecture and discussion.

MyDevelopmentLab (www.mydevelopmentlab.com)   The APA strongly recommends student self-assessment tools and the use of embedded questions and assignments (see www.apa.org/ed/eval_strategies.html for more information). In keeping with these recommendations, Pearson's MyDevelopmentLab offers students useful and engaging self-assessment tools and offers instructors flexibility in assessing and tracking student progress. For instructors, MyDevelopmentLab is a powerful tool for assessing student performance and adapting course content to students' changing needs—without investing additional time or resources. Students benefit from an easy-to-use site on which they can test themselves on key content, track their progress, and utilize an individually tailored study plan. MyDevelopmentLab includes an eBook plus multimedia tutorials, audio, video, simulations, animations, and controlled assessments to completely engage students and reinforce learning.

MyDevelopmentLab is designed with instructor flexibility in mind; you decide the extent of integration into your course—from independent self-assessment for students to total course management. By transferring faculty members' most time-consuming tasks—content delivery, student assessment, and grading—to automated tools, MyDevelopmentLab enables faculty to spend more quality time with students. Instructors are provided with the results of student diagnostic tests in a gradebook and can view performance of individual students or an aggregate report on their class. Instructors can access the remediation activities students receive within their customized study plans and can also link to extra lecture notes, video clips, and activities that reflect the content areas their class is struggling with. Instructors can bring these resources to class or easily post them on-line for students to access.

With the Twelfth Edition of *The Developing Child* comes a new generation of MyDevelopmentLab, with dozens of improvements and new features that make MyDevelopmentLab both more powerful and easier to use. Some highlights of the new MyDevelopmentLab course include the following:

- GradeTracker for the website version of MyDevelopmentLab, to track students' performance on quizzes.
- A new, more flexible, powerful, and intuitive platform for the course management version of MyDevelopmentLab.
- A redesigned eBook that gives students the option to highlight passages and access media content directly from the eBook page.

- A new interactive Timeline tool that vividly illustrates key dates in the history of psychology through text, audio, and video.
- Redesigned Flash Cards for reviewing key terms, with audio to help students with pronunciation of difficult terminology.
- Continued improvements to design, course content, and grading system based on direct customer feedback.

For technical support for any of your Pearson products, you and your students can contact http://247.pearsoned.com.

Course Management   Use these preloaded, customizable content and assessment items—available in Blackboard, WebCT, and other formats—to teach your on-line courses. Contact your Pearson representative for additional details.

Development: Journey through Childhood and Adolescence CD-ROM (ISBN: 0-205-39568-6)   This multimedia learning tool is available to be packaged with the text or sold separately. It includes eight units that cover development from the prenatal period through adolescence and introduce all of the biological, cognitive, and psychosocial changes that occur along the way. Clips include footage of live births, interviews with adolescents and the elderly, and toddlers learning to walk. In addition, audio clips, flash animations, and 3-D video animations accompany the footage. Written by Dr. Kelly Welch of Kansas State University, the CD-ROM includes several exercises for students, such as "drag-and-drop" activities, multiple-choice quizzes, flash cards of glossary terms, journal writing, and instant feedback exercises called "Mad Minutes."

Insights into Human Development Video (ISBN: 0-205-46624-9)   This video is available to accompany *The Developing Child*, Twelfth Edition. The video highlights important high-interest topics in human development, including imagination in early childhood, motivation and school success, and aggression in adolescent romantic relationships. A video user's guide, with critical thinking questions and Web resources, is available to support the use of the video in the classroom.

Study Card for Child Development (Topical) (ISBN: 0-205-43507-6)   Colorful, affordable, and packed with useful information, the Study Card makes studying easier, more efficient, and more enjoyable. Course information is distilled down to the basics, helping students quickly master the fundamentals, review a subject for understanding, or prepare for an exam. The Study Card is laminated for durability.

Acknowledgments

Thanks to the wonderful people at Allyn & Bacon who participated in the development and completion of this project, including Christina Lembo and Patrick Cash-Peterson. In addition, I am grateful to all of the reviewers who took time to comment on this and previous editions of *The Developing Child*. The following people provided invaluable feedback through their reviews for the Twelfth Edition:

Elizabeth M. Blunk, Texas State University
Megan E. Bradley, Frostburg State College
Richard Cavasina, California University of Pennsylvania
Emily Doolittle, George Washington University
Joann Farver, University of Southern California
Janet Gebelt, Westfield State College
Myra Heinrich, Mesa State College
Wendy Jordanov, Tennessee State University
Amanda Nolen, University of Arkansas at Little Rock
Brady J. Phelps, South Dakota State University
June Rosenberg, Lyndon State College
Diane Serafin, Luzerne County Community College
Delar K. Singh, Eastern Connecticut State University
Monica Sylvia, Le Moyne College
Gordon Lee Whitman, Tidewater Community College

Thanks also to the following people who provided thoughtful criticism and commentary on earlier editions and drafts:

Steven H. Baron, Montgomery County Community College
Janette B. Benson, University of Denver
Marvin W. Berkowitz, Marquette University
Katherine Black, University of Hartford
Elizabeth M. Blunk, Texas State University
Megan E. Bradley, Frostburg State University
Peter J. Byrne, Maria College
Tsu-Ming Chiang, Georgia College and State University
Saundra K. Ciccarelli, Gulf Coast Community College
Joan Cook, County College of Morris
Rita M. Curl, Minot State University
Wallace E. Dixon, Jr., Heidelberg College
Emily Doolittle, George Washington University
Jerome Dusek, Syracuse University
Cynthia Erdley, University of Maine
Donna Frick-Horbury, Appalachian State University
Gloria Gartner, Lakeland Community College
Janet Gebelt, Westfield State College
Betty K. Hathaway, University of Arkansas at Little Rock
Celia B. Hilber, Jacksonville State University
Patricia A. Jarvis, Illinois State University

Wendy Jordanov, Tennessee State University
Janice H. Kennedy, Georgia Southern University
Kee Jeong Kim, Virginia Technical University
Pamela Ludemann, Framingham State College
Philip J. Mohan, University of Idaho
Terese Morrow, Illinois Central College
Brady J. Phelps, South Dakota State University
Jane A. Rysberg, California State University
Donald Sanzotta, Cayuga Community College
Jane P. Sheldon, University of Michigan–Dearborn
Delar K. Singh, Eastern Connecticut State University
Nancy White, Youngstown State University
Gordon Lee Whitman, Tidewater Community College
Ric Wynn, County College of Morris
Sheri D. Young, John Carroll University

The Developing Child

Basic Issues in the Study of Development 1

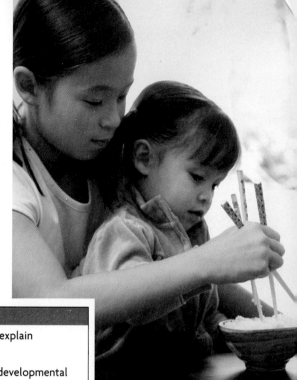

Like many new parents, Derrick and Tracy purchased an infant care book that included information about the normal sequence of infant development. They delighted in noting that their newborn son, Blake, seemed to be capable of doing everything that a newborn should be able to do. The book said that he should begin to try to roll over between 1 and 2 months of age. Right on schedule, 4-week-old Blake began to throw his right arm and leg over his body every time he was laid on his back, in a fruitless effort to roll over. When he reached his 2-month birthday, Blake still hadn't rolled over, but Derrick and Tracy were comforted by the book's emphasis on individual differences. A few days later, their concerns about Blake's development evaporated when he finally succeeded in turning from his back to his stomach.

As this brief peek into the world of newborn parenting suggests, research on child development has found its way out of the laboratory and into everyday life (Hulbert, 2003). You might be surprised to learn that this trend was already on the rise back in the 1920s, when psychologist John B. Watson (1878–1958) wrote popular magazine articles and best-selling books advocating rigid feeding, weaning, and toilet-training schedules and other practices that he believed would ensure emotional hardiness in children:

> Never hug and kiss them, never let them sit in your lap. If you must, kiss them once on the forehead when they say good night. Shake hands with them in the morning. Give them a pat on the head if they have made an extraordinarily good job of a difficult task. (1928, pp. 81–82)

Watson's ideas held sway until Dr. Benjamin Spock's (1903–1990) classic *The Commonsense Book of Baby and Child Care* became a runaway best-seller in 1946. Spock's advice was quite the opposite of Watson's. He warned parents against imposing excessive demands on children. Spock advised parents to nurse infants on demand and to wait until they displayed signs of readiness before weaning and toilet-training them.

Thanks to an ever-growing body of research, we know a great deal more about child development now than was the case in either Watson's or Spock's day. Consequently, most contemporary developmentalists view Watson's ideas as excessively rigid, if not downright abusive. Many also believe that the recommendations in Spock's original book (which has been revised many times since 1946) may have been a bit too lax. What today's developmental scientists share with Watson and Spock, however, is a desire to understand the processes that underlie human development and to find ways to help parents, teachers, therapists, and others who work with children do so effectively. To that end, they develop theories and conduct research aimed at describing, explaining, predicting, and influencing development.

Issues in the Study of Development

Centuries before researchers began to use scientific methods to study age-related changes, philosophers proposed explanations of development based on everyday observations. Many of their questions and assertions about the nature of human development continue to be central to modern-day **developmental science**.

Two Key Questions

Two important questions have shaped the scientific study of child development. First, philosophers and scientists alike have debated the degree to which inborn tendencies and environmental factors influence development. Second, there are differing opinions as to whether age-related change occurs in stages.

The Nature-Nurture Debate The argument about nature versus nurture, also referred to as heredity versus environment or *nativism* versus *empiricism*, is one of the oldest and most central theoretical issues within both psychology and philosophy. For example, have you ever heard someone say that "baby talk" will interfere with a child's language development? If so, then you have heard an argument for the nurture side of the debate. Such a statement assumes that language development is mostly a matter of imitation: The child must

developmental science The study of age-related changes in behavior, thinking, emotions, and social relationships.

hear language that is properly pronounced and grammatically correct in order to develop linguistic fluency. The nature side would counter that children possess some kind of internal mechanism to ensure that they develop fluent language, no matter how many "goo-goo-ga-gas" they hear from those around them. "Which side is right?" students invariably ask. If there were a simple answer to that question, the debate would have ceased long ago. Instead, the controversy continues today with regard to many developmental processes, including language development.

Philosophically, the nature side of the controversy was represented by the *idealists* and *rationalists*, principally Plato and René Descartes, both of whom believed that at least some knowledge is inborn. On the other side of the argument were a group of British philosophers called *empiricists*, including John Locke, who insisted that at birth the mind is a blank slate—in Latin, a *tabula rasa*. All knowledge, the empiricists argued, is created by experience. From this perspective, developmental change is the result of external, environmental factors acting on a child whose only relevant internal characteristic is the capacity to respond.

In contrast to both rationalists and empiricists, other philosophers believed that development involved an interaction between internal and external forces. For example, the Christian notion of *original sin* teaches that children are born with a selfish nature and must be spiritually reborn. After rebirth, children have access to the Holy Spirit, which helps them learn to behave morally through parental and church-based instruction in religious practice.

French philosopher Jean-Jacques Rousseau also believed in the idea of interaction between internal and external forces, but he claimed that all human beings are naturally good and seek out experiences that help them grow. For Rousseau, the goal of human development was to achieve one's inborn potential. "Good" developmental outcomes, such as a willingness to share one's possessions with others who are less fortunate, resulted from growing up in an environment that didn't interfere with the child's expression of his own innate characteristics. In contrast, "bad" outcomes, such as aggressive behavior, were learned from others or arose when a child experienced frustration in his efforts to follow the dictates of the innate goodness with which he was born.

The views of two of psychology's pioneers illustrate the way early psychologists approached the nature-nurture issue. Borrowing an idea from Darwin's theory of evolution, early childhood researcher G. Stanley Hall (1844–1924) believed that the milestones of childhood were dictated by an inborn developmental plan and were similar to those that had taken place in the development of the human species. He thought that developmentalists should identify **norms**, or average ages at which milestones happen. Norms, Hall said, could be used to learn about the evolution of the species as well as to track the development of individual children. So, for Hall, development was mostly about the nature side of the debate.

John Watson, whose views you read about at the beginning of the chapter, explained development in a way that was radically different from that of G. Stanley Hall. In fact, Watson coined a new term, behaviorism, to refer to his point of view (Watson, 1913). **Behaviorism** defines development in terms of behavior changes caused by environmental influences. Watson did not believe in an inborn developmental plan of any sort. Instead, he claimed that, through manipulation of the environment, children could be trained to be or do anything (Jones, 1924; Watson, 1930). As Watson put it,

John Watson's pioneering research on emotional learning in infants helped psychologists better understand the role of classical conditioning in child development.

> Give me a dozen healthy infants, well-formed, and my own specified world to bring them up in and I'll guarantee to take any one at random and train him to become any type of specialist I might select—doctor, lawyer, merchant, chief, and yes, even beggar-man and thief, regardless of his talents, penchants, abilities, vocations, and the race of his ancestors. (1930, p. 104)

In a famous study known as the "Little Albert" experiment, Watson conditioned a baby to fear white rats (Watson & Rayner, 1920). As the

Which photo represents *continuous* or *quantitative* change? Which illustrates *discontinuous* or *qualitative* change?

baby played with the rat, Watson made banging sounds that frightened the child. Over time, the baby came to associate the rat with the noises. He cried and tried to escape from the room whenever the rat was present. Based on the Little Albert study and several others, Watson claimed that all age-related changes are the result of learning (Watson, 1928).

Stages and Sequences   The nature-nurture controversy is not the only "big question" in developmental psychology. An equally central dispute concerns the *continuity-discontinuity issue*: Is a child's expanding ability just "more of the same," or does it reflect a new kind of activity? For example, a 2-year-old is likely to have no individual friends among her playmates, while an 8-year-old is likely to have several. We could think of this as a *quantitative* change (a change in amount) from zero friends to some friends, which suggests that the qualitative aspects of friendship are the same at every age—or, as developmentalists would express it, changes in friendships are *continuous* in nature. Alternatively, we could think of the difference in friendships from one age to another as a *qualitative* change (a change in kind or type)—from disinterest in peers to interest, or from one sort of peer relationship to another. In other words, in this view, changes in friendships are *discontinuous*, in that each change represents a change in the quality of a child's relationships with peers. Thus, friendships at 2 are quite different from friendships at 8 and differ in ways that cannot be captured by describing them solely in terms of the number of friends a child has.

Of particular significance is the idea that, if development consists only of additions (quantitative change), then the concept of stages is not needed to explain it. However, if development involves reorganization, or the emergence of wholly new strategies, qualities, or skills (qualitative change), then the concept of stages may be useful. Certainly, we hear a lot of "stagelike" language in everyday conversation about children: "He's just in the terrible twos" or "It's only a stage she's going through." Although there is not always agreement on just what would constitute evidence for the existence of discrete stages, the usual description is that a stage shift involves not only a change in skills but some discontinuous change in underlying structure (Lerner, Theokas, & Bobek, 2005). The child in a new stage approaches tasks differently, sees the world differently, is preoccupied with different issues.

Learning Objective 1.2
What are the internal and external variables that influence development?

Influences on Development

Modern developmental psychologists still debate the nature-nurture and continuity-discontinuity questions. But most agree that essentially every facet of a child's development is a product of some pattern of interaction of nature and nurture (Rutter, 2002). Further, most recognize that some aspects of development are continuous and others are more stagelike. Consequently, the discussions have become a bit more complex.

Maturation

Nature shapes development most clearly through genetic programming that may determine whole sequences of later development. Developmentalist Arnold Gesell (1880–1961) used the term **maturation** to describe genetically programmed sequential patterns of change, and this term is still uniformly used today (Gesell, 1925; Thelen & Adolph, 1992). Any maturational pattern is marked by three qualities: It is universal, appearing in all children, across cultural boundaries; it is sequential, involving some pattern of unfolding skill or characteristics; and it is relatively impervious to environmental influence. In its purest form, a maturationally determined developmental sequence occurs regardless of practice or training. You don't have to practice growing pubic hair; you don't have to be taught how to walk. In fact, only extreme conditions, such as severe malnutrition, prevent such sequences from unfolding. Yet even confirmed maturational theorists agree that experience plays a role.

The Timing of Experience

Modern research tells us that specific experience interacts with maturational patterns in intricate ways. For example, Greenough (1991) notes that one of the proteins required for the development of the visual system is controlled by a gene whose action is triggered only by visual experience. Moreover, experience is required to maintain the neural connections underlying vision (Briones, Klintsova, & Greenough, 2004). So some visual experience is needed for the genetic program to operate. The timing of specific experiences may matter as well. The impact of a particular visual experience may be quite different if it occurs at birth than if it occurs when a baby is older.

Developmentalists' thinking about the importance of timing was stimulated, in part, by research on other species that showed that specific experiences had different or stronger effects at some points in development than at others. The most famous example is that baby ducks will become imprinted on (become attached to and follow) any duck or any other quacking, moving object that happens to be around them 15 hours after they hatch. If nothing is moving or quacking at that critical point, they don't become imprinted at all (Hess, 1972). So the period just around 15 hours after hatching is a **critical period** for the duck's development of a proper following response.

In humans, we more often see sensitive periods than true critical periods. The difference is that a **sensitive period** is a time when a particular experience can be best incorporated into the maturational process, whereas a critical period is a time when an experience *must* happen or a particular developmental milestone will never occur. For example, infancy and early childhood are sensitive periods for language development. A child who is physically isolated from other humans by an abusive parent during these years will not develop normal language, but she will develop some language function once she is reintegrated into a normal social environment.

Inborn Biases and Constraints

Another kind of internal influence is described by the concepts of "inborn biases," or "constraints" on development. For instance, researchers such as Elizabeth Spelke (1991) have concluded that babies come into the world with certain "preexisting conceptions," or constraints on their understanding of the behavior of objects. Very young babies already seem to understand that unsupported objects will move downward and that a moving object will continue to move in the same direction unless it encounters an obstacle. Theorists do not propose that these built-in response patterns are the end of the story; rather, they see them as the starting point. Development is a result of experience filtered through these initial biases, but those biases constrain the number of developmental pathways that are possible (Campbell & Bickhard, 1992; Cole, 2005).

Behavior Genetics

The concept of maturation and the idea of inborn biases are both designed to account for patterns and sequences of development that are the same for all

maturation Sequential patterns of change that are governed by instructions contained in the genetic code and shared by all members of a species.

critical period Any time period during development when an organism is especially responsive to and learns from a specific type of stimulation. The same stimulation at other points in development has little or no effect.

sensitive period A period during which particular experiences can best contribute to proper development. It is similar to a critical period, but the effects of deprivation during a sensitive period are not as severe as during a critical period.

The study of identical twins, like these two girls, is one of the classic methods of behavior genetics. Whenever pairs of identical twins are more like each other in some behavior or quality than are pairs of fraternal twins, a genetic influence is likely at work.

children. At the same time, nature contributes to variations from one individual to the next. The study of genetic contributions to individual behavior, called **behavior genetics**, uses two primary research techniques—the study of identical and fraternal twins and the study of adopted children. If identical twins are more like each other on some dimension than other kinds of siblings are, despite having grown up in different environments, this is rather compelling evidence of a genetic contribution for that trait. In the case of adopted children, the strategy is to compare the degree of similarity between the adopted child and his birth parents (with whom he shares genes but not environment) with the degree of similarity between the adopted child and his adoptive parents (with whom he shares environment but not genes). If the child turns out to be more similar to his birth parents than to his adoptive parents, or if his behavior or skills are better predicted by the characteristics of his birth parents than by characteristics of his adoptive parents, that evidence would again demonstrate the influence of heredity. Behavior geneticists have shown that heredity affects a remarkably broad range of behaviors (Posthuma, de Geus, & Boomsma, 2003). These include intellectual as well as social and emotional functioning. Consequently, you will be reading about the results of twin and adoption studies in several future chapters.

Gene-Environment Interaction A child's genetic heritage may also affect his environment (Caspi & Moffitt, 2006), a phenomenon that could occur via either or both of two routes. First, the child inherits his genes from his parents, who also create the environment in which he is growing up. So a child's genetic heritage may predict something about his environment. For example, parents who themselves have higher IQ scores are not only likely to pass their "good IQ" genes on to their children, but also likely to create a richer, more stimulating environment for those children. Similarly, children who inherit a tendency toward aggression or hostility from their parents are likely to live in a family environment that is higher in criticism and negativity—because those are expressions of the parents' own genetic tendencies toward aggressiveness or hostility (Reiss, 1998).

Second, each child's unique pattern of inherited qualities affects the way she behaves with other people, which in turn affects the way adults and other children respond to her. A cranky or temperamentally difficult baby may receive fewer smiles and more scolding than a placid, even-tempered one; a genetically brighter child may demand more personal attention, ask more questions, or seek out more complex toys than would a less bright child (Saudino & Plomin, 1997). Furthermore, children's interpretations of their experiences are affected by all their inherited tendencies, including not only intelligence but also temperament or pathology (Plomin, Reiss, Hetherington, & Howe, 1994).

Internal Models of Experience Although we often associate experience exclusively with external forces, it's just as important to consider each individual's view of his or her experiences—in other words, the internal aspect of experience. For instance, suppose a friend says to you, "Your new haircut looks great. I think it's a lot more becoming when it's short like that." Your friend intends it as a compliment, but what determines your reaction is how you hear the comment, not what is intended. If your internal model of your self includes the basic idea "I usually look okay," you will likely hear your friend's comment as a compliment; but if your internal model of self or relationships includes some more negative elements, such as "I usually do things wrong, so other people criticize me," then you may hear an implied criticism in your friend's comment ("Your hair used to look awful").

behavior genetics The study of the genetic contributions to behavior or traits such as intelligence or personality.

Theorists who emphasize the importance of such meaning systems argue that each child creates a set of **internal models of experience**—a set of core ideas or assumptions about the world, about himself, and about relationships with others—through which all subsequent experience is filtered (Epstein, 1991; Reiss, 1998). Such assumptions are certainly based in part on actual experiences, but once they are formed into an internal model, they generalize beyond the original experience and affect the way the child interprets future experiences. A child who expects adults to be reliable and affectionate will be more likely to interpret the behavior of new adults in this way and will create friendly and affectionate relationships with others outside of the family. A child's self-concept seems to operate in much the same way, as an internal working model of "who I am" (Bretherton, 1991). This self-model is based on experience, but it also shapes future experience.

internal models of experience A theoretical concept emphasizing that each child creates a set of core ideas or assumptions about the world, the self, and relationships with others through which all subsequent experience is filtered.

Aslin's Model of Environmental Influence

Theoretical models are useful for attempting to organize ideas about how all these internal and environmental factors interact to influence development. One particularly good example of a theoretical approach that attempts to explain environmental influences is a set of models summarized by Richard Aslin (1981), based on earlier work by Gottlieb (1976a, 1976b) and shown schematically in Figure 1.1. Aslin and his colleagues have used these models to study infants' speech perception and other aspects of language development (e.g., Maye, Weiss, & Aslin, 2008). In each drawing the dashed line represents the path of development of some skill or behavior that would occur without a particular experience; the solid line represents the path of development if the experience were added.

For comparison purposes, the first of the five models shows a maturational pattern with no environmental effect. The second model, which Aslin calls *maintenance*, describes a pattern in which some environmental input is necessary to sustain a skill or behavior that has already developed maturationally. For example, kittens are born with full binocular vision, but if you cover one of their eyes for a period of time, their binocular skill declines.

The third model shows a *facilitation* effect of the environment, in which a skill or behavior develops earlier than it normally would because of some experience. For example, children whose parents talk to them more often in the first 18 to 24 months of life, using more complex sentences, appear to develop two-word sentences and other early grammatical forms somewhat earlier than do children who are talked to less. Yet less-talked-to children do eventually learn to create complex sentences and use most grammatical forms correctly, so the experience of being talked to more provides no permanent gain.

When a particular experience does lead to a permanent gain, or an enduringly higher level of performance, Aslin calls the model *attunement*. For example, children from poverty-level families who attend special enriched child care in infancy and early childhood have consistently higher IQ scores throughout childhood than do children from the same kinds of families who do not have such enriched experience (Ramey & Ramey, 2004). Aslin's final model, *induction*, describes a pure environmental effect: In the absence of some experience, a particular behavior does not develop at all. Giving a child tennis lessons or exposing him to a second language falls into this category of experience.

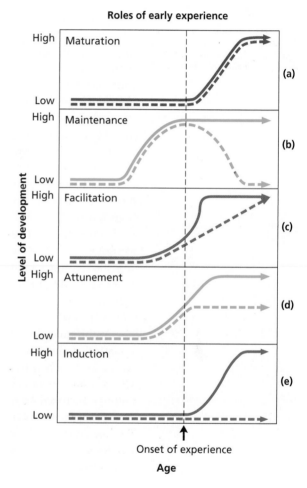

Figure 1.1   Aslin's Models of Environmental Influence

Aslin's five models of possible relationships between maturation and environment. The top model shows a purely maturational effect; the bottom model (induction) shows a purely environmental effect. The other three show interactive combinations: maintenance, in which experience prevents the deterioration of a maturationally developed skill; facilitation, in which experience speeds up the development of some maturational process; and attunement, in which experience increases the ultimate level of some skill or behavior above the "normal" maturational level.

(*Source*: Aslin, Richard N. "Experiential Influences and Sensitive Periods in Perceptual Development," *Development of perception. Psychobiological perspectives: Vol. 2. The visual system* (1981), p. 50. Reprinted by permission of Elsevier Science and the author.)

Learning Objective 1.3

How does the ecological perspective improve scientists' understanding of child development?

The Ecological Perspective

Until quite recently, most research on environmental influences focused on a child's family (frequently only the child's mother) and on the stimulation available in the child's home, such as the kinds of toys or books available to the child. If psychologists looked at a larger family context at all, it was usually only in terms of the family's economic status—its level of wealth or poverty. Since the early 1980s, however, there has been a strong push to widen the scope of research, to consider the *ecology*, or *context*, in which each child develops. Urie Bronfenbrenner, one of the key figures in this area of study (1979, 1989), emphasizes that each child grows up in a complex social environment (a social ecology) with a distinct cast of characters: brothers, sisters, one or both parents, grandparents, baby-sitters, pets, teachers, friends. And this cast is itself embedded within a larger social system: The parents have jobs that they may like or dislike; they may or may not have close and supportive friends; they may be living in a safe neighborhood or one full of dangers; the local school may be excellent or poor; and the parents may have good or poor relationships with the school. Bronfenbrenner's argument is that researchers not only must include descriptions of these more extended aspects of the environment but must also consider the ways in which all the components of this complex system interact with one another to affect the development of an individual child. (We will look more closely at Bronfenbrenner's theory in Chapter 13.)

One aspect of such a larger ecology is the still broader concept of *culture*, a system of meanings and customs, including values, attitudes, goals, laws, beliefs, morals, and physical artifacts of various kinds, such as tools and forms of dwellings. For a system of meanings and customs to be called a culture, it must be shared by some identifiable group, whether that group is the entire population of a country or a subsection of such a population; it must then be transmitted from one generation of that group to the next (Cole, 2005). Families and children are clearly embedded in culture, just as they are located within an ecological niche within the culture. The majority U.S. culture, for example, is strongly shaped by the values expressed in the Constitution and the Bill of Rights; it also includes a strong emphasis on "can-do" attitudes and on competition. In addition, U.S. cultural beliefs include the assumption that the ideal living arrangement is for each family to have a separate house—a belief that contributes to a more spread-out pattern of housing in the United States than what exists in Europe.

Anthropologists point out that a key dimension on which cultures differ from one another is that of *individualism* versus *collectivism* (e.g., Kashima et al., 2005). People in cultures with an individualistic emphasis assume that the world is made up of independent persons whose achievement and responsibility are individual rather than collective. Most European cultures are based on such individualistic assumptions, as is the dominant U.S. culture, created primarily by Whites who came to the United States from Europe. In contrast, most of the remainder of the world's cultures operate with a collectivist belief system in which the emphasis is on collective rather than individual identity, on group solidarity, sharing, duties and obligations, and group decision making (Kashima et al., 2005). A person living in a collectivist system is integrated into a strong, cohesive group that protects and nourishes that individual throughout his life. Collectivism is the dominant theme in most Asian countries, as well as in many African and South American cultures. Strong elements of collectivism are also part of the African American, Hispanic American, Native American, and Asian American subcultures.

Greenfield (1995) gives a wonderful example of how the difference between collectivist and individualist cultures can affect actual child-rearing practices as well as people's judgments of others' child-rearing. She notes that mothers from the Zinacanteco Maya culture maintain almost constant bodily contact with their young babies and do not feel comfortable when they are separated from their infants. They believe that their babies require this contact to be happy. When these mothers saw a visiting American anthropologist put her own baby down, they were shocked and blamed the baby's regular crying on the fact that he was separated from his mother so often. Greenfield argues that the constant bodily contact of the

Mayan mothers is a logical outgrowth of their collectivist approach, because their basic goal is interdependence rather than independence. The American anthropologist, in contrast, operates with a basic goal of independence for her child and so emphasizes more separation. Each group judges the other's form of child-rearing to be less optimal or even inadequate.

Such differences notwithstanding, researchers note that it is wrong to think of collectivism and individualism in either-or terms, because there are elements of both in every culture (Green, Deschamps, & Páez, 2005). Consequently, when researchers categorize a given culture as collectivist or individualist, they are referring to which of the two sets of values predominates. It is also true that there is a considerable amount of individual variation within cultures. Thus, people who live in individualistic societies may nevertheless, as individuals, develop a collectivist orientation. The same is true for their counterparts in collectivist societies.

Vulnerability and Resilience

Learning Objective 1.4

In what ways do the concepts of vulnerability and resilience help us better understand child development?

At this point, it should be clear to you that nature and nurture do not act independently in shaping each child's development; they interact in complex and fascinating ways. Consequently, the same environment may have quite different effects on children who are born with different characteristics. One influential research approach exploring such an interaction is the study of vulnerable and resilient children. In their long-term study of a group of children born in 1955 on the island of Kauai, Hawaii, Emmy Werner and Ruth Smith (Werner, 1993, 1995; Werner & Smith, 1992, 2001) found that only about two-thirds of the children who grew up in poverty-level, chaotic families turned out to have serious problems themselves as adults. The other third, described as *resilient*, turned out to be "competent, confident, and caring adults" (Werner, 1995, p. 82). Thus, similar environments were linked to quite different outcomes.

Theorists such as Norman Garmezy, Michael Rutter, Ann Masten, and others (Garmezy, 1993; Garmezy & Rutter, 1983; Masten & Coatsworth, 1995; Rutter, 1987, 2005b) argue that the best way to make sense out of results like Werner and Smith's is to think of each child as born with certain *vulnerabilities*, such as a difficult temperament, a physical abnormality, allergies, or a genetic tendency toward alcoholism. Each child is also born with some *protective factors*, such as high intelligence, good coordination, an easy temperament, or a lovely smile, which tend to make her more resilient in the face of stress. These vulnerabilities and protective factors then interact with the child's environment, and thus the same environment can have quite different effects, depending on the qualities the child brings to the interaction.

A more general model describing the interaction between the qualities of the child and the environment comes from Fran Horowitz (1987, 2003), who proposes that the key ingredients are each child's vulnerability or resilience and the "facilitativeness" of the environment. A highly facilitative environment is one in which the child has loving and responsive parents and is provided with a rich array of stimulation. If the relationship between vulnerability and facilitativeness were merely additive, the best outcomes would occur for resilient infants reared in optimal environments, and the worst outcomes for vulnerable infants in poor environments, with the two mixed combinations falling halfway between. But that is not what Horowitz proposes, as you can see represented schematically in Figure 1.2 on page 10. Instead, she is suggesting that a resilient child in a poor environment may do quite well, since such a child can take advantage of

Many children who grow up in poverty-stricken neighborhoods are high achievers who are well adjusted. Developmentalists use the term *resilient* to refer to children who demonstrate positive developmental outcomes despite being raised in high-risk environments.

Figure 1.2 Horowitz's Model of Vulnerability and Resilience

Horowitz's model describes one possible type of interaction between the vulnerability of the child and the quality of the environment. The height of the surface shows the "goodness" of the developmental outcome (such as IQ or skill in social relationships). In this model, only the combination of a vulnerable infant and a nonfacilitative environment will result in a really poor outcome.

(*Source: Exploring Developmental Theories: Toward a Structural/Behavioral Model of Development*, by Horowitz, F. D. Copyright 1987 by Taylor & Francis Group LLC-Books. Reproduced with permission of Taylor & Francis Group LLC-Books in the format Textbook via Copyright Clearance Center.)

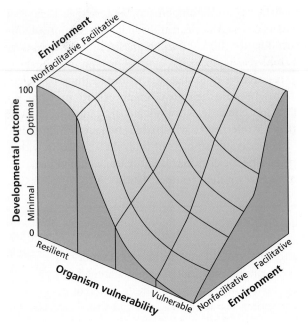

all the stimulation and opportunities available. Similarly, she suggests that a vulnerable child may do quite well in a highly facilitative environment. According to this model, it is only the "double whammy"—the vulnerable child in a poor environment—that leads to really poor outcomes.

In fact, as you will see throughout the book, a growing body of research shows precisely this pattern. For example, very low IQ scores are most common among children who were low-birth-weight babies and were reared in poverty-level families, while low-birth-weight children reared in middle-class families have essentially average IQs, as do normal-weight infants reared in poverty-level families (Werner, 1986). Further, among low-birth-weight children who are reared in poverty-level families, those whose families offer "protective" factors (such as greater residential stability, less crowded living conditions, and more acceptance, more stimulation, and more learning materials) achieve higher IQ scores than do equivalently low-birth-weight children reared in the least optimal poverty-level conditions (Bradley et al., 1994). The key point here is that the same environment can have quite different effects, depending on the qualities or capacities the child brings to the equation.

Three Kinds of Change

Age-related changes are a part of our everyday lives, so much so that we often give them little thought. Yet, consider the difference between a human being's first step and his or her first date. Clearly, both are related to age, but they represent fundamentally different kinds of change. Generally, developmental scientists think of each age-related change as falling into one of three categories.

Normative age-graded changes are universal; that is, they are common to every individual in a species and are linked to specific ages. Some universal changes, like a baby's first steps, happen because we are all biological organisms subject to a genetically programmed maturation process. The infant who shifts from crawling to walking and the older adult whose skin becomes progressively more wrinkled are both following a plan that is an intrinsic part of the physical body, most likely something in the genetic code itself. However, some changes are universal because of shared experiences. In each culture, the *social clock*, or a set of age norms, defines a sequence of normal life experiences, such as the right time to begin toilet-training, the age at which a child is expected to dress herself, and expectations regarding school-aged children's capacity for doing homework without adult supervision.

Equally important as a source of variation in life experience are historical forces, which affect each generation somewhat differently. Such changes are called **normative history-graded changes**. Social scientists use the word **cohort** to describe a group of individuals who are born within some fairly narrow span of years and thus share the same historical experiences at the same times in their lives. For instance, during the 1980s, a type of instruction called *whole language* was the dominant method of teaching reading in the United States. During the 1990s, *phonics* became the predominant teaching strategy. As a result, the cohort of adults who attended elementary school in the 1980s display different liter-

normative age-graded changes Changes that are common to every member of a species.

normative history-graded changes Changes that occur in most members of a cohort as a result of factors at work during a specific, well-defined historical period.

cohort A group of individuals who share the same historical experiences at the same times in their lives.

acy skills from those who received their early education in the 1990s. The differences stem from method-of-instruction-based variations in the normative history-graded changes that both cohorts went through when they were in elementary school.

Finally, **nonnormative changes**, or **individual differences**, result from unique, unshared events. One clearly unshared event in each person's life is conception; the combination of genes each individual receives at conception is unique. Thus, genetic differences—including physical characteristics such as body type and hair color as well as genetic disorders—represent one category of individual differences. Characteristics influenced by both heredity and environment, such as intelligence and personality, constitute another class of individual differences. Other individual differences are the result of the timing of a developmental event.

The shift from crawling to walking is an example of a normative age-graded change.

Theories of Development

Developmental theories are sets of statements that propose general principles of development. Students often say that they dislike reading about theories; what they want are the facts. However, theories are important, because they help us look at facts from different perspectives. A brief introduction to several important theories will help you understand some of the more detailed information about them presented in later chapters.

Psychoanalytic Theories

Learning Objective 1.6
What are the main ideas of the psychoanalytic theories?

The most distinctive and central assumption of the **psychoanalytic theories** is that behavior is governed by unconscious as well as conscious processes. Psychoanalytic theorists also see development as fundamentally stagelike, with each stage centered on a particular form of tension or a particular task. The child moves through these stages, resolving each task or reducing each tension as best he can. This emphasis on the formative role of early experience, particularly early family experience, is a hallmark of psychoanalytic theories. In this view, the first 5 or 6 years of life constitute a kind of sensitive period for the creation of the individual personality. Sigmund Freud (1856–1939) is usually credited with originating the psychoanalytic approach (1905, 1920), and his terminology and many of his concepts have become part of our intellectual culture. Another theorist in this tradition, Erik Erikson (1902–1994), has also had a large impact on the way psychologists think about personality development.

Freud's Theory Freud proposed the existence of a basic, unconscious, instinctual sexual drive he called the

When parents divorce, boys are more likely to show disturbed behavior or poorer school performance than are girls. But why? Theories can help to explain facts like this.

nonnormative changes (individual differences) Changes that result from unique, unshared events.

developmental theories Sets of statements that propose general principles of development.

psychoanalytic theories Developmental theories based on the assumption that age-related change results from maturationally determined conflicts between internal drives and society's demands.

libido The term used by Freud to describe the basic, unconscious, instinctual sexual energy in each individual.

id In Freudian theory, the inborn, primitive portion of the personality, the storehouse of libido, the basic energy that continually pushes for immediate gratification.

ego In Freudian theory, the portion of the personality that organizes, plans, and keeps the person in touch with reality. Language and thought are both ego functions.

superego In Freudian theory, the "conscience" part of personality, which contains parental and societal values and attitudes incorporated during childhood.

psychosexual stages The stages of personality development suggested by Freud: the oral, anal, phallic, latency, and genital stages.

psychosocial stages The stages of personality development suggested by Erikson, involving basic trust, autonomy, initiative, industry, identity, intimacy, generativity, and ego integrity.

libido. He argued that this energy is the motive force behind virtually all human behavior. Freud also proposed that unconscious material is created over time through the functioning of the various *defense mechanisms*, several of which are listed in Table 1.1. We all use defense mechanisms every day, and Freud's ideas about them continue to be influential among psychologists (Cramer, 2000).

A second basic assumption is that personality has a structure, which develops over time. Freud proposed three parts of the personality: the **id**, which is the source of the libido; the **ego**, a much more conscious element, the "executive" of the personality; and the **superego**, which is the center of conscience and morality, since it incorporates the norms and moral strictures of the family and society. In Freud's theory, these three parts are not all present at birth. The infant and toddler is all id—all instinct, all desire, without the restraining influence of the ego or the superego. The ego begins to develop in the years from age 2 to about 4 or 5, as the child learns to adapt her instant-gratification strategies. Finally, the superego begins to develop just before school age, as the child incorporates the parents' values and cultural mores.

Freud thought the stages of personality development were strongly influenced by maturation. In each of Freud's five **psychosexual stages**, the libido is centered in that part of the body that is most sensitive at that age. In a newborn, the mouth is the most sensitive part of the body, so libidinal energy is focused there. The stage is therefore called the *oral stage*. As neurological development progresses, the infant has more sensation in the anus (hence the *anal stage*) and later in the genitalia (the *phallic* and eventually the *genital stages*).

Erikson's Theory The stages Erikson proposed, called **psychosocial stages**, are influenced much less by maturation and much more by common cultural demands for children of a particular age, such as the demand that a child become toilet trained at about age 2 or that the child learn school skills at age 6 or 7. In Erikson's view, each child moves through a fixed sequence of tasks, each centered on the development of a particular facet of identity. For example, the first task, central to the first 12 to 18 months of life, is to develop a sense of *basic trust*. If the child's caregivers are not responsive and loving, however, the child may develop a sense of basic mistrust, which will affect his responses at all the later stages.

In both Freud's and Erikson's theories, the critical point is that the degree of success a child experiences in meeting the demands of these various stages will depend very heavily on the interactions he has with the people and objects in his world. This interactive element in

Table 1.1 Some Common Defense Mechanisms

Mechanism	Definition	Example
Denial	Behaving as if a problem doesn't exist	A pregnant woman fails to get prenatal care because she convinces herself she can't possibly be pregnant even though she has all the symptoms.
Repression	Intentionally forgetting something unpleasant	A child "forgets" about a troublesome bully on the bus as soon as he gets safely home from school every day.
Projection	Seeing one's own behavior or beliefs in others whether they are actually present or not	A woman complains about her boss to a co-worker and comes away from the conversation believing that the co-worker shares her dislike of the boss, even though the co-worker made no comment on what she said.
Regression	Behaving in a way that is inappropriate for one's age	A toilet-trained 2-year-old starts wetting the bed every night after a new baby arrives.
Displacement	Directing emotion to an object or person other than the one that provoked it	An elderly adult suffers a stroke, becomes physically impaired, and expresses her frustration through verbal abuse of the hospital staff.
Rationalization	Creating an explanation to justify an action or to deal with a disappointment	A man stealing money from his employer says to himself, "They won't give me a raise. So what if I took $50?"

Freud's and all subsequent psychoanalytic theories is absolutely central. Basic trust cannot be developed unless the parents or other caregivers respond to the infant in a loving, consistent manner. The oral stage cannot be fully completed unless the infant's desire for oral stimulation is sufficiently gratified. And when a stage is not fully resolved, the old pattern or the unmet need is carried forward, affecting the individual's ability to handle later tasks or stages. So, for example, a young adult who developed a sense of mistrust in the first years of life may have a more difficult time establishing a secure intimate relationship with a partner or with friends.

Cognitive Theories

Learning Objective 1.7

What are the main ideas of cognitive-developmental and information-processing theories?

In psychoanalytic theories, the quality and character of a child's relationships with a few key people are seen as central to the child's whole development. **Cognitive-developmental theories**, which emphasize primarily cognitive development rather than personality, reverse this order of importance, emphasizing the centrality of the child's actions on the environment and her cognitive processing of experiences.

Piaget's Theory   The central figure in cognitive-developmental theory has been Jean Piaget (1896–1980), a Swiss psychologist whose theories (1952, 1970, 1977; Piaget & Inhelder, 1969) shaped the thinking of several generations of developmental psychologists. Piaget was struck by the great regularities in the development of children's thinking. He noticed that all children seem to go through the same kinds of sequential discoveries about their world, making the same sorts of mistakes and arriving at the same solutions. For example, all 3- and 4-year-olds seem to think that if you pour water from a short, fat glass into a tall, thin one, there is more water in the thin glass, since the water level is higher there than in the fat glass. In contrast, most 7-year-olds realize that the amount of water is the same in either glass.

Piaget's detailed observations of such systematic shifts in children's thinking led him to several assumptions, the most central of which is that it is the nature of the human organism to adapt to its environment. This is an active process. In contrast to many theorists, Piaget did not think that the environment shapes the child. Rather, the child (like the adult) actively seeks to understand his environment. In the process, he explores, manipulates, and examines the objects and people in his world.

The process of adaptation, in Piaget's view, is made up of several important subprocesses—*assimilation*, *accommodation*, and *equilibration*—all of which you will learn more about in Chapter 6. What is important to understand at this preliminary point is that Piaget thought that the child develops a series of fairly distinct "understandings," or "theories," about the way the world works, based on her active exploration of the environment. Each of these "theories" corresponds to a specific stage. Piaget thought that virtually all infants begin with the same skills and built-in strategies and since the environments children encounter are highly similar in important respects, he believed that the stages through which children's thinking moves are also similar. Piaget pro-

Piaget based many of his ideas on naturalistic observation of children of different ages on playgrounds and in schools.

posed a fixed sequence of four major stages, each growing out of the one that preceded it, and each consisting of a more or less complete system or organization of concepts, strategies, and assumptions.

cognitive-developmental theories Developmental theories that emphasize children's actions on the environment and suggest that age-related changes in reasoning precede and explain changes in other domains.

Vygotsky's Theory   Russian psychologist Lev Vygotsky (1896–1934) is normally thought of as belonging to the cognitive-developmental camp because he, too, was primarily concerned with understanding the origins of the child's knowledge (1978/1930). Vygotsky differed from Piaget, however, in one key respect: He was convinced that complex forms of thinking have their origins in social interactions (Duncan, 1995). According to Vygotsky, a child's learning of new cognitive skills is guided by an adult (or a more skilled child, such as an older sibling), who models and structures the child's learning experience, a process Jerome Bruner later called **scaffolding** (Wood, Bruner, & Ross, 1976). Such new learning, Vygotsky suggested, is best achieved in what he called the **zone of proximal development**—that range of tasks which are too hard for the child to do alone but which she can manage with guidance. As the child becomes more skilled, the zone of proximal development steadily widens, including ever harder tasks. Vygotsky thought the key to this interactive process lay in the language the adult used to describe or frame the task. Later, the child could use this same language to guide her independent attempts to do the same kinds of tasks.

Information-Processing Theory   Although it is not truly a cognitive-developmental theory, many of the ideas and research studies associated with **information-processing theory** have increased psychologists' understanding of Piaget's stages and other age-related changes in thinking. The goal of information-processing theory is to explain how the mind manages information (Klahr, 1992). Information-processing theorists use the computer as a model of human thinking. Consequently, they often use computer terms such as *hardware* and *software* to talk about human cognitive processes.

Theorizing about and studying memory processes are central to information-processing theory (Birney, Citron-Pousty, Lutz, & Sternberg, 2005). Theorists usually break memory down into subprocesses of encoding, storage, and retrieval. *Encoding* is organizing information to be stored in memory. For example, you may be encoding the information in this chapter by relating it to your own childhood. *Storage* is keeping information, and *retrieval* is getting information out of memory.

Most memory research assumes that the memory system is made up of multiple components. The idea is that information moves through these components in an organized way (see Figure 1.3). The process of understanding a spoken word serves as a good example. First, you hear the word when the sounds enter your *sensory memory*. Your experiences with language allow you to recognize the pattern of sounds as a word. Next, the word moves into your *short-term memory*, the component of the memory system where all information is processed. Thus, short-term memory is often called *working memory*. Knowledge of the word's meaning is then called up out of *long-term memory*, the component of the system where information is permanently stored, and placed in short-term memory, where it is linked to the word's sounds to enable you to understand what you have just heard.

Each memory component manages information differently. Information flows through sensory memory as if in a stream. Bits of information that are not attended to drop out quickly. Short-term memory is extremely limited in capacity—an adult's short-term memory can hold about seven items at a time. However, information can be retained in short-term

scaffolding The term used by Bruner to describe the process by which a teacher (or parent, older child, or other person in the role of teacher) structures a learning encounter with a child, so as to lead the child from step to step—a process consistent with Vygotsky's theory of cognitive development.

zone of proximal development In Vygotsky's theory, the range of tasks that are slightly too difficult for a child to do alone but that can be accomplished successfully with guidance from an adult or more experienced child.

information-processing theories A set of theories based on the idea that humans process information in ways that are similar to those used in computers.

Figure 1.3
The Information-Processing System

Information-processing research on memory is based on the assumption that information moves into, out of, and through sensory, short-term, and long-term memories in an organized way.

memory as long as it is processed in some way—for example, when you repeat your grocery list to yourself on the way to the store.

Long-term memory is unlimited in capacity, and information is often stored in terms of meaningful associations. For example, suppose you read a sentence such as "Bill wrote a letter to his brother." When you think about the sentence later, you might mistakenly recall that it contained the word *pen*. This happens because information about the process of writing and the tools used to do it are stored together in long-term memory.

There are both age-related and individual differences in information processing. As you will learn in Chapter 6, the number of items that can be retained in short-term memory at one time is far more limited in young children than in adults and older children. In addition, among children of the same age, some use more efficient strategies for remembering and solving problems. Looking at differences of both kinds and examining children's thinking from Piaget's and Vygotsky's perspectives provide a more complete picture of how children acquire the ability to reason logically.

Learning Theories

Learning Objective 1.8
How do learning theorists explain development?

Learning theories represent a theoretical tradition very different from that of either the psychoanalysts or the cognitive-developmentalists, one in which the emphasis is much more on the way the environment shapes the child than on how the child understands his experiences. Learning theorists do not argue that genetics or built-in biases are unimportant, but they see human behavior as enormously plastic, shaped by predictable processes of learning. Three of the most important learning theories are Pavlov's classical conditioning model, Skinner's operant conditioning model, and Bandura's social cognitive theory.

Classical Conditioning
Classical conditioning, made famous by Ivan Pavlov's (1849–1936) experiments with his salivating dog, involves the acquisition of new signals for existing responses. If you touch a baby on the cheek, she will turn toward the touch and begin to suck. In the technical terminology of classical conditioning, the touch on the cheek is the *unconditional stimulus*; the turning and sucking are *unconditioned responses*. The baby is already programmed to do all that; these are automatic reflexes. Learning occurs when some new stimulus is introduced to the system.

The general model is that other stimuli that are present just before or at the same time as the unconditional stimulus will eventually trigger the same responses. In the typical home situation, for example, a number of stimuli occur at about the same time as the touch on the baby's cheek before feeding: the sound of the mother's footsteps approaching, the kinesthetic cues of being picked up, and the tactile cues of being held in the mother's arms. All these stimuli may eventually become *conditional stimuli* and may trigger the infant's response of turning and sucking, even without any touch on the cheek.

Classical conditioning is of special interest in the study of child development because of the role it plays in the development of emotional responses, as Watson's Little Albert experiment so aptly demonstrated. For example, things or people present when you feel good will become conditional stimuli for that same sense of well-being; things or people previously associated with some uncomfortable feeling may become conditional stimuli for a sense of unease or anxiety. This is especially important in infancy, since a child's mother or father is present so often when nice things happen—when the child feels warm, comfortable, and cuddled. Thus, mother and father usually come to be conditional stimuli for pleasant feelings, a fact that makes it possible for the parents' mere presence to reinforce other behaviors as well. A tormenting older sibling might come to be a conditional stimulus for angry feelings, even after the sibling has long since stopped the tormenting. Such classically conditioned emotional responses are remarkably powerful. They begin to be formed very early in life, continue to be created throughout childhood and adulthood, and profoundly affect each individual's emotional experiences. Moreover, therapists can use the principles of classical conditioning

learning theories
Psychological theories that explain development in terms of accumulated learning experiences.

classical conditioning One of three major types of learning. An automatic, or unconditional response such as an emotion or a reflex comes to be triggered by a new cue, called the conditional stimulus, after having been paired several times with that stimulus.

Laboratory research involving animals was important in the development of Skinner's operant conditioning theory.

to help children resolve a variety of emotional problems (see *Developmental Science in the Real World*).

Operant Conditioning   The second major type of learning is most often called operant conditioning, although you may also see it referred to as *instrumental conditioning*. **Operant conditioning** is the process through which the frequency of a behavior increases or decreases because of the consequences the behavior produces. When a behavior increases, it is said to have been *reinforced*; when it decreases, the behavior is said to have been *punished*. Psychologist B. F. Skinner (1904–1990) discovered the principles of operant conditioning in a series of animal studies. He believed that these principles strongly influence human development.

Reinforcement occurs when a consequence results in an increase in the frequency of a particular behavior. With **positive reinforcement**, an *added* stimulus or consequence increases a behavior. Certain kinds of pleasant stimuli—such as praise, a smile, food, a hug, or attention—serve as positive reinforcers for most people most of the time. But strictly speaking, a reinforcer is defined by its effect; we don't know that something is reinforcing unless we see that its presence increases the probability of some behavior. For example, if a parent gives a child dessert as a reward for good table manners, and the child's frequency of good table manners increases, then the dessert is a reinforcer. If the frequency does not increase, then the dessert is not a reinforcer.

Negative reinforcement increases a behavior because the reinforcement involves the termination or removal of an unpleasant stimulus. Suppose your little boy is whining and begging you to pick him up. At first you ignore him, but finally you do pick him up. What happens? He stops whining. So your picking-up behavior has been negatively reinforced by the cessation of his whining, and you will be more likely to pick him up the next time he whines. At the same time, his whining has probably been positively reinforced by your attention, so he will be more likely to whine on similar occasions.

Dr. Rawlins is a psychologist who works in a large urban school district. The children she works with suffer from a wide range of emotional problems, but one of the most common is *school refusal*, a condition in which a child refuses to go to school. You might be surprised to learn that the mechanisms at work in John Watson's classical conditioning experiment with Little Albert are similar to those that psychologists use to help children overcome school refusal.

Recall that Little Albert learned to associate a neutral stimulus (a rat) with a stimulus to which his inborn reflexes predisposed him to respond fearfully (a loud noise). Unless a child is attempting to avoid a specific threat, such as a bully, psychologists speculate that school refusal results from a similar pattern of associations. For some reason, the neutral stimulus of school has become associated with stimuli that naturally provoke anx-

ious responses in children. Thus, psychologists reason that children's fear of school can be unlearned through the same stimulus-response mechanism that produced it—a type of therapy called *systematic desensitization* (Kauffman, 2005; Wolpe, 1958).

To initiate a systematic desensitization intervention, a therapist begins by teaching the child how to control his respiration rate and muscular contractions in order to achieve a state of physical relaxation. Once the child has mastered this control, the therapist helps him learn to "switch on" his relaxation response in connection with each step in the sequence of events involved in getting to and staying in school. For example, the child first learns to intentionally relax while getting ready for school. Next, he practices intentionally relaxing while waiting for the bus, and then while he is on the bus. Once at school, the

child is encouraged to initiate his relaxation response in front of the school entrance. The final step is to learn to intentionally relax in the classroom and to initiate the relaxation response whenever he experiences feelings of anxiety during the school day. After repeating these steps several times, most children with school refusal learn to associate going to school with relaxation responses rather than with anxiety.

Questions for Reflection

1. How could systematic desensitization be used to help a child who was bitten by a dog overcome her subsequent fear of all dogs?
2. What actions on the part of parents, teachers, or peers might prevent a child with school refusal from benefiting from systematic desensitization?

In laboratory situations, experimenters can be sure to reinforce a behavior every time it occurs or to stop reinforcements completely so as to produce *extinction* of a response. In the real world, however, consistency of reinforcement is the exception rather than the rule. Much more common is a pattern of *partial reinforcement*, in which a behavior is reinforced on some occasions but not others. Studies of partial reinforcement show that children and adults take longer to learn behaviors under partial reinforcement conditions, but once established, such behaviors are much more resistant to extinction. If you smile at your daughter only every fifth or sixth time she brings a picture to show you (and if she finds your smile reinforcing), she'll keep on bringing pictures for a very long stretch, even if you quit smiling altogether.

Both positive and negative reinforcements strengthen behavior. **Punishment**, in contrast, weakens behavior. Sometimes punishments involve eliminating nice things (for example, "grounding" a child, taking away TV privileges, or sending her to her room). Often they involve administering unpleasant things such as a scolding or a spanking. What is confusing about such consequences is that they don't always do what they are intended to do: They do not always suppress the undesired behavior.

Say, for example, a parent suspends a teenager's driving privileges for coming home after curfew in the hope that the penalty will stop the behavior of coming home late. For some teens, this approach will be effective. Others, though, may respond with defiance, by staying out later and later each time their driving privileges are restored. To these teens, the parent's "punishment" is a form of recognition for the defiant attitude they hope to project. For them, the "punishment" is actually a positive reinforcement. Thus, punishment, like reinforcement, must be defined in terms of its effect on behavior; if a consequence doesn't weaken or stop a behavior, it isn't a punishment.

Bandura's Social Cognitive Theory

Albert Bandura, whose variation of learning theory is by far the most influential among developmental psychologists today, has built on the base of these traditional learning concepts but has added several other key ideas (1989, 2004, 2008). First, he argues that learning does not always require direct reinforcement. Learning may also occur merely as a result of watching someone else perform some action. Learning of this type, called *observational learning*, or *modeling*, is involved in a wide range of behaviors. Children learn how to hit from watching other people in real life and on television. They learn how to be generous by watching others donate money or share goods. Bandura also calls attention to another class of reinforcements called *intrinsic reinforcements*. These are internal reinforcements, such as the pride a child feels when she figures out how to draw a star or the sense of satisfaction you may experience after strenuous exercise.

Finally, and perhaps most importantly, Bandura has gone far toward bridging the gap between learning theory and cognitive-developmental theory by emphasizing important cognitive (mental) elements in observational learning. Indeed, he now calls his theory "social cognitive theory" rather than "social learning theory," as it was originally labeled (Bandura, 1986, 1989). For example, Bandura now stresses the fact that modeling can be the vehicle for learning abstract information as well as concrete skills. In abstract modeling, the observer extracts a rule that may be the basis of the model's behavior, then learns the rule as well as the specific behavior. A child who sees his parents volunteering one day a month at a food bank may extract a rule about the importance of "helping others," even if the parents never actually articulate this rule. Thus, through modeling, a child can acquire attitudes, values, ways of solving problems, even standards of self-evaluation.

Collectively, Bandura's additions to traditional learning theory make his theory far more flexible and powerful, although it is still not a strongly developmental theory. That is,

operant conditioning The type of learning in which the probability of a person's performing some behavior is increased or decreased because of the consequences it produces.

positive reinforcement The process of strengthening a behavior by the presentation of some pleasurable or positive stimulus.

negative reinforcement The process of strengthening a behavior by the removal or cessation of an unpleasant stimulus.

punishment The removal of a desirable stimulus or the administration of an unpleasant consequence after some undesired behavior in order to stop the behavior.

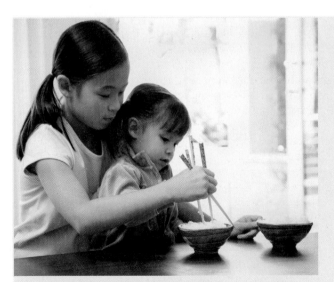

Using chopsticks is only one example of the myriad skills that are learned through modeling.

Bandura has little to say about any changes that may occur with age in what or how a child may learn from modeling. In contrast, both psychoanalytic and cognitive-developmental theories are strongly developmental, emphasizing sequential, often stagelike qualitative change that occurs with age.

Learning Objective 1.9
What are the criteria that developmental scientists use to compare theories?

Comparing Theories

After learning about theories of development, students usually want to know which one is right. However, developmentalists don't think of theories in terms of right or wrong but, instead, compare them on the basis of their assumptions and how useful they are to understanding human development.

Assumptions about Development   When we say that a theory assumes something to be true, we mean that it begins from a general perspective on development. We can think of a theory's assumptions in terms of its answers to three questions about development.

One question addresses the *active or passive issue*: Is a person active in shaping her own development, or is she a passive recipient of environmental influences? Theories that claim a person's actions on the environment are the most important determinants of her development are on the active side of this question. Cognitive-developmental theories, for example, typically view development this way. In contrast, theories on the passive side of the question, such as classical and operant conditioning, maintain that development results from the action of the environment on the individual.

As you learned earlier in the chapter, the *nature or nurture question* is one of the most important issues in developmental psychology. All developmental theories, while admitting that both nature and nurture are involved in development, make assumptions about their relative importance. Theories claiming that biology contributes more to development than environment are on the nature side of the question. Those that view environmental influences as most important are on the nurture side. Other theories assume that nature and nurture are equally important, and that it is impossible to say which contributes more to development.

Developmental theories also disagree on the *stability versus change issue*. Theories that have no stages assert that development is a stable, continuous process. Stage theories, on the other hand, emphasize change more than stability. They claim that development happens in leaps from lower to higher steps.

Table 1.2 lists the theories you have read about in this chapter and the assumptions each makes regarding these issues. Because each theory is based on different assumptions, each takes a different approach to studying development. Consequently, research derived from each reveals something different about development.

A theory's assumptions also shape the way it is applied in the real world. For example, a teacher who approached instruction from the cognitive-developmental perspective would create a classroom in which children can experiment to some degree on their own. He would also recognize that children differ in abilities, interests, developmental level, and other internal characteristics. He would believe that structuring the educational environment is important, but that what each student ultimately learns will be determined by his or her own actions on the environment. Alternatively, a teacher who adopted the learning theory perspective would guide and reinforce children's learning very carefully. Such a teacher would place little importance on ability differences among children. Instead, he would try to accomplish the same instructional goals for all children through proper manipulation of the environment.

Usefulness   Developmentalists also compare theories with respect to their usefulness. Before reading this section, you should understand that there is a fair amount of disagreement among psychologists on exactly how useful each theory is. Nevertheless, there are a few general criteria most psychologists use to evaluate the usefulness of a theory.

Table 1.2 Comparing Theories

	Theory	Main Ideas	Active or Passive?	Nature or Nurture?	Stages or No Stages?
Psychoanalytic Theories	Freud's Psychosexual Theory	Personality develops in five stages from birth to adolescence; in each stage, the need for physical pleasure is focused on a different part of the body.	Passive	Nature	Stages
	Erikson's Psychosocial Theory	Personality develops through eight life crises across the entire lifespan; a person finishes each crisis with either a good or a poor resolution.	Passive	Both	Stages
Cognitive Theories	Piaget's Cognitive-Developmental Theory	Reasoning develops in four universal stages from birth through adolescence; in each stage, the child builds a different kind of scheme.	Active	Both	Stages
	Vygotsky's Socio-Cultural Theory	Social interaction is critical to the development of thinking and problem-solving; stages in the development of reasoning reflect internalized language.	Active	Both	Stages
	Information-Processing Theory	The computer is used as a model for human cognitive functioning; encoding, storage, and retrieval processes change with age, causing changes in memory function.	Active	Both	Some theories have stages; others do not
Learning Theories	Classical Conditioning	Learning happens when neutral stimuli become so strongly associated with natural stimuli that they elicit the same responses.	Passive	Nurture	No stages
	Operant Conditioning	Development involves behavior changes that are shaped by reinforcement and punishment.	Passive	Nurture	No stages
	Bandura's Social Cognitive Theory	People learn from models; what they learn from a model depends on how they interpret the situation cognitively and emotionally.	Active	Nurture	No stages

One kind of usefulness has to do with a theory's ability to generate predictions that can be tested with scientific methods. For example, one criticism of Freud's theory is that many of his claims are difficult to test. In contrast, when Piaget claimed that most children can solve hypothetical problems by age 12 or so, he made an assertion that is easily tested. Thus, Piaget's theory is viewed by many developmentalists as more useful in this sense than Freud's. Vygotsky, the learning theorists, and the information-processing theorists have also proposed many testable ideas (Thomas, 2000).

Another criterion by which psychologists judge the usefulness of theories is their *heuristic value*, the degree to which they stimulate thinking and research. In terms of heuristic value, we would have to give Freud's and Piaget's theories equally high marks. Both are responsible for an enormous amount of theorizing and research on human development, often by psychologists who strongly disagree with them.

Yet another way of thinking about a theory's usefulness is in terms of practical value. In other words, a theory may be deemed useful if it provides solutions to real-life problems. On this criterion, the learning and information-processing theories seem to stand out because they provide tools that can be used to influence behavior. A person who suffers from anxiety attacks, for example, can learn to use biofeedback, a technique derived from classical conditioning theories, to manage them. Similarly, a student who needs to learn to study more effectively can get help from study-skills courses based on information-processing theories.

Ultimately, of course, no matter how many testable hypotheses or practical techniques a theory produces, it is of little or no value to developmentalists if it doesn't explain the basic facts of development. On this criterion, learning theories, especially those of classical and operant conditioning, are regarded by many developmentalists as somewhat less useful than other perspectives (Thomas, 2000). While they explain how specific behaviors may be learned, the complexity of human development can't be reduced to connections between stimuli and responses or behaviors and reinforcers.

Eclecticism As you can see, the point of comparing theories is not to conclude which one is true. Instead, we compare them to understand the unique contribution each can make to a comprehensive understanding of human development. Consequently, today's developmental scientists try to avoid the kind of rigid adherence to a single theoretical perspective that was characteristic of theorists such as Freud, Piaget, and Skinner. Instead, most adopt an approach known as **eclecticism**, the use of multiple theoretical perspectives to explain and study human development (Parke, 2004).

To better understand the eclectic approach, think about how ideas drawn from several theories might help us better understand a child's disruptive behavior in school. Observations of the child's behavior and her classmates' reactions may suggest that her behavior is being rewarded by the other children's responses (a behavioral explanation). Deeper probing of the child's family situation may indicate that her acting-out behavior reflects an emotional reaction to a family event such as divorce (a psychoanalytic explanation). The emotional reaction may arise from her inability to understand why her parents are divorcing (a cognitive-developmental explanation). When appropriately applied, each of these perspectives can help us gain insight into developmental issues. Moreover, we can integrate all of them into a more complete explanation than any of the perspectives alone could provide us with.

Finding the Answers: Research Designs and Methods

The easiest way to understand research methods is to look at a specific question and the alternative ways in which it can be answered. Suppose we wanted to answer the following question: "What causes children's attention spans to increase as they get older?" How might we go about answering this question?

Learning Objective 1.10
What are the goals of developmental science?

The Goals of Developmental Science

Developmental psychology uses the scientific method to achieve four goals: to *describe*, to *explain*, to *predict*, and to *influence* human development from conception to death. To describe development is simply to state what happens. "Children's attention spans get longer as they get older" is an example of a statement that represents the description goal of developmental psychology. All we would have to do is measure how long children of various ages pay attention to something to meet this objective.

Explaining development involves telling why a particular event occurs. As you learned earlier in this chapter, developmentalists rely on theories to generate explanations. Useful theories produce predictions researchers can test, or **hypotheses**, such as "If changes in the brain cause children's attention spans to increase, then children whose brain development is ahead of that of their peers should also have longer attention spans." To test this biological hypothesis, we would have to measure some aspect of brain structure or function as well as attention span. Then we would have to find a way to relate one to the other.

We could instead test an experiential explanation of attention-span increase by comparing children of the same age who differ in the amount of practice they get in paying attention. For example, we might hypothesize that the experience of learning to play a musical instrument enhances children's ability to attend. If we compare instrument-playing and non–instrument-playing children of the same age and find that those who have musical training do better on tests of attention than their agemates who have not had musical training, the experiential perspective gains support.

eclecticism The use of multiple theoretical perspectives to explain and study human development.

hypothesis A testable prediction based on a theory.

If both the biological and the experiential hypotheses are supported by research, they provide far more insight into age-related attention-span change than would either hypothesis alone. In this way, theories add tremendous depth to psychologists' understanding of the facts of human development and provide information that can be used to influence development. Let's say, for example, that a child is diagnosed with a condition that can affect the brain, such as epilepsy. If we know that brain development and attention span are related, we can use tests of attention span to make judgments about how much her medical condition may have already influenced her brain. At the same time, because we know that experience affects memory as well, we may be able to provide her with training that will help her overcome attention-span problems that are likely to arise in the future.

Studying Age-Related Changes

Learning Objective 1.11
What are the pros and cons of cross-sectional, longitudinal, and sequential research designs?

When researchers set out to study age-related change, they have basically three choices: (1) study different groups of people of different ages, using what is called a **cross-sectional design**; (2) study the *same* people over a period of time, using a **longitudinal design**; or (3) combine cross-sectional and longitudinal designs in some fashion in a **sequential design**.

Cross-Sectional Designs   To study attention cross-sectionally, we might select groups of participants at each of several ages, such as groups of 2-, 5-, 8-, and 11-year-olds. If we find that each group demonstrates a longer average attention span than all the groups that are younger, we may be tempted to conclude that attention span does increase with age, but we cannot say this conclusively with cross-sectional data, because these children differ not only in age, but in cohort. The differences in attention might reflect educational differences and not actually be linked to age or development. Furthermore, cross-sectional studies cannot tell us anything about sequences of change over age or about the consistency of individual behavior over time, because each child is tested only once. Still, cross-sectional research is very useful because it is relatively quick to do and can give indications of possible age differences or age changes.

Longitudinal Designs   Longitudinal designs seem to solve the problems that arise with cross-sectional designs, because they follow the same individuals over a period of time. For example, to examine our attention-span hypothesis, we could test a particular group of children first at age 2, then at age 5, next at age 8, and finally at age 11. Such studies look at sequences of change and at individual consistency or inconsistency over time. And because these studies compare the same people at different ages, they get around the cohort problems of cross-sectional designs. However, longitudinal designs have several major difficulties. One problem is that longitudinal designs typically involve giving each participant the same tests over and over again. Over time, people learn how to take the tests. Such practice effects may distort the measurement of any underlying developmental changes.

Another significant problem with longitudinal studies is that not everyone sticks with the program. Some participants drop out; others die or move away. As a general rule, the healthiest and best-educated participants are most likely to stick it out, and that fact biases the results, particularly if the study continues into adulthood.

Longitudinal studies also don't really get around the cohort problem. For example, one famous study, the Oakland Growth Study, followed individuals born between 1918 and 1928 into old age. Consequently, the study's participants experienced certain major historical events, such as the Great Depression and World War II, that probably influenced their development. So, we don't know whether the ways in which they changed across these years, when they were children and teenagers, were caused by developmental processes or by the unique historical period in which they were growing up.

Sequential Designs   One way to avoid the shortcomings of both cross-sectional and longitudinal designs is to use a sequential design. To study our attention-span question using

cross-sectional design A form of research study in which samples of participants from several different age groups are studied at the same time.

longitudinal design A form of research study in which the same participants are observed or assessed repeatedly over a period of months or years.

sequential design A form of research study that combines cross-sectional and longitudinal designs in some way.

Only by studying the same children over time (that is, longitudinally), such as this boy Eddie at three ages, can developmentalists identify consistencies (or changes) in behavior across age.

a sequential design, we would begin with at least two age groups. One group might include 2- to 4-year-olds, and the other might have 5- to 7-year-olds. We would then test each group over a number of years, as illustrated in Figure 1.4. Each testing point beyond the initial one provides two types of comparisons. Age-group comparisons provide the same kind of information as a cross-sectional study would. Comparisons of the scores or behaviors of participants in each group to their own scores or behaviors at an earlier testing point provide longitudinal evidence at the same time.

Sequential designs also allow for comparisons of cohorts. Notice in Figure 1.4, for example, that those in Group A are 5 to 7 years old at testing point 1, and those in Group B are 5 to 7 years old at testing point 2. Likewise, Group A members are 8 to 10 at point 2, and their counterparts in Group B are this age at point 3. If same-age comparisons of the two groups reveal that their average attention spans are different, the researchers have evidence that, for some reason, the two cohorts differ. Conversely, if the groups perform similarly, the investigators can conclude that their respective performances represent developmental characteristics rather than cohort effects. Moreover, if both groups demonstrate similar age-related patterns of change over time, the researchers can conclude that the developmental pattern is not specific to any particular cohort. Finding the same developmental pattern in two cohorts provides psychologists with stronger evidence than either cross-sectional or longitudinal data alone.

Figure 1.4
A Hypothetical Sequential Study

A hypothetical sequential study of attention span across ages 2 to 13.

		Age at testing point 1	Age at testing point 2	Age at testing point 3
Group	A	5 to 7	8 to 10	11 to 13
	B	2 to 4	5 to 7	8 to 10

Learning Objective 1.12
What descriptive methods are used by developmental scientists?

Descriptive Methods

A researcher interested in studying the relationship between age and attention span must decide how to go about finding relationships between *variables*. Variables are characteristics that vary from person to person, such as height, intelligence, and personality. When two or more variables vary together, there is some kind of relationship between them. The hypothesis that attention span increases with age involves two variables—attention span and age—and suggests a relationship between them. There are several ways of identifying and describing such relationships.

Case Studies and Naturalistic Observation **Case studies** are in-depth examinations of single individuals. To examine changes in attention span, a researcher could use a case study comparing an individual's scores on tests of attention at various ages in childhood. Such a study might tell a lot about the stability or instability of attention in the individual studied, but the researcher wouldn't know if the findings applied to others.

Still, case studies are extremely useful in making decisions about individuals. For example, to find out if a child has mental retardation, a psychologist can do an extensive case study involving tests, interviews of the child's parents, behavioral observations, and so on. Case studies are also frequently the basis of important hypotheses about unusual developmental events such as head injuries and strokes.

When psychologists use **naturalistic observation**, they observe people in their normal environments. For instance, to find out more about attention span in children of different ages, a researcher could observe them in their homes or child-care centers. Such studies provide developmentalists with information about psychological processes in everyday contexts.

The weakness of this method, however, is *observer bias*. For example, if a researcher observing 2-year-olds is convinced that most of them have very short attention spans, he is likely to ignore any behavior that goes against this view. Because of observer bias, naturalistic observation studies often use "blind" observers who don't know what the research is about. In most cases, such studies employ two or more observers for the sake of accuracy. This way, the observations of each observer can be checked against those of the other.

Like case studies, the results of naturalistic observation studies have limited generalizability. In addition, naturalistic observation studies are very time-consuming. They must be repeated in a variety of settings before researchers can be sure people's behavior reflects development and not the influences of a specific environment.

Correlations A **correlation** is a number ranging from −1.00 to +1.00 that describes the strength of a relationship between two variables. A zero correlation indicates that there is no relationship between those variables. A positive correlation means that high scores on one variable are usually accompanied by high scores on the other. The closer a positive correlation is to +1.00, the stronger the relationship between the variables. Two variables that move in opposite directions result in a negative correlation, and the nearer the correlation is to −1.00, the more strongly the two are inversely related.

To understand positive and negative correlations, think about the relationship between temperature and the use of air conditioners and heaters. Temperature and air conditioner use are positively correlated. As the temperature climbs, so does the number of air conditioners in use. Conversely, temperature and heater use are negatively correlated. As the temperature decreases, the number of heaters in use goes up.

If we want to test the hypothesis that greater attention span is related to increases in age, we can use a correlation. All we would need to do would be to administer attention-span tests to children of varying ages and to calculate the correlation between test scores and ages. If there was a positive correlation between the length of children's attention spans and age—if older children attended for longer periods of time—then we could say that our hypothesis had been supported. Conversely, if there was a negative correlation—if older children paid attention for shorter periods of time than younger children—then we would have to conclude that our hypothesis had not been supported.

case studies In-depth studies of individuals.

naturalistic observation A research method in which participants are observed in their normal environments.

correlation A statistic used to describe the strength of a relationship between two variables. It can range from −1.00 to +1.00. The closer it is to +1.00 or −1.00, the stronger the relationship being described.

Experimental Methods

Learning Objective 1.13
What is the primary advantage of the experimental method?

As useful as they are, case studies, naturalistic observations, and correlations reveal little about *causal* relationships between variables. For instance, the amount of time that children spend watching television is correlated with excessive weight gain, but it's highly doubtful that watching television causes a child to gain too much weight. Instead, the television-watching and weight gain are correlated because both are related to the actual causes of weight gain: too many calories (eating snacks while watching television) and too little exercise.

When developmental scientists seek to identify the cause of an age-related change, they turn to experiments. An **experiment** is a research method that tests a causal hypothesis. Suppose, for example, that we think age differences in attention span are caused by younger children's failure to use attention-maintaining strategies, such as ignoring distractions. We could test this hypothesis by providing attention training to one group of children and no training to another group. If the trained children got higher scores on attention tests than they did before training, and the no-training group showed no change, we could claim that our hypothesis had been supported.

A key feature of an experiment is that participants are assigned *randomly* to participate in one of several groups. In other words, chance determines the group in which the researcher places each participant. When participants are randomly assigned to groups, the groups have equal averages and equal amounts of variation with respect to variables such as intelligence, personality traits, height, weight, health status, and so on. Consequently, none of these variables can affect the outcome of the experiment.

Participants in the **experimental group** receive the treatment the experimenter thinks will produce a particular effect, while those in the **control group** receive either no special treatment or a neutral treatment. The presumed causal element in the experiment is called the **independent variable**, and the behavior on which the independent variable is expected to show its effect is called a **dependent variable** (or the *outcome variable*).

Applying these terms to the attention-training experiment may help you better understand them. The group that receives the attention training is the experimental group, while those who receive no instruction form the control group. Attention training is the variable that we, the experimenters, think will cause differences in attention span, so it is the independent variable. Performance on attention tests is the variable we are using to measure the effect of the attention training. Therefore, performance on attention tests is the dependent variable.

Experiments are essential for understanding many aspects of development. But two special problems in studying child development limit the use of experiments. First, many of the questions developmentalists want to answer have to do with the effects of unpleasant or stressful experiences—for example, abuse or prenatal exposure to alcohol or tobacco. For obvious ethical reasons, researchers cannot manipulate these variables. For example, they cannot ask one set of pregnant women to have two alcoholic drinks a day and others to have none. To study the effects of such experiences, developmentalists must rely on nonexperimental methods, like correlations.

Second, the independent variable developmentalists are often most interested in is age itself, and they cannot assign participants randomly to age groups. Researchers can compare the attention spans of 4-year-olds and 6-year-olds, but the children differ in a host of ways other than their ages. Older children have had more and different experiences. Thus, unlike psychologists studying other aspects of behavior, developmental psychologists *cannot* systematically manipulate many of the variables they are most interested in.

To get around this problem, developmentalists can use any of a number of strategies, sometimes called *quasi-experiments*, in which they compare groups without assigning the participants randomly. Cross-sectional comparisons are a form of quasi-experiment. So are studies in which researchers select naturally occurring groups that differ in some dimension of interest, such as children whose parents choose to place them in child-care programs compared with children whose parents keep them at home. Such comparisons have built-in problems, because groups that differ in one way are likely to be different in other ways as well. Families who place their children in child care are also likely to be poorer, more likely to have only a single parent, and may have different values or religious backgrounds than those who rear their children at home. If researchers find that the two groups of children differ in some fashion, is it because they have spent their daytime hours in different places or because of these other differences in their families? Such comparisons can

experiment A research method for testing a causal hypothesis, in which participants are assigned randomly to experimental and control groups and the experimental group is then provided with a particular experience that is expected to alter behavior in some fashion.

experimental group A group of participants in an experiment who receive a particular treatment intended to produce some specific effect.

control group A group of participants in an experiment who receive either no special treatment or some neutral treatment.

independent variable A condition or event that an experimenter varies in some systematic way in order to observe the impact of that variation on participants' behavior.

dependent variable The variable in an experiment that is expected to show the impact of manipulations of the independent variable; also called the *outcome variable*.

be made a bit cleaner if the comparison groups are initially selected so that they are matched on those variables that researchers think might matter, such as income, marital status, or religion. But a quasi-experiment, by its very nature, will always yield more ambiguous results than will a fully controlled experiment. However, as noted in the *Thinking about Research* discussion, media reports of research often do not provide consumers with sufficient information about research methods. Such information is vital to determining the validity of a research finding. Likewise, it can help parents and others who work with children determine the relevance of the research to their own lives.

THINKING ABOUT RESEARCH

Responding to Media Reports of Research

In today's information age, parents are bombarded with media reports about research nearly every day. Thinking about such reports can help you understand why it is important to learn about research methods even if you have no intention of ever doing research yourself. For purposes of illustration, consider the following: In 2004, the news media carried a number of reports warning parents of young children that watching too much television in the early years might lead to attention deficit hyperactivity disorder (ADHD) later in childhood (e.g., Clayton, 2004). These warnings were based, reporters said, on a scientific study that was published in the prestigious journal *Pediatrics*. How can a person who isn't an expert on the subject in question evaluate claims like these?

The thinking strategies used by psychologists and other scientists can help us sift through such information. *Critical thinking*, the foundation of the scientific method, is the process of objectively evaluating claims, propositions, and conclusions to determine whether they follow logically from the evidence presented. When we engage in critical thinking, we exhibit these characteristics:

- **Independent thinking.** When thinking critically, we do not automatically accept and believe what we read or hear.
- **Suspension of judgment.** Critical thinking requires gathering relevant and up-to-date information on all sides of an issue before taking a position.
- **Willingness to modify or abandon prior judgments.** Critical thinking involves evaluating new evidence, even when it contradicts pre-existing beliefs.

Applying the first of these three characteristics to the television-ADHD study involves recognizing that the validity of any study isn't determined by the authority of its source. In other words, prestigious journals—or psychology textbooks, for that matter—shouldn't be regarded as sources of fixed, immutable truths. In fact, learning to question accepted "truths" is important to the scientific method itself.

The second and third characteristics of critical thinking, suspension of judgment and willingness to change, may require changing some old habits. If you're like most people, you respond to media reports about research on the basis of your own personal experiences, a type of evidence scientists call *anecdotal evidence*. For instance, in response to the media report about television-watching and ADHD, a person might say "I agree with that study because my cousin has such severe ADHD that he had to drop out of high school, and he was always glued to the television when he was little." Another might counter with "I don't agree with that study because I watched a lot of television when I was a kid, and I don't have ADHD."

Suspension of judgment requires that you postpone either accepting or rejecting the study's findings until you have accumulated more evidence. This might involve determining what, if any, findings have been reported by other researchers regarding a possible link between television-watching and ADHD. Finding out about other relevant studies can help to form a comprehensive picture of what the entire body of research says about the issue. Ultimately, when enough evidence has been gathered, a critical thinker must be willing to abandon preconceived notions and prior beliefs that conflict with it.

The quality of the evidence is just as important as the quantity, however. Thus, a critical thinker would evaluate the findings of the television-ADHD study in terms of the methods used to obtain them. Did the researchers randomly assign young children to experimental and control groups who watched different amounts of television and then assess whether experimental and control children differed in ADHD symptoms several years later? If so, then the study was an experiment and media claims that television-watching in early childhood leads to ADHD might be justified. If, however, the researchers simply measured television-watching in early childhood and then correlated this variable with a measure of ADHD later on, then claims of a causal relationship between the two variables wouldn't be justified. Instead, the appropriate response would be to look for underlying variables, such as parental involvement, that might explain the connection. [The research cited in these reports was correlational in nature, so the strong causal claims implied by many media accounts of the study (Christakis, Zimmerman, Giuseppe, & McCarty, 2004) were inappropriate.]

Does a critique of this kind suggest that parents need not be concerned about how much time their toddlers spend in front of the television? Clearly not. Instead, it confirms a point made at the beginning of the chapter. Development is a complex process involving interactions among many variables. Thus, scientific studies can help parents better understand development, but they must be weighed along with other sources of information, including parents' own priorities and values, in the formulation of parenting decisions.

Questions for Critical Analysis

1. How could you apply the concepts of vulnerability and resilience to questions about the role of television-watching in the development of ADHD?
2. What variables other than parental involvement might contribute to a relationship between television-watching and ADHD?

Learning Objective 1.14

Why is cross-cultural research important to the study of human development?

Cross-Cultural Research

Cross-cultural research, or research comparing cultures or contexts, is becoming increasingly common in developmental psychology. Cross-cultural research is important to developmentalists for two reasons. First, developmentalists want to identify universal changes—that is, predictable events or processes that occur in the lives of individuals in all cultures. Developmentalists don't want to make a general statement about development—such as "Attention span increases with age"—if the phenomenon in question happens only in Western, industrialized cultures. Without cross-cultural research, it is impossible to know whether studies involving North Americans and Europeans apply to people in other parts of the world.

Second, one of the goals of developmental psychology is to produce findings that can be used to improve people's lives. Cross-cultural research is critical to this goal as well. For example, developmentalists know that children in cultures that emphasize the community more than the individual are more cooperative than children in cultures that are more individualistic. However, to use this information to help all children learn to cooperate, developmentalists need to know exactly how adults in collectivist cultures teach their children to be cooperative. Cross-cultural research helps developmentalists identify specific variables that explain cultural differences.

All of the methods you have learned about, which are summarized in Table 1.3, are used in cross-cultural research. Cross-cultural researchers borrow methods from other disciplines as well. One such strategy, borrowed from the field of anthropology, is to compile an *ethnography*—a detailed description of a single culture or context based on extensive observation. Often the observer lives within the culture for a period of time, perhaps as long as several years. Each ethnography is intended to stand alone, although it is sometimes possible to compare several different studies to see whether similar developmental patterns exist in varying contexts.

Alternatively, investigators may attempt to compare two or more cultures directly, by testing children or adults in each of several cultures with the same or comparable measures. Sometimes this involves comparisons across different countries. Sometimes the comparisons are between subcultures within the same country, as in the increasingly common research that compares children or adults from different ethnic groups or communities in the United States, such as African Americans, Hispanic Americans, Asian Americans, and European Americans.

Most of the studies in developmental science involve children in industrialized societies who attend school for several hours each day. By studying children, like this girl, whose cultures require them to spend much of their time working rather than going to school, developmentalists can determine which age-related changes in cognitive functioning are likely to be attributable to formal education and which arise from natural, presumably universal, developmental processes.

Learning Objective 1.15

What are the ethical standards that developmental researchers must follow?

Research Ethics

No matter which of the research strategies summarized in Table 1.3 a researcher chooses to use, she is ethically bound to conduct her research according to a well-established set of rules. *Research ethics* are the guidelines researchers follow to protect the rights of animals and humans who participate in studies. Ethical guidelines are published by professional organizations such as the American Psychological Association, the American Educational Research Association, and the Society for Research in Child Development. Universities, private foundations, and government agencies have review committees that make sure that all research these organizations sponsor is ethical. Guidelines for animal research include the requirement that animals be protected from unnecessary pain and suffering. Further, researchers must demonstrate that the potential benefits of their studies to either human or animal populations are greater than any potential harm to animal subjects.

Ethical standards for research involving human participants are based on the following major themes:

Protection from Harm. It is unethical to do research that may cause permanent physical or psychological harm to participants. Moreover, if there is a possibility of temporary harm, researchers must provide participants with some way of repairing the

cross-cultural research Any study that involves comparisons of different cultures or contexts.

Table 1.3 Research Methods and Designs

Method	Description	Advantages	Limitations
Cross-Sectional Designs	Participants of different ages studied at one time	Provide quick access to data about age differences	Ignore individual differences; cohort effects
Longitudinal Designs	Participants in one group studied several times	Track developmental changes in individuals and groups	Time-consuming; findings may apply only to the group that is studied
Sequential Designs	Study that combines both longitudinal and cross-sectional components	Yield cross-sectional and longitudinal data relevant to the same hypothesis	Time-consuming; different attrition rates across groups
Case Studies	In-depth study of one or a few individuals using observation, interviews, or psychological testing	Provide in-depth information; important in the study of unusual events	Results may not generalize beyond the case that is studied; time-consuming; subject to misinterpretation
Naturalistic Observation	Observation of behavior in natural settings	Participants behave naturally	Researchers' expectations can influence results; little control over conditions
Correlation Studies	Determination of mathematical relationship between two variables	Assess strength and direction of relationships	Cannot demonstrate cause and effect
Experiments	Random assignment of participants to control or experimental group; manipulation of independent variable	Identify cause-effect relationships	Results may not generalize to non-research settings; many variables cannot be studied in experiments
Cross-Cultural Research	Research that either describes culture or includes culture as a variable	Provides information about universality and culture-specificity of age-related changes	Time consuming; difficult to construct tests and methods that are equally valid in different cultures

damage. For example, if the study will remind participants of unpleasant experiences, like rape, researchers must provide them with counseling.

Informed Consent.   Researchers must inform participants of any possible harm and require them to sign a consent form stating that they are aware of the risks involved in participating. In order for children to participate in studies, their parents must give permission after the researcher has informed them of possible risks. If children are older than 7, they must also give consent themselves. If the research takes place in a school or child-care center, an administrator representing the institution must also consent. In addition, human participants, whether children or adults, have the right to discontinue participation in a study at any time. Researchers are obligated to explain this right to children in language they can understand.

Confidentiality.   Participants have the right to confidentiality. Researchers must keep the identities of participants confidential and must report data in such a way that no particular piece of information can be associated with any specific participant. The exception to confidentiality is when children reveal to researchers that they are being abused or have been abused in any way by an adult. In most states, all citizens are required to report suspected cases of child abuse.

Knowledge of Results.   Participants, their parents (if they are children), and administrators of institutions in which research takes place have a right to a written summary of a study's results.

Protection from Deception.   If deception has been a necessary part of a study, participants have the right to be informed about the deception as soon as the study is over.

Think Critically

- How have culture, religion, and science shaped your views of development?
- Researchers have found a positive correlation between a mother's age at the birth of her child and the child's later IQ: Very young mothers have children with lower IQs. How would an ecological approach help us understand this finding?

Conduct Your Own Research

Jenna is a 6-year-old who throws a temper tantrum every time she doesn't get her way. Describe her behavior to several people and ask them to explain it. Compare their explanations to those of the psychoanalytic, cognitive, and learning theorists.

Summary

ISSUES IN THE STUDY OF DEVELOPMENT

1.1 What answers have been proposed to the nature-nurture and continuity-discontinuity questions?

- The question of the degree to which development is influenced by nature and by nurture has been central to the study of development for thousands of years. Theorists on the nature side of the debate favor biological explanations, while those on the nurture side endorse experiential explanations of age-related changes. Psychologists who favor continuity emphasize the quantitative aspects of development, while those who view development as discontinuous often propose stage models to explain developmental change.

1.2 What are the internal and external variables that influence development?

- Internal variables that influence development include factors such as maturation, critical and sensitive periods, inborn biases, individual genetic variations, and internal models of experience. External variables include parent behaviors and characteristics of the physical environment. Theoretical models try to explain how internal and external variables interact.

1.3 How does the ecological perspective improve scientists' understanding of child development?

- The ecological perspective attempts to explain how external factors such as family and culture influence development. Bronfenbrenner proposed a contextual model highlighting the more extended aspects of a child's environment. Cultural influences filter down to the child through social institutions and through her neighborhood and family. All the components of this complex system interact to affect development.

1.4 In what ways do the concepts of vulnerability and resilience help us better understand child development?

- Developmental psychologists often discuss development in terms of vulnerability and resilience. The idea is that certain risk factors, such as poverty, predispose children to develop in undesirable ways. However, protective factors, such as high IQ, prevent some children from being negatively influenced by risk factors.

1.5 How do the three kinds of age-related change differ?

- Normative age-graded changes are those that are experienced by all human beings. Normative history-graded changes are common to individuals who have similar cultural and historical experiences. Nonnormative changes, such as the timing of experiences, can lead to individual differences in development.

THEORIES OF DEVELOPMENT

1.6 What are the main ideas of the psychoanalytic theories?

- Psychoanalytic theories suggest that internal drives strongly influence development. Both Freud and Erikson proposed stages to explain the process of personality development as people age.

1.7 What are the main ideas of cognitive-developmental and information-processing theories?

- Cognitive-developmental theories propose that basic cognitive processes influence development in all other areas. Piaget's theory has been especially influential, but interest in Vygotsky's ideas has grown in recent years. Information-processing theory also explains development in terms of cognitive processes.

1.8 How do learning theorists explain development?

- Learning theories emphasize the influence of the environment on children's behavior. Classical and operant conditioning principles explain learning in terms of links between stimuli and responses. Bandura's so-into two embryos. Thus they were identical with respect to the genes they received from their mother but were not identical with regard to their father's genes. To complicate matters, each boy received a different mix of genes from the two sperm. It was this different combination of genes from their father that led to the anatomical difference between the two boys' genitalia. (By the way, the boys were and continue to be completely normal in every other way.)

As you might guess, semi-identical twins are an extremely rare occurrence. In fact, before the twins' case came to light, laboratory studies with human reproductive cells had convinced experts that the combination of a single egg and multiple sperm could not possibly produce a living child. But technologies that are evolving at a breathtaking pace enabled the Good Samaritan researchers to trace each gene in the twins' bodies to the parent from whom it originated and to the two sperm that were involved in the boys' conception. The resulting evidence led the researchers to the inevitable conclusion that a feat that had proven to be impossible in the laboratory had been achieved through the natural process of conception.

Thanks to these same technologies, scientists are gaining insight into prenatal developmental processes that were shrouded in mystery just a few decades ago. In this chapter, you will become acquainted with some of these insights. As a result, we hope that you will gain a greater appreciation for the amazing process of prenatal development.

Conception and Genetics

The first step in the development of a human being is that moment of *conception*, when two single cells—one from a male and the other from a female—join together to form a new cell called a **zygote**. This event sets in motion powerful genetic forces that will influence the individual over the entire lifespan.

The Process of Conception

Ordinarily, a woman produces one **ovum** (egg cell) per month from one of her two ovaries. The ovum is released from an ovary roughly midway between two menstrual periods. If it is not fertilized, the ovum travels from the ovary down the **fallopian tube** toward the **uterus**, where it gradually disintegrates and is expelled as part of the next menstrual flow. If a couple has intercourse during the crucial few days when the ovum is in the fallopian tube, one of the millions of **sperm** ejaculated as part of each male orgasm may travel the full distance through the woman's vagina, cervix, and uterus into the fallopian tube and penetrate the ovum. A child is conceived. The zygote then continues on its journey down the fallopian tube and eventually implants itself in the wall of the uterus. (See the *Thinking about Research*.)

The Basic Genetics of Conception   Except in individuals with particular types of genetic abnormality, the nucleus of each cell in the human body contains a set of 46 **chromosomes**, arranged in 23 pairs. These chromosomes include all the genetic information for that individual, governing not only individual characteristics like hair color, height, body shape, temperament, and aspects of intelligence, but also all those characteristics shared by all members of our species, such as patterns of physical development and inborn biases of various kinds.

zygote The single cell formed from separate sperm and egg cells at conception.

ovum The cell released monthly from a woman's ovaries, which, if fertilized, forms the basis for the developing organism.

fallopian tube The tube between the ovary and the uterus down which the ovum travels to the uterus and in which conception usually occurs.

uterus The female organ in which the embryo/fetus develops (popularly referred to as the *womb*).

sperm The cells produced in a man's testes that may fertilize an ovum following intercourse.

chromosomes The structures, arrayed in 23 pairs, within each cell in the body that contain genetic information. Each chromosome is made up of many segments, called genes.

Assisted Reproductive Technology

Physicians define *infertility* as the failure to conceive after 12 consecutive months of unprotected intercourse (Mitchell, 2002). To help them conceive and deliver healthy babies, many infertile couples turn to *assisted reproductive techniques (ART)*. The use of *fertility drugs* to stimulate the ovaries to produce eggs is the most common approach to treating infertility. Increasing the number of eggs a woman produces increases the chances of a natural conception. Moreover, fertility drugs play an important role in other assisted reproductive techniques. They are often used along with *artificial insemination*, the process of injecting sperm into a woman's uterus at times when eggs are known to be present.

Fertility drugs are also employed in *in vitro fertilization* (*IVF; in vitro* is Latin for *glass*), popularly known as the "test-tube baby" method. The first step in IVF involves using fertility drugs to stimulate the woman's ovaries to produce multiple eggs. The eggs are then extracted from the ovaries and combined with

An eight-celled embryo is ideal for an IVF transfer. Pictured here is an embryo on the day of transfer into a woman's uterus.

sperm in a laboratory dish. If conception takes place, one or more embryos—ideally at the six-to-

eight-cell stage of development—are transferred to the woman's uterus in the hope that a normal pregnancy will develop. The eggs used in IVF can come from the woman who will carry the child or from a donor. Likewise, the sperm can be from the woman's partner or a donor.

However, IVF is not a highly successful procedure. Less than one-third of such procedures result in a live birth (Wright, Schieve, Reynolds, & Jeng, 2005). The older a woman is, the lower the probability that she will be able to have a successful IVF pregnancy. Roughly 35% of 20- to 29-year-old IVF patients achieve a live birth, but only 13% or so of IVF procedures involving women over age 40 are successful (SART, 2008). Moreover, IVF is expensive and is typically not covered by health insurance (Jain, Harlow, & Hornstein, 2002).

Successful IVF carries a different set of risks. Multiple births are more frequent among IVF patients, primarily because doctors typically transfer several zygotes at once in order to increase the likelihood of at least one live birth (Society for Assisted Reproductive Technology, 2004). Consequently, 13–33% of IVF patients deliver twins, and another 2–5% give birth to triplets (SART, 2008). Multiple births are associated with premature birth, low birth weight, and birth defects. Thus, reducing the frequency of multiple births among women undergoing treatment for infertility has become an important goal of re-

productive medicine (Jain, Missmer, & Hornstein, 2004).

Despite the risks associated with IVF, most women who achieve successful pregnancies as a result of this technique deliver babies who are healthy and normal. Further, both comparative (IVF infants and children versus non-IVF ones) and longitudinal studies have shown that children conceived through IVF who are of normal birth weight and who do not have any birth defects develop identically to peers who were conceived naturally (Levy-Shiff et al., 1998; van Balen, 1998). Such findings should give encouragement and hope to those couples who must turn to assisted reproductive technology to fulfill their desire to have children.

Questions for Critical Analysis

1. Look back at the discussion of research ethics in Chapter 1. Would it be ethical to use assisted reproductive technology to experimentally manipulate variables associated with conception, such as the timing of conception in relation to the seasons of the year, in order to determine the effects of such variables on development during infancy and childhood? Why or why not?
2. The use of assisted reproductive technology to help postmenopausal women get pregnant is controversial. What are the arguments for and against this practice?

This photo shows the moment of conception, when a single sperm has pierced the coating around the ovum.

The only cells that do not contain 46 chromosomes are the sperm and the ovum, collectively called **gametes**, or *germ cells*. In the early stages of development, gametes divide as all other cells do (a process called *mitosis*), with each set of 23 chromosome pairs duplicating itself. In the final step of gamete division, however, called *meiosis*, each new cell receives only one chromosome from each original pair. Thus, each gamete has only 23 chromosomes instead of 23 pairs. When a child is conceived, the 23 chromosomes in the ovum and the 23 in the sperm combine to form the 23 pairs that will be part of each cell in the newly developing body.

The chromosomes are composed of long strings of molecules of a chemical called **deoxyribonucleic acid (DNA)**. In an insight for which they won the Nobel Prize in 1953, James Watson and Francis Crick deduced that DNA is in the shape of a double helix, somewhat like a twisted ladder. The remarkable feature of this ladder is that the rungs are constructed so that the entire helix can "unzip"; then each half can guide the duplication of the missing part, thus allowing multiplication of cells so that each new cell contains the full set of genetic information.

The string of DNA that makes up each chromosome can be subdivided further into segments called **genes**, each of which controls or influences a particular feature of an organism or a portion of some developmental pattern. A gene controlling or influencing some specific characteristic, such as your blood type or your hair color, always appears in the same place (the *locus*; plural is *loci*) on the same chromosome in every individual of the same species. For example, the locus of the gene that determines whether you have type A, B, or O blood is on chromosome 9, and similar genes for blood type are found on chromosome 9 in every other human being. In February, 2001, scientists working on a remarkable group of studies known as the *Human Genome Project (HGP)* announced that they had identified the locus of every human gene (U.S. Department of Energy, 2001) (see Figure 2.1).

There are actually two types of chromosomes. In 22 of the chromosome pairs, called *autosomes*, the members of the pair look alike and contain exactly matching genetic loci. The 23rd pair, however, operates differently. The chromosomes of this pair, which determine the child's sex and are therefore called the *sex chromosomes*, come in two varieties, referred to as the X and the Y chromosomes.

A normal human female has two X chromosomes in this 23rd pair (an XX pattern), while a normal human male has one X and one Y chromosome (an XY pattern). The X chromosome is considerably larger than the Y chromosome and contains many genetic loci not found on the Y.

Note that the sex of the child is determined by the sex chromosome it receives from the sperm. Because a woman has only X chromosomes, every ovum carries an X. But because a man has both X and Y chromosomes, when the father's gametes divide, half the sperm will carry an X, and half a Y. If the sperm that fertilizes the ovum carries an X, then the child inherits an XX pattern and is a girl. If the fertilizing sperm carries a Y, then the combination is XY, and the child is a boy.

Geneticists have pushed this understanding a step further, discovering that only one very small section of the Y chromosome actually determines maleness—a segment referred to as *SRY* (*sex-determining region of the Y chromosome*). Sometime between 4 and 8 weeks after conception, SRY genetic codes signal the male embryo's body to begin secreting hormones called *androgens*. These hormones cause male genitalia to develop. If androgens are not present, female genitalia develop, no matter what the embryo's chromosomal status is.

gametes Sperm and ova. These cells, unlike all other cells of the body, contain only 23 chromosomes rather than 23 pairs.

deoxyribonucleic acid (DNA) The chemical of which chromosomes are composed.

gene A uniquely coded segment of DNA in a chromosome that affects one or more specific body processes or developments.

Creutzfeldt-Jakob disease	Diabetes insipidus, neurohypophyseal
Gerstmann-Straussler disease	SRY (sex-determining region Y)
Insomnia, fatal familial	McKusick-Kaufman syndrome
Hallervorden-Spatz syndrome	Cerebral amyloid angiopathy
Alagille syndrome	Thrombophilia
Corneal dystrophy	Myocardial infarction, susceptibility to
Inhibitor of DNA binding, dominant negative	Huntington-like neurodegenerative disorder
Facial anomalies syndrome	Anemia, congenital dyserythropoietic
Gigantism	Acromesomelic dysplasia, Hunter-Thompson type
Retinoblastoma	Brachydactyly, type C
Rous sarcoma	Chondrodysplasia, Grebe type
Colon cancer	Myeloid tumor suppressor
Galactosialidosis	Breast cancer
Severe combined immunodeficiency	Maturity onset diabetes of the young, type 1
Hemolytic anemia	Diabetes mellitus, noninsulin-dependent
Obesity/hyperinsulinism	Graves disease, susceptibility to
Pseudohypoparathyroidism, type 1a	Epilepsy, nocturnal frontal lobe and benign neonatal, type 1
McCune-Albright polyostotic fibrous dysplasia	Epiphyseal dysplasia, multiple
Somatotrophinoma	Electro-encephalographic variant pattern
Pituitary ACTH secreting adenoma	Pseudohypoparathyroidism, type 1b
Shah-Waardenburg syndrome	

Figure 2.1   Human Chromosome #20

This figure represents the genetic "map" of human chromosome #20; the map was produced by scientists associated with the Human Genome Project. Researchers have produced equally specific maps for all 23 human chromosomes. These maps include genes for normal traits (e.g., eye color) as well as for genetic disorders.

Genotypes, Phenotypes, and Patterns of Genetic Inheritance

When the 23 chromosomes from the father and the 23 from the mother come together at conception, they provide a mix of "instructions," which do not always match. When the two sets of instructions are the same at any given locus (such as genes for type A blood from both parents), geneticists say that the genetic pattern is **homozygous**. When the two sets of instructions differ, the genetic pattern is said to be **heterozygous**, such as a gene pair that includes a gene for type A blood from one parent and a gene for type O blood from the other. How are these differences resolved? Geneticists are still a long way from having a complete answer to this question, but some patterns are very clear. Table 2.1 gives a few examples of physical characteristics that follow the rules you'll be reading about in this section.

Genotypes and Phenotypes   First, it's important to know that geneticists (and psychologists) make an important distinction between the **genotype**, which is the specific set of "instructions" contained in a given individual's genes, and the **phenotype**, which is the set of actual observed characteristics of the individual. The phenotype is a product of three things: the genotype, environmental influences from the time of conception onward, and the interaction between the two. A child might have a genotype associated with high IQ, but if his mother drinks too much alcohol during the pregnancy, there may be damage to his nervous system, resulting in mild retardation. Another child might have a genotype including the mix of genes that contribute to a "difficult" temperament, but if his parents are particularly sensitive and thoughtful, he may learn other ways to handle himself.

Dominant and Recessive Genes   Whenever a given trait is governed by a single gene, as is true of some 1,000 individual physical characteristics, inheritance patterns follow well-understood rules. Figure 2.2 offers a schematic look at how the **dominant/recessive pattern of inheritance** works, using the genes for curly and straight hair as an example. Because straight hair is controlled by a recessive gene, an individual must inherit the straight-hair gene from both parents in order for her phenotype to include straight hair. A child who receives only one gene for straight hair will have curly hair, but she may pass the straight-hair gene on to her offspring.

Since curly hair is controlled by a dominant gene, a child who inherits a gene for curly hair from either parent will actually have curly hair. However, her hair may not be as curly as that of the parent from whom she received the gene. Genes vary in *expressivity*, a term that simply means that the same gene may be expressed differently in two individuals who have it.

The dominant/recessive pattern doesn't always work in such a straightforward way. For example, humans carry genes for three kinds of blood type: A (dominant), B (dominant), and O (recessive). Each individual has only two of these genes. If one gene is A and the other is O, then the individual's blood type is A. As you know, an individual must inherit two recessive O genes to have type O blood. But what happens if an individual receives an A and a B gene? Since both are dominant, the individual has type AB blood, and the genes are said to be *co-dominant*.

Polygenic and Multifactorial Inheritance   In the **polygenic pattern of inheritance**, many genes influence the phenotype. There are many polygenic traits in which the dominant/recessive pattern is also at work. For example, geneticists think that children get

Table 2.1   Normal Traits

Dominant	Recessive	Polygenic
Freckles	Flat feet	Height
Coarse hair	Thin lips	Body type
Dimples	Rh negative blood	Eye color
Curly hair	Fine hair	Skin color
Nearsightedness	Red hair	Personality
Broad lips	Blond hair	
Rh positive blood	Type O blood	
Types A and B blood		
Dark hair		

Source: Tortora and Grabowski, 1993.

homozygous Term describing the genetic pattern when the two genes in the pair at any given genetic locus both carry the same instructions.

heterozygous Term describing the genetic pattern when the two genes in the pair at any given genetic locus carry different instructions, such as a gene for blue eyes from one parent and a gene for brown eyes from the other parent.

genotype The pattern of characteristics and developmental sequences mapped in the genes of any specific individual, which will be modified by individual experience into the phenotype.

phenotype The expression of a particular set of genetic information in a specific environment; the observable result of the joint operation of genetic and environmental influences.

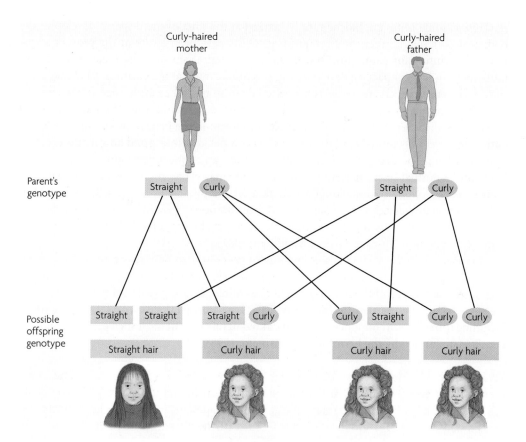

Figure 2.2
The Genetics of Hair Type

Examples of how the genes for curly and straight hair pass from parents to children.

three genes for skin color from each parent (Tortora & Derrickson, 2005). Dark skin is dominant over light skin, but blended skin colors are possible. Thus, when one parent has dark skin and the other has fair skin, their children most likely will have skin that is somewhere between the two. The dark-skinned parent's dominant genes will insure that the children are darker than the fair parent, but the fair-skinned parent's genes will prevent the children from having skin as dark as that of the dark-skinned parent.

Eye color is another polygenic trait with a dominant/recessive pattern (Tortora & Derrickson, 2005). Scientists don't know for sure how many genes influence eye color. They do know, however, that the genes don't cause specific colors. Instead, they cause the colored part of the eye to be dark or light. Dark colors (black, brown, hazel, and green) are dominant over light colors (blue and gray). However, blended colors are also possible. People whose chromosomes carry a combination of genes for green, blue, and gray eyes can have phenotypes that include blue-gray, blue-green, or gray-green eye color. Likewise, genes that cause different shades of brown can combine their effects to produce variations in children's phenotypes that are different from those of their brown-eyed parents.

Many genes influence height, and there is no dominant/recessive pattern of inheritance among them. Most geneticists think each height gene has a small influence over a child's size (Tanner, 1990) and that a child's height will be the sum of the effects of all of these genes.

Height, like most polygenic traits, is also a result of a **multifactorial pattern of inheritance**—that is, it is affected by both genes and environment. For this reason, doctors use a child's height as a measure of his general health (Sulkes, 1998; Tanner, 1990). If a child is ill, poorly nourished, or emotionally neglected, he will be smaller than others his age. Thus, when a child is shorter than 97% of his agemates, doctors try to determine if he is short because of his genes or because something is causing him to grow poorly (Tanner, 1990).

Genomic Imprinting and Mitochondrial Inheritance
Scientists have discovered some additional principles of genetic inheritance. Through a process called *genomic*

dominant/recessive pattern of inheritance The pattern of genetic transmission in which a single dominant gene influences a person's phenotype, but an individual must have two recessive genes to express a recessive trait.

polygenic pattern of inheritance Any pattern of genetic transmission in which multiple genes contribute to the outcome, such as is presumed to occur for complex traits such as intelligence or temperament.

multifactorial pattern of inheritance The pattern of genetic transmission in which both genes and environment influence the phenotype.

imprinting, some genes are biochemically marked at the time ova and sperm develop in the bodies of potential mothers and fathers. Geneticists have been aware of the process of genomic imprinting for some time, but recent technological advances have enabled them to more fully study its impact on development. A genomic imprint is a chemical label that identifies each gene in a person's body as having come from his father or mother. Research indicates that some genes are harmful only if they are tagged as having come from the father and others cause disorders only if they originated from the mother (Jirtle & Weidman, 2007). Scientists don't yet fully understand the process of genomic imprinting and how it affects development. It could be that genomic imprints "turn on" an atypical developmental process or "turn off" a normal one. Alternatively, the imprints may evoke responses in other genes or tissues in the developing individual's body that set the process of atypical development in motion. Some studies suggest that age-related deterioration of genomic imprints may be particularly important in diseases that appear later in life, including several kinds of cancer, Type II diabetes, and heart disease (Jirtle & Weidman, 2007).

In *mitochondrial inheritance*, children inherit genes located outside the nucleus of the zygote. These genes are carried in structures called *mitochondria* that are found in the fluid that surrounds the nucleus of the ovum before it is fertilized. Consequently, mitochondrial genes are passed only from mother to child. Geneticists have learned that several serious disorders, including some types of blindness, are transmitted in this way. In most such cases, the mother herself is unaffected by the harmful genes (Amato, 1998).

Twins and Siblings   In most cases, babies are conceived and born one at a time. However, 3 out of every 100 births in the United States today are multiple births (Martin et al., 2007). This number has risen dramatically in recent decades, in large part because widely prescribed new medications given to infertile women frequently stimulate multiple ovulation. The great majority of multiple births in the United States are twins; triplets or higher multiples occur only about once in every 1,000 births (Martin et al., 2007).

Roughly two-thirds of twins are **fraternal twins**. Fraternal twins develop when two ova have been produced and both have been fertilized, each by a separate sperm. Such twins, also called **dizygotic twins**, are no more alike genetically than any other pair of siblings and may not even be of the same sex. The remaining one-third of twins are **identical twins** (also called **monozygotic twins**). In such cases, a single fertilized ovum apparently initially divides in the normal way, but then for unknown reasons separates into two parts, with each part developing into a separate individual. Because identical twins develop from precisely the same original fertilized ovum, they have identical genetic heritages. You'll remember from Chapter 1 that comparison of the degree of similarity of these two types of twins is a major research strategy in the important field of behavior genetics.

Development from Conception to Birth

When we think about prenatal development, our thoughts often focus on the pregnant woman, because the pregnancy is visible. Until very recently, the process of prenatal development was almost completely shrouded in mystery. The only clues scientists had about the process came from examination of embryos and fetuses that were spontaneously aborted or from studies of animal embryology.

Because little was known about prenatal development, there was a lot of confusion about the connection between the experiences of the pregnant woman and the intrauterine development and experiences of the child. For example, pregnancy has traditionally been divided into three *trimesters* of equal length, so doctors as well as expectant couples tended to think of prenatal development as consisting of three analogous stages. One consequence of the confusion was that many people believed that when the mother first *felt* the fetus move, this was the first time the fetus actually had moved.

Of course, technology has changed all this. Thanks to a variety of techniques, scientists have learned that there are indeed three stages of prenatal development, but the developing

fraternal (dizygotic) twins Children carried in the same pregnancy but who develop from two separately fertilized ova. They are no more alike genetically than other pairs of siblings.

identical (monozygotic) twins Children carried in the same pregnancy who develop from the same fertilized ovum. They are genetic clones of each other.

germinal stage The first stage of prenatal development, beginning at conception and ending at implantation of the zygote in the uterus (approximately the first 2 weeks).

blastocyst Name for the mass of cells from roughly 4 to 10 days after fertilization.

embryo The name given to the developing organism during the period of prenatal development between about 2 weeks and 8 weeks after conception, beginning with implantation of the blastocyst in the uterine wall.

child has already reached the *third* stage before the mother ends her first trimester. Moreover, we know that spontaneous movement of the fetus begins within a few weeks of conception.

One of the most significant effects of improvements in technology has been to offer fathers greater awareness of the prenatal developmental process. Researchers have found that both the father's and the mother's feelings of attachment to the unborn child intensify when the parents can observe the fetus during an ultrasound examination (Sandelowski, 1994).

The Stages of Prenatal Development

Learning Objective 2.3
What happens in each of the stages of prenatal development?

The period of gestation of the human infant is 38 weeks (about 265 days). These 38 weeks are divided into three stages of unequal length, identified by specific changes within the developing organism (see Table 2.2 on page 38).

The Germinal Stage   The **germinal stage** begins at conception and ends when the zygote is implanted in the wall of the uterus. After conception, the zygote spends roughly a week floating down the fallopian tube to the uterus. Cell division begins 24 to 36 hours after conception; within 2 to 3 days, there are several dozen cells and the whole mass is about the size of the head of a pin. Approximately 4 days after conception, the mass of cells, now called a **blastocyst**, begins to subdivide, forming a sphere with two layers of cells around a hollow center. The outermost layer will form the various structures that will support the developing organism, while the inner layer will form the **embryo** itself. When it touches the wall of the uterus, the outer cell layer of the blastocyst breaks down at the point of contact. Small tendrils develop and attach the cell mass to the uterine wall, a process called *implantation*. When implantation is complete (normally 10 days to 2 weeks after conception), the blastocyst has perhaps 150 cells (Tanner, 1990). The sequence is illustrated schematically in Figure 2.3.

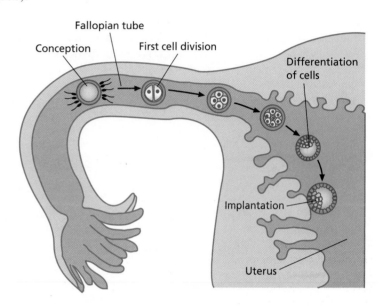

Figure 2.3   Migration of the Zygote

This schematic shows the normal progression of development for the first 10 days of gestation, from conception to implantation.

The Embryonic Stage   The **embryonic stage** begins when implantation is complete. The blastocyst's outer layer of cells specializes into two membranes, each of which forms critical support structures. The inner membrane becomes a sac or bag called the **amnion**, filled with liquid (amniotic fluid) in which the embryo floats. The outer membrane, called the **chorion**, develops into two organs, the **placenta** and the **umbilical cord**. The placenta, which is fully developed by about 4 weeks of gestation, is a platelike mass of cells that lies against the wall of the uterus. It serves as the liver and kidneys for the embryo until the embryo's own organs begin to function. It also provides the embryo with oxygen and removes carbon dioxide from its blood.

Connected to the embryo's circulatory system via the umbilical cord, the placenta also serves as a critical filter between the mother's circulatory system and the embryo's. Nutrients such as oxygen, proteins, sugars, and vitamins from the maternal blood can pass through to the embryo or fetus; digestive wastes and carbon dioxide from the infant's blood pass back through to the mother, whose own body can eliminate them. At the same time, many (but not all) harmful substances, such as viruses or the mother's hormones, are filtered out because they are too large to pass through the various membranes in the placenta. Most drugs and anesthetics, however, do pass through the placenta, as do some disease organisms.

While the support structures are developing, the mass of cells that will form the embryo itself is differentiating further into several types of cells that form the rudiments of skin, sense

embryonic stage The second stage of prenatal development, from week 2 through week 8, when the embryo's organs form.

amnion The sac, or bag, filled with liquid in which the embryo/fetus floats during prenatal life.

chorion The outer layer of cells of the blastocyst during prenatal development, from which both the placenta and the umbilical cord are formed.

placenta An organ that develops between the fetus and the wall of the uterus during gestation.

umbilical cord The cord connecting the embryo/fetus to the placenta, containing two arteries and one vein.

Table 2.2 Milestones in Prenatal Development

Stage/Time Frame	Milestones	
GERMINAL		
Day 1: Conception	Sperm and ovum unite, forming a zygote containing genetic instructions for the development of a new and unique human being.	 Sperm and egg
Days 10 to 14: Implantation	The zygote burrows into the lining of the uterus. Specialized cells that will become the placenta, umbilical cord, and embryo are already formed.	 Zygote
EMBRYONIC		
Weeks 3 to 8: Organogenesis	All of the embryo's organ systems form during the 6-week period following implantation.	 6-week fetus
FETAL		
Weeks 9 to 38: Growth and Organ Refinement	The fetus grows from 1 inch long and ¼ ounce to a length of about 20 inches and a weight of 7–9 pounds. By week 12, most fetuses can be identified as male or female. Changes in the brain and lungs make viability possible by week 24; optimum development requires an additional 14 to 16 weeks in the womb. Most neurons form by week 28, and connections among them begin to develop shortly thereafter. In the last 8 weeks, the fetus can hear and smell, is sensitive to touch, and responds to light. Learning is also possible.	

12-week fetus

14-week fetus

Well-developed fetus (age not given)

Sources: Kliegman, 1998; Tortora & Grabowski, 1993.

receptors, nerve cells, muscles, circulatory system, and internal organs—a process called *organogenesis*.

A heartbeat can be detected roughly 4 weeks after conception; the beginnings of lungs and limbs are also apparent at this time. By the end of the embryonic period, rudimentary fingers and toes, eyes, eyelids, nose, mouth, and external ears are all present, as are the basic parts of the nervous system; these and other developmental milestones are summarized in Table 2.2. The embryonic stage ends when organogenesis is complete and bone cells begin to form, typically about 8 weeks after conception.

The Fetal Stage   Once organogenesis is complete, the developing organism is known as a **fetus** and the final phase of prenatal development, the **fetal stage**, begins (lasting from approximately 8 weeks until birth). From a weight of about ¼ ounce and a length of 1 inch, the fetus grows to a baby weighing about 7 pounds and having a length of about 20 inches, who is ready to be born. In addition, this stage involves refinements of the organ systems that are essential to life outside the womb (see Table 2.3).

By the end of week 23, a small number of babies have attained **viability**, the ability to live outside the womb (Moore & Persaud, 1993). However, most babies born this early die, and those who do survive struggle for many months. Remaining in the womb just 1 week longer, until the end of week 24, greatly increases a baby's chances of survival. The extra week probably allows time for lung function to become more efficient. In addition, most brain structures are completely developed by the end of the 24th week. For these reasons, most experts accept 24 weeks as the average age of viability.

The Fetal Brain   As you learned earlier, the foundational structures of all of the body's organ systems are formed during the embryonic stage. Yet most of the formation and fine-tuning of the brain take place during the fetal stage (see Figure 2.4 on page 40). **Neurons**, the specialized cells of the nervous system, actually begin developing during the embryonic stage, in week 3. But the pace of neural formation picks up dramatically between the 10th and 18th weeks, a process known as **neuronal proliferation**.

Between the 13th and 21st weeks, **neuronal migration** takes place, a process in which newly formed neurons migrate to the specialized regions of the brain where they will

fetus The name given to the developing organism from about 8 weeks after conception until birth.

fetal stage The third stage of prenatal development, from week 8 to birth, when growth and organ refinement take place.

viability The fetus's capacity for survival outside the womb.

neurons The cells in the nervous system that are responsible for transmission and reception of nerve impulses.

neuronal proliferation The rapid development of neurons between the 10th and 18th week of gestation.

neuronal migration The movement of neurons to specialized regions of the brain.

Table 2.3	Milestones of the Fetal Stage
Period	What Develops
Weeks 9–12	Fingerprints; grasping reflex; facial expressions; swallowing and rhythmic "breathing" of amniotic fluid; urination; genitalia appear; alternating periods of physical activity and rest
Weeks 13–16	Hair follicles; responses to mother's voice and loud noises; 8–10 inches long; weighs 6 ounces
Weeks 17–20	Fetal movements felt by mother; heartbeat detectable with stethoscope; lanugo (hair) covers body; eyes respond to light introduced into the womb; eyebrows; fingernails; 12 inches long
Weeks 21–24	Vernix (oily substance) protects skin; lungs produce surfactant (vital to respiratory function); viability becomes possible, although most born now do not survive
Weeks 25–28	Recognition of mother's voice; regular periods of rest and activity; 14–15 inches long; weighs 2 pounds; good chance of survival if born now
Weeks 29–32	Very rapid growth; antibodies acquired from mother; fat deposited under skin; 16–17 inches long; weighs 4 pounds; excellent chance of survival if delivered now
Weeks 33–36	Movement to head-down position for birth; lungs mature; 18 inches long; weighs 5–6 pounds; virtually 100% chance of survival if delivered
Weeks 37+	Full-term status; 19–21 inches long; weighs 6–9 pounds

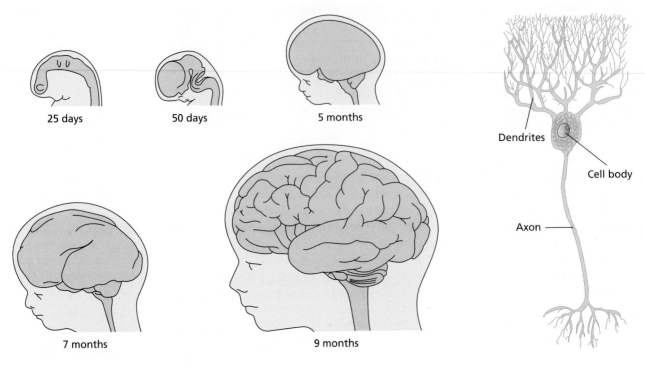

Figure 2.4   The Prenatal Brain

Stages in the prenatal development of the brain, beginning with the neural tube in the embryonic period.

(*Source*: From drawings by Tom Prentiss in "The Development of the Brain" by W. Maxwell Cowan in *Scientific American*, September 1979, pp. 112–114+. Adapted by permission of Nelson H. Prentiss.)

Figure 2.5   Structure of the Neuron

The structure of a single developed neuron. The cell bodies are the first to be developed, primarily between 10 and 20 weeks of gestation. Axons and dendrites begin to develop in the last 2 months of gestation and continue to increase in size and complexity for several years after birth.

cell body The part of the cell that contains the nucleus and in which all the cell's vital functions are carried out.

synapses Tiny spaces across which neural impulses flow from one neuron to the next.

axons Tail-like extensions of neurons.

dendrites Branchlike protrusions from the cell bodies of neurons.

glial cells The "glue" that holds neurons together to give form to the structures of the nervous system.

reside for the rest of the individual's life (Chong et al., 1996). While migrating, neurons consist only of **cell bodies**, the part of the cell that contains the nucleus and in which all the cell's vital functions are carried out (see Figure 2.5). Once they have reached their final destinations in the fetal brain, the neurons begin to develop connections. These connections, called **synapses**, are tiny spaces between neurons across which neural impulses travel from one neuron to the next. Several changes in fetal behavior signal that the process of synapse formation is under way. For instance, the fetus exhibits alternating periods of activity and rest and begins to yawn (Walusinski, Kurjak, Andonotopo, & Azumendi, 2005; see Figure 2.6). When observed, these changes tell physicians that fetal brain development is proceeding normally.

Synapse formation requires the growth of two neuronal structures. **Axons** are tail-like extensions that can grow to be several feet in length. **Dendrites** are tentaclelike branches that extend out from the cell body (see Figure 2.5). Dendrite development is thought to be highly sensitive to adverse environmental influences such as maternal malnutrition and defects in placental functioning (Dieni & Rees, 2003).

Simultaneously with neuronal migration, **glial cells** begin to develop. These cells are the "glue" that hold the neurons together to give shape to the brain's major structures. As glial cells develop, the brain begins to assume a more mature appearance, one that can be observed using magnetic resonance imaging (MRI) and other modern technologies that you will read more about later in the chapter (see Figure 2.7).

Figure 2.6   Fetal Yawning

Fetal yawning appears between the 10th and 15th week. Its presence signals the beginning of sleep stages in the fetal brain.

(*Source*: O. Walusinski et al., "Fetal yawning: A behavior's birth with 4D US revealed," *The Ultrasound Review of Obstetrics & Gynecology, 5* (2005), 210–217. Reprinted with permission.)

Figure 2.7
A Normal Third-Trimester Fetal Brain

Glial cells that develop during the last few months of prenatal development hold neurons together and give form and structure to the fetal brain.

(*Source*: S. Brown, J. Estroff, and C. Barnewolf, "Fetal MRI," *Applied Radiology,* 33 (2004): 9–25. Copyright © 2004 by Applied Radiology/Anderson Publishing. Reprinted with permission.)

Sex Differences in Prenatal Development

Learning Objective 2.4

How do male and female fetuses differ?

Because nearly all prenatal development is controlled by maturational sequences that are the same for all members of our species—male and female alike—there aren't very many sex differences in prenatal development. Still, there are a few, and they set the stage for some of the physical differences that are evident at later ages.

Sometime between 4 and 8 weeks after conception, the male embryo begins to secrete androgens, including the male hormone testosterone from the rudimentary testes. If this hormone is not secreted or is secreted in inadequate amounts, the embryo will be "demasculinized," even to the extent of developing female genitalia. Female embryos do not appear to secrete any equivalent hormone prenatally. However, the accidental presence of male hormone at the critical time (such as from some drug the mother may take, or from a genetic disorder called congenital adrenal hyperplasia) acts to "defeminize," or to masculinize, the female fetus, sometimes resulting in malelike genitalia and frequently resulting in masculinization of later behavior, such as more rough-and-tumble play (Collaer & Hines, 1995). Several hormones that affect the prenatal development of genitalia (particularly testosterone in males) also appear to affect the pattern of brain development, resulting in subtle brain differences between males and females and affecting patterns of growth-hormone secretions in adolescence, levels of physical aggression, and the relative dominance of the right and left hemispheres of the brain (Ruble & Martin, 1998; Todd et al., 1995). Although early research has raised some very intriguing questions, the evidence in this area is still fairly sketchy; it is clear that whatever role such prenatal hormones play in brain architecture and functioning is highly complex (Baron-Cohen, Lutchmaya, & Knickmeyer, 2006).

Girls progress a bit faster in some aspects of prenatal development, particularly skeletal development. They are 4 to 6 weeks ahead in bone development at birth (Tanner, 1990). Despite the more rapid development of girls, boys are slightly heavier and longer at birth, with more muscle tissue and fewer fat cells. For example, in the United States, the average birth length and weight for boys is 20 inches and just over 7 pounds, compared with slightly more than 19 inches and 7 pounds for girls (Needlman, 1996).

Boys are considerably more vulnerable to all kinds of prenatal problems. Many more boys than girls are conceived—on the order of about 120 to 150 male embryos for every 100 female ones—but more of the males are spontaneously aborted. At birth, there are about 105 boys for every 100 girls. Boys are also more likely to experience injuries at birth (perhaps because they are larger), and they have more congenital malformations (Zaslow & Hayes, 1986). Male fetuses also appear to be more sensitive to variables such as cocaine which may negatively affect prenatal development (Levine et al., 2008). The striking sex difference in vulnerability to certain problems seems to persist throughout the lifespan. Males have shorter life expectancy, higher rates of behavior problems, more learning disabilities, and usually more negative responses to stressors such as maternal insensitivity (Warren & Simmens, 2005). One possible explanation for at least some of this sex difference may lie in the basic genetic difference. Because many genes for problems or disorders are recessive and are carried on the X chromosome, the XX combination affords a girl more protection against "bad" recessive genes that may be carried on one X chromosome; the dominant gene on the corresponding X chromosome would be expressed instead. Because boys have only one X chromosome, such a recessive gene is much more likely to be expressed phenotypically in a boy.

Some studies suggest that male fetuses, on average, are more physically active than females (DiPietro, Hodgson, Costigan, Hilton, & Johnson, 1996; DiPietro, Hodgson, Costigan, & Johnson, 1996). However, other studies have shown that a sex difference in wakefulness is responsible for these findings (de Medina, Visser, Huizink, Buitelaar, & Mulder, 2003). That is, male fetuses are awake more often than female fetuses are and, as a result, appear to be more active. When activity levels are measured within periods of wakefulness, male and female fetuses are equally active. By contrast, research showing that female fetuses are more responsive to external stimuli does seem to indicate that there is a real sex difference in responsiveness (Groome et al., 1999).

Learning Objective 2.5

What behaviors have scientists observed in fetuses?

Prenatal Behavior

In recent years, techniques such as ultrasound imaging have provided researchers with a great deal of information about fetal behavior. Some researchers suggest that establishing norms for fetal behavior would help health-care providers better assess fetal health (Nijhuis, 2003). Thus, in recent years, the number of research studies examining fetal behavior has increased significantly. These studies have produced rather remarkable findings, some of which are shown in Figure 2.8.

For one thing, researchers have learned that the fetus responds to sounds with heart rate changes, head turns, and body movements as early as the 25th week of gestation (Joseph, 2000). Researchers have also shown that it is possible to observe fetal brain activity by scanning the mother's abdomen with the same kinds of techniques used to examine brain function postnatally—techniques such as magnetic resonance imaging (MRI). Studies using these techniques have found that late-term fetuses exhibit neurological as well as behavioral responses to sounds (Moore et al., 2001).

Research also suggests that the fetus can distinguish between familiar and novel stimuli by the 32nd or 33rd week (Sandman, Wadhwa, Hetrick, Porto, & Peeke, 1997). In one classic study, pregnant women recited a short children's rhyme out loud each day between weeks 33 and 37. In week 38, researchers played a recording of either the same rhyme the mother had been reciting or another rhyme and measured the fetal heart rate. Fetal heart rates dropped during the playing of the familiar rhyme, but not during the unfamiliar rhyme, suggesting that the fetuses had learned the sound patterns of the rhyme (DeCasper, Lecaneut, Busnel, Granier-DeFerre, & Maugeais, 1994). The ability to learn in this way seems to emerge between 24 and 38 weeks (Krueger, Holditch-Davis, Quint, & DeCasper, 2004; Pressman, DiPietro, Costigan, Shupe, & Johnson, 1998).

Evidence for fetal learning also comes from studies in which newborns appear to remember stimuli to which they were exposed prenatally: their mother's heartbeats, the odor of the amniotic fluid, and stories or pieces of music they heard in the womb (Righetti, 1996; Schaal, Marlier, & Soussignan, 1998). In another classic study of prenatal learning, pregnant women

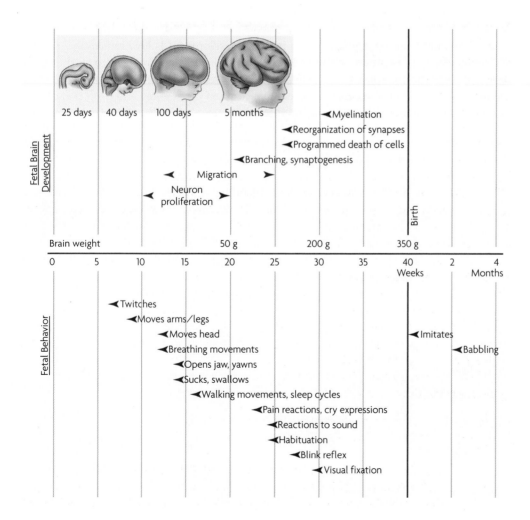

Figure 2.8
Correlations between Fetal Behavior and Brain Development

Researchers have discovered numerous correlations between fetal brain development and behavior.

(*Source*: O. Walusinski et al., "Fetal yawning: A behavior's birth with 4D US revealed," *The Ultrasound Review of Obstetrics & Gynecology*, 5 (2005), 210–217. Reprinted with permission.)

read a children's story such as Dr. Seuss's *The Cat in the Hat* out loud each day for the final 6 weeks of their pregnancies. After the infants were born, they were allowed to suck on special pacifiers that turned a variety of sounds off and on. Each kind of sound required a special type of sucking. Researchers found that the babies quickly adapted their sucking patterns in order to listen to the familiar story, but did not change their sucking in order to listen to an unfamiliar story (DeCasper & Spence, 1986). In other words, babies preferred the sound of the story they had heard in utero.

Developmentalists are trying to find out if prenatal learning affects later development, and if so, how (Bornstein et al., 2002). In one study, pregnant women wore waistbands equipped with speakers through which they exposed their fetuses to an average of 70 hours of classical music per week between 28 weeks of gestation and birth (Lafuente et al., 1997). By age 6 months, the babies who had heard the music were more advanced than control infants in many motor and cognitive skills. Of course, the exact meaning of this result is difficult to assess, but it does suggest that the prenatal sensory environment may be important in later development.

Researchers have also been able to identify individual differences in fetal behavior. You have already read about the sex difference in activity level. As is true of most sex differences, however, the range of individual differences within each gender is far greater than the difference in *average* activity levels between male and female fetuses. Longitudinal studies have shown that very active fetuses, both males and females, tend to become children who are very active. Moreover, these children are more likely to be labeled "hyperactive" by parents and teachers. In contrast, fetuses who are less active than average are more likely to have mental retardation (Accardo et al., 1997).

Problems in Prenatal Development

One of the most important points about prenatal development is how remarkably regular and predictable it is. However, this sequence of development is not immune to modification or outside influence, as you'll soon see in detail. The potential problems fall into two general classes: genetic and chromosomal problems that begin at conception, and problems caused by damaging substances or events called **teratogens**.

Learning Objective 2.6
What are the effects of the major dominant, recessive, and sex-linked diseases?

Genetic Disorders

Many disorders appear to be transmitted through the operation of dominant and recessive genes (see Table 2.4). *Autosomal* disorders are caused by genes

Table 2.4 Genetic Disorders

Autosomal Dominant	Autosomal Recessive	Sex-Linked Recessive
Huntington's disease	Phenylketonuria	Hemophilia
High blood pressure	Sickle-cell disease	Fragile-X syndrome
Extra fingers	Cystic fibrosis	Red-green color blindness
Migraine headaches	Tay-Sachs disease	Missing front teeth
Schizophrenia	Kidney cysts in infants	Night blindness
	Albinism	Some types of muscular dystrophy
		Some types of diabetes

Sources: Amato, 1993; Tortora and Grabowski, 1993.

teratogens Substances such as viruses and drugs or events that can cause birth defects.

located on the autosomes. The genes that cause *sex-linked* disorders are found on the X chromosome.

Autosomal Disorders   Most recessive autosomal disorders are diagnosed in infancy or early childhood. For example, one recessive gene causes a baby to have problems digesting the amino acid phenylalanine. Toxins build up in the baby's brain and cause mental retardation. This condition, called *phenylketonuria (PKU)*, is found in about 1 in every 15,000 babies in the United States (Arnold, 2007; Mijuskovic, 2006). If a baby consumes no foods containing phenylalanine, however, she will not become mentally retarded. Milk is one of the foods PKU babies can't have, so early diagnosis is critical. For this reason, most states require all babies to be tested for PKU soon after birth.

Like many recessive disorders, PKU is associated with race. Caucasian babies are more likely to have the disorder than infants in other racial groups. Similarly, West African and African American infants are more likely to suffer from *sickle-cell disease*, a recessive disorder that causes red blood cell deformities (Overby, 2002). In sickle-cell disease, the blood can't carry enough oxygen to keep the body's tissues healthy. Few children with sickle-cell disease live past the age of 20, and most who survive to adulthood die before they are 40.

Almost one-half of West Africans have either sickle-cell disease or sickle-cell trait (Amato, 1998). Persons with *sickle-cell trait* carry a single recessive gene for sickle-cell disease, which causes a few of their red blood cells to be abnormal. Doctors can identify carriers of the sickle-cell gene by testing their blood for sickle-cell trait. Once potential parents know that they carry the gene, they can make informed decisions about future childbearing. In the United States, about 1 in 600 African Americans has sickle-cell disease, and 1 in 12 African Americans has sickle-cell trait (Distenfeld & Woermann, 2007). Sickle-cell disease and sickle-cell trait also occur more frequently in people of Mediterranean, Caribbean, Indian, Arab, and Latin American ancestry than in those of European ancestry (Overby, 2002).

About 1 in every 3,000 babies born to Jewish couples of Eastern European ancestry suffers from another recessive disorder, *Tay-Sachs disease*. By the time he is 1 to 2 years old, a Tay-Sachs baby is likely to have severe mental retardation and blindness. Very few survive past the age of 3 (Painter & Bergman, 1998).

Disorders caused by dominant genes, such as *Huntington's disease*, are usually not diagnosed until adulthood (Amato, 1998). This disorder causes the brain to deteriorate and affects both psychological and motor functions. Until recently, children of people with Huntington's disease had to wait until they became ill themselves to know for sure that they carried the gene. Now, doctors can use a blood test to identify the Huntington's gene. Thus, people who have a parent with this disease can make better decisions about their own childbearing and can prepare for living with a serious disorder when they get older.

Sex-Linked Disorders   Most sex-linked disorders are caused by recessive genes (see Figure 2.9). One fairly common sex-linked recessive disorder is *red-green color blindness*. People with this disorder have difficulty distinguishing between the colors red and green when they are next to each other. The prevalence of red-green color blindness is 8% in men and 0.5% (½ percent) in women (U.S. National Library of Medicine Genetics Home Reference, 2008). Most people learn ways of compensating for the disorder and thus live perfectly normal lives.

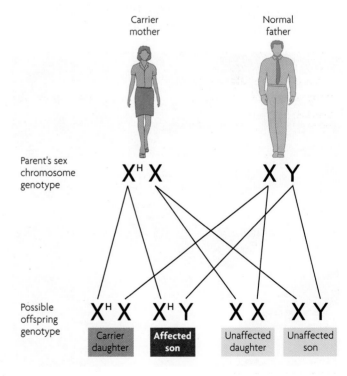

Figure 2.9   Sex-Linked Inheritance

Compare this pattern of sex-linked transmission of a recessive disease (hemophilia) with the pattern shown in Figure 2.2.

A more serious sex-linked recessive disorder is *hemophilia*. The blood of people with hemophilia lacks the chemical components that cause blood to clot. Thus, when a person with hemophilia bleeds, the bleeding doesn't stop naturally. Approximately 1 in 5,000 baby boys is born with this disorder, which is almost unknown in girls (Scott, 1998).

About 1 in every 1,500 males and 1 in every 2,500 females has a sex-linked disorder called *fragile-X syndrome* (Amato, 1998). A person with this disorder has an X chromosome with a "fragile," or damaged, spot. Fragile-X syndrome can cause mental retardation that becomes progressively worse as children get older (Adesman, 1996). In fact, experts estimate that 5–7% of all retarded males have fragile-X syndrome (Zigler & Hodapp, 1991). Fragile-X syndrome is also strongly associated with autism, a disorder that interferes with children's capacity to form emotional bonds with others (Cohen et al., 2005). Fortunately, fragile-X syndrome is one of several disorders that can be diagnosed before birth (see *Developmental Science in the Real World*).

DEVELOPMENTAL SCIENCE IN THE REAL WORLD

Fetal Assessment and Treatment

Shilpa and Rudy Patel are preparing for the birth of their first child. Like many other couples, they are hoping that their child will be healthy. In their case, however, there is real cause for concern because a genetic disorder known as *fragile-X syndrome* runs in Shilpa's family.

One procedure that can be used to test Shilpa's fetus is known as *chorionic villus sampling (CVS)*. CVS and another procedure, *amniocentesis*, can be used to identify chromosomal errors and many genetic disorders prior to birth (Curry, 2002). In CVS, cells are extracted from the placenta and subjected to a variety of laboratory tests during the early weeks of prenatal development. In amniocentesis, a needle is used to extract amniotic fluid containing fetal cells between weeks 14 and 16 of gestation. Fetal cells filtered out of the fluid are then tested in a variety of ways to diagnose chromosomal and genetic disorders. In addition, *ultrasonography* has become a routine part of prenatal care in the United States because of its usefulness in monitoring fetal growth in high-risk pregnancies. When an ultrasound test suggests that there may be some kind of brain or spinal cord abnormality, follow-up tests using magnetic resonance imaging are sometimes employed (Levine, 2002). These images are more detailed than those that are produced by ultrasonography.

Many laboratory tests that use maternal blood, urine, and/or samples of amniotic fluid also help health-care providers monitor fetal development. For example, the presence of a substance called *alpha-fetoprotein* in a mother's blood is associated with a number of prenatal defects, including abnormalities in the brain and spinal cord. Doctors can also use a laboratory test to assess the maturity of fetal lungs (Kliegman, 1998). This test is critical when doctors have to deliver a baby early because of a pregnant woman's health.

Fetoscopy involves insertion of a tiny camera into the womb to directly observe fetal development. Fetoscopy makes it possible for doctors to surgically correct some kinds of defects (Kliegman, 1998) and has made techniques such as fetal blood transfusions and bone marrow transplants possible. Specialists also use fetoscopy to take samples of blood from the umbilical cord. Fetal blood tests can help doctors identify a bacterial infection that is causing a fetus to grow too slowly (Curry, 2002). Once diagnosed, the infection can be treated by injecting antibiotics into the amniotic fluid to be swallowed by the fetus or by injecting drugs into the umbilical cord (Kliegman, 1998).

Questions for Reflection

1. How do you think you would respond to the news that a child you were expecting was carrying some kind of genetic defect?
2. Suppose Shilpa and Rudy learn that their baby is a girl. Will this news make them more or less concerned about the effect that carrying the fragile-X defect may have on their child's development? Why?

Ultrasound technology allows fathers to experience prenatal development in a more intimate way.

Chromosomal Errors

Over 50 different chromosomal anomalies have been identified, and most result in miscarriage. When babies do survive, the effects of chromosomal errors tend to be dramatic.

Trisomies   A *trisomy* is a condition in which an individual has three copies of a particular autosome. The most common is **Down syndrome** (also called **trisomy 21**), in which the child has three copies of chromosome 21. Roughly 1 in every 700 to 800 infants is born with this abnormality (CDC, 2006c). These children have distinctive facial features, most notably a flattened face and somewhat slanted eyes with an epicanthic fold on the upper eyelid (an extension of the normal eyelid fold), reduced total brain size, and often other physical abnormalities such as heart defects. Typically, they have mental retardation.

The risk of bearing a child with trisomy 21 varies with the age of the mother. Among women over 35, the chances of conceiving a child with the disorder are 1 in 385 (Chen, 2007). At 40, the risk rises to 1 in 106, and at 45, the chances are 1 in 30. Paternal age is a factor as well (Fisch et al., 2003). Interestingly, with mothers younger than 35, the father's age has no effect on trisomy 21 risk. However, a man over 40 who conceives a child with a woman over 35 is twice as likely to father a child with Down syndrome as a younger father is.

Scientists have identified children with trisomies of the 13th and 18th pairs of chromosomes as well (Amato, 1998). These disorders have more severe effects than trisomy 21. Few children with trisomy 13 or trisomy 18 live past the age of 1 year. As with trisomy 21, the chances of having a child with one of these disorders increase with a woman's age.

Note the distinctive facial characteristics of this Down syndrome child.

Sex-Chromosome Anomalies   A second class of anomalies, associated with an incomplete or incorrect division of either sex chromosome, occurs in roughly 1 out of every 400 births (Berch & Bender, 1987). The most common is an XXY pattern, called Klinefelter's syndrome, which occurs in approximately 1 out of every 1,000 males. Affected boys most often look quite normal, although they have characteristically long arms and legs and underdeveloped testes. Most do not have mental retardation, but language and learning disabilities are common. Somewhat rarer is an XYY pattern. These children also develop as boys; typically they are unusually tall, with mild retardation.

A single-X pattern (XO), called Turner's syndrome, and a triple-X pattern (XXX) may also occur, and in both cases the child develops as a girl. Girls with Turner's syndrome—perhaps 1 in every 3,000 live female births (Tanner, 1990)—show stunted growth and are usually sterile. Without hormone therapy, they do not menstruate or develop breasts at puberty. Neuroimaging studies show that Turner syndrome is associated with abnormal development in both the cerebellum and the cerebrum (Brown et al., 2002). These girls also show an interesting imbalance in their cognitive skills: They often perform particularly poorly on tests that measure spatial ability but usually perform at or above normal levels on tests of verbal skill (Golombok & Fivush, 1994). Girls with an XXX pattern are of normal size but are slow in physical development. In contrast to girls with Turner's syndrome, they have markedly poor verbal abilities and overall low IQ, and they do particularly poorly in school compared with other children with sex-chromosome anomalies (Bender et al., 1995; Rovet & Netley, 1983).

Down syndrome (trisomy 21) A genetic anomaly in which every cell contains three copies of chromosome 21 rather than two. Children born with this genetic pattern have characteristic physical features and usually have mental retardation.

Teratogens: Maternal Diseases

Deviant prenatal development can also result from variations in the environment in which the embryo and fetus is nurtured. A particular teratogen, such as a drug or a disease in the mother, will result in a defect in the embryo or fetus only if it occurs during a particular period of days or weeks of prenatal life. The general rule is that each organ system is most vulnerable to disruption at the time when it is developing most rapidly (Moore & Persaud, 1993). Figure 2.10 shows times when different parts of the body are most vulnerable to teratogens. As you can see, the first 8 weeks are the period of greatest vulnerability for all the organ systems.

Rubella The first few weeks of gestation comprise a critical period for a negative effect from rubella (also called German measles). Most infants exposed to rubella in the first 4 to 5 weeks show some abnormality, while only about 10% of those exposed in the final 6 months of pregnancy are affected negatively (Moore & Persaud, 1993). Deafness, cataracts, and heart defects are the most common abnormalities. These effects are observable immediately after birth. But recent research suggests that rubella may also be linked to developmental outcomes, such as the development of schizophrenia, that aren't apparent until adolescence or adulthood (Brown, 2000–2001). Fortunately, rubella is preventable. A vaccine is available,

NOTE: Dark portions denote highly sensitive periods; light portions denote less sensitive periods.

Figure 2.10   The Timing of Teratogen Exposure

The timing of teratogen exposure is crucial. Notice that teratogens have the most impact during the embryonic stage, except on certain body parts such as the brain and ears, which continue to be at risk for teratogenic effects because they continue to grow and develop during the fetal period.

(*Source*: From C. Moore, J. Barresi, and C. Thompson, "The cognitive basis of future-oriented prosocial behavior," *Social Development*, 7 (1998): 198–218. Copyright © 1998 by Blackwell Publishers, Inc. Reprinted with permission.)

and it should be given to all children as part of a regular immunization program (American College of Obstetrics and Gynecology [ACOG], 2002). Adult women who were not vaccinated as children can be vaccinated later, but the vaccination must be done at least 3 months before a pregnancy to provide complete immunity. Moreover, the vaccine itself can be teratogenic, another good reason to wait several weeks before attempting to conceive.

HIV/AIDS In the United States, over 6,000 babies are born to women with HIV/AIDS each year (CDC, 2007a). These grim numbers are counterbalanced by some good news, though. First, only about a quarter of infants born to mothers with HIV actually become infected (Mofenson, 2002). Even more encouraging is the finding that infected women who are treated with *antiretroviral drugs* during their pregnancies have a markedly lower risk of transmitting the disease to their children—as low as 2% (CDC, 2007a). Because most women with HIV are asymptomatic and are unaware they are infected, the Centers for Disease Control recommends routine HIV counseling and voluntary testing for all pregnant women early in their pregnancies so that they can begin taking antiretroviral drugs, should that be necessary.

In other parts of the world, HIV is much more prevalent among pregnant women. Unfortunately, many women with HIV in nonindustrialized countries know little or nothing about available treatments and possible health consequences of the virus for themselves, their babies, and their partners. For example, one study involving 79 pregnant women with HIV aged 18 to 38, in Burkina Faso, West Africa, found that most participants did not intend to inform their partners about their HIV status because they feared being stigmatized (Issiaka et al., 2001). Moreover, none were aware of community organizations from which individuals with HIV could obtain information and support. Such findings suggest that the need for basic HIV education in the developing world is critical.

Cytomegalovirus and Other Sexually Transmitted Diseases

A much less well known but remarkably widespread and potentially serious sexually transmitted disease (STD) is *cytomegalovirus (CMV)*, a virus in the herpes group. It is now thought to be the single most prevalent infectious cause of both congenital mental retardation and deafness. CMV typically has few, if any, symptoms in an adult. In most cases, an affected person doesn't even know she carries this virus, although in an active phase it sometimes creates symptoms that suggest mononucleosis, including swollen glands and low fever. In infants who are infected prenatally or during birth, however, the virus can sometimes produce crippling disabilities.

Roughly half of all women of childbearing age have antibodies to CMV (CDC, 2006a), indicating that they have been infected at some time. Perhaps 2% of babies whose mothers have CMV antibodies become infected prenatally, which means that approximately 1 out of every 150 babies is congenitally infected.

Like CMV, the herpes virus can be transmitted to the fetus during delivery if the mother's disease is in the active phase at that time. Not only will the child then periodically experience the genital sores characteristic of the disease, but he or she may suffer other complications, most notably meningoencephalitis, a potentially serious inflammation of the brain and spinal cord. Because of this increased risk, many physicians now recommend surgical delivery (cesarean section) of infants of mothers with herpes, although vaginal delivery is possible if the disease is inactive.

Two additional STDs, *syphilis* and *gonorrhea*, also cause birth defects (Di Mario, Say, & Lincetto, 2007). Unlike most teratogens, a syphilis infection is most harmful during the last 26 weeks of prenatal development and causes eye, ear, and brain defects. Gonorrhea, which can cause the infant to be blind, is also usually transmitted during birth. For this reason, doctors usually treat the eyes of newborns with a special ointment that prevents damage from gonorrhea.

Chronic Illnesses

Conditions such as heart disease, diabetes, lupus, hormone imbalances, and epilepsy can also negatively affect prenatal development (Adab, Jacoby, Smith, & Chadwick, 2001; Kliegman, 1998; McAllister et al., 1997; Sandman et al., 1997). And recent research indicates that prenatal exposure to some maternal health conditions, such as the fluctuations in metabolism rate characteristic of diabetes, may predispose infants to developmental delays (Levy-Shiff, Lerman, Har-Even, & Hod, 2002). One of the most important goals of the new specialty of *fetal-maternal medicine* is to manage the pregnancies of women who have such conditions so that the health of both mother and fetus will be supported. For example, pregnancy often affects a diabetic woman's blood sugar levels so drastically that it becomes impossible for her to keep them under control. In turn, erratic blood sugar levels may damage the fetus's nervous system or cause it to grow too rapidly (Allen & Kisilevsky, 1999; Kliegman, 1998). To prevent such complications, a fetal-maternal specialist must find a diet, a medication, or a combination of the two that will stabilize the mother's blood sugar but will not harm the fetus.

Environmental Hazards   There are a number of substances found in the environment that may have detrimental effects on prenatal development. For example, women who work with mercury (e.g., dentists, dental technicians, semiconductor manufacturing workers) are advised to limit their exposure to this potentially teratogenic substance (March of Dimes, 2008b). Consuming large amounts of fish may also expose pregnant women to high levels of mercury (because of industrial pollution of the oceans and waterways). Fish may also contain elevated levels of another problematic industrial pollutant known as polychlorinated biphenyls, or PCBs. For these reasons, researchers recommend that pregnant women limit their consumption of fish, especially fresh tuna, shark, swordfish, and mackerel (March of Dimes, 2008b).

There are several other environmental hazards that pregnant women are advised to avoid (March of Dimes, 2008b):

- *Lead*, found in painted surfaces in older homes, pipes carrying drinking water, lead crystal glassware, and some ceramic dishes
- *Arsenic*, found in dust from pressure-treated lumber
- *Cadmium*, found in semiconductor manufacturing facilities
- *Anesthetic gases*, found in dental offices, outpatient surgical facilities, and hospital operating rooms
- *Solvents*, such as alcohol and paint thinners
- *Parasite-bearing substances*, such as animal feces and undercooked meat, poultry, or eggs

Learning Objective 2.9
What are the potential adverse effects of tobacco, alcohol, and other drugs on prenatal development?

Teratogens: Drugs

There is now a huge literature on the effects of prenatal drugs, especially controlled substances such as cocaine and marijuana (Barth, 2001). Sorting out the effects of drugs has proved to be an immensely challenging task because many women use multiple substances: Women who drink alcohol are also more likely than nondrinkers to smoke; those who use cocaine are also likely to take other illegal drugs or to smoke or drink to excess, and so on. In addition, many women who use drugs have other problems, such as depression, that may be responsible for the apparent effects of the drugs they use (Pajulo, Savonlahti, Sourander, Helenius, & Piha, 2001). Furthermore, the effects of drugs may be subtle, visible only many years after birth in the form of minor learning disabilities or increased risk of behavior problems.

Smoking   Recent research suggests that smoking during pregnancy may cause genetic damage in the developing fetus (de la Chica, Ribas, Giraldo, Egozcue, & Fuster, 2005). In addition, the link between smoking and low birth weight is well established. Infants of mothers who smoke are on average about half a pound lighter at birth than infants of nonsmoking mothers (Mohsin, Wong, Baumann, & Bai, 2003) and are nearly twice as likely to be born with a weight below 2,500 grams (5 pounds 8 ounces), the common definition of low birth weight. The primary problem-causing agent in cigarettes is nicotine, which constricts the blood vessels, reducing blood flow and nutrition to the placenta.

The effects of smoking on both height and weight are still evident when the children of smoking and nonsmoking mothers reach school age (Cornelius, Goldschmidt, Day, & Larkby, 2002). Medical researchers have also found that prenatal smoking increases children's risk of a number of health problems (DiFranza, Aligne, & Weitzman, 2004). These problems include susceptibility to respiratory infections, asthma, and ear infections.

Prenatal exposure to tobacco also appears to have long-term effects on children's cognitive and social development. Some studies suggest that there are higher rates of learning problems and antisocial behavior among children whose mothers smoked during pregnancy (DiFranza, Aligne, & Weitzman, 2004). Moreover, children of women who smoked during pregnancy are more likely than their schoolmates to be diagnosed with attention-deficit hyperactivity disorder (Linnet et al., 2003; Thapar et al., 2003).

Drinking   The effects of alcohol on the developing fetus range from mild to severe. At the extreme end of the continuum are children who exhibit a syndrome called **fetal alcohol syndrome (FAS)**, which affects 1 to 2 of every 1,000 infants in the United States (Chambers & Vaux, 2006). Projecting these figures to all children born in the United States means that up to 12,000 children with FAS are born every year. These children, whose mothers were usually heavy drinkers or alcoholics, are generally smaller than normal, with smaller brains and often with distinct physical anomalies or deformities. They frequently have heart defects, and their faces have certain distinctive features (visible in the two photos below), including a somewhat flattened nose and nose bridge and often an unusually long space between nose and mouth. However, the disorder is often difficult to diagnose. Experts recommend that physicians who suspect that a child may have FAS carry out a multidisciplinary assessment, one that includes a comprehensive medical and behavioral history of both the mother and the child as well as neuropsychological testing (Chudley et al., 2005).

The best single study of the consequences of prenatal alcohol exposure has been done by Ann Streissguth and her colleagues (Baer, Sampson, Barr, Connor, & Streissguth, 2003), who followed a group of over 500 women who drank moderate to heavy amounts of alcohol while pregnant and their children. Streissguth tested the children repeatedly, beginning immediately after birth, again later in infancy, at age 4, at school age, and again at ages 11, 14, and 21.

fetal alcohol syndrome (FAS) A pattern of abnormalities, including mental retardation and minor physical anomalies, often found in children born to alcoholic mothers.

 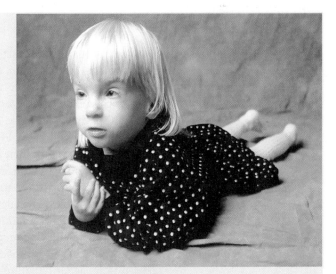

These two children, from different countries and different racial backgrounds, have both been diagnosed as having fetal alcohol syndrome (FAS). Both are mentally retarded and have relatively small heads. Note also the short nose and low nasal bridge typical of FAS children.

She found that the mother's alcohol consumption in pregnancy was associated with sluggishness and weaker sucking in infancy; lower scores on measures of intelligence at 8 months, 4 years, and 7 years; and problems with attention and vigilance at 4, 7, 11, and 14. Teachers also rated the 11-year-olds on overall school performance and on various behavior problems, and on both of these measures, children whose mothers had consumed the most alcohol during pregnancy were rated significantly worse. Streissguth also asked mothers about their diet, their education, and their life habits. She found that the links between a mother's alcohol consumption and poor outcomes for the child held up even when all these other variables were controlled statistically. These children are now all young adults, and investigators have found deficiencies in their information-processing skills, demonstrating that the effects of prenatal alcohol exposure persist into adulthood (Connor, Sampson, Bookstein, Barr, & Streissguth, 2001). Moreover, they are more likely than peers who were not prenatally exposed to alcohol to have alcohol abuse problems themselves (Baer et al., 2003).

Recent evidence also points to milder effects of moderate, or "social," drinking, such as two glasses of wine a day. Children of mothers who drink at this level during pregnancy are more likely to have IQ scores below 85 and to show poorer attention spans. They are also more likely than non-alcohol-exposed peers to have learning problems, both in social situations and in school (Kodituwakku, May, Clericuzio, & Weers, 2001). Thus, we do not yet know whether there is any safe level of alcohol consumption during pregnancy.

Cocaine   Significant numbers of pregnant women in the United States (and presumably elsewhere in the world) also take various illegal drugs, most notably cocaine. About a third of all cocaine-exposed babies are born prematurely, and among those carried to term, many are lower than normal in birth weight. In addition, cocaine-exposed infants are three times as likely to have a very small head circumference or to show some signs of neurological abnormalities (Needlman, Frank, Augustyn, & Zuckerman, 1995; Singer, Arendt, & Minnes, 1993). Some (but not all) also show significant drug withdrawal symptoms after birth, such as irritability, restlessness, shrill crying, tremors, and lower levels of responsiveness to their mothers (Ukeje, Bendersky, & Lewis, 2001).

A few studies suggest that prenatal cocaine exposure is associated with several kinds of deficits in preschool and school-aged children. These include reduced vocabulary at age 6, delayed cognitive and motor development at 3 to 5 years of age, and poor impulse control (Delaney-Black et al., 2000; Hurt, Malmus, Betancourt, Brodsky, & Giannetta, 2001; Savage, Brodsky, Malmud, Giannetta, & Hurt, 2005). As a result, children who were exposed to cocaine prenatally are more likely to require special education services in school (Levine et al., 2008).

Marijuana and Heroin   Prenatal exposure to marijuana appears to interfere with a child's growth. Even at age 6, children whose mothers used the drug during pregnancy are smaller on average than their non-drug-exposed peers (Cornelius et al., 2002). Researchers also now have evidence suggesting that prenatal exposure to marijuana adversely affects the developing brain (Wang et al., 2004). These findings may help explain why a number of studies have shown that the behavior of infants and children who were prenatally exposed to the drug differs from that of their agemates. For example, the infants of twice-weekly marijuana smokers suffer from tremors and sleep problems. Moreover, they seem to have little interest in their surroundings for up to 2 weeks after birth (Brockington, 1996). How these early differences affect babies' later development is unknown. However, some studies suggest that learning disabilities and attention problems are more common among children whose mothers used marijuana during pregnancy (Fried & Smith, 2001).

Both heroin and methadone, a drug often used in treating heroin addiction, can cause miscarriage, premature labor, and early death (Brockington, 1996; Dharan, Parviainen, Newcomb, & Poleshuck, 2006). Further, 60–80% of babies born to heroin- or methadone-addicted women are addicted to these drugs as well. Addicted babies have high-pitched cries and suffer from withdrawal symptoms, including irritability, uncontrollable tremors, vomiting, convulsions, and sleep problems. These symptoms may last as long as 4 months.

The degree to which heroin and methadone affect development depends on the quality of the environment in which babies are raised. Babies who are cared for by mothers who continue to be addicted themselves usually don't do as well as those whose mothers stop using drugs or who are raised by relatives or foster families (Brockington, 1996). By age 2, most heroin- or methadone-addicted babies in good homes are developing normally.

Other Teratogens and Maternal Factors

Learning Objective 2.10
What are the risks associated with legal drugs, maternal diet, age, emotional distress, and poverty?

A variety of additional factors, from vitamins to environmental pollutants to maternal emotions, can affect prenatal development. A few are listed in Table 2.5, and others are discussed in more detail in this section.

Prescription and Over-the-Counter Drugs
You may have heard about the thalidomide tragedy that occurred in the 1960s. The drug involved was a mild tranquilizer that doctors prescribed to pregnant women who were experiencing severe symptoms of morning sickness. Sadly, the drug caused serious malformations of the limbs in thousands of fetuses that were exposed to it (Vogin, 2005).

In general, doctors advise against taking any unnecessary medicines during pregnancy. But some pregnant women must take drugs in order to treat health conditions that may be threatening to their own and their unborn child's life. For instance, pregnant women with epilepsy must take antiseizure medication because the seizures themselves are potentially harmful to the unborn child. Other drugs that pregnant women may have to risk taking, even though they can be harmful, include medications that treat heart conditions and diabetes, those that control asthma symptoms, and some kinds of psychiatric drugs. In all such cases, physicians weigh the benefits of medication against potential teratogenic effects and look for a combination of drug and dosage that will effectively treat the mother's health condition while placing her unborn child at minimal risk.

Table 2.5 Some Important Teratogens

Teratogen	Possible Effects on Fetus
Maternal Diseases	
Cancer	Fetal or placental tumor
Toxoplasmosis	Brain swelling, spinal abnormalities
Chicken pox	Scars, eye damage
Parvovirus	Anemia
Hepatitis B	Hepatitis
Chlamydia	Conjunctivitis, pneumonia
Tuberculosis	Pneumonia or tuberculosis
Drugs	
Inhalants	FAS-like syndrome, premature labor
Accutane/vitamin A	Facial, ear, heart deformities
Streptomycin	Deafness
Penicillin	Skin disorders
Tetracycline	Tooth deformities
Diet pills	Low birth weight

Sources: Amato, 1998; Kliegman, 1998.

In contrast to prescription drugs, most people, pregnant or otherwise, take over-the-counter medicines on a casual, as-needed basis without consulting a doctor. Many of these drugs, such as acetaminophen, are safe for pregnant women unless taken to excess (Organization of Teratology Information Specialists, 2005). However, experts advise pregnant women to discuss the medicines they usually take with physicians at the outset of their pregnancies. These discussions should deal with both drugs and any vitamins or supplements that the pregnant woman usually takes. Their doctors will advise them as to which of the substances are safe and which are risky. Often, too, physicians can suggest safer alternatives; typically most look to older drugs that have been thoroughly tested (Vogin, 2005).

Diet Both the general adequacy of a pregnant woman's diet, measured in terms of calories, and the presence of certain key nutrients are critical to prenatal development. At a minimum, a mother needs sufficient overall calories and protein to prevent malnutrition. When a woman experiences severe malnutrition during pregnancy, particularly during the final 3 months, she faces a greatly increased risk of stillbirth, low infant birth weight, or infant death during the first year of life (Di Mario, Say, & Lincetto, 2007). Autopsies show that infants born to malnourished mothers have smaller brains, with fewer and smaller brain cells than normal (Georgieff, 1994).

A vital specific nutrient whose importance during pregnancy has become clear is folic acid, a B vitamin found primarily in liver, beans, leafy green vegetables, broccoli, orange juice, fortified breakfast cereals, and grain products, especially wheat germ. Inadequate amounts of this nutrient have been clearly linked to the risk of neural tube defects such as spina bifida, a deformity in which the lower part of the spine does not close (Mersereau, 2004). Many (but not all) such children are retarded; most have some lower-body paralysis. Because the neural tube develops primarily during the very earliest weeks of pregnancy, before a woman may even know she is pregnant, it is important for women who plan a pregnancy to ingest at least the minimum level of folic acid: 400 micrograms daily. To help raise the normal intake above the desired level, new regulations by the Food and Drug Administration in the United States now require that 140 micrograms of folic acid be added to each 100 grams of enriched flour, thus greatly increasing the likelihood that the majority of women will receive sufficient quantities of folic acid. Since the mandate was instituted, the number of infants born with spina bifida in the United States has been reduced by about one-third (Mersereau et al., 2004).

Dieticians recommend that expectant mothers take in about 300 calories more per day than before they were pregnant (March of Dimes, 2008a). Lack of financial resources may prevent women who live in poverty from getting the needed calories. However, poor nutrition during pregnancy also occurs among women who are not poor but who express concerns about weight gain both before and during pregnancy. For instance, one Japanese study found that weight-conscious young women who were underweight prior to pregnancy tended to remain so during their pregnancies (Takimoto, 2006). Researchers have also found that about 25% of middle-class pregnant women in the United States intentionally restrict caloric intake to avoid gaining what they consider to be an unacceptable amount of "baby weight" (Shearer, 2007). Researchers argue that the behavior of such women needlessly exposes their fetuses to the potentially devastating effects of poor nutrition (Franko & Spurrell, 2000). Thus, they say, doctors need to take steps to identify overly weight-conscious pregnant women and to educate them about the fetus's nutritional needs.

There are also risks associated with gaining too much. In particular, women who gain too much weight are more likely to have a cesarean section delivery (Takimoto, 2006); they are also prone to postpartum obesity, which carries a whole set of health risks, including heart disease and diabetes (Johnson & Yancey, 1996). Gains within the recommended ranges appear optimal, although there is wide variability from one woman to the next.

Finally, women who are obese before they become pregnant have some additional risks, regardless of the amount of weight they gain. Such women are about twice as likely to have infants with neural tube defects, regardless of their intake of folic acid (Scialli, 2007)—a finding that argues in favor of weight loss before pregnancy for women who are classed as obese.

The Mother's Age Have you heard sensationalized media reports about women giving birth in their 50s and even into their 60s? Such late-in-life births are very rare, but it is the case that the average age at which women give birth for the first time has increased over the past few decades. In 1970, the average age at which a woman in the United States delivered her first child was 21.4 years. By contrast, in 2003, the average age was 25.1 years (Martin et al., 2005). The shift is largely due to the increasing prevalence of first births among women in their late thirties and early forties.

In most cases, older mothers have uncomplicated pregnancies and deliver healthy babies, but the risks associated with pregnancy do increase somewhat as women get older

(Martin et al., 2005). Their babies are also at greater risk of weighing less than 5.5 pounds at birth, a finding that is partly explained by the greater incidence of multiple births among older mothers. Still, infants born to women over the age of 35, whether single or multiple births, are at higher risk of having problems such as heart malformations and chromosomal disorders.

At the other end of the age continuum, when comparing the rates of problems seen in teenage mothers with those seen in mothers in their 20s, almost all researchers find higher rates of problems among the teens. However, teenage mothers are also more likely to be poor and less likely to receive adequate prenatal care (Martin et al., 2005). Thus, it is very hard to sort out the causal factors. An unusually well-designed study, however, made the link between early pregnancy and poor outcomes quite clear.

Alison Fraser and her colleagues (1995) studied 135,088 White girls and women, aged 13 to 24, who gave birth in the state of Utah between 1970 and 1990. This is an unusual sample for studies on this subject: Almost two-thirds of the teenaged mothers in this group were married, and most had adequate prenatal care; 95% remained in school. These special conditions enabled Fraser to disentangle the effects of ethnicity, poverty, marital status, and the mother's age—all of which are normally confounded in studies of teenage childbearing. Overall, Fraser found higher rates of adverse pregnancy outcomes among mothers age 17 and younger than among the mothers age 20 and up. The rate of preterm births was twice as high; the incidence of low birth weight was almost twice as high. And these differences were found even among teenaged mothers who were married, in school, and had adequate prenatal care. Outcomes were riskier still among teenaged mothers who lacked adequate prenatal care, but good care alone did not eliminate the heightened risk of problems linked to teen births. Just why such a heightened risk should exist for teen mothers is not entirely clear. The most likely possibility is that there is some negative biological consequence of pregnancy in a girl whose own growth is not complete.

Stress and Emotional State   The idea that emotional or physical stresses are linked to poor pregnancy outcomes is firmly established in folklore, but "its foundation in science is much less secure" (DiPietro, 2004). Results from studies in animals are clear: Exposure of the pregnant female to stressors such as heat, light, noise, shock, or crowding significantly increases the risk of low-birth-weight offspring as well as later problems in the offspring (Schneider, 1992). Studies in humans are harder to interpret because women who experience high levels of stress are quite likely to be different in other ways from those who do not, so it is harder to uncover clear causal connections. Nonetheless, a number of careful studies do show that stressful life events, emotional distress, and physical stress are all linked to slight increases in problems of pregnancy, such as low birth weight (DiPietro, 2004). Moreover, studies involving experimentally induced stressors (e.g., requiring a pregnant woman to take some kind of cognitive test) show that they seem to cause short-term changes in fetal activity, heart rate, and other responses (DiPietro, Costigan, & Gurewitsch, 2003). Whether such changes are sufficient to affect development in any meaningful way is as yet unknown.

Similarly, maternal emotions are associated with measures of fetal response such as activity level. Researcher Janet DiPietro and her colleagues have found that the fetuses of women who have positive emotions toward their condition are less active than those of mothers who feel more negatively about their pregnancies (DiPietro, Hilton, Hawkins, Costigan, & Pressman, 2002). The long-term effects of this association, if there are any, have been difficult to identify. However, researchers have found that severe and prolonged emotional distress during pregnancy can have long-term associations with children's development. Likewise, researchers have found that children of mothers who reported high levels of psychological distress during pregnancy are more emotionally negative at both 6 months and 5 years of age than those of nondistressed mothers (Martin, Noyes, Wisenbaker, &

Huttunen, 1999). But critics of such studies claim that the real connection is a matter of maternal genes and/or parenting style; emotionally negative and depressed mothers may use ineffective parenting strategies or simply be more likely, for genetic reasons, to have children who are less emotionally positive than their peers (Lau, Riisdijk, Gregory, McGuffin, & Elev, 2007).

One fairly consistent finding, however, is that the fetuses of severely distressed mothers tend to grow more slowly than others (Linnet et al., 2003). Developmentalists hypothesize that this effect may result directly from emotion-related hormones or it may be an indirect effect of the mother's emotional state. A stressed or depressed mother may eat less, or her weakened immune system may limit her ability to fight off viruses and bacteria, either of which may retard fetal growth. Consequently, many psychologists suggest that providing stressed and/or depressed pregnant women with social support and counseling may lead to improvements in both maternal and fetal health (Brockington, 1996). Moreover, many studies suggest that antidepressant drugs do not harm the fetus and may be very helpful for pregnant women who are severely depressed (Rybakowski, 2001).

Poverty The basic sequence of fetal development is clearly no different for children born to poor mothers than for children born to middle-class mothers, but many of the problems that can negatively affect prenatal development are more common among the poor. For example, in the United States, mothers who have not graduated from high school are about twice as likely as mothers with a college education to have a low-birth-weight infant or a stillborn infant. Poor women are also likely to have their first pregnancy earlier and to have more pregnancies overall, and they are less likely to be immunized against such diseases as rubella. They are also less likely to seek prenatal care, and if they do, they seek it much later in their pregnancies. A significant portion of this difference could be overcome in the United States: Devoting the resources needed to provide good, universal prenatal care could significantly reduce not only the rate of infant death but also the rate of physical abnormalities and perhaps even mental retardation. Equal access to care is not the only answer. In Canada, for example, in which such care is universally available, social class differences in low-birth-weight deliveries and in infant mortality rates remain (Spencer, 2003).

Think Critically

- In your view, what are the advantages and disadvantages of genetic counseling for couples who want to have a child but who are concerned about a genetic or chromosomal disorder that runs in one or both of their families?
- With the advent of antiretroviral drugs, the rate of mother-to-fetus transmission of HIV has been greatly reduced. Do you think that these findings justify mandatory testing and treatment of pregnant women who are at high risk of having HIV/AIDS? Why or why not?

Conduct Your Own Research

In every culture, there are traditional beliefs about pregnancy, many of which are myths. For example, you may have heard that labor is more likely to begin during a full moon or that boys "carry high" but girls "carry low." Other once-popular ideas include the notion that eating spicy foods or having sex will bring on premature labor. Survey your classmates, friends, and relatives to find out what kinds of things they have heard about pregnancy. If you have access to people from different cultures, analyze the similarities and differences in these beliefs across groups.

Summary

CONCEPTION AND GENETICS

2.1 What are the characteristics of the zygote?

- At conception, 23 chromosomes from the sperm join with 23 from the ovum to make up the set of 46 that will be reproduced in each cell of the new baby's body. Each chromosome consists of a long string of deoxyribonucleic acid (DNA) made up of segments called genes. The baby's sex is determined by the 23rd pair of chromosomes, a pattern of XX for a girl and XY for a boy.

2.2 In what ways do genes influence development?

- Geneticists distinguish between the genotype, which is the pattern of inherited characteristics, and the phenotype, which is the result of the interaction of genotype and environment. Genes are transmitted from parent to child according to complex patterns of inheritance that include dominant/recessive, polygenic, multifactorial, and sex-linked.

DEVELOPMENT FROM CONCEPTION TO BIRTH

2.3 What happens in each of the stages of prenatal development?

- During the first days after conception, called the germinal stage of development, the zygote (the initial cell formed by egg and sperm) divides, travels down the fallopian tube, and is implanted in the wall of the uterus. The second stage, the period of the embryo, which lasts until 8 weeks after fertilization, includes the development of the various structures that support fetal development, such as the placenta, as well as primitive forms of all organ systems. The final 30 weeks of gestation, called the fetal period, are devoted primarily to enlargement and refinements in all the organ systems.

2.4 How do male and female fetuses differ?

- During the embryonic period, the XY embryo secretes the hormone testosterone, which stimulates the growth of male genitalia and shifts the brain into a "male" pattern. Boys are more active, have more slowly developing skeletons, are bigger at birth, and are more vulnerable to most forms of prenatal stress.

2.5 What behaviors have scientists observed in fetuses?

- The fetus is responsive to stimuli and appears to learn in the womb. Temperamental differences in the womb (such as activity level) persist into infancy and childhood, and some aspects of the prenatal sensory environment may be important to future development.

PROBLEMS IN PRENATAL DEVELOPMENT

2.6 What are the effects of the major dominant, recessive, and sex-linked diseases?

- Dominant disorders are not usually manifested until adulthood. Huntington's disease, a fatal affliction of the nervous system, is one such disorder. Recessive disorders affect individuals earlier in life, often leading to mental retardation and/or early death. These disorders include phenylketonuria, sickle-cell disease, and Tay-Sachs disease. A fairly common sex-linked disorder is red-green color blindness. Hemophilia and fragile-X syndrome are more serious sex-linked disorders that affect males far more often than females.

2.7 How do trisomies and other disorders of the autosomes and sex chromosomes affect development?

- Abnormal numbers of chromosomes or chromosomal damage cause a number of serious disorders, including Down syndrome.

2.8 How do maternal diseases and environmental hazards affect prenatal development?

- Some diseases contracted by the mother, including rubella, AIDS, sexually transmitted diseases like genital herpes and CMV, and chronic illnesses, may cause abnormalities or disease in the child. Environmental hazards include pollutants such as mercury and lead as well as parasite-bearing substances such as animal feces. Their effect on the fetus varies with the timing of the exposure.

2.9 What are the potential adverse effects of tobacco, alcohol, and other drugs on prenatal development?

- Drugs such as alcohol and nicotine appear to have harmful effects on the developing fetus; drug effects depend on the timing of exposure and the dosage.

2.10 What are the risks associated with legal drugs, maternal diet, age, emotional distress, and poverty?

- Some prescription and over-the-counter drugs have teratogenic effects. Physicians need to know what drugs pregnant women take regularly so that they can provide guidance as to the appropriate use of such drugs during pregnancy. If a mother suffers from poor nutrition, she faces an increased risk of stillbirth, low birth weight, and infant death during the first year of life. Older mothers and very young mothers also run increased risks, as do their infants. Long-term, severe depression or chronic physical illness in the mother may increase the risk of complications during pregnancy or difficulties in the infant. A number of prenatal risk factors are associated with poverty, including earlier age at first pregnancy and lack of access to prenatal care.

Key Terms

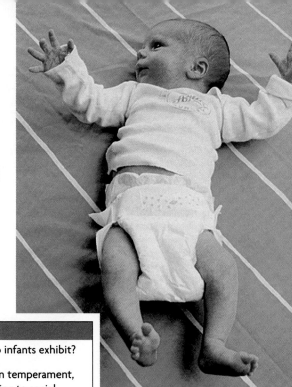

Birth and Early Infancy 3

When Mahajabeen Shaik gave birth to twins, the larger of the two, Hiba, weighed a robust 20 ounces, small but sufficient for her gestational age of 26 weeks. But the other twin, Rumaisa, weighed just 8.6 ounces, a birth weight that gave her the distinction of being the smallest surviving infant ever born. Remarkably, experts in neonatal medicine at Chicago's Loyola University told Mahajabeen and her husband, Mohammed Rahman, that the odds favored a normal infancy and childhood for both girls (Associated Press, 2005). Doctors told them the story of one of the "graduates" of Loyola's neonatal intensive care unit (NICU), Madeline Mann, who weighed just 9.9 ounces when she was born in 1989 (Muraskas & Hasson, 2004). The first four months of her life were spent in Loyola's NICU. In the years following her discharge from the hospital, Madeline blossomed into an energetic preschooler. As she progressed through the school years, it became clear that not only was she free from any serious disabilities, but she was quite gifted in a variety of areas. Madeline excelled in school, getting top scores on

Rumaisa Rahman is shown here at a few weeks old. The smallest surviving infant, she weighed just 8.6 ounces at birth.

standardized achievement tests, and learned to play the violin. She participated in sports as well. By her mid-teens, the only indication that she had been a premature baby was her small size. At age 14, Madeline was just 4 feet 7 inches tall and weighed only 60 pounds. Still, throughout her life, her rate of growth had been entirely normal, and she had been free of any major health problems.

Encouraged by Madeline's story, Mahajabeen and Mohammed watched hopefully as their twins grew stronger each day. By the time the girls reached 5 months of age, both were out of the hospital and developing normally. Their case, like that of Madeline Mann, is remarkable. In fact, there are only 58 documented cases of surviving newborns who weighed 13 ounces or less (Muraskas & Hasson, 2004). Further, most of those who do survive have life-long health or neurological problems.

Fortunately, most infants are born on time and do not require intensive care. In most cases, too, expectant mothers do not deliver under emergency circumstances and can choose the setting in which their babies will be born. We begin our discussion of birth and early infancy with an overview of the array of birth choices available today.

Birth

For parents, birth is an experience that combines great physical stress with a wide variety of emotions: the joy of seeing the baby for the first time, curiosity about what kind of individual she will be, worry about possible physical problems, anxiety about the ability to parent effectively, and so on. For the child, of course, birth marks her entrance into the family and community.

Birth Choices

In the industrialized world, parents must make a number of choices in advance of the delivery. Parents may worry about whether they are making the best choices both for themselves and for the baby.

Drugs during Labor and Delivery   Surveys indicate that about 40% of expectant mothers in the United States fear being in pain during childbirth (Geissbuehler & Eberhard, 2002). Thus, one key decision about the birth process concerns the use of pain-relieving drugs during delivery. Four types of pain relief are used (American College of Obstetricians and Gynecologists [ACOG], 2004). *Systemic analgesics* are usually given as injections. They relieve pain without causing loss of consciousness, much as an acetaminophen tablet (Tylenol) relieves a headache. *Local anesthetics* are also injected and cause numbness in a very small area, somewhat like the shot of novacaine that a dentist gives prior to filling a tooth. Local anesthetics are often given when a procedure called an *episiotemy* is necessary (a small incision that increases the size of the vagina). *Regional analgesics*, usually called *epidural blocks*, are the most commonly used form of pain relief. They cause a complete loss of sensation below the point in the spine where the pain-relieving drug is injected. *General anesthesia* both relieves pain and induces unconsciousness. Because general anesthesia is the fastest acting form of pain relief, it is most commonly used in emergency situations in which other forms of pain relief act too slowly.

Studying the causal links between such drug use and the baby's later behavior or development has proved to be monumentally difficult. Controlled experiments are obviously not possible, since women cannot be randomly assigned to specific drug regimens. In the real world, drugs are also given in myriad different combinations. However, there have been many studies of the immediate effects of obstetric anesthesia on newborns.

One important finding is that nearly all drugs given during labor pass through the placenta and enter the fetal bloodstream. Because the newborn lacks the enzymes necessary to break down such drugs quickly, the effect of any drug lasts longer in the baby than it does in the mother. Not surprisingly, then, drugged infants may show signs of being under the influence of such drugs (Sola, Rogido, & Partridge, 2002). For example, they may have slower or faster than normal heartbeats, depending on which drugs their mothers were given. In rare cases, infants of anesthetized mothers experience seizures.

Because of these risks, many women choose to avoid drugs altogether. The general term *natural childbirth* is commonly used to refer to this particular choice. This approach is also often called the *Lamaze method*, after the physician who popularized the notion of natural childbirth and devised a variety of pain management techniques. In natural childbirth, women rely on psychological and behavioral methods of pain management rather than on pain-relieving drugs.

Natural childbirth involves several components. First, a woman selects someone, usually the baby's father, to serve as a labor coach. *Prepared childbirth classes* psychologically prepare the woman and her labor coach for the experience of labor and delivery. For example, they learn to use the term *contraction* instead of *pain*. Further, believing that her baby will benefit from natural childbirth provides the woman with the motivation she needs to endure labor without the aid of pain-relieving medication. Finally, relaxation and breathing techniques provide her with behavioral responses that serve to replace the negative emotions that typically result from the physical discomfort of contractions. Aided by her coach, the woman focuses attention on her breathing rather than on the pain.

The Location of Birth   Another choice parents must make is where the baby is to be born. In the United States, there are typically four alternatives: (1) a traditional hospital maternity unit; (2) a hospital-based birth center or a birthing room located within a hospital, which provides a more homelike

These couples, like so many today, are taking a childbirth class together. Having the father present at the delivery as coach seems to reduce the mother's pain and even shorten the length of labor.

In the United States, the most common delivery setting is in a hospital, assisted by a physician. In other industrialized societies, home deliveries assisted by a midwife are quite common.

setting, with both labor and delivery completed in the same room and family members often present throughout; (3) a freestanding birth center, like a hospital birth center except not located in a hospital, with delivery typically attended by a midwife rather than (or in addition to) a physician; and (4) at home.

At the turn of the century, only about 5% of babies in the United States were born in hospitals; today, the figure is 99% (Martin et al., 2007). The remaining 1% are born at home or in freestanding birth centers. Limited research in Canada and the United States (e.g., Janssen, Holt, & Myers, 1994; Johnson & Daviss, 2005) indicates that such nonhospital deliveries, if planned and attended by a midwife or equivalent professional, are no riskier than deliveries in hospitals.

The Presence of Fathers at Delivery The father's presence during labor and delivery has become the norm in the United States, so much so, in fact, that it has become difficult to study this variable. Decades ago, when hospital policies varied greatly with regard to the presence of fathers in the delivery room, it was possible to compare father-present to father-absent deliveries. Such studies found that when fathers were present, laboring women experienced less pain, requested less medication, delivered sooner, and experienced fewer complications than when fathers were absent (Henneborn & Cogan, 1975). However, contrary to the expectations of some, researchers found that being present at the birth of a child had little effect on fathers' emotional bonds with infants (Palkovitz, 1985). These findings suggest that the practice of encouraging fathers to be present in North American labor and delivery rooms is part of a larger cultural trend toward increased father involvement during children's early years rather than the result of research on bonding.

Learning Objective 3.2
What are the events and risks associated with each stage of the birth process?

The Process of Birth

Labor typically progresses through three stages. Occasionally, complications occur, but most of these are managed by health-care providers in ways that ensure the health of both mother and baby. Once the child is born, her health is assessed, and the family begins getting to know its newest member.

The Stages of Labor Stage 1 covers the period during which two important processes occur: **dilation** and **effacement**. The cervix (the opening at the bottom of the uterus) must open up like the lens of a camera (dilation) and flatten out (effacement). At the time of actual delivery of the infant, the cervix must normally be dilated to about 10 centimeters (about 4 inches). This part of labor has been likened to what happens when you put on a sweater with a neck that is too tight. You have to pull and stretch the neck of the sweater with your head in order to get it on. Eventually, you stretch the neck wide enough so that the widest part of your head can pass through. A good deal of the effacement may actually occur in the last weeks of the pregnancy, as may some dilation. It is not uncommon for women to be 80% effaced and 1 to 3 centimeters dilated when they begin labor. The contractions of the first stage of labor, which are at first widely spaced and later more frequent and rhythmical, serve to complete both processes.

Customarily, stage 1 is itself divided into phases. In the early (or *latent*) phase, contractions are relatively far apart and are typically not very uncomfortable. In the *active* phase, which begins when the cervix is 3 to 4 centimeters dilated and continues until dilation has

dilation A key process in the first stage of childbirth, during which the cervix widens sufficiently to allow the infant's head to pass into the birth canal. Full dilation is 10 centimeters.

effacement The flattening of the cervix, which, along with dilation, is a key process of the first stage of childbirth.

reached 8 centimeters, contractions are closer together and more intense. The last 2 centimeters of dilation are achieved during a period usually called the *transition* phase. It is this period, when contractions are closely spaced and strong, that women typically find the most painful.

Fortunately, transition is relatively brief, especially in second or later pregnancies. Figure 3.1 shows the duration of the several subphases, although neither the figure nor the average numbers convey the wide individual variability that exists. Among women delivering a first child, stage 1 labor may last as little as 3 hours or as long as 20 (Biswas & Craigo, 1994; Kilpatrick & Laros, 1989). The average is about 8 hours for first births and 6 for subsequent deliveries (Albers, 1999). The times are generally longer for women receiving anesthesia than for those delivering by natural childbirth.

At the end of the transition phase, the mother will normally have the urge to help the infant come out by "pushing." When the birth attendant (physician or midwife) is sure the cervix is fully dilated, she or he will encourage this pushing, and the second stage of labor—the actual delivery—begins. The baby's head moves past the stretched cervix, into the birth canal, and finally out of the mother's body. Most women find this part of labor markedly less distressing than the transition phase. The average length of stage 2 is about 50 minutes for first infants and 20 minutes for later deliveries (Moore & Persaud, 1993). It rarely takes longer than 2 hours.

Most infants are delivered head first, facing down toward the mother's spine. Three to four percent, however, are oriented differently, either feet first or bottom first (called *breech* presentations) (ACOG, 2007). Several decades ago, most breech deliveries were accomplished with the aid of medical instruments such as forceps; today, nearly four-fifths of breech presentations are delivered by cesarean section—a procedure discussed more fully in the next section. Stage 3, typically quite brief, is the delivery of the placenta (also called the *afterbirth*) and other material from the uterus. You can see all these steps presented in Figure 3.2 on page 64.

Complications   Many complications are possible during birth. Researchers have found that life-threatening complications during birth (e.g., collapse of the umbilical cord) are associated with poor developmental outcomes, such as poor self-control later in childhood and adolescence (Beaver & Wright, 2005). It's important to note, however, that the association between birth complications and later developmental outcomes may not be a causal one. Instead, factors such as poverty and poor maternal health are probably linked to increased risk of both birth complications and poor developmental outcomes.

Still, birth complications that interfere with a child's vital functions can lead to brain damage and, as a result, cause a variety of later developmental problems. One such complication is an insufficiency of oxygen for the infant, a state called **anoxia**. During the period immediately surrounding birth, anoxia may occur because the umbilical circulation system fails to continue supplying blood oxygen until the baby breathes or because the umbilical cord has been squeezed in some way during labor or delivery. Long-term effects of anoxia have been hard to pin down. Prolonged anoxia is often (but not invariably) associated with such major consequences as cerebral palsy or mental retardation (Venerosi, Valanzano, Cirulli, Alleva, & Calamandrei, 2004). Briefer periods of oxygen deprivation appear to have little long-term effect, although that is still a tentative conclusion.

Infants may also dislocate their shoulders or hips during birth. Some experience fractures, and in others, nerves that control facial muscles are compressed, causing temporary paralysis on one side of the face. Such complications are usually not serious and resolve themselves with little or no treatment.

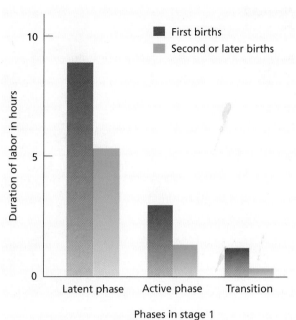

Figure 3.1
Phases of Labor

Typical pattern of timing of the phases of stage 1 of labor for first births and for subsequent births. The relatively long latent phase shown here counts from 0 centimeters dilated, which increases the total hours somewhat. The average length of stage 1 is about 8 hours for a first birth and 6 hours for later births.

(*Source*: Based on Biswas & Craigo, 1994, from Figures 10-16, p. 216, and 10-17, p. 217.)

anoxia A shortage of oxygen. This is one of the potential risks at birth, and it can result in brain damage if it is prolonged.

Figure 3.2
Phases of Delivery

The sequence of steps during delivery is shown clearly in these drawings.

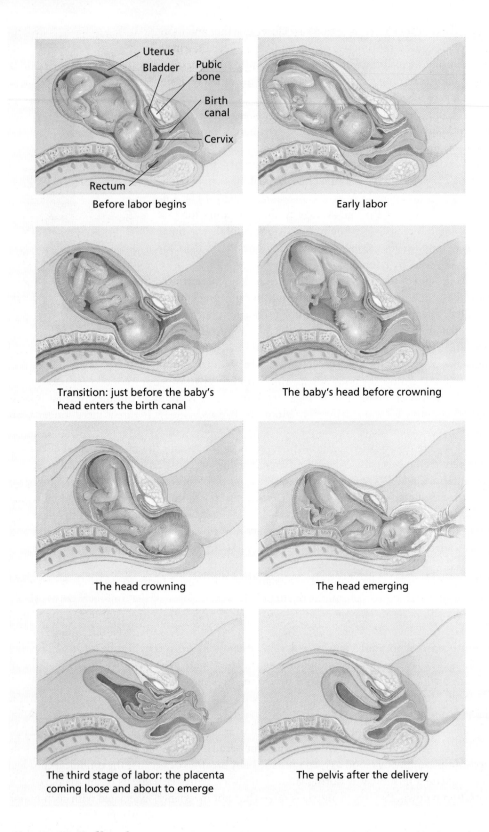

Before labor begins

Early labor

Transition: just before the baby's head enters the birth canal

The baby's head before crowning

The head crowning

The head emerging

The third stage of labor: the placenta coming loose and about to emerge

The pelvis after the delivery

cesarean section (c-section)
Delivery of the child through an incision in the mother's abdomen.

Cesarean Deliveries Sometimes it is necessary to deliver a baby surgically through incisions made in the abdominal and uterine walls. There are several situations that justify the use of this operation, called a **cesarean section** (or **c-section**). Factors that call for the procedure include fetal distress during labor, labor that fails to progress in a reasonable amount of time, a fetus that is too large to be delivered vaginally, and maternal health conditions that may be aggravated by vaginal delivery (e.g., cardiovascular disease, spinal injury) or may be dangerous to a vaginally delivered fetus (e.g., herpes) (ACOG, 2008a).

Many observers claim that the current rate of cesarean deliveries in the United States is too high. The National Center for Health Statistics (Martin et al., 2007) reports that just over 30% of all deliveries in 2005 in the United States involved a cesarean section. Critics of the frequency with which c-sections occur say that many of these operations are unnecessary. Are their claims justified?

One factor behind current c-section statistics is that, as you learned earlier, more older women are having babies (Joseph et al., 2003). These women are more likely to conceive twins and other multiples. In such cases, surgical delivery almost always increases the odds in favor of the babies' postnatal health. Thus, the benefits of cesarean delivery outweigh its risks.

By contrast, surveys suggest that as many as 14% of c-sections performed in the United States between 2000 and 2005 were entirely elective (McCourt et al., 2007). In these cases, women who had no medical problems, and who were carrying healthy fetuses, requested a surgical delivery, and their physicians complied. The ethics committee of the American College of Obstetrics and Gynecology (2008b) has ruled that elective surgical deliveries are ethical as long as the practitioner is certain that, for the patients who request them, vaginal deliveries carry equal risk.

But should cesarean delivery be thought of as just another birth option? Critics say that the possible benefits of elective cesareans do not justify exposing women to their risks (Hall, 2003). They claim that many obstetric patients do not realize that a c-section is major surgery and carries the same risks as other abdominal operations. These risks include allergic reactions to anesthetics, infection, accidental injuries to other organs (as well as to the fetus), and excessive blood loss. Consequently, these critics believe that elective cesarean delivery represents a poorly informed choice on the part of the patient, and an irresponsible practice on the part of the physician. Moreover, some researchers have begun to test the hypothesis that during labor the mother's body produces hormones that cross the placenta prior to the baby's birth and influence immune system functioning in the newborn (Malamitsi-Puchner et al., 2005). If future research provides support for this hypothesis, critics may have yet another reason, a very important one, to argue that cesarean deliveries be avoided except in situations in which vaginal delivery is dangerous to the baby or to the mother.

Assessing the Newborn It has become customary in most hospitals to evaluate an infant's status immediately after birth, and then again 5 minutes later, to detect any problems that may require special care. The most frequently used assessment system is the *Apgar score*, developed by a physician, Virginia Apgar (1953). The newborn is given a score of 0, 1, or 2 on each of the five criteria listed in Table 3.1 on page 66. A maximum score of 10 is fairly unusual immediately after birth, because most infants are still somewhat blue in the fingers and toes at that stage. At the 5-minute assessment, however, 85–90% of infants are scored as 9 or 10, meaning that they are getting off to a good start. Any score of 7 or better indicates that the baby is in no danger. A score of 4, 5, or 6 usually means that the baby needs help establishing normal breathing patterns; a score of 3 or below indicates a baby in critical condition, requiring active intervention, although babies with such low Apgar scores can and often do survive (Casey, McIntire, & Leveno, 2001).

Another test used to assess newborns, widely used by researchers, is the Brazelton Neonatal Behavioral Assessment Scale (Brazelton, 1984). In this test, a skilled examiner checks the neonate's responses to a variety of stimuli; his reflexes, muscle tone, alertness, and cuddliness; and his ability to quiet or soothe himself after being upset. Scores on this test can be helpful in identifying children who may have significant neurological problems. More interestingly, several investigators (e.g., Francis, Self, & Horowitz, 1987) have found that teaching parents how to administer this test to their own infants turns out to have beneficial effects on the parent-infant interaction, apparently because it heightens the parent's awareness of all the subtle cues the baby provides.

Table 3.1 Evaluation Method for Apgar Score

Aspect of Infant Observed	Score Assigned		
	0	1	2
Heart rate	Absent	<100/min.	>100/min.
Respiratory rate	No breathing	Weak cry and shallow breathing	Good strong cry and regular breathing
Muscle tone	Flaccid	Some flexion of extremities	Well flexed
Response to stimulation of feet	None	Some motion	Cry
Color	Blue; pale	Body pink, extremities blue	Completely pink

Source: Francis et al., 1987, pp. 731–732.

The First Greeting Many parents experience intense joy as they greet the infant for the first time, accompanied often by laughter, exclamations of delight at the baby's features, and first tentative and tender touching. Here are one mother's reactions to seeing her new daughter:

> She's big, isn't she? What do you reckon? (Doctor makes a comment.) Oh look, she's got hair. It's a girl—you're supposed to be all little. Gosh. Oh, she's lovely. Oh, she's opened her eyes (laughs). Oh lovely (kisses baby). (MacFarlane, 1977, pp. 64–65)

Most parents are intensely interested in having the baby look at them right away. They are delighted if the baby opens her eyes and will try to stimulate her to do so if she doesn't. The parents' initial tentative touches also seem to follow a pattern: The parent first touches the infant rather gingerly with the tip of a finger and then proceeds gradually to stroking with the full hand (MacFarlane, 1977). The tenderness seen in most of these early encounters is striking.

Learning Objective 3.3

What are some of the possible consequences of low birth weight?

low birth weight (LBW) Term for any baby born with a weight below 2,500 grams (5.5 pounds), including both those born too early (preterm) and those who are small for date.

very low birth weight (VLBW) Term for any baby born with a weight below 1,500 grams (3.3 pounds).

extremely low birth weight (ELBW) Term for any baby born with a weight below 1,000 grams (2.2 pounds).

preterm infant An infant born before 38 weeks gestational age.

Low Birth Weight

The optimal weight range for infants—the weight that is associated with the lowest risk of later death or disability—is between about 3,000 and 5,000 grams (6.6 to 11 pounds) (Rees, Lederman, & Kiely, 1996). Several different labels are used to describe infants whose weight falls below this optimal range. All babies below 2,500 grams (5.5 pounds) are described with the most general term of **low birth weight (LBW)**. Those below 1,500 grams (3.3 pounds) are usually called **very low birth weight (VLBW)**, and those below 1,000 grams (2.2 pounds) are called **extremely low birth weight (ELBW)**. The incidence of low birth weight has declined in the United States in the past decade but is still high: About 8% of all newborns weigh below 2,500 grams (Martin et al., 2007). About 19% of those small babies weighed less than 1,500 grams. Babies who weigh more than 1,500 grams and who receive good neonatal care have close to a 100% chance of survival. However, in the VLBW and ELBW groups, the more the infant weighs, the greater his chances of survival.

Causes of Low Birth Weight Low birth weight occurs for a variety of reasons, of which the most obvious and common is that the infant is born before the full 38 weeks of gestation. Any baby born before 38 weeks of gestation is labeled a **preterm infant**. Multiple births are especially likely to end in preterm delivery. In addition, mothers who suffer from chronic illnesses and those who develop a serious medical condition during pregnancy are more likely to deliver preterm infants (Sola, Rogido, & Partridge, 2002). In most cases of preterm delivery, labor begins spontaneously. However, because of a condition in the fetus or in the mother, physicians sometimes elect to deliver babies prior to 38 weeks of gestation via c-section.

It is also possible for an infant to have completed the full 38-week gestational period but still weigh less than 2,500 grams or to weigh less than would be expected for the number of weeks of gestation completed, however long that may have been. Such an infant is called a **small-for-date infant**. Infants in this group appear to have suffered from prenatal malnutrition, such as might occur with constriction of blood flow caused by the mother's smoking, or from other significant problems prenatally. Such infants generally have poorer prognoses than do equivalent-weight infants who weigh an appropriate amount for their gestational age, especially if the small-for-date infant is also preterm (Sola, Rogido, & Partridge, 2002).

Health Status of Low-Birth-Weight Infants All low-birth-weight infants share some characteristics, including markedly lower levels of responsiveness at birth and in the early months of life. Those born more than 6 weeks before term also often suffer from **respiratory distress syndrome**. Their poorly developed lungs lack an important chemical, called a *surfactant*, that enables the air sacs to remain inflated; some of the sacs collapse, resulting in serious breathing difficulties (Sola, Rogido, & Partridge, 2002). Beginning in 1990, neonatologists began treating this problem by administering a synthetic or animal-derived version of surfactant, a therapy that has reduced the rate of death among very low-birth-weight infants by about 30% (Hamvas et al., 1996; Schwartz, Anastasia, Scanlon, & Kellogg, 1994).

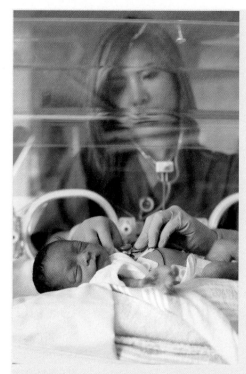

Low-birth-weight infants like this one are not only small; they are also more wrinkled and skinny, because the layer of fat under the skin has not fully developed. They are also more likely to have significant breathing difficulties, because their lungs lack surfactant.

Long-Term Consequences of Low Birth Weight Thankfully, two-thirds to three-fourths of premature infants are indistinguishable from peers by the time they reach school age (Bowen, Gibson, & Hand, 2002; Foulder-Hughes & Cooke, 2003a). But the remainder experience difficulties in school. The two critical predictive factors for such children seem to be birth weight and gestational age (Foulder-Hughes & Cooke, 2003b; McGrath & Sullivan, 2002). The lower a child's birth weight and the earlier the gestational age at which he was born, the greater the risk that he will exhibit school problems. Researchers have found that children who were born prior to the 27th week and who weighed less than 2.2 pounds are far more likely to suffer from problems in elementary school than LBW children who were born later and/or weighed more than 2.2 pounds (Shum, Neulinger, O'Callaghan, & Mohay, 2008). Moreover, this difference persists through fourth grade in many cases. However, research also shows that these children do show progress over time, indicating that their difficulties do not necessarily suggest the presence of a permanent disability (Fussell & Burns, 2007).

However, it is also important for parents to know that the type of care a premature infant receives contributes to how rapidly she develops (White-Traut et al., 2002). For example, a relatively recent innovation in the care of preterm newborns is an intervention called "kangaroo care" in which parents are shown how to increase the amount of skin-to-skin contact infants engage in with them. An important part of the intervention involves allowing parents to hold these tiny newborns for very long periods of time. Researchers have found that babies who receive kangaroo care grow and develop more rapidly than preterm infants given conventional neonatal care (Feldman & Eidelman, 2003; Tessier et al., 2003). An added bonus is that kangaroo care increases mothers' confidence in their ability to care for their premature newborns (Johnson, 2007).

small-for-date infant An infant who weighs less than is normal for the number of weeks of gestation completed.

respiratory distress syndrome A problem frequently found in infants born more than 6 weeks before term, in which the infant's lungs lack a chemical (surfactant) needed to keep air sacs inflated.

Advocates of massage therapy for preterm infants also cite the necessity for skin-to-skin contact. Their research shows that preterm newborns gain weight faster and are more responsive to their environment after a few sessions of massage therapy (Dieter, Field, Hernandez-Reif, Emory, & Redzepi, 2003). Surveys show that about 40% of newborn nurseries in the United States provide premature infants with some kind of massage intervention (Field, Hernandez-Reif, Feijo, & Freedman, 2006). Similarly, researchers have found that the physical contact that results from "double-bedding" of preterm twins increases such infants' chances for positive developmental outcomes (Diamond & Amso, 2008).

As preterm infants get older, Susan Landry and her colleagues have found, those whose mothers are good at identifying and shaping their attention behaviors develop more rapidly than those whose mothers are less so (Dieterich, Hebert, Landry, Swank, & Smith, 2004). Of course, responsive parenting is important for full-term babies' development as well. But Landry has found that consistent parental responsiveness over the first several years of life is more critical to preterm than to full-term infants' development (Landry, Smith, & Swank, 2006).

Behavior in Early Infancy

Who is this small stranger who brings both joy and strain? What qualities and skills does the newborn bring to the interaction process? He cries, breathes, looks around a bit. But what else can he do in the early hours and days? On what skills does the infant build?

Reflexes and Behavioral States

Learning Objective 3.4
What reflexes and behavioral states are exhibited by infants?

One important part of the infant's repertoire of behaviors is a large collection of **reflexes**, which are physical responses triggered involuntarily by specific stimuli. In addition, newborns typically display a behavioral cycle that includes periods of alertness, sleepiness, and hunger.

Reflexes   Some reflexes persist into adulthood, such as your automatic eyeblink when a puff of air hits your eye or the involuntary narrowing of the pupil of your eye when you're in a bright light. Others, sometimes referred to as **adaptive reflexes**, are essential to the infant's survival but gradually disappear in the first year of life. Sucking and swallowing reflexes are prominent in this category, as is the **rooting reflex**—the automatic turn of the head toward any touch on the cheek, a reflex that helps the baby get the nipple into his mouth during nursing. These reflexes are no longer present in older infants or adults but are clearly highly adaptive for the newborn.

Finally, newborns have a large collection of **primitive reflexes**, controlled by the medulla and the midbrain, both of which are close to being fully developed at birth. For example, if you make a loud noise or startle a baby in some other way, you'll see her throw her arms outward and arch her back, a pattern that is part of the **Moro reflex** (also called the *startle reflex*). Stroke the bottom of her foot, and she will splay out her toes; this reaction is called the **Babinski reflex**.

These various primitive reflexes disappear over the first year of life (see Table 3.2), apparently superseded by the action of the cortex, which by this age is much more fully developed. Yet, even though these reflexes represent neurologically primitive patterns, they are nonetheless linked to important later behavior patterns. The tonic neck reflex (described in Table 3.2), for example, forms the foundation for the baby's later ability to reach for objects, because it focuses the baby's attention on the hand; the grasp reflex, too, is linked to the later ability to hold onto objects.

In a similar way, the walking reflex may be linked to later voluntary walking. In an early study, Zelazo and his colleagues (1972) stimulated the walking reflex repeatedly in

The Moro reflex

The Babinski reflex

Table 3.2 Examples of Primitive and Adaptive Reflexes

Reflex	Stimulation	Response	Developmental Pattern
Tonic neck	While baby is on his back and awake, turn his head to one side.	Baby assumes a "fencing" posture, with arm extended on the side toward which the head is turned.	Fades by 4 months
Grasping	Stroke the baby's palm with your finger.	Baby will make a strong fist around your finger.	Fades by 3 to 4 months
Moro	Make a loud sound near the baby, or let the baby "drop" slightly and suddenly.	Baby extends legs, arms, and fingers, arches his back, and draws back his head.	Fades by about 6 months
Walking	Hold baby under arms with feet just touching a floor or other flat surface.	Baby will make step-like motions, alternating feet as in walking.	Fades by about 8 weeks in most infants
Babinski	Stroke sole of the baby's foot from toes toward heel.	Baby will fan out his toes.	Fades between 8 and 12 months
Rooting	Stroke baby's cheek with finger or nipple.	Baby turns head toward the touch, opens mouth, and makes sucking movements.	After 3 weeks, transforms into a voluntary head-turning response

some babies every day from the 2nd to the 8th week after birth. By 8 weeks, these stimulated babies took many more steps per minute when they were held in the walking position than did nonstimulated babies. And at the end of the first year, the stimulated babies learned to walk alone about a month sooner than did comparison babies who had not had their walking reflex stimulated.

The late Esther Thelen (1941–2004) cited Zelazo's findings regarding the walking reflex as an example of her **dynamic systems theory**, the notion that several factors interact to influence development (Thelen, 1996). Thelen noted that infants gain a proportionately substantial amount of weight at about the same time that they no longer show the walking reflex. Consequently, Thelen claimed that infants no longer exhibit the walking reflex because their muscles are not yet strong enough to handle the increased weight of their legs. True walking, according to Thelen, emerges both as a result of a genetic plan for motor skill development and because of a change in the ratio of muscle strength to weight in infants' bodies. This latter change is strongly influenced by environmental variables, especially nutrition. Thus, the streams of influence that are incorporated into dynamic systems theory include inborn genetic factors and environmental variables such as the availability of adequate nutrition.

Wayne Dennis's (1960) classic study of children raised in Iranian orphanages presaged Thelen's theory. His work demonstrated that babies who were routinely placed on their backs in cribs learned to walk eventually, but they did so about a year later than babies in less restrictive settings. Research involving infants living in normal environments supports the notion that experience influences motor development. In one study, very young babies who were given more practice sitting were able to sit upright longer than those without such practice (Zelazo, Zelazo, Cohen, & Zelazo, 1993). Opportunities to practice motor skills seem to be particularly important for young children who have disorders, such as cerebral palsy, that impair motor functioning (Kerr, McDowell, & McDonough, 2007). Consequently, developmentalists are fairly certain that severely restricting a baby's movement slows down acquisition of motor skills, and many are beginning to accept the idea that a baby's movement experiences in normal environments may also influence motor skill development.

reflexes Automatic body reactions to specific stimulation, such as the knee jerk or the Moro reflex. Adults have many reflexes, but the newborn also has some primitive reflexes that disappear as the cortex develops.

adaptive reflexes Reflexes that are essential to the infant's survival but that disappear in the first year of life.

rooting reflex The reflex that causes an infant to automatically turn toward a touch on the cheek, open the mouth, and make sucking movements.

primitive reflexes Collection of reflexes seen in young infants that gradually disappear during the first year of life, including the Moro and Babinski reflexes.

Moro reflex The reflex that causes infants to extend their legs, arms, and fingers, arch the back, and draw back the head when startled (for example, by a loud sound or a sensation of being dropped).

Babinski reflex A reflex found in very young infants that causes them to splay out their toes in response to a stroke on the bottom of the foot.

dynamic systems theory The view that several factors interact to influence development.

Thus, primitive reflexes are not just curiosities. They can be informative, as when a baby fails to show a reflex that ought to be there or displays a reflex past the point at which it normally disappears. For example, infants exposed to narcotics or those suffering from anoxia at birth may show only very weak reflexes; infants with Down syndrome have only very weak Moro reflexes and sometimes have poor sucking reflexes. When a primitive reflex persists past the normal point, it may suggest some neurological damage or dysfunction (Scerif et al., 2005; Schott & Rossor, 2003). Reflexes are also the starting point for many important physical skills, including reaching, grasping, and walking.

Behavioral States   Researchers have described five different states of sleep and wakefulness in neonates, referred to as **states of consciousness**, summarized in Table 3.3. Most infants move through these states in the same sequence: from deep sleep to lighter sleep to fussing and hunger and then to alert wakefulness. After they are fed, they become drowsy and drop back into deep sleep. The cycle repeats itself about every 2 hours.

Neonates sleep as much as 90% of the time—as much in the daytime as at night (Sola, Rogido, & Partridge, 2002). By 6 or 8 weeks of age, most infants somewhat decrease their total amount of sleep per day and show signs of day/night sleep rhythms (called *circadian rhythms*). Babies this age begin to string two or three 2-hour cycles together without coming to full wakefulness; at which point, we say that the baby can "sleep through the night." By 6 months, babies are still sleeping a bit over 14 hours per day, but the regularity and predictability of the sleep are even more noticeable (Iglowstein, Jenni, Molinari & Largo, 2003). Most 6-month-olds have clear nighttime sleep patterns and nap during the day at more predictable times. Of course, babies vary a lot around these averages (see Figure 3.3).

Cultural beliefs play an important role in parents' responses to infants' sleep patterns. For example, parents in the United States typically see a newborn's erratic sleep cycle as a behavior problem that requires "fixing" through parental intervention (Harkness, 1998). Put differently, parents in the United States live by the clock themselves and are thus motivated to train their infants to adapt to the cultural context into which they have been born (Cole, 2005). As a result, American parents focus a great deal of attention on trying to force babies to sleep through the night.

By contrast, in the majority of cultures in the world (and in Western cultures until perhaps 200 years ago), babies sleep in the same bed with their parents, typically until they are weaned, a pattern often called *cosleeping*. Such an arrangement is established for any of a number of reasons, including lack of alternative sleeping space for the infant. More often, cosleeping seems to reflect a basic collectivist value, one that emphasizes contact and interdependence rather than separateness (Harkness & Super, 1995). The practical advantages of cosleeping, such as ease of breastfeeding, have led to an increase in its popularity in the United States and in other Western nations, a trend that has fostered a number of new stud-

states of consciousness The periodic shifts in alertness, sleepiness, crankiness, and so on that characterize an infant's behavior.

Table 3.3   The Basic States of Infant Sleep and Wakefulness

State	Characteristics
Deep sleep	Eyes closed, regular breathing, no movement except occasional startles
Active sleep	Eyes closed, irregular breathing, small twitches, no gross body movement
Quiet awake	Eyes open, no major body movement, regular breathing
Active awake	Eyes open, with movements of the head, limbs, and trunk; irregular breathing
Crying and fussing	Eyes may be partly or entirely closed; vigorous diffuse movement with crying or fussing sounds

Sources: Based on the work of Hutt, Lenard, and Prechtl, 1969; Parmelee, Wenner, and Schulz, 1964; Prechtl and Beintema, 1964.

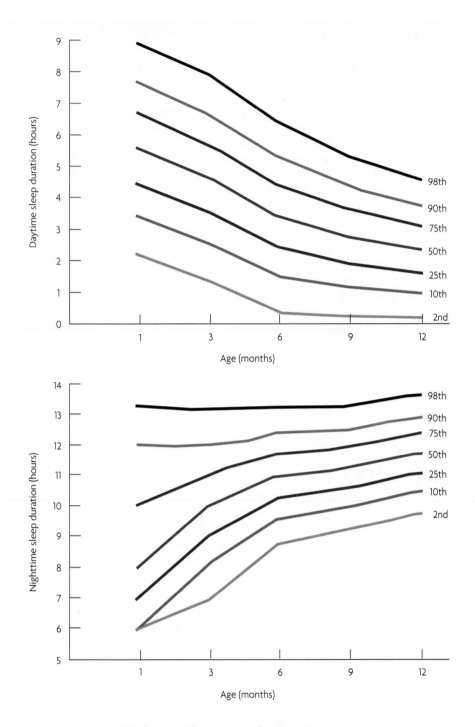

Figure 3.3 **Daytime and Nighttime Sleep across the First Year**

This figure shows the percentile ranks among infants for various amounts of sleep (e.g., the 98th percentile means that 98% of babies sleep less; the 2nd percentile means that 2% of babies sleep less). As you can see daytime napping declines as the duration of nighttime sleep increases over the first year of life.

(*Source*: From Ivo Iglowstein, Oskar G. Jenni, Luciano Molinari, and Remo H. Largo, Sleep Duration from Infancy to Adolescence: Reference Values and Generational Trends, *Pediatrics*, Feb. 2003; *111*, 302–307. Copyright © 2003 by the American Academy of Pediatrics. Adapted with permission.)

ies on the practice. One finding is that mothers who cosleep with infants breastfeed their babies for a longer period of time than mothers who do not cosleep (Taylor, Donovan, & Leavitt, 2008).

Crying is yet another normal part of an infant's cycle of behavioral states (see *Thinking about Research* on page 72). One researcher studying normal newborns found that they cried

Variations in Infants' Cries

Parents have always known that some babies have cries that are particularly penetrating or grating; other babies seem to have much less irritating crying sounds. Researchers have confirmed this parental observation in a wide range of studies (Soltis, 2004). Many groups of babies with known medical abnormalities have different-sounding cries, including those with Down syndrome, encephalitis, meningitis, and many types of brain damage. This observation has been extended to babies who appear physically normal but who are at risk for later problems because of some perinatal problem, such as preterm or small-for-date babies. Such babies typically make crying sounds that are acoustically distinguishable from those of a normal, low-risk baby. In particular, the cry of such higher-risk babies has a more grating, piercing quality. Interestingly, the cries of babies with

colic also have some of these same qualities.

On the assumption that the baby's cry may reflect some basic aspect of neurological integrity, Lester wondered whether one could use the quality of the cry as a diagnostic test. Among a group of high-risk babies, for example, could one predict later intellectual functioning from a measure of the pitch of the baby's cry? The answer seems to be yes. In a classic research study, Lester (1987) found that among preterm babies, those with higher-pitched cries in the first days of life had lower scores on an IQ test at age 5 years. The same kind of connection has also been found among both normal babies and those exposed to methadone prenatally. In all these groups, the higher the pitch and more grating the cry, the lower the child's later IQ or motor development (Huntington, Hans, & Zeskind, 1990).

Eventually, it may be possible for physicians to use the presence of such a grating or piercing cry as a signal that the infant may have some underlying physical problem or as a way of making better guesses about the long-term outcomes for babies at high risk for later problems (Soltis, 2004).

Questions for Critical Analysis

1. Suppose you did a study showing that the more irritable the infant's cries are, the more likely parents are to develop hostile attitudes toward their infant. What would be the implications of this finding for neurological explanations of the correlation between the quality of infants' cries and later developmental problems?
2. What kind of research would be necessary to establish norms for infant crying?

---

from 2% to 11% of the time (Korner, Hutchinson, Koperski, Kraemer, & Schneider, 1981). The percentage frequently increases over the first few weeks, peaking at 2–3 hours of crying a day at 6 weeks and then dropping off to less than 1 hour a day by 3 months (Needlman, 1996). Such a peak in crying at 6 weeks has been observed in infants from a number of different cultures, including cultures in which mothers have almost constant body contact with the infant (St. James-Roberts, Bowyer, Varghese, & Sawdon, 1994), which suggests that this crying pattern is not unique to the United States or to other Western cultures. Initially, infants cry most in the evening; later, their most intense crying occurs just before feedings.

Moreover, parents across a variety of cultures use very similar techniques to soothe crying infants. Most babies stop crying when they are picked up, held, and talked or sung to. Encouraging them to suck on a pacifier also usually helps. Parents sometimes worry that picking up a crying baby will lead to even more crying. But research suggests that prompt attention to a crying baby in the first 3 months actually leads to less crying later in infancy (Cecchini, Lai, & Langher, 2008). It is important for health-care professionals to make new parents aware of these findings, because studies suggest that parents of newborns who learn to effectively manage bouts of crying have more confidence in their new roles. Such confidence, in turn, contributes to marital relationship satisfaction (Meijer & Wittenboer, 2007).

The basic function of a baby's cry, obviously, is to signal need. Because babies can't move to someone, they have to bring someone to them, and crying is the main way they have to attract attention. In fact, infants have a whole repertoire of cry sounds, with different cries for pain, anger, or hunger. The anger cry, for example, is typically louder and more intense, and the pain cry normally has a very abrupt onset—unlike the more basic kinds of hunger or distress cries, which usually begin with whimpering or moaning.

For the 15–20% of infants who develop **colic**, a pattern involving intense bouts of crying totaling 3 or more hours a day, nothing seems to help (Coury, 2002). Typically, colic appears at about 2 weeks of age and then disappears spontaneously at 3 or 4 months of age. The crying is generally worst in late afternoon or early evening. Neither psychologists nor physicians know why colic begins, or why it stops without any intervention. It is a difficult pattern to live with, but the good news is that it does go away.

colic A pattern of persistent and often inconsolable crying, totaling more than 3 hours a day, found in some infants in the first 3 to 4 months of life.

Finally, the infant behavioral state most enjoyed by many caregivers is the one in which babies are awake and alert. However, neonates are in this state only 2 to 3 hours each day, on average, and the total amount of waking time is unevenly distributed over a 24-hour period. In other words, 15 minutes of waking time may happen at 6:00 a.m., then 30 minutes at 1:00 p.m., another 20 minutes at 4:00 p.m., and so on. Over the first 6 months, advances in neurological development enable infants to remain awake and alert for longer periods of time as their patterns of sleeping, crying, and eating become more regular.

Motor, Sensory, and Perceptual Abilities

Learning Objective 3.5
What kinds of motor, sensory, and perceptual abilities do newborns have?

Although the motor abilities of newborns are extremely limited, they enter the world with all of the equipment they need to begin taking in information from the world around them. As you learned in Chapter 2, some aspects of **sensation**, the process of taking in raw information through the senses, are well established prior to birth (e.g., hearing). Others require some refinement over the early months and years. **Perception**, the attribution of meaning to sensory information, develops rapidly during the early months and years as well.

Motor Skills   The infant's motor skills emerge only gradually in the early weeks. By 1 month, a baby can hold her chin up off the floor or mattress. By 2 months, she can hold her head steady while she's being held and is beginning to reach for objects near her. These improving motor skills follow two broad patterns originally identified by Gesell: Development proceeds from the head downward, in a pattern called **cephalocaudal**, and from the trunk outward, in another pattern called **proximodistal** (Gesell, 1952). Thus, the baby can hold up her head before she can sit or roll over and can sit before she can crawl.

Another interesting feature of young babies' motor skills is how repetitively they perform their limited range of movements (Adolph & Berger, 2005). They kick, rock, wave, bounce, bang, rub, scratch, or sway repeatedly and rhythmically. These repeated patterns become particularly prominent at about 6 or 7 months of age, although you can see instances of such behavior even in the first weeks, particularly in finger movements and leg kicking. These movements do not seem to be totally voluntary or coordinated, but they also do not appear to be random. For instance, Thelen (1995) has observed that kicking movements peak just before the baby begins to crawl, as if the rhythmic kicking were a part of the preparation for crawling. Thelen's work has revealed certain patterns and order in the seemingly random

Young Lucy was 5 months old when this photo was taken, showing her "airplaning." You can see that by this age, she is able to hold up not only her head but also part of her chest—a big advance over the motor skills seen in newborns.

sensation The process of taking in raw information through the senses.

perception The attribution of meaning to sensory information.

cephalocaudal One of two basic patterns of physical development in infancy (the other is proximodistal), in which development proceeds from the head downward.

proximodistal One of two basic patterns of physical development in infancy (the other is cephalocaudal), in which development proceeds from the center outward—that is, from the trunk to the limbs.

movements of the young infant, but even this understanding does not alter the fact that, by contrast with perceptual abilities, the baby's initial motor abilities are quite limited.

Sensory and Perceptual Abilities   Babies come equipped with a surprisingly mature set of perceptual skills. The newborn can do several things:

- Focus both eyes on the same spot, with 8–10 inches being the best focal distance; discriminate his mother's face from other faces almost immediately; and, within a few weeks, follow a moving object with his eyes—although not very efficiently.

- Easily hear sounds within the pitch and loudness range of the human voice; roughly locate objects by their sounds; discriminate some individual voices, particularly his mother's voice.

- Taste the four basic tastes (sweet, sour, bitter, and salty) plus a fifth taste called umami, which is elicited by an amino acid found in meat, fish, and legumes.

- Identify familiar body odors, including discriminating his mother's smell from the smell of a strange woman.

Brief as this summary is, several points stand out. First of all, newborns' perceptual skills are a great deal better than most parents believe—better than most psychologists or physicians believed until a few years ago. The better research techniques have become, the more we have understood just how skillful the newborn baby really is—important evidence for the significance of nature in the nature-nurture interaction.

Even more striking is how well adapted the baby's perceptual skills are for the interactions he will have with the people in his world. He hears best in the range of the human voice, and he can discriminate his mother (or other regular caregiver) from others on the basis of smell, sight, or sound almost immediately. The distance at which he can focus his eyes best, about 8–10 inches, is approximately the distance between his eyes and his mother's face during nursing.

As you'll see in Chapter 5, a newborn has a long way to go in the development of sophisticated perceptual abilities, but the infant begins life able to make key discriminations and to locate objects through various perceptual cues.

Learning Objective 3.6
What types of learning do infants exhibit?

Learning

Infants use their motor, sensory, and perceptual skills to act on the people and objects in their environment. Such actions enable them to establish a foundational understanding of the world upon which to construct their future cognitive and social development. Thus, all three types of skills facilitate early **learning**, or change due to experience.

Classical Conditioning   The bulk of the research on learning in newborns suggests that they can be classically conditioned, although it is difficult (Herbert, Eckerman, Goldstein, & Stanton, 2004). Conditioning that relates to feeding in some way is most likely to be successful, perhaps because this activity is so critical for the infant's survival. As one example, Elliott Blass and his colleagues (1984) gave 1- and 2-day-old infants sugar water in a bottle (the unconditional stimulus), which prompted sucking (the unconditioned response). Then, just before they were given the sugar water, the babies' foreheads were stroked (the conditional stimulus). After several such repetitions, the experimenters stroked the infants' foreheads without giving the sugar water to see if the infants would begin sucking—which they did, thus showing classical conditioning.

By the time infants are 3 or 4 weeks old, classical conditioning is no longer difficult to establish; it occurs easily with many different responses. In particular, this means that the conditioned emotional responses you read about in Chapter 1 may begin to develop as early as the first week of life. Thus, the mere presence of Mom or Dad or another favored person may trigger the sense of "feeling good," a response that may contribute to the child's later attachment to the parent.

learning Change due to experience.

Operant Conditioning   Newborns also clearly learn by operant conditioning. Both the sucking response and head turning have been successfully increased by the use of reinforcements, such as sweet-tasting liquids or the sound of the mother's voice or heartbeat (Moon & Fifer, 1990). At the least, the fact that conditioning of this kind can take place means that the neurological basis for learning to occur is present at birth. Results like this also tell us something about the sorts of reinforcements that are effective with very young children. It is surely highly significant for the whole process of mother-infant interaction that the mother's voice is an effective reinforcer for virtually all babies.

Schematic Learning   The fact that babies can recognize voices and heartbeats in the first days of life is also important, because it suggests that another kind of learning is going on as well. This third type of learning, sometimes referred to as **schematic learning**, draws both its name and many of its conceptual roots from Piaget's theory. The basic idea is that from the beginning the baby organizes her experiences into expectancies, or known combinations. These expectancies, often called *schemas*, are built up over many exposures to particular experiences but thereafter help the baby to distinguish between the familiar and the unfamiliar. Carolyn Rovee-Collier (1986) has suggested that we might think of classical conditioning in infants as being a variety of schematic learning. When a baby begins to move her head as if to search for the nipple as soon as she hears her mother's footsteps coming into the room, this is not just some kind of automatic classical conditioning, but the beginning of the development of expectancies. From the earliest weeks, the baby seems to make connections between events in her world, such as between the sound of her mother's footsteps and the feeling of being picked up or between the touch of the breast and the feeling of a full stomach. Thus, early classical conditioning may be the beginnings of the process of cognitive development.

Habituation   A concept related to schematic learning is habituation. **Habituation** is the automatic reduction in the strength or vigor of a response to a repeated stimulus. For example, suppose you live on a fairly noisy street, where the sound of cars going by is repeated over and over during each day. After a while, you not only don't react to the sound, you quite literally do not perceive it as being loud. The ability to do this—to dampen down the intensity of a physical response to some repeated stimulus—is obviously vital in our everyday lives. If we reacted constantly to every sight and sound and smell that came along, we'd spend all our time responding to these repeated events, and we wouldn't have energy or attention left over for things that are new and deserve attention. The ability to dishabituate is equally important. When a habituated stimulus changes in some way, such as a sudden extra-loud screech of tires on the busy street by your house, you again respond fully. The reemergence of the original response strength is a sign that the perceiver—infant, child, or adult—has noticed some significant change.

A rudimentary capacity to habituate and to dishabituate is built in at birth in human babies, just as it is in other species. In 10-week-old babies, this ability is well developed. An infant will stop looking at something you keep putting in front of her face; she will stop showing a startle reaction (Moro reflex) to loud sounds after the first few presentations but will again startle if the sound is changed; she will stop turning her head toward a repeating sound (Swain, Zelazo, & Clifton, 1993). Such habituation itself is not a voluntary process; it is entirely automatic. Yet in order for it to work, the newborn must be equipped with the capacity to recognize familiar experiences. That is, she must have, or must develop, schemas of some kind.

The existence of these processes in the newborn has an added benefit for researchers: It has enabled them to figure out what an infant responds to as "the same" or "different." If a baby is habituated to some stimulus, such as a sound or a specific picture, the experimenter can then present slight variations on the original stimulus to see the point at which dishabituation occurs. In this way, researchers have begun to get an idea of how the newborn baby or young infant experiences the world around him—a point you'll read more about in Chapter 5.

schematic learning The development of expectancies concerning what actions lead to what results or what events tend to go together.

habituation An automatic decrease in the intensity of a response to a repeated stimulus, enabling a child or adult to ignore the familiar and focus attention on the novel.

Learning Objective 3.7

How do newborns differ in temperament, and what skills do they bring to social interactions?

Temperament and Social Skills

Clearly, many aspects of early development are universal, such as reflexes and the capacity to respond to conditioning. However, there are also important individual differences among infants. All babies cry, but some cry more than others; some are easily irritated by a wet diaper, while others seem to be more tolerant of physical discomforts. Moreover, human newborns, unlike those in many other species, are a very long way from being independent. If they are to survive, someone must provide consistent care over an extended period. So the infant's capacity to entice others into the caregiving role is critical. It is here that the "social" skills of infants, along with the ability of parents to adapt to the caregiving role, come into play.

Of course, you can't evaluate a baby's temperament on the basis of one picture, but you might guess that young Benjamin, smiling delightedly, has an easier temperament than Eleanor, who is pushing away her food and who may have a slow-to-warm-up temperament.

Temperament   Babies vary in the way they react to new things, in their typical moods, in their rate of activity, in their preference for social interactions or solitude, in the regularity of their daily rhythms, and in many other ways. Developmentalists collectively call these differences **temperament**. You'll be reading a great deal more about temperament in Chapter 9, but because the concept will come up often as we go along, it is important at this early stage to introduce some of the basic terms and ideas.

In classic research, developmentalists Alexander Thomas and Stella Chess (1977) described three categories of infant temperament, the **easy child**, the **difficult child**, and the **slow-to-warm-up child**. Easy children, who comprised approximately 40% of Thomas and Chess's original study group, approach new events positively. They try new foods without much fuss, for example. They also exhibit predictable sleeping and eating cycles, are usually happy, and adjust easily to change.

By contrast, the difficult child is less predictable with regard to sleep and hunger cycles and is slow to develop regular cycles. These children react vigorously and negatively to new things, are more irritable, and cry more. Thomas and Chess point out, however, that once the difficult baby has adapted to something new, he is often quite happy about it, even though the adaptation process itself is trying. In Thomas and Chess's original sample, about 10% of children were clearly classifiable in this group.

Children in the slow-to-warm-up group are not as negative in responding to new things or new people as are the difficult children. They show instead a kind of passive resistance. Instead of spitting out new food violently and crying, the slow-to-warm-up child may let the food drool out and may resist mildly any attempt to feed her more of the same. These infants show few intense reactions, either positive or negative, although once they have adapted to something new, their reaction is usually fairly positive. Approximately 15% of Thomas and Chess's sample followed this pattern.

While these differences in style or pattern of response tend to persist through infancy into later childhood, no psychologist studying temperament suggests that such individual differences are absolutely fixed at birth. Inborn temperamental differences are shaped, strengthened, bent, or counteracted by the child's relationships and experiences. Infants enter the world with somewhat different repertoires or patterns of behavior, and those differences not only affect the experiences an infant may choose, but also help to shape the emerging pattern of interaction that develops between infant and parents. For example, toddlers and preschoolers with difficult temperaments are more often criticized or physically punished by their parents than are easy children, presumably because their behavior is more troublesome (Vitaro, Barker, Boivin, Brendgen, & Tremblay, 2006). Yet once it is established, such a pattern of criticism and punishment itself is likely to have additional consequences for a child. Nonetheless, not all parents of difficult children respond in this way. A skilled parent, especially one who correctly perceives that the child's "difficultness" is a temperamental quality

temperament Inborn predispositions that form the foundations of personality.

easy child An infant who adapts easily to change and who exhibits regular patterns of eating, sleeping, and alertness.

difficult child An infant who is irritable and irregular in behavior.

slow-to-warm-up child An infant who may seem unresponsive but who simply takes more time to respond than other infants do.

and not a result of the child's willfulness or the parent's ineptness, can avoid some of the pitfalls and can handle the difficult child more adeptly.

The Emergence of Emotional Expression There is really no way to know just what emotion a baby actually feels. The best we can do is to try to judge what emotion a baby appears to express through his body and face. Researchers have done this by confronting babies with various kinds of events likely to prompt emotions, photographing or videotaping those encounters, and then asking adult judges to say which emotion the baby's face expresses (Izard, 2007).

Table 3.4 summarizes the current thinking about the ages at which various important emotional expressions first appear. As you can see, some rudimentary emotional expressions are visible at birth, including a sort of half-smile that delights parents even though they cannot figure out how to elicit it consistently. Within a few weeks, though, babies begin to show a full social smile. Happily, one of the earliest triggers for this wonderful baby smile is the kind of high-pitched voice that all adults seem to use naturally with infants. So adults seem to be preprogrammed to behave in just the ways that babies will respond to positively. Within a few weeks, babies will also smile in response to a smiling face, especially a familiar face.

Within a few months, babies' emotional expressions differentiate even further, so that they express sadness, anger, and surprise. Four-month-olds also begin to laugh—and there are few things in life more delightful than the sound of a giggling or laughing baby! Fear appears as a discrete emotional expression at about 7 months.

A baby's smile and laughter are an utter delight for parents. Laughing is one of the important social/emotional responses that contribute to the emerging parent-child bond, part of the "glue" that cements the relationship together.

Table 3.4 The Emergence of Emotional Expressions in Infancy and Toddlerhood

Age	Emotion Expressed	Examples of Stimuli That Trigger That Expression
At birth	Interest	Novelty or movement
	Distress	Pain
	Disgust	Offensive substances
	Neonatal smile (a "half smile")	Appears spontaneously for no known reason
3 to 6 weeks	Pleasure/social smile (precursor to joy)	High-pitched human voice; clapping the baby's hands together; a familiar voice; a nodding face
2 to 3 months	Sadness	Painful medical procedure
7 months	Wariness (precursor to fear)	A stranger's face
	Frustration (precursor to anger)	Being restrained; being prevented from performing some established action
	Surprise	Jack-in-the-box
	Fear	Extreme novelty; heights (such as in the visual cliff experiment)
	Anger	Failure or interruption of some attempted action, such as reaching for a ball that has rolled under a couch
	Joy	Immediate delighted response to an experience with positive meaning, such as the caregiver's arrival or a game of peekaboo

Sources: Izard and Malateste, 1987; Mascolo and Fischer, 1995; Sroufe, 1996.

Taking Turns   Yet another social skill the baby brings to interactions is the ability to take turns. As adults, we take turns all the time, most clearly in conversations and eye contacts. In fact, it's very difficult to have any kind of social encounter with someone who does not take turns. Kenneth Kaye (1982) argues that the beginnings of this turn-taking can be seen in very young infants in their eating patterns. As early as the first days of life, a baby sucks in a "burst-pause" pattern. He sucks for a while, pauses, sucks for a while, pauses, and so on. Mothers enter into this process, such as by jiggling the baby during the pauses, thus creating an alternating pattern: suck, pause, jiggle, pause, suck, pause, jiggle, pause. The rhythm of the interaction is really very much like a conversation. It is not clear whether this conversational quality of very early interaction occurs because the adult figures out the baby's natural rhythm and adapts her own responses to the baby's timing or whether some mutual adaptation is going on. Nonetheless, it is extremely intriguing that this apparent turn-taking is seen in infants only days old.

Health and Wellness in Early Infancy

You may have heard references to the increasing life expectancy in the United States. At the beginning of the 20th century, Americans' average life expectancy was only about 49 years, but by the century's end, it was 76 years. One of the most significant factors behind this statistic is the reduction in infant mortality that occurred in industrialized societies during the 20th century. Improved medical technology and better understanding of newborns' nutritional and health-care needs are responsible for this trend. Sadly, though, many infants die in the first year of life. In fact, infancy continues to be associated with a higher death rate than any other period of life except old age. Many such deaths are due to genetic disorders, but others result from causes that are more easily preventable.

Learning Objective 3.8
What are the infant's nutritional, health-care, and immunization needs?

Nutrition, Health Care, and Immunizations

Newborns, of course, are completely physically dependent on their caretakers. To develop normally, they need adequate nutrition, regular medical care, and protection against diseases.

Nutrition   Eating is not among the states listed in Table 3.3 on page 70, but it is certainly something that newborn babies do frequently! Given that a newborn's natural cycle seems to be about 2 hours long, she may eat as many as ten times a day. Gradually, the baby takes more and more milk at each feeding and doesn't have to eat so often. By 2 months, the average number is down to five or six feedings each day, dropping to about three feedings by age 8 to 12 months (Overby, 2002). Breast-fed and bottle-fed babies eat with the same frequency, but these two forms of feeding do differ in other important ways (see *Developmental Science in the Real World*).

Up until 6 months, babies need only breast milk or formula accompanied by appropriate supplements (American Academy of Pediatrics [AAP], 2005). For example, pediatricians usually recommend vitamin B_{12} supplements for infants whose nursing mothers are vegetarians (Moilanen, 2004). Doctors may recommend supplemental formula feeding for infants who are growing poorly, but breast milk meets the nutritional needs of most infants.

There is no evidence to support the belief that solid foods encourage babies to sleep through the night. In fact, early introduction of solid food can actually interfere with nutrition. Pediatricians usually recommend withholding solid foods until 4 to 6 months of age (Overby, 2002). The first solids should be single-grain cereals, such as rice, with added iron. Parents should introduce their baby to no more than one new food each week. If parents follow a systematic plan, food allergies can be easily identified (Tershakovec & Stallings, 1998).

Health Care and Immunizations   Infants need frequent medical check-ups. While much of *well-baby care* may seem routine, it is extremely important to babies' development. For example, babies' motor skills are usually assessed during routine visits to a doctor's office

Breast or Bottle?

Expectant mother Suzanne found it easy to decide where she wanted to give birth and whom she wanted to serve as her labor coach. Now, her greatest worries centered around how she would feed her baby. She had heard that breast-feeding was best, but she expected to return to work within a few weeks after the birth. Consequently, she was leaning toward bottle-feeding but was seeking information that would reassure her that her baby would develop properly on formula.

All parents, like Suzanne, want to do what's best for their babies, and developmentalists today generally agree that breast-feeding is superior to bottle-feeding for meeting infants' nutritional needs (Overby, 2002). However, not all mothers *can* breast-feed. Some have an insufficient milk supply. Others suffer from medical conditions that require them to take drugs that may filter into breast milk and harm the baby. Furthermore, viruses, including HIV, can be transmitted from mother to child through breast milk. And what about adoptive mothers?

Developmentalists are quick to reassure mothers who can't nurse that their babies will most likely develop as well as breast-fed infants. However, it is important to understand that several decades of extensive research in many countries comparing large

groups of breast- and bottle-fed infants make it clear that breast-feeding is nutritionally superior to bottle-feeding. All of the research was summarized in an official policy statement that was issued by the American Academy of Pediatrics in 2005 (AAP, 2005). On average, breast-fed infants are less likely to suffer from such problems as diarrhea, gastroenteritis, bronchitis, ear infections, and colic, and they are less likely to die in infancy (AAP, 2005). Breast milk also appears to promote the growth of nerves and the intestinal tract, to contribute to more rapid weight and size gain, and to stimulate better immune system function. Research also suggests that breast-feeding may protect infants from becoming overweight in later years. For these reasons, physicians strongly recommend breast-feeding if it is at all possible, even if the mother can nurse for only a few weeks after birth or if her breast milk must be supplemented with formula feedings (Tershakovec & Stallings, 1998).

For those who cannot breast-feed at all, nutrition experts point out that infants who are fed high-quality, properly sterilized formula typically thrive on it (AAP, 2005). Moreover, there are a wide variety of formulas available today to fulfill the requirements of infants who have special needs, such as those who are lactose-intolerant. It

is also reassuring to know that the social interactions between mother and child seem to be unaffected by the type of feeding. Bottle-fed babies are held and cuddled in the same ways as breast-fed babies, and their mothers appear to be just as sensitive and responsive to their babies and just as bonded to them as are mothers of breast-fed infants (Field, 1977).

Questions for Reflection

1. If Suzanne were your friend and asked you for advice regarding this important decision, what would you tell her?
2. The research linking breast-feeding to obesity protection was correlational. What other variables might explain this relationship?

---

or a health clinic. An infant whose motor development is less advanced than expected for his age may require additional screening for developmental problems such as mental retardation (Sulkes, 1998).

One of the most important elements of well-baby care is vaccination of the infant against a variety of diseases (see Table 3.5 on page 80). Although immunizations later in childhood provide good protection against these diseases, the evidence suggests that immunization is most effective when it begins in the first month of life and continues across childhood and adolescence (AAP, 2008). Even adults need occasional "booster" shots to maintain immunity.

Illnesses

Learning Objective 3.9
What kinds of illnesses typically occur in infancy?

Virtually all babies get sick, most of them repeatedly. Among infants around the world, three types of illnesses are most common: diarrhea, upper respiratory infections, and ear infections.

Diarrhea Worldwide, one of the most common and deadly illnesses of infancy and early childhood is diarrhea, accounting for the deaths of an estimated 3.5 million infants and children each year. In developing countries, 1 out of 4 deaths of children under age 5 is due to diarrhea; in some countries, the rate is even higher (Cheng, McDonald, & Thielman, 2005). In the United States, diarrhea rarely leads to death in infants, but virtually every infant or young child has at least one episode of diarrhea each year; about 1 in 10 cases is severe enough for the child to be taken to a doctor (Kilgore, Holman, Clarke, & Glass, 1995). In most cases,

Table 3.5 Recommended Immunization Schedule for Children from Birth to 6 Years

Vaccine	Recommended Age
Hepatitis B	Birth–18 months
Rotavirus	2–6 months
Diphtheria, Tetanus, Pertussis	Four doses: 2 months, 4 months, 6 months, 16–18 months
Haemophilus Influenzae Type b (Hib)	Four doses: 2 months, 4 months, 6 months, 12–15 months
Pneumococcal	Four doses: 2 months, 4 months, 6 months, 12–15 months
Polio	Three doses: 2 months, 4 months, 6–18 months
Influenza	6 months to 6 years
Measles, Mumps, Rubella	12–15 months
Varicella	12–15 months
Hepatitis A	Two doses: 12 months–2 years
Meningococcal	2–6 years

Source: AAP, 2008.

the cause of the illness is a viral or bacterial infection, the most common of which is *rotavirus*, a microorganism that is spread by physical contact with others who are infected with the disease (Laney, 2002).

Virtually all deaths from diarrhea could be prevented by giving fluids to rehydrate the child (Laney, 2002). In serious cases, this rehydration should involve a special solution of salts (oral rehydration salts, or ORS). The World Health Organization has for some years been involved in a program of training health professionals around the world in the use of ORS, with some success (Muhuri, Anker, & Bryce, 1996). Still, diarrhea remains a very serious illness for infants and children in many parts of the world.

Upper Respiratory Infections A second common illness during infancy is some kind of upper respiratory infection. In the United States, the average baby has seven colds in the first year of life. (That's a lot of nose-wipes!) Interestingly, research in a number of countries shows that babies in child-care centers have about twice as many such infections as do those reared entirely at home, presumably because babies in group-care settings are exposed to a wider range of germs and viruses (e.g., Lau, Uba, & Lehman, 2002). In general, the more different people a baby is exposed to, the more colds she is likely to get. This is not as bad as it may seem at first. The heightened risk of infection among infants in child care drops after the first few months, while those reared entirely at home have very high rates of illness when they first attend preschool or kindergarten. Attendance at child care thus simply means that the baby is exposed earlier to the various microorganisms typically carried by children.

Ear Infections Otitis media (OM), an inflammation of the middle ear that is caused by a bacterial infection, is the leading cause of children's visits to physicians' offices in the United States (Waseem, 2007). More than 90% of children have had at least one episode of OM in the first year of life, and about one-third have 6 or more bouts before age 7. Thanks to antibiotic drugs, most cases of OM clear up quickly. However, physicians have become concerned in recent years about the increasing resistance of the bacteria that cause otitis media to antibiotics. As a result, many physicians now recommend a "wait-and-see" response to cases of OM (AAP, 2004). If the child develops a high fever or the infection continues for 3 to 4 days, then antibiotics are prescribed. Placebo-controlled studies suggest that 75% of cases of OM clear up on their own within 7 days of initial diagnosis (AAP, 2004).

In a few children, OM becomes chronic, defined as an episode of otitis media that re-

otitis media (OM) An inflammation of the middle ear that is caused by a bacterial infection.

mains uncured after 6 months of antibiotic treatment (Waseem, 2007). In such cases, some physicians recommend that children undergo surgery to insert tubes in the ears. The tubes allow fluid to escape from the middle ear through the ear drum. Such drainage is needed because chronic fluid in the ears not only increases the frequency of infections but also interferes with hearing. Researchers have found that even mild hearing losses cause children to have difficulties with speech perception and can slow down the pace of language development. As a result, children in whom chronic fluid in the ears goes untreated are more likely to fail in school than are those with normal hearing (Tharpe, 2006).

Infant Mortality

Learning Objective 3.10
What factors contribute to infant mortality?

A small minority of babies face not just a few sniffles but the possibility of death. In the United States, about 7 babies out of every 1,000 die before age 1 (Heron, Hoyert, Xu, Scott, & Tejada-Vera, 2008). The rate has been declining steadily for the past few decades (down from 20 per 1,000 in 1970), but the United States continues to have a higher infant mortality rate than other industrialized nations. Almost two-thirds of these infant deaths occur in the first month of life and are directly linked to either congenital anomalies or low birth weight (Heron et al., 2008). Fewer than 3 deaths per 1,000 births occur in the remainder of the first year.

Sudden Infant Death Syndrome   A sizeable fraction of deaths in the first year are attributable to **sudden infant death syndrome (SIDS)**, in which an apparently healthy infant dies suddenly and unexpectedly. In the United States, SIDS is the leading cause of death in infants more than 1 month of age (Task Force on Sudden Infant Death Syndrome, 2005). SIDS occurs worldwide; for unexplained reasons, however, the rate varies quite a lot from country to country. For example, rates are particularly high in Australia and New Zealand and particularly low in Japan and Sweden (Hoffman & Hillman, 1992).

Physicians have not yet uncovered the basic cause of SIDS, although they have learned a fair amount about the groups that are at higher risk: babies with low birth weight, male babies, African American babies, and babies with young mothers. SIDS is also more common in the winter and among babies who sleep on their stomachs (Task Force on Sudden Infant Death Syndrome, 2005), especially on a soft or fluffy mattress, pillow, or comforter. The growing evidence on the role of sleeping position persuaded pediatricians in many countries to change their standard advice to hospitals and families about the best sleeping position for babies. The American Academy of Pediatrics, for example, has been recommending since 1992 that healthy infants should be positioned on their sides or backs when they are put down to sleep. Physicians in many other countries have made similar recommendations, a change in advice that has been followed by a significant drop in SIDS cases in every country involved (Fein, Durbin, & Selbst, 2002; Willinger, Hoffman, & Hartford, 1994). In the United States, for example, the number of SIDS cases has dropped by nearly 30% since 1992. Still, sleeping position cannot be the full explanation, because, of course, most babies who sleep on their stomachs do not die of SIDS.

Smoking by the mother during pregnancy or by anyone in the home after the child's birth is another important contributor to SIDS. Babies exposed to such smoke are about four times as likely as are babies with no smoking exposure to die of SIDS (CDC, 2006d). Thus, in addition to advising pregnant women not to smoke, health-care professionals warn parents against allowing smoking in the home after the baby is born.

Imaging studies of the brains of infants at high risk for SIDS, such as those who display apnea in the early days of life, suggest that neuronal development progresses at a slower rate in these children than in others who do not exhibit such risk factors (Morgan et al., 2002). Babies' patterns of sleep reflect these neurological differences and also predict SIDS risk. Infants who show increasingly lengthy sleep periods during the early months are at lower risk of dying from SIDS than babies whose sleep periods do not get much longer as they get older (Cornwell & Feigenbaum, 2006). Likewise, autopsies of SIDS babies have revealed that their brains often show signs of delayed myelination.

sudden infant death syndrome (SIDS) The unexpected death of an infant who otherwise appears healthy; also called crib death. The cause of SIDS is unknown.

Figure 3.4
Infant Mortality across Ethnic Groups

As you can see, infant mortality rates vary widely across U.S. racial and ethnic groups.

(*Sources*: Heron et al., 2008; MacDorman & Atkinson, 1999; Matthews, 2005.)

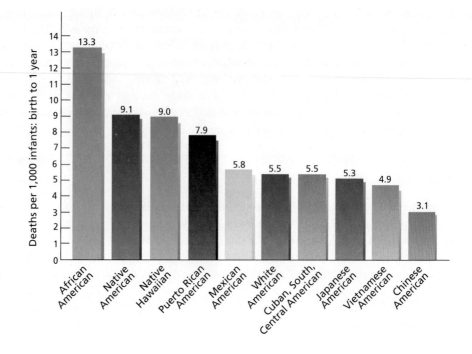

Figure 3.5
Early Prenatal Care and Ethnicity

Wide disparities exist across ethnic groups wth regard to access to prenatal care, although this factor cannot fully explain group differences in infant mortality. Note, for instance, that African Americans and Mexican Americans have similar rates of early prenatal care but vary widely in infant mortality.

(*Source*: National Center for Health Statistics (NCHS). (2007). *Health, United States, 2007*. Hyattsville, MD: Author.)

Ethnic Differences in Infant Mortality   Large variations in infant mortality rates exist across ethnic groups in the United States, as shown in Figure 3.4 (Heron et al., 2008; MacDorman & Atkinson, 1999; Matthews, 2005). Rates are lowest among Asian American infants; about 5 of every 1,000 die each year. Among White American babies, the rate is approximately 5.5 deaths per 1,000. The three groups with the highest rates of infant death are Native Americans (9.1 deaths per 1,000), Native Hawaiians (9 deaths per 1,000), and African Americans (13.3 deaths per 1,000). One reason for these differences is that Native American and African American infants are two to three times more likely to suffer from congenital abnormalities and low birth weight—the two leading causes of infant death—than babies in other groups. Furthermore, SIDS is two to three times as common among them.

Because babies born into poor families, regardless of race or ethnicity, are more likely to die than those whose families are better off economically, some observers have suggested that

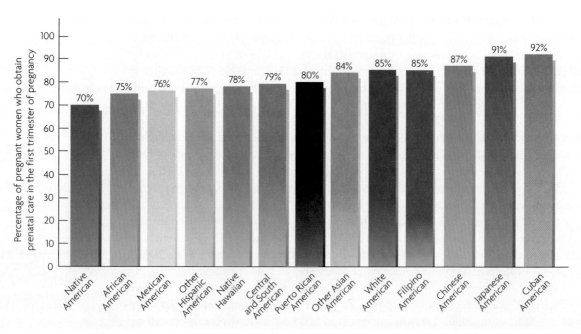

poverty explains the higher rates of infant death among Native Americans and African Americans, the two groups with the highest rates of poverty. However, infant mortality rates among Hispanic American groups suggest that the link between poverty and infant mortality is not so straightforward. The infant mortality rate among Mexican American babies is 5.8 per 1,000, and the mortality rate for infants of Cuban, South, and Central American ancestry is only 5.5 per 1,000 (MacDorman & Atkinson, 1999). These groups are almost as likely to be poor as African Americans and Native Americans. In contrast, Puerto Rican families are not likely to be poorer than other Hispanic American families, but the mortality rate is 7.9 per 1,000 among their infants. Similarly, rates of early prenatal care—defined as consulting a doctor or midwife during the first trimester of pregnancy—are nearly identical for African American women and Hispanic American women (National Center for Health Statistics [NCHS], 2007). Consequently, access to prenatal care cannot explain differences in infant mortality across these groups (see Figure 3.5).

Interestingly, mortality rates among the babies of immigrants of all racial and ethnic groups are lower than those among babies of U.S.-born mothers. This finding also challenges the poverty explanation for racial and ethnic group differences in infant mortality, because immigrant women are more likely to be poor and less likely to receive prenatal care than women born in the United States (MacDorman & Atkinson, 1999). Many researchers suggest that lower rates of tobacco and alcohol use among women born outside the United States may be an important factor.

Think Critically

- How would you go about raising public awareness of the advantages of breastfeeding, the importance of early immunizations, and the developmental risks associated with ear infections?
- Generate your own hypothesis to explain group differences in infant mortality. What kind of information would you need to test your hypothesis?

Conduct Your Own Research

You can find out more about women's childbearing-related worries by carrying out what researchers call a *free-response* study. Simply ask several women, both pregnant and nonpregnant if you can, to express their concerns in their own words. Write down what they say. When you have collected a number of responses, analyze them for common themes.

Summary

BIRTH

3.1 What decisions must parents make about the birth process in industrialized societies?

- Parents must decide whether to use pain-relieving drugs during delivery, whether their baby should be born in a hospital or other setting, and whether the father should be present for the delivery. Most drugs given to a woman during delivery pass through to the infant's bloodstream and have short-term effects on infant responsiveness. In uncomplicated, low-risk pregnancies, delivery at home or in a birth center may be as safe as hospital delivery. The presence of the father during delivery has a variety of positive consequences, including reducing the mother's experience of pain, but being present for the birth does not appear to affect the father's attachment to the infant.

3.2 What are the events and risks associated with each stage of the birth process?

- The normal birth process has three stages: dilation and effacement, delivery, and placental delivery. Several types of problems may occur at birth, including reduced oxygen supply to the infant (anoxia). Slightly more than one-quarter of all deliveries in the United States today are by cesarean section. Newborns are typically assessed using the Apgar score, which is a rating on five dimensions. Most parents show intense interest in the new baby's features, especially the eyes.

3.3 What are some of the possible consequences of low birth weight?

- Infants born weighing less than 2,500 grams are designated as low birth weight (LBW); those below 1,500 grams are very low birth weight (VLBW); those below 1,000 grams are extremely low birth weight (ELBW). The lower the weight, the greater the risk of neonatal death or of significant lasting problems, such as low IQ score or learning disabilities.

BEHAVIOR IN EARLY INFANCY

3.4 What reflexes and behavioral states are exhibited by infants?

- Infants have a wide range of reflexes. Some, such as the sucking reflex, are essential for life. Other primitive reflexes are present in the newborn but disappear in the first year. Cycles of sleeping, waking, and crying are present from the beginning.

3.5 What kinds of motor, sensory, and perceptual abilities do newborns have?

- Motor skills are only rudimentary at birth. Perceptual skills include the ability to focus both eyes; visually track slowly moving objects; discriminate the mother by sight, smell, and sound; and respond to smells, tastes, and touch.

3.6 What types of learning do infants exhibit?

- Within the first few weeks of life, babies are able to learn through association of stimuli (classical conditioning), from pleasant and unpleasant consequences (operant conditioning), from categorization of stimuli (schematic learning), and from repeated exposure to stimuli (habituation).

3.7 How do newborns differ in temperament, and what skills do they bring to social interactions?

- Babies differ from one another on several dimensions, including vigor of response, general activity rate, rest-lessness, irritability, and cuddliness. Thomas and Chess identified three temperamental categories: easy, difficult, and slow-to-warm-up. Infants develop the ability to express a range of emotions, such as pleasure and distress, over the first year.

HEALTH AND WELLNESS IN EARLY INFANCY

3.8 What are the infant's nutritional, health-care, and immunization needs?

- Breast milk or formula supplies all of an infant's nutritional needs until 6 months of age. Babies require periodic check-ups to track their growth and development. They also need to be immunized against a variety of diseases.

3.9 What kinds of illnesses typically occur in infancy?

- Common illnesses of childhood include diarrhea, upper respiratory infections, and ear infections. In the developing world, diarrhea is the leading cause of infant death. In the industrialized world, ear infections are the most serious of these illnesses, although they are rarely fatal. All forms of upper respiratory illness are more common among children in day care than among those reared at home.

3.10 What factors contribute to infant mortality?

- In the United States and other industrialized countries, most infant deaths in the first weeks are due to congenital anomalies or low birth weight; after the first weeks, sudden infant death syndrome (SIDS) is the most common cause of death in the first year. African American, Native Hawaiian, and Native American infants display higher rates of infant mortality than White Americans and other ethnic groups in the United States. Poverty may be a factor, but other groups with similar rates of poverty, such as Hispanic Americans, have lower infant mortality rates than African Americans, Native Hawaiians, and Native Americans.

Key Terms

adaptive reflexes (p. 68)
anoxia (p. 63)
Babinski reflex (p. 68)
cephalocaudal (p. 73)
cesarean section (c-section) (p. 64)
colic (p. 72)
difficult child (p. 76)
dilation (p. 62)
dynamic systems theory (p. 69)
easy child (p. 76)
effacement (p. 62)
extremely low birth weight (ELBW) (p. 66)

habituation (p. 75)
learning (p. 74)
low birth weight (LBW) (p. 66)
Moro reflex (p. 68)
otitis media (OM) (p. 80)
perception (p. 73)
preterm infant (p. 66)
primitive reflexes (p. 68)
proximodistal (p. 73)
reflexes (p. 68)
respiratory distress syndrome (p. 67)
rooting reflex (p. 68)
schematic learning (p. 75)

sensation (p. 73)
slow-to-warm-up child (p. 76)
small-for-date infant (p. 67)
states of consciousness (p. 70)
sudden infant death syndrome (SIDS) (p. 81)
temperament (p. 76)
very low birth weight (VLBW) (p. 66)

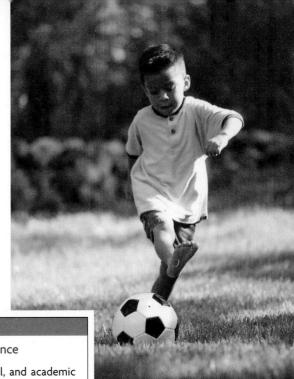

Physical Development 4

Have you ever tried to water ski? If you spent more time treading water than you did gliding over its surface, you might feel somewhat embarrassed to learn about the skiing prowess of 2-year-old Cole Marsolek of Menomonie, Wisconsin. Cole became something of a local celebrity when a Minneapolis television station featured video of the tyke confidently skiing on Wisconsin's Tainter Lake, holding the ski rope in one hand and enthusiastically waving to his admirers on shore with the other. Lest you think Cole's accomplishment was unique, a quick search of YouTube.com will yield

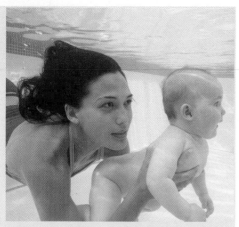

Most children who learn to water ski as toddlers are exposed to multiple experiential elements, such as infant swimming classes..

numerous links to video clips of skiing toddlers, some of whom are several months younger than Cole.

Learning to ski in the early years of life isn't really all that remarkable when you think of it as a developmental event that involves the types of interactions between maturation and experience that Aslin's model captures so well (see Figure 1.1 on page 7). Children possess the necessary neurological subsystem for skiing, the *vestibular sense*, at birth, but their nervous systems have not yet developed all of the connections that are required to control the body. Likewise, their skeletal and muscular systems must pass through several critical maturational milestones before skiing is possible. In addition, as infants grow, their body proportions change such that they become less top-heavy, a basic requirement for maintaining an upright position on land or water.

As all of these maturational processes are evolving, an experiential foundation is being laid. Most children who learn to ski as toddlers observe their parents having fun skiing before they can walk. Boat rides accustom them to the sound of the motor and the feeling of being in an unstable environment. Infant swimming classes help them learn how to maneuver in the water with a life jacket on.

All of these maturational and experiential elements come together between the first and second birthday when parents choose this particular point in their children's development to introduce them to water skiing, as most such parents do. That is, as soon as children can walk well, parents interested in fostering this skill put their children on skis for the first time. Further, parents use specially designed training skis that are easier to balance on than adult skis. During children's first attempts, parents give them hands-on physical support, much as parents of older children do when they help them learn to ride a bicycle. Once children can reliably remain upright on skis, parents provide them with plenty of opportunities to practice their skills. Moreover, parents applaud and cheer for water-skiing tots as the distances they can travel without falling gradually increase.

Sometimes explaining an unusual outcome helps us better understand the factors that work together to produce more typical developmental events. Thus, the point that you should take away from this brief explanation of the phenomenon of early water skiing is that the milestones of physical development that all children share—maturation of the brain, acquisition of motor skills, puberty, and the like—result from interactions between maturational and experiential factors that are similar to those that enable toddlers to ski. These common milestones are the subject of this chapter. As you read about them, you will gain a better understanding of the ways in which internal and external variables interact to produce them.

The Brain and Nervous System

Figure 4.1 shows the main structures of the brain. At birth, the **midbrain** and the **medulla** are the most fully developed. These two parts, both in the lower part of the skull and connected to the spinal cord, regulate vital functions such as heartbeat and respiration as well as attention, sleeping, waking, elimination, and movement of the head and neck—all tasks a newborn can perform at least moderately well. The least developed part of the brain at birth is the **cerebral cortex**, the convoluted gray matter that wraps around the midbrain and is involved in perception, body movement, thinking, and language. Changes in the brain and nervous system continue throughout childhood and adolescence. There are several critical processes that contribute to these changes.

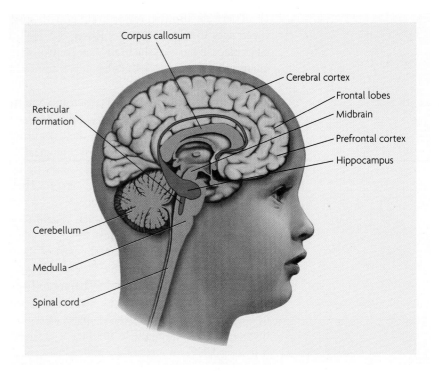

Figure 4.1 **Major Structures of the Brain**

The medulla and the midbrain are largely developed at birth. In the first 2 years after birth, it is primarily the cortex that develops, although the dendrites continue to grow and synapses continue to form throughout the nervous system. The prefrontal cortex is the last part of the brain to mature.

Growth Spurts

Learning Objective 4.1
What are the major growth spurts in the brain?

One of the most important principles of neurological development is that the brain grows in spurts rather than in a smooth, continuous fashion (Fischer & Rose, 1994). Each of these spurts involves all of the major developmental processes you'll read about in the sections that follow, and each is followed by a period of stability. In infancy, the intervals of growth and stability are very short. There are short growth spurts at approximately 1-month intervals until the baby is about 5 months old. As the infant gets older, the periods of both growth and stability become longer, with spurts occurring at about 8, 12, and 20 months of age. Between ages 2 and 4, growth proceeds very slowly, and then there is another major spurt at age 4.

Interestingly, many growth spurts are *localized*; that is, they are restricted to one or a few parts of the brain rather than applying to the whole brain (Thompson et al., 2000). Neuropsychologists have correlated some of these localized brain growth spurts with milestones of cognitive development (Fischer & Rose, 1994). For example, the spurt at 20 months of age happens at the same time as most infants show evidence of goal-directed planning in their behavior. A toddler may move a chair from one location to another so that he can climb high enough to reach a forbidden object. Similarly, the spurt around age 4 is accompanied by attainment of an impressive level of fluency in both speaking and understanding language.

Two major growth spurts happen in the brain during middle childhood (Spreen, Risser, & Edgell, 1995). The first is linked to the striking improvements in fine motor skills and eye-hand coordination that usually emerge between 6 and 8 years of age. During the spurt experienced by 10- to 12-year-olds, the frontal lobes of the cerebral cortex (see Figure 4.1) become the focus of developmental processes (van der Molen & Molenaar, 1994). Predictably, logic and planning, two cognitive functions that improve dramatically during this period, are carried out primarily by the frontal lobes. In addition, this spurt is associated with improvements in memory function (Hepworth, Rovet, & Taylor, 2001).

midbrain A section of the brain lying above the medulla and below the cortex that regulates attention, sleeping, waking, and other automatic functions; it is largely developed at birth.

medulla A portion of the brain that lies immediately above the spinal cord; it is largely developed at birth.

cerebral cortex The convoluted gray portion of the brain, which governs perception, body movement, thinking, and language.

There are also two major brain growth spurts in the teenage years. The first occurs between ages 13 and 15 (Spreen, Risser, & Edgell, 1995). For the most part, this growth spurt takes place in parts of the brain that control spatial perception and motor functions. Consequently, by the mid-teens, adolescents' abilities in these areas far exceed those of school-aged children.

Neuropsychologists Kurt Fischer and Samuel Rose believe that a qualitatively different neural network also emerges during this brain growth spurt, a network that enables teens to think abstractly and to reflect on their cognitive processes (Fischer & Rose, 1994). As evidence, they cite neurological and psychological research, from study after study, revealing that major changes in brain organization show up between ages 13 and 15 and qualitative shifts in cognitive functioning appear after age 15. They claim that the consistency of these research findings is too compelling to ignore.

The brain growth spurt between 13 and 15 years of age is also associated with profound changes in the **prefrontal cortex (PFC)** (Gogtay et al., 2004; Kanemura, Aihara, Aoki, Araki, & Nakazawa, 2004). The PFC is the part of the frontal lobe that is just behind the forehead (see Figure 4.1). It is responsible for *executive processing*, a set of information processing skills that you will read more about in Chapter 6. These skills enable us to consciously control and organize our thought processes. Just prior to puberty, the neurons in the PFC rapidly form new synapses with those in other parts of the brain. Over the first few years of adolescence, the brain prunes away the least efficient of these synapses (Giedd, 2004; Giedd, Blumenthal, & Jeffries, 1999). As a result, by mid-adolescence, teenagers' executive processing skills far exceed those that they exhibited during middle childhood.

The second brain growth spurt begins around age 17 and continues into early adulthood (van der Molen & Molenaar, 1994). This time, the frontal lobes of the cerebral cortex are the focus of development (Davies & Rose, 1999). You may recall that this area of the brain controls logic and planning. Thus, it is not surprising that older teens perform differently from younger teens when dealing with problems that require these cognitive functions.

prefrontal cortex (PFC) The part of the frontal lobe just behind the forehead that is responsible for executive processing.

Learning Objective 4.2

What are synaptogenesis and pruning?

Synaptic Development

One of the processes that contribute to brain growth is called **synaptogenesis**, or the process of creating connections (*synapses*) between neurons (Johnson, 2005). Recall from Chapter 2 that the brain is composed of two basic types of cells: neurons and glial cells. Virtually all of both types of cells are already present at birth. The developmental process after birth primarily involves the creation of synapses, or connections between neurons. Synapse development results from growth of both dendrites and axons (see Figure 4.2).

Both play a role in neuronal communication, which is accomplished with chemicals called **neurotransmitters**, such as serotonin, dopamine, or endorphins. Neurotransmitters are stored in sacs at the ends of the terminal buttons and released when needed. They are picked up by *receptor sites* on the dendrites. So, as you can see, the synapses are where the action is, so to speak, in everything that goes on in the brain.

Synaptogenesis occurs at a rapid rate in the cortex during the first 2 years after birth, resulting in a tripling of the overall weight of the brain during those years (Johnson, 2005). This burst in synaptogenesis, as well as other spurts that occur later in development, is followed by a period of **pruning**, when unnecessary connections are eliminated, making the whole system operate more efficiently.

For example, early in development, each muscle cell seems to develop synaptic connections with several motor

Figure 4.2 The Neuron

A typical neuron has three major parts: (1) a cell body, which carries out the metabolic functions of the neuron; (2) branched fibers called dendrites, which are the primary receivers of impulses from other neurons; and (3) a slender, tail-like extension called an axon, the transmitting end of the neuron, which ends in many branches, each with an axon terminal. The axon is covered with myelin, a fatty substance that makes the transmission of neural impulses more efficient.

neurons in the spinal cord. But after the pruning process has occurred, each muscle fiber is connected to only one neuron. Some neurophysiologists have suggested that the initial surge of synapse formation follows a built-in pattern (Greenough, Black, & Wallace, 1987). The organism seems to be programmed to create certain kinds of neural connections and does so in abundance, creating redundant pathways. According to this argument, the pruning that takes place beginning at around 18 months is a response to experience, resulting in selective retention of the most efficient pathways. However, neurophysiologists point out that some synapses are formed entirely as a result of experience, and that synaptogenesis continues throughout our lives as we learn new skills.

Consistent with the overall "start-and-stop" pattern of brain development, pruning does not occur at the same time in all parts of the brain. For example, the maximum density of synapses in the portions of the brain that have to do with language comprehension and production occurs at about age 3 years. In contrast, the part of the cortex devoted to vision is maximally dense at 4 months of age, with rapid pruning thereafter (Huttenlocher, 1994).

One of the most intriguing points about this process of synaptogenesis is that the combination of the early surge of synaptic growth and then pruning means that the 1-year-old actually has a greater density of dendrites and synapses than an adult does—a piece of information that has surprised many psychologists. Even at age 4, when the early burst of pruning has occurred in all areas of the brain, synaptic density is about twice that in an adult's brain. Pruning continues in spurts throughout childhood and adolescence.

Research on synaptogenesis and pruning supports the old dictum "Use it or lose it" (Nelson, de Haan, & Thompson, 2006). A child growing up in a rich or intellectually challenging environment will retain a more complex network of synapses than a child growing up with fewer forms of stimulation—a variation of the nature-nurture interaction that Aslin calls *attunement* (see Figure 1.1). The evidence to support this proposal comes from several kinds of research, including work with animals. For example, rats that are reared in highly stimulating environments as infants will have a denser network of neurons, dendrites, and synaptic connections as adults than rats that do not receive as much stimulation (Escorihuela, Tobena, & Fernández-Teruel, 1994). Animal studies also show that enriched environments help the young brain overcome damage caused by teratogens such as alcohol (Hannigan, O'Leary-Moore, & Berman, 2007). Also, in both nonhuman primates and humans, infants who experience significant sensory deprivation, such as from being blind in one eye, develop (or retain) less dense synaptic networks in the part of the brain linked to that particular function (Gordon, 1995). Thus, the early months appear to be a sensitive period for the retention of synapses; neural complexity that is not retained in these early years does not redevelop later. Love and affection, while critical to an infant for other reasons, are not enough to optimize brain organization; the baby needs patterned visual and auditory stimulation, particularly language.

A second basic point is that the **plasticity** of the brain, its capacity to respond to experience, is at its height in the first few years of life (Nelson, de Haan, & Thomas, 2006). However, it is important to note that the brain possesses some degree of plasticity throughout the lifespan. Equally important is the point that the implications of the association between plasticity and age are complex. For one thing, precisely because the brain is so plastic in the early years, it is also more vulnerable to deprivation than it is later in life. The brain of an adolescent who has a history of adequate nutrition is much better able to withstand the stress of a temporary period of malnutrition than the brain of an infant is. At the same time, though, if a teenager is malnourished so severely that his brain is damaged, he will probably be able to overcome the damage once adequate nutrition is restored, but he will do so at a slower pace than he would have under the same conditions earlier in life.

Finally, we must raise one additional point about plasticity. Nearly everything scientists know about the role of experience in brain development is derived from studies of children whose environments are characterized by deficiencies (Nelson, de Haan, & Thomas, 2006). For instance, we know that inadequate nutrition can slow brain development and, consequently, interfere with both cognitive and social development (Liu, Raine, Venables,

synaptogenesis The process of synapse formation.

neurotransmitters Chemicals that accomplish the transmission of signals from one neuron to another at synapses.

pruning The process of eliminating unused synapses.

plasticity The ability of the brain to change in response to experience.

& Mednick, 2004). However, these findings do not imply that *supernutrition*, or a diet that provides nutrition beyond what is required for normal growth, accelerates brain growth and cognitive development. Indeed, this kind of fallacious conclusion, often inferred from studies emphasizing the importance of experience to brain development, leads to inappropriate beliefs.

Similarly, in recent years many educators have suggested that teachers should employ instructional strategies that are geared toward the developmental processes going on in the brains of their students (e.g., Berninger & Richards, 2002). It is probably beneficial for teachers to understand brain development. However, research aimed at establishing milestones for normal brain development, such as those that have long been known for motor skills (crawling precedes standing, standing precedes walking, and so on), has only just begun (Giedd et al., 1999). Thus, most neuroscientists agree that it is far too soon to form conclusions about how knowledge of brain development might inform "brain-based" teaching strategies for students of different ages.

| Learning Objective 4.3 |
| How does the process of myelination influence brain function? |

Myelination

A second crucial process in neuronal development is the creation of sheaths, or coverings, around individual axons, which insulate them from one another electrically and improve the conductivity of the nerves. These sheaths are made of a substance called *myelin* (see Figure 4.2 on page 88); the process of developing the sheaths is called **myelination**.

The sequence of myelination follows both cephalocaudal and proximodistal patterns. Thus, nerves serving muscle cells in the hands are myelinated earlier than those serving the feet. Myelination is most rapid during the first 2 years after birth, but it continues at a slower pace throughout childhood and adolescence. For example, the parts of the brain that are involved in vision reach maturity by the second birthday (Lippé, Perchet, & Lassonde, 2007). By contrast, the parts of the brain that govern motor movements are not fully myelinated until about age 6 (Todd, Swarzenski, Rossi, & Visconti, 1995).

Myelination leads to improvement in brain functions. For example, the **reticular formation** (see Figure 4.1) is the part of the brain responsible for keeping your attention on what you're doing and for helping you sort out important and unimportant information. Myelination of the reticular formation begins in infancy but continues in spurts across childhood and adolescence. In fact, the process isn't complete until the mid-20s (Spreen et al., 1995). So, teenagers have longer attention spans than children, who, in turn, have longer attention spans than infants.

Also of importance is the myelination of the neurons that link the reticular formation to the frontal lobes. It is well documented that **selective attention**, the ability to focus cognitive activity on the important elements of a problem or situation, increases significantly during middle childhood (Wetzel, Widmann, Berti, & Schröger, 2006). It seems likely that myelination of linkages between the frontal lobes and the reticular formation work together to enable school-aged children to develop this important kind of concentration (Sowell et al., 2003).

To understand the importance of selective attention, imagine that your psychology instructor, who usually hands out tests printed on white paper, gives you a test printed on blue paper. You won't spend a lot of time thinking about why the test is blue instead of white; this is an irrelevant detail. Instead, your selective attention ability will prompt you to ignore the color of the paper and focus on the test questions. In contrast, some younger elementary school children might be so distracted by the unusual color of the paper that their test performance would be affected. As the nerves connecting the reticular formation and frontal lobes become more fully myelinated during the school years, children begin to function more like adults in the presence of such distractions.

The neurons of the **association areas**—parts of the brain where sensory, motor, and intellectual functions are linked—are myelinated to some degree by the time children enter school. However, from age 6 to age 12, the nerve cells in these areas become almost com-

myelination The process by which an insulating layer of a substance called myelin is added to neurons.

reticular formation The part of the brain that regulates attention.

selective attention The ability to focus cognitive activity on the important elements of a problem or situation.

association areas Parts of the brain where sensory, motor, and intellectual functions are linked.

pletely myelinated. Neuroscientists believe that this progression of the myelination process contributes to increases in information-processing speed. For example, suppose you were to ask a 6-year-old and a 12-year-old to identify pictures of common items—a bicycle, an apple, a desk, a dog—as rapidly as possible. Both would have equal knowledge of the items' names, but the 12-year-old would be able to produce the names of the items much more rapidly than the 6-year-old. Such increases in processing speed probably contribute to improvements in memory function you'll read about later in Chapter 6 (Johnson, 2005; Kail 1991).

Neurons in other parts of the brain, such as the **hippocampus** (see Figure 4.1) are also myelinated in childhood (Tanner, 1990). The hippocampus is involved in the transfer of information to long-term memory. Maturation of this brain structure probably accounts for improvements in memory function, spatial cognition, and the ability to navigate (Nelson, de Haan, & Thomas, 2006). Moreover, maturation of the connections between the hippocampus and the cerebral cortex is probably responsible for the common finding that people's earliest memories involve events that happened when they were about 3 years old (Zola & Squire, 2003).

hippocampus A brain structure that is involved in the transfer of information to long-term memory.

corpus callosum The structure that connects the right and left hemispheres of the cerebral cortex.

lateralization The process through which brain functions are divided between the two hemispheres of the cerebral cortex.

Lateralization

Learning Objective 4.4
What are the milestones of the lateralization process?

Equal in importance to synapse formation and myelination is the specialization in function that occurs in the two hemispheres of the brain. The **corpus callosum** (see Figure 4.1), the brain structure through which the left and right sides of the cerebral cortex communicate, grows and matures more during the early childhood years than in any other period of life. The growth of this structure accompanies the functional specialization of the left and right hemispheres of the cerebral cortex. This process is called **lateralization**.

Left- and Right-Brain Dominance   Figure 4.3 illustrates how brain functions are lateralized in 95% of humans, a pattern known as *left-brain dominance*. In a small proportion of the remaining 5 percent, the functions are reversed, a pattern called *right-brain dominance*. However, most people who are not left-brain dominant have a pattern of *mixed dominance*, with some functions following the typical pattern and others reversed. (By the way, the terms *left-brain* and *right-brain* are sometimes used to describe personality or learning style. Such usage has nothing to do with the physical lateralization of functions in the two hemispheres of the brain.)

Neuroscientists suspect that our genes dictate which functions will be lateralized and which will not, because some degree of lateralization is already present in the human fetus (Gupta et al., 2005). For example, both fetuses and adults turn their heads in order to be able to listen to language with the right ear. Because sounds entering the right ear are routed to the left side of the brain for interpretation, such findings suggest that language begins to be lateralized in most fetuses. Full lateralization of language function, though, doesn't happen until near the end of the early childhood period (Spreen et al., 1995).

It appears that the experience of learning and using language, not simply genetically programmed maturation of the brain, is the impetus behind hemispheric specialization. Young children whose language skills are the most advanced also show the strongest degree of lateralization (Mills, Coffey-Corina, & Neville, 1994). Neuroscientists have not determined whether some children advance rapidly in language acquisition because their brains are lateralizing at a faster pace. It could also be that some children's brains are lateralizing language function more rapidly because they are learning it faster.

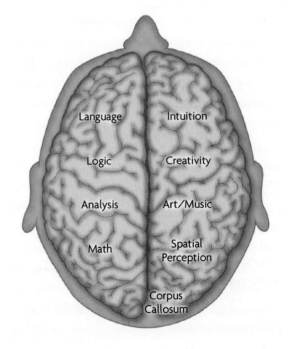

Figure 4.3   Lateralization of Brain Functions

Brain functions are lateralized, as shown in the figure. Neurologists think that the basic outline of lateralization is genetically determined, whereas the specific timing of the lateralization of each function is determined by an interaction of genes and experiences.

Studies of children who are deaf and who are learning sign language also suggest that experience contributes to brain development (Johnson, 2005; Mills et al., 1994). These children use the same area of the brain to process sign meanings as children who can hear use for spoken word meanings. Likewise, the sign vocabularies of children who are deaf grow at about the same rate as the vocabularies of children learning spoken language. However, the processing of sign language grammar by children who are deaf happens in an entirely different area of the brain from that used by children who can hear to understand the structure of spoken language. In addition, grammatical knowledge is acquired at a slower pace by children who are deaf. These observations indicate that some aspects of brain development are linked more to the kinds of linguistic stimuli to which the brain is exposed—in other words, to experience—than to a rigid genetic plan.

Spatial Perception   Lateralization is also linked to the development of **spatial perception**, the ability to identify and act on relationships of objects in space. For example, when you use a map to get from one place to another, you are using spatial perception to read the map and to relate it to the real world. Across early and middle childhood, spatial perception is lateralized to the right hemisphere of the brain in most people. Perception of objects such as faces lateralizes in the preschool years. However, complex spatial perception, such as map-reading, isn't strongly lateralized until after age 8 (Roberts & Bell, 2000). At the same time, the areas of the corpus callosum that are involved in interhemispheric communication related to spatial perceptual tasks grow rapidly (Thompson et al., 2000). As a result of both lateralization and corpus callosum growth, children beyond age 8 exhibit spatial perceptual skills that are superior to those of younger children.

A behavioral test of spatial perception lateralization that neuroscientists often use involves **relative right-left orientation**, the ability to identify right and left from multiple perspectives. Such tests usually show that most children younger than 8 know the difference between their own right and left. Typically, though, only those older than 8 understand the difference between statements like "it's on *your* right" and "it's on *my* right." Lateralization of spatial perception may also be related to the increased efficiency with which older children learn math concepts and problem-solving strategies. In addition, it is somewhat correlated to progress through Piaget's stages of cognitive development (van der Molen & Molenaar, 1994).

Differences in visual experiences have been postulated to explain sex differences in spatial perception and in a related function called **spatial cognition**, the ability to infer rules from and make predictions about the movement of objects in space. For example, when you are driving on a two-lane road and you make a judgment about whether you have enough room to pass the car ahead of you, you are using spatial cognition. From an early age, boys score much higher than girls, on average, when asked to perform spatial cognition tasks, perhaps because of boys' play preferences (Hyde, 2005). Some researchers argue that boys' greater interest in constructive activities such as building with blocks helps them develop more acute spatial perception. Research showing that the gender difference in spatial cognition is larger among children from middle- and high-income families than from low-income families seems to support this view, presumably because families with greater economic resources are better able to provide boys with the play materials that they specifically request (Bower, 2005).

Handedness   **Handedness**, the tendency to rely primarily on the right or the left hand, is another important aspect of neurological lateralization (Tanner, 1990). Studies relating brain lateralization to handedness suggest that a common neurological process may be involved in both. About 96% of right-handers possess the typical pattern of language-on-the-left (Pujol, Deus, Losilla, & Capdevila, 1999). However, only 75% of left-handers are left-brain dominant. About 1% of left-handers have complete right-brain language specialization, and the rest have a mixed pattern of dominance (Pujol et al., 1999).

It used to be thought that right-handedness increased among humans as societies became more literate. The idea was that, when teaching children how to write, parents and

spatial perception The ability to identify and act on relationships of objects in space; in most people, this skill is lateralized to the right cerebral hemisphere.

relative right-left orientation The ability to identify right and left from multiple perspectives.

spatial cognition The ability to infer rules from and make predictions about the movement of objects in space.

handedness A strong preference for using primarily one hand or the other; it develops between 3 and 5 years of age.

teachers encouraged them to use their right hands. In this way, right-handedness became sort of a custom that was passed on from one generation to the next through instruction. By examining skeletons that predate the invention of writing, archaeologists have determined that the proportions of right- and left-handedness were about the same in illiterate ancient populations as they are among modern humans: 83% right-handed, 14% left-handed, and 3% ambidexterous (Steele & Mayes, 1995). These findings suggest that the prevalence of right-handedness is likely to be the result of genetic inheritance. Moreover, geneticists at the National Cancer Institute (NCI) have identified a dominant gene for right-handedness that they believe to be so common in the human population that most humans receive a copy of it from both parents (Klar, 2003).

Further evidence for the genetic hypothesis can be found in studies demonstrating that handedness appears very early in life—often before the first birthday—although it doesn't become well established until the preschool years (Stroganova, Posikera, Pushina, & Orekhova, 2003). Research comparing children's right-hand and left-hand performance on manual tasks, such as moving pegs from one place to another on a pegboard, also supports the genetic hypothesis. Most of these studies show that older children are better at accomplishing fine-motor tasks with the nondominant hand than younger children are (Dellatolas et al., 2003; Roy, Bryden, & Cavill, 2003). Findings from studies comparing nondominant hand use in children and adults follow the same pattern (Annett, 2003; Cavill & Bryden, 2003). Thus, experience in using the hands appears to moderate, rather than strengthen, the advantage of the dominant over the nondominant hand.

Of course, what developmentalists ultimately want to know is how being left- or right-handed affects a child's development. At one time, left-handedness was regarded as a highly undesirable developmental outcome. This was due to superstitions about associations between left-handedness and the presence of evil spirits. As a result, parents and teachers encouraged left-handers to switch to right-handedness. Today, developmentalists and parents alike tend to believe that it is best to allow a child to follow her natural tendencies with regard to handedness.

Nevertheless, research does suggest that left-handedness is associated with poor developmental outcomes in both the cognitive and the socioemotional domain (Johnston, Nicholls, Shah, & Shields, 2008). But this association is probably the result of an underlying factor that influences both handedness and developmental outcomes. It's important to remember, too, that only a small proportion of left-handed children ever display these deficits. Consequently, parents should avoid pushing a left-handed child to be right-handed in the interest of preventing developmental problems. Even if parents succeed in switching the child's hand preference, if there is a hidden risk factor present, it will still be there. Thus, research aimed at finding and moderating the effects of the underlying cause of the correlation between handedness and poor developmental outcomes is needed, rather than a campaign to change children's hand preferences.

Size, Shape, and Skills

As you've seen, changes in children's nervous system have powerful influences on their development. But changes in other systems are influential as well.

Growth

<table>
<tr><td>Learning Objective 4.5</td></tr>
<tr><td>What patterns of growth are evident in childhood and adolescence?</td></tr>
</table>

By age 2, a toddler is about half as tall as he will be as an adult (hard to believe, isn't it?). You may also find it surprising that growth from birth to maturity is neither continuous nor smooth.

During the first phase, which lasts for about the first 2 years, the baby gains height very rapidly, adding 10 to 12 inches in length in the first year and tripling his body weight in the same span. At about age 2, the child settles down to a slower but steady addition of 2 to 3 inches and about 6 pounds a year until adolescence.

During the second phase, children's growth becomes more predictable from one point of measurement to the next. When health-care professionals measure children's height and weight, they use a statistic called a *percentile rank* to describe how the child compares to others of the same age. A percentile rank is the percentage of individuals whose measurements are equal to or less than those of the individual child who is being described. For example, if a child's weight is at the 25th percentile, 25% of children of his age weigh less than he does and 75% weigh more. In other words, a child who is at the 25th percentile is on the small side, compared to peers. One who is at the 50th percentile is about average, and another who is at the 75th percentile is larger than most children her age.

Individual children's height and weight percentile ranks can vary a great deal in the first 2 years of life. Thus, a child might accurately be described as "small for her age" at one check-up and "big for her age" at another check-up. But beginning around the age of 2 years, children's percentile ranks for height and weight begin to stabilize. When a child's percentile ranks for height and weight become stable, the child is said to have established his individual **growth curve**, or rate of growth. Figure 4.4, which is based on longitudinal data derived from several hundred children (Mei, Grummer-Strawn, Thompson, & Dietz, 2004), illustrates this pattern. As you can see, few children change ranks after 30 to 36 months of age. Thus, if a 3-year-old's growth curve is at the 25th percentile, his adult height will also be very near the 25th percentile.

The third phase is the dramatic adolescent "growth spurt," when the child may add 3 to 6 inches a year for several years, after which the rate of growth again slows until final adult size is reached. This growth spurt is, on average, larger for boys than for girls, but virtually all children show a period of more rapid growth sometime between the ages of about 9 and 15.

The shape and proportions of the child's body also change. In an adult, the head is about an eighth to a tenth of the total height. In a toddler, the head is proportionately far larger in order to accommodate the nearly adult-sized brain of the infant. And a child's hands and feet

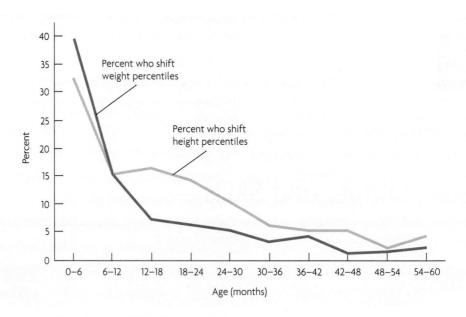

Figure 4.4   Growth Curve Shifts from Birth to 5 Years

This figure shows the percentage of children in each age group who show changes in the percentile ranks for their height and weight from one check-up to the next.

(*Source*: Mei, Grummer-Strawn, Thompson, & Dietz, 2004.)

growth curve The pattern and rate of growth exhibited by a child over time.

normally reach full adult size sometime in late elementary school or early adolescence, causing his appearance to be somewhat awkward. However, researchers have found no point in the adolescent growth process at which teenagers become consistently less coordinated or less skillful in physical tasks (Butterfield, Lehnhard, Lee, & Coladarci, 2004).

Bones, Muscles, and Fat

Learning Objective 4.6
In what ways do bones, muscles, and fat change?

The hand, wrist, ankle, and foot all have fewer bones at birth than they will have at full maturity. An adult has nine separate bones in his wrist, while a 1-year-old has only three; the remaining six bones develop over the period of childhood. Like many aspects of physical development, this process occurs earlier in girls than in boys. For example, the nine adult wrist bones are normally visible on x-rays, though not yet fully hardened or completely "articulated" (meaning they don't yet work as well together as they will in adulthood), by 51 months in girls but not until 66 months in boys (Needlman, 1996). Consequently, in the early years of school, girls display more advanced coordination in skills such as handwriting than boys do.

In one part of the body, though, the bones fuse rather than differentiate. The skull of a newborn is made up of several bones separated by spaces called **fontanels**. Fontanels allow the head to be compressed without injury during the birth process, and they give the brain room to grow. In most children, the fontanels are filled in by bone by 12 to 18 months, creating a single connected skull bone.

Bones also change in quality as well as in number over the course of development. An infant's bones are softer, with a higher water content, than an adult's bones. The process of bone hardening, called **ossification**, occurs steadily from birth through puberty, following such a regular and predictable pattern that physicians use **bone age** as the best single measure of a child's physical maturation; x-rays of the hand and wrist show the stage of development of wrist and finger bones. In infancy and toddlerhood, the sequence of development generally follows the cephalocaudal and proximodistal patterns. For example, bones of the hand and wrist harden before those in the ankles or feet.

Muscles—like bones—change in quality from infancy through adolescence, becoming longer and thicker and developing a higher ratio of muscle to water at a fairly steady rate throughout childhood. At adolescence, muscles go through a growth spurt, just as height does, so that adolescents become quite a lot stronger in just a few years. Both boys and girls show this increase in strength, but the increase is much greater in boys (Malina, 2007). For example, in a classic cross-sectional study in Canada involving 2,673 children and teenagers, Smoll and Schutz (1990) measured strength by having each child hang as long as possible from a bar, keeping his or her eyes level with the bar. As you can see in Figure 4.5, 9-year-old boys could maintain this flexed arm hang for about 40% longer than could girls of the same age; by age 17, boys could sustain it almost three times as long as girls. Similar results have been found for other measures of strength (Butterfield et al., 2004). This substantial difference in strength is one reflection of the sex difference in muscle mass. In adult men, about 38% of total body mass is muscle, compared to only about 31% in adult women (Janssen, Heymsfield, Wang, & Ross, 2000). Such a sex difference in muscle mass (and accompanying strength) seems to be largely a result of hormone differences, although sex differences in exercise patterns or fitness may also play some role (Gabbard, 2008).

Another major component of the body is fat, most of which is stored immediately under the skin. This subcutaneous fat first develops beginning at about 34 weeks prenatally and has an early peak at about 9 months after birth (the so-called baby fat); the

fontanel One of several "soft spots" in the skull that are present at birth but disappear when the bones of the skull grow together.

ossification The process of hardening by which soft tissue becomes bone.

bone age A measure of physical maturation based on x-ray examination of bones, typically the wrist and hand bones. Two children of the same chronological age may have different bone age because their rates of physical maturation differ.

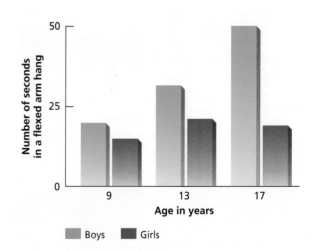

Figure 4.5   **Sex Differences in Strength**

Both boys and girls get stronger between childhood and adolescence, but boys gain much more strength.

(*Source*: Smoll & Schutz, 1990, from Table 1, p. 363.)

thickness of this layer of fat then declines until about age 6 or 7, after which it rises until adolescence. Once again, there is a sex difference in these patterns. From birth, girls have slightly more fat tissue than boys do, and this difference becomes gradually more marked during childhood. At adolescence, the difference grows still further. The size of the change is illustrated in results of the Canadian study cited earlier (Smoll & Schutz, 1990). Between ages 13 and 17, the percentage of body weight made up of fat rose from 21.8% to 24.0% among the girls in this study but dropped from 16.1% to 14.0% among the boys. So during and after puberty, proportions of fat rise among girls and decline among boys, while the proportion of weight that is muscle rises in boys and declines in girls.

Learning Objective 4.7
How does children's ability to use their bodies change?

Using the Body

The ability to use the body to carry out physical activities involves interactions of several separate systems.

Stamina *Stamina* is the capacity to sustain motor activity. For example, if you observe children on playgrounds, you will notice that preschoolers display short bursts of physical activity followed by periods of rest. School-aged children show a similar pattern, but their periods of activity are longer and their periods of rest are shorter than those of younger children because they possess more stamina (Gabbard, 2008).

Changes in stamina are linked to growth of the heart and lungs, which is especially evident during puberty. As the heart and lungs increase in size, the heart rate drops. Both of these changes are more marked for boys than for girls—another of the factors that increases boys' capacity for sustained effort relative to that of girls. Before puberty, boys and girls are fairly similar in physical strength, speed, and stamina, although even at these earlier ages, when a difference exists, it favors the boys. After puberty, boys have a clear advantage in all three areas (Smoll & Schutz, 1990).

Motor Development **Motor development** includes both movement skills, often called *gross motor skills*, such as crawling, walking, running, and bike riding, and manipulative skills, often called *fine motor skills*, such as grasping or picking up objects, holding a crayon or a pencil, or threading a needle. Both gross motor and fine motor skills are present in some form at every age, as you can see in Table 4.1. As a general rule, however, gross motor

By age 1, Nellie (left) not only can walk; she can navigate stairs. By age 5 or 6, most children have developed very good gross motor skills, needed to run and kick (middle). Yet a 5- or 6-year-old will approach a task requiring fine motor skills, such as using scissors, with tense concentration and slow, still imprecise body movements (right).

motor development Growth and change in ability to perform both gross motor skills (such as walking or throwing) and fine motor skills (such as drawing or writing).

Table 4.1 Sequences of Development of Various Motor Skills

Age	Locomotor (Gross Motor) Skills	Manipulative (Fine Motor) Skills
1–3 mos.	Stepping reflex; lifts head; sits with support	Holds object if placed in hand; begins to swipe at objects
4–6 mos.	Rolls over; sits with self-support by 6 months; creeps	Reaches for and grasps objects, using one hand to grasp
7–9 mos.	Sits without support	Transfers objects from one hand to the other; can grasp with thumb and finger ("pincer grasp") by 9 months
10–12 mos.	Pulls self up to standing; walks grasping furniture, then walks without help; squats and stoops	Grasps a spoon across palm, but has poor aim of food at mouth
13–18 mos.	Walks backward and sideways; runs (14–20 months)	Stacks two blocks; puts objects into small containers and dumps them out
2–4 yrs.	Runs easily; walks up stairs using one foot per step; skips on both feet; pedals and steers a tricycle	Picks up small objects (e.g., Cheerios); holds crayon with fingers (age 2–3), then between thumb and first two fingers (age 3–4); cuts paper with scissors
4–6 yrs.	Walks up and down stairs using one foot per step; walks on tiptoe; walks a thin line; jumps, throws, and catches fairly well	Threads beads but not needle (age 4–5); threads needle (age 5–6); grasps pencil maturely but writes or draws with stiffness and concentration
6–9 yrs.	Kicks and hits stationary objects (e.g., ball) with force; intercepts moving objects on the run but must stop to hit, kick, or catch; running speed 4 to 5 yards per second	Uses mature grip when writing or drawing; uses downward motion to strike object with implement (e.g., hammer); bounces object with one hand with limited control
9–12 yrs.	Kicks, hits, and catches moving objects on the run; substantial increase in vertical jump; running speed 5 to 6 yards per second	Uses downward or horizontal motion to strike object with implement as appropriate (e.g., hammer versus baseball bat); bounces object with one hand with good control

Sources: Capute et al., 1984; Connolly and Dalgleish, 1989; Den Ouden, Rijken, Brand, Verloove-Vanhorick, and Ruys, 1991; Fagard and Jacquet, 1989, Gabbard, 2008; Gallahue and Ozmun, 1995; Hagerman, 1996; Needlman, 1996; Overby, 2002; Thomas, 1990.

skills develop earlier, with fine motor skills lagging behind. Thus, 6-year-olds can run, hop, skip, jump, and climb well; many can ride a two-wheeled bike. But children this age are not yet skilled at using a pencil or crayon or cutting accurately with scissors (see Figure 4.6). When they use such tools, their whole body gets involved—the tongue moving and the whole arm and back involved in the writing or cutting motion—a pattern plainly evident in the photograph of the girl cutting on page 96. In the elementary school years, fine motor skills improve rapidly, making it possible for most children not only to write more clearly and easily, but also to play a musical instrument, draw, and develop sports skills that require fine motor coordination.

The Endocrine and Reproductive Systems

One of the most obvious sets of physical changes involves the development of sexual maturity. The whole process is controlled by special chemical signals and is somewhat different in girls and boys.

Figure 4.6 Stages in Children's Drawings

Examples of drawings in each category of two object forms.

(*Source*: Toomela, A. (1999). Drawing Development: Stages in the Representation of a Cube and a Cylinder. *Child Development*, 70, 1141–1150. Reprinted with permission from the Society for Research in Child Development.)

Learning Objective 4.8

What are the contributions of the various hormones to physical development?

Hormones

Hormones, which are secretions of the various **endocrine glands** in the body, govern pubertal growth and physical changes in several ways, which are summarized in Table 4.2. The **pituitary gland** provides the trigger for release of hormones from other glands; thus, it is sometimes called the *master gland*. For example, the thyroid gland secretes thyroxine only when it receives a signal from the pituitary in the form of a secretion of a specific thyroid-stimulating hormone.

Gains in coordination, strength, and stamina enable these adolescent girls to perform far better on the basketball court than was possible just a couple of years earlier.

The rate of growth of children is governed largely by thyroid hormone and pituitary growth hormone. Thyroid hormone is secreted in greater quantities for the first 2 years of life and then falls to a lower level and remains steady until adolescence (Tanner, 1990). Secretions from the testes and ovaries, as well as adrenal androgen, are also at very low levels in the early years of childhood. As Figure 4.7 shows, this changes at age 7 or 8, when adrenal androgen begins to be secreted in greater amounts—the first signal of the changes of puberty (Rosenthal & Gitelman, 2002).

Although **puberty** is often thought of as a single event, it is actually a series of milestones that culminate in the ability to reproduce. After the initial hormonal changes that happen around age 7 or 8, there is a complex sequence of additional hormonal changes. The pituitary gland begins secreting increased levels of **gonadotrophic hormones**. These in turn stimulate the development of glands in the testes and the ovaries that then secrete more of the so-called *sex hormones*—testosterone in boys and a form of estrogen called *estradiol* in girls.

Along with the gonadotrophic hormones, the pituitary gland secretes three other hormones that interact with the sex hormones and affect growth: *ACTH*, which signals the adrenal glands to secrete adrenal androgen; *thyroid-stimulating*

Table 4.2 Major Hormones Involved in Physical Growth and Development

Gland	Key Hormone(s) Secreted	Aspects of Growth Influenced
Thyroid	Thyroxine	Normal brain development and overall rate of growth
Adrenal	Adrenal androgen (chemically very similar to testosterone)	Some pubertal changes as well as the development of skeletal and muscular maturity
Leydig cells in the testes (in boys)	Testosterone	Crucial in the formation of male genitals prenatally; triggers the sequence of primary and secondary sex characteristic changes at puberty; stimulates increased output of growth hormone and affects bones and muscles
Ovaries (in girls)	Several estrogens, the most critical of which is estradiol	Development of the menstrual cycle, breasts, and pubic hair
Pituitary	Growth hormone (GH), thyroid-stimulating hormone (TSH), ACTH, and the gonadotrophic hormones	Growth hormone governs the rate of physical maturation; other pituitary hormones signal the respective sex glands to secrete; gonadotrophic hormones help control the menstrual cycle

Source: Tanner, 1990.

Figure 4.7 Hormone Changes in Childhood and Adolescence

Changes in hormones prior to and at adolescence. The top graph shows changes in adrenal androgen, which are equivalent in boys and girls; the bottom graphs show increases in estradiol for girls in picograms per milliliter, and testosterone for boys in nanograms per milliliter.

(*Sources*: Androgen data from M. K. McClintock and G. Herdt, from "Rethinking Puberty: The Development of Sexual Attraction," *Current Directions in Psychological Science*, Vol. 5, No. 6 (December 1996), p. 181, Fig. 2. © 1996 American Psychological Association. By permission of Cambridge University Press. Estradiol and testosterone data from Elizabeth Susman, Fig. 2 from "Modeling Developmental Complexity in Adolescence: Hormones and Behavior in Context," p. 291, *Journal of Research on Adolescence*, 7, 1997. © 1997 by Lawrence Erlbaum Associates, Inc. By permission of the publisher and author.)

hormone; and general *growth hormone*. Adrenal androgen, which is chemically very similar to testosterone, plays a particularly important role for girls, triggering the growth spurt and affecting pubic hair development. For boys, adrenal androgen is less significant, presumably because they already have so much male hormone in the form of testosterone in their bloodstreams. The increased levels of sex and growth hormones trigger two sets of body changes: development of the sex organs, and a much broader set of changes in the brain, bones, muscles, and other body organs.

The most obvious changes of puberty are those associated with sexual maturity. Changes in *primary sex characteristics* include growth of the testes and penis in the male and of the ovaries, uterus, and vagina in the female. *Secondary sex characteristic* changes include breast development in girls, changing voice pitch and beard growth in boys, and the growth of body hair in both sexes. These physical developments occur in a defined sequence, customarily divided into five stages following a system originally suggested by J. M. Tanner (1990) (see Table 4.3). Stage 1 describes the preadolescent stage, stage 2 the first signs of a pubertal change, stages 3 and 4 the intermediate steps, and stage 5 the final adult characteristic.

endocrine glands Glands (including the adrenals, the thyroid, the pituitary, the testes, and the ovaries) that secrete hormones governing overall physical growth and sexual maturing.

pituitary gland Gland that provides the trigger for release of hormones from other glands.

puberty The series of hormonal and physical changes at adolescence that bring about sexual maturity.

gonadotrophic hormones Hormones secreted by the pituitary gland at the beginning of puberty that stimulate the development of glands in the testes and ovaries, which then begin to secrete testosterone or estrogen.

Table 4.3 Examples of Tanner's Stages of Pubertal Development

Stage	Female Breast Development	Male Genital Development
1	No change except for some elevation of the nipple.	Testes, scrotum, and penis are all about the same size and shape as in early childhood.
2	Breast bud stage: elevation of breast and the nipple as a small mound. Areolar diameter increases compared to stage 1.	Scrotum and testes are slightly enlarged. Skin of the scrotum reddens and changes texture, but little or no enlargement of the penis.
3	Breast and areola both enlarged and elevated more than in stage 2, but no separation of their contours.	Penis slightly enlarged, at first mainly in length. Testes and scrotum are further enlarged.
4	Areola and nipple form a secondary mound projecting above the contour of the breast.	Penis further enlarged, with growth in breadth and development of glans. Testes and scrotum further enlarged, and scrotum skin still darker.
5	Mature stage. Only the nipple projects, with the areola recessed to the general contour of the breast.	Genitalia achieve adult size and shape.

Source: Petersen and Taylor, 1980, p. 127.

Learning Objective 4.9

What are the sequences of pubertal changes in boys and girls?

Sequence of Changes in Girls and Boys

Studies of preteens and teens in both Europe and North America show that in girls, the various sequential changes are interlocked in a particular pattern, shown schematically in Figure 4.8 (Malina, 1990). The first steps are the early changes in breasts and pubic hair, followed by the peak of the growth spurt and by the beginnings of stages 4 and 5, which involve further breast and pubic hair development. Usually, only after the growth spurt does first menstruation occur, an event called **menarche** (pronounced men-ARE-kee). Menarche typically occurs 2 years after the beginning of other visible changes and is succeeded only by the final stages of breast and pubic hair development. Among girls in industrialized countries today, menarche occurs, on average, between ages 12½ and 13½; 95% of all girls experience this event between the ages of 11 and 15 (Adelman & Ellen, 2002).

Interestingly, the timing of menarche changed rather dramatically from the mid-19th to the mid-20th century. In 1840, the average age of menarche in Western industrialized countries was roughly 17; the average dropped steadily from that time until the 1950s at a rate of about 4 months per decade among European populations, an example of what psychologists call a **secular trend** (Roche, 1979). The change was most likely caused by significant changes in lifestyle and diet, particularly increases in protein and fat intake along with reductions in physical exercise, that resulted in an increase in the proportion of body fat in females.

The stability of the average age of menarche at about 12.5 years over the past half century supports the notion that there is a genetic limit on the age range within which menarche may

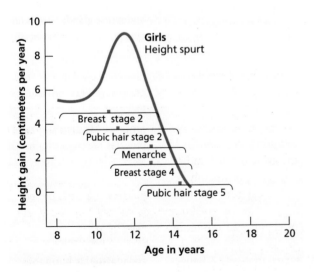

Figure 4.8 Sequence of Pubertal Changes in Girls

The figure shows the normal sequence and timing of pubertal changes for girls. The red box on each black line represents the average age when the change occurs; the line indicates the range of normal times. Note the wide range of normality for all of these changes. Also note how relatively late in the sequence the growth spurt and menarche occur.

(*Sources:* Malina, 1990; Tanner, 1990.)

occur (Viner, 2002). Nevertheless, trends in the dietary habits of children over this same period have led to some important changes in endocrine system development among girls. Increased consumption of fats has led to higher proportions of body fat among today's girls, which, in turn, have triggered hormonal changes. Although these changes have had little impact on the average age of menarche, they have led to declines in the average ages at which girls show secondary sex characteristics, such as the appearance of breast buds and pubic hair (Anderson, Dallal, & Must, 2003; Wang, 2002). On average, girls nowadays show these signs 1 to 2 years earlier than their mothers and grandmothers did, resulting in a lengthening of the average time between the appearance of secondary sex characteristics and menarche (Parent et al., 2003). Little is known about how these early hormonal shifts affect girls' later health. Several studies are under way to determine whether overweight girls who exhibit early secondary sex characteristic development are at increased risk for breast cancer, adult obesity, and heart disease (National Cancer Institute, 2006; Pierce & Leon, 2005). Interestingly, too, researchers are also investigating why overweight delays pubertal development in boys and whether such delays affect boys' health later in life (Wang, 2002).

For about 2 years after menarche, ovulation occurs in only 30% of girls' menstrual cycles (Adelman & Ellen, 2002). Over the next 2 years, that ovulation percentage rises to the adult rate of 80%. Such irregularity no doubt contributes to the widespread (but false) assumption among girls in their early teens that they cannot get pregnant because they are too young.

In boys, as in girls, the peak of the growth spurt typically comes fairly late in the sequence, as you can see in Figure 4.9. These data suggest that, on average, a boy completes stages 2 and 3 of genital development and stages 2 and 3 of pubic hair development before he reaches his growth peak. The development of a beard and the lowering of the voice occur near the end of the sequence. Precisely when in this sequence the boy begins to produce viable sperm is very difficult to determine. It appears that a boy can attain fertility as early as age 12 or as late as age 16 and still be within the normal range (Adelman & Ellen, 2002). Sequentially, fertility usually occurs just before a boy reaches his full adult height.

While the order of pubertal development seems to be highly consistent, there is quite a lot of individual variability. Figures 4.8 and 4.9 depict the normative, or average, pattern, but individual teenagers often deviate from the norm. For instance, a girl might move through several stages of pubic hair development before the first clear changes in the breasts become evident or might experience menarche much earlier in the sequence than normal. It is important to keep this variation in mind if you are trying to make a prediction about an individual teenager.

menarche Onset of menstruation.

secular trend A pattern of change in some characteristic over several cohorts, such as systematic changes in the average timing of menarche or in average height or weight.

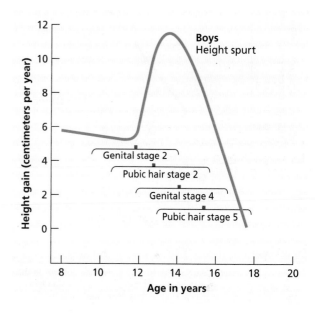

Figure 4.9　Sequence of Pubertal Changes in Boys

The sequence of pubertal changes begins about 2 years later for boys than for girls, but as with girls, the height spurt occurs relatively late in the sequence.

(*Sources*: Malina, 1990; Tanner, 1990.)

The Timing of Puberty

Learning Objective 4.10
How does the timing of puberty affect teens' development?

In any random sample of 12- and 13-year-olds, you will find some who are already at stage 5, and others still at stage 1 in the steps of sexual maturation. In U.S. culture today, most young people seem to share the expectation that pubertal changes will happen sometime between ages 12 and 14. Coincidentally, most girls acquire a culturally undesirable *endomorphic*, or somewhat flabby, body type, as a result of puberty. Thus, early-developing girls should have more adjustment problems than average- or late-developing girls. Similarly, puberty provides most boys with a culturally admired *mesomorphic*, or lean and muscular, body type. Thus, early-developing boys should display better psychological and social adjustment than average- or late-developing boys.

Research in the United States indicates that girls who are early developers (who experience major body changes before age 10 or 11) show consistently more negative body images, such as thinking of themselves as too fat (Sweeting & West, 2002). Such girls are also more likely to get into trouble in school and at home, more likely to become sexually active, and more likely to be depressed than are girls who are average or late developers (Kaltiala-Heino, Kosunen, & Rimpela, 2003). Among boys, both very early and very late puberty are associated with depression (Kaltiala-Heino, Kosunen, & Rimpela, 2003). However, researchers have also consistently found that boys who are slightly ahead of their peers in pubertal development often occupy leadership roles and are more academically and economically successful in adulthood (Taga, Markey, & Friedman, 2006). In addition, substance use is associated with early puberty in both girls and boys, because, based on their appearance, early maturers are often invited to join groups of older teens among whom substance use is an important social activity (Costello, Sung, Worthman, & Angold, 2007). Moreover, parenting moderates the effects of pubertal timing such that early-maturing boys and girls are both more likely to become involved in sexual activity and substance abuse if their parents are permissive.

In nearly all studies examining pubertal timing, though, earliness or lateness has been defined in terms of the actual physical changes. The results have been somewhat clearer when researchers have instead asked teenagers about their internal models of earliness or lateness. The link between the internal model and the outcome is especially vivid in a classic study of ballet dancers by Jeanne Brooks-Gunn (Brooks-Gunn, 1987; Brooks-Gunn & Warren, 1985). She studied 14- to 18-year-old girls, some of whom were serious ballet dancers studying at a national ballet company school. A very lean, almost prepubescent body is highly desirable among such dancers. Brooks-Gunn therefore expected that dancers who were very late in pubertal development would actually have a better image of themselves than those who were on time. And that is exactly what she found (see Figure 4.10). Among the nondancers, menarche at the biologically average time was associated with a better body image than was late menarche, but exactly the reverse was true for the dancers. Thus, as predicted, it is the discrepancy between a teenaged girl's internal model of puberty and her experiential reality that predicts the effects of pubertal timing. Research has yet to examine the relationship between boys' internal models of puberty and their actual experiences.

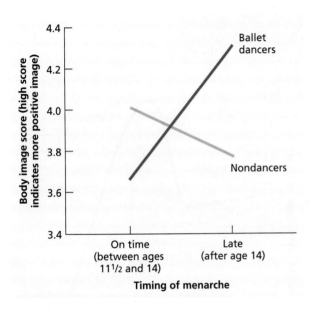

Figure 4.10   Timing of Puberty and Body Image

Serious ballet dancers clearly prefer to have a very late puberty. In this study, dancers whose menarche was "on time" by ordinary standards actually had poorer body images than those who were objectively quite late, while the reverse was true for nondancers. Thus, it is perception of timing and not actual timing that is critical.

(*Source*: Brooks-Gunn & Warren, 1985, from Table 1, p. 291.)

Sexual Behavior in Adolescence

In the United States, most people become sexually active sometime before age 20, about half before they leave high school (see Figure 4.11). For some teens, being "sexually active" constitutes a single act of intercourse sometime during the high school years. However, many others have multiple partners and frequently engage in unprotected sex acts.

Learning Objective 4.11

What are the ethnic, social, and academic factors that predict early sexual behavior?

Prevalence and Predictors of Sexual Behavior

Figure 4.11 shows findings from a large-scale national survey of high school students in the United States (Centers for Disease Control [CDC], 2006f). As you can see from the figure, high school boys were found to be more sexually active than girls. Furthermore, the proportion of sexually experienced teens increased across grades 9 to 12. One statistic illustrated by the figure that is particularly worrisome to public health

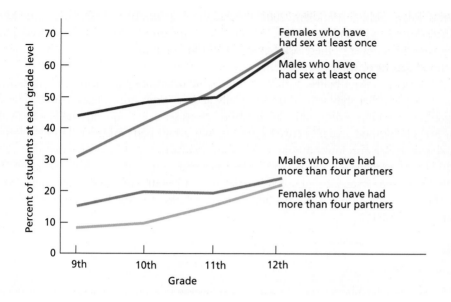

Figure 4.11
Sexual Experience among High School Students in the United States

The graph illustrates the data from a representative sample of more than 15,000 high school students interviewed in 2005. As you can see, the number of students who have had sex at least once increases substantially from ninth to twelfth grade, and an alarming percentage of teens have had four or more partners by the end of the high school years.

(*Source*: CDC, 2006f.)

officials is the proportion of teens who have had multiple partners before leaving high school. Research has shown that the more partners a teenager (or an adult, for that matter) has, the more likely he or she is to contract a sexually transmitted disease.

Sexual experience varies across ethnic groups (CDC, 2006f). About 67% of African American high school students report having had sexual intercourse at least once in their lives. The rates among Hispanic American and White students are 51% and 44%, respectively. African American students are also more likely than Hispanic Americans and White teens to have had their first sexual encounter before age 13 (17% versus 7% and 4%, respectively).

There are also age and ethnic differences among students who are sexually active—defined as having had sex at least once within 3 months of responding to the survey. For example, roughly 41% of eleventh-grade females report recent sexual activity, while 20% of ninth-grade females do so. With respect to ethnic differences, 49% of African American students, as compared to 35% of Hispanic Americans and 32% of Whites, report being currently sexually active.

Among students who are sexually active, 63% say that they use condoms (CDC, 2006f). African Americans are more likely than students in other groups to report using condoms (69% versus 57% for Hispanic Americans and 63% for Whites). Birth control pills are used even less frequently. Only 21% of sexually active females report being on the pill. In addition, pill usage is far more common among White high school girls (27%) than among their African American and Hispanic American peers (9% and 11%, respectively).

Although sexual activity of boys is somewhat correlated with the amount of testosterone in their blood, social factors are much better predictors of teenagers' sexual activity than hormones (Halpern, Udry, Campbell, & Suchindran, 1993; Udry & Campbell, 1994). Those who begin sexual activity early are more likely to live in poor neighborhoods in which young people are not closely monitored by adults. They come from poorer families or from families in which sexual activity is condoned and dating rules are lax. They are more likely to use alcohol. Many were abused and/or neglected in early childhood (Herrenkohl, Herrenkohl, Egolf, & Russo, 1998).

Among girls, those who are sexually active are also more likely to have had early menarche, to have low interest in school, to have had their first date at a relatively early age, and to have a history of sexual abuse (Buzi,

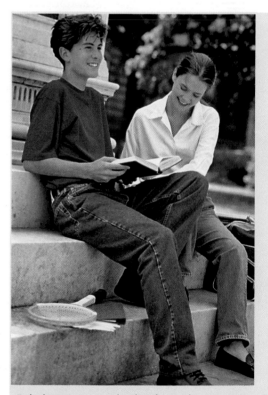

Early dating is associated with early sexual activity.

Roberts, Ross, Addy, & Markham, 2003; Ompad et al., 2006). In general, these same factors predict sexual activity among Whites, African Americans, and Hispanics. And in every group, the greater the number of these risk factors present for an individual teenager, the greater the likelihood that he or she will be sexually active.

Adolescents' moral beliefs and the activities in which they participate also predict to some extent whether they will become sexually active. For example, teens who believe premarital sex is morally wrong and who attend religious services frequently are less likely than their peers to become sexually active before reaching adulthood (Miller et al., 1998). Rates of sexual activity are also lower among teens who are involved in sports or other after-school pursuits than among their peers who do not participate in such activities (Savage & Holcomb, 1999). Moreover, alcohol use is associated with 25–30% of adolescent sexual encounters; thus, teens who do not use alcohol are less likely to be sexually active than those who drink (CDC, 2000).

Learning Objective 4.12

Which sexually transmitted diseases are common among sexually active teens?

Sexually Transmitted Diseases

Predictably, as rates of sexual behavior increase among teenagers, so do the rates of **sexually transmitted diseases (STDs)**, diseases spread by sexual contact. STD rates tend to be higher among younger sexually active individuals than among those who are older. In fact, more than half of all new STD cases each year in the United States occur in 15- to 24-year-olds. The rate of one STD, *chlamydia*, is higher among teenagers than in any other age group. About 3% of sexually active 15- to 19-year-old females in the United States have chlamydia (CDC, 2007c). But chlamydia rates pale in comparison to those associated with the *human papilloma virus (HPV)*. About half of sexually active 15- to 19-year-old girls test positive for HPV (Quick Stats, 2007). If you read the entries in Table 4.4, you can readily see that the effects of STDs can be quite severe, especially "silent" infections such as chlamydia and HPV that often do not produce symptoms until they have caused a great deal of damage.

Many teens are also woefully ignorant of sexually transmitted diseases and their potential consequences, although about 90% of high school students report having learned about sexually transmitted diseases (STDs) in school (CDC, 2000; Rosenthal, Lewis, Succop, & Burklow, 1997; Sharma & Sharma, 1997). Even when they are knowledgeable about STDs, many teens lack the assertiveness necessary to resist sexual pressure from a romantic partner or to discuss condom use.

Recently, the Food and Drug Administration approved a vaccine that officials believe will protect young women against four types of HPV (CDC, 2006b). The vaccine is recommended

sexually transmitted diseases (STDs) Category of disease spread by sexual contact, including chlamydia, genital warts, syphilis, gonorrhea, and HIV; also called venereal diseases.

Table 4.4   Common Sexually Transmitted Diseases

Disease	Symptoms	Treatment	Long-Term Consequences
Chlamydia	Painful urination; discharge; abdominal discomfort; one-third have no symptoms	Antibiotics	Pelvic inflammatory disease; sterility
Genital warts (HPV)	Painless growths on genitalia and/or anus	Removal of warts; no known cure	Increased risk of cervical cancer
Genital herpes	Painful blisters on genitalia	No known cure; can be controlled with various drugs	Risk of transmission to partners and to infants during birth
Gonorrhea	Discharge; painful urination	Antibiotics	Pelvic inflammatory disease
Syphilis	Sores on mouth, genitals	Antibiotics	Paralysis; brain damage; death
HIV/AIDS	Fatigue; fever; frequent infections	Antiretroviral drugs	Chronic infections; death

for all females between the ages of 9 and 26. However, researchers do not yet know how long the vaccine's protective effects will last. Moreover, officials point out that there are other forms of HPV against which the vaccine offers no protection. For these reasons, public health officials state that girls and women who get the vaccine should continue to use condoms.

Male teens who engage in same-sex intercourse are at higher risk of contracting HIV/AIDS than other groups. Among male teens who test positive for HIV, 60% acquired the virus in this way (CDC, 2007b). Moreover, about 60% of female adolescents who test positive for HIV became infected through sexual contact with a male who engaged in same-sex intercourse at some time in the past. Surveys showing that the disease is virtually nonexistent among homosexual male teens before age 15 but is present in about 10% of them by age 22 have prompted public health officials to heighten their efforts to educate young teens about HIV/AIDS (Valleroy et al., 2000). In addition, they have recommended universal screening for HIV for teens who engage in same-sex intercourse so that antiretroviral drugs can be prescribed as early in the course of the disease as possible. Education and screening programs are especially important among African American male teens, who account for 69% of all new cases of HIV/AIDS among 13- to 19-year-olds in the United States (CDC, 2007b).

To combat the spread of STDs among teens, many developmentalists and public health advocates say that more effective sex education programs are needed. Most suggest that programs that include social and decision-making skills training, along with information about STDs and pregnancy, are more likely to reduce the prevalence of sexual activity and increase the number of teens who protect themselves against disease and pregnancy when they do have sex than are information-only approaches. However, no clear consensus about the effectiveness of various approaches to sex education has emerged (Hovell et al., 1998). Moreover, researchers have found that students prefer to get information about sex from their parents (Measor, 2004; Somers & Surmann, 2004). Information provided by peers and young adults who have had personal experiences with unplanned pregnancy and sexually transmitted diseases may also influence teens' sexual decision-making to a greater degree than formal educational programs (Kidger, 2004).

Teenage Pregnancy

Learning Objective 4.13
What are the factors associated with pregnancy in adolescence?

The rate of teenage pregnancy is higher in the United States than in any other Western industrialized country (Ambuel, 1995; Singh & Darroch, 2000). For example, the overall annual rate is about 40 pregnancies per 1,000 teens in the United States; it is only 17 pregnancies per 1,000 in Israel and 4 per 1,000 in Japan (Martin et al., 2006; Merrick & Morad, 2002). Ethnic differences exist within the United States as well (Hamilton, Martin, & Ventura, 2007). Among Asian Americans, the teen pregnancy rate is about 15 per 1,000, while the rate among Whites is 25 per 1,000. Among Hispanic Americans and African Americans, the rates are 83 and 65 per 1,000, respectively.

However, teen pregnancy statistics can be confusing, because they usually refer to all pregnancies among women under age 20. To clarify the extent of the teen pregnancy problem, it is useful to break down the statistics by adolescent subgroups. For example, in the United States, the annual pregnancy rate is 1 pregnancy per 1,000 for girls younger than 15; 22 per 1,000 among girls aged 15 to 17; and 70 per 1,000 among 18- to 19-year-olds (Martin et al., 2006). Looking at the numbers this way shows that teen pregnancy is far more frequent among older adolescents and, in fact, is most likely to happen after a girl leaves high school.

The age at which an adolescent becomes a parent is only one aspect of the teen pregnancy issue. Birth rates among teenagers have actually dropped in the entire U.S. population since the 1960s, including among 15- to 19-year-olds. What has increased is the rate of births to unmarried teens. In 1970, about three-quarters of teen mothers were married, whereas in 2004, a similar proportion, some 80% or so, were unmarried (Martin et al., 2006).

The proportion of teenaged mothers who eventually marry the baby's father has also declined in recent years, and, again, there are ethnic differences. Less than 5% of African American teen mothers marry the baby's father, compared to 26% of Hispanics and 41% of Whites

(Population Resource Center, 2004). Moreover, across ethnic groups, 17% of teen mothers maintain romantic relationships with their babies' fathers beyond the first few months after birth (Gee & Rhodes, 1999, 2003).

Whether a girl becomes pregnant during her teenage years depends on many of the same factors that predict sexual activity in general (Miller, Benson, & Galbraith, 2001). The younger a girl is when she becomes sexually active, the more likely she is to become pregnant. Among teenaged girls from poor families, from single-parent families, or from families with relatively uneducated parents, pregnancy rates are higher (Vikat, Rimpela, Kosunen, & Rimpela, 2002). Likewise, girls whose mothers became sexually active at an early age and bore their first child early are likely to follow a similar path.

In contrast, the likelihood of pregnancy is lower among teenaged girls who do well in school and have strong educational aspirations. Such girls are both less likely to be sexually active at an early age and more likely to use contraception if they are sexually active. Girls who have good communication about sex and contraception with their mothers are also less likely to get pregnant (Dogan-Até & Carrión-Basham, 2007).

When teenaged girls become pregnant, in most cases, they face the most momentous set of decisions they have encountered in their young lives. About one-third of teen pregnancies across all ethnic groups end in abortion, and about 14% result in miscarriages (Alan Guttmacher Institute, 2004). Among Whites, 7% of teens carry the baby to term and place it for adoption, while 1% of African American teens relinquish their babies to adoptive families.

The children of teenaged mothers are more likely than children born to older mothers to grow up in poverty, with all the accompanying negative consequences for the child's optimum development (Burgess, 2005). For instance, they tend to achieve developmental milestones more slowly than infants of older mothers (Pomerleau, Scuccimarri, & Malcuit, 2003). However, the children of teenaged mothers whose own parents help with child care, finances, and parenting skills are less likely to suffer such negative effects (Birch, 1998; Uno, Florsheim, & Uchino, 1998). Moreover, social programs that provide teenaged mothers with child care and the support they need to remain in school positively affect both these mothers and their babies. Such programs also improve outcomes for teenaged fathers (Kost, 1997).

Learning Objective 4.14
In what ways are gay, lesbian, bisexual, and transgendered teens different from and similar to their peers?

Sexual Minority Youth

The emergence of a physical attraction to members of the opposite sex, or *heterosexuality*, is one of the defining features of adolescence for the great majority of teenagers. For some, though, adolescence is the time when they discover— or confirm a long-standing suspicion—that they are attracted to people of the same sex (*homosexuality*) or to both sexes (*bisexuality*). Still others become increasingly convinced that their psychological gender is inconsistent with their biological sex (*transgenderism*).

Gay, Lesbian, and Bisexual Adolescents Surveys involving thousands of teens have found that about 92% identify themselves as exclusively heterosexual in *sexual orientation*, a person's preference for same- or opposite-sex partners (Austin et al., 2004; Remafedi, Resnick, Blum, & Harris, 1998). About 7% of teens report that they are still unsure of their sexual orientation, and 1% say that they classify themselves as exclusively gay, exclusively lesbian, or bisexual. By adulthood, 94% report being exclusively heterosexual, and just over 5% describe themselves as gay, lesbian, or bisexual, leaving only a very small proportion who are still undecided as to their sexual orientation (Langer, Arnedt, & Sussman, 2004).

Several twin studies have suggested a genetic basis for homosexuality (Lippa, 2005). Most of these studies indicate that when one identical twin is homosexual, the probability that the other twin will also be homosexual is 50–60%, whereas the concordance rate is only about 20% for fraternal twins and only about 11% for pairs of biologically unrelated boys adopted into the same family (Dawood, Pillard, Horvath, Revelle, & Bailey, 2000; Kendler, Thornton, Gilman, & Kessler, 2000). Family studies also suggest that male homosexuality runs in families—that is, the families of most gay men have a higher proportion of homosexual males

The process through which an individual comes to realize that he or she is homosexual appears to be a gradual one. Groups such as this one provide teens with the social support they need to cope with their own feelings and with the negative responses of some peers to their sexual orientation.

than do the families of heterosexual men (Kirk, Bailey, & Martin, 2000). Such findings strengthen the hypothesis that homosexuality has a biological basis (Dawood et al., 2000).

Additional studies suggest that prenatal hormone patterns may also be a causal factor in homosexuality (Lippa, 2005). For example, women whose mothers took the drug diethyl-stilbestrol (DES, a synthetic estrogen) during pregnancy are more likely to be homosexual as adults than are women who were not exposed to DES in the womb (Meyer-Bahlburg et al., 1995). Moreover, there is evidence that many boys who demonstrate strong cross-sex play preferences in early childhood show homosexual preferences when they reach adolescence (Bailey & Zucker, 1995). Interestingly, too, studies show that the long bones in the legs and arms of school-aged children who grow up to be homosexual do not grow as rapidly as those of children who eventually become heterosexual (Martin & Nguyen, 2004). These findings indicate that maturational differences between homosexuals and heterosexuals are evident before puberty and involve body systems other than the sexual organs themselves. Taken together, prenatal hormone exposure studies, research examining early childhood activity preferences, and studies comparing the processes of physical maturation in heterosexuals and homosexuals are consistent with the hypothesis that homosexuality is programmed in at birth.

Such evidence does not mean that environment plays no role in homosexuality. For example, when one of a pair of identical twins is homosexual, the other twin does *not* share that sexual orientation 40–50% of the time. Something beyond biology must be at work, although developmentalists do not yet know what environmental factors may be involved.

Whatever the cause of variations in sexual orientation, the process through which an individual comes to realize that he or she is homosexual appears to be a gradual one (Diamond, 2007). Some researchers think that the process begins in middle childhood as a feeling of doubt about one's heterosexuality (Carver, Egan, & Perry, 2004). Retrospective studies have found that many gay men and lesbians recall having had homosexual fantasies during their teen years, but few fully accepted their homosexuality while still in adolescence (Wong & Tang, 2004). Instead, the final steps toward full self-awareness and acceptance of one's homosexuality appear to take place in early adulthood.

As homosexual teens grapple with questions about their sexual orientation, many report feeling isolated from and unaccepted by their peers (Galliher, Rostosky, & Hughes

2004; Martin & D'Augelli, 2003). This may help explain why a higher proportion of homosexual than heterosexual teens suffer from depression and attempt suicide (Cato & Canetto, 2003; Savin-Williams & Ream, 2003). Many mental health professionals suggest that, to respond to these adolescents' needs, school officials provide emotional and social support for homosexual teens (Rostosky, Owens, Zimmerman, & Riggle, 2003; van Wormer & McKinney, 2003).

While homosexual adolescents clearly face unique challenges, they share many of the same concerns as their heterosexual peers. For example, both homosexual and heterosexual girls are more likely than boys to be dissatisfied with their physical appearance (Saewyc, Bearinger, Heinz, Blum, & Resnick, 1998). Consequently, dieting is more common among both homosexual and heterosexual girls than among boys of either sexual orientation. Like their heterosexual counterparts, homosexual male adolescents drink alcohol more often and engage in more risky behavior than do female teenagers.

Transgendered Teens   *Transgendered* teens and adults are those whose psychological gender is the opposite of their biological sex. Some studies suggest that transgendered individuals may have been exposed to atypical amounts of androgens in the womb (Lippa, 2005). However, most do not have such histories, so the cause of transgenderism remains a mystery. Nevertheless, transgendered adolescents usually report that, since early childhood, they have been more interested in activities that are associated with the opposite sex than in those that are typical for their own (Lippa, 2005). However, most children who are attracted to cross-gender activities, and even those who express a desire to be the opposite gender, do not exhibit transgenderism after puberty (Cohen-Kettenis & van Goozen, 1997). Thus, such behaviors on the part of children are not considered to be predictive of the development of transgenderism in adolescence.

Because of their fear of being stigmatized, most teens who suspect that they are transgendered keep their feelings to themselves. The denial and anger that are often expressed by family members when transgendered adolescents do venture to "come out" amplify these teens' distress (Zamboni, 2006). As a result, like gay, lesbian, and bisexual teens, transgendered teens are more likely to suffer from depression and are at higher risk of suicide than heterosexual adolescents are (Rosenberg, 2003).

Health and Wellness

You read about infants' physical health in Chapter 3, and children have many of the same needs. However, their needs, and the focus of concerns about their health, change significantly after puberty, so it's important to separate our discussion of health issues and look first at childhood and then at adolescence.

Learning Objective 4.15
What are the health needs and concerns of children and adolescents?

Health in Childhood

Typically, childhood is a fairly healthy period of life. However, children have many accidents, and the health habits formed during these years can persist for a lifetime, influencing individual health for good or for ill.

Health-Care Needs   Just as infants do, young children continue to require periodic medical check-ups and a variety of immunizations (Overby, 2002). At yearly check-ups, doctors monitor preschoolers' growth and motor development. At the same time, doctors and nurses often serve as parents' first source of help with children who have sensory or developmental disabilities that were not diagnosed in infancy (Coury, 2002). Moreover, health-care professionals provide parents with strategies for dealing with everyday parenting issues. For example, parents frequently ask for advice regarding young children's sleeping habits (see *Developmental Science in the Real World*).

A Good Night's Sleep for Kids (and Parents, Too!)

Every night Luis and Ramona go through the same ordeal when they put their 3-year-old son, Manny, to bed. The boy begs to sleep with them, but they always refuse. After four or five cycles of begging and sobbing, usually spread over at least an hour, Manny finally becomes so exhausted that he can no longer stay awake. Despite his parents' consistency, Manny often gets his way. He wakes up every night around 2:00 a.m. and attempts to slip into his parents' bed without their noticing. Sometimes Luis or Ramona awakens and takes him back to bed and, in the process, initiates another round of the begging-sobbing cycle that Manny exhibits at bedtime. Other times, they are sleeping so soundly that Manny's late-night invasion goes unnoticed, and they awaken to find him in their bed the next morning.

Manny's nighttime behavior is all too familiar to many parents of preschoolers. Here are the bedtime strategies that most health-care professionals recommend:

• Provide the child with a structured, predictable daytime schedule, and stick to it as closely as possible every day.
• Set a regular bedtime that is 8 to 10 hours before the desired waking time.
• Discontinue daytime naps for a child who has difficulty getting to sleep or who awakens too early in the morning.
• Establish a routine set of "settling activities," such as a bath, story book, and goodnight kiss, and resist the child's efforts to prolong or modify the routine.
• Provide the child with a *transitional object* such as a doll or stuffed animal that is reserved especially for bedtime.

Making such adjustments can be challenging, especially when the child actively resists them. However, research confirms that these kinds of changes can significantly reduce sleep-related conflicts (Borkowski, Hunter, & Johnson, 2001). Thus, a few days or even weeks of persistence on the parents' part may pay off in years of undisturbed sleep for parents and children alike.

Questions for Reflection

1. If you were Manny's parent, what strategies would you use to try to prevent him from awakening at night and getting into your bed?
2. In your opinion, to what extent are parental concerns about where children sleep driven by cultural beliefs and standards of behavior?

School-aged children benefit from regular medical care as well. For one thing, there are a few important immunizations that are usually administered during this period (Umetsu, 1998). In addition, many school-aged children have undiagnosed health problems. For example, 10–20% have difficulty sleeping (Owens, Spirito, McGuinn, & Nobile, 2000; Sadeh, Gruber, & Raviv, 2002). In most cases, parents of school children are unaware of such problems until a physician or nurse specifically asks a child about sleep patterns as part of a routine check-up. Sleep difficulties are associated with attention, concentration, and behavioral problems, so picking up on an undetected sleep problem, and correcting it, may improve a child's life considerably (Sadeh et al., 2002).

Growth Curves and Health   Earlier in the chapter you learned that stabilization of a child's growth curve enables health-care professionals to predict her height at later ages. For this reason, the growth curve is critical to assessments of children's health (Overby, 2002). A downward deviation away from an established growth curve for height may be a sign that a child is suffering from an undiagnosed illness (Styne & Glaser, 2002). An upward deviation for weight may mean that the child is trending toward becoming overweight. The importance of growth curve assessment is one reason most health-care professionals assert that it is critical to young children's health that they be examined by the same physician, or at least in the same clinic, at each check-up (Children's Hospital of Philadelphia, 2008).

Illnesses and Accidents   In the United States, the average child has four to six brief bouts of sickness each year, most often colds or the flu (Sulkes, 1998). Children who are experiencing high levels of stress or family upheaval are more likely to become ill (Guttman & Dick, 2004). Another danger for children is accidents. In any given year, about a quarter of all

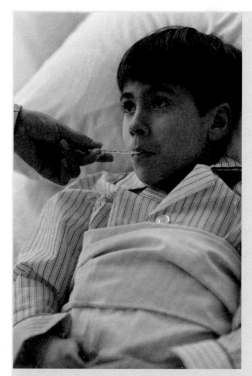

Most kids in the United States are sick in bed about 5 days a year, most often with a cold or the flu.

children under 5 in the United States have at least one accident that requires some kind of medical attention, and accidents are the major cause of death in preschool and school-aged children (Fein, Durbin, & Selbst, 2002). At every age, accidents are more common among boys than among girls, presumably because of their more active and daring styles of play. The majority of accidents among children occur at home—falls, cuts, accidental poisonings, and the like. Automobile accidents are the second leading source of injuries to school-aged children in the United States, followed by bicycle-related mishaps (National Center for Injury Prevention and Control [NCIPC], 2000). In fact, 80% of bicycle-related head injuries involve children. Research suggests that wearing a helmet while riding a bike reduces the chances of head injury by more than 85%. Consequently, many cities and states have enacted laws requiring both children and adult bicyclists to wear helmets. Finally, some "accidents" are actually the result of parental abuse (see *Thinking about Research*).

Nutrition   Because children grow more slowly during the early childhood years than in infancy, they may seem to eat less than when they were babies. Moreover, food aversions often develop during the preschool years. For example, a child who loved carrots as an infant may refuse to eat them at age 2 or 3. Consequently, conflicts between young children and their parents often focus on the child's eating behavior (Overby, 2002).

Nutritionists point out that it is important that parents keep in mind that young children eat only half as much food as adults. Thus, parents should not become so concerned about the quantity of food a child consumes that they cater to her preferences for sweets and other high-calorie, high-fat foods (Wong, 1993). Although young children are rarely overweight, many children acquire eating habits during these years that lead to later weight problems. Nutrition-

---

THINKING ABOUT RESEARCH

Causes and Consequences of Child Abuse and Neglect

Figuring out what qualifies as abuse is not always simple; most psychologists today tend to follow definitions proposed by Douglas Barnett and his colleagues (1993) as well as other researchers (Rogosch, Cicchetti, Shields, & Toth, 1995): *Physical abuse* involves the nonaccidental infliction of bodily injury on the child—anything from a bruise to injuries so extreme that the child requires hospitalization or dies; *sexual abuse* involves any kind of sexual contact between a child and a responsible adult that is for the purpose of the adult's gratification or gain; *physical neglect* includes either failure to provide adequately for the child's nurturance and basic care or failure to provide supervision adequate for the child's age, or both.

About 1 million cases of abuse and neglect in the United States each year come to the attention of law enforcement officials and/or health-care professionals (Fein, Durbin, & Selbst, 2002; Lamb & Lewis, 2005). Two-thirds involve physical injuries, another quarter involve sexual abuse, and 5% are the result of neglect, such as underfeeding an infant (Sulkes, 1998). Sadly, 2,000 infants and children die as a result of abuse or neglect each year (CDC, 2006e).

Certain risk factors predispose parents to abuse and/or neglect their children, but abuse does not normally occur unless several of these risk factors occur in the same family at the same time. First, the risk of abuse is higher in any family experiencing significant stress, whether that stress arises from unemployment, poverty, neighborhood violence, a lack of social support, or an especially difficult or demanding infant (CDC, 2006e). Second, some parents, particularly those who were themselves abused, simply know no other way to deal with frustration and stress or with disobedience in their child, other than striking the child in some way. Other parents are depressed or unable to form the kind of emotional bond to the child that would help to prevent abuse (Wiehe, 2003). Parental alcohol and drug dependence, too, play a significant role in a great many cases (Eiden, Foote & Schuetze, 2007). A third key element is a lack of social support or some degree of social isolation.

Some children who are frequently or severely abused develop *post-traumatic stress disorder (PTSD)*. This disorder involves extreme levels of anxiety, flashback memories of episodes of abuse, nightmares, and other sleep disturbances. For

some, these symptoms persist into adulthood (Koenen, Moffitt, Poulton, Martin, & Caspi, 2007). Abused children are also more likely than nonabused peers to exhibit delays in all domains of development (Cicchetti, Rogosch, Maughan, Toth, & Bruce, 2003). On the positive side, in studies involving abused and/or neglected children who were placed in foster care, developmentalists have found that differences between abused and nonabused children in physical, cognitive, and social development disappear within 1 year (Olivan, 2003). As you might suspect, though, these studies suggest that the critical factor in the catching-up process is the quality of the post-abuse environment.

Questions for Critical Analysis

1. As a researcher, how might you set up a study to determine the qualities that distinguish abuse victims who experience long-term negative consequences from those who appear to experience no lasting effects?

2. What underlying factor or factors might explain the correlation between family stressors such as parental unemployment and child abuse?

---

ists recommend keeping a variety of nutritious foods on hand and allowing a child's appetite to be a good guide to how much food she should eat. Of course, this approach only works if young children's access to sweets and other attractive, but nonnutritious, foods is limited.

During the school years, children become more open to new foods, but different kinds of nutritional problems arise. Many school-aged children make food choices without adult supervision for the first time in their lives. They use their allowances to purchase items from vending machines at school, or they stop at a corner store on the way to or from school. Not surprisingly, school-aged children's food choices in such circumstances are not always wise, and many consume a great deal of "junk" food—sodas, candy bars, and the like—of which their parents may not be aware.

Excessive Weight Gain

Excessive weight gain is one of the most serious health issues of childhood and adolescence. It is a pattern in which children gain more weight in a year than is appropriate for their height, age, and sex. If a child gains excessive amounts of weight over a number of years, she is at risk of having weight problems and a number of serious health problems in adulthood.

A word about terminology is in order here, because you are probably familiar with the term *obesity* with regard to weight problems. For adults, obesity has a fixed definition that is based on the **body mass index (BMI)**, a measure that estimates a person's proportion of body fat. Adults whose BMIs exceed 30 are classified as obese (CDC, 2007e). When referring to children, public health officials speak in terms of excessive weight gain, as defined above, because some degree of increase in BMI occurs naturally in growing children as the ratio of fat to muscle in their bodies changes. Moreover, when prepubertal hormonal changes occur in the later years of middle childhood, girls' BMIs can become temporarily distorted as the accompanying accumulation of fat tissue outpaces the growth of other kinds of tissue. Thus, it would be wrong to conclude that a 10- or 11-year-old girl was obese when what was really happening was that her body was in a transitional stage. Using different terminology helps to

This overweight child not only has different kinds of encounters with his peers—he is also more likely to be overweight as an adult, with all the increased health risks that accompany being overweight.

excessive weight gain A pattern in which children gain more weight in a year than is appropriate for their age height, and sex.

body mass index (BMI) A measure that estimates a person's proportion of body fat.

BMI-for-age Comparison of an individual child's BMI against established norms for his or her age group and sex.

overweight Describes a child whose BMI is at the 95th percentile.

at-risk-for-overweight Describes a child whose BMI is between the 85th and 95th percentiles.

get across the idea that the process of diagnosing weight problems is not the same for children as for adults.

To determine whether an individual child's weight gain is appropriate, health-care professionals use a measure called **BMI-for-age**, a variation on the BMI that applies to adults (CDC, 2007e). A child's BMI-for-age is determined by calculating her BMI and comparing it to those of others her age. Different standards are used for boys and girls, because their BMIs do not increase at the same rate.

Children whose BMIs fall at the 95th percentile (the top 5%) are considered **overweight**, and those whose BMIs fall between the 85th and 95th percentiles are classified as **at-risk-for-overweight** (CDC, 2007e). Because of growth spurts and the inherent instability of physical variables in childhood, multiple assessments are required before a child is actually classified as either, however. As you can see in Figure 4.12, the numbers of overweight children and adolescents in the United States have grown at an alarming rate over the past two decades (NCHS, 2007). Similar increases have been documented in every country in the world that tracks the prevalence of overweight among children and teenagers (Wang & Lobstein, 2006).

The older a child gets without stopping the pattern of excessive weight gain, the more likely the child is to be overweight into the adult years (Magarey, Daniels, Boulton, & Cockington, 2003; Singh, Mulder, Twisk, van Mechelen, & Chinapaw, 2008). Only a fifth of overweight babies become overweight adults, but half of those who are overweight in elementary school continue to be overweight in adulthood (Serdula et al., 1993). In addition, more than half of overweight children have one or more risk factors, such as elevated levels of cholesterol or high blood pressure, that predispose them to heart disease later in life (National Center for Chronic Disease Prevention and Health Promotion [NCCDPHP], 2000).

As you might suspect, overeating or eating too much of the wrong foods causes excessive weight gain in children just as it does in adults (NCCDPHP, 2000). However, both twin and adoption studies suggest that the tendency to gain excessive amounts of weight in childhood probably results from an interaction between a genetic predisposition for obesity and environmental factors that promote overeating or low levels of activity (Stunkard, Harris, Pedersen, & McClearn, 1990; Wardle, Carnell, Haworth, & Plomin, 2008). Whatever the genetic contribution might be, research suggests that a cultural pattern of decreases in physical activity and increases in the consumption of high-calorie convenience foods has led to the current epidemic of overweight children and adults (NCCDPHP, 2000).

It's important to keep in mind, though, that weight-loss diets for children can be fairly risky. Because they are still growing, the nutritional needs of overweight children differ from those of overweight adults (Tershakovec & Stallings, 1998). Consequently, overweight children require special diets developed and supervised by nutritional experts. Moreover, increasing the amount of exercise children get is just as important as changing their eating habits (NCCDPHP, 2000). Experts on weight management in childhood recommend that parents of overweight and at-risk children take the following steps (CDC, 2007e):

Figure 4.12
Prevalence of Overweight among Children and Teens in the United States

The percentages of children and teens who are overweight have increased dramatically over the past two decades.

(*Source*: NCHS, 2007b.)

PART 3 ■ THE PHYSICAL CHILD

- Provide plenty of vegetables, fruits, and whole-grain products.
- Include low-fat or non-fat milk or dairy products.
- Choose lean meats, poultry, fish, lentils, and beans for protein.
- Serve reasonably sized portions.
- Encourage everyone in the family to drink lots of water.
- Limit sugar-sweetened vegetables.
- Limit consumption of sugar and saturated fat.
- Limit children's TV, video game, and computer time.
- Involve the whole family in physical activities such as walking and bicycling.

The prevalence of overweight is somewhat less among adolescents than it is among school-aged children (NCHS, 2007b).One factor that may explain this age difference is that more teens than younger children actively try to lose weight, including those who do not have weight problems. Dieting in adolescence represents the culmination of a trend toward increasing awareness of the social desirability of thinness and knowledge of popular methods of weight loss that is evident among both boys and girls as early as age 7 (Kostanski, Fisher, & Gullone, 2004). Among teenagers, surveys suggest that 40% diet regularly, and 20% use extreme measures such as taking diet pills and fasting (CDC, 2006f; Neumark-Sztainer, Wall, Eisenberg, Story, & Hannan, 2006). As you will learn in Chapter 15, such extreme measures can be indicative of an *eating disorder*, a serious psychological disorder involving distortions of thinking and behavior that go far beyond habitual dieting. In most teens, however, habitual dieting is probably the result of an increased capacity for self-reflection (more on this in Chapter 6).

Poverty and Children's Health

As Table 4.5 suggests, children who live in poverty are at greater risk for a number of health problems than are their peers who are better off (Burgess,

Table 4.5 Comparison of Health Problems of Poor and Nonpoor Children

Problem	Rate for Poor Children Compared to Nonpoor Children
Low birth weight	1.5 to 2 times higher
Delayed immunization	3 times higher
Asthma	Somewhat higher
Lead poisoning	3 times higher
Neonatal mortality	1.5 times higher
Deaths from accidents	2 to 3 times higher
Deaths from disease	3 to 4 times higher
Number reported to be in fair or poor health (rather than good health)	2 times higher
Percentage with conditions limiting school activity	2 to 3 times higher
Physical stunting (being in the 5th percentile or lower for height)	2 times higher
Days sick in bed or lost school days	40 percent higher
Severely impaired vision	2 to 3 times higher
Severe iron-deficiency anemia	2 times higher

Sources: Brooks-Gunn, J., and Duncan, G. J., "The Effect of Poverty on Children," *The Future of Children, 7*(2), 1997, pp. 55–71; Starfield, B., "Childhood Morbidity: Comparisons, Clusters, and Trends," *Pediatrics, 88*, 1991, pp. 519–526.

Table 4.6   Correlates of Poverty and Health

Parent Characteristics	Environmental Characteristics
Health status and history	Child-proofing of environment (e.g., safety latches on cabinets)
Depression	
Parenting skills (e.g., consistent bedtime)	Cleanliness of home, neighborhood, child-care facilities
Health habit instruction (e.g., teaching children how to brush their teeth)	Types of food available in the home
Smoking	Types of foods sold in neighborhood grocery stores
Substance abuse	Medicines available in neighborhood drug stores
Obesity	Seat belts, child safety seats in vehicles
Prenatal care compliance	Mold, pollution, and other respiratory irritants
Knowledge of child development	Access to health care
Enrollment in available health insurance, nutritional support programs	Safe, appropriate sites for motor play in neighborhood
Work schedule	Safe, appropriate toys in home
Unemployment	Access to high-quality child-care programs
Nonparental care arrangements	Level of violence in neighborhood
Education	

Source: Ashiabi & O'Neal, 2007; Burgess, Propper, & Rigg, 2004; Dowd, 2007.

Propper, & Rigg, 2004; Case, Lubotsky, & Paxson, 2002; Currie, Shields, & Wheatley Price, 2004; Currie & Stable, 2003). Nevertheless, researchers typically do not study income in isolation from other variables. Instead, most examine the effects of **socioeconomic status (SES)**—a collective term that includes the economic, occupational, and educational factors that influence a family's relative position in society—on children's health. Such studies show that variables such as employment status, occupation, and parental educational levels predict children's health better than income alone does. Still, identifying risk factors tells us little about why those factors are important.

One possible explanation for this association is access to health care. Yet recent studies comparing poor families in the United States to those in Canada and the United Kingdom, where all citizens have access to free health care, have failed to fully support this hypothesis (Case, Lee, & Paxson, 2007). Children in poor families across all three nations have more health problems than those in more affluent households do. Thus, access to medical care is one piece of the SES-health relationship puzzle in the United States, but it isn't the whole story.

Looking beyond access to care, researchers have identified a number of other variables that may help to explain the association between poverty and children's health (Chen, 2004). For instance, tobacco use is more frequent among adults in low-income households (Gilman, Abrams, & Buka, 2003). As a result, children in lower SES homes are more likely to be exposed to nicotine prior to birth and to second-hand smoke in the early years. Table 4.6 lists several other such factors.

None of the factors in Table 4.6 alone, especially if it is experienced only temporarily, is sufficient to explain the relationship between poverty and children's health. But the presence of several of them in a child's life significantly increases the chances that the child will develop a health problem. However, there are a number of factors that help to protect children from the detrimental effects of the cumulative stressors associated with poverty. These factors in-

socioeconomic status (SES) A collective term that includes the economic, occupational, and educational factors that influence a family's relative position in society.

sensation-seeking A strong desire to experience the emotional and physical arousal associated with risky behaviors such as fast driving and unprotected sex.

clude parental knowledge of child development and a strong social support network (Barrow, Armstrong, Varga, & Boothroyd, 2007; Seo, 2006). Thus, the ultimate effect that living in poverty has on the health of an individual child will depend on the combined effects of the risk and protective factors that are present in the child herself and in her environment. Poverty does not guarantee bad outcomes, but it stacks the deck against many children.

Risky Behavior in Adolescence

Learning Objective 4.18
How do psychologists explain risky behavior in adolescence?

For most individuals, adolescence is one of the healthiest periods of life. However, as adolescents gain independence, they encounter numerous health risks as a result of their own behavioral choices.

Sensation-Seeking   Many teenagers appear to have what developmentalists describe as a heightened level of **sensation-seeking**, or a desire to experience high levels of arousal such as those that accompany high-speed driving or the highs that are associated with drugs. Sensation-seeking leads to recklessness (what most developmental researchers call "risky" or "high-risk" behavior), which, in turn, leads to markedly increased rates of accidents and injuries in this age range. For example, adolescents drive faster and use seat belts less often than adults do (CDC, 2000). To reduce the number of accidents among teenaged drivers, many states in the United States have enacted laws that allow only "graduated" driver's licenses (Cobb, 2000). Sixteen-year-olds can drive in most such states, but they must remain accident- and ticket-free for a certain period of time before they can have privileges such as driving at night.

Risky behaviors may be more common in adolescence than in other periods because such behaviors help teenagers gain peer acceptance and establish autonomy from parents and from other authority figures (Jessor, 1992). However, neurological factors may be important as well. Developmental psychologist Laurence Steinberg suggests that sensation-seeking increases in adolescence because of changes in the brain that prompt teens to focus more on emotional gratification than they did in earlier years (Steinberg, 2008). Sensation-seeking declines, Steinberg says, as the prefrontal cortex matures and enables teens to gain better control of their impulses and to be better able to delay emotional gratification in favor of constructive goals such as academic achievement.

Alcohol and Drug Use   As you can see in Figure 4.13, illicit drug use is somewhat less common among recent cohorts than in past cohorts of teenagers (Johnston, O'Malley, Bachman, & Schulenberg, 2007). Researchers attribute this trend to declining approval of drug use among adolescents and to contemporary teens' better understanding of the negative consequences of taking drugs. Still, experts agree that drug use among teens continues to be a significant problem because of the risks to which teens expose themselves, such as drunk driving and the possibility of life-long addiction, when they use these substances.

Table 4.7 lists the percentages of eighth-, tenth-, and twelfth-grade students who reported using each drug listed in the 12 months preceding the survey. Clearly, as was true in earlier cohorts, marijuana is the illicit substance that teens use most often, but a surprising number of teenagers are using prescription drugs such as Ritalin, OxyContin, and Vicodin. Similar percentages of teens use over-the-counter drugs such as cough medicines. (Note: The figures in the

Figure 4.13
Illicit Drug Use Trends among Teenagers

This figure shows the percentage of teens who admitted to using illicit drugs in the previous 12 months. As you can see, drug use rates have declined since the 1970s.

(*Source*: Johnston, O'Malley, Bachman, & Schulenberg, 2007.)

Table 4.7 Percentages of Teens Who Have Used Illicit Drugs in the Past 12 Months

Drug	8th-graders	10th-graders	12th-graders
Alcohol	34%	56%	67%
Marijuana	12%	25%	32%
Vicodin*	3%	7%	10%
Diet pills*	5%	8%	8%
Tranquilizers*	3%	5%	7%
Over-the-counter cold medicines*	4%	5%	7%
Cocaine	2%	3%	5%
OxyContin*	3%	4%	4%
MDMA (Ecstasy)	1%	3%	4%
Crack cocaine	1%	1%	2%
Ritalin*	3%	4%	4%
Methamphetamine	2%	2%	3%
LSD	<1%	2%	2%
Heroin	1%	1%	1%

*Recreational usage outside the scope of the purpose for which drug is medically approved.

Source: Johnston et al., 2007.

table for such drugs refer only to their use for purposes other than those for which they have been medically approved.) Nevertheless, illicit drug use is far less prevalent than alcohol use among teenagers. Nearly one-third of twelfth-graders reported having been drunk in the month prior to the survey.

Teens who express the most interest in sensation-seeking are those who are most likely to use drugs and consume alcohol (Donohew et al., 1999). Furthermore, teens who are high sensation-seekers choose friends who are similar. Once such groups are formed, sensation-seeking becomes a central feature of their activities. So, for example, if one member tries marijuana or alcohol, others do so as well. However, teens who spend a lot of time alone may also be vulnerable to substance abuse. Researchers have found that shy adolescents, particularly those who are high in neuroticism, are more likely to use alcohol and drugs than are peers who are more outgoing (Kirkcaldy, Siefen, Surall, & Bischoff, 2004).

The use of alcohol and other substances by teens leads to lowered inhibitions, just as it does in adults. However, the degree of disinhibition and the riskiness of the sensation-seeking activities that result from alcohol-induced disinhibition are greater in adolescents (Breyer & Winters, 2005). Furthermore, some studies suggest that the adolescent brain requires more alcohol, marijuana, and other drugs to experience a "high," thereby heightening the risk of immediate adverse responses and long-term dependence on these drugs. Once they become addicted to alcohol or drugs, the effects of these substances on the development of the prefrontal cortex may cause adolescents to lose the ability to judge the value of non-drug rewards, such as grades (Goldstein & Volkow, 2002). For this reason, alcohol and drugs represent enormous threats to a teenager's developmental pathway—yet another reason for parents to be vigilant in monitoring their adolescent children's activities and supporting their development in positive ways.

Smoking Sensation-seeking seems to be less important in tobacco use. Surveys suggest that 12% of U.S. adolescents are regular smokers, and 30% have tried smoking (Johnston, O'Malley, Bachman, & Schulenberg, 2007). Smoking rates have dropped considerably since the mid-1970s, when about 30% of older teenagers were regular smokers. Researchers argue that, thanks to public education campaigns and the inclusion of antismoking information in school curricula, more teenagers are aware of the health consequences of smoking than in earlier cohorts. Moreover, many teens report that they oppose smoking because of its possible effect on their attractiveness to potential romantic partners.

Teenagers who believe they are already in poor health are more likely to smoke than those who think of themselves as healthy (Kirkcaldy, Siefen, Surall, & Bischoff, 2004; Leff et al., 2003). Note, however, that *perceptions* of one's health can be very different from one's actual health status. So, the key here is that teens who begin smoking *believe* their health is poor, regardless of how healthy they may actually be. They also seem to think they have little or no power to affect their future health. In other words, adolescent smokers of this kind have a fatalistic "What have I got to lose?" attitude about smoking because they view themselves as doomed to a future of poor health no matter what they do.

Peer influence plays an important role in teen smoking. When a nonsmoking teenager begins associating with a cohesive group of adolescents among whom smoking is a prominent behavior and a sign of group membership, he is likely to take up the habit too. In fact, some developmentalists advise parents that if their teenaged child's friends smoke, especially close friends with whom the child spends a lot of time, parents should probably assume that their child smokes as well (Urberg, Degirmencioglu, & Pilgrim, 1997). Moreover, the period between ages 15 and 17 seems to be the time during which a teenager is most susceptible to peer influences with regard to smoking (West, Sweeting, & Ecob, 1999). Clearly, then, by monitoring the friends of their 15- to 17-year-olds and discouraging them from associating with smokers, parents may help prevent their teens from smoking (Mott, Crowe, Richardson, & Flay, 1999).

Parental influence is important, too—a pattern that is especially clear for mothers and daughters (Kandel & Wu, 1995). When an adult stops smoking, the likelihood that her children will smoke decreases. Thus, another way to prevent teenaged smoking is to encourage parents to give up the habit. In addition, having a family rule against substance use—including drugs, alcohol, and tobacco—has a lot more influence on teenagers' decisions about using such substances than most parents think (Abdelrahman, Rodriguez, Ryan, French, & Weinbaum, 1998; Mott et al., 1999). Similarly, teens who view smoking as morally wrong are less likely to smoke than peers who do not think of smoking as a moral issue (Taylor et al., 1999). Thus, parents who think tobacco use is morally wrong should discuss their beliefs with their children.

Mortality

Learning Objective 4.19
What are the major causes of death among children and teenagers?

Those of us who live in countries with relatively low rates of infant and childhood mortality are accustomed to thinking of childhood as a basically healthy time. Yet worldwide, over 10% of children die before age 5; in many countries, the rate is higher than 20% (Public Health Policy Advisory Board, 2001). In less developed countries, the most common cause of death is diarrhea, confounded by malnutrition (Dillingham & Guerrant, 2004). In contrast, the leading cause of children's deaths in the United States is accidents, particularly motor vehicle accidents (Hoyert, Kung, & Smith, 2005).

Happily, the rate of childhood deaths in the United States has been declining an average of about 2% every year for the past five decades (Hoyert et al., 2005; Singh & Yu, 1996), suggesting that, as a society, we have begun to control at least some of the causes of mortality, particularly through the use of car seats, seat belts, and bicycle helmets. However, the United States continues to have wide ethnic variation in mortality rates among children. African American children—especially African American boys—have the highest death rates, primarily because of much higher rates of accidents and homicides; Asian American children have the lowest rates, with White American children falling in between (Heron, 2007).

During the teen years, accidents continue to be the most frequent cause of death in most groups in the United States. However, among African Americans, homicide surpasses accidents as the leading cause of death after age 15 (Heron, 2007). In fact, African American teenaged boys are nearly ten times as likely as their White peers to die as a result of homicide. The ratio of African American to White teenaged girls who die as a result of homicide is almost as high, although homicide rates are a great deal lower among females than among males across all ethnic groups. Suicide and accident rates are lower among African American teens than in other ethnic groups. And deaths due to disease occur about as often among African Americans as among other teens. However, the very high incidence of homicide deaths raises the overall mortality rates for African American adolescents higher than that of teens in other groups.

Think Critically

- In this chapter you learned that boys develop fine motor skills at a slower pace than girls do. How do you think this sex difference affects boys' experiences in school?
- What would you say to the parent of an overweight child who said she believed that her son was just carrying some "baby fat" that he was sure to outgrow later in life?

Conduct Your Own Research

Studies of dieting behavior have shown that school-aged and teenaged girls are five or six times as likely as boys to have dieted at least ten times in the past year. Try asking about 20 male and 20 female students how many times they have deliberately tried to lose weight in the past year. Compare your findings to sex differences in dieting rates among children and teenagers. Develop a theory to explain any age differences that you find.

Summary

THE BRAIN AND NERVOUS SYSTEM

4.1 What are the major growth spurts in the brain?

- The brain develops in spurts. Several short spurts occur in the first years, followed by longer periods of growth at about ages 4, 6, 10, 13, and 17.

4.2 What are synaptogenesis and pruning?

- In most parts of the brain, synaptic development (synaptogenesis) reaches its first peak between 12 and 24 months, after which there is an eliminating (pruning) of unnecessary synapses. Periods of synaptic growth followed by pruning of redundant pathways continue to occur throughout childhood and adolescence.

4.3 How does the process of myelination influence brain function?

- Myelination of nerve fibers occurs rapidly in the early years but continues throughout childhood and adolescence. Myelination increases the efficiency of neural transmission. It is a gradual process; only the structures that are needed to support basic life functions are myeli-

nated at birth. Brain structures that are critical to memory and other forms of complex information processing become myelinated later in childhood.

4.4 What are the milestones of the lateralization process?

- Significant changes in brain lateralization happen in early childhood. Some aspects of language function are lateralized. Others are not lateralized until the end of early childhood. Object perception is lateralized in early childhood, but complex spatial perception is not lateralized until age 8. Handedness is weakly related to brain lateralization, but the association between the two is poorly understood at the present time.

SIZE, SHAPE, AND SKILLS

4.5 What patterns of growth are evident in childhood and adolescence?

- Changes in height and weight are rapid during the first 2 years and then level off to a steady pace until adolescence, when a sharp growth spurt occurs.

4.6 In what ways do bones, muscles, and fat change?

- Bones increase in number in some joints (e.g., the wrist) but decrease in quantity in others (e.g., the skull). Bone hardening, or ossification, contributes to development of motor skills. Muscle tissue increases primarily in density and length of fibers, with a much larger increase at adolescence for boys than for girls. Fat cells are added in the early years and then again rapidly at adolescence, in this case more for girls than for boys.

4.7 How does children's ability to use their bodies change?

- Children of 6 or 7 have confident use of most gross motor skills, although there are refinements still to come; fine motor skills needed for many school tasks are not fully developed until sometime in the elementary school years.

THE ENDOCRINE AND REPRODUCTIVE SYSTEMS

4.8 What are the contributions of the various hormones to physical development?

- The physical changes of adolescence are triggered by a complex set of hormonal changes, beginning at about age 8. Very large increases in gonadotrophic hormones, which in turn trigger increased production of estrogen and testosterone, are central to the process.

4.9 What are the sequences of pubertal changes in boys and girls?

- In girls, sexual maturity is achieved in a set of changes beginning as early as age 8 or 9. Menarche occurs relatively late in the sequence. Boys achieve sexual maturity later, with the growth spurt occurring a year or more after the start of genital changes.

4.10 How does the timing of puberty affect teens' development?

- Variations in the rate of pubertal development have some psychological effects. In general, children whose physical development is markedly earlier or later than they expect or desire show more negative effects than do those whose development is "on time."

SEXUAL BEHAVIOR IN ADOLESCENCE

4.11 What are the ethnic, social, and academic factors that predict early sexual behavior?

- Sexual activity among teens has increased in recent decades in the United States. Compared to teens who delay sexual activity until leaving high school, teens who begin sexual activity earlier are less interested in school and more likely to come from poorer families or from families in which sexual activity is condoned, more likely to use alcohol, and more likely to have been abused.

4.12 Which sexually transmitted diseases are common among sexually active teens?

- Adolescents in the United States suffer from a variety of sexually transmitted diseases. The most common STDs among teens are chlamydia and the human papilloma virus (HPV). Most adults support sex education programs to combat the spread of STDs, but there is no consensus regarding the effectiveness of various approaches.

4.13 What are the factors associated with pregnancy in adolescence?

- The risk factors for teen pregnancy include early sexual activity, a low level of parental education, coming from a single-parent home, and being the daughter of a woman who gave birth in adolescence. Long-term consequences for girls who bear children during adolescence are negative on average, although a significant minority of such girls are able to overcome their early disadvantages.

4.14 In what ways are gay, lesbian, bisexual, and transgendered teens different from and similar to their peers?

- Research suggests that both heredity and environment contribute to the development of sexual orientation. Sexual attraction emerges in the early teens for both heterosexual and homosexual teens. Some gay and lesbian teens experiment with both same- and opposite-sex relationships before settling on a homosexual identity. Transgendered teens are those whose psychological gender does not match their biological sex. The cause of transgenderism is unknown, but prenatal hormones may be a factor.

HEALTH AND WELLNESS

4.15 What are the health needs and concerns of children and adolescents?

- Like infants, older children benefit from regular medical check-ups. Many immunizations are required for initial and continued school enrollment. Acute illnesses are a normal part of children's early lives, and accidents are fairly common. Children of all ages need regular check-ups and immunizations.

4.16 In what ways does excessive weight gain threaten the immediate and future health of children and adolescents?

- Excessive weight gain is a pattern in which children gain more weight in a year than is appropriate for their height, age, and sex. If a child gains excessive amounts of weight over a number of years, she is at risk of having weight problems and a number of serious health problems in adulthood.

4.17 How does poverty affect children's health?

- Virtually all forms of physical disability, chronic illness, acute illness, and accidents are more frequent among children living in poverty. Explanations focus on limited access to health care and on more dangerous home and neighborhood situations among the poor, as well as on the effects of parental behaviors such as smoking and substance abuse on children's health.

4.18 How do psychologists explain risky behavior in adolescence?

- Increases in sensation-seeking in adolescence may be caused by changes in the brain. Peer influences and the desire to establish autonomy may also be contributing factors. Sensation-seeking behaviors (e.g., driving too fast) are a significant health risk for this age group. Tobacco, alcohol, and drug use are additional risks for some teens.

4.19 What are the major causes of death among children and teenagers?

- After early infancy, mortality rates are low among children, with most deaths being due to accidents. Among teens, homicide is a significant cause of death, especially for African American males.

Key Terms

association areas (p. 90)
at-risk-for-overweight (p. 112)
BMI-for-age (p. 112)
body mass index (BMI) (p. 111)
bone age (p. 95)
cerebral cortex (p. 87)
corpus callosum (p. 91)
endocrine glands (p. 98)
excessive weight gain (p. 111)
fontanel (p. 95)
gonadotrophic hormones (p. 98)
growth curve (p. 94)
handedness (p. 92)

hippocampus (p. 91)
lateralization (p. 91)
medulla (p. 87)
menarche (p. 100)
midbrain (p. 87)
motor development (p. 96)
myelination (p. 90)
neurotransmitters (p. 88)
ossification (p. 95)
overweight (p. 112)
pituitary gland (p. 98)
plasticity (p. 89)
prefrontal cortex (PFC) (p. 88)

pruning (p. 88)
puberty (p. 98)
relative right-left orientation (p. 92)
reticular formation (p. 90)
secular trend (p. 100)
selective attention (p. 90)
sensation-seeking (p. 115)
sexually transmitted diseases (STDs) (p. 104)
socioeconomic status (SES) (p. 114)
spatial cognition (p. 92)
spatial perception (p. 92)
synaptogenesis (p. 88)

Perceptual Development 5

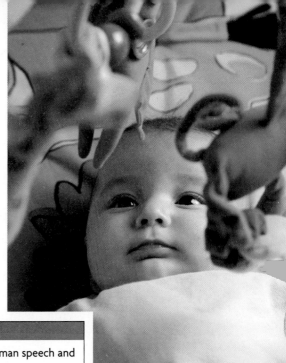

As Julio's school bus drove the familiar route from school to home, the kindergartner thought about how proud he was of himself for learning to recite the Pledge of Allegiance. His kindergarten class had worked on it for weeks, and he couldn't wait to get home and recite it for his mother. When the bus pulled to a stop in front of Julio's family's apartment building, he bounded out of the door and said to his waiting mother, "Mama, I can say the whole pledge. Wanna hear it?"

Julio's mother answered, "Sure, but let's wait until we're inside."

Once inside the apartment, Julio put his backpack down on the sofa and squared his shoulders, clearing his throat as he straightened his shirt a bit. He beamed with pride as he began:

> I pledge allegiance to the flag of the newnited steaks of America and to the republic . . .

When Julio finished, his mother applauded and praised him, but she felt compelled to correct his errors. "That's wonderful, son. I think it could still use a little more practice. For one thing, it's 'united', not 'newnited'," she said.

"What's 'united'?" Julio asked, looking puzzled.

"It means separate things are joined into one, like when you put a puzzle together and the pieces make one big picture," his mother replied.

"Oh, I get it . . . 'united'," Julio said, trying out the new word.

Julio's mother carefully explained each word that he had misunderstood in the pledge and helped him practice reciting it until he could say it perfectly.

We have all heard children make errors like Julio's, and most of us find them to be endearing. You should recall from Chapter 3 that *sensation* is the process of taking in raw sensory information, and *perception* is the process of giving meaning to that information. To put it differently, sensory input comes into the brain from the outside, and we use information that is already stored in the brain to make sense of it. In Julio's case, he was unfamiliar with the word "united," so he connected the sensory information contained in the "ew" sound to a word that he did know, "new." Thus, for Julio, "united" became "newnited."

Julio's mother was able to explain the meanings of the words in the pledge so that he could properly perceive them. But how does the environment explain to babies what they need to know to give meaning to what they see, hear, smell, taste, and feel? As you will learn, some developmentalists argue that babies acquire such knowledge through observing and acting on the world. Others say that there are a few basic perceptual mechanisms that are present in the brain at birth. In this chapter, you will read about this debate, and you will learn what researchers on both sides have discovered about infants' and young children's ability to make sense of the world.

Thinking about Perceptual Development

The study of perceptual development has been significant because it has been a key battleground in the dispute about nature versus nurture—though theorists who study perceptual development refer instead to the contrast between *nativism* and *empiricism*. **Nativism** is the view that most perceptual abilities are inborn. **Empiricism** argues that these skills are learned. This issue has been so central in studies of perception that researchers have focused almost all their attention on young infants; only by observing infants can they observe the organism when it is relatively uninfluenced by specific experience (Bornstein, Arterberry, & Nash, 2005).

nativism The view that perceptual abilities are inborn.

empiricism The view that perceptual abilities are learned.

Learning Objective 5.1
What are the three approaches to studying infants' perceptual skills?

Ways of Studying Early Perceptual Skills

It took a while for psychologists to figure out how to study infants' perceptual skills. Babies can't talk and can't respond to ordinary questions, so how were researchers to decipher just what they could see, hear, or discriminate? Eventually, clever researchers figured out three basic methods for "asking" a baby about what he experiences. With the preference technique, devised by Robert Fantz (1956), the baby is simply shown two pictures or two objects, and the researcher keeps track of how long the baby looks at each one. If many infants shown the same pair of pictures consistently look longer at one picture than the other, this result not only indicates that babies see some difference between the two but also may reveal something about the kinds of objects or pictures that capture babies' attention.

Another strategy takes advantage of the processes of habituation and dishabituation you learned about in Chapter 3. Researchers first present a baby with a particular sight or sound over and over until he habituates—that is, until he stops looking at it or showing interest in it. Then experimenters present another sight or sound or object that is slightly different from the original one and watch to see if the baby shows renewed interest (dishabituation). If the baby does show renewed interest, they know he perceives the slightly changed sight or sound as "different" in some way from the original.

The third option is to use the principles of operant conditioning described in Chapter 1. For example, an infant might be trained to turn her head when she hears a particular sound, using the sight of an interesting moving toy as a reinforcement. After the learned response is well established, the experimenter can vary the sound in some systematic way to see whether the baby still turns her head.

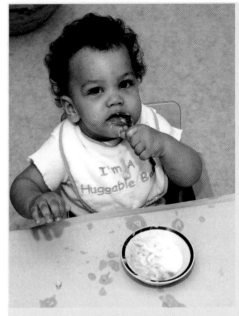

Success! The spoon is in the mouth! At 1 year, Genevieve isn't very skillful yet, but she is already able to coordinate the perceptual and motor skills involved in this complex task at least a bit.

Explanations of Perceptual Development

Learning Objective 5.2
What are the arguments for the nativist and empiricist views of perceptual development?

We noted earlier that the study of perception, more than any other topic in developmental psychology except perhaps intelligence, has been dominated by questions of nature versus nurture, or nativism versus empiricism. Certainly there are other theoretical issues worthy of study, but given the importance of the historical argument between the nativists and the empiricists, it's worthwhile to take a closer look at current understanding of this question about perceptual development.

Arguments for Nativism   It is not hard to find strong arguments for a nativist position on perceptual development. As researchers have become more and more clever in devising ways to test infants' perceptual skills, they have found more and more skills already present in newborns or very young infants: Newborns have good hearing, poor but adequate eyesight, and excellent touch and taste perception. They have at least some color vision and at least a rudimentary ability to locate the source of sounds around them. More impressive still, they are capable of making quite sophisticated discriminations from the earliest days of life, including being able to identify their mothers by sight, smell, or sound.

Newborn or very young babies also do not have to be taught what to look at. There are "rules" for looking, listening, and touching that can be detected at birth. As Kagan puts it: "Nature has apparently equipped the newborn with an initial bias in the processing of experience. He does not, as the 19th-century empiricists believed, have to learn what he should examine" (1971, p. 60). Furthermore, studies on babies' object understanding point to the strong possibility that other "assumptions," or biases about the way the world is organized, may also be built-in.

The fact that the "rules" seem to change with age can also be explained in nativist terms, since the nervous system is undergoing rapid maturation during the early months of life, much of it apparently in an automatic way, as preprogrammed synapses are formed rapidly. Furthermore, these rule changes seem to occur in bursts. One such set of changes seems to occur at about 2 to 3 months, when infants appear to shift away from focusing their eyes on contours or edges and toward more detailed visual analysis of objects or figures. At about the same age, a baby becomes able to track objects smoothly. Another shift seems to occur at about 4 months, when a whole host of discrimination skills, including depth perception and coordination of auditory and visual information, first become evident.

Of course, it is possible that this apparent pileup of changes at 4 months reflects the accidental fact that many researchers have chosen to study babies of this age rather than younger babies. Perhaps, though, one major reason why researchers choose to study babies this age is that they are significantly easier to test—because there has been some underlying maturational shift that makes them more attentive, more able to focus, more stable in state.

Finally, we can find support for a nativist position in comparisons of the perceptual development of babies born after the normal gestational period versus those born preterm or at the normal term. In one such study, Yonas (1981) compared the response of two groups of 6-week-old babies: a group of normal-term babies and a group of babies born 3 to 4 weeks late (postterm). Both sets of infants were tested for depth perception using the method of looming objects. Yonas found that the postterm infants showed more consistent reactions to the looming objects, even though both groups had had precisely the same number of weeks of experience with objects since birth. Thus, it looks as if it is maturational age, and not experience, that matters in this case, which strengthens a nativist, or biological, position.

Arguments for Empiricism

On the other side of the ledger, however, we can find a great deal of evidence from research with other species that some minimum level of experience is necessary to support the development of the perceptual systems—the pattern of environmental effect Aslin calls *maintenance* (see Figure 1.1). For example, animals deprived of light show deterioration of the whole visual system and a consequent decrease in perceptual abilities (Hubel & Weisel, 1963). Likewise, animals deprived of auditory stimuli display delayed or no development of auditory perceptual skills (Dammeijer, Schlundt, Chenault, Manni, & Anteunis, 2002).

It is also possible to find support for the negative version of Aslin's facilitation effect: Infants lacking sufficient perceptual stimulation may develop more slowly. Wayne Dennis's study of orphanage babies in Iran (1960) illustrates this possibility. The infants who didn't have a chance to look at things, to explore objects with hands and eyes and mouth, and who were deprived of the opportunity to move around freely were retarded in the development of both perceptual and motor skills.

Attunement may also occur. Evidence from studies of other species suggests that animals that are completely deprived of visual experiences in the early months of life never develop the same degree of depth perception as do those with full visual experience (Gottlieb, 1976b). The ability to integrate information from different senses also depends on early experience. For instance, you have a good idea about what a particular fabric feels like just by looking at it. That's because of experiences you have had in which you have used both vision and your sense of touch to take in information about fabrics. So, when you see different kinds of fabrics, your brain can make an educated guess about what they feel like without actually touching them. Studies with primates show that the capacity to create links among the various senses fails to develop unless information that requires multiple sensory modalities is present in the environment in the first few months after birth (Batterson, Rose, Yonas, Grant, & Sackett, 2008).

Integrating the Nativist and Empiricist Positions

We can best understand the development of perceptual skills by thinking of it as the result of an interaction between inborn and experiential factors. The relationship between the built-in process and the role of the environment is a little like the difference between a computer's hardware and its software. The perceptual hardware (specific neural pathways, rules for examining the world, a bias toward searching for patterns, and the like) may be preprogrammed, while the software (the program that governs the child's response to a particular real environment) depends on specific experience. A child is able to make visual discriminations between people or among objects within the first few days or weeks of life. That's built into the hardware. The specific discriminations she learns and the number of separate objects she learns to recognize, however, will depend on her experience. She is initially able to discriminate all the sound contrasts that exist in any spoken language, but the specific sound contrasts she eventually focuses on and the actual language she learns depend on the language she hears. The basic system is thus adapted to the specific environment in which the child finds herself. A perfect example of this, of course, is the newborn's ability to discriminate her mother's face from a very similar woman's face. Such a discrimination must be the result of experience, yet the capacity to make the distinction must be built in. Thus, as is true of virtually all dichotomous theoretical disputes, both sides are correct. Both nature and nurture are involved.

Sensory Skills

When developmentalists study sensory skills, they are asking just what information the sensory organs receive. Does the structure of the eye permit infants to see color? Are the structure of the ear and the cortex such that a very young infant can discriminate among different pitches? The common theme running through all of what you will read about sensory skills in this section is that newborns and young infants have far more sensory capacity than physicians or psychologists thought even as recently as a few decades ago. Perhaps because babies' motor skills are so obviously poor, we assumed that their sensory skills were equally poor. But we were wrong.

visual acuity How well one can see.

tracking Following a moving object with the eyes.

Seeing

Learning Objective 5.3
How do infants' visual skills change across the first months of life?

Until 25 or 30 years ago, many medical texts stated that newborn infants were blind. Now we know that the newborn has poorer visual skills than older children but is quite definitely not blind.

Visual Acuity In adults, the usual standard for **visual acuity**—how well one can see—is 20/20 vision. If you have 20/20 vision, you can see and identify something that is 20 feet away that the average person can also see at 20 feet. A person with 20/100 vision, in contrast, has to be as close as 20 feet to see something that the average person can see from 100 feet. In other words, the higher the second number, the poorer the person's visual acuity. At birth, an infant's visual acuity is in the range from 20/200 to 20/400, but it improves rapidly during the first year as a result of all the swift changes occurring in the brain described in Chapter 4, including myelination, dendritic development, and pruning. Most infants reach the level of 20/20 vision by about 2 years of age (Keech, 2002).

The fact that the newborn sees so poorly is not so negative a thing as it might seem at first. Of course, it does mean that a baby doesn't see faraway things very clearly; he probably can't see well enough to distinguish two people standing nearby. But he sees quite well close up, which is all that is necessary for most encounters with the people who care for him or with objects immediately at hand, such as breast, bottle, or mobiles hanging above his crib.

Tracking Objects in the Visual Field When an infant tries to get a spoon in her mouth, one of the things she needs to do is keep her eyes on her hand or the spoon as she moves it toward herself. This process of following a moving object with your eyes is called **tracking**, and you do it every day in a variety of situations. You track the movement of other cars when you are driving; you track as you watch a friend walk toward you across the room; a baseball outfielder tracks the flight of the ball so that he can catch it. Because a newborn infant can't yet move independently, a lot of her experiences with

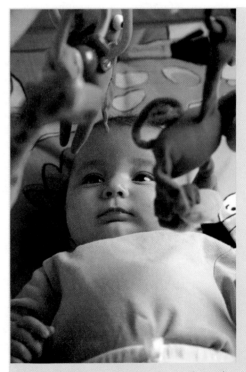

At 2 months, Eleanor's visual acuity is good enough that she can clearly see the colorful mobile hanging above her crib..

6-week-old   **10-week-old**

Figure 5.1 **Infants' Tracking Skills**

The red line in each figure shows the trajectory of the moving line that babies tried to follow with their eyes in Aslin's experiment. The black line represents one baby's eye movements at 6 weeks and again at 10 weeks. At 6 weeks, the baby more or less followed the line, but not smoothly. By 10 weeks, the same baby's tracking skill was remarkably smooth and accurate.

(*Source:* Aslin, Richard N., "Motor Aspects of Visual Development in Infancy," *Handbook of Infant Perception: Vol. 1, From Sensation to Perception*, P. Salapatek and L. Cohen, eds. © 1987 by Academic Press. Adapted by permission.)

objects are with things that move toward her or away from her. If she is to have any success in recognizing objects, she has to be able to keep her eyes on them as they move; she must be able to track.

Studies by Richard Aslin (1987) and others show that tracking is initially fairly inefficient but improves quite rapidly. Infants younger than 2 months show some tracking for brief periods if the target is moving very slowly, but a shift occurs somewhere around 6 to 10 weeks, and babies' tracking becomes skillful rather quickly. You can see the change graphically in Figure 5.1, taken from a study by Aslin.

Color Vision   Researchers have established that the types of cells in the eye necessary for perceiving red and green (the cones) are clearly present by 1 month, perhaps at birth; the cones required for perceiving blue are probably present by then as well (Bornstein et al., 1992). Thus, infants can and do see and discriminate among various colors (Pereverzeva, Hui-Lin Chien, Palmer, & Teller, 2002).

Taken together, research findings on tracking and color vision certainly do not support the notion that an infant is blind at birth. While it is true that the infant's visual acuity is initially poor, it improves rapidly, and other visual capacities are remarkably well developed early on. There are also some interesting hints that some kind of "shifting of gears" may take place at approximately 2 months; a number of skills, including the scanning of objects and tracking, improve incrementally at about that age (Bronson, 1994). But we don't yet know whether such changes are the result of such neurological changes as the rapid proliferation of synapses and the growth of dendrites, of changes in the eye itself, or perhaps of the child's experience.

Hearing and Other Senses

As you learned in Chapter 2, babies can hear long before they are born. However, like vision, hearing improves considerably in the early months of life. The other senses follow a similar course.

Auditory Acuity   Although children's hearing improves up to adolescence, newborns' **auditory acuity**—how well they hear—is actually better than their visual acuity. Research evidence suggests that within the general range of pitch and loudness of the human voice, newborns hear nearly as well as adults do. Only with high-pitched sounds is their auditory acuity less than that of an adult; high-pitched sounds must be louder for a newborn to hear them than for older children or adults (Werner & Gillenwater, 1990).

Detecting Locations   Another basic auditory skill that exists at birth and improves with age is the ability to determine the location of a sound. Because your two ears are separated from one another, sounds arrive at one ear slightly before the other, which allows you to judge location. Only if a sound comes from a source equidistant from the two ears (along the midline) does this system fail. In this case, the sound arrives at the two ears at the same time and you know only that the sound is somewhere on your midline. Newborns can judge at least the general direction from which a sound has come because they turn their heads in roughly the right direction toward some sound. More specific location of sounds, however, is not well developed at birth. For example, Barbara Morrongiello has observed babies' reactions to sounds played at the midline and then sounds coming from varying degrees away from the midline. Among infants 2 months old, it takes a shift of about 27 degrees off midline before the baby shows a changed response; among 6-month-olds, only a 12-degree shift is needed, while by 18 months, discrimination of a 4-degree

auditory acuity How well one can hear.

shift is possible—nearly the skill level seen in adults (Morrongiello, 1988; Morrongiello, Fenwick, & Chance, 1990).

Smelling and Tasting   Babies' senses of smell and taste have been studied much less than other senses. However, we do have some basic knowledge about them. As in adults, the two senses are intricately related—that is, if you cannot smell for some reason (for example, when you have a cold), your taste sensitivity is also significantly reduced. Smell is registered in the mucous membranes of the nose, which can discriminate nearly unlimited variations. The cells of these membranes are present very early on in prenatal development, even before the embryonic phase is complete (Elmas, Erdogan, & Özogul, 2003). Thus, babies come into the world with the equipment they need for smell and are apparently able to use the sense of smell to learn about the world even before they are born. Researchers have found that newborns recognize the odor of their own amniotic fluid and that babies as young as 1 week old can discriminate between their mother's and other women's odors (Doty, 2003; Rattaz, Goubet, & Bullinger, 2005).

Taste is detected by the taste buds on the tongue, which register four basic tastes—sweet, sour, bitter, and salty—and a fifth taste called *umami*—the taste elicited by glutamate, an amino acid in meat, fish, and legumes. Newborns appear to respond differentially to the four basic tastes (Crook, 1987). Some of the clearest demonstrations of this fact come from an elegantly simple set of early studies by Jacob Steiner (Ganchrow, Steiner, & Daher, 1983; Steiner, 1979). Newborn infants who had never been fed were photographed before and after flavored water was put into their mouths. By varying the flavor, Steiner could determine whether the babies reacted differently to different tastes. As you can see in Figure 5.2, babies responded quite differently to sweet, sour, and bitter flavors. Newborns can also taste umami. Generally, they express pleasure when researchers test them for sensitivity to this flavor

| Normal | Sweet | Sour | Bitter |

Figure 5.2   Newborns' Responses to Tastes

These are three of the newborns Steiner observed in his experiments on taste response. The left-hand column shows each baby's normal expression; the remaining columns show the change in expression when they were given sweet, sour, and bitter tastes. What is striking is how similar the expressions are for each taste.

(*Source*: Steiner, J. E., "Human Facial Expressions in Response to Taste and Smell Stimulation," in *Advances in Child Development and Behavior*, Vol. 13, H. W. Reese and L. P. Lipsitt, eds. © 1979 by Academic Press. By permission.)

(Nicklaus, Boggio, & Issanchou, 2005). Some researchers speculate that newborns' preferences for umami-flavored and sweet foods explain their attraction to breast milk, a substance that is naturally rich in sugars and glutamates.

Senses of Touch and Motion The infant's senses of touch and motion may well be the best developed of all. The research you read about in Chapter 3 on the effects of massage on preterm infants illustrates that even the youngest infants are sensitive to touch (Dieter, Field, Hernandez-Reif, Emory, & Redzepi, 2003). Motion perception is clearly present even in the youngest infants, although a considerable degree of fine-tuning takes place over the first year of life (Bosworth & Birch, 2005).

Perceptual Skills

In studies of perceptual skills, developmentalists are asking what the individual does with the sensory information—how it is interpreted or combined. Researchers have found that very young infants are able to make remarkably fine discriminations among sounds, sights, and physical sensations, and they pay attention to and respond to patterns, not just to individual events.

Learning Objective 5.5
How does visual perception change over the first months and years of life?

Looking

One important question to ask about visual perception is whether the infant perceives his environment in the same way as older children and adults. Can he judge how far away an object is by looking at it? Does he visually scan an object in an orderly way? Developmentalists believe that infants' patterns of looking at objects tell a great deal about what they are trying to gain from visual information.

Depth Perception One of the perceptual skills that has been most studied is depth perception. You need this ability any time you reach for something or decide whether you have room to make a left turn before an oncoming car gets to you. Similarly, an infant needs to be able to judge depth in order to perform all kinds of simple tasks, including judging how far away an object is so that he can reach for it, or how far it is to the floor if he has ideas about crawling off the edge of the couch, or how to aim a spoon toward a bowl of chocolate pudding.

It is possible to judge depth using any (or all) of three rather different kinds of information: First, *binocular cues* involve both eyes, each of which receives a slightly different visual image of an object; the closer the object is, the more different these two views are. In addition, information from the muscles of the eyes also tells you something about how far away an object may be. Second, pictorial information, sometimes called *monocular cues*, requires input from only one eye. For example, when one object is partially in front of another one, you know that the partially hidden object is farther away—a cue called *interposition*. The relative size of two similar objects, such as telephone poles or two people you see in the distance, may also indicate that the smaller-appearing one is farther away. Linear perspective (the visual effect that makes railroad tracks seem to get closer together at a distance) is another monocular cue. Third, *kinetic cues* come from either your own motion or the motion of some object: If you move your head, objects near you seem to move more than objects farther away (a phenomenon called *motion parallax*). Similarly, if you see some object moving, such as a person walking across a street or a train moving

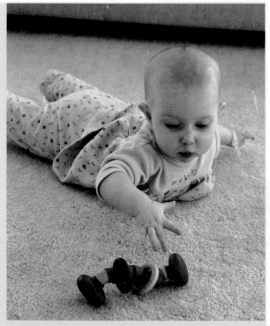

One of the many skills 5-month-old Lucy has to have in order to reach for and grasp her toy is the ability to judge depth. She must determine how far away the toy is and whether it is near enough for her to reach with her hand.

along a track, the closer it is, the more distance it appears to cover in a given time.

How early can an infant judge depth, and which of these cues does he use? This is still an active area of research, so scientists do not have any final answers. The best conclusion at the moment seems to be that kinetic information is used first, perhaps by about 3 months of age; binocular cues are used beginning at about 4 months; and pictorial (monocular) cues are used last, perhaps at 5 to 7 months (Bornstein et al., 1992; Frichtel & Lécuyer, 2006).

In a remarkably clever early study, Eleanor Gibson and Richard Walk (1960) devised an apparatus called a visual cliff. You can see from the photo that it consists of a large glass table with a checkerboard pattern immediately below the glass; on the other side—the "cliff" side—the checkerboard is several feet below the glass. A baby placed on the apparatus could judge depth by several means, but it is primarily kinetic information that

In an experiment using a "visual cliff" apparatus, like the one used by Gibson and Walk, mom tries to entice her baby out onto the "cliff" side. But because the infant can perceive depth, he fears that he will fall if he comes toward her, so he stays put, looking concerned.

would be useful, since the baby in motion would see the nearer surface move more than the farther surface. If a baby has no depth perception, she should be equally willing to crawl on either side of the table, but if she can judge depth, she should be reluctant to crawl out on the "cliff" side.

Since an infant had to be able to crawl in order to be tested in Gibson and Walk's procedure, the babies they studied were all 6 months old or older. Most of these infants did not crawl out on the cliff side but were quite willing to crawl out on the shallow side. In other words, 6-month-old babies have depth perception.

However, the development of depth perception, or *stereopsis*, as the mature form of this visual perceptual skill is called, is far from complete at age 6 months. In order to exhibit adult levels of stereopsis, children's brains must be able to fully fuse the images they receive from the eyes into a single image. This process, called *binocular fusion*, develops over the first 10 years of life (Gabbard, 2008). The attainment of binocular fusion, and the improvements in stereopsis that accompany it, is the main reason that children's throwing and catching skills improve markedly in later childhood.

What Babies Look At   Even though a baby cannot judge depth right away, her behavior is governed by visual information from the very first minutes of life. From the beginning, babies look at the world around them in a nonrandom way. In Marshall Haith's phrase (1980), there are "rules babies look by." Furthermore, those rules seem to change with age.

In the first 2 months, a baby's visual attention is guided by a search for meaningful patterns (Bornstein, Arterberry, & Nash, 2005). Babies scan the world around them—not very smoothly or skillfully, to be sure, but nonetheless regularly, even in the dark. This general scanning continues until they come to a sharp light/dark contrast, which typically signals the edge of some object. Once she finds such an edge, a baby stops searching and moves her eyes back and forth across and around the edge. Thus, the initial rule seems to be: Scan till you find an edge and then examine the edge. Motion also captures a baby's attention at this age, so she will look at things that move as well as things with a noticeable light/dark contrast.

These rules seem to change between 2 and 3 months of age, perhaps because by then the cortex has developed more fully. At about this time, the baby's attention seems to shift from where an object is to what an object is. To put this another way, the baby seems to move from a strategy designed primarily for finding things to a strategy designed primarily for identifying things. Babies this age begin to scan rapidly across an entire figure rather than concentrating on edges. As a result, they spend more time looking at the internal features of some object or array of objects and are thus better able to identify the objects.

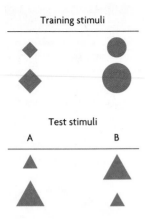

Training stimuli

Test stimuli

A   B

Figure 5.3
Pattern Recognition

In the Carons' study, the researchers first habituated each baby to a set of training stimuli (all "small over large" in this case). Then they showed each baby two test stimuli: one that had the same pattern as the training stimuli (A) and one that had a different pattern (B). Babies aged 3 and 4 months showed renewed interest in stimulus B but not stimulus A, indicating that they were paying attention to the pattern and not just specific stimuli.

(*Source*: This figure was published in *Pre-Term Birth and Psychological Development*, by S. Friedman and M. Sigman, "Processing of relational information as an index of infant risk," in A. J. Caron and R. F. Caron (Eds.), *Pre-Term Birth and Psychological Development*, pp. 227–228, © 1981 by Academic Press. Reprinted by permission.)

What is amazing about this shift at about 3 months is the degree of detail infants seem to be able to take in and respond to. They notice whether two pictures are placed horizontally or vertically, they can tell the difference between pictures with two things in them and pictures with three things in them, and they clearly notice patterns, even such apparently abstract patterns as "big thing over small thing."

One early study that illustrates this point particularly well was done by Albert and Rose Caron (1981), who used "training stimuli" in a habituation procedure. The babies were first shown a series of pictures that shared some particular relationship, such as "small over big." After the baby stopped being interested in the training stimuli (that is, after he habituated), the Carons showed him another figure (the "test stimulus") that either followed the same pattern or followed some other pattern, such as those in Figure 5.3. If the baby had really habituated to the pattern of the original pictures (small over big), he should show little interest in a picture like test stimulus A ("Ho hum, same old boring small over big thing"), but he should show renewed interest in test stimulus B ("Hey, here's something new!"). Caron and Caron found that 3- and 4-month-old children did precisely that. So even at this early age, babies find and pay attention to patterns, not just to specific stimuli.

Researchers have also been interested in babies' perception of faces. Brain-imaging studies suggest that there is an area of the brain dedicated to face processing in both adults and infants as young as 3 months of age (Johnson, 2005). Moreover, among faces, babies clearly prefer some to others. They prefer attractive faces (an intriguing result discussed in *Thinking about Research*), and it now seems apparent that they prefer the mother's face from the earliest hours of life (Bushnell, 2001). Recent research indicates that recognition of the mother's voice directs the newborn's attention to her face (Sai, 2005). Recall from Chapter 3 that maternal voice recognition happens prenatally. After birth, once the association between the mother's voice and her face has happened, the newborn spends more time looking at her face than at other visual stimuli, setting the stage for the formation of a memory for the face.

Beyond the issue of preference, there is also the question of just what it is that babies are looking at when they scan a face. Before about 2 months of age, babies seem to look mostly at the edges of the faces (the hairline and the chin), a conclusion buttressed by the finding by Pascalis and his colleagues (1995) that newborns could not discriminate mom's face from a stranger's if the hairline was covered. After 4 months, however, covering the hairline did not affect the baby's ability to recognize mom. In general, babies appear to begin to focus on the internal features of a face, particularly the eyes, at about 2 to 3 months.

THINKING ABOUT RESEARCH

Langlois's Studies of Babies' Preferences for Attractive Faces

Many studies on infant perception seem to point toward the conclusion that more perceptual rules are built-in than had been supposed. One such built-in rule appears to be a preference for attractive faces. In the first study in an important series of experiments, Langlois and her colleagues (1987) tested 2- to 3-month-olds and 6- to 8-month-olds. Each baby was shown color slides of adult Caucasian women, half rated by adult judges as attractive, half rated as unattractive. On each trial, the baby saw two slides simultaneously, with each face approximately life-size, while the experimenter peeked through a hole in the screen to count the number of seconds the baby looked at

each picture. Each baby saw some attractive/attractive pairs, some unattractive/unattractive pairs, and some mixed pairs. With mixed pairs, even the 2- and 3-month-old babies consistently looked longer at the attractive faces. Several later studies, including some in which pictures of individuals of different races were used, produced similar findings (Langlois, Ritter, Roggman, & Vaughn, 1991; Langlois, Roggman, & Rieser-Danner, 1990).

It is hard to imagine what sort of learning experiences could account for such a preference in a 2-month-old. Instead, these findings raise the possibility that there is some inborn template for the "correct" or "most desired" shape and configura-

tion for members of our species, and that we simply prefer those who match this template better.

Questions for Critical Analysis

1. If there is an inborn template that is used as a standard against which faces are compared, how might such a template affect our interactions with others?

2. How would researchers determine the degree to which attractiveness affects adults' perceptions of infants' faces? Why would such research be unable to tell us whether the concept of attractiveness is inborn?

Listening

When we turn from looking to listening, we find similarly intriguing indications that very young infants not only make remarkably fine discriminations among individual sounds but also pay attention to patterns. Early studies established that babies as young as 1 month old can discriminate between speech sounds such as *pa* and *ba* (Trehub & Rabinovitch, 1972). Studies using conditioned head-turning responses have shown that by perhaps 6 months of age, babies can discriminate between two-syllable "words" such as *bada* and *baga* and can even respond to a syllable that is hidden inside a string of syllables, as in *tibati* or *kobako* (MacWhinney, 2005).

Even more striking is the finding that babies are actually better at discriminating some kinds of speech sounds than adults are. Each language uses only a subset of all possible speech sounds. Japanese, for example, does not use the *l* sound that appears in English; Spanish makes a different distinction between *d* and *t* than occurs in English. It turns out that up to about 6 months of age, babies can accurately discriminate all sound contrasts that appear in any language, including sounds they do not hear in the language spoken to them. At about 6 months of age, they begin to lose the ability to distinguish pairs of vowels that do not occur in the language they are hearing; by age 1, the ability to discriminate nonheard consonant contrasts begins to fade (Dietrich, Swingley, & Werker, 2007).

Some of the best evidence on this point comes from the work of Janet Werker and her colleagues (Werker & Desjardins, 1995; Werker & Tees, 1984). They have tested 6- and 10-month-old infants on various consonant pairs, including one pair that is meaningful in English (*ba* versus *da*); a pair that occurs in a North American Indian language, Salish (*ki* versus *qi*); and one from Hindi, a language from the Indian subcontinent (*t.a* versus *ta*). Other infants were tested with both English and German vowel contrasts. Figure 5.4 shows the results on contrasts that do not occur in English for babies growing up in English-speaking families. You can see that at 6 months, these babies could still readily hear the differences between pairs of foreign consonants but were already losing the ability to discriminate foreign vowels. Infants aged 10 and 12 months could not readily hear either type of contrast. Similarly, Werker has found that 12-month-old Hindi infants can easily discriminate a Hindi contrast but not an English contrast. So each group of infants loses only the ability to distinguish pairs that do not appear in the language they are hearing.

Researchers have also found that babies are sensitive to the intonational and stress patterns of the speech they are listening to. For example, Anne Fernald (1993) has found that 5-month-olds will smile more when they hear tapes of adults saying something in a positive or approving tone than when they hear someone speaking in a negative tone, whether the words are in Italian, German, or English. By 8 months, babies demonstrate clear preferences for the language most often spoken by their mothers (MacWhinney, 2005). Even more impressive is a study showing that by 9 months of age, babies listening to English prefer to listen to words that use the typical English pattern of stress on the first syllable (such as *fal*ter, *com*et, or *gen*tle) rather than those that stress the second syllable (e.g., com*ply* or as*sign*) (Jusczyk & Hohne, 1997). Presumably, babies listening to another language would prefer listening to whatever stress pattern was typical of that language. All this research shows that very early on—from birth and perhaps even before birth—the baby is paying attention to crucial features of the language she hears, such as stress and intonation.

Figure 5.4 Werker's Studies of Speech Perception

These data from Werker's studies are for babies growing up in English-speaking families, but she has similar results from infants in families that speak Hindi and families that speak Salish. In every case, 6-month-olds can still "hear" the distinctions between consonant pairs that do not occur in their family's language, but by 12 months that ability has largely disappeared. Discrimination of nonheard vowel pairs disappears even earlier.

(*Source:* "Listening to Speech in the First Year of Life: Experimental Influences on Phoneme Perception" by Werker and Desjardins, *Current Directions in Psychological Science*, Vol. 4, No. 3 (June 1995), p. 80, Fig. 2. By permission of Blackwell Publishers.)

Pattern perception is also evident; research shows that, by 5 months of age, infants can recognize their own names (Newman, 2005). Studies that examine infants' responses to music show that babies have an uncanny ability to recognize patterns of sounds as well (Trehub, 2003). Infants respond to dissonant notes (i.e., tones that don't sound pleasant when played together) just as adults do (Trainor, Tsang, & Cheung, 2002). Likewise, they recognize familiar melodies, no matter what key they are played in. They also notice when a familiar melody is played on an instrument that differs from the one with which they were familiarized with the song (Trainor, Anonymous, & Tsang, 2004). Likewise, they can discriminate between songs that have different meters, such as waltzes and marches.

Interestingly, too, infants are able to recognize another universal in infant-directed singing—the distinction between play songs (e.g., "The Itsy-Bitsy Spider") and lullabies (e.g., "Rock-a-Bye Baby"). Babies respond to lullabies by turning their attention toward themselves and playing with their hands or sucking their thumbs (Rock, Trainor, & Addison, 1999). In contrast, they display externally directed responses to play songs and behave in ways that seem to encourage adults to continue singing (Rock et al., 1999). This ability to discriminate song type may arise out of the capacity to recognize the emotional characteristics of a piece of music, another aspect of musical perception that appears early in life (Adachi, Trehub, & Abe, 2004; Schmidt, Trainor, & Santesso, 2003).

Learning Objective 5.7

What is intermodal perception, and when does it develop?

Combining Information from Several Senses

If you think about the way you receive and use perceptual information, you'll realize that you rarely have information from only one sense at a time. Ordinarily, you have both sound and sight, touch and sight, or still more complex combinations of smell, sight, touch, and sound. Psychologists have been interested in knowing how early an infant can combine such information. For example, how early can an infant integrate information from several senses, such as knowing which mouth movements go with which sounds? Even more complex, how early can a baby learn something via one sense and transfer that information to another sense (for example, at what age can a child recognize solely by feel a toy he has seen but never felt before)? This skill is usually called **intermodal perception**.

Piaget believed that intermodal perception was not present until quite late in the first year of life, after the infant had accumulated many experiences with specific objects and how they simultaneously looked, sounded, and felt. Other theorists, including the eminent perceptual psychologists James J. Gibson (1904–1979) and Eleanor J. Gibson (1910–2002), have argued that some intersensory integration or even transfer is built in at birth (Gibson, 2002). The baby then augments that inborn set of skills with specific experience with objects. Research favors the Gibsonian view: Empirical findings show that intermodal perception is possible as early as 1 month and becomes common by 6 months (Rose & Ruff, 1987; Schweinle & Wilcox, 2004). Moreover, research comparing these skills in children born prematurely and those born at term suggests that basic maturational processes play an important role in their development (Espy et al., 2002).

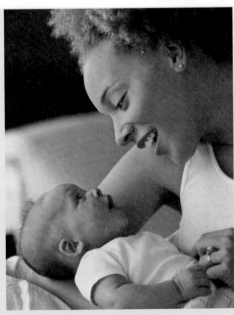

At 3 weeks, this infant can already discriminate her mother's face from the face of another woman; she can also identify mom by voice and smell.

intermodal perception
Formation of a single perception of a stimulus that is based on information from two or more senses.

Research also suggests that intermodal perception is important in infant learning. One group of researchers found that babies who habituated to a combined auditory-visual stimulus were better able to recognize a new stimulus than infants who habituated to either the auditory or the visual stimulus alone (Bahrick & Lickliter, 2000). For example, suppose you played a videotape of someone singing for one baby, played the videotape without the sound for another, and played an audio recording of the song for a third. Research suggests that the first baby would recognize a change in either the singer (visual stimulus) or the song (auditory stimulus) more quickly than either of the other two infants.

In older children, intermodal perception can be readily demonstrated. For instance, in several delightfully clever early experiments, Elizabeth Spelke showed that 4-month-old infants can connect sound rhythms with movement (1979). She showed babies two films simultaneously, one showing a toy kangaroo bouncing up and down, the other a donkey bouncing up and down, with one of the animals bouncing at a faster rate. Out of a loudspeaker located between the two films, the infant heard a tape recording of a rhythmic bouncing sound that matched the bounce pattern of one of the two animals. In this situation, babies showed a preference for looking at the film showing the bounce rate that matched the sound.

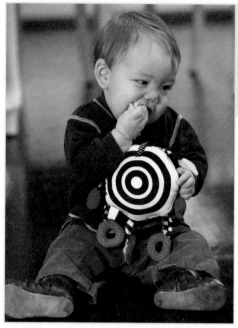

Even though 7-month-old Leslie is not looking at this toy while she chews on it, she is nonetheless learning something about how it ought to look based on how it feels in her mouth and in her hands—an example of intermodal perception.

An even more striking illustration of the same basic process comes from the work of Jeffery Pickens (1994). He showed 5-month-old babies two films side by side; each film showed a train moving along a track. Then out of a loudspeaker he played various sequences of engine sounds, such as getting gradually louder (thus appearing to come closer) or getting gradually fainter (thus appearing to be moving away). The babies in this experiment looked longer at the film of the train whose movement matched the pattern of engine sounds. That is, they appeared to have some understanding of the link between the pattern of sound and the pattern of movement—knowledge that demonstrates not only intermodal perception but also surprisingly sophisticated understanding of the accompaniments of motion.

perceptual constancies A collection of mental rules that allow humans to perceive shape, size, and color as constant even when perceptual conditions (such as amount of light, angle of view, and the like) change.

size constancy The ability to see an object's size as remaining the same despite changes in size of the retinal image; a key element in size constancy is the ability to judge depth.

Ignoring Perceptual Information

Learning Objective 5.8
What are perceptual constancies, and when are they important to perception?

Although babies are remarkably skillful at making perceptual discriminations of various kinds, they must acquire another, very different, kind of perceptual skill: the ability to ignore some kinds of perceptual data. Specifically, the child must acquire a set of rules called **perceptual constancies**.

When you see someone walking away from you, the image of the person on your retina actually becomes smaller. Yet you don't see the person getting smaller, but rather as the same size and moving farther away. When you do this, you are demonstrating **size constancy**; you are able to see the size as constant even though the retinal image has changed. Other constancies include the ability to recognize that shapes of objects are the same even though you are looking at them from different angles, called (logically enough) **shape constancy**, and the ability to recognize that colors are constant even though the amount of light or shadow on them changes, called **color constancy**.

Taken together, the several specific constancies add up to the larger concept of **object constancy**, which is the recognition that objects remain the same even when the sensory information you have about them has changed in some way. Babies begin to show signs of these constancies at 3 or 4 months of age and become more skilled over the first several years (Kavšek, 2002). Think about shape constancy as an illustration.

Shape constancy has perhaps the most obvious day-to-day relevance for a baby. She has to realize that her bottle is still her bottle even though it is turned slightly and thus presents

shape constancy The ability to see an object's shape as remaining the same despite changes in the shape of the retinal image; a basic perceptual constancy.

color constancy The ability to see the color of an object as remaining the same despite changes in illumination or shadow.

object constancy The general phrase describing the ability to see objects as remaining the same despite changes in sensory information about them.

a different shape to her eyes; she has to figure out that her toys are the same when they are in different positions. The beginnings of this understanding seem to be present by about 2 or 3 months of age. The classic study was done by Thomas Bower (1966), who first trained 2-month-old babies to turn their heads when they saw a particular rectangle. He then showed them tilted or slightly turned images of the same rectangle to see if the babies would respond to these as "the same," even though the retinal image cast by these tilted rectangles was actually a trapezoid and not a rectangle at all. Two-month-olds did indeed continue to turn their heads to these tilted and turned rectangles, showing that they had some shape constancy.

The Object Concept

Acquiring the various perceptual constancies is only part of a larger task facing the child; he must also figure out the nature of objects themselves. First of all, an infant must somehow learn to treat some combinations of stimuli as "objects" but not others, a process usually referred to as *object perception*. A still more sophisticated aspect of the infant's emerging concept of objects is the understanding that objects continue to exist even when they are out of view, an understanding usually referred to as **object permanence**.

object permanence The understanding that objects continue to exist even when they cannot be directly viewed.

Learning Objective 5.9
What kinds of rules do infants appear to use in perceiving objects?

Object Perception

The most thorough and clever work on object perception in infants has been done by Elizabeth Spelke and her colleagues (Spelke & Kinzler, 2007). Spelke believes that babies are born with certain built-in assumptions about the nature of objects. One of these is the assumption that when two surfaces are connected to each other, they belong to the same object; Spelke calls this the *connected surface principle*. To study this (Spelke, 1982), she first habituated some 3-month-old babies to a series of displays of two objects; other babies were habituated to the sight of one-object displays. Then the babies were shown two objects touching each other, such as two square blocks placed next to each other so that they created a rectangle. Under these conditions, the babies who had been habituated to two-object displays showed renewed interest, clearly indicating that they "saw" this as different, presumably as a single object. Babies who had seen the one-object displays during habituation showed no renewed interest. Spelke has also shown that babies as young as 2 and 3 months old are remarkably aware of the kinds of movements objects are capable of, even when the objects are out of sight. They expect an object to continue to move on its initial trajectory, and they show surprise if the object's movement violates this expectancy. They also seem to have some awareness that solid objects cannot pass through other solid objects.

In one experiment, Spelke (1991) used the procedure shown schematically in the upper part of Figure 5.5. Two-month-old babies were repeatedly shown a series of events like that in the

Figure 5.5   Spelke's Classic Study of Object Perception

The top part of the figure shows a schematic version of the three conditions Spelke used. The graph below the conditions shows the actual results. You can see that the babies stopped looking at the ball and screen after a number of familiarization trials, but they showed renewed interest in the inconsistent version—a sign that the babies saw this as somehow different or surprising. The very fact that the babies found the inconsistent trial surprising is itself evidence that infants as young as 2 months have far more knowledge about objects and their behavior than most developmentalists had thought.

(*Source: Epigenesis of Mind: Essays on Biology and Cognition* by E. S. Spelke. Copyright 1991 by Taylor & Francis Group LLC-Books. Reproduced with permission of Taylor & Francis Group LLC-Books and the author in format Textbook via Copyright Clearance Center. © 1991 by Lawrence Erlbaum Associates, Inc. By permission of the publisher and author.)

"familiarization" section of the figure: A ball was rolled from the left-hand side to the right and disappeared behind a screen (the dashed line in Figure 5.5). The screen was then taken away and the baby could see that the ball was stopped against the wall on the right. After the baby got bored looking at this sequence (habituated), he or she was tested with two variations, one "consistent" and one "inconsistent." In the consistent variation, a second wall was placed behind the screen and the sequence was conducted as before, except now when the screen was removed, the ball could be seen resting up against the nearer wall. In the inconsistent variation, the ball was surreptitiously placed on the far side of the new wall. When the screen was removed, the ball was visible in this presumably impossible place. Babies in this experiment were quite uninterested in the consistent condition but showed sharply renewed interest in the inconsistent condition, as you can see in the lower part of Figure 5.5, which shows the actual results of the experiment.

Spelke is not suggesting that all of a child's knowledge of objects is built-in; she is suggesting that some rules are built-in and that others are learned through experience. Other researchers, such as Renée Baillargeon (1994, 2008), argue that basic knowledge is not built-in, but that strategies for learning are innate. According to this view, infants initially develop basic hypotheses about the way objects function—how they move, how they connect to one another. These early basic hypotheses are quite rapidly modified, based on the baby's experience with objects. For example, Baillargeon finds 2- to 3-month-old infants are already operating with a basic hypothesis that an object will fall if it isn't supported by something, but they have no notion of how much support is required. By about 5 months of age, this basic hypothesis has been refined, and they understand that the smiling-face block in the upper arrangement of Figure 5.6 (condition a) will stay supported, but the block in the bottom arrangement (condition b) will not (Baillargeon, 1994). However, other psychologists question Baillargeon's conclusions. For example, developmental psychologist Leslie Cohen and his associates have conducted similar experiments with 8-month-olds, and they argue that infants respond to the stimuli used in such studies on the basis of novelty rather than because of an understanding of stable and unstable block arrangements (Cashon & Cohen, 2000). Such varying interpretations demonstrate just how difficult it is to make inferences about infants' thinking from their interactions with physical objects.

Recent research has also examined the degree to which infants can make practical use of their understanding of objects and object movements. For example, several studies have shown that 2-year-olds experience difficulty when they are required to use this understanding to search for a hidden object (Kloos, Haddad, & Keen, 2006). In one study, 2-, 2.5-, and 3-year-olds were shown a display similar to that in the top portion of Figure 5.5 and responded in exactly the same way as younger infants to the consistent and inconsistent displays (Berthier, DeBlois, Poirier, Novak, & Clifton, 2000). Next, a board in which there were several doors took the place of the screen; however, the barrier protruded several inches above this board (see Figure 5.7). Across several trials, children were shown the ball rolling behind the board and were asked to open the door behind which they thought the ball would be found. Even though the children could clearly see behind which door the barrier was placed in every trial, none of the 2-year-olds and only a few of the 2.5-year-olds were able to succeed on this task, in contrast to the large majority of 3-year-olds. Developmentalists

Figure 5.6
Baillargeon's Study of Object Perception

Renée Baillargeon's research suggests that 2- and 3-month-old babies think that the smiling-face block will not fall under either of these conditions, but by 5 months, they realized that only the condition shown in (a) is stable. In condition (b), the block will fall.

(*Source*: "How Do Infants Learn About the Physical World?" by Baillargeon, R., *Current Directions in Psychological Science*, Vol. 3, No. 5 (October 1994), p. 134, Fig. 1. By permission of Blackwell Publishers.)

Figure 5.7   Toddlers' Understanding of Object Movement

Researchers use devices such as this one to find out whether toddlers can predict that a moving object will be stopped by the barrier that protrudes above the wall of doors. Children younger than 3 typically fail to identify the door behind which the object will be found.

interpret such results to mean that young infants' understanding of objects is the foundation upon which the object concept is gradually constructed and applied to real-world interaction with objects over the first 3 years of life (Mash, Novak, Berthier, & Keen, 2006).

Learning Objective 5.10
What is object permanence, and how does it develop?

Object Permanence

The study of object perception is a rather new area of research. In contrast, object permanence has been extensively studied. This has happened in large part because this particular understanding was strongly emphasized in Piaget's theory of infant development (Piaget & Inhelder, 1969).

Stages in the Development of Object Permanence According to Piaget's observations, replicated frequently by later researchers, the first sign that a baby is developing object permanence comes at about 2 months of age. Suppose you show a toy to a child of this age and then put a screen in front of the toy and remove the toy. When you then take away the screen, the baby shows some indication of surprise, as if she knew that something should still be there. The child thus seems to have a rudimentary schema, or expectation, about the permanence of an object. However, infants of this age show no signs of searching for a toy they may have dropped over the edge of the crib or that has disappeared beneath a blanket or behind a screen—a pattern of reaction that parents take advantage of when an infant is fussing for some toy or object he can't reach or when they want him to stop fooling with some object. So, with young infants, there is a fleeting concept of the permanence of objects, but it isn't yet well developed enough to motivate them to search for a hidden object.

At about 6 or 8 months of age, this begins to change. Babies of this age look over the edge of the crib for the dropped toy or over the edge of the high chair for food that was spilled. (In fact, babies of this age may drive their parents nuts playing "dropsy" in the high chair.) Infants this age will also search for partially hidden objects. If you put a favorite toy under a cloth but leave part of it sticking out, the infant will reach for the toy, which suggests that in some sense the infant recognizes that the whole object is there even though she can see only part of it. Yet if you cover the toy completely with the cloth or put it behind a screen, the infant will stop looking at it and will not reach for it, even if she has seen you put the cloth over it.

This changes again somewhere between 8 and 12 months. At this age, the "out of sight, out of mind" parental strategy no longer works at all. Infants this age will reach for or search for a toy that has been covered completely by a cloth or hidden by a screen. Thus, by 12 months, most infants appear to grasp the basic fact that objects continue to exist even when they are no longer visible.

Object constancy has intrigued researchers and theorists in part because it forms one kind of bridge between studies of perception and studies of early cognitive development. Many developmentalists have also been struck by a possible link between the emergence of object constancy and the infant's earliest attachment. It seems reasonable to assume that some kind of object permanence is required before a baby can become attached to an individual person, such as his mother or father. Since clear single attachments don't appear much before 5 months, right about the time that the baby is showing signs of object permanence, the connection seems very reasonable.

Interestingly, and surprisingly to a lot of developmentalists, most direct tests of this hypothesis have not shown much sign of such a causal link. Still, the problem may be with the research techniques rather than the hypothesis. As John Flavell (1985, p. 135) wonders, "However could a child persistently yearn and search for a specific other person if the child were still cognitively incapable of mentally representing that person in the person's absence?" Flavell's logic is persuasive, but as usual we will have to wait for further research evidence to be sure.

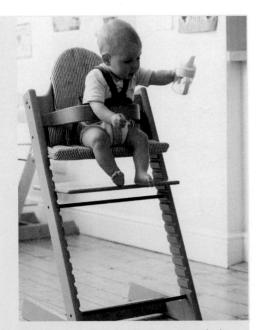

Piaget proposed that infants' experiments with objects, like playing "dropsy," help them acquire object permanence.

Object Permanence and Cultural Practices It might seem that experiences manipulating objects contribute to the development of object permanence. However, Susan Goldberg's classic longitudinal study of 38 Zambian infants (1972) indicated that this is not the case. From shortly after birth, Zambian babies are carried about in slings on their mothers' backs. They spend very little time on the floor or in any position in which they have much chance of independent movement until they are able to sit up at about 6 months. At that point they are usually placed on a mat in the yard of the house. From this vantage the baby can watch all the activity around the house and in the neighborhood, but he has few objects to play with.

Yet despite this very limited experience manipulating objects, tests of object permanence showed that, on average, the Zambian babies were ahead of U.S. babies on a measure of the object concept at 6 months of age. At 9 and 12 months of age, the Zambian babies were slightly behind U.S. babies, but Goldberg believes that this difference is due not to any cognitive failure but to the fact that at these ages the Zambian babies were quite unresponsive and passive toward objects and thus were very difficult to test. She observed that Zambian adults actively discourage older infants from touching and manipulating objects, and so, she hypothesized, the infants may have interpreted the objects in the experiment to be things that they weren't supposed to respond to. Nevertheless, Goldberg's research revealed a clear progression toward object permanence across the first 18 months of life that was quite similar to that observed in Western infants.

Infants who are carried in slings for several hours each day have limited opportunities to manipulate objects, yet researchers have found that they better understand objects and their movements at 6 months of age than babies in other cultures do. However, in later infancy, these babies develop object concepts more slowly, because, according to researchers, adults actively discourage them from touching and manipulating objects.

Perception of Social Signals

The description of the infant's ability to discriminate faces presented earlier in this chapter treats faces as if they were purely physical objects, with fixed properties such as eye characteristics, hairlines, and so forth. But, of course, other people's faces also provide social signals in the form of varying emotional expressions. Variations in vocal intonations and body language similarly provide social cues. These are important bits of information for a baby to detect and decipher. Parents, teachers, and other adults convey a great deal of information through their emotional expression. In peer interactions, too, the ability to read another's emotion is essential for any kind of sustained cooperative play or for the subtle adaptations required for the formation of enduring friendships.

Early Discrimination of Emotional Expressions

Research evidence suggests that infants begin to pay attention to social/emotional cues in faces at about 2 or 3 months of age. For example, at that age, infants begin to smile more to human faces than to a doll's face or another inanimate object, suggesting that at this early stage, the baby is already responding to the added social signals available in the human face (Nelson, de Haan, & Thomas, 2006). The orientation of the face seems to be one critical ingredient in this early preferential smiling. Albert Caron and his colleagues (1997) found that babies smile more only when the face is turned toward them; if the face is turned aside, the baby does not smile more.

Infants this age are also beginning to notice and respond differently to variations in others' emotional expressions. Initially, they discriminate emotions best when they receive information on many channels simultaneously—such as when they see a particular facial expression and hear the corresponding emotion expressed in the adult's voice

Infant Responses to Maternal Depression

Marsha, a new mother, had just been diagnosed with postpartum depression. Her doctor assured her that there was a good chance that the antidepressants she had begun taking, along with the psychotherapist he had recommended, would enable her to pull out of the depression in a few weeks. Still, Marsha told her psychotherapist that she worried about how her depression might affect her 1-month-old's development. In response, the therapist encouraged Marsha to participate in a training program designed to help depressed mothers recognize how their illness was affecting their parenting behaviors. Further, the program would help Marsha learn how to exhibit more effective parenting behaviors in their place.

Marsha was right to be concerned about the effects of her own depression on her baby's development. For one thing, one of the characteristics of people who suffer from depression is the exhibition of sad facial expressions even in situations in which they feel happy. And, as you've learned, babies use parents' facial expressions to guide them in the expression of their own emotions. So, what are the effects on babies of day-to-day interactions with a depressed mother?

Developmentalists have found that babies who interact regularly with depressed mothers express more negative and fewer positive emotions. They smile less, show more sad and angry facial expressions, and are more disorganized and distressed (Dawson, Panagiotides, Klinger, & Spieker, 1997; Field, Healy, Goldstein, & Guthertz, 1990; Pickens & Field, 1993). Recent findings, though, suggest that the relationship between maternal and infant depression may derive from babies' prenatal exposure to the biochemical features of their mothers' emotional state. Further, studies have shown that stress- and depression-related hormones are passed from mother to infant prenatally or via breast-feeding (Hart et al., 2004).

Whether the link between maternal and infant depression arises from babies' ability to perceive facial expression or is biochemical in nature, it seems clear that maternal behaviors are important as well. Infants whose depressed mothers exhibit sensitive parenting behaviors are less likely to display long-term negative effects than babies of other depressed mothers (NICHD Early Child Care Research Network, 1999). In other words, when depressed mothers exhibit the same kinds of parenting behaviors as most nondepressed mothers,

their emotional status doesn't appear to have negative effects on their babies' development. Thus, because the link between maternal depression and its effects on infants is a behavioral one, parent training may provide an avenue through which the potential negative effects of maternal depression can be moderated. Indeed, several studies have shown that training can increase the frequency of sensitive behaviors in depressed mothers (Doesum, Hosman, & Riksen-Walraven, 2005). Moreover, antidepressant medications positively affect many aspects of depressed mothers' behavior, including making the tone of their verbal interactions with infants more like that of nondepressed mothers (Kaplan, Bachorowski, Smoski, & Zinser, 2001).

Questions for Reflection

1. How might researchers study whether genetics plays a role in the correlation between maternal and infant depression?
2. Based on this discussion, what items might be included in a brief observational checklist that health-care professionals could use to identify problem behaviors in depressed mothers?

(Flom & Bahrick, 2007). For example, in one classic study Haviland and Lelwica (1987) found that when mothers expressed happiness with both face and voice, 10-week-old babies looked happy and interested and gazed at the mother; when the mothers expressed sadness, babies showed increased mouth movements or looked away; when the mothers expressed anger, some babies cried vigorously, while others showed a kind of still or "frozen" look.

By 5 to 7 months, babies can begin to "read" one channel at a time, responding to facial expression alone or vocal expression alone, even when the emotions are displayed by a stranger rather than mom or dad (Flom & Bahrick, 2007). Specifically, they can tell the difference between happy and sad voices and between happy, surprised, and fearful faces. They also seem to have some preliminary understanding that vocal and facial emotional expressions typically go together.

Late in the first year of life, infants take another important step and link the information about a person's emotional expression with the environmental context. For example, a 12-month-old, faced with some new and potentially fearful event such as a new toy or a strange adult, may first look at mom's or dad's face to check for the adult's emotional expression. If mom looks pleased or happy, the baby is likely to explore the new toy with more ease or to accept the stranger with less fuss. If mom looks concerned or frightened, the baby responds to those cues and reacts to the novel situation with equivalent concern or fear. Researchers have described this as a process of **social referencing** (Thompson & Goodwin, 2005; Walker-Andrews, 1997). Not only do babies use the emotions of others to

social referencing Using another person's emotional reaction to some situation as a basis for deciding one's own reaction. A baby does this when she checks her parent's facial expression or body language before responding positively or negatively to something new.

guide their own responses, but recent research suggests that, by 12 months of age, they can use nonverbal cues to identify the cause of another person's emotional response (Moses, Baldwin, Rosicky, & Tidball, 2001). Moreover, 1-year-olds can calm themselves when their caregivers behave in expected ways (Cole, Martin, & Dennis, 2004). For example, a baby who is frustrated by hunger will calm down when she sees her caregiver preparing to nurse her or to provide her with some other kind of nourishment. However, infants' basic ability to perceive emotions carries potential risks for those whose mothers are depressed (see *Developmental Science in the Real World*).

Cross-Cultural Commonalities and Variations

Learning Objective 5.12

What cross-cultural differences in emotional perception have been noted?

It is reasonable to ask whether children in every culture learn about emotions in this same way. The Utka, an Inuit band in northern Canada, have two words for fear, distinguishing between fear of physical disaster and fear of being treated badly. Some African languages have no separate words for fear and sorrow. Samoans use the same word for love, sympathy, and liking, and Tahitians have no word at all that conveys the notion of guilt. These examples, drawn by James Russell (1989) from the anthropological literature, remind us that we need to be very careful when we talk about the "normal" process of a child learning about emotional expression and emotional meaning. From an English-speaking, Western perspective, emotions such as fear and anger seem like "basic" emotions that all infants understand early and easily. But what would be the developmental sequence for a child growing up in a culture in which fear and sorrow are not distinguished?

Figure 5.8
Basic Emotions

What emotion is being expressed in each of these photos? If you said happiness, sadness, fear, surprise, disgust, and anger, you agree with virtually all observers, in many countries, who have looked at these pictures.

(Copyright Paul Ekman.)

The work of Paul Ekman (1972, 1973, 1989, 2007) has provided evidence of a strong cross-cultural similarity in people's facial expressions when conveying certain of these same "basic" emotions, such as fear, happiness, sadness, anger, and disgust. (Figure 5.8 shows two such common expressions.) In all cultures studied so far, adults understand these facial expressions as having the same core meaning. Cultural variations are laid on top of these basic expressive patterns, and cultures have different rules about which emotions may be expressed and which must be masked. One could hypothesize that infants and toddlers are quite good at discriminating and understanding the core, shared patterns; even 2-year-olds can recognize and categorize happy and sad expressions. Beyond that basic understanding, the child must then slowly learn all the cultural overlays—the links between emotion and situation that hold for each culture, the specific meanings of emotional language, and the scripts that govern the appropriate expression of emotion in a given culture. This is no small task. What is remarkable is just how much of this information the preschooler already comprehends and reflects in his own behavior.

Think Critically

- How would nativists and empiricists explain infants' responses to music?
- Research shows that infants lack object permanence prior to about 8 months of age. How might this feature of infant perception be useful to caregivers?

Conduct Your Own Research

If you have access to a 3- to 6-month-old infant, you can replicate the research findings showing that infants respond differently to play songs and lullabies. Ask the baby's mother or father to sing the two types of songs and note whether the infant displays the kinds of behavior described in the text. Recall that researchers have found that lullabies elicit inwardly directed behaviors, such as thumb-sucking, and play songs elicit externally directed behaviors, such as babbling and smiling.

Summary

THINKING ABOUT PERCEPTUAL DEVELOPMENT

5.1 What are the three approaches to studying infants' perceptual skills?

- Studies of perceptual development have been greatly aided by methodological advances, such as Fantz's preference technique and the use of habituation or operant conditioning techniques with very young infants.

5.2 What are the arguments for the nativist and empiricist views of perceptual development?

- A central issue in the study of perceptual development continues to be the nativism-empiricism debate. Many basic perceptual abilities, including strategies for examining objects, appear to be built into the system at birth or to develop as the brain develops over the early years. But specific experience is required both to maintain the underlying system and to learn fundamental discriminations and patterns.

SENSORY SKILLS

5.3 How do infants' visual skills change across the first months of life?

- Color vision is present at birth, but visual acuity and tracking ability are relatively poor at birth. These skills develop rapidly during the first few months.

5.4 How do infants' senses of hearing, smell, taste, touch, and motion compare to those of older children and adults?

- Basic auditory skills are more fully developed at birth; auditory acuity is good for the range of the human voice, and the newborn can locate at least the approximate direction of a sound. The sensory capacities for smelling and tasting and the senses of touch and motion are also well developed at birth.

PERCEPTUAL SKILLS

5.5 How does visual perception change over the first months and years of life?

- Depth perception is present in at least rudimentary form by 3 months of age. The baby initially uses kinetic cues, then binocular cues, and finally pictorial cues by about 5 to 7 months. Visual attention appears to follow definite rules, even in the first hours of life. Babies can discriminate the mother's face from other faces, and the mother's voice from other voices, almost immediately after birth.

5.6 How do infants perceive human speech and other auditory stimuli?

- From the beginning, babies appear to attend to and discriminate among all possible speech sound contrasts; by the age of 1 year, the infant makes fine discriminations only among speech sounds that occur in the language she is actually hearing. Babies also attend to and discriminate among different patterns of sounds, such as melodies or speech inflections.

5.7 What is intermodal perception, and when does it develop?

- Intermodal perception, the ability to coordinate information from two or more senses, has been demonstrated in infants as young as 1 month old and is found reliably in 4-month-olds.

5.8 What are perceptual constancies, and when are they important to perception?

- Perceptual constancies are mental rules that enable humans to perceive the features of objects in the same way under varying conditions (e.g., viewing angle). Perceptual constancies such as size constancy, shape constancy, and color constancy are all present in at least rudimentary form by 4 months of age.

THE OBJECT CONCEPT

5.9 What kinds of rules do infants appear to use in perceiving objects?

- Young babies have quite complex understanding of objects, their properties, and their possible movements. They use the connected surface principle, the assumption that two connected surfaces belong to the same object, and also seem to know that objects fall when they are not supported. They also appear to discriminate between stable and unstable arrangements of objects such as block towers.

5.10 What is object permanence, and how does it develop?

- The understanding of object permanence (the realization that objects exist even when they are out of sight) begins at 2 or 3 months of age and is quite well developed by 10 months.

PERCEPTION OF SOCIAL SIGNALS

5.11 How does infants' ability to perceive emotions change over the first year?

- Babies' ability to discriminate among emotional expressions appears early in the first year. By 6 months of age, most infants can discriminate between emotional information contained in facial expressions and that represented by vocal tone. By 12 months, babies not only recognize nonverbal indicators of others' emotions but also change their own to match those of their caregivers (social referencing).

5.12 What cross-cultural differences in emotional perception have been noted?

- Cross-cultural research has shown that facial expressions are given the same meaning in every culture studied so far. What varies across cultures to some degree is the situations associated with various emotions as well as social rules for expressing them.

Key Terms

auditory acuity (p. 126)
color constancy (p. 133)
empiricism (p. 122)
intermodal perception (p. 132)
nativism (p. 122)

object constancy (p. 133)
object permanence (p. 134)
perceptual constancies (p. 133)
shape constancy (p. 133)
size constancy (p. 133)

social referencing (p. 138)
tracking (p. 125)
visual acuity (p. 125)

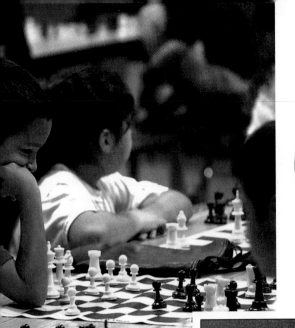

6

Cognitive Development 1: Structure and Process

When the last birthday party guest finally left, Sheilah busied herself with cleaning up the cake crumbs while the birthday boy, 7-year-old Rudy, looked through his gifts. One of them was an intriguing board game. "Mom," he said, "can you play this game with me now?"

Sheilah replied that she was busy and suggested that Rudy play the game with his 4-year-old sister, Marcella. "She's too little," protested Rudy.

"Give her a chance," his mother replied. Rudy reluctantly agreed and set off in search of his sister.

Rudy found Marcella in her room and began explaining the game to her. "You get one of these little guys and I get one. Which color do you want?" he asked. The two decided that Rudy would have a red playing piece and Marcella would have a blue one. "You put the guys on this square, and then you spin the spinner. Then you have to move your guy however many spaces it says on the spinner. If you land on one of these squares," he explained, pointing to a square with a star on it, "you get another turn. If you land on one with a stop sign, you have to skip a turn."

Marcella seemed to understand, so Rudy decided to let her go first. She flicked the spinner, and the arrow landed on four. "Okay," said Rudy, "you have to move your guy four spaces."

Marcella picked up her piece and began to count off the spaces, "1, 2, 3," when she suddenly stopped. "Four is a stop sign. I don't want to be on a stop sign. I'm gonna do the spinner again."

At this, Rudy became indignant. "You can't do it again; that's cheating," he yelled. "Mom," Rudy called loudly so that Sheilah could hear him in the other room, "I can't play with her 'cause she's a cheater." Marcella began to sob as Rudy packed up the game and said, "Go play with your baby toys."

Scenes like this one are all too familiar to parents whose children are on either side of the transition from, in Piaget's terms, the preoperational stage to the concrete operational stage. Concrete operational 7-year-olds like Rudy have a strong preference for structured experiences with outcomes that depend on rules. They can imagine how much fun it would be to win a board game, but they know that to achieve a legitimate victory a player must abide by the rules. For preoperational 4-year-olds like Marcella, the world is more fluid. Like 7-year-olds, they can imagine winning a game, but they don't yet understand that the legitimacy of the outcome depends on the rules. That is, without rules, a game isn't a game at all. Thus, they prefer pretend play activities in which rules are easily changed and depend primarily on the whim of the player.

Piaget's Basic Ideas

Piaget set out to answer a fundamental question: How does a child's knowledge of the world change with age? In answering this question, Piaget's most central assumption was that the child is an active participant in the development of knowledge, constructing his own understanding. This idea, perhaps more than any other, has influenced the thinking of all developmentalists who have followed Piaget. In addition, after three decades of research devoted to challenging his assertion that cognitive functioning develops in stages, the whole concept of cognitive stages is enjoying a resurgence of interest among developmental psychologists (Feldman, 2004; Homer & Hayward, 2008; Kuhn, 2008; Shayer, 2008). Of course, the hundreds of studies that have been done since Piaget first proposed the stages have revealed a number of shortcomings in his original account of cognitive development. Still, the basic outline he first sketched more than 70 years ago of cognitive changes from infancy to adolescence appears to be fairly accurate.

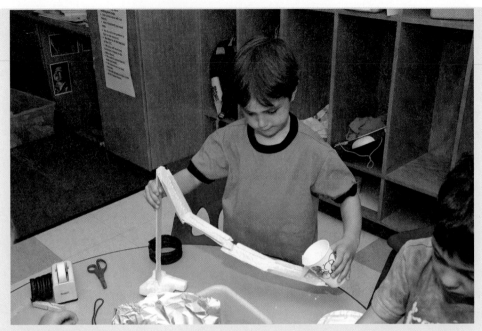

The metaphor of the child as a "little scientist," constructing his understanding of the world, comes directly from Piaget's theory.

Learning Objective 6.1

What is the role of schemes in cognitive development?

Schemes

A pivotal Piagetian concept—and one of the hardest to grasp—is that of a **scheme** (sometimes called a *schema*). This term is often used as a rough synonym for the word *concept* or the phrases *mental category* or *complex of ideas*, but Piaget used it even more broadly than that. He saw knowledge not as merely passive mental categories but as actions, either mental or physical; each of these actions is what he meant by a scheme. So a scheme is not really a category, but the *action* of categorizing in some particular fashion. Some purely physical or sensory actions are also schemes. If you pick up and look at a ball, you are using your "looking scheme," your "picking-up scheme," and your "holding scheme."

Piaget proposed that each baby begins life with a small repertoire of simple sensory or motor schemes, such as looking, tasting, touching, hearing, and grasping. For the baby, an object is a thing that tastes a certain way, feels a certain way when touched, or has a particular color. Later, the toddler develops mental schemes as well, such as categorizing or comparing one object to another. Over the course of development, the child gradually adds extremely complex mental schemes, such as deductive analysis or systematic reasoning. In fact, humans continue to add new schemes, both physical and mental, throughout the lifespan. So where, you might be wondering, do these new schemes come from?

According to Piaget, as people act on their environments, an inborn mental process called **organization** causes them to derive generalizable schemes from specific experiences. For example, when an infant handles a spherical object, such as a ball, the scheme she constructs will be applied to all similar objects. So, when she observes a decorative glass ball, she will attempt to handle it in the same way she would a rubber ball. Schemes organize our thinking according to categories that help us determine what kinds of actions to take in response to variations in environmental characteristics.

According to Piaget, **figurative schemes** are mental representations of the basic properties of objects in the world. For instance, a child uses figurative schemes when she correctly labels dogs and cats, lists their characteristics (e.g., wet noses, fur, whiskers), and describes their typical behaviors (e.g., barking, wagging tails, mewing). Knowing that dogs and cats are different kinds of animals and that animals represent a category that is distinct from others

scheme Piaget's word for the basic actions of knowing, including both physical actions (sensorimotor schemes, such as looking or reaching) and mental actions (such as classifying, comparing, and reversing). An experience is assimilated into a scheme, and the scheme is created or modified through accommodation.

organization The process of deriving generalizable schemes from specific experiences.

figurative schemes Mental representations of the basic properties of objects in the world.

(e.g., clothes, food, etc.) also involves figurative schemes. By contrast, **operative schemes** enable children to understand the logical connections among objects in the world and to reason about or operate on them. For example, operative schemes come into play when children understand that collies are dogs, dogs are mammals, mammals are animals, and so on.

Adaptation

Learning Objective 6.2
How do assimilation, accommodation, and equilibration change schemes?

Our schemes don't always work the way we expect them to. So, according to Piaget, the mental process he called **adaptation** complements organization by working to change schemes that don't quite fit the challenges offered by our environments. Three subprocesses are involved in adaptation.

Assimilation is the process of taking in, of absorbing some event or experience and making it part of a scheme. Piaget would say that when a baby handles a decorative glass ball in the same way she learned to manipulate a rubber ball, she has assimilated the ball to her ball-handling scheme. The key here is that assimilation is an active process. For one thing, we assimilate information selectively. We don't behave like a blotter, absorbing everything we experience; instead, we pay attention only to those aspects of any experience for which we already have schemes. For example, when you listen to an instructor give a lecture, you may try to write everything down in your notebook or store it in your brain, but in fact you assimilate only the thoughts you can connect to some concept or model you already have.

The process complementary to assimilation is **accommodation**, which involves changing a scheme as a result of new information taken in by assimilation. The baby who grasps a glass ball for the first time will respond to the slipperiness of the surface, compared to what she expected based on her experience with rubber balls, and will accommodate her ball-handling scheme. In this way, she will develop a ball-handling scheme that can take into account different surface characteristics of different kinds of balls. Thus, in Piaget's theory, the process of accommodation is the key to developmental change. Through accommodation, we reorganize our thoughts, improve our skills, and change our strategies.

The third aspect of adaptation is **equilibration**, the process of bringing assimilation and accommodation into balance. This is not unlike what a scientist does when she develops a theory about some body of information. The scientist wants to have a theory that will make sense out of every observation—that is, one that has internal coherence. When new research findings come along, she assimilates them into her existing theory; if they don't fit perfectly, she makes modifications (accommodations) in the theory so that it will assimilate information that previously did not fit. However, if enough nonconfirming evidence accumulates, the scientist may have to throw out her theory altogether or change some basic theoretical assumptions; either response is a form of equilibration.

A road map analogy may be helpful. Suppose you have just moved to a new city, and instead of buying a local map, you try to learn your way around with only a hand-drawn map given to you by a friend. As you make your way through the new city, you make corrections on your map—redrawing it and writing notes to yourself. The redrawn and revised map is certainly an improvement over the original version, but eventually you will find that it is both impossible to read and still seriously flawed. So you start over and draw a new map, based on all your information. You carry this around with you, revising it and writing on it until it, too, is so full of annotations that you need to start over. The corrections and annotations you make to your map are analogous to accommodations in Piaget's theory; the process of starting over and drawing a new map is analogous to equilibration. Each modification of an existing map or drawing of a new map allows you to more easily assimilate your driving or walking experiences. Put more simply, with each modification, your map works better than before.

Piaget thought that a child operated in a similar way, creating coherent, more or less internally consistent schemes. However, since the infant starts with a very limited repertoire of schemes (a very primitive initial map), the early structures the child creates are simply not going to be adequate. Such inadequacies, Piaget thought, force the child to make periodic major changes in the internal schemes.

operative schemes Mental representations of the logical connections among objects in the world.

adaptation The processes through which schemes change.

assimilation That part of the adaptation process proposed by Piaget that involves absorbing new experiences or information into existing schemes. Experience is not taken in "as is," however, but is modified (or interpreted) somewhat so as to fit the preexisting schemes.

accommodation That part of the adaptation process proposed by Piaget by which a person modifies existing schemes as a result of new experiences or creates new schemes when old ones no longer handle the data.

equilibration The third part of the adaptation process proposed by Piaget, involving a periodic restructuring of schemes to create a balance between assimilation and accommodation.

Piaget saw three particularly significant reorganization, or equilibration, points in childhood, each ushering in a new stage of development. The first occurs at about 18–24 months, when the toddler shifts from the dominance of simple sensory and motor schemes to the use of the first symbols. The second equilibration point normally falls between ages 5 and 7, when the child adds a whole new set of powerful operative schemes Piaget calls **operations**. These are far more abstract and general mental actions, such as mental addition or subtraction. The third major equilibration point is in adolescence, when the child figures out how to "operate on" ideas as well as on events or objects.

The three major equilibration points yield four stages during which children use different ways of acting on the world around them. During the **sensorimotor stage**, from birth to 24 months, infants use their sensory and motor schemes to act on the world around them. In the **preoperational stage**, from 24 months to about 6 years, youngsters acquire symbolic schemes, such as language and fantasy, that they use in thinking and communicating. Next comes the **concrete operations stage**, during which 6- to 12-year-olds begin to think logically. The last phase is the **formal operations stage**, in which adolescents learn to think logically about abstract ideas and hypothetical situations.

operation Term used by Piaget for a complex, internal, abstract scheme, first seen at about age 6.

sensorimotor stage Piaget's term for the first major stage of cognitive development, from birth to about 24 months, when the child uses sensory and motor skills to act on the environment.

preoperational stage Piaget's term for the second major stage of cognitive development, from about 24 months to about age 6, marked by the ability to use symbols.

concrete operations stage Piaget's term for the stage of development between ages 6 and 12, during which children become able to think logically.

formal operations stage Piaget's name for the fourth and final major stage of cognitive development, occurring during adolescence, when the child becomes able to manipulate and organize ideas or hypothetical situations as well as objects.

Causes of Cognitive Development

Since Piaget's stages represent a fixed sequence, you might think that they are controlled by an inborn genetic plan, much like the sequence of motor skill development you read about in Chapter 4. Piaget suggested that just such an inborn plan for cognitive development exists, but that it depends on environmental factors for its full expression. He proposed four main causes of cognitive development: two that are internal, and two that are found in a child's environment (Piaget & Inhelder, 1969).

As you learned in the preceding section, Piaget believed that equilibration was the chief process through which new stages of cognitive development are reached. He hypothesized that the process of equilibration is an inborn, automatic response to conflicts between a child's current schemes and the challenges of her environment. Likewise, he assumed that the basic pattern of brain maturation common to all human beings that you learned about in Chapter 4 contributed to cognitive development. So, he claimed, individual differences in the pace at which children proceed through the four stages of cognitive development may be partly explained by different rates of brain maturation, which may be the result of either inborn differences or environmental factors such as nutrition.

The two environmental factors Piaget posited to explain progression through the stages were social transmission and experience. *Social transmission* is simply information the child gets from other people. According to Piaget, parents, teachers, and others provide children with information, such as the names and characteristics of objects, as well as with models of more mature cognitive development. Say, for example, a preschooler believes that her dresser turns into a monster every night when the light is turned off. To reassure her, her parent turns the light on and off repeatedly to demonstrate that the dresser remains a piece of furniture whether the light is on or off. In so doing, the parent is demonstrating use of a logical scheme that has many applications to the physical world: "If this object was a dresser with the light on, it must still be a dresser when the light is off. Darkness cannot change the 'dresserness' of the dresser; it can't change one object into another." The parent's logical scheme conflicts with the magical scheme on which the child bases her belief that pieces of furniture can change into monsters in the dark. As a result, the experience stimulates the process of equilibration for the child. Piaget suggested that adults contribute a great deal to children's progression from one stage to the next through these kinds of informal demonstrations.

By *experience*, Piaget meant the child's own opportunities to act on the world and to observe the results of those actions. If you watch preschoolers playing on the beach or in a sandbox, you will notice that one of their favorite activities is to fill containers with sand, empty them out, and fill them up again. You might see a group of children making a "mountain" out of sand in this way. In so doing, they notice that the mountain doesn't hold together very well unless a little water is mixed with the sand, but then they see that too much water also prevents the mountain from holding together. Through this kind of experimentation and modification of actions, Piaget believed, children often stimulate their own cognitive development.

One place where children are exposed to many opportunities for both social transmission and experience is in school. In fact, studies all over the world have shown that children who attend school progress through Piaget's stages more rapidly than those who do not (Mishra, 2001). These studies lend weight to Piaget's claim that movement from one cognitive stage to another is not simply a matter of maturation but is the result of a complex interaction between internal and environmental variables. Each of these variables, Piaget suggested, is *necessary but not sufficient* to produce movement from one cognitive stage to the next. In other words, a certain degree of brain maturation is required for each stage, but brain development by itself cannot cause a child to progress to the next stage. All of the causal factors—equilibration, maturation, social transmission, and experience—must interact and support one another in order for cognitive development to proceed.

Infancy

Piaget's theory assumes that the baby assimilates incoming information into the limited array of sensory and motor schemes she is born with—such as looking, listening, sucking, and grasping—and accommodates those schemes based on her experiences. This is the starting point for the entire process of cognitive development.

Piaget's View of the Sensorimotor Period

| Learning Objective 6.4 |
| How did Piaget describe cognitive development in the first 2 years of life? |

In the beginning, in Piaget's view, the baby is entirely tied to the immediate present, responding to whatever stimuli are available. She does not remember events or things from one encounter to the next and does not appear to plan or intend. John Flavell summarizes all of this very nicely:

> [The infant] exhibits a wholly practical, perceiving-and-doing, action-bound kind of intellectual functioning; she does not exhibit the more contemplative, reflective, symbol-manipulating kind we usually think of in connection with cognition. The infant "knows" in the sense of recognizing or anticipating familiar, recurring objects and happenings, and "thinks" in the sense of behaving toward them with mouth, hand, eye, and other sensory-motor instruments in predictable, organized, and often adaptive ways. (1985, p. 13)

This pattern gradually changes during the first 24 months as the baby comes to understand that objects continue to exist even when they are out of sight (see Chapter 5) and as she becomes able to remember objects, actions, and individuals over periods of time. Yet Piaget insisted that in the sensorimotor period, the infant is not yet able to manipulate these early mental images or memories. Nor does she use symbols to stand for objects or events. It is the new ability to manipulate internal symbols, such as words or images, that marks the beginning of the next stage, the stage of preoperational thought, which emerges in most children some time between 18 and 24 months.

The change from the limited repertoire of schemes available to the newborn to the ability to use symbols between 18 and 24 months is gradual, although Piaget identified six substages, summarized in Table 6.1 on page 149. Each substage represents some specific advance. Substage 2 is marked by the beginning of those important coordinations between looking and listening, reaching and looking, and reaching and sucking that are such central features of the 2-month-old's means of exploring the world. The term **primary circular reactions** refers to the many simple repetitive actions seen at substage 2, each organized around the infant's own body. The baby accidentally sucks his thumb one day, finds it pleasurable, and repeats the action. **Secondary circular reactions**, in substage 3, differ only in that the baby is now repeating some action in order to trigger a reaction outside his own body. The baby coos

primary circular reactions Piaget's phrase to describe a baby's simple repetitive actions in substage 2 of the sensorimotor stage, organized around the baby's own body; the baby repeats some action in order to have some desired outcome occur again, such as putting his thumb in his mouth to repeat the good feeling of sucking.

secondary circular reactions Repetitive actions in substage 3 of the sensorimotor period, oriented around external objects; the infant repeats some action in order to have some outside event recur, such as hitting a mobile repeatedly so that it moves.

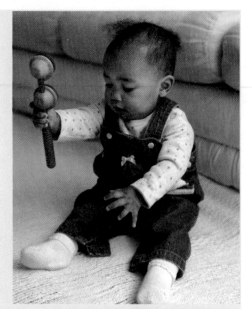
Three-month-old Andrea may be showing a secondary circular reaction here, shaking her hand repeatedly to hear the sound of the rattle. A learning theorist would say that the pleasure she experiences from hearing the sound is reinforcing her hand-shaking behavior.

and mom smiles, so the baby coos again, apparently in order to get mom to smile again; the baby accidentally hits the mobile hanging above his crib, it moves, and he then repeats his arm wave, apparently with some intent to make the mobile move again. These initial connections between bodily actions and external consequences are fairly automatic, very like a kind of operant conditioning. During this substage, infants build the important schemes that underlie the *object concept*, a set of milestones discussed extensively in Chapter 5. Recall that **object permanence**, or the understanding that objects continue to exist even when they are out of sight, is one of the most important of these milestones.

Substage 4 brings with it the beginnings of a real understanding of causal connections. At this point, the infant moves into exploratory high gear. In substage 5, this exploratory behavior becomes even more marked with the emergence of what Piaget called **tertiary circular reactions**. In this substage, the baby is not content merely to repeat the original triggering action but tries out variations. He might try out many other sounds or facial expressions to see if they will trigger mom's smile or try moving his hand differently or in new directions in order to make the mobile move in new ways. At this stage, the baby's behavior has a purposeful, experimental quality. Nonetheless, Piaget thought that even in substage 5 the baby does not have internal symbols to stand for objects. The development of such symbols is the mark of substage 6.

Piaget's descriptions of this sequence of development, largely based on remarkably detailed observations of his own three children, provoked a very rich array of research, some that confirms the general outlines of his proposals and some that does not. Research results described in Chapter 5, along with other research on infant memory and imitation, point to the conclusion that in a number of important respects, Piaget underestimated the ability of infants to store, remember, and organize sensory and motor information.

Learning Objective 6.5
What have researchers discovered about infants' ability to remember and to imitate others' actions?

Challenges to Piaget's View of Infancy

Although research has generally supported the sequence of cognitive development discovered by Piaget, there are many findings that challenge his view. As you learned in Chapter 5, research by Elizabeth Spelke and Renée Baillargeon, among others, has given us a more detailed account of infants' understanding of objects than Piaget's studies did. Their work suggests that infants have a much more sophisticated understanding of objects than Piaget concluded. Likewise, research examining infants' memory functioning and their capacity for imitation also suggests that Piaget may have underestimated their capabilities.

Memory   One hint that infants are capable of greater feats of memory than Piaget proposed is research showing that habituation and dishabituation are already present at birth—research you read about in Chapter 3. Habituation, you'll recall, involves a lessening of response to a repeated stimulus. For instance, a newborn stops exhibiting a startle response to a sound after she has been exposed to it several times. For habituation to be possible, the baby must have at least some ability to store (remember) information about the previous occurrences. Similarly, for dishabituation to occur, the baby must recognize that a new event is somehow different, which suggests that the baby's memory contains a fairly detailed image or template of the original event (Schneider & Bjorklund, 1998).

A second source of evidence that quite young babies can remember specific events over periods of time comes from a series of clever studies by Carolyn Rovee-Collier and her colleagues (Bhatt & Rovee-Collier, 1996; Gerhardstein, Adler, & Rovee-Collier, 2000; Hartshorn & Rovee-Collier, 1997; Hayne & Rovee-Collier, 1995; Rovee-Collier, 1993). In her most widely used procedure, Rovee-Collier uses an ingenious variation of an operant conditioning strategy. She first hangs an attractive mobile over a baby's crib and watches to see how the baby re-

object permanence The understanding that objects continue to exist even when they cannot be directly perceived.

tertiary circular reactions The deliberate experimentation with variations of previous actions, characteristic of substage 5 of the sensorimotor period, according to Piaget.

Table 6.1 Substages of Piaget's Sensorimotor Stage

Substage	Age	Piaget's Label	Characteristics
1	Birth–1 month	Reflexes	Use of built-in schemes or reflexes such as sucking or looking; no imitation; no ability to integrate information from several senses
2	1–4 months	Primary circular reactions	Accommodation of basic schemes (grasping, looking, sucking), as baby practices them endlessly. Beginning coordination of schemes from different senses, such as looking toward a sound; baby does not yet link bodily actions to some result outside the body.
3	4–8 months	Secondary circular reactions	Baby becomes much more aware of events outside his own body and makes them happen again, in a kind of trial-and-error learning. Imitation may occur, but only of schemes already in the baby's repertoire. Beginning understanding of the "object concept."
4	8–12 months	Coordination of secondary schemes	Clear intentional means-ends behavior. The baby not only goes after what she wants, but may combine two schemes to do so, such as knocking a pillow away to reach a toy. Imitation of novel behaviors occurs, as does transfer of information from one sense to the other (cross-modal transfer).
5	12–18 months	Tertiary circular reactions	"Experimentation" begins, in which the infant tries out new ways of playing with or manipulating objects. Very active, very purposeful trial-and-error exploration.
6	18–24 months	Beginning of representational thought	Development of use of symbols to represent objects or events. Child understands that the symbol is separate from the object. Deferred imitation first occurs at this stage.

sponds. In particular, she is interested in how often the baby normally kicks her legs while looking at the mobile. After 3 minutes of this "baseline" observation, she attaches a string from the mobile to the baby's leg, as you can see in Figure 6.1, so that each time the baby kicks her leg, the mobile moves. Babies quickly learn to kick repeatedly in order to make this interesting new thing happen (what Piaget would call a secondary circular reaction). Within 3 to 6 minutes, 3-month-olds double or triple their kick rates, showing that learning has clearly occurred. Rovee-Collier then tests the baby's memory of this learning by coming back some days later and hanging the same mobile over the crib, but not attaching the string to the baby's foot. If the baby remembers the previous occasion, she should kick at a higher rate than she did when she first saw the mobile, which is precisely what 3-month-old babies do, even after a delay of as long as a week.

Such studies show that the young infant is cognitively a whole lot more sophisticated than developmentalists (and Piaget) had once supposed. At the same time, Rovee-Collier's work also offers some support for Piaget's views, since she observes systematic gains over the months of infancy in the baby's ability to remember. A 2-month-old can remember the kicking action for only 1 day; a 3-month-old can remember for over a week; and by 6 months, a baby can remember for more than 2 weeks. Rovee-Collier has also found that all these early infant memories are strongly tied to the specific context in which the original experience occurred. Even 6-month-olds do not recognize or remember the mobile if the investigator makes even a very small change, such as hanging a different cloth around the crib in which the child was originally tested. Thus, babies do remember far more than Piaget believed—but their memories are highly specific. With age, their memories become less and less tied to

Figure 6.1
Rovee-Collier's Studies of Infant Learning

This 3-month-old baby in one of Rovee-Collier's memory experiments will quickly learn to kick her foot in order to make the mobile move. And several days later, she will remember this connection between kicking and the mobile.

(*Source:* Rovee-Collier, 1993, p. 131.)

Figure 6.2
Imitation

Although researchers still disagree on just how much young infants will imitate, everyone agrees that they will imitate the gesture of tongue protrusion.

specific cues or contexts (DeFrancisco & Rovee-Collier, 2008; Hsu & Rovee-Collier, 2006; Learmonth, Lamberth, & Rovee-Collier, 2004).

Imitation   Another active area of study has been the ability of the infant to imitate. If you look again at Table 6.1 on page 149, you'll see that Piaget thought that the ability to imitate emerged quite gradually over the early months. In broad terms, Piaget's proposed sequence has been supported. For example, imitation of someone else's hand movements or their actions with objects seems to improve steadily during the months of infancy, starting at 1 or 2 months of age; imitation of two-part actions develops only in toddlerhood, perhaps at 15 to 18 months (Poulson, Nunes, & Warren, 1989). In two areas, however, Piaget may have been wrong about infants' imitative abilities.

First, although Piaget thought babies could not imitate other people's facial gestures until about substage 4 (8–12 months), quite a lot of research now shows that newborns are able to imitate at least some facial gestures, particularly tongue protrusion (Nagy & Molnar, 2004), as shown in the photo in Figure 6.2. Nevertheless, newborns' capacity for imitation appears to be quite limited. Researchers have found that neonates imitate tongue-protrusion but not mouth-opening (Anisfeld et al., 2001). Taken together, studies of imitative behavior in newborns indicate that Piaget was probably wrong in his assertion that very young infants are incapable of imitation. However, it seems likely that he was accurate in his view that imitation is not a general strategy infants use for developing their understanding of the world until they are a bit older.

Piaget also argued that *deferred imitation*, in which a child sees some action and then imitates it at a later time when the model is no longer visible, became possible only in substage 6 (at about 18 months of age), since deferred imitation requires some kind of internal representation. Once again, more recent research points to earlier development of this ability (Learmonth et al., 2004; Learmonth, Lamberth, & Rovee-Collier, 2005). At least one study (Meltzoff, 1988) shows that babies as young as 9 months can defer their imitation for as long as 24 hours. By 14 months, toddlers can recall and later imitate someone's actions over a period of 2 days (Hanna & Meltzoff, 1993). This finding makes it clear that children of this age can and do learn specific behaviors through modeling, even when they have no chance to imitate the behavior immediately.

egocentrism A cognitive state in which the individual (typically a child) sees the world only from his own perspective, without awareness that there are other perspectives.

The Preschool Years

Piaget's theory and research findings suggest that preschoolers' ability to use symbols such as words significantly enhances their ability to understand and act on the world around them. But their ability to reason about the world is still fairly poor.

Learning Objective 6.6

What are the characteristics of children's thinking during the preoperational stage?

Piaget's View of the Preoperational Stage

Piaget saw evidence of symbol use in many aspects of the behavior of children aged 2 to 6. For example, children this age begin to pretend in their play. Such symbol use is also evident in the emergence of language and in the preschooler's primitive ability to understand scale models or simple maps (DeLoache, 1995). Thus, children's figurative schemes grow by leaps and bounds during this stage. By contrast, operative schemes develop slowly. As a result, the fragmentary, "in-progress" nature of preschoolers' operative schemes usually prevents them from generating valid conclusions to logical problems.

Other than symbol use, Piaget's description of the preoperational stage focused on all the other things the preschool-aged child still cannot do, giving an oddly negative tone to his description of this period. Piaget saw the preschooler's thinking as rigid, captured by appearances, insensitive to inconsistencies, and tied to her own perspective—a quality Piaget (1954) called **egocentrism**. The child is not being selfish; rather, she simply thinks (assumes) that everyone sees the world as she does.

Figure 6.3 illustrates a classic technique used to measure this egocentrism. The child is shown a three-dimensional scene with mountains of different sizes and colors. From a set of drawings, she picks out the one that shows the scene the way she sees it. Most preschoolers can do this without much difficulty. Then the examiner asks the child to pick out the drawing that shows how someone else sees the scene, such as a doll or the examiner. At this point, preschoolers have difficulty. Most often, they again pick the drawing that shows their own view of the mountains (Gzesh & Surber, 1985). In Piaget's view, for a child to be able to succeed at this task, she must shift from using herself as the only frame of reference to seeing things from another perspective. Piaget thought that preschool children could not yet do this.

The preschool child's focus on the appearance of objects is an equally important part of Piaget's description of this period, evident in some of the most famous of his studies, those on conservation (see Figure 6.4 on page 152). **Conservation** is the understanding that the quantity of a substance remains the same even when its appearance changes. Piaget's measurement technique involved first showing the child two equal objects or sets of objects, getting the child to agree that they were equal in some key respect, such as weight, quantity, length, or number, and then shifting, changing, or deforming one of the objects or sets and asking the child if they were still equal. Next, Piaget asked how the child knew the answer was correct. Children who were using preoperational schemes would give justifications, such as "the sausage has more clay because it is longer now." This kind of thinking reflects the child's tendency to think of the world in terms of one variable at a time, a type of thought Piaget called **centration**. By contrast, concrete operational thinkers are capable of **decentration**, a process in which multiple dimensions are considered. Thus, the older child says, "the sausage looks like more because its longer now, but you didn't add any clay or take any away so it must still be the same." Piaget insisted, based on his evaluations of both children's solutions and their reasoning, that children rarely exhibit a true understanding of conservation before age 5 or 6.

Figure 6.3   Piaget's Three Mountains Task

The experimental situation shown here is similar to one Piaget used to study egocentrism in children. The child is asked to pick out a picture that shows how the mountains look to her, and then to pick out a picture that shows how the mountains look to the doll.

conservation The understanding that the quantity or amount of a substance remains the same even when there are external changes in its shape or arrangement.

centration The young child's tendency to think of the world in terms of one variable at a time.

decentration Thinking that takes multiple variables into account.

Challenges to Piaget's View of Early Childhood

Learning Objective 6.7
How has recent research challenged Piaget's view of this period?

Studies of conservation have generally confirmed Piaget's predictions. Although younger children can demonstrate some understanding of conservation if the task is made very simple, most children cannot consistently solve conservation problems until age 5 or 6 or later (e.g., Andreucci, 2003). Nevertheless, evidence suggests that preschoolers are somewhat more cognitively sophisticated than Piaget thought.

Egocentrism and Perspective Taking   Children as young as 2 and 3 appear to have at least some ability to understand that another person sees things or experiences

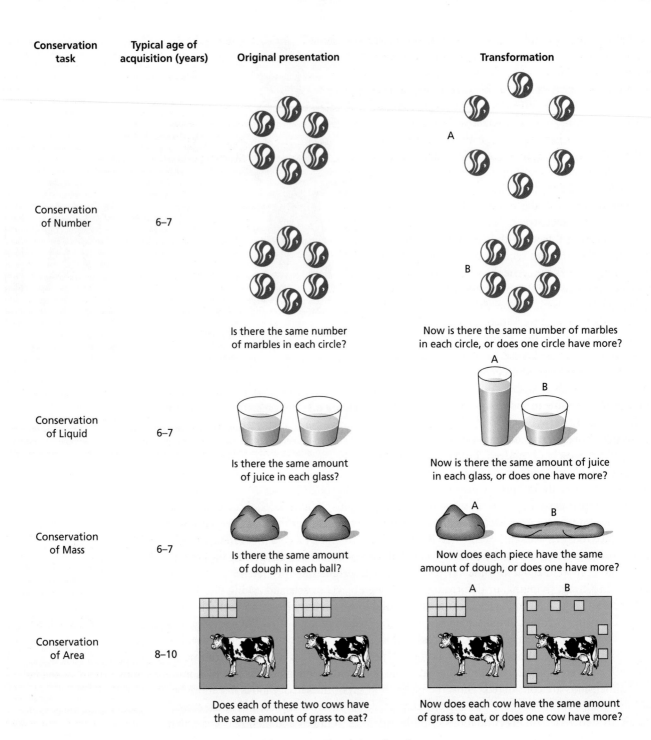

Conservation task	Typical age of acquisition (years)	Original presentation	Transformation

Conservation of Number — 6–7

Is there the same number of marbles in each circle?

Now is there the same number of marbles in each circle, or does one circle have more?

Conservation of Liquid — 6–7

Is there the same amount of juice in each glass?

Now is there the same amount of juice in each glass, or does one have more?

Conservation of Mass — 6–7

Is there the same amount of dough in each ball?

Now does each piece have the same amount of dough, or does one have more?

Conservation of Area — 8–10

Does each of these two cows have the same amount of grass to eat?

Now does each cow have the same amount of grass to eat, or does one cow have more?

Figure 6.4   Piaget's Concrete Operational Tasks

Piaget's research involved several kinds of conservation tasks. He classified children's thinking as concrete operational with respect to a particular task if they could correctly solve the problem and provide a concrete operational reason for their answer. For example, if a child said, "The two circles of marbles are the same because you didn't add any or take any away when you moved them," the response was judged to be concrete operational. Conversely, if a child said, "The two circles are the same, but I don't know why," the response was not classified as concrete operational.

things differently than they do. For example, children of this age will adapt their play or their speech to the demands of their companions. They play differently with older and younger playmates and talk differently to a younger child (Brownell, 1990; Guralnick & Paul-Brown, 1984).

However, such understanding is clearly not perfect at this young age. Developmental psychologist John Flavell has proposed two levels of perspective-taking ability. At level 1, the child knows that another person experiences something differently. At level 2, the child develops a whole series of complex rules for figuring out precisely what the other person sees or experiences (Flavell, Green, & Flavell, 1990). Two- and 3-year-olds have level 1 knowledge but not level 2 knowledge; the latter only begins to emerge in 4- and 5-year-olds. For example, a child of 4 or 5 understands that another person will feel sad if she fails or happy if she succeeds. The preschool child also begins to figure out that unpleasant emotions arise in situations in which the relationship between desire and reality is unequal. Sadness, for example, normally occurs when someone loses something or fails to acquire some desired object (Harris, 1989).

Appearance and Reality   The child's movement away from egocentrism seems to be part of a much broader change in her understanding of appearance and reality. Flavell has studied this understanding in a variety of ways (Flavell, 2004). In the most famous Flavell procedure, the experimenter shows the child a sponge that has been painted to look like a rock. Three-year-olds will say either that the object looks like a sponge and is a sponge or that it looks like a rock and is a rock. But 4- and 5-year-olds can distinguish the two; they realize that it looks like a rock but is really a sponge (Flavell, 1986). Thus, the older child understands that an object may not be what it seems.

Using similar materials, investigators have also asked whether a child can grasp the **false belief principle** (Lamb & Lewis, 2005). Individuals who understand the false belief principle can look at a problem or situation from another person's point of view in order to discern what kind of information can cause that person to believe something that isn't true. For example, after a child has felt the sponge/rock and has answered questions about what it looks like and what it "really" is, a researcher might ask something like this: "John [one of the child's playmates] hasn't touched this; he hasn't squeezed it. If John just sees it over here like this, what will he think it is? Will he think it's a rock or will he think that it's a sponge?" (Gopnik & Astington, 1988, p. 35). Most 3-year-olds think that the playmate will believe the object is a sponge because they themselves know that it *is* a sponge. By contrast, 4- and 5-year-olds realize that, because the playmate hasn't felt the sponge, he will have a false belief that it is a rock. Some studies show that 3-year-olds can perform more accurately if they are given a hint or clue. For example, if experimenters tell them that a "naughty" person is trying to fool their playmate, more of them will say that he will falsely think the sponge is rock (Bowler, Briskman, & Grice, 1999). But the child of 4 or 5 more consistently understands that someone else can believe something that isn't true and act on that belief.

Theories of Mind

Learning Objective 6.8
What is a theory of mind, and how does it develop?

Evidence like that just described has led researchers to examine children's understanding of others' thoughts and feelings in a new way. In the past 15 years, a number of developmentalists have examined a theoretical notion known as **theory of mind**, or a set of ideas that explain other people's ideas, beliefs, desires, and behavior (Flavell, 1999, 2000, 2004). As you might suspect, research indicates that adolescents and adults have a much more fully developed theory of mind than children do (Flavell & Green, 1999; Flavell, Green, & Flavell, 1998, 2000; Flavell, Green, Flavell, & Lin, 1999). However, research also suggests that the degree of sophistication in young children's theory of mind is probably greater than either Piaget or casual observers of children would expect.

Understanding Thoughts, Desires, and Beliefs   As early as 18 months, toddlers begin to have some understanding of the fact that people (but not inanimate objects) operate with goals and intentions (Meltzoff, 1995). By age 3, they understand some aspects of the links between people's thinking or feeling and their behavior. For example, they know that a person who wants something will try to get it. They also know that a person may still want something even if she can't have it (Lillard & Flavell, 1992). But 3-year-olds do not yet understand the basic principle that each person's actions are based on his or her own representation of reality and that a person's representation may differ from what is "really" there. For

false belief principle The understanding that another person might have a false belief and the ability to determine what information might cause the false belief. A child's understanding of the false belief principle is one key sign of the emergence of a representational theory of mind.

theory of mind Ideas that collectively explain other people's ideas, beliefs, desires, and behavior.

example, a person's *belief* about how popular she is has more influence on her behavior than her actual popularity. It is this new aspect of the theory of mind that clearly emerges at about age 4 or 5.

Furthermore, not until about age 6 do most children realize that knowledge can be derived through inference. For example, researchers in one study showed 4- and 6-year-olds two toys of different colors (Pillow, 1999). Next, they placed the toys in opaque containers. They then opened one of the containers and showed the toy to a puppet. When asked whether the puppet now knew which color toy was in each container, only the 6-year-olds said yes.

Understanding of the reciprocal nature of thought seems to develop between age 5 and age 7 for most children. This is a particularly important development, because it is probably necessary for the creation of genuinely reciprocal friendships, which begin to become evident in the elementary school years (Sullivan, Zaitchik, & Tager-Flusberg, 1994). In fact, an individual preschooler's rate of development of theory of mind is a good predictor of her ability to judge others' trustworthiness (Maas, 2008).

Influences on Theory of Mind Development
Brain-imaging studies suggest that the development of a specific neural network in the cerebral cortex is strongly related to theory of mind development (Costa, Torriero, Oliveri, & Caltagirone, 2008). Moreover, developmentalists have found that a child's theory of mind is correlated with his performance on conservation tasks as well as egocentrism and understanding of appearance and reality (Melot & Houde, 1998; Yirmiya & Shulman, 1996). In addition, pretend play seems to contribute to development of theory of mind. Shared pretense with other children, in particular, is strongly related to theory of mind (Dockett & Smith, 1995; Schwebel, Rosen, & Singer, 1999). However, recent longitudinal research indicates that the link between theory of mind and pretend play may be in the opposite direction from what some psychologists have assumed. That is, development of a theory of mind may precede and, to some extent, cause the emergence of sophisticated forms of pretend play, such as the kind of role-play observed when children play house (Jenkins & Astington, 2000).

Recent findings suggest that interactions with siblings may be more important than those with peers (Deneault et al., 2008; Hughes et al., 2005). In one study, researchers compared children with either older or younger siblings to those who had only co-twins or no siblings (Wright, Fineberg, Brown, & Perkins, 2005). They found that only children and twin-only children performed more poorly on theory of mind tasks than those who had either older or younger siblings. Various explanations have been proposed for what is called the *sibling advantage* in theory of mind development. To date, the best such theory focuses on the mentor-apprentice roles that often characterize siblings of different ages. You will learn more about these roles in Chapter 11.

Language skills, such as knowledge of words for feelings, desires, and thoughts—for example, *want*, *need*, *think*, and *remember*—are also related to theory of mind (Green, Pring, & Swettenham, 2004; Hughes et al., 2005). Furthermore, children whose parents discuss emotion-provoking past events with them develop a theory of mind more rapidly than their peers do (Ontai & Thompson, 2008). Indeed, some level of language facility may be a necessary condition for the development of theory of mind. Developmentalists have found that preschool children simply do not succeed at tests of false-belief skills until they have reached a certain threshold of general language skill (Milligan, Astington, & Dack, 2007). Differences in rate of language development may also explain why preschool-aged girls, whose language skills are, on average, more advanced than those of boys, demonstrate higher levels of success on tests of false-belief skills (Charman, Ruffman, & Clements, 2002).

Further support for this point comes from the finding that children with disabilities that affect language development, such as congenital deafness, mental retardation, or autism, develop a theory of mind more slowly than others (Best, Moffat, Power, Owens, & Johnstone, 2008). Research has also demonstrated that, among such children, development of theory of mind is better predicted by language skills than by disability category (Porter, Coltheart, & Langdon, 2008).

False Belief and Theory of Mind Across Cultures

Learning Objective 6.9

What does research indicate about the correlation between culture and theory of mind?

Research suggests that the false belief principle develops between ages 3 and 5 across a variety of cultures. For example, in one classic study Jeremy Avis and Paul Harris (1991) adapted the traditional false belief testing procedure for use with children in a pygmy tribe, the Baka, in Cameroon. The Baka are hunters and gatherers who live together in camps. Each child was tested in his or her own hut, using materials with which he or she was completely familiar. The child watched one adult named Mopfana (a member of the tribe) put some mango seeds into a bowl. Mopfana then left the hut, and a second adult (also a tribe member) told the child that they were going to play a game with Mopfana: They were going to hide the seeds in a cooking pot. Then the second adult asked the child what Mopfana was going to do when he came back. Would he look for the seeds in the bowl or in the pot? The second adult also asked the child whether Mopfana's heart would feel good or bad before he lifted the lid of the bowl. Younger children— 2- and 3-year-olds and those who had recently turned 4—were much more likely to say that Mopfana would look for the seeds in the pot or to say that he would be sad before he looked in the bowl; older 4-year-olds and 5-year-olds were nearly always right on both questions.

In another classic study, when Flavell used his sponge/rock task with children in mainland China, he found that Chinese 3-year-olds are just as confused about this task as are American or British 3-year-olds, whereas 5-year-old Chinese children had no difficulty with it (Flavell, Zhang, Zou, Dong, & Qi, 1983). In these very different cultures, then, something similar seems to be occurring between ages 3 and 5. In these years, all children seem to understand something general about the difference between appearance and reality.

Research also suggests that certain aspects of theory of mind development may be universal. For example, similar sequences of such development have been found in the United States, China, Europe, and India (Cole, 2005; Liu, Wellman, Tardif, & Sabbagh, 2008). Figure 6.5 shows the results of one study comparing the performance of children from five

Research indicates that the sequence of development of theory of mind is highly similar across cultures.

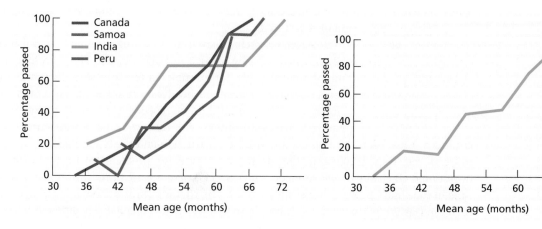

Figure 6.5 False Belief Tasks across Cultures

Percentage of children passing the false-belief test as a function of age. In the left panel, data are plotted separately for Canada, Samoa, India, and Peru. In the right panel, results for these four cultures are combined. Data from 13 Samoan and all Thai children were excluded from this analysis because their birth dates were not available.

(*Source:* Callaghan et al. (2005). "Synchrony in the Onset of Mental State." *Psychological Science, 16*(5), 378–384, Fig. 1, p. 382, copyright © 2005 by Blackwell Publishers, Inc. Reprinted with permission.)

cultures on a false-belief task (Callaghan et al., 2005). Moreover, participation in shared pretending has also been shown to be related to theory of mind development cross-culturally (Tan-Niam, Wood, & O'Malley, 1998).

Learning Objective 6.10

How do the theories of the neo-Piagetians and Vygotsky explain cognitive development?

Alternative Theories of Early Childhood Thinking

In recent years, a number of interesting theoretical approaches have attempted to explain both Piaget's original results and more recent findings that appear to contradict them.

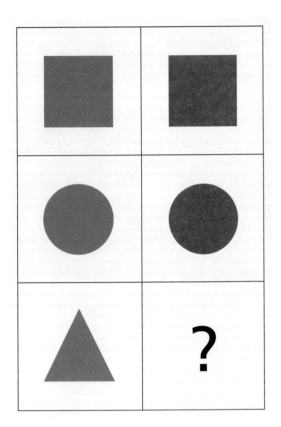

Figure 6.6   Neo-Piagetian Matrix Task

Neo-Piagetians have used Piaget's matrix classification task in strategy training studies with young children. Before training, most preschoolers say that a green triangle or an orange circle belongs in the box with the question mark. After learning a two-step strategy in which they are taught to classify each object first by shape and then by color, children understand that an orange triangle is the figure that is needed to complete the matrix.

Neo-Piagetian Theories   One set of alternative proposals is based on the information-processing model (explained in Chapter 1). These are called **neo-Piagetian theories** because they expand on, rather than contradict, Piaget's views (Morral, Gobbo, Marini, & Sheese, 2008). For example, the late neo-Piagetian Robbie Case explained age differences in cognitive development as a function of changes in children's use of their short-term memories (Case, 1985, 1992). Case used the term **short-term storage space (STSS)** to refer to working memory capacity. According to Case, there is a limit on how many schemes can be attended to in STSS. He referred to the maximum number of schemes that may be put into STSS at one time as **operational efficiency**. Improvements in operational efficiency occur through both practice (through tasks that require memory use, such as learning the alphabet) and brain maturation as the child gets older. Thus, a 7-year-old is better able to handle the processing demands of conservation tasks than a 4-year-old because of improvements in the operational efficiency of the STSS.

A good example of the function of STSS may be found by examining *matrix classification*, a task Piaget often used with both preschool and school-aged children (see Figure 6.6). Matrix classification requires the child to place a given stimulus in two categories at the same time. Young children fail at such tasks because, according to neo-Piagetian theory, they begin by processing the stimulus according to one dimension (either shape or color) and then either fail to realize that it is necessary to reprocess the stimulus along the second dimension or forget to do so.

However, researchers have trained young children to perform correctly on such tasks by using a two-step strategy. They are taught to think of a red triangle, for example, in terms of shape first and color second. Typically, instruction involves a number of training tasks in which researchers remind children repeatedly that it is necessary to remember to reclassify stimuli with respect to the second variable. According to Case, both children's failure prior to instruction and the type of strategy training to which they respond illustrate the constraints imposed on problem-solving by the limited operational efficiency of the younger child's STSS. There is only room for one scheme at a time in the child's STSS, either shape or color. The training studies show that younger children can learn to perform correctly but do so in a way that is qualitatively different from the approach of older children. The older child's more efficient STSS allows her to think about shape and color at the same time and therefore to perform matrix classification successfully without any training.

However, it appears that children must be exposed to multiple training sessions that take place over a fairly extended period of time, as long as an entire year, in order to effect permanent changes in their matrix completion behaviors (Siegler & Svetina, 2002). Comparative research has shown that children who develop these skills on their own do so over an equivalent period of time and demonstrate transitional behaviors that are quite similar to those of children who are trained by experimenters. Thus, some developmentalists have suggested that there is no advantage to be gained by training children to exhibit skills that they are known to acquire in the natural course of cognitive development. Moreover, with regard to research methodology, when children must be trained over long periods of time, it becomes impossible to distinguish between the effects of training and those of the natural developmental processes that are occurring contemporaneously with such training.

Vygotsky's Socio-Cultural Theory   In Chapter 1, you learned that psychologists' interest in Russian psychologist Lev Vygotsky's views on development has grown recently. Vygotsky's theory differs from both Piagetian and neo-Piagetian theory in its emphasis on the role of social factors in cognitive development. For example, two preschoolers working on a puzzle together discuss where the pieces belong. After a number of such dialogues, the participants internalize the discussion. It then becomes a model for an internal conversation the child uses to guide himself through the puzzle-solution process. In this way, Vygotsky suggested, solutions to problems are socially generated and learned. Vygotsky did not deny that individual learning takes place. Rather, he suggested that group learning processes are central to cognitive development. Consequently, from Vygotsky's perspective, social interaction is required for cognitive development (Thomas, 2005).

You'll recall that two important general principles of Vygotsky's theory are the *zone of proximal development* and *scaffolding*. Vygotsky also proposed specific stages of cognitive development from birth to age 7. Each stage represents a step toward the child's internalization of the ways of thinking used by adults in his society.

In the first period, called the *primitive stage*, the infant possesses mental processes that are similar to those of lower animals. He learns primarily through conditioning until language begins to develop in the second year. At that point, he enters the *naive psychology stage*, in which he learns to use language to communicate but still does not understand its symbolic character. For example, he doesn't realize that any collection of sounds could stand for the object "chair" as long as everyone agrees on the sounds; that is, if all English speakers agreed to substitute the word *blek* for *chair*, they could do so because they would all understand what *blek* meant.

Once the child begins to appreciate the symbolic function of language, near the end of the third year of life, he enters the *egocentric speech stage*. In this stage, he uses language as a guide to solving problems. In effect, he tells himself how to do things. For example, a 3-year-old walking down a flight of stairs might say to himself "Be careful." Such a statement would be the result of his internalization of statements made to him by more mature individuals in his environment.

Piaget also recognized the existence and importance of egocentric speech. However, he believed that egocentric speech disappeared as the child approached the end of the preoperational stage. In contrast, Vygotsky claimed that egocentric speech becomes completely internalized at age 6 or 7, when children enter the final period of cognitive development, the *ingrowth stage*. Thus, he suggested that the logical thinking Piaget ascribed to older children resulted from their internalization of speech routines they had acquired from older children and adults in the social world rather than from schemes they had constructed for themselves through interaction with the physical world.

At present, there is insufficient evidence to support or contradict most of Vygotsky's ideas (Miller, 2002). However, some intriguing research on children's construction of theory of mind ideas during social interactions lends weight to Vygotsky's major propositions. It seems that children in pairs and groups do produce more sophisticated theory of mind ideas than individual children who work on problems alone. For this reason, educators have used Vygotsky's theory as the basis for recommending that school children do assignments and work on projects in groups rather than individually (Norton & D'Ambrosio, 2008). However, the

neo-Piagetian theory A theory of cognitive development that assumes that Piaget's basic ideas are correct but that uses concepts from information-processing theory to explain children's movement from one stage to the next.

short-term storage space (STSS) A neo-Piagetian term for working memory capacity.

operational efficiency A neo-Piagetian term for the number of schemes an individual can place into working memory at one time.

sophistication of a group's ideas appears to depend on the presence of at least one fairly advanced individual child in the group (Tan-Niam, Wood, & O'Malley, 1998). Thus, Vygotsky's theory may ignore the important contributions of individual thought to group interaction.

The School-Aged Child

Like their younger counterparts, school-aged children develop figurative schemes at an impressive pace, especially when formal schooling introduces them to a breadth of ideas and basic facts about the world that take them beyond everyday experience. What is different about this stage, though, is that children's operative schemes begin to take shape and to provide them with a network of rules that provide logical frameworks for their figurative schemes. Consequently, the child develops a set of immensely powerful, abstract, general rules or strategies for examining and interacting with the world. Piaget called these new rules *concrete operations*.

Learning Objective 6.11
What are concrete operations, and how do they represent an advance over earlier forms of thought?

Piaget's View of Concrete Operations

Piaget defined concrete operations as a set of powerful, abstract schemes that are critical building blocks of logical thinking, providing internal rules about objects and their relationships.

Reversibility   Piaget thought that the most critical of all the concrete operations was **reversibility**—the understanding that both physical actions and mental operations can be reversed. The clay sausage in a conservation experiment can be made back into a ball; the water can be poured back into the shorter, fatter glass. This understanding of the basic reversibility of actions lies behind many of the gains made during this period.

For example, if you understand reversibility, then knowing that A is larger than B also tells you that B is smaller than A. The ability to understand hierarchies of classes, such as "Fido," "spaniel," "dog," and "animal," also rests on this ability to go backward as well as forward in thinking about relationships. Both Piaget's original observations and more recent research have demonstrated that at about age 7 or 8 the child first grasps the principle of **class inclusion**, the idea that subordinate classes are included in larger, superordinate classes. Bananas are included in the class "fruit," fruits are included in the class "food," and so forth. Preschool children understand that bananas are also fruit, but they do not yet fully understand the relationship between the classes—that the class "fruit" is superordinate, including all bananas as well as all other types of fruit, such as oranges and apples.

Piaget also proposed that reversibility underlies the school-aged child's ability to use **inductive logic**: She can reason from her own experience to a general principle. For example, she can move from the observation that when you add another toy to a set and then count the set, it has one more toy than it did before, to a general principle that adding always makes more.

Elementary school children are pretty good observational scientists and enjoy cataloging, counting species of trees or birds, or figuring out the nesting habits of guinea pigs. What they are not yet good at is **deductive logic**, which requires starting with a general principle and then predicting some outcome or observation, like going from a theory to a hypothesis. For example, suppose someone asked you to think of all the ways human relationships and societies would be different if women were physically as strong as men. Answering this question requires deductive, not inductive, logic; the problem is hard because you must imagine things that you have not experienced. The concrete operational child is good at dealing with things he knows or can see and physically manipulate—that is, he is good with concrete, or actual things; he does not do well with mentally manipulating ideas or possibilities. Piaget thought that deductive reasoning did not develop until the stage of formal operations in adolescence.

reversibility One of the most critical of the operations Piaget identified as part of the concrete operations period: the understanding that actions and mental operations can be reversed.

class inclusion The principle that subordinate classes of objects are included in superordinate classes.

inductive logic Reasoning from the particular to the general, from experience to broad rules, characteristic of concrete operational thinking.

deductive logic Reasoning from the general to the particular, from a rule to an expected instance or from a theory to a hypothesis, characteristic of formal operational thinking.

Horizontal Decalage Note that Piaget did *not* argue that all concrete operational skills popped out at the same moment, as if a light bulb had gone on in the child's head. He used the term **horizontal decalage** to refer to children's tendency to be able to solve some kinds of concrete operational problems earlier than others. The French word *decalage* means "shift." The shift into concrete operational thinking is "horizontal" because it involves applying the same kind of thinking—concrete operational logic—to new kinds of problems. A "vertical" decalage would be a shift from one kind of thinking to another, as happens when children move from the preoperational to the concrete operational stage.

Because elementary school students are good at observational science and inductive reasoning, field trips like this fossil-hunting expedition are a particularly effective way of teaching.

An early longitudinal study of concrete operations tasks by Carol Tomlinson-Keasey and her colleagues (1979) demonstrated just how long the period of horizontal decalage may actually be. They followed a group of 38 children from kindergarten through third grade, testing them with five tasks each time: conservation of mass, weight, and volume; class inclusion; and hierarchical classification. You can see from Figure 6.7 that the children got better at all five tasks over the 3-year period, with a spurt between the end of kindergarten and the beginning of first grade (at about the age Piaget thought that concrete operations really developed) and another spurt during second grade. However, even at the end of third grade, not every child had mastered all of the concrete operations tasks.

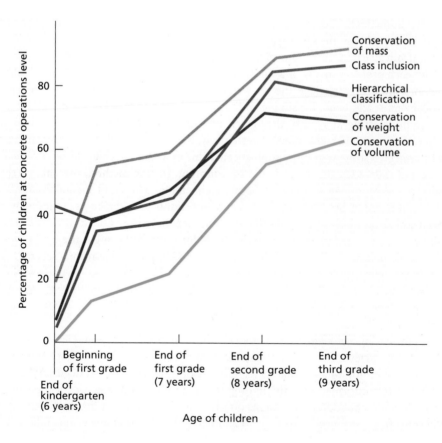

Figure 6.7   Longitudinal Study of Concrete Operations

In this longitudinal study, children were tested with the same set of concrete operations tasks five different times, beginning in kindergarten and ending in the third grade.

(*Source*: Tomlinson-Keasey, Eisert, Kahle, Hardy-Brown, & Keasey, 1979, adapted from Table 2, p. 1158.)

horizontal decalage Piaget's term for school-aged children's inconsistent performance on concrete operations tasks.

Understanding the concept of horizontal decalage is especially important for teachers, parents, and others who interact with children every day. For example, a 9-year-old may grasp the logic of some mathematical relationships (e.g., If 6 + 2 = 8 and 4 + 4 = 8, then 6 + 2 = 4 + 4). Her understanding of such relationships demonstrates concrete operational thought. However, the same child, when asked by a parent to recall where she left her backpack, has difficulty applying concrete operational logic to the problem. As adults, we might use our concrete operations schemes to think of the problem this way: "If I had my backpack when I came in the door after school, and I didn't have it when I sat down in the living room, then it must be somewhere between the door and the living room." However, a 9-year-old who can grasp the concrete operational logic of mathematical relationships may demonstrate horizontal decalage by responding to the lost backpack problem with preoperational thinking: "I don't know where my backpack is; someone must have stolen it." In such situations, teachers or parents may think a child is being difficult or lazy; in reality, she simply may not yet be capable of using concrete operational thinking to solve everyday problems that seem simple to adults but are actually quite complex.

Learning Objective 6.12

What does Siegler's research suggest about concrete operational thinking?

Different Approaches to Concrete Operational Thought

Some psychologists have suggested that the problem of horizontal decalage calls into question Piaget's assertion that concrete operational thinking is a stage of cognitive development.

Siegler's Wave Theory   The work of Robert Siegler (1996; Siegler & Chen, 2002) has shown that individual children may use a wide variety of types of rules—from very simple to quite sophisticated—on the same type of problem in different attempts on the same day. For example, if you give first- or second-graders simple addition problems (3 + 6, 9 + 4, etc.), they may solve each problem in any of a variety of ways. If they have committed a particular sum to memory, they may retrieve the answer directly from memory without calculation—the strategy most adults use for simple addition problems. On other problems, children may simply count, starting at 1, until they reach the sum. So 6 + 3 becomes "One, two, three, four, five, six, . . . seven, eight, nine." Alternatively, they may use what some researchers call the *min strategy*, a somewhat more sophisticated rule in which the child starts with the larger number and then adds the smaller one by counting. In this method, the child arrives at the sum 3 + 6 by saying to herself, "Seven, eight, nine." The child mentally counts each number as it is added. So, when she begins at 6 and counts to 7, she knows that one number has been added. Similarly, she knows that two numbers have been added when she gets to 8, and three have been added when she arrives at 9. Finally, a child might use a still more sophisticated *decomposition strategy*, which involves dividing a problem into several simpler ones. For example, a child might add 9 + 4 by thinking, "10 + 4 = 14, 9 is one less than 10, 14 − 1 = 13, so 9 + 4 = 13" (Siegler, 1996, p. 94). (You may use this method for more complicated problems, such as multiplying 16 × 9. You might think, "9 × 10 = 90; 9 × 6 = 54; 54 + 90 = 144.")

With increasing age, elementary school children use counting less and less while increasing their use of retrieval, the min strategy, and decomposition—a finding that is entirely consistent with the notion of a gradual increase in use of more complex strategies. What Siegler has added to this information is the finding that the same child may use all these different strategies on different addition problems on the same day. So, it isn't that each child systematically shifts from one level of strategy to another, but rather that any given child may have a whole variety of strategies and may use some or all of them on different problems. Over time, the child's repertoire of likely strategies does indeed shift toward more and more complex or sophisticated ones, just as Piaget and others have described. But the process is not steplike; instead, it is more like a series of waves, as shown in Figure 6.8. When children add a new strategy, they do not immediately give up old ones; instead, they continue to use the old and the new for a while. Gradually, as the new strategies become more firmly established and better rehearsed, the less efficient or less effective strategies are dropped.

Relational Complexity   Other theorists have explained children's success and failure on Piaget's concrete operational tasks as a result of variations in the **relational complexity** of the tasks themselves (Andrews & Halford, 2002). They argue that success on Piaget's tasks is determined by how many elements a problem has and how complicated the relationships among the elements are. Performance on Piaget's tasks improves across middle childhood, they claim, because improvements in the efficiency of the child's working memory enable him to cognitively manage more elements and more complex relationships among the elements of a problem.

One line of research on relational complexity deals with **transitivity**, the ability to make inferences about logical relationships in an ordered set of stimuli (Andrews & Halford, 1998). A simple example of a transitivity task is one in which a child is shown a stick *A* and asked to compare it to a slightly shorter stick *B*. Through questioning and discussion with the experimenter, the child concludes that *A* is longer than *B*. He is then asked to compare *B* to a slightly shorter stick *C*. Once he concludes that *B* is longer than *C*, he is asked whether *A* is longer or shorter than *C*. Children who infer that *A* must be longer than *C*, even though they did not directly compare *A* to *C*, exhibit transitivity. Researchers whose studies span 3 decades have found that few children younger than 6 can solve simple transitivity problems (Murray & Youniss, 1968; Andrews & Halford, 1998). When the complexity of transitivity problems is increased, as when sticks *B* and *C* are of equal length, even 8-year-olds have difficulty with transitivity (Andrews & Halford, 1998; Murray & Youniss, 1968). Thus, contrary to Piaget's view, there may not be a single transitivity scheme that is universally applicable to all such problems. Instead, a child's success on a transitivity problem may depend on how well the problem fits the capabilities of his information processing system at a particular point in development.

Relational complexity studies also focus on **seriation** tasks, problems that require children to use a rule to put an array of objects in order (Piaget & Inhelder, 1969). In Piaget's classic version of the seriation task, the researcher asks the child to arrange ten sticks of varying length from shortest to longest. Most children younger than 8 create ordered sets that include only three or four sticks rather than a single ordered array that includes all of them. In other words, they simplify the task by breaking it down into several less complex subtasks that they can accomplish (Halford, Bunch, & McCredden, 2007). In the process, however, they end up with an incorrect solution to the original problem.

Adolescence

Piaget's research led him to conclude that a new level of thinking emerges fairly rapidly in early adolescence that enables teens to think logically about ideas that are not tied to concrete referents in the real world. Called *formal operations*, this stage is typically defined as the period during which adolescents learn to reason logically about abstract concepts.

Figure 6.8   Siegler's Wave Theory

Siegler's "overlapping wave" model of cognitive development is probably a better description of the way children move toward more complex forms of thinking than the steplike stage model Piaget originally proposed.

(*Source: Emerging Minds: The Process of Change in Children's Thinking* by Robert S. Siegler, © 1996 by Oxford University Press, Inc. Used by permission of Oxford University Press.)

relational complexity The number of elements in a problem and the complexity of the relationships among the elements.

transitivity The ability to make inferences about logical relationships in an ordered set of stimuli.

seriation The ability to use a rule to put an array of objects in order.

Piaget's View of Formal Operations

The formal operations stage has a number of key elements.

Systematic Problem Solving   One important feature of formal operational thinking is the ability to search systematically and methodically for the answer to a problem. To study this ability, Piaget and his colleague Barbel Inhelder (Inhelder & Piaget, 1958) presented adolescents with complex tasks, mostly drawn from the physical sciences. In one of these tasks, participants were given various lengths of string and a set of objects of various weights that could be tied to one of the strings to make a swinging pendulum. They were shown how to start the pendulum by pushing the weight with differing amounts of force and by holding the weight at different heights. The participants' task was to figure out whether the length of the string, the weight of the object, the force of the push, or the height of the push (or a combination of these factors) determines the period of the pendulum, that is, the amount of time for one swing. (In case you've forgotten your high school physics, the answer is that only the length of the string affects the period of the pendulum.)

If you give this task to a concrete operational child, she will usually try out many different combinations of length, weight, force, and height in an inefficient way. She might try a heavy weight on a long string and then a light weight on a short string. Because she has changed both string length and weight in these two trials, however, there is no way she can draw a clear conclusion about either factor. In contrast, an adolescent using formal operational thinking is likely to be more organized, attempting to vary just one of the four factors at a time. She may try a heavy object with a short string, then with a medium string, then with a long one. After that, she might try a light object with the three lengths of string. Of course, not all adolescents (or all adults, for that matter) are quite this methodical in their approach. Still, there is a very dramatic difference between the overall strategy used by 10-year-olds and that used by 15-year-olds, which marks the shift from concrete to formal operations.

Logic   Another facet of the shift from concrete to formal operations is the appearance of what Piaget called hypothetico-deductive reasoning in the child's repertoire of skills. Piaget

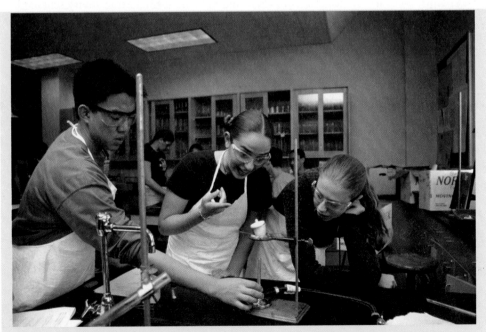

One aspect of formal operations is the use of deductive logic, which is normally required first in high school, especially in math and science classes like this chemistry class.

suggested that the concrete operational child can use inductive reasoning, which involves arriving at a conclusion or a rule based on a lot of individual experiences. **Hypothetico-deductive reasoning**, a more sophisticated kind of reasoning, involves using deductive logic, considering hypotheses or hypothetical premises, and then deriving logical outcomes. For example, the statement "If all people are equal, then you and I must be equal" involves logic of this type. Although children as young as 4 or 5 can understand some deductive relationships if the premises given are factually true, both cross-sectional and longitudinal studies support Piaget's assertion that only at adolescence are young people able to understand and use the basic principles of logic (Mueller, Overton, & Reene, 2001; Ward & Overton, 1990).

A great deal of the logic of science is hypothetico-deductive logic. Scientists begin with a theory and propose, "If this theory is correct, then we should observe such and such." In doing this, they are going well beyond their observations; they are conceiving of things they have never seen that ought to be true or observable. We can think of the change to this type of thinking at adolescence as part of a general decentering process that began much earlier. The preoperational child gradually moves away from his egocentrism and comes to be able to view things from the physical or emotional perspective of others. During the formal operations stage, the child takes another step by freeing himself even from his reliance on specific experiences.

Piaget also suggested that in many adolescents, hypothetico-deductive thinking leads to an outlook he called *naive idealism* (Piaget & Inhelder, 1969). Adolescents can use this powerful intellectual tool to think of an ideal world and to compare the real world to it. Not surprisingly, the real world often falls short of the ideal. As a result, some adolescents become so dissatisfied with the world that they resolve to change it. For many, the changes they propose are personal. For example, a teen whose parents have been divorced for years may suddenly decide she wants to live with the noncustodial parent because she expects that her life will be better. Another may express naive idealism by becoming involved in a political or religious organization.

The two compositions in Figure 6.9 illustrate how concrete operational and formal operational thinking lead to very different results when children are asked to reason deductively

hypothetico-deductive reasoning Piaget's term for the form of reasoning that is part of formal operational thought and involves not just deductive logic but also the ability to consider hypotheses and hypothetical possibilities.

Figure 6.9
Concrete versus Formal Operational Thinking

The same boy wrote both of these compositions. The one on the left was written when the boy was 10, and the other when he was 13. The compositions illustrate the difference between concrete operational and formal operational thinking in response to the hypothetical question "What would you do if you became president of the United States?"

(*Source*: Author.)

If I become president, I would create a program called "Houston 2020". It would be a whole new Houston that would orbit around the Earth, but there would still be a Houston on Earth. I would get all the trained men of high offices in the Air Force to "litterally" go up into space and build this production. It would be Houston's twin. Houston 2020 would have a huge iron, steel, aluminum, and titanium dome over it, which would have a door that only opened to let ships in. It would have an oxygen supply that would last for two billion years. Yes I would do this and I would do the same for every major city in the United States of America!

If I were president, I would not be able to make or abolish laws on my own. So I would just make suggestions to Congress and the public because they make and unmake the laws. One suggestion would be to lower taxes so that people would like me. I would use this popularity to try and make the country a better place. I would be a loyal husband, a fantastic father, and a great brother. I would hope that people would follow my example so there would not be so much hatred. If there was less hatred, there would not be as much crime which would make this country a happier place to live.

from an untrue premise. Both essays were written by the same boy, one at age 10 and the other at age 13, in response to the question "What would you do if you became president of the United States?" The 10-year-old boy's response is full of ideas about the president's ability to manipulate the concrete world. Significantly, it proposes building replicas of American cities in space, nicely illustrating the concrete operational thinker's tendency to replicate concrete reality when asked to think hypothetically. By contrast, the composition written at age 13 reflects both better deductive thinking and Piaget's notion of naive idealism. Moreover, it contains abstract ideas, such as the hypothesized relationship between hatred and crime, that are completely absent from the composition written at age 10. Thus, as Piaget's theory suggests, at 13, this boy not only knew more about the office of the president (e.g., that the president doesn't make laws singlehandedly), but he also thought quite differently about the world than he did at age 10.

Learning Objective 6.14

What does post-Piagetian research suggest about this stage?

Post-Piagetian Work on Adolescent Thought

A good deal of post-Piagetian research confirms Piaget's basic observations. Adolescents, much more than elementary school children, operate with possibilities in addition to reality, and they are more likely to use deductive logic. As Flavell puts it, the thinking of the elementary school child "hugs the ground of . . . empirical reality" (1985, p. 98), while the teenager is more likely to soar into the realm of speculation and possibility. An 8-year-old thinks that "knowing" something is a simple matter of finding out the facts; a teenager is more likely to see knowledge as relative, as less certain (Bartsch, 1993). Deanna Kuhn and her colleagues (1995) have also found that teenagers and young adults, faced with disconfirming evidence, are more likely than younger children are to change their theories or their initial guesses; they are also more systematic in seeking out new information that will help hone their hypotheses—both hallmarks of formal operational reasoning.

A research illustration clearly illustrates the change in thinking. In an early cross-sectional study, Susan Martorano (1977) tested 20 girls at each of four grades (6th, 8th, 10th, and 12th) on 10 different tasks that required one or more of what Piaget called *formal operations skills*. Indeed, many of the tasks Martorano used were those Piaget himself had devised. Results from two of these tasks are shown in Figure 6.10. The pendulum problem is the same one described earlier; the balance problem requires a youngster to predict whether two different weights, hung at varying distances on either side of a scale, will balance. To solve this problem using formal operations, the teenager must consider both weight and distance simultaneously. You can see from the graph that a significant improvement in scores occurred between 8th and 10th grades (between ages 13 and 15).

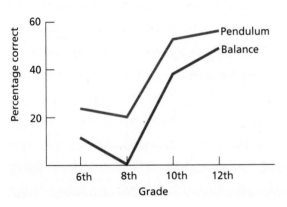

Figure 6.10

Performance on Two Formal Operations Tasks

These are the results from 2 of the 10 different formal operations tasks used in Martorano's cross-sectional study.

(*Source*: Martorano, 1977, p. 670. Copyright by the American Psychological Association.)

Formal Operations and Adolescent Decision Making In a more practical vein, Catherine Lewis (1981) has shown that teenagers' new cognitive abilities alter the ways in which they go about making decisions. Older teenagers are more focused on the future, on possibilities, and on options when they consider decisions. Lewis asked 8th-, 10th-, and 12th-grade students to respond to a set of dilemmas, each of which involved a person facing a difficult decision, such as whether to have an operation to remove a facial disfigurement or how to decide which doctor to trust when different doctors give differing advice. Forty-two percent of the 12th graders, but only 11% of the 8th graders, mentioned future possibilities in their answers to these dilemmas. In answer to the cosmetic surgery dilemma, for example, a 12th grader said, "Well, you have to look into the different things . . . that might be more important later on in your life. You should think about, will it have any ef-

Elkind's Adolescent Egocentrism

Psychologist David Elkind hypothesized that another common manifestation of hypothetico-deductive reasoning is a type of thought he called adolescent egocentrism, the belief that one's thoughts, beliefs, and feelings are unique. One component of adolescent egocentrism, Elkind said, is the *personal fable*, the belief that the events of one's life are controlled by a mentally constructed autobiography (Elkind, 1967). For example, a sexually active teenage girl might be drawing upon such a personal fable when she says "I just don't see myself getting pregnant" in response to suggestions that she use contraception. In contrast to this inappropriately rosy view of the future, a teen who is involved in a violent street gang may say "I'll probably get shot before I make 18" when advised to leave the gang and focus on graduating from high school.

Elkind also proposed that adolescent egocentrism drives teenagers to try out various attitudes, behaviors, and even clothing choices in front of an *imaginary audience*, an internalized set of behavioral standards usually derived from a teenager's peer group. Think about the example of a

teenaged girl who is habitually late for school because she changes clothes two or three times every day before leaving home. Each time the girl puts on a different outfit, she imagines how her peers at school will respond to it. If the imaginary audience criticizes the outfit, the girl feels she must change clothes in order to elicit a more favorable response. Similarly, a boy may spend hours in front of the mirror trimming his sideburns in an effort to achieve a look he thinks his peers will approve of.

Many developmentalists have found Elkind's personal fable and imaginary audience to be helpful in explaining a variety of adolescents' risky behaviors. For example, both types of thinking come into play when teens decide to start smoking (Bright, McKillop, & Ryder, 2008). As Elkind suggests, then, the personal fable and imaginary audience may lead adolescents to make poor decisions about risky behaviors.

However, adolescent egocentrism seems to serve a protective function for some teens. For instance, research suggests that teens who use this

kind of thinking as a coping mechanism when faced with a lack of support from parents are less likely to be depressed than peers who do not cope in this way (Goossens, Beyers, Emmen, & van Aken, 2002). Thus, in contrast to Elkind's negative characterization of the personal fable and imaginary audience, both may actually be facilitators of, rather than hindrances to, a teenager's identity development. Moreover, what Elkind called adolescent egocentrism may actually turn out to be one of many manifestations of the identity development process you will learn about in Chapter 10.

Questions for Critical Analysis

1. In what ways might the personal fable and imaginary audience positively influence a teenager's decisions about risky behaviors such as drug use and unsafe sex? How might they negatively influence such decisions?
2. What are the roles of the imaginary audience and the personal fable in adults' perceptions of themselves?

---

fect on your future and with, maybe, the people you meet . . . " (Lewis, 1981, p. 541). An 8th grader, in response to the same dilemma, said, "The different things I would think about in getting the operation is like if the girls turn you down on a date, or the money, or the kids teasing you at school" (Lewis, 1981, p. 542). The 8th grader, as is characteristic of the preadolescent or early adolescent, is focused on the here and now, on concrete things. The teenager is considering things that might happen in the future.

Note, though, that even among the 12th graders in Lewis's study, nearly three-fifths did not show this type of future orientation. And take another look at Figure 6.10; only about 50–60% of 12th graders solved the two formal operations problems. In fact, only 2 of the 20 12th graders in Martorano's study used formal operational logic on all 10 problems. These findings reflect a common pattern in research on adolescent thinking: By no means do all teenagers (or adults) use these more abstract forms of logic and thought. Keating (1980) estimates that only about 50–60% of 18- to 20-year-olds in industrialized countries use formal operations at all, let alone consistently. In nonindustrialized countries, the rates are even lower.

There are several possible explanations for such low levels of formal operational thought. One is that the parts of the brain needed to connect hypothetico-deductive thought to everyday problems may not be sufficiently developed to make these connections until the late teens. Neuroimaging studies comparing the brain activity of children, teens, and adults while they were engaged in a gambling task provide support for this hypothesis (Crone & van der Molen, 2004).

Expertise may also be a crucial factor. That is, most of us have some formal operational ability, but we can apply it only to topics or tasks with which we are highly familiar. Willis

Overton and his colleagues (1987) have found considerable support for this possibility in their research. They have found that as many as 90% of adolescents can solve quite complex logic problems if the problems are stated using familiar content, while only half can solve identical logic problems when they are stated in abstract language.

Another possibility is that most everyday experiences and tasks do not require formal operations. Inductive reasoning or other simpler forms of logic are quite sufficient most of the time. We can elevate our thinking a notch under some circumstances, especially if someone reminds us that it would be useful to do so, but we simply don't rehearse formal operations very much.

Finally, psychologist David Elkind (1967) has proposed that, paradoxically, it is formal operational thinking itself that impairs adolescents' ability to make sound decisions about everyday matters. Elkind has proposed that the hypothetico-deductive capabilities associated with formal operational thought enable teenagers to construct unrealistic ideas about both the present and the future. In effect, these ideas lead teens to view their lives with either excessive optimism or excessive pessimism. Elkind's ideas have had a great deal of influence on the approaches taken by researchers to understanding teens' decisions with regard to risky behaviors such as drug use (see *Thinking about Research*).

Culture and Formal Operational Thinking   The fact that formal operational thinking is found more often among young people or adults in Western or other industrialized cultures can be interpreted as being due to the fact that such cultures include high levels of technology and complex life-styles that demand more formal operational thought. By this argument, all nonretarded teenagers and adults are thought to have the capacity for formal logic, but only those of us whose lives demand its development will actually acquire it (Kuhn, 2008).

Notice that all these explanations undermine the very notion of a universal "stage" of thinking in adolescence. Yes, more abstract forms of thinking may develop in adolescence, but they are neither universal nor broadly used by individual teenagers or adults. Whether one develops or uses these forms of logic depends heavily on experience, expertise, and environmental demand.

Development of Information-Processing Skills

Human memory does not function as a mental tape recorder. Instead, memory is a constructive process, one that sometimes leads to errors and can even result in the invention of pseudomemories depicting events that never actually happened (Loftus, 1993). The constructive aspect of memory can begin quite early in life, as discussed in *Developmental Science in the Real World*. Further, constructive memories can be made more vivid, and our confidence in their veracity increased, by repetition, even when such memories are partially or entirely false (Thomas, Bulevich, & Loftus, 2003). Moreover, false memories that carry deep personal significance, are more likely to become embedded in our minds than those that concern less important matters (Kronlund & Whittlesea, 2005).

You may recall from Chapter 1 that the information-processing perspective is the view that has most often been used to study human memory. The information-processing model of memory postulates that information is processed, stored, and retrieved in different ways by the various components of the memory system, each of which has unique characteristics (see Figure 1.4). Although information-processing theory is not truly a developmental theory, research derived from this perspective has shed considerable light on age-related changes in memory and other aspects of cognitive development (Lamb & Lewis, 2005).

Leading Questions and Children's Memory

Ari was alarmed when his 3-year-old son, Micah, told him about an incident involving a neighbor that Ari believed to be a possible case of sexual molestation, so he immediately called the police. Before the police arrived, Ari received a telephone call from a social worker, who advised Ari to write down everything that his son said spontaneously about the event but to avoid questioning him directly. Puzzled, Ari wondered, Who might be better than a parent to question a child about such a potentially traumatic event?

The social worker explained that preschoolers' memories are more suggestible than those of older children or adults (Ceci & Bruck, 1995; Hardy & Van Leeuwen, 2004). One common way that researchers study the suggestibility factor is to show the same film to children and adults. Then, while asking questions about what the participants saw, the investigators inject a question that assumes something that didn't really happen (e.g., "He was carrying a pipe wrench when he came into the room, wasn't he?"). Young children are more affected than

adults are by such misleading suggestions (Leichtman & Ceci, 1995).

Research shows that young children are susceptible to misleading questions of this type because they have poor *source monitoring skills*, the ability to keep track of where a piece of information originated (Bright-Paul, Jarrold, & Wright, 2008). As a result, a young child who is being questioned has difficulty distinguishing between ideas that originated in his own memory and those that are contained in or implied by the interviewers' questions. Source monitoring is linked to theory of mind development. Consequently, many developmentalists hypothesize that theory of mind development accounts for improvements that emerge around age 6 or so in children's source monitoring skills and ability to resist interviewers' leading questions (Melinder, Endestad, & Magnussen, 2006).

Studies of children's vulnerability to suggestive questions have led professionals who work with children who have been molested to advise parents to avoid directly questioning their children. Instead, say experts, parents

should encourage children to speak spontaneously about what happened. When parents follow this advice, trained interviewers who know how to question preschoolers without unduly influencing them can have confidence in the information that they gain (Bruck, Ceci, & Hembrooke, 1998).

Questions for Reflection

1. Suppose when you pick your child up from child care, the teacher tells you that your child hit one of his classmates and asks you to talk to him about it. Based on the research regarding young children's memories, how should you proceed if you want to get the most accurate report possible about the incident from your child?

2. Think about possible conflicts between the rights of individuals who are accused of crimes and those of children who must be protected from people who would exploit them. How might research-based interviewing techniques help to protect both?

Changes in Processing Capacity and Efficiency

Learning Objective 6.15
How do cognitive processing capacity and efficiency change with age?

One obvious place to look for an explanation of developmental changes in memory skills is in the "hardware" itself. With any computer, there are physical limits on the number of different operations that can be performed simultaneously or in a given space of time. In the human memory system, the limiting factor is the short-term memory, as you'll recall from Chapter 1. It seems likely that as the brain and nervous system develop in the early years of life, the capacity of short-term memory increases (Johnson, 2005).

This has turned out to be a very difficult hypothesis to test. The most commonly cited evidence in support of an increase in short-term memory capacity is the finding that over the years of childhood, children are able to remember longer and longer lists of numbers, letters, or words, a pattern clear in the data shown in Figure 6.11. The difficulty with these results, however, is that they could also be simply another reflection of age differences in experience, because older children naturally have more experience with numbers, letters, and words. Thus, the memory-span data don't give a clear-cut answer to the question of whether basic processing capacity increases with age. Nevertheless, most developmental psychologists today agree that it is plausible to assume that short-term memory capacity increases across childhood, although most also admit that measuring such capacity is difficult (Cowan, Nugent, Elliott, Ponomarev, & Saults, 1999).

Figure 6.11

Memory Span across Age

Psychologists have tried to measure basic memory capacity by asking research participants to listen to a list of numbers, letters, or words and then repeat the list items in order. This figure shows the number of such items that children of various ages are able to remember and recall accurately.

(*Source*: Dempster, 1981, from Figures 1–3, pp. 66–68.)

automaticity The ability to recall information from long-term memory without effort.

Researchers have also produced persuasive evidence that processing efficiency increases steadily with age. Indeed, most developmentalists now see such a change in efficiency as the basis on which cognitive development rests (Swanson & Kim, 2007). The best evidence on this point is that cognitive processing gets steadily faster with age. Robert Kail (2007a) has found an exponential increase with age in processing speed on a wide variety of tasks, including such perceptual-motor tasks as tapping out a given rhythm or responding to a stimulus (for example, by pressing a button when you hear a buzzer) and cognitive tasks such as mental addition. He has found virtually identical patterns of speed increases in studies in Korea and the United States, adding a bit of cross-cultural validity to his results.

One plausible explanation for this common pattern is that over time, the brain and nervous system change physically in some fundamental way that allows increases in both response speed and mental processing. The most likely sources for such a basic change are the "pruning" of synapses and the myelination of the nerves, both of which you learned about in Chapter 4 (Hale, Fry, & Jessie, 1993). For example, assuming that pruning begins at about 12 to 18 months of age and then continues steadily throughout childhood, one effect is to make the "wiring diagram"—the connections within the nervous system—ever more efficient and thus able to operate faster.

However, experience using the memory system also contributes to increases in processing efficiency. For example, one of the most important ways in which processing becomes more efficient is through the acquisition of **automaticity**, or the ability to recall information from long-term memory without using short-term memory capacity. For example, when children can respond to the question "How much is 7 times 7?" by saying "49" without thinking about it, they have achieved automaticity with respect to that particular piece of information.

Automaticity is achieved primarily through practice (Meisinger & Bradley, 2008). It is critical to efficient information-processing because it frees up short-term memory space for more complex processing. Thus, the child or teenager who knows automatically what 7 × 7 is can use that fact in a complex multiplication or division problem without giving up any of the short-term memory space he is using to solve the problem. As a result, he is better able to concentrate on the "big picture" instead of expending effort trying to recall a simple multiplication fact. Not surprisingly, researchers have found that elementary school children who have automatized basic math facts in this way learn complex computational skills more rapidly (Kail & Hall, 1999). Similarly, kindergartners who display automaticity with regard to naming letters and objects are more likely to be fluent readers by the end of second grade than peers who require more time and effort to produce such names (Schatschneider, Fletcher, Francis, Carlson, & Foorman, 2004). Likewise, children who have practiced their handwriting skills to the point of automaticity can focus on the ideas they are writing about instead of the mechanical process of forming letters (Medwell & Wray, 2007). As a result, their compositions are longer, are better organized, and contain more elaboration.

Learning Objective 6.16

What kinds of improvements in strategy use happen across childhood and adolescence?

Memory Strategies

As we have noted, teenagers' and adults' working memories function more efficiently than those of children do. However, one of the most important principles in memory functioning is that the working memory, regardless of age or level of cognitive development, is limited in capacity. In order to deal with this limitation, the system creates **memory strategies**, ways of manipulating information that increase the chances that

PART 4 ■ THE THINKING CHILD

it will be remembered. Several common strategies are listed in Table 6.2. They emerge slowly over the entire course of childhood and adolescence, and even when children are familiar with a particular strategy, they often fail to use it.

Rehearsal Strategies   Suppose you need to run the following errands: stop at the dry cleaner; buy some stamps; copy your IRS forms; and buy milk, bread, orange juice, carrots, lettuce, spaghetti, and spaghetti sauce at the grocery store. To remember such a list, you might use any one of several possible strategies, some of which are listed in Table 6.2. In this particular case, one option would be to rehearse the list over and over in your mind. Do children do this when they try to remember? One classic early study (Keeney, Cannizzo, & Flavell, 1967) indicated that school-aged children do but younger children do not. Keeney showed children a row of seven cards with pictures on them and told the children to try to remember all the pictures in the same order they were laid out. A helmet was then placed over the child's head to prevent the child from seeing the cards but allow the experimenter to see if the child seemed to be rehearsing the list by muttering under his or her breath. Children under 5 almost never showed any rehearsal, but 8- to 10-year-old children usually did. Interestingly, when 5-year-olds were taught to rehearse, they were able to do so and their memory scores improved. Yet when these same 5-year-olds were given a new problem without being reminded to rehearse, they stopped rehearsing. That is, they could use the strategy if they were reminded to, but they did not produce it spontaneously—a pattern described as a **production deficiency**.

More recent work suggests that preschool-aged children show some kinds of strategies in their remembering if the task is quite simple, such as the game of hide-and-seek that Judy De-Loache (DeLoache, 1989; DeLoache, Simcock, & Marzolf, 2004) has used in her studies. In one of DeLoache's studies, the child watches the experimenter hide an attractive toy in some obvious place (e.g., behind a couch) and is then told that when a buzzer goes off she can go and find the toy. While playing with other toys during the 4-minute delay interval before the buzzer sounded, 2-year-olds often talked about, pointed to, or looked at the toy's hiding place—all of which seem clearly to be early forms of memory strategies.

These results and others like them indicate that there is no magic shift from nonstrategic to strategic behavior at age 5 or 6 or 7. Children as young as 2 use primitive strategies, but

memory strategies Ways of manipulating information that increase the chances that it will be remembered.

production deficiency A pattern whereby an individual can use some mental strategy if reminded to do so but fails to use the strategy spontaneously.

Table 6.2   Some Common Strategies for Remembering

Strategy	Description
Rehearsal	Perhaps the most common strategy, which involves either mental or vocal repetition or repetition of movement (as in learning to dance). May be used by children as young as 2 years under some conditions.
Clustering	Grouping ideas, objects, or words into clusters to help in remembering them, such as "all animals," or "all the ingredients in the lasagna recipe," or "the chess pieces involved in the move called castling." This is one strategy that clearly benefits from experience with a particular subject or activity, since possible categories are learned or are discovered in the process of exploring or manipulating a set of materials. Primitive clustering is used by 2-year-olds.
Elaboration	Finding shared meaning or a common referent for two or more things to be remembered. The helpful mnemonic for recalling the names of the lines on the musical staff ("Every Good Boy Does Fine") is a form of elaboration, as is associating the name of a person you have just met with some object or other word. This form of memory aid is not used spontaneously by all individuals and is not used skillfully until fairly late in development, if then.
Systematic Searching	Scanning the memory for the whole domain in which something might be found. Children aged 3 and 4 can begin to do this to search for actual objects in the real world but are not good at doing this in memory. Search strategies may be first learned in the external world and then applied to inner searches.

Source: Flavell, 1985.

school-aged children seem to have larger repertoires of strategies and to use them more flexibly and efficiently, a quality of thinking that becomes increasingly evident in older school-children (Kron-Sperl, Schneider, & Hasselhorn, 2008). For example, when learning a list of words, 8-year-olds are likely to practice the words one at a time ("cat, cat, cat"), while older children practice them in groups ("desk, lawn, sky, shirt, cat"). The 8-year-olds, tested again a year later, show signs of a shift toward the more efficient strategy (Guttentag, Ornstein, & Siemens, 1987).

Clustering Another strategy that helps improve memory involves putting the items to be learned or remembered into some meaningful organization. For example, in trying to remember a list of items you need to buy at the grocery store, you could aid your memory by thinking of the items as ingredients in a recipe (e.g., "what I need to make spaghetti and meatballs"). Another common strategy is to mentally group the items into categories such as "fruits and vegetables" and "canned goods," a strategy called clustering, or chunking.

Studies of clustering often involve having children or adults learn lists of words that have potential categories built into them. For example, in a study of categorical clustering, a researcher would ask you to remember this list of words: *chair, spaghetti, lettuce, cat, desk, chocolate, duck, lion, table.* You would be given 2 minutes to try to memorize the list, using whatever method(s) you wished. Then the researcher would ask you to list the words you could recall. If you used some kind of clustering technique, you would be likely to list the same-category words together (*cat, duck, lion; chair, desk, table;* and *spaghetti, chocolate, lettuce*).

School-aged children show this kind of internal organization strategy when they recall things, while preschoolers generally do not. And among school-aged children, older children use this strategy more efficiently, using a few large categories rather than many smaller ones (Bjorklund & Muir, 1988; Schlagmüller & Schneider, 2002). Interestingly, research shows that children often spontaneously use such a strategy but derive no apparent memory benefit from it, a pattern called a **utilization deficiency** (Bjorklund, Miller, Coyle, & Slawinski, 1997; Schneider & Bjorklund, 1998)—in a sense the opposite pattern from a production deficiency, in which a child will use and benefit from a strategy if reminded to do so but will not use it spontaneously. Utilization deficiencies are intriguing to theorists because they suggest that the child assumes that using some kind of strategy is a good thing to do but does not fully understand how to go about it. This form of deficiency is more common in children younger than 6 or 7, but it occurs among older children and teenagers as well (Kron-Sperl, Schneider, & Hasselhorn, 2008).

Strategy Training Training studies, in which children and adolescents are taught to use a particular memory strategy, suggest that teens benefit more from training than younger children do (Ghetti, Papini, & Angelini, 2006). For example, in one of the early strategy training studies, researchers taught elementary school and high school students a strategy for memorizing the manufacturing products associated with different cities, for example, "Detroit—automobiles" (Pressley & Dennis-Rounds, 1980). Once participants had learned the strategy and were convinced of its effectiveness, researchers presented them with a similar task: memorizing Latin words and their English translations. Experimenters found that only the high school students made an effort to use the strategy they had just learned to accomplish the new memory task. The elementary school children used the new strategy only when researchers told them to and demonstrated to them how it could be applied to the new task. The high school students' success seemed to be due to their superior ability to recognize the similarity between the two tasks—an aspect of metamemory, which will be discussed in the next section.

The differences between elementary school children's and adolescents' ability to learn strategies for processing meaningful text, such as newspaper articles or material in textbooks, are even more dramatic. In a classic study of text processing, experimenters asked 10-, 13-, 15-, and 18-year-olds to read and summarize a 500-word passage (about 1 page in a typical college textbook). The researchers (Brown & Day, 1983) hypothesized that participants would use four rules in writing summaries. First, they would delete trivial information. Sec-

utilization deficiency Using some specific mental strategy without deriving benefit from it.

ond, their summaries would show categorical organization; that is, they would use terms such as *animals* rather than specific names of animals mentioned in the text. Researchers also speculated that participants would use topic sentences from the text in their summaries and would invent topic sentences for paragraphs that didn't have them.

The results of the research suggested that participants of all ages used the first rule, because all of their summaries included general rather than detailed or trivial information about the passage. However, the 10- and 13-year-olds used the other rules far less frequently than did the 15- and 18-year-olds. There were also interesting differences between the two older groups. Fifteen-year-olds used categories about as frequently as 18-year-olds did, but the oldest group used topic sentences far more effectively. This pattern of age differences in strategy use suggests that complex information-processing skills such as text summarizing improve gradually during the second half of adolescence.

Studies of text outlining reveal a similar pattern (Drum, 1985). Both elementary school and high school students know that an outline should include the main ideas of a passage along with supporting details. However, research suggests that 17-year-olds generate much more complete outlines than do 14-year-olds. Moreover, 11-year-olds' outlines usually include only a few of the main ideas of a passage and provide little or no supporting details for the main ideas they do include.

Metamemory and Metacognition

One way in which a child's information-processing "software" changes is in her increasing awareness of her own mental processes. If a memory researcher had you learn a list of everyday words (*chair*, *spaghetti*, *lettuce*, and so on) and asked you afterward what techniques you used to remember them, you could describe your mental processes. You could also relate other things about the way your mind works, such as good ways to study particular subjects or which kinds of tasks are hardest for you, and why. These are examples of **metamemory** and **metacognition**—knowing about remembering and knowing about knowing. Such skills are a part of a larger category that information-processing theorists refer to as **executive processes**, cognitive skills that allow a person to devise and carry out alternative strategies for remembering and solving problems.

Research suggests that such skills emerge in early childhood. For example, John Flavell's appearance/reality research has demonstrated that children between ages 3 and 5 know that in order to tell if a rock painted like a sponge is really a sponge or a rock, a person needs to touch or hold the object. Just looking at it doesn't give enough information (Flavell, 1993; O'Neill, Astington, & Flavell, 1992). In a similar vein, 4-year-olds (but not 3-year-olds) understand that to remember or forget something, one must have known it at a previous time (Lyon & Flavell, 1994). Flavell's research also suggests that by age 4, a child understands that there is a process called *thinking* that people do and that is distinct from knowing or talking (Flavell, Green, & Flavell, 1995). They also understand in some preliminary way that people can think about imaginary objects or events as well as real ones. Despite these major advances, however, 4- and 5-year-olds do not yet understand that thinking occurs continuously (Wellman & Hickling, 1994). In particular, they don't realize that other people are thinking all the time, and when asked, they are bad at guessing what another person might be thinking about, even when the clues are quite clear—such as when the other person is reading or listening to something. All of these skills are much more highly developed in 7- and 8-year-olds, who seem to have figured out that their own and other people's thinking goes on constantly and follows certain rules.

These skills are of particular interest because performance on a whole range of everyday tasks is better if the child can monitor her own performance or can recognize when a particular strategy is called for and when it is not. Four- and 5-year-olds do show some such monitoring, but it is rarely seen earlier than that, and it clearly improves fairly rapidly across the elementary school years. For example, 10-year-olds are more likely than 8-year-olds to know

metamemory Knowledge about one's own memory processes.

metacognition General and rather loosely used term describing knowledge of one's own thinking processes: knowing what one knows, and how one learns.

executive processes Cognitive skills that allow a person to devise and carry out alternative strategies for remembering and solving problems.

that understanding a story requires that the reader or listener exert mental effort to prevent his or her mind from wandering (Parault & Schwanenflugel, 2000).

Among other things, some metacognitive ability is critical for learning to read skillfully. A child learning to read needs to recognize which words he knows and which he does not, or which sentences he understands and which he does not, and needs to have some idea of how to get the information he needs. He needs to be able to recognize the difference between easy sentences and hard ones so that he can concentrate more and put more effort into the harder ones. A variety of research reveals that younger and poorer readers are less adept at all these metacognitive tasks, while better or older readers can do them more readily and skillfully (Martini & Shore, 2008).

By age 14 or 15, the executive processing skills of an adolescent far exceed those of a younger child. These gains result from improvements in working memory efficiency and increases in knowledge, which are largely attributable to the maturation of the prefrontal cortex (Giedd, 2004). As a result, teenagers outperform school-aged children on even simple memory tasks, such as remembering faces, and are far better than younger children at using complex strategies that aid memory (Gathercole, Pickering, Ambridge, & Wearing, 2004; Itier & Taylor, 2004). For example, one classic study of metamemory involved offering fifth-graders, eighth-graders, and college students the opportunity to earn money by remembering words (Cuvo, 1974). Researchers designated to-be-recalled words as being worth either 1 cent or 10 cents. Fifth-graders rehearsed 1-cent and 10-cent words equally. In contrast, eighth-graders and college students put more effort into rehearsing 10-cent words than 1-cent words. At the end of the rehearsal period, fifth-graders recalled equal numbers of 1- and 10-cent words, while older participants remembered more 10-cent items. Further, college students outperformed eighth-graders in both rehearsal and recall. These findings suggest that the capacity to apply memory skills selectively based on the characteristics of a memory task appears early in the teen years and continues to improve throughout adolescence.

Another important skill that is facilitated by the development of executive processes is **response inhibition**, the ability to control responses to stimuli (Luna, Garver, Urban, Lazar, & Sweeney, 2004). Response inhibition is evident in situations that call for carefully considering the impact of your answer before responding to a question, such as in a job interview. Consequently, teens are less likely than school-aged children to immediately jump to a conclusion regarding the solution to a problem. Teens are likely to mentally work through the problem and be certain that they have taken into account all of the details involved in its solution before announcing that they have solved it.

Learning Objective 6.18
How does expertise influence memory function?

Expertise

All of the apparent developmental changes that we have discussed may well turn out to be as much a function of expertise as they are of age. Piaget thought that children apply broad forms of logic to all their experiences in any given stage. If that's true, then the amount of specific experience a child has had with some set of materials shouldn't make a lot of difference. A child who understands hierarchical classification but who has never seen pictures of different types of dinosaurs still ought to be able to create classifications of dinosaurs about as well as a child who has played a lot with dinosaur models. A child who understands the principle of transitivity (if A is greater than B and B is greater than C, then A is greater than C) ought to be able to demonstrate this ability with sets of strange figures as well as she could with a set of toys familiar to her. But, in fact, that seems not to be the case.

Developmentalists now have a great deal of research showing that specific knowledge makes a huge difference (Kail, 2007b). Children and adults who know a lot about some subject or some set of objects (dinosaurs, baseball cards, mathematics, or whatever) not only categorize information in that topic area in more complex and hierarchical ways, but also are better at remembering new information on that topic and better at applying more advanced forms of logic to material in that area. Furthermore, such expertise seems to generalize very little to other tasks (Ericsson & Crutcher, 1990). A child who is a devout soccer fan will be

response inhibition The ability to control responses to stimuli.

These school-aged chess players, unless they are rank novices, would remember a series of chess moves or the arrangement of pieces on a chessboard far better than would nonplayers, regardless of their ages.

better than a nonfan at recalling lists of soccer words or the content of a story about soccer, but the two children are likely to be equally good at remembering random lists of words (Schneider & Bjorklund, 1992; Schneider, Reimers, Roth, & Visé, 1995).

Research on expertise also shows that even the typical age differences in strategy use or memory ability disappear when the younger group has more expertise than the older. For example, Michelene Chi, in her now-classic early study (1978), showed that expert chess players can remember the placement of chess pieces on a board much more quickly and accurately than can novice chess players, even when the expert chess players are children and the novices are adults—a finding since replicated several times (e.g., Schneider, Gruber, Gold, & Opwis, 1993). To paraphrase Flavell (1985), expertise makes any of us look very smart, very cognitively advanced; lack of expertise makes us look very dumb.

Think Critically

- Think of a common infant behavior such as a baby's repeatedly throwing a toy on the floor. How does the behavior seem to fit with Piaget's ideas about primary, secondary, and tertiary circular reactions?
- How does reversibility come into play when you watch a magician perform? Do you think an understanding of reversibility makes the performance more or less interesting for you than for a young child who has yet to develop reversibility?
- How would Piaget's theory be used to explain the finding that younger children do not benefit from memory strategy training as much as older children and teens do?

Conduct Your Own Research

You can use a deck of playing cards to examine memory improvement. Do your research with a 7-year-old and a 10-year-old, testing each child separately. For the first trial, select 12 cards, 3 from each suit, making sure that the cards are all of different values. Arrange the cards in front of the child randomly and allow 1 minute for the child to memorize the cards. When the minute has passed, take up the cards and ask the child to recall them. For the second trial, repeat the experiment with a different set of 12 cards, but tell the children that they may rearrange the cards if they think it will help their memory. The 7-year-old probably won't rearrange the cards by suit, but the 10-year-old will. This shows that the older child is attempting to use categories as a memory aid.

Summary

PIAGET'S BASIC IDEAS

6.1 What is the role of schemes in cognitive development?

- Piaget assumed that the child was an active agent in his own development, constructing his own understandings and adapting to the environment through his actions on the world. Cognitive structures called schemes underlie the stages of cognitive development. Each stage involves a different type of scheme. The schemes are hierarchical in that each stage builds on the schemes that were constructed in earlier stages.

6.2 How do assimilation, accommodation, and equilibration change schemes?

- The complementary processes of assimilation (adding new information to an existing scheme) and accommodation (changing schemes to take in new information), as well as the process of equilibration by which they are balanced, are the means by which schemes adapt to the world.
- Conflict between a child's existing schemes and his observations of the world leads to actions that eventually result in resolution of such conflicts, or equilibration, as Piaget called the process. Each stage of development represents a more adaptive equilibration.

6.3 What are the four causes of cognitive development proposed by Piaget?

- Equilibration interacts with maturation, social transmission, and experience to produce changes in children's thinking.

INFANCY

6.4 How did Piaget describe cognitive development in the first 2 years of life?

- Piaget's first stage is the sensorimotor period; the infant begins with a small repertoire of basic schemes, from which she moves toward symbolic representation in a series of six substages. In each stage, the infant uses sensory and motor abilities to act on the world and to test hypotheses about the results of such actions. These tests involve repetitive behaviors, or circular reactions. The major milestones of this stage include object permanence, means-end behavior, and representational thought.

6.5 What have researchers discovered about infants' ability to remember and to imitate others' actions?

- Post-Piagetian studies of infant cognition show infants' memory skills to be far more advanced than Piaget thought. Infants can imitate in the earliest weeks but do not show deferred imitation for several months.

THE PRESCHOOL YEARS

6.6 What are the characteristics of children's thinking during the preoperational stage?

- In Piaget's preoperational period, from 2 to 6 years, the child is able to use mental symbols to represent objects to himself internally. Despite this advance, the preschool-aged child still lacks many sophisticated cognitive characteristics. In Piaget's view, such children are still egocentric, rigid in their thinking, and generally captured by appearances.

6.7 How has recent research challenged Piaget's view of this period?

- Research on the cognitive functioning of preschoolers makes it clear that they are much less egocentric than Piaget thought. By age 4, children can distinguish between appearance and reality in a variety of tasks.

6.8 What is a theory of mind, and how does it develop?

- Preschoolers develop a surprisingly sophisticated theory of mind—that is, ideas of how other people's minds work. They understand that the actions of others are often based on thoughts and beliefs. The development of a theory of mind is influenced by general cognitive and language development. Engaging in pretend play with others seems to facilitate its development as well.

6.9 What does research indicate about the correlation between culture and theory of mind?

- Cross-cultural studies suggest that the development of the false belief principle and other features of theory of mind may be universal milestones of early childhood cognitive development.

6.10 How do the theories of the neo-Piagetians and Vygotsky explain cognitive development?

- Recent theorizing about the preschool period has been influenced by neo-Piagetian theories that explain Piaget's stages in information-processing terms. Vygotsky's socio-cultural theory emphasizes the role of social interactions in children's cognitive development. Moreover, Vygotsky suggested that language provides the framework necessary to support many of the general concepts children acquire in the preschool years.

THE SCHOOL-AGED CHILD

6.11 What are concrete operations, and how do they represent an advance over earlier forms of thought?

- In Piaget's third stage—concrete operations—occurring from age 6 to age 12, the child acquires powerful new mental tools called operations, such as reversibility.

6.12 What does Siegler's research suggest about concrete operational thinking?

- Recent research on this period confirms many of Piaget's descriptions of sequences of development but calls into question his basic concept of stages. Siegler's work shows that cognitive development is less steplike than Piaget proposed; children may use a variety of different strategies, varying in complexity, on the same kind of problem. Still, the repertoire of strategies does become more complex with age.

ADOLESCENCE

6.13 What are the key elements of formal operational thinking?

- Piaget's fourth stage—formal operations—is said to develop from age 12 onward and is characterized by the ability to apply basic operations to ideas and possibilities as well as to actual objects and by the emergence of systematic problem solving and hypothetico-deductive logic.

6.14 What does post-Piagetian research suggest about this stage?

- Researchers have found clear evidence of such advanced forms of thinking in at least some adolescents.

DEVELOPMENT OF INFORMATION-PROCESSING SKILLS

6.15 How do cognitive processing capacity and efficiency change with age?

- Most theorists agree that there are age-related changes in the capacity of the mental "hardware" as well as improvements in speed and efficiency.

6.16 What kinds of improvements in strategy use happen across childhood and adolescence?

- Processing efficiency improves because of increasing use of various types of processing strategies with age, including strategies for remembering. Preschoolers use some strategies, but school-aged children use them more often and more flexibly. In adolescence, the number of strategies and the efficiency with which they are used improve substantially.

6.17 What are metamemory and metacognition, and what is their importance in cognitive development?

- Children's capacities to think about their own mental processes (metacognition) and to select appropriate memory strategies (metamemory) also contribute to improvements in memory functioning.

6.18 How does expertise influence memory function?

- Studies of expertise show that prior knowledge contributes to both individual and age-related differences in memory functioning and strategy use.

Key Terms

accommodation (p. 145)
adaptation (p. 145)
assimilation (p. 145)
automaticity (p. 168)
centration (p. 151)
class inclusion (p. 158)
concrete operations stage (p. 146)
conservation (p. 151)
decentration (p. 151)
deductive logic (p. 158)
egocentrism (p. 151)
equilibration (p. 145)
executive processes (p. 171)
false belief principle (p. 153)
figurative schemes (p. 144)

formal operations stage (p. 146)
horizontal decalage (p. 159)
hypothetico-deductive reasoning (p. 163)
inductive logic (p. 158)
memory strategies (p. 168)
metacognition (p. 171)
metamemory (p. 171)
neo-Piagetian theory (p. 156)
object permanence (p. 148)
operation (p. 146)
operational efficiency (p. 156)
operative schemes (p. 145)
organization (p. 144)
preoperational stage (p. 146)
primary circular reactions (p. 147)

production deficiency (p. 169)
relational complexity (p. 161)
response inhibition (p. 172)
reversibility (p. 158)
scheme (p. 144)
secondary circular reactions (p. 147)
sensorimotor stage (p. 146)
seriation (p. 161)
short-term storage space (STSS) (p. 156)
tertiary circular reactions (p. 148)
theory of mind (p. 153)
transitivity (p. 161)
utilization deficiency (p. 170)

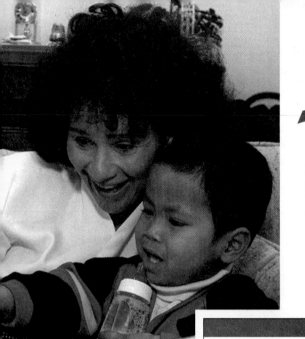

7 Cognitive Development II: Individual Differences in Cognitive Abilities

Japanese novelist Kenzaburo Oe and his wife were devastated when they learned that their newborn son had been born with part of his brain outside of the skull (Cameron, 1998). The doctors informed them that there was a risky surgical procedure that might save the boy's life, but the operation would leave him with mental retardation and other developmental problems. Inspired by the tenacity with which his tiny son clung to life, Oe named the boy Hikari, the Japanese word for "light," and agreed to the surgery.

Although the operation saved Hikari's life, it was clear within a few years that he would always lag far behind others in cognitive and social development and that the chances of his ever being able to live independently were remote. Despite Hikari's limited ability to speak and understand language, however, he displayed a remarkable ability to memorize songs. His parents decided to give him piano lessons and found a teacher who was willing to take on the challenging student. As the teacher worked with Hikari, it became apparent that the child had remarkable musical gifts. Within months, he was playing difficult classical pieces with ease. Moreover, he began to create his own pieces. Though she doubted the effort would be successful, Hikari's piano teacher decided to try to teach him how to write his compositions. To her surprise, he mastered the difficult skill of writing music in a relatively short time. Today, as a middle-aged man, Hikari Oe is an accomplished and celebrated composer of classical music. Yet his scores on standardized tests of intelligence are far below average, and he is unable to live independently.

Hikari Oe is just one of the thousands of individuals with mental retardation and other severe mental disabilities who display *savant syndrome*, the exhibition of remarkable talents in the context of a severe disability. Psychologists have studied savants such as Hikari for more than a hundred years, yet do not yet know why some abilities in these individuals become accentuated while others are destroyed. But studying savants has led to the development of new theories of normal intellectual functioning, theories that have led psychologists to look beyond conventional intelligence tests in the quest for an accurate definition of human intelligence.

In this chapter, you will learn about the history of intelligence testing and the study of human intelligence. You will also learn about the range of individual differences in intelligence and some of the controversies surrounding group differences. At the end of the chapter, you will read about a theory of intelligence that is based on studies of savants such as Hikari Oe.

Measuring Intellectual Power

Psychologists have argued for decades about whether test performance is an adequate definition of intelligence. At a conceptual level, though, most psychologists agree that **intelligence** includes the ability to reason abstractly, the ability to profit from experience, and the ability to adapt to varying environmental contexts. Consequently, most tests of intelligence include tasks that require examinees to use these abilities.

Still, most of us have a greatly inflated notion of the permanence or importance of an IQ score. To acquire a more realistic view, it helps to know something about what such tests were designed to do and something about the beliefs and values of those who devised them.

intelligence A set of abilities defined in various ways by different psychologists but generally agreed to include the ability to reason abstractly, the ability to profit from experience, and the ability to adapt to varying environmental contexts.

The First IQ Tests

Learning Objective 7.1
What were Binet's and Terman's approaches to measuring intelligence?

The first modern intelligence test was published in 1905 by two Frenchmen, Alfred Binet and Theodore Simon (1905). From the beginning, the test had a practical purpose—to identify children who might have difficulty in school. For this reason, the tasks that made up the test Binet and Simon devised were very much like some school tasks, including measures of vocabulary, comprehension of facts and relationships, and mathematical and verbal reasoning. For example, could a child describe the difference between wood and glass? Could a young child touch his nose, his ear, his head? Could he tell which of two weights was heavier?

Figure 7.1
The Distribution of IQ Scores

The approximate distribution of scores on most modern IQ tests, along with the labels typically used for scores at various levels. The tests are designed and the scoring is standardized so that the average score is 100 and two-thirds of the scores fall between 85 and 115. Because of brain damage and genetic anomalies, there are slightly more children with low IQs than there are children with very high IQs.

Lewis Terman and his associates at Stanford University modified and extended many of Binet and Simon's original tasks when they translated and revised the test for use in the United States (Terman, 1916; Terman & Merrill, 1937). The several Terman revisions, called the **Stanford-Binet**, consist of six sets of tests, one set for children of each of six consecutive ages. A child taking the test begins with the set of tests for the age below his actual age, then takes the set for his age, then those for each successively older age until he has either completed all the tests for older ages or has reached a point where the remaining tests are too difficult for him.

Terman initially described a child's performance in terms of a score called an **intelligence quotient**, later shortened to **IQ**. This score was computed by comparing the child's chronological age (in years and months) with his **mental age**, defined as the level of questions he could answer correctly. For example, a child who could solve the problems for a 6-year-old but not those for a 7-year-old would have a mental age of 6. Terman devised a formula to calculate the IQ score:

$$\frac{\text{Mental Age}}{\text{Chronological Age}} \times 100$$

This formula results in an IQ score above 100 for children whose mental age is higher than their chronological age and an IQ score below 100 for children whose mental age is below their chronological age.

This old system for calculating IQ scores is not used any longer, even in the modern revisions of the Stanford-Binet. IQ score calculations are now based on a direct comparison of a child's performance with the average performance of a large group of other children of the same age, with a score of 100 still typically defined as average.

The majority of children achieve Stanford-Binet scores that are right around the average of 100, with a smaller number scoring very high or very low. Figure 7.1 shows the distribution of IQ scores that will result when the test is given to thousands of children. You can see that 67% (about two-thirds) of all children achieve scores between 85 and 115, while 96% achieve scores between 70 and 130. The groups that developmentalists refer to as "children who are gifted" or "children with mental retardation," both of which you'll read about in some detail in Chapter 15, clearly represent only very small fractions of the distribution.

One advantage of the modern method of calculating IQ scores is that it allows the test makers to restandardize the test periodically, so that the average remains at 100. Such readjustments are needed because IQ test scores have been rising steadily over the past 50 or 60 years. If the same standards were used today as were applied in 1932, when tests such as the Stanford-Binet were first devised, the average score would be 115 and not 100—an increase that has been found among children and adults all over the world (Dickens & Flynn, 2001; Flynn, 1994, 1999). That is, the average child today can solve problems that only an above-average child could solve 60 years ago. This historical shift upward in scores on cognitive ability tests is known as the *secular trend* in IQ scores. You may recall this term from Chapter 4, where you read about its use in relation to historical changes in the timing of menarche. The secular trend in IQ scores is also sometimes called the *Flynn effect*, because it was discovered by psychologist James Flynn (2007) (see *Thinking about Research*).

IQ test scores

The Flynn Effect

When thinking about the ways in which children's IQ scores have changed over the past 70 years, it's important to keep in mind that both maturational and experiential variables influence IQ scores. For instance, most IQ tests include measures of processing speed and of vocabulary. Processing speed is strongly influenced by maturation, but vocabulary depends on experience. Most observers attribute gains in the maturational component of IQ scores to improvements in health and nutrition (Williams, 1998), most of which took place during the first half of the 20th century. Studies of test score changes in nations that have experienced significant improvements in the physical environment over the same period (e.g., Singapore, Estonia, and rural Kenya) lend weight to this hypothesis. These studies reveal that children's performance on maturationally loaded tasks has risen dramatically along with improvements in diet and health (Cocodia et al., 2003; Daley, Whaley, Sigman, Espinosa, & Neumann, 2003; Must, Must, & Raudik, 2003).

By contrast, scores on tests that reflect the experiential elements of the Flynn effect are continuing to increase in some industrialized societies (Nettelbeck & Wilson, 2004). This increase is usually attributed to children's increased preschool attendance. In addition, test scores attained by today's children may reflect their tendency to be a bit more "testwise" than earlier cohorts simply because they take more tests and do more test-like activities in the early years of school (Cocodia et al., 2003).

Research also suggests that the experiential component of the Flynn effect can be reversed; that is, some types of experience can have negative effects on IQ scores (Teasdale & Owen, 2005). Studies in some European countries suggest that IQ scores may actually be falling, a finding that researchers attribute to declining enrollments in secondary schools in these countries (Teasdale & Owen, 2005, 2008). Thus, while questions about the secular trend in IQ scores are interesting in and of themselves, the greatest value of research on the phenomenon may be the light it sheds on the contributions of schooling to intelligence test scores.

Questions for Critical Analysis

1. What are some possible alternative explanations for the finding that IQ scores may be falling in some European countries?
2. What are the advantages and disadvantages of intelligence tests that include both maturationally loaded and experientially based items?

Modern IQ Tests

Learning Objective 7.2

What intelligence tests are used today, and how do they differ from earlier tests?

The three tests most frequently used by psychologists today are the Stanford-Binet V (the fifth revision of the original Stanford-Binet), the third edition of the Wechsler Preschool and Primary Scale of Intelligence (the **WPPSI-III**), and the fourth edition of the Wechsler Intelligence Scales for Children (the **WISC-IV**). The two Wechsler tests are derived from an intelligence test for children originally developed by psychologist David Wechsler (1974). The WPPSI-III is designed for children between the ages of 2½ and 7. Norms for the WISC-IV begin at age 6 and progress to age 16. (Several other well-known tests are listed in Table 7.1 on page 180.) All three tests feature both verbal and nonverbal problems ranging from very easy to very difficult. Children begin with the easiest problems of each type, continue with that type of item until they can go no further, and then go on to the next type of problem.

The WISC-IV is the test most often used in schools to diagnose children's learning problems. It consists of 15 different tests. Five of these tests, those that comprise the **verbal comprehension index**, rely strongly on verbal skills (for example, vocabulary, describing similarities between objects, general information). The remaining 10 tests demand nonverbal types of thinking, such as arranging pictures to tell a story and repeating digits back to the examiner. The nonverbal tests are divided among the **perceptual reasoning index**, **processing speed index**, and **working memory index**. Each of these groups of tests measures a different kind of nonverbal intelligence and generates its own IQ score. The WISC-IV also provides a comprehensive **full scale IQ** score that takes all four types of tests into account. Many psychologists find comparisons of the different kinds of IQ scores generated by the WISC-IV to be helpful in determining a child's intellectual strengths and weaknesses.

Infant Tests   Neither the Stanford-Binet nor either of the Wechsler tests can be used with children much younger than about 3. Infants and toddlers don't talk well, if at all, and most childhood tests rely heavily on language. (Even the Peabody Picture Vocabulary Test, described in Table 7.1, requires that the child understand individual words.) So how do developmentalists measure "intelligence" in an infant? This becomes an important question if they

WPPSI-III The third revision of the Wechsler Preschool and Primary Scale of Intelligence.

WISC-IV The most recent revision of the Wechsler Intelligence Scales for Children, a well-known IQ test developed in the United States that includes both verbal and performance (nonverbal) subtests.

verbal comprehension index Tests on the WISC-IV that tap verbal skills such as knowledge of vocabulary and general information.

perceptual reasoning index Tests on the WISC-IV, such as block design and picture completion, that tap nonverbal visual-processing abilities.

processing speed index Timed tests on the WISC-IV, such as symbol search, that measure how rapidly an examinee processes information.

Table 7.1 Intelligence Tests That May Be Used in Place of the Stanford-Binet and the WISC

Test	Description	
Peabody Picture Vocabulary Test (PPVT)	Not originally designed as an IQ test, but widely used as a quick measure of intelligence because the scores correlate so highly with Binet or Wechsler scores. Includes 150 pages, each page with four pictures, the pages arranged in order of increasing difficulty. The examiner says a word and asks the child to point to the appropriate picture, as in the example to the right. Widely used with preschool children.	 PPVT item (word is *emerge*)
Raven's Progressive Matrices	Each of the 36 items shows a pattern on a rectangular space, such as a set of dots covering the space. One section of the rectangle is blanked out, and the child must choose which of six alternative fill-in options will match the original matrix, as in the example to the right. Designed as a nonverbal measure of intelligence.	 Raven item
Kaufman Assessment Battery for Children (KABC)	Kaufman himself does not call this an intelligence test, although it is often used in this way. Suitable for children aged 2½ to 12, it includes three tests of *sequential processing* (such as number recall) and seven tests of *simultaneous processing* (including face recognition), combined to provide an overall score based primarily on nonverbal measures. Six achievement subtests can also be given, including vocabulary, riddles, and reading. The test also allows flexible testing procedures, including the use of other languages, alternative wording, and gestures, all of which make the test one of the fairest for ethnic minorities and children from poverty-level families.	
Cognitive Abilities Test (COGAT)	The COGAT is one of several intelligence tests that are administered to groups of children rather than in one-on-one testing sessions. These tests include items similar to those on individual tests, but they tend to be less reliable. Thus, they are typically used to screen children to determine who should be tested individually rather than to make decisions that require a great deal of precision, such as those associated with placing children in special education classes.	

Sources: Portions adapted with the permission of The Free Press, a Division of Simon & Schuster, Inc., from *Bias in Mental Testing* by Arthur R. Jensen. Copyright © 1980 by Arthur R. Jensen. All rights reserved. Other portions from Sattler, 2008.

working memory index Tests on the WISC-IV, such as digit span, that measure working memory efficiency.

full scale IQ The WISC-IV score that takes into account verbal and nonverbal scale scores.

Bayley Scales of Infant Development The best-known and most widely used test of infant "intelligence."

want to be able to identify, during infancy, those children who are not developing normally or to predict later intelligence or school performance.

Most "infant IQ tests," such as the widely used **Bayley Scales of Infant Development** (Bayley, 1969, 1993), have been constructed rather like IQ tests for older children in that they include sets of items of increasing difficulty. However, instead of testing school-like skills—skills an infant does not yet have—the items measure primarily sensory and motor skills, such as reaching for a dangling ring (an item for a typical baby at 3 months), putting cubes in a cup on request (9 months), or building a tower of three cubes (17 months). Some more clearly cognitive items are also included, such as uncovering a toy hidden by a cloth, an item used with 8-month-old infants to measure an aspect of object permanence.

Bayley's test and others like it, such as the Denver Developmental Screening Test, have proved helpful in identifying infants and toddlers with serious developmental delays (Gardner et al., 2006). As a more general predictive tool to forecast later IQ scores or school performance, however, such tests have not been nearly as useful as many had hoped. On the whole, it looks as if what is being measured on typical infant tests is not the same as what is tapped by the commonly used intelligence tests for children and adults (Birney, Citron-Pousty, Lutz, & Sternberg, 2005; Colombo, 1993).

Achievement Tests Another kind of test of intellectual skill with which you are probably familiar is the achievement test, which nearly all of you have taken in elementary and high school. **Achievement tests** are designed to test specific information learned in school, using items like those in Table 7.2. The child taking an achievement test doesn't end up with an IQ score, but his performance is compared to that of other children in the same grade across the country.

How is an achievement test different from an IQ test? An IQ test is intended to reveal something about how well a child can think and learn, while an achievement test tells something about

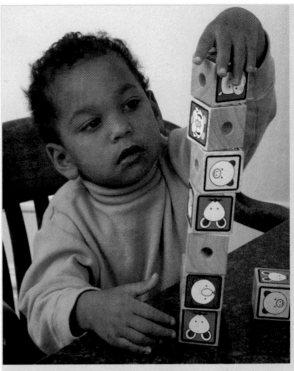

At 22 months, James would clearly pass the 17-month item on the Bayley Scales of Infant Development that calls for the child to build a tower of three blocks.

Table 7.2   Some Sample Items from a Fourth-Grade Achievement Test

Vocabulary	Reference Skills
jolly old man 1. angry 2. fat 3. merry 4. sorry	Which of these words would be first in ABC order? 1. pair 2. point 3. paint 4. polish
Language Expression	**Spelling**
Who wants _____ books? 1. that 2. these 3. them 4. this	Jason took the *cleanest* glass. right _____ wrong _____
Mathematics	**Mathematics Computation**
What does the "3" in 13 stand for? 1. 3 ones 2. 13 ones 3. 3 tens 4. 13 tens	79 149 62 +14 −87 ×3

Source: From Comprehensive Tests of Basic Skills, Form S, Reprinted by permission of the publisher, CTB/McGraw-Hill, Del Monte Research Park, Monterey, CA 93940. Copyright © 1973 by McGraw-Hill, Inc. All rights reserved. Printed in the USA.

achievement test Test designed to assess a child's learning of specific material taught in school, such as spelling or arithmetic computation; in the United States, achievement tests are typically given to all children in designated grades.

In the United States, virtually all fourth-graders—like these in Austin, Texas—are given achievement tests so that schools can compare their students' performance against national norms.

what a child has already learned. Or to put it another way: Designers of IQ tests thought they were measuring a child's basic capacity (underlying **competence**), while an achievement test is intended to measure what the child has actually learned (**performance**). This is an important distinction. Each of us presumably has some upper limit of ability—what we could do under ideal conditions if we were maximally motivated, healthy, and rested. Yet, since everyday conditions are rarely ideal, people typically perform below their hypothetical ability.

The creators of the widely used IQ tests believed that by standardizing the procedures for administering and scoring the tests, they could come close to measuring competence. But because scientists can never be sure that they are assessing any ability under the best of all possible circumstances, they have to settle for measuring performance at the time the test is taken. What this means in practical terms is that the distinction between IQ tests and achievement tests is one of degree rather than of kind. IQ tests include items that are designed to tap fairly fundamental intellectual processes such as comparison and analysis; achievement tests call for specific information the child has learned in school or elsewhere. Thus, the strong link between IQ and performance on achievement tests calls into question the notion that such tests are good measures of what has been taught and learned in a particular school. High scores in one school may simply mean that the students are brighter rather than indicating anything about the quality of the school's curriculum or the methods used by its teachers.

College entrance tests, such as the SAT, fall somewhere in between IQ and achievement tests. They are designed to measure basic "developed abilities," such as the ability to reason with words, rather than specific knowledge. But all three types of tests measure aspects of a child or young person's performance and not his or her competence.

Learning Objective 7.3
How stable are IQ scores throughout childhood and adolescence?

Stability of Test Scores

One of the bits of folklore about IQ tests is that a particular IQ score is something you "have," like blue eyes or red hair—that a child who achieves a score of, say, 115 at age 3 will continue to score in about the same range at age 6 or 12 or 20. Psychologists use the term **reliability** to refer to the stability of a test score. By definition, a reliable test yields scores that are stable over time. That is, if a child takes a reliable test several times, her scores will be very similar at each testing. In this sense, IQ scores are, in fact, very stable, although there are also some exceptions to this general rule. One such exception is the weak link between scores on infant IQ tests such as the Bayley Scales and later IQ scores. The typical correlation between a Bayley score at 12 months and a Stanford-Binet IQ score at 4 years is only about .20 to .30 (Bee et al., 1982)—significant but not robust. Newer tests of infant intelligence, such as those based on habituation rates or other basic processes, may ultimately prove to be more helpful predictors of later IQ scores (Gaultney & Gingras, 2005); currently, however, there is no widely used method that allows developmentalists to predict with any reliability which 1-year-olds will later have high or low IQ scores.

However, beginning at about age 3, consistency in performance on IQ tests such as the Stanford-Binet or the WISC-IV increases markedly (Birney et al., 2005). If such a test is taken twice, a few months or a few years apart, the scores are likely to be very similar. The correlations between adjacent-year IQ scores in middle childhood, for example, are typically in the range of .65 to .80 (Bartels, Rietveld, Van Baal, & Boomsma, 2002; Honzik, 1986). Moreover, correlations among IQ scores measured in late childhood, early adolescence, and adulthood are also quite high, typically ranging from .70 to .85, including adult IQs that are measured when people are in their 70s and 80s (Deary, Whiteman, Starr, Whalley, & Fox, 2004;

competence A person's basic, underlying level of skill, displayed under ideal circumstances. It is not possible to measure competence directly.

performance The behavior shown by a person under real-life rather than ideal circumstances. Even when researchers are interested in competence, all they can ever measure is performance.

reliability The stability of a test score over multiple testing sessions.

PART 4 ■ THE THINKING CHILD

Mortensen, Andresen, Kruuse, Sanders, & Reinisch, 2003). However, many children show quite wide fluctuations in their scores. When children are given IQ tests repeatedly over a period of years, the common finding is that about half show little or no significant fluctuation in their scores while the remaining half show at least small changes from one testing to another, with perhaps 15% showing rather substantial change (Sattler, 2008).

One example comes from a New Zealand longitudinal study in which all 1,037 children born in the town of Dunedin over a 1-year period in the 1970s were followed through childhood and adolescence. Among many other measures, the researchers measured the children's IQs with the WISC every 2 years starting at age 7. They found that over any 2-year period, 10% of the children's IQ scores changed as much as 15 points—a very large change (Caspi, Harkness, Moffitt, & Silva, 1996). Another 13% showed major changes over longer periods; 15 of the children showed cumulative shifts of more than 50 points over 6 years. In most cases, however, these large shifts represented "bounce" or "rebound" rather than permanent shifts upward or downward. That is, some children seemed to respond to specific life experiences—stresses or special advantages—with a decline or a rise in IQ score. A few years later, their IQ score returned to something closer to the original score.

Such fluctuations, while intriguing, occur against a background of increasing IQ test score stability with age. The general rule of thumb is that the older the child, the more stable the IQ score becomes. Older children may show some fluctuation in scores in response to major stresses such as parental divorce, a change in schools, or the birth of a sibling, but by age 10 or 12, IQ scores are normally quite stable.

Despite the evidence for stability, it is worth pointing out that IQ scores are not etched on a child's forehead at birth. Although these scores do become quite stable in late childhood, individual children can and do shift in response to especially rich or especially impoverished environments or to any stress in their lives (Sattler, 2008).

What IQ Scores Predict

The information on long-term stability of IQ test scores reveals something about the reliability of the tests. What about their validity? **Validity** has to do with whether a test is measuring what it is intended to measure. One way to assess a test's validity is to see whether scores on that test predict real behavior in a way that makes sense. In the case of IQ tests, the most central question is whether IQ scores predict school performance. That was what Binet originally intended his test to do; that is what all subsequent tests were

validity The degree to which a test measures what it is intended to measure.

designed to do. The research findings on this point are quite consistent: The correlation between a child's IQ test score and her grades in school or performance on other school tests typically falls between .45 and .60 (Brody, 1997; Peterson, Pihl, Higgins, Seguin, & Tremblay, 2003). A correlation in this range suggests a strong but by no means perfect relationship. It indicates that, on the whole, children with high IQ scores are more likely than their peers with average and low scores to be among the high achievers in school, and those who score low are likely to be among the low achievers. Still, some children with high IQ scores don't shine in school while some children with lower scores do.

IQ scores predict future grades as well as current grades. Preschool children with high IQ scores tend to do better when they enter school than those with lower scores; elementary school children with higher IQ scores do better later in high school. Further, IQ scores predict the total number of years of education a child is likely to complete. Higher-IQ elementary school children

Among these high school students, those with higher IQs are not only likely to get better grades, but also more likely to go on to college. Intelligence also adds to a child's resiliency—his ability to survive stress, including poverty.

are more likely to complete high school and are more likely to decide to go on to college (Brody, 1997).

It is important to point out that these predictive relationships hold within each social class and ethnic group in the United States. Among the poor, among African Americans and Hispanic Americans, and among middle-class White Americans, children with higher IQs are most likely to get good grades, complete high school, and go on to college (Birney et al., 2005; Brody, 1992; Rushton & Jensen, 2005). Such findings have led a number of theorists to argue that intelligence adds to the child's *resilience*—a concept you learned about in Chapter 1. At the other end of the scale, low intelligence is associated with a number of negative long-term outcomes, including adult illiteracy, delinquency in adolescence, and criminal behavior in adulthood (Birney et al., 2005; Stattin & Klackenberg-Larsson, 1993).

Clearly, then, IQ tests can be said to be valid: They measure what they purport to measure, which is school performance. However, they do not measure everything. Later in the chapter, you will read about two models, those of Robert Sternberg and Howard Gardner, that place the kind of intelligence measured by IQ tests into a much broader framework that encompasses many other aspects of cognition. And in Chapter 12, you will learn about *emotional intelligence*, a theoretical approach that represents a new way of thinking about children's understanding of their own and others' emotions.

Most importantly, intelligence tests cannot tell you (or a teacher or anyone else) that a child has some specific, fixed, underlying intellectual capacity. IQ tests were originally designed to measure only the specific range of skills that are needed for success in school. They do this reasonably well, so, for this limited purpose, they are valid. But these tests do not predict how well a particular person may perform other cognitive tasks requiring skills such as creativity, insight, "street smarts," or ability to read social cues.

Explaining Individual Differences in IQ Scores

You will not be surprised to discover that the arguments about the origins of differences in IQ test scores nearly always boil down to a dispute about nature versus nurture. When Binet and Simon wrote the first IQ test, they did not assume that intelligence as measured on an IQ test was fixed or inborn. However, many of the American psychologists who revised and promoted the use of IQ tests did believe that intellectual capacity is inherited and largely fixed at birth. Those who hold this view and those who believe that the environment is crucial in shaping a child's intellectual performance have been arguing—often vehemently—for at least 60 years. Both groups can muster research to support their views.

Learning Objective 7.5
What do twin and adoption studies suggest about the effects of heredity and environment on IQ scores?

Twin and Adoption Studies

Both twin studies and studies of adopted children show strong hereditary influences on IQ scores. Identical twins are more like one another in IQ scores than are fraternal twins, and the IQs of adopted children are better predicted from the IQs of their natural parents than from those of their adoptive parents (Brody, 1992; Loehlin, Horn, & Willerman, 1994; Rushton & Jensen, 2005; Scarr, Weinberg, & Waldman, 1993). This is precisely the pattern of correlations we would expect if there were a strong genetic element at work.

Further, as Figure 7.2 shows, correlations between the IQ scores of identical twins are stronger than those between the scores of fraternal twins throughout childhood, adolescence, and adulthood (Posthuma, de Geus, & Boomsma, 2003). Neuroimaging studies suggest that these correlations arise from genes that affect the distribution of *gray matter* (nonmyelinated neurons) in the frontal lobes of the brain (Thompson et al., 2001).

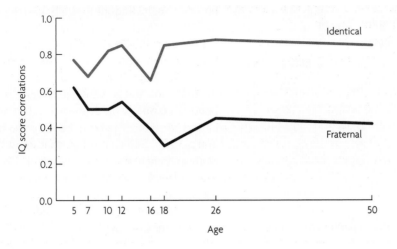

Figure 7.2   IQs of Fraternal and Identical Twins

This figure illustrates the combined findings of several longitudinal and cross-sectional studies of Dutch twins (Posthuma, de Geus, & Boomsma, 2003). You will notice that in childhood, when fraternal twins share the same environment, their IQ scores are more strongly correlated than in adulthood, when they presumably no longer live together. By contrast, the IQ scores of identical twins are even more strongly correlated in adulthood than during the childhood years. This pattern suggests conclusions about both heredity and environment. Specifically, at least with regard to IQ scores, the influence of heredity appears to increase with age, while that of the environment declines.

Remember, however, that if individual differences in IQ scores were fully attributable to heredity, the correlation between the scores of twins would be 1.0. Recent longitudinal studies suggest that heredity explains, at best, 80% of individual variation in IQ scores (Polderman et al., 2006). Thus, the take-away message from twin studies is that both heredity and environment contribute to IQ score differences. The importance of the environment is further highlighted by studies involving *virtual twins*, children of the same age who are adopted and raised as twins. As you can see in Figure 7.3, the IQ scores of virtual twins are more strongly correlated than those of biological siblings who are raised in separate homes (Segal, McGuire, Havelena, Gill, & Hershberger, 2007).

Adoption studies provide support for an environmental influence on IQ scores, because the IQ scores of adopted children are clearly affected by the environment in which they have grown up (van IJzendoorn, Juffer, & Poelhuis, 2005). Early studies of adopted children involved mostly children born to poverty-level parents who were adopted into middle-class

**Figure 7.3
IQ Correlations**

Twin and adoption studies show that both heredity and environment influence IQ scores.

(*Sources*: Bouchard & McGue, 1981; Scarr, Weinberg, & Waldman, 1993; Segal et al., 2007.)

Table 7.3	IQ Scores at Adolescence for Capron and Duyme's Adopted Children		
		Socioeconomic Status of Adoptive Parents	
		High	Low
Socioeconomic Status of Biological Parents	High	119.60	107.50
	Low	103.60	92.40

Source: From Capron, C., and Duyme, M., "Assessment of Effects of Socio-Economic Status on IQ in a Full Cross-fostering Study," *Nature, 340,* 1989, p. 553. By permission of the publisher, Macmillan Magazines, Ltd. and the authors.

families. Such children typically have IQ scores 10 to 15 points higher than those of their birth mothers (Scarr et al., 1993), suggesting that the effect of being brought up by a middle-class adoptive family is to raise the child's IQ score. What this finding doesn't indicate is whether a less stimulating adoptive family would lower the test score of a child whose birth parents had average or above-average IQs. Information on that question comes from a French study by Christiane Capron and Michel Duyme (1989), who studied a group of 38 French children, all adopted in infancy. Approximately half of the children had been born to better-educated parents of higher social class, while the other half had been born to working-class or poverty-level parents. Some of the children in each group had then been adopted by higher-social-class parents, and the others by poorer families. Table 7.3 shows the children's IQ scores in adolescence. If you compare the two columns in the table, you can see the effect of rearing conditions: The children reared in upper-class homes had IQ scores that were about 11 points higher than those of children reared in lower-class families, regardless of the social class or education of the birth parents. At the same time, you can see a genetic effect if you compare the two rows in the table: The children born to upper-class parents had higher IQ scores than children from lower-class families, no matter what kind of environment they were reared in.

Learning Objective 7.6

How do shared and nonshared family characteristics affect IQ scores?

Family Characteristics and IQ Scores

Adoption studies suggest that families make important contributions to children's intellectual development. Such factors are collectively known as the **shared environment**, because they affect all of the children in a household. Researchers have discovered a number of risk and protective factors in shared environments that are correlated with children's IQ scores.

Risk Factors Perhaps the most important risk factor in the shared environment is low socioeconomic status (SES). In Chapter 4 you learned that certain characteristics of low SES affect children's health (look back at Table 4.6, on page 114). Many of these factors, such as the mother's level of education, are correlated with children's scores on IQ tests as well (Gale, O'Callaghan, Godfrey, Law, & Martyn, 2004; Harden, Turkheimer, & Loehlin, 2007).

You can see this effect particularly vividly in Figure 7.4, which is based on data from a huge national study of more than 50,000 children born in 12 different hospitals around the United States between 1959 and 1966 (Broman, Nichols, & Kennedy, 1975). In order to make sure that the effects are due to SES and not ethnic differences, the figure shows only the results for White children who were tested with the Stanford-Binet at age 4, a total sample of more than 11,800 children. As

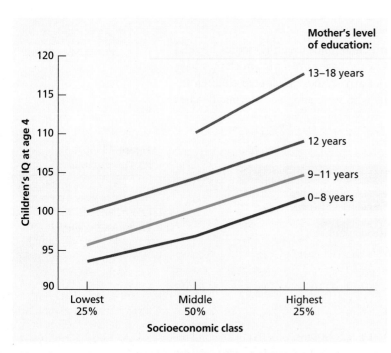

Figure 7.4 Socioeconomic Class, Maternal Education, and IQ

Each line represents the IQ scores of 4-year-old White children whose mothers had a particular level of education, and whose families fit in one of three broad socioeconomic class levels. Both elements are obviously related to the child's IQ.

(*Source*: Broman et al., 1975, p. 47.)

you can see, the average IQ score of the children rises as the family's SES rises and as the mother's education rises.

Such differences are not found in the results of standardized tests of infant intelligence such as the Bayley Scales (Golden & Birns, 1983). Later in childhood, test score differences associated with SES appear in most studies (Cox, 1983; Misra, 1983), producing what is sometimes called a **cumulative deficit**. That is, the longer a child lives in poverty, the more negative the effect on IQ test scores and other measures of cognitive functioning (Turkheimer et al., 2003).

Protective Factors   When you read about correlations between poverty and IQ scores, it's easy to get the idea that children in low-income homes are doomed to have below-average intellectual abilities. However, there are several factors that help protect children against the risks associated with poverty. In fact, researchers have found that the quality of parent-child interactions may be a more important factor than income in determining a child's IQ (Robinson, Lanzi, Weinberg, Ramey, & Ramey, 2002). Research has shown that, no matter what the economic status of a child's family is, there are at least five dimensions of family interaction or stimulation that influence her IQ. Parents of children who have higher IQ scores or scores that increase with age tend to do several things:

This kind of rich, complex, stimulating environment is consistently linked to higher IQ scores in children.

- They provide an interesting and complex physical environment for their children, one that includes play materials that are appropriate for each child's age and developmental level (Englund, Luckner, Whaley, & Egeland, 2004; Luster, Lekskul & Oh, 2004).

- They are emotionally responsive to and involved with their children. They respond warmly and appropriately to a child's behavior, smiling when the child smiles, reacting when the child speaks, answering the child's questions, and responding to the child's cues in myriad other ways (La Paro, Justice, Skibbe, & Pianta, 2004).

- They talk to their children often, using language that is diverse, descriptive, and accurate (Fewell & Deutscher, 2003; Hart & Risley, 1995; Sigman et al., 1988).

- When they play with or interact with their children, they operate in what Vygotsky referred to as the *zone of proximal development* (described in Chapter 1), aiming their conversation, their questions, and their assistance at a level that is just above the level the children could manage on their own, thus helping the children to master new skills (e.g., Tamis-LeMonda, Shannon, Cabrera, & Lamb, 2004).

- They expect their children to do well and to develop rapidly. They emphasize and encourage school achievement (Englund et al., 2004; Murray et al., 2006).

You may have figured out the methodological problem in research on parent-child interactions: the same problem that surfaces in comparisons of the IQs of children in families that differ in SES. Because parents provide both the genes and the environment, it isn't clear that these environmental factors are really causally important. Perhaps these are simply the environmental features provided by brighter parents, and it is their genes and not the environment that cause the higher IQ scores in their children. The way around this problem is to look at the link between environmental factors and IQ in adopted children. In fact, the few studies of this type do point to the same critical environmental features. That is, adoptive parents who behave in the ways listed above have adopted children who score higher on IQ tests (Plomin, Leohlin, & DeFries, 1985; van IJzendoorn et al., 2005).

Differences within Families   Within families, the experiences of individual children also differ in ways that affect IQ test scores. Taken together, such characteristics constitute the **nonshared environment**, factors that affect one child but not others in a family. Being the oldest of a large family, for example, is a very different experience from being the youngest or being in the middle; being the only girl in a family of boys is different from being a girl with only sisters. Psychologists are just beginning to study these within-family variables. Thus far,

shared environment
Characteristics of a family that affect all children in the household.

cumulative deficit Any difference between groups in IQ or achievement test scores that becomes larger over time.

nonshared environment
Characteristics of a family that affect one child but not others in the household.

Figure 7.5
Family Size and IQ

These data from the 1965 National Merit Scholarship Examination show the commonly found relationship between test scores and family size and birth order. Within each family size, the average score is highest for the first-born and declines with each position in the birth-order sequence.

(*Sources*: Data from Breland, 1974, recalculated by Storter, 1990, Table 7, p. 32.)

they have been looking mostly at obvious differences, such as the number of children in a family or the child's position within the family, both of which seem to be at least slightly related to a child's IQ score. On average, the more children in a family, the lower the IQ scores of the children. And, on average, first-born children have the highest IQ scores, with average scores declining steadily down the birth order (Abdel-Khalek & Lynn, 2008; Zajonc & Sulloway, 2007). One fairly typical set of data is illustrated in Figure 7.5, which is based on scores of nearly 800,000 students who took the National Merit Scholarship Examination in 1965, with the scores converted to the equivalent of IQ scores.

These differences are found consistently when IQ scores are averaged over many children or adults. However, when you look at individual families, the pattern is much weaker or not obvious at all. So you should be careful about extrapolating the aggregated data illustrated in Figure 7.5 to your own family or to other individual families. Some significant effect of birth order is detectable with large samples, but that particular effect may or may not be present in an individual family.

Another point about birth-order comparisons is that the absolute differences in IQ scores are not huge, even in the aggregated data. Still, this pattern has been observed repeatedly in the United States and in several other nations, leaving developmentalists to wonder why such a pattern occurs. Robert Zajonc's hypothesis is that, on average, the birth of each succeeding child "dilutes" the intellectual climate of the home (Zajonc & Sulloway, 2007). The oldest child initially interacts only with adults (parents) and thus has the most complex and enriching environment possible in that family at that time. Second or later children, in contrast, experience a lower average intellectual level simply because they interact with both other children and adults.

However, critics claim that Zajonc's theory, because it narrowly focuses on correlations between birth order and scores on conventional IQ tests, overlooks aspects of the environment that are unique to later-borns (Gillies & Lucey, 2006). These critics argue that later-borns must sometimes find ways to overcome the privileged position that first-borns occupy in the family system. For example, they may need to find a distinctive area of achievement to gain the same level of attention that parents give to first-borns. Moreover, in conflicts with first-borns, younger siblings must deal with older siblings' age-related advantages in physical and cognitive development. Thus, we might expect that later-borns would have opportunities to become skilled negotiators with (or manipulators of) near-age peers that first-borns do not have. In fact, this is exactly what the research shows (Gillies & Lucey, 2006). Thus, some aspects of the family environment may indeed be "diluted" by the time later-borns come along, but others are enhanced.

Some developmentalists have suggested that cultural beliefs about the significance of birth order may be just as important as any "dilution" that may occur as family size increases (Herrera, Zajonc, Wieczorkowska, & Cichomski, 2003). For example, among the Balinese, standard syllables signifying children's birth rank are added to their names. The rationale for this practice is that the higher a child's birth rank, the greater the status he or she must be afforded by members of the culture. As a result, every person a child meets instantly knows his or her status and the cultural prescriptions regarding how he or she is to be treated.

Learning Objective 7.7

In what ways do early interventions affect IQ scores and school performance?

Early Interventions and IQ Scores

Home environments and family interactions are not the only sources of environmental influence. Many young children also spend a very large amount of time in child care, special programs like Head Start, or preschool. How much effect do these environments have on a child's intellectual performance?

Attempts to answer this question have led to a messy body of research (Ripple & Zigler, 2003). Still, researchers agree generally on the effects. Children enrolled in Head Start or other enriched preschool programs show a gain of about 10 IQ points during the year of the Head Start experience compared to similar children without such experience. This IQ gain typically fades and then disappears within the first few years of elementary school (Ripple & Zigler, 2003; Zigler & Styfco, 1993). However, research also suggests that the contributions made by Head Start teachers to children's beliefs about their ability to attain educational goals continue to be evident in adolescence (Slaughter-Defoe & Rubin, 2001).

Children who have attended Head Start programs like this one are less likely to repeat a grade or to be assigned to special education classes.

On other measures, a clear residual effect can be seen as well. Children with Head Start or other quality preschool experience are less likely to be placed in special education classes, somewhat less likely to repeat a grade, and somewhat more likely to graduate from high school (Darlington, 1991; Haskins, 1989). They also are healthier, have better immunization rates, and show better school adjustment than their peers (Ripple & Zigler, 2003; Zigler & Styfco, 1993). In addition, Head Start programs provide a useful context for identifying and helping children who exhibit behavior patterns, such as aggression, that put them at risk for adjustment difficulties in elementary school (Kamps, Tankersley, & Ellis, 2000).

Furthermore, one study that looked at adult outcomes of preschool attendance suggested lasting effects. Young adults who had attended a particularly good experimental preschool program, the Perry Preschool Project in Milwaukee, had higher rates of high school graduation, lower rates of criminal behavior, lower rates of unemployment, and a lower probability of being on welfare than did their peers who did not have the advantage of the preschool experience (Barnett, 1993). Thus, the potential effects of such early education programs may be broad—even though the programs appear to have no lasting effect on standardized IQ test scores (Ripple & Zigler, 2003).

More promising still—although far more expensive and complex—are enrichment programs that begin in infancy rather than at age 3 or 4. The best-designed and most meticulously reported of such infancy interventions has been carried out by Craig Ramey and his colleagues at the University of North Carolina (Ramey, Ramey, & Lanzi, 2007). Infants from poverty-level families whose mothers had low IQ scores were randomly assigned either to a special child-care program, 8 hours a day, 5 days a week, or to a control group that received nutritional supplements and medical care but no special enriched child care. The special child-care program, which began when the infants were 6 to 12 weeks of age and lasted until they began kindergarten, involved the kinds of optimal stimulation described earlier. When they reached kindergarten age, half the children in each group were enrolled in a special supplemental program that focused on family support and increasing educational activities at home. The remaining children had only the normal school experience.

The average IQ scores of the children at various ages are shown in Figure 7.6 on page 190. You can see that the IQ scores of the children who had been enrolled in the special child-care program were higher at every age, whether they were in the school-age supplementary program or not, although the scores for both groups declined in the elementary school years. What is not shown in the figure but is perhaps more practically significant is the fact that 44.0% of the control group children had IQ scores classified as borderline or retarded (scores below 85), compared to only 12.8% of the children who had been in the special child-care program. In addition, the enriched infant-care group had significantly higher scores on both reading and mathematics achievement tests at age 12 and were only half as likely to have repeated a grade (Campbell & Ramey, 1994). And a follow-up study of the participants at age 21 revealed that the early advantage associated with participation in the program persisted into young adulthood (Campbell, Pungello, Miler-Johnson, Burchinal, & Ramey, 2001).

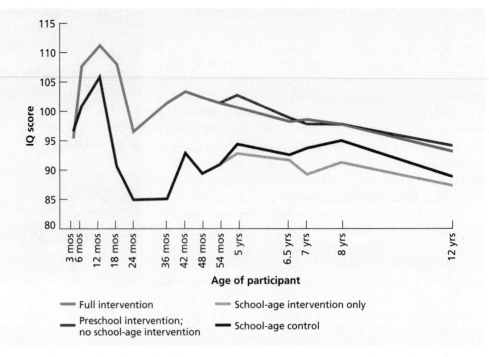

Figure 7.6   Ramey's Studies of Early Intervention

In the Ramey study, children were randomly assigned in infancy to an experimental group with special child care (the "full intervention" group) or to a control group. From kindergarten through third grade, half of each group received supplementary family support, while the other half received none. Thus, the "preschool intervention" group had the intervention for 5 years, but nothing beyond that; the "school-age intervention" group had no intervention before school age but did have assistance in early elementary school. The difference in IQ between the intervention and control groups remained statistically significant even at age 12.

(*Source*: Campbell, F. A., and Ramey, C. T., "Effects of achievement: A follow-up study of children from low-income families," Fig. 1, p. 690, *Child Development*, 65 (1994), 684–698. By permission of the Society for Research in Child Development.)

Ramey also gained insight from the varying experiences of the children in the control group. Some of them had been reared primarily at home; others had spent periods of time in other types of child-care or preschool programs. When he compared the IQ scores of these two groups with those who had been in the special child-care program, he found a consistent rank order: Children in the special program had the highest scores, followed by those who had had some kind of child-care experience, with those reared entirely at home having the lowest. The IQ scores at age 4 for these three groups were 101.1, 94.0, and 84.2, respectively (Burchinal, Lee, & Ramey, 1989). So the length and quality of the intervention appeared to be directly related to the size of the effect. Other researchers have confirmed the basic conclusion that the most effective programs are those that begin early and provide consistent, frequent stimulation (Ramey & Ramey, 1998, 2004).

reaction range Term used by some psychologists for the range of possible outcomes (phenotypes) for some variable, given basic genetic patterning (the genotype). In the case of IQ scores, the reaction range is estimated at 20 to 25 points.

Learning Objective 7.8
In what ways do heredity and environment interact to influence IQ scores?

Interactions of Heredity and Environment

Putting together all the information about the influence of heredity and environment on IQ scores makes it clear that both factors are highly significant. Studies around the world and across several decades consistently yield estimates that at least half the variation in IQ scores within any population is due to heredity (Neisser et al., 1996; Plomin & Rende, 1991; Rogers, Rowe, & May, 1994; Rushton & Jensen, 2005; van Leeuwen, van den Berg, & Boomsma, 2008). The remaining half is clearly due to environment or to interactions between environment and heredity.

One useful way to think about this interaction is with the idea of a **reaction range**—a range within upper and lower boundaries of possible functioning established by one's genes.

Where a child's IQ score falls within those boundaries is determined by environment. Richard Weinberg (1989) estimates that the reaction range for IQ scores is about 20 to 25 points. That is, given a specific genetic heritage (a genotype), a child's actual IQ test performance (the phenotype) may vary by as much as 20 or 25 points, depending on the richness or poverty of the environment in which the child grows up. When a child's environment is improved, the child moves closer to the upper end of his reaction range. When the environment becomes worse, the child's effective intellectual performance falls toward the lower end of his reaction range. Thus, even though a reaction range of intelligence (as measured with an IQ test) is highly heritable, the IQ score within that range is determined by environment. Research showing that the IQ scores of identical twins are more weakly correlated in poor families than in those with more economic resources amply demonstrates this idea (Turkheimer, Haley, Waldron, D'Onofrio, & Gottesman, 2003).

We could also think about the interaction between heredity and environment in terms rather like those Horowitz used in his model (recall Figure 1.2, page 10), or we could use Aslin's concept of maintenance. Some theorists (Turkheimer & Gottesman, 1991) have argued that within the normal range of environments, IQ scores may be largely a function of heredity, not because environment is unimportant but simply because most environments are sufficiently rich to support or maintain normal intellectual development. It is only when environmental quality falls below some crucial threshold that it has a major effect on the level of measured IQ, as might be true for children reared in an orphanage or in a severely impoverished environment. This view does not necessarily contradict the concept of a reaction range. Rather, the argument is that the lower end of any given child's reaction range is likely to be manifested only if the child is reared in an environment that falls below the critical threshold. If we think about the effect of environment in this way, it makes sense that special programs like Ramey's are effective for children from poverty-level environments, since such a program improves the child's environment to the point that it adequately supports normal intellectual development. The same program provided to a child from a more enriched family environment, however, should have little or no effect on IQ scores—which is essentially what researchers have found.

Explaining Group Differences in IQ or Achievement Test Scores

So far, we have sidestepped a difficult issue: group differences in IQ or achievement test scores. Because group differences have powerful personal and political ramifications and can easily be blown out of proportion, it's important not to place too much emphasis on them and to point out that individual variation in IQ and achievement is far greater than variation across groups. But you should be aware of what psychologists know, what they don't know, and how they explain these group differences.

Ethnic Differences

Learning Objective 7.9
What ideas have theorists proposed to explain ethnic group differences in IQ scores?

Evidence points to several ethnic group differences in intellectual performance (Rushton & Jensen, 2005). First, Asian and Asian American students typically test 3 to 6 points higher on IQ tests and do consistently better on achievement tests (especially math and science tests) than do Caucasian children (Rushton & Jensen, 2005). More troubling for researchers and theorists is the finding that in the United States, African American children consistently score lower than Caucasian children on standard measures of intelligence. This difference, which is on the order of 12 IQ points, is not found on infant tests of intelligence or on measures of infant habituation rate (Fagan & Singer, 1983), but it becomes apparent by the time children are 2 or 3 years old (Brody, 1992; Peoples, Fagan, &

Drotar, 1995; Rushton & Jensen, 2005). There is some indication that the size of the IQ difference between African American and Caucasian children declined during the 1970s and 1980s and may now be less than 10 points (Neisser et al., 1996; Williams & Ceci, 1997). A noticeable difference persists.

Some scientists, while acknowledging that the environments of the two groups are, on average, substantially different, nonetheless argue that the IQ score difference must reflect some genetic differences between ethnic groups (Jensen, 1980; Lynn & Harvey, 2008; Rushton & Jensen, 2005). Other scientists, even granting that IQ is highly heritable, point out that a 10- or 12-point difference falls well within the presumed reaction range of IQ. They emphasize that there are sufficiently large differences in the environments in which African American and White American children are typically reared to account for the average difference in score (Brody, 1992). African American children are more likely to be born with low birth weight, more likely to suffer from inadequate nutrition, more likely to have high blood levels of lead, and less likely to be read to or provided with a wide range of intellectual stimulation. Each of these environmental variations is known to be linked to lower IQ scores.

Further evidence for the environmental hypothesis comes from studies of Asian American families, who tend to emphasize academic achievement more than either African American or White families. As teens, Asian Americans prioritize their time differently than do adolescents in other groups: Family and school take precedence over social activities with peers (Fuligni, Yip, & Tseng, 2002). Such differences have been cited in explanations of Asian American children's higher IQ scores.

Cultural differences also clearly contribute to observed differences between African American and Caucasian children's test scores, as African American psychologists have long pointed out (Fagan & Holland, 2007; Ogbu, 1994, 2004). One such cultural effect is discussed in *Developmental Science in the Real World*. We can see such differences at work in the way children from different subcultures respond to the testing situation itself. For example, in a classic study of adopted African American children, Moore (1986) found that those who

DEVELOPMENTAL SCIENCE IN THE REAL WORLD

Stereotype Threat

Dr. Jones is a clinical psychologist who works at a large children's hospital. One of her duties is to administer individual intelligence tests to children who are patients in the hospital's neurology department. When she administers a test to a child, Dr. Jones doesn't refer to it as an "intelligence" test. Instead, she says, "I'm going to ask you some questions about words" or "I'm going to ask you to solve some problems." Dr. Jones uses this approach because her goal is to get the best performance possible out of each child she tests. She believes that if children are worried about the type of test they are taking or how their performance will be judged, they aren't likely to do their best. Dr. Jones is particularly concerned about how the performance of a child who is a member of a minority group might be affected by what she says about a test, because she is familiar with the research on *stereotype threat*.

Psychologists Claude Steele and Joshua Aronson (Steele & Aronson, 1995) define *stereotype threat* as a subtle sense of pressure members of a particular group feel when they are attempting to perform well in an area in which their group is characterized by a negative stereotype. According to Steele and Aronson, African American students experience stereotype threat whenever they are faced with an important cognitive test, such as a college entrance exam or an IQ test, because of the general cultural stereotype that African Americans are less intellectually able than members of other groups. In order to avoid confirming the stereotype, says the theory, African Americans avoid putting forth their best effort, because to fail after having put forth one's best effort would mean that the stereotype was true.

Numerous studies have confirmed the existence of stereotype threat among both children and adults (McKown & Weinstein, 2003; Nussbaum & Steele, 2007; Steele & Aronson, 2004; Suzuki & Aronson, 2005). However, stereotype threat appears to have a smaller effect on children's test performance than it does on that of adults. Nevertheless, Dr. Jones believes that it is best to err on the side of caution with respect to stereotype threat. Her conclusion is that refraining from using the term "intelligence test" does not harm children or threaten their performance, whereas using that term might cause them to be more anxious than they would be otherwise.

Questions for Reflection

1. Do you agree with Dr. Jones's conclusion regarding erring on the side of caution?
2. How might parents and teachers moderate the effects of stereotype threat on children's test performance?

had been reared in White families (and thus imbued with the values of the majority culture) not only had a higher average IQ score than those adopted into African American families (117 versus 103) but also approached the IQ-testing situation quite differently. They stayed more focused on the tasks and were more likely to try some task even if they didn't think they could do it. African American children adopted into middle-class African American families did not show this pattern of persistence and effort. They asked for help more often and gave up more easily when faced with a difficult task. When Moore then observed each adoptive mother teaching her child several tasks, he could see parallel differences. The White mothers were more encouraging and less likely to give the child the answer than were the African American mothers.

Findings like these suggest that the observed IQ differences among racial or ethnic groups are at least to some degree a reflection of cultural bias. Such bias arises from the fact that IQ tests and schools alike are designed by the majority culture to promote a particular form of intellectual activity, and many African American or other minority families rear their children in ways that do not promote or emphasize this particular set of skills (Guthrie, 2004). Consequently, some developmentalists have argued for banning intelligence testing altogether. However, most psychologists agree that there are still some good reasons for using IQ tests, as long as their limitations are understood. Likewise, studies examining a new approach to individualized assessment suggest that it may be possible for psychologists who are testing children from disadvantaged backgrounds to duplicate the test-familiarity advantage of middle-class children in the testing situation itself. In *dynamic assessment*, children are informed about the purpose of an intelligence test and are given a chance to practice with each kind of problem-solving task on the test prior to actually being tested. Studies show that dynamic assessment significantly increases the proportion of minority children who attain above-average scores (Lidz & Macrine, 2001). Further, whenever possible, intelligence testing of ethnic minority children should be carried out by testing professionals with ethnic backgrounds similar to those of the children being tested. Research has shown that children from minority groups get better scores under such conditions (Kim, Baydar, & Greek, 2003). Moreover, as we noted in Table 7.1, the Kaufman Assessment Battery for Children (KABC) (Kaufman & Kaufman, 2004) has been praised for its lack of bias. Minority group children tend to get higher scores on the KABC than they do on the Wechsler tests (Kaufman, Kaufman, Kaufman-Singer, & Kaufman, 2005). Thus, the KABC is used by many preschools, elementary schools, and clinicians to assess intelligence in minority group children.

Cross-Cultural Differences

Learning Objective 7.10

What factors contribute to cross-cultural differences in IQ and achievement test scores?

Many cross-cultural psychologists have argued that comparisons of IQ scores across cultures are meaningless, because each culture emphasizes different aspects of intelligence in child-rearing practices (Mishra, 2001). Further, each develops its own methods of assessing individual differences in these aspects of intelligence, which are tied to the society's beliefs about the relative importance of different kinds of skills. Consequently, in the industrialized world, tests of intelligence look very much like achievement tests (as you learned earlier), because school performance is the primary arena in which children are expected to apply their intellectual abilities. Thus, using such tests to measure intelligence in a culture where children are expected to use their cognitive gifts differently is invalid.

Because of the difficulty inherent in developing tests that provide comparable scores across very different cultures, research attempting to directly compare the intelligence of individuals in one culture to that of those in another has generally been restricted to comparisons of industrialized societies. For example, several studies have found that Chinese, Japanese, and Korean children tend to score slightly higher on traditional intelligence tests than do their American and European counterparts (Lynn, 1991; Lynn & Song, 1992; Rushton & Jensen, 2005).

Cross-national comparisons of intellectual skills have focused more on the domains of math and science achievement than on IQ scores. Such studies have often found that children in the United States demonstrate substantially lower levels of performance in these areas than children in other industrialized nations (Gonzales et al., 2004). These comparisons have focused on Asian children because their scores have been found to be significantly higher than those of children in other nations. Harold Stevenson and others have argued that the differences between Asian and American children in performance on mathematics achievement tests result not from genetic differences in capacity, but from differences in cultural emphasis on the importance of academic achievement, in the number of hours spent on homework, and in the quality of math instruction in the schools (Chang & Murray, 1995; Geary, 1996; Schneider, Hieshima, Lee, & Plank, 1994; Stevenson & Lee, 1990; Stigler, Lee, & Stevenson, 1987). For example, Singaporean parents start teaching their children about numbers and mathematical reasoning long before the children begin school (Sharpe, 2002).

Moreover, teachers in Asian nations take a different approach to mathematics instruction than do teachers in the United States. For example, James Stigler and Harold Stevenson (1991) observed teaching practices in 120 classrooms in Japan, Taiwan, and the United States. Asian teachers typically devoted an entire class period to a single type of problem. In U.S. classrooms, in contrast, teachers rarely spent 30 or 60 minutes on a single coherent math or science lesson involving the whole class of children and a single topic. Instead, they shifted often from one topic to another during a single math or science lesson. They might do a brief bit on addition, then talk about measurement, then about telling time, and then shift back to addition. Stigler and Stevenson also found striking differences in the amount of time teachers spent leading instruction for the whole class. In the U.S. classrooms they observed, group instruction occurred only 49% of the time; it occurred 74% of the time in Japan and 91% of the time in Taiwan. More recent studies have produced similar findings (NCES, 2003).

Asian and American math instruction also differs with respect to emphasis on *computational fluency*, the degree to which an individual can automatically produce solutions to simple calculation problems (Geary et al., 1999). A number of mathematicians and professors of mathematics have claimed that American math instruction has been influenced more by fads than by a sound understanding of the role of computational fluency in mathematical problem-solving (Murray, 1998). They point out that research has demonstrated that computational fluency is related both to calculation skills and to facility in solving word problems (Geary et al., 1999; Kail & Hall, 1999).

Asian and American cultures differ with respect to beliefs about achievement as well. For example, developmentalists have found that North American parents and teachers emphasize innate ability, which they assume to be unchangeable, more than they emphasize effort. For Asians, the emphasis is just the opposite: They believe that people can become more capable by working harder (Serpell & Hatano, 1997). Because of these differences in beliefs, some developmentalists claim, Asian parents and teachers have higher expectations for children and are better at finding ways to motivate them to do schoolwork.

Another difference between Asian and American schools, especially at the elementary level, involves the use of rewards. Because of the influence of Skinner's operant conditioning theory on education in the United States, teachers commonly use material rewards, such as stickers, to motivate children. Such rewards may be effective when they are unexpected and tied to high standards (Deci, Koestner, & Ryan, 1999; Eisenberger, Pierce, & Cameron, 1999). Giving a sur-

Asian and Asian American children tend to get higher scores on math and science tests than their peers in other groups do. What explanations can you think of for such a difference?

prise sticker to the only child in a class who gets a grade of 100 on a spelling test is an example of this approach to using rewards. However, when teachers use such rewards routinely to try to motivate children to do everyday tasks, such as turning in homework, they clearly undermine both intrinsic motivation and interest in the tasks to which the stickers are linked (Deci et al., 1999). So, Asian students may be more intrinsically motivated to achieve because they are provided with fewer material rewards; achievement itself is their reward.

Sex Differences

Learning Objective 7.11

How do males and females differ with respect to IQ and achievement test performance?

Comparisons of overall IQ test scores for boys and girls do not reveal consistent differences (Camarata & Woodcock, 2006). It is only when researchers break down the overall score into several subscores that reflect separate skills that some patterns of sex differences emerge (Lippa, 2005). On average, girls are slightly better at verbal tasks and tasks that are timed. Boys, on the other hand, are somewhat better at numerical reasoning, a difference that becomes clearer on tests in high school, when reasoning problems make up a larger portion of math exams.

Sex differences in spatial abilities are also found regularly and are evident in the early preschool years (Levine, Huttenlocher, Taylor, & Langrock, 1999). Boys have somewhat higher average scores on tests of spatial visualization, such as those illustrated in Figure 7.7. On measures of mental rotation, like that illustrated in part (c) of the figure, the sex difference is substantial and becomes larger with age (Hyde, 2005). Differences in such abilities are manifested in everyday tasks such as route learning. In learning to follow a new way to get from one place to another, both preschool and elementary school boys make fewer errors than girls (Beilstein & Wilson, 2000).

Of course, even on tests of mental rotation, the two distributions overlap. That is, some girls and women are good at this type of task, while some boys and men are not. Still, the average difference is quite large. The fact that girls score lower on such tests does not mean that no women are qualified for occupations that demand such skill, such as being an architect or engineer. Indeed, there are many girls who display exceptional levels of spatial ability, and the link between spatial ability and skills such as model building is just as strong for girls as for boys (Brosnan, 1998). However, the difference in boys' and girls' averages on tests of spatial ability does mean that fewer girls or young women will be able to meet the training requirements for such jobs.

Where might such differences come from? The explanatory options should be familiar by now. Biological influences have been most often suggested as the cause of sex differences in spatial abilities (Hyde, 2005). Specifically, boys show greater coherence in brain function in areas of the brain devoted to spatial tasks, while girls display more organized functioning in parts of the brain where language and social information are processed (Hanlon, Thatcher, & Cline, 1999). Advocates of this position also point out that research with adults has demonstrated that hormonal differences between men and women, as well as hormonal variations among women, are linked to performance on spatial tasks (Halpern & Tan, 2001; Josephs, Newman, Brown, & Beer,

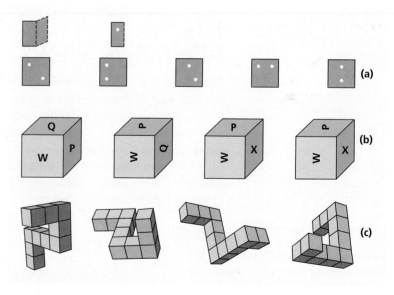

Figure 7.7 **Spatial Ability Tasks**

Three examples of spatial ability tasks. (a) *Spatial visualization.* The figure at the top represents a square piece of paper being folded. A hole is punched through all the thicknesses of the folded paper. Which figure shows what the paper looks like when it is unfolded? (b) *Spatial orientation.* Compare the three cubes on the right with the one on the left. No letter appears on more than one face of a given cube. Which of the three cubes on the right could be a different view of the cube on the left? (c) *Mental rotation.* In each pair, can the three-dimensional objects be made congruent by rotation?

(*Source: Sex Differences in Cognitive Abilities,* by D. Halpern. Copyright 1986 by Taylor & Francis Group LLC-Books. Reproduced with permission of Taylor & Francis Group LLC-Books in the format Presentation via Copyright Clearance Center.)

2003). As a result, some argue that hormonal differences between boys and girls or hormonal variations in the prenatal environment may affect spatial abilities.

More purely environmental explanations have also been prominent in discussions of the sex differences in mathematical or verbal reasoning. For instance, longitudinal studies have shown that parents' beliefs about their children's talents at age 6 predict those children's beliefs about their own abilities at age 17 (Fredricks & Eccles, 2002). Thus, findings regarding parental attitudes towards sons' and daughters' performance on mathematics tests may help explain sex differences in this area. For one, parents are more likely to describe sons as competent in mathematics (Furnham 2000; Tiedemann, 2000). Parents are also more likely to characterize a daughter who performs well in math classes as a "hard worker," while a son who does well in mathematics is often described as "talented" (Räty, Vänskä, Kasanen, & Kärkkäinen, 2002). Not surprisingly, when children reach high school age, their self-descriptions mirror the beliefs expressed by parents of young children. That is, boys say that natural ability enables them to get good scores on math tests, while girls say that they "work hard" to do so (Reis & Park, 2001). Thus, it isn't surprising that even the most mathematically talented girls are far less likely to aspire to careers in math and science than are boys (Webb, Lubinski, & Benbow, 2002).

Environmental explanations notwithstanding, it is clear that males far outnumber females at the highest levels of mathematical giftedness, often quantified as scores in the top 1% on tests of quantitative reasoning, such as the math portion of the SAT (Lippa, 2005). Researchers have yet to find an adequate explanation for this sex difference. However, recent findings suggest that the disproportionate male to female ratio among the mathematically gifted may be but one manifestation of a larger phenomenon, that of greater variability among males than females. In other words, there are more males than females at the highest levels of mathematical ability, but the same is probably true of the lowest levels (Deary, Thorpe, Wilson, Starr, & Whalley, 2003). Such findings do not constitute an explanation for sex differences in mathematical giftedness. However, they do help us conceptualize these differences more dispassionately—that is, as "differences" rather than some form of "superiority" or "advantage" that has been unjustly conferred upon males.

Alternative Views of Intelligence

Using IQ tests to define and explain individual and group differences in intelligence is called the *psychometric approach* (Birney et al., 2005; Shayer, 2008). Recently, developmentalists of diverse theoretical orientations have argued that this approach is too narrow. That is, many are beginning to believe that psychologists have placed too much emphasis on defining intelligence in terms of correlations between IQ tests and school achievement. Moreover, a number of developmentalists have suggested that we still do not really know what it is that intelligence tests measure. Thus, several alternative approaches to defining and measuring intelligence have been proposed in recent years.

Learning Objective 7.12

How do information-processing theorists explain individual differences in IQ scores?

Information-Processing Theory

In Chapter 6, you read about developmental changes in information-processing strategies. Several developmentalists have argued that some of the same concepts can be used to explain what specific processes are measured on IQ tests.

Speed of Information Processing As you learned in Chapter 6, it is becoming increasingly clear that increases in speed or efficiency of processing underlie age-related changes in cognitive skills (Edmonds et al., 2008). Thus, it makes sense to hypothesize that differences in processing speed may also underlie individual differences in IQ scores (Thomas & Karmiloff-Smith, 2003). A number of investigators have found just such a link: Participants with faster reaction times or speed of performance on a variety of simple tasks also have higher average IQ scores on standard tests (McRorie & Cooper, 2004; Rinderman & Neubauer, 2004). A few studies have even linked speed of processing directly to central nervous system functioning and to IQ. For example, it is now possible to measure the speed of conduction of impulses along individual nerves, such as nerves in the arm. Philip Vernon (1993; Vernon & Mori, 1992) has found a correlation of about .45 between such a measure and IQ test score.

Most of this research has been done with adults, but a link between speed of reaction time and IQ scores has also been found in a few studies with children (Rindermann & Neubauer, 2004). Furthermore, there are some pretty clear indications that such speed-of-processing differences may be built in at birth. Indeed, the link between infant habituation (or recognition memory) and later IQ score seems to be primarily a result of basic variations in speed of processing (Rose & Feldman, 1997).

Other Links between IQ and Information Processing

Other researchers have explored the connections between IQ and information processing by comparing the information-processing strategies used by typically developing children with those used by children with mental retardation. In one classic study, Judy DeLoache compared the searching strategies of groups of 2-year-olds who were either developing normally or showed delayed development (DeLoache & Brown, 1987). When the search task was very simple, such as looking for a toy hidden in an obvious location in a room, the two groups did not differ in search strategies or skill. But when the experimenter surreptitiously moved the toy before the child was allowed to search, typically developing children were able to search in alternative plausible places, such as in nearby locations; delayed children simply persisted in looking in the place where they had seen the toy hidden. They either could not change strategies once they had settled on a particular approach or did not have alternative, more complex strategies in their repertoires.

Other research underlines this difference in the flexibility of strategy use (Pretz & Sternberg, 2005). In several early studies, Joseph Campione and Ann Brown (1984; Campione, Brown, Ferrara, Jones, & Steinberg, 1985) found that both children with mental retardation and children with average and above-average IQs could learn to solve problems such as those in parts (a), (b), and (c) of Figure 7.8, but the children with mental retardation could not transfer this learning to a more complex problem of the same general type, such as part (d), whereas children with average and above-average IQs could. Both sets of studies suggest that flexibility of use of any given strategy may be another key dimension of individual differences in intelligence.

Evaluating the Information-Processing Approach

The information-processing approach offers some important bridges between testing approaches to intelligence and cognitive-developmental theories such as those of Piaget and the neo-Piagetians (Anderson, 2005). It now looks as if children are born with some basic, inborn cognitive strategies (such as noting differences or similarities). It is also clear that these strategies or rules change during the early years of life, with more complex ones emerging and old ones being used more flexibly. Plain old experience is a key part of the process of change. The more a child plays with blocks, the better she will be at organizing and classifying blocks; the more a person plays chess, the better he will be at seeing and remembering relationships among pieces on the board. So some of the changes that Piaget thought of as changes in the underlying structure of intelligence are instead specific task learning. But there does seem to be some structural change as well, such as the emergence of new strategies, particularly metacognitive strategies.

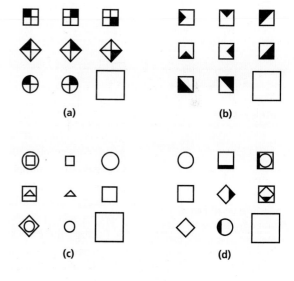

Figure 7.8   Flexibility of Strategy Use

For parts (a) through (d), the child must figure out the "system" in each set and then describe what pattern should go in the empty box in the bottom right-hand corner. Part (a) shows rotation; part (b) shows addition of two elements; part (c) shows subtraction. The figure in part (d) is harder because the child must apply *two* principles at once, in this case both addition and rotation. Children with mental retardation and children with average and above-average IQs could do problems like those in parts (a), (b), and (c), but children with mental retardation did much more poorly on problems like the one in part (d).

(*Source*: Campione et al., 1985, Figure 1, p. 302, and Figure 4, p. 306.)

Individual differences in what is normally thought of as intelligence can then be conceived of as resulting both from inborn differences in the speed or efficiency of the basic processes (differences in the hardware, perhaps) and from differences in expertise or experience. The child with a slower or less efficient processing system will move through all the various steps and stages more slowly; he will use the experience he has less efficiently or effectively and may never develop as complete a range of strategies as the child who is initially quicker. But when this less innately gifted child has sufficient expertise in some area, that specialized knowledge can compensate for the lower IQ.

This point is nicely illustrated in a study of expertise done in Germany (Schneider & Bjorklund, 1992). School-aged children who were experts (very knowledgeable) about soccer had better recall of soccer-related lists than did nonexperts. But high-IQ novices did as well as low-IQ experts on these same tasks. So rich knowledge in some area can compensate somewhat for lower IQ, but it does not result in equality. High-IQ experts will still be better than medium- or low-IQ experts in any given area.

The information-processing approach may also have some practical applications. Studies of recognition memory in infancy, for example, may give developmentalists a way to identify children with mental retardation very early in life or to sort out from among low-birth-weight infants those who seem at particular risk for later problems. Identifying the aspects of information processing that distinguish children with cognitive disabilities from typically developing peers may also allow developmentalists to identify specific kinds of training that would be useful for a child with mental retardation or for a child with a learning disability.

It is well to remember, though, that developmentalists do not yet have any tests of information-processing ability that could realistically replace the careful use of IQ tests in schools and clinics, although a few psychologists believe that a clinically useful biological measure of intelligence will be available within several decades (Tasbihsazan, Nettelbeck, & Kirby, 2003). Nor are the sequential theories of information-processing development yet able to explain all the observed differences among infants, preschoolers, and older children in performance on various Piagetian tasks. In short, information-processing theory is an important addition to psychologists' understanding of cognitive development, but it does not replace all the other approaches.

triarchic theory of intelligence A theory advanced by Robert Sternberg, proposing the existence of three types of intelligence: analytical, creative, and practical.

Learning Objective 7.13

What is the triarchic theory of intelligence?

Sternberg's Triarchic Theory of Intelligence

Some developmentalists say that the problem with relying on IQ tests as the primary means of understanding and studying intelligence is that these tests fail to provide a complete picture of mental abilities. Psychologist Robert Sternberg, while conceding that conventional tests are good predictors of academic performance and other important outcomes (Sternberg, Grigorenko, & Bundy, 2001), argues that there are components of intellectual functioning that these tests measure poorly. He suggests that there are actually three aspects, or types, of intelligence (1985, 2003; Sternberg & Wagner, 1993). Consequently, Sternberg's theory is known as the **triarchic theory of intelligence**.

Sternberg has developed a test, the Sternberg Triarchic Abilities Test, to measure the three aspects of intelligence he hypothesizes (Sternberg, Castejon, Prieto, Hautamaeki, & Grigorenko, 2001). The first of the three, which Sternberg calls **analytical intelligence** (originally called *componential intelligence*), includes what is normally measured by IQ and achievement tests. Planning, organizing, and remembering facts and applying them to new situations are all part of analytical intelligence.

The second aspect Sternberg calls **creative intelligence** (originally labeled *experiential intelligence*). A person with well-developed creative intelligence can see new connections between things, is insightful about experiences, and questions what is sometimes called the "conventional wisdom" about various kinds of problems (Sternberg, 2001). A graduate student who comes up with good ideas for experiments, who can see how a theory could be applied to a totally different situation, who can synthesize many facts into a new organization,

analytical intelligence One of three types of intelligence in Sternberg's triarchic theory of intelligence; the type of intelligence typically measured on IQ tests, including the ability to plan, remember facts, and organize information.

creative intelligence One of three types of intelligence described by Sternberg in his triarchic theory of intelligence; includes insightfulness and the ability to see new relationships among events or experiences.

or who critically examines ideas that most professionals in the field accept as true is high in creative intelligence.

The third aspect Sternberg calls **practical intelligence** (originally labeled *contextual intelligence*), sometimes called "street smarts." People who have a high degree of practical intelligence are good at seeing how some bit of information may be applied to the real world or at finding some practical solution to a real-life problem—such as coming up with shortcuts for repetitive tasks or figuring out which of several different-sized boxes of cereal is the best buy. Practical intelligence may also involve being skilled at reading social cues or social situations, such as knowing not to give your boss bad news when she is clearly angry about something else or knowing how to persuade your supervisor to invest a large amount of money in your proposed sales plan (Sternberg, Wagner, Williams, & Horvath, 1995).

Sternberg's most basic point about these several types of intelligence is not just that standard IQ tests do not measure all three, but that in the world beyond the school walls, creative or practical intelligence may be required as much as or more than the type of skill measured on an IQ test (Sternberg & Grigorenko, 2006). These are important points to keep in mind when considering the origins of individual differences in IQ scores. What developmentalists know about "intelligence" is almost entirely restricted to information about analytical intelligence—the kind of intelligence most often demanded (and tested) in school. They know almost nothing about the origins or long-term consequences of variations in creative or practical intelligence.

Gardner's Multiple Intelligences

Learning Objective 7.14
What are the various types of intelligence proposed by Gardner?

Developmental psychologist Howard Gardner has also argued that a multidimensional view of intelligence provides both a better understanding of individual differences and, at least potentially, strategies for measuring these differences in more meaningful ways. Accordingly, he has proposed a theory of **multiple intelligences** (Gardner, 1983). This theory claims there are eight types of intelligence:

- Linguistic: People who are good writers or speakers, learn languages easily, or possess a lot of knowledge about language have greater than average linguistic intelligence.
- Logical/mathematical: Logical/mathematical intelligence enables individuals to learn math and to generate logical solutions to various kinds of problems.
- Spatial: Spatial intelligence is used in the production and appreciation of works of art such as paintings and sculpture.
- Bodily kinesthetic: Professional athletes possess high levels of this kind of intelligence.
- Musical: Musicians, singers, composers, and conductors possess musical intelligence.
- Interpersonal: Those in the "helping professions"—counselors, social workers, ministers, and the like—have high levels of interpersonal intelligence.
- Intrapersonal: People who are good at identifying their own strengths and choosing goals accordingly have high levels of intrapersonal intelligence.
- Naturalistic: Scientists are high in this type of intelligence involving the ability to recognize patterns in nature.

Gardner's theory is based on observations of people with brain damage, mental retardation, and other conditions, such as the savant syndrome displayed by Hikari Oe. Gardner points out that brain damage usually causes disruption of functioning in very specific mental abilities rather than a general decline in intelligence. He also notes that many individuals with mental deficits have remarkable talents: some are gifted in music; others can perform complex mathematical computations in their heads. Gardner continues to refine his model. In recent years, he has proposed that a ninth type of intelligence, one that he calls *existential intelligence*, deals with the spiritual realm and enables us to contemplate the meaning of life

practical intelligence One of three types of intelligence in Sternberg's triarchic theory of intelligence; often called "street smarts," this type of intelligence includes skill in applying information to the real world or solving practical problems.

multiple intelligences Eight types of intelligence (linguistic, logical/mathematical, spatial, bodily kinesthetic, musical, interpersonal, intrapersonal, and naturalistic) proposed by Howard Gardner.

(Halama & Strízenec, 2004). Critics claim that Gardner's view, while intuitively appealing, has little empirical support (Aiken, 1997).

Creativity

Finally, conventional intelligence tests do not measure **creativity**, the ability to produce original, appropriate, and valuable ideas and/or solutions to problems. While children's capacity for creativity appears to greatly depend on how much knowledge they have about a topic (Sak & Maker, 2006), researchers have found that creativity is only weakly related to IQ (Lubart, 2003).

Some developmentalists agree with the ideas proposed by psychologist J. P. Guilford (1897–1987) (Silvia et al., 2008). Guilford defined creativity as **divergent thinking** (Guilford, 1967). A child who uses divergent thinking can provide multiple solutions to problems that have no clear answer. In one creativity test, the Alternative Uses Test (Guilford, 1967), children are prompted to think of unusual uses of everyday objects such as bricks.

However, other theorists base their views on a model that was proposed by noted creativity researcher Paul Torrance (1915–2003). He argued that tests such as the Alternative Uses Test fail to capture all of the dimensions of creativity. To test

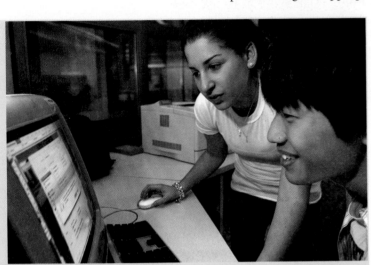

Conventional intelligence tests do not measure creativity. Moreover, the creative skills that students learn when they work on school publications, as these teens are doing, are not measured by achievement tests.

his theory, Torrance devised the Torrance Tests of Creative Thinking (Torrance, 1998). The test examines how individuals respond to problems that involve interpretations of pictures, interpretations of verbal scenarios, and producing drawings in response to prompts (Torrance, 1998). Test-takers receive scores on four dimensions of creativity:

- Fluency: The total number of ideas generated
- Flexibility: Number of different categories represented in ideas
- Originality: The degree to which ideas are unusual, statistically speaking
- Elaboration: The amount of detail in ideas

Evidence for the validity of Torrance's test among adults was found in his own longitudinal study in which children who received high scores on the test in the 1950s were found to have a greater number of creative accomplishments in adulthood some 40 years later (Plucker, 1999). Moreover, the Torrance test proved to be more strongly correlated with life achievements of a creative nature than were research participants' childhood IQ scores.

creativity The ability to produce original, appropriate, and valuable ideas and/or solutions to problems.

divergent thinking The ability to produce multiple solutions to problems that have no clear answer.

Think Critically

- Given the variability in individual IQ scores, does it make sense to select children for special classes, such as those for the gifted, on the basis of a single test score? How else could you go about choosing students?
- A lot of effort has been expended trying to explain possible sex differences in mathematical ability. What are the practical implications of viewing such differences as genetic versus viewing them as caused by environmental factors?

Conduct Your Own Research

You can use Figure 7.8 on page 197 in a simple study that will help you learn more about stereotype threat. Randomly assign equal numbers of your male and female classmates or friends to "stereotype-threat" and "no-stereotype-threat" conditions. Tell those in the threat condition that the tasks in the figure measure sex differences in cognitive ability. Point out that men often outperform women on such tasks. Tell participants in the nonthreat condition that you have to collect data on the tasks for your psychology class. Score participants' responses to sets (a) through (d) as correct or incorrect according to the explanations provided in the figure caption. You should find that women in the threat condition make more errors than those in the nonthreat condition. Men should score about the same in both.

Summary

MEASURING INTELLECTUAL POWER

 What were Binet's and Terman's approaches to measuring intelligence?

- Early tests of intelligence, such as that devised by Binet, were designed to identify children who might have difficulty in school. Scores were based on a child's mental age. Terman adapted Binet's test for use in the United States (the Stanford-Binet) and introduced the term *intelligence quotient (IQ)*. Modern intelligence tests compare a child's performance to that of others of the same age. Scores above 100 represent better than average performance; scores below 100 represent poorer than average performance.

7.2 What intelligence tests are used today, and how do they differ from earlier tests?

- The most commonly used individually administered tests for children are the current revisions of the Stanford-Binet and the Wechsler Intelligence Scales for Children (WISC). The WISC-IV provides separate IQ scores for verbal comprehension, perceptual reasoning, processing speed, and working memory. The Bayley Scales of Infant Development and other developmental screening instruments measure a variety of motor and cognitive milestones in the first 2 to 3 years. Standardized achievement tests are similar to intelligence tests but measure only information that is learned in school.

7.3 How stable are IQ scores throughout childhood and adolescence?

- IQ scores are quite stable from one testing to the next, especially as a child gets older. But individual children's scores may still fluctuate or shift over the course of childhood.

7.4 What do IQ scores predict?

- IQ test scores are quite good predictors of school performance and years of education, a correlation that gives one piece of evidence for the validity of the tests. An important limitation of IQ tests is that they do not measure many other facets of intellectual functioning that might be of interest.

EXPLAINING INDIVIDUAL DIFFERENCES IN IQ SCORES

7.5 What do twin and adoption studies suggest about the effects of heredity and environment on IQ scores?

- Studies of identical twins and of adopted children clearly show a substantial genetic influence on measured IQ scores. These studies also show that environment contributes to IQ scores.

7.6 How do shared and nonshared family characteristics affect IQ scores?

- Poor children consistently score lower on IQ tests than do children from middle-class families; children whose families provide appropriate play materials and encourage intellectual development score higher on IQ tests. Children in large families may be subject to a dilution of family resources that produces successively lower IQ scores in each child.

7.7 In what ways do early interventions affect IQ scores and school performance?

- Environmental influence is shown by increases in test performance or school success among children who have been in enriched preschool or infant-care programs. Children who participate in these programs are also less likely to require special education services and more likely to graduate from high school.

7.8 In what ways do heredity and environment interact to influence IQ scores?

- One way to explain the interaction of heredity and environment is with the concept of reaction range: Heredity

...nes some range of potential; environment ...ermines the level of performance within that range. In addition, parents' levels of intelligence shape the environments they create for children. The child is exposed to parental influence both genetically and environmentally.

EXPLAINING GROUP DIFFERENCES IN IQ OR ACHIEVEMENT TEST SCORES

7.9 What ideas have theorists proposed to explain ethnic group differences in IQ scores?

- A consistent difference in IQ scores of about 10 to 12 points is found between African American and Caucasian children in the United States. It seems most likely that this difference is due to environmental and cultural differences between the two groups, such as differences in health and prenatal care and in the type of intellectual skills taught and emphasized at home.

7.10 What factors contribute to cross-cultural differences in IQ and achievement test scores?

- Some researchers have argued that the differences between Asian and American children in performance on mathematics achievement tests result not from genetic differences in capacity but from differences in cultural emphasis on the importance of academic achievement, the number of hours spent on homework, and the type (or approach) of math instruction in the schools.

7.11 How do males and females differ with respect to IQ and achievement test performance?

- Males and females do not differ on overall IQ test scores, but they do differ in some subskills. The largest differences are on measures of spatial reasoning, on which males are consistently better.

ALTERNATIVE VIEWS OF INTELLIGENCE

7.12 How do information-processing theorists explain individual differences in IQ scores?

- Information-processing theory provides developmentalists with an alternative approach to explaining individual differences in intelligence. Higher-IQ individuals, for example, appear to process information more quickly and to apply strategies or knowledge more broadly.

7.13 What is the triarchic theory of intelligence?

- Sternberg's triarchic theory of intelligence suggests that IQ tests measure only analytical intelligence, one of three aspects of intellectual ability. According to his theory, these tests measure neither creative nor practical intelligence.

7.14 What are the various types of intelligence proposed by Gardner?

- Gardner has proposed eight distinct types of intelligence: linguistic, logical/mathematical, spatial, bodily kinesthetic, musical, interpersonal, intrapersonal, and naturalistic.

7.15 How do theorists explain creativity?

- Guilford suggested that creativity involves divergent thinking. Torrance proposed four dimensions of creativity: fluency, flexibility, originality, and elaboration. Both devised tests to measure creativity that are still used by researchers.

Key Terms

achievement test (p. 181)
analytical intelligence (p. 198)
Bayley Scales of Infant Development (p. 180)
competence (p. 182)
creative intelligence (p. 198)
creativity (p. 200)
cumulative deficit (p. 187)
divergent thinking (p. 200)
full scale IQ (p. 179)

intelligence (p. 177)
intelligence quotient (IQ) (p. 178)
mental age (p. 178)
multiple intelligences (p. 199)
nonshared environment (p. 187)
perceptual reasoning index (p. 179)
performance (p. 182)
practical intelligence (p. 199)
processing speed index (p. 179)
reaction range (p. 190)

reliability (p. 182)
shared environment (p. 186)
Stanford-Binet (p. 178)
triarchic theory of intelligence (p. 198)
validity (p. 183)
verbal comprehension index (p. 179)
WISC-IV (p. 179)
working memory index (p. 179)
WPPSI-III (p. 179)

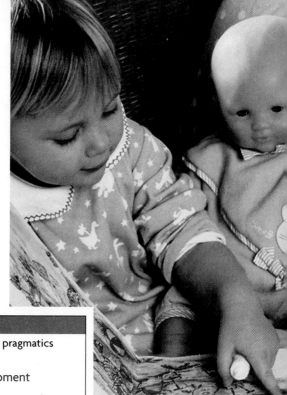

The Development of Language 8

In recent years, countless programs geared toward teaching sign language to infants who can hear have been developed. The authors and publishers of these programs claim that acquiring sign language will speed up the language development process, enabling children to acquire larger vocabularies and more complex grammatical structures than others their age. As a result, in the future they will be better readers and better academic learners. Anecdotal reports about the benefits of teaching babies to sign are found on the dozens of Internet sites that market sign-language training products to eager parents (e.g., babysigns. com, sign2me.com). You learned in Chapter 1 that developmental scientists approach such claims by asking whether evidence supports them.

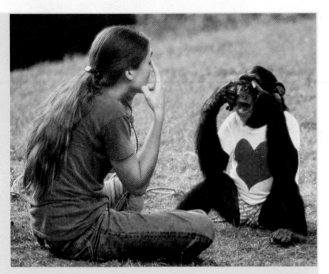

Chimpanzees can fairly easily learn signs for individual objects or actions and can understand and follow quite complex instructions. Here Nim Chimpsky, one of the first chimps trained to use signs to communicate, signs "I see." But is it advisable to teach human infants to use sign language?

Researcher Cyne Johnston and her colleagues at the Universities of Ottawa and Waterloo carried out an extensive review of sign-language training programs for hearing infants (Johnston, Durieux-Smith, & Bloom, 2005). They identified dozens of such programs and found that most included training aids such as videotapes and flash cards. Moreover, all of the programs claimed to enhance language development and cited research in support of their claims.

Next, Johnston's team examined the methods and findings of the cited studies to determine whether the authors' claims of support were justified. Johnston and her colleagues concluded that almost all of the studies had been carried out in ways that made it impossible to determine whether any of the training programs actually influenced language development. For the most part, the studies lacked experimental methods, such as random assignment, that would support claims of causality. Further, many failed to control variables, such as parental enthusiasm, that might account for program effects. Some involved very small numbers of participants and purely descriptive research methods such as naturalistic observation and case studies.

Based on their analysis, Johnston and her colleagues concluded that there is no evidence that teaching hearing babies to use sign language enhances their language development. The researchers did note, however, that teaching sign language to infants does not appear to be harmful to the process of spoken language development. Consequently, if parents find it useful or enjoyable to do so, there doesn't appear to be any reason why they shouldn't.

Do such conclusions mean that parents have no influence on infants' language development? Clearly not, because, at a minimum, a child must have linguistic input and be able to engage in linguistic interactions with other people in order to acquire language. Thus, as you'll see throughout this chapter, both maturation and experience are critical to language development.

Before the First Word: The Prelinguistic Phase

phonology The sound patterns of a particular language and the rules for combining them.

semantics A particular language's system of meaning and the rules for conveying meaning.

syntax The rules for forming sentences in a particular language.

Before delving into the topic of language development, we need to be clear about just what it is we're studying. Language has several dimensions. The sound patterns that a particular language uses and the rules that govern those patterns are its **phonology**. **Semantics** refers to how language represents meaning. The rules a language uses for combining words into sentences is known as **syntax**. You will see each of these terms again as we trace the development of language from its early, preverbal beginnings to the emergence of true linguistic fluency many years later.

Chimpanzees can learn to communicate by using sign language or by pointing to sequences of symbols. However, in most cases, it takes a good deal of effort to teach them to use **expressive language**—sounds, signs, or symbols that communicate meaning (Savage-Rumbaugh et al., 1993). In contrast, as Flavell puts it, "Draconian measures would be needed to prevent most children from learning to talk" (1985, p. 248). And as any parent can tell you, once children do learn, it is virtually impossible to shut them up! The process of language development actually begins in the months before the baby speaks his first word, a period called the **prelinguistic phase.**

Early Sounds and Gestures

Learning Objective 8.1
What are the characteristics of cooing and babbling?

A baby's early perceptual skill is not matched right away by much skill in producing sounds. From birth to about 1 month of age, the most common sound an infant makes is a cry, although infants also make other fussing, gurgling, and satisfied sounds. This sound repertoire expands at about 1 or 2 months with the addition of some laughing and **cooing**—making repetitive vowel sounds, like *uuuuuu*. Sounds like this are usually signals of pleasure in babies and may show quite a lot of variation, including increases and decreases in volume or pitch.

Consonant sounds appear only at about 6 or 7 months of age, when for the first time the baby has the muscle control needed to combine a consonant sound with a vowel sound. From 6 months on, there is a rapid increase in the amount of vowel-consonant combinations. This type of vocalization, called **babbling**, makes up about half of babies' noncrying sounds from about 6 to 12 months of age (Mitchell & Kent, 1990).

Much early babbling involves repetitive strings of the same syllables, such as *dadadada* or *nananana* or *yayayaya*. Adults find babbling delightful to listen to; Lois Bloom (1998), one of the foremost theorists and observers of children's language, points out that these new sound combinations are also much easier for adults to imitate than are the earlier baby sounds, because babbling has more of the rhythm and sound of adult speech. The imitative game that may then develop between parent and child is not only a pleasure for both but may help the baby to learn language.

Babbling is an important part of the preparation for spoken language in other ways as well. For one thing, developmentalists have observed that infants' babbling gradually acquires some of the intonational patterns of the language they are hearing—a process Elizabeth Bates refers to as "learning the tune before the words" (Bates, O'Connell, & Shore, 1987). At the very least, infants do seem to develop at least two such "tunes" in their babbling. Babbling with a rising intonation at the end of a string of sounds seems to signal a desire for a response; a falling intonation requires no response.

A second important thing about babbling is that when babies first start babbling, they typically babble all kinds of sounds, including some that are not part of the language they are hearing. Then, beginning at about 9 or 10 months of age, the sound repertoire of infants gradually begins to shift toward the set of sounds they are listening to, with the nonheard sounds dropping out—a pattern that clearly parallels the findings of Werker's research, illustrated in Figure 5.4 (page 131), and that reflects what psychologists know about early synaptic development and pruning (Werker & Tees, 2005). Findings like these do not prove that babbling is necessary for language development, but they certainly make it look as if babbling is part of a connected developmental process that begins at birth.

Another part of that connected developmental process appears to be a kind of gestural language that develops near the end of the first year (Goldin-Meadow, 2007a) (see *Thinking about Research* on page 206). Pointing is the most common

expressive language Sounds, signs, or symbols used to communicate meaning.

prelinguistic phase The period before a child speaks his or her first words.

cooing Making repetitive vowel sounds, particularly the *uuu* sound; the behavior develops early in the prelinguistic period, when babies are between about 1 and 4 months of age.

babbling The repetitive vocalizing of consonant-vowel combinations by an infant, typically beginning at about 6 months of age.

What do you think this young girl is "saying" with her pointing gesture? Before they speak their first words, babies successfully use gestures and body language in consistent ways to communicate meaning.

Sign Language and Gestures in Children Who Are Deaf

As you have learned, gestures play an important communicative role in the lives of babies who are approaching their first birthdays (Goldin-Meadow, 2007a). But consider the case of children who cannot hear and whose parents use sign language to communicate with them. You might think that children who acquire sign language would not also learn to use gestures, but that is not the case.

The milestones of both verbal and nonverbal language development in children who are deaf are highly similar to those of children who can hear. Children who are deaf show a kind of sign babbling that emerges between 5 and 7 months of age, much as children who can hear begin to babble sounds in these same months (Takei, 2001). Interestingly, children who are deaf also vocalize in ways that sound very much like the babbling of infants who can hear, an indication that babbling is more strongly influenced by maturation than by the environment. Then, a couple of months shy of their first birthdays, children who are deaf begin using simple gestures, such as pointing; this is just about the same time that we

see such gestures in babies who can hear (Goldin-Meadow, 2007b). At about 12 months of age, babies who are deaf display their first referential signs, which are analogous to the first spoken words of babies who can hear. Interestingly, though, these referential signs do not replace the gestures that appeared a few months earlier. Instead, like babies who can hear and who are just learning to speak, infants who are learning to sign use both referential signs and gestures to communicate.

Researcher Susan Goldin-Meadow (2007b) argues that, in both babies who can hear and babies who are deaf, gestural communication assumes a subordinate role to structured language once it begins to develop. Thus, at 1 year of age, infants who cannot hear use two forms of manual communication: the beginnings of structured sign language and gestures that amplify signed messages or communicate information that cannot be expressed in sign language. Similarly, infants who can hear are just beginning to develop structured spoken language, and they, too, use gestures as

aids to communication. This marked similarity in the sequence and timing of the steps of early language in infants who are deaf and infants who can hear provides strong support for the argument that the human infant is somehow primed to learn language. Moreover, this priming involves both the referential, grammatical components (words, signs) and nonverbal components (gestures) of communication.

Questions for Critical Analysis

1. We noted that the emergence of vocalization in infants who are deaf at the same time that babbling appears in infants who can hear supports the idea that maturation strongly influences language development. Does the appearance of gestures in children who are deaf at about the same time as in children who can hear also support this hypothesis? Why or why not?

2. In your view, what are the benefits and risks associated with being the hearing child of parents who are deaf?

---

gesture infants use. However, it is not unusual to see a baby of this age ask for things by using a combination of gestures and sounds. A 10-month-old baby who apparently wants you to hand her a favorite toy may stretch and reach for it, opening and closing her hand, making whining sounds or other heartrending noises. There is no mistaking the meaning. At about the same age, babies enter into those gestural games much loved by parents, like "patty-cake," "soooo-big," or "wave bye-bye" (Bates et al., 1987).

Learning Objective 8.2

What have researchers learned about infants' receptive language skills?

Receptive Language

Interestingly, the first signs that an infant understands the meaning of individual words spoken to her (which linguists call **receptive language**) also become evident at about 9 or 10 months (MacWhinney, 2005). Larry Fenson and his colleagues (1994) asked hundreds of mothers about their babies' understanding of various words. The mothers of 10-month-olds identified an average of about 30 words their infants understood; for 13-month-olds, that number was up to nearly 100 words. Since infants of 9 to 13 months of age typically speak few, if any, individual words, findings like these make it clear that receptive language comes before expressive language. Children understand before they can speak. Babies as young as 9 or 10 months old are already actively learning the language they are listening to. Not only can they understand some simple instructions, but they can benefit from being exposed to a rich array of language.

These bits of information point to a whole series of changes that seem to come together at 9 or 10 months: the beginning of meaningful gestures, the drift of babbling toward the heard language sounds, the first participation in imitative gestural games, and the first comprehension of individual words. It is as if the child now understands something about the process of communication and is intending to communicate to the rest of the world.

receptive language
Comprehension of spoken language.

Learning Words and Word Meanings

Somewhere in the midst of all the babbling, the first words appear, typically at about 12 or 13 months (Fenson et al., 1994). Once she has learned the first few words, the infant begins the work of identifying specific links between words and the objects or actions for which they stand.

The First Words

Learning Objective 8.3
What are the trends in word learning over the first 2 years?

A *word*, as linguists usually define it, is any sound or set of sounds that is used consistently to refer to some thing, action, or quality. But for a child, a word can be any sound; it doesn't have to be a sound that matches words adults are using. Brenda, a little girl studied by Ronald Scollon (1976), used the sound *nene* as one of her first words. It seemed to mean primarily liquid food, since she used it for "milk," "juice," and "bottle," but she also used it to refer to "mother" and "sleep." (Some of Brenda's other early words are listed in the left-hand column of Table 8.1.)

Often, a child's earliest words are used only in one or two specific situations and in the presence of many cues. The child may say "doggie" or "bow-wow" only in response to such promptings as "What's that?" or "How does the doggie go?" Typically, this early word learning is very slow, requiring many repetitions for each word. In the first 6 months of word usage (roughly between 12 and 18 months of age), children may learn to say as few as 30 words. Most linguists (e.g., Nelson, 1985) have concluded that in this earliest word-use phase, the child learns each word as something connected to a set of specific contexts. The toddler has apparently not yet grasped that words are symbolic—that they refer to objects or events regardless of context.

Somewhere between 16 and 24 months, after the early period of very slow word learning, most children begin to add new words rapidly, as if they have figured out that things have names. According to Fenson's very large cross-sectional study, based on mothers' reports, the average 16-month-old has a speaking vocabulary of about 50 words (a shift you can see illustrated by young Brenda's 19-month vocabulary in Table 8.1); by 24 months of age, this speaking vocabulary has multiplied more than sixfold to about 320 words (Fenson et al., 1994). A parallel study in Italy by Elizabeth Bates and her colleagues (Caselli, Casadio, & Bates, 1997) showed that this rapid rate of vocabulary growth is not unique to children learning English. In this new phase, children seem to learn new words after very few repetitions and to generalize these new words to many more situations.

For the majority of children, the naming explosion is not a steady, gradual process; instead, a vocabulary spurt begins once the child has acquired about 50 words. You can see this pattern in Figure 8.1 on page 208, which shows the vocabulary growth curves of six children studied longitudinally by Goldfield and Reznick (1990); the same pattern has been found by other researchers as well (e.g., Bloom, 1993). Not all children show precisely this pattern (Ganger & Brent, 2001). In Goldfield and Reznick's study, for example, 13 children showed a

Table 8.1 Brenda's Vocabulary at 14 Months and 19 Months

14 Months	19 Months*		
aw u (I want, I don't want)	baby	nice	boat
nau (no)	bear	orange	bone
d di (daddy, baby)	bed	pencil	dimb
d yu (down, doll)	big	write	checkers
nene (liquid food)	blue	paper	cut
e (yes)	Brenda	pen	I do
ada (another, other)	cookie	see	jump
	daddy	shoe	met
	eat	sick	Pogo
	at	swim	Ralph
	(hor)sie	tape	you too
	mama	walk	
	mommy	wowow	

*Brenda did not actually pronounce all these words the way an adult would. The columns show the adult version, since that is easier to read.

Source: R. Scollon, *Conversations with a one-year-old*. Honolulu: University of Hawaii Press, 1976, pp. 47, 57–58.

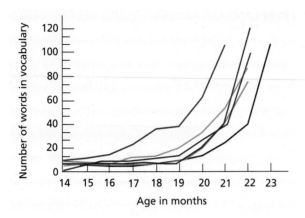

Figure 8.1
Early Vocabulary Growth

Each line in this figure represents the vocabulary growth of one of the children followed by Goldfield and Reznick in their longitudinal study.

(*Source*: B. A. Goldfield and J. S. Reznick, Figure 3, p. 177, "Early lexical acquisition: Rate, content, and the vocabulary spurt," *Journal of Child Language*, 17 (1990), 171–183. By permission of Cambridge University Press.)

vocabulary spurt; 11 other children in the study followed varying growth patterns, including several who showed no spurt at all but only gradual acquisition of vocabulary. Still, a rapid increase over a period of a few months is the most common pattern.

During this early period of rapid vocabulary growth, the majority of new words are names for things or people. Verblike words tend to develop later, perhaps because they label relationships between objects rather than just individual objects (Bates et al., 1994; Gleitman & Gleitman, 1992). For example, in Fenson's large cross-sectional study (1994), 63% of the words mothers said their children knew by age 2 were nouns, while only 8.5% were verbs. Studies of children learning other languages show very similar patterns, as you can see in Table 8.2.

Some studies suggest that noun learning may precede verb learning because infants lack the ability to consistently associate words with actions until about 18 months of age (Casasola & Cohen, 2000). However, recent cross-linguistic research also suggests that English-speaking parents, compared to Korean-speaking parents, for example, emphasize nouns more than verbs in speaking and reading to infants (Choi, 2000). Thus, the noun-before-verb learning pattern may be influenced by the characteristics of the language being learned as well as by the behavior of mature speakers toward the infant.

underextension The use of words to apply only to specific objects, such as a child's use of the word *cup* to refer only to one particular cup.

overextension The inappropriate use of a word to designate an entire category of objects, such as when a child uses the word *kitty* to refer to all animate objects.

Table 8.2 Early Words Acquired by Children in Four Cultures

	German Boy	English Girl	Turkish Girl	Chinese Girl
Words for people or things	Mommy	Mommy	Mama	Momma
	Papa	Daddy	Daddy	Papa
	Gaga	babar	Aba	grandmother
	baby	baby	baby	horse
	dog	dog	food	chicken
	bird	dolly	apple	uncooked rice
	cat	kitty	banana	cooked rice
	milk	juice	bread	noodles
	ball	book	ball	flower
	nose	eye	pencil	wall clock
	moon	moon	towel	lamp
Nonnaming words	cry	run	cry	go
	come	all gone	come	come
	eat	more	put on	pick up
	sleep	bye-bye	went pooh	not want
	want	want	want	afraid
	no	no	hello	thank you
Total percentage of naming words	67%	69%	57%	59%

Source: Gentner, 1992.

Research indicates that **underextension**—use of a word for only one specific object or in a single context—is most common at the earliest stages of vocabulary development, particularly before the naming explosion (MacWhinney, 2005), which suggests that most children initially think of words as belonging to only one thing, rather than as names for categories.

Once the naming explosion starts, however, the child appears to grasp the idea that words go with categories, and **overextension**—the use of a single word for an entire category of objects or in multiple contexts—becomes more common. At that stage, we're more likely to hear the word *kitty* applied to dogs or guinea pigs than we are to hear it used for just one animal or for a very small set of animals or objects (Clark, 1983). All children seem to show overextension, but the particular classes a child creates are unique to that child. One child Eve Clark observed used the word *ball* to refer not only to toy balls but also to radishes and stone spheres at park entrances. Another child used the word *ball* to refer to apples, grapes, eggs, squash, and a bell clapper (Clark, 1975).

These overextensions may reveal something about the way young children think—for example, that they have broad classes. However, linguists such as Clark point out that these children don't know very many words. A child who wants to call attention to a horse may not know the word *horse* and so may say *dog* instead. Overextension may thus arise from the child's desire to communicate and may not be evidence that the child fails to make the particular discriminations. As the child learns the separate labels that are applied to the different subtypes of furry four-legged creatures, overextension disappears.

For most toddlers, the word *ball* stands for a variety of round objects: balls of various kinds, round fruits such as oranges and peaches, and decorative objects such as globes and paperweights.

Later Word Learning

Learning Objective 8.4

How does word learning proceed in early and middle childhood?

During the preschool years, children continue to add words at remarkable speed. At age 2½, the average vocabulary is about 600 words, about a quarter of which are verbs (Bates et al., 1994); by age 5 or 6, total vocabulary has risen to perhaps 15,000 words—an astonishing increase of 10 words a day (Pinker, 1994). What accounts for this amazing rate of word learning? Researchers have found that a momentous shift in the way children approach new words happens around age 3. As a result of this shift, children begin to pay attention to words in whole groups, such as words that name objects in a single class (e.g., types of dinosaurs or kinds of fruit) or words with similar meanings. In a sense, understanding of the categorical nature of words helps children develop what we might think of as mental "slots" for new words. Once the slots are in place, children seem to automatically organize the linguistic input they receive from parents, teachers, peers, books, television programs, advertisements, and every other source of language to extract new words and fill the slots as quickly as possible.

fast-mapping The ability to categorically link new words to real-world referents.

Psychologists use the term **fast-mapping** to refer to this ability to categorically link new words to real-world referents (Carey & Bartlett, 1978). (*Referents* are the real objects and events to which words refer.) At the core of fast-mapping, say researchers, is a rapidly formed hypothesis about a new word's meaning (Behrend, Scofield, & Kleinknecht, 2001). The hypothesis is based on information derived from the child's prior knowledge of words and word categories and from the context in which the word is used. Once formed, the hypothesis is tested through use of the word in the child's own speech, often immediately after learning it. The feedback the child receives in response to use of the word helps him judge the accuracy of the hypothesis and the appropriateness of the category to which he has assumed that the word belongs. Perhaps this helps explain why preschoolers do so much talking and why they are so persistent at getting their listeners to actively respond to them.

Does this toddler know the word *doll* because she first had a concept of doll and later learned the word, or did she learn the word first and then create a category or concept to go with the word?

Experimental studies have demonstrated that fast-mapping is evident as early as 18 months of age. In these studies, researchers teach toddlers new words that represent easily identifiable categories and then, after a period of time, measure their learning of related words. For example, fast-mapping should enable a child who has been taught the word *table* to acquire the word *chair* on her own more rapidly than a child who is unfamiliar with the word *table*. Such studies show that when children are tested a few weeks after receiving vocabulary instruction, they are more likely than children who were not instructed to understand and to use words that are related to, but are distinct from, those they were taught (e.g., Gershkoff-Stowe & Hahn, 2007).

In middle childhood, children continue to add vocabulary at the rate of 5,000 to 10,000 words a year. This figure comes from several careful studies by Jeremy Anglin (1993, 1995; Skwarchuk & Anglin, 2002), who estimates children's total vocabularies by testing them on a sample of words drawn at random from a large dictionary. Figure 8.2 shows Anglin's estimates for first-, third-, and fifth-grade children. Anglin finds that the largest gain from third to fifth grade occurs in knowledge of the type of words he calls "derived words"—words such as *happily* or *unwanted*, which have a basic root to which some prefix or suffix is added. Anglin argues that at about age 8 or 9, the child shifts to a new level of understanding of the structure of language, figuring out relationships between whole categories of words, such as between adjectives and adverbs (*happy* and *happily*, *sad* and *sadly*) and between adjectives and nouns (*happy* and *happiness*). Once he understands such relationships, the child can understand and create whole sets of new words, and his vocabulary thereafter increases rapidly.

Figure 8.2
Vocabulary Growth in Middle Childhood

Anglin's estimates of the total vocabulary of first-, third-, and fifth-graders.

(*Source*: From "Word Learning and the Growth of Potentially Knowable Vocabulary" by Jeremy M. Anglin (1995), p. 7, Fig. 6. By permission of Jeremy M. Anglin.)

Constraints on Word Learning

Learning Objective 8.5

What are some proposed constraints on word learning?

A subject of hot debate among linguists in recent years is just how a child figures out which part of some scene a word may refer to. The classic example: A child sees a brown dog running across the grass with a bone in its mouth. An adult points and says "doggie." From such an experience, the toddler is somehow supposed to figure out that *doggie* refers to the animal and not to "running," "bone," "dog with bone," "brownness," "grass," or any other combination of elements in the whole scene.

Many linguists have proposed that a child could cope with this monumentally complex task only if he operated with some built-in biases, or **constraints** (e.g., Golinkoff, Mervis, & Hirsh-Pasek, 1994; Waxman & Kosowski, 1990; Woodward & Markman, 1998). For example, the child may have a built-in assumption that words refer to whole objects and not to their parts or attributes—this is referred to as the *whole object constraint* (Hollich, Golinkoff, & Hirsh-Pasek, 2007). The *mutual exclusivity constraint* leads children to assume that objects have only one name (Markman, Wasow, & Hansen, 2003).

Another built-in constraint is the **principle of contrast**, which is the assumption that every word has a different meaning. Thus, if a new word is used, it must refer to some different object or a different aspect of an object (Clark, 1990). For example, in a widely quoted early study, Carey and Bartlett (1978) interrupted a play session with 2- and 3-year-old children by pointing to two trays and saying, "Bring me the chromium tray, not the red one, the chromium one." These children already knew the word *red* but did not know the word *chromium*. Nonetheless, most of the children were able to follow the instruction by bringing the tray that was not red. Furthermore, a week later, about half of the children remembered that the word *chromium* referred to some color and that the color was "not red." Thus, they learned some meaning by contrast.

constraint As used in discussions of language development, an assumption that is presumed to be built-in or learned early (a "default option") by which a child figures out what words refer to. Examples include the principle of contrast and the whole object constraint.

principle of contrast The assumption that every word has a different meaning, which leads a child to assume that two or more different words refer to different objects.

Early proponents of constraints argued that such biases are innate—built into the brain in some fashion. Another alternative is that the child learns the various constraints over time. For example, Carolyn Mervis and Jacquelyn Bertrand (1994) found that not all children between the ages of 16 and 20 months use the principle of contrast to learn the name of a new, unknown object. Children in their sample who did use this principle had larger vocabularies and were more likely to be good at sorting objects into categories. Results like these suggest that constraints may be a highly useful way for children to learn words quickly but that they may be a product of cognitive/linguistic development rather than the basis for it.

A more sweeping argument against the notion of built-in constraints comes from Katherine Nelson (1988), who points out that a child rarely encounters a situation in which an adult points vaguely and gives some word. Other theorists also emphasize that the situations in which children hear new words are rich with cues to help the children figure out what the words may refer to—including the parents' facial expressions, the emphasis in their words, and the entire context in which the new word is given (MacWhinney, 2005). To the extent that this is true, then, the child doesn't need a collection of constraints in order to figure out new words.

Suppose this little girl already knows the word *flower*. If her mother points to the flower and says "petal," is the girl likely to think that *flower* and *petal* mean the same thing? According to the principle of contrast, she will not be confused, because children approach word learning with the assumption that each word has a different meaning. Thus, she will assume that *petal* refers to some aspect of the flower whose name she doesn't yet know.

Learning the Rules: The Development of Grammar and Pragmatics

After learning the first words, the next big step the child takes is to begin to string words into sentences. Children begin by combining single words, gestures, and vocal intonations. Next, they put two words together, then three, four, and more. The first two-word sentences are usually formed between the ages of 18 and 24 months.

Holophrases and First Sentences

Learning Objective 8.6
How do children's first sentences differ from holophrases?

Just as the first spoken words are preceded by apparently meaningful gestures, the first two-word sentences have gestural precursors as well. Toddlers often combine a single word with a gesture to create a "two-word meaning" before they actually use two words together in their speech. Bates suggests an example: A child may point to daddy's shoe and say "daddy," as if to convey "daddy's shoe." Or she may say "cookie!" while simultaneously reaching out her hand and opening and closing her fingers, as if to say "Give cookie!" (Bates et al., 1987). In both cases, the meaning conveyed by the use of a gesture and body language combined with a word is more than that of the word alone. Linguists call these word-and-gesture combinations **holophrases**; they are common between the ages of 12 and 18 months.

Once children actually begin speaking two-word sentences, they move rapidly through a series of steps or stages. The first sentences—which Roger Brown, a famous observer of child language, called *stage 1 grammar*—have several distinguishing features: They are short (generally two or three words), and they are simple. Nouns, verbs, and adjectives are usually included, but virtually all purely grammatical markers (which linguists call *inflections*) are missing. At the beginning, for example, children learning English do not normally add -s to the ends of nouns to make them plural, put the -ed ending on verbs to make the past tense,

holophrase A combination of a gesture and a single word that conveys more meaning than just the word alone; often seen and heard in children between 12 and 18 months old.

Table 8.3 Some Meanings Children Express in Their Earliest Simple Sentences

Meaning	Examples
Agent-action	Sarah eat; Daddy jump
Action-object	Eat cookie; read book
Possessor-possessed object	Mommy sock; Timmy lunch
Action-location	Come here; play outside
Object-location	Sweater chair; juice table
Attribute-object	Big book; red house
Nomination	That cookie; it dog
Recurrence	More juice; other book

Source: Maratsos, 1983.

or use -'s for the possessive or auxiliary verbs such as *am* or *do*. For example, they might say "I tired" or "Me tired" rather than "I am tired," or "I not want it" rather than "I don't want it." Because only the really critical words are present in these early sentences, Brown (1973; Brown & Bellugi, 1964) described them as **telegraphic speech**. The child's language sounds rather like old-fashioned telegrams, in which people included all the essential words—usually nouns, verbs, and modifiers—but left out all the prepositions, auxiliary verbs, and the like because they had to pay for each word in a telegram.

Interestingly, linguists are no longer sure that precisely this form of telegraphic speech occurs in children learning all languages. Some research seems to show that what determines the words children use in their early sentences is the amount of stress normally placed on such words when that particular language is spoken. In English and in many other languages, nouns, verbs, and adjectives are stressed in speech, whereas inflections are not. In some languages, however, such as Turkish, inflections are stressed, and children growing up hearing Turkish seem to use inflections much earlier (Gleitman & Wanner, 1988). Findings like these certainly raise some interesting questions about the universality of some of the patterns Brown and others have described.

In contrast, there is no dispute about the assertion that even at this earliest stage, children create sentences following rules—not adult rules, to be sure, but rules nonetheless. Children focus on certain types of words and put them together in particular orders. They also manage to convey a variety of different meanings with their simple sentences.

For example, young children frequently use a sentence made up of two nouns, such as "mommy sock" or "sweater chair" (Bloom, 1973). We might conclude from this that a two-noun form is a basic grammatical characteristic of early language, but such a conclusion misses the complexity. For instance, the child in Bloom's classic study who said "mommy sock" said it on two different occasions. The first time was when she picked up her mother's sock, and the second was when the mother put the child's own sock on the child's foot. In the first case, "mommy sock" seemed to mean "mommy's sock," which is a possessive relationship. In the second instance, the child was conveying that "mommy is putting a sock on me," which is an agent-object relationship.

Table 8.3 lists some other meanings that children convey with their earliest sentences. Not all children express all these relationships or meanings in their early word combinations, and there does not seem to be a fixed order in which these meanings or constructions are acquired, but all children appear to express at least a few of these patterns in their earliest, simplest sentences (Maratsos, 1983).

telegraphic speech Term used by Roger Brown to describe the earliest sentences created by most children, which sound a bit like telegrams because they include key nouns and verbs but generally omit all other words and grammatical inflections.

Learning Objective 8.7
What is the significance of the grammar explosion?

The Grammar Explosion

Just as a vocabulary explosion follows an early, slow beginning, so a grammar explosion follows several months of short, simple sentences. One sign of this change is that children's sentences get longer, as you can see in Figure 8.3, which shows the maximum sentence length reported by parents of toddlers of various ages, drawn from Fenson's study. Most 18- to 20-month-olds are still using one- and two-word sentences. By 24 months, children include four and five words in their longest sentences; by 30 months, their maximum sentence length has almost doubled again.

overregularization Young children's applications of basic rules to irregular words.

Vocabulary and the Grammar Explosion The grammar explosion is strongly linked to vocabulary development. Fenson finds a correlation of .84 between the complexity of a child's sentences and the size of her speaking vocabulary—an astonishingly high correlation for behavioral research (Fenson et al., 1994). That is, children whose grammar is more complex and advanced also have larger vocabularies. Just what such a link may indicate about how children learn language is still a matter of debate. Is a large vocabulary necessary for grammar development? Alternatively, perhaps having begun to understand how to construct sentences, a child can also understand new words better and hence learn them more readily. Whatever the eventual explanation, Fenson's research gives developmentalists important data to work with.

During the grammar explosion, children's speech ceases to be telegraphic, as they rather quickly add many of the inflections and function words. Within a few months, they use plurals, past tenses, auxiliary verbs such as *be* and *do*, prepositions, and the like. You can get a feeling for the sound of the change from Table 8.4, which lists some of the sentences spoken by a boy named Daniel, recorded by David Ingram (1981). The left-hand column lists some of Daniel's sentences at about 21 months of age, when he was still using the simplest forms; the right-hand column lists some of his sentences only 2½ months later (age 23 months), when he had shifted into a higher gear. As you can see, stage 2 grammar includes longer sentences and a few inflections, such as "doggies."

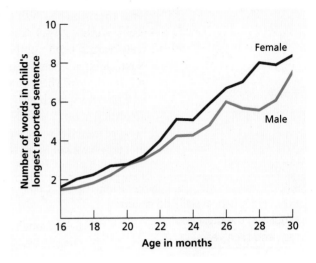

Figure 8.3
Early Sentences

In their cross-sectional study, Fenson and his colleagues asked 1,130 parents of toddlers (aged 16 to 30 months) to describe the longest sentence used by their child.

(*Source*: From "Variability in Early Communicative Development" by Fenson, Dale, Reznick, Bates, Thal, and Pethick, *Monographs of the Society for Research in Child Development*, 59, No. 242 (1994), p. 82, Fig. 27. By permission of the Society for Research in Child Development.)

Adding Inflections Daniel obviously did not add all the inflections to his sentences at once. As you can see in Table 8.4, he uses only a few, such as -*s* for plural, although the beginning of a negative construction is apparent in "No book," and the beginning of a question form shows in "Where going?" even though he has not yet added the auxiliary verb to the question.

Within each language community, children seem to add inflections and more complex word orders in fairly predictable sequences. In a classic early study, Roger Brown (1973) found that the earliest inflection used by children learning English is most often -*ing* added onto a verb, as in "I playing" or "doggie running." Then come (in order) prepositions such as *on* and *in*; the plural -*s* on nouns; irregular past tenses such as *broke* or *ran*; possessives; articles (*a* and *the*); the -*s* on third-person verb forms, as in *he wants*; regular past tenses such as *played* and *wanted*; and the various forms of auxiliary verbs, as in *I am going*.

Questions and Negatives There are also predictable sequences in the child's developing use of questions and negatives. In each case, the child seems to go through periods when he creates types of sentences that he has not heard adults use but that are consistent with the particular set of rules he is using. For example, in the development of questions in English, there is a point at which the child puts a *wh* word (*who*, *what*, *when*, *where*, or *why*) at the beginning of a sentence but doesn't yet put the auxiliary verb in the right place, as in "Why it is resting now?" Similarly, in the development of negatives, there is a stage in which the child uses *not* or -*n't* or *no* but omits the auxiliary verb, as in "I not crying," "There no squirrels," or "This not fits" (Bloom, 1991). Then children rather quickly figure out the correct forms and stop making these mistakes.

Overregularization Another intriguing phenomenon of this second phase of sentence construction is **overregularization**. What English-speaking 3- to 4-year-olds do is apply the basic rules to irregular words, thus making the language more regular than it really is (Maratsos, 2000). You can hear this phenomenon in children's creation of past

Table 8.4	Examples of Daniel's Stage 1 and Stage 2 Sentences
Stage 1 (Simple) Sentences, Age 21 Months	Stage 2 (More Complex) Sentences Age 23 Months
A bottle	A little boat
Here bottle	Doggies here
Hi Daddy	Give you the book
Horse doggie	It's a boy
Broke it	It's a robot
Kitty cat	Little box there
Poor Daddy	No book
That monkey	Oh cars
Want bottle	That flowers
	Where going?

Source: Reprinted by permission of the publisher. D. Ingram, Early patterns of grammatical development, in R. E. Stark (Ed.), *Language behavior in infancy and early childhood*, tables 6 and 7, pp. 344–345. Copyright © 1981 by Elsevier Science Publishing Co., Inc.

tense forms such as "wented," "blowed," or "sitted," and plurals such as "teeths" or "blockses" (Fenson et al., 1994; Kuczaj, 1977, 1978). Stan Kuczaj has pointed out that young children initially learn a small number of irregular past tenses and use them correctly for a short time. Next, children rather suddenly seem to discover the rule of adding -ed and overgeneralize this rule to all verbs. Then, they relearn the exceptions one at a time. Even among preschoolers, this type of error is not hugely common, comprising only about 2–3% of all past tenses in English, according to one study (Marcus et al., 1992). These overregularizations nonetheless stand out because they are so distinctive and because they illustrate yet again that children create forms that they have not heard but that are logical within their current understanding of grammar.

Learning Objective 8.8

What grammatical skills do children acquire in the preschool, elementary, and teen years?

Later Grammar Learning

Even though most children are reasonably fluent in their first language (or languages) by age 3 or 4, there are still many refinements to be made. These refinements gradually appear in children's language over the course of the later preschool, elementary, and even early teen years.

Complex Sentences   Soon after young children have figured out inflections and basic sentence forms such as negation and questions, they begin to create remarkably complex sentences, using conjunctions such as *and* and *but* to combine two ideas or using embedded clauses. Here are some examples, taken from the speech of 3- and 4-year-olds, from de Villiers and de Villiers (1992):

> I didn't catch it but Teddy did!
> I'm gonna sit on the one you're sitting on.
> Where did you say you put my doll?
> Those are punk rockers, aren't they?

Children add still more complex and difficult sentence forms to their repertoires throughout elementary school, and recurrent overregularization errors are eliminated (Bowerman, 1985). (However, children have trouble understanding and using passive forms, such as "The food is eaten by the cat" and do not use them much in spontaneous speech until they are 8 or 9.) But these are refinements. The really giant strides occur between ages 1 and about 4, as the child moves from single words to complex questions, negatives, and commands.

Further Refinements   During middle childhood, children become skilled at managing the finer points of grammar (Prat-Sala, Shillcock, & Sorace, 2000; Ragnarsdottir, Simonsen, & Plunkett, 1999). For example, by the end of middle childhood, most children understand various ways of saying something about the past such as *I went, I was going, I have gone, I had gone, I had been going,* and so on. Moreover, they use such tenses correctly in their own speech. During the middle childhood years, children also learn how to maintain a topic of conversation, how to create unambiguous sentences, and how to speak politely or persuasively (Anglin, 1993).

pragmatics The rules for the use of language in communicative interaction, such as the rules for taking turns and the style of speech that is appropriate for different listeners.

Pragmatics

For about a decade, linguists have also been interested in a third aspect of children's language—the way children learn to use speech, either to communicate with others (an aspect of language called **pragmatics**) or to regulate their own behavior. How early do children know what kind of language to use in specific situations? How early do they learn the "rules" of conversation—for example, that people conversing take turns?

Children seem to learn the pragmatics of language at a remarkably early age. For example, children as young as 18 months show adult patterns of gazing when they are talking with a parent: They look at the person who is talking, look away at the beginning of their own speaking turn, and then look at the listener again when they are signaling that they are about to stop talking (Rutter & Durkin, 1987).

Furthermore, a child as young as 2 years old adapts the form of his language to the situation he is in or the person he is talking to—a point made in Chapter 6 in the discussion of children's egocentrism. A child might say "Gimme" to another toddler as he grabs the other child's cup but say "More milk" to an adult. Among older children, language is even more clearly adapted to the listener: 4-year-olds use simpler language when they talk to 2-year-olds than when they talk to adults (Tomasello & Mannle, 1985); first-graders explain things more fully to a stranger than to a friend (Sonnenschein, 1986) and are more polite to adults and strangers than to peers. Both of these trends are even clearer among fourth-graders. Thus, very early on—probably from the beginning—the child recognizes that language is meant to communicate, and he adapts the form of his language in order to achieve better communication.

These children already know many of the social rules about how language is used, including rules about who is supposed to look at whom during a conversation.

Children also use language to help control or monitor their own behavior. Such *private speech*, which may consist of fragmentary sentences, muttering, or instructions to the self, is detectable from the earliest use of words and sentences. For example, when 2- or 3-year-olds play by themselves, they give themselves instructions, stop themselves with words, or describe what they are doing: "No, not there," "I put that there," or "Put it" (Furrow, 1984).

Piaget thought that this was egocentric speech, but Vygotsky believed that Piaget was quite wrong in this case. Vygotsky insisted instead that the child uses private speech to communicate with herself for the explicit purpose of guiding her own behavior. He believed that such self-directing use of language is central to all cognitive development.

In young children, such self-directing speech is audible. In older children, it is audible only when the child is facing a challenging task; in other situations, it goes "underground." For example, you may recall from Chapter 6 that Flavell found that young elementary school children muttered to themselves while they were trying to remember lists; among 9- or 10-year-olds, this behavior is much less common (Bivens & Berk, 1990). Thinking of this set of findings in terms of the work on information processing described in Chapter 6 leads to the view that the child uses language audibly to remind himself of some new or complex processing strategy; as the child rehearses the strategy and learns it more flexibly, audible language is no longer needed. Such an interpretation is bolstered by the observation that even adults use audible language in problem solving when they are faced with especially difficult tasks.

Even this brief foray into the research on children's use of language points out that a full understanding of language development requires knowledge of both cognitive development and children's social skills and understanding. Lois Bloom argues that "children learn language in the first place because they strive to . . . share what they and other persons are feeling and thinking" (1993, p. 245). From birth, the child is able to communicate feelings and thoughts through facial expressions, and somewhat later through gestures. But these are imperfect vehicles for communication; language is much more efficient. Such an argument reminds us once again that child development is not divided into tidy packages labeled "physical development," "social development," and "language development" but is instead a coherent, integrated process.

Explaining Language Development

If merely describing language development is difficult, explaining it is still harder. Indeed, explaining how a child learns language has proved to be one of the most compelling challenges in developmental psychology.

Environmental Theories

The earliest theories of language were based either on learning theory or on the commonsense idea that children learn language by imitation. Imitation obviously has to play some part, because a child learns the language she hears. Still, imitation alone can't explain all language acquisition, because it cannot account for children's tendency to create words and expressions they have never heard, such as "footses" and "I goed."

Reinforcement theories such as Skinner's (1957) fare no better. Skinner argued that in addition to the role they play in imitation, parents shape language through systematic reinforcements, gradually rewarding better and better approximations of adult speech (the process of *shaping*). Yet when researchers have listened to parents talking to children, they find that parents don't seem to do anything like what Skinner proposed. Instead, parents are remarkably forgiving of all sorts of peculiar constructions and meaning (Brown & Hanlon, 1970; Hirsh-Pasek, Trieman, & Schneiderman, 1984); they reinforce children's sentences on the basis of whether the sentence is true rather than whether it is grammatically correct. Still, it seems obvious that what is said to a child has to play some role in the process of language formation.

The Linguistic Environment   Children who are exposed to less (and less varied) language in their earliest years don't seem to catch up later in vocabulary, a point illustrated with the data in Table 8.5. These numbers come from the National Longitudinal Survey of Labor Market Experience of Youth (NLSY), a 12-year longitudinal study of a large sample of young women in the United States, begun when they were still teenagers. Table 8.5 shows one piece of information about the preschool-aged children of these young women: the percentage who had vocabulary scores below the 30th percentile on the most commonly used measure of vocabulary—the Peabody Picture Vocabulary Test (PPVT). Developmentalists know that the amount and quality of language a child hears varies with the mother's income level: Poor mothers talk to their children less, use less complex sentences, and read to their children less. The data in Table 8.5 reveal that one consequence of poverty for children is a considerably higher risk of poor language skills.

By age 4, the difference in vocabulary between poor and better-off children is already substantial, and the gap only widens over the school years. Similarly, Catherine Snow (1997) has found that 4-year-old children reared in poverty use shorter and less complex sentences

Table 8.5   Percentage of Children Aged 4 to 7 Who Score Below the 30th Percentile on the Peabody Picture Vocabulary Test, as a Function of Poverty

Type of Family	Number of Cases	Observed Percentage	Adjusted Percentage*
Recipients of Federal Aid to Families with Dependent Children, or AFDC ("welfare" families)	196	60%	52%
Poor but not receiving AFDC	116	47%	42%
Not poor	659	27%	30%

*These percentages have been adjusted statistically to subtract out the effects of differences in parents' education, family structure, family size, and age, sex, and ethnicity of the child.

Source: From "The life circumstances and development of children in welfare families: A profile based on national survey data" by Zill, Moore, Smith, Stief, and Coiro, *Escape from poverty: What makes a difference for children*, P. L. Chase-Lansdale and J. Brooks-Gunn, eds., p. 45, Table 2.3. © 1995 by Cambridge University Press. By permission of Cambridge University Press.

than do their better-off peers. Many factors no doubt contribute to these differences, but the richness and variety of the language a child hears are obviously highly significant (Pan, Rowe, Singer, & Snow, 2005). Of all these factors, being read to may be one of the most critical (Patterson, 2002).

Motherese Beyond the mere quantity of language directed at the child, the quality of the parents' language may also be important in helping the child learn language (Soderstrom, 2007). In particular, developmentalists know that adults talk to children in a special kind of very simple language, originally called **motherese** by many linguists and now more scientifically described as **infant-directed speech**. This simple language is spoken in a higher-pitched voice and at a slower pace than is speech to older children or other adults. The sentences are short and grammatically simple, with concrete vocabulary. When speaking to children, parents also repeat a lot, introducing minor variations ("Where is the ball? Can you see the ball? Where is the ball? There's the ball!"). They may also repeat the child's own sentences but in slightly longer, more grammatically correct forms—a pattern referred to as an *expansion* or a *recasting*. For example, if a child said "mommy sock," the mother might recast it as "Yes, this is mommy's sock," or if a child said "Doggie not eat," the parent might say "The doggie is not eating."

Developmentalists also know that babies as young as a few days old can discriminate between motherese and speech directed to other adults and that they prefer to listen to motherese, whether it is spoken by a female or a male voice (Cooper & Aslin, 1994; Pegg, Werker, & McLeod, 1992). This preference exists even when the motherese is being spoken in a language other than the one normally spoken to the child. Janet Werker and her colleagues (1994), for example, have found that both English and Chinese infants prefer to listen to infant-directed speech, whether it is spoken in English or in Cantonese (one of the major languages of China).

The quality of motherese that seems to be particularly attractive to babies is its higher pitch. Once the child's attention is drawn by this special tone, the very simplicity and repetitiveness of the adult's speech may help the child to pick out repeating grammatical forms. Children's attention also seems to be drawn to recast sentences. For example, Farrar (1992) found that a 2-year-old was two or three times more likely to imitate a correct grammatical form after he had heard his mother recast his own sentences than he was when the mother used that same correct grammatical form in her normal conversation. Experimental studies confirm this effect of recastings. Children who are deliberately exposed to higher rates of specific types of recast sentences seem to learn the modeled grammatical forms more quickly than do those who hear no recastings (Nelson, 1977).

Recent studies suggest that mothers' conversations with other adults also play a special role in language development. However, these conversations don't appear to interest an infant until she begins using language to communicate herself, usually between 18 and 24 months of age (Soderstrom & Morgan, 2007). Listening to them helps infants learn non-object words such as those that refer to colors and quantities (Tare, Shatz, & Gilbertson, 2007).

Nativist Theories

Learning Objective 8.11
What kind of evidence supports the nativist theories?

On the other side of the theoretical spectrum are the nativist theorists, who argue that much of what the child needs for learning language is built into the organism (Matthews, 2006). Early nativist theorists such as Noam Chomsky (1965, 1975, 1986, 1988) were especially struck by two phenomena: the extreme complexity of the task the child must accomplish, and the apparent similarities in the steps and stages of children's early language development across languages and among all children. Newer cross-language comparisons make it clear that there is more variability than at first appeared, as will be described in the next section of this chapter. Nonetheless, nativist theories are alive and well and are becoming increasingly accepted.

One particularly influential nativist is Dan Slobin (1985a, 1985b), who assumes that every child is born with a basic language-making capacity, made up of a set of fundamental operating principles. Slobin argues that just as the newborn infant seems to come

motherese (infant-directed speech) The simplified, higher-pitched speech that adults use with infants and young children.

programmed with "rules to look by," infants and children are programmed with "rules to listen by." You've already encountered a good deal of evidence consistent with this proposal in earlier sections. Researchers have established that very young infants focus on individual sounds and syllables in the stream of sounds they hear, that they pay attention to sound rhythm, and that they prefer speech of a particular pattern (motherese). Slobin also proposes that babies are preprogrammed to pay attention to the beginnings and endings of strings of sounds and to stressed sounds—a hypothesis supported by research (e.g., Morgan, 1994). Together, these operating principles help to explain some of the features of children's early grammar. In English, for example, the stressed words in a sentence are normally the verb and the noun—precisely the words that English-speaking children use in their earliest sentences. In Turkish, on the other hand, prefixes and suffixes are stressed, and Turkish-speaking children learn both very early. Both of these patterns make sense if we assume that the preprogrammed rule is not "pay attention to verbness" or "nounness" or "prefixness" but "pay attention to stressed sounds."

Learning Objective 8.12

How do constructivist theories differ from other approaches?

Constructivist Theories

The fact that the nativist model is consistent with growing knowledge of apparently built-in perceptual skills and processing biases is certainly a strong argument in its favor. Even so, this is not the only compelling theoretical option. In particular, some theorists argue persuasively that what is important is not the built-in biases or operating principles but the child's construction of language as part of the broader process of cognitive development (Akhtar, 2004).

One prominent proponent of this view, Melissa Bowerman, puts the proposition this way: "When language starts to come in, it does not introduce new meanings to the child. Rather, it is used to express only those meanings the child has already formulated independently of language" (1985, p. 372). However, Bowerman (2007) also notes that as the child starts to use language to express the ideas he is beginning to grasp, the very act of creating linguistic frameworks for them helps him better understand them. Thus, from the constructivist perspective, cognitive and language development are interdependent processes, and research in the constructivist tradition looks for linkages between advances in the two domains. For example, symbolic play (such as pretending to drink from an empty cup) and imitation of sounds and gestures both appear at about the same time as the child's first words, suggesting some broad "symbolic understanding" that is reflected in a number of behaviors.

Another example reinforces this argument: At about the point at which two-word sentences appear, children begin to combine several gestures into a sequence in their pretend play, such as pouring imaginary liquid, drinking, and then wiping the mouth. Children who are the first to show such sequencing in their play are also the first to show two- or three-word sentences in their speech (e.g., McCune, 1995; Shore, 1986).

We need not choose between Slobin's and Bowerman's approaches. Both may be true. The child may begin with built-in operating principles that aim her attention at crucial features of the language input. The child then processes that information according to her initial (perhaps built-in) strategies or schemes. Then she modifies those strategies or schemes as she receives new information, such as by arriving at some of the constraints about word meanings. The result is a series of rules for understanding and creating language. The strong similarities observed among children in their early language constructions come about both because all children share the same initial processing rules and because most children are exposed to very similar input from the people around them. But because the input is not identical, because languages differ, language development follows less and less similar pathways as the child progresses.

Finally, it seems clear that, as the nativists claim, some kind of capacity for processing linguistic information is "hard-wired" into the infant brain. However, many developmentalists have argued that this phenomenon is best understood when it is integrated into a constructivist view of language development. This integrated view proposes that the child begins with built-in operating principles that aim the child's attention at crucial features of the language input. The child then processes that information according to her initial (perhaps built-in) strategies or schemes. Then she modifies those strategies or rules as she receives new information—for example, arriving at some of the constraints on word meanings. The result is a series of rules for understanding and creating language. The strong similarities we see among children in their early language constructions come about both because all children share the same initial processing rules and because most children are exposed to very similar input from the people around them. But because the input is not identical, because languages differ, language development follows less and less common pathways as the child progresses.

Individual and Group Differences in Language Development

The description you've read of the sequence of language development is accurate on the average, but the speed with which children acquire language skill varies widely. There also seem to be important style differences.

Differences in Rate

Learning Objective 8.13
Are differences in the rate of language development related to later measures of proficiency?

There is a great deal of individual variation in language development. Some children begin to use words at 8 months, while others do not do so until 18 months. Similarly, the normal range of variation in vocabulary size among 2-year-olds is from a low of 10 words to a high of several hundred (MacWhinney, 2005).

You can see the range of normal variation in sentence construction very clearly in Figure 8.4, which shows the average number of meaningful units per sentence [referred to by linguists as the **mean length of utterance (MLU)**] of 10 children, from longitudinal studies by Roger Brown (1973), Ira Blake (1994), and Lois Bloom (1991). The figure includes a line at the MLU level that normally accompanies a switch from simple, uninflected two-word sentences to more complex forms.

mean length of utterance (MLU) The average number of meaningful units in a sentence. Each basic word is one meaningful unit, as is each inflection.

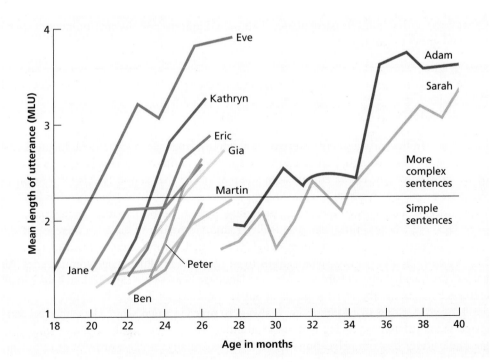

Figure 8.4
Classic Studies of Mean Length of Utterance

The 10 children whose language is charted here, studied by three different linguists, moved at markedly different times from simple one- and two-word sentences to more complex sentences.

(*Sources*: Reprinted and adapted by permission of the publisher from (1) *A First Language: The Early Stages*, by Roger Brown, p. 55, Cambridge, Mass.: Harvard University Press, Copyright © 1973 by the President and Fellows of Harvard College; (2) Lois Bloom, *Language Development from Two to Three*, Cambridge University Press, 1991, p. 92, Table 3.1; (3) I. K. Blake, "Language Development and Socialization in Young African-American Children," in Greenfield and Cocking (eds.), *Cross-Cultural Roots of Minority Children*, Lawrence Erlbaum Associates, 1994, p. 169, Table 9.1 and p. 171, Fig. 9.1.)

You can see that Eve was the earliest to make this transition, at about 20 months, while Adam and Sarah passed over this point nearly a year later. These variations are confirmed in Fenson's much larger cross-sectional study of more than 1,000 toddlers whose language was described by their parents. In this group, the earliest age at which parents reported more complex sentences than simple sentences was about 22 months, with an average of about 27 months. However, as many as a quarter of children had not reached this point by 30 months (Fenson et al., 1994).

At present, MLU is frequently used by physicians, teachers, and others to identify children who need additional screening to determine whether they have some kind of language disability (Hewitt, Hammer, Yount, & Tomblin, 2005). More than half of children who are behind schedule during the early months of language development eventually catch up to their agemates without any special interventions. *Speech-language therapy (SLT)* can help many of those who don't catch up on their own, especially when SLT is targeted to the specific elements (e.g., verb tenses) that are lacking in these children's expressive language (e.g., Leonard, Camarata, Pawtowska, Brown, & Camarata, 2008). The subset who do not catch up is primarily made up of children who also have poor receptive language (Bates, 1993; Thal, Tobias, & Morrison, 1991). Research suggests that some kind of defect in the fast-mapping process may be responsible for the leveling off in vocabulary growth that many of these children exhibit around the age of 3 (Alt, Plante, & Creusere, 2004). Such children appear to remain behind in language development and perhaps in cognitive development more generally. In practical terms, this means that parents of a child who is significantly delayed in understanding as well as speaking language should seek professional help to try to diagnose the problem and begin appropriate intervention.

How can these variations in speed of early language development be explained? The alternative possibilities should be familiar by now. One possibility is that the rate of language development may be something one inherits—in the same way that intelligence or the rate of physical development may be affected by heredity. Twin studies designed to test this possibility show that vocabulary size (but not grammatical complexity) is more similar in identical twins than in fraternal twins (Mather & Black, 1984). However, adoption studies show that 2-year-olds' language skill can be predicted about equally well from the IQ scores or the language skills of either their biological or their adoptive parents (Plomin & DeFries, 1985). So it seems that parents who talk more, who read to their children more and elicit more language from them, and who respond appropriately to their children's language may have children who develop language more rapidly, regardless of genetic inheritance. Overall, as with IQ, it seems obvious that both the particular genes the child inherits and the environment in which the child grows up contribute to her rate of language development.

Learning Objective 8.14
In what ways does language vary across cultural groups?

Cross-Cultural Differences in Language Development

In the early years of research on children's language development, linguists and psychologists were strongly impressed by the apparent similarities across languages in children's early language. You've already seen some evidence that supports this impression in Table 8.2 on page 208, which illustrated large similarities in early vocabularies. Studies in a wide variety of language communities, including Turkish, Serbo-Croatian, Hungarian, Hebrew, Japanese, a New Guinean language called Kaluli, German, and Italian, have revealed important similarities in young children's language (Maitel, Dromi, Sagi, & Bornstein, 2000). For example, the prelinguistic phase seems to be identical in all language communities. All babies coo, then babble; all babies understand language before they can speak it; babies in all cultures begin to use their first words at about 12 months.

Moreover, a one-word phase seems always to precede a two-word phase in every language, with the latter appearing at about 18 months. Likewise, across all languages studied so far, prepositions describing locations are added in essentially the same order. Words for "in," "on," "under," and "beside" are learned first; then the child learns the words for "front" and "back" (Slobin, 1985b). Finally, children everywhere seem to pay more attention to the ends of words than to the beginnings, so they learn suffixes before they learn prefixes.

Interestingly, the universal tendency of children to attend to the ends of statements produces cross-cultural differences in language learning. Such differences happen because different languages use different kinds of words at the ends of sentences. In English, the last word in a statement is most likely to be a noun. However, in Mandarin (spoken in China) and Korean, the last word is often a verb. Consequently, while children who are learning English tend to use more nouns than verbs in their first attempts at speaking, children learning Mandarin and Korean produce just as many verbs as nouns (MacWhinney, 2005). Further, this linguistic difference is associated with cross-cultural variations in the way mothers speak to their babies. Those who speak languages that often use verbs at the ends of statements talk about verbs more to their babies. By contrast, mothers who speak English and other noun-focused languages more often explain nouns to infants.

Parents who talk a lot to their babies and ask them questions, as this man appears to be doing, have children who learn to talk sooner.

Another interesting cross-linguistic difference is that the specific word order a child uses in early sentences is not the same for all children in all languages. In some languages, a noun/verb sequence is fairly common; in others, a verb/noun sequence may be heard. In addition, particular inflections are learned in highly varying orders from one language to another. Japanese children, for example, begin very early to use a special kind of marker, called a *pragmatic marker*, which tells something about the feeling or the context of what is being said. For instance, the word *yo* is used at the end of a sentence when the speaker is experiencing some resistance from the listener; the word *ne* is used when the speaker expects approval or agreement. Japanese children begin to use these markers very early, much earlier than children whose languages contain inflections.

Most strikingly, children learning certain languages do not appear to go through a stage of using simple two-word sentences with no inflections. Children learning Turkish, for example, use essentially the full set of noun and verb inflections by age 2 and never go through a stage of using uninflected words. Their language is simple, but it is rarely ungrammatical from the adult's point of view (Aksu-Koc & Slobin, 1985; Maratsos, 1998).

Finally, cross-cultural studies of language development provide us with several good examples of how such research informs our understanding of universals in human development. For example, researchers at one time thought that individual differences in the types of words babies use might be universal (e.g., Shore, 1995). This difference was termed a *style* of language acquisition. Early studies suggested that some toddlers exhibited a *referential* style that focused on labeling objects, while others showed an *expressive* style that concentrated more on social and emotional words. Further research, however, demonstrated that these differences, while somewhat useful for describing the development of English-speaking children, were not manifested in the development of children who were learning other languages (Camaioni & Longobardi, 1995). As a result, researchers took a closer look at English-speaking toddlers, and they found that the apparent style difference disappears with age and has no impact on later language development (Bates et al., 1994).

Learning to Read and Write

Finally, throughout the industrialized world, and increasingly in developing nations, using language to read and write is just as critical to a child's development as using spoken language. Certainly, spoken language forms the foundation on which children build literacy skills. However, learning to read and write taps into children's cognitive and motor skills as well.

Learning Objective 8.15
What is the role of phonological awareness in learning to read?

The Early Foundation: Phonological Awareness

Certain aspects of early childhood language development, such as rate of vocabulary growth, predict how easily a child will learn to read and write when she enters school (Wood & Terrell, 1998). However, one specific component of early childhood language development—phonological awareness—seems to be especially important (Anthony & Lonigan, 2004; Boscardin, Muthén, Francis, & Baker, 2008; Schatschneider, Fletcher, Francis, Carlson, & Foorman, 2004). **Phonological awareness** is a child's awareness of the rules governing sound patterns that are specific to his or her own language. It also includes the child's knowledge of that particular language's system for representing sounds with letters. Researchers measure English-speaking children's phonological awareness with questions like these: "What would *bat* be if you took away the [b]? What would *bat* be if you took away the [b] and put [r] there instead?"

Developmentalists now have abundant evidence that children who are more phonologically aware at age 3, 4, or 5 later learn to read much more easily (Adams, Trieman, & Pressley, 1998; Bryant, MacLean, Bradley, & Crossland, 1990; Hansen & Bowey, 1994; Wagner et al., 1997; Whitehurst, 1995). Furthermore, if you train preschoolers or kindergartners in phonological awareness, their reading skills in first grade improve—a result that has been found in studies in Scandinavia and Germany as well as the United States (Al Otaiba et al., 2008).

Young children can learn phonological awareness skills either through formal means, as these preschoolers are doing, or informally through word games and rhymes.

Of course, a child doesn't have to acquire phonological awareness in early childhood. Phonological skills can be learned in elementary school through formal instruction (Ball, 1997; Bus & van IJzendoorn, 1999; Segers & Verhoeven, 2004). However, numerous studies have shown that the greater a child's phonological awareness *before* he enters school, the faster he learns to read (Christensen, 1997; Gilbertson & Bramlett, 1998; Schatschneider, Francis, Foorman, Fletcher, & Mehta, 1999; Wood & Terrell, 1998). In addition, phonological awareness in the early childhood years is related to rate of literacy learning for languages as varied as Korean, English, Punjabi, and Chinese (Chiappe, Glaeser, & Ferko, 2007; Chiappe & Siegel, 1999; Ho & Bryant, 1997; Huang & Hanley, 1997; McBride-Chang & Ho, 2000). Large gains in phonological awareness appear to take place between children's fourth and fifth birthdays, just before most children enter kindergarten (Justice et al., 2005).

Researchers have also found that many of the everyday activities preschoolers engage in foster the development of phonological awareness. For example, among English-speaking children, learning and reciting nursery rhymes contributes to phonological awareness (Bryant, MacLean, & Bradley, 1990; Bryant, MacLean, Bradley, & Crossland, 1990; Layton, Deeny, Tall, & Upton, 1996; MacLean, Bryant, & Bradley, 1987). For Japanese children, a game called *shiritori*, in which one person says a word and another comes up with a word that begins with its ending sound, helps children develop these skills (Kobayashi, Haynes, Macaruso, Hook, & Kato, 2005; Norboru, 1997; Serpell & Hatano, 1997). Educators have also found that using such games to teach phonological awareness skills to preschoolers is just as effective as using more formal tools such as flash cards and worksheets (Brennan & Ireson, 1997). *Shared reading*, or *dialogic reading*, has also been found to contribute to growth in phonological awareness (Burgess, 1997).

phonological awareness
Understanding of the rules governing the sounds of a language as well as knowledge of the connection between sounds and the way they are represented in written language.

Young children with good phonological awareness skills often use a strategy called **invented spelling** when they attempt to write (see Figure 8.5). In spite of the many errors they make, children who use invented spelling before receiving formal instruction in reading and writing are more likely to become good spellers and readers later in childhood (Dixon & Kaminska, 2007). Thus, the evidence suggests that one of the best ways parents and preschool teachers can help young children prepare for formal instruction in reading is to engage them in activities that encourage word play and invented spelling.

Figure 8.5   Invented Spelling

Translation: *A snake came to visit our class.*
A 5-year-old used a strategy called "invented spelling" to write this sentence about a snake's visit (hopefully accompanied by an animal handler!) to her kindergarten class. Invented spelling requires a high level of phonological awareness. Research suggests that children who have well-developed phonological awareness skills by the time they reach kindergarten learn to read more quickly.

(*Source*: Author.)

Becoming Literate in School

Learning Objective 8.16

What strategies do educators use to help children learn how to read?

Children who are learning to read a language that is based on the *alphabetic principle*, the principle that letters stand for sounds, benefit from specific instruction in sound-letter correspondences, a type of instruction called **systematic and explicit phonics** (Armbruster, Lehr, & Osborn, 2003). *Systematic* means that instruction must follow a plan, beginning with simple, one-letter/one-sound correspondences (e.g., the letter *b* for the sound /b/) and moving to those that involve two or more letters. The plan must be carefully developed so that instruction corresponds in meaningful ways to the spelling system of the language that is being learned. *Explicit* means that letter-sound correspondences are taught intentionally.

Effective phonics curricula also provide beginning readers with ample opportunities for daily practice in using their knowledge of sound-symbol correspondences so that they can develop automaticity. Phonics researchers argue that children cannot comprehend written language easily until they can decode it automatically and fluently (Rego, 2006). Their view is based on the finding that working memory is limited in capacity. Therefore, when decoding words is automatic, working memory capacity is freed up for the task of comprehending what has been read.

Advocates for the **whole language approach**, an approach to reading instruction that places more emphasis on the meaning of written language than on its structure, say that most children are capable of inferring letter-sound correspondences on their own as long as they have enough exposure to print (Strauss & Altwerger, 2007). The key, say these educators, is to motivate children to interact with written language in meaningful and enjoyable ways. Thus, they argue that reading curricula should include high-quality children's literature rather than phonics workbooks. Moreover, they recommend that teachers directly instruct children in phonics skills only when children ask questions about letters and sounds.

Research suggests that thinking that reading instruction must follow *either* the phonics *or* the whole language approach is a mistake. Instead, advocates of the **balanced approach** argue for comprehensive reading instruction that includes systematic and explicit phonics along with other instructional strategies derived from the whole language approach (Iaquinta, 2006). They argue that exposing children to good literature and helping them acquire a love of reading are important elements in any reading curriculum. And, precisely because phonics is so important, teachers have an obligation to find ways of teaching these skills in enjoyable ways. For instance, some strategies for teaching phonics take advantage of children's love of games.

Once children have learned the basic reading process, learning about meaningful word parts, such as prefixes and suffixes, helps them become more efficient readers and to better understand what they read (Adams & Henry, 1997; McBride-Chang, Shu, Zhou, & Wagner, 2004; Nagy, Berninger, Abbott, Vaughan, & Vermeulen, 2004). Instruction in comprehension

invented spelling A strategy young children with good phonological awareness skills use when they write.

systematic and explicit phonics Planned, specific instruction in sound-letter correspondences.

whole language approach An approach to reading instruction that places more emphasis on the meaning of written language than on its structure.

balanced approach Reading instruction that combines explicit phonics instruction with other strategies for helping children acquire literacy.

strategies, such as identifying the purpose of a particular text, also helps improve reading skill and understanding (Pressley & Wharton-McDonald, 1997; Van den Broek, Lynch, Naslund, Ievers-Landis, & Verduin, 2004). Of course, all along the way, children need to be exposed to good literature, both by reading on their own and by having teachers and parents read to them.

Some of the strategies used to teach reading also help children learn writing—the other component of literacy. For example, instruction in sound-symbol connections helps children learn to spell as well as to read (Rego, 2006). Of course, good writing is far more than just spelling; it requires instruction and practice, just as reading does. Specifically, children need to learn about writing techniques such as outlining and paragraph development in order to become good writers. They also need to learn about language mechanics, such as grammar and appropriate uses of words, as well as how to edit their own and others' written work (Graham & Harris, 1997).

Despite educators' best efforts, many children fall behind their classmates in literacy during the early school years. In general, reading researchers have found that poor readers have problems with sound-letter combinations (Agnew, Dorn, & Eden, 2004). Thus, many children who have reading difficulties benefit from highly specific phonics approaches that provide a great deal of practice in translating letters into sounds and vice versa (Koppenhaver, Hendrix, & Williams, 2007; Ryder, Tunmer, & Greaney, 2008).

However, curriculum flexibility is also important in programs for poor readers. Some do not improve when phonics approaches are used. In fact, programs such as the *Reading Recovery* program, which combine sound-letter practice and comprehension training, have proven to be highly successful in helping poor readers catch up, especially when the programs are implemented in the early elementary years (Hurry & Sylva, 2007). Consequently, teachers need to be able to assess the effectiveness of whatever approach they are using and change it to fit the needs of individual students.

English-language learners (ELLs) School children who do not speak English well enough to function in English-only classes.

bilingual education As practiced in the United States, a school program for students who are not proficient in English in which instruction in basic subject matter is given in the children's native language during the first 2 or 3 years of schooling, with a gradual transition to full English instruction over several years.

Learning Objective 8.17

What instructional strategies do educators use to help English-language learners?

Learning a Second Language

Worldwide patterns of population growth and movement have led to tremendous increases in the number of children attending school in the United States, Canada, Great Britain, and Australia whose first language is not English. About two-thirds of these children speak English well enough to function in school, but the rest essentially do not speak English. Educators in English-speaking countries use the term **English-language learners (ELLs)** to refer to non–English-speaking children—either immigrant children or native-born children.

About 11% of school-aged children in the United States are classified as ELL (National Center for Education Statistics [NCES], 2006). However, as you probably realize, these children are not equally distributed across schools. Some systems have relatively few, while others, as Table 8.6 shows, enroll a large number of such pupils. Furthermore, in many urban areas in North America, ELL children come from widely varying linguistic backgrounds. In Toronto, for example, school children speak more than 80 different languages (Toronto District School Board, 2001). In the U.S. cities of Los Angeles, New York, Chicago, and Washington, DC, more than 100 languages are spoken in the homes of children (NCES, 2008). Because the issues involved in educating ELL children are so diverse across nations and even across regions within nations, there is no one-size-fits-all instructional strategy for helping these children learn to speak, read, and write English.

In the United States, some ELL children, mostly those whose first language is Spanish, participate in a bilingual education program (Osorio-O'Dea, 2001). In **bilingual education**, instruction is presented in the children's native language during the first 2 or 3 years of schooling, and teachers make a gradual transition to instructing totally in English

Table 8.6 Percentage of ELL Students in Some of North America's Largest School Systems

Los Angeles	42%
Toronto	41%
Dallas	33%
Houston	28%
San Diego	27%
Denver	25%
Miami	19%
Albuquerque	18%
Chicago	14%
New York City	14%
District of Columbia	12%
Vancouver	12%

Sources: British Columbia Ministry of Education, 2001; NCES, 2003b; Toronto District School Board, 2001.

One Language or Two?

Chan, a Chinese American, and Luisa, a Mexican American, are the proud parents of a 3-month-old girl. Chan is fluent in Mandarin and English, and Luisa is a Spanish-English bilingual. Their own experiences have convinced them that being bilingual is a great asset. They hope to provide their daughter with an even greater asset—that of being fluent in three languages. However, they are somewhat worried about the advisability of raising a child with more than one language in the home.

Knowing two or more languages clearly provides social and economic benefits to an adult. However, research suggests that there are cognitive advantages *and* disadvantages to growing up bilingual. On the positive side, children who are bilingual have a clear advantage in *metalinguistic ability*, the capacity to think about language (Bialystok, Shenfield, & Codd, 2000). In addition, most bilingual children display more advanced executive processing skills on language tasks than do monolingual children (Carlson & Meltzoff, 2008). These

two advantages enable bilingual children to more easily grasp the connection between sounds and symbols in the beginning stages of learning to read (Bialystok, 1997; Oller, Cobo-Lewis, & Eilers, 1998).

On the negative side, infants in bilingual homes reach some milestones later than those learning a single language. For example, bilingual infants' receptive and expressive vocabularies are as large as those of monolingual infants, but the words they know are divided between two languages (Patterson, 1998). Consequently, they are behind monolingual infants in word knowledge no matter which language is considered, a difference that persists into the school years. In addition, children growing up in bilingual homes in which the two languages vary greatly in how they are written (e.g., English and Chinese) may acquire reading skills in both languages more slowly than peers in monolingual homes (Bialystok, Majumder, & Martin, 2003; Guglielmi, 2008).

However, research indicates that bilingual children who are equally fluent in both languages encounter few, if any, learning problems in school (Vuorenkoski, Kuure, Moilanen, & Peninkilampi, 2000). Still, most children do not attain equal fluency in both languages (Hakansson, Salameh, & Nettelbladt, 2003). When the language in which they are less fluent is the language in which their schooling is conducted, they are at risk for learning problems (Anderson, 1998; Thorn & Gathercole, 1999).

Questions for Reflection

1. What kind of linguistic environment would you provide for your child if you were in the same position as Chan and Luisa?
2. In your opinion, how likely is it that the little girl will achieve her parents' goal of fluency in three languages? What factors will influence her eventual level of fluency in each of the three languages?

---

over the next few years. Such programs have been developed for Spanish-speaking children because they constitute by far the largest group of ELL students in U.S. schools (Planty et al., 2008). In other English-speaking countries, bilingual education is available to children from large non–English-speaking groups as well. For example, schools in Canada have provided both English- and French-speaking students in Quebec, a primarily French-speaking province, with bilingual education for decades. (See *Developmental Science in the Real World*.)

An alternative to bilingual education is **structured immersion**, used in classrooms in which all the children speak the same non-English native language and the teacher speaks both English and the children's native language. In such classrooms, the basic instruction is in English, paced so that the children can comprehend, with the teacher translating only when absolutely necessary. French language programs of this kind for English-speaking children have been very successful in Quebec (Allen, 2004; Holobow, Genesee, & Lambert, 1991).

In many North American cities, a substantial proportion of school children come from homes in which a language other than English is spoken. With support, these children can become fluent in English and can excel in school.

In these programs, students are taught exclusively in French for 2 years of elementary school. During the remaining elementary years, they receive bilingual instruction. Research shows that, in the early grades, these pupils are somewhat behind monolingual English-speakers in literacy skills. However, when these children reach high school age, they get higher scores on reading achievement tests than their monolingual peers.

However, it is often logistically impossible to provide bilingual education or structured immersion for most ELL children. For one thing, if a school system has only a handful of students who speak a particular language, it is not financially feasible to establish a separate curriculum for them. In addition, it may be impossible to find bilingual teachers for children whose language is spoken by very few people outside their country of origin. For these

structured immersion An alternative to traditional bilingual education used in classrooms in which all children speak the same non-English native language. All basic instruction is in English, paced so that the children can comprehend, with the teacher translating only when absolutely necessary.

reasons, most ELL school children in the United States, about 85%, are enrolled in **English-as-a-second-language (ESL)** programs (Osorio-O'Dea, 2001). In ESL programs, children attend academic classes that are conducted entirely in English and spend part of each day in English-language classes.

Research has shown that no particular approach to second-language learning is more successful than any other (Mohanty & Perregaux, 1997). There is some indication that programs that include a home-based component, such as those that encourage parents to learn the new language along with their children, may be especially effective (Koskinen et al., 2000). But it seems that any structured program, whether bilingual education or ESL, fosters higher achievement among non–English-speaking children than simply integrating them into English-only classes, an approach called **submersion**. Although most children in submersion programs eventually catch up to their English-speaking peers, many educators believe that instruction that supports children's home language and culture as well as their English-language skills enhances their overall development (Bougie, Wright, & Taylor, 2003).

With respect to overall achievement, ELL students' performance in school is very similar to that of English-speaking children (NCES, 2008). In fact, in U.S. schools, native-born English-speaking children are more likely to fail one or more grades than children whose home language is either Asian or European. Native-born Spanish-speaking children fail at about the same rate as English speakers. And in U.S. schools, adolescents who are recent immigrants are more likely to complete high school than peers who entered the United States at younger ages or who are native-born (White & Glick, 2000). In fact, studies suggest that, with the help of special programs designed to ease their transition into a new language, ELL children can outperform their monolingual peers on standardized tests of reading achievement as early as second grade, even if they enter school with no knowledge whatever of English (Lesaux & Siegel, 2003). Thus, there is no evidence that a child who enters school with limited English skills has any greater risk of failure than a child whose first language is English.

One cautionary note is important, however: An ELL student does not have an increased risk of failure as long as the school provides some kind of transition to English-only instruction *and* school officials take care to administer all standardized tests in the language with which the child is most familiar (Bernardo & Calleja, 2005). The first is necessary to optimize the ELL child's potential for achievement. The second ensures that non–English-speaking children are not misclassified as having mental retardation or learning disablities because of their limited English skills.

Think Critically

- Much of the research that you read about in this chapter was based on a very small number of case studies. Why do you think the researchers chose to use the case study method? What are the advantages and disadvantages of the case study method with regard to the study of language development?
- In what way are studies of animal communication useful in the study of human language development?

Conduct Your Own Research

As noted in this chapter, Vygotsky and Piaget differed about the function of private speech. You can observe children using private speech in a preschool, kindergarten, or first-grade classroom. (Remember to get permission from school officials and from the children's parents.) Focus on one child at a time, keeping a record of the child's self-directed statements. Determine the proportion of such statements that appear to be for the purpose of guiding behavior, as Vygotsky suggested. An example of such a statement might be a preschooler's utterance of "this goes here" while putting a puzzle together. After you have collected data on several children, decide whether you agree with Vygotsky.

English-as-a-second-language (ESL) An alternative to bilingual education; children who are not proficient in English attend academic classes taught entirely in English but then spend several hours in a separate class to receive English-language instruction.

submersion An approach to education of non–English-speaking students in which they are assigned to a classroom where instruction is given in English and are given no supplemental language assistance; also known as the "sink or swim" approach.

Summary

BEFORE THE FIRST WORD: THE PRELINGUISTIC PHASE

8.1 What are the characteristics of cooing and babbling?

- Cooing is the first type of communicative sound that a baby produces. It is made up of repetitive vowel sounds. Vocalizations that include strings of consonant and vowel sounds appear around 6 months of age and are called babbling. Babbling gradually changes until it reflects only those sounds that are included in the language that the baby is learning to speak.

8.2 What have researchers learned about infants' receptive language skills?

- By 10 months of age, infants understand 30 or more words, though their speaking vocabulary is still extremely limited. By 13 months, an infant's receptive vocabulary increases to 100 words. Babies as young as 9 to 12 months understand simple instructions.

LEARNING WORDS AND WORD MEANINGS

8.3 What are the trends in word learning over the first 2 years?

- The earliest words appear at about 1 year of age. The first words are simple and are typically used only for specific objects or situations. Vocabulary grows slowly at first and then usually spurts in a naming explosion. By 16 months of age, most children have a vocabulary of about 50 words. The earliest words are typically highly specific and context-bound in meaning; later, children typically overextend word usage.

8.4 How does word learning proceed in early and middle childhood?

- Children continue to learn new words throughout the preschool years and add approximately 10 words a day by the time they are ready to begin elementary school. Fast-mapping, the use of categories to learn new words, enables them to acquire new words rapidly.

8.5 What are some proposed constraints on word learning?

- Many (but not all) linguists have concluded that in determining word meanings, a child has built-in constraints or biases, such as the assumption that words refer to objects or actions but not both and the principle of contrast. Others linguists believe that such constraints exist but are acquired rather than built-in.

LEARNING THE RULES: THE DEVELOPMENT OF GRAMMAR AND PRAGMATICS

8.6 How do children's first sentences differ from holophrases?

- Linguists use the term *holophrase* to refer to infants' use of single words, or single words combined with gestures, as sentences. As holophrases become less frequent around age 18 months, two-word sentences begin to appear in the child's speech. The young child can use these simple sentences to convey many different meanings, including location, possession, and agent-object relationships.

8.7 What is the significance of the grammar explosion?

- During the grammar explosion, the child quickly adds many grammatical inflections and learns to create questions and negative sentences.

8.8 What grammatical skills do children acquire in the preschool, elementary, and teen years?

- By age 3 or 4, most children can construct remarkably complex sentences. Later skills are primarily refinements of established skills, such as learning to understand and use passive sentences.

8.9 What are the milestones of pragmatics development?

- As early as age 2, children adapt their language to the needs of the listener and begin to follow culturally specific customs of language usage. Children also use language to regulate their own behavior.

EXPLAINING LANGUAGE DEVELOPMENT

8.10 How do environmental theories explain language development?

- Several theories have been offered to explain language development. Two early environmental explanations, one based on imitation and one on reinforcement, have been largely set aside. More recently, emphasis has been placed both on the helpful quality of the simpler form of adult-to-child language called *motherese*, or infant-directed speech, and on the role of expansions and recastings of children's sentences.

8.11 What kind of evidence supports the nativist theories?

- Nativist theories assume that the child is born with a set of operating principles that focus him on relevant aspects of language input. Children's production of words that suggest the use of rules (e.g., "feets" rather than "feet"; "breaked" rather than "broke") rather than imitation of mature speech supports the nativist view.

8.12 How do constructivist theories differ from other approaches?

- Constructivist approaches differ from the learning and nativist perspectives in that they argue that language development is guided by the same processes that shape general cognitive development. Constructivist theorists hold that a child constructs language at the same time and in the same way as he constructs all cognitive understandings.

INDIVIDUAL AND GROUP DIFFERENCES IN LANGUAGE DEVELOPMENT

8.13 Are differences in the rate of language development related to later measures of proficiency?

- Children show differences in the rate of development of both vocabulary and grammar, differences explained by both heredity and environmental influences. Despite these variations in rate of early development, however, most children eventually learn to speak skillfully.

8.14 In what ways does language vary across cultural groups?

- The sequence of language development is remarkably consistent across all languages. There are a few exceptions, however. For example, children learning Turkish produce sentences during the two-word stage that differ with regard to the use of inflections from those of children learning other languages.

LEARNING TO READ AND WRITE

8.15 What is the role of phonological awareness in learning to read?

- Development of an awareness of the sound patterns of a particular language during early childhood is important in learning to read and write. Children seem to acquire this skill through word play. Phonological awareness helps children establish connections between spoken and written language.

8.16 What strategies do educators use to help children learn how to read?

- In school, children need specific instruction in sound-letter correspondences, word parts, and comprehension strategies to become good readers. They also need to be exposed to good literature and to have lots of appropriate practice in using literacy skills.

8.17 What instructional strategies do educators use to help English-language learners?

- Children with limited English perform as well as English-speaking peers when they receive specific kinds of support in school. In bilingual education classes, academic instruction takes place in children's first language and English is taught as a separate subject. In ESL programs, children receive academic instruction in English along with specific instruction in English. In structured immersion programs, a bilingual teacher provides most instruction in English and translates only when absolutely necessary. Research has not produced a clear answer as to which approach is most effective.

Key Terms

babbling (p. 205)
balanced approach (p. 223)
bilingual education (p. 224)
constraint (p. 210)
cooing (p. 205)
English-as-a-second-language (ESL) (p. 226)
English-language learners (ELLs) (p. 224)
expressive language (p. 205)
fast-mapping (p. 209)
holophrase (p. 211)

invented spelling (p. 223)
mean length of utterance (MLU) (p. 219)
motherese (infant-directed speech) (p. 217)
overextension (p. 209)
overregularization (p. 213)
phonological awareness (p. 222)
phonology (p. 204)
pragmatics (p. 214)
prelinguistic phase (p. 205)
principle of contrast (p. 210)

receptive language (p. 206)
semantics (p. 204)
structured immersion (p. 225)
submersion (p. 226)
syntax (p. 204)
systematic and explicit phonics (p. 223)
telegraphic speech (p. 212)
underextension (p. 209)
whole language approach (p. 223)

Personality Development: Alternative Views

9

Learning Objectives

Defining Personality

9.1 What are the dimensions of temperament that most psychologists agree on?

9.2 How do advocates for the Big Five approach define personality?

Genetic and Biological Explanations of Personality

9.3 What is the focus of the biological approach to personality?

9.4 What are some important criticisms of the biological approach?

Learning Explanations of Personality

9.5 What are the basic propositions of learning explanations of personality?

9.6 What are some criticisms of the learning perspective?

Psychoanalytic Explanations of Personality

9.7 What are the major points of the psychoanalytic approach to personality?

9.8 How does Freud's theory explain personality development?

9.9 How does Erikson's theory explain personality development?

9.10 What evidence is there to support the psychoanalytic perspective on personality?

9.11 What are some criticisms of psychoanalytic theories?

A Possible Synthesis

9.12 How can elements of the biological, learning, and psychoanalytic approaches be combined into a comprehensive explanation of personality?

Have you ever watched preschoolers and their families wait in line at a fast food restaurant where there is an attractive play area? When their children ask to go to the play area, most parents follow a script that goes something like this: "As soon as we get our food, we'll go over there, but you have to finish eating before you can play." In response, some children look longingly at the play area but remain steadfastly at their parents' side. Others whine a bit but soon distract themselves from their unfulfilled desire to play by focusing on their anticipation of the toy they will get with their food. Still others behave as if they had just been told the world as they know it was coming to an end. They cry loudly and may even scream in frustration. Many of these children fall onto the floor and injure themselves, adding more drama to the display. Some even hit or kick the refusing parent. Others defiantly run to the play area, seemingly oblivious to their parents' instructions to stay in line. Remarkably, these variations often occur among children from the same family.

Thinking about the differences that appear when children are in frustrating situations captures the essence of what psychologists mean when they use the term *personality*. Formally, this term is defined as the individual's enduring patterns of responses to and interactions with others and the environment. Practically, it pervades all of children's relationships, thereby exerting just as powerful an influence on developmental outcomes as their cognitive abilities. What causes such differences? When we look for answers to this question, whether in the countless books on child-rearing that are available today or in the professional literature, we inevitably encounter the debate that pervades every discussion of human development: the nature-nurture controversy. Of course, as interesting as the nature-nurture debate is to developmental scientists, what parents want to know is how they should respond to children's personalities. They wonder, too: If personality is indeed inherited, then to what degree will their responses matter? That is, can the behavior of a child who throws a tantrum every time she doesn't get her way be changed, or do family members simply have to resign themselves to tolerating her disruptive behavior?

As we have noted with regard to other characteristics, most developmentalists would say that it is the interaction between a child's inborn traits and the characteristics of his or her environment, not one or the other, that determines personality. In other words, parenting practices should be based on an understanding of all the factors that influence children's personalities. As you will learn in this chapter, there is little doubt that heredity is an important factor. However, learning influences personality as well. Thus, parenting that relies solely on either the notion that personality is inborn or the idea that it is learned is likely to be ineffective. Instead, parents need to have a better idea of how and when inborn traits and learning, as well as a number of other factors, come into play.

In this chapter, we will review how various theorists have approached the explanation of personality development. When you finish reading this chapter, you will have a better appreciation for the complexities of human personality. You will see that, like most developmental variables, it isn't simply a matter of *either* inborn traits *or* environmental influences.

Defining Personality

personality The collection of relatively enduring patterns of reacting to and interacting with others and the environment that distinguishes each child or adult.

Like the concept of intelligence, the concept of personality has been hard to define clearly. Most theorists and researchers have thought of **personality** in terms of variations on a set of basic traits or dimensions, such as shyness versus gregariousness or activity versus passivity. If researchers could identify the basic dimensions of personality, they could then describe any individual's personality as a profile of those key traits. That sounds straightforward, but coming to agreement on the nature of the key dimensions has been no simple task. Over the years, researchers and theorists have disagreed vehemently about how many such dimensions there might be, how they should be measured, or even whether there are any stable personality traits at all. However, in the past decade, somewhat to the surprise of many psychologists, a consensus has emerged on certain principles. The first is that infant temperament makes a sizeable contribution to later personality. The second principle is that five basic dimensions emerge as the core of an individual's personality during early and middle childhood and the ways in which these dimensions are manifested in an individual's life are fairly stable across adolescence and adulthood.

Temperament

Learning Objective 9.1
What are the dimensions of temperament that most psychologists agree on?

You read about temperament in Chapters 1 and 3, so the concept is not completely new. Mary Rothbart and John Bates, two of the leading researchers in this area, define temperament as "individual differences in emotional, motor, and attentional reactivity and self-regulation" that children consistently display in all kinds of settings and situations (1998, p. 109) (see *Developmental Science in the Real World*). These authors, and most others who study temperament, conceive of these qualities as the emotional substrate of personality—the set of core qualities or response patterns that are visible in infancy and reflected in such things as typical activity level, irritability or emotionality, "soothability," fearfulness, and sociability (Hartup & van Lieshout, 1995, p. 658; Rothbart, Ahadi, & Evans, 2000).

Three Views of Temperament   One of the most influential temperament category systems has been Stella Chess and Alexander Thomas's (1984) description of *difficult*, *easy*, and *slow-to-warm-up* temperaments, reflecting profiles on nine different dimensions—a system described in Chapter 3. In contrast, Arnold Buss and Robert Plomin originally proposed

DEVELOPMENTAL SCIENCE IN THE REAL WORLD
Temperamental Surgency in the Toddler Classroom

Benita works in a child-care center and is assigned to the toddler room. She has noticed that one of the tykes, an 18-month-old boy named Thomas, seems to dominate the others. The little boy is bright, cheerful, and physically active, and he makes friends easily. However, when Benita plays naming games with the toddlers, Thomas blurts out an answer whenever Benita asks "What's this?" before his peers have a chance to answer. Benita wonders whether she should make a special effort to reduce Thomas's domineering behavior.

Developmental scientists often employ Chess and Thomas's (1984) goodness-of-fit model—the notion that the appropriateness of the environment for a given child's temperament is more important than the temperament itself—to explain interactions between infants' temperaments and their capacity to adjust to different settings. For instance, some temperamental profiles predispose infants to adjust easily to the structure of a child-care center, whereas others increase the chances

that they will develop behavior problems (De Schipper et al., 2004). In general, infants who are classified as easy according to Chess and Thomas's system more readily adjust to child-care centers than do infants in the difficult category. Such research suggests that what Benita may be seeing in Thomas's behavior is a conflict between his temperament and the demands of the environment in which he is being cared for.

Thomas possesses an above-average level of a dimension of temperament that researchers call *surgency*—a cluster of traits that includes sociability, high activity level, generally positive emotional states, and impulsiveness (Rothbart & Putnam, 2002). Some studies suggest that surgency is observable in infants as young as 3 months of age. Moreover, surgency is a highly stable facet of temperament that persists throughout childhood and into adulthood. Surgent children's impulsiveness predisposes them to develop behavior problems in structured set-

tings such as child-care centers. Despite their generally positive emotional state, surgent children can become frustrated when they are prevented from behaving impulsively. In some cases, this frustration leads them to behave aggressively toward their peers. Thus, Benita's challenge is to find a way to encourage Thomas to allow the other children to respond to her questions without causing him to become so frustrated that he expresses his impulsiveness in less positive ways.

Questions for Reflection

1. How might Benita use the principles of operant conditioning that you learned about in Chapter 1 to reduce Thomas's behavior of blurting out answers?
2. If you were Thomas's parent, how would you respond if Benita expressed her concerns about his impulsive behavior to you?

Even in the early years of life, differences in personality are evident.

only three key dimensions: activity level, emotionality (primarily negative emotionality), and sociability (Buss, 1989; Buss & Plomin, 1984, 1986). The questionnaire they devised to measure these three qualities has been widely used by researchers studying infants, children, and adults. Yet another key figure has been Jerome Kagan, who has focused on only a single dimension, which he calls *behavioral inhibition*—an aspect of what most people mean by "shyness" (Kagan, Reznick, & Snidman, 1990; Kagan, Snidman, & Arcus, 1993). None of these conceptualizations has been universally accepted.

An Emerging Consensus Temperament researchers are still struggling to define the key dimensions and have not reached a clear agreement (Thompson & Goodvin, 2005). However, over the past decade, a consensus has emerged, one that is reflected in the writings of the leading researchers in the field (Caspi & Shiner, 2006; Kagan & Herschkowitz, 2005; Rothbart, 2007). Many theorists are now emphasizing the following five key dimensions of temperament:

- *Activity level.* A tendency to move often and vigorously, rather than to remain passive or immobile.

- *Approach/positive emotionality.* A tendency to move toward rather than away from new people, situations, or objects, usually accompanied by positive emotion. This dimension is similar to what Buss and Plomin call *sociability*.

- *Inhibition and anxiety.* The flip side of approach is a tendency to respond with fear or to withdraw from new people, situations, or objects.

- *Negative emotionality/irritability/anger.* A tendency to respond with anger, fussiness, loudness, or irritability; a low threshold of frustration. This dimension appears to be what Thomas and Chess are tapping with their concept of the "difficult" child and what Buss and Plomin call *emotionality*.

- *Effortful control/task persistence.* An ability to stay focused, to manage attention and effort.

Temperament across Cultures Despite knowing something about temperament, researchers are still left with several huge questions to answer. One such question concerns the universality of these dimensions of temperament. Early research by Daniel Freedman (1979) suggested that Chinese and Native American infants were less active than Caucasian American or Japanese babies. Kagan and his colleagues (1994) replicated part of these results in their comparison of Chinese, Irish, and Caucasian American 4-month-olds. They found that the Chinese infants were significantly less active, less irritable, and less vocal than were babies in the other two groups. The Caucasian American infants showed the strongest reactions to new sights, sounds, or smells. Similarly, Chisholm (1989) has replicated Freedman's research on Native American babies, finding them to be significantly less irritable, less excitable, and more able to quiet themselves than Caucasian American babies.

Since such differences are evident in newborns, they cannot be the result of systematic shaping by the parents. But the parents bring their temperaments as well as their cultural training to interactions with their newborns, which may tend to strengthen or perpetuate the babies' temperamental differences. For instance, Freedman and other researchers have observed that both Japanese and Chinese mothers talk to their infants much less than Caucasian mothers do. These differences in mothers' behavior were present from the mothers' first encounters with their infants after delivery, so the pattern is not a response to the babies' quieter behavior. Nonetheless, a correspondence between a mother's culturally defined behaviors and a baby's temperamental pattern is likely to strengthen the pattern in the child, which would tend to make the cultural differences larger over time (Chen, Wang, & De Souza, 2006).

Big Five The five primary dimensions of adult personality identified by researchers: extraversion, agreeableness, conscientiousness, neuroticism, and openness/intellect.

extraversion One of the Big Five personality traits; a person who scores high on this trait is characterized by assertiveness, energy, enthusiasm, and outgoingness.

The distinction between temperament and personality is a little like the difference between a genotype and a phenotype. The genotype sets the basic pattern, but the eventual outcome depends on the way the basic pattern is affected by specific experience. What is measured as personality later in childhood or adulthood reflects how the basic pattern has been affected by myriad life experiences. For example, recent longitudinal research suggests that mothers' responses to toddlers' temperaments can serve to either strengthen or weaken inborn temperamental variables such as shyness (Rubin, Burgess, & Hastings, 2002; Rubin & Coplan, 2004). Toddlers of mothers who are critical of their shy behavior display more shyness as preschoolers than children of mothers who are accepting of this trait in their children. If this interactive model is correct, then variations in temperament ought to bear some (perhaps even considerable) resemblance to personality in adulthood, although the matchup will probably not be perfect.

agreeableness One of the Big Five personality traits; a person who scores high on this trait is characterized by trust, generosity, kindness, and sympathy.

openness/intellect One of the Big Five personality traits; a person who scores high on this trait is characterized by curiosity, imagination, insight, originality, and wide interests.

The Big Five

Learning Objective 9.2
How do advocates for the Big Five approach define personality?

If temperament is the foundation for later personality, then we should expect to find some consistency in characteristics across the lifespan. As this view would predict, researchers now agree that personality in childhood and later in life can be adequately described as a set of variations across five dimensions—the so-called **Big Five** (see Table 9.1). If you compare these five traits to the dimensions of infant temperament that you read about earlier, you will notice similarities. **Extraversion**, along with its opposite *introversion*, for instance, is quite similar to the temperamental dimensions of approach/positive emotionality and inhibition. **Agreeableness** and **openness/intellect** also draw on approach/positive emotionality as well as effortful control. **Conscientiousness** has much in common with effortful control, and **neuroticism** resembles negative emotionality.

The usefulness of the Big Five for describing personality has been demonstrated in studies of adults in a variety of countries, including some non-Western cultures, which lends some cross-cultural validity to this list. At the very least, researchers know that this set of dimensions is not unique to American adults (Lüdtke, Trautwein, & Köller, 2004; McCrae & Terracciano, 2005).

conscientiousness One of the Big Five personality traits; a person who scores high on this trait is characterized by efficiency, organization, planfulness, and reliability.

neuroticism One of the Big Five personality traits; a person who scores high on this trait is characterized by anxiety, self-pity, tenseness, and emotional instability.

Table 9.1 The Big Five Personality Traits

Trait	Basic Feature(s)	Qualities of Individuals High in the Trait
Extraversion	The extent to which a person actively engages the world versus avoiding social experiences	Active, assertive, enthusiastic, outgoing, talkative
Agreeableness	The extent to which a person's interpersonal interactions are characterized by warmth and compassion versus antagonism	Affectionate, forgiving, generous, kind, sympathetic, trusting
Openness/Intellect	Reflects the depth, complexity, and quality of a person's mental and experiential life	Artistic, curious, imaginative, insightful, original, having wide interests
Conscientiousness	The extent and strength of a person's impulse control	Efficient, organized, planful, reliable, responsive, thorough, able to delay gratification in the service of more distant goals
Neuroticism; also called emotional (in)stability	The extent to which a person experiences the world as distressing or threatening	Anxious, self-pitying, tense, touchy, unstable, worrying

Sources: Caspi, 1998, p. 316; John et al., 1994, Table 1, p. 161; McCrae and Costa, 1994.

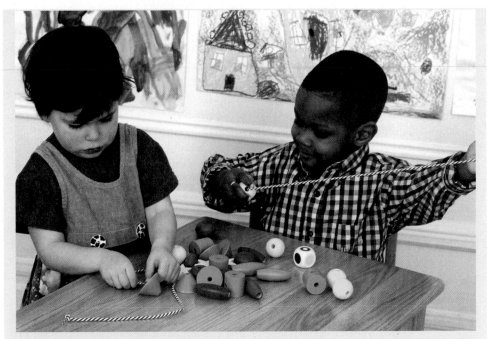

The temperamental characteristic of effortful control, which these preschoolers seem to have, is linked to the Big Five trait of conscientiousness.

There is also good evidence that the Big Five are stable traits: Among adults, personality test scores on these five dimensions have been shown to be stable over periods as long as a decade or more (Caspi et al., 2003; Costa & McCrae, 1994). In addition, the usefulness of the Big Five as a description of personality has been validated by a variety of studies linking scores on these dimensions to behavior in a wide variety of real-life situations (Caspi et al., 2005; Furnham, Petrides, Tsaousis, Pappas, & Garrod, 2005). For example, college students who score high on the dimensions of conscientiousness and openness to experience tend to have higher GPAs than their peers who score lower on these traits. Those high in neuroticism have poorer health habits (they more often smoke, for example) and complain more about their health than do those low in neuroticism (Costa & McCrae, 1984). Thus, the Big Five, as measured either through self-reports or through reports by observers, appear to be both reliable and valid descriptions of personality.

A growing body of research suggests that the Big Five provide a useful description of personality structure in late childhood and adolescence as well as adulthood (e.g., Baker, Victor, Chambers, & Halverson, 2004; Deal, Halverson, Martin, Victor, & Baker, 2007; Soto, John, Gosling, & Potter, 2008). For example, Cornelis van Lieshout and Gerbert Haselager (1994), in a large study of children and adolescents in the Netherlands, found that the five clearest dimensions on which they could characterize their young participants matched the Big Five very well, and this was true for both boys and girls and for preschoolers as well as adolescents. In this sample, agreeableness and emotional (in)stability (the equivalent of the neuroticism dimension) were the most evident dimensions of personality, followed by conscientiousness, extraversion, and openness.

Similar results have come from longitudinal studies in the United States, in which researchers have found that measures of the Big Five in childhood predict academic achievement and a variety of social variables in adolescence (Asendorpf, Denissen, & van Aken, 2008; Bilalic, McLeod, & Gobet, 2007; Laidra, Pullmann, & Allik, 2007). In one particularly influential study, Oliver John and his colleagues (1994) studied a random sample of nearly 500 boys initially selected from among all fourth-graders in the Pittsburgh public school system and followed until age 13. Like the Dutch researchers, John found strong evidence that the five-factor model captured the personality variations among these preteen boys.

John's study was also helpful as a test of the validity of the five-factor model because he gathered information on other aspects of the boys' behavior, such as their school success or their delinquent behavior. By comparing the personality profiles of boys who differed in some other way, he could check to see if their personality patterns differed in ways that made theoretical and conceptual sense. For example, Figure 9.1 contrasts the personality profiles of boys who reported delinquent activity versus boys who reported none. As John predicted, delinquent boys were markedly lower than nondelinquent boys in both agreeableness and conscientiousness. John also found that boys higher in conscientiousness did slightly better in school, just as would be expected. Subsequent studies supported John's findings. However, some of these studies also found a positive correlation between neuroticism and delinquency (e.g., Retz et al., 2004). Likewise, research examining relationships among the Big Five and delinquency in adolescent girls shows that neuroticism predicts criminal behavior among them as well (ter Laak et al., 2003). In addition, the link between a low level of conscientiousness and delinquency holds for girls. However, researchers have not found a correlation between a low level of agreeableness and delinquency among females.

These results are impressive and point to the usefulness of the five-factor model, but it is still too soon to tell whether the Big Five will turn out to be the optimal way of describing children's personality. In particular, researchers may need more than five dimensions to describe children. For example, both John and his colleagues in their U.S. study and van Lieshout and Haselager in their Dutch study found two additional dimensions that describe children's personality: irritability and activity level. With regard to activity level, longitudinal studies have provided support for the hypothesis that this particular dimension of temperament persists through childhood and gradually becomes subsumed by the extraversion dimension of the Big Five during the adolescent years (Eaton, 1994; Soto et al., 2008). Such studies point to the need for long-term studies in which links between early temperament and later personality can be more clearly identified.

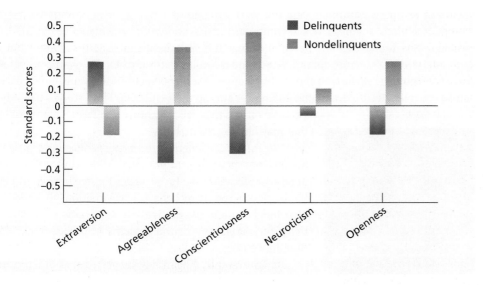

Figure 9.1 John's Study of the Big Five and Delinquency

Twelve-year-olds who report more delinquent acts have personality profiles quite different from those of nondelinquent 12-year-olds—a set of results that helps to validate the usefulness of the Big Five personality traits as a description of children's personality.

(*Source*: O. P. John et al., from "The 'little five': Exploring the nomological network of the five factor model of personality in adolescent boys," *Child Development, 65*, 160–178.)

Genetic and Biological Explanations of Personality

Many researchers, such as Robert Plomin, maintain that the evidence that heredity plays a strong role in the determination of personality is powerful and must be taken into account in any theoretical explanation of individual differences (Plomin, 2001, 2004). The genetic approach includes a number of persuasive propositions. However, there are many critics of this perspective.

Learning Objective 9.3

What is the focus of the biological approach to personality?

The Biological Argument

Broadly expressed, the argument that the origins of personality are biological is based on four major propositions.

Proposition 1: Each individual is born with genetically determined characteristic patterns of responding to the environment and to other people. Virtually every researcher who studies temperament shares the assumption that temperamental qualities are inborn, carried in the genes. This idea is not so very different from the notion of "inborn biases," or "constraints," you have read about in earlier chapters, except that in this case the focus is on individual rather than shared behavioral dispositions.

There is clear, strong evidence to support this assertion (Ganiban, Saudino, Ulbricht, Neiderhiser, & Reiss, 2008), both in studies of adult personality and in studies of childhood temperament. Studies of twins in many countries show that identical twins are much more alike in their temperament or personality than are fraternal twins (Rose, 1995). Hill Goldsmith and his colleagues (1997) combined the results from many studies in which twins have been rated by their parents on some version of the Buss and Plomin temperament categories. Their research shows that the correlations on each dimension are a great deal higher for pairs of identical twins than for pairs of fraternal twins, indicating a strong genetic effect. Further support for the genetic hypothesis comes from researchers who have found that non-twin siblings are far more similar in personality than many parents believe them to be. Developmentalist Kimberly Saudino (Saudino, Wertz, Gagne, & Chawla, 2004) compared parents' ratings of siblings' activity levels to computerized assessments of videotapes of the children's behavior. She found that the parental ratings differed significantly across siblings but the computerized assessments did not. She found a similar pattern when she compared parents' ratings of siblings' shyness to those of objective observers. Such findings mean that parents tend to exaggerate temperamental differences among their children. Thus, studies that rely on parental ratings may fail to capture similarities across siblings that may have a genetic basis.

Proposition 2: Genetic differences operate via variations in fundamental physiological processes. Many (but not all) temperament theorists take Proposition 1 a step further and trace the basic differences in behavior to variations in underlying physiological patterns, particularly to variations in the reactivity of underlying neural systems (Gunnar et al., 2003; Plomin, 2004).

As an example, Kagan has suggested that differences in behavioral inhibition are based on differing thresholds for arousal in those parts of the brain—the amygdala and the hypothalamus—that control responses to uncertainty (Schwartz, Wright, Shin, Kagan, & Rauch, 2003). Arousal of these parts of the brain leads to increases in muscle tension and heart rate. Shy or inhibited children are thought to have a low threshold for such a reaction. That is, they more readily

This 1-year-old may just be having a bad day. But if this is typical behavior, one sign of a "difficult" temperament, she will be at higher risk for a variety of problems at later ages.

become tense and alert in the presence of uncertainty, perhaps even interpreting a wider range of situations as uncertain. What we inherit, according to this view, is not "shyness" or some equivalent behavioral pattern but a tendency for the brain to react in particular ways.

In support of this argument, Kagan reports correlations in the range of .60 between a measure of behavioral inhibition in children aged 2 to 5 and a series of physiological measures, such as muscle tension, heart rate, dilation of the pupil of the eye, and chemical composition of both urine and saliva, which strongly suggest that temperament is based on physiological responses and is not simply a set of learned habits (1994; Kagan et al., 1990). Moreover, Kagan and his associates have found that behavioral measures of inhibition taken in infancy are correlated with measures of brain reactivity to stimuli at ages 10 to 12; the correlation held for adults as well (Schwartz et al., 2003; Woodward et al., 2001). Other researchers have demonstrated that temperamental differences are associated with different levels of activity in the left and right hemispheres of the brain (Fox, Henderson, Rubin, Calkins, & Schmidt, 2001; McManis, Kagan, Snidman, & Woodward, 2002).

Proposition 3: Temperamental dispositions persist through childhood and into adulthood. No theorist in the biological camp proposes that initial temperamental dispositions remain unchanged by experience. Still, if temperamental patterns create a bias toward particular behaviors, temperament ought to exhibit at least some stability over time. Such stability ought to show itself in the form of at least modest correlations between measures of a given temperamental dimension at different ages.

Although the research evidence is somewhat mixed, there is growing evidence of consistency in temperamental ratings over rather long periods of infancy and childhood (Kagan & Fox, 2006; Rothbart, Ahadi, Hersey, & Fisher, 2001). In one study involving a group of 450 Australian children, researchers found that mothers' reports of children's irritability, cooperation/manageability, inflexibility, rhythmicity, persistency, and tendency to approach (rather than to avoid) contact were all quite consistent from infancy through age 8 (Pedlow, Sanson, Prior, & Oberklaid, 1993). Similarly, in a longitudinal study of American children from age 1 to age 12, Diana Guerin and Allen Gottfried (1994a, 1994b) found strong consistency in parents' reports of their children's overall "difficultness" as well as approach versus withdrawal, positive versus negative mood, and activity level. In fact, research suggests that temperament differences are stable from the preschool years into adulthood (Caspi, 1998, 2000; Caspi & Shiner, 2006).

Kagan has also found considerable consistency over the childhood years in his measure of inhibition, which is based on direct observation of the child's behavior rather than on the mother's or father's ratings of the child's temperament. He reports that half of the babies in his longitudinal study who had shown high levels of crying and motor activity in response to a novel situation when they were 4 months old were still classified as highly inhibited at age 8, while three-fourths of those rated as uninhibited at 4 months remained in that category 8 years later (Kagan et al., 1993). Furthermore, the inhibited toddlers in Kagan's sample were less likely than their more uninhibited peers to be rated as highly aggressive or delinquent at age 11 (Schwartz, Snidman, & Kagan, 1996).

Thus, babies who readily and positively approach the world around them continue to be more positive as young teenagers; cranky, temperamentally difficult babies continue to show many of the same temperamental qualities 10 years later; and strongly behaviorally inhibited babies are quite likely to continue to show such "shyness" at later ages. Such consistency is probably stronger among children whose temperamental patterns are initially fairly extreme, such as highly inhibited youngsters or those with particularly clear patterns of negative emotionality (e.g., Rubin, Hastings, Stewart, Henderson, & Chen, 1997), but even among children with less extreme patterns, researchers find some degree of consistency.

Proposition 4: Temperamental characteristics interact with the child's environment in ways that may either strengthen or modify the basic temperamental pattern. Despite all the clear evidence for genetic/biological influences on temperament, genetics is clearly not destiny; there is still a good deal of room for environmental influences. For example, the extent to which parents direct the behavior of their children and express warmth toward them seems to be a significant factor in shaping the children's tendency toward positive affect and approach rather than withdrawal (Degnan, Henderson, Fox, & Rubin, 2008; Rubin, Cheah, & Fox, 2001; Rubin & Coplan, 2004). In most cases, the resultant personality develops through some interaction between the child's temperamental tendencies and the environment the child encounters or creates. One factor that tends to strengthen a child's built-in qualities is the fact that we all—including young children—choose our experiences. Highly sociable children seek out contact with others; children low on the activity dimension are more likely to choose sedentary activities like working puzzles or playing board games rather than baseball. Similarly, temperament may affect the way a child interprets a given experience—a factor that helps to account for the fact that two children in the same family may experience the family pattern of interaction quite differently.

Imagine, for example, a family that moves often, such as a military family. If one child in this family has a strong built-in pattern of behavioral inhibition, the myriad changes and new experiences will likely trigger repeated fear responses. This child comes to anticipate each new move with dread and is likely to interpret his family life as highly stressful. A second child in the same family, with a more strongly approach-oriented temperament, finds the many moves stimulating and energizing and is likely to think of his childhood in a much more positive light.

A third environmental factor that often reinforces built-in temperamental patterns is the tendency of parents (and others in the child's world) to respond differently to children with different temperaments. The sociable child, who may smile often, is likely to elicit more smiles and more positive interactions with adults, simply because she has reinforced their behavior by her positive temperament. Buss and Plomin (1984) have proposed the general argument that children in the middle range on temperament dimensions typically adapt to their environment, while those whose temperament is extreme—for example, extremely difficult children—force their environment to adapt to them. Parents of difficult children, for example, adapt to the children's negativity by punishing them more, although often less consistently, than do parents of more adaptable children (Lengua & Kovacs, 2005). This pattern may well contribute to the higher rates of significant emotional problems in such children.

Buss and Plomin's proposal, while it may be accurate, doesn't convey the additional complexities of the process. First, sensitive and responsive parents can moderate the more extreme forms of infant or child temperament; a particularly nice example comes from the work of Megan Gunnar (1994) and her colleagues, who studied a group of highly inhibited toddlers who differed in the security of their attachment to their mothers. As you will learn in Chapter 11, *securely attached* infants use their caregivers as a "safe base" for exploring the world and are easily consoled after a separation from them. *Insecurely attached* infants do not consistently use the caregivers as a safe base and may even avoid them after a period of separation. In a classic series of studies, Gunnar found that insecurely attached inhibited toddlers showed the usual physiological responses to challenging or novel situations. Securely attached temperamentally inhibited toddlers, on the other hand, showed no such indications of physiological arousal in the face of novelty or challenge. Thus, secure attachment appears to have modified a basic physiological/temperamental response. Another example, also involving inhibited/fearful children, comes from the work of Kenneth Rubin and his colleagues (1997), who found that highly inhibited children with oversolicitous mothers showed more persistent inhibition across situations than did those whose mothers were more relaxed and less intrusive or intense.

Thus, while many forces within the environment tend to reinforce a child's basic temperament and thus create stabil-

This child, clinging to her mom's leg, might be rated as relatively high in "behavioral inhibition." She may also be being reinforced for her clinging or shy behavior by her mother's approval of the behavior.

ity and consistency of temperament/personality over time, environmental forces can also push a child toward new patterns or aid a child in controlling extreme forms of basic physiological reactions.

Critique of Biological Theories

Learning Objective 9.4
What are some important criticisms of the biological approach?

The biological approach to the origins of personality has two great strengths. First, it is strongly supported by a large body of empirical research. There is simply no refuting the fact that built-in genetic and physiological patterns underlie what we think of as temperament or personality. This approach thus provides a powerful counterweight to the longtime dominance of psychoanalytic and learning theories of personality development, both of which strongly emphasized environmental influences.

Paradoxically, the second strength of this approach is that it is not purely biological; it is an interactionist approach, very much in keeping with much of the current theorizing about development. The child is born with certain behavioral tendencies, but his eventual personality depends on the transactions between his initial characteristics and the responses of his environment.

On the other side of the ledger, though, there appear to be a number of problems, not the least of which is the continuing lack of agreement on the basic dimensions of temperament. Researchers have used such varying definitions and measures that it is often difficult to compare the results of different investigations.

A second problem has been that many biologically oriented temperament theories have not been fundamentally developmental theories. They allow for change through the mechanism of interaction with the environment, but they do not address the question of whether there are systematic age differences in children's responses to new situations or to people; they do not focus on whether the child's emerging cognitive skills have anything to do with changes in the child's temperamental patterns. They do not, in a word, address how the shared developmental patterns may interact with inborn individual differences. A few theorists have begun to talk about such developmental patterns (e.g., Rothbart & Bates, 1998), but this remains a set of questions in need of exploration.

Neither of these concerns constitutes a refutation of any of the basic tenets of this theoretical approach. Clearly, genetic differences and basic biology are important in shaping individual differences in temperament or personality.

Learning Explanations of Personality

Instead of focusing on what the child brings to the equation, learning theorists have looked at the reinforcement patterns in the environment as the primary cause of differences in children's personality patterns. Of course, theorists in this tradition do not reject biology. Albert Bandura, arguably the most influential theorist in this group, agrees that biological factors (such as hormones) or inherited propensities (such as temperament, presumably) also affect behavior. But he and others of this persuasion look to the environment as the major source of influence.

The Learning Argument

Learning Objective 9.5
What are the basic propositions of learning explanations of personality?

The learning camp includes several distinct schools of thought. Some investigators, often called *radical behaviorists*, argue that only the basic principles of classical and operant conditioning are needed to account for variations in behavior, including personality. Others, among them Bandura, emphasize not only observational learning but also important cognitive elements. However, like the biological explanations, all of the learning approaches are organized around a set of basic propositions. Both groups of learning theorists agree with the first two propositions listed below; the remaining propositions emerge primarily from Bandura's work.

Proposition 1: Behavior is strengthened by reinforcement. If this rule applies to all behavior, then it should apply to attachment patterns, shyness, sharing behavior, and competitiveness. Children who are reinforced for clinging to their parents, for example, should show more clinging than children who are not reinforced for it. Similarly, a nursery school teacher who pays attention to children only when they get rowdy or aggressive should find that the children in her care get steadily more rowdy and aggressive over the course of weeks or months.

Proposition 2: Behavior that is reinforced on a partial schedule should be even stronger and more resistant to extinction than behavior that is consistently reinforced. You read about partial reinforcement in Chapter 1, so you have some idea of what is involved. Most parents are inconsistent in their reinforcement of their children, so most children are on partial schedules of some kind, whether the parents intend that or not. That is, they are sometimes reinforced for a particular behavior, but not every time. Because behavior that is rewarded in this way is highly persistent—highly resistant to extinction, in the language of learning theory—partial reinforcement is a major factor in the establishment of those distinctive and stable patterns of behavior defined as personality.

An immense collection of studies supports these first two propositions. For example, in several studies, experimenters systematically rewarded some children for hitting an inflated rubber clown on the nose. When the researchers later watched the children in free play with peers, they found that the children who had been rewarded showed more hitting, scratching, and kicking than did children who hadn't been rewarded for punching the clown (Walters & Brown, 1963). Partial reinforcement in the form of inconsistent behavior from parents also has the expected effect. For example, one study (Sears, Maccoby, & Levin, 1977) found that parents who permit fairly high levels of aggression in their children, but who occasionally react by punishing them quite severely, have children who are more aggressive than do parents who neither permit nor punish aggression.

Proposition 3: Children learn new behaviors largely through modeling. Bandura has argued that the full range of social behaviors, from competitiveness to nurturance, is learned not just by direct reinforcement but also by watching others behave in those ways. Thus, the child who sees her parents taking a casserole next door to the woman who has just been widowed will learn generosity and thoughtful behavior. The child who sees her parents hitting each other when they are angry will most likely learn violent ways of solving problems.

Children learn from television, too, and from their peers, their teachers, and their brothers and sisters. A boy growing up in an environment where he observes playmates and older boys hanging around street corners, shoplifting, or selling drugs is going to learn those behaviors. His continuous exposure to such antisocial models makes it that much harder for his parents to reinforce more constructive behavior.

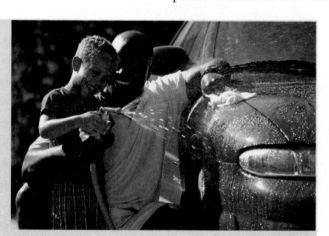

By observing and working next to his dad, this 3-year-old is not only learning how to wash a car; he's also learning his father's attitudes about work and perhaps the beginnings of self-efficacy.

These many effects of observational learning have been demonstrated experimentally in literally hundreds of studies (Bandura, 1973, 1977, 2008). One interesting—and very practical—sidelight to the process of modeling has been the repeated finding that modeling works better than preaching. So, parents' displaying of desired behavior—such as generosity, fairness, or diligent work—is more effective than simply telling children that it is good to be generous, fair, or hardworking. For example, in one early study, Joan Grusec and her colleagues (1978) had elementary school children play a miniature bowling game, ostensibly to test the game. The children first observed an adult "test" the game and saw the adult win 20 marbles. Near the bowling game was a poster that said "Help poor children. Marbles buy gifts." Under the poster was a bowl with some marbles in it. Half of the participants saw the adult model donate half his newly won marbles to this bowl; the other half of the children did not see the model donating marbles. In addition, the model either "preached" about donating marbles or said nothing. To some of the children, the adult preached in specific terms, saying that the child should donate half his marbles when he played the game, since it would be good to make poor children happy by doing that. To the other children, the adult preached in more general terms, saying that the child should donate half his marbles because it is a good thing to make other people happy by helping them any way one can. After demonstrating the game, the adult model then left the room, and the child had an opportunity to play the bowling game and to decide whether to donate any marbles. You can see in Figure 9.2 how many children in each group (out of a maximum of 16) donated marbles. Clearly, modeling increased the effectiveness of preaching. The results also illustrate the point that when a conflict exists between what a model says and what the model does—such as when parents smoke but tell their children not to—children generally follow the behavior and not the verbal message. So the old adage "Do what I say and not what I do" doesn't seem to work.

However, learning from modeling is not an entirely automatic process. Bandura points out that what a child (or adult) learns from watching someone else will depend on four things: what she pays attention to and what she is able to remember (both cognitive processes), what she is physically able to copy, and what she is motivated to imitate. Because attentional abilities, memory, and other cognitive processes change with age through infancy and childhood, what a baby or child can or will learn from any given modeled event also changes through development (Grusec, 1992).

Proposition 4: From reinforcement and modeling, children learn not only overt behavior but also ideas, expectations, internal standards, and self-concepts. The child learns standards for his own behavior and expectancies about what he can and cannot do—which Bandura (1997) calls **self-efficacy**—from specific reinforcements and from modeling. In this way, the child internalizes what he has learned. Once those standards and those expectancies or beliefs are established, they affect the child's behavior in consistent and enduring ways and form the core of what can be called personality (Bandura, Caprara, Barbaranelli, Gerbino, & Pastorelli, 2003).

Figure 9.2
Modeling, Preaching, and Sharing

These results from Grusec's modeling study illustrate the general finding that modeling is more powerful than preaching in changing children's behavior.

(*Source*: Grusec, Saas-Kortsaak & Simutis, 1978, from Table 1, p. 922.)

Critique of Learning Models

Learning Objective 9.6
What are some criticisms of the learning perspective?

Several implications of the learning approach to personality are worth emphasizing. First of all, learning theories can explain either consistency or inconsistency in children's behavior. The behavior of a child who is friendly and smiling both at home and at school, for example, could be explained by saying that the child is being reinforced for that behavior in both settings rather than by assuming that the child has strong "approach tendencies" or a "gregarious temperament." Similarly, if the child is helpful at school but defiant at home, learning theorists invoke the principle that different reinforcement contingencies are at work in the two settings. To be sure, because individuals tend to choose settings that support or reward their accustomed behavior and because a person's behavior tends to elicit similar responses (reinforcements) from others in many settings, there is a bias toward consistency. But learning theorists have less trouble accounting for normal "situational variability" in behavior than do other theorists.

A related implication is that learning theorists are supremely optimistic about the possibility of change. Children's behavior can change if the reinforcement system (or their beliefs about themselves) changes, so problem behavior can be modified. In contrast, biologically oriented temperament theorists, while agreeing that environmental variations can alter or shift the child's built-in temperamental tendencies, are more pessimistic about the likelihood

self-efficacy Bandura's term for an individual's belief in his or her ability to accomplish tasks.

This girl may be excited about learning how to throw a pot (yet another example of modeling), but there is no guarantee that she will be equally interested in learning to cook or to throw a football—a kind of inconsistency that learning theorists can explain more easily than biological temperament theorists can.

of change, particularly for children whose temperamental pattern is extreme. Extremely inhibited children, for example, tend to remain that way, even in supportive environments; extremely irritable, angry, inattentive children ("difficult" children in Chess and Thomas's conceptualization) are highly likely to become aggressive, difficult schoolchildren with a higher-than-normal likelihood of developing antisocial or delinquent patterns later, unless they learn extremely good strategies for self-control (e.g., Eisenberg et al., 2005; Moffitt & Harrington, 1996).

The great strength of the learning view of personality and social behavior is that it gives an accurate picture of the way in which many specific behaviors are learned. It is perfectly clear that children *do* learn through modeling; it is equally clear that children (and adults) will continue to perform behaviors that "pay off" for them.

The cognitive elements in Bandura's theory add further strength, offering a beginning integration of learning models and cognitive-developmental approaches (Mischel, 2007). Bandura's concept of **reciprocal determinism**, shown in Figure 9.3, attempts to explain how the different sets of factors emphasized in these theories interact to influence personality. Each of the three components of Bandura's model influences—and is influenced by—the other two. Moreover, the personal factors include cognitive elements, such as the child's stage of cognitive development, that earlier learning theories ignored (see *Thinking about Research*).

If we were to apply Piaget's language to Bandura's theory, we might refer to the acquisition of a "self-scheme"—a concept of one's own capacities, qualities, standards, and experiences. New experiences are then assimilated to that scheme. You will recall from Chapter 6 that one of the characteristics of the process of assimilation as Piaget proposed it is that new information or experiences are modified as they are taken in. Similarly, Bandura is saying that once the child's self-concept is established, it affects what behaviors he chooses to perform, how he reacts to new experiences, whether he persists or gives up on some new task, and the like. If a child believes he is unpopular, for example, then he will not be surprised if others do not choose to sit by him in the lunchroom; if someone does sit next to him, he's likely to explain it in such a way that he retains his central belief, such as by saying to himself, "There must have been no place else to sit." In this way, the underlying scheme isn't modified (accommodated) very much.

Just as biological temperament theorists argue that inborn temperament serves as a central mediating force, shaping the child's choices and behavior, so in social learning theory the self-concept (or self-scheme) acts as a central mediator, leading to stable differences in behavior of the kind we typically call personality. The self-concept can be modified (accommodated) if the child accumulates enough experience or evidence that doesn't fit with the existing scheme (that is, in learning theory language, if the reinforcement contingencies change in some dramatic way). If an "unpopular" child noticed that classmates regularly chose to sit next to him at lunch even when there were other seats available, he might eventually change his self-scheme, coming to think of himself as "somewhat popular." However, since the child (like an adult) will choose activities or situations that fit his self-concept, such as sitting in the corner where no one is likely to see him, he will be partially protected from such nonconfirming experiences.

To be sure, Bandura and Piaget would not agree on how this self-concept develops. Piaget emphasizes internal processes, while Bandura emphasizes reinforcement and modeling as causal factors. What they agree on is the impact that such a scheme will have once it has developed.

reciprocal determinism
Bandura's model in which personal, behavioral, and environmental factors interact to influence personality development.

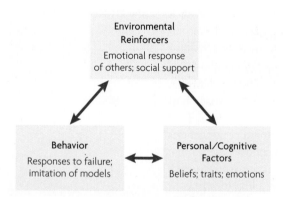

Figure 9.3 **Bandura's Reciprocal Determinism**

Bandura suggests that three components—the external environment, individual behaviors, and cognitive factors such as beliefs, expectancies, and personal dispositions (i.e., personality traits)—are all influenced by each other and play reciprocal roles in shaping personality.

Locus of Control and Adolescent Health

You may have noticed that the same outcome can have quite different effects on two individual children. For instance, one child responds to getting a bad grade in school by studying harder, while another concludes that studying is of no use because school is just too hard. In Bandura's model of reciprocal determinism, an outcome produces different expectations in individuals because it is interpreted differently by them. Varying interpretations result from many factors. A trait called *locus of control*, a set of beliefs about the causes of events, is one of the most influential of these factors (Rotter, 1990).

Locus of control develops across the middle childhood and early teen years and is well established by mid-adolescence. An individual with an *external locus of control* attributes the causes of experiences (for example, school failure) to factors outside herself. A high school student with an external locus of control might claim that she failed a class because it was too difficult, an explanation that implies that she believes she has no control over what happens to her. A person with an

internal locus of control views variables inside a person as responsible for outcomes. A high school student with an internal locus of control would say that he failed a class because he didn't study enough, a judgment that suggests that he believes he has control over academic outcomes.

An external locus of control predisposes a teenager to procrastinate, to avoid confronting problems, and to develop a self-defeating form of perfectionism (i.e., unwillingness to pursue a goal unless success is guaranteed) (Janssen & Carton, 1999; Periasamy & Ashby, 2002). Not surprisingly, research shows that adolescents with an external locus of control are less successful in school than their peers with an internal locus of control (Pennington, 2000). Perhaps more striking, though, are the associations that have been found between locus of control and health outcomes. One such finding is that teens with an external locus of control are less likely than those with an internal locus to follow medical advice when they are diagnosed with a serious medical condition, such as a sexually transmitted disease (Kahn et al., 2005). Girls

with an external locus of control are also more likely than their peers are to engage in unsafe sex practices and to get pregnant (Young, Turner, Denny, & Young, 2004).

These findings suggest that having an external locus of control increases teenagers' vulnerability to a variety of health threats. Moreover, researchers have found that an external locus of control is quite resistant to change. Thus, they are searching for more effective strategies for identifying and intervening with teens who exhibit an external locus of control (Young & Bradley, 1998).

Questions for Critical Analysis

1. What kind of research would be required to test the effectiveness of an intervention program aimed at changing teenagers' locus of control?
2. How would a social cognitive theorist, such as Bandura, explain the process through which individuals develop locus of control beliefs?

The learning theories, particularly the more radical versions, also have significant weaknesses. First, from the perspective of many psychologists, these theories still place too much emphasis on what happens to the child and not enough on what the child is doing with the information she has (Thomas, 2000). Bandura's theory is much less vulnerable to this charge, but most learning theories of personality are highly mechanistic and focused on external events. Second, like biological temperament theories, learning theories are not really developmental. They can say how a child might acquire a particular behavior pattern or belief, but they do not take into account the underlying developmental changes that are occurring. Do 3-year-olds and 10-year-olds develop a sense of self-efficacy in the same way? Do they learn the same amount or in the same way from modeling? Given Bandura's emphasis on the cognitive aspects of the modeling process, a genuinely developmental social learning theory could emerge in the coming years. Still, despite these limitations, all the theories in this group offer useful descriptions of one source of influence on the child's developing pattern of behavior.

Psychoanalytic Explanations of Personality

Like many temperament theorists and those social learning theorists like Bandura, psychoanalytic theorists believe that the interaction between the child's inborn characteristics and the environment plays a central role in shaping differences in personality. However, unlike most temperament or learning approaches, psychoanalytic theories are clearly developmental as well, describing systematic changes in children's sense of self, in their needs or drives, and in their relationships with others.

Learning Objective 9.7

What are the major points of the psychoanalytic approach to personality?

The Psychoanalytic Argument

You read about psychoanalytic theories in Chapter 1, so the major propositions of this approach should be familiar.

Proposition 1: Behavior is governed by unconscious as well as conscious motives and processes. Freud emphasized three sets of instinctual drives: the sexual drive (libido); life-preserving drives, including avoidance of hunger and pain; and aggressive drives. Erikson emphasizes a more cognitive process, the drive for identity.

Proposition 2: Personality structure develops over time, as a result of the interaction between the child's inborn drives and needs and the responses of the key people in the child's world. Because the child is often prevented from achieving instant gratification of his various drives, he is forced to develop new skills—planning, talking, delaying, and other cognitive techniques that allow gratification of the basic needs in more indirect ways. Thus, the ego is created, and it remains the planning, organizing, thinking part of the personality. The superego, in turn, develops because parents and other adults try to restrain certain kinds of gratification; the child eventually incorporates these adult standards into his own personality.

Proposition 3: Development of personality is fundamentally stagelike, with each stage centered on a particular task or a particular basic need. You'll read about both Freud's and Erikson's stages in some detail below. The key point is simply that there are stages in these theories.

Proposition 4: The specific personality a child develops depends on the degree of success the child has in moving through the various stages. In each stage, the child requires a particular kind of supportive environment in order to successfully resolve that particular dilemma or meet that need. A child lacking the needed environment will have a very different personality from one whose environment is partially or wholly adequate. However, while each stage is important, all the psychoanalytic theorists strongly emphasize the crucial significance of the very earliest stages and focus especially on the adequacy of the relationship between the baby and the central caregiver, usually the mother. This is not quite like saying that infancy is a sensitive period for personality development; rather, Freud and later psychoanalytic theorists argue that the earliest relationship establishes a pattern and sets the child on a particular pathway through the remainder of the stages.

All four of these general propositions are contained in both Freud's and Erikson's theories, but both the details and the emphases differ in important respects. In Freud's theory, for example, cognitive skills develop only because the child needs them to obtain gratification; they have no independent life. In Erikson's theory (and in many other variations of psychoanalytic theory), cognitive skills are part of a set of ego functions that are presumed to develop independently, rather than arising entirely in the service of basic gratification.

Basic physical maturation is also more central to Freud's theory than to Erikson's. In Freud's theory, the stages shift from one to the next in part because of maturation of the nervous system. In each stage, the child is attempting to gratify basic physical ("sexual") needs through stimulation of a particular part of the body—that part of the body that is most sensitive at that time. As neurological development proceeds, maximum body sensitivity shifts from the mouth to the anus to the genitals, and this maturational change is part of what drives the stage changes. Erikson acknowledges such physical changes but places greater emphasis on shifts in the demands of the social environment. For Erikson, each stage centers on a specific social conflict, resulting in a psychosocial crisis. For example, stage 4 ("industry versus inferiority") begins at about age 6, because that is when the child goes off to school; in a culture in which schooling is delayed, the timing of the developmental task might be delayed as well.

Because of such theoretical differences, Erikson and Freud have described the stages of development differently. Because both sets of stages have become part of the vocabulary of developmental psychology, you need to be conversant with both.

Freud's Psychosexual Stages

Freud proposed five **psychosexual stages**, which are summarized in Table 9.2.

The Oral Stage: Birth to 1 Year   The mouth, lips, and tongue are the first centers of pleasure for the baby, and his earliest attachment is to the one who provides pleasure in the mouth, usually his mother. For normal development, the infant requires some optimal amount of oral stimulation—not too much and not too little. If the optimal amount of stimulation is unavailable, then some libidinal energy may remain attached to ("fixated on," in Freud's terms) the oral mode of gratification. Such an individual, Freud thought, will continue to have a strong preference for oral pleasures in later life, as you can see in the right-hand column in Table 9.2.

The Anal Stage: 1 to 3 Years   As the body matures, the baby becomes more and more sensitive in the anal region. And as she matures physically, her parents begin to place great emphasis on toilet training and express approval when she manages to perform in the right place at the right time. These two forces together help to shift the major center of physical and sexual sensitivity from the oral to the anal region.

The key to the child's successful completion of this stage (according to Freud) is how parents manage toilet training. If toilet training becomes a major battleground, then some fixation of energy at this stage may occur—with the possible adult consequences of excessive orderliness and stinginess or the opposite of these.

The Phallic Stage: 3 to 5 Years   At about 3 or 4 years of age, the genitals become increasingly sensitive, ushering in a new stage. One sign of this new sensitivity is that children of both sexes normally begin to masturbate at about this age. In Freud's view, the most important event that occurs during the phallic stage is the so-called **Oedipus conflict**. He described the sequence of events more fully (and slightly more believably!) for boys.

According to Freud, during the phallic stage, the boy, having discovered his penis, rather naively wishes to use this newfound source of pleasure to please his oldest source of pleasure, his mother. He becomes envious of his father, who has access to the mother's body in a way that the boy does not. The boy also sees his father as a powerful and threatening figure who has ultimate power—the power to castrate. The boy is caught between desire for his mother and fear of his father's power.

psychosexual stages The stages of personality development suggested by Freud, consisting of the oral, anal, phallic, latency, and genital stages.

Oedipus conflict The pattern of events that Freud believed occur between ages 3 and 5, when the child experiences a sexual desire for the parent of the opposite sex; the resulting fear of possible reprisal from the parent of the same sex is resolved when the child identifies with that parent.

Table 9.2   Freud's Stages of Psychosexual Development

Stage	Age (years)	Sensitive Zones	Major Developmental Task (potential source of conflict)	Personality Traits of Adults "Fixated" at This Stage
Oral	0–1	Mouth, lips, tongue	Weaning	Oral behavior, such as smoking and overeating; passivity and gullibility
Anal	1–3	Anus	Toilet training	Orderliness, stinginess, obstinacy, or the opposites
Phallic	3–5	Genitals	Oedipus conflict; identification with same-sex parent	Vanity, recklessness, or the opposites
Latency	5–12	No specific area; sexual energy is latent	Development of ego defense mechanisms	None; fixation does not normally occur
Genital	12–18 and adulthood	Genitals	Mature sexual intimacy	None; adults who have successfully integrated earlier stages should emerge with a sincere interest in others and mature sexuality.

In elementary school, boys play with boys, girls play with girls. How would Freud explain this?

Most of these feelings and the resultant conflict are unconscious. The boy does not have overt sexual feelings or behave sexually toward his mother. But unconscious or not, the result of this conflict is anxiety. How can the little boy handle this anxiety? In Freud's view, the boy responds with a defensive process called *identification*: The boy "incorporates" his image of his father and attempts to match his own behavior to that image. By trying to make himself as much like his father as possible, the boy not only reduces the chance of an attack from the father; he takes on some of the father's power as well. Furthermore, it is the "inner father," with his values and moral judgments, that serves as the core of the child's superego.

According to Freud, a parallel process occurs in girls. The girl sees her mother as a rival for her father's sexual attentions and has some fear of her mother (though less than the boy has of his father, since the girl may assume she has already been castrated). In this case, too, identification with the mother is thought to be the "solution" to the girl's anxiety.

The Latency Stage: 5 to 12 Years Freud thought that after the phallic stage came a sort of resting period before the next major change in the child's sexual development. The child has presumably arrived at some preliminary resolution of the Oedipus conflict and now experiences a kind of calm after the storm. One of the obvious characteristics of this stage is that the identification with the same-sex parent that defined the end of the phallic stage is now extended to others of the same sex. So it is during these years that children's peer interactions are almost exclusively with members of the same sex and that children often have "crushes" on same-sex teachers or other adults.

The Genital Stage: 12 to 18 and Older The further changes in hormones and the genital organs that take place during puberty reawaken the sexual energy of the child. During this period, a more mature form of sexual attachment occurs. From the beginning of this period, the child's sexual objects are people of the opposite sex. Freud placed some emphasis on the fact that not everyone works through this period to a point of mature heterosexual love. Some people have not had a satisfactory oral period and thus do not have a foundation of basic love relationships. Some have not resolved the Oedipus conflict and arrived at a complete or satisfactory identification with the same-sex parent, a failure that may affect their ability to cope with rearoused sexual energies in adolescence.

Optimal development at each stage, according to Freud, requires an environment that satisfies the unique needs of each period. The baby needs sufficient oral and anal stimulation; the 4-year-old boy needs a father present with whom to identify and a mother who is not too seductive. An inadequate early environment will leave a residue of unresolved problems and unmet needs, which are then carried forward to subsequent stages. This emphasis on the formative role of early experience, particularly early family experience, is a hallmark of psychoanalytic theories. In this view, the first 5 or 6 years of life are critical for the development of the individual personality.

Learning Objective 9.9
How does Erikson's theory explain personality development?

Erikson's Psychosocial Stages

Erikson shared most of Freud's basic assumptions, but there are some crucial differences between the two theories. First, Erikson placed less emphasis on the centrality of sexual drive and instead focused on a stepwise emergence of a sense of identity. Second, although he agreed with Freud that the early years are highly important, Erikson argued that identity is not fully formed at the end of adolescence but continues to move through further developmental stages in adult life. You can see in Table 9.3 the eight **psychosocial stages** that Erikson proposed, three of which are reached only in adulthood.

In Erikson's view, maturation plays a relatively small role in the sequence of stages. Far more important are common cultural demands on children of a particular age, such as the demand that the child become toilet trained at about age 2, that the child learn school skills at age 6 or 7, or that the young adult form an intimate partnership. Each stage, then, centers on a particular *dilemma*, or social task. Thus, Erikson called his stages psychosocial stages rather than psychosexual stages.

Basic Trust versus Basic Mistrust: Birth to 1 Year

The first task (or dilemma) occurs during the first year of life, when the child must develop a sense of basic trust in the predictability of the world and in his ability to affect the events around him. Erikson believed that the behavior of the major caregiver (usually the mother) is critical to the child's successful or unsuccessful resolution of this task. Children who reach the end of the first year with a firm sense of trust are those whose parents are loving and respond predictably and reliably to the child. A child who has developed a sense of trust will go on to other relationships, carrying this sense with him. Those infants whose early care has been erratic or harsh may develop mistrust, and they too carry this sense with them into later relationships.

Erikson never said, by the way, that the ideal or "correct" resolution to any of the dilemmas was to arrive at the ego quality at one end of the continuum. In the first stage, for example, there is some risk in being too trusting. The child also needs to develop some healthy mistrust, such as learning to discriminate between dangerous and safe situations.

Autonomy versus Shame and Doubt: 2 to 3 Years

Erikson saw the child's greater mobility during the toddler years as forming the basis for the sense of independence or autonomy. But if the child's efforts at independence are not carefully guided by the parents and she experiences repeated failures or ridicule, then the results of all the new opportunities for exploration may be shame and doubt instead of a basic sense of self-control and self-worth. Once again, the ideal is not for the child to have *no* shame or doubt; some doubt is needed for the child to understand which behaviors are acceptable and which

psychosocial stages The stages of personality development suggested by Erikson, involving tasks centered on trust, autonomy, initiative, industry, identity, intimacy, generativity, and ego integrity.

Table 9.3 Erikson's Eight Psychosocial Stages of Development

Approximate Age (years)	Ego Quality to Be Developed	Some Tasks and Activities of the Stage
0–1	Basic trust versus basic mistrust	Develop trust in mother or central caregiver and in one's own ability to make things happen, a key element in an early secure attachment
2–3	Autonomy versus shame, doubt	Develop walking, grasping, and other physical skills that lead to free choice; complete toilet training; child learns control but may develop shame if not handled properly
4–5	Initiative versus guilt	Learn to organize activities around some goal; become more assertive and aggressive
6–12	Industry versus inferiority	Absorb all the basic cultural skills and norms; including school skills and tool use
13–18	Identity versus role confusion	Adapt sense of self to physical changes of puberty, make occupational choice, achieve adultlike sexual identity, and search for new values
19–25	Intimacy versus isolation	Form one or more intimate relationships that go beyond adolescent love; marry and form family groups
26–40	Generativity versus stagnation	Bear and rear children, focus on occupational achievement or creativity, and train the next generation
41+	Ego integrity versus despair	Integrate earlier stages and come to terms with basic identity; accept self

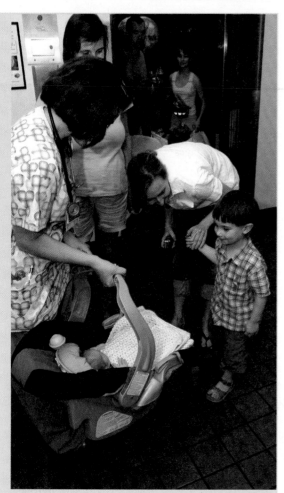

This preschooler, who is in the stage Erikson calls initiative versus guilt, may develop resentful or aggressive thoughts about his new baby brother. If so, the guilt he feels may help him inhibit any actions that may arise from these feelings.

are not, which are safe and which are dangerous. But the ideal does lie toward the autonomy end of the continuum.

Initiative versus Guilt: 4 to 5 Years   This phase, roughly equivalent to Freud's phallic stage, is also ushered in by new skills or abilities in the child. The 4-year-old is able to plan a bit, to take the initiative in reaching particular goals. The child tries out these new cognitive skills and attempts to conquer the world around him. He may try to go out into the street on his own; he may take a toy apart, and then find he can't put it back together and throw the parts at his mother. It is a time of vigorous action and of behaviors that parents may see as aggressive. The risk is that the child may go too far in his forcefulness or that the parents may restrict and punish too much—either of which can produce guilt. Some guilt is needed, since without it the child would develop no conscience and no self-control. The ideal interaction between parent and child is certainly not total indulgence, but too much guilt can inhibit the child's creativity and interactions with others.

Industry (Competence) versus Inferiority: 6 to 12 Years   The beginning of schooling is a major force in ushering in this stage. The child is now faced with the need to win approval by developing specific competences—learning to read, to do math, and to succeed at other school skills. The task of this period is thus simply to develop the repertoire of abilities society demands of the child. If the child is unable to develop the expected skills, she will develop instead a basic sense of inferiority. Yet some failure is necessary so that the child can develop some humility; as always, balance is an issue. Ideally, the child must have sufficient success to encourage a sense of competence but should not place so much emphasis on competence that failure is unacceptable or that she becomes a "workaholic."

Identity versus Role Confusion: 13 to 18 Years   The task that faces the child during puberty is a major one in which the adolescent reexamines his identity and the roles he must occupy. Erikson suggested that two "identities" are involved—a sexual identity and an occupational identity. What should emerge for the adolescent from this period is a reintegrated sense of self, of what one wants to do and be, and of one's appropriate sexual role. The risk is that the child may suffer confusion, arising from the profusion of roles opening up at this age.

Learning Objective 9.10

What evidence is there to support the psychoanalytic perspective on personality?

Evidence and Applications

Empirical explorations of Freud's or Erikson's theories are relatively rare, largely because both theories are so general that specific tests are very difficult to perform. For example, to test Freud's notion of fixation, researchers would need much more information about how to determine whether a given child is fixated at some stage. What is a sign that a child is fixated at the oral or the anal stage? Is there some automatic connection between how early a child is weaned and such ostensibly oral adult behavior as smoking or overeating? When researchers have searched for such direct linkages, they have not found them.

Despite these difficulties, researchers have managed to observe instances of some of Freud's psychosexual stages. For instance, one 4-year-old boy, after his mother told him that she loved him, said, "And I love you too, and that's why I can't ever marry someone else" (Watson & Getz, 1990a, p. 29). In their studies of Oedipal behavior, Malcolm Watson and

Kenneth Getz (1990a, 1990b) have indeed found that children of about 4 or 5 are likely to make comments like this. More generally, they have found that 4-year-olds, more than any other age group, show more affectionate behavior toward the opposite-sex parent and more aggressive or antagonistic behavior toward the same-sex parent. You can see the results of a study of aggressive and antagonistic behavior in Figure 9.4. Whether Freud's explanation of this phenomenon is the correct one remains to be seen, but these observations are certainly consistent with his theory.

A second research area that has its roots in psychoanalytic theory is the current work on the security or insecurity of children's early attachments. Both Erikson and Freud argued that the quality of the child's first relationship with the central caregiver will shape her relationships with other children and other adults at later ages. You'll be reading a great deal more about early attachments in Chapter 11, but here it is sufficient to note that research in this area provides a good deal of support for the basic psychoanalytic hypothesis that the quality of the child's earliest relationship affects the whole course of her later development. Dozens of longitudinal studies have assessed children's attachment security at age 1 or 2 and then followed them over a period of years—in some cases throughout childhood and adolescence. The consistent finding is that children who had a more secure attachment in infancy have more positive relationships with others and are more socially skillful later on (Thompson, 1998). Thus, the relationship formed during the earliest stage of psychosocial development seems to create a prototype for later relationships, as Erikson proposed. Recall, too, the result from the study by Gunnar (1994) described earlier: Temperamentally inhibited toddlers who have formed a secure attachment to their mothers show little or no physiological sign of fearfulness in a novel setting. Thus, the quality of the child's early attachment can at least partially override basic temperamental tendencies as the personality is formed.

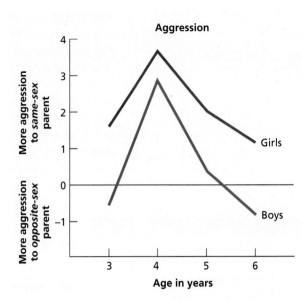

Figure 9.4   Age and Parent-Directed Aggression

This figure graphs data from the detailed reports of parents on their children's affectionate and aggressive behavior toward them. Scores above 0 mean that the child was more aggressive toward the same-sex parent than toward the opposite-sex parent; scores below 0 mean the reverse.

(*Source*: Watson & Getz, 1990b, from Table 3, p. 499.)

Critique of Psychoanalytic Theories

Learning Objective 9.11

What are some criticisms of psycho-analytic theories?

Freud's and Erikson's psychoanalytic theories are attractive for several reasons. Perhaps their greatest strength is that they provide us with a better account of the complexities of personality development than other perspectives, especially the learning theories (Seligman, 2005). In psychoanalytic theory, a particular characteristic of the environment, such as inconsistent parenting, is not hypothesized to have a specific effect on development. Instead, psychoanalysts predict that the effects of such factors depend on how individual children perceive them, the stage of development in which children experience them, and, in Erikson's case, the cultural context in which they occur.

Moreover, psychoanalytic theories focus on the importance of the emotional quality of the child's relationship with caregivers. These theories suggest that the child's needs or tasks change with age, so that the parents must constantly adapt to the changing child. One of the implications of this observation is that "good parenting" should not be thought of as if it were a global quality. Some parents may be very good at meeting the needs of an infant but terrible at dealing with a teenager's identity struggles; others may have the opposite pattern. The child's eventual personality and her overall emotional health thus depend on the interaction, or *transaction*, that develops in a particular family. This is an attractive element of psychoanalytic theories, because research within developmental psychology is increasingly supporting a transactional conception of the process of development (Blatt, 2008).

Psychoanalytic theory has also given psychologists a number of helpful concepts, such as defense mechanisms and identification, that have been so widely adopted that they have become a part of everyday language as well as theory. These strengths have led to a resurgence of influence of both Erikson's theory and several related psychoanalytic approaches.

The great weakness of all the psychoanalytic approaches is the fuzziness of many of the concepts. Identification may be an intriguing theoretical notion, but how can it be measured? How do researchers detect the presence of specific defense mechanisms? Without more precise operational definitions, it is impossible to test the theories. The general concepts of psychoanalytic theories have furthered an understanding of development only when other theorists or researchers have offered more precise definitions or clearer methods for measuring some psychoanalytic construct, such as the concept of security of attachment that you will read about in Chapter 11. Psychoanalytic theory may thus sometimes offer a provocative way of thinking about personality, but it is not a precise theory of development.

Learning Objective 9.12

How can elements of the biological, learning, and psychoanalytic approaches be combined into a comprehensive explanation of personality?

A Possible Synthesis

You have read about three different views of the origins of those unique, individual patterns of behavior we call personality. Each view can be at least partially supported with research evidence; each has clear strengths. Do developmentalists need to choose just one of them, or can the views be combined in a way that makes sense? Some argue that theories as different as these cannot ever be combined, because they make such different assumptions about the child's role in the process of personality development (Lerner, Theokas, & Bobek, 2005; Overton & Reese, 1973). Nonetheless, combinations of these varying perspectives, like the one shown in Figure 9.5, may still be fruitful. This model suggests that the child's inborn temperament is a beginning point—an initial, highly significant bias in the system. Arrow 1 suggests a direct relationship between that inborn temperament and the eventual personality seen in the child and later in the adult.

Arrow 2 suggests a second direct effect, between the pattern of the child's environment and his eventual personality and social behavior. Whether the parents respond reliably and

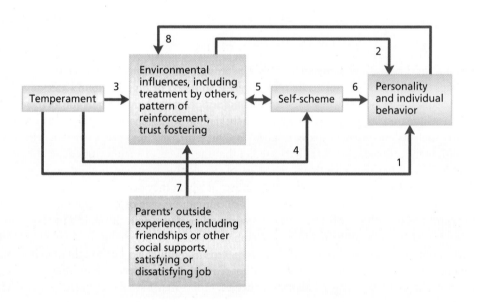

Figure 9.5   An Interactive Model of Personality

Here is one version of a complex interactive model describing the formation of individual personality. The effects of inborn temperament and environmental influences are not merely additive. That is, the whole is greater than the sum of its parts. Each affects the other, helping to create the child's unique self-scheme, which in turn affects the child's experiences. All this occurs within the context of the family, which is itself influenced by the parents' own life experiences. What developmentalists think of as personality is a complex product of all these forces.

appropriately to the infant will affect his trust, or the security of his attachment, which will show up in a range of behaviors later; whether the parents reinforce aggressive or friendly behavior will influence the child's future as well.

These direct effects are straightforward, even obvious, but most of what happens is much more complicated than that. The way the child is treated is influenced by her temperament (arrow 3), and both that basic temperament and the family environment affect the child's self-scheme, or self-concept—her expectations for others and herself, her beliefs about her own abilities (arrows 4 and 5). This self-scheme (including the child's sense of self-efficacy), in turn, helps to shape the child's overt behavior, which reflects her "personality" (arrow 6).

This system does not exist in a vacuum. In keeping with the ecological approach of Bronfenbrenner and others, arrow 7 suggests that the parents' ability to maintain a loving and supportive relationship with their child is influenced by the parents' own outside experiences, such as whether they like their jobs or whether they have enough emotional support to help them weather their own crises.

For example, Mavis Hetherington (1989) reports that children with difficult temperaments show more problem behavior in response to their parents' divorce than do children with easier temperaments, but this difference exists only if the mother is also depressed and has inadequate social support. In this study, those difficult children whose divorcing mothers were not depressed did not show heightened levels of problems. Thus, the child's temperament clearly seems to have an impact, but the effect of temperament can be and is modified by the parents' pattern of response.

Another illustration of the intricacy of the system comes from the work of Susan Crockenberg (e.g., Crockenberg & Leerkes, 2004). In one early study (1981), Crockenberg studied a group of 48 mothers and infants over the first year of life. She measured each child's irritability (an aspect of temperament) when the baby was 5 to 10 days old and assessed the security of the child's attachment to the mother when the child was 12 months old. We might expect that irritable babies would be more likely to be insecurely attached, merely because they are more difficult to care for. In fact, Crockenberg found a small effect of this kind (see Table 9.4). But Crockenberg didn't stop there. She also measured the level of the mother's social support—the degree of help she received from family and friends in dealing with the strains of having a new child or other life changes she might be experiencing. The results of the study show that insecure attachment in the child was most likely when the mother had an irritable infant and low levels of support. If the baby was irritable, but the mother had good support, the child nearly always developed secure attachment. Only when two difficult conditions occurred together did a poor outcome result for the child.

In a later study, Crockenberg (1987) found that a higher level of anger and noncompliant behavior (perhaps reflections of what is called *neuroticism* in the Big Five) was common in toddlers who had been irritable as infants and whose mothers were angry and punitive

Table 9.4 Influence of Child's Temperament and Mother's Social Support on the Child's Secure or Insecure Attachment

Child Irritability	Mother's Social Support	Securely Attached Children	Insecurely Attached Children
High	Low	2	9
High	High	12	1
Low	Low	7	2
Low	High	13	2

Source: From S. B. Crockenberg, Table 5, 862, "Infant Irritability, Mother Responsiveness, and Social Support Influences on the Security of Infant-Mother Attachment," *Child Development, 52,* 1981, p. 857–865. By permission of the Society for Research in Child Development.

toward them. Furthermore, such angry and punitive behavior by the mother was more likely if the mother had experienced rejection in her own childhood and if she experienced little support from her partner. Clearly, Crockenberg's work reveals a system of effects.

Returning to Figure 9.5, you'll see that arrow 8 emphasizes the transactional elements of the system. Once the child's unique pattern of behaviors and attitudes (personality) is formed, this pattern affects the environment she will encounter, the experiences she will choose, and the responses of the people around her, which in turn affect her behavior (Feinberg, Reiss, Niederhiser, & Hetherington, 2005).

No doubt even this fairly complex system underestimates the intricacy of the process of personality development in the child. Most research does not yet encompass all the pieces of the puzzle. But the very fact that developmental psychologists are turning toward such complex models is a very good thing. Development *is* complex, and developmentalists will not be able to describe it or explain it until they begin to examine and try to measure all these separate forces.

Think Critically

- Suppose that parents received an "owners' manual" for their children at birth, and that one of the features of the owners manual was a complete description of the child's temperament. In what way would having such information so early in a child's life affect parents' responses to children? How might parental access to such information facilitate or impede the development of children's personalities?
- As you learned in the chapter, children with difficult temperaments are punished more often than those who are more easy-going. How would you explain this finding using the interactive model in Figure 9.5 on page 250?

Conduct Your Own Research

As Freud's description of the latency stage would predict, researchers have found that the tendency for school-aged children to segregate themselves by gender is universal. There also appear to be universal rules defining socially acceptable contact between preadolescent boys and girls (Sroufe, Bennett, England, Urban, & Schulman, 1993). Some examples of acceptable girl-boy interactions are (1) accidental contact; (2) contact compelled by an adult, as when a teacher forces a boy to work with a girl in class; (3) and contact accompanied by verbal taunts, insults, or mild physical aggression such as pushing. You can observe both gender-segregated play and rule-governed cross-gender contact on any school playground. As you watch children at play, note the following: (1) the number of contacts between boys and girls; (2) the type of contact (accidental, compelled, or aggressive); (3) children's comments to or about a boy or girl who violates gender segregation rules; and (4) the kinds of activities exhibited by boys' groups and girls' groups. Use your data to hypothesize some additional rules governing children's relations with peers of the same sex and of the opposite sex.

Summary

DEFINING PERSONALITY

9.1 What are the dimensions of temperament that most psychologists agree on?

- Researchers studying infants and young children have studied temperament rather than personality. Temperament is now widely seen as a set of built-in, behavior tendencies that form the emotional substrate of personality. There are sizeable differences among temperament theorists regarding how best to characterize the basic dimensions of temperament, but there is general agreement on five key dimensions: activity level, approach/positive emotionality, inhibition and anxiety, negative emotionality/irritability/anger, and effortful control/task persistence.

9.2 How do advocates for the Big Five approach define personality?

- Researchers studying adult personality have agreed on a set of five dimensions (the Big Five) that capture most of the variation among individuals: extraversion, agreeableness, conscientiousness, neuroticism, and openness/intellect. Recent research suggests that the same five dimensions may give an accurate picture of variations in children's and adolescents' personalities as well.

GENETIC AND BIOLOGICAL EXPLANATIONS OF PERSONALITY

9.3 What is the focus of the biological approach to personality?

- Biological explanations of temperament and personality, focusing on genetic differences in patterns or styles of reacting to people and the environment, are well supported by research. Evidence is also accumulating that specific differences in neurological and chemical responses underlie many observed variations in behavior. However, temperament is clearly not totally determined by heredity or ongoing physiological processes, although the child's built-in temperament does shape her interactions with the world and affect others' responses to her.

9.4 What are some important criticisms of the biological approach?

- Critics point out that theorists do not agree on the basic dimensions of temperament. In addition, biological theories ignore important factors such as children's cognitive interpretations of events.

LEARNING EXPLANATIONS OF PERSONALITY

9.5 What are the basic propositions of learning explanations of personality?

- Traditional learning theorists emphasize the role of basic learning processes, such as reinforcement, in shaping individual behaviors, including patterns of interaction with others. Social/cognitive learning theorists such as Bandura also emphasize the role of observational learning as well as the role of the child's learned expectancies, standards, and self-efficacy beliefs in creating more enduring patterns of response.

9.6 What are some criticisms of the learning perspective?

- Critics argue that learning theories place too much importance on what is happening to the child and pay too

little attention to how the child acts on his environment. They also suggest that learning theories explain only how children acquire specific behaviors, not the underlying processes that drive personality development.

PSYCHOANALYTIC EXPLANATIONS OF PERSONALITY

9.7 What are the major points of the psychoanalytic approach to personality?

- Psychoanalytic theorists emphasize the importance of unconscious motives and processes as well as the stagelike emergence of personality. This approach views the relationship of the child with significant adults, particularly in early infancy, as critical. While Freud's and Erikson's theories share a common set of assumptions, they differ with respect to the importance of the libido. In addition, Freud proposed that personality development was completed in childhood, while Erikson claimed that change continued throughout the lifespan.

9.8 How does Freud's theory explain personality development?

- Freud emphasized the unconscious emotional struggles that arise as a child adapts to the demands of the family environment. In addition, his psychosexual stages are strongly affected by maturation. Particularly significant is the phallic stage, beginning at about age 3 or 4, when the Oedipus conflict arises and is resolved through the process of identification.

9.9 How does Erikson's theory explain personality development?

- Erikson agreed with Freud that the struggle that takes place between the child's desires and needs and the demands of the environment shapes personality. However, he placed more emphasis on the culture at large than did Freud, who emphasized primarily the child's immediate family. Erikson's psychosocial stages are influenced both by social demands and by the child's physical and intellectual skills. Each of the major stages has a central task, or dilemma, relating to some aspect of the development of identity.

9.10 What evidence is there to support the psychoanalytic perspective on personality?

- Psychoanalytic theories have been broadly confirmed in some aspects, such as the impact of early attachment on later functioning.

9.11 What are some criticisms of psychoanalytic theories?

- Critics point out that psychoanalytic theories are difficult to test because of their imprecision.

A POSSIBLE SYNTHESIS

9.12 How can elements of the biological, learning, and psychoanalytic approaches be combined into a comprehensive explanation of personality?

- Elements of all three views can be combined into a transactional, or interactionist, view of personality de-velopment. Temperament may serve as the base from which personality grows, both by affecting behavior directly and by affecting the way others respond to the child. Both the child's temperament and the specific pattern of response from the people in the child's environment affect the child's self-concept, or self-scheme, which then helps to create stability in the child's unique pattern of behavior.

Key Terms

agreeableness (p. 233)

Big Five (p. 233)

conscientiousness (p. 233)

extraversion (p. 233)

neuroticism (p. 233)

Oedipus conflict (p. 245)

openness/intellect (p. 233)

personality (p. 230)

psychosexual stages (p. 245)

psychosocial stages (p. 247)

reciprocal determinism (p. 242)

self-efficacy (p. 241)

the various sources of information he has about his own actions and their impact. In particular, over the first year, the infant develops a sense of himself as an agent in the world—as able to make things happen. The delight the baby shows when he is able to make a mobile move or create a noise by squeezing a squeaky toy is evidence of the baby's emerging sense of himself as an agent—the first step in the formation of a self-concept. Albert Bandura argues that the roots of the sense of self-efficacy are found during this first year, when the infant realizes he can control certain events in the world.

This sense of efficacy or control occurs not just with inanimate objects but perhaps even more centrally in interactions with adults, who respond appropriately to the child's behavior—smiling back when the baby smiles, making funny faces when the baby does particular things, playing repetitive games like peek-a-boo while changing diapers or feeding the baby. Of course the baby is not "causing" these things to happen in most cases; it is the parents who are initiating the games or patterns. But within these games and patterns are myriad repetitions of sequences in which the baby does something and the parent responds with some predictable behavior. From the baby's perspective, he has "made it happen," and his sense of self, of efficacy or agency, is established.

Piaget also argued that a critical element in the development of the subjective self is the understanding of object permanence that develops at about 9 to 12 months. Just as the infant is figuring out that mom and dad continue to exist when they are out of sight, he is figuring out—at least in some preliminary way—that he exists separately and has some permanence.

The Objective Self

Learning Objective 10.2
What does acquisition of an objective self add to the infant's self-concept?

The second major step in the development of a self-concept is for the toddler to come to understand that she is also an object in the world. Just as a ball has properties—roundness, the ability to roll, a certain feel in the hand—so the self also has properties, such as gender, size, a name, and qualities like shyness or boldness, coordination or clumsiness. It is this self-awareness that is the hallmark of the "me" self.

Studying Self-Awareness Babies as young as 4 months old respond differently to live video or still photographic images of themselves and others (Rochat & Striano, 2002). For example, they look longer at images of others than they do at images of themselves. They also smile more in response to pictures of other babies. However, developmentalists believe that this type of discrimination is only a precursor to true self-awareness.

The most common procedure psychologists use to measure self-awareness involves a mirror. First the baby is placed in front of a mirror, just to see how she behaves. Most infants of about 9 to 12 months will look at their own images, make faces, or try to interact with the baby in the mirror in some way. After allowing this free exploration for a time, the experimenter, while pretending to wipe the baby's face with a cloth, puts a spot of rouge on the baby's nose and then again lets the baby look in the mirror. The crucial test of self-recognition, and thus of awareness of the self, is whether the baby

At 4 months, Lucy's pleasure at looking at herself in a mirror comes from the fact that this is an interesting moving object to inspect—not from any understanding that this is herself in the mirror.

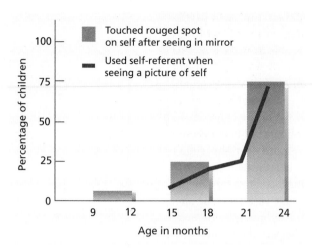

Figure 10.1   Self-Recognition in Infancy

Mirror recognition and self-naming develop at almost exactly the same time.

(*Source*: Lewis & Brooks, 1978, pp. 214–215.)

reaches for the spot of rouge on her own nose rather than for the spot on the nose in the mirror.

The results from one of Michael Lewis's studies using this procedure are shown in Figure 10.1. As you can see, very few of the 9- to 12-month-old children in this study touched their noses, but by 21 months, three-quarters of the children showed that level of self-recognition. The figure also shows the rate at which children refer to themselves by name when they are shown a picture of themselves, which is another commonly used measure of self-awareness. You can see that this development occurs at almost exactly the same time as self-recognition in a mirror. Both are present by about the middle of the second year of life (Lewis & Ramsay, 2004).

Once the toddler achieves such self-awareness, his behavior is affected in a wide range of ways. Self-aware toddlers begin to insist on doing things for themselves and show a newly proprietary attitude toward toys or other treasured objects ("Mine!"). Looked at this way, much of the legendary behavior in the "terrible twos" can be understood as an outgrowth of self-awareness. In a quite literal sense, toddlers are self-willed for the first time.

Another behavioral change ushered in by the toddler's newly emerging self-awareness is the expression of such self-conscious emotions as embarrassment, pride, or shame. These emotions are not normally expressed until late in the second year of life, presumably because they all involve some aspect of self-evaluation, not present until the toddler has achieved at least minimal self-awareness (Lewis, Allesandri, & Sullivan, 1992; Lewis, Sullivan, Stanger, & Weiss, 1989; Thompson & Goodvin, 2005). According to Lewis, emotions such as shame or pride require the child to be aware of some standards of conduct and to compare himself to those standards—a development that also occurs late in the second year of life. It is only at this age, for example, that children begin to use words like *dirty* to describe themselves or an object, suggesting that they are judging themselves or others against some standard. The child then expresses shame when he feels he has not met the standard, or pride when he is able to meet the standard—to build the block tower as high as the teacher wants, say, or to wash his hands so that they are clean, or the like. One aspect of this phase of development is that after age 2, children become increasingly eager for adult approval, using the adult's response to gauge whether they have met some standard or lived up to some expectation. By school age, children are beginning to internalize those standards and expectations and thus become more autonomous in their self-judgments (Combrinck-Graham & Fox, 2007). Likewise, they internalize their parents' rules and regulations, thereby becoming better able to regulate their emotional expression and behavior.

Early Self-Definitions   Having achieved an initial self-awareness, the preschool child begins to define "who I am" by learning about her own qualities and her social roles. The 2-year-old not only knows her own name; she can probably also tell you if she is a girl or a boy and whether she is big or little. By about age 5 to 7, a child can give you quite a full description of herself on a whole range of dimensions. For example, Susan Harter (2006b) has found that children of this age have clear notions of their own competence on a variety of specific tasks, such as solving puzzles, counting, knowing a lot in school, climbing or skipping or jumping rope, or being able to make friends.

Beginning in the second year, children also seem to become aware of themselves as players in the social game. By age 2, the toddler has already learned a variety of social "scripts"—routines of play or interaction with others. Case (1991) points out that the toddler next begins to develop an implicit understanding of her own roles in these scripts. So she begins to think of herself as a "helper" in some situations or as "the boss" when she is telling another child what to do. You can see this clearly in sociodramatic play among preschoolers, who begin to take explicit roles: "I'll be the daddy and you be the mommy" or "I'm the teacher." As part of the same process, the preschool child also gradually understands her place in the network of family roles—she knows that she has sisters, brothers, father, mother, and so on.

These are major advances in the child's understanding. Yet the self-definition is still tied to concrete characteristics. For one thing, each facet of a preschool child's self-concept seems to be quite separate, rather like a list: "I'm good at running"; "I don't like to play with dolls"; "I live in a big house"; "I have blue eyes" (Harter, 2006b). These separate aspects of the self-scheme, or internal working model of the self, have not yet coalesced into a global sense of self-worth (Harter, 2006a). Children this age do not say "I am a terrible person" or "I really like myself." Their perceptions of themselves are more tied to specific settings and specific tasks. Moreover, a preschooler's self-concept tends to focus on his own visible characteristics—whether he's a boy or girl, what he looks like, what or who he plays with, where he lives, what he is good or bad at doing—rather than on more enduring, inner qualities.

The Emotional Self

Another facet of self that emerges during the early years is the child's ability to understand and regulate her own expressions of emotion (Dunn, 1994; Hoeksma, Oosterlaan, & Schipper, 2004). Part of this process is the development of *impulse control*, sometimes called *inhibitory control*—the growing ability to inhibit a response, for example, to wait rather than to weep, to yell rather than to hit, to go slowly rather than to run (Kochanska & Aksan, 2006). When an infant is upset, it is the parents who help to regulate that emotion by cuddling, soothing, or removing the child from the upsetting situation. Over the preschool years, this regulation process is gradually taken over more and more by the child as the various prohibitions and instructions are internalized. A 2-year-old is only minimally able to modulate feelings or behavior in this way; by age 5 or 6, however, most children have made great strides in controlling the intensity of their expressions of strong feelings, so they don't automatically hit someone or something when they are angry, cry inconsolably when they are frustrated, or sulk when they are denied (Sroufe, 1996).

A second aspect of the child's regulation of emotion—one that is clearly linked to the cognitive processes discussed in Chapter 6—is the need to learn the social rules of specific emotional expressions. For example, as early as age 3, children begin to learn that there are times when they ought to smile—even when they do not feel completely happy (Liew, Eisenberg, & Reiser, 2004). Thus, they begin to use the "social smile," a facial expression that is quite distinct from the natural, delighted smile. Similarly, children gradually learn to use abbreviated or constricted forms of other emotions, such as anger or disgust (Izard & Abe, 2004; Izard & Malatesta, 1987), and they learn to conceal their feelings in a variety of situations. An ability to conceal feelings appears to rest on the child's emerging theory of mind. For example, for a child to conceal some emotion in order not to hurt someone else's feelings requires that she have some sense of what will cause the other person's feelings to be hurt. Equally, the preschool child learns to use her own emotional expressions to get things she wants, crying or smiling as needed. This control of emotions, in turn, rests at least partially on her grasp of the links between her behavior and others' perception of her behavior, an understanding that develops rapidly between ages 3 and 4 as a consequence of the child's growing theory of mind (see Chapter 6).

Developmentalist Nancy Eisenberg argues that emotion regulation is the foundation on which a child's entire repertoire of social skills is built (Eisenberg, Hofer, & Vaughan, 2007). Research lends some support for this notion, as the ability to regulate emotions during the preschool years is strongly predictive of a wide variety of social skills later in life (Rubin, Burgess, Dwyer, & Hastings, 2003). For instance, self-control in early childhood is related to children's ability to obey moral rules and to think about right and wrong during the school years (Kochanska & Aksan, 2006). Further, young children who are skilled in controlling negative emotions, such as anger, are less likely to display behavior problems during the school years (Eisenberg et al., 1999; Eisenberg et al., 2005). Emotional regulation skills appear to be particularly important for children whose temperaments include high levels of anger proneness (Diener & Kim, 2004). Research also suggests that children who poorly control their negative emotions are less popular with peers (Denham et al., 2003; Eisenberg, Liew, & Pidada, 2001; Fantuzzo, Sekino, & Cohen, 2004).

The process of acquiring emotional control is one in which control shifts slowly from the parents to the child (Houck & Lecuyer-Marcus, 2004). Here again, the child's temperament is a factor. For example, preschoolers who have consistently exhibited "difficult" behavior since infancy are more likely to have self-control problems in early childhood (Schmitz et al., 1999). Similarly, preschoolers who were born prematurely or who were delayed in language development in the second year of life experience more difficulties with self-control during early childhood (Carson, Klee, & Perry, 1998; Schothorst & van Engeland, 1996).

However, parents' age-based expectations and parenting behaviors are also important. For instance, most parents know that it is unreasonable to expect toddlers to wait for long periods of time, so they provide external control mechanisms such as reminding them of prohibitions and repeating requests. Over the years from 3 to 6, children gradually internalize such parental standards and expectations and take on more of the control task for themselves. For example, if you were to observe parents and children in a doctor's waiting room, you would see that parents of bored toddlers often physically direct and redirect their behavior. A parent of a 2-year-old might take the child onto his lap and read to her. In contrast, you would notice that older preschoolers look for things to do on their own. In response to such evidence of emotional maturity, parents expect more control from older preschoolers and use verbal instructions, rather than physical control, to help them manage their behavior.

In addition to parenting behavior, the way parents express emotions themselves is related to their children's ability to regulate emotions. Generally, parents who are very expressive of their negative emotions tend to have children who poorly control their negative feelings (Eisenberg, Gershoff et al., 2001; Eisenberg, Liew, & Pidada, 2001). Interesting, too, is the finding that positive emotional expressivity in parents does not predict children's emotional self-regulation as consistently as negative emotional expressivity.

Learning Objective 10.4

How do school-aged children describe themselves?

Self-Concept at School Age

Over the elementary school years, the child's concrete self-concept gradually shifts toward a more abstract, more comparative, more generalized self-definition. A 6-year-old might describe herself as "smart" or "dumb"; a 10-year-old is more likely to say he is "smarter than most other kids" or "not as good at baseball as my friends" (Harter, 2006b). The school-aged child also begins to see her own (and other people's) characteristics as relatively stable and, for the first time, develops a global sense of her own self-worth.

A number of these themes are illustrated nicely in a classic study by Montemayor and Eisen (1977) of self-concepts in 9- to 18-year-olds. Using the question "Who am I?" these researchers found that the younger children they studied were still using mostly surface qualities to describe themselves, as in the description by this 9-year-old:

My name is Bruce C. I have brown eyes. I have brown hair. I have brown eyebrows. I am nine years old. I LOVE! Sports. I have seven people in my family. I have great! eye site. I have lots! of friends. I live on 1923 Pinecrest Dr. I am going on 10 in September. I'm a boy. I have a uncle that is almost 7 feet tall. My school is Pinecrest. My teacher is Mrs. V. I play Hockey! I'm almost the smartest boy in the class. I LOVE! food. I love fresh air. I LOVE school. (pp. 317–318)

In contrast, look at the self-description of this 11-year-old girl in the sixth grade:

My name is A. I'm a human being. I'm a girl. I'm a truthful person. I'm not very pretty. I do so-so in my studies. I'm a very good cellist. I'm a very good pianist. I'm a little bit tall for my age. I like several boys. I like several girls. I'm old-fashioned. I play tennis. I am a very good swimmer. I try to be helpful. I'm always ready to be friends with anybody. Mostly I'm good, but I lose my temper. I'm not well-liked by some girls and boys. I don't know if I'm liked by boys or not. (pp. 317–318)

This girl, like other youngsters of her age in Montemayor and Eisen's study, not only describes her external qualities but also emphasizes her beliefs, the quality of her relationships, and her general personality traits. Thus, as the child moves through the elementary school years (Piaget's concrete operations period), her self-definition becomes more complex, more comparative, less tied to external features, and more focused on feelings and ideas.

The increasingly comparative self-assessments seen in middle childhood are particularly visible in the school context. Kindergarten and first-grade children pay relatively little attention to how well others do at a particular task; in fact, the great majority will confidently tell you that they are the smartest kid in their class—an aspect of a general tendency at this age to identify self-qualities as positive (Harter, 2006b). By third grade, however, children begin to notice whether their classmates finish a test sooner than they do or whether someone else gets a better grade or more corrections on his spelling paper (Eccles & Roeser, 2005). Their self-judgments begin to include both positive and negative elements.

These fourth-graders are already developing fairly clear ideas about their academic abilities, comparing their own successes and failures to those of other children in their class. These ideas then become incorporated in the children's self-schemes, affecting their choices and sense of self-efficacy.

Teachers' behavior shows a related progression: In the first few grades, teachers emphasize effort and work habits. Gradually, they begin to use more comparative judgments. By junior high, teachers compare children not only to each other but to fixed standards, students at other schools, or national norms (Eccles & Roeser, 2005). These comparisons are sometimes subtle, but they can be powerful. Robert Rosenthal (1994), in a famous series of studies, has shown that a teacher's belief about a given student's ability and potential has a small but significant effect on his or her behavior toward that student and on the student's eventual achievement. This set of results has now been replicated many times. Rosenthal's standard procedure is to tell teachers at the beginning of a school year that some of the children in the class are underachievers and just ready to "bloom" intellectually, although in fact the children labeled in this way are chosen randomly. At the end of the year, those students labeled as having more potential have typically shown more academic gains than those who have not been labeled in this way.

Similarly, parents' judgments and expectations also play a role. For example, you may recall from Chapter 7 that parents in the United States are more likely to attribute a daughter's good performance in math to hard work but a son's good math grades to ability. Children absorb these explanations and adjust their behavior accordingly (Fredricks & Eccles, 2005).

The beliefs about their own abilities that students develop through this process of self-assessment are usually quite accurate. Students who consistently do well in comparison to others come to believe that they are academically competent. Further, and perhaps more important, they come to believe that they are in control of academic outcomes—in Bandura's terms, they have a strong sense of their own academic self-efficacy.

Self-Concept and Identity in Adolescence

| Learning Objective 10.5 |
How do Erikson's and Marcia's theories explain adolescent identity development?

The trend toward greater abstraction in self-definition continues during adolescence, and the self-concept blossoms into a mature sense of identity.

Self-Descriptions   Compare the answers of this 17-year-old to the "Who am I?" question with the ones you read earlier:

> I am a human being. I am a girl, I am an individual. I don't know who I am. I am a Pisces. I am a moody person. I am an indecisive person. I am an ambitious person. I am a very curious person. I am not an individual. I am a loner. I am an American (God help me). I am a Democrat.

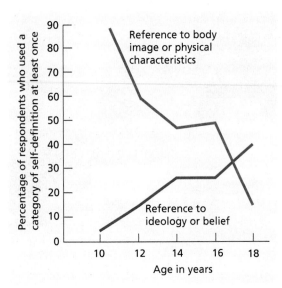

Figure 10.2

Age-Related Change in Self-Definitions

As they get older, children and adolescents define themselves less by what they look like and more by what they believe or feel.

(*Source*: Montemayor & Eisen, 1977, from Table 1, p. 316.)

I am a liberal person. I am a radical. I am a conservative. I am a pseudoliberal. I am an atheist. I am not a classifiable person (i.e., I don't want to be). (Montemayor & Eisen, 1977, p. 318)

Obviously, this girl's self-concept is even less tied to her physical characteristics or even her abilities than is that of the 11-year-old. She is describing abstract traits or ideology. Figure 10.2 shows this shift from concrete to abstract self-definitions, based on the answers of all 262 participants in Montemayor and Eisen's study. Participants' answers to the "Who am I?" question were placed in one or more specific categories, such as references to physical properties ("I am tall," "I have blue eyes") or references to ideology ("I am a Democrat," "I believe in God"). Figure 10.2 makes it clear that physical appearance was still a highly significant dimension of self-concept in the preteen and early teen years but became less dominant in late adolescence.

The adolescent's self-concept also becomes more differentiated as the teenager comes to see herself somewhat differently in each of several roles: as a student, with friends, with parents, and in romantic relationships (Harter, 2006b). Once these ideas are formed, they begin to influence adolescents' behavior. For example, teens whose academic self-concepts are strong take more difficult courses in high school than those who believe themselves to be less academically able. Further, they tend to select courses in disciplines in which they believe they have the greatest ability and to avoid courses in perceived areas of weakness (Marsh & Yeung, 1997). Further, as you might suspect, teens with weak academic self-concepts are more likely to get into trouble in school than those who have more confidence in their ability to succeed academically (Pisecco, Wristers, Swank, Silva, & Baker, 2001).

Adolescents' academic self-concepts seem to come both from internal comparisons of their performance to a self-generated ideal and from external comparisons to peer performance (Bong, 1998). It also appears that perceived competency in one domain affects how a teenager feels about his ability in other areas. For example, if a high school student fails a math course, it is likely to affect his self-concept in other disciplines besides math. This sug-

If you asked them to define themselves, these teenagers would surely give much more abstract and comparative answers than you would hear from a 6-year-old.

PART 5 ▪ THE SOCIAL CHILD

gests that teens' self-concepts are hierarchical in nature. Perceived competencies in various domains serve as building blocks for creating a global academic self-concept (Harter, 2006b).

Erikson's Identity Crisis   A somewhat different way to look at adolescent self-concept is through the lens of Erikson's theory. In this model, the central task (or dilemma) of adolescence is that of **identity versus role confusion**. Erikson argued that the child's early sense of identity comes partly "unglued" at puberty because of the combination of rapid body growth and the sexual changes of puberty. He described this period as a time when the adolescent mind is in a kind of moratorium between childhood and adulthood.

During this stage, the adolescent's old identity will no longer suffice; a new identity must be forged, one that allows a place for the young person in each of the myriad roles of adult life—occupational roles, sexual roles, religious roles. Confusion about all these role choices is inevitable. The teenage clique, or crowd, thus forms a base of security from which the young person can move toward a unique solution of the identity process. Ultimately, each teenager must achieve an integrated view of himself, including his own pattern of beliefs, occupational goals, and relationships.

Marcia's Identity Statuses   Nearly all the current work on the formation of adolescent identity has been based on James Marcia's descriptions of *identity statuses* (Marcia, 1966, 1980), which are rooted in but go beyond Erikson's general conception of the adolescent identity crisis. Following one of Erikson's ideas, Marcia argues that the formation of an adolescent identity has two key parts: a crisis and a commitment. By a "crisis," Marcia means a period of decision making when old values and old choices are reexamined. This may occur in a sort of upheaval (the classic notion of a crisis), or it may occur gradually. The outcome of the reevaluation is a commitment to some specific role, some particular ideology.

If you chart the two elements of crisis and commitment together, as in Figure 10.3, you can see that four different "identity statuses" are possible:

- **Identity achievement:** The young person has been through a crisis and has reached a commitment to ideological or occupational goals.
- **Moratorium:** A crisis is in progress, but no commitment has yet been made.
- **Foreclosure:** A commitment has been made without the person's having gone through a crisis. No reassessment of old positions has been made. Instead, the young person has simply accepted a parentally or culturally defined commitment.
- **Identity diffusion:** The young person is not in the midst of a crisis (although there may have been one in the past), and no commitment has been made. Diffusion may represent either an early stage in the process (before a crisis) or a failure to reach a commitment after a crisis.

Evidence for Erikson's and Marcia's Theories

Erikson's and Marcia's theories assume that some kind of identity crisis is both normal and healthy. These assumptions have not been entirely supported by the evidence. Researchers have found evidence for the beginnings of identity development in early adolescence (Crocetti, Rubini, Luyckx, & Meeus, 2008); however, the whole process of identity formation may occur later than Erikson thought (Kroger, 2007). In one combined analysis of eight separate cross-sectional studies, Alan Waterman (1985) found that most young people attained the identity achievement status in college, not during high school. Waterman also found that the moratorium status was relatively uncommon, except in the early years of college. So if most young people are going through an identity crisis, the crisis is occurring fairly late in adolescence and is not lasting terribly long.

identity versus role confusion As hypothesized by Erikson, the psychosocial stage in which a teenager must develop a sense of personal identity or else enter adulthood with a sense of confusion about his or her place in the world.

identity achievement One of four identity statuses proposed by Marcia, involving the successful resolution of an identity "crisis" and resulting in a new commitment.

moratorium One of four identity statuses proposed by Marcia, involving an ongoing reexamination of identity but no new commitment.

foreclosure One of four identity statuses proposed by Marcia, involving an ideological or occupational commitment without a previous reevaluation.

identity diffusion One of four identity statuses proposed by Marcia, involving neither a current reevaluation of identity nor a firm personal commitment.

Figure 10.3   Marcia's Identity Statuses

Marcia's four proposed identity statuses, based on Erikson's theory. To come to a fully achieved identity, according to this model, the young person must examine his or her values or goals and reach a firm commitment.

(*Source:* Marcia, 1980.)

What's more, about a third of the young people at every age were in the foreclosure status, which may indicate that many young people simply do not go through a crisis at all, but follow well-defined grooves.

As a further caveat, all the participants in the studies Waterman analyzed were either in college or in college-preparatory high school programs. This may give a false impression of the process of identity formation for young people who do not go to college, who do not have the luxury of a long period of questioning but must work out some kind of personal identity while still in their teens (Munro & Adams, 1977).

In addition, cognitive development may be more strongly related to identity formation than either Erikson or Marcia believed. Research suggests that teens who are most advanced in the development of logical thinking and other information-processing skills are also the most likely to have attained Marcia's identity achievement status (Peterson, Marcia, & Carpendale, 2004). This may help to explain why the process takes place at somewhat later ages than Erikson's and Marcia's theories predict. There is also evidence that the quest for personal identity continues throughout the lifespan, with alternating periods of instability and stability (Marcia, 2002). Consequently, adolescence may be only one such period among several.

Finally, the conception of an adolescent identity crisis is also strongly influenced by cultural assumptions in industrialized Western societies, in which full adult status is postponed for almost a decade after puberty. In such cultures, young people do not normally or necessarily adopt the same roles or occupations as their parents. Indeed, they are encouraged to choose for themselves. In such a cultural system, adolescents are faced with what may be a bewildering array of options, a pattern that might well foster the sort of identity crisis Erikson described. As this hypothesis would predict, the proportion of study participants who fall within the identity diffusion category has increased substantially over the past 2 decades. Researchers interpret this trend as a natural consequence of contemporaneous increases in the amount of time that young people spend in college and other transitional settings, in the age at which they marry, in the age at which they have their first child, and so on (Born, 2007). Further, these studies suggest that, in the context of such dramatic historical and cultural shifts, it may be wrong to view identity diffusion as a negative developmental outcome.

For all these reasons, both Marcia and Waterman now agree that the various identity statuses do not form a clear developmental progression that all or most teenagers and young adults follow, even in Western cultures. Instead, the four identity statuses may more reasonably be thought of as different approaches young people may take to the task of identity formation, depending on culture as well as on the young person's individual situation (Marcia, 1993; Waterman, 1988). In this view, it is not correct to say that a young person who is in the foreclosure status has not achieved any identity. She has an identity, which she has adopted from parental or other societal rules without significant questioning.

Thus, the developmental aspect of the Erikson or Marcia model is very likely not correct. In contrast, the other implication of the model—the notion that experiencing an identity crisis and its resolution is a psychologically healthy process—is confirmed by a variety of research. In Western cultures, at least, young people who have made a commitment to some identity (that is, those who are classed in either identity achievement or foreclosure status) have higher self-esteem and lower levels of depression and are more goal-directed. Those in a foreclosure status tend to be more stereotyped in their approach to relationships, while those in identity diffusion status have the most difficulties with intimacy (Waterman, 1992). All this evidence suggests that while a variety of roads may lead to some kind of personal identity, not all roads are psychologically equivalent.

Learning Objective 10.6

What is the process of ethnic identity development, according to Phinney?

Ethnic Identity in Adolescence

Minority teenagers, especially those of color in a predominantly White culture, face another task in creating an identity in adolescence: They must also develop an ethnic identity, including self-identification as a member of some specific group, commitment to that group and its values and attitudes, and some evaluative attitudes (positive or negative) about the group to which they belong. Some of this self-identification occurs in middle childhood (Aboud & Doyle, 1995): 7- and 8-year-old minority children already understand the differences between themselves and majority children, and most often prefer their own subgroup.

Further steps in the ethnic identity process occur in adolescence as minority teens' general sense of identity grows (Cross & Cross, 2008). Jean Phinney (1990; Phinney, Ferguson, & Tate, 1997; Phinney & Rosenthal, 1992) proposes that the development of a complete ethnic identity moves through three rough stages during adolescence. The first stage is an *unexamined ethnic identity*, equivalent to what Marcia calls a foreclosed status. For some subgroups in U.S. society, such as African Americans and Native Americans, this unexamined identity typically includes the negative images and stereotypes common in the wider culture. Indeed, it may be during adolescence, with the advent of the cognitive ability to reflect and interpret, that the young person becomes keenly aware of the way in which his own group is perceived by the majority.

In addition to establishing a sense of personal identity, minority teens must also develop an ethnic identity. Some resolve this developmental task by creating a bicultural identity for themselves, one that allows them to interact comfortably with members of the majority group, individuals who belong to other minority groups, and members of their own group.

The second stage in Phinney's model is the *ethnic identity search*, parallel to the crisis in Marcia's analysis of adolescent identity. This search is typically triggered by some experience that makes ethnicity relevant—perhaps an example of blatant prejudice or merely the wider realm of experience offered by high school. At this point, the minority teenager begins to arrive at her own judgments.

This exploration stage is eventually followed by a *resolution of the conflicts and contradictions*—analogous to Marcia's status of identity achievement. This is often a difficult process, as teenagers become aware of what Prentice and Miller (2002) call *homegrown stereotypes*. These stereotypes involve instructions for how a group member is supposed to present herself to other members of the same group. They often include the notion that one's own beliefs are at variance with those of the group, but that certain behaviors are required when presenting oneself to the group in order to maintain their acceptance. For example, an African American teen might learn that she is supposed to behave in certain ways toward White peers in order to continue to be accepted by African American peers. Hispanic teens often report similar experiences. Some resolve this pressure by keeping their own ethnic group at arm's length. Some search for a middle ground, adopting aspects of both the majority and minority cultures, a pattern Phinney calls a "blended bicultural identity" (Phinney & Devich-Navarro, 1997). Others deal with it by creating essentially two identities (a pattern Phinney calls an "alternating bicultural identity"), as expressed by one young Hispanic teen interviewed by Phinney:

> Being invited to someone's house, I have to change my ways of how I act at home, because of culture differences. I would have to follow what they do. . . . I am used to it now, switching off between the two. It is not difficult. (Phinney & Rosenthal, 1992, p. 160)

Still others resolve the dilemma by wholeheartedly choosing their own racial or ethnic group's patterns and values, even when that choice may limit their access to the larger culture.

In both cross-sectional and longitudinal studies, Phinney has found that African American teens and young adults do indeed move through these steps or stages toward a clear ethnic identity. Furthermore, there is evidence that African

Cultures determine the kinds of behaviors that signify the transition from childhood to adulthood. For example, European American families might consider teenagers' quest for independence to be a sign of normal, healthy development. By contrast, to Asian American parents, increased willingness to fulfill family obligations would be considered a more appropriate way for teenagers to express their growing understanding of the adult roles they will shortly assume.

American, Asian American, and Mexican American teens and college students who have reached the second or third stage in this process—those who are searching for or who have reached a clear identity—have higher self-esteem and better psychological adjustment than do those who are still in the "unexamined" stage (Phinney, 1990). In contrast, among Caucasian American students, ethnic identity has essentially no relationship to self-esteem or adjustment.

Further, Phinney has found that ethnic identity seems to provide African American teens with an important protective factor. For one thing, those who possess a strong sense of ethnic identity get better grades than peers who do not (Oyserman, Harrison, & Bybee, 2001). The "bicultural" pattern of Phinney's last stage has been found to be a consistent characteristic of adolescents and adults who have high self-esteem and enjoy good relations with members of both the dominant culture and their own ethnic group (Farver, Bhadha, & Narang, 2002; Phinney, Horenczyk, Liebkind, & Vedder, 2001; Yamada & Singelis, 1999). Further, African American teens are more likely than Asian American and Caucasian American youths to choose friends whose ethnic identity statuses are the same as their own (Hamm, 2000). As the discussion in *Developmental Science in the Real World* indicates, such research has led some developmentalists to propose programs aimed at helping African American teens acquire a strong sense of ethnic identity (Phinney, Kim-Jo, Osorio, & Vilhjalmsdottir, 2005).

Of course, the search for identity is affected by cultural norms. It is likely that parent-teen conflict is common and even socially acceptable in North American and European families because these individualistic cultures associate separation from parents with psychological and social maturity. As a result, parents in North America and Europe expect to experience

DEVELOPMENTAL SCIENCE IN THE REAL WORLD

Adolescent Rites of Passage

An expression of intense concentration appeared on 13-year-old Aisha's face as she stood before a mirror, wrapping a brightly colored cloth around her head. She had learned the art of Gele head-wrapping just a few hours earlier and wanted to demonstrate it for her mother and younger sister. Headwrapping is just one of many traditional African skills Aisha has learned in the rites of passage program she is attending at a local community college. The purpose of the program, one of hundreds across the United States, is to help Aisha and other African American teens develop a sense of ethnic identity.

Many developmentalists argue that the fuzziness of the adolescent-to-adult transition in U.S. culture is more problematic for African American teens than for other American teens. They point out that other minority groups practice rites of passage that connect their young people with centuries-long cultural heritage—such as the Jewish *bar mitzvah* and *bat mitzvah* and the *quinceañera* for young Hispanic girls. By contrast, the institution of slavery separated African Americans from the traditions of their ancestors.

Consequently, many African American churches and other institutions have devised formal initiation rites preceded by a period of instruction in traditional African cultural values and practices, typically called *rites of passage programs*. The goal of such programs is to enhance African American teens' sense of ethnic identity and self-esteem, thereby making them less vulnerable to institutional racism as well as drug abuse, pregnancy, and other risks associated with adolescence (Alford, 2007; Harvey & Rauch, 1997; Warfield-Coppock, 1997).

Research indicates that rites of passage programs can make a difference (Harvey & Hill, 2004). After participating in one such program, boys and girls in the fifth and sixth grades showed

a number of positive effects (Cherry et al., 1998). They exhibited higher self-esteem, a stronger sense of racial identity, a lower incidence of school behavior problems, and greater knowledge of African culture.

The experiences of many African American youth in rites of passage programs suggest that there may be some real advantage to providing teens with formal instruction and initiation into adult roles. What many see as a vestige of a by-gone era may actually serve a very important function in adolescent identity development.

Questions for Reflection

1. Rites of passage programs include three separate components that may explain their positive effects on teenagers: contact with adults, contact with peers, and information about ethnicity. Which factor do you think is most important and why?

2. When you were a teenager, did you participate in any formal rites of passage, such as a confirmation, *bar mitzvah*, or *quinceañera*? If so, what effect did it have on you? If not, in what way do you think such a program might have been helpful to you?

these conflicts and endorse adolescents' efforts to demonstrate independence. For example, many American parents think that part-time jobs help teens mature. Thus, if an American parent prohibits a teenager from getting a job, but the adolescent presents a good argument as to why he should be allowed to work, the conflict is seen as a sign of maturity. In contrast, cultures that emphasize the community rather than the individual view teens' acceptance of family responsibilities as a sign of maturity. An issue such as whether a teen should get a job is decided in terms of family needs. If the family needs money, the adolescent might be encouraged to work. However, if the family needs the teenager to care for younger siblings while the parents work, then a part-time job will be forbidden. If the teenager argues about the parents' decision, the conflict is seen as representing immaturity rather than maturity.

Research involving Asian American teenagers helps to illustrate this point. Psychologists have found that first-generation Asian American teens often feel guilty about responding to the individualistic pressures of North American culture. Their feelings of guilt appear to be based on their parents' cultural norms, which suggest that the most mature adolescents are those who take a greater role in the family rather than try to separate from it (Chen, 1999). Thus, for many Asian American adolescents, achievement of personal and ethnic identity involves balancing the individualistic demands of North American culture against the familial obligations of their parents' cultures (Kiang, Harter, & Whitesell, 2007).

Phinney's stage model is a useful general description of the process of ethnic identity formation, but as research involving Asian American teens demonstrates, the details and content of ethnic identity differ markedly from one subgroup to another. Further, those groups that encounter more overt prejudice will have a different set of experiences and challenges than will those who may be more easily assimilated (Quintana, 2007); those whose own ethnic culture espouses values that are close to those of the dominant culture will have less difficulty resolving the contradictions than will those whose subculture is at greater variance with the majority. Whatever the specifics, young people of color and those from clearly defined ethnic groups have an important additional identity task in their adolescent years.

Self-Esteem

Our discussion thus far has treated self-concept as if there were no values attached to the categories by which we define ourselves. Yet clearly one's self-concept contains an evaluative aspect, usually called *self-esteem*. Note, for example, the differences in tone in the answers to the "Who am I?" question quoted earlier in the chapter. The 9-year-old makes a lot of positive statements about himself, whereas the two older respondents offer more mixed evaluations.

The Development of Self-Esteem

Learning Objective 10.7
How does self-esteem develop?

Over the years of elementary school and high school, children's evaluations of their own abilities become increasingly differentiated, with quite separate judgments about skills in academics or athletics, physical appearance, peer social acceptance, friendships, romantic appeal, and relationships with parents (Harter, 2006b). A consistent feature of self-competence judgments across domains is that they become less positive as children get older. The declines may be based on children's experiences. For example, social self-esteem, the assessment of one's own social skills, is higher in popular children than in those who are rejected by their peers (Jackson & Bracken, 1998).

Another striking feature of self-competence judgments is that they differ for boys and girls. Developmentalists believe that these differences are influenced both by cultural expectations and by children's own experiences. To fully understand this sex difference, it's important to understand that each component of self-esteem is valued differently by different children. Initially, the standards and beliefs of the larger culture influence these values, so almost all young boys rate themselves as competent in sports, because they know that the culture values sports achievement in males. However, over time, children come to value domains in which they experience real achievements. So, as children get older, both boys and girls who view themselves as highly competent in sports, because of their own actual successes, also value sports achievement very highly (Jacobs et al., 2002). And lack of demonstrated skill in sports leads to a decline in the value placed on sports achievement among children of both genders.

As children develop domain-specific self-competence judgments, they also create for themselves a global self-evaluation that stands alongside these self-judgments. It is this global evaluation of one's own worth that is usually referred to as **self-esteem**. However, self-esteem is not merely the sum of all the separate assessments the child makes about his skills in different areas.

Instead, as Susan Harter's extremely interesting research on self-esteem reveals, each child's level of self-esteem is a product of two internal assessments (Harter, 1987, 1990, 1999). First, each child experiences some degree of discrepancy between what he would like to be and what he thinks he is—a gap between his ideal self and what he perceives to be his real self (Harter, 2006a). When that discrepancy is small, the child's self-esteem is generally high. When the discrepancy is large—when the child sees himself as failing to live up to his own goals or values—self-esteem is much lower. The standards are not the same for every child. Some value academic skills highly; others value sports skills or having good friends. The key to self-esteem, Harter proposes, is the amount of discrepancy between what the child desires and what the child thinks he has achieved. Thus, being good at something—singing, playing chess, or being able to talk to one's parents—won't raise a child's self-esteem unless the child values that particular skill.

Another major influence on a child's self-esteem, according to Harter, is the over-all sense of support the child feels from the important people around her, particularly parents and peers (DuBois et al., 2002; Franco & Levitt, 1998). Both these factors are clear in the results of Harter's own research. She asked third-, fourth-, fifth-, and sixth-graders how important it was to them to do well in each of five domains and how well they thought they actually did in each. The total discrepancy between these sets of judgments made up the discrepancy score. (A high discrepancy score indicates that the child reported that she was not doing well in areas that mattered to her.) The social support score was based on children's replies to a set of questions about whether they thought others (parents and peers) liked them as they were, treated them as a person, or felt that they were important. The findings for the fifth- and

Playing ball with dad is a classic father-daughter activity in American culture. One of the side effects is likely to be that the daughter comes to believe that her father values skill in playing ball.

self-esteem A global evaluation of one's own worth; an aspect of self-concept.

sixth-graders were virtually identical, and both sets of results strongly supported Harter's hypothesis, as does other research, including studies of African American youth (DuBois, Felner, Brand, Phillips, & Lease, 1996; Luster & McAdoo, 1995): A low discrepancy score alone does not protect the child completely from low self-esteem if she lacks sufficient social support. And a loving and accepting family and peer group do not guarantee high self-esteem if the youngster does not feel she is living up to her own standards.

A particularly risky combination occurs when the child perceives that parental support is contingent on good performance in some area—getting good grades, making the first-string football team, being chosen to play the solo with the school orchestra, being popular with classmates. If the child does not measure up to the standard, he experiences both an increased discrepancy between ideal and achievement and a loss of support from the parents.

If we accept Harter's model and assume that self-esteem is a product of a person's comparison of her desired or valued qualities with her actual qualities, we still have to ask where each child's values and self-judgments come from. First, of course, a child's own direct experience with success or failure in various arenas plays an obvious role. Second, the value a child attaches to some skill or quality is obviously affected fairly directly by peers' and parents' attitudes and values. Peer standards (and general cultural standards) for appearance establish benchmarks for all children and teens. A child who is "too tall" or "too fat" or who deviates in some other way from the accepted norms is likely to feel a sense of inadequacy. Similarly, the degree of emphasis parents place on the child's performing well in some domain—whether schoolwork, athletics, or playing chess—is an important element in forming the child's aspirations in each area.

Consistency of Self-Esteem over Time

Learning Objective 10.8
How consistent is self-esteem across childhood and adolescence?

A number of longitudinal studies of elementary school children and teenagers show that self-esteem is moderately stable in the short term but somewhat less so over periods of several years. The correlation between two self-esteem scores obtained a few months apart is generally about .60. Over several years, this correlation drops to something more like .40 (Alsaker & Olweus, 2002), a level that has been found over periods as long as a decade, from early adolescence into early adulthood (Block & Robins, 1993). So while it is true that a child with high self-esteem at age 8 or 9 is likely to have high self-esteem at age 10 or 11, it is also true that there is a good deal of variation around that stability.

Self-esteem seems to be particularly unstable in the years of early adolescence, especially at the time of the shift from elementary school to junior high school (Seidman & French, 2004). In one study, Edward Seidman and his colleagues (1994) followed a group of nearly 600 Hispanic, Black, and White youngsters over the 2 years from sixth grade through junior high. Seidman found a significant drop in average self-esteem between the last year of elementary school and the first year in junior high, a decline that occurred in each of the three ethnic groups. Similarly, David DuBois and his colleagues (1996), in a cross-sectional study of 1,800 children in grades 5 through 8, found that eighth-graders had significantly lower self-esteem than did fifth-graders.

On average, self-esteem tends to rise in the later teen years (Harter, 2006a). However, both the decline in average self-esteem in the early teen years and the average increase that follows can obscure important individual differences (Harter & Whitesell, 2003). Underlying the averages, researchers often find four patterns of self-esteem change among adolescents (Diehl, Vicary, & Deike, 1997; Zimmerman, Copeland, Shope, & Dielman, 1997). The largest group of teens, about half in most studies, display consistently high self-esteem throughout adolescence. The second group exhibit low self-esteem early in adolescence, but it rises steadily as they get older. The self-esteem ratings of the third group are low in both early and late adolescence. Teens in the fourth group enjoy moderate to high self-esteem at the beginning of the period but exhibit steady declines as adolescence progresses. As you might suspect, differences in self-esteem are related to some important developmental outcomes, such as academic achievement (Valentine, DuBois, & Cooper, 2004).

Harter and others have found that a child who has low self-esteem is more likely than are her high self-esteem peers to suffer from depression in both middle childhood and adolescence, especially when she also exhibits high levels of neuroticism (Harter, 1987; Renouf & Harter, 1990). Bear in mind, though, that this is correlational evidence. These findings don't prove that there is a causal connection between low self-esteem and depression. They only indicate that the two tend to go together.

The Development of the Concepts of Gender and Sex Roles

As noted at the beginning of this chapter, biological sex and psychological gender are integral components of each individual's sense of self. Thus, in this final section, we turn our attention to the process through which sex and gender become woven into each child's self-concept. We begin by examining how children come to understand several important concepts that are associated with sex and gender.

Learning Objective 10.9
How do ideas about gender and sex roles change across childhood?

Developmental Patterns

Those of us who want to understand ourselves—and developmentalists who may wish to advise parents about child-rearing—need to know more about the ways in which children learn about gender and sex roles.

What Must Be Learned   Acquiring an understanding of sex roles involves several related tasks. On the cognitive side, a child must learn the nature of the sex/gender category itself—that *boyness* or *girlness* is permanent, unchanged by such things as modifications in clothing or hair length. This understanding is usually called the **gender concept**. On the social side, the child has to learn what behaviors go with being a boy or a girl. That is, the child must learn the **sex role** (sometimes called the *gender role*) defined as appropriate for his or her gender in the particular culture.

All roles involve sets of expected behaviors, attitudes, rights, duties, and obligations. Teachers are supposed to behave in certain ways, as are employees, mothers, or baseball managers—all roles in our culture. Gender roles are somewhat broader than most other roles, but they are nonetheless roles—sets of expected behaviors, attitudes, rights, duties, and obligations involved in filling the role of "girl," "woman," "boy," or "man." Put another way, a gender role is a "job description" for being a male or a female in a given culture.

Sex-typed behavior is behavior exhibited by a child or an adult that matches culturally defined gender-role expectations for that person's gender (see *Thinking about Research*). A girl may know quite well that she is a girl and be able to describe the cultural sex roles for girls accurately but may still behave in a tomboyish way. Such a girl's sex-role behavior is less sex-typed than the behavior of a girl who adopts more traditional behavior patterns.

This mother is not only teaching her daughter how to cook; she is also transmitting information about sex roles and reinforcing traditional sex typing.

gender concept The full understanding that gender is constant and permanent, unchanged by appearance.

sex role The set of behaviors, attitudes, rights, duties, and obligations that are seen as appropriate for being male or female in any given culture.

sex-typed behavior Behavior that matches a culturally defined sex role.

The Gender Concept   Research suggests that gender is a highly significant variable for children from the earliest days of life. For example, infants as young as 3 months of age distinguish between photos of male and female infants (Shirley & Campbell, 2000). Curiously, these young infants pay more attention to male babies and to male infant activities than to females. As you'll read later, by as early as 18 months of age, children prefer playmates of the same sex. By 4, children can readily identify the gender of a speaker of their own age on the basis of vowel sounds in speech patterns (Perry, Ohde, & Ashmead, 2001).

How soon does a child apply gender categorization to herself or himself? Research suggests that the process of self-categorization is linked to cognitive development (Trautner, Gervai, & Nemeth, 2003). In other words, a child's understanding of gender progresses along with his or her general understanding of the world. Moreover, like general cognitive develop-

Gender Differences in Temperament: Real or Imagined?

What kinds of temperamental differences come to mind when you think about boys and girls? You may think of boys as more irritable and girls as more fearful. But are these differences real, or are they simply stereotypes? In some studies, researchers have found that boys are more emotionally intense and less fearful than girls and that girls are generally more sociable (Calkins, Dedmon, Gill, Lomax, & Johnson, 2002; Gartstein & Rothbart, 2003). Nevertheless, temperamental differences between boys and girls are much smaller than the differences perceived by parents and other adults.

In one classic study, researchers found that adults viewing a videotape of an infant interpreted the baby's behavior differently depending on the gender label experimenters provided. Participants who were told the baby was a girl interpreted a particular behavior as expressing fear. Amazingly, participants who believed the infant was a boy labeled the same behavior anger (Condry & Condry, 1976).

Research on another dimension of temperament, emotionality, provides further examples of how perceived differences in temperament may affect parental responses to children's behavior. Most studies have found that, even in infancy, girls are more responsive to others' facial expressions (McClure, 2000). This difference often leads to the perception that girls are more emotionally sensitive. However, studies of actual behavior reveal that boys are just as affectionate and empathetic as girls during infancy (Melson, Peet, & Sparks, 1991; Zahn-Waxler, Radke-Yarrow, Wagner, & Chapman, 1992).

Temperamental stereotyping may affect the quality of the parent-infant relationship. For example, parents of a calm, quiet girl may respond positively to her because they perceive her behavior to be consistent with their concept of "girlness." In contrast, parents of a physically active girl may develop a rejecting, disapproving attitude toward her because they view her behavior as excessively masculine. As a result of these judgments, parents may behave more affectionately toward a girl whom they perceive to be feminine than they do toward a daughter whom they view as masculine.

You should recognize these issues as yet another example of the nature-nurture debate. As you learned in Chapter 9, individual differences in temperament are inborn. Yet it is also clear that parents treat boys and girls differently beginning very early in infancy. Thus, as children get older, gender differences in temperament are likely to be the result of both their inborn characteristics and the gender-based expectations and response patterns exhibited by their parents.

Questions for Critical Analysis

1. In what ways might stereotypes influence the methods that researchers use to study gender differences in temperament?
2. How do differences between men and women, which have evolved over many years, contribute to expectations about how male and female infants differ in temperament? In other words, in your view, do adults engage in what might be called backward generalization from adults to infants with regard to their opinions about the existence of gender differences early in life?

---

ment, understanding of gender appears to involve a universal sequence of stages (Munroe, Shimmin, & Munroe, 1984).

The first stage is **gender identity**, which is simply a child's ability to label his own sex correctly and to identify other people as men or women, boys or girls. By 9 to 12 months, babies already treat male and female faces as if they were different categories, apparently using hair length as the primary differentiating clue (Ruble, Martin, & Berenbaum, 2006). Within the next year, they begin to learn the verbal labels that go with these different categories. By age 2, if you show children a set of pictures of a same-sex child and several opposite-sex children and ask "Which one is you?" most children can correctly pick out the same-sex picture (Thompson, 1975). Between ages 2 and 3, children learn to identify and label others correctly by sex, such as by pointing out "which one is a girl" or "which one is a boy" in a set of pictures (Ruble, Martin, & Berenbaum, 2006). Hair length and clothing seem to be especially important cues in these early discriminations.

Next comes **gender stability**, the understanding that people stay the same gender throughout life. Researchers have measured this understanding by asking children such questions as "When you were a little baby, were you a little girl or a little boy?" or "When you grow up, will you be a mommy or a daddy?" Slaby and Frey, in their classic study (1975), found that most children understand this aspect of gender by about age 4, as Figure 10.4 on page 272 suggests.

The final stage in development of a gender concept, usually referred to as **gender constancy**, is the understanding that someone's biological sex stays the same even though he may appear to change by wearing different clothes or changing his hair length. For example, boys don't change into girls by wearing dresses. This is an appearance/reality problem very much like Flavell's sponge/rock test described in Chapter 6. The child must figure out that although a boy wearing a dress may look like a girl, he is really still a boy, just as the sponge painted to look like a rock may look like a rock but is really still a sponge. When children are asked the

gender identity The first stage in the development of gender concept, in which a child labels self and others correctly as male or female.

gender stability The second stage in the development of gender concept, in which the child understands that a person's gender stays the same throughout life.

gender constancy The final stage in development of gender concept, in which the child understands that gender doesn't change even though there may be external changes (in clothing or hair length, for example).

Figure 10.4
Early Sex-Role Stereotypes

In describing this self-portrait, the 5-year-old artist said, "This is how I will look when I get married to a boy. I am under a rainbow, so beautiful with a bride hat, a belt, and a purse." The girl knows she will always be female and associates gender with externals such as clothing (gender stability). She is also already quite knowledgeable about gender role expectations.

(*Source*: Author.)

gender constancy question in this way, many 4-year-olds and most 5-year-olds can answer correctly, just as 4- and 5-year-olds understand other appearance/reality distinctions (Martin & Ruble, 2004). Sandra Bem has found that to reach this level of understanding, a child must have at least some grasp of the basic genital differences between boys and girls and some understanding that genital characteristics are what make a child "really" a boy or a girl. In her study, 4-year-olds who did not yet understand genital differences also did not show gender constancy (Bem, 1989). In sum, children as young as 2 or 3 know their own sex and that of people around them, but children do not have a fully developed concept of gender until they are 5 or 6.

Sex-Role Concepts and Stereotypes

Obviously, figuring out your gender and understanding that it stays constant is only part of the story. Learning what goes with, or ought to go with, being a boy or a girl is also a vital part of the child's task.

Sex-Role Stereotypes Studies of children show that stereotyped ideas about sex roles develop early, even in families that espouse gender equality (Lippa, 2005). Even 2-year-olds already associate certain tasks and possessions with men and women, such as vacuum cleaners and food with women and cars and tools with men. By age 3 or 4, children can assign stereotypic occupations, toys, and activities to each gender (Ruble, Martin, & Berenbaum, 2006). By age 5, children begin to associate certain personality traits with males or females, and such knowledge is well developed by age 8 or 9 (Martin, 1993; Serbin, Powlishta, & Gulko, 1993).

Studies of children's ideas about how men and women (or boys and girls) ought to behave add an interesting further refinement to what developmentalists know about sex-role stereotypes, and an early study by William Damon (1977) illustrates this element particularly nicely. Damon told children aged 4 through 9 a story about a little boy named George who likes to play with dolls. George's parents tell him that only little girls play with dolls; little boys shouldn't. The children were then asked a batch of questions about the story, such as "Why do people tell George not to play with dolls?" or "Is there a rule that boys shouldn't play with dolls?" Four-year-olds in this study thought it was okay for George to play with dolls. There was no rule against it, and he should do it if he wanted to. Six-year-olds, in contrast, thought it was wrong for George to play with dolls. By about age 9, children had differentiated between what boys and girls usually do and what is "wrong." One boy said, for example, that breaking windows was wrong and bad, but that playing with dolls was not bad in the same way: "Breaking windows you're not supposed to do. And if you play with dolls, well you can, but boys usually don't."

What seems to happen is that the 5- or 6-year-old, having figured out that she is permanently a girl or he is a boy, is searching for a rule about how boys and girls behave (Martin & Halverson, 1981; Martin & Ruble, 2004). The child picks up

Four-year-olds and 9-year-olds think it is okay for a boy to play with dolls, but many 6-year-olds think it is simply wrong for boys to do girl things or for girls to do boy things.

information from watching adults, from watching television, from hearing evaluations of different activities (e.g., "Boys don't cry"). Initially they treat these as absolute, moral rules. Later they understand that these are social conventions, at which point sex-role concepts become more flexible (Katz & Ksansnak, 1994) (see Figure 10.5).

In a similar way, many kinds of fixed, biased ideas about other people—such as biases against obese children, against those who speak another language, or against those of other races—are at their peak in the early school years and then decline throughout the remaining years of childhood and into adolescence (Doyle & Aboud, 1995; Powlishta, Serbin, Doyle, & White, 1994). Another way to put it is that children of 5 to 7 years of age have a strong sense of "us" versus "them," of in-group versus out-group. They classify other children as "like me" or "not like me" on some dimension, and they develop strong preferences for those who are like themselves and highly stereotyped (often negative) ideas about those who are not like themselves (Bennett & Sani, 2008a).

This entire stereotyping process seems to be totally normal, part of the child's attempt to create rules and order, to find patterns that can guide his understanding and his behavior. In fact, children's beliefs about the degree to which they "fit in" with peers of the same sex may be an important component of healthy psychological adjustment during the elementary school years (Egan & Perry, 2001). Thus, just as an English-speaking 2- or 3-year-old discovers the rule about adding -ed to a verb to make the past tense and then overgeneralizes that rule, so the 6- or 7-year-old discovers the "rules" about boys and girls, men and women, "us" and "them," and overgeneralizes. In fact, most 6- and 7-year-olds believe that gender-role differences are built-in along with biological gender differences. By age 9, they understand that at least some differences in behavior between boys and girls are the result of training or experience (Taylor, 1996).

Sex-Role Stereotypes across Cultures

The content of sex-role stereotypes is remarkably similar in cultures around the world. John Williams and Deborah Best (1990), who have studied adults' gender stereotypes in 28 different countries and children's gender stereotypes in 24 countries, find that the most strongly stereotyped traits are weakness, gentleness, appreciativeness, and softheartedness for women and aggression, adventurousness, cruelty, and coarseness for men. There are a few differences, naturally. German children, for instance, choose "adventurous," "confident," and "steady" as female items, although these are more normally male items in other cultures. Pakistani children identify "emotional" with men; Japanese children associate independence and severity with neither sex. But these are variations on a common theme. Researchers have presented children with a story in which the sex of the main character was not explicitly stated. When asked to tell whether the character was better represented by a male or a female doll, in all 24 countries, 8-year-olds chose the male figure for stories about aggression, strength, cruelty, coarseness, and loudness, and they chose the female figure for stories about weakness. In 23 of 24 countries, 8-year-olds also chose the female character for gentleness, appreciativeness, and softheartedness. Thus, not only does every culture appear to have clear sex-role stereotypes, but the content of those stereotypes is remarkably similar across cultures.

Another of the interesting revelations of cross-cultural research is that the male stereotype and sex-role concept seem to develop a bit earlier and to be stronger than the female stereotype and sex-role concept—and this is true in virtually all countries studied. Whatever the reason for this phenomenon, it is clear that in Western societies, the qualities attributed to males are more highly valued than are female traits (Broverman, Broverman, Clarkson, Rosenkrantz, & Vogel, 1970; Lippa, 2005). Research has demonstrated that children assign

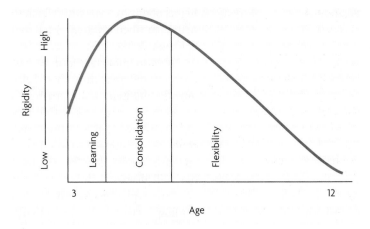

Figure 10.5
Age-Related Change in Gender Stereotypes

As children learn about and consolidate their knowledge of gender-related phenomena, their stereotypes become more rigid. Once they have a better understanding of gender, their stereotypes become more flexible.

(*Source*: From Martin, C., Ruble, D. (2004), Children's search for gender cues: Cognitive perspectives on gender development, *Current Directions in Psychological Science*, 13, 67–70, fig. 1, p. 69, copyright © 2004 by Blackwell Publishers, Inc. Reprinted with permission.)

higher status to a job with which they are unfamiliar when it is portrayed as being done by a man than when researchers tell them the job is usually performed by a woman (Liben, Bigler, & Krogh, 2001).

It's also important to note that children's stereotypical beliefs about men and women are probably different from their beliefs about boys and girls (Bennett & Sani, 2008b). Consequently, children do not attribute higher status to boys in the same way as they do to men. For example, psychologist Gail Heyman showed second- and third-graders pictures of unfamiliar children and told them about behaviors the children had exhibited—behaviors that could be interpreted in several different ways (Heyman, 2001). Heyman found that both boys and girls were likely to classify the behavior as "bad" or "naughty" if the pictured child was a boy. Still, despite their beliefs about the gender-based status of adult occupations and apparent stereotypical negative bias toward boys, children as young as 4 years old recognize that excluding someone from an activity strictly on the basis of gender is morally wrong (Killen, Pisacane, Lee-Kim, & Ardila-Rey, 2001).

Sex-Role Behavior The final element in the development of a sex-role concept is the actual behavior children show with those of their own sex and of the opposite sex. The unexpected finding here is that children's behavior is sex-typed earlier than are their ideas about sex roles or stereotypes. For example, by 18 to 24 months, children begin to show some preference for sex-stereotyped toys, such as dolls for girls or trucks or building blocks for boys, which is some months before they can normally identify their own gender (Miller, Trautner, & Ruble, 2006).

A similar pattern exists for playmate preference. Long before age 3, girls and boys begin to show a preference for same-sex playmates and are much more sociable with playmates of the same—at a time when they do not yet have a concept of gender stability (Lippa, 2005; Maccoby, 1988, 1990; Maccoby & Jacklin, 1987). By school age, peer relationships are almost exclusively same-sex. You can see the early development of this preference in Figure 10.6, which shows the results of a seminal study of preschool play groups. The researchers counted how often children played with same-sex or opposite-sex playmates (La Freniere, Strayer, & Gauthier, 1984). You can see that by age 3, over 60% of play groups were same-sex groupings, and the rate rose for older children.

Not only are preschoolers' friendships and peer interactions increasingly sex-segregated, it is also becoming clear that boy-boy interactions and girl-girl interactions differ in quality, even in these early years. One important part of same-sex interactions seems to involve instruction and modeling of sex-appropriate behavior. In other words, older boys teach younger boys how to be "masculine," and older girls teach younger girls how to be "feminine" (Danby & Baker, 1998).

Sex Roles and Adolescent Identity Development

In adolescence, teens' understanding of and attitudes toward sex roles become central to the search for identity that you read about earlier in the chapter. Certainly, the physical changes of puberty contribute to the significance of gender issues for teens. Indeed, as you learned in Chapter 4, the timing of puberty can have a profound impact on individual teenagers' perceptions of themselves. Unlike younger children, adolescents understand that sex roles are social conventions, so their attitudes toward them are more flexible (Katz & Ksansnak, 1994). And, by the mid-teens, most adolescents have largely abandoned the automatic assumption that whatever their own gender does is better or preferable (Powlishta et al., 1994).

Figure 10.6   La Freniere's Classic Study of Playmate Preference

Same-sex playmate preference among preschoolers.

(*Source*: P. La Freniere, F. Strayer, and R. Gauthier, "The emergence of same-sex affiliative preference among pre-school peers: A developmental/ethological perspective," *Child Development*, 55. Society for Research in Child Development (1984): p. 1961, Fig. 1. By permission of the Society for Research in Child Development.)

However, increased flexibility may mean that teens experience more anxiety about how they should or should not behave, since cultural stereotypes are no longer seen as rigid dictates that must be followed. Because teens are actively searching for ways to incorporate gender into their own identities, parental attitudes as well as behavior become increasingly important in shaping teens' ideas about gender and sex roles (Castellino, Lerner, Lerner, & von Eye, 1998; Cunningham 2001; Ex & Janssens, 1998; Jackson & Tein, 1998; Raffaelli & Ontai, 2004).

Explaining Sex-Role Development

Learning Objective 10.11

How do social learning, cognitive-developmental, and gender schema theories explain sex-role development?

Theorists from most of the major traditions have tried their hand at explaining these patterns of sex-role development. Freud relied on the concept of identification to explain the child's adoption of appropriate sex-role behavior, but his theory founders on the fact that children begin to show clearly sex-typed behavior long before age 4 or 5, when Freud thought identification occurred.

Social Learning Theory   Social learning theorists, such as Albert Bandura (1977) and Walter Mischel (1966, 1970; Bandura & Bussey, 2004), have naturally emphasized the role of both direct reinforcement and modeling in shaping children's sex-role behavior and attitudes, as well as the availability of stereotypical sex-role models in the various media to which children are exposed. This approach has been far better supported by research than have Freud's ideas.

Social learning theorists point out that children are exposed to sex-role stereotypes in entertainment media. In both commercials and regular programming, women are more often shown at home or in romantic situations; men more often appear in work settings, with cars, or playing sports. Men are shown solving problems and being more active, aggressive, powerful, and independent. Women are most often portrayed as submissive, passive, attractive, sensual, nurturing, emotional, and less able to deal with difficult situations (Golombok & Fivush, 1994; Huston & Wright, 1998; Leaper, Breed, Hoffman, & Perlman, 2002).

Advocates of the social learning perspective also point out that parents reinforce sex-typed activities in children as young as 18 months old, not only by buying different kinds of toys for boys and girls, but by responding more positively when their sons play with blocks or trucks or when their daughters play with dolls (Bussey & Bandura, 2004; Fagot & Hagan, 1991; Lytton & Romney, 1991). Some evidence also suggests that toddlers whose parents are more consistent in rewarding sex-typed toy choice or play behavior, and whose mothers favor traditional family sex roles, learn accurate gender labels earlier than do toddlers whose parents are less focused on the gender-appropriateness of the child's play (Fagot & Leinbach, 1989; Fagot, Leinbach, & O'Boyle, 1992)—findings clearly consistent with the predictions of social learning theory.

Similarly, parents of school-aged children are often guided by gender stereotypes when they select leisure-time activities for their children. For instance, parents more strongly encourage boys to participate in sports and in computer-based activities than they do girls (Fredricks & Eccles, 2005; Simpkins, Davis-Kean, & Eccles, 2005). They do so because of their beliefs about gender differences in various abilities. Research shows that, over time, children's own views about gender differences in athletic talent come into line with those of their parents and influence their activity preferences.

Still, helpful as it is, a social learning explanation is probably not sufficient. In particular, parents differentially reinforce "boy" versus "girl" behavior less than you'd expect, and probably not enough to account for the very early and robust discrimination children seem to make on the basis of gender (Fagot, 1995; Gauvain, Fagot, Leve, & Kavanagh, 2002). Moreover, parents' reinforcement of gender-typed behavior is far from consistent (Power, 2000). Experimental studies have shown that parents neither encourage girls to engage in stereotypically female play behaviors nor discourage them from

Social learning theorists argue that little boys prefer to play with trucks because parents buy them more trucks and reinforce them directly for such play.

Social attitudes toward "tomboys," as these young female hockey players might be labeled, have changed a great deal in recent decades. As a result, girls are often encouraged to take up traditionally male activities. By contrast, boys who express interest in traditionally female activities, such as ballet, are still discouraged from participating in them.

engaging in stereotypically male activities. By contrast, fathers, but not mothers, take more interest in the gender-appropriateness of boys' play behaviors. For the most part, though, parents treat boys and girls similarly.

Even children whose parents seem to treat their young sons and daughters in highly similar ways nonetheless learn gender labels and show same-sex playmate choices. Moreover, once they reach adulthood, the gender-related behavior of the large majority of girls who exhibited male-stereotypical behavior in childhood is indistinguishable from that of other women (Burn, O'Neil, & Nederend, 1996; Carr, 2007), despite the relative lack of discouragement girls experience when they exhibit tomboyish behavior. So, there seems to be something more to sex-role development than modeling and reinforcement.

Cognitive-Developmental Theories A second alternative, based strongly on Piagetian theory, is Lawrence Kohlberg's suggestion that the crucial aspect of the process of sex-role development is the child's understanding of the gender concept (1966; Kohlberg & Ullian, 1974). Once the child realizes that he is a boy or she is a girl forever, he or she becomes highly motivated to learn to behave in the way that is expected or appropriate for that gender. Specifically, Kohlberg predicted that systematic same-sex imitation should become evident only after the child has shown a full understanding of gender constancy. Most studies designed to test this hypothesis have supported Kohlberg: Children do seem to become much more sensitive to same-sex models after they understand gender constancy (Martin & Ruble, 2004). What Kohlberg's theory cannot easily explain, however, is the obvious fact that children show clearly differentiated sex-role behavior, such as toy preferences, long before they have achieved full understanding of the gender concept.

Gender Schema Theory The most fruitful current explanation of sex-role development is usually called **gender schema theory** (Bem, 1981; Martin, 1991; Martin & Halverson, 1981; Martin & Ruble, 2004), a model that has its roots in information-processing theories of cognitive development as well as in Kohlberg's theory. Just as the self-concept can be thought

gender schema theory A theory of the development of gender concept and sex-role behavior that proposes that, between about 18 months and age 2 or 3, a child creates a fundamental schema by which to categorize people, objects, activities, and qualities by gender.

of as a "self-scheme" or "self-theory," so the child's understanding of gender can be seen in the same way. The gender schema begins to develop at about 18 months, once the child notices the differences between male and female, knows his own gender, and can label the two groups with some consistency; the gender schema is generally fully developed by age 2 or 3.

Why would children notice gender so early? Why is it such a significant characteristic? One possibility, suggested by Maccoby (1988), is that because gender is clearly an either/or category, children seem to understand very early that this is a key distinction. Thus, the category serves as a kind of magnet for new information. Another alternative is that young children pay a lot of attention to gender differences because their environment provides so many gender references. Adults and other children emphasize gender distinctions in innumerable small ways. The first question we ask about a new baby is "Is it a boy or a girl?" We buy blue baby clothes for boys and pink for girls; we ask toddlers whether their playmates are boys or girls. A preschool teacher emphasizes gender if she says "Good morning, boys and girls" or divides her charges into a boys' team and a girls' team (Bigler, 1995). In all these ways, adults signal to children that this is an important category and thus further the very early development of a gender scheme that matches cultural norms and beliefs. Whatever the origin of this early scheme, once it is established, a great many experiences are assimilated to it, and children may begin to show preferences for same-sex playmates or for gender-stereotyped activities (Martin, Ruble, & Berenbaum, 2006).

The key difference between gender-schema theory and Kohlberg's cognitive-developmental theory is that for the initial gender schema to be formed, children need not understand that gender is permanent. When they come to understand gender constancy at about 5 or 6, children develop a more elaborated rule, or schema, about "what people who are like me do" and they treat this "rule" the same way they treat other rules—as absolute. By early adolescence, teenagers understand that sex-role concepts are social conventions, and not rigid rules (Katz & Ksansnak, 1994). Indeed, a significant minority of teenagers and youths begin to define themselves as having both masculine and feminine traits—a point we'll return to in a moment.

Many of us, committed to the philosophical goal of equality for women, have taken the rigidity of children's early sex stereotypes ("Mommy, you can't be a psychology doctor, you have to be a psychology nurse") as evidence that there has been little progress toward gender equality. Gender schema theorists emphasize that such rule learning is absolutely normal, and so is the rigid stereotyping seen in children's ideas about sex roles between ages 5 and 8 or 9. Children are searching for order, for rules that help to make sense of their experiences. And a rule about "what men do" and "what women do" is a helpful schema for them.

Individual Gender Schemas   A different approach to the study of sex-role development can be found in research on individual gender schemas, or orientations. Researchers can ask, about any given child, adolescent, or adult, not only how closely the individual's behavior matches the sex-role stereotype, but also how the person thinks of herself or himself and gender-related qualities. In the early years of this research, the issue was usually phrased as masculinity versus femininity, and these were thought of as being on opposite ends of a single continuum. A person could be masculine or feminine but couldn't be both. Following the lead of Sandra Bem (1974) and Janet Spence and Robert Helmreich (1978), psychologists today most often conceive of masculinity and femininity as two separate dimensions, with masculinity centered around agentic/instrumental (assertive) qualities and femininity centered around expressive/communal (nurturing) qualities. A person can be high or low on either or both. Indeed, categorizing people as high or low on each of these two dimensions, based on each individual's self-description, yields four basic sex-role types, called masculine, feminine, androgynous, and undifferentiated—as you can see in Figure 10.7. The masculine and feminine types are the traditional combinations in which a person sees himself or

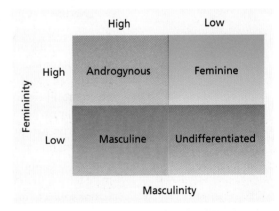

Figure 10.7   Sex-Role Orientation Categories

Thinking of masculinity and ferminity as separate dimensions rather than as two ends of the same dimension leads to the creation of four sex-role types.

masculine One of four sex-role types suggested by the work of Bem and others; a type characterized by high scores on masculinity measures and low scores on femininity measures.

feminine One of four sex-role types suggested by the work of Bem and others; a type characterized by high scores on femininity measures and low scores on masculinity measures.

androgynous One of four sex-role types suggested by the work of Bem and others; a type characterized by high levels of both masculine and feminine qualities.

undifferentiated One of four sex-role types suggested by the work of Bem and others; a type characterized by low scores on both masculinity and femininity measures.

herself as high in one quality and low in the other. A **masculine** person, according to this conceptualization, is one who perceives himself or herself as having many traditional masculine qualities and few traditional feminine qualities. A **feminine** person shows the reverse pattern. In contrast, **androgynous** individuals see themselves as having both masculine and feminine traits; **undifferentiated** individuals describe themselves as lacking both kinds of traits—a group that sounds a lot like those with a "diffuse" identity in Marcia's system.

This categorization system says nothing about the accuracy of the child's or the adult's general sex-role schema. A teenaged girl, for example, could have a clear notion of the norms for male or female behavior and still perceive herself as having some stereotypically masculine qualities. In some sense, then, when developmentalists study masculinity, femininity, and androgyny, they are studying the intersection between the self-scheme and the gender scheme.

Either an androgynous or a masculine sex-role self-concept is associated with higher self-esteem among both boys and girls (Gurnáková & Kusá, 2004). This finding makes sense if we assume that there is a "masculine bias" in the United States and other Western societies, in that traditionally masculine qualities such as independence and competitiveness are more valued by both men and women than are many traditionally female qualities. If such a bias exists—and there is plenty of evidence that it does—then the teenaged boy's task is simpler than the teenaged girl's. He can achieve high self-esteem and success with his peers by adopting a traditional masculine sex role, whereas a girl who adopts a traditional feminine sex role is adopting a less valued role, with attendant risks of lower self-esteem and a reduced sense of competence (Massad, 1981; Rose & Montemayor, 1994).

Findings like these suggest the possibility that while the creation of rigid rules (or schemas) for sex roles is a normal and even essential process in young children, a blurring of those rules may be an important process in adolescence, particularly for girls, for whom a more masculine or androgynous self-concept is associated with more positive outcomes.

Learning Objective 10.12

In what ways might hormones influence gender-related behavior?

Biological Approaches

The theories we have discussed so far flourished in an era when most developmentalists had turned away from the idea that hormonal differences between males and females contributed to sex-role development. Today, developmentalists are taking another look at decades-old experimental studies with animals showing that prenatal exposure to testosterone powerfully influences behavior after birth (Lippa, 2005; Zuloaga, Puts, Jordan, & Breedlove, 2008). Female animals exposed to testosterone behave more like male animals; for instance, they are more aggressive than females who do not experience prenatal exposure to testosterone. Similarly, when experimenters block the release of testosterone during prenatal development of male animal embryos, the animals exhibit behavior that is more typical of the females of their species.

Nature has provided some important evidence regarding the behavioral effects of prenatal exposure to testosterone in humans. Normally developing female embryos produce miniscule amounts of testosterone. Occasionally, however, genetic defects cause unusually large amounts of testosterone to be produced (Rosenthal & Gitelman, 2002). These defects can cause physical defects in the genitalia. In addition, girls with these conditions are more likely to exhibit stereotypically male behavior than are girls who do not have them (Lippa, 2005).

Hormonal influences have been proposed to explain the outcomes of cases involving sex reassignment of infants (like the one you read about at the beginning of the chapter) (Bostwick & Martin, 2007). Many sex reassignments arise from a genetic defect that causes male fetuses to develop deformed genitalia. This defect, however, interferes only with testosterone's effects on the sex organs (Rosenthal & Gitelman, 2002). The brains of these fetuses are exposed to normal amounts of testosterone throughout prenatal development. The hormonal hypothesis asserts that boys with this kind of genetic defect develop a masculine gender identity, despite being raised as girls, because their brains have been exposed prenatally to amounts of testosterone that are typical for male fetuses. As a result, like other boys, they come into the world with the tendency to look for "boy" things and to subtly incorporate such things into their developing self-concepts. According to this view, one could not reasonably expect to inculcate a sense of "femaleness" into these boys' self-concepts by raising them to believe they were girls. Moreover, research indicates that even when these individuals elect to retain the feminine identity with which they have been raised, they possess many attri-butes and exhibit a number of behaviors that are more typical of males than of females (Reiner & Gearhart, 2004).

Finally, note that our discussion of biological approaches has focused largely on research aimed at explaining the role played by biological factors in atypical development. It is always legitimate to question the degree to which findings based on such cases can be generalized to the more common course of development experienced by the majority of children. Although we must keep this caution in mind, research examining how variations in prenatal hormones caused by genetic defects influence behavior after birth suggests that hormones may be far more important in normal sex-role development than theorists once believed.

Think Critically

- The finding that children with difficult temperaments are punished more often than children with easy-going temperaments are could be interpreted several ways. What alternative explanations can you think of?
- If you were to create a mathematical model to explain gender-role development, how much weight (in percentages) would you give to each of these factors: hormones, imitation, reinforcement, models, peer influence, and cognitive development? Explain the reasons behind your weighting of the factors.

Conduct Your Own Research

You can replicate the classic study of Montemayor and Eisen simply by asking children and teenagers from 10 to 18 years of age to answer the question "Who am I?" (Remember to get parents' permission before involving children in any research project.) In each participant's response, count the number of references to physical characteristics and the number to beliefs or ideology. Plot your results on a graph like the one in Figure 10.2 on page 262. If your results differ from those of Montemayor and Eisen, try to determine what may have influenced your results. It may help to think about how the children you questioned might be different from those in the original study or how children's ideas about the self may have been influenced by historical and cultural changes in the three decades since Montemayor and Eisen's data were collected.

Summary

THE CONCEPT OF SELF

10.1 What is the subjective self?

- The child's emerging self-concept has several elements, including the awareness of the self as separate from others and the understanding of self-permanence (which may collectively be called the subjective self). The subjective self develops in the first year of life.

10.2 What does acquisition of an objective self add to the infant's self-concept?

- During the second year of life, the infant's self-concept expands beyond the subjective self to include an objective self, or a sense of self-awareness. As the objective self becomes better refined in early childhood, the child begins to classify herself according to easily identifiable categories such as gender ("boy" or "girl") and age ("little kids" and "big kids").

10.3 In what way is the ability to regulate emotions related to social functioning?

- Children gain an understanding of their emotions during early childhood. The ability to regulate emotion during early childhood predicts how well children function in social settings during the school years.

10.4 How do school-aged children describe themselves?

- The self-concept becomes steadily more abstract in the elementary and high school years, coming to include not only actions but also likes and dislikes, beliefs, and more general personality characteristics.

10.5 How do Erikson's and Marcia's theories explain adolescent identity development?

- During adolescence, there may be a reevaluation of the self, a process Erikson called the identity crisis. In theory, adolescents move from a diffuse sense of future occupational or ideological identity, through a period of reevaluation, to a commitment to a new self-definition. Marcia's theory proposes four identity statuses that may be exhibited as a result of the identity formation process: identity achievement, moratorium, foreclosure, and identity diffusion. Research findings raise doubts about whether the identity-formation process has such a clear developmental aspect.

10.6 What is the process of ethnic identity development, according to Phinney?

- Minority-group adolescents construct an ethnic identity. For many, a sense of belonging to two cultures, the dominant society as well as their own ethnic group, appears to be the most adaptive resolution of this process.

SELF-ESTEEM

10.7 How does self-esteem develop?

- Beginning at about age 7 or 8, the child develops a global evaluation of his or her self-worth (self-esteem). Self-esteem is shaped both by the degree of discrepancy between a child's goals and his accomplishments and by the degree of emotional support the child perceives from parents and peers. Self-esteem develops out of a child's experiences with success and failure, the value he ascribes to the activities at which he succeeds or fails, and the feedback he gets from peers and parents about his performance.

10.8 How consistent is self-esteem across childhood and adolescence?

- Self-esteem is fairly stable across childhood but somewhat less so in early adolescence. Children with high self-esteem and greater feelings of self-efficacy show lower levels of depression.

THE DEVELOPMENT OF THE CONCEPTS OF GENDER AND SEX ROLES

10.9 How do ideas about gender and sex roles change across childhood?

- Children generally acquire gender identity (the ability to correctly identify their own gender and that of others) by about age 2 or 3. They develop gender stability (knowing that people stay the same gender throughout life) by about 4, and they understand gender constancy (that people don't change gender by changing appearance) by about 5 or 6.

10.10 What is the connection between gender stereotypes and sex-typed behavior?

- In early elementary school, children create quite rigid rules about what boys and girls ought to do or are allowed to do. Older children are aware that such rules are social conventions and do not treat them as incontrovertible. Sex-typed behavior is evident from about 18 months of age.

10.11 How do social learning, cognitive-developmental, and gender schema theories explain sex-role development?

- Theorists of several different traditions have attempted to explain observed patterns in sex-role development. Learning theories emphasize modeling and parental expectations. Cognitive-developmental theories propose that gender development occurs in stages. The most widely accepted theory is gender schema theory, which proposes that children begin to acquire a rule about what boys do and what girls do as soon as they figure out the difference between boys and girls, and that this schema forms the basis of both stereotyping and sex-typed behavior. Young people also differ in the extent to which they see themselves as having feminine or masculine qualities or traits. Those who describe themselves with qualities from both sets are said to be androgynous. Both girls and boys who describe themselves as androgynous or masculine have somewhat higher self-esteem, at least in U.S. culture.

10.12 In what ways might hormones influence gender-related behavior?

- Animal studies show that prenatal exposure to testosterone leads to masculine behavior in females, while lack of exposure to this hormone causes male animals to behave in ways that are more typical of females. Research involving children with genetic defects suggests that testosterone may also influence sex-typed behavior in humans.

Key Terms

androgynous (p. 278)

feminine (p. 278)

foreclosure (p. 263)

gender concept (p. 270)

gender constancy (p. 271)

gender identity (p. 271)

gender schema theory (p. 276)

gender stability (p. 271)

identity achievement (p. 263)

identity diffusion (p. 263)

identity versus role confusion (p. 263)

masculine (p. 278)

moratorium (p. 263)

objective self (p. 256)

self-concept (p. 256)

self-esteem (p. 268)

sex role (p. 270)

sex-typed behavior (p. 270)

subjective self (p. 256)

undifferentiated (p. 278)

11 The Development of Social Relationships

During the late 1980s, a tragic saga began to unfold in the Sudan. Over the course of the next 10 years, government-backed forces bent on imposing Islamic law on the entire population drove millions of Christian and animist families from their homes. These desperate families headed for the Kenyan and Ethiopian borders in hopes of finding refuge. Sadly, tens of thousands of the refugees died, and their deaths left many children without parents. These children, some as young as 4 years of age, knew that they faced certain death if they returned home. Lacking adults to support them, the children banded together, the older children protecting the younger ones, and kept on the move. Little did they know that they would spend years walking in the hostile East African desert, a deadly hot and dry land more than twice the size of Texas. Many starved to death or died from disease, bad water, or tainted or poisonous food. At night, howling packs of hyenas would sometimes stalk the groups. On some occasions, as many as five children from a group would be lost to these predators. The terrified survivors could do nothing but climb trees and watch.

Miraculously, thousands of these children, referred to as "Lost Boys" despite the fact that many were girls, made it to refugee camps in Kenya and Ethiopia. There relief workers fed them, treated their injuries, and set up makeshift schools to educate them. Ultimately, international relief agencies helped many of the children resettle in the United States. Many of them were successful in school, graduated from college, and went on to establish careers and families of their own, showing few hints of the degree of hardship and deprivation that they suffered earlier in their lives (Geltman et al., 2005).

It is likely that none of the Lost Boys would have survived alone. Undoubtedly, the capacity of the older children to provide protection and sustenance for the younger ones was vital to their physical survival. However, developmental scientists attribute the intellectual and psychosocial resilience that the Lost Boys displayed later in life to the intense bonds that they developed with one another during their ordeal (Geltman et al., 2005). These bonds helped the children compensate emotionally for the loss of their parents. Thus, the Lost Boys' story serves as a reminder that socioemotional connections can be just as important to development as physical care.

In this chapter, you will be introduced to the important ideas and discoveries of John Bowlby, Mary Ainsworth, and other developmental scientists regarding emotional bonds between infants and caregivers. We will next discuss the impact of these early relationships on those that come along later in life. A look at peer relationships, along with positive and negative patterns of peer interaction, rounds out our discussion of social relationships.

Relationships with Parents

The parent-child relationship has been at the center of much theorizing and research in developmental psychology. To understand the major research findings, you need a basic knowledge of the theoretical foundation on which most research studies have been based.

In this relationship, the son is attached to his dad, but (in Ainsworth's terms) the father's relationship to his son is an affectional bond rather than an attachment.

Attachment Theory

The strongest theoretical influence in studies of infant-parent relationships is attachment theory, particularly the work of John Bowlby and Mary Ainsworth (Ainsworth & Bowlby, 1991). Bowlby's thinking had roots in psychoanalytic thought, particularly in the emphasis on the significance of the earliest relationship between mother and child. To this theoretical base, he added important evolutionary and ethological concepts. In his view, "the propensity to make strong emotional bonds to particular individuals [is] a basic component of human nature, already present in germinal form in the neonate" (Bowlby, 1988a, p. 3). Such a relationship has survival value because it ensures that the infant will receive nurturance. The relationship is built and maintained by an interlocking repertoire of instinctive behaviors that create and sustain proximity between parent and child. For example, children are born with a repertoire of built-in behaviors, such as crying, smiling, and making eye contact, that elicit caregiving from others. Similarly, there are universal ways in which parents, particularly mothers, respond to these behaviors—for example, picking the infants up when they cry or speaking to them in a high-pitched voice.

Affectional Bonds and Attachments   In Bowlby's and Ainsworth's writings, this mutual pattern of responding is key to the development of affectional bonds and attachments. Ainsworth defines an **affectional bond** as "a relatively long-enduring tie in which the partner is important as a unique individual and is interchangeable with none other. In an affectional bond, there is a desire to maintain closeness to the partner" (1989, p. 711). An **attachment** is a subvariety of affectional bond in which a person's sense of security is bound up in the relationship. When you are attached, you feel (or hope to feel) a special sense of security and comfort in the presence of the other, and you can use the other as a safe base from which to explore the rest of the world.

In these terms, the child's relationship with the parent is an attachment, but the parent's relationship with the child is usually not, since the parent presumably does not feel a greater sense of security in the presence of the infant or use the infant as a safe base. A relationship with one's adult partner or with a very close friend, however, is an attachment in the sense Ainsworth and Bowlby meant the term. Of course, adults aren't as dependent on their partners or friends as children are on their parents. Still, there is a certain kind of security that an adult draws from being in such a relationship; knowing that one can rely on the acceptance and support of a romantic partner or a close friend no matter what happens in many ways parallels the safe base function attachment relationships serve for children.

Because affectional bonds and attachments are internal states, developmentalists cannot observe them directly. Instead, they deduce their existence by observing **attachment behaviors**, which are all those behaviors that allow a child or an adult to achieve and retain physical proximity to someone else to whom he is attached. These could include smiling, making eye contact, calling out to the other person across a room, touching, clinging, or crying.

It is important to make clear that there is no one-to-one correspondence between the number of different attachment behaviors a child (or adult) shows on any one occasion and the strength of the underlying attachment. Attachment behaviors are elicited primarily when the individual has need of care or support or comfort. An infant is needy a good deal of the time; an older child would be likely to show attachment behaviors only when he was frightened, tired, or otherwise under stress. It is the pattern of these behaviors, not the frequency, that reveals something about the strength or quality of the attachment or the affectional bond. To understand the early relationship between the parent and the child, developmentalists look at both sides of the equation—at the development of the parent's bond to the child and at the child's attachment to the parent.

Internal Working Models   According to Bowlby, once an attachment to another person has been established, the child begins to construct a mental representation of the relationship that becomes a set of expectations that the child has for future interactions with the same person. Bowlby coined the term **internal working model** to describe this mental representation and suggested that it includes such elements as the child's confidence (or lack of it) that the attachment figure will be available or reliable, the child's expectation of rebuff or affection, and the child's sense of assurance that the attachment figure is really a safe base for exploration. The internal model begins to be formed late in the child's first year of life and becomes increasingly elaborated and better established over the first 4 or 5 years. By age 5,

affectional bond A "relatively long-enduring tie in which the partner is important as a unique individual and is interchangeable with none other" (Ainsworth, 1989, p. 711).

attachment A subtype of affectional bond in which the presence of the partner adds a special sense of security, a "safe base," for the individual.

attachment behaviors The collection of (probably) instinctive behaviors of one person toward another that bring about or maintain proximity and caregiving, such as the smile of the young infant; behaviors that reflect an attachment.

internal working model As applied to social relationships, a cognitive construction of the workings of relationships, such as expectations of support or affection, trustworthiness, and so on. The earliest relationships may form the template for such a cognitive construction.

most children have clear internal models of the mother (or other caregiver), a self-model, and a model of relationships (Schermerhorn, Cummings, & Davies, 2008).

Once formed, such models shape and explain experiences and affect memory and attention. Children notice and remember experiences that fit their model and miss or forget experiences that don't match it. More importantly, the model affects the child's behavior: The child tends to re-create, in each new relationship, the pattern with which he is familiar. Alan Sroufe gives an example that may make this point clearer:

> What is rejection to one child is benign to another. What is warmth to a second child is confusing or ambiguous to another. For example, a child approaches another and asks to play. Turned down, the child goes off and sulks in a corner. A second child receiving the same negative reaction skips on to another partner and successfully engages him in play. Their experiences of rejection are vastly different. Each receives confirmation of quite different inner working models. (1988, p. 23)

In a sense, these internal models are not unlike the social scripts that the preschooler develops in other areas (Bretherton, 1993). They contain expectations for sequences of behavior, rules for behavior with various individuals, and interpretations of others' actions; they help shape what the child pays attention to and what she remembers (Kirsh & Cassidy, 1997).

The Parent's Bond to the Child

Learning Objective 11.2
What factors influence the parent's bond to the child?

If you read any popular magazines, you have probably come across articles proclaiming that mothers (or fathers) must have immediate contact with their newborn infant if they are to become properly bonded with the baby. As you'll see, the formation of an attachment relationship to a child is far too complex to be completely dependent on a single, early experience.

The Development of Interactive Skill What is essential in the formation of an early bond is the opportunity for the parent and infant to develop a mutual, interlocking pattern of attachment behaviors, a smooth "dance" of interaction. The baby signals her needs by crying or smiling; she looks at her parents when they look at her. The parents, in their turn, enter into this interactive dance with their own repertoire of caregiving behaviors. They pick the baby up when she cries, wait for and respond to her signals of hunger or some other need, and so on. Some researchers and theorists have described this as the development of *synchrony* (Feldman, 2007; Isabella, Belsky, & von Eye, 1989).

One of the most intriguing things about this process is that all humans seem to know how to do this particular dance—and do it in very similar ways. In the presence of a young infant, most adults will automatically display a distinctive pattern of interactive behaviors, including a smile, raised eyebrows, and very wide-open eyes. Adults also use their voices in special ways with babies, as you'll remember from the discussion of motherese in Chapter 8. Parents all over the world use the characteristic high-pitched and lilting pattern of motherese; they also use similar intonation patterns. For example, in a study of mother-infant interactions, Hanus and Mechthild Papousek (1991) found that Chinese, German, and American mothers all tended to use a rising voice inflection when they wanted the baby to "take a turn" or contribute to the interaction and a falling intonation when they wanted to soothe the baby.

Yet even though people show these behaviors with many infants, they do not form a bond with every baby they coo at in a restaurant or a grocery store. For an adult, the critical ingredient for the formation of a bond seems to be the opportunity to develop real synchrony—to practice the dance until the partners follow one another's lead smoothly and pleasurably. This takes time and many rehearsals, and some parents (and infants) become more skillful at it than others. In general, the smoother and more predictable the process becomes, the more satisfying it seems to be to the parents and the stronger their bond to the infant becomes.

Father-Child Bonds Most of the research you have read about so far has involved studies of mothers. Still, many of the same principles seem to hold for fathers as well (Lewis & Lamb, 2003). In particular, fathers seem to direct the same repertoire of attachment behaviors toward their infants as do mothers (Figueiredo, Costa, Pacheco, & Pais, 2007). In the early weeks of a baby's life, dad touches, talks to, and cuddles the baby in the same ways mom does; both mothers and fathers show the same physiological responses when they interact with their new infant, including increased heart rate and blood pressure (Corter & Fleming, 1995).

After the earliest weeks of life, however, signs of some specialization of parental behaviors with infants become evident (Brown, McBride, Shin, & Bost, 2007). Studies in the United States show that fathers spend more time playing with a baby, using more physical rough-

Ryan's dad, like most fathers, is far more likely to play with him by tossing him around than is his mom.

housing. Mothers spend more time in routine caregiving, and they talk to and smile at the baby more (Parke, 1995; Walker, Messinger, Fogel, & Karns, 1992). This does not mean that fathers have a weaker affectional bond with the infant; it does mean that the behaviors they show toward the infant are typically somewhat different from those mothers show. Nevertheless, by 6 months of age, infants are just as likely to show signs of attachment to their fathers as to their mothers (Feldman, 2003). These signs include laughing and wriggling with delight in short, intense bursts while interacting with their fathers. By contrast, the signs of attachment to mothers are more likely to include slow, gradual smiles. It isn't a matter of liking one parent more than the other. Babies demonstrate through these signs that the specific features of synchronous interaction are different for mothers and fathers.

However, we should not leap to the conclusion that this sex difference is somehow built-in; instead, it appears to rest on cultural patterns. Researchers in England and in India have found higher levels of physical play by fathers than by mothers, but other researchers in Sweden, Israel, Italy, China, and Malaysia have not (Parke & Buriel, 1998). Findings like this nicely illustrate the usefulness of cross-cultural research for identifying patterns of behavior that are influenced by varying cultural expectations or training.

The Child's Attachment to the Parent

Like the parent's bond to the baby, the baby's attachment emerges gradually. Bowlby (1969) suggested three phases in the development of the infant's attachment; these are presented schematically in Figure 11.1. Once formed, the attachment relationship changes somewhat as the child gets older.

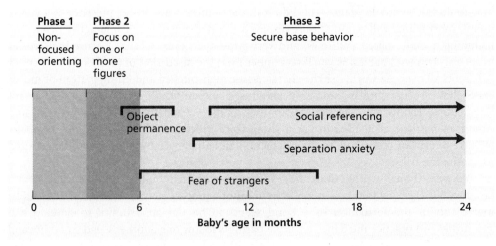

Figure 11.1   Attachment in Developmental Context

This schematic shows how the various threads of development of attachment are woven together.

Phase 1: Nonfocused Orienting and Signaling   Bowlby believed that a baby begins life with a set of innate behavior patterns that orient him toward others and signal his needs. Mary Ainsworth described these as *proximity-promoting* behaviors: They bring people closer. In the newborn's repertoire, these behaviors include crying, making eye contact, clinging, cuddling, and responding to caregiving efforts by being soothed.

At this stage, there is little evidence that the baby is attached to the parents. Nonetheless, the roots of attachment are established. The baby is building up expectancies and schemas about interaction patterns with the parents, as well as developing the ability to discriminate mom and dad from others in many contexts.

Phase 2: Focus on One or More Figures   By 3 months of age, the baby begins to aim her attachment behaviors somewhat more narrowly. She may smile more at the people who regularly take care of her and may not smile readily at a stranger. The infant does not yet have a complete attachment, though. The child still favors a number of people with her proximity-promoting behaviors, and no one person has yet become the "safe base." Children in this phase show no special anxiety at being separated from their parents and no fear of strangers.

Phase 3: Secure Base Behavior   Only at about 6 months of age, according to Bowlby, does the baby form a genuine attachment—about the same time that he develops some preliminary understanding that objects and people continue to exist when they are out of sight (object permanence). For the first time, the infant uses the "most important" person as a safe base from which to explore the world around him—one of the key signs that an attachment exists. Because the 6- to 7-month-

A few months ago, this baby probably would have let himself be held by just about anyone without a fuss; now all of a sudden he's afraid of strangers. Parents are often puzzled by this behavior, but it is absolutely normal.

old begins to be able to move about the world more freely by creeping and crawling, he can move toward the caregiver as well as entice the caregiver to come to him. Attachment behaviors therefore shift from mostly "come here" (proximity-promoting) signals to what Ainsworth calls *proximity-seeking* behaviors, which might be thought of as "go there" behaviors.

Once the child has developed a clear attachment, several related behaviors also appear. One of these is social referencing, which you read about in Chapter 5. The 10-month-old uses his ability to discriminate among various facial expressions to guide his safe-base behavior. He begins to check out mom's or dad's facial expression before deciding whether to venture forth into some novel situation. At about the same age or a little earlier, babies also typically show both fear of strangers and separation anxiety.

Fear of Strangers and Separation Anxiety   Fear of strangers and separation anxiety are two forms of distress that are rare before 5 or 6 months; they appear sometime between 6 and 9 months, rise in frequency until about 12 to 16 months, and then decline after about 24 months. The research findings are not altogether consistent, but it looks as though fear of strangers normally appears first, at about the same time as babies show fearful reactions in other situations. Anxiety at separation starts a bit later but continues to be visible for a longer period, a pattern diagrammed in Figure 11.1.

Such increases in stranger fear and separation anxiety have been observed in children from a number of different cultures and in both home-reared and child-care-reared children in the United States, which suggests that some basic age-related developmental timetables underlie this pattern (Kagan & Herschkowitz, 2005; Kagan, Kearsley, & Zelazo, 1978). Virtually all children show at least mild forms of these two types of distress, although the intensity of the reaction varies widely. Some babies protest briefly; others are virtually inconsolable. Some of this variation undoubtedly reflects basic temperamental differences in behavioral inhibition

(Kagan et al., 1994). Heightened fearfulness may also be a response to some upheaval or stress in the child's life, such as a recent move or a change in the daily schedule. Whatever the origin of such variations in fearfulness, the pattern does eventually diminish in most toddlers, typically by the middle of the second year.

Attachments to Mothers and Fathers   From the age of 7 or 8 months, when strong attachments are first seen, infants prefer either the father or the mother to a stranger. And when both the father and the mother are available, an infant will smile at or approach either or both, except when she is frightened or under stress. When that happens, especially between the ages of 8 and 24 months, the child typically turns to the mother rather than the father (Lamb, Bornstein, & Teti, 2002).

As you might expect, the strength of the child's attachment to the father at this early age seems to be related to the amount of time dad has spent with the child. In one early study, for example, Gail Ross found she could predict a baby's attachment to the father by knowing how many diapers the dad changed in a typical week. The more diapers, the stronger the attachment (Caldera, 2004; Ross, Kagan, Zelazo, & Kotelchuk, 1975). But greatly increased time with the father does not seem to be the only element, since Michael Lamb and his Swedish colleagues (1983) found that infants whose fathers were their major caregivers for at least a month in the first year of the child's life were nonetheless more strongly attached to their mothers than to their fathers. For the father to be consistently preferred over the mother would probably require essentially full-time paternal care. As this option becomes more common, it will be possible to study such father-child pairs to see whether babies develop a preference for the father.

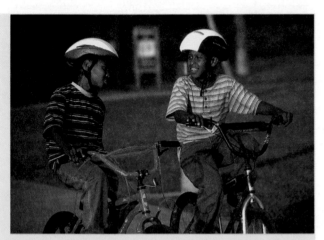

Because school-aged children roam farther from home, spending more and more time with peers, it is tempting to assume that they are less strongly attached to their parents. But this assumption is wrong. Children this age still depend on their parents to be a safe base.

Cultures with Shared Infant Caretaking   You may be wondering whether attachment patterns vary when an infant has more than one primary caretaker (Tronick, 2007). In one classic study, Edward Tronick and his colleagues (1992) studied a pygmy group called the Efe, who forage in the forests of Zaire. They live in small groups of perhaps twenty individuals in camps, each consisting of several extended families. Infants in these communities are cared for communally in the early months and years of life. They are carried and held by all the adult women, and they interact regularly with many different adults. They may even be nursed by women other than their mothers, although they normally sleep with their mothers.

Tronick and his colleagues report two things of particular interest about early attachment in this group. First, Efe infants seem to use virtually any adult or older child in their world as a safe base, which suggests that they may have no single central attachment. Second, beginning at about 6 months of age, the Efe infant nonetheless seems to insist on being with his mother more and to prefer her over other women, although other women continue to help care for the child. Thus, even in an extremely communal rearing arrangement, some sign of a central attachment is evident, although it may be less dominant.

Attachments in Early Childhood   By age 2 or 3, although the child's attachment to the mother and father remains powerful, most attachment behaviors have become less continuously visible. Children of this age are cognitively advanced enough to understand mom if she explains why she is going away and says that she will be back, so their anxiety at separation wanes. They can even use a photograph of their mother as a "safe base" for exploration in a strange situation (Passman & Longeway, 1982), which reflects another cognitive advance. By age 3 or 4, a child can also use shared plans offered by parents ("I'll be home after your nap time") to lessen her potential anxiety at separation (Crittenden,

1992). Attachment behaviors have naturally not completely disappeared. Two-year-olds still want to sit on mom's or dad's lap; they are still likely to seek some closeness or proximity when mom returns from some absence. But in nonfrightening or nonstressful situations, toddlers and preschoolers are able to move farther and farther from their safe base without apparent distress.

Bowlby referred to this new form of attachment as a **goal-corrected partnership** (Bowlby, 1969). The infant's goal, to put it most simply, is always to have the attachment figure within sight or touch. The preschooler's goal is also to be "in contact" with the parent, but "contact" no longer requires constant physical presence. The preschooler not only understands that his mother will continue to exist when she isn't there; he now also understands that the relationship continues to exist even when the partners are apart. This enables the toddler or preschooler to modify ("correct") her goal of contact with her attachment figure by engaging in collaborative planning: agreeing on when and how the two will be together, for example, or what the child will do if she gets scared or anxious, or who the replacement security person will be.

Although teens have more conflicts with parents than do younger children, they continue to maintain strong attachments to them.

Attachments in Middle Childhood   In elementary school, overt attachment behaviors such as clinging and crying are even less visible, so it is easy to lose sight of the fact that children this age are still strongly attached to their parents. The elementary school child may take primary responsibility for maintaining contact with the parent (Kerns, 1996), but she wants to know that mom and dad are there when she needs them. Such a need is most likely to arise when the child faces some stressful situation, perhaps the first day of school, an illness or upheaval in the family, or the death of a pet. Because fewer experiences are new and potentially stressful to the 7- or 8-year-old than to the preschooler, there is much less obvious safe-base behavior and less open affection expressed by the child to the parent (Maccoby, 1984). These changes do not, however, signify that the child's attachment to the parent has weakened. In fact, extended separations from parents can be extremely stressful for school-aged children (Smith, Lalonde, & Johnson, 2004).

Parent-Child Relationships in Adolescence

Learning Objective 11.4
What are the characteristics of parent-child relationships in adolescence?

In adolescence, the form of attachment behaviors shifts somewhat, because teenagers have two apparently contradictory tasks in their relationships with their parents: to establish autonomy from the parents and to maintain their sense of relatedness (attachment) with their parents. The push for autonomy shows itself in increasing conflict between parent and adolescent; the maintenance of connection is seen in the continued strong attachment of child to parent.

Increases in Conflict   The rise in conflict with parents as children enter adolescence has been repeatedly documented (e.g., Steinberg & Silk, 2002). In the great majority of families, there is an increase in mild bickering or conflicts over everyday issues such as chores or personal rights—whether the adolescent should be allowed to wear a bizarre hair style or certain clothing or whether and when the teen should be required to do family chores. Teenagers and their parents also interrupt one another more often and become more impatient with one another. They may also argue about the age at which privileges such as dating should be granted (Cunningham, Swanson, Spencer, & Dupree, 2003).

This increase in discord is widely found, but it is important not to assume that it signifies a major disruption of the quality of the parent-child relationship. Laurence Steinberg,

goal-corrected partnership Term used by Bowlby to describe the form of the child-parent attachment in the preschool years, in which the two partners, through improved communication, negotiate the form and frequency of contact between them.

one of the key researchers in this area, estimates that relatively few families in the United States experience a substantial or pervasive deterioration in the quality of parent-child relationships in the years of early adolescence (Steinberg & Silk, 2002). Those families at highest risk for persistently heightened conflict are those in which the parents have a history of low levels of warmth and supportiveness toward their child in earlier years and continue this pattern during adolescence (Rueter & Conger, 1995; Silverberg & Gondoli, 1996). When parents express warmth and supportiveness and are open to hearing the teenager's opinions and disagreements, the period of heightened conflict seems to be relatively brief.

If the rise in conflict doesn't signal that the relationship is falling apart, what does it mean? A variety of theorists have suggested that the temporary discord, far from being a negative event, may instead be a developmentally healthy and necessary part of the adolescent's identity formation. In order to become his own person, the teenager needs to push away from the parents, disagree with them, try out his own limits—a process of **individuation** not unlike that seen in the toddler who begins to say "no" to parents during that famous period called the terrible twos (Grotevant & Cooper, 1985).

The pattern of causes for parent-teen conflict is obviously complex. Hormonal changes may be causally linked to increases in assertiveness, perhaps especially among boys. Parents' reactions to pubertal changes may also be highly important parts of the mix. Visible pubertal changes, including menarche, alter parents' expectations of the teenager and increase their concern about guiding and controlling the adolescent to help her avoid the pitfalls of too great a level of independence.

Attachment to Parents Paradoxically, in the midst of this distancing and temporarily heightened family conflict, teenagers' underlying emotional attachment to their parents remains strong. Results from a classic study by Mary Levitt and her colleagues (1993) illustrate the point. Levitt interviewed African American, Hispanic American, and Caucasian American children aged 7, 10, and 14. All the children were shown a drawing with a set of three concentric circles. They were asked to place in the innermost circle the names of those "people who are the most close and important to you—people you love the most and who love you the most." In the next circle outward, children were asked to place the names of "people who are not quite as close but who are still important—people you really love or like, but not quite as much as the people in the first circle." The last circle contained names of somewhat more distant members of this personal "convoy." For each person listed, the interviewer then asked about the kind of support that person provided.

Levitt found that for all three racial or ethnic groups, at all three ages, parents and other close family were by far the most likely to be placed in the inner circle. Even 14-year-olds rarely placed friends in this position. So the parents remain central. At the same time, it is clear from Levitt's results that peers become increasingly important sources of support, as you can see in Figure 11.2. This figure shows the total amount of support the children and adolescents described from each source. Friends clearly provided more support for the 14-year-olds than they did for the younger children, a pattern that is clear for all three groups.

In general, a teenager's sense of well-being or happiness is more strongly correlated with the quality of his attachment to his parents than to the quality of his attachments to his peers (Raja, McGee, & Stanton, 1992; van Brakel, Muris, Bögels, & Thomassen, 2006). In fact, good relationships with parents and peers seem to go hand in hand during the teen years. Teenagers who are

individuation The process of psychological, social, and physical separation from parents that begins in adolescence.

Figure 11.2
The Social Convoy

African American (Af), Caucasian American (Cs), and Hispanic American (Hs) children and teens were asked about the amount and type of support they received from various members of their "social convoy." Note that for teens, friends become more significant sources of support, but parents do not become substantially *less* important.

(*Source*: M. Levitt, N. Guacci-Franco, and J. Levitt. "Convoys of social support in childhood and early adolescence: Structure and function," *Developmental Psychology*, 29 (1993): p. 815. Copyright © 1993 by the American Psychological Association. Reprinted with permission of the American Psychological Association and M. Levitt.)

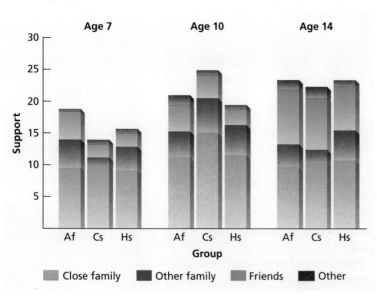

close to their parents are also more likely to enjoy positive relationships with their peers than are adolescents who are not close to their parents (Allen, Porter, McFarland, Marsh, & McElhaney, 2005; Turnage, 2004; Weimer, Kerns, & Oldenburg, 2004; Zimmermann, 2004). Furthermore, the stronger the sense of connectedness (attachment) a teenager has with his parents, the less likely he is to engage in any of the risky or delinquent behaviors you learned about in Chapter 4 (Brook, Whiteman, Finch, & Cohen, 2000; Resnick et al., 1997). Thus, even while the teenager is becoming more autonomous, the parents continue to provide a highly important psychological safe base.

Variations in the Quality of Attachments

Go to a child-care center and watch the way the babies or toddlers greet their parents at the end of the day. Some are calmly pleased to see mom or dad; others may run to the parent, crying and clinging; still others may show little interest. These children may all have formed an attachment to their parents, but the quality of those attachments differs markedly.

Secure and Insecure Attachments

All attachment theorists share the assumption that the first attachment relationship is the most influential ingredient in the creation of the child's working model. Variations in this first attachment relationship are almost universally described using Mary Ainsworth's category system (Ainsworth et al., 1978). She distinguished between *secure attachment* and two types of *insecure attachment*, which she assessed using a procedure called the Strange Situation.

The **Strange Situation** consists of a series of episodes in a laboratory setting, typically used when the child is between 12 and 18 months of age. The child first spends time with the mother and then with the mother and a stranger; then the child is left alone with the stranger, then completely alone for a few minutes, then reunited with the mother, then left alone again, and finally reunited first with the stranger and then with the mother. Ainsworth suggested that children's reactions to these situations indicated one of three types of attachment: **secure attachment**, shown by a child who uses the parent as a safe base and is readily consoled after separation, and two types of **insecure attachment**, shown by a child who either shows little preference for mother over a stranger (the *insecure/detached* or *insecure/avoidant* child) or is wary of strangers and upset at separation but is not reassured by the mother's return (the *insecure/resistant* or *insecure/ambivalent* child). Mary Main has suggested a fourth type of attachment, which she calls *insecure/disorganized/disoriented* (Main & Solomon, 1990).

Some of the characteristics of the different types of attachment are listed in Table 11.1 on page 292. As you read the descriptions, note that whether the child cries when he is separated from his mother is not a helpful indicator of the security of his attachment. It is the entire pattern of the child's responses to the Strange Situation that is critical, not any one response.

Origins of Secure and Insecure Attachments

Studies of parent-child interactions suggest that one crucial ingredient for a secure attachment is *emotional availability* on the part of the caregiver (Biringen, 2000). An emotionally available caregiver is one who is able and willing to form an emotional attachment to the infant. For example, economically or emotionally distressed parents may be so distracted by their own problems that they can't invest emotion in the parent-infant relationship. Such parents may meet the baby's physical needs—feeding, changing diapers, and so on—but be unable to respond emotionally.

A number of studies (including some cross-cultural research) further suggest that both acceptance of the infant by the parents and some aspect of sensitivity to the child—a quality that has been measured and given various labels, including *synchrony*, *mutuality*, and *contingent responsiveness*—are also necessary for the formation of an attachment relationship

Strange Situation A series of episodes used by Mary Ainsworth and others in studies of attachment. The child is observed with the mother, with a stranger, alone, when reunited with the stranger, and when reunited with the mother.

secure attachment An internal working model of relationships in which the child uses the parent as a safe base and is readily consoled after separation, when fearful, or when otherwise stressed.

insecure attachment An internal working model of relationships in which the child does not as readily use the parent as a safe base and is not readily consoled by the parent if upset. Includes three subtypes of attachment: avoidant, ambivalent, and disorganized/disoriented.

Table 11.1 Categories of Secure and Insecure Attachment in Ainsworth's Strange Situation

Category	Behavior
Secure attachment	Child readily separates from mother and easily becomes absorbed in exploration; when threatened or frightened, child actively seeks contact and is readily consoled; child does not avoid or resist contact if mother initiates it. When reunited with mother after absence, child greets her positively or is easily soothed if upset. Clearly prefers mother to stranger.
Insecure attachment (detached/avoidant)	Child avoids contact with mother, especially at reunion after an absence. Does not resist mother's efforts to make contact, but does not seek much contact. Shows no preference for mother over stranger.
Insecure attachment (resistant/ambivalent)	Child shows little exploration and is wary of stranger. Greatly upset when separated from mother, but not reassured by mother's return or her efforts at comforting. Child both seeks and avoids contact at different times. May show anger toward mother at reunion, and resists both comfort from and contact with stranger.
Insecure attachment (disorganized/disoriented)	Dazed behavior, confusion, or apprehension. Child may show contradictory behavior patterns simultaneously, such as moving toward mother while keeping gaze averted.

Sources: Ainsworth et al., 1978; Carlson and Sroufe, 1995; Main and Solomon, 1990.

(Posada et al., 2002). This key quality is more than merely love and affection. To be rated as sensitive, or high in contingent responsiveness, the parents must be attuned to the child's signals and cues and respond appropriately. They smile when the baby smiles, talk to the baby when he vocalizes, pick him up when he cries, and so on (Ainsworth & Marvin, 1995; Sroufe, 1996). Developmentalists' certainty that this type of responsiveness is a key ingredient in the formation of secure attachment has been strengthened by experimental studies showing that training mothers who demonstrate insensitivity to become more sensitive is highly effective. Such studies show long-term effects on both mothers' behavior and infants' attachment security (van Doesum, Riksen-Walraven, Hosman, & Hoefnagels, 2008).

Each of the several subvarieties of insecure attachment also has additional distinct antecedents. For example, a disorganized/disoriented pattern of attachment seems especially likely when the child has been abused or has parents who had some trauma in their own childhoods, such as either abuse or the early death of a parent (Cassidy & Berlin, 1994; Main & Hesse, 1990). An insecure pattern is more common when the mother is inconsistently or unreliably available to the child. Mothers may show such unavailability or periodic neglect for a variety of reasons, but a common one is depression (van Doesum et al., 2008). When the mother rejects the infant or regularly (rather than intermittently) withdraws from contact with the infant, the infant is more likely to show an avoidant pattern of attachment.

Attachment Quality across Cultures Studies in a variety of countries have pointed to the possibility that secure attachments may be influenced by culture as well (Carlson & Harwood, 2003) The most thorough analyses have come from a Dutch psychologist, Marinus van IJzendoorn, who has examined the results of 32 separate studies in 8 different countries. Table 11.2 shows the percentage of babies classified in each category for each country. We need to be cautious about overgeneralizing the information in this table, because in most cases there are only one or two studies from a given country, normally with quite small samples. The single study from China, for example, included only 36 babies. Still, the findings are thought-provoking.

The most striking thing about the data in Table 11.2 is their consistency. In each of the eight countries, a secure attachment is the most common pattern, found in more than half of all babies studied; in five of the eight countries, an avoidant pattern is the more common of the two forms of insecure attachment. Only in Israel and Japan is this pattern significantly reversed. How can such differences be explained?

Table 11.2 Secure and Insecure Attachments in Different Cultures

Country	Number of Studies	Percentage of Children Showing Each Type of Attachment		
		Secure	Avoidant	Ambivalent
West Germany	3	56.6	35.3	8.1
Great Britain	1	75.0	22.2	2.8
Netherlands	4	67.3	26.3	6.4
Sweden	1	74.5	21.6	3.9
Israel	2	64.4	6.8	28.8
Japan	2	67.7	5.2	25.0
China	1	50.0	25.0	25.0
United States	18	64.8	21.1	14.1
Overall average		65%	21%	14%

Source: Based on Table 1 of van IJzendoorn and Kroonenberg, 1988, pp. 150–151.

One possibility is that the Strange Situation is simply not an appropriate measure of attachment security in all cultures. For example, because Japanese babies are rarely separated from their mothers in the first year of life, being left totally alone in the midst of the Strange Situation may be far more stressful for them, which might result in more intense, inconsolable crying and hence a classification of ambivalent attachment. The counterargument is that comparisons of toddlers' reactions in the Strange Situation suggest few cultural differences in such behaviors as proximity-seeking or avoidance of the mother, all of which lead to more confidence that the Strange Situation is tapping similar processes among children in many cultures (Sagi, van IJzendoorn, & Koren-Karie, 1991).

It is also possible that the meaning of a "secure" or "avoidant" pattern is different in different cultures, even if the percentages of each category are similar. German researchers, for example, have suggested that, in their culture, an insecure-avoidant classification may reflect not indifference by the mother but rather explicit training toward greater independence in the baby (Grossmann, Grossmann, Spangler, Seuss, & Unzner, 1985).

On the other hand, research in Israel (Sagi, 1990) shows that the attachment classification derived from the Strange Situation predicts the baby's later social skills in much the same way as it does for samples in the United States, which suggests that the classification system is valid in both cultures. The most plausible hypothesis is that the same factors in mother-infant interaction contribute to secure and insecure attachments in all cultures and that these patterns reflect similar internal models. But it will take more research like the Israeli work, in which the long-term outcomes of the various categories are studied, before developmentalists can be sure if this is correct.

Japanese babies spend more time with their mothers than do infants in Western cultures. As a result, they may exhibit more distress during the Strange Situation and be inappropriately classified as ambivalently attached.

Temperament and Attachment

Learning Objective 11.6

How does infant temperament influence the attachment process?

The general timing of the development of attachment behaviors is the same in virtually all children. However, the emotional intensity of the relationship varies considerably from child to child. For example, infants differ widely in how much fear they show toward strangers or toward novel situations. Some of this difference may reflect basic temperamental variations (Kagan, 1994). Heightened fearfulness may also be a response to some upheaval or stress in the child's life, such as a recent move or a parent's job change.

Individual differences in infant temperament may also be related to security of attachment (Zeanah & Fox, 2004). Generally speaking, easy infants, as defined by the Thomas and Chess system (which you read about in Chapter 9), are more likely to be securely attached than babies in the other two categories (Goldsmith & Alansky, 1987; Seifer, Schiller, Sameroff, Resnick, & Riordan, 1996; Vaughn et al., 1992). The relationship makes sense if you think about the traits of infants in the difficult and slow-to-warm-up groups. Difficult infants actively resist comfort; consequently, a parent may be discouraged from establishing a nurturing relationship with a difficult infant. Likewise, slow-to-warm-up babies are less responsive to parental behaviors directed toward them, and the parents of these infants may reduce the frequency of behaviors directed to their unresponsive babies. The result is that the kind of give-and-take relationships most easy infants experience with their parents may never develop for babies who are difficult or slow-to-warm-up (Laible, Panfile, & Makariev, 2008).

It's important to remember, however, that a correlation is just a correlation and certainly does not suggest that all easy infants develop secure attachment or that all babies of the other two temperamental types are insecurely attached. In fact, the majority of infants in all three temperament categories are securely attached (van IJzendoorn et al., 1992). In addition, if infant temperament dictated attachment quality, it would be highly unlikely to see infants who are securely attached to one parent but insecurely attached to the other. In reality, this is a very common research finding (e.g., Goossens & van IJzendoorn, 1990).

For these reasons, developmentalists propose that it is not temperament, per se, that influences attachment. Rather, attachment is influenced by the **goodness-of-fit** between the infant's temperament and his or her environment (Thomas & Chess, 1977). For example, if the parents of an irritable baby boy are good at tolerating his irritability and persist in establishing a synchronous relationship with him, then his irritability doesn't lead to the development of an insecure attachment.

goodness-of-fit The degree to which an infant's environment and his or her temperament work together.

Learning Objective 11.7

To what degree are attachment classifications stable, and what are their long-term consequences?

Stability and Long-Term Consequences of Attachment Quality

Do variations in the quality of a child's early attachment persist over time? This question is a particularly important one for those researchers and therapists who are concerned that the effects of early abuse or neglect or other sources of insecure attachment might be permanent.

Stability of Attachment Classification   Both consistency and inconsistency are evident in attachment relationships over time (Ranson & Urichuk, 2008). According to a review of the relevant research carried out by Judith Crowell and Stuart Hauser (2008), one important finding that has surfaced in many longitudinal studies is that secure attachments seem to be more stable than insecure attachments. In addition, the stability of an attachment classification appears to depend on an individual's life circumstances. When the child's family environment or life circumstances are reasonably consistent, the security or insecurity of attachment usually remains constant as well, even over many years (Weinfield & Egeland, 2004).

The very fact that a child's security can change from one time to another does not refute the notion of attachment as an internal working model. Bowlby suggested that for the first 2 or 3 years of life, the particular pattern of attachment shown by a child is in some sense a property of each specific relationship. For example, studies of toddlers' attachments to mothers and fathers show that, in many cases, the child is securely attached to one parent and insecurely attached to the other, with both possible combinations equally represented (Schoppe-Sullivan et al., 2006). It is the quality of the particular relationship that determines the child's security with that specific adult. If that relationship changes markedly, the security of the baby's attachment to that individual may change, too. However, Bowlby argued that by age 4 or 5, the internal

This elementary school child appears to be securely attached to her parent. Research on the stability of attachment classifications suggests that the secure quality of the relationship was established when the girl was an infant.

working model becomes more general, more a property of the child, more generalized across relationships, and thus more resistant to change. At that point, the child tends to impose her working model on new relationships, including relationships with teachers and peers. Thus, a child may "recover" from an initially insecure attachment or lose a secure one. Consistency over time is more typical, however, both because children's relationships tend to be reasonably stable for the first few years and because once the internal model is clearly formed, it tends to perpetuate itself.

Long-Term Consequences of Secure and Insecure Attachment Ainsworth's classification system has proved to be extremely helpful in predicting a remarkably wide range of other behaviors in children, both toddlers and older children. Dozens of studies (e.g., Carlson, Sampson, & Sroufe, 2003; Diener, Isabella, Behunin, & Wong, 2008) show that, compared to children rated as insecurely attached, children rated as securely attached to their mothers in infancy are later more sociable, more positive in their behavior toward friends and siblings, less clinging and dependent on teachers, less aggressive and disruptive, more empathetic, and more emotionally mature in their approach to school and other settings outside the home.

At adolescence, those who were rated as securely attached in infancy or who are classed as secure on the basis of recent interviews have more intimate friendships (Bauminger, Finzi-Dottan, Chason, & Har-Even, 2008). Those with insecure attachments—particularly those with avoidant attachments—not only have less positive and supportive friendships in adolescence but are also more likely to become sexually active early and to practice riskier sex (Carlson, Sroufe, & Egeland, 2004; O'Beirne & Moore, 1995).

One particularly clear demonstration of some of these links comes from a longitudinal study by Alan Sroufe and his colleagues (Sroufe, Egeland, Carlson, & Collins, 2005). These researchers assessed the security of attachment of a group of several hundred infants and then followed the children through childhood and adolescence, testing and observing them at regular intervals. Some of their observations were of participants who had been invited to attend a specially designed summer camp during early adolescence. The counselors rated each child on a range of characteristics, and observers noted how often children spent time together or with the counselors. Naturally, neither the counselors nor the observers knew what the children's initial attachment classification had been. Those children with histories of secure attachment in infancy were rated as higher in self-confidence and social competence. They complied more readily with requests from counselors, expressed more positive emotions, and had a greater sense of their ability to accomplish things. Secure children created more friendships, especially with other securely attached youngsters, and engaged in more complex activities when playing in groups. In contrast, the majority of the children with histories of insecure attachment showed some kind of deviant behavior pattern, such as isolation from peers, bizarre behavior, passivity, hyperactivity, or aggressiveness. Only a few of the originally securely attached children showed any of these patterns.

Quality of Attachment in Adulthood Longitudinal studies show that the effects of attachment status persist into adulthood (Jones, 2008; Tideman, Nilsson, Smith, & Stjernqvist, 2002). Adults who were securely attached as infants perceive their relationships with their mothers differently than do adults who were insecurely attached. Attachment security in childhood may even find its way into romantic relationships in adulthood. Some studies show that men and women who were securely attached to their parents are more sensitive to their partners' needs (Mikulincer & Shaver, 2005).

Adults' internal models of attachment affect the way they behave with their own children as well. To assess the degree to which they do so, psychologist Mary Main and her colleagues developed a standardized attachment status interview for use with adults (Main, Hesse, & Goldwyn, 2008; Main, Kaplan, & Cassidy, 1985). They found that an adult's internal working model of attachment can be classified as one of three types:

- *Secure/autonomous/balanced.* These individuals value attachment relations and see their early experiences as influential, but they are objective in describing both good and bad qualities. They speak coherently about their early experiences and have thoughts about what motivated their parents' behavior.

- *Dismissing or detached.* These adults minimize the importance or the effects of 0early family experience. They may idealize their parents, perhaps even denying the existence of any negative childhood experiences. They emphasize their own personal strengths.
- *Preoccupied or enmeshed.* These adults often talk about inconsistent or role-reversed parenting. They are still engrossed with their relationship with their parents, still actively struggling to please them or very angry at them. They are confused and ambivalent, but still engaged.

When adults' models of attachment are related to the security of attachment displayed by their children, the expected pattern emerges strongly: Adults with secure models of attachment to their own parents are much more likely to have infants or toddlers with secure attachments. Those adults with dismissing models are more likely to have infants with avoidant attachments; those with preoccupied attachments are more likely to have infants with ambivalent attachments. Across 20 studies, the typical finding is that three-quarters of the mother-infant pairs share the same attachment category (van IJzendoorn, 1995, 1997). Diane Benoit has even found marked consistency across three generations: grandmothers, young mothers, and infants (Benoit & Parker, 1994).

The cross-generational similarity appears to be a result of each mother's own behavior toward her child, which varies as a function of her own internal working model of attachment (Steele, Hodges, Kaniuk, Hillman, & Henderson, 2003). Mothers who are themselves securely attached are more responsive and sensitive in their behavior toward their infants or young children. By contrast, mothers with dismissing or preoccupied attachments display behaviors that may interfere with the development of secure attachment in their children. When Emma Adam and her colleagues observed interactions between mothers and their 2-year-old children in a variety of settings (Adam, Gunnar, & Tanaka, 2004), they found that preoccupied mothers tended to display more anger, intrusiveness (actions that interfered with a child's goals), and negative emotions in interactions with their children than did mothers in the secure category. Moreover, dismissing mothers were less likely than secure mothers to exhibit positive emotions when interacting with their toddlers.

Crowell and Feldman (1988) also noted that mothers with dismissing or preoccupied internal working models interpreted the child's behavior very differently than did the secure moms: One dismissing mother observed her crying child through the observation window and said, "See, she isn't upset about being left." At reunion, she said to the child, "Why are you crying? I didn't leave" (1991, p. 604). Thus, the mother's own internal model not only affects her actual behavior but also affects the meaning she ascribes to the child's behavior, both of which will affect the child's developing model of attachment.

Relationships with Peers

Because most theories of social and personality development have strongly emphasized the centrality of parent-child interactions, most psychologists thought of relationships with peers as much less important, until recently. That view is now changing as it becomes clear that peer relationships play a unique and significant role in a child's development. We now know that children's relationships with parents and peers are interactive (Chen, He, Chang, & Liu, 2005). That is, good parenting is most effective when children associate with peers who exhibit social competence. Conversely, antisocial peers can undermine the potentially positive effects of good parenting. Thus, developmentalists no longer think of parental and peer relationships as independent sets of influences. Of course, children have relationships with parents before they develop them with peers. In this section, we'll discuss how peer relationships change over the years of childhood and adolescence.

Peer Relationships in Infancy and the Preschool Years

Learning Objective 11.8

What are the characteristics of infants' and preschoolers' peer interactions?

Children first begin to show some positive interest in other infants as early as 6 months of age. If you place two babies of that age on the floor facing each other, they will touch each other, pull each other's hair, and reach for each other's clothing. In 10-month-olds, these behaviors are even more evident. By 14 to 18 months of age, two or more children can play together with toys—occasionally cooperating, but more often simply playing side by side with different toys, a pattern Mildred Parten (1932) first described as **parallel play**. Toddlers of this age express interest in one another, gazing at or making noises at each other. Only at around 18 months of age, however, do toddlers show evidence of coordinated play, such as when one toddler chases another or imitates the other's action with some toy. By 3 or 4, children appear to prefer to play with peers rather than alone, and their play with one another is much more cooperative and coordinated, including various forms of group pretend play.

The first signs of playmate preferences or friendships also emerge in the toddler and preschool years (Hay, Payne, & Chadwick, 2004). A few children show signs of specific playmate preferences as early as age 18 months; by age 3 or 4, more than half of children have at least one mutual friendship, and many have already developed an enduring "best friend" relationship (Sebanc, Kearns, Hernandez, & Galvin, 2007).

To be sure, these early "friendships" are not nearly as deep or intimate as those between pairs of older children or adolescents. Toddler friends ignore each other's bids for interaction as often as not. Still, these pairs show unmistakable signs that their relationship is more than merely a passing fancy. They display more mutual liking, more reciprocity, more extended interactions, more positive and less negative behavior, more forgiveness, and more supportiveness in a novel situation than is true of nonfriend pairs at this same age. When they quarrel, they are more likely than nonfriends to try to patch it up (Dunn, 1993; Hartup, Laursen, Stewart, & Eastenson, 1988; Newcomb & Bagwell, 1995).

There is every reason to believe that early play with such a friend is a highly important arena for children to practice a host of social skills (Sebanc, 2003). As John Gottman says, in order to play collaboratively, friends "must coordinate their efforts with all the virtuosity of an accomplished jazz quartet" (1986, p. 3). Often, they must subdue their own desires in the interests of joint play, which requires some awareness of the other's feelings and wishes as well as an ability to modulate one's own emotions. You already know that these cognitive and control skills emerge during the preschool years; what the research on friendships reveals is that play with peers, especially play with friends, may be a crucial ingredient in that development.

By age 3, most children actually play together with one another in coordinated ways, rather than merely playing side by side.

Peer Relationships at School Age

Learning Objective 11.9

How do peer relationships change during the school years?

Over the past few decades, peer relationships have become increasingly important among school-aged children. Gradually, the amount of time that they spend interacting in school, in after-school care settings, and via electronic communication has come to exceed the amount of time that they spend in other activities (Neufeld & Maté, 2005). As a result, controversies have emerged regarding the degree to which this shift toward increased time with peers and decreased time with parents is beneficial or harmful to children. For instance, clinical psychologist Gordon Neufeld (Neufeld & Maté, 2005) has argued that spending more time with parents than with peers is essential for children's mental health. By contrast, researcher Judith Rich Harris has suggested precisely the opposite (1998).

Friendships While many things have changed, one feature of school-aged children's peer relationships has remained unchanged over the years. Compared to preschoolers, school-aged children develop a larger collection of **reciprocal friendships**—pairs in which each child names the other as a friend or as a "best friend." Thomas Berndt, in several studies (e.g., Berndt & Hoyle, 1985), has found that most first-graders have only one such reciprocal

parallel play Form of play seen in toddlers, in which children play next to, but not with, one another.

reciprocal friendship A friendship in which each partner identifies the other as a friend; also, a quality of friendship in school-aged children, when friendship is for the first time perceived as being based on reciprocal trust.

friendship. This number gradually rises through elementary school, so that by eighth grade, the average child has two or three reciprocal friendships. If researchers simply ask children to name their friends—ignoring the question of whether the friendship is reciprocated—the numbers are still higher. Second-graders name about four friends each, and seventh-graders name about seven (Reisman & Shorr, 1978). Cross-cultural studies show that best-friend relationships and the belief that having a best friend is important are universal features of school-aged children's social development (Schraf & Hertz-Lazarowitz, 2003).

Children in this age range also behave differently with friends than they do with strangers, just as preschoolers do. They are more open and more supportive with chums, smiling and looking at each other, laughing and touching each other more than nonfriends; they talk more with friends and cooperate with and help each other more. Pairs of friends are also more successful than are nonfriend pairs at solving problems or performing some task together (Newcomb & Bagwell, 1995). Yet school-aged children are also more critical of friends and have more conflicts with them than they do with strangers (Hartup, 1996). At the same time, when such conflicts with friends occur, children are more concerned about resolving them than they are disagreements with nonfriends. Thus, friendships constitute an arena in which children can learn how to manage conflicts (Newcomb & Bagwell, 1995).

Sex Differences in Friendship Quality

As you learned in Chapter 10, children's preference for same-sex playmates emerges early in life. Over the elementary school years, this preference increases. By third grade or so, almost all of children's relationships involve others of the same sex (Maccoby, 2002). Gender differences in interaction patterns both contribute to and are reinforced by the phenomenon of gender segregation in middle childhood.

Waldrop and Halverson (1975) refer to boys' relationships as *extensive* and to girls' relationships as *intensive*. Boys' friendship groups are larger and more accepting of newcomers than are girls'. Boy friends play more outdoors and roam over a larger area in their play. Girl friends are more likely to play in pairs or in smaller groups, and they spend more playtime indoors or near home or school (Benenson, 1994; Gottman, 1986).

Interestingly, the ability to regulate emotion is associated with sex differences in friendship patterns (Dunsmore, Noguchi, Garner, Casey, & Bhullar, 2008). Among girls, those who are best able to manage their emotions have the greatest number of friends. For boys, the association is the opposite: skilled emotional management is linked to having fewer friends. These findings help to explain sex differences in social interactions among school-aged children. Compared to those of girls, boys' groups and boys' friendships appear to be focused more on competition and dominance, patterns in which open displays of emotions are often advantageous (Maccoby, 1995). By contrast, the ability to restrain emotions is critical to interactions among girls, which typically emphasize agreement, compliance, and self-disclosure.

None of these observed differences should obscure the fact that the interactions of male and female friends have a great many characteristics in common. For example, collaborative and cooperative exchanges are the most common forms of communication in both boys' and girls' friendships in these years. Nor should we necessarily conclude that boys' friendships are less important to them than are girls'. Nevertheless, it seems clear that there are differences in form and style that may well have enduring implications for the patterns of friendship over the life span.

Learning Objective 11.10
What are the characteristics and consequences of variations in social status?

Social Status

One important aspect of individual differences in peer relationships is the degree to which peers like an individual child. Typically, this variable is called **social status**. Psychologists know a great deal about children in the three traditional status categories—popular, neglected, and rejected. **Popular children** are those who are most often described as well-liked and who are selected as playmates by peers. **Neglected children** are seldom described by peers as either liked or disliked, and **rejected children** are those who are actively disliked and avoided by their peers.

Popular and Neglected Children Some of the characteristics that differentiate popular children from others are things outside a child's control. In particular, attractive children and physically larger children are more likely to be popular. However, being very different from one's peers may also cause a child to be neglected or rejected. For example, shy children usually have few friends (Fordham & Stevenson-Hinde, 1999). Similarly, highly creative children are often rejected, as are those who have difficulty controlling their emotions (Aranha, 1997; Maszk, Eisenberg, & Guthrie, 1999).

However, children's social behavior seems to be more important than looks or temperament. Most studies show that popular children behave in positive, supporting, nonpunitive, and nonaggressive ways toward most other children. They explain things, take their playmates' wishes into consideration, take turns in conversation, and are able to regulate the expression of their strong emotions. In addition, popular children are usually good at accurately assessing others' feelings (Underwood, 1997). Most are also good at looking at situations from others' perspectives (Fitzgerald & White, 2003).

However, the degree to which popularity represents good adjustment depends on the peer context in which it occurs. Teenagers popular with peers who approve of and value inappropriate behavior—skipping school, for instance—are likely to exhibit such behavior (Allen, Porter, McFarland, Marsh, & McElhaney, 2005). In such cases, popularity may work against the achievement of positive developmental outcomes.

Neglected children share many characteristics of peers who are popular. They often do quite well in school, but they are more prone to depression and loneliness than are popular children (Cillessen, van IJzendoorn, van Lieshout, & Hartup, 1992; Rubin, Hymel, Mills, Rose-Krasnor, 1991; Wentzel & Asher, 1995). This is especially true for girls, who seem to value popularity more than boys do (Oldenburg & Kerns, 1997). Peer neglect may be associated with depression because recent brain-imaging studies show that peer neglect stimulates the same areas of the brain as physical pain (Eisenberger, 2003). In addition, some neglected children have unrealistic expectations about adults' ability to "fix" their situation (Galanaki, 2004). They may think, "Why doesn't the teacher *make* them be my friends?" Such thoughts may lead to feelings of hopelessness.

Nevertheless, many neglected children and teens aren't the least bit concerned about their lack of popularity (McElhaney, Antonishak, & Allen, 2008). Many such children are shy and prefer solitary activities; thus, their neglected status may simply be a function of their own personalities. However, a child's neglected status can change, suggesting that it is a function of both the social context and an individual child's personality. In fact, neglected children often move to the popular category when they become part of a new peer group.

Some children prefer solitary activities and are not distressed about their lack of inclusion in peer groups.

Rejected Children There are two types of rejected children. *Withdrawn/rejected* children realize that they are disliked by peers (Harrist, Zaia, Bates, Dodge, & Pettit, 1997). After repeated attempts to gain peer acceptance, these children eventually give up and become socially withdrawn. As a result, they often experience feelings of loneliness.

Aggressive/rejected children are often disruptive and uncooperative but usually believe that their peers like them (Zakriski & Coie, 1996). Many appear to be unable to control the expression of strong feelings (Eisenberg, Fabes, et al., 1995; Pettit, Clawson, Dodge, & Bates, 1996). They interrupt their play partners more often and fail to take turns in a systematic way.

Causes and Consequences of Peer Rejection A growing body of research shows that rejection by one's peers in elementary school—especially when the rejection is because of excessive aggressiveness—is one of the very few aspects of childhood functioning that consistently predicts behavior problems or emotional disturbances later in childhood, in adolescence, and in adulthood (e.g., Ladd & Troop-Gordon, 2003). For example, Melissa DeRosier

social status A term used by psychologists to refer to how well an individual child is liked by his or her peers.

popular children Children who are described as well-liked by a majority of peers.

neglected children Children who are seldom described by peers as either liked or disliked.

rejected children Unpopular children who are explicitly avoided and not chosen as playmates or friends.

A pattern of persistent aggression, and the peer rejection that so often accompanies it, is linked to a variety of long-term problems for children.

and her colleagues (1994) followed one group of over 600 children over a 4-year period in the early elementary grades. She found that those children who were most chronically rejected by their peers later showed higher rates of several types of problems, including more absences from school, more depression or sadness, and more behavior problems.

Similarly, John Coie and his colleagues (1995) followed a group of over 1,000 children from the third to the tenth grade. Among the boys, those who were both aggressive and rejected in third grade were far more likely to show delinquency or other behavior problems in high school than were any other group of boys. Among girls, aggressiveness (but not peer rejection) was linked to later behavior problems.

Such a link between early unpopularity and later behavior problems might be explained in any of several ways. Early problems with peers might be merely the most visible reflection of a general maladjustment that later manifests itself as delinquency or emotional disturbance. Alternatively, developmentalists might hypothesize that a failure to develop friendships itself causes problems that later become more general. Or, the basic difficulty could lie in a seriously warped internal working model of relationships that leads to peer rejection in elementary school and to delinquency. Or, all of the above might be true.

Happily, not all rejected children remain rejected, and when a rejected child's status changes, the negative outcomes associated with rejection diminish (Ladd, Herald-Brown, & Reiser, 2008). Moreover not all rejected children develop serious behavior problems or delinquency. And not all aggressive children are rejected. Research gives a few hints about what may differentiate these several subgroups. For example, some aggressive children also show fairly high levels of altruistic or prosocial behavior, and this mixture of qualities carries a much more positive prognosis than does aggression unleavened by helpfulness (Coie & Cillessen, 1993; Newcomb et al., 1993). Distinctions like these may help developmentalists not only to refine their predictions but to design better intervention programs for rejected/aggressive children.

Learning Objective 11.11

What is the significance of peer groups and romantic relationships in adolescence?

Peer Relationships in Adolescence

Many of the friendship patterns just discussed change at adolescence. For example, personality traits become more important in friend selection (Tani, Rossi, & Smorti, 2005). Adolescent friendships are also increasingly intimate, in the sense that the friends share more of their inner feelings and secrets and are more knowledgeable about each other's feelings. Loyalty and faithfulness become centrally valued characteristics of friendship. These adolescent friendships are also more likely to endure for a year or longer (Bowker, 2004). Mixed-sex groups begin to appear, conformity to peer group values and behaviors increases, and parents' influence on the child wanes, even though the child's attachment to the parents remains strong.

Functions of Adolescent Peer Groups   Just as individual relationships change, the function of the peer group changes in adolescence. In elementary school, peer groups primarily serve as a setting for mutual play (and for all the learning about relationships and the natural world that is part of such play). For teenagers, the peer group has another function. The teenager is struggling to make a slow transition from the protected life of the family to the independent life of adulthood; the peer group becomes the vehicle for that transition.

One sign of this shift is that teenagers begin to confide primarily in their peers, rather than in their parents. You've seen one illustration of this change in Figure 11.2 (see page 290). An equally striking set of findings comes from research by Duane Buhrmester (1996). Figure 11.3 shows the combined findings from several studies in which children, teenagers, or adults were asked to rate the level of intimate disclosure they experienced with parents, friends, and a romantic partner. You can see three clear stages. Before adolescence, children report higher levels of self-disclosure with their parents. At adolescence, this changes in a major way: Self-disclosure with parents declines dramatically, while self-disclosure with friends becomes dominant. Then in adulthood, a second shift occurs as a romantic partner takes the role of primary confidant.

Another aspect of this change in the centrality of peer relationships is a strong clannishness and intense conformity to the group. Such conformity, which Erikson saw as an entirely normal aspect of adolescence, seems to peak at about age 13 or 14 (at about the same time that developmentalists observe a drop in self-esteem); conformity then wanes as the teenager begins to arrive at a sense of identity that is more independent of the peer group.

It is also very clear that peers do indeed put pressure on each other to conform to peer group behavior standards. However, it is also true that peer group pressures are less potent and less negative than popular cultural stereotypes might suggest (Teitelman, Ratcliffe, & Cederbaum, 2008). Adolescents, like adults, choose their friends, and they are likely to choose to associate with a group that shares their values, attitudes, and behaviors. If the discrepancy between their own ideas and those of their friends becomes too great, teens are more likely to move toward a more compatible group of friends than to be persuaded to shift toward the first group's values or behaviors. Furthermore, teenagers report that explicit peer pressure is most likely to be pressure toward positive activities, such as school involvement, and away from misconduct. Thus, while Erikson appears to be quite correct in saying that peers are a major force in shaping a child's identity development in adolescence, peer influence is neither monolithic nor uniformly negative (Berndt & Keefe, 1995; Brown, Dolcini, & Leventhal, 1995).

One important exception to this rather rosy view of the impact of peer pressure occurs among teens who spend time with peers who lean toward aggressive, delinquent, or disruptive behavior (Véronneau, Vitaro, Pedersen, & Tremblay, 2008). Such peer subgroups often do provide explicit pressure toward misconduct or lawbreaking, to which some teens are susceptible. Whether an adolescent will be drawn to such a group in the first place, and whether he will be pushed toward more deviant behavior once he begins to "hang out" with such a group, appears to depend a good deal on his individual qualities—such as whether he has good social skills or has already shown some disruptive behavior before adolescence. For example, Frank Vitaro and his colleagues (1997) found that among a group of 868 boys they studied from age 11 to 13, those who had been moderately disruptive at age 11 were more likely to be delinquent at age 13 if they had had aggressive or disruptive friends at ages 11 and 12 than if their friends had been less aggressive or disruptive.

Changes in Peer Group Structure in Adolescence

The structure of the peer group also changes over the years of adolescence. The classic, widely quoted early study is Dexter Dunphy's observation of the formation, dissolution, and interaction of teenage groups in a high school in Sydney, Australia, between 1958 and 1960 (Dunphy, 1963). Dunphy identified two important subvarieties of groups. The first type, which he called a **clique**, is made up of four to six young people who appear to be strongly attached to one another. Cliques have strong cohesiveness and high levels of intimate sharing. In the early years of adolescence, cliques are almost entirely same-sex groups—a residual of the preadolescent pattern. Gradually, however, cliques combine into larger sets Dunphy called **crowds**, which include both males and females. Finally, the crowd breaks down again into heterosexual cliques and then into loose associations of couples. In Dunphy's study, children associated with their peers in crowds between approximately ages 13 and 15—the very years when researchers have observed the greatest conformity to peer pressure.

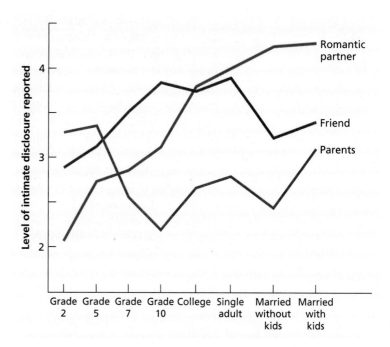

Figure 11.3
Time Spent with Parents and Peers

Before adolescence, parents are most often a child's closest confidants; in adolescence, it is peers in whom the young person confides.

(*Source*: From "Need fulfillment, interpersonal competence, and the developmental context of early adolescent friendship" by D. Buhrmester, *The Company They Keep: Friendship in Childhood and Adolescence*, W. M. Bukowski, A. F. Newcomb, and W. W. Hartup (eds.), p. 168, Fig. 8.2. © 1996 Cambridge University Press. By permission of Cambridge University Press.)

clique A group of four to six friends with strong affectional bonds and high levels of group solidarity and loyalty; the term is used by researchers to describe a self-chosen group of friends.

crowd A larger and looser group of friends than a clique, normally made up of several cliques that have joined together; a reputation-based group, common in adolescent subculture, with widely agreed-upon characteristics.

Bradford Brown and other researchers have changed Dunphy's labels somewhat (Brown, 1990; Brown, Mory, & Kinney, 1994). Brown uses the word *crowd* to refer to the "reputation-based" group with which a young person is identified, either by choice or by peer designation. In most U.S. schools, there are any number of crowds—"jocks," "brains," "nerds," "dweebs," "punks," "druggies," "toughs," "normals," "populars," "preppies," or "loners." Studies in junior and senior high schools in the United States make it clear that teenagers can readily identify each of the major crowds in their school, and they offer quite stereotypic—even caricatured—descriptions of them (e.g., "The partiers goof off a lot more than the jocks do, but they don't come to school stoned like the burnouts do"). Each of these descriptions serves as what Brown calls an "identity prototype" (Brown et al., 1994, p. 133): Labeling others and labeling oneself as belonging to one or more of these groups help to create or reinforce the adolescent's own identity. Such labeling also helps the adolescent identify potential friends or foes. Thus, being identified as a member of one crowd or another channels each adolescent toward particular activities and particular relationships. Furthermore, within any given school, the various crowds are organized into a fairly clear, widely understood pecking order—that is, more status is attributed to some groups than to others. In U.S. schools, the groups labeled "jocks," "populars," or "normals" (or the equivalent) are typically at the top, with "brains" somewhere in the middle, and "druggies," "loners," and "nerds" at the bottom (Brown et al., 1994).

In one study of sixth-graders, researchers found that individual differences in achievement and overall academic motivation were predictable from crowd membership at the beginning of the year (Kindermann, 2007). Cross-group variations in school engagement—as measured by participation in extracurricular activities, interest in school subjects, and so on—appeared to explain this relationship. That is, students who were members of highly engaged crowds tended to be higher achievers and to be more strongly motivated to achieve than those who belonged to crowds that were less engaged.

In a study of peer group effects at the high school level, researchers found that teens who belong to a "brains" crowd are more likely to graduate from college, and those who belong to a "criminals" group are more likely to engage in antisocial behavior after leaving high school (Barber, Eccles, & Stone, 2001). Thus, the high school crowd with which a given individual adolescent chooses to associate may be indicative of the sense of personal identity he or she will build on in adulthood.

Within (and sometimes across) these crowds, adolescents create smaller friendship groups Brown calls *cliques* (with a definition that is very similar to Dunphy's meaning for the same term). Brown, like Dunphy, notes that in early adolescence, cliques are almost entirely same-sex; by late adolescence, they have become mixed in gender, often composed of groups of dating couples.

At a certain age, children move from one kind of clique to another.

Whatever specific clique or crowd a teenager may identify with, theorists agree that the peer group performs the highly important function of helping the teenager shift from friendships to "partner" social relationships. The 13- or 14-year-old can begin to try out her new relationship skills in the wider group of the clique or crowd. Only after the adolescent develops some confidence do the beginnings of dating and of more committed pair relationships become evident.

Heterosexual Relationships   Of all the changes in social relationships in adolescence, perhaps the most profound for most teens is the shift from the total dominance of same-sex friendships to heterosexual relationships (Richards, Crowe, Larson, & Swarr, 1998).

By age 15 or 16, most teens in the United States have begun dating. The change happens gradually but proceeds at a somewhat more rapid pace in girls.

At the beginning of adolescence, teens are still fairly rigid about their preferences for same-sex friends (Bukowski, Sippola, & Hoza, 1999). Over the next year or two, they become more open to opposite-sex friendships (Harton & Latane, 1997; Kuttler, LaGreca, & Prinstein, 1999). The skills they gain in relating to opposite-sex peers in such friendships and in mixed-gender groups enable them to participate in romantic relationships (Feiring, 1999). Thus, while post-pubertal sexual desires are often assumed to be the basis of emergent romantic relationships, it appears that social factors are just as important. In fact, research suggests that social competence across a variety of relationships—with parents, peers, and friends—predicts the ease with which teens move from exclusive same-sex relationships to opposite-sex friendships and romantic relationships (Theriault, 1998).

Besides their social importance, these new relationships are clearly part of the preparation for assuming a full adult sexual identity. Physical sexuality is part of that role, but so are the skills of personal intimacy with the opposite sex, including flirting, communicating, and reading the form of social cues used by the other gender. In Western societies, adolescents learn these skills first in larger crowds or cliques and then in dating pairs (Zani, 1993). In fact, some studies suggest that engaging in such behaviors in group settings contributes more to the development of competence in romantic relationships than dating does (Laursen & Mooney, 2007).

By age 12 or 13, most adolescents have a prototypical understanding of what it means to be "in love." Interestingly, even though the actual progression toward romantic relationships happens faster for girls, boys report having had the experience of falling in love for the first time at an earlier age. Moreover, by the end of adolescence, the average boy believes he has been in love several more times than the average girl (Montgomery & Sorell, 1998).

The sense of being in love is an important factor in adolescent dating patterns (Montgomery & Sorell, 1998). In other words, teenagers prefer to date those with whom they believe they are in love, and they view falling out of love as a reason for ending a dating relationship. In addition, for girls but not for boys, romantic relationships are seen as a context in which self-disclosure can take place. Put another way, girls seem to want more psychological intimacy from these early relationships than their partners do (Feiring, 1999).

Homosexual Teens   Romantic relationships emerge somewhat differently in the lives of homosexual teens. Researchers have found that homosexual teenagers today are more comfortable than those in past cohorts about revealing their sexual orientation to their parents and to their peers (Floyd & Bakeman, 2006). Consequently, developmentalists have learned a great deal about the development of a homosexual orientation in the past couple of decades.

One thing that researchers have learned is that homosexual teenagers become aware of same-sex attraction at around age 11 or 12, roughly the same age when their heterosexual peers begin to notice their attraction to the opposite sex (Rosario, Scrimshaw, & Hunter, 2004). In contrast to the case among heterosexual teens, boys notice and act on same-sex attraction at somewhat earlier ages than girls do (Grov, Bimbi, Nanin, & Parsons, 2006). However, girls who ultimately commit to a homosexual orientation express more certainty about their sexual identity than boys do (Rosario, Scrimshaw, Hunter, & Braun, 2006).

There are many boys and girls, however, who experience some degree of attraction to both sexes prior to self-identifying as gay or lesbian. Thus, many homosexual teens go through a period of sexual discovery that begins with experimentation with heterosexual relationships. Shortly thereafter, these teenagers begin to experiment with same-sex relationships. By age 15 or so, most have classified themselves as primarily heterosexual or committed to a gay, lesbian, or bisexual orientation (Rosario, Scrimshaw, & Hunter, 2004). Many of those who are gay, lesbian, or bisexual participate in clubs and extracurricular activities that are designed to help sexual minority youth form social connections. In the company of these like-minded peers, gay, lesbian, and bisexual teens meet potential romantic partners and find important sources of social support (Rosario, Scrimshaw, & Hunter, 2004).

Sibling Relationships

Playmates and friends play a highly significant role in children's development, but so too can brothers and sisters. The Biblical story of Cain and Abel might lead us to believe that rivalry or jealousy is the key ingredient of sibling relationships. Certainly the birth of a new brother or sister radically changes the life of the older sibling. The parents have less time for the older child, who may feel neglected and angry; such feelings may lead both to more confrontations between the older child and the parents and to feelings of rivalry with the new baby (Furman, 1995).

Yet rivalry is not the only quality of early sibling relationships; observations of preschoolers interacting with their siblings point toward other ingredients as well. Toddlers and preschoolers help their brothers and sisters, imitate them, and share their toys. Judy Dunn, in a detailed longitudinal study of a group of 40 families in England, observed that the older child often imitated a baby brother or sister; by the time the younger child was a year old, however, he or she began imitating the older sibling, and from then on most of the imitation consisted of the younger child copying the older one (Dunn & Kendrick, 1982).

Young brothers and sisters also hit each other, snatch toys, and threaten and insult each other. The older child in a pair of preschoolers is likely to be the leader and is therefore likely to show more of both aggressive and helpful behaviors (Abramovitch, Pepler, & Corter, 1982). For both members of the pair, however, the dominant feature seems to be ambivalence. Both supportive and negative behaviors are evident in about equal proportions. In Abramovitch's research, such ambivalence occurred whether the pair were close in age or further apart and whether the older child was a boy or a girl. Naturally there are variations on this theme; some pairs show mostly antagonistic or rivalrous behaviors, and some show mostly helpful and supportive behaviors. Most sibling pairs show both types of behaviors.

How do those themes play out in middle childhood? As a general rule, sibling relationships seem to be less central in the lives of school-aged children than are relationships with either friends or parents (Buhrmester, 1992). Children of elementary school age are less likely to turn to a sibling for affection than to parents, and they are less likely to turn to a brother or sister for companionship or intimacy than they are to a friend. Nevertheless, research indicates that sibling interactions—especially those that involve resolution of conflicts—strongly influence children's understanding of social relationships and equip them with skills that are important in adult relationships (Bettner, 2007; Thompson & Halberstadt, 2008).

Sibling relationships also vary enormously. On the basis of direct studies of young children as well as retrospective reports by young adults about their sibling relationships when they were of school age, researchers have identified several patterns or styles of sibling relationships: (1) a *caregiver relationship*, in which one sibling serves as a kind of quasi-parent for the other, a pattern that seems to be more common between an older sister and younger brother than for any other combination of siblings; (2) a *buddy relationship*, in which both members of the pair try to be like one another and take pleasure in being together; (3) a *critical* or *conflictual relationship*, which includes attempts by one sibling to dominate the other, teasing, and quarreling; (4) a *rival relationship*, which contains many of the same elements as a critical relationship but is also low in any form of friendliness or support; and (5) a *casual* or *uninvolved relationship*, in which the siblings have relatively little to do with one another (Murphy, 1993; Stewart, Beilfuss, & Verbrugge, 1995). Rivalrous or critical relationships seem to be more common between siblings who are close together in age (4 or fewer years apart) and in families in which the parents are less satisfied with their marriage (Buhrmester & Furman, 1990; McGuire, McHale, & Updegraff, 1996). Buddy relationships appear to be somewhat more common in pairs of sisters (Buhrmester & Furman, 1990), while rivalry seems to be highest in boy-boy pairs (Stewart et al., 1995).

These patterns appear to vary somewhat when children care for themselves after school while their parents are working. The caregiver relationship predominates, with the older sibling typically given the caregiver role. Longitudinal research suggests that older siblings in such situations can help younger brothers and sisters acquire self-reliance skills (Brody, Kim,

Murry, & Brown, 2003). Research also indicates that parents' ability to cope with work-related stress is enhanced by having an older child who is capable of caring for a younger sibling.

Behavior with Peers

The broad sketch of peer relationships from toddlerhood through adolescence that you have just read makes clear the various roles that peers play in children's development over these years. It also points out how central such relationships are. What it does not convey are all the changes in the actual content and quality of children's peer interactions. To fill in some of the gaps, we will consider two specific categories of behavior representing two ends of a continuum: prosocial behavior and aggression.

Prosocial Behavior

Learning Objective 11.13
What is prosocial behavior, and when does it appear?

Prosocial behavior is defined by psychologists as "intentional, voluntary behavior intended to benefit another" (Eisenberg, 1992, p. 3). In everyday language, prosocial behavior is essentially what we mean by *altruism*, and it changes with age, just as other aspects of peer behavior change.

Prosocial behaviors first become evident in children of about 2 or 3—at about the same time they begin to show real interest in play with other children. They will offer to help another child who is hurt, offer a toy, or try to comfort another person (Eisenberg & Fabes, 1998; Zahn-Waxler & Radke-Yarrow, 1982; Zahn-Waxler, Radke-Yarrow, Wagner, & Chapman, 1992). As pointed out in Chapter 6, children this young are only beginning to understand that others feel differently than they do, but they obviously understand enough about the emotions of others to respond in supportive and sympathetic ways when they see other children or adults hurt or sad.

After these early years, researchers have noted a number of trends. One such trend is the appearance of prosocial reciprocity in the later preschool years. For example, a 4- or 5-year-old child is more likely to offer to share a toy with a child who has previously offered a toy to her (Fujisawa, Kutsukake, & Hasegawa, 2008). Older children and adolescents are more likely than preschoolers to provide physical and verbal assistance to someone in need (Eisenberg, 1992). However, not all prosocial behaviors show this pattern of increase with age. Comforting another child, for example, appears to be more common among children in preschool and early elementary grades than among older children (Eisenberg, 1988, 1990).

Developmentalists also know that children vary a lot in the amount of altruistic behavior they show, and that young children who show relatively more empathy and altruism are also those who regulate their own emotions well. They show positive emotions readily and negative emotions less often (Eisenberg et al., 1996). They are also more popular with peers (Mayeux & Cillissen, 2003). These variations in children's levels of empathy or altruism seem to be related to specific kinds of child rearing (see *Developmental Science in the Real World* on page 306).

prosocial behavior Voluntary behavior intended to benefit another, such as giving away or sharing possessions, money, or time, with no obvious self-gain; altruism.

Aggression

Learning Objective 11.14
In what ways do boys and girls of different ages differ in the exhibition of aggression?

If you have watched children in pairs or groups, you know that all is not sweetness and light in the land of the young. Children do support and share with their friends, and they do show affectionate and helpful behaviors toward one another, but they also tease, fight, yell, criticize, and argue over objects and territory. Researchers who have studied this more negative side of children's interactions have looked mostly at **aggression**, which can be defined as behavior apparently intended to injure some other person or object.

aggression Behavior that is aimed at harming or injuring another person or object.

Instrumental and Hostile Aggression   Every child shows at least some aggression, but the form and frequency of aggression change over the years of childhood. When 2- or

Rearing Helpful and Altruistic Children

Eight-year-old Marisol, perched on a kitchen stool that allowed her to reach the counter, slowly poured cake mix from the box into a large mixing bowl, taking care not to spill any. Her father, Rick, stood by her side ready to assist if his daughter needed help. "Good job," he said as the last of the mix fell into the bowl. "Now we add the eggs." With that, Rick painstakingly showed Marisol how to break an egg. Rick thought to himself that the cake would be finished a lot sooner if he did it himself, without Marisol. But Rick was committed to help-

ing his daughter learn the skills needed to be a contributing member of the Ruiz household.

Teaching children to be helpful can be time-consuming. Helping them learn to be altruistic—that is, to want to help others even when there is no reward involved—can be even more difficult. However, research on the development of prosocial behavior can provide insights into the process (Eisenberg & Fabes, 1998):

• **Capitalize on the child's capacity for empathy.** If your child injures someone, point out

the consequences of that injury for the other person: "When you hit Susan, it hurts her."
• **Create a loving and warm family climate.** When parents express affection and warmth regularly toward their children, the children are more likely to be generous and altruistic.
• **Provide rules or guidelines about helpful behavior.** Direct instructions foster prosocial behavior: "I'd like you to help Keisha with her puzzle" or "Please share your candy with John."
• **Provide prosocial attributions.** Attribute your child's helpful or altruistic action to the child's own internal character: "You're such a helpful child!"
• **Have children do helpful things.** Assign them regular household tasks such as helping to cook or clean, taking care of pets, or watching younger siblings.
• **Model thoughtful and generous behavior.** Stating the rules will do little good if parents' own behavior does not match what they say! Children (and adults) are simply much more likely to do generous or thoughtful things if they see other people—especially other people in authority, such as parents—being generous and thoughtful.

Questions for Reflection

1. How might teachers and parents model generosity?
2. Why do you think that a loving and warm family climate promotes altruistic behavior?

Having children do helpful things, as these third-graders are doing by sorting recyclable material, is one way to increase altruistic behavior in kids.

3-year-old children are upset or frustrated, they are more likely to throw things or to hit each other. Typically, children of this age behave aggressively in order to achieve a goal, such as getting a toy from another child. This kind of aggression is known as **instrumental aggression**. Once the goal is achieved, the aggression stops.

As their verbal skills improve, children shift away from overt physical aggression toward greater use of verbal aggression, such as taunting or name-calling. The purpose of aggression changes as well. Among older preschoolers, **hostile aggression**, the goal of which is to hurt another's feelings rather than to do physical harm, becomes more common. In the elementary school and adolescent years, physical aggression becomes still less common, and children learn the cultural rules about when it is acceptable to display anger or aggression and how much one can acceptably display. In most cultures, this means that anger is increasingly disguised and aggression is increasingly controlled with increasing age (Underwood, Coie, & Herbsman, 1992).

instrumental aggression
Aggressive behavior intended to achieve a goal, such as obtaining a toy from another child.

hostile aggression Aggressive verbal behavior intended to hurt another's feelings.

306   **PART 5 ■ THE SOCIAL CHILD**

Sex Differences in Aggression One interesting exception to the general pattern of declining physical aggression with age is that in all-boy pairs or groups, at least in the United States, physical aggression seems to remain both relatively high and constant over the years of childhood. Indeed, at every age, boys show more physical aggression and more assertiveness than do girls, both within friendship pairs and in general (Coie & Dodge, 1998). Table 11.3 gives some highly representative data from a very large, careful survey in Canada (Offord, Boyle, & Racine, 1991) in which both parents and teachers completed checklists describing each child's behavior. Table 11.3 lists only the information provided by teachers, but parent ratings yielded parallel findings. It is clear that boys were described as far more aggressive on nearly any measure of physical aggressiveness.

The social consequences of aggressive behavior vary with gender as well. For girls, aggression seems to lead consistently to peer rejection. Among boys, however, aggression may result in either popularity or rejection (Rodkin, Farmer, Pearl, & Van Acker, 2000; Xie, Cairns, & Cairns, 1999). In fact, aggressiveness seems to be a fairly common characteristic of popular African American boys. In addition, irrespective of their general popularity, the close friends of aggressive boys tend to be aggressive as well. Furthermore, aggressiveness seems to precede these relationships. In other words, boys who are aggressive seek out other boys like themselves as friends (Hanish, Martin, Fabes, & Barcelo, 2008). Yet being friends doesn't seem to make either member of an aggressive friendship pair more aggressive (Poulin & Boivin, 2000). Research also suggests that children have more positive attitudes toward aggressive peers whose aggressive acts are seen as mostly retaliatory in nature and toward those who engage in prosocial as well as aggressive behaviors (Coie & Cillessen, 1993; Newcomb, Bukowski, & Pattee, 1993; Poulin & Boivin, 1999). Social approval may not increase boys' aggressiveness, but it does seem to help maintain it, because interventions to reduce aggressive behavior typically have little effect on aggressive boys who are popular (Phillips, Schwean, & Saklofske, 1997). Moreover, the behavior of aggressive boys is often linked to the availability of socially weak and passive peers to serve as victims (see *Thinking about Research* on page 308).

Relational Aggression The findings of studies examining sex differences in aggression have been so clear and so consistent that most psychologists have concluded that boys are simply "more aggressive" in every possible way. But that conclusion may turn out to be wrong, or at least misleading. Instead, it appears that girls express aggressiveness in a different way, using what has been labeled relational aggression instead of either physical aggression or nasty words (Putallaz et al., 2007). Physical aggression hurts others through physical damage or threat of such damage; **relational aggression** is aimed at damaging another person's self-esteem or peer relationships, such as by cruel gossiping, by making facial expressions of disdain, or by ostracizing or threatening to ostracize the other ("I won't invite you to my birthday party if you do that"). Another important difference between hostile and relational aggression is that acts of hostile aggression are more likely to draw adult attention, especially when they involve hitting or other actions that can cause physical harm. Consequently, they may occur less frequently than acts of relational aggression. By contrast, children can engage in relational aggression in ways that escape the notice of adults—such as passing notes containing derogatory statements about peers or subtly moving away from a child who is the target of aggression during recess. As a result, some children may become habitual victims of relational aggression.

Girls are much more likely to use relational aggression than are boys, especially toward other girls, a difference that begins as early as the preschool years and becomes very marked by the fourth or fifth grade. For example, in one study of nearly 500 children in the third through sixth grades, Nicki Crick found that 17.4% of the girls but only 2% of the boys were

Table 11.3 Percentage of Boys and Girls Aged 4 to 11 Rated by Their Teachers as Displaying Aggressive Behavior

Behavior	Boys	Girls
Mean to others	21.8	9.6
Physically attacks people	18.1	4.4
Gets in many fights	30.9	9.8
Destroys own things	10.7	2.1
Destroys others' things	10.6	4.4
Threatens to hurt people	13.1	4.0

Source: Offord et al., 1991, from Table 2.3, p. 39.

relational aggression
Aggression aimed at damaging another person's self-esteem or peer relationships, such as by using ostracism or threats of ostracism, cruel gossiping, or facial expressions of disdain.

Bullies and Victims

At first glance, aggressive interactions among children might appear to be fairly simple: One child hurts another child. However, research shows that, across the middle childhood years, aggressive interactions become increasingly complex (Hay, Payne, & Chadwick, 2004). As children get older, they tend to take on consistent roles across aggressive interactions–perpetrator, victim, assistant to the perpetrator, reinforcing onlooker, nonparticipant onlooker, defender of the victim, and so on (Andreou & Metallidou, 2004). Children's personality traits to some degree determine the roles they assume. For example, shy children usually occupy the nonparticipant onlooker role, while children who are emotionally unstable are more likely to serve as assistants to the perpetrator or as reinforcing onlookers (Tani, Greenman, Schneider, & Fregoso, 2003). Until fairly recently, both research on and interventions aimed at reducing aggression focused on the habitual perpetrators, or bullies. However, most developmentalists now believe that changing the behavior of children who are habitual victims of aggression may be just as important as intervening with aggressive children themselves (Green, 2001).

Studies show that certain characteristics are found among habitual victims across a wide variety of cultural settings (Eslea et al., 2004). Among boys, victims are often physically smaller or weaker than their peers. Whether boys or girls, victims seldom assert themselves with their peers, making neither suggestions for play activities nor prosocial actions. Instead, they submit to whatever suggestions others make. Other children do not like this behavior and thus do not like the victims (Crick & Grotpeter, 1996; Schwartz, Dodge, & Coie, 1993). The consequences of such victimization can include loneliness, school avoidance, low self-esteem, and significant depression at later ages (Kochenderfer & Ladd, 1996; Olweus, 1995).

Still, not all children faced with a passive and unresponsive playmate turn into bullies. Bullies are distinctive because they are more aggressive toward adults than nonbullies, cannot empathize with their victims' pain or unhappiness, feel little or no guilt or shame about their actions, and are often impulsive (Menesini et al., 2003). However, bullying is a complex phenomenon that must be understood as resulting from characteristics of bul-

lies themselves, the family environments in which they are being raised, and the social settings in which bullying incidents occur (Ahmed & Braithwaite, 2004; Rigby, 2005). Studies suggest that four factors lie behind the development of bullying behavior (Olweus, 1995):

- Indifference toward the child and lack of warmth from the parents in the early years
- Failure by parents to set clear and adequate limits on aggressive behavior
- The parents' use of physical punishment
- A difficult, impulsive temperament in the child

Questions for Critical Analysis

1. How might a child's temperament influence parents to exhibit the kinds of parental behaviors found to be associated with bullying?
2. Based on the research discussed above, what characteristics should be included in a checklist designed to help teachers and parents identify children who are at high risk of becoming perpetual victims?

---

high in relational aggression—almost precisely the reverse of the rates of physical aggression (Crick & Grotpeter, 1995).

What might be the origins of such sex differences in the form of aggression used? One obvious possibility is that hormone differences play a part. For one thing, higher rates of physical aggression in males have been observed in every human society and in all species of primates. There is some evidence of a link between rates of physical aggression and testosterone levels in males (e.g., Susman et al., 1987), particularly in adolescence and later. Thus, differing rates of physical aggression appear to have at least some biological basis. However, peer reinforcement may also play a role. Researchers have found that children as young as 3 years of age believe that girls are more likely to display relational aggression and boys are more likely to show physical aggression (Giles & Heyman, 2005). Thus, just as children encourage their peers to engage in other types of stereotypical behavior, they may provide rewards for boys and girls who display gender-appropriate aggressive behaviors. Likewise, they may actively sanction peers of both sexes for engaging in gender-inappropriate forms of aggression.

Learning Objective 11.15
What is trait aggression, and how does it differ from typical age-related forms of aggression?

Trait Aggression

Earlier in this chapter, you learned that aggressive behavior tends to decrease with age. However, there are a few children, most of them boys, for whom a high level of aggressive behavior in early childhood is predictive of a lifelong pattern of antisocial behavior, a finding that has been supported by cross-cultural research (Derzon, 2001; Hart, Olsen, Robinson, & Mandleco, 1997; Henry, Caspi, Moffitt, & Silva, 1996; Kosterman, Graham, Hawkins, Catalano, & Herrenkohl, 2001; Newman, Caspi, Moffitt, & Silva, 1997). Researchers have searched for causes of this kind of aggression, which psychologists often refer to as *trait aggression*, to distinguish it from developmentally normal forms of aggression.

Some psychologists have looked for a genetic basis for trait aggression and have produced some supportive data (Brendgen et al., 2008; Hudziak et al., 2003; Rowe, 2003; van Beijsterveldt, Bartels, Hudziak, & Boomsma, 2003). Others suggest that trait aggression is associated with being raised in an aggressive environment, such as an abusive family (Dodge, 1993). Family factors other than abuse, such as lack of affection and the use of coercive discipline techniques, also appear to be related to trait aggression, especially in boys (Chang, Schwartz, Dodge, & McBride-Chang, 2003).

Still other developmentalists have discovered evidence that aggressive children may shape their environments in order to gain continuing reinforcement for their behavior. For example, as early as 4 years of age, aggressive boys tend to prefer other aggressive boys as playmates and to form stable peer groups with them. These groups develop their own patterns of interaction and reward each other with social approval for aggressive acts (Hanish et al., 2008). This pattern of association among aggressive boys continues through middle childhood and adolescence.

Finally, a large body of research suggests that highly aggressive children lag behind their peers in understanding others' intentions (Crick & Dodge, 1994). Research demonstrating that teaching aggressive children how to think about others' intentions reduces aggressive behavior also supports this conclusion (Crick & Dodge, 1996; Webster-Stratton & Reid, 2003). Specifically, this research suggests that aggressive school-aged children seem to reason more like 2- to 3-year-olds about intentions. For example, they are likely to perceive a playground incident (such as one child accidentally tripping another during a soccer game) as an intentional act that requires retaliation. Training helps aggressive school-aged children acquire an understanding of others' intentions that most children learn between the ages of 3 and 5. Thus, trait aggression may originate in some kind of deviation from the typical developmental path during the early childhood period.

Think Critically

- Compare and contrast the interaction patterns of adolescents in high schools to those of adults on campus or in workplaces. To what degree do crowds and cliques develop in such settings, and what roles do they play in academic and workplace functioning?
- In what ways do adults exhibit relational aggression? Do gender differences in types of aggression appear to persist into the adult years?

Conduct Your Own Research

A playground where toddlers and preschoolers play while their parents watch would be an ideal place to carry out a naturalistic observation of safe base behavior. Before you observe any children and parents, be sure to introduce yourself to the parents and explain that you are doing an assignment for your child development class. For a set period of time—say, 15 minutes—observe an individual child and note how many times he or she looks at, speaks to, or moves toward the parent. Repeat the procedure for several other children. Categorize the children as younger or older and compare the number of safe base behaviors for each age group. You should find that the younger the children are, the more frequently they make contact with their parent (their safe base).

Summary

RELATIONSHIPS WITH PARENTS

11.1 How did Bowlby and Ainsworth characterize affectional bonds, attachments, and internal working models?

- Bowlby and Ainsworth distinguished between an affectional bond (an enduring tie to a partner viewed as unique) and an attachment, which involves feelings of security and having a safe base. An attachment is deduced from the existence of attachment behaviors. Once established, an attachment relationship becomes the basis of an internal working model that the child applies to future interactions with the attachment figure and with others.

11.2 What factors influence the parent's bond to the child?

- For parents to form a strong bond to their infant, what is most crucial is not immediate contact at birth but the development and repetition of mutually reinforcing and interlocking attachment behaviors.

11.3 How does the child's attachment to the parent change across infancy, early childhood, and middle childhood?

- Bowlby proposed that the child's attachment to the caregiver develops through a series of steps, from rather indiscriminate aiming of attachment behaviors toward anyone within reach, through a focus on one or more figures, to secure base behavior, beginning at about 6 months of age, which signals the presence of a clear attachment. Attachment behaviors become less visible during the preschool years, except when the child is stressed. School-aged children exhibit less safe base behavior than infants and preschoolers do, but extended separations can still be stressful.

11.4 What are the characteristics of parent-child relationships in adolescence?

- The child's basic attachment to the parents remains strong in adolescence, despite an increase in parent-child conflict, the greater independence of the teenager, and the increased role of the peer group.

VARIATIONS IN THE QUALITY OF ATTACHMENTS

11.5 How does the behavior of securely and insecurely attached infants differ?

- Children differ in the security of their first attachments. The secure infant uses the parent as a safe base for exploration and can be readily consoled by the parent. Insecurely attached infants display a variety of patterns, including ambivalence toward and avoidance of parents. Some insecurely attached infants exhibit a disorganized pattern in which they sometimes move toward and sometimes move away from parents. Differences in attachment classification are correlated with patterns of parental responsiveness.

11.6 How does infant temperament influence the attachment process?

- An infant's temperament may affect attachment. Behaviorally inhibited infants exhibit more stranger and separation anxiety than other infants. Infants with difficult temperaments often actively resist the kinds of comfort that foster the development of secure attachments. As a result, they are more likely than other infants to develop insecure attachments.

11.7 To what degree are attachment classifications stable, and what are their long-term consequences?

- The security of an initial attachment is reasonably stable and is fostered by sensitivity and contingent responsiveness by the parent. Securely attached children appear to be more socially skillful, more curious and persistent in approaching new tasks, and more mature. An adult's internal working model of attachment, based on the security of his or her own attachment to parents in childhood, influences parenting behavior.

RELATIONSHIPS WITH PEERS

11.8 What are the characteristics of infants' and preschoolers' peer interactions?

- Cooperative play emerges around 18 months, although infants still typically play by themselves. By 3 or 4, children would rather play with peers than alone.

11.9 How do peer relationships change during the school years?

- By the time they reach school age, most children have formed individual friendships and show preferential positive behavior toward their friends. Friendships become more common and more stable in the elementary school years, and more intimate in adolescence. In elementary school, peer interactions are focused mostly on common activities; in adolescence, peer groups also become a vehicle for the transition from dependence to independence.

11.10 What are the characteristics and consequences of variations in social status?

- Popularity among peers, in elementary school or later, is most consistently based on the amount of positive and supportive social behavior shown by a child toward peers. Socially rejected children are often characterized by high levels of aggression or bullying and low levels of agreement and helpfulness. Aggressive/rejected children are likely to show behavior problems in adolescence and a variety of disturbances in adulthood.

11.11 What is the significance of peer groups and romantic relationships in adolescence?

- Reputation-based groups, or crowds, are an important part of adolescent social relationships, particularly in the early high school years. Smaller groups of friends, or cliques, are also significant and gradually shift from being same-sex groups to mixed-sex groups to dating pairs. On average in Western cultures, dating begins at about age 15, but there is wide variability.

11.12 What are the characteristics of sibling relationships?

- Sibling relationships are often thought of as rivalrous, but there are many variations. Siblings in caregiver relationships act as surrogate parents for brothers and sisters. Those in buddy relationships try to act alike and enjoy being together. Rival relationships are characterized by conflict, and siblings in uninvolved relationships have little to do with one another.

BEHAVIOR WITH PEERS

11.13 What is prosocial behavior, and when does it appear?

- Prosocial behavior, such as helpfulness or generosity, is apparent as early as age 2 or 3 and generally increases throughout childhood.

11.14 In what ways do boys and girls of different ages differ in the exhibition of aggression?

- Physical aggression decreases as children's language skills improve. Thus, older preschoolers and school-aged children are more likely than toddlers to use verbal aggression rather than physical aggression. At all ages, boys exhibit more physical aggression than girls do; girls show more relational aggression.

11.15 What is trait aggression, and how does it differ from typical age-related forms of aggression?

- Some children develop a pattern of aggressive behavior, known as trait aggression, that continues to cause problems for them throughout childhood and adolescence. Unlike more typical forms of aggression, trait aggression changes little with age.

Key Terms

affectional bond (p. 284)
aggression (p. 305)
attachment (p. 284)
attachment behaviors (p. 284)
clique (p. 301)
crowd (p. 301)
goal-corrected partnership (p. 289)
goodness-of-fit (p. 294)

hostile aggression (p. 306)
individuation (p. 290)
insecure attachment (p. 291)
instrumental aggression (p. 306)
internal working model (p. 284)
neglected children (p. 298)
parallel play (p. 297)
popular children (p. 298)

prosocial behavior (p. 305)
reciprocal friendship (p. 297)
rejected children (p. 298)
relational aggression (p. 307)
secure attachment (p. 291)
social status (p. 298)
Strange Situation (p. 291)

12 Thinking about Relationships: Social-Cognitive and Moral Development

One rarely turns on the television or picks up a newspaper nowadays without encountering some kind of discussion of moral decline. Increases in the frequency of heinous crimes, together with examples of rude behavior in everyday life, are cited in support of the proposition that society, at least in the West, is less civil than in days gone by. The answer to this problem, some say, is to incorporate *character education* into our schools.

A number of educators have developed character education curricula that can be used by any school, regardless of the cultural make-up of its student body. One curriculum has been authored by developmental psychologist Thomas Lickona of the State University of New York at Cortland. For more than 20 years, Lickona has been writing books designed to help parents and teachers apply the findings of developmental research to the task of educating for character (e.g., Lickona, 1994). Over the same period, he has participated in numerous studies of the effects of character education on school climate and on individual behavior.

Most recently, Lickona has advocated an approach to character education based on the assumption that ten essential virtues comprise character (Lickona, 2004). The ten virtues are wisdom, justice, fortitude, self-control, love, a positive attitude, hard work, integrity, gratitude, and humility. Lickona claims that, although maturational and developmental processes play important roles in the development of character, for the most part it must be deliberately and systematically transmitted to children by caring adults. His research has shown that when character education is implemented in a school, the frequency of undesirable behaviors declines. And as an added bonus, academic achievement tends to go up.

As a developmental scientist, Lickona argues that character education, like any other kind of instruction, must be based on a sound understanding of child development. A developmentally appropriate approach to character education, whether it occurs in one's family home or in a school with hundreds of pupils, begins with an understanding that how individuals think about relationships, a process called social cognition, is at the heart of character. Thus, we begin this chapter with a discussion of how thinking about social relationships changes over the years of childhood and adolescence and end with an examination of moral development, the process of learning to distinguish between right and wrong in accordance with cultural values.

The Development of Social Cognition

The topic of **social cognition** should not be entirely new to you. You have read about many facets of social cognition in previous chapters. The infant's emerging ability to recognize individuals and to use facial expressions and other body language for social referencing is one kind of social cognition, as is the growing understanding of others' emotions and the development of a theory of mind in the preschool years. One could also argue that an internal working model of attachment is a kind of social cognition, as is the child's self-scheme. However, there are a few other important components of social cognition. Before we consider them, it's important that you understand a few basic principles.

social cognition Thinking about and understanding the emotions of and interactions and relationships among people.

Some General Principles and Issues

Learning Objective 12.1
What are the general principles of social-cognitive development?

One way to think about social cognition is simply to conceive of it as the application of general cognitive processes or skills to a different topic—in this case, people or relationships. In Chapter 6, you learned about how children's thinking changes from infancy through adolescence. At any given age, a child might simply apply her current ways of thinking to her relationships and to people as well as to objects. In this view, the child's understanding of self and others, of social relationships, reflects or is based on her overall level of cognitive development, such as her level of perspective-taking skills (Rubin, Coplan, Chen, Baskirk, & Wojslawowica, 2005; Selman, 1980).

This approach has a powerful intuitive appeal. After all, as John Flavell points out (1985), it is the same head doing the thinking whether a child works on a conservation problem or tries to understand people. Furthermore, as you will see very clearly as we go through the evidence, many of the same principles that seem to apply to general cognitive development hold for social cognitive development as well; that is, children's social cognition develops in certain directions:

- *From outer to inner characteristics.* Younger children pay attention to the surface of things, to what things look like; older children look for principles, for causes.

- *From observation to inference.* Young children initially base their conclusions only on what they can see or feel; as they grow, they make inferences about what ought to be or what might be.
- *From definite to qualified.* Young children's "rules" are very definite and fixed (such as sex-role rules); by adolescence, rules begin to be qualified.
- *From observer's view to general view.* Children become less egocentric with time—less tied to their own individual views, more able to construct a model of some experience or some process that is true for everyone.

All of these dimensions of change describe children's emerging social cognition, just as they describe the development of thinking about objects. But thinking about people or relationships also has some special features that makes it different from thinking about physical objects.

One obvious difference is that people, unlike rocks or glasses of water, behave intentionally. In particular, people often attempt to conceal information about themselves; thus, the ability to "read" other people's cues is a key social-cognitive skill. Further, unlike relationships with objects, relationships with people are mutual and reciprocal. Dolls, sets of blocks, or bicycles don't talk back, get angry, or respond in unexpected ways, but people do all these things. In learning about relationships, children must learn enough about other people's motives and feelings to predict such responses.

Children also have to learn special rules about particular forms of social interactions—such as rules about politeness, about when you can and cannot speak, and about power or dominance hierarchies—all of which are forms of social scripts (Schank & Abelson, 1977). The existence of such scripts allows children to develop strong expectations about how people will behave, in what order, in which settings. Furthermore, these scripts probably change with age, not just because children's cognitive skills change, but also simply because the rules (scripts) themselves change from one social setting to another. One obvious example is the set of changes that occurs when children start school. The script associated with the role of "student" is quite different from the one connected with the role of "little kid." Classrooms are more tightly organized, expectations for obedience are higher, and there are more drills and routines to be learned than was probably true at home or even in child care or nursery school. The school script changes when the young adolescent moves into junior high school and then again when she enters high school.

These illustrations make it clear that the development of sophisticated social cognition is more than a simple process of applying basic cognitive processes and strategies to the arena of social interaction. The child must also come to understand the ways in which social relationships are different from interactions with the physical world, and she must learn special rules and strategies. Let's begin with the child's growing ability to describe other people.

Learning Objective 12.2

In what ways do children's descriptions of other people change across childhood and adolescence?

Describing Other People

Research suggests that there is a shift from observation (what children see) to inference (how they interpret what they see) in children's descriptions of others, as well as a clear change in focus from outer to internal characteristics. There seem to be at least three steps. Up to perhaps ages 6 to 8, children's descriptions of others are focused almost exclusively on external features. Children in this age range describe others' hair color, their relative size, their gender, where they live, and what they like to do. Race is another characteristic that frequently crops up in such descriptions (see *Developmental Science in the Real World*). This description by a 7-year-old boy, taken from a classic study in England by Livesley and Bromley, is typical:

> He is very tall. He has dark brown hair, he goes to our school. I don't think he has any brothers or sisters. He is in our class. Today he has a dark orange [sweater] and gray trousers and brown shoes. (1973, p. 213)

Learning and Unlearning Prejudice

Mara was excited about her new job teaching first grade in a public school that had a multi-ethnic student population. She became concerned on her first day, however, when she overheard many of the 6-year-olds in her class making remarks about one another's ethnicity. Even more alarming to her was her young pupils' tendency to sort themselves according to ethnicity and to express dismay when a child of a different ethnicity sat by them or tried to join their games. Mara wanted to know how she could help her students learn to be more tolerant.

Research suggests that ethnic group schemas are well established by age 5 (Pezdek, Blandon-Gitlin, & Moore, 2003). Once these schemas are formed, children use them to make judgments about others. These early judgments probably reflect young children's egocentric thinking. Essentially, children view those like themselves as desirable companions and those who are unlike them—in gender, ethnicity, and other categorical variables—as undesirable (Doyle & Aboud, 1995). There is some evidence that these judgments increase in strength as children move through the elementary school years (Nesdale, Durkin, Maass, & Griffiths, 2005). These findings suggest that the characteristics of Piaget's concrete operational stage, the goal of which is to construct a mental model of the outside world, may contribute to school-aged children's tendency to attribute an inappropriate amount of importance to external traits such as ethnicity.

Of course, cognitive development doesn't happen in a social vacuum, and by age 5, most White children in English-speaking countries have acquired an understanding of their culture's ethnic stereotypes and prejudices (Bigler & Liben, 1993). Likewise, African American, Hispanic American, and Native American children become sensitive very early in life to the fact that people in their own groups are viewed negatively by many Whites. Some studies suggest that this early awareness of stereotypes negatively influences minority children's self-esteem (Jambunathan & Burts, 2003).

Psychologists speculate that the combination of immature cognitive development, acquisition of cultural stereotypes, and teachers' lack of awareness may foster prejudicial attitudes. The key to preventing the development of prejudice, they say, is for preschool teachers to discuss ethnicity openly and to make conscious efforts to help children acquire nonprejudiced attitudes (Cushner, McClelland, & Safford, 1992). For example, they can assign children of different ethnic groups to do projects together.

Ideally, all children should learn to evaluate their own and others' behavior according to individual criteria rather than group membership, and minority children need to be especially encouraged to view their ethnicity positively. Preschool teachers are in a position to provide young children with a significant push toward these important goals.

Questions for Reflection

1. How might Mara implement some of the strategies suggested here for reducing prejudice in her classroom?

2. In your view, what is the role of entertainment media in the development of ethnic prejudice?

When young children do use internal or evaluative terms to describe people, they are likely to use quite global terms, such as *nice* or *mean* and *good* or *bad*. Further, young children do not seem to see these qualities as lasting or general traits of the individual, applicable in all situations or over time (Rholes & Ruble, 1984). In other words, the young child has not yet developed a concept that might be thought of as "conservation of personality."

Then, beginning at about age 7 or 8, at just about the time children seem to develop a global sense of self-esteem, a rather dramatic shift occurs in their descriptions of others. They begin to focus more on the inner traits or qualities of another person and to assume that those traits will be apparent in many situations (Gnepp & Chilamkurti, 1988). Children this age still describe others' physical features, but such descriptions seem to be intended more as examples or elaborations of more general points about internal qualities. You can see the change when you compare the 7-year-old's description on page 314 with this (widely quoted) description by a child who is nearly 10:

> He smells very much and is very nasty. He has no sense of humour and is very dull. He is always fighting and he is cruel. He does silly things and is very stupid. He has brown hair and cruel eyes. He is sulky and 11 years old and has lots of sisters. I think he is the most horrible boy in the class. He has a croaky voice and always chews his pencil and picks his teeth and I think he is disgusting. (Livesley & Bromley, 1973, p. 217)

This description still includes many external, physical features, but it goes beyond such concrete surface qualities to the level of personality traits, such as a lack of humor or cruelty.

In adolescence, young people's descriptions begin to include more comparisons of one trait with another or one person with another, more recognition of

A preschool child would no doubt label this boy's emotion as "sad." A teenager would understand that the emotion might be much more complicated, such as sadness mixed with anger at himself or some other form of ambivalence.

inconsistencies and exceptions, more shadings of gray (Shantz, 1983), as in this description by a 15-year-old:

> Andy is very modest. He is even shyer than I am when near strangers and yet is very talkative with people he knows and likes. He always seems good tempered and I have never seen him in a bad temper. He tends to degrade other people's achievements, and yet never praises his own. He does not seem to voice his opinions to anyone. He easily gets nervous. (Livesley & Bromley, 1973, p. 221)

Some findings from two early studies by Carl Barenboim illustrate these changes (1977, 1981). He asked children ranging in age from 6 to 16 to describe three people. Any descriptions that involved comparing a child's behaviors or physical features with another child, or with a norm, he called *behavioral comparisons* (such as "Billy runs a lot faster than Jason" or "She draws the best in our whole class"). Statements that involved some internal personality construct he called *psychological constructs* (such as "Sarah is so kind" or "He's a real stubborn idiot!"); any that included qualifiers, explanations, exceptions, or mentions of changes in character he called *organizing relationships* (e.g., "He's only shy around people he doesn't know" or "Usually she's nice to me, but sometimes she can be quite mean"). Figure 12.1 shows the combined findings from the two studies. You can see that behavioral comparisons were most common at around age 8 or 9, psychological constructs increased with age, and organizing relationships did not appear at all until age 10 and were still increasing at age 16.

You may have noticed the strong resemblance between this series of changes and the development of children's self-descriptions outlined in Chapter 10 (Figure 10.2). This parallel illustrates Flavell's basic point, that it is the same head doing the thinking about self and about others.

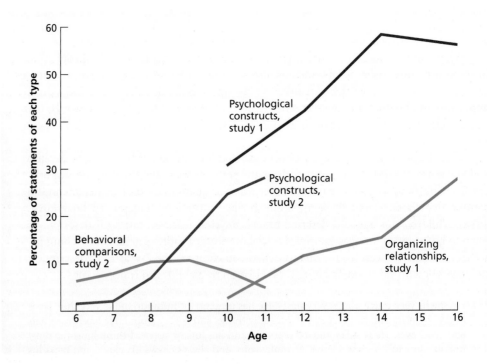

Figure 12.1   Children's Descriptions of Others

Barenboim's two studies of children's descriptions of others show clear shifts toward greater emphasis on psychological constructs. Study 1 involved children aged 10 to 16; study 2 involved children 6 to 11.

(*Source*: From C. Barenboim, "The development of person perception in childhood and adolescence: From behavioral comparisons to psychological constructs to psychological comparisons," *Child Development*, 52, Society for Research in Child Development (1981): p. 134, Fig. 1. By permission of the Society for Research in Child Development.)

Reading Others' Feelings

Learning Objective 12.3

How do children vary individually and across age with regard to understanding others' emotions?

Both cognitive skill and social information are obviously involved in understanding others' emotions. You need to be able to identify various body signals, including facial expressions; you need to understand various kinds of emotions and know that it is possible for people to feel several emotions at the same time; you need to understand the social context; and you need to have a theory of mind that helps you link the context with the other person's likely feelings. For example, you need the basic understanding that another person will be happy or sad depending on how well he does at something important to him.

Research on children's understanding of others' emotions suggests that they acquire these various forms of knowledge gradually over the years from about age 1 to adolescence (Pons, Harris, & de Rosnay, 2004; Thompson & Goodvin, 2005). You already know from Chapter 5 that by 10 to 12 months of age, babies can tell the difference between positive and negative facial and vocal expressions—at that age, they already show social referencing behavior. By age 3 or 4, the child's emotion-recognition repertoire has expanded considerably, and she has some preliminary understanding of the links between other people's emotions and their situations, such as that someone would be sad if she failed. And by age 10, the child understands and can read some emotional blends, even expressions of ambivalence.

Individual Differences in Emotion Knowledge Not all children (or all adults) are equally skilled in their ability to read other people's emotions, a point emphasized in Daniel Goleman's popular book *Emotional Intelligence* (1995b). These individual differences turn out to be quite significant for a child's overall social development and social competence. For example, preschoolers who know and use more emotion-related words (*angry*, *sad*, and so on) are more popular with peers (Fabes, Eisenberg, Hanish, & Spinrad, 2001).

Carol Izard and her colleagues (1997) have shown such a linkage longitudinally. In a group of economically disadvantaged children, Izard found that those who had better and more accurate emotion knowledge in preschool later showed greater social competence and fewer behavior problems in first grade. Such a linkage suggests the possibility that an intervention program designed to improve children's basic emotional competence—their ability both to read others and to control their own emotional expressions—might have wide-ranging benefits. One such intervention, the PATHS program, is described in *Thinking about Research* on page 319.

The Development of Empathy To explore the development of children's ability to read the emotions and cues of others, psychologists have also studied the development of empathy. **Empathy** involves two aspects: apprehending another person's emotional state or condition and then matching that emotional state oneself. An empathizing person experiences the same feeling he imagines the other person to feel, or a highly similar feeling. Sympathy involves the same process of apprehending another's emotional state, but it is accompanied not by a matching emotion but by a general feeling of sorrow or concern for the other person (Eisenberg & Fabes, 1998; Eisenberg, Fabes, Schaller, & Miller, 1989). Generally speaking, empathy seems to be the earlier response developmentally; among older children and adults, sympathy often seems to grow out of an initial empathetic response (Eisenberg et al., 2007).

The most thorough analysis of the development of empathy and sympathy has been offered by Martin Hoffman (2007), who describes four broad steps, summarized in Table 12.1 on page 318. The first stage, *global empathy*, which seems to be a kind of automatic empathetic distress response, is visible in quite young infants. Hoffman describes one example:

> An 11-month-old girl, on seeing a child fall and cry, looked as if she was about to cry herself, and then put her thumb in her mouth and buried her head in her mother's lap, which is what she would do if she herself were hurt. (1988, pp. 509–510)

empathy As defined by Hoffman, "a vicarious affective response that does not necessarily match another's affective state but is more appropriate to the other's situation than to one's own" (1982, p. 285).

Table 12.1   Stages in the Development of Empathy Proposed by Hoffman

Stage	Description
Stage 1: Global empathy	Observed during the first year. If the infant is around someone expressing a strong emotion, he may match that emotion–for example, by beginning to cry when he hears another infant crying.
Stage 2: Egocentric empathy	Beginning at about 12 to 18 months of age, when children have developed a fairly clear sense of their separate selves, they respond to another's distress with some distress of their own, but they may attempt to "cure" the other person's problem by offering what they themselves would find most comforting. They may, for example, show sadness when they see another child hurt, and go get their own mother to help.
Stage 3: Empathy for another's feelings	Beginning as young as age 2 or 3 and continuing through elementary school, children note others' feelings, partially match those feelings, and respond to the other's distress in nonegocentric ways. Over these years, children become able to distinguish a wider (and more subtle) range of emotions.
Stage 4: Empathy for another's life condition	In late childhood or adolescence, some children develop a more generalized notion of others' feelings and respond not just to the immediate situation but to the other individual's general situation or plight. Thus, a young person at this level may become more distressed by another person's sadness if she knows that the sadness is chronic or that the person's general situation is particularly tragic than if she sees it as a more momentary problem.

Sources: Hoffman, 1982, 1988, 2000.

This initial response changes as early as 12 or 18 months, as soon as the child has a clear understanding of the difference between self and others. The toddler still shows a matching emotion but understands that the distress is the other person's and not her own. Nonetheless, her solution to the other's distress is still likely to be egocentric, such as offering the distressed person a teddy bear (Eisenberg & Fabes, 1998).

Children's empathetic and sympathetic responses become more and more subtle over the preschool and elementary school years, as they become better readers of others' emotions. By middle childhood, many children can even empathize with several different emotions at once, as when they see another child make a mistake and fall down during a game. The observing child may see and empathize with both the hurt and the sense of shame or embarrassment, and she may be aware that the child may prefer not to be helped. In adolescence, a still more abstract level emerges, when the child moves beyond the immediate situation and empathizes (or sympathizes) with another person's general plight.

Notice that both developmental progressions—reading others' emotions and empathizing with them—reflect several of the general principles listed earlier in this chapter and parallel the changes Piaget described. In particular, there is a shift from observation to inference: With increasing age, the child's empathetic response is guided less by just the immediate, observed emotions seen in others, such as facial expressions or body language, and more by the child's inferences or deductions about the other person's feelings. This is not a swift change. For example, research in England by Paul Harris and his associates (1981) showed that not until

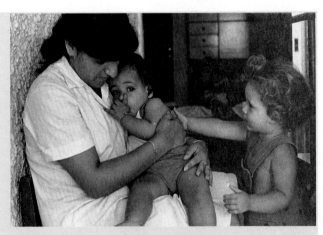

Children as young as 2 or 3 show this kind of empathetic response to other people's distress or delight

Preventing Violence by Increasing Children's Emotional Competence

Research reveals that most violent youths have poor social-reasoning skills and a poor understanding of others' emotions (Gleason, Jensen-Campbell, & Richardson, 2004). Although programs aimed at improving these skills in teenagers have met with limited success (Armstrong, 2003), research indicates that addressing such deficits in younger children may help to prevent violence in the teen years (DeRosier & Marcus, 2005). One violence prevention initiative geared toward younger children uses the PATHS (Promoting Alternative THinking Strategies) program, a set of 60 lessons designed to teach elementary school children about emotions and how to read them (Kusché & Greenberg, 1994).

Researchers used the PATHS curriculum with a group of 900 excessively aggressive early elementary school children in 395 different classrooms in four U.S. cities in a project known as the Fast Track Project (Conduct Problems Prevention Research Group, 2007). The children were divided into experimental and control groups. In special class sessions, children in the experimental group learned how to recognize others' emotions. They also learned strategies for controlling their own feelings, managing aggressive impulses, and resolving conflicts with peers.

After several years of implementation, the program produced the following effects among children in the experimental group:

- Better recognition of emotions
- More competence in social relationships
- Lower ratings of aggressiveness by peers
- Lowered risk of being placed in special education classes
- Less use of physical punishment by parents

This project provides support for the linkage between emotion knowledge and social competence. It also gives psychologists, teachers, parents, and law enforcement officials some degree of optimism about the prospects for changing the developmental trajectories of aggressive children (Foster, Jones, & Conduct Problems Prevention Research Group, 2007).

Questions for Critical Analysis

1. Was the Fast Track Project a true experiment? Why or why not?
2. Suppose you were a researcher who wanted to replicate the results of the Fast Track Project. Which of its several components would you choose to manipulate if you had only enough resources to study one of the independent variables? Explain why.

---

adolescence do young people become fully aware that other people may hide their emotions or act differently from the way they feel "inside."

As you might expect, not all children show equal amounts of such empathetic responses. Some biological disposition toward empathy appears to be part of the story, as evidenced by the greater similarity in levels of empathy among identical twins than among fraternal twins (Volbrecht, Lemery-Chalfant, Aksan, Zahn-Waxler, & Goldsmith, 2007). On the environmental side, many of the same factors that contribute to greater altruistic behavior (described in *Developmental Science in the Real World* in Chapter 11 on page 306) also appear to contribute to more empathetic responses in young children. For example, greater maternal response to distress is linked to increased empathy among toddlers (e.g., Davidov & Grusec, 2006). Like altruistic or kind behavior, empathy is also fostered by parental explanations about the consequences of the child's actions for others and by parental discussions of emotions (e.g., Miller, Eisenberg, Fabes, Shell, & Gular, 1989). Finally, developmentalists have some preliminary evidence that temperamental variables are linked to empathy. Specifically, children who are high in effortful control, the capacity to regulate emotion in order to accomplish goals, are also high in empathy (Valiente et al., 2004). Whatever its source, empathy appears to be critical to controlling aggressive impulses, as children who are high in empathy tend to be low in aggressiveness (Strayer & Roberts, 2004).

Describing Friendships

Preschool children seem to understand friendships mostly in terms of common activities. If you ask a young child how people make friends, the answer is usually that they "play together" or spend time physically near each other (Hartup, 2006). Children this age think of friendship as something that involves sharing toys or giving things to one another.

> **Learning Objective 12.4**
>
> How does children's understanding of friendship change as they get older?

During the preschool years, friendships are based on shared activities. As children get older, reciprocal trust becomes more important than activities.

Gradually, this view of friendship begins to shift away from an emphasis on activities (Dunn, Cutting, & Fisher, 2002). Extensive studies by Thomas Berndt (1983, 1986, 2004) show that the key ingredient of friendships for elementary school children seems to be reciprocal trust: Friends are seen as special people with desired qualities other than mere proximity, as people who are generous with one another, who help and trust one another. Children this age also understand that friendship has a temporal dimension: Friends are people with whom one has a history of connection and interaction, rather than people one has just met or played with once, as Figure 12.2 suggests. Likewise, over the elementary school years, children develop an understanding of gradations in friendships. That is, they understand the difference between "best friends" and other kinds of friends (Schraf & Hertz-Lazarowitz, 2003). Important, too, is the finding that improvements in children's understanding of peer relationships are linked to the quantity and quality of children's friendships (Rose & Asher, 2004).

By about age 11 or 12, children begin to talk about intimacy as an important ingredient in friendship; by middle adolescence, they expect a friend to be a confidant and to be supportive and trustworthy (Hartup, 2006). Understanding of friendship also becomes more qualified, more shaded. Research suggests that in late adolescence, young people understand that even very close friendships cannot fill every need and that friendships are not static: They change, grow, or dissolve as each member of the pair changes (Damon, 1977). A really good friendship, then, is one that adapts to these changes. Young people of this age say things about friendship like this: "Trust is the ability to let go as well as to hang on" (Selman, 1980, p. 141).

Some research findings from an early cross-sectional study by Brian Bigelow and John La Gaipa (1975) illustrate this pattern of change. These researchers asked several hundred children in Canada to write an essay about how their expectations of friends differed from their expectations of other acquaintances. The answers were scored along many dimensions, three of which are shown in Figure 12.3. You can see that references to demographic similarity (e.g.,

> My definition of a good friend is someone who you can trust. They will never turn their back on you. They will always be there for you. when you are feeling down in the dumps. They'll try to cheer you up. They will never forget about you. They'll always sit next to you at lunch,

Figure 12.2   A 10-Year-Old's Explanation of Friendship

This essay on friendship written by a 10-year-old illustrates the way older school-aged children think about friends. (*Source*: Author.)

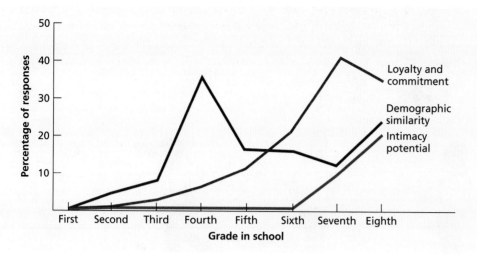

Figure 12.3   Changes in Children's Ideas about Friendship

Some of the changes in children's ideas about friendship are clear from these findings from Bigelow and La Gaipa's study.

(*Source*: Bigelow & La Gaipa, 1975, from Table 1, p. 858.)

"We live in the same neighborhood") were highest among fourth-graders, whereas comments about loyalty and commitment were highest among seventh-graders. References to intimacy potential (e.g., "I can tell her things about myself I can't tell anyone else") did not appear at all until seventh grade but then increased in eighth grade.

From what you have read so far, you can see that the patterns of developmental change in children's understanding of themselves, of others, and of relationships are strikingly similar, shifting in all the ways listed at the beginning of the chapter: from outer to inner characteristics, from observation to inference, from definite to qualified, and from an egocentric to a general view.

Understanding Rules and Intentions

What changes in children's understanding of rules and intentions emerge during the elementary school years?

A somewhat different facet of the child's emerging social cognition is her understanding of different categories for social rules. Beginning some time in the elementary school years, children understand the important distinction between what Elliot Turiel (1983) calls conventional rules and moral rules. **Conventional rules** are arbitrary, created by a particular group or culture. School rules about wearing uniforms, not running in the hall, and asking permission before you leave the room are all conventional rules, as are cultural rules about appropriate dress for boys and girls. By age 7 or 8, children begin to grasp the fact that such rules are arbitrary and may vary from one group to another or from one situation to another. Children know that they should follow such rules when in the specified group or situation but need not follow them at other times. **Moral rules**, in contrast, are seen as universal and obligatory, reflecting basic principles that guarantee the rights of others. Not running in the hall is a conventional rule; not hitting other people is a moral rule. Children judge the breaking of moral rules as far more serious than the breaking of conventional rules (Nucci & Nucci, 1982). Breaking conventional rules is seen as impolite or disruptive but is not typically condemned. Children's judgments of moral transgressions, however, are harsher.

Of course, as adults, we distinguish between intentional and unintentional rule violations, but do children make this same distinction? Working from his assumptions about young children's egocentrism, Piaget suggested that young children are incapable of such discriminations.

conventional rules As defined by Turiel, arbitrary, socially defined rules specific to a particular culture, subculture, group, or setting, such as "Don't run in the halls" or "Smoking allowed only in designated areas."

moral rules As defined by Turiel, universal and obligatory rules reflecting basic principles that guarantee the rights of others.

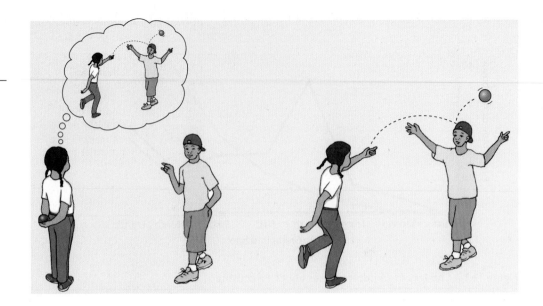

...een ...ess young children's understanding of an actor's intentions.

However, more recent research has demonstrated that young children do understand intentions to some degree (Zhang & Yu, 2002). For one thing, it's quite common for preschoolers to say "It was an accident . . . I didn't mean to do it" when they are punished. Such protests suggest that children understand that intentional wrongdoing is punished more severely than unintentional transgressions of the rules. Likewise, researchers have pointed out that children must understand intentions in order to determine whether a promise has been fulfilled. Studies show that children as young as 4 years can make such judgments (Maas, 2008).

Several studies suggest that children can make judgments about actors' intentions both when presented with abstract problems and when motivated by a personal desire to avoid punishment (Feinfield, Lee, Flavell, Green, & Flavell, 1999). In one classic study, 3-year-olds listened to stories about children playing ball (Nelson, 1980). Pictures were used to convey information about intentions (see Figure 12.4). The children were more likely to label a child who intended to harm a playmate as "bad" or "naughty" than to judge negatively a child who accidentally hit another child in the head with the ball. However, children's judgments were also influenced by outcomes. In other words, they were more likely to say a child who wanted to hurt his playmate was "good" if he failed to hit the child with the ball. These results suggest that children know more about intentions than Piaget thought, but they are still limited in their ability to base judgments entirely on intentions.

Moral Development

moral development The process of learning to distinguish between right and wrong in accordance with cultural values.

One of parents' and teachers' greatest concerns is helping children learn to be good people, to do the "right" thing according to the standards and values of their culture. **Moral development** is very complex. It has been explained in terms of psychoanalytic, learning, and cognitive-developmental theories. The cognitive-developmental theories, especially that of Lawrence Kohlberg, have been the most influential for the past several decades.

Learning Objective 12.6

How do psychoanalytic, learning, and cognitive-developmental theories differ in their explanations of moral development?

Dimensions of Moral Development

The psychoanalytic, learning, and cognitive-developmental theories each focus on a different aspect of moral development.

Moral Emotions Psychoanalytic theory emphasizes emotions in explaining moral development. According to Freud, the child learns moral rules by identifying with the same-sex parent during the phallic stage. The rules a child learns from her same-sex parent form her *superego*, or her internal moral judge. The superego has two parts: a conscience and an ego ideal. The **conscience** is a list of things that "good boys" and "good girls" don't do, such as telling lies. The **ego ideal** is a list of things that "good boys" and "good girls" do, such as obeying parents. When a child disobeys her conscience, she feels guilt. When she fails to live up to the standards set by the ego ideal, she feels shame. Freud believed children learn to obey the rules of their consciences and ego ideals to avoid these uncomfortable feelings.

To better understand Freud's idea about how the superego works, think about a hungry 7-year-old at the grocery store. He can figure out how to take a candy bar without anyone noticing. However, his superego classifies this behavior as stealing, and thinking about stealing a candy bar makes him feel guilty. This creates a conflict for him. If he steals the candy, he'll feel guilty. If he doesn't, he'll be hungry. If he has a healthy personality, Freud believed, he will obey his superego even though doing so will mean remaining hungry.

Erikson's views on moral development were similar to Freud's. However, Erikson believed that children learn moral rules from both parents. Erikson's theory also claimed that pride is just as important for moral development as guilt and shame. For example, if the boy decides not to take the candy, he will not only avoid feeling guilty but also feel pride in his ability to resist temptation.

Recently, there has been a resurgence of interest in moral emotions among developmentalists (Eisenberg, 2000; Nunner-Winkler, 2007). Research has shown, as Freud and Erikson predicted, that feelings of guilt, shame, and pride develop before age 6 (Kochanska & Aksan, 2006). Moreover, as both theorists predicted, the quality of parent-child relationships contributes to the development of moral emotions. For instance, children who have been abused display less understanding than do nonabused children of situations that produce guilt and pride in most people (Koenig, Cicchetti, & Rogosch, 2004).

Researchers infer that children are experiencing shame when they try to hide an act they know to be wrong. In fact, most school-aged children define shame as the emotion people experience when others find out they have done something wrong (Levorato & Donati, 1999). However, it is not until the later school years, at age 10 or so, that children connect shame exclusively to moral wrongs (Olthof, Ferguson, Bloemers, & Deij, 2004). Adolescents' understanding of shame, predictably, is more complex. They tell researchers that people experience shame when they fail to live up to their own standards of behavior as well as when their wrongdoing is exposed to others.

Some research suggests that connections between moral emotions and moral behavior are weaker than Freud believed, because they depend on cognitive development (Hoffman, 2007). Younger children connect moral feelings with adult observation. They seem to think they should feel guilty or ashamed only if a parent or teacher sees them commit a violation of a moral rule. Thus, a 7-year-old candy thief is unlikely to feel guilty unless he gets caught in the act. Later, after age 9 or 10, when children better understand moral feelings, they are more likely to make behavioral choices based on how guilty, ashamed, or proud they think they will feel. For example, when the boy who wants the candy is older, he will be more likely to choose not to take the candy because he knows resisting temptation will make him feel proud of himself.

By contrast, researcher Grazyna Kochanska has found that the guilt-behavior connection is linked to temperament in young children. Children who have a fearful temperament exhibit more signs of guilt, such as body tension, when they believe they have done something wrong (Kochanska et al., 2002). Another contributing factor may be parenting style. Kochanska's research indicates that children of mothers who rely heavily on power-assertive discipline techniques such as yelling and spanking display less guilt.

Moral Behavior Another way of looking at moral development is through the lens of learning theorist B. F. Skinner's operant conditioning model, which proposes that

conscience The list of "don'ts" in the superego; violation of any of these leads to feelings of guilt.

ego ideal The list of "dos" in the superego; violation of any of these leads to feelings of shame.

consequences teach children to obey moral rules. According to Skinner, adults reward children for morally acceptable behavior with praise. At the same time, they punish children for morally unacceptable behavior. As a result, acceptable behavior increases and unacceptable behavior decreases as children get older.

Consequences certainly do influence children's behavior. However, punishment may actually interfere with moral development. For example, if a child's parent spanks him in the grocery store parking lot for having a stolen a candy bar, the parent hopes that the spanking will teach him that stealing is wrong. But the child may learn only that he can't steal when he's with the parent. Similarly, when punishment is severe or embarrassing, children may be distracted from making the connection between their behavior and the punishment. A child who has stolen candy may be so angry at his parent for embarrassing him with a public spanking that he concentrates all his attention on his anger. As a result, he fails to realize that his choice to steal caused the spanking (Hoffman, 1988).

An approach that combines punishment with reasoned explanations may be more effective. On discovering that a 7-year-old had stolen a candy bar, a parent using this approach would respond by telling the child privately that it is wrong to take things that don't belong to you even if you are very hungry. Next, the parent would require the child to right the wrong by admitting his crime, apologizing to the cashier or manager, and paying for the candy. Finally, the 7-year-old would probably have to repay his parents in some way if they gave him the money to pay for the stolen candy. Such a process allows the child to learn both that it is wrong to steal and that, when he breaks a moral rule, he must do something to set things right (Zahn-Waxler, Radke-Yarrow, & King, 1979).

As you may recall from Chapter 1, social-learning theorist Albert Bandura claims that children learn more from observing others than from either rewards or punishments. His theory states that, when a child sees someone rewarded for a behavior, he believes that he will also be rewarded if he behaves in the same way. Similarly, when he sees a model punished, he assumes that he will also experience punishment if he imitates the model's behavior (Bandura, 1977, 1989). For example, a story about a child who was praised by a parent for resisting the temptation to steal may teach the child who hears or reads it that resisting temptation is praiseworthy. Conversely, when a child is exposed to a story about a boy or girl who steals and doesn't get caught, he may learn that it's possible to steal without getting caught.

As Bandura's theory predicts, children learn a lot about moral behavior, both acceptable and unacceptable, from models' behavior. Models can even influence children to change their moral behavior. For example, if a 7-year-old sees another child steal candy after he decides not to, he may change his mind.

Moral Reasoning *Moral reasoning* is the process of making judgments about the rightness or wrongness of specific acts. As you learned earlier in this chapter, children learn to discriminate between intentional and unintentional acts in early childhood. However, using this understanding to make moral judgments is another matter. Piaget claimed that the ability to use reasoning about intentions to make judgments about the moral dimensions of behavior appears to emerge along with concrete operational thinking.

Piaget studied moral development by observing children playing games. As he watched them play, Piaget noticed that younger children seemed to have less understanding of the games' rules. Following up on these observations, Piaget questioned children of different ages about rules. Their answers led him to propose a two-stage theory of moral development (Piaget, 1932).

Children in Piaget's **moral realism stage**, which he found to be typical of children younger than 8, believe that the rules of games can't be changed because they come from authorities, such as parents, government officials, or religious figures. For example, one 6-year-old told Piaget that the game of marbles was invented on Noah's ark. He went on to explain that the rules can't be changed because the "big ones," meaning adults and older children, wouldn't like it (Piaget, 1965, p. 60).

moral realism stage The first of Piaget's stages of moral development, in which children believe that rules are inflexible.

Moral realists also believe that all rule violations result in punishment. For example, Piaget told children a story about a child who fell into a stream when he tried to use a rotten piece of wood as a bridge. Children younger than 8 told him that the child was being punished for something "naughty" he had done in the past.

After age 8, Piaget proposed, children move into the **moral relativism stage**, in which they learn that people can agree to change rules if they want to. They realize that the important thing about a game is that all the players follow the same rules, regardless of what those are. For example, 8- to 12-year-olds know that a group of children playing baseball can decide to give each batter four strikes rather than three. They understand that their agreement doesn't change the game of baseball and that it doesn't apply to other people who play the game. Children in this stage also get better at following the rules of games.

Eight- to twelve-year-olds also know that rule violations don't result in punishment unless you get caught. As a result, they view events like falling into a stream because of using a rotten piece of wood as a bridge as accidents. They understand that accidents are not caused by "naughty" behavior. Children older than 8 also understand the relationship between punishment and intentions. For example, looking back at the situation of a 7-year-old taking a candy bar from a store, Piaget's research suggests that children over 8 would distinguish between a child who unintentionally left without paying for the candy and another who deliberately took it. Older children would likely say that both children should return or pay for the candy, but only the one who intentionally stole it should be punished.

Research supports Piaget's claim that children over 8 give more weight to intentions than to consequences when making moral judgments (Zelazo, Helwig, & Lau, 1996). Although their thinking is more mature than that of preschoolers, school-aged children's moral reasoning is still highly egocentric. For example, every parent has heard the exclamation "It's not fair!" when a child fails to receive the same treat or privilege as a sibling. However, it is rare, if not completely unknown, for a child to protest the fairness of his receiving something that was not also given to a sibling. Thus, school-aged children still have a long way to go before they are capable of mature moral reasoning. To understand this developmental process, we must turn to the work of Lawrence Kohlberg (1927–1987).

Kohlberg's Stages of Moral Development

Learning Objective 12.7
What kinds of moral reasoning do people use at Kohlberg's preconventional, conventional, and postconventional levels?

Piaget (1932) was the first to offer a description of the development of moral reasoning, but Kohlberg's work has had the most powerful impact on developmentalists' thinking (Colby, Kohlberg, Gibbs, & Lieberman, 1983; Dawson, 2002; Kohlberg, 1964, 1976, 1980, 1981). Building on and revising Piaget's ideas, Kohlberg pioneered the practice of assessing moral reasoning by presenting children with a series of hypothetical dilemmas in story form, each of which highlighted a specific moral issue, such as the value of human life. One of the most famous is the dilemma of Heinz:

> In Europe, a woman was near death from a special kind of cancer. There was one drug that the doctors thought might save her. It was a form of radium that a druggist in the same town had recently discovered. The drug was expensive to make, but the druggist was charging ten times what the drug cost him to make. He paid $200 for the radium and charged $2000 for a small dose of the drug. The sick woman's husband, Heinz, went to everyone he knew to borrow the money, but he could only get together about $1000, which is half of what it cost. He told the druggist that his wife was dying, and asked him to sell it cheaper or let him pay later. But the druggist said, "No, I discovered the drug and I'm going to make money from it." So Heinz got desperate and broke into the man's store to steal the drug for his wife. (Kohlberg & Elfenbein, 1975, p. 621)

After hearing this story, the child or young person is asked a series of questions, such as whether Heinz should have stolen the drug. What if Heinz didn't love his wife? Would that change anything? What if the person dying was a stranger? Should Heinz steal the drug anyway?

moral relativism stage The second of Piaget's stages of moral development, in which children understand that many rules can be changed through social agreement.

On the basis of answers to dilemmas like this one, Kohlberg concluded that there were three main levels of moral reasoning, each with two stages, as summarized briefly in Table 12.2.

Levels and Stages At Level I, **preconventional morality**, the child's judgments of right and wrong are based on sources of authority who are close by and physically superior to her—usually the parents. Just as the elementary school child's descriptions of others are largely external, her standards for judging rightness or wrongness are also external rather than internal. In particular, it is the outcome or consequences of actions that determine the rightness or wrongness of those actions.

In stage 1 of this level—*the punishment and obedience orientation*—the child relies on the physical consequences of some action to decide whether it is right or wrong. If she is punished, the behavior was wrong; if she is not punished, it was right. She is obedient to adults because they are bigger and stronger.

In stage 2—*individualism, instrumental purpose, and exchange*—the child begins to do things that are rewarded and to avoid things that are punished. (For this reason, the stage is sometimes referred to as *naive hedonism*.) If something feels good or brings pleasant results, it is good. Some beginning of concern for other people is apparent during this stage, but only if that concern can be expressed as something that benefits the child herself as well. So she can enter into agreements such as "If you help me, I'll help you." The following responses to variations of the Heinz dilemma, drawn from studies of children and teenagers in a number of different cultures, illustrate stage 2:

> He should steal the food for his wife because if she dies he'll have to pay for the funeral, and that costs a lot. (Taiwan)

preconventional morality
The first level of moral development proposed by Kohlberg, in which moral judgments are dominated by consideration of what will be punished and what feels good.

Table 12.2 Kohlberg's Stages of Moral Development

Stage	Description
LEVEL I: Preconventional Morality	
Stage 1: Punishment and obedience orientation	The child decides what is wrong on the basis of what is punished. Obedience is valued for its own sake, but the child obeys because adults are physically more powerful.
Stage 2: Individualism, instrumental purpose, and exchange	The child follows rules when it is in her immediate interest. What is good is what brings pleasant results.
LEVEL II: Conventional Morality	
Stage 3: Mutual interpersonal expectations, relationships, and interpersonal conformity	Moral actions are those that live up to the expectations of the family or other significant group. "Being good" becomes important for its own sake.
Stage 4: Social system and conscience	Moral actions are those so defined by larger social groups or the society as a whole. One should fulfill duties one has agreed to and uphold laws, except in extreme cases.
LEVEL III: Principled or Postconventional Morality	
Stage 5: Social contract orientation (or utility and individual rights)	Acting so as to achieve the "greatest good for the greatest number." The teenager or adult is aware that most values are relative and laws are changeable, although rules should be upheld in order to preserve the social order. Still, there are some basic nonrelative values, such as the importance of each person's life and liberty.
Stage 6: Universal ethical principles	The adult develops and follows self-chosen ethical principles in determining what is right. These ethical principles are part of an articulated, integrated, carefully thought-out, and consistently followed system of values and principles.

Sources: Kohlberg, 1976; Lickona, 1978.

He should steal the drug because "he should protect the life of his wife so he doesn't have to stay alone in life." (Puerto Rico)

Researcher: Suppose it wasn't his wife who was starving but his best friend. Should he steal the food for his friend?

Child: Yes, because one day when he is hungry his friend would help. (Turkey) (Snarey, 1985, p. 221)

At Level II, **conventional morality**, the young person shifts from judgments based on external consequences and personal gain to judgments based on rules or norms of a group to which he or she belongs, whether that group is the family, the peer group, a church, or the nation. What the chosen reference group defines as right or good is right or good in the child's view, and the child internalizes these norms to a considerable extent.

The majority of teenagers use stage 3 moral reasoning: What is good is what family or peers define as good and right. Do you think that the level of moral reasoning a teenager shows has any connection to his or her conformity to peers?

Stage 3 (the first stage of Level II) is the stage of *mutual interpersonal expectations, relationships, and interpersonal conformity* (sometimes also called the *good boy/nice girl stage*). Children at this stage believe that good behavior is what pleases other people. They value trust, loyalty, respect, gratitude, and maintenance of mutual relationships. Andy, a boy Kohlberg interviewed who was at stage 3, said:

I try to do things for my parents, they've always done things for you. I try to do everything my mother says, I try to please her. Like she wants me to be a doctor and I want to, too, and she's helping me get up there. (Kohlberg, 1964, p. 401)

Another mark of stage 3 is that the child begins to make judgments based on intentions as well as on outward behavior. If someone "means well" or "didn't mean to do it," the wrongdoing is seen as less serious than if the person did it "on purpose."

In stage 4, the second stage of conventional morality, the child turns to larger social groups for her norms. Kohlberg labeled this the stage of *social system and conscience*. Children reasoning at this stage focus on doing their duty, respecting authority, following rules and laws. The emphasis is less on what is pleasing to particular people (as in stage 3) and more on adhering to a complex set of regulations. The regulations themselves are not questioned.

The transition to Level III, **principled morality** (also called **postconventional morality**), is marked by several changes, the most important of which is a shift in the source of authority. At Level I, children see authority as totally outside themselves; at Level II, the judgments or rules of external authority are internalized, but they are not questioned or analyzed; at Level III, a new kind of personal authority emerges and allows a person to make individual judgments and choices based on self-chosen principles.

In stage 5 at this level—called the *social contract orientation* by Kohlberg—people show evidence of the beginning of such self-chosen principles. Rules, laws, and regulations are still seen as important because they ensure fairness, and they are seen as logically necessary for society to function. However, people operating at this level also recognize that rules, laws, and regulations sometimes need to be ignored or changed. The system of government in the United States is based on moral reasoning of this kind, since it provides means for changing laws and for allowing personal protests against a given law, such as the civil rights protests of the 1960s and the Vietnam War protests of the 1960s and 1970s.

Stage 6, the second stage in Level III, is simply a further extension of this same pattern, with the individual searching for the highest level of moral principles possible and then trying to live in a way that is consistent with them. Kohlberg referred to this stage as the *universal ethical principles orientation*. People who reason in this way assume personal responsibility for their own actions on the basis of fundamental and universal principles, such as justice and basic respect for persons (Kohlberg, 1978; Kohlberg, Boyd, & Levine, 1990). In their case studies of modern adults who reason and act at this level, Ann Colby and William Damon

conventional morality The second level of moral development proposed by Kohlberg, in which a person's judgments are dominated by considerations of group values and laws.

principled (postconventional) morality The third level of moral development proposed by Kohlberg, in which considerations of justice, individual rights, and social contracts dominate moral judgment.

Kohlberg thought that there were at least a few people, such as Mother Teresa, whose moral reasoning was based on universal ethical principles.

Figure 12.5
Responses to Kohlberg's Moral Dilemmas across Age

These findings are from Colby and Kohlberg's long-term longitudinal study of a group of boys who were asked about Kohlberg's moral dilemmas every few years from age 10 through early adulthood. Note that post-conventional, or principled, reasoning was quite uncommon, even in adulthood.

(*Source*: From Colby et al., "A longitudinal study of moral judgment," *Monographs of the Society for Research in Child Development*, 48 (1–2, Serial No. 200), Society for Research in Child Development (1983): p. 46, Fig. 1. By permission of the Society for Research in Child Development.)

(1992) note that another quality such people share is "open receptivity"—a willingness to examine their ideas and convictions, even while they act firmly and generously in support of their ideals. Such people are not common. Two famous examples are Mahatma Gandhi and Mother Teresa, both of whom devoted their lives to humanitarian causes.

It is very important to understand that what defines the stage or level of a person's moral development is not the specific moral choices the person makes but the form of reasoning used to justify the choices. For example, either choice—that Heinz should steal the drug or that he should not—can be justified with logic at any given stage. You have already read some examples of stage 2 justifications for Heinz's stealing the drug; the following is a stage 5 justification of the same choice, drawn from a study in India:

> What if Heinz was stealing to save the life of his pet animal instead of his wife? If Heinz saves an animal's life his action will be commendable. The right use of the drug is to administer it to the needy. There is some difference, of course—human life is more evolved and hence of greater importance in the scheme of nature—but an animal's life is not altogether bereft of importance. . . . (Snarey, 1985, p. 223, drawn originally from Vasudev, 1983, p. 7)

If you compare this answer to those presented earlier, you can clearly see the difference in the form of reasoning used, even though the action being justified is precisely the same.

Kohlberg argued that this sequence of moral development is both universal and hierarchically organized, just as Piaget thought his proposed stages of cognitive development were universal and hierarchical. That is, each stage follows and grows from the preceding one and has some internal consistency. Individuals should not move backward, or "down" the sequence, but only upward through the stages, if they move at all. Kohlberg did not suggest that all individuals eventually progress through all six stages or even that the stages are always associated with specific ages, but he insisted that their order is invariant and universal.

Age and Moral Reasoning   Kohlberg's own findings, confirmed by many other researchers (e.g., Walker, de Vries, & Trevethan, 1987), show that preconventional moral reasoning (stages 1 and 2) is dominant in elementary school, with stage 2 reasoning still evident among many early adolescents. Conventional reasoning (stages 3 and 4) emerges in middle adolescence and remains the most common form of moral reasoning in adulthood. Postconventional reasoning (stages 5 and 6) is relatively rare, even in adults. For example, in one study of men in their forties and fifties, only 13% were rated as using stage 5 moral reasoning (Gibson, 1990).

Two research examples illustrate these overall age trends. The first, illustrated in Figure 12.5, comes from Kohlberg's own longitudinal study of 58 boys, first interviewed when they were 10, and followed for more than 20 years (Colby et al., 1983). Table 12.3 shows cross-sectional data from a study by Lawrence Walker and his colleagues (1987). They studied 10 boys and 10 girls at each of four ages, interviewing the parents of each child as well. Note that Walker scored each response on a 9-point scale rather than using just the five main stages. This system, which has become quite common, allows for the fact that many people's reasoning falls between two specific stages.

The results of these two studies, although not identical, point to remarkably similar conclusions about the order of emergence of the various stages and about the approximate ages at which they predominate. In both studies, stage 2 reasoning dominates at ages 9 to 10, and stage 3 reasoning is most common at about ages 15 to 16.

Sequence of Stages   The evidence also seems fairly strong that Kohlberg's stages occur in the sequence he proposed. For example, in three long-term longitudinal studies of

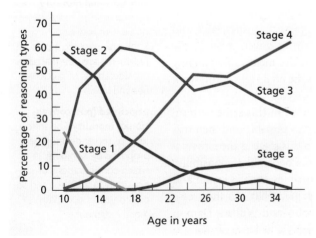

Table 12.3 Percentages of Children and Parents Who Show Moral Reasoning at Each of Kohlberg's Stages

Age	Stage 1	1–2	2	2–3	3	3–4	4	4–5	5
6 (grade 1)	10%	70%	15%	5%	–	–	–	–	–
9 (grade 4)	–	25%	40%	35%	–	–	–	–	–
12 (grade 7)	–	–	15%	60%	25%	–	–	–	–
15 (grade 10)	–	–	–	40%	55%	5%	–	–	–
Parents	–	–	–	1%	15%	70%	11%	3%	–

Source: From Walker et al., "Moral stages and moral orientations in real-life and hypothetical dilemmas," *Child Development*, 60 (1987): p. 849, Table 1. By permission of the Society for Research in Child Development.

teenagers and young adults, one in the United States (Colby et al., 1983), one in Israel (Snarey, Reimer, & Kohlberg, 1985), and one in Turkey (Nisan & Kohlberg, 1982), the changes in participants' reasoning nearly always occurred in the hypothesized order. Participants did not skip stages, and only about 5–7% of them showed any indication of regression (movement down the sequence of stages rather than up). Similarly, when Walker (1989) retested the participants in his study 2 years later, he found that only 6% had moved down (most only half a stage), while 22% had moved up, and none had skipped a stage. Such a rate of regression is about what researchers would expect to find, given the fact that the measurements of stage reasoning are not perfect. On the whole, the available evidence suggests that moral judgment changes over time in the sequence Kohlberg described (Rest, 1983).

Moral Reasoning Stages across Cultures   Variations of Kohlberg's dilemmas have been presented to children or adults in numerous countries and subcultures, both Western and non-Western, industrialized and nonindustrialized (Boom, Wouters, & Keller, 2007; Gibbs, Basinger, Grime, & Snarey, 2007; Monga, 2007). John Snarey, who has reviewed and analyzed these many studies, notes several things in support of Kohlberg's claim that the stages are universal: (1) Studies of children consistently find an increase in stage of reasoning with age; (2) the few longitudinal studies report "strikingly similar findings" (1985, p. 215), with participants progressing through the stage sequence with few reversals; and (3) cultures differ in the highest level of reasoning observed. In urban societies (both Western and non-Western), stage 5 is typically the highest stage observed, while in those cultures Snarey calls "folk societies," stage 4 is typically the highest. Collectively, this evidence provides quite strong support for the universality of Kohlberg's stage sequence.

Causes and Consequences of Moral Development

Learning Objective 12.8

What are the causes and consequences of age-related changes in moral reasoning?

The most obvious reason for the correlations between Kohlberg's stages and chronological age and for a consistent sequence of stages is that moral reasoning is strongly tied to cognitive development. Further, although the stages have often been criticized for failing to predict moral behavior, research does suggest that there is a link between moral reasoning and moral behavior.

Moral Reasoning and Cognitive Development   It appears that children must have a firm grasp of concrete operational thinking before they can develop or use conventional moral reasoning. Likewise, formal operational thinking appears to be necessary for advancement to the postconventional level. To be more specific, Kohlberg and many other theorists suggest that the decline of egocentrism that occurs as an individual moves through Piaget's concrete and formal operations stages is the cognitive-developmental variable that matters most in the development of moral reasoning. The idea is that the greater a child's or adolescent's ability to look at a situation from another person's perspective, the more advanced she is likely to be in moral reasoning. Psychologists use the term **role-taking** to refer to this ability (Selman, 1980). Research has provided strong support for the hypothesized links between role-taking and moral development (Kuhn, Kohlberg, Languer, & Haan, 1977; Walker, 1980).

Nevertheless, cognitive development isn't enough. Kohlberg thought that the development of moral reasoning also required support from the social environment. Specifically, he claimed, to foster mature moral reasoning, a child's or teenager's social environment must provide him with opportunities for meaningful, reciprocal dialogue about moral issues. Research showing that media portrayals of morally deviant behavior, especially violent behavior, negatively influence children's moral reasoning suggests that environmental factors may also interfere with moral development (Krcmar & Vieira, 2005). Thus, Kohlberg agreed with advocates of character education, as described at the beginning of the chapter, that moral development must be deliberately and systematically encouraged by parents and teachers.

Longitudinal research relating parenting styles and family climate to levels of moral reasoning suggests that Kohlberg was right (Pratt, Arnold, & Pratt, 1999). Parents' ability to identify, understand, and respond to children's and adolescents' less mature forms of moral reasoning seems to be particularly important to the development of moral reasoning. It is important because individuals of all ages have difficulty understanding and remembering moral arguments that are more advanced than their own level (Narvaez, 1998). Thus, a parent who can express her own moral views in terms of a child's level of understanding is more likely to be able to influence that child's moral development.

Moral Reasoning and Moral Behavior   Level of moral reasoning appears to be positively correlated with prosocial behavior and negatively related to antisocial behavior (Schonert-Reichl, 1999). In other words, higher levels of prosocial behavior are found among children and teens who are at higher levels of moral reasoning (compared to their peers). Alternatively, the highest levels of antisocial behavior are found among adolescents at the lowest levels of moral reasoning. Moreover, attitudes toward the acceptability of violence also vary with levels of moral reasoning. Individuals at lower levels have more tolerant attitudes toward violence (Sotelo & Sangrador, 1997).

Another connection between moral reasoning and behavior proposed by Kohlberg is that the higher the level of moral reasoning a young person shows, the stronger the link to behavior. For example, Kohlberg and others simply asked participants whether there is a link between one's stage of moral reasoning and the probability of making some moral choice, such as not cheating. In one early study, Kohlberg (1975) found that only 15% of college students reasoning at stage 5 of the principled level cheated when they were given an opportunity, while 55% of those at the conventional level and 70% of those at the preconventional level cheated.

A similar result comes from studies in which the moral reasoning of highly aggressive or delinquent youngsters is compared to that of nondelinquent peers. The repeated finding is that delinquents (male or female) have lower levels of moral reasoning than do nondelinquents, even when the two groups are carefully matched for levels of education, social class, and IQ (Chudzik, 2007; Ma, 2003; Smetana, 1990). In one study of this type, Virginia Gregg and her colleagues (1994) found that only 20% of a group of incarcerated male and female delinquents were reasoning at stage 3 or higher, while 59% of a carefully matched comparison group of nondelinquents were reasoning at this level. Like younger children who act out more in school, delinquents are most likely to use highly self-oriented reasoning, at Kohlberg's stage 2 (Richards, Bear, Stewart, & Norman, 1992).

role-taking The ability to look at a situation from another person's perspective.

Delinquents appear to be behind their peers in moral reasoning because of deficits in role-taking skills. For example, researchers have found that teenagers who can look at actions they are contemplating from their parents' perspective are less likely to engage in delinquent behavior than adolescents who cannot do so (Wyatt & Carlo, 2002). Most delinquent teens also seem to be unable to look at their crimes from their victims' perspectives or to assess hypothetical crimes from the victims' perspectives. Thus, programs aimed at helping delinquents develop more mature levels of moral reasoning usually focus on heightening their awareness of the victim's point of view. However, few such programs have been successful (Armstrong, 2003; Moody, 1997; Putnins, 1997).

Finally, despite the abundance of evidence for a link between moral reasoning and behavior, no one has found the correspondence to be perfect. After all, in Kohlberg's studies, 15% of the stage 5 moral reasoners did cheat, and a quarter of stage 4 and stage 5 reasoners who thought it morally right to participate in a sit-in did not do so. As Kohlberg says, "One can reason in terms of principles and not live up to those principles" (1975, p. 672).

Alternative Views

Learning Objective 12.9

How do Eisenberg's and Gilligan's approaches to moral development differ from Kohlberg's?

Most of the moral dilemmas Kohlberg posed for participants in his studies deal with wrongdoing—with stealing, for example, or disobeying laws. Few of the dilemmas reveal anything about the kind of reasoning children use in justifying prosocial behavior. You learned in Chapter 11 that altruistic behavior is evident in children as young as 2 and 3, but how do children explain and justify such behavior?

Eisenberg's Model of Prosocial Reasoning   Nancy Eisenberg and her colleagues evaluated children's empathy and prosocial behavior by gaining their responses to dilemmas involving self-interest (1989). One story for younger children, for example, involves a child walking to a friend's birthday party. On the way, he comes upon another child who has fallen and hurt himself. If the party-bound child stops to help, he will probably miss the cake and ice cream. What should he do? In response to dilemmas like this, preschool children most often use what Eisenberg calls **hedonistic reasoning**, in which the child is concerned with self-oriented consequences rather than moral considerations. Preschoolers asked about what they would do if they came upon an injured child on their way to a birthday party say things like "I'd help because he'd help me the next time" or "I wouldn't help because I'd miss the party." This approach gradually shifts to one Eisenberg calls **needs-oriented reasoning**, in which the child expresses concern rather directly for the other person's need, even if the other's need conflicts with the child's own wishes or desires. Children operating on this basis say things like "He'd feel better if I helped." These children do not express their choices in terms of general principles or indicate any reflectiveness about generalized values; they simply respond to the other's needs.

Still later, typically in adolescence, children say they will do good things because it is expected of them, a pattern highly similar to Kohlberg's stage 3. Finally, in late adolescence, some young people give evidence that they have developed clear, internalized values that guide their prosocial behavior: "I'd feel a responsibility to help because of my values" or "If everyone helped, society would be a lot better."

Some sample data from Eisenberg's longitudinal study of a small group of U.S. children illustrate the shift from hedonistic to needs-oriented reasoning; see Figure 12.6 on page 332. By early adolescence, hedonistic reasoning has virtually disappeared and needs-oriented reasoning has become the dominant form. However, when Eisenberg and her colleagues conducted follow-up studies of participants in early adulthood, they found that age-related changes in pro-social reasoning reflected individual differences in personality as well as a universal developmental process (Eisenberg et al., 2007).

Culture also contributes to the development of prosocial reasoning. In one study, Eisenberg and her team of researchers (Eisenberg, Hertz-Lazarowitz, & Fuchs, 1990; Boehnke,

hedonistic reasoning A form of prosocial moral reasoning described by Eisenberg in which the child is concerned with consequences to self rather than moral considerations, roughly equivalent to Kohlberg's stage 2.

needs-oriented reasoning A form of prosocial moral reasoning proposed by Eisenberg in which the child expresses concern directly for the other person's need, even if the other's need conflicts with the child's own wishes or desires.

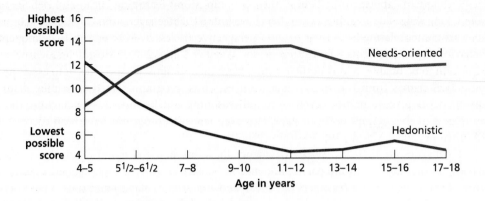

Figure 12.6   Eisenberg's Longitudinal Study of Prosocial Reasoning

Every 2 years Eisenberg asked the same group of children what a person should do when confronted with each of a series of dilemmas about doing good, such as helping someone who is hurt. She then analyzed their form of reasoning, using a measure for which the minimum score was 4 and the maximum was 16.

(*Source*: Eisenberg et al., "Pro-social development in late adolescence," *Child Development*, 66, 1995, pp. 1179–1197.)

Silbereisen, Eisenberg, & Reykowski, 1989) found a pattern of prosocial reasoning development among German, Polish, Italian, and city-dwelling Israeli children resembling the one shown in Figure 12.6. However, kibbutz-reared Israeli elementary school children showed little needs-oriented reasoning (Eisenberg, 1986). Instead, this particular group of Israeli children was more likely to reason on the basis of internalized values and norms and the humanness of recipients, a pattern consistent with the strong emphasis on egalitarianism and communal values in the kibbutzim. These findings suggest that culture may perhaps play a larger role in children's moral reasoning than in their reasoning about justice, although that is still a highly tentative conclusion.

There are obviously strong parallels between the sequences of changes in prosocial reasoning Eisenberg has described and Kohlberg's levels and stages of moral reasoning. Children seem to move from a self-centered orientation ("What feels good to me is right") to a stance in which social approval guides reasoning about both justice and moral behavior ("What is right is what other people define as right; I should do good things because others will approve of me if I do"). Much later, some young people seem to develop internalized, individualized norms to guide both kinds of reasoning. Despite these obvious parallels, though, researchers have typically found only moderate correlations between children's reasoning about prosocial dilemmas such as Eisenberg's and their reasoning about Kohlberg's justice or fairness dilemmas. The sequences of steps may be similar, but as was true of so much of the cognitive development you read about in Chapter 6, children's reasoning in one area doesn't necessarily generalize to a related area.

Eisenberg's research, as well as the work of others in the same field, helps to broaden Kohlberg's original conception, without changing the fundamental arguments. In contrast, Carol Gilligan has questioned some of the basic tenets of Kohlberg's model.

Gilligan's Ethic of Caring   Carol Gilligan (1982; Gilligan & Wiggins, 1987) is fundamentally dissatisfied with Kohlberg's focus on justice and fairness as the defining elements of moral reasoning. Gilligan argues that there are at least two distinct "moral orientations": justice and caring. Each has its own central injunction: not to treat others un-

Gilligan argues that these young women are much more likely to use an "ethic of caring" than an "ethic of justice" as a basis for their moral judgments, while the reverse is true among boys and men. Such a difference may exist among adults, but research on children and adolescents shows no such pattern.

fairly (justice), and not to turn away from someone in need (caring). Boys and girls learn both of these injunctions, but Gilligan has hypothesized that girls are more likely to operate from an orientation of caring or connection, while boys are more likely to operate from an orientation of justice or fairness. Because of these differences, she argues, they tend to perceive moral dilemmas quite differently.

Given the emerging evidence on sex differences in styles of interaction and in friendship patterns, which you read about in Chapter 11, Gilligan's hypothesis makes some sense. Perhaps girls, focusing more on intimacy in their relationships, judge moral dilemmas by different criteria. In fact, however, research on moral dilemmas has not shown that boys are more likely to use justice as the basis for their moral reasoning or that girls more often use caring. Several studies of adults have shown such a pattern (e.g., Lollis, Ross, & Leroux, 1996; Lyons, 1983; Mitchell, 2002), but studies of children, adolescents, and college students generally have not (Jadack, Hyde, Moore, & Keller, 1995; Smetana, Killen, & Turiel, 1991; Walker, 1991). What matters far more than gender in determining whether a given child or adult will use a caring or a justice orientation in addressing a moral dilemma is the nature of the dilemma itself. Dilemmas relating to interpersonal relationships, for example, are more likely to be addressed using a caring orientation, whereas dilemmas explicitly involving issues of fairness are more likely to be addressed with a justice orientation. It may be that adult women are more likely than men to interpret moral dilemmas as personal, but both men and women use both caring and justice arguments in resolving moral dilemmas (Turiel, 1998).

For example, Lawrence Walker scored children's answers to moral dilemmas using both Kohlberg's fairness scheme and Gilligan's criteria for a caring orientation. He found no sex difference either for hypothetical dilemmas like the Heinz dilemma or for real-life dilemmas suggested by the children themselves (Walker et al., 1987). Only among adults did Walker find a difference in the direction that Gilligan hypothesized.

Gilligan's arguments have often been quoted in the popular press as if they were already proven, when in fact the empirical base is really quite weak. Gilligan herself has done no systematic studies of children's (or adults') caring orientation. Yet despite these weaknesses, most developmentalists are not ready to discard all of her underlying points (Sherblom, 2008). Most agree to credit Gilligan's model with helping to broaden the study of moral development beyond the cognitively oriented perspective offered by Kohlberg.

Think Critically

- How might an understanding of social-cognitive development affect parental responses to children's misbehavior?
- Suppose that Gilligan's view of moral development is correct, and adult women focus on an ethic of caring when thinking about moral issues while men focus on an ethic of justice. What do you think the implications of such a difference would be for male-female relationships, for men and women as political leaders, or for other social phenomena?

Conduct Your Own Research

You can replicate Carl Barenboim's classic research by asking children of different ages to describe three specific people. You might begin by asking children to name the three peers they like best. Next, ask them to describe these children. Try to interview children across the same age range as those who participated in Barenboim's studies (6–16 years). Using the examples on page 316 in the text as a guide, count the number of physical/behavioral, psychological, and organizing relationship remarks made by the children you interview. Sum the remarks across the ages of the children you interview, and use the sums to create a graph like the one in Figure 12.1 on page 316.

Summary

THE DEVELOPMENT OF SOCIAL COGNITION

12.1 What are the general principles of social-cognitive development?

- Many of the general principles that describe overall cognitive development also describe developmental changes in social cognition, including a shift in focus from outer to inner characteristics, from observation to inference, from definite to qualified judgment, and from a particular to a general view. Social and moral reasoning differ from other aspects of cognition, however, in that a child must learn that unlike objects, people behave with intention, mask feelings, and operate by special socially defined scripts or rules.

12.2 In what ways do children's descriptions of other people change across childhood and adolescence?

- Children's descriptions of other people shift from a focus on external features to a focus on personality traits and to more qualified, comparative descriptions during adolescence; this progression parallels the shifts in children's self-descriptions.

12.3 How do children vary individually and across age with regard to understanding others' emotions?

- Children learn to interpret many basic emotional expressions fairly early, but they can correctly read more complex emotions and emotional blends only later. The ability to read others' emotions and intentions is an important element in a child's general social competence; those who are less skilled, who have less "emotion knowledge," are more likely to be rejected by their peers. Empathy—the ability to match or approximate the emotion of another—is seen in young infants, but it becomes less egocentric and more subtle through the preschool and elementary school years.

12.4 How does children's understanding of friendship change as they get older?

- Children's thinking about their relationships, especially friendships, also changes developmentally, moving from definitions of friends as people who share physical space or activities, to definitions emphasizing trust, and finally, during adolescence, to definitions emphasizing intimacy.

12.5 What changes in children's understanding of rules and intentions emerge during the elementary school years?

- In elementary school, children begin to understand the distinction between conventional rules and moral rules. They also distinguish between intentional and unintentional acts.

MORAL DEVELOPMENT

12.6 How do psychoanalytic, learning, and cognitive-developmental theories differ in their explanations of moral development?

- Psychoanalytic theories of moral development emphasize emotions, whereas learning theories focus on reinforcement and modeling. Cognitive-developmental theorists study moral reasoning and assert that moral development is strongly related to general cognitive development.

12.7 What kinds of moral reasoning do people use at Kohlberg's preconventional, conventional, and postconventional levels?

- Kohlberg described six distinct stages in children's (and adults') reasoning about moral issues. These six stages are divided into three levels. The child moves from preconventional morality (dominated by punishment and "what feels good"), to conventional morality (dominated by group norms or laws), to postconventional or principled morality (dominated by social contracts and basic ethical principles).

12.8 What are the causes and consequences of age-related changes in moral reasoning?

- Both cognitive-developmental and environmental variables, such as the opportunity to discuss moral issues, contribute to advancement through Kohlberg's stages. A child's or adult's stage predicts prosocial and antisocial behavior and attitudes to some degree.

12.9 How do Eisenberg's and Gilligan's approaches to moral development differ from Kohlberg's?

- Alternative models of moral reasoning include Eisenberg's stages of prosocial reasoning (reasoning about why to do something good) and Gilligan's proposed caring orientation. Gilligan's hypothesis that girls are more likely than boys to use caring, rather than justice, as a basis for moral judgments has not been supported by research with children, adolescents, and college students.

Key Terms

13

The Ecology of Development: The Child within the Family System

I f you have read William Golding's novel *The Lord of the Flies* or have seen one of the film versions, you know that the former teacher put forward a rather pessimistic view of human nature. In the story, a group of boys ranging in age from 6 or so to early adolescence are stranded on an island with no adult supervision. The hero, Ralph, attempts to establish a civilized community for the boys, based on the rules of the English society from which they have come. Exploiting the tendency of the younger boys toward fearfulness and superstition, his nemesis, Jack, sets up a "culture" in which he enjoys absolute power. Although there have been many interpretations of Golding's work, one message seems clear: Children need adults to become civilized, or, to put it differently, to channel their natural impulses into behaviors that will enhance both their own development and the collective good of humankind.

While most developmentalists would probably find Golding's characterization of unsupervised children and adolescents a bit too pessimistic, they would probably, nonetheless, agree with the basic premise that children require relationships with adults in order to develop optimally. But will just any adult do, or is there a need for a special adult-child relationship to serve as a context in which culture is transmitted from one generation to the next? In other words, do children really need families?

Questions like these are the subject of this chapter. We will begin with an examination of the complex theories that have been proposed to explain interactions among family members and the larger social contexts within which families exist. Afterward, we will turn our attention to the characteristics of family relationships and the contributions of individuals to them. Finally, you will read about changes in family structure and other aspects of family life that influence children's development.

Understanding the Family System

Family influences on children's development are often studied within the broader context of a *systems perspective*. The primary idea behind the systems approach is that multiple factors work together holistically. That is, the combined interactive effects of all the variables included in the catch-all term *family influences* are greater than the sum of any of the individual factors. For example, a parent's approach to discipline influences a child's development. At the same time, the child's own temperament influences her development. But when the two factors are combined, a different, or *interactive*, effect is produced that is more important than either factor alone. So, a particular approach to discipline may have one effect on a child with an easygoing temperament and a completely different effect on a child with a difficult temperament. Before we discuss Bronfenbrenner's *bioecological theory*, which is arguably the most important developmental systems theory that has been proposed, we will consider a few of the basic principles of the systems perspective as it has been applied to the study of families.

Family Systems Theory

Learning Objective 13.1
How does family systems theory explain family interactions?

In search of a comprehensive explanation of the family and how it shapes individuals, developmental scientists have turned to *systems theory* (Lamb & Lewis, 2005). Systems theorists emphasize that any system—biological, economic, or psychological—has two key properties. First and foremost, a system has "wholeness and order," which is another way of saying that the whole is greater than the sum of its parts. The whole consists of the parts and their relationship to one another. Often an analogy is made between a system and a melody. A melody is far more than a set of individual notes; it is the relationship of notes to one another that creates the melody. Thus, **family systems theory** is the view that the family is an integrated network of factors that work together to influence a child's development. Thus, the influence of the system as a whole on development is greater than the sum of the individual factors that make up the family.

A second feature of any system is that it is adaptive in precisely the same way as Piaget theorized that the child's cognitive system is. When any part of a system changes or some new element is added, the system "assimilates" if it can but "accommodates" if it must. So systems resist change as much as they can by absorbing new data or new parts into the existing structure; if that doesn't work—as it often doesn't—only then will the system change. For example, when a family's second child is born, the parents may try to keep to their old routines as much as possible; the presence of this new individual in the family system will, however, inevitably force accommodations. This will be particularly true if

family systems theory The view that the family is an integrated network of factors that work together to influence a child's development.

**Figure 13.1
Belsky's Model of Family
Interaction**

Developmentalist Jay Belsky proposed this model of family interaction to illustrate the system
of mutual influences that work
together to affect children's
development.

(*Source*: From fig. 1, p. 6, Belsky, J.
(1981). Early human experience: A family perspective. *Developmental Psychology, 17*, 3–23. Reprinted with
permission.)

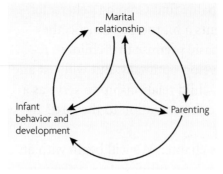

the new baby is temperamentally very different
from the first child.

You can see that these two features of
systems—wholeness and adaptability—cause
change in any one part of a system to affect every
other part. This was suggested in a systems model
of family functioning proposed by developmental
psychologist Jay Belsky (1981). As Figure 13.1 illustrates, systems such as the one proposed by Belsky have feedback loops. For example, a husband
who is suffering from depression is likely to be
more negative toward his wife than he used to be, and this negativity will put a strain on their
relationship. The worsening of the relationship, coupled with the man's depression, will cause
these parents to treat their children differently—they will be less attentive in general, and
more critical and strict when they do pay attention. The children will react with changes of
their own, perhaps becoming defiant, and in response the parents will then become more
strict and demanding. In this way, a cycle is set in motion.

Learning Objective 13.2

How do the various systems in
Bronfenbrenner's model interact to
influence children's development?

Bronfenbrenner's Bioecological Approach

Of all the various systems theories, none has been more influential than that of
the late developmental psychologist Urie Bronfenbrenner (1917–2005) (1979,
1989, 2001). For Bronfenbrenner, the family is the filter through which the larger
society influences child development. As such, the family can help the larger culture achieve
the goal of socializing new members, but it can also serve as a buffer against harmful elements
in the culture-at-large. Thus, according to Bronfenbrenner, although other institutions can
substitute for it to some degree, the family is "the most efficient means of making human beings human" (Bronfenbrenner, quoted in EBC, 1991).

Of course there are many developmental theories, such as Freud's psychoanalytic theory, that emphasize the importance of the child's family.
What distinguishes Bronfenbrenner's bioecological approach from other developmental theories is his attempt to explain how all of the various environmental influences on children's development are related to one another.
Moreover, Bronfenbrenner also provides an explanation for how all of these
interrelated influences mesh with the child's own biological make-up. For
this reason, his theory is now known as the *bioecological approach*.

Just how does Bronfenbrenner achieve such a comprehensive account of
the role played by environmental factors in individual development? The
fundamental premise of his theory is that the bioecological system in which
the child develops can be thought of as a series of layers, or concentric
circles. The innermost circle, made up of elements Bronfenbrenner calls
microsystems, includes all those settings in which the child has direct personal
experience, such as the family, a child-care center or a school, and a job setting (for a teenager).

The next layer, which Bronfenbrenner calls *exosystems*, includes a whole
range of system elements that the child does not experience directly but that
influence the child because they affect one of the microsystems, particularly
the family. The parents' work and workplace is one such element, as is the
parents' network of friends.

Finally, Bronfenbrenner describes a *macrosystem* that includes the larger
cultural or subcultural setting in which both the microsystems and the exosystems are embedded. The poverty or wealth of the family, the neighborhood in which the family lives, the ethnic identity of the family, and the larger
culture in which the entire system exists are all parts of this macrosystem.

The late Urie Bronfenbrenner changed the way developmentalists think about the complexity of the
contexts in which children grow up. His bioecological model was influenced by his life history. At the
age of 6, Bronfenbrenner came to the United States
from Russia with his parents. With his wife, Liese,
he raised six children. He was one of the founders
of the Head Start program in the 1960s. At the time
of his death, he had thirteen grandchildren and one
great-grandchild.

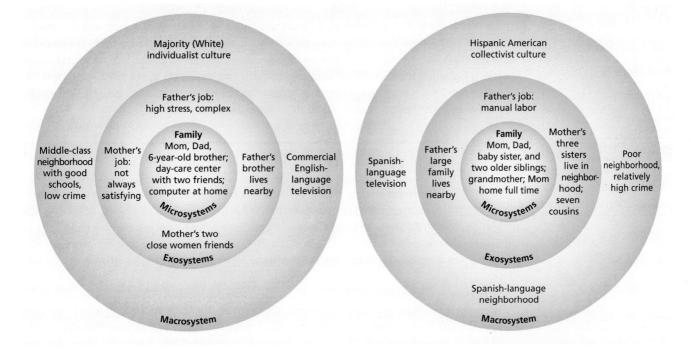

Figure 13.2 presents these three layers schematically for two hypothetical 4-year-old American children—one from the majority White culture living in an intact middle-class family with two employed parents, the other a Hispanic American child living with both parents and a grandmother in a working-class, largely Spanish-speaking neighborhood, whose mother stays at home full-time. If you try to imagine yourself living within each of these systems, you can get a feeling for the many complex ways in which they differ and how all their pieces interact with one another. Bronfenbrenner's point is that until developmentalists really understand the ways in which all the elements in such complex systems interact to affect the child, they will not understand development.

It is probably obvious that trying to understand child development in this way is immensely difficult. It is hard to keep all the elements of a system in mind at once, let alone to try to study all the relevant parts simultaneously. Perhaps frustrated by that difficulty, or perhaps because of the long tradition of examining family and cultural effects in more linear ways, psychologists have continued to design research that explores only small pieces of the total ecological system. Thus, much of what is known about family and cultural influences on children is piecemeal rather than systemic. Nonetheless, let's plunge in, using Bronfrenbrenner's model as a general framework. In this chapter, we will focus on the most important element of the microsystem: the family itself. In Chapter 14, we will move beyond the family to consider other dimensions of the microsystem such as nonparental care settings and schools. We will also examine some of the factors in the exosystem, such as parental employment, and in the larger cultural context, or the macrosystem.

Dimensions of Family Interaction

Researchers who have focused most directly on patterns of parent-child interaction have identified several major dimensions on which families differ and which seem to be significant for the child. These include the

Figure 13.2
Bronfenbrenner's Bioecological Model

Two hypothetical children, growing up in widely different ecological settings, illustrate the layers in Bronfenbrenner's model. To understand how the environment affects a child, developmentalists would need to study every aspect of this complex system simultaneously—a tall order.

It is probably obvious that loving a child is a critical ingredient in the child's optimum development—but sometimes it doesn't hurt to restate the obvious.

individual characteristics of children and parents, the emotional tone and responsiveness of parents, the manner in which parents exercise control of children's behavior, and the quality and amount of communication. Remember that all of these factors, though they are found in the microsystem, reflect the influences of factors outside the family as well as within it. So, while it is useful for instructional purposes to focus exclusively on the family system for a bit, keep in mind that we are only temporarily ignoring the larger contexts within which the family exists in order to better understand its unique characteristics.

Learning Objective 13.3

What are the individual characteristics of children and parents that contribute to family interactions?

Individuals in the Family System

Each individual in the family system carries within himself or herself a variety of factors that are relevant to how he or she interacts with others in the system. Some of these factors—a child's or parent's temperament, a child's age or gender—are contained within the individuals themselves. Others, such as birth order, are imposed upon members by the family system itself.

Children's Characteristics You should remember from Chapter 9 that children's temperaments influence the ways in which others interact with them. In Chapter 11, you read about the link between temperament and attachment in infancy and its contribution to peer relations later in childhood. Thus, it should come as no surprise to you at this point to learn that children's temperaments contribute to the general tenor of the family system (Burt, McGue, Krueger, & Iacono, 2005). For example, in a family in which one child has a very difficult temperament, a great deal of time and energy may be devoted to keeping the child happy (Turecki, 2000). As a result, parents may be too frazzled to meet the needs of other children, and the difficult child's siblings may become resentful of her.

Children's relationships with their parents and siblings may also be affected by their place in the family sequence (referred to as **birth order**, or ordinal position). Parents generally have higher expectations for maturity in their first-born child and may well be more responsive to or more child-centered with that child. First-borns are also punished more, in part because parents are simply less skilled in using noncoercive forms of control with their first child. Perhaps responding to the higher expectations, oldest children (first-borns or only children) have higher average IQ scores and are somewhat more achievement-oriented (Zajonc & Sulloway, 2007). However, historian Frank Sulloway has suggested that later-borns enter the family as social "underdogs," a status that motivates them to be more rebellious and, perhaps, more open to new experiences (Sulloway, 1996). The underdog status of later-borns may also help to explain research findings we noted in Chapter 7 regarding later-borns' superior conflict management skills (Gillies & Lucey, 2006).

Differential treatment of siblings goes beyond parental expectations based on birth order, a point you may remember from the discussion of the *nonshared environment* in Chapter 7. Several studies by Judy Dunn (2007) in both the United States and England have shown that parents may express warmth and pride toward one child and scorn toward another. Similarly, parents may be very strict with one child and very lenient with her siblings. Children recognize and respond to these differences quite early in life. Responses may include resentment and increased hostility toward siblings from children who are treated more harshly than their brothers and sisters are. However, the causes and effects of differential treatment of siblings are difficult to study, because they are confounded with children's ages, their gender, and their temperaments.

Children's ages are an especially important influence on parent-child relationships, as we noted in Chapter 11's discussion of *goal-corrected partnerships*, a pattern in which parents expect older preschoolers to accept more responsibility for themselves than they did when they were infants and toddlers. Similarly, parents' expectations rise when children enter school, and the goal of parenting often becomes training the child to regulate his or her own behavior (Lamb & Lewis, 2005). Researchers have learned that there are several parenting variables

birth order A child's position in the sequence of children within a family, such as first-born, later-born, or only child.

that contribute to the development of this kind of self-regulation. First, the parents' own ability to self-regulate is important, perhaps because they are providing the child with models of good or poor self-regulation (Prinstein & La Greca, 1999). Also, the degree of self-regulation a parent expects influences the child's self-regulatory behavior. Higher expectations, together with parental monitoring to make certain that expectations are met, are associated with greater self-regulatory competence (Rodrigo, Janssens, & Ceballos, 1999).

It is also clear that parents treat boys and girls differently, beginning in infancy, as we noted in Chapter 10. Some of these differences depend on both the parent's and the baby's sex. For example, parents sing more expressively to same-sex than to opposite-sex infants (Trehub, Hill, & Kamenetsky, 1997). Likewise, mothers of infants maintain more physical and visual contact with daughters than with sons (Lindahl & Haimann, 1977). Differences such as these may contribute in some way to the formation of same-sex alliances between parents and children that may be important later in childhood.

Other kinds of variations in parents' interactions with boys and girls are demonstrated by both mothers and fathers. For example, in one classic study, researchers found that adults viewing a videotape of an infant interpreted the baby's behavior differently depending on the gender label provided by the researchers. Participants who were told that the baby was a girl interpreted a particular behavior as expressing "fear." Amazingly, those who believed the infant to be male labeled the same behavior "anger" (Condry & Condry, 1976). More recent research employing this technique suggests that the current cohort of adults is somewhat less likely to stereotype infant behavior in this way, although, like their counterparts in the 1970s, they attend to and comment on motor activity more when they believe a target infant is a boy (Pomerleau, Malcuit, Turgeon, & Cossette, 1997). Thus, temperamental stereotyping may affect the quality of the parent-child relationship.

Some studies also suggest that there are sex differences in parents' expectations with respect to school-aged children's self-regulatory behavior. For example, mothers make different kinds of demands on boys and girls. They appear to provide both with the same types of guidance, but they are more likely to give boys more autonomy over their own behavior than they give girls. Nevertheless, they are also more likely to hold girls to a higher standard of accountability for failure (Pomerantz & Ruble, 1998). Developmentalists speculate that this difference may lead to stronger standards of behavior for girls later in development.

However, the opposite may be true with regard to children who have behavioral difficulties, such as those associated with attention deficit hyperactivity disorder (ADHD). Parents are more likely to attribute such problems to causes outside the child's control when the child is a girl (Maniadaki, Sonuga-Barke, & Kakouros, 2005). By contrast, parents of boys with ADHD are likely to view their sons' behavior as intentional. As a result, the strictness of rules and the harshness of disciplinary techniques is more likely to be increased in response to a son's ADHD symptoms than to a daughter's. Researchers speculate that this pattern, rather than producing higher behavioral standards among boys than among girls, may set up a pattern of hostile and manipulative interactions between parents and sons. Thus, again, we see that parent-child relationships are bidirectional in nature. That is, the effects of any pattern of parent behavior depend to some degree on the characteristics of children. Likewise, children's characteristics influence how parents respond to them.

The Parents' Characteristics   The parents bring their own life histories, their own personalities, and their relationship with each other into the family dynamics as well. Not surprisingly, for example, parents who are high in the trait of neuroticism tend to view their children's behavior more negatively than parents who are more optimistic (Kurdek, 2003). Similarly, significant depression in either parent has a profound effect on the entire family system. You already know from Chapter 11 that an insecure attachment is more likely when the mother is depressed. Parents who are depressed also perceive their children as more difficult and problematic and are more critical of them, even when objective observers cannot identify any difference in the behavior of such children and the children of mothers who are not depressed (Richters & Pellegrini, 1989; Webster-Stratton & Hammond,

1988). Thus, a parent's depression changes not only her behavior but her perception of the child's behavior, both of which alter the family system.

The parent's own internal working model of attachment also seems to have a very strong effect on the family system and thus on the child. You'll also recall from Chapter 11 that those adults who are themselves securely attached are much more likely to have a child who is also securely attached.

Perhaps most broadly, the quality of the parents' own relationship with each other spills over into their relationship with their children. Couples with satisfying marital relationships are more warm and supportive toward their children; those whose marriage is full of discord also have more negative relationships with their children (Erel & Burman, 1995; Parke & Buriel, 1998). Their children show heightened risks of anxiety, depression, and delinquent behavior (Harold & Conger, 1997). In general, fathers' relationships with their children seem to be more strongly affected by the quality of their marital relationship than do mothers' relationships, but the spillover occurs for both parents.

Learning Objective 13.4

How do emotional warmth and parental responsiveness influence parent-child relationships?

Warmth and Responsiveness

One key family dimension that has an effect on the child is the relative **warmth versus hostility** of the home. "Warmth" has been difficult to define and measure, but it seems intuitively obvious that it is highly important for the child, and research has supported this intuition. A warm parent cares about the child, expresses affection, frequently or regularly puts the child's needs first, shows enthusiasm for the child's activities, and responds sensitively and empathetically to the child's feelings (Maccoby, 1980). On the other end of this continuum are parents who overtly reject their children—saying in words or by their behavior that they do not love or want them.

Such differences have profound effects. Psychologists have found that children in warm and loving families are more securely attached in the first 2 years of life; have higher self-esteem; are more empathetic, more altruistic, and more responsive to others' hurts or distress; and have higher IQ scores in preschool and elementary school and do better in school (Domitrovich & Bierman, 2001; Maccoby, 1980; Pettit, Bates, & Dodge, 1997; Simons, Robertson, & Downs, 1989). They are also less likely to show high levels of aggression or delinquent behavior in later childhood or in adolescence (Goldstein, Davis-Kean, & Eccles, 2005; Hipwell et al., 2008). In addition, teens who were reared in low-warmth families are more likely to have suicidal thoughts and other mental health problems (Lai & McBride-Chang, 2001; Xia & Qian, 2001).

As Bronfenbrenner's model would predict, high levels of affection can even buffer a child against the negative effects of otherwise disadvantageous environments (Stansfield, Head, Bartley & Fonagy, 2008). Several studies of children and teens growing up in poor, dangerous neighborhoods show that the single ingredient that most clearly distinguishes the lives of those who do not become delinquent from those who do is a high level of maternal love (Glueck & Glueck, 1972; McCord, 1982). Similarly, in a longitudinal study, Gregory Pettit and his colleagues (Pettit, Bates, & Dodge, 1997) found that children who were growing up in poverty but whose parents provided more "supportive parenting" (including warmth) were less likely to develop aggressive or delinquent behavior than equally poor children in less emotionally supportive families.

At the other end of the continuum from parental warmth, parental hostility is linked to declining school performance and higher risk of delinquency (Melby & Conger, 1996). When such hostility is expressed as physical abuse or neglect, the consequences for the child may be even more severe, as we discussed in Chapter 4.

Fostering a secure attachment of the child to the parent appears to be one of the key consequences of emotional warmth (Stansfield et al., 2008). You already know from Chapter 11 that securely attached children are more skillful with their peers, more exploratory, more sure of themselves. Warmth also makes children generally more responsive to guidance, so the

warmth versus hostility The key dimension of emotional tone used to describe family interactions.

parents' affection and warmth increase the potency of the things they say to their children as well as the efficiency of their discipline (MacDonald, 1992).

A second key element of family interaction patterns is **responsiveness** by the parent to the child, a concept you've encountered in earlier chapters. Responsive parents are those who pick up on the child's signals appropriately and then react in sensitive ways to the child's needs (Ainsworth & Marvin, 1995; Sroufe, 1996). Children of parents who do more of this learn language somewhat more rapidly, show higher IQ scores and more rapid cognitive development, and are more likely to be securely attached, more compliant with adult requests, and more socially competent (e.g., Bornstein, 1989; Kochanska, 1997; van den Boom, 1994). Further evidence for the importance of responsiveness comes from research showing that training new parents to be more responsive reduces the odds that an infant will develop an insecure or disorganized attachment (Juffer, Bakermans-Kranenburg, & van IJzendoorn, 2005).

Neuroimaging studies have shed new light on the importance of parental warmth and responsiveness. These studies suggest that the cerebral cortex contains networks of **mirror neurons**, specialized cells that allow the brain to mentally simulate behaviors and emotions that primates observe in others (Rizzolatti, Sinigaglia, & Anderson, 2008). *Simulation theory* proposes that these mental models shape children's understanding of others' emotions and behavior (Gallese, 2005). Thus, according to this perspective, a child whose parents exhibit warmth develops a neurological model for parental warmth that may carry over to his other social relationships and to his own parenting behavior in adulthood.

responsiveness An aspect of parent-child interaction; a responsive parent is sensitive to the child's cues and reacts appropriately, following the child's lead.

mirror neurons Specialized cells in the cerebral cortex that simulate the behavior and emotions of others.

Methods of Control and Communication Patterns

How do parents' methods of control and communication affect development?

It is the nature of children to do things their parents do not want them to do, ask for things they cannot have, or refuse to obey their parents' requests or demands. Parents are inevitably faced with the task of controlling the child's behavior and training the child to follow basic rules, a process popularly known as *discipline*. Parental control of children's behavior, a third aspect of family interaction, relies on several elements.

One element of control is the consistency of rules—making it clear to the child what the rules are, what the consequences are of disobeying (or obeying) them, and then enforcing them consistently. Some parents are very clear and consistent; others waver or are fuzzy about what they expect or will tolerate. Studies of families show that parents who are clear and consistent have children who are much less likely to be defiant or noncompliant, more competent and sure of themselves, and less likely to become delinquent or show significant behavior problems than are children from families with less consistent rules.

One piece of research that illustrates this pattern nicely is Lawrence Kurdek and Mark Fine's study of 850 junior high school students (Kurdek & Fine, 1994). They measured the level of control in the family by asking the young adolescents to rate the accuracy of each of the following three statements:

Someone in my family makes sure that my homework is done.

Generally, someone in my family knows where I am and what I'm doing.

Someone in my family keeps a close eye on me.

Kurdek and Fine also had information about each child's self-esteem and sense of self-efficacy, which they combined into a measure of "psychosocial competence." You can see the relationship between these two pieces of information in Figure 13.3: Greater family control was clearly associated with greater psychosocial competence.

Figure 13.3
Parental Control and Self-Esteem

Junior high school students who report higher levels of parental control and supervision also describe themselves as having higher self-esteem and self-efficacy.

(*Source:* From Kurdek, L., and Fine, M., fig. 1, p. 1143. "Family acceptance and family control as predictors of adjustments in young adolescents," *Child Development*, 65 (1994), 1137–1146. By permission of the Society for Research in Child Development.)

This dad seems to be willing to listen carefully to his son, even though the boy is angry and may be accusatory.

Such a link between good parental control and positive outcomes for the child has been found among African American as well as White and Hispanic American youth (Mogro-Wilson, 2008). For example, Craig Mason and his colleagues (1996; Walker-Barnes & Mason, 2004) have found that among working-class Black families, those in which the parents maintained the most consistent monitoring and control over their adolescents had teenagers who were least likely to show problem behavior. Interestingly and importantly, the link between parental control and lower rates of problem behavior in Mason's study was especially clear in cases in which the child had many peers who were engaging in problem behavior. Thus, the parents, by applying consistent rules and monitoring the child's activities, could at least partially counteract the negative effects of their children's "hanging out" with misbehaving peers (Darling, Cumsille, & Martínez, 2008).

To understand the process of control, you must understand the role of punishment, the technique that most parents use to enforce their rules. Punishment is most often aimed at getting a child to stop doing something prohibited, such as writing on the wall, hitting his brother, or staying out past a curfew, but it may also be used to try to push a child to do something that he is resisting, such as cleaning his room. Punishments almost invariably involve some negative consequence for the child, ranging from withholding privileges or treats, assigning extra chores, sending a child to his room, or "grounding" the child to more severe forms of verbal scolding and even spanking. The most controversial of these is spanking. Because of the importance of the question, the pros and cons of physical punishment are explored in *Thinking about Research*, but there are two points about punishment strategies in general that you should understand.

First, as developmentalist Gerald Patterson says, "Punishment 'works.' If you use it properly it will produce rapid changes in the behavior of other people" (1975, p. 19). The operative word here, though, is *properly*. The most effective punishments—those that produce long-term changes in a child's behavior without unwanted or negative side effects—are those used early in some sequence of misbehavior, with the lowest level of emotion possible and the mildest level of punishment possible. Taking a desired toy away when the child first hits a sibling with it or consistently removing small privileges when a child misbehaves will produce the desired results, especially if the parent is also warm, clear about the rules, and consistent. It is far less effective to wait until the sibling's screams have reached a piercing level or until the fourth time a teenager has gone off without telling you where she's going and then weigh in with yelling, critical comments, and strong punishment.

Second, to a considerable degree, parents "get back what they put in" with respect to punishment. As you learned in Chapter 9, children learn by observation as well as by doing, so they learn the adults' ways of coping with stress and their forms of punishment. Yelling at children to get them to stop doing something, for example, may bring a brief change in their behavior (which reinforces the parent for yelling, by the way), but it also increases the chances that the children will yell back on other occasions.

Yet another dimension of the family system is the quality of the communication between parent and child. Developmentalists have conducted much less research on the quality of communication within families than on some of the other dimensions, so they are a long way from understanding all the ramifications of communication style. However, in general, children from families with open communication are seen as more emotionally or socially mature (Baumrind, 1971; Bell & Bell, 1982). Some studies also show that children in such families attain higher levels of academic achievement (Scott, 2004). Moreover, individuals who grow up in families characterized by open communication have good social skills in adulthood (Koesten, 2004).

To Spank or Not to Spank?

In keeping with Bronfenbrenner's model, parents' beliefs regarding the best way to discipline children are influenced by the larger culture (Giles-Sims & Lockhart, 2005). In the United States, many parents believe that spanking is the most effective form of punishment.

In the short term, spanking a child usually does get the child to stop a behavior, and it seems to temporarily reduce the chance that the child will repeat the behavior (Gershoff, 2002). But, even in the short term there are some negative side effects. The child may stop misbehaving, but after a spanking he is likely to be crying, which may be almost as distressing as the original misbehavior. Another short-term side effect is that the parent is being negatively reinforced for spanking whenever the child stops misbehaving. Thus, the parent is being "trained" to use spanking the next time, and a cycle is being built up.

In the longer term, the effects of spanking are clearly negative (Gershoff, 2002). The child observes the parent using physical force as a method of solving problems or getting people to do what she wants. By repeatedly pairing her presence with

the unpleasant or painful event of spanking, the parent is undermining her own positive value for the child. Spanking also frequently carries a strong underlying emotional message—anger, rejection, irritation, dislike of the child. Even very young children read such emotional messages quite clearly (Rohner, Kean, & Cournoyer, 1991). Spanking thus helps to create a family climate of rejection instead of warmth, with all the attendant negative consequences.

Finally, research evidence suggests that children who are spanked—like children who are abused—at later ages are less popular with their peers and show higher levels of aggression, lower self-esteem, more emotional instability, higher rates of depression and distress, and higher levels of delinquency and later criminality (Christie-Mizell, Pryor, & Grossman, 2008; Fine, Trentacosta, Izard, Mostow, & Campbell, 2004). As adults, children who have been spanked regularly are more likely to be depressed than are those who were never or rarely spanked (Straus, 1995), and they also have higher risks of various other types of adult problems, including unemployment, divorce

or violence within a relationship, and criminality (Maughan, Pickles, & Quinton, 1995). All these negative effects are especially clear if the physical punishment is harsh and erratic, but the risks for these poor outcomes are increased even with fairly mild levels of physical punishment.

Developmentalists who oppose spanking do not mean to suggest that parents should never punish a child. They are saying that physical punishment, such as spanking, is not a good way to go about it. Yelling at the child is not a good alternative strategy, either. Strong verbal aggression by a parent toward a child is also linked to many poor outcomes in the child, including increased risk of delinquency and adult violence (Straus, 1991b).

Questions for Critical Analysis

1. Why would it be unethical to use the experimental method to study the effects of spanking?
2. What kinds of variables (e.g., parents' personality traits) might explain the correlation between spanking and poor developmental outcomes?

Open communication may also be important for the functioning of the family as a unit. For example, in a study of a national sample of families with adolescents, Howard Barnes and David Olson (1985) measured communication by asking the parents and teenagers to agree or disagree with statements such as "It is easy for me to express all my true feelings to my (mother/father/child)." As you can see in Figure 13.4, the investigators found that compared to those reporting poorer communication, parents and children who reported good, open communication also described their families as more adaptable in the face of stress or change and said that they were more satisfied with their families.

Parenting Styles

Each of the dimensions of family interaction discussed in the previous section has a demonstrable effect on the child, but if psychologists want to use a systems theory approach, it is not enough to look at each dimension independently. They also have to think about how the dimensions interact to create styles or patterns of child rearing.

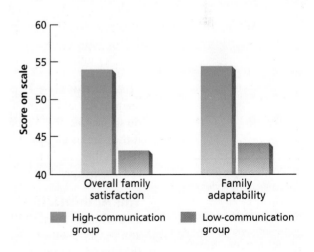

Figure 13.4 Communication, Satisfaction and Adaptability

Good family communication was associated with both satisfaction and adaptability in this study of over 400 adolescents and their parents.

(*Source*: Barnes & Olson, 1985, Table 3, page 445.)

Types of Parenting Styles

The most influential proposal about styles of child rearing has come from Diana Baumrind (1973), who has looked at combinations of the various dimensions of parenting: (1) warmth, or nurturance; (2) level of expectations, which she calls "maturity demands"; (3) the clarity and consistency of rules, referred to as control; and (4) communication between parent and child. Baumrind saw three specific combinations of these characteristics:

- The **permissive style** is high in nurturance but low in maturity demands, control, and communication.
- The **authoritarian style** is high in control and maturity demands but low in nurturance and communication.
- The **authoritative style** is high in all four.

Figure 13.5   Maccoby and Martin's Parenting Styles

Maccoby and Martin expanded on Baumrind's categories of parenting style in this two-dimensional typology.

(*Source*: Adapted from E. E. Maccoby and J. A. Martin. "Socialization in the context of the family: Parent-child interaction." In E. M. Hetherington (Ed.), *Handbook of Child Psychology*. Wiley, 1983, p. 39, Fig. 2. © 1983 by Wiley. By permission.)

Eleanor Maccoby and John Martin (1983) extended Baumrind's category system, proposing a model that has been widely influential. They emphasized two dimensions, as you can see in Figure 13.5: the degree of control or demand and the level of acceptance/responsiveness. The intersection of these two dimensions creates four parenting types, three of which correspond fairly closely to Baumrind's authoritarian, authoritative, and permissive types. Maccoby and Martin's fourth type, the uninvolved **neglecting style**, was not identified by Baumrind in her early work, although their research shows clearly that this is a parenting style that deserves more study.

The Authoritarian Type   Authoritarian parents, as Kristan Glasgow and her colleagues describe them, are highly demanding of their children but at the same time quite unresponsive: "These parents attempt to mold and control the behavior and attitudes of their children according to a set of standards. They tend to emphasize obedience, respect for authority, and order. [They] also discourage verbal give-and-take with their children, expecting rules to be followed without further explanation" (Glasgow, Dornbush, Troyer, Steinberg, & Ritter, 1997, p. 508). Children growing up in such families do less well in school, are typically less skilled with peers, and have lower self-esteem than children from other types of families (Baumrind, 1991; Maccoby & Martin, 1983). Some of these children appear subdued; others may show high levels of aggressiveness or other indications of being out of control (Caputo, 2004).

The Permissive Type   Children growing up with indulgent or permissive parents, who are tolerant and warm but exercise little authority, also show some negative outcomes. They do slightly less well in school in adolescence, and they are likely to be aggressive—particularly if the parents are specifically permissive toward aggressiveness—and to be somewhat immature in their behavior with peers and in school. They are less likely to take responsibility and are less independent (Maccoby & Martin, 1983).

The Authoritative Type   The most consistently positive outcomes have been associated with the authoritative parenting pattern, in which the parents are high in both control and warmth, setting clear limits, expecting and reinforcing socially mature behavior, and at the same time responding to the child's individual needs. Note that parents who use this style of parenting do not let the child rule the roost. Authoritative parents are quite willing to discipline the child appropriately if the child misbehaves. They are less likely to use physical punishment than are authoritarian parents, preferring instead to use time out or other mild punishments, but it is important to understand that such parents are not wishy-washy. Children reared in such families typically show higher self-esteem. They are more independent but at the same time are more likely to comply with parental requests, and they may show more altruistic behavior as well. They are self-confident and achievement-oriented in school

permissive style One of the three parenting styles described by Baumrind, characterized by high levels of nurturance and low levels of control, maturity demands, and communication.

authoritarian style One of the three parental styles described by Baumrind, characterized by high levels of control and maturity demands and low levels of nurturance and communication.

and get better grades in elementary school, high school, and college (e.g., Crockenberg & Litman, 1990; Dornbusch, Ritter, Liederman, Roberts, & Fraleigh, 1987; Jackson, Pratt, Hunsberger, & Pancer, 2005; Steinberg, Elmen, & Mounts, 1989; Weiss & Schwarz, 1996).

The Neglecting Type The most consistently negative outcomes are associated with the fourth parenting pattern, the neglecting or uninvolved type. You may remember from the discussion of secure and insecure attachments in Chapter 11 that one of the characteristics often found in the families of children rated as insecurely attached is the "psychological unavailability" of the mother. The mother may be depressed or may be overwhelmed by problems in her life, or she simply may not have made any deep emotional connection with the child. Whatever the reason, such children continue to show disturbances in their relationships with peers and with adults for many years. At adolescence, for example, youngsters from neglecting families are more impulsive and antisocial and much less achievement-oriented in school (Block, 1971; Caputo, 2004; Lamborn, Mounts, Steinberg, & Dornbusch, 1991; Pulkkinen, 1982). Lack of parental monitoring appears to be critical: Children and teens whose neglecting parents show poor monitoring are far more likely to become delinquent and to engage in sexual activity in early adolescence (Patterson, Reid, & Dishion, 1992; Pittman & Chase-Lansdale, 2001; Walker-Barnes & Mason, 2004).

Parenting Styles and Development

Learning Objective 13.7
What did Steinberg and Dornbusch's study reveal about parenting styles?

The best single piece of research demonstrating the effects of the several parenting styles is a study of nearly 11,000 high school students in California and Wisconsin that was conducted by Laurence Steinberg and Sanford Dornbusch and their colleagues. Of this sample, 6,902 were followed over a 2-year period, providing valuable longitudinal information (Steinberg, Lamborn, Darling, Mounts, & Dornbusch, 1994). The researchers measured parenting styles by asking the teenagers to respond to questions about their relationship with their parents and their family life, including questions about both parental acceptance/responsiveness and parental control or demand—the dimensions that define Maccoby and Martin's category system. For example, the teenagers were asked to indicate the extent to which each of the following statements was true for them:

> I can count on my parents to help me out if I have some kind of problem.
>
> When [my father] wants me to do something, he explains why.
>
> My parents know exactly where I am most afternoons after school.

On the basis of participants' answers to such questions, Steinberg and Dornbusch were able to classify most of their families in the Maccoby and Martin category system and could then look at the relationship between these family styles and a variety of behaviors in the teenagers. They found that teenagers from authoritative families showed the most optimal pattern on every measure they used. These teenagers had higher self-reliance, higher social competence, better grades, fewer indications of psychological distress, and lower levels of school misconduct, drug use, and delinquency. Teenagers from authoritarian families had the lowest scores on the several measures of social competence and self-reliance; those from neglecting families had the least optimal scores on measures of problem behaviors and school achievement (Steinberg et al., 1994). Figure 13.6 on page 348 illustrates two of these results: variations in grade point average and self-reported delinquent acts (including carrying a weapon, stealing, and getting into trouble with the police).

In an analysis of the data for the nearly 7,000 students on whom they had 2 years of information, Steinberg and Dornbusch found that students who described their parents as most authoritative at the beginning of the study showed more improvement in academic competence and self-reliance and the smallest increases in psychological symptoms and delinquent behavior over the 2 years, suggesting that the family style has a causal and continuing effect. These results have been replicated by many other researchers across a variety of cultures (e.g., Álvarez, Martín, Vergeles, & Martín, 2003).

authoritative style One of the three parental styles described by Baumrind, characterized by high levels of control, nurturance, maturity demands, and communication.

neglecting style A fourth parenting style suggested by Maccoby and Martin, involving low levels of both acceptance and control.

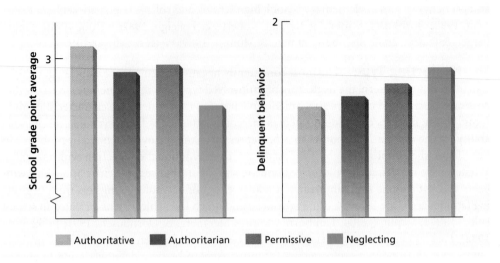

Figure 13.6 Steinberg and Dornbusch's Study of Parenting Style and Delinquency

School grades and delinquency both varied as a function of parental style in Steinberg and Dornbusch's large sample of teenagers. Delinquent behavior in this case reflected the adolescent's own report of the frequency with which he or she carried a weapon, stole, or got into trouble with the police.

(*Source*: Steinberg et al., 1994, from Table 5, p. 762.)

These results are impressive, and they have been replicated in more recent cohorts of adolescents (Steinberg, Blatt-Eisengart, & Cauffman, 2006). However, the family system is in fact more complex than the simple comparison of the four parenting types may make it sound. For example, authoritative parents not only create a good family climate and thereby support and motivate their child optimally; they also behave differently toward the child's school. They are much more likely to be involved with the school, attending school functions or talking to teachers, and this involvement seems to play a crucial role. When an otherwise authoritative parent is not also involved with the school, the outcomes for the student are not so clearly positive. Similarly, a teenager whose parent is highly involved with the school but is not authoritative shows less optimal outcomes. It is the combination of authoritativeness and school involvement that is associated with the best results (Steinberg, Lamborn, et al., 1992).

Learning Objective 13.8

How do parenting styles differ across ethnic and socioeconomic groups?

Ethnic and Socioeconomic Differences in Parenting Styles

An additional complexity appears in analyses of relationships between parenting styles and developmental outcomes within each of several ethnic groups. Steinberg and Dornbusch's sample was large enough to allow them to do this for subgroups of African American, Hispanic American, and Asian American youth and their families, as well as for Whites (Steinberg et al., 1991). The results suggest both common processes and unique cultural variations.

Figure 13.7 shows the percentage of families from each of the four ethnic groups involved in this study that could be classed as authoritative, broken down further by social class and by the intactness of the family. The authoritative pattern was most common among Whites and least common among Asian Americans, but in each group, authoritative parenting was more common among the middle class and (with one exception) more common among intact families than in single-parent or stepparent families.

The more important question is whether the same predictive relationships between family style and child outcomes apply to all the groups. For some outcomes, the answer is "yes." In all four groups, for example, teenagers from authoritative families showed more self-reliance and less delinquency than did those from nonauthoritative families (Steinberg et al., 1991).

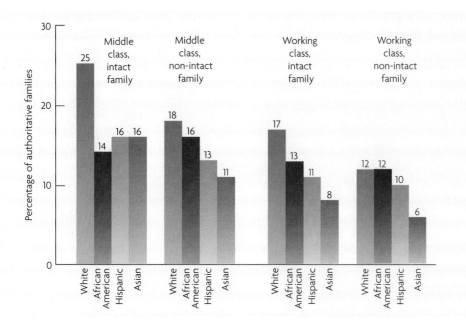

Figure 13.7   Social Class, Ethnicity, and Parenting Style

As this figure suggests, authoritative parenting is more common among middle-class parents as well as in intact families (in which the child lives with both natural parents) of all ethnicities.

(*Source*: Steinberg et al., 1991.)

On the other hand, school performance was not linked to authoritative parenting in the same ways in all four groups. In this study, good grades were linked to such a parenting style for Whites and for Hispanic Americans, but only very weakly for Asian Americans—a group of students who do extremely well in school even though their parents are among the least authoritative. However, other researchers have found that the pattern of outcomes associated with authoritative and authoritarian parenting among other groups does hold true for Asian families (Chen, Dong, & Zhou, 1997). Among African American families, research results have been inconsistent with regard to linkages between parenting styles and academic achievement (Lamborn, Dornbusch, & Steinberg, 1996; Norwood, 1997).

How can developmentalists explain these differences? Taking a cue from Bronfenbrenner's model, Steinberg and Dornbusch hypothesized that ethnic differences in beliefs about the importance of education (part of the macrosystem) play a part in producing variations in educational outcomes across groups (Steinberg, Dornbusch, & Brown, 1992). They found that an additional key element is the belief students and parents hold about the importance of education for later success in life. All four ethnic groups studied share a belief that doing well in school will lead to better chances later, but the groups disagree on the consequences of doing poorly in school. Asian American students, more than any other group, believe that a good job is unlikely to follow a bad education, whereas Hispanic Americans and African Americans are more optimistic about the risks associated with poor school performance. Perhaps as a result of their greater fear of academic failure, Asian American students spend much more time on homework than do other groups.

Another possibility is that the four styles suggested by Maccoby and Martin are themselves ethnocentric and simply

Asian parents very often score high on measures of authoritarian parental style. But their high level of strictness and control is embedded in a particular set of cultural values, and it thus has a different meaning for the child and a different effect on the child's behavior than such a style might have in a non-Asian family. This is yet another illustration of the fact that psychologists must be careful in generalizing theories and results across cultures.

do not (perhaps cannot) capture the elements that make individual cultural patterns unique (Parke & Buriel, 1998). For example, Ruth Chao (Chao & Tseng, 2002) notes that Chinese American parents, who require obedience, usually score high on traditional measures of authoritarian parenting. But in Asian cultures, strictness and a demand for obedience are perceived as aspects of concern and caring, not as reflections of lack of warmth. For the Chinese, says Chao, the key concept in parenting is training, which means teaching or educating, and training carries with it not only the element of control but also high involvement and closeness to the child. Chinese parents control their children not in order to dominate them—a motivation implicit in the authoritarian style as Baumrind described it—but rather to ensure that harmonious relations within the family and the culture will be maintained. According to Chao, the traditional measures of the authoritarian style simply fail to capture these values and thus badly misrepresent the quality of parent-child interactions within Chinese families.

Similarly, authoritative parenting may be less common in African American families because such families are more likely to be poor than those in other groups. One-third of African American children live in poverty, compared to 10% of Whites, 12% of Asian Americans, and 27% of Hispanic Americans (Douglas-Hall & Chau, 2007). As Figure 13.7 shows, authoritative parenting is less common among poor parents than among middle-class parents in all four major U.S. ethnic groups. Moreover, in Chapter 4 you learned that poverty is associated with a number of risk factors that threaten children's physical and psychological well being (see Table 4.5 on page 113). Thus, it seems possible that African American parents believe that authoritarian parenting, rather than authoritative parenting, is an optimal adaptation to the circumstances in which they are bringing up their children (Pezzella, 2006).

Family Structure, Divorce, and Parental Employment

So far, we haven't considered how the structure of a child's family influences interaction patterns and individual development. To fully understand how families influence development, we need to consider whether **family structure** (the configuration of individuals in a particular child's household) matters and how changes in family structure, such as divorce, contribute.

Family Structure

Most of you probably know that the proportion of two-parent families in the United States has declined over the past 30 years. In 1970, almost 95% of children lived in such families, but by the end of the 20th century, only about 74% of children were living in two-parent homes (U.S. Census Bureau, 2008a). However, as you'll see, two-parent homes are quite diverse. Most of the remaining 26% of children live in single-parent homes that are headed by women. Some children are being raised by same-sex couples.

Families Headed by Two Natural Parents   The broadest statement psychologists can make about the effects of family structure is that the optimal situation for children, at least in the United States, appears to include two natural parents who are married (Scott, 2004). Among Whites, children of married natural parents fare somewhat better than those of cohabiting biological parents (Manning & Brower, 2006). However, African American and Hispanic American children seem to be just as likely to thrive in homes headed by long-term cohabiting biological parents as in households headed by married natural parents.

As you probably know, though, many two-parent homes are far from happy and harmonious. Researchers have found that, among other variables, hostility in the parents' relationship is associated with a higher incidence of behavior problems in children (Katz & Woodin, 2002). Conversely, the greater the parents' satisfaction with their relationship, the better able their children are to regulate feelings of sibling rivalry (Volling, McElwain, & Miller, 2002).

family structure The configuration of individuals in a child's household.

Such findings underscore the concept of the family as a system in which each relationship affects all others in some way.

Blended Families

Blended families are established when a divorced or never-married single parent marries a parent or nonparent. Because children in such families are likely to have experienced periods during which they were living in single-parent homes, it's impossible to say whether any associated developmental outcomes are the result of the family structure itself or of the number of changes in living arrangements that the children have had to deal with over the years. Nevertheless, it's important to note that children living in such families have higher rates of delinquency and lower school grades than do those who live with two natural parents who are married (Lee, Burkham, Zimiles, & Ladewski, 1994) (see Figure 13.8). As a general rule, among preschoolers and school-aged children these negative effects are more pronounced for boys than for girls.

In adolescence, the pattern of gender differences shifts. Associations between blended family status and poor developmental outcomes are stronger for teenaged girls than for teenaged boys (Brown & Amatea, 2000). The structure that has been studied most involves a divorced or never-married mother who marries after a period of singlehood. In such families, girls seem to have a great deal more difficulty getting along with a new stepfather than their brothers do. Many are critical of the new stepfather and treat him as an intruder. Others sulk and try to avoid contact with him. Girls in this situation are more likely to become depressed. They are also more likely than boys to become involved with drugs.

The reasons for this pattern are unknown. Some developmentalists speculate that the daughter may feel displaced from a special or more responsible position in the family system that she held when her mother was single (Brown & Amatea, 2000). In contrast, the teenaged boy may have more to gain by the addition of the stepfather because he acquired a male role model. Whatever the explanation, findings like these remind us once again that family systems are astonishingly complex.

Single-Parent Families

Single-parent households are quite diverse. As you can see in Figure 13.9 on page 352, female-headed households are far more common than those headed by males. Consequently, most research on single-parent families focuses on female-headed households.

In contrast to stereotypes, some single mothers are very financially secure. In fact, beginning in the early 1990s, the proportion of births to single mothers increased most rapidly among middle-class professional women who actively decided to become single parents (Ingrassia, 1993). However, on average, female-headed families are far more likely to be poor than two-parent households are. Approximately 26% of female-headed families live in poverty, compared to just 4% of two-parent households (U.S. Census Bureau, 2008a). Thus, the developmental outcomes that are found among the children of single mothers may be due to poverty, to family structure, or to an interaction between the two.

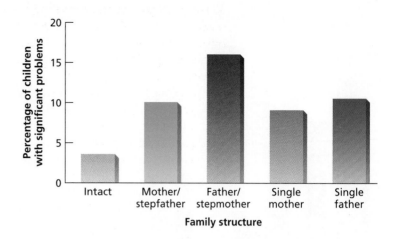

Figure 13.8 Family Structure and Behavior Problems

Children living with a stepparent, especially those living with their father and a stepmother, are more likely than those in intact families to show behavior problems of one type or another.

(*Source*: Lee, Burkham, Zimilies, & Ladewski, 1994, from Table 1, p. 417.)

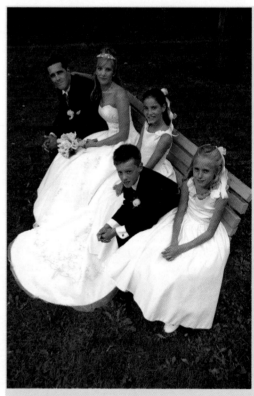

In the United States, many two-parent homes are formed when a single parent marries another single parent or a nonparent.

blended family A family that is established when a single parent marries a nonparent or parent.

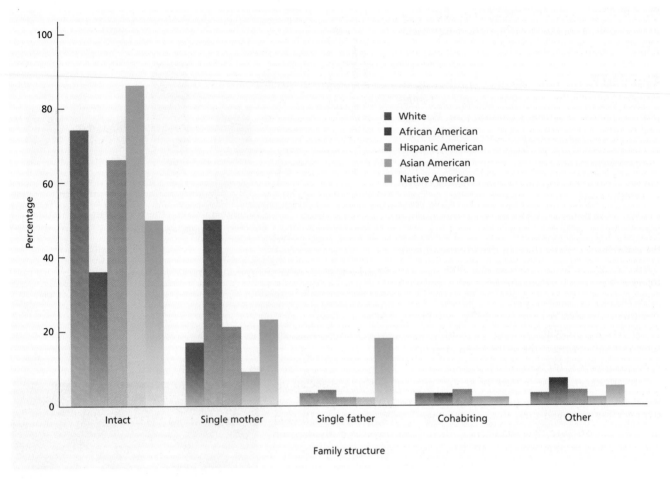

Intact   Single mother   Single father   Cohabiting   Other

Family structure

- White
- African American
- Hispanic American
- Asian American
- Native American

Figure 13.9
Family Structure and Ethnicity

Household types for U.S. children under 18 years of age.

(*Source*: U.S. Census Bureau, 2003, 2007, 2008a.)

When they think of "the family," many people think of a configuration with a father and mother and several children. Although it is still true that most children in the United States live with two biological parents, the percentage of children who spend their entire childhood and adolescence in such a family system has decreased substantially over the past several decades.

Children of single mothers are about twice as likely as other children to drop out of high school, twice as likely to have a child before age 20, and less likely to have a steady job in their late teens or early 20s (McLanahan & Sandefur, 1994). Children of adolescent mothers are particularly at risk. Differences between children of teenagers and those whose mothers are older are evident in early childhood. Some studies suggest that preschoolers whose mothers are single teenagers display less advanced cognitive and social development than their peers (Furstenberg, Brooks-Gunn, & Chase-Lansdale, 1989). Other research indicates that, when the children of teen mothers become teens themselves, they are more likely to exhibit behaviors such as truancy, fighting with peers, and early sexual activity than peers whose mothers are older (Levine, Pollack, & Comfort, 2001).

As gloomy as these findings may seem, keep in mind that many single mothers (and fathers, too) maintain strong links with an **extended family**, a family structure that includes parents, grandparents, aunts, uncles, cousins, and so on. Extended families seem to serve a protective function for children who are growing up in single-parent homes (Wilson, 1995). Grandmothers, for example, appear to be important sources of emotional warmth for the children of teenaged mothers (Coley & Chase-Lansdale, 1998). Moreover, extended family members often help single and divorced mothers with financial and emotional support as well as with child care. In the United States, such networks are more common among minorities than among Whites (Harrison, Wilson, Pine, Chan, & Buriel, 1990).

Gay and Lesbian Families Questions about children's sex-role identity and sexual orientation have dominated research on gay and lesbian parenting (Bailey, Brobow, Wolfe, & Mikach, 1995). Studies have generally shown that children raised by gay and lesbian parents develop sex-role identities in the same way as children of heterosexual parents. They are also just as likely to be heterosexual (Golombok & Tasker, 1996).

To help answer general questions about cognitive and social development among the children of gay and lesbian parents, researchers have conducted comprehensive reviews of the small number of studies that have been done. Such reviews have typically found that the majority of studies suggest that children raised by gay and lesbian parents do not differ from those raised by heterosexuals (Fitzgerald, 1999; Lambert, 2005; Patterson, 1997). However, most such studies have involved a very small number of families and children (Schumm, 2004). Moreover, in almost all cases, the children involved have been conceived and reared in heterosexual relationships prior to being parented by a same-sex couple. Thus, the findings of these studies can't be attributed conclusively to the effects of being raised by a gay or lesbian parent.

One study, though, involved 80 school-aged children who had been conceived by artificial insemination (Chan, Raboy, & Patterson, 1998). Researchers compared these children across four types of family structures: lesbian couples, single lesbian mothers, heterosexual couples, and single heterosexual mothers. The study found no differences in either cognitive or social development among the children. However, it did find that the same variables—parenting stress, parental conflict, parental affection—predicted developmental outcomes in all four groups. These findings, much like those contrasting two-parent and single-parent families, suggest that children's development depends more on how parents interact with them than on family configuration.

The same factors that influence interactions in families headed by a man and a woman contribute to the well being of children who are being raised by same-sex couples.

Family Structure and Ethnicity Looking at family structure across ethnic groups further illustrates family diversity in the United States. You can get some feeling for the degree of variation from Figure 13.9. The figure graphs estimates of the percentages of four family types among White, African American, Hispanic American, Asian American, and Native American children in the United States.

You can see that single-parent families are far more common among African Americans and Native Americans than among other groups. A difference in the proportion of births to unmarried women is one contributing factor. As Figure 13.10 on page 354 shows, births to single women have increased rather dramatically across all ethnic groups in the United States in the past few decades. However, the rates of such births are much higher among African American and Native American women than in other groups. (By the way, in all groups, more than three-quarters of single women giving birth are over the age of 20. Thus, teenage pregnancy contributes very little to the statistics on single motherhood.)

A second factor is that, although many African American and Native American single mothers eventually marry, adults in these groups—whether parents or not—are less likely to marry. Among 45- to 49-year-olds in the United States, just 9% of White and Asian American and 11% of Hispanic American women have never married, compared to 28% of African Americans and 27% of Native Americans (U.S. Census Bureau, 1998, 2008b). As a result, African American and Native American children are far more likely than children in other groups to spend all of their childhood years living in poverty. In both groups, as well as among Hispanic Americans, nearly half of all female-headed households live in poverty (U.S. Census Bureau, 2003).

Of course, statistics can't explain why African American and Native American families are more likely than those of other groups to be headed by single parents. Sociologists speculate that, in the case of African Americans, lack of economic opportunities for men renders them

extended family A family structure that includes parents, grandparents, aunts, uncles, cousins, and so on.

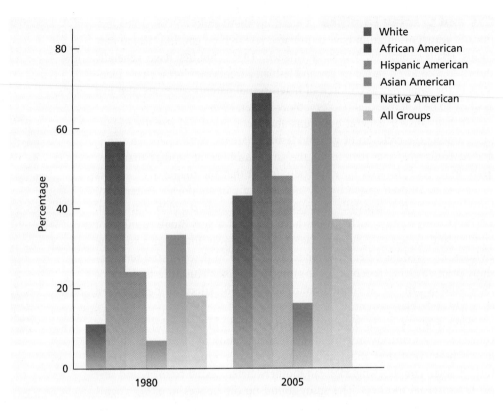

Figure 13.10   Births to Unmarried Women

Percentage of births to unmarried women across ethnic groups in the United States. The rate of births to unmarried women has increased across all groups in the United States over recent decades. These statistics are one reason for the growing number of school-aged and teenaged children who live in single-parent homes.

(*Source*: Martin et al., 2007.)

less able to take on family responsibilities (Cherlin, 1992). Others add that grandparents and other relatives in both groups traditionally help support single mothers. For instance, among Native Americans, a traditional cultural value sociologists call *kin orientation* views parenting as the responsibility of a child's entire family, including grandparents and aunts and uncles. As a result, Native American single parents, especially those who live in predominantly Native American communities, receive more material and emotional support than do single parents in other groups and may feel less pressure to marry (Ambert, 2001).

<table>
<tr><td>Learning Objective 13.10</td><td rowspan="2"># Divorce</td></tr>
<tr><td>How does divorce affect children's behavior?</td></tr>
</table>

There can be little doubt that divorce is traumatic for children. However, this statement must be followed by a note of caution. Some of the negative effects of divorce are due to factors that were present *before* the divorce, such as difficult temperament in the child or excessive marital conflict between the parents (Cherlin, Chase-Lansdale, & McRae, 1998). It's also important to keep in mind that divorce is not a unitary variable; children are probably affected by a multitude of divorce-related factors: parental conflict, poverty, disruptions of daily routine, and so on (Bailey & Zvonkovic, 2003; Hetherington, Bridges, & Insabella, 1998). For this reason, children whose parents separate or stay in conflict-ridden marriages, even if they do not actually divorce, may experience many of the same effects (Ingoldsby, Shaw, Owens, & Winslow 1999).

Children and Divorce   In the first few years after a divorce, children typically show declines in school performance and show more aggressive, defiant, negative, or depressed behavior (Bonde, Obel, Nedergard, & Thomsen, 2004). By adolescence, the children of divorced parents are more likely than peers to become sexually active at an early age, to experiment with drugs and alcohol, and to engage in criminal behavior (Price & Kunz, 2003; Wallerstein & Lewis, 1998).

The negative effects of divorce seem to persist for many years. For example, children whose parents divorce have a higher risk of mental health problems in adulthood (Chase-Lansdale, Cherlin, & Kiernan, 1995; Cherlin et al., 1998; Wallerstein & Lewis, 1998). Many young adults whose parents are divorced lack the financial resources and emotional support needed to succeed in college, and a majority report that they struggle with fears of intimacy in relationships (Wallerstein & Lewis, 1998). Not surprisingly, adults whose parents were divorced are themselves more likely to divorce.

As a general rule, these negative effects are more pronounced for boys than for girls. However, some researchers have found that the effects are delayed in girls, making it more difficult to associate the effects with the divorce. Consequently, longitudinal studies often find that girls show equal or even greater negative effects (Amato, 1993; Hetherington, 1991a, 1991b). Age differences in the severity of the reaction have been found in some studies but not others. For example, one longitudinal study found that the effects of parental divorce were most severe in a group of 12-year-olds who experienced the divorce in early childhood rather than during the school years (Pagani, Boulerice, Tremblay, & Vitaro, 1997).

Ethnicity, incidentally, does not appear to be a causal factor. Yes, a larger percentage of African American children grow up in single-parent families. But the same negative outcomes occur in Caucasian American single-parent families, and the same positive outcomes are found in two-parent minority families. For example, the school dropout rate for Caucasian American children from single-parent families is higher than that for Hispanic American or African American children reared in two-parent families (McLanahan & Sandefur, 1994).

Understanding the Effects of Divorce How are developmentalists to understand all these various findings? First, divorce reduces the financial and emotional resources available to support the child. With only one parent, the household typically has only one income and only one adult to respond to the child's emotional needs. Data from the United States indicate that a woman's income drops an average of 40–50% after a divorce (Bradbury & Katz, 2002).

Second and perhaps most importantly, single parenthood, divorce, and stepparenthood all increase the likelihood that the family climate or style will shift away from authoritative parenting (Barber & Demo, 2006). This is evident in the first few years after a divorce, when the custodial parent (usually the mother) is distracted or depressed and less able to manage warm control; it is evident in families with a stepparent as well, where rates of authoritative parenting are lower than in intact families (look back at Figure 13.7 on page 349).

Remember, an authoritarian or neglecting parenting style is linked to poor outcomes whether the parenting style is triggered by a divorce, a stressful remarriage, the father's loss of a job, or any other stress (Goldberg, 1990). Ultimately, it is this process within the family, rather than any particular type of disruption, that is significant for the child (see *Developmental Science in the Real World* on page 356). Predictably, studies show that children whose parents maintain high levels of warmth and responsiveness during and shortly after a divorce are far less likely to show negative effects (Sandler, Miles, Cookston, & Braver, 2008).

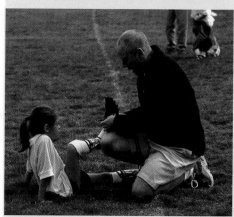

Many single parents manage to overcome substantial obstacles and give their children the support and supervision they need.

When Divorce Is Unavoidable

Adriana and Martin have decided to end their marriage, but they are concerned about how their divorce might affect their two children. Like most parents, they know that divorce can be traumatic for children, and they want to do their best to minimize such effects. They have gone to a family therapist to find out how best to achieve this goal. After determining that the couple was sure that their differences could not be reconciled and that there was no alternative to divorce, the therapist advised them that they would not be able to eliminate all of the short-term disruptive effects of such an event on their children. However, the therapist did suggest some specific things that Adriana and Martin could do to soften or reduce the effects:

• *Try to keep the number of separate changes the child has to cope with to a minimum.* If at all possible, keep the children in the same school or child-care setting and the same house or apartment (Austin, 2008).
• *If the children are teenagers, consider having each child live with the parent of the same*

gender. The data are not totally consistent, but it looks as if this may be a less stressful arrangement (Lee et al., 1994).
• *The custodial parent should help the children stay in touch with the noncustodial parent.* Likewise, the noncustodial parent should maintain as much contact as possible with the children, calling and seeing them regularly, attending school functions, and so on (Cashmore, Parkinson, & Taylor, 2008).
• *Keep the conflict to a minimum.* Most of all, try not to fight in front of the children. Open conflict has negative effects on children whether the parents are divorced or not (Sandler, Miles, Cookston & Braver, 2008). Thus, divorce is not the sole culprit—divorce combined with open conflict between the adults has worse effects.
• *Parents should not use the children as go-betweens or talk disparagingly about their ex-spouses to them.* Children who feel caught in the middle between the two parents are more likely to show various kinds of negative symptoms, such as depression or

behavior problems (Buchanan, Maccoby, & Dornbusch, 1991).
• *Older children should be included in the decision-making process.* When children participate in deciding where and with whom they will live, how often they will see the noncustodial parent, and so on, families experience less postdivorce conflict and agreements tend to be more stable than when children's input is not sought (Cashmore & Parkinson, 2008; McIntosh, Wells, Smyth, & Long, 2008).

In the midst of the emotional upheaval that accompanies divorce, these are not easy prescriptions to follow. However, if divorcing parents are able to do so, their children will probably suffer less.

Questions for Reflection

1. What specific strategies can Adriana and Martin employ to achieve the goal of reducing conflict?
2. If you were in this situation, where would you turn for emotional and moral support? Why?

Learning Objective 13.11

How do parents' employment patterns affect children?

Parents' Jobs

The existing research on the effects of parents' work on children contains an odd quirk. Nearly all the research on mothers' employment compares mothers who work with those who do not, while nearly all the work on the impact of fathers' employment focuses on fathers who have lost their jobs. Little research has studied mothers who lose their jobs or compared stay-at-home fathers with employed fathers. Given the cultural history of most Western industrialized societies, this pattern of research makes sense, although it certainly leaves some significant gaps in developmentalists' knowledge. Fortunately, a new body of work is beginning to emerge that asks a very different kind of question: What is the impact of the quality of the parents' work experience on family life?

Mothers' Employment   How is life different for children whose mothers work outside the home, compared to those whose mothers stay home? Do these two groups of children differ in any systematic way? These questions are obviously not entirely separable from all the issues about child care you'll be reading about in Chapter 14, since it is precisely because the mother is working that most children are in alternative care. But the question is also relevant for families with school-aged children, where the impact of the mother's work is not as confounded with the effects of alternative child care.

Most of the research on the impact of mothers' employment points to a neutral or slightly positive effect for most children (Parke & Buriel, 1998; Scott, 2004). Girls whose mothers work are more independent and admire their mothers more than do girls whose mothers do not

In the United States today, nearly two-thirds of women with children under age 6 and three-quarters of women with school-aged or adolescent children work at least part-time (NICHD Early Child Care Research Network, 2003). In general, the effects seem to be neutral or beneficial for the children.

work. And both boys and girls whose mothers work have more egalitarian sex-role concepts. The effects of the mother's employment on children's academic performance are less clear. Many studies show no gender differences (e.g., Gottfried, Bathurst, & Gottfried, 1994).

Curiously, some studies suggest that maternal employment in the first year of life has negative effects on White children but positive effects on African American children. In one longitudinal study, researchers examined cognitive and social development in 3- to 4-year-olds of both races whose mothers had been employed between the children's birth and first birthday (Brooks-Gunn, Han, & Waldfogel, 2002; Han, Waldfogel, & Brooks-Gunn, 2001). They found that the White children exhibited negative effects in both domains. Further, when the children were tested again at ages 7 to 8, White children continued to display less advanced development than peers whose mothers had not been employed during the first year after birth. In contrast, African American children whose mothers had been employed during the first year of their lives did not differ from peers whose mothers had not been employed.

One large study (Muller, 1995), involving a nationally representative sample of 24,599 eighth-graders, suggested that these effects may continue into early adolescence. Participants in this study showed a very small negative effect from the mother's employment on their math grades and test scores. However, this difference appeared to result from the fact that mothers who work are less involved with the child's school and are less likely to supervise the child's schoolwork during after-school hours, rather than from a long-lasting deficit brought about by maternal employment in the early years. Thus, working mothers who find ways to provide such supervision and who remain involved with their children's schools have kids who do as well as children whose mothers are homemakers.

These findings point to the fact that it is not the mother's job per se that produces the various effects that are linked to maternal employment. Rather, the mother's employment causes changes in daily routines and in interaction patterns, simply because she is not at home for as many hours. Fathers in two-earner families spend somewhat more time in child care and household tasks than do fathers with homemaker wives, although it is still true that working mothers do about twice as much of this labor as do fathers (Blair & Johnson, 1992; Parke & Buriel, 1998). This change in the division of labor may then have an effect on the quality of the father's interactions with the children, as well as altering the role model each parent provides for the child. Finally, of course, when the mother works, she has less time available for one-on-one interaction with the children, including

Parents' working conditions represent one of the most important ways in which institutions outside the home influence families and, as a result, influence the development of individual children. Therefore, when workers succeed in improving the conditions under which they work, their efforts may produce long-term benefits for the entire society as well as immediate benefits for themselves and their families.

supervision of their homework. Perhaps, then, it isn't surprising that research shows that the effects of maternal employment on infant development depend on how working mothers allocate their time (Huston & Aronson, 2005). Those who compensate for the time they spend at work by reducing the amount of time they devote to other activities that do not involve their children increase the chances that their employment status will have either positive or neutral effects on their babies' development.

Fathers' Employment or Unemployment   Research evidence reveals what you might guess intuitively, that when a man loses his job, it puts enormous strain on his marriage; marital conflict rises, and both parents show more symptoms of depression. The resulting effects on family dynamics look much like those seen in divorcing families or in families facing other sorts of stresses. Both parents become less consistent in their behavior toward their children, less affectionate, and less effective at monitoring them (Conger, Patterson, & Ge, 1995). The children respond to this deterioration in their parents' behavior as they do during a divorce, by exhibiting a variety of symptoms, sometimes including depression, aggression, or delinquency. Often their school performance declines (Conger, Ge, Elder, Lorenz, & Simons, 1994; Conger et al., 1992; Flanagan & Eccles, 1993). The likelihood of maltreatment, including both neglect and abuse, increases somewhat during periods of paternal unemployment as well (Berger, 2004). Fortunately, these negative effects usually disappear when the father again finds work. But the sequence illustrates nicely how an event outside the family can affect the child through its impact on the parents' behavior toward each other and toward the child.

Social Support for Parents

Learning Objective 13.12
What is the importance of social support to the family system?

A second aspect of parents' lives that affects the family system is the quality of their network of relationships and their satisfaction with the social support they receive from that network. The general point is fairly self-evident: Parents who have access to adequate emotional and physical support—from each other or from friends and family—are able to respond to their children more warmly, more consistently, and with better control (Crnic, Greenberg, Ragozin, Robinson, & Basham, 1983; Parke & Buriel, 1998; Taylor, Casten, & Flickinger, 1993). Children whose parents have access to more assistance from friends complete more years of school than do children whose parents have less support of this type (Hofferth, Boisjoly, & Duncan, 1995). The effect of social support on parents is particularly evident when they are experiencing stress of some kind, such as job loss, chronic poverty, teenage childbirth, a temperamentally difficult child or an infant with a handicap, divorce, or even just fatigue.

You may recall that Chapter 9 mentioned a study by Susan Crockenberg (1981) that illustrates the point nicely. She found that temperamentally irritable infants had an increased likelihood of ending up with an insecure attachment to their mothers only when the mother lacked adequate social support. When the mother felt that she had enough support, similarly irritable children were later securely attached. There are many other examples of this "buffering effect" of social support:

- New mothers who lack social and emotional support are more likely to suffer from postpartum depression than are those with adequate support (Cutrona & Troutman, 1986).

- Divorced parents who have help and emotional support from friends or family members are much more able to maintain a stable and affectionate environment for their children than are those who grapple with divorce in isolation (Hetherington, 1989).
- Among African American single mothers, those who have enough aid and emotional support from kin show a more authoritative style of parenting than do single mothers lacking such aid (Taylor et al., 1993).

As a general rule, social support seems to allow parents to mobilize the best parenting skills they have in their repertoire. Of course, not all "help" from family or friends feels like support. (You have probably received unwanted advice from your parents, in-laws, or friends.) The key is not the objective amount of contact or advice received, but rather the parent's satisfaction with the level and quality of the support he or she is experiencing. The moral seems to be that at times of greatest difficulty or stress, you need the emotional and physical support of others the most. Yet if you wait until that difficult moment to look around and see who is there to help, you may not find what you need. Social networks must be developed and nurtured over time. But they certainly seem to pay dividends for parents, and thus for children.

Think Critically

- What other variables might account for the relationships among parenting style, ethnicity, socioeconomic status, and developmental outcomes?
- Given what you have learned in this chapter, how would you answer someone who asked you whether it is worse for an unhappy couple to get divorced or to stay together even though they fight all the time?

Conduct Your Own Research

It is likely that a significant proportion of your friends and classmates have experienced a parental divorce. Recruit a few of them to participate in a study of young adults' memories regarding parental divorce. Ask volunteers to tell you how old they were when their parents divorced. Then ask them each to write a brief summary of how the divorce affected them immediately and in the long term. Categorize the summaries by age to determine whether volunteers' experiences vary according to the age at which they confronted parental divorce.

Summary

UNDERTAKING THE FAMILY SYSTEM

13.1 How does family systems theory explain family interactions?

- Family systems theory proposes that the family is an integrated network of factors that work together to influence a child's development. Changing one aspect of family life changes all the others. The influence of the system as a whole on development is greater than the sum of the individual factors that make up the family.

13.2 How do the various systems in Bronfenbrenner's model interact to influence children's development?

- Bronfenbrenner conceives of the child's bioecological system as composed of three layers: microsystems, such as the family or the school, in which the child is directly involved; exosystems, such as the parent's jobs, which affect the child indirectly by influencing some aspect of a microsystem; and the macrosystem, including the ethnic subculture and the broader society or culture within which the family exists.

DIMENSIONS OF FAMILY INTERACTION

13.3 What are the individual characteristics of children and parents that contribute to family interactions?

- The family system is affected by a child's temperament, birth order, age, and gender. Parental characteristics that affect the family system include a parent's depression, the parent's working model of attachment, and the quality of the parents' relationship.

13.4 How do emotional warmth and parental responsiveness influence parent-child relationships?

- Children in families that provide high levels of warmth and affection have more secure attachments and better peer relationships than children in families that are more cold or rejecting. Parents who are responsive to children's needs also positively affect children's development.

13.5 How do parents' methods of control and communication affect development?

- Parents who have clear rules and standards and enforce those rules and expectations consistently have children with the greatest self-esteem and the greatest competence across a broad range of situations. Open communication in the family system is associated with social maturity in children.

PATTERNS OF CHILD REARING

13.6 What are the four parenting styles proposed by Maccoby and Martin?

- Four styles of parenting suggested by several theorists are authoritarian, authoritative, permissive, and neglecting. The authoritative style appears to be the most generally effective for producing confident, competent, independent, and affectionate children. The most negative outcomes are found with the neglecting style.

13.7 What did Steinberg and Dornbusch's study reveal about parenting styles?

- Research by Steinberg and Dornbusch suggests that parenting styles are related to a variety of developmental outcomes, including academic achievement, social functioning, mental health, and delinquency.

13.8 How do parenting styles differ across ethnic and socioeconomic groups?

- Research has revealed ethnic differences in the ways in which parenting style affects children. In particular, Asian American children generally do very well in school despite low rates of authoritative parenting, which may indicate that the categorization of family styles is culture-specific.

FAMILY STRUCTURE, DIVORCE, AND PARENTAL EMPLOYMENT

13.9 How is family structure related to development?

- The structure of the family has an impact on family functioning, which in turn affects children's behavior. Children reared in single-parent families are at higher risk for a variety of negative outcomes, including dropping out of school, teen parenthood, and delinquency. Having a stepparent is also associated with heightened risks of poorer outcomes for children. Family interaction variables that predict developmental outcomes function in the same ways in gay and lesbian families as in other types of families.

13.10 How does divorce affect children's behavior?

- For most children, divorce results in a decline in standard of living and a decrease in authoritative parenting. Some of the negative effects of divorce may be attributable to family conflict that occurred prior to the divorce itself.

13.11 How do parents' employment patterns affect children?

- Parents' employment status may affect children directly by increasing or decreasing the family's economic resources, but it may also affect them indirectly through its influence on the parents themselves. For example, employment changes the mother's self-image, increasing her economic power and altering the distribution of labor. Loss of job by a father disrupts the family system, increasing authoritarian parenting and reducing marital satisfaction.

13.12 What is the importance of social support to the family system?

- Having adequate physical and emotional support from a network of friends and/or relatives enables parents to employ effective parenting strategies. Such support is especially critical for families exposed to stressors such as job loss, chronic poverty, teenage parenthood, children with difficult temperaments or disabilities, and divorce.

Key Terms

authoritarian style (p. 346)
authoritative style (p. 346)
birth order (p. 340)
blended family (p. 351)

extended family (p. 352)
family structure (p. 350)
family systems theory (p. 337)
mirror neurons (p. 343)

neglecting style (p. 346)
permissive style (p. 346)
responsiveness (p. 343)
warmth versus hostility (p. 342)

Beyond the Family: The Impact of the Broader Culture

14

Learning Objectives

Nonparental Care

14.1 Why is it difficult to study the effects of nonparental care?

14.2 How does early nonparental care affect infants' and young children's development?

14.3 How does self-care affect school-aged children's development?

The Impact of Schools

14.4 How do the various approaches to early childhood education differ, and how does preschool affect children's development?

14.5 What factors contribute to effective schooling at the elementary level, and how does elementary school influence children's development?

14.6 How do children's achievement goals change during the transition to secondary school?

14.7 What have researchers learned about disengaged and engaged students?

14.8 Why do some parents choose to homeschool their children?

The Impact of Entertainment Media

14.9 What are the effects of television and video games on children's development?

14.10 What are the roles of computers and electronic multitasking in children's development?

Macrosystem Effects: The Impact of the Larger Culture

14.11 What are the effects of poverty on children and families?

14.12 How do the values of African Americans, Hispanic Americans, and Asian Americans differ?

14.13 In what way does the culture as a whole affect children's development?

D o you know what momentous event happened on November 10, 1969? Here's a hint. It seemed relatively insignificant at the time, but it influenced the lives of millions of children and continues to do so today. In fact, there's a good chance that it influenced your own daily routine when you were a preschooler.

November 10, 1969, was the date on which *Sesame Street* made its debut (Palmer, 2003). When the program hit the airwaves, it was an instant success. Incredibly, by the end of its first year, fully half of the 12 million children in the United States were watching *Sesame Street* every day. Still, critics pointed out that the popularity of the show gave no indication as to whether it was achieving its educational goals. In response, psychologists began to study the program's effects on its young viewers. To date, many such studies have been done, and there is little doubt that *Sesame Street* has a positive impact on children's development in both the cognitive and the social-emotional domains (e.g., Wright et al., 2001). Moreover, the creators of *Sesame Street* demonstrated that psychological research can serve as a solid foundation on which to build entertainment media for children that are both effective and commercially successful.

Given these positive findings, you might be surprised to learn that *Sesame Street* has been criticized by some developmentalists, including the late Urie Bronfenbrenner, whose bioecological model of development you learned about in Chapter 13. Although they recognized the value of the program for children's cognitive development, Bronfenbrenner and others criticized the disconnect between the urban setting in which the live characters and muppets interact on the show and the characteristics—poverty, crime, lack of educational and job opportunities—of real-world urban neighborhoods (Morrow, 2005). However, the larger, more general criticism that Bronfenbrenner (1967) expressed about television was its capacity for diminishing the importance of the family. Simply put, more time with television means less time with mother, father, siblings, grandparents, and so on. For Bronfenbrenner, the threat or promise of any factor outside the child's immediate environment depends on how it affects the family system. Thus, as you read about the effects of nonparental care, schooling, socioeconomic status, and culture, keep in mind that these factors affect children both directly and indirectly through their impact on the family system itself.

Nonparental Care

In 1970, only 18% of married women with children under age 6 were in the U.S. labor force; by 2005, 60% of mothers in this group were employed (Federal Interagency Forum on Child and Family Statistics, 2008). More than half of women with children under age 1—including more than half of women living with a husband—now work outside the home at least part-time (Han, Ruhm, Waldfogel, & Washbrook, 2008). It is now typical for infants as well as school-aged children to spend a significant amount of time being cared for by someone other than a parent.

Learning Objective 14.1

Why is it difficult to study the effects of nonparental care?

Difficulties in Studying Nonparental Care

It might seem that the effect on development of nonparental care could easily be determined by comparing children who receive nonparental care to those who are cared for entirely by their parents. However, both "nonparental care" and "parental care" are among those variables that are actually complex interactions among numerous variables rather than single factors whose effects can be studied independently. Thus, interpretation of research on nonparental care has to take into account a variety of issues.

First, an enormous variety of different care arrangements are all lumped together in the general category of "nonparental care" (see Figure 14.1). Children who are cared for by grandparents in their own homes as well as those who are enrolled in child-care centers both receive nonparental care. In addition, these care arrangements begin at different ages for different children and last for varying lengths of time. Some children have the same nonparental caregiver

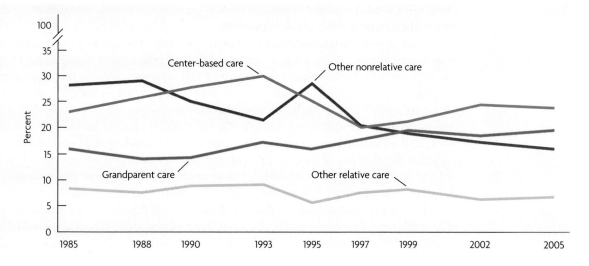

Figure 14.1 **Nonparental Care Arrangements for Children under Age 4 in the United States**

For children under 4 whose mothers are employed, multiple nonparental care arrangements have been the norm for the past two decades. Many children are cared for in more than one type of setting.

(*Source*: FIFCFS, 2008.)

over many years; others shift often from one care setting to another. Moreover, nonparental care varies widely in quality. Furthermore, distinguishing among the various types of care arrangements still does not begin to convey the enormous variety of solutions parents arrive at in seeking alternative care for their children (Clarke-Stewart, Gruber, & Fitzgerald, 1994).

Not only are there a wide variety of child-care arrangements across families, but it is common for children to experience more than one type of arrangement. For example, a child may attend a center-based program 2 days a week and be cared for by a relative on the other days. One-third of 1-year-olds in the large national sample studied by the National Institute of Child Health and Development (NICHD Early Child Care Research Network, 1997) had experienced at least three different nonparental care arrangements; more than half had been placed in two different situations.

Child-care arrangements also vary by ethnicity (U.S. Census Bureau, 2001). Hispanic American children are half as likely to be enrolled in child-care centers as African American and Caucasian American children. Among children who are not enrolled in center care, African American and Hispanic American youngsters are more likely to be cared for by relatives than by nonrelatives; the opposite is true of Caucasian American children.

Families who place their children in nonparental care are also different in a whole host of ways from those who care for their children primarily at home. How can researchers be sure that effects attributed to nonparental care are not the result of these other family differences instead? Mothers also differ in their attitudes toward the care arrangements they have made. Some mothers with children in nonparental care would rather be at home taking care of their children; others are happy to be working. The reverse is also true: Some mothers who are at home full time would rather be working, and some are delighted to be at home.

Most of the research developmentalists have to draw on does not take these complexities into account. Researchers have frequently compared children "in child care" with those "reared at home" and assumed that any differences between the two groups were attributable to the child-care experience. Recent studies are often better, but developmentalists are still

The number of infants in the United States who experience center-based care is increasing.

a long way from having clear or good answers to even the most basic questions about the impact of child care on children's development.

Finally, it is important to understand that, on average, the differences between children in nonparental care and their home-reared peers, both positive and negative, are very small (NCIHD Early Child Care Research Network, 2003). Moreover, studies that have attempted to examine all of the complex variables associated with parental and nonparental care, such as parents' level of education, have shown that family variables are more important than the type of child-care arrangements a family chooses (NCIHD Early Child Care Research Network, 2003). Developmental psychologist Sandra Scarr, a leading child-care researcher, has suggested that the kind of child care parents choose is an extension of their own characteristics and parenting styles (Scarr, 1997). For example, poorly educated parents may choose child-care arrangements that do not emphasize infant learning. Similarly, parents whose focus is on intellectual development may not place a high priority on the emotional aspects of a particular child-care arrangement. Thus, Scarr claims, child-care effects are likely to be parenting effects in disguise.

Learning Objective 14.2

How does early nonparental care affect infants' and young children's development?

Effects of Early Nonparental Care on Development

Despite the difficulties involved in studying nonparental care, researchers have provided developmentalists and parents alike with at least some information about how nonparental care affects children's development. Studies have looked at a number of important outcomes. Attachment, for example, has been the focus of numerous studies. Developmental scientists have also examined the effects of nonparental care on children's cognitive and social functioning.

Attachment   One vital question is whether an infant or toddler can develop a secure attachment to her mother and father if she is repeatedly separated from them (Bowlby, 2007). Researchers know that the majority of infants develop secure attachments to parents who go to work every day, so it is clear that regular separations do not preclude secure attachment. Still, the early research created enough concern that psychologist Jay Belsky, in a series of papers and in testimony before a congressional committee, sounded an alarm (Belsky, 1985, 1992; Belsky & Rovine, 1988). Combining data from several studies, he concluded that there was a slightly heightened risk of insecure attachment among infants who entered child care before their first birthday, compared with those cared for at home throughout the first year. Subsequent analyses supported Belsky's conclusion (Lamb, Sternberg, & Prodromidis, 1992).

To search for answers to the questions raised by Belsky's research, 25 researchers at 14 universities got together in 1991 to design and carry out a very large study that would address all these questions (NICHD Early Child Care Research Network, 2006). They enrolled over 1,300 infants and their families in the study, including African American and Hispanic American families, mothers with little education as well as those with college or graduate degrees, and both single mothers and two-parent families.

The results of the study are surprisingly clear: Child care, in itself, is unrelated to the security of the child's attachment. Only among infants whose mothers are relatively insensitive to their needs at home does child care or nonparental care potentially have some negative effects. For these children, low-quality care is linked to less secure attachment. Only the infants who experience the combination of two poor conditions—an insensitive mother and poor care—have a higher risk of being insecurely attached. Infants with insensitive mothers whose nonparental care is of good quality are just as likely as any other child to be securely attached.

Cognitive Development   In a large study by the NICHD Early Child Care Research Network (2006), researchers found a small but significant positive effect of high-quality care on children's overall cognitive and language skills. Other research suggests that this positive effect is even larger among infants and children from poor families, who show significant and lasting gains in IQ scores and later school performance after attending highly enriched child care throughout infancy and early childhood—research you'll recall from Chapter 7 (Loeb, Fuller, Kagan, & Carrol, 2004).

Even middle-class children sometimes show cognitive benefits when they are in good care (e.g., Peisner-Feinberg, 1995). For example, Alison Clarke-Stewart found that regardless of the economic situation of the child's parents, the more cognitively enriched the child's daytime experience was, the higher the child's later cognitive performance (Clarke-Stewart et al., 1994). Children who were read to, talked to, and explicitly taught showed greater cognitive gains than did children who spent their days in less stimulating environments—and this was true whether the children were cared for entirely at home or in some other care setting. Several longitudinal studies in Sweden confirm such a positive effect of high-quality child care (Andersson, 1992; Broberg, Wessels, Lamb, & Hwang, 1997).

Personality   When researchers look at the impact of nonparental child care on children's personality, they find yet another somewhat confusing story. A number of investigators have found that children in child care are more sociable and more popular and have better peer-play skills than do those reared primarily at home. Bengt-Erik Andersson found this in his longitudinal study in Sweden (1989, 1992), as have researchers in the United States (Scarr & Eisenberg, 1993). However, this is by no means the universal finding. Many other researchers find nonparental care linked to heightened aggression with peers and lower compliance with teachers and parents, both during the preschool years and at later ages (NICHD Early Child Care Research Network, 2004; Nomaguchi, 2006).

For example, in one very well-designed large study, John Bates and his colleagues (1994) found that kindergarten children who had spent the most time in child care—in infancy, as toddlers, or during the preschool years—were more aggressive and less popular with their peers at school age than were children who had been reared entirely at home or who had spent fewer years in child care. Bates did not find that those who had entered child care early in infancy were worse off; the critical variable was the total length of time in nonparental care, not the timing of that care. These negative effects were fairly small. A child's level of aggressiveness in elementary school is influenced by a wide variety of things, including temperament and the effectiveness of the parents' disciplinary techniques (Degnan, Henderson, Fox, & Rubin, 2008). Yet the fact that nonparental care is implicated in this equation certainly raises a cautionary flag.

Confusing, isn't it? By some measures, child-care children seem to be more socially competent than home-reared children; by other measures, they seem less so. One possible way to resolve this discrepancy is once again to look at the relative quality of care at home or in child care. Consistent with this argument is a finding by Tiffany Field (1991) that the beneficial effects of child-care experience on the child's social competence hold only for good-quality care. Similarly, Alison Clarke-Stewart, in a study comparing various types of nonparental care with home care (Clarke-Stewart et al., 1994), found that what is critical for the child's level of aggression is whether the child spends the daytime hours in an organized, well-structured situation or a messy, unstimulating one—and that it does not matter if the unstructured and messy setting is at home or in child care. If this argument holds, then it is not child care per se that is at issue, but the child's actual day-to-day experiences. Yet even if this turns out to be the best explanation of the observed negative effects, it is hardly cause for cheering. The children in Bates's study, for example, were in ordinary, everyday types of child-care situations. If such run-of-the-mill care is of sufficiently poor quality that it has even small negative effects on children's later behavior, parents and developmentalists ought to be concerned.

What is it about nonparental care that predisposes infants to become aggressive, disobedient kindergartners? Perhaps an examination of what Bronfenbrenner would call the *biological context* can provide an answer. Researchers have found that levels of the stress hormone *cortisol* increase from morning to afternoon in infants who are enrolled in center-based care (Watamura, Donzella, Alwin, & Gunnar, 2003). By contrast, cortisol levels decrease over the course of the day in home-reared infants. Interestingly, cortisol levels of home-reared and center-care infants are identical on weekends and holidays. Thus, some developmentalists argue that the higher levels of cortisol experienced by center-care infants affect their rapidly developing brains in ways that lead to problem behaviors. However, there is no direct evidence yet to support this hypothesis.

Some developmentalists argue that nonparental care arrangements probably vary in the degree to which they induce stress in infants and young children. In other words, they say, quality of care may be just as important as quantity of care (Maccoby & Lewis, 2003). For example, some researchers have found that, when infants are cared for in high-quality centers, the amount of time they spend in such care is unrelated to social behavior (Love et al., 2003). Thus, developmentalists urge parents, especially those who must leave their infants in center-based care for extended periods of time, to make every effort to ensure that the arrangement they choose has the characteristics discussed in *Developmental Science in the Real World*.

Another point to keep in mind is that individual differences have been found to interact with nonparental care. For example, infants who are behaviorally inhibited, in Jerome Kagan's terms, may be more sensitive to the stresses associated with center-based care (Watamura et al., 2003). For this reason, more research that takes temperament into account is needed before we can say for certain that nonparental care has uniformly negative effects on children's social and personality development (Crockenberg, 2003).

Learning Objective 14.3
How does self-care affect school-aged children's development?

Before- and After-School Care

Once children reach school age, the issues surrounding nonparental care change to some degree, for both parents and researchers. Many families require care arrangements only for brief periods of time before and after school. Parents of most younger school children provide such arrangements, but as children get older, many families allow children to supervise themselves. In the United States, more than 7 million children are at home by themselves after school for an hour or more each weekday (Crockett, 2003). They

DEVELOPMENTAL SCIENCE IN THE REAL WORLD

Choosing a Child-Care Center

Rey is a single father who needs to find someone to care for his 14-month-old son while he is at work. Up until now, Rey's mother has been caring for the boy, but she has decided to return to work herself. Rey has heard about studies showing that high-quality care can enhance children's development, but he isn't exactly sure what is meant by the term "high-quality." Here are a few pointers Rey could use to find a high-quality child-care center (NICHD Early Child Care Research Network, 2006).

- *A low teacher/child ratio.* For children younger than 2, the ratio should be no higher than 1:4; for 2- to 3-year-olds, ratios between 1:4 and 1:10 appear to be acceptable.

- *A small group size.* The smaller the number of children cared for together—whether in one room in a child-care center or in a home—the better for the child. For infants, a maximum of 6 to 8 per group appears best; for 1- to 2-year-olds, between 6 and 12 per group; for older children, groups as large as 15 or 20 appear to be acceptable.

- *A clean, colorful space, adapted to child play.* It is not essential to have lots of expensive toys, but the center must offer a variety of activities that children find engaging, organized in a way that encourages play.

- *A daily plan.* The daily curriculum should include some structure, some specific teaching, and some supervised activities. However, too much regimentation is not ideal.

- *Sensitive caregivers.* The adults in the child-care setting should be positive, involved, and responsive to the children, not merely custodial.

- *Knowledgeable caregivers.* Training in child development and infant curriculum development helps caregivers provide a child-care setting that meets criteria for good quality.

Questions for Reflection

1. What do you think Rey should do to ease his son's transition from his mother's care to a child-care center?
2. One of the criteria is "sensitive caregivers." What kinds of caregiver behaviors might be indicative of this criterion?

are often referred to as *self-care children*. Self-care arrangements differ so much from child to child that it is impossible to say whether, as a group, self-care children differ from others. For example, some self-care children are home alone but are closely monitored by neighbors or relatives, while others are completely without supervision of any kind (Brandon, 1999). Consequently, the global category "self-care children" isn't very useful in research. To compare self-care children to others and to make predictions, investigators have to focus on variables that may affect self-care—such as the crime rate of the neighborhood in which self-care occurs. Thus, developmentalists have learned that the effects of self-care on a child's development depend on behavioral history, age, gender (with girls less negatively affected), the kind of neighborhood the child lives in, and how well parents monitor the child during self-care periods (Casper & Smith, 2002; NICHD Early Child Care Research Network, 2004; Posner & Vandell, 1994; Steinberg, 1986).

Research consistently demonstrates that self-care children are more poorly adjusted in terms of both peer relationships and school performance. They tend to be less socially skilled and to have a greater number of behavior problems. However, some of these differences between self-care children and others arise from the effect of self-care on children who already have social and behavioral difficulties before self-care begins. Investigators have found that children who have such problems in the preschool years, before they experience any self-care, are the most negatively affected by the self-care experience (Pettit, Laird, Bates, & Dodge, 1997).

With respect to age, most developmentalists agree that children under the age of 9 or 10 should not care for themselves. In fact, most cities and/or states have laws specifying the age at which a child may be legally left at home alone for long periods of time. In some areas, this age is in the mid-teens. Thus, parents considering self-care should check with local child protective services to find out the specific regulations in their area.

From a developmental perspective, children younger than 9 do not have the cognitive abilities necessary to evaluate risks and deal with emergencies. Children who start self-care in the early elementary years are vulnerable to older self-care children in their neighborhoods who may hurt or even sexually abuse them and are more likely to have adjustment difficulties in school (Pettit et al., 1997). High-quality after-school programs can help these younger children attain a higher level of achievement (Peterson, Ewigman, & Kivlahan, 1993; Zigler & Finn-Stevenson, 1993).

Children older than 9 may be cognitively able to manage self-care, but they, too, benefit from participation in well-supervised after-school programs. Even part-time participation in supervised activities after school seems to make a difference in the adjustment of self-care children (Pettit et al., 1997). Good programs provide children with opportunities to play, do homework, and get help from adults (Posner & Vandell, 1994).

Self-care has the most negative effects for children in low-income neighborhoods with high crime rates (Marshall et al., 1997). Self-care children in such areas may use after-school time to "hang out" with socially deviant peers who are involved in criminal activity or who have negative attitudes about school. Predictably, then, the positive effects of organized after-school programs on academic achievement are greater for children in low-income neighborhoods (Mason & Chuang, 2001; Posner & Vandell, 1994).

When everything is taken into consideration, the most important factor in self-care seems to be parental monitoring. Many parents, particularly single mothers, enlist the help of neighbors and relatives to keep an eye on their self-care children (Brandon & Hofferth, 2003). Most require children to call them at work when they get home from school to talk about their school day and get instructions about homework and chores. For example, a working mother might tell a fifth-grader, "By the time I get home at 5:00, you should be finished with your math and spelling. Don't work on your history project until I get home and can help you with it. As soon as you finish your math and spelling, start the dishwasher." Research suggests that children whose periods of self-care are monitored in this way are less likely to experience the potential negative effects of self-care (Galambos & Maggs, 1991).

The Impact of Schools

School is another vitally important microsystem experienced by virtually all children in the great majority of cultures. School normally begins between ages 5 and 7, and in industrialized countries, it typically continues through age 16 or older. During these 10 or more years, the child learns an enormous number of facts and develops new and much more complex forms of thinking. What role does the schooling itself play in this set of cognitive changes and in other changes in the social domain?

How do the various approaches to early childhood education differ, and how does preschool affect children's development?

Early Childhood Education

The term **early childhood education** applies to programs that provide instruction to children between birth and age 8. There are many theoretical models in the field of early childhood education. In general, such models fall into two broad categories: *developmental approaches* and *academic approaches*.

Developmental Approaches   The goal of **developmental approaches** is to support children through the natural course of physical, cognitive, and socioemotional development. Examples of developmental approaches with which you may be familiar are the *Waldorf* approach, the *Reggio Emilia* model, and the *Montessori* method. All of these approaches place more emphasis on the natural course of child development than they do on teaching children specific skills such as letter identification. As a result, children who attend preschools that take these approaches spend a great deal of time exploring and experimenting with educational materials.

Although there are thousands of "Montessori" schools in the United States, including some that are operated by public school systems, a true Montessori school is one that is staffed by teachers who have been specifically trained in the methods and materials that are unique to the Montessori approach. The goal of the Montessori method, founded by Italian physician Maria Montessori in the early years of the 20th century, is to enable each child to achieve his or her full developmental potential. The main idea behind the Montessori classroom is that the child is allowed to freely choose his activities, but the range of activities available is limited to those which support the child's development. In other words, Montessori educators control the environment in ways that support the child's natural development rather than trying to control the child herself. For example, Montessori classrooms provide young children with materials that strengthen the small muscles in their hands and fingers, thereby supporting the development of fine motor skills.

Because Montessori materials look like toys to children, teachers never have to say, "Susie, you need to work on your fine motor skills today." Instead, teachers monitor children's progress toward developmental goals and encourage children to choose activities that support the goals. For example, they might give children a few spring-type clothespins and something to clip them on, such as a piece of cardboard or a paper plate. In addition, Montessori teachers help children learn to cooperate and take turns using learning materials.

Academic Approaches   **Academic approaches** to early childhood education focus on teaching young children the skills they need to succeed in elementary school. Academically oriented preschool programs employ curricula that are based on learning goals. Instruction tends to be teacher-directed, and the activities in which children engage are highly similar to those that are found in elementary schools.

For instance, one common goal in academic prekindergarten programs is that children will learn to associate letters with the sounds they represent. Children are instructed in letter-sound relationships by teachers in a variety of ways. On one day, a teacher might conduct a whole-class session in which she holds up flash cards with letters and demonstrates the sounds they represent. The children imitate her a few times, and then she asks them to pro-

early childhood education Educational programs for children between birth and 8 years.

developmental approach An approach to early childhood education that supports children's development of naturally occurring milestones.

academic approach An approach to early childhood education that provides children with instruction in skills needed for success in school.

vide the sound for each letter as she holds up the card. On another day, a teacher might work with children in groups of three or four and ask them to look through a story book and find all the letters that represent the /m/ sound.

It is important to point out that the developmental and academic approaches are not mutually exclusive. A preschool program can include elements of both. In fact, as you might guess because of the developmental characteristics of young children, it would be practically impossible to design a preschool program in which every minute of the day was taken up with academic activities. For example, recall from Chapter 4 that the reticular formation, the brain structure that controls attention, is far from mature during these years. As a result, young children simply cannot be expected to sit still, receive instruction, and complete academic tasks such as filling in blanks on worksheets for several hours each day.

Developmentally Appropriate Practices   The National Association for the Education of Young Children (NAEYC) is an organization that evaluates early childhood programs and accredits those that meet its standards. The NAEYC standards do not endorse any particular approach to early childhood education. Instead, they focus on **developmentally appropriate practices**, an approach to curriculum development that takes into account the universal features of child development, individual differences across children, and the social and cultural contexts in which development occurs (NAEYC, 2006). According to these broad criteria, any kind of preschool program, regardless of its purpose or theoretical foundation, can be judged as either developmentally appropriate or developmentally inappropriate.

For example, the fact noted earlier—that the reticular formation in the brains of young children is still immature—is a universal that, according to the NAEYC standards, must be considered when early childhood educators design preschool programs. Thus, such programs should not depend on children's ability to pay attention to external stimuli, such as a teacher's lecture, for long periods of time. In addition, teachers should expect young children to be easily distracted and should be tolerant of their need for a great deal of repetition. Moreover, children differ in the rate at which their reticular formations mature. So, the standard of developmental appropriateness also requires that teachers be tolerant of such individual differences. Even among children of similar ages, one child may require an instruction to be repeated twice, for instance, while another may require it to be repeated seven times. The social and cultural contexts in which children are developing affect their capacity to pay attention, too, and developmentally appropriate practices require that this factor be considered in the design of the curriculum. For example, parents who are high school graduates are more likely than parents who did not complete high school to provide their children with the kinds of activities that encourage them to develop the attention skills required in preschool (Suizzo & Stapleton, 2007). Thus, when early childhood educators design programs for children whose parents are likely to be poorly educated, they should assume that such children will require a bit more time to develop needed attention skills than would be required in a program in which most children's parents were high school graduates.

The Effects of Early Childhood Education   In Chapter 7, you learned that early childhood programs have positive effects on the cognitive development of economically disadvantaged children. Similarly, early interventions are critical to the development of children with disabilities that affect cognitive functioning, and they help prepare young English-language learners for the task of acquiring academic skills in a new language (Fuller, 2007). Such programs are also instrumental in helping children who were born prematurely catch up with their peers (Blair, 2002).

Despite these positive findings, sociologist Bruce Fuller (2007), who conducted an extensive review of preschool programs across the United States, argues that research does not support the assumption that research on early education programs for children with disadvantages applies to nondisadvantaged children. Fuller points to studies showing that, while typically developing children from middle- and upper-income homes tend to display cognitive gains as a result of attending preschool, the magnitude of these gains is quite small and

developmentally appropriate practices Early childhood education practices based on an understanding of developmental universals, individual differences, and contextual variables.

the gains have not always been found to persist over the elementary years. In addition, universal preschool programs that were implemented in the early 1990s in Oklahoma and Georgia and that have been attended by tens of thousands of children from homes across the socioeconomic spectrum have failed to improve academic performance at the elementary school level in those states. Fuller warns that the studies you read about earlier, showing that time spent in child care is linked to aggressive behavior, also apply to academically oriented preschools. Thus, he and others ask whether the cognitive benefits of preschool outweigh its social risks for nondisadvantaged children.

One approach to the benefits/risk question is to determine whether there is an optimal amount of time for preschool attendance—that is, a number of hours that ensures cognitive gains without enhancing social risks. Fuller cites research showing that 15 hours a week is about the right amount of time to achieve the goal of balancing cognitive gains and social risks for 2- to 4-year-olds.

Explaining the Effects of Preschool

What explains this pattern of findings? It may be that the nature of the young brain's executive functioning and self-regulatory abilities gives preschoolers less ability than older children to benefit from formal educational experiences (Blair, 2002). This assertion does not mean that early education is pointless, but what it does imply is that expectations for the effects of early education must take into account the developmental characteristics of young children.

Research also suggests that a neurological transition occurs between the fifth and sixth birthdays, precisely when most children in the United States are enrolled in kindergarten, that enables children to benefit much more from formal education than they did at earlier ages (Tsujimoto, Yamamoto, Kawaguchi, Koizumi, & Sawaguchi, 2004). Even so, there may be limits on the effectiveness of time spent in kindergarten as well. One team of researchers tracked reading and math achievement in a nationally representative sample of more than 14,000 full-day and part-day kindergarten students across the elementary school years (Votruba-Drzal, Li-Grining, & Maldonado-Carreño, 2008). As you can see in Figure 14.2, they found that children who attended full-day kindergarten displayed no long-term advantages over those who attended part-day programs. Moreover, by fifth grade, the researchers found that children who had attended part-day kindergartens displayed slightly higher levels of achievement than those who had been enrolled in full-day programs. However, as the researchers noted, disadvantaged children were more likely to attend full-day kindergartens than nondisadvantaged children were. As a result, instead of calling into question the effectiveness of full-day kindergarten, these findings may be yet another indicator that intensive educational interventions are vital to minimizing the achievement gap between disadvantaged youngsters and their nondisadvantaged peers.

Taken together, the research on the effects of preschool suggests that parents of typically developing children who have adequate economic resources should probably not assume that formal preschool is essential for their children's academic success (Fuller, 2007). Nor does full-day kindergarten appear to be critical for such children (Votruba-Drzal, Li-Grining, & Maldonado-Carreño, 2008). Furthermore, learning experiences in the home and in nonparental care settings that are less structured than preschool and kindergarten classrooms may contribute as much—or more—to children's intellectual development as formal educational experiences do (Morrison, Bachman, & Connor, 2005). From a policy perspective, Fuller argues that public resources are likely to yield the greatest dividends when they are focused on high-quality preschool

Figure 14.2

Reading Achievement and Kindergarten Program

Researchers found that children who attended part-day and full-day kindergarten did not differ in reading achievement across kindergarten, first, second, and third grade.

(*Source*: Votruba-Drzal, E., Li-Grining, C., & Maldonado-Carreño, C. (2008). A developmental perspective on full- versus part-day kindergarten and children's academic trajectories through fifth grade. *Child Development, 79*, 957–978, Fig. 1, p. 967. Copyright © 2008 by Blackwell Publishers, Ltd. Reproduced with permission Blackwell Publishers, Ltd.)

Other cross-cultural studies—in Hong Kong and in Mexico, Peru, Colombia, Liberia, Zambia, Nigeria, Uganda, and many other countries—support the conclusion that school experiences are indeed causally linked to the emergence of some advanced cognitive skills. The links are both indirect and direct. One example of an indirect effect is that mothers in non-Western cultures who have attended Western-style schools engage in more teacher-like behavior with their children than their peers who have little or no formal education (Chavajay & Rogoff, 2002). Such a shift in a mother's role and behavior is likely to affect a child's cognitive development. A direct effect of schooling is that children who attend school acquire complex concepts and information-processing strategies that their nonschooled peers do not develop (Kagan & Herschkowitz, 2005). Schooled children are also better at generalizing a concept or principle they have learned to some new setting than those who do not attend school.

Schooling also affects the rate at which children move through Piaget's concrete operations stage (Mishra, 2001). You might think that rate of cognitive development doesn't matter, so long as everyone ends up in the same place. However, longitudinal studies show that the rate of progression through concrete operations predicts how well children will reason in adolescence and adulthood (Bradmetz, 1999). Thus, the cognitive-developmental advantage a child gains by attending school is one that probably lasts a lifetime.

A different way to measure the impact of schooling on cognitive development is to compare children whose birthdays fall just before the arbitrary school district cutoff date for entrance into kindergarten or first grade to those whose birthdays fall after the cutoff date. If a particular school district sets September 15 as the cutoff, for example, then a child born on September 10 is eligible for first grade 5 days after he turned 6, whereas a child born on September 20 is not eligible for another year, even though he is only 10 days younger. A year later, these two children are still essentially the same age, but one has had a year of school and the other has not, so investigators can look at the effect of schooling with age held constant (e.g., Morrison, Smith, & Dow-Ehrensberger, 1995; Stelzl, Merz, Ehlers, & Remer, 1995).

Studies comparing early versus late school starters in the United States show that schooling itself, rather than merely age, has a direct effect on some kinds of cognitive skills, such as the ability to use good memory strategies. In one such study, Fred Morrison and his colleagues (1995) found that a big improvement in the use of memory strategies occurred in first grade; children of the same age who spent the year in kindergarten because they just missed the cutoff did not show the same gain in memory skill—although these children would of course acquire such skill in the following year, when they were in first grade.

The Transition to Secondary School

Learning Objective 14.6
How do children's achievement goals change during the transition to secondary school?

There are many places in the world, including some in North America, where children attend a lower school for 8 years before moving on to a high school. Such an arrangement is known as an 8-4 system. Because students typically show achievement declines after entering high school, educators have developed two models that include a transitional school—a junior high, middle school, or intermediate school—between elementary and high school. The junior high model typically includes 6 years of elementary school followed by 3 years of junior high and 3 years of high school. The middle school model comprises 5 elementary grades, 3 middle school grades, and 4 years of high school.

However, neither the junior high nor the middle school model seems to have solved the transition problem. Students show losses in both achievement and self-esteem across both transition points in the 6-3-3 and 5-3-4 systems. Further, students in both systems show greater losses during the transition to high school than those in 8-4 systems (Alspaugh, 1998; Anderman, 1998). Consequently, educators and developmentalists are searching for explanations and practical remedies.

One potential explanation for transition-related achievement declines is that students' academic goals change once they enter middle school. Researchers classify such goals into two very broad categories: task goals and ability goals. **Task goals** are based on personal standards and a desire to become more competent at something. For example, a runner who wants to improve her time in the 100-meter dash has a task goal. An **ability goal** is one that defines success in competitive terms. A person pursuing an ability goal wants to be better than another person at something. For example, a runner who wants to be the fastest person on his team has an ability goal. Longitudinal research shows that most fifth-graders have task goals, but by the time children have been in sixth grade a few months, most have shifted to ability goals (Anderman & Anderman, 1999; Anderman & Midgley, 1997).

A student's goal approach influences her behavior in important ways. Task goals are associated with a greater sense of personal control and positive attitudes about school (Anderman, 1999). A student who takes a task-goal approach to her schoolwork tends to set increasingly higher standards for her performance and attributes success and failure to her own efforts. For example, a task-goal–oriented student is likely to say she received an A in a class because she worked hard or because she wanted to improve her performance.

In contrast, students with ability goals adopt relative standards—that is, they view performance on a given academic task as good so long as it is better than someone else's. Consequently, such students are more strongly influenced by the group with which they identify than by internal standards that define good and bad academic performance. Ability-goal–oriented students are also more likely than others to attribute success and failure to forces outside themselves. For example, such a student might say he got an A in a class because it was easy or because the teacher liked him. Moreover, such students are likely to have a negative view of school (Anderman, 1999).

Because middle schools emphasize ability grouping more than elementary schools, it is likely that many middle-school students change their beliefs about their own abilities during these years (Anderman, Maehr, & Midgley, 1999; Roeser & Eccles, 1998). Thus, high-achieving elementary students who maintain their levels of achievement across the sixth-grade transition gain confidence in their abilities (Pajares & Graham, 1999). In contrast, high achievers, average achievers, and low achievers who fail to meet expectations in middle school undergo a change in self-concept that likely leads to a decline in self-esteem. Once an ability-goal–oriented student adopts the belief that his academic ability is less than adequate, he is likely to stop putting effort into his schoolwork. In addition, such students are likely to use ineffective cognitive strategies when attempting to learn academic material (Young, 1997). Consequently, achievement suffers along with self-esteem.

Educators have devised a number of strategies to address this shift in goal structure. One such approach is based on research demonstrating that the availability of supportive adults outside a child's family makes the transition easier (Galassi, Gulledge, & Cox, 1997; Wenz-Gross, Siperstein, Untch, & Widaman, 1997). For example, some schools pair students with an adult mentor, either a teacher or a volunteer from the community, either for a transitional period or throughout the middle-school years. In one such program, a homeroom teacher monitors several students' daily assignment sheets, homework, grades, and even school supplies. The homeroom teacher also maintains communication with each child's parents regarding these issues. So, if a student in this program isn't doing his math homework or doesn't have any pencils, it is the homeroom teacher's responsibility to tell his parents about the problem. The parents are then responsible for follow-up.

Research suggests that programs of this level of intensity are highly successful in improving middle-schoolers' grades (Callahan, Rademacher, Hildreth, & Hildreth, 1998). Their success probably lies in the fact that the homeroom teacher functions very much like an elementary school teacher—and despite cultural expectations to the contrary, a sixth-grader is developmentally a child, whether he is in elementary school or middle school. It isn't surprising that a strategy that makes a middle school more like an elementary school—a school designed for children, not adolescents—is successful. In fact, some observers think that middle schools have failed to meet their goal of easing the transition to secondary schooling because they have simply duplicated high school organization and imposed it on students who are not developmentally ready for it, rather than providing them with a real transition (Alspaugh, 1998).

task goal A goal orientation associated with a desire for self-improvement.

ability goal A goal orientation associated with a desire to be superior to others.

One approach aimed at making middle schools truly transitional involves organizing students and teachers into teams. For example, in some schools, sixth, seventh, and eighth grades are physically located in different wings of the school building. In such schools, each grade is like a school-within-a-school. Teachers in each grade-level team work together to balance the demands of different subject-area classes, assess problems of individual students, and devise parent involvement strategies. Preliminary research suggests that the team approach helps to minimize the negative effects of the middle-school transition. As a result, it has become the recommended approach of the National Middle School Association in the United States (Loonsbury, 1992).

Regardless of the type of school they attended prior to high school—middle school, junior high, or grade school—for many teens, a general pattern of success or failure that continues into the adult years is set early in high school. For example, a teen who fails one or more courses in the first year of high school is far less likely than his or her peers to graduate (Roderick & Camburn, 1999). It appears that minority students have a particularly difficult time recovering from early failure.

However, some psychologists emphasize the positive aspects of transition to high school, claiming that participation in activities that are usually offered only in high school allows students opportunities to develop psychological attributes that can't be acquired elsewhere. To demonstrate the point, researchers asked high school students to use pagers to signal them whenever they were experiencing high levels of intrinsic motivation along with intense mental effort (Larson, 2000). The results showed that students experienced both states in elective classes and during extracurricular activities far more often than in required academic classes (Larson, 2000). In other words, a student engaged in an art project or sports practice is more likely to experience this particular combination of states than one who is in a history class. Consequently, educators may be able to ease the transition to high school for many students by offering a wide variety of elective and extracurricular activities and encouraging students to participate.

Engagement in and Disengagement from Secondary School

Some secondary school students benefit little from extracurricular and elective activities because they choose not to be involved in them. For some, the demands of part-time jobs limit the time they have to participate, causing some developmentalists to question the value of these work experiences (see *Thinking about Research*). Such concerns arise out of research showing that secondary school students fall into two distinct groups. Some students are highly "engaged" in the schooling process, to use Laurence Steinberg's term. They not only enjoy school but are involved in all aspects of it, participating in extracurricular and elective activities, doing their homework, and so on. Others are "disengaged" from schooling, particularly from the academic part of the process. Steinberg argues that a child's level of engagement or disengagement is critical for the child and her future.

This high school girl has quite firmly developed beliefs about her abilities and potentials, based on her past school successes and failures. These beliefs contribute significantly to her level of engagement in schooling and will affect important life choices, such as whether to go to college or whether to drop out of school altogether.

Disengaged Students   Steinberg (1996) paints quite a gloomy picture of the typical level of engagement of U.S. high school students, based on interviews with and observations of over 20,000 teenagers and their families. A high proportion don't take school or their studies seriously; outside of class, they don't often participate in activities that reinforce what they are learning in school (such as doing their homework); the peer culture denigrates academic success and scorns those students who try to do well in school. Some of the specifics that support these conclusions are summarized in Table 14.1 on page 377.

Furthermore, a great many U.S. parents are just as disengaged from their children's schooling as their teenagers are. In Steinberg's large study, more than half the high school students said they could bring home grades of C or worse without their parents getting upset; a third said their parents didn't know what they were studying at school; only about a fifth of the parents in this study consistently attended school programs. To use the terminology presented in Chapter 13, parents of disengaged students are most likely to be classed as permissive or authoritarian; parents of engaged students are most likely to be rated as authoritative (Steinberg, 1996).

Those Who Drop Out   At the extreme end of the continuum of uninvolvement are teenagers who drop out before completing high school. The good news is that the dropout rate has declined significantly over the past several decades. Nevertheless, surveys show that about 10% of 16- to 24-year-olds in the United States left school prior to graduating and do not intend to return (National Center for Education Statistics [NCES], 2005a). If this cohort is like others before it, about 12% will eventually obtain a general equivalency diploma (GED) (Federal Interagency Forum on Child and Family Statistics [FIFCFS], 2000).

About 90% of high school students in the United States receive a diploma (NCES, 2008). Hispanic Americans have the highest drop-out rate at 22%, compared with 11% for African Americans and 6% for Whites (NCES, 2008). Just under 4% of Asian Americans leave high school, and about 15% of Native American students do so (Freeman & Fox, 2005). Kids growing up in poor families—especially poor families with a single parent—are considerably more likely to drop out of high school than are those from more economically advantaged or intact families. The relationship between social class and dropping out is at least partly ex-

THINKING ABOUT RESEARCH

The Effects of Teenaged Employment

In the United States, surveys of teenagers suggest that deciding on a career is one of the central themes of adolescent identity development (Mortimer, Zimmer-Gembeck, Holmes, & Shanahan, 2002). Moreover, many teens believe that engaging in part-time work during high school will help them with this aspect of identity achievement. Parents, too, often encourage their adolescent children to obtain part-time employment on the grounds that it "builds character" and teaches young people about "real life."

Are American teens and parents right about such beneficial effects of work? Longitudinal research involving individuals who graduated from high school in the late 1980s revealed that the more hours participants worked during high school, the more likely they were to use drugs (alcohol, cigarettes, marijuana, cocaine), to display aggression toward peers, to argue with parents, to get inadequate sleep, and to be dissatisfied with life (Bachman & Schulenberg, 1993). More recent studies have shown a similar pattern among teenagers who were in high school during the late 1990s (Bachman, Safron, Sy, & Schulenberg, 2003). Moreover, as adults, individuals who worked while in high school are less likely than peers who did not work to go to college. Thus, working may actually decrease teens' chances for successful careers during adulthood, precisely the opposite of what many adolescents and parents believe.

A quite different answer to the question of the impact of teenaged employment comes from research that takes into consideration the kind of work teenagers do, as well as how many hours they spend on the job (Mortimer & Harley, 2002). These findings indicate that unskilled work that affords little opportunity for independence and little chance to learn long-term job skills is much more likely to be associated with poor outcomes than is complex, skilled work. They also suggest that adolescents who have skill-based work experiences develop increased feelings of competence. In addition, those students who see themselves as gaining useful skills through their work also seem to develop confidence in their ability to achieve economic success in adulthood (Grabowski, Call, & Mortimer, 2001).

It is not clear how we should add up the results of these several studies. At the very least, this mixture of results should make parents think twice before encouraging teenagers to work. However, parents need to consider the quality of work a teen will do before assuming that a job will negatively affect his or her development.

Questions for Critical Analysis

1. Teenaged employment may be correlated with developmental outcomes because teens who work differ from those who do not in ways that are also related to such outcomes. What variables do you think might distinguish teens who choose to work from their peers who don't?

2. Are there developmental outcomes not addressed by the research described in this discussion that you think might be positively affected by teenaged employment?

plained by the quality of the schools in poor neighborhoods (Cappella & Weinstein, 2001).

Longitudinal studies have found three strong predictors of dropping out: a history of academic failure, a pattern of aggressive behavior, and a tendency to engage in risky behaviors (Farmer et al., 2003). With respect to risky behaviors, decisions about sexual intercourse seem to be especially critical. For girls, giving birth and getting married are strongly linked to dropping out.

Another risky behavior, adolescent drug use, is also a strong predictor of dropping out (Garnier, Stein & Jacobs, 1997). In fact, alcohol and drug use are better predictors of a high school student's grades than are his grades in elementary or middle school. Consequently, decisions about such behaviors seem to be one factor that can cause a teen to deviate from a previously positive developmental pathway.

Peer influence may also be a factor in dropping out. Teens who quit school are likely to have friends who have dropped out or who are contemplating leaving school (Ellenbogen & Chamberland, 1997). Similarly, family variables are linked to dropping out. For example, children whose families move a lot when they are in elementary or middle school are at increased risk for dropping out of high school (Worrell, 1997).

One group of researchers has explored the possibility that by taking into consideration several relevant factors they can devise a general profile of high school students who are potential dropouts. Their research has led to identification of a "type" of high school student who is likely to drop out—one who is quiet, disengaged, low-achieving, and poorly adjusted (Janosz, LeBlanc, Boulerice, & Tremblay, 2000). Many such students show a pattern of chronic class-cutting just prior to dropping out (Fallis & Opotow, 2003).

Table 14.1	Steinberg's Evidence for Widespread Disengagement from Schooling among U.S. Teenagers

- Over one-third of students said they get through the school day mostly by "goofing off with their friends."
- Two-thirds of students said they had cheated on a school test in the past year; nine out of ten said they had copied homework from someone else.
- The average U.S. high school student spends only about 4 hours a week on homework, compared with students in other industrialized countries, who spend 4 hours a *day*.
- Half the students said they did not do the homework they were assigned.
- Two-thirds of U.S. high school students hold paying jobs; half work 15 or more hours a week.
- Only about 20% of students said their friends think it is important to get good grades in school.
- Nearly 20% of students said they do not try as hard as they can in school because they are afraid of what their friends might think.

Source: L. Steinberg, *Beyond the Classroom* (New York: Simon & Schuster, 1996).

Based on the U.S. average, about a tenth of these ninth-graders will drop out before finishing high school.

Researchers have also asked young adults to explain why they chose to leave school. Across all ethnic and income groups, young adults (16- to 25-year-olds) who dropped out of high school report that their primary reason for doing so was that their classes were uninteresting (Bridgeland, DiIulio, & Morison, 2006). Dropouts also say that the feeling that they had fallen behind and could not catch up contributed to their decision to leave school. They report that peers who were planning to drop out influenced them, and that lack of parental monitoring also played a role. Nearly three-quarters say that they regret the decision to quit school.

Engaged Students: Those Who Achieve

The other side of the coin are those engaged students who do well in school. Engaged students spend more time on homework, cut class less often, pay more attention in class, and don't cheat.

While engaged students like these are likely to have the advantage of higher IQ, they are also interested in school and expend effort to do well.

They also tend to spend their time with other students who are engaged or who at least do not ridicule them for making some effort in school, and they are likely to have authoritative parents who expect them to get good grades and who are involved with them and with the school (Furlong & Christenson, 2008).

You might argue that all the relationships just described exist simply because brighter kids have an easier time with schoolwork, and there is some truth to that. In fact, the best single predictor of a student's academic performance in high school is his or her IQ score (Matarazzo, 1972). Bright students also have the advantage of many years of successful schooling. Such academic success fosters a greater sense of self-efficacy in these intellectually more able students, in turn increasing their sense of involvement with schooling. Yet the sense of involvement has many other ingredients, which jointly have a strong impact on a teenager's effort and success in school.

Effort and success, in turn, predict more years of subsequent education, a link that exists among children reared in poverty as well as among the middle class (Barrett & Depinet, 1991). Those extra years of education then have a powerful effect on the career path a young person enters in early adulthood, influencing lifetime income and job success (Featherman, 1980; Rosenbaum, 1984). These are not trivial effects, which is why Steinberg's conclusions about the typical level of school engagement among U.S. high school students are so disturbing.

<table>
<tr><td>Learning Objective 14.8</td></tr>
<tr><td>Why do some parents choose to homeschool their children?</td></tr>
</table>

Homeschooling

A growing number of parents in the United States are educating their children at home. In 1965, there were only about 2,500 homeschooled children in the United States; by the end of the 20th century, there were more than 1 million homeschooled children (NCES, 2005b). In recent years, homeschooling has grown at a particularly rapid pace among minority families, especially African Americans (Jonsson, 2003). In 1997, there were only about 20,000 homeschooled African American children in the United States. In 2002, the number had grown to approximately 120,000. Homeschooling movements in other nations have experienced similar growth rates. In Canada, for example, homeschool associations estimate that more than 80,000 students are now being educated at home (Basham, 2001). By contrast, in the late 1970s, there were only a few thousand such students. In New Zealand, the number of families involved in homeschooling more than doubled between 1993 and 2003 (New Zealand Ministry of Education, 2003). And in the United Kingdom, homeschooling has been referred to as the "quiet revolution" (Meighan, 1995).

Why would parents want to take on the daunting task of teaching their children at home? Surveys show that the most frequent reason for homeschooling is parents' belief that they can do a better job of educating their children than public or private schools can (Basham, 2001). In addition, many homeschool parents want to be sure that their own religious and moral values are included in their children's education. Many also want to protect their children from negative peer influences or school-based crime.

Special circumstances contribute to the decision to homeschool as well. For instance, some parents who must travel frequently for business reasons choose homeschooling because it allows their families to travel with them. Others want to include activities such as gardening in their children's formal education, and homeschooling allows them the time to do so. Homeschooling also works well for children who are involved in time-consuming pursuits such as elite-level athletic training.

About 8% of homeschool parents have children with disabilities and prefer teaching them at home to having them receive special-education services from local schools (Basham, 2001). The one-on-one teaching these children get at home often helps them achieve more than their peers with disabilities in public schools are able to (Duvall, Delquadri, & Ward, 2004; Ensign, 1998). In addition, children with disabilities who are homeschooled don't have to deal with teasing from peers.

Research on homeschooling is sparse. Advocates point to a small number of studies showing that homeschooled children are socially competent and emotionally well adjusted and score above average on standardized achievement tests (Ray, 1999). College entrance exam scores of homeschooled students are particularly impressive, ranging from an average score at the 59th percentile for students who were educated at home for one year to an average at the 92nd percentile for those who spent all of their school years in home education (Ray, 1999). However, opponents of homeschooling, a group that includes most professional educators, claim that comparisons of homeschooling and public education are misleading (Jonsson, 2003). They point out that researchers have studied only homeschooled children whose families volunteered to participate in research studies. In contrast, most public school achievement test data are based on representative samples or on populations of entire schools.

When comparing homeschooled children to those who attend school, it is also important to know that parents who choose homeschooling differ in significant ways from other families (American Demographics, 2001). One such difference is that 80% of homeschool families have two parents in the home, while among public school families the two-parent-household rate is about 66%. Homeschool parents also tend to have more education; about half possess college degrees, compared to only a third of public school parents. As a result, homeschooling households tend to have higher incomes than those of children who attend public school (Basham, 2001).

Professional educators also argue that homeschooled children miss out on the kinds of socialization opportunities that school attendance provides (Jonsson, 2003). However, advocates of homeschooling counter that homeschooled children have the opportunity to become closer to their parents than children who attend conventional schools. Moreover, homeschoolers typically band together to create music, art, athletic, and social programs for their children. Consequently, most homeschooled children have as many opportunities for socializing with peers as children who attend school (Jonsson, 2003).

The Impact of Entertainment Media

Entertainment media—television, movies, MP3 players, video games, computers, and the like—are a pervasive part of most children's environments. Of all of these, children and teens devote the most time to television and to video games (Kaiser Family Foundation, 2004). In Chapter 4, you learned that the sedentary nature of these activities contributes to the development of obesity in many children. In this section, we will more closely examine the effects of these forms of entertainment on cognitive and social development.

Television and Video Games

Learning Objective 14.9
What are the effects of television and video games on children's development?

"But the kids on TV look so happy when they eat it! Don't you want me to be happy?" the 7-year-old son of one of the authors sobbed when his request for a sugary cereal was denied. The effect of advertising on children's food preferences is well documented (Chapman, Nicholas, & Supramaniam, 2006; Livingstone &

Helsper, 2006). However, it is just one of many effects that television has on children's lives. Video games carry risks as well.

Television and Development   Albert Bandura demonstrated the effects of televised violence on children's behavior in his classic "Bobo doll" studies (Bandura, Ross, & Ross, 1961). In these experiments, children were found to imitate adults' violent treatment of an inflatable clown that was depicted on film. Recent research suggests that such effects persist into the adult years. Psychologist L. Rowell Huesmann and his colleagues (2003) found that individuals who had watched the greatest number of violent television programs in childhood were the most likely to engage in actual acts of violence as young adults. Brain-imaging studies suggest that these long-term effects may be the result of patterns of neural activation that underlie emotionally laden behavioral scripts that children learn while watching violent programming (Murray et al., 2006). These patterns of neural activation may also explain the finding that repeated viewing of TV violence leads to emotional desensitization regarding violence and to the belief that aggression is a good way to solve problems (Donnerstein, Slaby, & Eron, 1994; Funk, Bechtoldt-Baldacci, Pasold, & Baumgardner, 2004; Van Mierlo & Van den Bulck, 2004).

Of course, television isn't all bad. Researchers have found that science-oriented programs such as *Bill Nye the Science Guy* and *The Magic School Bus* are effective teaching tools (Calvert & Kotler, 2003). Likewise, programs designed to teach racial tolerance to school-aged children have consistently shown positive effects on children's attitudes and behavior (Persson & Musher-Eizenman, 2003; Shochat, 2003). However, such programs are far less popular among boys than they are among girls (Calvert & Kotler, 2003). Moreover, even among girls, their popularity declines as children progress through middle childhood years. Perhaps these findings are best summed up by adapting an old cliché: "You can lead a child to quality TV programming, but you can't make him watch it." Thus, parental regulation of television viewing is the key to ensuring that exposure to TV will have more positive than negative effects on a child's development.

Television and Risky Behavior   The messages conveyed in the popular media about sex, violence, and drug and alcohol use may influence teens' risky behavior. In the United States, 13- to 17-year-olds spend more time watching television, listening to music, and

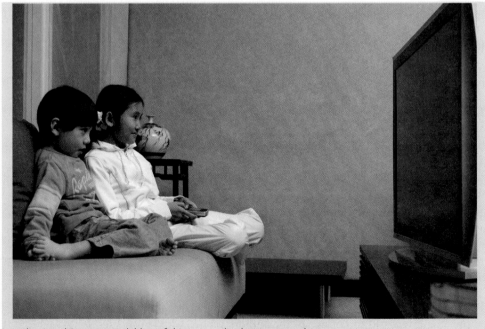

In the United States, most children of this age watch television every day.

playing video games than they do in school (Collins et al., 2004). Surprisingly, most teenagers report that their parents have few, if any, rules regarding media use (Mediascope Press, 2000). However, research indicates that media messages interact with individual differences in sensation-seeking (Greene, Krcmar, Rubin, Walters, & Hale, 2002). Thus, teens who are highest in sensation-seeking are those who are most strongly influenced by media portrayals of risky behavior.

Prime-time television programs contain about five sexual incidents per hour, and only 4% of these impart information about the potential consequences of sex (Kaiser Family Foundation, 2005). Drugs and alcohol are even more prevalent than sex in the popular media. One survey found that 98% of 200 movies surveyed portrayed characters using drugs, alcohol, or tobacco, and in most cases characters used more than one (Mediascope Press, 1999). Another group of researchers found that 51% of the films they surveyed depicted teenagers smoking, 46% showed teenagers consuming alcohol, and 3% contained images of teens using illegal drugs (Mediascope Press, 1999). Again, references to the consequences of drug or alcohol use were rare; they occurred in only 13% of the films surveyed.

Video Games   Some sources claim that families spend more money on video game systems and on the games themselves than they do on any other form of entertainment ("Children spend more time . . . ," 2004). Developmentalists have looked at how these games affect children's cognitive and social/emotional development. Some studies suggest that video game playing enhances children's spatial-cognitive skills and may even eliminate the well-documented gender difference in this domain (Feng, Spence, & Pratt, 2007; Greenfield, Brannon, & Lohr, 1994).

Nevertheless, research suggests even short-term exposure to violent video games in laboratory settings increases research participants' general level of emotional hostility (Anderson & Dill, 2000; Bushman & Huesmann, 2006). Apparently, increases in emotional hostility and decreases in the capacity to empathize with others, which are engendered by violent video games, are the motivating forces behind the increases in aggressive behavior that often result from playing such games for extended periods of time (Funk, Buchman, Jenks, & Bechtoldt, 2003; Gentile, Lynch, Linder, & Walsh, 2004).

Computers and Electronic Multitasking

Learning Objective 14.10
What are the roles of computers and electronic multitasking in children's development?

Surveys show that more than 90% of school-aged children and adolescents in the United States use computers on a regular basis. About 60% regularly use the Internet (DeBell & Chapman, 2006). Remarkably, adolescents spend an average of 6 hours each day using multiple electronic devices (Foehr, 2006).

Computers   Computer and Internet use rates are nearly identical for boys and girls. However, a "digital divide" exists across income groups. Among 8- to 18-year-olds who live in the poorest households, 54% use the Internet at home every day, compared to 57% of those in middle-income homes and 71% of children in upper-income families (Kaiser Family Foundation, 2004). However, nearly 100% of children in all three groups regularly use the Internet at school. Moreover, the proportions of children who use computers and the Internet at home have increased dramatically among all income groups over the past decade, and there is good evidence that the digital divide is shrinking (Kaiser Family Foundation, 2004). Most children use computers for school work, to play games, and to engage in electronic communication such as email and instant messaging.

Apart from teacher-directed activities such as homework, children use computers in much the same ways as they use other environments (Kaiser Family Foundation, 2004). For the most part, children play when they are on a computer. Consequently, educators and parents need to keep an eye on children who are supposed to be doing school work on their computers and to be aware of the tendency of children to test digital boundaries, such as prohibitions against visiting chat rooms, just as they do physical boundaries. Studies show that when children focus on academic tasks, computers can help to raise achievement test scores and grades (Jackson et al., 2006). In addition, many developmental psychologists see in children's propensity for digital play an opportunity to learn more about the natural course of child development (Sandvig, 2006). For instance, studying children's virtual communications can help developmentalists better understand their face-to-face interactions.

Like television, however, the Internet is a mixed blessing. One issue is that advertising occurs in far more subtle forms online than it does on television. If a child working on a school report enters the term "nutrition" in a search engine, for example, many of the links that show up will appear to be informational but, on closer inspection, will be found to have been designed to sell some kind of food product (Moore & Rideout, 2007). Others will lead children to online games that are nothing more than ploys to introduce children to new products. Similarly, a child who is searching for information on a health topic may stumble onto sexually explicit materials. Once again, adult monitoring is essential when children are using computers.

Electronic Multitasking

Computers are an important element in the *electronic multitasking environment* in which many adolescents immerse themselves these days (Foehr, 2006). In one observational study of school computer labs, researchers found that many students worked on papers and other assignments in a split-screen format, with one part of the screen devoted to their work and another to a game (Jones, 2003). And many of these students were listening to music on their MP3 players at the same time. Some may also have been instant-messaging friends on the computers they were using.

Interestingly, neuroscientists have located a network of neurons in the prefrontal cortex of the adult brain that allows humans to rapidly shift their focus from one task to another while keeping multiple goals in mind—the essence of multitasking (Koechlin, Basso, Pietrini, Panzer, & Grafman, 1999). As you learned in Chapter 4, the prefrontal cortex is an important site of brain development in the teen years. Thus, multitasking may emerge in adolescence along with the other newly developed forms of cognitive functioning that teens delight in exercising (e.g., Piaget's *naive idealism*). Still, research shows that, although multitasking may be a good temporary strategy for managing information overload, it is an inefficient approach for processing information in meaningful ways (Law, Logie, & Pearson, 2006). Something, and often something quite important, inevitably gets lost in the mix.

Some studies suggest that children in the United States now spend more time playing video games than they do watching television.

Moreover, developmentalists fear that habitual multitasking increases levels of sensation-seeking, thereby increasing teens' chances of engaging in risky behavior (Foehr, 2006). In fact, multitasking itself can be quite a risky behavior when it takes the form of text-messaging while driving. Multitasking is also linked to increased anxiety levels (Bailey & Konstan, 2006). For these reasons, mental health professionals such as psychiatrist Edward Hallowell have developed therapeutic interventions to help teens and adults break the multitasking habit (Hallowell, 2007).

Macrosystem Effects: The Impact of the Larger Culture

Finally, we consider explicitly the question of contexts and cultures. Each family, and thus each child, is embedded in a series of overlapping contexts, each of which affects the way the family itself interacts as well as all other parts of the system.

Socioeconomic Status and Development

Learning Objective 14.11
What are the effects of poverty on children and families?

In Chapter 4, you learned about the effects of *socioeconomic status (SES)*—a collective term that includes the economic, occupational, and educational factors that influence a family's relative position in society—on children's health. We discussed the impact of socioeconomic status on children's cognitive development in Chapter 7, and the association between poverty and single-parenthood in Chapter 13. In this chapter, we deal with SES as a factor that operates at both the microsystem and the exosystem levels of Bronfenbrenner's model. For instance, when poverty prevents a child from getting enough to eat, it operates as part of the microsystem. When the stores in the neighborhood in which the child lives do not offer a variety of healthy foods because of the low incomes of the residents, poverty functions at the exosystem level. Likewise, when parents' lack of transportation prevents them from obtaining employment, poverty not only functions as an exosystem factor but also becomes part of a self-perpetuating developmental context in which a child's development is hindered by a lack of material resources.

Characteristics of Child Poverty   In the United States, *poverty* is defined as a yearly income of less than $21,200 for a family of four (U.S. Department of Health and Human Services, 2008). As you can see in Figure 14.4 on page 384, the child poverty rate in the United States declined from 22% in 1993 to 17.4% in 2006 (DeNavas-Walt, Proctor, & Smith, 2007). However, you will notice that children are more likely than those in other age groups to live in poor households. In addition, another 39% of children in the United States live in *low-income* households, those in which the total family income is between 100% and 200% of the official federal poverty level (Douglas-Hall & Chau, 2007). Thus, more than half of all children in the United States live in families that have either insufficient funds or just enough to get by.

Child poverty rates vary across ethnic groups, as you can see in Figure 14.5 on page 384 (Douglas-Hall & Chau, 2007). Children reared by single mothers are far more likely than other children to be living in poverty. About 26% of single parents have incomes below the poverty line, compared to just 4% of two-parent families (U.S. Census Bureau, 2008b). Research shows that children in low-income and poor households are at greater risk of a number of health problems than are their peers who are better off financially. This association exists in other countries as well (Currie, Shields, & Wheatley Price, 2004; Currie & Stabile, 2003).

For most children, the deleterious effects of low income are transient, because most families do not remain in poverty throughout their children's early years. Long-term studies suggest that about 8% of families with children in the United States experience chronic low-income status (U.S. Department of the Treasury, 2008). Similar results have been obtained in longitudinal studies in the United Kingdom (Burgess, Propper, & Rigg, 2004).

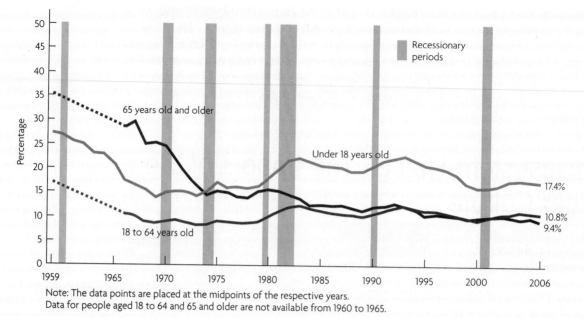

Figure 14.4 Poverty and Age

The graph shows the percentage of people in the United States living in poverty from 1959 to 2006, including children under 18.

(*Source*: DeNavas-Walt, Proctor, & Smith, 2007.)

The Effects of Poverty on Families Among many other things, poverty reduces options for parents. They may not be able to afford prenatal care, so their children are more likely to be born with some sort of disability. When the mother works, she is likely to have fewer choices of affordable child care. Poor children spend more time in poor-quality child care and shift more from one care arrangement to another. Poor families also live in smaller and less adequate housing, often in decaying neighborhoods with high rates of violence, and many of them move frequently, so their children change schools often. The parents are less likely to feel they have adequate social support, and the children often lack a stable group of playmates (Dodge, Pettit, & Bates, 1994). Overall, poor environments are more chaotic, and people living in poverty are more highly stressed with fewer psychological and social resources (Brooks-Gunn, 1995; McLoyd & Wilson, 1991).

Mothers and fathers living in poverty also interact with their children differently than parents in working-class or middle-class families in the United States. Poverty-level parents talk and read to their children less, provide fewer age-appropriate toys, spend less time with them in intellectually stimulating activities, explain things less often and less fully, are less warm, and are stricter and more physical in their discipline (Dodge et al., 1994; Evans, 2004; Sampson & Laub, 1994). In the terms introduced in Chapter 13, in poor families, the parents are more likely to be either neglecting or authoritarian and are less likely to be authoritative.

Some of this pattern of parental behavior is clearly a response to the extraordinary stresses and special demands of the poverty environment—a

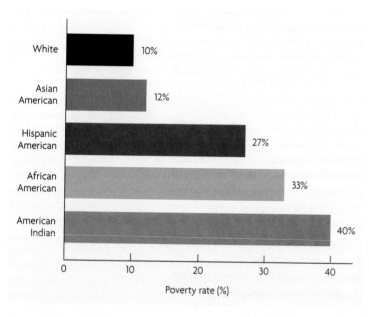

Figure 14.5 Child Poverty Rates across Ethnic Groups in the United States, 2006

Although overall poverty rates have declined considerably in the United States over the past three decades, the rate among some ethnic groups continues to be alarmingly high.

(*Source*: From A. Douglas-Hall and M. Chau, 2007. *Basic Facts about Low-Income Children, Birth to Age 18*. Reprinted by permission of NCCP (National Center for Children in Poverty).)

point buttressed by the repeated observation that those parents living in poverty who nonetheless feel they have enough social support are much less likely to be harshly punitive or unsupportive toward their children (Hashima & Amato, 1994; Taylor & Roberts, 1995). To some extent, the stricter discipline and emphasis on obedience observed among poor parents may be thought of as a logical response to the realities of life in a very poor neighborhood.

Some of the differences in child-rearing patterns between poor and nonpoor parents may also result from straightforward modeling of the way these individuals themselves were reared; some inadequate practices may be a product of ignorance of children's needs. Poor parents with relatively more education, for example, typically talk to their children more, are more responsive, and provide more intellectual stimulation than do equally poor parents with lower levels of education (Kelley, Sanchez-Hucles, & Walker, 1993). Whatever the cause, children reared in poverty experience both different physical conditions and quite different interactions with their parents.

The Effects of Poverty on Children   Not surprisingly, children raised in poverty turn out differently. Children from poverty environments have higher rates of illness and disabilities, as you saw in Chapter 4. And, as you learned in Chapter 7, they also typically have lower IQ scores and move through the sequences of cognitive development more slowly—effects that have been found in studies in which researchers controlled for many possible confounding factors, such as the mother's IQ and the family structure (McLoyd, 1998). Children living in poverty are half as likely as their more well-off peers to know the alphabet and to be able to count before they enter school (U.S. Census Bureau, 2001). They are twice as likely as nonpoor children to repeat a grade and are less likely to go on to college (Brooks-Gunn, 1995; Huston, 1994; Zill, Moore, Smith, Steif, & Coiro, 1995). Children from low-income homes also exhibit more behavior problems than their better-off peers (Qi & Kaiser, 2003). As adults, children from low-income families are more likely to be poor, thus continuing the cycle through another generation. All these effects are greater for those children who live in poverty in infancy and early childhood and for those who have lived in poverty continuously than for children who have experienced some mixture of poverty and greater affluence (Bolger, 1997; Duncan et al., 1994; Shanahan, Sayer, Davey, & Brooks, 1997; Smith, Brooks-Gunn, & Klebanov, 1997).

Figure 14.6 shows one of these effects, drawn from research by Greg Duncan and his colleagues (1994). Duncan collected information on family income for a large sample of families over the years from the child's birth to age 5. He looked at the child's IQ score at age 5 as a function of whether the family had been poor in every one of those 5 years or in only some years. The figure compares the IQ scores of each of these groups to the benchmark IQ of children who never lived in poverty. It's clear that constant poverty has a greater negative effect than occasional poverty, and both are worse than not being poor. In this analysis, Duncan controlled for the mother's education and the structure of the household (single mother versus two parents, for example), so the differences observed seem to be real effects of poverty.

The Special Case of Inner-City Poverty   All of the effects of poverty are probably much worse for children growing up in poverty-ravaged urban areas, and most such children are African Americans, Hispanic Americans, or other minorities (Brooks-Gunn, Duncan, & Aber, 1997). They are exposed to street gangs and street violence, to drug pushers, to overcrowded homes, and to higher risks of abuse. Entire communities have become like war zones. Predictably, children who are victimized or who witness violent crimes are more likely to suffer from emotional problems than are peers who are spared these experiences (Purugganan, Stein, Johnson Silver, & Benenson, 2003).

Surveys in a number of large cities indicate that nearly half of inner-city elementary and high school students have witnessed at least one violent crime in the past year (Osofsky, 1995); nearly all have heard gunfire, seen someone being beaten up, or observed a drug deal (White, Bruce, Farrell, & Kliewer, 1997); as many as 30% have seen a homicide by the time they are 15 (Garbarino &

Figure 14.6
Duration of Poverty and IQ Scores

In this analysis, the zero line represents the average IQ score of a group of 5-year-old children in Duncan's study who had never lived in poverty. Average IQ scores of children who had lived in poverty some of the time or all of the time are compared to that benchmark. You can see that children who spent all of their first 5 years living in poverty had considerably lower average IQs than those who lived in poverty only part of the time, and both groups were significantly lower than the benchmark group.

(*Source*: Duncan et al., 1994, from Table 3, p. 306.)

Kostelny, 1997). In a 1993 national survey by the Centers for Disease Control, 22.1% of high school students reported that they had carried a weapon (gun, knife, or club) some time in the previous 30 days; 7.9% had carried a gun (Kann et al., 1995). Psychologist James Garbarino, who has written extensively about urban poverty, points out that "these figures are much more like the experience of children in the war zones . . . in other countries . . . than they are of what we should expect for our own children, living in 'peace' " (Garbarino & Kostelny, 1997, p. 33).

A growing body of evidence shows that the effect of living in a concentrated pocket of poverty is to intensify all of the ill effects of family poverty (Klebanov, Brooks-Gunn, Hofferth, & Duncan, 1995; Kupersmidt, Griesler, DeRosier, Patterson, & Davis, 1995). Individual family characteristics are still the most important determinants of the child's development, but when the whole neighborhood is poor, especially when the residents of the neighborhood are in constant flux, the negative effects for children are intensified (Brooks-Gunn et al., 1997). In such situations, parents have fewer nonfamily resources to rely on, and children have more violent and fewer supportive adult models; rates of child abuse rise, as do rates of aggression and delinquency by the children (Coulton, Korbin, Su, & Chow, 1995; McLoyd, 1997). When the whole neighborhood also lacks what sociologist William Wilson calls "connectedness and stability"—when the adults do not collaborate to monitor the children and do not provide practical or emotional support to one another—the effects are still worse (Sampson, 1997; Wilson, 1995).

Many children living in such neighborhoods show all the symptoms of posttraumatic stress disorder (Garbarino, 2002; Garbarino, Dubrow, Kostelny, & Pardo, 1992; Jenkins & Bell, 1997), including sleep disturbances, irritability, inability to concentrate, angry outbursts, and hypervigilance. Many experience flashbacks or intrusive memories of traumatic events. And because they are likely to have missed out on many of the forms of intellectual stimulation and consistent family support that would allow them to succeed in school, they have high rates of behavior problems and academic failure. Fewer than half of urban poor children graduate from high school (Garbarino, Kostelny, & Dubrow, 1991). The reasons for such school failure are complex, but there is little doubt that the chronic stress experienced by these children is one highly significant component.

It's not hard to see why some refer to scenes of urban poverty like this as "war zones."

The Roles of Stress and Protective Factors   Arnold Sameroff and his colleagues (1987) have argued that the effects of various different kinds of stress accumulate. A child may be able to handle one or two, but as the stresses and risks pile up, the probability that the child will thrive intellectually, emotionally, or socially declines steadily. For a child growing up in poverty, perhaps especially urban poverty, the chances of experiencing multiple separate types of stress are very high indeed.

At the same time, studies of resilient and vulnerable children suggest that certain characteristics or circumstances may help to protect some children from the detrimental effects of repeated stresses and upheavals (Cederblad, Pruksachatkunakorn, Boripunkul, Intraprasert, & Hook, 2003; Easterbrooks, Davidson, & Chazan, 1993; Furstenberg & Hughes, 1995; Garmezy & Masten, 1991; Masten, Best, & Garmezy, 1990; Masten & Coatsworth, 1998; Runyan et al., 1998; Townsend & Belgrave, 2003; Winfield, 1995). Table 14.2 lists the key qualities of resilient children suggested by Ann Masten and Douglas Coatsworth in a review (1998). Note that the qualities listed in Table 14.2 are the same qualities that are linked to competence in children who are not growing up in poverty or in other risky environments. As Masten and Coatsworth put it:

> Resilient children do not appear to possess mysterious or unique qualities; rather, they have retained or secured important resources representing basic protective systems in human development. . . . Competence develops in the midst of adversity when, despite the situation at hand, fundamental systems that generally foster competence in development are operating to protect the child or counteract the threats to development. (1998, p. 212)

The results of Emmy Werner's long-term longitudinal study on the Hawaiian island of Kauai demonstrate that these factors operate in real lives (Werner & Smith, 1992). The families of the resilient children and adults in her sample were clearly more authoritative, more cohesive, and more loving than were the equally poor families whose children had worse outcomes. Similarly, studies of boys reared in high-crime inner-city neighborhoods show that high intelligence and at least a minimum level of family cohesion are key ingredients

Table 14.2   Characteristics of Resilient Children and Adolescents

Source	Characteristic
Individual	Good intellectual functioning
	Appealing, sociable, easygoing disposition
	Self-efficacy, self-confidence, high self-esteem
	Talents
	Faith
Family	Close relationship to caring parent figure
	Authoritative parenting: warmth, structure, high expectations
	Socioeconomic advantages
	Connections to extended supportive family networks
Extrafamilial Context	Bonds to prosocial adults outside the family
	Connections to prosocial organizations
	Attending effective schools

Source: From "The development of competence in favorable and unfavorable environments" by Ann S. Masten, *American Psychologist*, 53, p. 212 (1998). Copyright © 1998 by the American Psychological Association. Reprinted within the guidelines of the American Psychological Association and by permission of the author.

affecting a boy's chance of attaining a successful adult life pattern (Long & Vaillant, 1984; Mc-Cord, 1982; Sampson & Laub, 1994). Boys reared in poverty-level families plagued by alcoholism, or who had parents with strong antisocial tendencies or low IQs, were simply much less likely to develop the competence needed to bootstrap themselves out of their difficult circumstances. Thus, the outcome depends on some joint effect of the number of stresses the child must cope with and the range of competencies or advantages the child brings to the situation. Poverty does not guarantee bad outcomes, but it stacks the deck against most children.

Learning Objective 14.12

How do the values of African Americans, Hispanic Americans, and Asian Americans differ?

Race and Ethnicity

In the United States, because poverty is so much more common among some ethnic groups than others, socioeconomic status and ethnic group membership are strongly linked. Because of this overlap, it is sometimes tempting to focus attention solely on socioeconomic status as the most powerful factor, ignoring the additional impact of ethnicity. For example, what difference does it make to a child to grow up in a family whose cultural roots emphasize collectivism rather than individualism? You have learned something about these questions throughout the book, but here we will take one final look at what is known about ethnic effects, using the several major groups in the United States as illustration.

We should begin with a definition of **ethnicity**. According to Parke and Buriel, "Ethnicity refers to an individual's membership in a group sharing a common ancestral heritage based on nationality, language, and culture" (1998, p. 496); the group is an **ethnic group**. Ethnicity may include a biological or racial component, but that is not an essential part of the definition. Thus, race and ethnicity are not the same. Ethnicity refers primarily to social and cultural characteristics, whereas race normally designates a group with specific physical characteristics. Thus, African Americans and Asian Americans may be viewed as both ethnic and racial categories, whereas Hispanic Americans, Polish Americans, or Italian Americans would be regarded only as ethnic groups.

These Irish Americans marching in a St. Patrick's Day parade fit the definition of an ethnic group, but they are not a race.

ethnicity An individual's membership in an ethnic group.

ethnic group "A subgroup whose members are perceived by themselves and others to have a common origin and culture, and shared activities in which the common origin or culture is an essential ingredient" (Porter & Washington, 1993, p. 140).

African Americans   African Americans, who make up about 14% of the total population (U.S. Census Bureau, 2008), have a culture that has been shaped by their African heritage, their experience of slavery, and a continuing experience of discrimination and segregation. The central values of this culture include the following (Hill, Soriano, Chen, & LaFromboise, 1994):

- Collectivism or communalism, as opposed to individualism; identity is collective as well as personal.
- Person-centered rather than object-centered values; relationships with people are more important than material possessions.
- Mutuality and reciprocity; a belief that "what goes around, comes around," that each person's actions will eventually have repercussions for that individual.
- A strong religious or spiritual orientation, involving acknowledgment of a higher power.
- An emphasis on the importance of children for family continuity.

- Harmony and a sense of connection with nature, including a belief in the "oneness of being" of all humanity.
- Role flexibility.

These values, especially the emphasis on collectivism or communalism and the importance of children, have contributed to a pattern of family structure that is quite different from that of the majority Caucasian American culture. Caucasian Americans think of "the family" as a father, a mother, and several children. Within the African American culture, "family" has a much broader definition, including many variations of extended family structures—a pattern that likely has its roots in West African culture (Stewart, 2007; Sudarkasa, 1993). Martin and Martin, in their book *The Black Extended Family*, defined the African American family as a multigenerational, interdependent kinship system that is welded together by

Some African Americans teach their children about African culture by celebrating Kwanzaa. The Kwanzaa candles represent unity, self-determination, collective work and responsibility, cooperative economics, purpose, creativity, and faith.

a sense of obligation to relatives; is organized around a dominant figure; extends across geographic boundaries to connect family units to an extended family network; and has a built-in mutual aid system for the welfare of its members and the maintenance of the family as a whole (1978, p. 1). Thus, the key is not just that three or more generations often live in the same household but that contact with nonresident kin is frequent and integral to the functioning of the family unit. When asked, African Americans overwhelmingly report a strong sense of family solidarity (Hatchett & Jackson, 1993; Wilson, 1986, 1989).

Within this subculture, marriage does not play the dominant role in family formation that it does among Caucasian Americans: Fewer African American adults marry, and divorce is more common (U.S. Census Bureau, 2008b). One result is that a much larger percentage of African American children are born to or reared by unmarried mothers (Martin et al., 2007). However, because of the cultural emphasis on the importance of children and on communalism, these single mothers occupy a different niche within the African American culture than do single mothers in the majority culture. The latter group are more likely to receive financial help from their parents but to live independently; an African American single mother is more likely to live in an extended family with her own mother or grandmother (DeLeire & Kalil, 2002).

These extended family structures allow individuals to pool their economic resources; they also provide important social and emotional support to the members of the household. The presence of the children's grandmother seems to provide especially helpful support for the young single mother; African American children from such three-generation families do better in school and show fewer behavior problems than do African American children reared by single mothers in households without a grandmother (DeLeire & Kalil, 2002). There is also some evidence that the presence of the grandmother increases the chance that an infant will develop a secure rather than an insecure attachment (Egeland & Sroufe, 1981). Thus, the extended family not only has a cultural history but also seems to be a successful adaptive strategy for many African American families.

Religion also appears to play a special, positive role within the African American culture. The church is a place for participation and belonging, an institution in which those who take on specific roles achieve prestige and status, as well as an institution that can provide help in times of physical or emotional need (Dupree, Watson, & Schneider, 2005). For African American children, participation in church activities seems to be a plus as well; a few studies suggest that those who are more active in a church are more likely to be successful in other arenas, such as in school or on the job (Lee, 1985).

The culture of African American families is also profoundly shaped by the persistence of prejudice. African American adolescents who are most aware of such prejudice are most likely to see school achievement as irrelevant (Taylor, Casten, Flickinger, Roberts, & Fulmore, 1994). Even the process of grieving for lost loved ones appears to be complicated by this consciousness of historical racial prejudice. Researchers have found that African Americans' memories of relatives who have passed away are often framed in terms of how racial prejudice interfered with the individual's pursuit of life goals (Rosenblatt & Wallace, 2005). When these memories are shared with children, it is likely that they increase children's awareness of the notion that African Americans often encounter obstacles in life that members of other groups do not. On a positive note, though, these stories may also enhance children's feelings of pride in their family histories and sense of ethnic identity.

Because so many African American families and children live in poverty or near-poverty, it is very difficult to sort out which patterns are due to economic conditions and which are due to distinctive African American cultural processes. These factors obviously interact and are further embedded within the larger culture, in which prejudice and discrimination against African Americans are still a part of everyday life.

Hispanic Americans   Some of the statements made above about African Americans are also true of Hispanic Americans, for whom poverty is also endemic. The term *Hispanic* was chosen by the Department of Commerce to denote any person with family roots in Spanish-speaking countries or from Central or South America. The term *Latino*, which many people prefer, is the Spanish word for the same group. Hispanic people represent the fastest-growing minority group in the United States. In 1980, only 6% of the population was Hispanic. By 2006, the proportion had grown to 15% (U.S. Census Bureau, 2008b).

A number of subgroups, differing somewhat in values and cultural traditions, comprise the Hispanic population in the United States. Just over 60% are Mexican, 12% are Puerto Rican, and 4% are Cuban in origin (U.S. Census Bureau, 2001). The rest are from other Central and South American countries. Within this diverse group, Puerto Ricans have the highest poverty rates; their divorce rates are comparable to those among African Americans. Both Mexican Americans and Cuban Americans have divorce rates closer to the rate among White Americans.

These subgroups, however, share a number of cultural values, all of which are aspects of a basic collectivist world view (Hill et al., 1994; Parke & Buriel, 1998):

- Preference for group participation or group work rather than individual effort (*allocentrism*).
- Strong commitment to and adherence to family; placing the family before the individual; self-identity is embedded in the family (*familia*).
- Avoidance of personal conflict; keeping the peace at all costs (*simpatía*).
- Respect for and deference to authority, such as parents, elders, teachers, or government officials (*respeto*).
- High value placed on personal relationships, which are seen as more important than reputation or material gain; feelings and needs of others are paramount; competition is discouraged (*personalismo*).

In addition, of course, there is also the common thread of the Spanish language. The great majority of Hispanic Americans today either speak only Spanish or are bilingual. Because of recent rapid immigration, more than half of Hispanic American school-aged children have only limited English proficiency; a shift toward English as the dominant language generally occurs among second- or third-generation Hispanic

This Hispanic American family has obviously assimilated some of the larger American culture: They are celebrating Thanksgiving. At the same time, they have doubtless retained many features of their own culture, including the centrality of family loyalty.

Americans, but many if not most continue to speak Spanish in the home (Hakimzadeh & Cohn, 2007). Many Hispanic American communities also have Spanish-language newspapers and radio and TV stations; in many neighborhoods, Spanish is the dominant tongue.

The significance of family life within Hispanic American culture is hard to exaggerate. The nuclear family is the core of this kin system, although contact with extended family members and with "fictive kin" is frequent (Howes, Guerra, & Zucker, 2007). *Fictive kin*, also common in extended African American family systems, might include a child's godparents or other friends who develop a long-term connection with the family and with each child (Keefe & Padilla, 1987).

This pattern seems to be stronger in first-generation immigrants, who rely almost exclusively on family members for emotional support and problem solving. The children of immigrants seem to have more extensive nonkin networks, and many shift somewhat toward an individualist set of values—with accompanying increases in intrafamily stress (Delgado-Gaitan, 1994; Parke & Buriel, 1998). In both newly immigrant and second-generation families, however, the extended family clearly plays a more central role in the daily life of Hispanic Americans than it does in the majority culture.

This emphasis on the central role of the family is reflected in the values taught to children so that they will become *bien educado*. Literally translated, *bien educado* means "well educated"; the phrase does not primarily connote formal education, however, but rather the ability to function well in any social setting without disrespect or rudeness. Thus, *bien educado* includes politeness, respect, loyalty, and attachment to the extended family and cooperation with others. Hispanic American mothers emphasize the importance of a child's showing proper demeanor in public; a Caucasian American mother, in contrast, is likely to be pleased or even proud when her child behaves in some independent and even slightly naughty way (Harwood, 1992).

These values are taught in the home through all the mechanisms you have read about throughout this book: modeling, direct reinforcement, and style of family interaction. A number of studies suggest that the more fully Hispanic American parents identify with their ethnic heritage, the more likely it is that the child will show these valued qualities, such as concern for others (Knight, Cota, & Bernal, 1993). Moreover, when children of Hispanic immigrants achieve a bicultural identity that includes a strong identification with their parents' culture, along with a sense of belonging in the dominant culture of the United States, they attain higher levels of both social adjustment and academic achievement (Coatsworth, Maldonado-Molina, Pantin, & Szapocznik, 2005).

Asian Americans   Asian American culture, too, places great stress on obedience to family, on respect for elders, and on family honor. Asian American families also resemble Hispanic American families in some respects: They often include three generations in the same household; they are generally hierarchically organized, with the father as the obvious head; and there is a strong emphasis on the interdependence of family members. Despite these surface similarities to other ethnic groups, the mixture of values in Asian American families includes several that are distinct (American Psychological Association, 1993; Park, 2005; Parke & Buriel, 1998):

- Pacifism, self-discipline, and self-control—all values linked to Confucianism, and thus common among Asian groups with a strong Confucian heritage (Chinese, Korean, and Vietnamese particularly, with lesser influence among Japanese).

- An emphasis on hierarchy and respect in social systems and personal relationships (parents are superior to children, men to women), also based on Confucianism.

- Strong family links; young people are expected to obey elders; family solidarity and harmonious relationships are highly valued; family needs come before individual needs.

- A strong belief that each person controls his or her own destiny.

- A powerful work ethic and belief in the importance of achievement.

Nine-year-old Brian gets help with his homework from his dad—a common event in Asian American households, in which parents typically emphasize the importance of hard work in reaching academic goals.

The Asian American family model includes a striking combination of indulgence, physical contact, comfort, and care on the one hand and high expectations for both obedience and achievement on the other. Children are taught that empathy for others is highly important and yet respecting the privacy of others is also critical (Barry, Bernard, & Beitel, 2008). Overall, children are highly valued, although the family's collective needs normally take precedence over the child's individual needs (Paiva, 2008; Rothbaum, Pott, & Morelli, 1995).

Asian Americans also believe in individual effort as one of the primary roads to success (Harrison et al., 1990; Stevenson, 1988). In Caucasian American culture, ability rather than hard work is seen as the key to success. This difference is not trivial. If you believe in ability as the key ingredient, then there is not much point in pressing for greater effort, and you will accept mediocre performance from your child. An Asian American parent, in contrast, believing in the centrality of effort, takes a very different attitude toward both success and failure by a child: The parent takes success more or less for granted but responds to failure by insisting on more effort. Because of these different belief systems, Asian American parents spend more time tutoring their children and have higher standards for their children's achievement. They are also less likely to be satisfied with their children's schools, believing that schools, too, can always do better. Yet despite what (to Caucasian American eyes) seems like strong pressure to achieve, Asian and Asian American students do not report high feelings of stress or anxiety, whereas high-achieving Caucasian American adolescents do report frequent feelings of stress (Crystal et al., 1994).

Given all these differences, it isn't surprising that Asian American children as a group achieve at higher levels in schools than any other U.S. ethnic group, just as Asian children from Japan, China, Taiwan, and Korea regularly outperform U.S. children and teenagers on standardized tests of math and science, as you learned in Chapter 7. Similarly, you should recall from the discussion of schooling earlier in the chapter that a greater proportion of Asian Americans than any other group in the United States complete high school and college.

Ethnicity in Perspective   What conclusions can be drawn about the role of ethnicity (or, more broadly, culture) in children's development from these three brief (and necessarily simplistic) sketches? Sadly, not many. First and foremost, of course, you have been reading almost entirely about subgroups within U.S. culture, which tells little about other cultural systems. And even within these limits, most research involves comparisons of each ethnic group with children or families in the majority culture. Until recently, most of this research assumed that the dominant culture was right or "normal" and that all other variations were inferior or "deviations" from the standard. That assumption has faded, but developmentalists have very little concurrent information about these groups and even less data about whether the same processes operate in each subgroup. What they are left with is a kind of snapshot of each group, with no way to tell which characteristics are the most crucial, which attitudes or values the most significant.

For example, if developmentalists look for reasons for good or poor school performance in different subcultures, what conclusions can they draw? Bilingualism cannot be the sole factor, because both Asian Americans and Hispanic Americans are typically bilingual; child-rearing style cannot be the sole factor, because Asian American parents are likely to be authoritarian (by current research definitions), yet their children do well in school. Doubtless it is the pattern of values and parental behavior that is crucial, and not any single variable (Knafo, Daniel, & Khoury-Kassabri, 2008). Cultures and subcultures are incredibly complex systems; their effects come from the combinations of factors, not merely from the adding up of a set of separate variables. In addition, of course, it's essential to try to understand how each subculture, each set of values, combines or conflicts with the values of the majority culture. For a child growing up with one foot in one culture and one in another culture, these are highly important issues.

The Culture as a Whole

Learning Objective 14.13

In what way does the culture as a whole affect children's development?

A culture as a whole is also a system, made up of values, assumptions, and beliefs, a political and an economic system, patterns of personal relationships, and so forth. Each piece of that system affects all the other parts; changing one part changes the whole. The wide cultural consequences of the rapid increase in the number of women in the labor force in the United States and other industrialized countries is a very good example. It has led, among many other things, to a fast-growing demand for non-parental care (with consequent changes in children's lives), to changes in male-female relationships, to new political alignments, and to shifts in patterns of interactions within families, which in turn affect children in still other ways.

Throughout this text, you have learned about sequences of children's development that seem to occur regardless of cultural context. At the same time, examples of cultural differences are also evident. At the most visible and measurable level are cultural variations in children's specific beliefs, the social scripts they learn, and the pattern of family and kin relationships they experience.

An interesting example comes from the work of Giyoo Hatano and his colleagues (1993; Inagaki & Hatano, 2004), who compared beliefs about the nature of plants and animals among Japanese, Israeli, and American kindergarten, second-grade, and fourth-grade children. Piaget noted, and others have confirmed, that young children typically view the world through the lens of *animism*, which leads them to attribute not only life but also feelings and self-awareness to inanimate objects, to plants, and to animals. Later, they differentiate among these several facets of life and understand that plants are alive but have no self-awareness. Hatano's study confirms the broad features of this shift: Younger children in all three cultures had much stronger beliefs in animism. But Hatano also found differences in the developmental pattern, depending on the specific cultural beliefs about life.

Japanese culture includes the belief that plants are much like humans; in the Buddhist system, even a blade of grass is thought to have a mind. In contrast, in Israeli language and culture, plants are put into a quite different category from animals and humans. When children in Japan and Israel were asked whether a tree or a tulip was alive, 91% of the Japanese—but only 60% of the Israeli fourth-graders said that it was. One-fifth of Japanese fourth-graders attributed sensory properties to plants, saying that a tree or a tulip could feel chilly or could feel pain if it was hit with a stick. Overall, because of their stronger distinction between plants and animals, Israeli children were much slower than either Japanese or American children to come to the understanding that people, animals, and plants are all alive. This study thus illustrates both an underlying developmental pattern that seems to be shared across cultures and the cultural variations laid over that basic pattern.

It is not hard to generate similar examples. For instance, cultures may vary in the proportion of securely and insecurely attached children because of variations in their typical child-rearing styles or beliefs, even though the process by which a child becomes securely or insecurely attached is much the same from one culture to another. In a similar way, adolescents in all cultures need to change their identity to at least some extent in order to move into the adult world, but cultures that provide initiation rituals at puberty may make the process much simpler and less confusing.

Certainly, developmentalists need to know a great deal more about how cultural variations affect development. But as you learned in Chapter 1, they also have to ask a more subtle set of questions. In particular, they need to know whether the relationship between environmental events or a child's characteristics and some outcome for the child is the same in every culture. Is authoritative child-rearing optimal in all cultures, or is some other style better for preparing children for adult life in some settings? Are aggressive children unpopular in every culture, or are there some settings in which aggression is highly valued? Indeed, is unpopularity in childhood a major risk factor for adult dysfunction in every culture? As yet there are no answers, although researchers are beginning to ask the questions.

Think Critically

- What are some of the implications of Sandra Scarr's view that parents' choices regarding nonparental care are an extension of their values and parenting styles?
- Suppose a child's birthday is a few days after his local school district's cutoff date for enrolling in first grade. In light of the evidence about the effects of schooling that you read about in this chapter, what would be the pros and cons of sending the child to a private school for first grade so that he would be eligible for second grade in a public school the following year?

Conduct Your Own Research

In the section on nonparental care, you learned that many children are placed in multiple care settings. You can find out how frequently such arrangements occur in your own area by surveying parents at a local child-care center. First, explain your project to the center director and get his or her permission to interview parents as they pick up their children each evening. Next, spend a few late afternoons at the center conducting your interviews. Ask parents how many days a week their children attend the center and whether they are also in other kinds of nonparental care. Also ask how many different kinds of care each child has experienced since birth. Keep records of both the number and the types of care arrangements each child is currently experiencing and has been exposed to in the past.

Summary

NONPARENTAL CARE

14.1 Why is it difficult to study the effects of nonparental care?

- Nonparental care is difficult to study because it involves so many variables. In addition, care arrangements interact with family variables such as income and parents' educational level. Often, it is impossible to separate the effects of nonparental care from the effects of these variables.

14.2 How does early nonparental care affect infants' and young children's development?

- A major study showed that child care has no overall negative effect on the security of children's attachment to their parents. Child care often has positive effects on the cognitive development of less advantaged children, but it may have negative effects on advantaged children if there is a large discrepancy between the home environment and the level of stimulation in child care. How child care affects a child's personality depends on the quality of the care. An organized, structured situation is preferable. Infants' physiological responses to the stresses associated with nonparental care may underlie its association with developmental outcomes.

14.3 How does self-care affect school-aged children's development?

- Self-care is associated with several negative effects. Girls, children who live in safe neighborhoods, and children whose parents closely monitor their activities after school are the least likely to be negatively affected by self-care.

THE IMPACT OF SCHOOLS

14.4 How do the various approaches to early childhood education differ, and how does preschool affect children's development?

- Developmental approaches, such as the Montessori method, seek to support the attainment of naturally occurring developmental goals. Academic approaches instruct preschoolers in the skills necessary for success in elementary schools. Developmentally appropriate practices are based on an understanding of developmental universals, individual differences, and the social and cultural contexts of development. Preschool and full-day kindergarten programs may have limited benefits for children who do not have disabilities and who come from homes with adequate economic resources. Learning experiences in less formal settings may contribute as much to such children's development as structured educational programs do.

14.5 What factors contribute to effective schooling at the elementary level, and how does elementary school influence children's development?

- Teaching style, class size, and parental involvement contribute to children's achievement in elementary school. A child's adaptation to school is affected by his readiness to learn to read as well as by his parents' involvement in the school and in his educational attainment. Experience with school appears to be causally linked to some aspects of cognitive development.

14.6 How do children's achievement goals change during the transition to secondary school?

- Children demonstrate achievement losses at every school transition. Most children are motivated by task goals in elementary school, but ability goals become more common after the transition to middle school, where ability grouping is more evident than in earlier grades. When children fail to meet the demands of middle school, they lose confidence in their abilities and show lower levels of self-esteem. Likewise, students who perform poorly in the first year or two of high school are less likely to graduate, an outcome that affects their chances for academic and economic success in adulthood.

14.7 What have researchers learned about disengaged and engaged students?

- By adolescence, children have a clearly developed idea of their comparative skills and abilities. These beliefs are a significant element in decisions about whether to finish high school or drop out. Disengaged students exhibit a pattern of behavior that includes academic failure, lack of participation in extracurricular activities, and increased rates of risky behavior. Engaged students are more interested in school and invest personal effort in school work and extracurricular activities.

14.8 Why do some parents choose to homeschool their children?

- Some parents choose to homeschool their children for religious reasons. Others want to provide one-on-one instruction for a child with disabilities. Some parents choose homeschooling in order to protect their children from negative peer influences. Generally, homeschooled children exhibit few differences from their schooled peers, but research has been sparse and includes only those homeschooled children whose families have volunteered to participate.

THE IMPACT OF ENTERTAINMENT MEDIA

14.9 What are the effects of television and video games on children's development?

- Children who watch specifically educational TV programming can gain skills or positive attitudes. Experts agree that watching violence on television increases the level of aggression shown by a child. Video games may enhance children's spatial cognitive skills; however, those that are violent may also contribute to aggressive behavior.

14.10 What are the roles of computers and electronic multitasking in children's development?

- Children use computers for school work and to play games. Computer and Internet use can raise children's grades and achievement test scores. Multitasking may interfere with learning, lead to increases in sensation-seeking, and increase anxiety.

MACROSYSTEM EFFECTS: THE IMPACT OF THE LARGER CULTURE

14.11 What are the effects of poverty on children and families?

- Children growing up in poverty, perhaps especially urban poverty, are markedly disadvantaged in many ways, including having lower access to medical care and greater exposure to multiple stresses. They do more poorly in school and drop out of school at far higher rates. Some protective factors, including a secure attachment, higher IQ, authoritative parenting, and effective schools, can help to counterbalance poverty effects for some children.

14.12 How do the values of African Americans, Hispanic Americans, and Asian Americans differ?

- African American subculture includes a strong emphasis on extended family households and contact and on religion. Hispanic Americans, too, place great emphasis on family ties; their emphasis on family honor and solidarity is heightened by the use of a shared language. In their collectivist cultural system, kin contact is frequent and central to daily life. Asian Americans emphasize respect and loyalty to family as well, but they stress the central importance of effort (rather than inherent ability) as the path to achievement.

14.13 In what way does the culture as a whole affect children's development?

- Developmentalists have very little understanding of how cultural variations influence development. Some patterns of development and some basic developmental processes (such as moral development and attachment) appear to be independent of culture. Other processes and patterns are affected by cultural variation.

Key Terms

ability goals (p. 374)
academic approaches (p. 368)
developmental approaches (p. 368)

developmentally appropriate practices (p. 369)
early childhood education (p. 368)

ethnic group (p. 388)
ethnicity (p. 388)
task goals (p. 374)

15 Atypical Development

As always, Winnie was in a rush on the day she had to take her 14-year-old daughter, Lynn, to the pediatrician's office after school for a measles booster shot. Thoughts of how she could possibly get Lynn's 10-year-old brother to soccer practice on time were running through her mind as the nurse weighed and measured Lynn prior to giving her the injection. Thus, Winnie was somewhat annoyed when the nurse told her that Lynn would have to see the doctor before she could get her shot.

When the pediatrician came in, he asked Winnie to leave the examining room so that he could speak to Lynn alone. A few minutes later, the doctor called her back into the room. Winnie was shocked when he asked her if she was aware that Lynn had lost 15 pounds since her last visit to the doctor's office just 6 months earlier. He pointed out that Lynn's weight, at 93 pounds, was far below that which was appropriate for her 65-inch height. Together, Lynn, Winnie, and the pediatrician discussed the possibility that Lynn might be suffering from an eating disorder.

Many parents, like Winnie, are taken aback when they learn that their adolescent has a serious behavioral or emotional problem. Their surprise is derived from years of having observed the child following what appears to be a normal developmental pathway in which all of the anticipated developmental milestones have appeared as expected. Yet Winnie's experience and that of parents like her represent just one of several patterns in which nonnormative changes that threaten a child's well being, or *atypical developmental changes*, make their appearance in a child's life. (Recall from Chapter 1 that nonnormative changes are those developmental changes which result from unique, unshared events.) Some nonnormative changes of this kind are evident from the earliest months of life. For example, Down syndrome, which you learned about in Chapter 2, is identified before birth. Others can be readily identified before a child's second birthday. Still others do not become known until a child enters school.

These nonnormative pathways are the topic of this chapter. Each such pathway presents parents with a unique set of challenges. The fact that many (even most) of them manage to adapt effectively to the presence of child who displays atypical development is testimony to the devotion and immense effort expended.

Understanding Atypical Development

Perhaps the best starting point for our discussion is to develop a working definition of *atypical development*. There are many behaviors that might be called *atypical* if we went by the literal definition of the term—that is, *not typical*. Most children do things that others would view as unusual, but in most cases these behaviors fall within the normal range of variation. By contrast, **atypical development** involves behaviors that are not only unusual, but also part of an enduring pattern that interferes with a child's development in significant ways.

atypical development An enduring pattern of behavior that is unusual, compared to the behavior of others of the child's age, and that interferes with the child's development in some significant way.

Types of Problems

Learning Objective 15.1
What kinds of problems fall within the domain of atypical development?

As we have noted, at one time or another most children show some kind of behavior that their parents would describe as "unusual" or "abnormal" (Klass & Costello, 2003). For example, about 10% of school-aged children wet their pants frequently enough that their parents express concern about it to pediatricians (Coury, 2002). Such problems, although worthy of further investigation, almost always fall within the range of typical development and are not indicative of a deeper problem (see *Developmental Science in the Real World* on page 398). Usually, developmentalists label a child's development as atypical only if a problem persists for 6 months or longer or if the problem is at the extreme end of the continuum for that behavior.

Within the domain of atypical development, *psychological disorders* constitute one important category of problems. A **psychological disorder** is a pattern of behavior that is

psychological disorder A pattern of behavior that is unusual in a person's culture and interferes with his or her psychological, social, and/or educational functioning.

Knowing When to Seek Professional Help

Lucinda is a 4-year-old girl who is currently engaged in an ongoing battle with her parents. The proper arrangement of spaghetti is the central dispute in this battle. Lucinda is convinced that spaghetti and spaghetti sauce should touch each other only in a person's mouth. Consequently, she insists on having her spaghetti served in two separate bowls, one for the pasta and another for the sauce. Furthermore, she requires a spoon for the sauce and a fork for the pasta. She becomes hysterical at even the slightest suggestion that she try having her spaghetti in its more conventional form. Her parents have begun to worry that she might have some kind of serious mental disorder and wonder whether they should consult a child psychologist. Their response is typical of today's parents, many of whom are well informed about child development (Klass & Costello, 2003). But many kinds of difficult behavior can be well within the bounds of normal individual differences. So, it's understandable that parents might fear they are overreacting if they conclude that their child may have a serious problem.

Checklists developed by experts in developmental psychopathology can be helpful in distinguishing behavior that is difficult to manage from behavior that may indicate a disorder for which professional care is appropriate. One such checklist has been published by the National Mental Health Association (available at http://www.nmha .org). Here are a few of the warning signs for children and teenagers:

Parents often worry that their children may have some kind of serious mental disorder. However, most problematic behaviors, such as this child's temper tantrum, fall within the range of normal behavior.

- Changes in grades or behavior reports from teachers
- Changes in patterns of sleeping or eating
- Frequent stomachaches or other minor physical symptoms
- Obsessive concern with weight loss
- A sad facial expression that persists over a period of weeks
- Outbursts of rage that lead to destruction of property or aggression toward others
- Activity far in excess of that exhibited by children of the same age
- Frequent unyielding defiance of parental or teacher authority

Of course, every child or teenager who exhibits such behavior doesn't have a serious psychological disorder. Still, when a child's pattern of difficult behavior matches one or more of these signs, parents should probably adopt the "better safe than sorry" approach and consult a mental health professional.

Questions for Reflection

1. According to the checklist, is Lucinda's spaghetti-eating behavior likely to be a sign of a psychological disorder? Why or why not?
2. What strategies might Lucinda's parents use to get her to try eating spaghetti the way most people do?

---

attention problems A category of psychopathologies that impair one's ability to concentrate, including attention deficit hyperactivity disorder, attention deficit disorder, and hyperkinetic disorder.

externalizing problems A category of psychopathologies that includes any deviant behavior primarily directed toward others, such as conduct disorders.

unusual in a child's culture and interferes with his or her psychological, social, and/or educational functioning. There are three main categories of psychological disorders in children and adolescents. The first two are **attention problems** (most particularly, attention deficit hyperactivity disorder), which impair the ability to concentrate, and **externalizing problems** (also described as *disruptive behavior disorders*), including both delinquency and excessive aggressiveness or defiance, in which the deviant behavior is directed outward. The third category, **internalizing problems** (also called *emotional disturbances*), includes such problems as depression, anxiety, or eating disorders, in which the deviant behavior is largely directed internally, against the individual herself. You will be reading more about each of these categories later in the chapter.

There are several other types of atypical development that fall outside these three basic categories. For example, individuals at both extremes of the IQ scale are atypical when compared to others of their age. Likewise, children who have average intelligence but who are several years behind their peers in school achievement are considered to be atypical. Children with severe social impairments constitute yet another group of children whose development is atypical. You will also learn about these groups of children.

Theoretical Perspectives on Atypical Development

Learning Objective 15.2

How do the biological, psychodynamic, learning, and cognitive perspectives explain atypical development?

Many of the theoretical perspectives that you read about in earlier chapters have been invoked to explain atypical development (see Table 15.1). For instance, the *biological perspective* views atypical development as a symptom of an underlying physical cause, such as genetic inheritance, biochemical abnormalities or imbalances, structural abnormalities within the brain, and/or infection. Consequently, those taking the biological perspective generally favor biological treatments such as drugs.

Originally proposed by Freud, the *psychodynamic (psychoanalytic) perspective* maintains that atypical development stems from early childhood experiences and unresolved, unconscious emotional conflicts. The cause assumed by the psychodynamic approach also suggests the cure, psychoanalysis, which Freud developed to uncover and resolve such unconscious conflicts. More recent psychodynamic approaches do not adhere strictly to Freud's accounts of atypical development, but they do emphasize the role of psychological processes and the importance of psychotherapy in addressing behavioral problems that arise from atypical development.

In stark contrast to both the biological and the psychodynamic perspective, the *learning perspective* suggests that atypical behaviors do not result from any underlying cause. That is, the behaviors themselves are the problem, and such behaviors are thought to be learned and sustained in the same way as any other behavior. According to this view, children and adolescents who exhibit atypical development are victims of faulty learning. Behavior therapists use learning principles to eliminate distressing behavior and to establish new, more appropriate behavior in its place.

The *cognitive perspective* suggests that faulty thinking or distorted perceptions can contribute to some types of atypical development. For example, pessimistic thinking is involved in depression and anxiety. Treatment consistent with this perspective is aimed at changing thinking and perceptions (i.e., cognitive therapy), which presumably will lead to a change in behavior.

internalizing problems A category of psychopathologies that includes anxiety and depression and other conditions in which deviant behavior is directed inwardly, against the self.

Table 15.1 Perspectives on Atypical Development

Perspective	Causes of Psychological Disorders	Treatment
Biological perspective	Atypical development is a symptom of an underlying physical disorder caused by a structural or biochemical abnormality in the brain, by genetic inheritance, or by infection.	Diagnose and treat like any other physical disorder Drugs or other physical treatment
Psychodynamic perspective	Atypical development stems from early childhood experiences and unresolved, unconscious sexual or aggressive conflicts.	Bring disturbing repressed material to consciousness and help patient work through unconscious conflicts Psychotherapy
Learning perspective	Atypical behaviors are learned and sustained like any other behaviors, or there is a failure to learn adaptive behaviors.	Use classical and operant conditioning and modeling to extinguish atypical behavior and to increase adaptive behavior Behavior therapy Behavior modification
Cognitive perspective	Faulty thinking or distorted perceptions can cause atypical development.	Change faulty, irrational, and/or negative thinking Cognitive therapy

Source: Wood et al., WORLD OF PSYCHOLOGY, © 2008. Reproduced by permission of Pearson Education, Inc.

Developmental Psychopathology

<table>
<tr><td>

Learning Objective 15.3

What is developmental psychopathology, and how has it changed the way psychologists approach questions about atypical development?

</td></tr>
</table>

In recent years, psychologists have changed the way they think about atypical development. Instead of searching for a single grand theory that can explain everything, they focus on factors that seem to predispose children to problems as well as on variables that appear to protect them (Beauchaine & Hinshaw, 2008). Developmentalists' knowledge about the dynamics of deviant development in general, and psychopathology in particular, has been enormously enhanced by an approach called **developmental psychopathology** (Achenbach, 1974; Cicchetti, 2008). This approach has strongly influenced how both researchers and practitioners think about children's and teenagers' psychological problems (Munir & Beardslee, 2001). It emphasizes several key points.

Developmental psychopathology integrates perspectives from a variety of disciplines in order to better understand atypical development. Researchers who study cultural differences, such as anthropologists, have contributed much to developmental psychopathologists' understanding of atypical development (Achenbach, 2008). For example, as you learned in Chapter 13, authoritarian parenting may be a risk factor in one setting and a protective factor in another.

Similarly, the work of behavior geneticists and neuroscientists has become increasingly important in the study of atypical development, especially when their findings are combined with those of developmental psychologists. For example, behavior geneticists have known for some time that heredity contributes to atypical development, and developmental psychologists have been aware of the roles that abuse plays in poor developmental outcomes for some time as well (Phares & Compas, 1993). Neuroscience has enabled them to get a better idea of just how inherited risks interact with environmental risks. In one study, Dante Cicchetti and his colleagues found evidence that the genes that children inherit from parents who suffer from conditions such as depression produce patterns of neurotransmitter functioning that differ from those of children whose parents do not have such conditions (Cicchetti, Rogosch, & Sturge-Apple, 2007). These neurotransmitter differences produce variations in how children respond to abuse. Such findings suggest that inherited risks may produce atypical development only in the presence of high-risk environmental factors such as abuse. Similarly, factors such as abuse may produce atypical development only in children who have inherited vulnerabilities. At the same time, protective factors—such as loving relationships with caregivers—may moderate the interaction between inherited and environmental risk factors such that a child's development does not differ from that of other children (Charuvastra & Cloitre, 2008).

This kind of complex interplay between risk and protective factors is another hallmark of developmental psychopathology. Consider the risks associated with a difficult temperament, for example (Rothbart, 2007). These risks are magnified when they are combined with harsh parenting, an approach to child-rearing that parents have usually learned from their own parents. Yet parents who have higher levels of education than their own parents usually do not model the harsh child-rearing strategies of their own parents (Serbin & Karp, 2003). Thus, the developmental pathway that a child with the internal risk factor of difficult temperament follows is influenced by how his parents respond to him, a factor that can serve to either increase or decrease the chances of a poor developmental outcome. At the same time, the parents' own experiences as children and those that they have had since contribute to how they respond to the child. As this example illustrates, developmental psychopathology provides explanations of atypical development that are far more comprehensive than those derived from the classical theories.

Developmental psychopathologists also include normative age-graded changes, developmental milestones that all children experience, in their explanations of atypical development. For example, a child's stage of cognitive development influences how she interprets an event that can increase her risk of an atypical developmental outcome. A teenager and a preschooler,

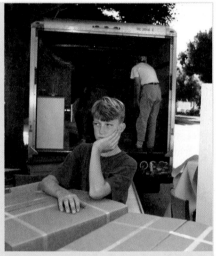

Whether a child or teenager will show a behavior problem in response to stress such as moving to a new home will depend in part on whether he faces other stresses or life changes at the same time—such as perhaps his parents' divorce.

developmental psychopathology A relatively new approach to the study of deviance that emphasizes that normal and abnormal development have common roots and that pathology can arise from many different pathways.

for example, may be affected quite differently by a risk factor such as abuse because of their cognitive-developmental differences (Abela & Hankin, 2008; Walker, 2002). Moreover, experiencing such a risk may lead to neurological changes that can affect the subsequent cognitive development of both the teenager and the preschooler (Gillespie & Nemeroff, 2007).

Finally, the *lifespan perspective*, the view that change occurs throughout life, is fundamental to developmental psychopathology (Wicks-Nelson & Israel, 1997). A maladaptive change at one point in development may be moderated or even reversed later on. Likewise, an adaptive change at one point in life can be threatened by later events. For example, a child's need for physical and emotional support in infancy may lead her to develop the sense of trust that Erikson described in his account of psychosexual development. However, if someone violates her trust at a later point, she may become generally distrustful of others. This distrust may lead to changes in behavior that increase the risk of some kind of maladaptive outcome. For instance, she may isolate herself for fear of being disappointed again.

Attention Problems and Externalizing Problems

You will recall that attention problems include disorders in which children's ability to concentrate seems to be impaired. Externalizing problems are disorders that involve outwardly directed inappropriate behaviors, such as aggression.

Attention Deficit Hyperactivity Disorder

Learning Objective 15.4
What diagnostic labels are given to children who have attention problems?

A glance at the diagnostic criteria for **attention deficit hyperactivity disorder (ADHD)**, listed in Table 15.2 on page 402, reveals that the hallmarks of this disorder are physical restlessness and problems with attention—precisely what the name implies. Russell Barkley (1997), one of the major researchers and theorists on ADHD, suggests that the underlying problem is a deficit in the child's ability to inhibit behavior—to keep himself from starting some prohibited or unhelpful behavior or from reacting to some compelling stimulus or to stop behaving in some fashion once he has started. In busy, complex environments with many stimuli (such as a classroom), children with ADHD are unable to inhibit their reactions to all the sounds and sights around them, so they appear restless and cannot focus sustained attention on a single activity.

Defining the Problem Whether this constellation of problems constitutes a single syndrome or several distinct subvarieties is still a matter of active debate. You'll note that the criteria in Table 15.2 are divided into two sets, those dealing with attention problems and those dealing with hyperactivity, suggesting the existence of two subtypes of ADHD: (1) **ADHD/hyperactive/impulsive type**, in which a high activity level is the main problem, and (2) **ADHD/inattentive type**, in which an inability to sustain attention is the major difficulty (DSM-IV TR, 2000). In addition, some children are diagnosed with **ADHD/combined type**, signifying that they meet the criteria for both the hyperactive/impulsive and the inattentive type.

Diagnosing ADHD is made all the more difficult by the fact that a great many children are inattentive or overactive at least some of the time. Both teachers and parents can be tempted to label a boisterous or obstreperous child as having ADHD. There is no doubt that a good deal of mislabeling of this kind does occur. Further, experimental studies have shown that, on many attention tasks, children diagnosed with ADHD do not differ from nondiagnosed children at all (Lawrence et al., 2004). Where children with ADHD do seem to differ markedly from other children is in their capacity to sustain attention when engaged in boring, repetitive tasks (DSM-IV TR, 2000). They also seem to be less able than other children of the same age to control impulses.

attention deficit hyperactivity disorder (ADHD) A disorder in which a child shows both significant problems in focusing attention and physical hyperactivity.

ADHD/hyperactive/ impulsive type ADHD in which hyperactivity is the main problem.

ADHD/inattentive type ADHD in which inattention is the main problem.

ADHD/combined type ADHD in which both hyperactivity and inattention are problems.

Table 15.2   Diagnostic Criteria for Attention Deficit Hyperactivity Disorder

- The child must show either significant *inattention* or significant *hyperactivity-impulsivity* (or both).

- Inattention is indicated by any six or more of the following:
    1. Often fails to give close attention to details or makes careless mistakes in schoolwork or other activities.
    2. Often has difficulty sustaining attention in tasks or play.
    3. Often does not seem to listen when spoken to directly.
    4. Often does not follow through on instructions and fails to finish chores, homework, or duties.
    5. Often has difficulty organizing tasks and activities.
    6. Often avoids, dislikes, or is reluctant to engage in tasks that require sustained mental effort.
    7. Often loses things necessary for tasks or activities (e.g., toys, pencils, books, tools).
    8. Is often easily distracted by extraneous stimuli.
    9. Is often forgetful in daily activities.

- Hyperactivity-impulsivity is indicated by the presence of six of the following, persisting over a period of at least six months:
    1. Often fidgets with hands or feet or squirms in seat.
    2. Often leaves seat in classroom or in other situations in which remaining seated is expected.
    3. Often runs about or climbs excessively or reports feeling of restlessness.
    4. Often has difficulty playing quietly.
    5. Is often "on the go" or often acts as if "driven by a motor."
    6. Often talks excessively.
    7. Often blurts out answers before questions are completed.
    8. Often has difficulty waiting for a turn.
    9. Often interrupts or intrudes on others.

- The onset of the problem must be before age 7.

- At least some of the symptoms must be present in two or more settings, such as home and school or school and play with peers.

- The behavior must interfere with developmentally appropriate social, academic, or occupational functioning.

Source: Reprinted with permission from the *Diagnostic and Statistical Manual of Mental Disorders*, 4th edition, Text Revision (Copyright © 2000). American Psychiatric Association.

Culture, Age, Gender, and Ethnicity   ADHD is diagnosed less frequently in other cultures than it is in the United States (Polanczyk, de Lima, Horta, Biederman, & Rohde, 2007). Some developmentalists suggest that this cross-national difference is the result of over-use of the diagnosis in the United States, an assertion that has been refuted by research (Cuffe, Moore, & McKeown, 2005). Others suggest that educators and mental health professionals in other nations have failed to recognize the degree to which ADHD is prevalent in their children (Polanczyk et al., 2007). One very thorough review of cross-national differences in ADHD prevalence suggested that underlying rates of ADHD-like behavior are highly similar around the world, but variations in the way the disorder is diagnosed lead to differences in ADHD rates across nations (Polanczyk et al., 2007).

Age is also related to ADHD prevalence. The data in Table 15.3 reveal that rates of ADHD diagnosis increase over the elementary school years (Visser & Lesesne, 2005). As school becomes more difficult, the characteristics of the disorder cause problems for more children. Many of those who are diagnosed in the later grades were able to succeed at the less challenging work in the early grades without additional help. Declines in diagnosis rates in adolescence may be attributable to maturational factors that help some children with ADHD compensate for attention difficulties.

The table also clearly shows the striking gender difference in ADHD diagnosis and treatment. Part of this difference is due to the finding that girls are more likely to exhibit symptoms of the inattentive and combined types of ADHD than the hyperactive type (Biederman et al., 1999). Boys show the opposite pattern; that is, they are more likely to be hyperactive and disruptive. Thus, teachers and parents may be more likely to notice boys' problems and seek help for them. Girls' symptoms, by contrast, may be attributed to laziness, moodiness, or a lack of interest in school. However, the gender difference may also represent an overreaction to boys' greater general rowdiness. Thus, some speculate that gender differences in ADHD diagnosis result from "medicalization" of typical male behavior, a view that remains controversial (Timimi & Leo, 2009).

Table 15.3 also shows that ADHD diagnosis and medication rates in the United States are consistent across White, African American, and multiracial groups. However, rates are far lower among Hispanic American children (Visser & Lesesne, 2005). This difference could be due to a real difference in children's behavior across groups, overdiagnosis in non-Hispanic groups, or underdiagnosis in Hispanic Americans. With regard to the first of these possibilities, surveys of teachers suggest that the kinds of behavior problems that lead to a diagnosis of ADHD occur just as frequently among Hispanic American children as they do in others (Ham, 2004). As for the second possible explanation, extensive surveys of parents, teachers, and health-care professionals, together with the high degree of consistency in diagnosis rates across non-Hispanic subgroups, suggest that ADHD is not overdiagnosed among them (Cuffe, Moore, & McKeown, 2005). The data shown in the table regarding language and ADHD diagnosis support the third possibility: that ADHD is underdiagnosed among Hispanic American children. It is likely that language differences among parents, teachers, and health-care professionals prevent the establishment of the kind of communication among them that is needed to diagnose ADHD. In other words, Hispanic American children whose parents speak English are more likely to be diagnosed with ADHD, or, put differently, those whose families do not speak English are at increased risk of not being diagnosed and treated for this troubling condition. These findings highlight the need for multilingual professionals in schools and health-care settings.

Table 15.3 Age, Gender, Ethnicity, and ADHD

	Percentage Diagnosed with ADHD		Percentage Taking Medication for ADHD	
	Male	Female	Male	Female
Age				
4–8	6	2	4	2
9–12	14	10	9	4
13–17	14	10	7	2
Race				
White	12	5	7	3
Black	12	4	6	2
Multiracial	14	6	7	3
Other	7	2	3	1
Ethnicity				
Hispanic	5	3	2	1
Non-Hispanic	12	2	7	3
Primary Language in the Home				
English	12	5	7	3
Other	2	1	<1	<1

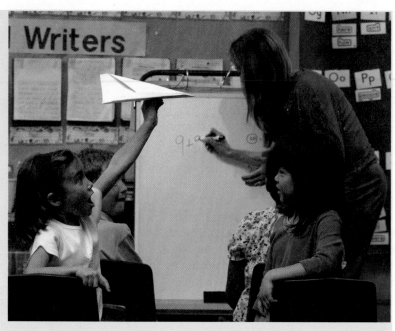
Children with ADHD are more physically active than peers. Many, like this girl, are also exceptionally adventurous.

Origins of the Problem   Where might ADHD come from? Because the behavioral pattern begins so early and has such a strong physical component, most clinicians have assumed that this problem has some kind of biological origin. Early research failed to confirm a biological hypothesis, but more recent evidence makes clear that ADHD is a neuropsychiatric disorder (Goldman, Genel, Bezman, & Slanetz, 1998; Kagan & Herschkowitz, 2005). Three converging lines of evidence support that conclusion.

First, physicians and psychologists have known for some time that a biological treatment is very often effective in reducing or eliminating the deviant behavior. Many children with ADHD in the United States are treated with a stimulant medication called methylphenidate (the most commonly used brand-name drug is Ritalin). The drug works by stimulating the part of the brain that maintains attention. About 70–90% of children treated with this drug show improvement, including decreases in demanding, disruptive, and noncompliant behaviors; lessened aggressiveness and noncompliance; more attentiveness in the classroom; and improved performance on many academic tasks (Pelham et al., 2002; Ridderinkhof, Scheres, Oosterlaan, & Sergeant, 2005). This evidence is consistent with a biological explanation for ADHD. More specifically, it suggests that the problem may lie in one of the brain's neurotransmitters, because stimulant medications of the type used with children with ADHD act by altering the action of monoamine, one of the key neurotransmitters (Kado & Takagi, 1996).

Additional evidence for an underlying biological cause comes from research in behavior genetics, which suggests that a pattern of hyperactivity is inherited, at least in certain families (Thapar, 2003). About one-quarter of the parents of hyperactive children themselves have a history of hyperactivity. Studies of twins also suggest there is a genetic contribution. Among identical twins, if one is diagnosed as hyperactive, the other is highly likely to have the same diagnosis; among fraternal twins, this concordance rate is much lower (Kado & Takagi, 1996). Evidence suggesting that inheritance may also indirectly influence the development of ADHD comes from research showing that temperament is related to ADHD. Children who are low in *effortful control* (look back at Chapter 9) are more likely to be diagnosed with the disorder than are their peers who get higher ratings on scales that measure this aspect of temperament (Chang & Burns, 2005). Likewise, longitudinal research has shown that infants who are very outgoing are more likely to be diagnosed with externalizing disorders, including ADHD, when they enter preschool than are infants who are less outgoing (Putnam & Stifter, 2005).

Finally, brain-imaging diagnostic methods have begun to reveal subtle differences in brain structure and brain function between individuals with and without ADHD (Kagan & Herschkowitz, 2005). For example, studies using magnetic resonance imaging (MRI) suggest that in the majority of children with ADHD, the right hemisphere of the brain is larger than the left hemisphere, while the majority of children without ADHD show the reverse (Hynd et al., 1993). Other researchers using positron emission tomography (PET) have found slight differences in brain metabolism (e.g., Zametkin et al., 1990).

Treating and Managing ADHD   We noted earlier that 70–90% of children with ADHD respond to treatment with stimulant drugs (Pelham et al., 2002; Ridderinkhof, Scheres, Oosterlaan, & Sergeant, 2005). As Table 15.3 shows, about half of children with

ADHD take these medications. Differences between diagnosis and medication rates are due partly to some parents' initial choices regarding treatment for the disorder. However, nonadherence to medical advice is probably a larger factor. Longitudinal studies show that one in five children who are prescribed medication for ADHD stops taking it within 4 to 6 months (Sanchez, Crismon, Barner, Bettinger, & Wilson, 2005). The primary reason for treatment termination is parents' view that their children should not be taking psychiatric medications.

Recently, too, researchers have warned against the routine prescribing of stimulant drugs for children who exhibit mild symptoms of ADHD. These researchers point to studies showing that methylphenidate increases the risk of cardiovascular disease and that newer medications (e.g., Adderall) are associated with changes in thinking that may increase a child's risk of developing a more serious psychological disorder (Gardner, 2007). As a result, physicians are prescribing drugs for mild cases of ADHD less often than in the past.

Oppositional Defiant Disorder

Learning Objective 15.5
What behaviors are associated with oppositional defiant disorder?

Children with **oppositional defiant disorder (ODD)** display a pattern of negative, defiant, disobedient, and hostile behavior toward their parents and other authority figures, established prior to age 8 (DSM-IV TR, 2000). Many children who suffer from ADHD are also diagnosed with ODD. Estimates of the prevalence of ODD among children with ADHD range from 21% to 60% (Austin, Reiss, & Burgdorf, 2007). Among children who are not diagnosed with ADHD, the prevalence of ODD has been estimated to fall between 2% and 16% (DSM-IV TR, 2000).

Children with ODD are difficult to manage, as you might guess. They tend to display defiant behaviors most often with the people they know best, such as their parents, siblings, teachers, and classmates. When interacting with people whom they do not know well, children with ODD often behave appropriately. For instance, many children with this disorder seem to be quite easy-going the first time they are interviewed by a psychologist or other mental health professional. Thus, diagnosing a child with ODD can be challenging. Diagnostic procedures must include assessments of the child's behavior across a variety of settings. Even so, it is not unusual for a child's parent and regular classroom teacher to report that his behavior fits the ODD profile, while others who interact less often with the child, such as a physical education or music teacher, report having no problems with the child.

The cause of ODD is unknown, but researchers have identified several important themes in its manifestation (Tynan, 2008). One is that, as is true of ADHD, males are diagnosed with ODD more often than females are. Temperament is a factor as well; most children with ODD displayed difficult temperaments in infancy. Some studies suggest that prenatal exposure to alcohol, nicotine, and other teratogens increases a child's chances of being diagnosed with ODD. Many parents of children with ODD suffer from emotional disturbances such as anxiety disorders and depression. A high degree of marital conflict is also often found among the parents of children with ODD.

If a child has both ADHD and ODD, medication may be prescribed for her ADHD symptoms, but the symptoms of ODD are treated with parent training (Tynan, 2008). Training is the treatment of choice because, by the time they consult with a mental health professional, parents of children with ODD have usually established a pattern for responding to their children's troublesome behavior that serves only to perpetuate it. Most such parents respond to their children's behavior by giving in to their demands in order to obtain brief reprieves from the perpetual hostility, argumentativeness, and disobedience. You should recognize this response pattern as negative reinforcement: The symptoms of ODD are an aversive stimulus that subsides temporarily when the parent gives the child whatever she wants. Thus, the behaviors of both the child and the parent are reinforced, and a maladaptive cycle is repeated each time the child misbehaves. In parent training sessions, therapists teach parents of children with ODD to break the cycle. They learn to set concrete limits for the child's behavior and

oppositional defiant disorder (ODD) A pattern of negative, defiant, disobedient, and hostile behavior toward parents and other authority figures, established prior to age 8.

to stick to promised consequences, no matter how difficult or outrageous the child's behavior becomes.

Learning Objective 15.6

What are childhood-onset and adolescent-onset conduct disorders, and how do they differ from delinquency?

Conduct Disorder

The broadest category of externalizing problems is what might be referred to in everyday speech as "antisocial behavior." The American Psychiatric Association's *Diagnostic and Statistical Manual of Mental Disorders* (or DSM) defines **conduct disorder** (CD) as a pattern of behavior that includes high levels of aggression, argumentativeness, bullying, disobedience, irritability, and threatening and loud behavior.

Childhood-Onset Conduct Disorder The features of oppositional defiant disorder are associated with **childhood-onset conduct disorder**, a pattern of behavior that includes high levels of aggression, argumentativeness, bullying, disobedience, irritability, and threatening and loud behavior and begins before a child is 10 years of age. Essentially, childhood-onset conduct disorder is diagnosed if a child has all the characteristics of ODD and also engages in threatening and/or aggressive behavior toward others and repetitively violates important social rules (e.g., stealing).

Very often, children who are diagnosed with childhood-onset conduct disorder begin life with a range of vulnerabilities, including difficult temperament, lower intelligence, or both (McCabe, Hough, Wood, & Yeh, 2001). In infancy, they are likely to have formed insecure/disorganized or insecure/avoidant attachments (Lynam, 1996; Lyons-Ruth, Easterbrooks & Cibelli, 1997; D. Shaw et al., 1996; van IJzendoorn, 1997). In the preschool years, these children very often throw tantrums and defy parents. They are very difficult children to handle. If the parents are not up to the task of controlling the child, the child's behavior worsens and becomes overt aggression toward others, who then reject the child.

During the school years, these children are less likely than peers to be able to empathize with others' feelings, a social-cognitive deficit that leads to peer rejection (Rey, 2001). Such peer rejection aggravates the problem, pushing the seriously aggressive child in the direction of other children with similar problems, who become the child's only supportive peer group (Shaw, Kennan, & Vondra, 1994). By adolescence, these youngsters are firmly established in delinquent or antisocial behavior, and their friends are drawn almost exclusively from among other delinquent teens (Tremblay, Mâsse, Vitaro, & Dobkin, 1995). They are also highly likely to display a cluster of other problem behaviors, including drug and alcohol use, truancy or dropping out of school, and early and risky sexual behavior, including having multiple sexual partners (Dishion et al., 1995; Kuperman et al., 2001; Wiesner, Kim, & Capaldi, 2005).

There is also some indication that childhood-onset conduct disorder has a strong genetic component (Deater-Deckard & Plomin, 1997; Oosterlaan, Geurts, Knol, & Sergeant, 2005). Thus, the preschooler who already shows defiant and oppositional behavior as well as aggressiveness may have strong inborn propensities for such behavior. Moreover, brain imaging studies indicate that the brain structures that regulate emotion and planning in children with CD are less fully developed than those of children who do not have the disorder (Huebner et al., 2008). But whether that propensity develops into a full-fledged, persisting conduct disorder will depend on the interactions between the inborn tendency and other aspects of the child's life, including the parents' ability to handle the child's early defiance as well as the general environment in which the child lives, such as inner city versus small town (Gottesman & Goldsmith, 1994; Loeber, Tremblay, Gagnon, & Charlebois, 1989). Parenting style matters as well; research suggests that children who develop conduct disorder have more permissive parents than do their peers (Rey, 2001).

Adolescent-Onset Conduct Disorder When a child exhibits the features of conduct disorder at age 11 or later, he is given the diagnosis of **adolescent-onset conduct disorder**. In contrast to those with childhood-onset conduct disorder, teens who are diagnosed with the adolescent-onset form of the disorder tend to manifest antisocial behaviors that are

conduct disorder Diagnostic term for a pattern of deviant behavior including high levels of aggressive, antisocial, or delinquent acts.

childhood-onset conduct disorder Conduct disorder beginning in childhood; the pattern is linked to rejection by peers and to conduct problems that persist into adolescence and adulthood.

milder, more transitory, and more a function of hanging out with bad companions than a deeply ingrained behavior problem (DSM-IV TR, 2000). Moreover, the antisocial behavior patterns of those with adolescent-onset conduct disorder often change as their relationships change. Consequently, peer influence seems to be the most important factor in the development of adolescent-onset conduct disorder.

Parenting style and other relationship variables seem to be additional factors in this type of antisocial behavior. Several studies show that authoritarian parenting increases the risk of adolescent-onset conduct disorder (Smith & Farrington, 2004). Thus, it may be that parents who do not balance strict supervision with recognition of teenagers' need to understand the reasons behind parents' rules incite rebellion in some children. However, the cultural context in which parenting occurs matters as well. It seems that the combination of authoritarian parenting and a culture that endorses strict

In 2002, about 7% of children and teenagers were arrested in the United States.

rules and strong enforcement of those rules does not increase the risk of conduct disorder in teens. For example, in most Middle Eastern societies, children whose parents display the authoritarian style are less likely to develop conduct disorder than peers whose families' approaches to discipline do not match the larger culture (Dwairy, 2008).

Permissive parenting is also associated with adolescent-onset conduct disorder. Most teens who develop the disorder have parents who do not monitor them sufficiently, often because there is only one parent in the home (Office of Juvenile Justice and Delinquency Prevention [OJJDP], 2006). Regardless of family structure, when parents provide good monitoring and emotional support, their adolescent children are unlikely to exhibit antisocial behavior even if they hang around with a tough crowd or have close friends who engage in such behavior (Mounts & Steinberg, 1995).

Delinquency **Delinquency** is a narrower category of externalizing problems than conduct disorder; it refers only to intentional lawbreaking. Clearly, many children who break laws also show other forms of conduct disorder, so the two categories overlap a great deal. Still, the overlap is not total, so it is useful to look at delinquency separately.

Low IQ scores appear to be an important risk factor for delinquency, particularly for children with childhood-onset conduct disorder, for those who show more serious or violent forms of offenses, and for those who experience some school failure (Hämäläinen & Pulkkinen, 1996). The argument offered by Donald Lynam and others (1993) is that school failure reduces a young person's engagement with school and the values it represents. School failure also increases the child's or adolescent's frustration, which raises the likelihood of aggression of some kind. Thus, for many less intelligent young people, the social constraint on delinquent behavior offered by education is simply weaker.

In addition to IQ, variations in self-esteem are related to delinquent behavior. However, there is considerable debate as to whether low or high self-esteem predisposes an adolescent to engage in delinquent behavior. On one side, Brent Donnellan and his colleagues argue that children who develop low self-esteem in elementary school, perhaps brought on by school failure or peer rejection, are more prone to delinquency in later years (Donnellan, Trzesniewski, Robins, Moffitt, & Caspi, 2005). By contrast, Roy Baumeister and others have claimed that the development of an inappropriately high level of self-esteem during childhood, given an individual's real accomplishments, is associated with delinquency (Baumeister, Bushman, & Campbell, 2000; Baumeister, Campbell, Krueger, & Vohs, 2003; Baumeister, Smart, & Boden, 1996). Put differently, Baumeister hypothesizes that *narcissism*, the view that one is the center of the world, is more likely to be at the center of a delinquent teen's sense of self-worth than is low self-esteem. To date, both sides have produced evidence in support of their views. As a result, Donnellan has argued that researchers should probably think of the kind of low self-esteem he measures as being qualitatively distinct from the narcissism that

adolescent-onset conduct disorder A conduct disorder that begins only in adolescence; it is typically less severe and persistent than childhood-onset conduct disorder.

delinquency A subcategory of conduct disorder involving explicit lawbreaking.

has been studied by Baumeister's group (Donnellan et al., 2005). He says that it is possible for a delinquent teen both to be narcissistic and to have low self-esteem when he judges himself against the criteria he knows to be part of a cultural definition of "good" people. What seems clear is that teens who display delinquent behavior have views of themselves that distinguish them from adolescents who do not engage in such behaviors.

It is important to emphasize, however, that unlike the broader category of conduct disorders, which are quite stable from childhood to adulthood, the milder forms of delinquency do not invariably or even commonly persist into adulthood. Many teens commit only occasional delinquent acts and show no further problem in adulthood. For them, mild delinquent behavior is merely a phase. It is those who show a syndrome of delinquent acts plus high-risk behavior and come from families with low warmth and ineffective control who are quite likely to engage in criminal acts as adults.

Internalizing Problems

As you learned earlier, internalizing problems are so named because they involve deviations from the typical developmental pathway that are directed internally, against the self. Such problems include disturbances of self-concept, as in eating disorders, and disturbances of emotions, as in depression.

Learning Objective 15.7

How do developmentalists define and explain eating disorders?

Eating Disorders

Eating disorders are among the most significant mental health problems of adolescence. Many psychologists argue that these disorders are in fact only the extreme end of a continuum of problems relating to dieting and obsession about body shape and size that appear to be epidemic among White teenaged (and increasingly preteen) girls in the United States and in Britain and some other European countries (e.g., Smolak, Levine, & Streigel-Moore, 1996).

Bulimia Bulimia (sometimes called *bulimia nervosa*) involves three elements: (1) a preoccupation with eating and an irresistible craving for food, leading to episodes of binge eating; (2) an intense fear of fatness; and (3) some method of purging to counteract the effects of the binge eating so as to avoid weight gain. Typical purging methods are self-induced vomiting, excessive use of laxatives, or excessive exercise (Garfinkel, 1995). Alternating periods of normal eating and binge eating are common among individuals in all weight groups.

Only when binge eating occurs as often as twice a week and is combined with repeated episodes of some kind of purging is the syndrome properly called bulimia. People with bulimia are ordinarily not exceptionally thin, but they are obsessed with their weight, feel intense shame about their abnormal behavior, and often experience significant depression. The physical consequences of bulimia can include marked tooth decay (from repeated vomiting), stomach irritation, dehydration, lowered body temperature, disturbances of body chemistry, loss of hair, and, in extreme cases, cardiovascular problems (Mitchell, 1995; Muscari, 1996).

It has been estimated that 1% of men and 7% of women show the full syndrome of bulimia; as many as 20% of teenaged girls in Western industrialized countries show at least some bulimic behaviors, such as occasional purging (Makino, Tsuboi, & Dennerstein, 2004; National Institute of Mental Health [NIMH], 2001b). Many more are sufficiently concerned about their weight to diet regularly or constantly. None of these behaviors is found in countries where food is scarce (Gordon, 2001). Adolescents most at risk for bulimia are those who live in cultures where slenderness is strongly emphasized, particularly those who wish to pursue a career that demands thinness, such as dance, gymnastics, modeling, or acting (Brownell & Fairburn, 1995).

Anorexia Nervosa Anorexia nervosa is less common than bulimia but potentially more deadly. About 1 in every thousand women in the United States suffers from the disorder (Makino, Tsuboi, & Dennerstein, 2004). Anorexia nervosa is characterized by extreme di-

bulimia Eating disorder characterized by alternating periods of bingeing and purging.

anorexia nervosa Eating disorder characterized by self-starvation.

eting, intense fear of gaining weight, and obsessive exercise. The weight loss eventually produces a variety of physical symptoms associated with starvation: sleep disturbance, cessation of menstruation, insensitivity to pain, loss of hair, low blood pressure, a variety of cardiovascular problems, and reduced body temperature. Perhaps as many as 10% of people with anorexia literally starve themselves to death; others die because of some type of cardiovascular dysfunction (Litt, 1996).

Causes of Eating Disorders   Of the two eating disorders, bulimia is considerably easier to treat; people who have anorexia frequently have relapses, even after extensive treatment. Explaining either disorder has proved to be exceptionally difficult. Both bulimia and anorexia typically begin with persistent dieting, reinforcing the idea that eating disorders represent the extreme end of a continuum that includes other forms of concern about weight (Cooper, 1995; Polivy & Herman, 1995). Such a link between dieting and eating disorders is further strengthened by evidence that in countries such as Taiwan, Singapore, and China, where dieting has become a recent fad, eating disorders, which were almost never seen in the past, are becoming more common (Goleman, 1995a; Lai, Tang, & Tse, 2005). Yet a great many young women (and some young men) diet regularly, even obsessively, but never develop an actual eating disorder. Indeed, surveys suggest that only 14% of adolescent girls are actually overweight, but 36% believe that they are too fat (Centers for Disease Control, 2000). So, what moves a dieter from "normal" dieting into bulimia or anorexia?

Girls who suffer from anorexia nervosa often have a distorted body image. They see themselves as too fat even when they are severely emaciated.

Some theorists have proposed biological causes for eating disorders, such as some kind of brain dysfunction in the case of bulimia. Others argue for a psychoanalytic explanation, perhaps a fear of growing up. Childhood sexual abuse also appears to predispose girls to develop eating disorders (Perkins & Luster, 1997; Wonderlich et al., 2001). Family variables, such as the quality of a girl's parents' marriage, may also be important factors (Wade, Bulik, & Kendler, 2001).

The most promising explanation of eating disorders, however, may lie in the discrepancy between the young person's internal image of a desirable body and her perception of her own body (McGee, Hewitt, Sherry, Parkin, & Flett, 2005). This explanation is supported by cross-cultural research demonstrating that adolescents in Western societies, who have the highest rates of eating disorders, are more likely to have negative body images than adolescents in non-Western societies (Makino, Tsuboi, & Dennerstein, 2004). Moreover, some developmentalists suggest that Western culture's emphasis on thinness as a requirement for attractiveness in a woman contributes to the prevalence of eating disorders.

Recent thinking, however, has placed more emphasis on the pre-existing psychological health of people who develop eating disorders than on cultural influences. Some researchers assert that the body images of individuals who suffer from eating disorders are the result of a general tendency toward distorted thinking (Dyl, Kittler, Phillips, & Hunt, 2006). In other words, these researchers say that people who have eating disorders tend to think in distorted ways about many things, not just their bodies. From this perspective, internalized images of the "perfect" body fuel the sales of diet products among psychologically healthy people, but they trigger a far more serious outcome, a true eating disorder, in individuals who have a tendency toward thought distortion. Thus, advertising may have a more powerful effect on an adolescent who has a general tendency toward distorted perceptions of herself and others than it does on teens who tend to view themselves and others more realistically. For instance, many young women who suffer from bulimia have also been diagnosed with *borderline personality disorder*, a psychiatric disorder in which individuals have irrational, unfounded fears that those they love will abandon them, as well as a host of other distorted perceptions (Halmi, 2003).

Longitudinal evidence seems to support this view. One study of young women who had been diagnosed with anorexia in adolescence, 94% of whom had recovered from their eating disorders, found that they were far more likely than the general population to suffer from a variety of mental disorders (Nilsson, Gillberg, Gillberg, & Rastam, 1999). Estimates of the proportion of young women who suffer from eating disorders and who also meet the criteria for some other type of psychiatric disorder range as high as 74% (Milos, Spindler, & Schnyder, 2004). An unusually high proportion of them, nearly 25%, have been diagnosed with *obsessive-compulsive disorder*, a disorder that involves an excessive need for control (American Psychiatric Association, 2000; Milos, Spindler, Ruggiero, Klaghofer, & Schnyder, 2002). These findings suggest that, for many teens, eating disorders may be a manifestation of some larger problem.

Learning Objective 15.8
What factors predispose teens to major depressive disorder?

Depression

You might be surprised to learn that, in some cases, emotional disorders in children are manifested as behaviors that are consistent with the criteria for attention deficit hyperactivity disorder and oppositional-defiant disorder (see *Thinking about Research*). Consequently, when children have behavior problems, mental health professionals often must rule out an emotional disorder as a possible cause before giving the child a diagnosis of ADHD, ODD, or childhood-onset conduct disorder. In addition, a child can be suffering from both a behavior disorder and **depression**, or feelings of sadness and despair that persist for more than 6 months (DSM-IV TR, 2000)

Defining the Problem   For many years, psychiatrists took the position that children or adolescents did not experience significant depression. This turned out to be quite wrong. Researchers have found abundant evidence that depression is actually quite common in adolescence and occurs at least occasionally among younger children. When a depressed mood lasts 6 months or longer and is accompanied by other symptoms, such as disturbances of sleeping and eating and difficulty concentrating, it is usually referred to as **clinical depression** or **major depressive disorder** (MDD). Although about 10% of children express feelings of deep sadness at some time or another, true clinical depression is very rare prior to adolescence. However, surveys and case studies suggest that, at any given time, 18% to 30% of adolescents in the United States are in the midst of an enduring depression, with about 6% meeting the criteria for MDD (CDC, 2006; Saluja et al., 2004).

depression A combination of sad mood and difficulty carrying out daily functions.

clinical depression (major depressive disorder) A combination of sad mood, sleeping and eating disturbances, and difficulty concentrating that lasts 6 months or longer.

Both depressed mood and significant clinical depressions rise in frequency in adolescence.

Pediatric Bipolar Disorder

As you may know, 1% to 3% of adults suffer from a mood disorder called *bipolar disorder (BD)*. Adults who have BD alternate between periods of deep despair and *mania*. A person in a manic state has a great deal of energy, tends to be impulsive, has a reduced need for sleep, and exhibits high activity levels.

While it is generally agreed that BD is sometimes found in adolescents, the notion that school-aged children can be diagnosed with BD is controversial (Harris, 2005). The difficulty with applying the BD diagnosis to children is that mania has been found to exist only in individuals who have completed pubertal development (Harris, 2005). However, over the past 15 years, a robust debate has arisen among mental health professionals about the claim that, in childhood, mania is manifested as episodes of explosive rage (Faedda, Baldessarini, & Suppes, 1995; NIMH, 2001a; Wozniak et al., 2005). Children who exhibit such episodes along with periods of depression are said to suffer from a form of BD called *pediatric*

bipolar disorder (PBD). However, there are many professionals who doubt the validity of the PBD diagnosis.

Developmentalists who are skeptical of the PBD diagnosis argue that most children who exhibit bouts of destructive rage are simply reeling from the effects of multiple risk factors rather than exhibiting a childhood form BD. Specifically, say critics, children who are diagnosed with PBD are those who have difficult temperaments, suffer from extreme forms of developmental problems such as ADHD and/or ODD, and have been exposed to stress-inducing traumas such as family disruption (Harris, 2005). Moreover, they point out that, in adulthood, bipolar disorder is stable over the lifespan, but longitudinal studies show that children who are diagnosed with PBD rarely grow into adults who fit the criteria for BD (Harris, 2005).

The strongest arguments against PBD are proposed by developmentalists who object to the use of powerful psychiatric drugs such as lithium to treat children who are diagnosed with the pro-

posed disorder (Harris, 2005; Olfman, 2006). These critics note that little is known about the effects of these drugs on the developing brain. Moreover, they point out that reliance on medications may cause parents not to receive other therapeutic interventions that might be helpful in managing their children's difficult behavior. They strongly believe that a great deal more research is needed both on proposed diagnostic criteria and on the effects of psychiatric drugs on development before mental health professionals begin to routinely apply the PBD diagnosis.

Questions for Critical Analysis

1. What is the significance of the finding that children with PBD rarely display BD in adulthood?
2. What kind of study would have to be done to determine how psychiatric drugs affect the developing brain? Look back at the discussion of research ethics in Chapter 1 and make a determination regarding the ethical requirements of such a study.

As many as 90% of teens who suffer a major depressive episode experience a recurrence within 2 years (Cicchetti & Toth, 1998). Further, depression has serious consequences. For one thing, depression can interfere with learning by slowing down the speed at which the brain processes information (Calhoun & Dickerson Mayes, 2005). Depressed teens are more likely than their nondepressed peers to use drugs (Rey, Sawyer, Raphael, Patton, & Lynskey, 2002). And a significant portion of teens with depression also say that they think about suicide (Fennig et al., 2005). In one longitudinal study of youths growing up in a working-class neighborhood in the United States, one-fifth of those who had had a period of serious depression by age 18 had also attempted suicide (Reinherz et al., 1993).

Interestingly, during the preadolescent years, boys and girls are about equally likely to be unhappy or depressed; however, beginning somewhere between ages 13 and 15, girls are twice as likely to report high or chronic levels of depression. This sex difference persists throughout adulthood and has been found in a number of industrialized countries and among African Americans, Hispanic Americans, and Caucasian Americans (DSM-IV TR, 2000).

Causes of Depression   Where does such depression come from, and why do girls experience more of it? The search for the developmental pathways leading to later depression begins with the clear finding that children growing up with depressed parents are much more likely than are those growing up with nondepressed parents to develop depression themselves (Eley et al., 2004). Of course, this finding could indicate a genetic factor, a possibility supported by at least a few studies of twins and adopted children (Petersen et al., 1993). Or, this link between parental and child depression could be explained in terms of the changes in the parent-child interaction that are caused by the parent's depression.

However, family and twin studies do not explain why the risk of depression increases in adolescence. Neuroimaging studies show that the sudden spike in depression rates in early adolescence may be related to some kind of dysfunction in the pituitary gland that is associated with the onset of puberty (McMaster & Kusumakar, 2004). Pituitary dysfunction, in turn, may cause adolescents to be more sensitive to family stressors than younger children are. Any combination of stresses—such as the parents' divorce, the death of a parent or another loved person, the father's loss of job, a move, a change of schools, or lack of sleep—increases the likelihood of depression or other kinds of emotional distress to a greater degree among adolescents than among children (Compas, Ey, & Grant, 1993; Fredriksen, Rhodes, Reddy, & Way, 2004).

Learning Objective 15.9

What risk factors are associated with teen suicide?

Adolescent Suicide

In some teens, sadly, the suicidal thoughts that often accompany depression lead to action. Surveys suggest that 17% of high school students in the United States have thought seriously about taking their own lives, and 2–8% have actually attempted suicide (CDC, 2007). A very small proportion of teens, about 10 out of every 100,000, succeed in killing themselves (CDC, 2007). However, public health experts point out that many teen deaths, such as those that result from single-car crashes, may be counted as accidental but are actually suicide (NCIPC, 2000).

Even though depression is more common among girls than boys, the likelihood of succeeding in committing suicide is almost five times as high among adolescent boys as among adolescent girls (Heron, 2007). In contrast, suicide *attempts* are estimated to be three times more common in girls than in boys (CDC, 2007). Girls, more often than boys, use less successful methods, such as self-poisoning.

The suicide rate is also nearly twice as high among Whites as among non-Whites, except for Native American youth, who attempt and commit suicide at higher rates than any other group (Heron, 2007). The rate among Native American teen males is 26.3 per 100,000 per year, compared with about 13 per 100,000 among Caucasian American teen males. Similarly, Hispanic American teen males are more likely to attempt suicide than Whites, although the rate of completed suicide among them is lower (NCIPC, 2000).

It is obviously very difficult to uncover the contributing factors in completed suicides, because the individuals are no longer available to be interviewed. Nonetheless, it does seem clear that some kind of significant psychopathology is virtually a universal ingredient, including but not restricted to depression. Behavior problems such as aggression are also common in the histories of completed suicides, as is a family history of psychiatric disorder or suicide, or a pattern of drug or alcohol abuse (Fennig et al., 2005; Garland & Zigler, 1993; Glowinski et al., 2001). In addition, psychologists suggest at least three other important elements (Shaffer, Garland, Gould, Fisher, & Trautman, 1988; Swedo et al., 1991):

- *Some triggering stressful event.*   Studies of suicides suggest that the triggering event is often a disciplinary crisis with the parents or some rejection or humiliation, such as breaking up with a girlfriend or boyfriend or failure in a valued activity.

- *An altered mental state.*   Such a state might be an attitude of hopelessness, reduced inhibitions from alcohol consumption, or rage.

- *An opportunity.*   For example, a loaded gun available in the house or a bottle of sleeping pills in the parents' medicine cabinet creates an opportunity for a teen to carry out suicidal plans.

Suicide prevention efforts have focused on education, such as providing training to teachers or to teenagers on how to identify students who are at risk for suicide, in the hope that vulnerable individuals might be helped before they make an attempt. For example, self-mutilating behavior such as carving the skin with sharp objects is correlated with extreme feelings of loneliness and hopelessness, two emotions that often lead to suicide (Guertin, Lloyd-Richardson, Spirito, Donaldson, & Boergers, 2001). Thus, teachers who observe such behavior or its effects should refer students to school counselors.

Other professionals who work with teenagers should also take an active role in suicide prevention. For example, checklists have been developed to help physicians and nurses screen adolescents for potential suicide risk when they visit clinics for routine health care (Gould et al., 2005). Further, because teens who have been arrested attempt and complete suicide at higher rates than their peers, many experts on youth suicide recommend that adolescents be formally screened for suicide risk by a mental health professional within 24 hours of an arrest (Gallagher & Dobrin, 2005).

Special training in coping skills has also been offered to students, so that they might be able to find a nonlethal solution to their problems. Unfortunately, most such programs appear to be ineffective in changing student attitudes or knowledge (Shaffer, Garland, Vieland, Underwood, & Busner, 1991). These discouraging results are not likely to improve until psychologists know a great deal more about the developmental pathways that lead to this particular form of psychopathology.

Antidepressants are often prescribed for depressed teens who are considered to be at high risk for suicide (de Angelis, 2004). Most studies have shown that these medications can be just as effective in treating depression in adolescents as in adults (Findling, Feeny, Stansbrey, Delporto-Bedoya, & Demeter, 2004). However, in the United States, these drugs have yet to be approved by the Food and Drug Administration for treatment of depression in teenagers (de Angelis, 2004). Further, a large-scale British study found that antidepressants may actually increase the risk of suicide in some teens. These findings prompted the FDA to issue a warning against the routine use of these drugs with adolescents (U.S. Food and Drug Administration, 2004).

Atypical Intellectual and Social Development

You may recall that, earlier in this chapter, we noted that some types of atypical development involve children's intellectual abilities. Some cause children to lag behind their peers. Others cause children to outpace them in cognitive functioning.

Mental Retardation

Learning Objective 15.10
What are the characteristics of children with mental retardation?

Mental retardation, or MR (also referred to by many educators today as *intellectual disability* or more generally as *developmental disability*), is normally diagnosed when a child has an IQ score below 70 and significant problems in adaptive behavior, such as an inability to dress or feed himself or a problem getting along with others or adjusting to the demands of a regular school classroom (MacMillan & Reschly, 1997). Thus, a low IQ score is a necessary but not sufficient condition for a diagnosis of mental retardation. Low IQ scores are customarily divided into several ranges, and different labels are attached to children in each range, as you can see in Table 15.4 on page 414.

Cognitive Functioning of Children with Mental Retardation

Some researchers interested in information processing have tried to understand normal intellectual processing by looking at the ways in which the thinking of children with mental retardation differs from that of children with normal IQs (Bray, Fletcher, & Turner, 1997; Calhoun & Dickerson Mayes, 2005; Campione, Brown, & Ferrara, 1982; DeLoache & Brown, 1987). This research leads to several major conclusions about children with MR:

- They think and react more slowly than children with normal IQs.
- They think concretely and have difficulty with abstract reasoning.

mental retardation An intellectual disability defined most often as an IQ below 70 combined with poor adaptive behavior.

Table 15.4 Categories of Mental Retardation

Classification	IQ Range	Percentage of Those with Mental Retardation	Characteristics of Persons at Each Level
Mild	55–70	90%	Are able to grasp learning skills up to sixth-grade level. May become self-supporting and can be profitably employed in various vocational occupations.
Moderate	40–55	6%	Probably are not able to grasp more than second-grade academic skills but can learn self-help skills and some social and academic skills. May work in sheltered workshops.
Severe	25–40	3%	Can be trained in basic health habits; can learn to communicate verbally. Learn through repetitive habit training.
Profound	Below 25	1%	Have rudimentary motor development. May learn very limited self-help skills.

Those with mental retardation (1–3%)

Moderate, severe, and profound (10%)

Mild (90%)

Total U.S. population

Total population of people with mental retardation

Source: Wood et al., WORLD OF PSYCHOLOGY, © 2008. Reproduced by permission of Pearson Education, Inc.

- They require much more complete and repeated instruction in order to learn new information or a new strategy. (Children with normal IQs may discover a strategy for themselves or be able to proceed with only incomplete instruction.)

- They do not generalize or transfer something they have learned in one situation to a new problem or task. They thus appear to lack those "executive" functions that enable older children and adults with normal IQs to compare a new problem to familiar ones or to scan through a repertoire of strategies until they find one that will work.

- Intellectual deficits often interfere with the development of social skills, such as the ability to recognize and respond to facial expressions (Moore, 2001).

On simple, concrete tasks, children with mental retardation learn in ways and at rates similar to those of younger children with normal IQs. The more significant deficit is in higher-order processing. These children can learn, but they do so more slowly and require far more exhaustive and task-specific instruction.

It's important to note, too, that many of the things you have learned about child development apply to children with mental retardation. Children with intellectual disabilities go through the same Piagetian stages, although at a slower rate, and their motivational characteristics are very much like those of normal children (Blair, Greenberg, & Crnic, 2001). For example, on tasks that normal children are highly intrinsically motivated to learn, such as learning how to play a new video game, children with mental retardation are just as likely to display high levels of intrinsic motivation. And for tasks for which normal children often require extrinsic motivation, such as doing homework, children with intellectual disabilities are also likely to require parent- or teacher-provided incentives.

Causes of Retardation   Children with mental retardation can be divided into two distinct subgroups, depending on the cause of the retardation. The smaller subset, making up about 15–25% of the total, includes children whose retardation is caused by some evident physical damage. Included in this group are those with a genetic anomaly, such as Down syndrome, that probably causes parts of the brain associated with learning to function poorly (Pennington, Moon, Edgin, Stedron, & Nadel, 2003). Damage resulting in retardation can also be caused by a disease, a teratogen such as prenatal alcohol, or severe prenatal malnutrition; it can occur during the birth itself, such as from prolonged anoxia. A small subset of children acquire mental retardation as a result of an injury suffered after birth, often in an auto accident or a fall.

The majority of children with mental retardation show no obvious signs of brain damage or other physical disorder. In these cases, the cause of the retardation is some combination of genetic and environmental conditions. Typically, these children come from families in which the parents have low IQs or mental illness or the home life is highly disorganized or emotionally or cognitively deprived. To be sure, in these cases, too, the child's intellectual disability might have been exacerbated by the effects of teratogens or other hazards, such as prenatal alcohol or elevated levels of prenatal or postnatal lead, but it is not thought to be attributable solely to such physical causes.

Large-scale studies have shown quite conclusively that the several causes of retardation are not distributed evenly across the range of low IQ scores. The lower the IQ, the more likely it is that the cause is physical rather than environmental (Broman et al., 1987). One implication of this conclusion is that interventions such as the enriched child care and preschool Ramey devised (see Figure 7.7 on page 195) are more likely to be effective in countering the effects of family culture in causing milder retardation. This is not to say that educators should ignore environmental enrichment or specific early training for children whose retardation has a physical cause. Greater breadth of experience will enrich their lives and may help to bring their level of functioning closer to the top end of their "reaction range," allowing them to function much more independently (Baumeister, 2006).

Learning Disabilities

Learning Objective 15.11
How do learning disabilities affect children's development?

Some children with normal IQs and essentially good adaptive functioning nonetheless have difficulty learning to read, write, or do arithmetic. The typical label for this problem is **learning disability (LD)**. Psychologists' definition of this problem includes the presumption that the difficulty arises from some kind of central nervous system dysfunction or damage, in much the same way that many definitions of ADHD assume some kind of biological underpinning. In fact, some children with attention deficit disorder are also diagnosed with learning disabilities so these two sets of problems overlap (Brook & Boaz, 2005). This overlap is far from complete, however, as most children diagnosed with learning disabilities do not suffer from ADHD.

Diagnosing Learning Disabilities Diagnosing a learning disability is extremely tricky, and such a diagnosis is always a residual one—that is, a diagnosis arrived at only by eliminating other possible explanations of a problem. "Disability" is the label normally applied to the problem experienced by a child of average or above average intelligence, with normal vision and hearing, who has significant difficulty absorbing, processing, remembering, or expressing some type of information, such as written words or numbers. Children diagnosed with learning disabilities do not show persistent or obvious emotional disturbance, and their difficulties cannot be attributed to any clear cultural or educational deprivation. Thus, the working definition focuses on what learning disability is not, rather than what it is. Furthermore, the specific form of a learning disability may vary widely, with some children displaying difficulties in reading only, some having trouble with reading and spelling (such as the boy whose writing sample is shown in Figure 15.1 on page 416), and others having more difficulty with arithmetic.

Because of such fuzziness in the definition, there is a good deal of dispute about just how many children really have a learning disability. Practically speaking, however, the learning disability label is used very broadly within school systems (at least in the United States) to describe children who have unexpected or otherwise unexplainable difficulty with schoolwork, particularly reading. About 6.5% of all children in the United States are currently labeled in this way (Herring, McGrath, & Buckley, 2007).

learning disability (LD) A term broadly used to describe an unexpected or unexplained problem in learning to read, spell, or calculate and more precisely used to refer to a neurological dysfunction that causes such effects.

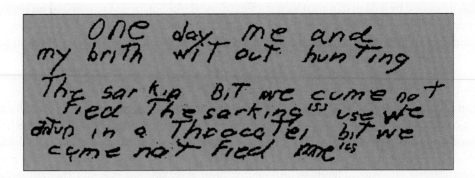

Figure 15.1 Writing Sample by a Child with a Learning Disability

This is part of a story written by 13-year-old Luke, who has a significant and persistent learning disability. The little numbers next to some of the words are Luke's word counts. They show that despite his severe writing handicap, his counting abilities are intact.

(*Source*: From *Learning Disabilities: A Psychological Perspective* by Sylvia Farnham-Diggory, p. 61, Copyright © 1978 by Sylvia Farnham-Diggory. By permission of the author.)

Causes of Learning Disabilities   Given such problems with the definition, it's not surprising that the search for causes of learning disabilities has been fraught with difficulties. The most central problem has been with the fundamental assumption that learning disabilities have a neurological basis. The difficulty is that children so labeled (like children with ADHD) rarely show signs of major brain damage on standard neurological tests—perhaps because many of the children are mislabeled or perhaps because the brain dysfunction is too subtle to detect with standard tests.

School can be a discouraging and frustrating place for a child with a learning disability.

Happily, brain-imaging techniques now may make it possible to uncover subtle, but very real and significant, neurological differences between children with learning disabilities and those who are good readers. A study by Sally Shaywitz and her colleagues (1998) used functional magnetic resonance imaging (fMRI) to identify the parts of the brain that become active when an individual is performing various reading-related tasks. When skillful adult readers in the study were working on these tasks, Shaywitz found that a series of brain regions were activated in turn, beginning with sections of the frontal lobe and then moving backward in the brain. Among the adults with learning disabilities who participated in this study, however, only the frontal lobe was fully activated, suggesting that their brains functioned quite differently on these tasks. This difference in brain activation patterns was especially vivid when the participants were working on tasks that required them to identify individual sounds, such as in a rhyming task—a finding that makes very good sense in light of all the research you read about in Chapter 8 that links good reading to phonological awareness.

In subsequent research, Shaywitz and her colleagues have found similar patterns of neurological activity in the brains of children with reading disabilities (Shaywitz, Mody, & Shaywitz, 2006). Such studies suggest that the brains of both children and adults with learning disabilities may not be "wired" in a way that allows them to efficiently analyze sounds into their phonological components. These findings may explain why interventions that provide explicit information about sound-symbol connections (which are typically not emphasized in conventional reading curricula), along with ample opportunities to practice newly acquired skills, have been found to be highly effective in helping people with learning disabilities become more fluent readers (Shaywitz, 2008).

Giftedness

Learning Objective 15.12

What are the characteristics of gifted children?

Some children lie at the other end of the intellectual continuum and are considered gifted. Finding good programs for such children is a continuing dilemma. A child named Michael, described by Halbert Robinson, is an extreme example of a gifted child:

> When Michael was 2 years and 3 months old, the family visited our laboratory. At that time, they described a youngster who had begun speaking at age 5 months and by 6 months had exhibited a vocabulary of more than 50 words. He started to read English when he was 13 months old. In our laboratory he spoke five languages and could read in three of them. He understood addition, subtraction, multiplication, division, and square root, and he was fascinated by a broad range of scientific constructs. He loved to make puns, frequently bilingual ones. (1981, p. 63)

> Michael's IQ score on the Stanford-Binet was in excess of 180 at age 2; 2 years later, when Michael was 4½, he performed as well as a 12-year-old on the test and was listed as having an IQ score beyond 220.

Definitions and Labels   We can certainly all agree that Michael should be labeled as gifted, but defining the term precisely is difficult (Cramond, 2004). A number of authors (e.g., Gardner, 2002) have argued that people with exceptional specific talents, such as musical, artistic, mathematical, or spatial abilities, should be classed as gifted, along with those with very high IQ scores. This broadening of the definition of giftedness has been widely accepted among theorists, who agree that there are many kinds of exceptional ability, each of which may reflect unusual speed or efficiency with one or another type of cognitive function.

Within school systems, however, giftedness is still typically defined entirely by IQ test scores, such as all scores above 130 or 140. Some developmentalists suggest that it may be useful to divide the group of high-IQ children into two sets, the "garden-variety gifted," who have high IQ scores (perhaps 130 to 150) but no extraordinary ability in any one area,

Elizabeth Lovance of Hartland, Wisconsin (on the right) skipped several grades and graduated from high school at age 14. She said of her experience of being accelerated through school: "I would have had a mental breakdown if I had remained where I was."

and the "highly gifted" (like Michael) with extremely high IQ scores and/or remarkable skill in one or more areas—a group Ellen Winner (von Károlyi & Winner, 2005) calls the profoundly gifted. These two groups may have quite different experiences at home and in school.

Cognitive and Social Functioning   Gifted children show speedy and efficient processing on simple tasks and flexible use of strategies on more complex tasks. They learn quickly and transfer that learning broadly, and they have remarkably good problem-solving skills—they often leap directly to a solution that requires less gifted individuals many intermediate steps to figure out (von Károlyi & Winner, 2005). Further, they seem to have unusually good metacognitive skills: They know what they know and what they don't know, and they spend more time than average-IQ children in planning how to go about solving some problem (Shore & Dover, 2004). Winner also notes that profoundly gifted children also have a "rage to master," a powerful drive to immerse themselves in learning in some area.

Whether such advanced intellectual abilities transfer to social situations is not so well established. Many parents are concerned about placing their gifted child in a higher grade in school because of fears that the child will not be able to cope socially; others have assumed that rapid development in one area should be linked to rapid development in all areas.

One famous and remarkable early study of gifted children, by Lewis Terman, pointed to the latter conclusion. In the 1920s, Terman selected 1,500 children with high IQ scores from the California school system. These children—now adults in their 90s—have been followed regularly throughout their lives (e.g., Feldhusen, 2003; Holahan, 1988; Terman, 1925; Terman & Oden, 1959). Terman found that the gifted children he studied were better off than their less gifted classmates in many ways other than school performance. They were healthier, they had wider-ranging interests, and they were more successful in later life. Both the boys and the girls in this study went on to complete many more years of education than was typical in their era, and most had successful careers as adults.

Most research suggests that gifted children have about the same risk of social or emotional problems as normal-IQ children, which means that most are well adjusted and socially adept (Gottfried, Gottfried, Bathurst, & Guerin, 1994; Vida, 2005). Optimism about the social robustness of gifted children may have to be tempered somewhat, however, in the case of the profoundly gifted subgroup, such as those with IQs above 180. These children are so different from their peers that they are likely to be seen as strange or disturbing. They are often socially solitary and introverted as well as fiercely independent and nonconforming; they have difficulties finding peers who can play at their level and are often quite unpopular with classmates (Kennedy, 1995). Also on the negative side of the ledger is the fact that many gifted children are so bored by school that they become disengaged and even drop out, often because their school district does not allow acceleration in grade or has no special programs for the gifted. Given the fact that skipping grades does not seem to be linked to social maladjustment (and is linked to better achievement among the gifted), it seems to make very good sense to encourage accelerated schooling, if only to help ward off extreme boredom in the gifted child.

Pervasive Developmental Disorders

Many of the atypical patterns of development we have discussed so far may indirectly cause difficulties in children's social relationships. Children with mental retardation, for example, may have problems keeping up with the play interests of children their age. For instance, they may develop the capacity for pretend play at a later age than other children. Thus, a child with mental retardation may be able to build social relationships by playing with other children, but in most cases the children he plays with will be younger than he is.

By contrast, the defining feature of the group of disorders known as **pervasive developmental disorders (PDDs)**, or *autism spectrum disorders*, is the inability to form social relationships. In PDDs, the lack of social skills is itself the disorder rather than an indirect consequence of another atypical developmental pattern. The social difficulties of individuals with PDDs usually derive from their poor communication skills and inability to understand the reciprocal, or give-and-take, aspects of social relationships. Many of these children also exhibit odd, repetitive behaviors, such as hand-flapping. Some develop attachments to objects and become extremely anxious—or even enraged—when separated from them. Others engage in self-injurious behaviors such as head-banging. In the United States, just under 1% of all children have some kind of PDD (Kagan & Herschkowitz, 2005; NIMH, 2001b). The rates are similar in European countries (Lauritsen et al., 2004). The two most frequently diagnosed PDDs are *autistic disorder* and *Asperger's disorder*.

The distinguishing symptoms that are exhibited by children with **autistic disorder** include limited or nonexistent language skills, an inability to engage in reciprocal social relationships, and a severely limited range of interests (DSM-IV TR, 2000). Most are also mentally retarded, easily distracted, slow to respond to external stimuli, and highly impulsive (Calhoun & Dickerson Mayes, 2005). Some children are helped with symptoms of distractibility and impulsivity by the kinds of stimulant medications that are often prescribed for children with ADHD (Posey, Puntney, Sasher, Kem, & McDougle, 2004).

pervasive developmental disorders (PDDs) A group of disorders in which children exhibit severe disturbances in social relationships.

autistic disorder A disorder in which children have much more limited language skills than others of the same age, an inability to engage in reciprocal social relationships, and a severely limited range of interests.

Many parents of children with autism report having noticed their children's peculiarities during the first few months of life. What strikes these parents is their infants' apparent lack of interest in people. However, in most cases, the disorder is not definitively diagnosed until children's failure to develop normal language skills makes it apparent that they are on an atypical developmental path. This usually occurs between the first and second birthday.

Children with autism who are capable of some degree of normal verbal communication and whose cognitive impairments are minimal are often called *high-functioning*. However, these children's communicative abilities are quite poor because of their limited ability to engage in social cognition. For example, most never fully develop a theory of mind (Peterson, Wellman, & Liu, 2005). As a result, they typically fail to understand how their statements are perceived by listeners and are incapable of engaging in normal conversations. In addition, the pitch and intonation of their speech is often abnormal. Some utter repetitive phrases, often in robot-like fashion, that are inappropriate for the situation in which they occur.

Many children with autism display impulsive, bizarre behaviors such as the writhing behavior in which this boy appears to be engaged. They are often unresponsive to the outside world while exhibiting these behaviors, and some injure themselves during these episodes.

Asperger's disorder is often thought of as a mild form of autistic disorder. The diagnostic criteria for it are highly similar to those for autistic disorder (DSM-IV TR, 2000). However, children with Asperger's disorder have age-appropriate language and cognitive skills and often obtain high scores on IQ tests. Despite their normal language skills, children with Asperger's disorder are incapable of engaging in normal social relationships because, like children with autism who are high-functioning, they usually do not develop the capacity to understand others' thoughts, feelings, and motivations (a theory of mind).

Because of their normal language and cognitive skills, most children with Asperger's disorder don't stand out from their peers until their second or third birthday, when other children begin to engage in cooperative play. However, normal children of this age vary widely, so children with Asperger's disorder are often assumed to be "late bloomers" or "going through a phase." Some are misdiagnosed with ADHD (Pozzi, 2003). Upon entering school, though, many begin to exhibit the odd behaviors that most people associate with pervasive developmental disorders. For example, they may become intensely focused on memorizing things that have little meaning to them, such as airline flight schedules. They may also engage in obsessive behaviors, such as counting and recounting the number of squares on a checkered tablecloth. By school age, their inability to form friendships like those of other children their age is usually quite apparent.

Like ADHD, pervasive developmental disorders were once thought to be the result of poor parenting. However, it is now well established that all of these disorders are of neurological origin (Kagan & Herschkowitz, 2005). However, there is no single brain anomaly or dysfunction that is associated with PDDs. Even for the individual disorders within this category, researchers have not found a single definitive neurological marker. In a few cases, specific genetic defects are known to lead to atypical neurological development and, in turn, cause children to develop pervasive developmental disorders. For instance, *fragile-X syndrome*, as you may recall from Chapter 2, can cause autistic disorder. For the most part, however, the cause of PDDs remains a mystery (Kagan & Herschkowitz, 2005).

Whatever the neurological mechanisms involved in PDDs, twin studies suggest that these disorders are hereditary. When one identical twin is diagnosed with a PDD, there is a 70% to 90% chance that the other twin will be diagnosed as well (Zoghbi, 2003). A wide variety of factors interact with genetic predispositions to trigger the appearance of these disorders (Rutter, 2005). When mothers are depressed, for example, infants have an increased risk of developing the symptoms of a PDD (Pozzi, 2003). However, media reports suggesting that immunizations may cause PDDs have proven to be unfounded (Rutter, 2005a).

Asperger's disorder A disorder in which children possess the other characteristics of autistic disorder but have intact language and cognitive skills.

You may have heard that vaccines containing a form of mercury called *thimerosal* are suspected of causing autism. However, researchers generally agree that the vaccine hypothesis is unfounded (Rutter, 2005a). In one important study, researchers tracked the development of more than half a million Danish children for several years in order to compare rates of autism among those who received vaccines with thimerosal and those who did not receive such immunizations (Madsen et al., 2002). Rates of autism were found to be nearly identical in the two groups. Furthermore, these researchers found that autism rates actually increased in Denmark after thimerosal was removed from all vaccines in the late 1990s (Madsen et al., 2003). Studies in the United States and Canada show a similar pattern. Although thimerosal has been removed from the vaccines that are routinely administered to infants and children, the prevalence of autism in both countries has continued to increase (Fombonne, Zakarian, Bennett, Meng, & McLean-Heywood, 2006; Schechter & Grether, 2008). Nevertheless, sensational media reports about the hypothesized link between immunizations and autism have contributed to the kinds of fears of vaccines that you read about earlier in the chapter.

Among some children with pervasive developmental disorders, symptoms actually get worse as the children get older (Sigman & McGovern, 2005). Sadly, the minimal language and social skills they appear to acquire through intensive educational programs in the early years of life sometimes deteriorate markedly before they reach adulthood. Many adults with these disorders live in sheltered environments and are employed in jobs that require minimal competencies.

The language skills of a child with a PDD are the best indicator of his or her prognosis in adulthood (DSM-IV TR, 2000). Consequently, children with Asperger's disorder have the best hope of attaining independence in adulthood. Thanks to their language and cognitive skills, many are capable of high levels of academic achievement. Indeed, expert reviews of the medical records of one of the most eminent German writers of the 20th century, Robert Walser, suggest that he probably suffered from Asperger's disorder (Fitzgerald, 2004). His social relationships, however, like those of almost all individuals with this disorder, continued to be impaired throughout his life.

Learning Objective 15.14
What have researchers learned about the effectiveness of inclusive education for children with disabilities?

Schooling for Atypical Children

Children who display atypical development require teachers and schools to make special adaptations. In 1975, largely as a result of pressure from parents of atypical or disabled children, Congress passed Public Law (PL) 94-142, called the Education for All Handicapped Children Act. It specifies that every child in the United States must be given access to an appropriate education in the least restrictive environment possible. PL 94-142 does not say that every child with a disability must be educated full-time in a regular classroom. The law allows schools to offer a continuum of services, including separate schools or special classrooms, although it also indicates that a child should be placed in a regular classroom as a first choice and removed from that setting only if her disability is such that she cannot be satisfactorily educated there. Table 15.5 lists the categories of disabilities covered by the law as well as the percentage of school children with disabilities in each category.

PL 94-142 and the supplementary laws that followed it (including the Education of the Handicapped Act of 1986 and the Individuals with Disabilities Education Act of 1990, renewed in 2004) rest most centrally on the philosophical view that children with disabilities have a right to participate in normal school environments (e.g., Stainback & Stainback, 1985). Proponents have further argued that such **inclusive education** aids the child with a disability by integrating him into the nondisabled world, thus facilitating the development of important social skills as well as providing more appropriate academic challenges than are often found in separate classrooms or special programs for the disabled (Friend & Bursuck, 2006). Advocates of inclusion are convinced that children with mild mental retardation and those with learning disabilities will show greater academic achievement if they are in regular classrooms.

Schools and school districts differ widely in the specific model of inclusion they use, although virtually all models involve a team of educators, including the classroom teacher, one

inclusive education General term for education programs that assign children with physical, mental, or emotional disabilities to regular classrooms and that provide any special services required by the child in that classroom.

Table 15.5   Disabilities for Which Children in the United States Received Special Education Services

Disability Category	Percentage of Special Education Students in the Category	Description of Disability
Learning Disability	46	Achievement 2 or more years behind expectations based on intelligence tests Example: A fourth-grader with an average IQ who is reading at a first-grade level
Communication Disorder in Speech or Language	19	A disorder of speech or language that affects a child's education; can be a problem with speech or an impairment in the comprehension or use of any aspect of language Example: A first-grader who makes errors in pronunciation like those of a 4-year-old and can't connect sounds and symbols
Mental Retardation	9	IQ below 70, together with impairments in adaptive functions Example: A school-aged child with an IQ lower than 70 who is not fully toilet-trained and who needs special instruction in both academic and self-care skills
Other Health Impairments	9	A health problem that interferes with a child's education Example: A child with severe asthma who misses several weeks of school each year
Serious Emotional Disturbance	8	An emotional or behavior disorder that interferes with a child's education Example: A child whose severe temper tantrums cause him to be removed from the classroom every day
Autistic Spectrum Disorders	3	Behavior consistent with the criteria for any of the various autistic spectrum disorders in the DSM-IV TR (2000) Example: A child with Asperger's syndrome who can manage the cognitive demands of regular classes but who needs help with communication and social skills
Multiple Disabilities	2	Need for special instruction and ongoing support in two or more areas to benefit from education Example: A child with cerebral palsy who is also deaf, who thus requires both physical and instructional adaptations
Hearing Impairment	1.2	A hearing problem that interferes with a child's education Example: A child who needs a sign-language interpreter in the classroom
Orthopedic Impairment	1	An orthopedic handicap that requires special adaptations Example: A child in a wheelchair who needs a special physical education class
Visual Impairment	0.4	Impaired visual acuity or a limited field of vision that interferes with education Example: A blind child who needs training in the use of Braille to read and write

Source: U.S. Census Bureau, 2008b.

or more special education teachers, classroom aides, and sometimes volunteers. Some schools follow a plan called a *pull-out program*, in which the student with a disability is placed in a regular classroom only part of each day, with the remainder of the time spent working with a special education teacher in a special class or resource room. More common are full-inclusion systems in which the child spends the entire school day in a regular class but receives help from volunteers, aides, or special education teachers who come to the classroom to work with the child there. In some districts, a group of children with disabilities may be

David, the child with Down syndrome on the left, is in an inclusive elementary school classroom, participating as fully as possible in all activities and assignments.

assigned to a single regular classroom; in others, no more than one such child is normally assigned to any one class (Friend & Bursuck, 2006).

There is little argument about the desirability of the overall goal: to provide every child with the best education possible, one that challenges the child and gives her the best possible chance to learn the basic intellectual and social skills needed to function in society. Thus, you may be surprised by the finding that teachers who have the most positive attitudes toward inclusion also have the highest burnout rates (Talmor, Reiter, & Feigin, 2005). Researchers speculate that teachers with idealistic views of inclusion probably work very hard to help students with disabilities succeed. When their efforts meet with limited success, they may suffer from feelings of failure and incompetence and may feel emotionally drained. In some schools, teachers are provided with co-teachers who carry some of the extra burdens involved in teaching a class that includes both typically developing children and children with disabilities. This practice appears to protect some teachers against burnout (Magiera & Zigmond, 2005). Moreover, students with disabilities receive much more direct instruction when both a regular teacher and a co-teacher are available.

Those of you who plan to be teachers should take note of such findings. In addition, be aware that, whatever your views on inclusion, it is a practice that is consistent with current law. Therefore, it is here to stay (Putnam, Spiegel, & Bruininks, 1995). In addition, recent changes in educational law, such as the landmark 2001 *No Child Left Behind* legislation, have raised standards with regard to what all children, including those with disabilities, are expected to learn. As a result, a growing number of children with special needs are being educated in classrooms with children who do not have disabilities (Friend & Bursuck, 2006).

Among the many varieties of inclusion programs, can features that are consistently associated with better results or poorer results be identified? This question is extremely hard to answer. For all kinds of perfectly understandable reasons, developmentalists have little of the kind of research needed to answer it. Inclusion programs vary widely in design and serve children with diverse problems. The teachers who implement them range from highly skilled and inventive to overwhelmed and unskilled. If a particular program pattern appears to work in one school, it is often difficult to tell whether it is successful because of the particular teachers involved, because of the specific characteristics of the children being served, or because the program itself is especially well designed.

Given all this, it is not surprising that clear answers to many of the questions about inclusion are still lacking. Still, educators and psychologists have struggled to summarize the information they do have, and most would agree with the following conclusions:

- Children with physical disabilities but no learning problem—such as blind children or some children with spina bifida—make the best academic progress when they are taught in the same way and in the same settings as children who do not have disabilities (Jenks, van Lieshout, & de Moor, 2008).

- For children with learning disabilities, however, full-inclusion programs may be less academically supportive than pull-out programs or resource rooms, because success for children with learning disabilities in a regular classroom depends heavily on the ability of the teacher to implement an individualized program. Co-teaching arrangements appear to be particularly helpful to children with learning disabilities (Magiera & Zigmond, 2005).

- Effective inclusion programs require that teachers be given additional training and substantial support from specialists, aides, or volunteers (Friend & Bursuck, 2006)—conditions that are sometimes not met because of budgetary or other reasons.

The above list of conclusions should convince you that there is no "magic bullet," no single solution for educators, for parents, or for children with disabilities. If you are planning to become a teacher, you will need to learn as much as possible about the needs of children with various kinds of disabilities as well as about successful strategies for teaching them; if you are a parent, you will need to inform yourself about all the educational alternatives so that you can become your child's consistent advocate within the school system.

Think Critically

- What implications for social and educational policy (if any) do you see in the fact that childhood-onset conduct disorders are likely to persist and ultimately to involve adult criminality and violence?
- Why do you think teenaged girls are more vulnerable to depression than teenaged boys are? What theory would you propose to explain the fact that girls attempt suicide more often than boys but are less likely to complete it?

Conduct Your Own Research

When a child is referred to a psychologist because her parents and teacher think she may have ADHD, the psychologist often compares the child's behavior to that of other children in the context in which it occurs. To get a feeling for how informative peer comparisons can be, ask an elementary school teacher to allow you to observe his or her class at a time when the children are supposed to be working independently. Observe a randomly selected sample of five children for a fixed period of time—say, 10 minutes each—and count the number of minutes each child spends working during the period. Be sure to watch only one child at a time. Convert your observations to percentages and average them. Next, follow the same procedure for every other child in the class. Prepare a chart showing how much each child's percentage of on-task behavior deviated from the average percentage of your randomly selected sample.

Summary

UNDERSTANDING ATYPICAL DEVELOPMENT

15.1 What kinds of problems fall within the domain of atypical development?

- Psychopathologies are most often divided into three broad groups: disorders of attention, including attention deficit hyperactivity disorder (ADHD); externalizing problems, including conduct disorders; and internalizing problems, including eating disorders and depression. Other types of atypical development affect children's intellectual and social functioning.

15.2 How do the biological, psychodynamic, learning, and cognitive perspectives explain atypical development?

- Biological theories emphasize physical causes such as genetics, hormones, and neurological functioning. Psychodynamic theorists focus on unresolved emotional conflicts, while learning theorists propose that atypical behaviors are learned. Cognitive perspectives assert that atypical development is associated with faulty thinking.

15.3 What is developmental psychopathology, and how has it changed the way psychologists approach questions about atypical development?

- Studies of psychopathology are more often being cast in a developmental framework, with emphasis on the complex pathways that lead to deviance or normality. Such an approach also emphasizes the importance of risk and protective factors, context, and a lifespan perspective.

ATTENTION PROBLEMS AND EXTERNALIZING PROBLEMS

15.4 What diagnostic labels are given to children who have attention problems?

- Attention deficit hyperactivity disorder (ADHD), the most common type of disorder of attention, includes both problems in focusing attention and excessive restlessness and activity. Long-term problems are greatest when ADHD is combined with a conduct disorder. ADHD appears to have an initial biological cause, but deviant behavioral patterns are aggravated or improved by subsequent experiences.

15.5 What behaviors are associated with oppositional defiant disorder?

- Children with oppositional defiant disorder are disobedient and hostile toward authority figures. Many children with ODD also have ADHD. Parent training is important in the treatment of ODD.

15.6 What are childhood-onset and adolescent-onset conduct disorders, and how do they differ from delinquency?

- Conduct disorders include patterns of both excess aggressiveness and delinquency. Childhood-onset conduct disorders appear to have a genetic component and are exacerbated by poor family interactions and subsequent poor peer relations. Adolescent-onset conduct disorders are less serious and often result from peer influence. Delinquent acts (lawbreaking) increase in adolescence and are found not only among children with early-onset conduct disorders but also among some teens who show a brief period of delinquency but no long-term negative consequences.

INTERNALIZING PROBLEMS

15.7 How do developmentalists define and explain eating disorders?

- Eating disorders, including bulimia and anorexia nervosa, probably result from a disordered body image. These disorders are most common in adolescent girls.

15.8 What factors predispose teens to major depressive disorder?

- Depression is another type of internalizing problem, relatively uncommon in childhood but common in adolescence. Depressed youngsters are more likely to have a family history of parental depression, to have low self-esteem, or to have a history of being ignored by peers. Depression in adolescence is about twice as common among girls as among boys. No consensus has yet been reached on the explanation for this sex difference.

15.9 What risk factors are associated with teen suicide?

- Depression sometimes leads to suicidal thoughts. Teenaged girls are more likely to attempt suicide, but teenaged boys are more likely to complete it. Risk factors for suicide include hopelessness, a triggering event, and an opportunity.

ATYPICAL INTELLECTUAL AND SOCIAL DEVELOPMENT

15.10 What are the characteristics of children with mental retardation?

- Children with mental retardation, normally defined as having an IQ below 70 combined with significant problems of adaptation, show slower development and more immature or less efficient information-processing strategies. Two types of retarded children can be identified: those whose retardation has a clear physical cause, who are overrepresented among the severely retarded, and those without physical abnormalities, whose retardation is a result of genetic causes, such as low-IQ parents and/or deprived environments, and who are overrepresented among the mildly retarded.

15.11 How do learning disabilities affect children's development?

- About 6.5% of school children in the United States are labeled as learning disabled. There is still considerable dispute about how to identify a genuine learning disability, and many children may be misclassified as learning disabled. Recent research supports the hypothesis that learning disabilities have their roots in atypical brain function, although this conclusion remains tentative.

15.12 What are the characteristics of gifted children?

- *Gifted* is a term applied to children with very high IQ or to those with unusual creativity or exceptional specific talents. Their information processing is unusually flexible and generalized. Gifted children appear to be socially well-adjusted, except for a small group who are unusually gifted and have a higher risk of psychopathology.

15.13 What behaviors are exhibited by children with pervasive developmental disorders?

- Children with pervasive developmental disorders (PDDs), also known as autism spectrum disorders, have impaired social relationships. Those who have autistic disorder have limited language skills and are often mentally retarded. Asperger's disorder is a milder form of autistic disorder in which children have normal language and cognitive skills.

SCHOOLING FOR ATYPICAL CHILDREN

15.14 What have researchers learned about the effectiveness of inclusive education for children with disabilities?

- Inclusive education, in which children with disabilities are primarily educated in regular classrooms alongside nondisabled children, is consistent with special education law in the United States. Successful programs are those that focus on including children who most benefit from learning with nondisabled peers, provide co-teachers for children with learning disabilities, and provide regular teachers with training in inclusive teaching strategies.

Key Terms

adolescent-onset conduct disorder (p. 406)

anorexia nervosa (p. 408)

Asperger's disorder (p. 419)

attention deficit hyperactivity disorder (ADHD) (p. 401)

ADHD/hyperactive/impulsive type (p. 401)

ADHD/inattentive type (p. 401)

ADHD/combined type (p. 401)

attention problems (p. 398)

atypical development (p. 397)

autistic disorder (p. 418)

bulimia (p. 408)

childhood-onset conduct disorder (p. 406)

clinical depression (major depressive disorder) (p. 410)

conduct disorder (p. 406)

delinquency (p. 407)

depression (p. 410)

developmental psychopathology (p. 400)

externalizing problems (p. 398)

inclusive education (p. 420)

internalizing problems (p. 398)

learning disability (LD) (p. 415)

mental retardation (p. 413)

oppositional defiant disorder (p. 405)

pervasive developmental disorders (PDDs) (p. 418)

psychological disorder (p. 397)

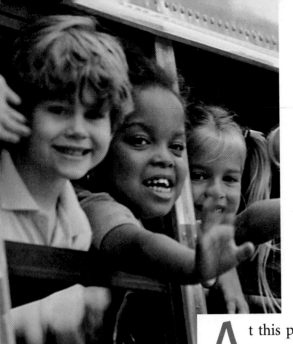

Epilogue

Putting It All Together: The Developing Child

At this point, it is likely that you know a good deal about the sequence of development of language and about sequential changes in cognitive functioning and in attachment, but you may not have a clear idea of how these different developmental sequences connect to one another. If your professor asked you to describe other developmental advances a child is making at the same time as she is first using two-word sentences, you might have a difficult time answering. This epilogue will help to "put the child back together" by looking at how aspects of development fit together chronologically.

Transitions, Consolidations, and Systems

The process of development can be thought of as being made up of a series of alternating periods of rapid growth (accompanied by disruption, or disequilibrium) and periods of comparative calm, or consolidation. Change is obviously going on all the time, from conception to death, but the evidence suggests that there are particular times when the changes pile up or when one highly significant change occurs. The change might be a major physiological development such as puberty, a highly significant cognitive change such as the beginning of symbol usage at about 18 months, or some other major shift.

Such a significant change has two related effects. First, in systems theory terms, any change inevitably affects the entire system. Thus, a rapid increase in skill in one area, such as language, demands adaptation in all parts of the developing system. Because a child learns to talk, her social interactions change, her thinking changes, and no doubt even her nervous system changes as new synapses are created and redundant or underused ones are pruned. Similarly, a child's early attachment may affect her cognitive development by altering the way she approaches new situations, and the hormonal changes of puberty often affect parent-child relations.

Second, when the system changes in such a major way, the child sometimes seems to come "unglued" for a while. The old patterns of relationships, of thinking, of talking, don't work very well anymore, and it takes a while to work out new patterns. Erikson frequently used the word *dilemma* to refer to such a period of semiupheaval. Klaus Riegel (1975) once suggested the term *developmental leaps*, which conveys nicely the sense of energy that often accompanies these pivotal periods. This epilogue will use the less vivid term *transition* to describe a time of change or upheaval and the term *consolidation* to describe an in-between time when change is more gradual. Together, these concepts may help you understand what is happening during each of the major age periods.

From Birth to 24 Months

Figure E.1 shows the various changes during the first 24 months of life. The rows of the figure correspond roughly to the chapters of this book; what you need to do now is read up and down the columns rather than just across the rows.

The overriding impression one gets of the newborn infant—despite her remarkable skills and capacities—is that she is very much on "automatic pilot." There seem to be built-in rules, or schemes, that govern the way an infant looks, listens, explores the world, and relates to others.

One of the really remarkable things about these rules, as you learned in Chapters 3 and 5, is how well designed they are to lead both the child and the caregivers into the "dance" of interaction and attachment. Think of an infant being breast-fed. The baby has the needed rooting, sucking, and swallowing reflexes to take in the milk; when the baby is nursing, the

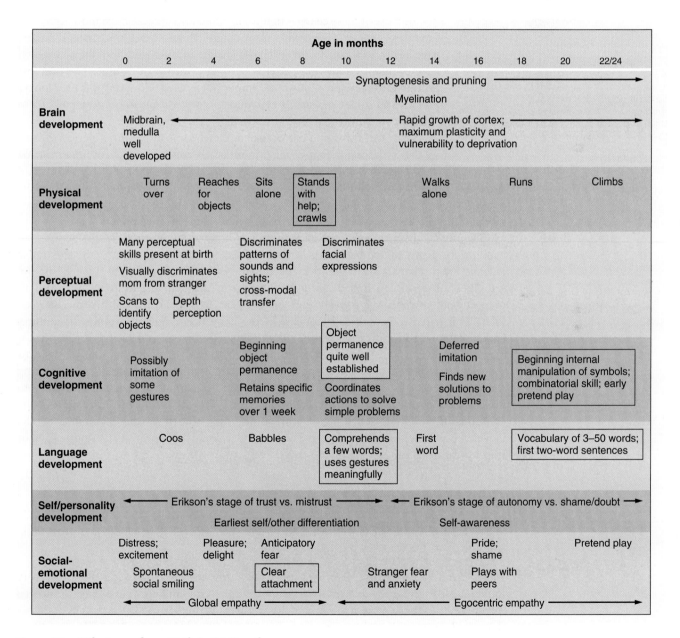

Figure E.1 Milestones from Birth to 24 Months

This summary chart shows some of the simultaneous developments during infancy. The several developmental changes that seem to be pivotal—transitional changes—are outlined in boxes.

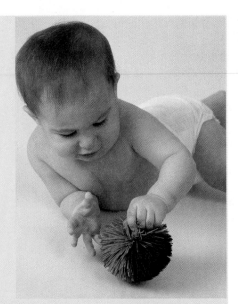

Eight-month-old Laura has a whole set of new skills and understandings: She can crawl, she has a firm attachment to both parents, she can perhaps understand a few words, and she has a beginning understanding of object permanence. All these more or less simultaneous changes profoundly alter the system that is the child.

mother's face is at the optimum distance from the baby's eyes for the infant to focus on it; the mother's facial features, particularly her eyes and mouth, are just the sort of visual stimuli that the baby is most likely to look at; the baby is particularly sensitive to the range of sounds of the human voice, especially the upper register, so the infant can easily hear the higher-pitched, lilting voice virtually all mothers use; and during breast-feeding the release of a hormone called cortisol in the mother has the effect of relaxing her and making her more alert to the baby's signals. Both the adult and the infant are thus "primed" to interact with one another.

Sometime around 6 to 8 weeks, there seems to be a change, when these automatic, reflexive responses give way to behavior that appears to be more volitional. The child now looks at objects differently, apparently trying to identify what an object is rather than merely where it is; at this age, she also begins to reliably discriminate one face from another, she smiles more, she sleeps through the night, and she generally becomes a more responsive creature.

Because of these changes in the baby (and also because most mothers by this time have recovered physically from childbirth and most mothers and fathers have begun to adjust to the immense change in their routines), big changes in mother-infant interaction patterns become evident at this time. The need for routine care-taking continues, of course, but as the child stays awake for longer periods and smiles and makes eye contact more, exchanges between parent and child become more playful and smoother.

Once this transition has occurred, there seems to be a brief period of consolidation lasting perhaps 5 or 6 months. Of course, change continues during this consolidation period. Neurological change, in particular, is rapid, with the motor and perceptual areas of the cortex continuing to develop. The child's perceptual skills also show major changes in these months, with depth perception becoming stronger and clear cross-modal transfer and identification of patterns of sounds and sights emerging.

Despite all these changes, however, there is a kind of equilibrium in this period—an equilibrium that is altered by a series of changes that occur between about 7 and 9 months: (1) The infant forms a strong central attachment, followed a few months later by the development of separation anxiety and fear of strangers; (2) the infant begins to move around independently (albeit very slowly and haltingly at first); (3) communication between infant and parents changes substantially, as the baby begins to use meaningful gestures and to comprehend individual words; (4) the infant begins to understand object permanence, that objects and people can continue to exist even when they are out of sight. At the very least, these changes profoundly alter the parent-child interactive system, requiring the establishment of a new equilibrium (a new consolidation). The infant continues to build gradually on this set of new skills—learning a few spoken words, learning to walk, consolidating the basic attachment—until some time between 18 and 24 months of age, at which point the child's language and cognitive development appear to take another major leap forward.

Central Processes

What causes all of these changes? Any short list of such causes will inevitably be a gross oversimplification, but four key processes seem to be at work.

Physical Maturation First and most obviously, the biological clock is ticking very loudly indeed during the early months. Only at adolescence and again in old age is such an obvious maturational pattern at work. In infancy, it is the prepatterned growth of neural dendrites and synapses that appears to be the key. The shift in behavior at 2 months, for example, seems to be governed by just such built-in changes, as synapses in the cortex develop sufficiently to control behavior more fully.

Important as this built-in program is, it nonetheless depends on the presence of a specific factor environment (Greenough, Black, & Wallace, 1987). The brain may be "programmed" to create certain synapses, but the process has to be triggered by exposure to particular kinds of experience. Because virtually all infants encounter such a minimum environment, perceptual, motor, and cognitive developments are virtually identical from one baby to the next. But that does not mean that the environment is unimportant.

The Child's Explorations   A second key process is the child's own exploration of the world around her. She is born ready to explore, to learn from her experience, but she still has to learn the specific connections between seeing and hearing, to tell the differences between mom's face and someone else's, to pay attention to the sounds emphasized in the language she is hearing, to discover that her actions have consequences, and so on.

Clearly, physiological maturation and the child's own explorations are intimately linked in a kind of perpetual feedback loop. The rapid changes in the nervous system, bones, and muscles permit more and more exploration, which in turn affects the child's perceptual and cognitive skills, and these in turn affect the architecture of the brain. For example, researchers have a good deal of evidence that the ability to crawl—a skill that rests on a host of maturationally based physical changes—profoundly affects a baby's understanding of the world. Before the baby can move independently, he seems to locate objects only in relation to his own body; after he can crawl, he begins to locate objects with reference to fixed landmarks. This shift, in turn, probably contributes to the infant's growing understanding of himself as an object in space.

Attachment   A third key process is obviously the relationship between infant and caregiver. It seems likely that Bowlby was right about the built-in readiness of all infants to create an attachment, but the quality of the specific experience the child encounters seems to have a more formative effect on attachment formation than is true for other aspects of development. A wide range of environments are "good enough" to support physical, perceptual, and cognitive growth in these early months. For the establishment of a secure central attachment, however, the acceptable range seems to be narrower.

Still, attachment does not develop along an independent track. Its emergence is linked both to maturational change and to the child's own exploration. For example, the child's understanding of object permanence may be a necessary precondition for the development of a basic attachment. As John Flavell puts it, "How ever could a child persistently yearn and search for a specific other person if the child were still cognitively incapable of mentally representing that person in the person's absence?" (1985, p. 135).

This hypothesis might be turned on its head with the argument that the process of establishing a clear attachment may cause, or at least affect, the child's cognitive development. For example, securely attached youngsters appear to persist longer in their play and to develop object permanence more rapidly (Bates, Bretherton, Beeghly-Smith, & McNew, 1982). Such a connection might exist because the securely attached child is simply more comfortable exploring the world around him from the safe base of his attachment figure. He thus has a richer and more varied set of experiences, which may stimulate more rapid cognitive (and neurological) development.

Internal Working Models   Attachment might also be thought of as a subcategory of a broader process—the creation of internal working models. Seymour Epstein (1991) proposes that what the baby is doing is nothing less than beginning to create a *theory of reality*. In Epstein's view, such a theory includes at least four elements:

- A belief about the degree to which the world is a place of pleasure or pain
- A belief about the extent to which the world is predictable, controllable, and just versus chaotic, uncontrollable, and capricious
- A belief about whether people are desirable or threatening to relate to
- A belief about the worthiness or unworthiness of the self

The roots of this theory of reality, so Epstein and others argue (Bretherton, 1991), lie in the experiences of infancy, particularly experiences with other people. Indeed, Epstein suggests that beliefs created in infancy are likely to be the most basic and therefore the most durable and resistant to change at later ages. Not all psychologists agree with Epstein about the broadness of the infant's theory of reality. However, virtually all agree that the baby begins to create at least two significant internal models, one of the self and one of relationships with others (attachment). Of the two, the attachment model seems to be the most fully developed at 18 or 24 months; the model of the self undergoes many elaborations in the years that follow. You'll recall from Chapter 10 that it is only at about age 6 or 7 that the child seems to have a sense of her global worth (Harter, 2006b).

Influences on the Basic Processes

The process of creating these two internal models is universal. Nonetheless, infants can be deflected from the common trajectory by several kinds of influences.

Organic Damage   The most obvious potential deflector of development is some kind of damage to the physical organism, from genetic anomalies, inherited disease, or teratogenic effects in utero. Yet even when damage does occur, nature and nurture interact: Recall from Chapter 2 that the long-term consequences of such damage may be more or less severe, depending on the richness and supportiveness of the environment the baby grows up in.

Family Environment   The specific family environment in which the child is reared also affects the developmental trajectory. On one end of the continuum are beneficial effects from an optimal environment that includes a variety of objects for the baby to explore, at least some opportunity to explore freely, and loving, responsive, and sensitive adults who talk to the infant often and respond to his cues (Bradley et al., 1989). Among other things, such enriched environments may contribute to the development and retention of a more elaborate and complex network of neural connections. On the other end of the continuum are some environments that fall outside of the "good enough" range and thus fail to support the child's most basic development. A family that subjected an infant to severe neglect or abuse would fall into this category, as might one in which a parent suffered deep or lasting depression or one characterized by persisting upheaval or stress. In between these extremes are many variations in enrichment, in responsiveness, and in loving support, all of which seem to have at least some impact on the child's pattern of attachment, his motivation, the content of his self-concept, his willingness to explore, and his specific knowledge. The consequences of such differences become evident later in life, when the child faces the challenging tasks of school and the demands of relating to other children.

Influences on the Family   As you've already read many times before, the child is embedded in the family, and the family is part of a larger economic, social, and cultural system, all of which can have both direct and indirect effects on the child. The most obvious example is the impact of poverty or wealth: The parents' overall economic circumstances may have a very wide-ranging impact on a child's life experience. Poor families are less able to provide a safe and secure environment. Their infants are more likely to be exposed to environmental toxins such as lead; less likely to have regular health care, including immunizations; and more likely to have nutritionally inadequate diets. If they must place their infant in child care, poor parents may be unable to afford good quality care, and they are more likely to have to shift the baby from one care arrangement to another. Collectively, these are large differences. The effects do not become evident immediately; babies being reared in poverty-level families do not look much different from babies being reared in more affluent circumstances. By age 2, 3, or 4, though, the differences begin to be obvious.

The Preschool Years

The main theme of the preschool period, as summarized in Figure E.2, is that the child is making a slow but immensely important shift from dependent baby to independent child. The toddler and then the preschooler can move around easily, can communicate more and more clearly, has a growing sense of himself as a separate person with specific qualities, and has the beginning of cognitive and social skills that allow him to interact more fully and successfully with playmates. In these years, the child's thinking is decentering, to use Piaget's term: He shifts away from using himself as the only frame of reference and becomes less tied to physical appearances.

In the beginning, these newfound skills and this new independence are not accompanied by much impulse control. Two-year-olds are pretty good at doing; they are terrible at *not* doing. If frustrated, they hit things, and wail, scream, or shout (isn't language wonderful?). A

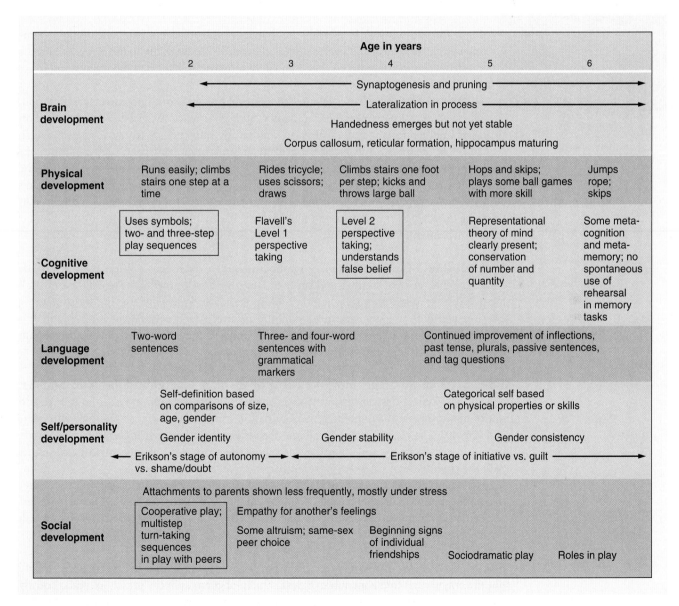

Figure E.2 Early Childhood Milestones

A brief summary of parallel developments during the preschool years.

Pride and independence!

large part of the conflict parents experience with children of this age arises because the parent must limit the child, not only for the child's own survival but also to help teach the child impulse control (Escalona, 1981).

The preschool years also stand out as the period in which the seeds of the child's (and perhaps the adult's) social skills and personality are sown. The attachment process that began in infancy continues to be formative, because it helps to shape the child's internal working model of social relationships. However, in the years from age 2 to 6, this early model is revised, consolidated, and established more firmly. The resultant interactive patterns tend to persist into elementary school and beyond. The 3-, 4-, or 5-year-old who develops the ability to share, to read others' cues well, to respond positively to others, and to control aggression and impulsiveness is likely to be a socially successful, popular 8-year-old. In contrast, the noncompliant, hostile preschooler is far more likely to become an unpopular, aggressive schoolchild (Caspi, 2000).

Central Processes

Many forces are at play in creating the changes of the preschool years, including two immense cognitive advances in this period: the toddler's new ability to use symbols, and the rapid development, between ages 3 and 5, of a more sophisticated theory of mind.

Physical Maturation   Synaptogenesis and pruning continue into early childhood, although at a slower pace than in infancy. Still, experience is crucial, as all the work on early interventions for disadvantaged children demonstrates (Ramey, Ramey, & Lanzi, 2007). In the midst of its growth spurts, the brain is organizing itself such that functions are beginning to show the pattern of lateralization that is found in adults. As a result, the brain becomes more efficient. The maturing of the reticular formation enhances the child's ability to pay attention, and that of the hippocampus leads to improved memory abilities. At the same time, advances in gross and fine motor skills enable the preschooler to function far more independently than in infancy.

Symbol Use   The development of symbol use is reflected in many different aspects of the child's life. It is evident in the rapid surge of language development, in the child's approach to cognitive tasks, and in play, when the child pretends and has objects stand for something else. The ability to use language more skillfully, in turn, affects social behavior in highly significant ways. For example, the child increasingly uses verbal rather than physical aggression and negotiates with parents instead of having tantrums or using defiant behavior.

Theory of Mind   The emergence of the child's more sophisticated theory of mind has equally broad effects, especially in the social arena, where her newfound abilities to read and understand others' behaviors form the foundation for new levels of interactions with peers and parents. It is probably not accidental that friendships between individual children are first visible at about the time that they also show the sharp drop in egocentrism that occurs with the emergence of the theory of mind.

The seminal role of cognitive changes is also evident in the growing importance of several basic schemes. Not only does the 2- or 3-year-old have an increasingly generalized internal model of attachment; she also develops a self-scheme and a gender scheme, each of which forms part of the foundation of both social behavior and personality.

Social Contacts   Important as the physical and cognitive changes are, they are clearly not the only factors that contribute to developmental changes in the preschool years. Equally important are the child's contacts with adults and peers. When young children play together, they expand each other's experience with objects and suggest new ways of pretending to one another, thus fostering still further cognitive growth. When two children disagree about how to explain something or insist on their own different views, each child gains awareness that there are other ways of thinking or playing, thus creating opportunities to learn about others' mental processes. Just as Vygotsky suggested, social interactions are the arena in which much cognitive growth occurs. For example, in one study, Charles Lewis found that children who have many siblings or who interact regularly with a variety of adult relatives show more rapid understanding of other people's thinking and acting than do children with fewer social partners (Lewis, Freeman, & Maridaki-Kassotaki, 1995). Similarly, Jenkins and Astington (1996) found that children from larger families show more rapid development of a representational theory of mind. Research also shows that children with secure attachments show a more rapid shift to understanding false belief and other aspects of a representational theory of mind than do children with insecure attachments (Charman, Redfern, & Fonagy, 1995; Steele, Holder, & Fonagy, 1995)—a result that points to the importance of the quality of social interactions as well as their quantity for the child's cognitive development.

Play with other children also forms the foundation of the child's emerging gender scheme. Noticing whether other people are boys or girls and what toys boys and girls play with is the first step in the long chain of sex-role learning.

Naturally enough, it is also social interactions, especially those with parents, that modify or reinforce the child's pattern of social behaviors. The parents' style of discipline becomes critical here. Gerald Patterson's work shows clearly that parents who lack the skills to control the toddler's impulsivity and demands for independence are likely to end up strengthening noncompliant and disruptive behavior (Patterson, Capaldi, & Bank, 1991).

Influences on the Basic Processes

The family's ability to support the child's development in the preschool years is affected not only by the skills and knowledge the parents bring to the process but also by the amount of stress they are experiencing from outside forces and the quality of support they have in their own lives. In particular, mothers who are experiencing high levels of stress are more likely to be punitive and negative toward their children, with resulting increases in the children's defiant and noncompliant behavior. Maternal negativity, in turn, is implicated in the persistence of noncompliant behavior into elementary school. This link is clear, for example, in Susan Campbell's longitudinal study of a group of noncompliant children (Campbell & Ewing, 1990; Campbell, Pierce, March, & Ewing, 1991). Campbell finds that among a group of 3-year-olds who were labeled "hard to manage," those who had improved by age 6 had mothers who had been less negative.

Stress is obviously not the only factor in the mother's level of negativity toward the child. Mothers with depression are also more likely to show negativity (Thompson & Goodvin, 2005), as are mothers from working-class or poverty-level families, who may well have experienced negativity and harsh discipline in their own childhoods. Even so, stress and lack of personal social support are both part of the equation. Thus, preschoolers, like children of every age, are affected by broader social forces outside the family as well as by the family interaction itself.

The Elementary School Years

Figure E.3 on page 434 summarizes the changes and continuities of middle childhood. There are obviously many gradual changes: increasing physical skill, less reliance on appearance, more attention to underlying qualities and attributes, and a greater role of peers. Major milestones in brain development include major growth spurts between ages 6 and 8 and again between ages 10 and 12, the gradual myelination of the association areas that occurs throughout this period, the full lateralization of spatial perception around age 8, improvements in reticular formation and hippocampus functioning, and the beginning of the final phase of prefrontal maturation at age 9 or so. Clearly, a great deal happens developmentally during the school years. But the momentous conjunction of neurological, physical, cognitive,

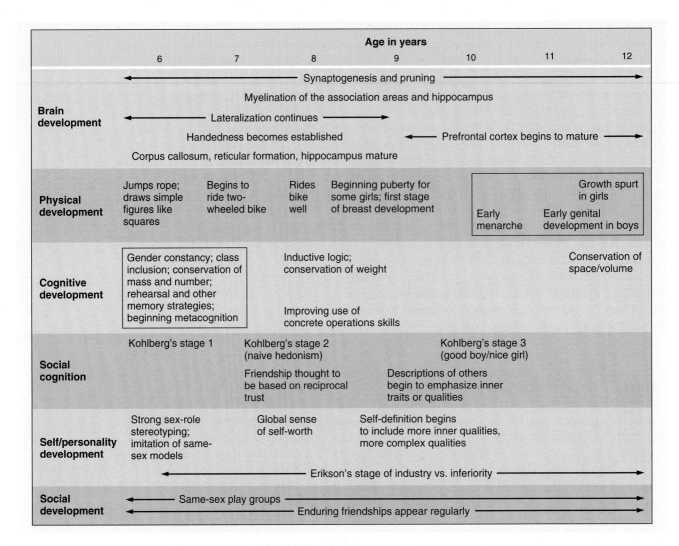

	Age in years						
	6	7	8	9	10	11	12
Brain development	Synaptogenesis and pruning						
	Myelination of the association areas and hippocampus						
	Lateralization continues						
	Handedness becomes established			Prefrontal cortex begins to mature			
	Corpus callosum, reticular formation, hippocampus mature						
Physical development	Jumps rope; draws simple figures like squares	Begins to ride two-wheeled bike	Rides bike well	Beginning puberty for some girls; first stage of breast development			Growth spurt in girls
					Early menarche	Early genital development in boys	
Cognitive development	Gender constancy; class inclusion; conservation of mass and number; rehearsal and other memory strategies; beginning metacognition		Inductive logic; conservation of weight				Conservation of space/volume
			Improving use of concrete operations skills				
Social cognition	Kohlberg's stage 1	Kohlberg's stage 2 (naive hedonism)		Kohlberg's stage 3 (good boy/nice girl)			
		Friendship thought to be based on reciprocal trust		Descriptions of others begin to emphasize inner traits or qualities			
Self/personality development	Strong sex-role stereotyping; imitation of same-sex models	Global sense of self-worth		Self-definition begins to include more inner qualities, more complex qualities			
	Erikson's stage of industry vs. inferiority						
Social development	Same-sex play groups						
	Enduring friendships appear regularly						

Figure E.3   Middle Childhood Milestones

A brief summary of parallel changes during the elementary school years.

and socioemotional development happening between ages 5 and 7, which enables the child to gain far more from educational experiences than she could in earlier years, merits special attention. This one interval during these years in which there seems to be a more rapid change is right at the beginning of middle childhood, at the point of transition from being a preschooler to being a schoolchild.

The Transition between 5 and 7

Some kind of transition into middle childhood has been noted in a great many cultures. There seems to be widespread recognition that a 6-year-old is somehow qualitatively different from a 5-year-old: more responsible, more able to understand complex ideas. Among the Kipsigis of Kenya, for example, the age of 6 is said to be the first point at which the child has *ng'omnotet*, translated as "intelligence" (Harkness & Super, 1985). The fact that schooling begins at this age seems to reflect an implicit or explicit recognition of this fundamental shift.

Psychologists who have studied development across this transition have pointed to a series of changes children undergo:

• Cognitively, there is a shift to what Piaget calls *concrete operational thinking*. The child now understands conservation problems, seriation, and class inclusion. More generally, the child seems to pay less attention to surface properties of objects and more to underlying continuities and patterns, to be captured less by appearance and to focus on the underlying reality. This can be seen not only in children's understanding of physical objects but also in their understanding of others, of relationships, and of themselves.

- Studies of information processing reveal a parallel rapid increase in the child's use of executive strategies.
- In terms of self-concept, a global judgment of self-worth first emerges at about age 7 or 8.
- In peer relationships, gender segregation becomes virtually complete by age 6 or 7, especially in individual friendships.

The confluence of these changes is impressive and seems to provide some support for the existence of the kind of stage Piaget hypothesized. There appears to be some kind of change in the basic structure of the child's thinking that is reflected in all aspects of the child's functioning. Still, impressive as these changes are, it is not so clear that what is occurring is a rapid, pervasive, structural change to a whole new way of thinking and relating. Children don't make this shift all at once in every area of their cognitive or social functioning. For example, while the shift from a concrete to a more abstract self-concept may become noticeable at age 6 or 7, it occurs quite gradually and is still going on at ages 11 and 12. Similarly, a child may grasp conservation of quantity at age 5 or 6 but typically does not understand conservation of weight until several years later.

Going to school is a hugely formative experience for children.

Furthermore, expertise, or lack of it, strongly affects the pattern of a child's cognitive progress. Thus, while most psychologists agree that a set of important changes normally emerges together at about this age, most also agree that they do not represent a rapid or abrupt reorganization of the child's basic mode of operating.

Central Processes

There seem to be three sets of developmental processes at work in the elementary school years: cognitive, social, and physical.

Cognitive Influences   Of the developmental shifts seen during middle childhood, the cognitive changes seem to many psychologists the most central, comprising a necessary but not sufficient condition for the alterations in relationships and in the self-scheme that also occur during this period. A good illustration is the emergence of a global sense of self-worth, which seems to require not only a tendency to look beyond or behind surface characteristics but also the use of inductive logic. The child appears to arrive at a global sense of self-worth by some summative, inductive process.

Similarly, the quality of the child's relationships with peers and parents seems to rest, in part, on a basic cognitive understanding of reciprocity and perspective taking. The child now understands that others read him as much as he reads them. Children of 7 or 8 will say of their friends that they "trust each other," something you would be very unlikely to hear from a 5-year-old.

Peer Group Influences   A bias toward seeing cognitive changes as central has dominated theories and research on middle childhood for many decades, largely as a result of the powerful influence of Piaget's theory. This imbalance has begun to be redressed in recent years as the importance of the peer group and the child's social experience has become better understood. There are two reasons for this change in thinking. First, developmentalists have reawakened to the (obvious) fact that a great deal of the experience on which the child's cognitive progress is based occurs in social interactions. Second, they have realized that social relationships present the child with a unique set of demands, both cognitive and interactive, and have unique consequences for the child's social and emotional functioning. It is in the elementary school years, for example, that patterns of peer rejection or acceptance are consolidated, with reverberations through adolescence and into adult life.

Physical Influences   It is not completely clear just what role physical change plays in the various developmental changes of the elementary school years. Clearly, there are physical changes going on. Girls, in particular, begin the early steps toward puberty during elementary school. What developmentalists don't yet know is whether the rate of physical development in these years is connected in any way to the rate of the child's progress through the sequence of cognitive or social understandings. One thing is true: Bigger, more coordinated, early-developing children are likely to have slightly faster cognitive development and to be somewhat more popular with peers. Obviously, this is an area in which developmentalists need far more knowledge.

Influences on the Basic Processes: The Role of Culture

Most of what you have read about middle childhood (and about other periods as well) is based on research on children growing up in Western cultures. Investigators must ask, therefore, whether the patterns they see are specific to particular cultures or whether they reflect underlying developmental processes common to all children everywhere.

With respect to middle childhood, there are some obvious differences in the experiences of children in Western cultures compared to those growing up in villages in Africa, in Polynesia, or in other parts of the world where families live by subsistence agriculture and schooling is not a dominant force in children's lives (Weisner, 1984). In many such cultures, children of 6 or 7 are thought of as "intelligent" and responsible and are expected to play almost adult-like roles. They are highly likely to be given the task of caring for younger siblings and to begin their apprenticeships in the skills they will need as adults, such as agricultural or animal husbandry skills, learning by working alongside the adults. In some West African and Polynesian cultures, it is also common for children of this age to be sent out to foster care with relatives or to apprentice with a skilled worker.

Such children obviously have a very different set of social tasks to learn in the middle childhood years than do children growing up in industrialized countries. They do not need to learn how to relate to or make friends with same-age strangers in a new environment (school). Instead, from an early age, they need to learn their place in an existing network of roles and relationships. For the Western child, the roles are less prescribed; the choices for adult life are far more varied.

Yet the differences in the lives of children in industrialized and nonindustrialized cultures should not obscure the very real similarities. In all cultures, middle childhood is the period in which children develop individual friendships, segregate their play groups by gender, develop the cognitive underpinnings of reciprocity, learn the beginnings of what Piaget called *concrete operations*, and acquire some of the basic skills that will be required for adult life. These are not trivial similarities. They speak to the power of the common process of development, even in the midst of obvious variations in experience.

Adolescence

Figure E.4 summarizes the various threads of development during adolescence. A number of experts on this developmental period argue that it makes sense to divide the years between 12 and 20 into two subperiods, one beginning at 11 or 12, the other perhaps at 16 or 17. Some label these periods "adolescence" and "youth" (Keniston, 1970); others call them "early" and "late" adolescence (Brooks-Gunn, 1988). However they are labeled, there are distinct differences.

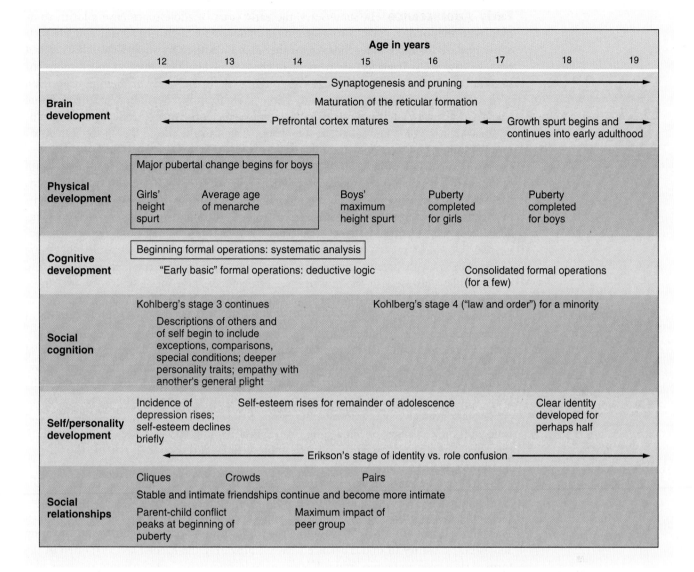

Figure E.4 Milestones of Adolescence

A brief summary of parallel developments during adolescence.

Early and Late Adolescence

Early adolescence, almost by definition, is a time of transition, of significant change in virtually every aspect of the child's functioning. Late adolescence is more a time of consolidation, when the young person establishes a cohesive new identity, with clearer goals and role commitments. Norma Haan (1981), borrowing Piaget's concepts, suggests that early adolescence is a time dominated by assimilation, whereas late adolescence is primarily a time of accommodation.

The 12- or 13-year-old is assimilating an enormous number of new physical, social, and intellectual experiences. While all this absorption is going on, but before the experiences have been digested, the young person is in a more or less continuous state of disequilibrium. Old patterns, old schemes no longer work very well, but new ones have not been established. It is during this early period that the peer group is so centrally important. Ultimately, the 16- or 17- or 18-year-old begins to make the needed accommodations, pulls the threads together, and establishes a new identity, new patterns of social relationships, new goals and roles.

Early Adolescence   In some ways, the early years of adolescence have a lot in common with the toddler years. Two-year-olds are famous for their negativism and for their constant push for more independence. At the same time, they are struggling to learn a vast array of new skills. Teenagers show many of these same qualities, albeit at much more abstract levels, thanks to the maturing of the prefrontal cortex. Many of them go through a period of negativism, particularly with parents, right at the beginning of the pubertal changes. And many of the conflicts with parents center on issues of independence—adolescents want to come and go when they please, listen to the music they prefer (at maximum volume), and wear the clothing and hair styles that are currently "in."

As is true of the negativism of 2-year-olds, it is easy to overstate the depth or breadth of the conflict between young teenagers and their parents. For the great majority of teenagers, there is no major turmoil—simply a temporary increase in the frequency of disagreements or disputes. The depiction of adolescence as full of storm and stress is as much an exaggeration as the stereotype of the "terrible twos." What is true is that both ages are characterized by a new push for independence, which is inevitably accompanied by more confrontations with parents over limits. While this push for independence is going on, young adolescents are also facing a new set of demands: new social skills, new and more complex school tasks, a need to form an adult identity. The sharp increase in the rate of depression (especially among girls) and the drop in self-esteem seen at the beginning of adolescence seem to be linked to this surplus of demands and changes. A number of investigators have found that those adolescents who must deal with the greatest number of simultaneous changes at the beginning of puberty—changing to junior high school, moving to a new town or new house, perhaps a parental separation or divorce—also show the greatest loss in self-esteem, the largest rise in problem behavior, and the biggest drop in grade point average (e.g., Simmons, Burgeson, & Reef, 1988). Young adolescents who can cope with these changes one at a time (for example, youngsters who are able to remain in the same school through eighth or ninth grade before shifting to high school) show fewer symptoms of stress.

Facing major stressful demands, the 2-year-old uses mom (or some other central attachment figure) as a safe base for exploring the world, returning for reassurance when she is fearful. Young adolescents seem to do the same with the family, using it as a safe base from which to explore the rest of the world, including the world of peer relationships. Parents of young adolescents must try to find a balance between providing the needed security, often in the form of clear rules and limits, and still allowing independence—just as parents of 2-year-olds must walk a fine line between allowing exploration and ensuring safety. Among teenagers, as among toddlers, the most confident and successful are those whose families manage this balancing act well.

Drawing a parallel between early adolescents and toddlers also makes sense in that both age groups face the task of establishing a separate identity. The toddler must separate herself from the symbiotic relationship with mom or another central caregiver. The child must figure out not only that she is separate but also that she has abilities and qualities. Physical maturation also allows her new levels of independent exploration. The young adolescent must separate himself from his family and from his identity as a child and begin to form a new identity as an adult.

Late Adolescence   To carry the analogy we've been using further, late adolescence is more like the later preschool years. Major changes have been weathered, and a new balance has been achieved. The physical upheavals of puberty are mostly complete, the family system has changed to allow the teenager more independence and freedom, and the beginnings of a new identity have been created. This period is not without its strains, however. Most young people do not achieve a clear identity until college age, if then, so the identity process continues. And the task of forming emotionally intimate partnerships (whether sexual or not) is a key task of late adolescence. Nonetheless, Haan seems to be correct that this later period is more one of accommodation than assimilation. It is definitely accompanied by rising levels of self-esteem and declining levels of family confrontation or conflict.

Central Processes and Their Connections

It seems clear that changes in one or another of the facets of development may be central to the constellation of transformations seen at a given age. In infancy, underlying physiological change and the creation of a first central attachment appear to have such key causal roles; in the preschool years, cognitive changes seem especially dominant; among school-aged children, both cognitive and social changes appear to be formative. In adolescence, every domain shows significant change. At this point, developmentalists simply do not have the research data to clarify the basic causal connections among the transformations in these various areas. Nevertheless, they have some information about linkages.

Independence of a new and different kind.

The Role of Puberty   One obvious factor to emphasize in discussions of adolescence is puberty itself. Puberty not only defines the beginning of early adolescence; it clearly affects all other facets of the young person's development, either directly or indirectly. There are several direct effects. Most clearly, the surges of pubertal hormones stimulate sexual interest while triggering body changes that make adult sexuality and fertility possible. These changes seem inescapably and causally linked to the gradual shift (for the great majority of teens) from same-sex peer groupings to mixed-sex crowds and finally to romantic relationships.

Hormone changes may also be directly implicated in the increases in confrontation or conflict between parents and children and in various kinds of aggressive or delinquent behavior. Lawrence Steinberg's research (1988) suggests such a direct link; he found pubertal stage and not age to be the critical variable in predicting the level of adolescents' conflict with their parents. Other investigators have found that in girls, the rise in estradiol at the beginning of puberty is associated with increases in verbal aggression and a loss of impulse control, while in boys, increases in testosterone are correlated with increases in irritability and impatience (Paikoff & Brooks-Gunn, 1990). However, many studies find no such connections (e.g., Coe, Hayashi, & Levine, 1988), so most theorists conclude that the links between pubertal hormones and changes in adolescent social behavior are considerably more complicated than they had first imagined.

One factor that complicates the analysis is that the physical changes of puberty have highly significant indirect effects as well as direct consequences. When a child's body grows and becomes more like that of an adult, the parents begin to treat the child differently, and the child begins to see himself as a soon-to-be-adult. Both of these changes may be linked to the brief rise in parent-adolescent confrontation and may help to trigger some of the searching self-examinations that are part of this period of life.

Physiological changes might conceivably also play some role in the shift to formal operations. There is some indication, for example, that synaptic and dendritic pruning continues through early adolescence, so a final reorganization of the brain may be occurring in these years. At the same time, any link between formal operational thinking and pubertal change cannot be inevitable, because all adolescents experience puberty, but not all make the transition to formal operations. The best guess at the moment is that neurological or hormonal

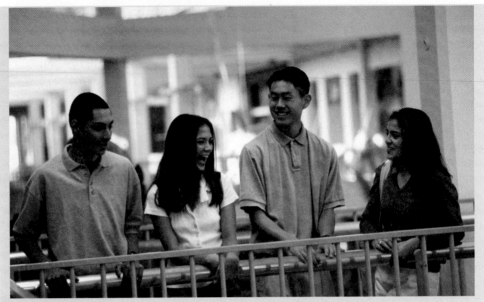

By late adolescence, the form of peer interaction has shifted from mixed-sex cliques to loose associations of pairs.

changes at adolescence may be necessary for further cognitive gains, but they cannot be sufficient conditions for such developments.

The Role of Cognitive Changes   An equally attractive possibility to many theorists is the proposition that it is the cognitive changes that are pivotal in adolescent development. Of course, two important milestones in brain development make these changes possible: the maturation of the prefrontal cortex and the surge in development in the frontal lobes around age 17. So, the division between cognitive and physical changes is a somewhat artificial one. Nevertheless, it is clear that cognitive development facilitates many of the other changes seen in adolescence, including changes in self-concept, the process of identity formation, increases in level of moral reasoning, and changes in peer relationships.

There is ample evidence, for example, that the greater abstractness in the adolescent's self-concept and in her descriptions of others is intimately connected to the broader changes in cognitive functioning (Harter, 1990). You will also remember from Chapter 12 that the shift in the child's thinking from concrete operations to at least beginning formal operations seems to be a necessary precondition for the emergence of more advanced forms of social cognition and moral judgment. Finally, some ability to use formal operations may also be necessary but not sufficient for the formation of a clear identity. One of the characteristics of formal operational thinking is the ability to imagine possibilities that you have never experienced and to manipulate ideas in your head. These new skills may help to foster the questioning of old values and old patterns that is a central part of identity formation. For example, several studies show that among high school and college students, those in Marcia's status of identity achievement or moratorium are much more likely also to be using formal operations reasoning than are those in the status of diffusion or foreclosure. In Rowe and Marcia's study (1980), the only individuals who showed full identity achievement were those who were also using full formal operations. But the converse was not true. That is, there were a number of participants in the study who used formal operations but had not yet established a clear identity. Thus, formal operational thinking may enable the young person to rethink many aspects of her life, but it does not guarantee that she will do so.

Overall, both the physical changes of puberty and the potential cognitive changes of formal operations appear to be central to the phenomena of adolescence, but the connections between them, and their impact on social behavior, remain unclear.

Influences on the Basic Processes

There is not enough space in this epilogue (or perhaps in this entire text) to detail all the factors that influence the teenager's experience of adolescence. You have already read about many of these factors, including the timing of the child's pubertal development, the degree of personal or familial stress, and such cultural variations as the use of initiation rites. But one more general point is worth repeating: Adolescence, like every other developmental period, does not begin as a clean slate. The individual youngster's own temperamental qualities, behavioral habits, and internal models of interaction, established in earlier years of childhood, obviously have a profound effect on the experience of adolescence. Examples are easy to find:

- Teens who are high in neuroticism and introversion, who have low self-esteem, and who tend to blame external agents for their problems are at higher risk for mental health problems than are peers who have a more optimistic outlook on life (Beautrais, Joyce, & Mulder, 1999).
- Alan Sroufe's longitudinal study (1989), described in Chapter 11, showed that those who had been rated as having a secure attachment in infancy were more self-confident and more socially competent with peers at the beginning of adolescence.
- Delinquency and heightened aggressiveness in adolescence are most often preceded by earlier behavior problems and by inadequate family control as early as the child's toddler years (Dishion, French, & Patterson, 1995). Even those who show such antisocial behavior for the first time as teenagers enter adolescence with different qualities, including poorer-quality friendships (Berndt & Keefe, 1995).
- Depression in the teenage years is more likely among those who enter adolescence with low self-esteem (Harter, 1987).

Avshalom Caspi and Terrie Moffitt (1991) make the more general point that any major life crisis or transition, including adolescence, has the effect of accentuating earlier personality or behavioral patterns rather than creating new ones. This is not unlike the observation that the child's attachment to the parent is revealed only when the child is under stress. As one example of the more general process, Caspi and Moffitt point out that girls who experience very early puberty have higher rates of psychological problems, on average, than do those who experience puberty at a more normal or average age. However, closer analysis reveals that it is only the early-maturing girls who already had social problems before puberty began whose pubertal experience and adolescence are more negative. Very early puberty does not induce psychological problems in girls who were psychologically healthier to begin with.

Caspi and Moffitt's observation appears to be important for understanding the various transitions of adult life as well as those of adolescence. Not only do we "carry ourselves with us" as we move through the roles and demands of adult life, but existing patterns may be most highly visible when we are under stress. This does not mean that we never change or learn new and more effective ways of responding—obviously many of us do. Still, it is important not to lose sight of the fact that by adolescence, and certainly by adulthood, people's internal working models and repertoires of coping behaviors are already established, creating a bias in the system. Another way of putting it is that while change is possible, continuity is the default option.

A Return to Some Basic Questions

With this brief overview in mind, let's now go back to some of the questions raised in Chapter 1 and see if the answers can be made any clearer.

What Are the Major Influences on Development?

Throughout this text, you have read about the arguments for and against both nature and nurture, or nativism and empiricism, as basic explanations of developmental patterns. In every instance, you learned that the real answer lies in the interaction between the two. To make the point more clearly, we might go back to Aslin's five models of environmental and internal influences on development, illustrated in Figure 1.1. You'll recall that Aslin proposed one purely physical model (which he calls maturation), according to which some particular development occurs regardless of environmental input, and one purely environmental pattern (which he calls induction), according to which some development is entirely a function of experience. These two "pure" alternatives make logical sense, but in actuality, probably neither occurs at all. All of development is a product of various forms of interaction between internal and external influences.

Even in the case of development that appears to be the most clearly biologically determined or influenced, such as physical development or early perceptual development, normal development can occur only if the child is growing in an environment that falls within an adequate or sufficient range. The fact that the vast majority of environments fall within that range in no way reduces the crucial importance of the environment. As John Flavell puts it, "Environmental elements do not become any less essential to a particular form of development just because they are virtually certain to be available for its use" (1985, p. 284). Similarly, even those aspects of development that seem most obviously to be products of the environment, such as the quality of the child's first attachment, rest on a physiological foundation and on instinctive patterns of attachment behaviors. The fact that all normal children possess that foundation and those instincts makes them no less essential for development.

The fact that virtually all babies have some chance to reach for and examine objects does not mean that such experience is unimportant in the child's emerging perceptual or motor skills. Most (if not all) so-called maturational sequences require particular kinds of environmental inputs if they are to occur at all.

Rutter's Five Principles of the Interaction of Nature and Nurture

It is not enough merely to say that all development is a product of interaction between nature and nurture. Developmentalists want to be able to specify much more clearly just how that interaction operates. Michael Rutter and his colleagues (1997) have proposed a set of five general principles governing the interplay between nature and nurture; these go beyond Aslin's models and provide a helpful summary analysis:

- *"Individuals differ in their reactivity to the environment"* (p. 338). Some babies, children, and adults are highly reactive, highly sensitive to stress or strangeness; others react with much less volatility. Variations in such reactivity may rest on basic inborn temperamental differences, or they may be the product of cumulative experience.

- *"There is a two-way interplay between individuals and their environments"* (p. 338). It is important not to think of the influences of the environment as a one-way street. Influences go back and forth.

- *"The interplay between persons and their environments needs to be considered within an ecological framework"* (p. 339). Although research nearly always treats environmental events (for example, divorce) as if they were the same for everyone, they are not. The event itself will differ as a function of culture, poverty, family structure, and a whole host of other variables.

- *"People process their experiences rather than just serve as passive recipients of environmental forces"* (p. 339). It is the meaning each child attaches to an experience that governs the effect, not the experience itself. Thus, the "same" experience can have widely differing effects, depending on how the child (or adult) processes or interprets it.

- *"People act on their environment so as to shape and select their experiences"* (p. 339). Experiences are not distributed randomly and independently of how the child or adult behaves. We each choose behaviors and niches within the family or within other social groups.

A Continuum of Environmental Influences   Another point, not included in Rutter's list, is that the form and extent of the interaction between nature and nurture may well vary as a function of the aspect of development in question. It may help to think of different facets of development along a continuum, with those most fully internally programmed on one end and those most externally influenced on the other.

Physical development defines one end of this continuum, since it is very strongly shaped by internal forces. Given the minimum necessary environment, physical maturational timetables are extremely powerful and consistent, particularly during infancy and adolescence. Next along the continuum is probably language (although some experts might argue with this conclusion, given the possible dependence of language development on prior cognitive developments). Language seems to emerge with only minimal environmental support—though again, the environment must fall within some acceptable range. At the very least, the child must hear language spoken (or see it signed). Still, specific features of the environment seem to matter a bit more in the case of language development than is true for physical development. For example, parents who respond appropriately to their children's vocalizations seem to be able to speed up the process, an example of what Aslin calls *facilitation*.

Cognitive development falls somewhere in the middle of the continuum. Clearly, powerful internal forces are at work here. As John Flavell expressed it, "There is an impetus to childhood cognitive growth that is not ultimately explainable by this environmental push or that experiential shove" (1985, p. 283). Developmentalists don't yet know whether the impressive regularity of the sequences of cognitive development arises from built-in processes such as assimilation and accommodation or from physiological changes such as synapse formation and pruning, or from some combination of causes. However, developmentalists do know that specific qualities of the environment affect both cognitive power and structure. Children with varied and age-appropriate toys, who receive encouragement for exploration and achievement, whose parents are responsive to their overtures—who experience, in Aslin's terms, not just facilitation but attunement—show faster cognitive development and higher IQ scores.

Social and emotional development lie at the other end of the continuum, where the impact of the environment seems to be the greatest, although even here genetic factors are obviously at work. Some aspects of temperament seem clearly to be built-in, or genetic, and attachment behaviors may be instinctive; both of these inborn factors certainly shape the child's earliest encounters with others. In this developmental area, however, the balance of nature and nurture seems to lean more toward nurture. In particular, the security of the child's attachment and the quality of the child's relationships with others outside of the family seem to be powerfully affected by the specific quality of the interactions within the family.

Does Timing Matter?

It's also important to remember that the impact of any experience can vary depending on when it occurs during development. This issue has been explored in a variety of ways throughout the book.

Early Experience as Critical   The most pervasive version of the timing question has asked whether the early years of life are a critical or sensitive period for the establishment of many of the trajectories of the child's later development. To borrow Ann Clarke's analogy (Clarke & Clarke, 1976): In the construction of a house, does the shape of the foundation determine the final structure partially or completely, or can later structures be built on the original foundation? Are any flaws or weaknesses in the original foundation permanent, or can they be corrected later, after the house is completed?

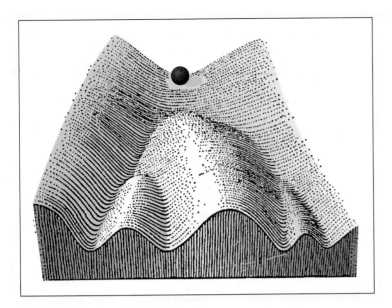

Figure E.5
Canalization

Waddington's visual depiction of the concept of canalization. A narrow and deep gully depicts strong canalization. If infancy is highly canalized, it means that almost any environment will support or sustain that development.

(*Source*: From C. H. Waddington, "A catastrophic theory of evolution," *Annals of the New York Academy of Science*, 231 (1974): 32–42. By permission.)

There are arguments on both sides. Some psychologists, such as Sandra Scarr, point to the fact that virtually all children successfully complete the sensorimotor period, and even children with mild and moderate retardation achieve some form of Piaget's concrete operations. The term that has been widely used to describe such developmental patterns is *canalization*, a notion borrowed from embryologist C. H. Waddington (1957). He suggested that development can be thought of metaphorically as a marble rolling down a gully on a hillside, as in Figure E.5. When a gully is narrow and deep, development is said to be highly canalized. The marble will roll down that gully with little deviation. Other aspects of development, in contrast, might be better depicted with much flatter or wider gullies, with many side branches, where the marble will be more likely to deviate from a given path. Scarr and others argue that in the early years of life, development is highly canalized, with strong "self-righting" tendencies. Even if deflected, the baby's pattern of development rapidly returns to the bottom of the gully and proceeds along the normal track. Such self-righting is illustrated, for example, by the large percentage of low-birth-weight or other initially vulnerable babies who nonetheless catch up to their normal-birth peers in physical and cognitive development by age 2 or 3.

Michael Lewis, in his book *Altering Fate* (1997), makes an even more sweeping argument against the primacy of early experience:

> I wish to argue against the idea that development is a sequence of small progressions that are gradual but accumulative, that it has clear directionality, that it is causal—earlier events are connected to later ones—and that prediction therefore is possible. Instead, I would like to argue for the idea that development is based on the pragmatic needs of the present, that the contextual flow of our lives determines our development through adaptation to the current. (pp. 15–16)

Lewis makes the point that chance encounters, upheavals, joys, and stresses change each of us; in a sense, he is saying that we remake ourselves moment to moment and that it is simply a mistake to think of development as if it were a cumulative process, with the earliest steps determining the trajectory of all that follows. Some developmentalists believe that Lewis has taken this argument too far, but he has certainly raised some important and provocative issues.

On the other side of the argument are a whole group of psychologists—much of whose thinking is rooted in psychoanalytic theory—who see infancy and early childhood as especially formative (e.g., Sroufe, 1983). They note that some prenatal influences are permanent; some effects of early cognitive impoverishment, malnutrition, or abuse may also be long-lasting. There is also a good deal of evidence that early psychological adaptations, such as the quality of the earliest attachment or the child's tendency toward aggressive behavior, tend to persist and shape the child's later experiences in a cumulative way.

It seems likely that both of these perspectives are valid: The early years of life are a sensitive period for some kinds of development and at the same time highly canalized. How can such an ap-

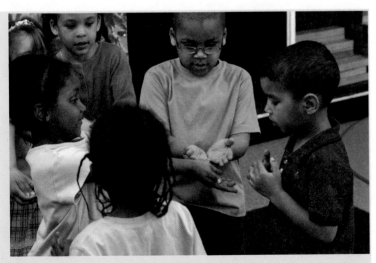

If infancy is a critical period for some aspects of personality development, then these preschoolers' characters are already well formed. Whether or not this is true remains one of the most crucial theoretical and practical issues in developmental psychology.

parent paradox be resolved? There are at least two possible ways. First, canalization could be seen not just as a product of powerful built-in programming but as the result of such programming being expressed in a sufficiently supportive environment. Viewed this way, a good deal of the apparent paradox disappears (Turkheimer & Gottesman, 1991). It is only when a child's particular environment falls outside the range of sufficiently supportive environments that there is a so-called environmental effect. So, for a child reared in an extremely impoverished orphanage setting or a child who is regularly physically abused, environmental effects can be strongly negative and long-lasting. The earlier such a deviation from a sufficiently supportive environment occurs, the more pervasive the effects seem to be. In this way of looking at critical periods versus canalization, a normally supported infancy may be less pivotal in the pattern of the child's development than minor deviations during toddlerhood or the preschool years. But if the deviations in infancy are extreme enough to deflect the infant from the normal developmental path—as in the case of severe abuse or malnutrition—the effect is larger than for deviations at any other age.

Robert Cairns (1991) offers a second resolution to the paradox when he points out that in any given period, some facets of development may be highly canalized and other facets may be strongly responsive to environmental variation. In infancy, for example, physical, perceptual, and perhaps linguistic development may be strongly canalized, but the development of internal working models of attachment is clearly affected by the child's specific family experiences. Indeed, all internal working models—whether of attachment, of gender identity and self-concept, or of peer relations—are likely to be more powerfully affected by early than by later experiences, simply because the model, once formed, affects and filters all later experience.

A particularly nice example of this kind of early effect comes from one of Alan Sroufe's studies of the long-term consequences of attachment security. Sroufe and his colleagues (Sroufe, Egeland, & Kreutzer, 1990) compared two groups of elementary school children. One group had formed secure attachments in infancy but for various reasons had not functioned well in the preschool years. The second group had shown poor adaptation at both ages. When these two groups of children were assessed at elementary school age, Sroufe found that those who had had a good early start "rebounded" better. They had better emotional health and social skills than did those who had had poor adaptation in infancy, even though both groups had functioned poorly as preschoolers. The infancy experience is not totally formative; the child's current circumstances also have a major impact. But, at least with respect to attachment security, early experience leaves a lingering trace.

Psychological Tasks at Different Ages

Another way to think about timing is to identify specific psychological tasks to be dealt with at different ages. Erikson's theory, for example, emphasizes a series of psychological dilemmas. Any experience that affects the way a child resolves a particular task will be formative at that time; at an earlier or later time, the same experience might have much less effect. Alan Sroufe and Michael Rutter (1984) have offered a broader list of age-related tasks, presented in Table E.1. In this way of looking at things, the child is seen as focusing on different aspects of the environment at different times. Thus, during the period from age 1 to 2½, when the child is focused on mastery of the world of objects, the quality and range of inanimate experiences to which the child has access may be of special importance.

Table E.1   Issues or Tasks in Each of Several Age Periods

Age in Years	Issues or Tasks
0–1	Biological regulation; harmonious interactions with parents and/or caregivers; formation of an effective attachment relationship
1–2½	Exploration, experimentation, and mastery of the world of objects (caregiver as secure base); individuation and autonomy; responding to external control of impulses
3–5	Flexible self-control; self-reliance; initiative; gender identification and gender concept; establishing effective peer contacts (empathy)
6–12	Social understanding (equity, fairness); gender constancy; same sex friendships; sense of "industry" (competence); school adjustment
13+	Formal operations (flexible perspective taking, "what-if" thinking); loyal friendships (same sex); beginning romantic relationships; emancipation; identity

Source: From L. A. Sroufe and M. Rutter, "The domain of developmental psychopathology," *Child Development*, 55 (1984): p. 22, Table 1. By permission of the Society for Research in Child Development.

Overall, most developmentalists today do not think that any specific age is "critical" for all aspects of development; most do think, though, that for any aspect of development, some ages are more critical than others, and that patterns that affect later experience are set during those times. As Alan Sroufe says, "Development is hierarchical; it is not a blackboard to be erased and written upon again. Even when children change rather markedly, the shadows of the earlier adaptation remain" (1983, pp. 73–74).

What Is the Nature of Developmental Change?

On balance, it seems likely that developmental change is more qualitative than quantitative. Certainly, over the years of development, the child acquires more vocabulary words, more information-processing strategies. But these tools and skills are used in different ways by older children than they are by younger ones. Further, it seems clear that these qualitative changes occur in sequences. Such sequences are apparent in physical development, in cognitive development, and in social and moral development.

Stages   Whether it is meaningful to speak of stages of development, however, is still an open question. Some hierarchically organized stages have certainly been identified, the most obvious example being Kohlberg's stages of moral reasoning. And researchers can certainly find examples of apparently stagelike changes across several developmental areas—for example, at about 18 to 24 months, the child seems to discover the ability to combine symbols, a change that is evident in two-word sentences, in thinking, and in multistep play with other children. There also appears to be a quite stagelike shift between ages 3 and 4, of which the theory of mind is the centerpiece. Nevertheless, each new skill or understanding seems to be acquired in a fairly narrow area first and is generalized more fully only later. In fact, one of the things that differentiates the gifted or higher-IQ child from the child with a lower IQ or mental retardation is how quickly and broadly the child generalizes some new concept or strategy to new instances.

Despite this nonstagelike quality of most developmental change, it is nonetheless true that the patterns of relationships, of thinking, and of problem solving of two children of widely different ages (say, a 5-year-old and an 11-year-old) differ in almost every respect. So there is certainly orderliness in the sequences, and there are some links between them, but there probably are not major stages as Piaget proposed them.

Continuities   In the midst of all this change, all these sequences, all the new ways of relating and thinking, there is also continuity. Each child carries forward some core of individuality. The notion of temperament certainly implies such a core, as does the concept of an internal working model. Alan Sroufe once again offers an elegant way of thinking about this central core. Continuity in development, he says, "takes the form of coherence across transformations" (1983, p. 51). Thus, the specific behavior exhibited by a child may change—the clinging toddler may not become a clinging 9-year-old—but the underlying attachment model or the temperament that led to the clinging will still be at least partially present, manifesting itself in new ways. In particular, it has become increasingly clear that maladaptations often persist over time, as seen in the consistency of high levels of aggression or tantrum behavior and in the persistence of some of the maladaptive social interactions that flow from insecure attachments. The task of developmental psychologists is to understand both coherence (consistency) and the underlying patterns of transformation (development).

What Is the Significance of Individual Differences?

The issue of individual continuities emphasizes the fact that development is individual as well as collective. By definition, and as the core of its basic approach, developmental psychology concerns itself with the typical rather than with deviations from what is expected. Still, you have read about individual differences in virtually every chapter, so you know that both in-born differences and emergent or environmentally produced variations are present for children in every aspect of development. It seems instructive to tie together many of the threads woven throughout this epilogue by returning to the dimension of individual difference you have read about several times—vulnerability versus resilience.

It may be useful to define these concepts somewhat differently than we did in earlier chapters, in terms of the range of environments that will be sufficiently supportive for optimal development. By this definition, a vulnerable infant is one with a narrow range of potentially supportive environments. For such a child, only the most stimulating, the most responsive, the most adaptive environment will do. When the child's environment falls outside that range, the probability of a poor outcome is greatly increased. A resilient child, in contrast, is one for whom any of a very wide range of environments will support optimal development. A resilient child may thus be more strongly canalized, and a vulnerable child less so.

Some kinds of vulnerabilities are inborn, caused by genetic abnormalities, prenatal trauma or stress, preterm birth, or malnutrition. Any child suffering from these problems will thrive only in a highly supportive environment. You've encountered this pattern again and again through the chapters of this book:

- Low-birth-weight infants typically have normal IQs if they are reared in middle-class homes, but they have a high risk of retardation if they are reared in nonstimulating poverty-level homes (Bradley et al., 1994).

- Prenatally malnourished infants or those who suffered other complications in utero or during delivery develop more or less normally if they attend highly stimulating special preschools, but they have significantly lower IQs if reared at home by mothers with limited education (Breitmayer & Ramey, 1986; Zeskind & Ramey, 1981).

- Children born with cytomegalovirus are much more likely to have learning problems in school if they are reared in poverty-level environments than if they are reared in middle-class families (Hanshaw et al., 1976).

These examples are fairly straightforward. But "vulnerability" in this sense does not remain constant throughout life. A more general proposition, which you might think of as a working hypothesis, is that each time a given child's environment falls outside the range of acceptable supportiveness (that is, each time a mismatch occurs between the child's needs and what is available), the child becomes more vulnerable; on the other hand, every time the child's needs are met, the child becomes more resilient. For example, a temperamentally difficult child whose family environment is nonetheless sufficient to foster a secure attachment will become more resilient, more able to handle the next set of tasks; a temperamentally easy child who for some reason developed an insecure attachment would become more vulnerable to later stress or environmental insufficiency.

Furthermore, the qualities of the environment that are critical for a child's optimal development no doubt change as the child passes from one age to another. Responsive and warm interactions with parents seem particularly important in the period from perhaps 6 months to 18 months; richness of cognitive stimulation seems particularly critical between perhaps 1 year and 4 years; opportunity for practicing social skills with peers may be especially crucial at a later age. Thus, as the tasks change with age, the optimal environment changes also. Among other things, this means that the same family may be very good with a child of one age and not so good with a child of another age.

Most generally, the vulnerability/resilience model leads to the conclusion that even the most "vulnerable" child can show improvement if her environment improves markedly. Because some congenitally vulnerable children do not encounter sufficiently supportive environments, their vulnerability continues to increase. For this reason, early problems often persist.

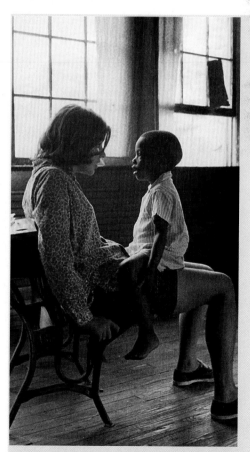

This photo has been used at the end of every edition of this text because it speaks so eloquently of the joy and discovery that are so much a part of development.

At the same time, improvement is possible, even likely. Most children manage to survive and thrive, despite stresses and vulnerabilities. As Emmy Werner puts it, "We could not help being deeply impressed by the resilience of most children and youth and their capacity for positive change and personal growth" (1986, p. 5).

A Final Point: The Joy of Development

To end both this epilogue and the text on an optimistic note, remember that in the midst of all the "crises" and "transitions" and "vulnerabilities," development has a special joyous quality. When a child masters a new skill, she is not just pleased—she is delighted and will repeat that new skill at length, quite obviously getting vast satisfaction from it. A 5-year-old who learns to draw stars may draw them on everything in sight, including paper, walls, clothes, and napkins, simply because it is so much fun to draw stars. A 10-year-old who learns to do cartwheels will delightedly display this new talent to anyone who will watch and will practice endlessly.

The same joyous quality can be part of the family's development as well. Confronting and moving successfully through any of the periodic and inevitable upheavals in family life can be immensely pleasing. Watching your child progress, liking your child, and enjoying being together are all deeply satisfying parts of rearing children. When parents cry at their son's or daughter's high school graduation or wedding, it is not merely sentiment. It is an expression of that sense of love, pride, and wonderment that they and their children have come so far.

Glossary

ability goal A goal orientation associated with a desire to be superior to others.

academic approach An approach to early childhood education that provides children with instruction in skills needed for success in school.

accommodation That part of the adaptation process proposed by Piaget by which a person modifies existing schemes as a result of new experiences or creates new schemes when old ones no longer handle the data.

achievement test Test designed to assess a child's learning of specific material taught in school, such as spelling or arithmetic computation; in the United States, achievement tests are typically given to all children in designated grades.

adaptation The processes through which schemes change.

adaptive reflexes Reflexes that are essential to the infant's survival but that disappear in the first year of life.

ADHD/combined type ADHD in which both hyperactivity and inattention are problems.

ADHD/hyperactive/impulsive type ADHD in which hyperactivity is the main problem.

ADHD/inattentive type ADHD in which inattention is the main problem.

adolescent-onset conduct disorder A conduct disorder that begins only in adolescence; it is typically less severe and persistent than childhood-onset conduct disorder.

affectional bond A "relatively long-enduring tie in which the partner is important as a unique individual and is interchangeable with none other" (Ainsworth, 1989, p. 711).

aggression Behavior that is aimed at harming or injuring another person or object.

agreeableness One of the Big Five personality traits; a person who scores high on this trait is characterized by trust, generosity, kindness, and sympathy.

amnion The sac, or bag, filled with liquid in which the embryo/fetus floats during prenatal life.

analytical intelligence One of three types of intelligence in Sternberg's triarchic theory of intelligence; the type of intelligence typically measured on IQ tests, including the ability to plan, remember facts, and organize information.

androgynous One of four sex-role types suggested by the work of Bem and others; a type characterized by high levels of both masculine and feminine qualities.

anorexia nervosa Eating disorder characterized by self-starvation.

anoxia A shortage of oxygen. This is one of the potential risks at birth, and it can result in brain damage if it is prolonged.

Asperger's disorder A disorder in which children possess the other characteristics of autistic disorder but have intact language and cognitive skills.

assimilation That part of the adaptation process proposed by Piaget that involves absorbing new experiences or information into existing schemes. Experience is not taken in "as is," however, but is modified (or interpreted) somewhat so as to fit the preexisting schemes.

association areas Parts of the brain where sensory, motor, and intellectual functions are linked.

at-risk-for-overweight Describes a child whose BMI is between the 85th and 95th percentiles.

attachment A subtype of affectional bond in which the presence of the partner adds a special sense of security, a "safe base," for the individual.

attachment behaviors The collection of (probably) instinctive behaviors of one person toward another that bring about or maintain proximity and caregiving, such as the smile of the young infant; behaviors that reflect an attachment.

attention deficit hyperactivity disorder (ADHD) A disorder in which a child shows both significant problems in focusing attention and physical hyperactivity.

attention problems A category of psychopathologies that impair one's ability to concentrate, including attention deficit hyperactivity disorder, attention deficit disorder, and hyperkinetic disorder.

atypical development An enduring pattern of behavior that is unusual, compared to the behavior of others of the child's age, and that interferes with the child's development in some significant way.

auditory acuity How well one can hear.

authoritarian style One of the three parental styles described by Baumrind, characterized by high levels of control and maturity demands and low levels of nurturance and communication.

authoritative style One of the three parental styles described by Baumrind, characterized by high levels of control, nurturance, maturity demands, and communication.

autistic disorder A disorder in which children have much more limited language skills than others of the same age, an inability to engage in reciprocal social relationships, and a severely limited range of interests.

automaticity The ability to recall information from long-term memory without effort.

axons Tail-like extensions of neurons.

babbling The repetitive vocalizing of consonant-vowel combinations by an infant, typically beginning at about 6 months of age.

Babinski reflex A reflex found in very young infants that causes them to splay out their toes in response to a stroke on the bottom of the foot.

balanced approach Reading instruction that combines explicit phonics instruction with other strategies for helping children acquire literacy.

Bayley Scales of Infant Development The best-known and most widely used test of infant "intelligence."

behavior genetics The study of the genetic contributions to behavior or traits such as intelligence or personality.

behaviorism The theoretical view that defines development in terms of behavior changes caused by environmental influences.

Big Five The five primary dimensions of adult personality identified by researchers: extraversion, agreeableness, conscientiousness, neuroticism, and openness/intellect.

bilingual education As practiced in the United States, a school program for students who are not proficient in English in which instruction in basic subject matter is given in the children's native language during the first 2 or 3 years of schooling, with a gradual transition to full English instruction over several years.

birth order A child's position in the sequence of children within a family, such as first-born, later-born, or only child.

blastocyst Name for the mass of cells from roughly 4 to 10 days after fertilization.

blended family A family that is established when a single parent marries a nonparent or parent.

BMI-for-age Comparison of an individual child's BMI against established norms for his or her age group and sex.

body mass index (BMI) A measure that estimates a person's proportion of body fat.

bone age A measure of physical maturation based on x-ray examination of bones, typically the wrist and hand bones. Two children of the same chronological age may have different bone age because their rates of physical maturation differ.

bulimia Eating disorder characterized by alternating periods of bingeing and purging.

case studies In-depth studies of individuals.

cell body The part of the cell that contains the nucleus and in which all the cell's vital functions are carried out.

centration The young child's tendency to think of the world in terms of one variable at a time.

cephalocaudal One of two basic patterns of physical development in infancy (the other is proximodistal), in which development proceeds from the head downward.

cerebral cortex The convoluted gray portion of the brain, which governs perception, body movement, thinking, and language.

cesarean section (c-section) Delivery of the child through an incision in the mother's abdomen.

childhood-onset conduct disorder Conduct disorder beginning in childhood; the pattern is linked to rejection by peers and to conduct problems that persist into adolescence and adulthood.

chorion The outer layer of cells of the blastocyst during prenatal development, from which both the placenta and the umbilical cord are formed.

chromosomes The structures, arrayed in 23 pairs, within each cell in the body that contain genetic information. Each chromosome is made up of many segments, called genes.

class inclusion The principle that subordinate classes of objects are included in superordinate classes.

classical conditioning One of three major types of learning. An automatic, or unconditional, response such as an emotion or a reflex comes to be triggered by a new cue, called the conditional stimulus, after having been paired several times with that stimulus.

clinical depression (major depressive disorder) A combination of sad mood, sleeping and eating disturbances, and difficulty concentrating that lasts 6 months or longer.

clique A group of four to six friends with strong affectional bonds and high levels of group solidarity and loyalty; the term is used by researchers to describe a self-chosen group of friends.

cognitive-developmental theories Developmental theories that emphasize children's actions on the environment and suggest that age-related changes in reasoning precede and explain changes in other domains.

cohort A group of individuals who share the same historical experiences at the same times in their lives.

colic A pattern of persistent and often inconsolable crying, totaling more than 3 hours a day, found in some infants in the first 3 to 4 months of life.

color constancy The ability to see the color of an object as remaining the same despite changes in illumination or shadow.

competence A person's basic, underlying level of skill, displayed under ideal circumstances. It is not possible to measure competence directly.

concrete operations stage Piaget's term for the stage of development between ages 6 and 12, during which children become able to think logically.

conduct disorder Diagnostic term for a pattern of deviant behavior including high levels of aggressive, antisocial, or delinquent acts.

conscience The list of "don'ts" in the superego; violation of any of these leads to feelings of guilt.

conscientiousness One of the Big Five personality traits; a person who scores high on this trait is characterized by efficiency, organization, planfulness, and reliability.

conservation The understanding that the quantity or amount of a substance remains the same even when there are external changes in its shape or arrangement. Typically, children do not have this understanding until after age 5.

constraint As used in discussions of language development, an assumption that is presumed to be built-in or learned early (a "default option") by which a child figures out what words refer to. Examples include the principle of contrast and the whole object constraint.

control group A group of participants in an experiment who receive either no special treatment or some neutral treatment.

conventional morality The second level of moral development proposed by Kohlberg, in which a person's judgments are dominated by considerations of group values and laws.

conventional rules As defined by Turiel, arbitrary, socially defined rules specific to a particular culture, subculture, group, or setting, such as "Don't run in the halls" or "Smoking allowed only in designated areas."

cooing Making repetitive vowel sounds, particularly the *uuu* sound; the behavior develops early in the prelinguistic period, when babies are between about 1 and 4 months of age.

corpus callosum The structure that connects the right and left hemispheres of the cerebral cortex.

correlation A statistic used to describe the strength of a relationship between two variables. It can range from −1.00 to +1.00. The closer it is to +1.00 or −1.00, the stronger the relationship being described.

creative intelligence One of three types of intelligence described by Sternberg in his triarchic theory of intelligence; includes insightfulness and the ability to see new relationships among events or experiences.

creativity The ability to produce original, appropriate, and valuable ideas and/or solutions to problems.

critical period Any time period during development when an organism is especially responsive to and learns from a specific type of stimulation. The same stimulation at other points in development has little or no effect.

cross-cultural research Any study that involves comparisons of different cultures or contexts.

cross-sectional design A form of research study in which samples of participants from several different age groups are studied at the same time.

crowd A larger and looser group of friends than a clique, normally made up of several cliques that have joined together; a reputation-based group, common in adolescent subculture, with widely agreed-upon characteristics.

cumulative deficit Any difference between groups in IQ or achievement test scores that becomes larger over time.

decentration Thinking that takes multiple variables into account.

deductive logic Reasoning from the general to the particular, from a rule to an expected instance or from a theory to a hypothesis, characteristic of formal operational thinking.

delinquency A subcategory of conduct disorder involving explicit lawbreaking.

dendrites Branchlike protrusions from the cell bodies of neurons.

deoxyribonucleic acid (DNA) The chemical of which chromosomes are composed.

dependent variable The variable in an experiment that is expected to show the impact of manipulations of the independent variable; also called the *outcome variable*.

depression A combination of sad mood and difficulty carrying out daily functions.

developmental approach An approach to early childhood education that supports children's development of naturally occurring milestones.

developmental psychopathology A relatively new approach to the study of deviance that emphasizes that normal and abnormal development have common roots and that pathology can arise from many different pathways.

developmental science The study of age-related changes in behavior, thinking, emotions, and social relationships.

developmental theories Sets of statements that propose general principles of development.

developmentally appropriate practices Early childhood education practices based on an understanding of developmental universals, individual differences, and contextual variables.

difficult child An infant who is irritable and irregular in behavior.

dilation A key process in the first stage of childbirth, during which the cervix widens sufficiently to allow the infant's head to pass into the birth canal. Full dilation is 10 centimeters.

divergent thinking The ability to produce multiple solutions to problems that have no clear answer.

dominant/recessive pattern of inheritance The pattern of genetic transmission in which a single dominant gene influences a person's phenotype, but an individual must have two recessive genes to express a recessive trait.

Down syndrome (trisomy 21) A genetic anomaly in which every cell contains three copies of chromosome 21 rather than two. Children born with this genetic pattern have characteristic physical features and usually have mental retardation.

dynamic systems theory The view that several factors interact to influence development.

early childhood education Educational programs for children between birth and 8 years.

easy child An infant who adapts easily to change and who exhibits regular patterns of eating, sleeping, and alertness.

eclecticism The use of multiple theoretical perspectives to explain and study human development.

effacement The flattening of the cervix, which, along with dilation, is a key process of the first stage of childbirth.

ego In Freudian theory, the portion of the personality that organizes, plans, and keeps the person in touch with reality. Language and thought are both ego functions.

ego ideal The list of "dos" in the superego; violation of any of these leads to feelings of shame.

egocentrism A cognitive state in which the individual (typically a child) sees the world only from his own perspective, without awareness that there are other perspectives.

embryo The name given to the developing organism during the period of prenatal development between about 2 weeks and 8 weeks after conception, beginning with implantation of the blastocyst in the uterine wall.

embryonic stage The second stage of prenatal development, from week 2 through week 8, when the embryo's organs form.

empathy As defined by Hoffman, "a vicarious affective response that does not necessarily match another's affective state but is more appropriate to the other's situation than to one's own" (1982, p. 285).

empiricism The view that perceptual abilities are learned.

endocrine glands Glands (including the adrenals, the thyroid, the pituitary, the testes, and the ovaries) that secrete hormones governing overall physical growth and sexual maturing.

English-as-a-second-language (ESL) An alternative to bilingual education; children who are not proficient in English attend academic classes taught entirely in English but then spend several hours in a separate class to receive English-language instruction.

English-language learners (ELLs) School children who do not speak English well enough to function in English-only classes.

equilibration The third part of the adaptation process proposed by Piaget, involving a periodic restructuring of schemes to create a balance between assimilation and accommodation.

ethnic group "A subgroup whose members are perceived by themselves and others to have a common origin and culture, and shared activities in which the common origin or culture is an essential ingredient" (Porter & Washington, 1993, p. 140).

ethnicity An individual's membership in an ethnic group.

excessive weight gain A pattern in which children gain more weight in a year than is appropriate for their age and height.

executive processes Cognitive skills that allow a person to devise and carry out alternative strategies for remembering and solving problems.

experiment A research method for testing a causal hypothesis, in which participants are assigned randomly to experimental and control groups and the experimental group is then provided with a particular experience that is expected to alter behavior in some fashion.

experimental group A group of participants in an experiment who receive a particular treatment intended to produce some specific effect.

expressive language Sounds, signs, or symbols used to communicate meaning.

extended family A family structure that includes parents, grandparents, aunts, uncles, cousins, and so on.

externalizing problems A category of psychopathologies that includes any deviant behavior primarily directed toward others, such as conduct disorders.

extraversion One of the Big Five personality traits; a person who scores high on this trait is characterized by assertiveness, energy, enthusiasm, and outgoingness.

extremely low birth weight (ELBW) Term for any baby born with a weight below 1,000 grams (2.2 pounds).

fallopian tube The tube between the ovary and the uterus down which the ovum travels to the uterus and in which conception usually occurs.

false belief principle The understanding that another person might have a false belief and the ability to determine what information might cause the false belief. A child's understanding of the false belief principle is one key sign of the emergence of a representational theory of mind.

family structure The configuration of individuals in a child's household.

family systems theory The view that the family is an integrated network of factors that work together to influence a child's development.

fast-mapping The ability to categorically link new words to real-world referents.

feminine One of four sex-role types suggested by the work of Bem and others; a type characterized by high scores on femininity measures and low scores on masculinity measures.

fetal alcohol syndrome (FAS) A pattern of abnormalities, including mental retardation and minor physical anomalies, often found in children born to alcoholic mothers.

fetal stage The third stage of prenatal development, from week 8 to birth, when growth and organ refinement take place.

fetus The name given to the developing organism from about 8 weeks after conception until birth.

figurative schemes Mental representations of the basic properties of objects in the world.

fontanel One of several "soft spots" in the skull that are present at birth but disappear when the bones of the skull grow together.

foreclosure One of four identity statuses proposed by Marcia, involving an ideological or occupational commitment without a previous reevaluation.

formal operations stage Piaget's name for the fourth and final major stage of cognitive development, occurring during adolescence, when the child becomes able to manipulate and organize ideas or hypothetical situations as well as objects.

fraternal (dizygotic) twins Children carried in the same pregnancy but who develop from two separately fertilized ova. They are no more alike genetically than other pairs of siblings.

full scale IQ The WISC-IV score that takes into account verbal and nonverbal scale scores.

gametes Sperm and ova. These cells, unlike all other cells of the body, contain only 23 chromosomes rather than 23 pairs.

gender concept The full understanding that gender is constant and permanent, unchanged by appearance.

gender constancy The final stage in development of gender concept, in which the child understands that gender doesn't change even though there may be external changes (in clothing or hair length, for example).

gender identity The first stage in the development of gender concept, in which a child labels self and others correctly as male or female.

gender schema theory A theory of the development of gender concept and sex-role behavior that proposes that, between about 18 months and age 2 or 3, a child creates a fundamental schema by which to categorize people, objects, activities, and qualities by gender.

gender stability The second stage in the development of gender concept, in which the child understands that a person's gender stays the same throughout life.

gene A uniquely coded segment of DNA in a chromosome that affects one or more specific body processes or developments.

genotype The pattern of characteristics and developmental sequences mapped in the genes of any specific individual, which will be modified by individual experience into the phenotype.

germinal stage The first stage of prenatal development, beginning at conception and ending at implantation of the zygote in the uterus (approximately the first 2 weeks).

glial cells The "glue" that holds neurons together to give form to the structures of the nervous system.

goal-corrected partnership Term used by Bowlby to describe the form of the child-parent attachment in the preschool years, in which the two partners, through improved communication, negotiate the form and frequency of contact between them.

gonadotrophic hormones Hormones secreted by the pituitary gland at the beginning of puberty that stimulate the development of glands in the testes and ovaries, which then begin to secrete testosterone or estrogen.

goodness-of-fit The degree to which an infant's environment and his or her temperament work together.

growth curve The pattern and rate of growth exhibited by a child over time.

habituation An automatic decrease in the intensity of a response to a repeated stimulus, enabling a child or adult to ignore the familiar and focus attention on the novel.

handedness A strong preference for using primarily one hand or the other; it develops between 3 and 5 years of age.

hedonistic reasoning A form of prosocial moral reasoning described by Eisenberg in which the child is concerned with consequences to self rather than moral considerations, roughly equivalent to Kohlberg's stage 2.

heterozygous Term describing the genetic pattern when the two genes in the pair at any given genetic locus carry different instructions, such as a gene for blue eyes from one parent and a gene for brown eyes from the other parent.

hippocampus A brain structure that is involved in the transfer of information to long-term memory.

holophrase A combination of a gesture and a single word that conveys more meaning than just the word alone; often seen and heard in children between 12 and 18 months old.

homozygous Term describing the genetic pattern when the two genes in the pair at any given genetic locus both carry the same instructions.

horizontal decalage Piaget's term for school-aged children's inconsistent performance on concrete operations tasks.

hostile aggression Aggressive verbal behavior intended to hurt another's feelings.

hypothesis A testable prediction based on a theory.

hypothetico-deductive reasoning Piaget's term for the form of reasoning that is part of formal operational thought and involves not just deductive logic but also the ability to consider hypotheses and hypothetical possibilities.

id In Freudian theory, the inborn, primitive portion of the personality, the storehouse of libido, the basic energy that continually pushes for immediate gratification.

identical (monozygotic) twins Children carried in the same pregnancy who develop from the same fertilized ovum. They are genetic clones of each other.

identity achievement One of four identity statuses proposed by Marcia, involving the successful resolution of an identity "crisis" and resulting in a new commitment.

identity diffusion One of four identity statuses proposed by Marcia, involving neither a current reevaluation of identity nor a firm personal commitment.

identity versus role confusion As hypothesized by Erikson, the psychosocial stage in which a teenager must develop a sense of personal identity or else enter adulthood with a sense of confusion about his or her place in the world.

inclusive education General term for education programs that assign children with physical, mental, or emotional disabilities to regular classrooms and that provide any special services required by the child in that classroom.

independent variable A condition or event that an experimenter varies in some systematic way in order to observe the impact of that variation on participants' behavior.

individuation The process of psychological, social, and physical separation from parents that begins in adolescence.

inductive logic Reasoning from the particular to the general, from experience to broad rules, characteristic of concrete operational thinking.

information-processing theories A set of theories based on the idea that humans process information in ways that are similar to those used in computers.

insecure attachment An internal working model of relationships in which the child does not as readily use the parent as a safe base and is not readily consoled by the parent if upset. Includes three subtypes of attachment: avoidant, ambivalent, and disorganized/disoriented.

instrumental aggression Aggressive behavior intended to achieve a goal, such as obtaining a toy from another child.

intelligence A set of abilities defined in various ways by different psychologists but generally agreed to include the ability to reason abstractly, the ability to profit from experience, and the ability to adapt to varying environmental contexts.

intelligence quotient (IQ) Originally defined in terms of a child's mental age and chronological age, IQ is now computed by comparing a child's performance with that of other children of the same chronological age.

intermodal perception Formation of a single perception of a stimulus that is based on information from two or more senses.

internal models of experience A theoretical concept emphasizing that each child creates a set of core ideas or assumptions about the world, the self, and relationships with others through which all subsequent experience is filtered.

internal working model As applied to social relationships, a cognitive construction of the workings of relationships, such as expectations of support or affection, trustworthiness, and so on. The earliest relationships may form the template for such a cognitive construction.

internalizing problems A category of psychopathologies that includes anxiety and depression and other conditions in which deviant behavior is directed inwardly, against the self.

invented spelling A strategy young children with good phonological awareness skills use when they write.

lateralization The process through which brain functions are divided between the two hemispheres of the cerebral cortex.

learning Change due to experience.

learning disability (LD) A term broadly used to describe an unexpected or unexplained problem in learning to read, spell, or calculate and more precisely used to refer to a neurological dysfunction that causes such effects.

learning theories Psychological theories that explain development in terms of accumulated learning experiences.

libido The term used by Freud to describe the basic, unconscious, instinctual sexual energy in each individual.

longitudinal design A form of research study in which the same participants are observed or assessed repeatedly over a period of months or years.

low birth weight (LBW) Term for any baby born with a weight below 2,500 grams (5.5 pounds), including both those born too early (preterm) and those who are small for date.

masculine One of four sex-role types suggested by the work of Bem and others; a type characterized by high scores on masculinity measures and low scores on femininity measures.

maturation Sequential patterns of change that are governed by instructions contained in the genetic code and shared by all members of a species.

mean length of utterance (MLU) The average number of meaningful units in a sentence. Each basic word is one meaningful unit, as is each inflection.

medulla A portion of the brain that lies immediately above the spinal cord; it is largely developed at birth.

memory strategies Ways of manipulating information that increase the chances that it will be remembered.

menarche Onset of menstruation.

mental age Term used by Binet and Simon and Terman in the early calculation of IQ scores to refer to the age level of IQ test items a child could successfully answer. Used in combination with the child's chronological age to calculate an IQ score.

mental retardation An intellectual disability defined most often as an IQ below 70 combined with poor adaptive behavior.

metacognition General and rather loosely used term describing knowledge of one's own thinking processes: knowing what one knows, and how one learns.

metamemory Knowledge about one's own memory processes.

midbrain A section of the brain lying above the medulla and below the cortex that regulates attention, sleeping, waking, and other automatic functions; it is largely developed at birth.

mirror neurons Specialized cells in the cerebral cortex that simulate the behavior and emotions of others.

moral development The process of learning to distinguish between right and wrong in accordance with cultural values.

moral realism stage The first of Piaget's stages of moral development, in which children believe that rules are inflexible.

moral relativism stage The second of Piaget's stages of moral development, in which children understand that many rules can be changed through social agreement.

moral rules As defined by Turiel, universal and obligatory rules reflecting basic principles that guarantee the rights of others.

moratorium One of four identity statuses proposed by Marcia, involving an ongoing reexamination of identity but no new commitment.

Moro reflex The reflex that causes infants to extend their legs, arms, and fingers, arch the back, and draw back the head when startled (for example, by a loud sound or a sensation of being dropped).

motherese (infant-directed speech) The simplified, higher-pitched speech that adults use with infants and young children.

motor development Growth and change in ability to perform both gross motor skills (such as walking or throwing) and fine motor skills (such as drawing or writing).

multifactorial pattern of inheritance The pattern of genetic transmission in which both genes and environment influence the phenotype.

multiple intelligences Eight types of intelligence (linguistic, logical/mathematical, spatial, bodily kinesthetic, musical, interpersonal, intrapersonal, and naturalistic) proposed by Howard Gardner.

myelination The process by which an insulating layer of a substance called myelin is added to neurons.

nativism The view that perceptual abilities are inborn.

naturalistic observation A research method in which participants are observed in their normal environments.

needs-oriented reasoning A form of prosocial moral reasoning proposed by Eisenberg in which the child expresses concern directly for the other person's need, even if the other's need conflicts with the child's own wishes or desires.

negative reinforcement The process of strengthening a behavior by the removal or cessation of an unpleasant stimulus.

neglected children Children who are seldom described by peers as either liked or disliked.

neglecting style A fourth parenting style suggested by Maccoby and Martin, involving low levels of both acceptance and control.

neo-Piagetian theory A theory of cognitive development that assumes that Piaget's basic ideas are correct but that uses concepts from information-processing theory to explain children's movement from one stage to the next.

neuronal migration The movement of neurons to specialized regions of the brain.

neuronal proliferation The rapid development of neurons between the 10th and 18th week of gestation.

neurons The cells in the nervous system that are responsible for transmission and reception of nerve impulses.

neuroticism One of the Big Five personality traits; a person who scores high on this trait is characterized by anxiety, self-pity, tenseness, and emotional instability.

neurotransmitters Chemicals that accomplish the transmission of signals from one neuron to another at synapses.

nonnormative changes (individual differences) Changes that result from unique, unshared events.

nonshared environment Characteristics of a family that affect one child but not others in the household.

normative age-graded changes Changes that are common to every member of a species.

normative history-graded changes Changes that occur in most members of a cohort as a result of factors at work during a specific, well-defined historical period.

norms Average ages at which developmental events happen.

object constancy The general phrase describing the ability to see objects as remaining the same despite changes in sensory information about them.

object permanence The understanding that objects continue to exist even when they cannot be directly perceived.

objective self The component of the self-concept that involves awareness of the self as an object with properties.

Oedipus conflict The pattern of events that Freud believed occur between ages 3 and 5, when the child experiences a sexual desire for the parent of the opposite sex; the resulting fear of possible reprisal from the parent of the same sex is resolved when the child identifies with that parent.

openness/intellect One of the Big Five personality traits; a person who scores high on this trait is characterized by curiosity, imagination, insight, originality, and wide interests.

operant conditioning The type of learning in which the probability of a person's performing some behavior is increased or decreased because of the consequences it produces.

operation Term used by Piaget for a complex, internal, abstract scheme, first seen at about age 6.

operational efficiency A neo-Piagetian term for the number of schemes an individual can place into working memory at one time.

operative schemes Mental representations of the logical connections among objects in the world.

oppositional defiant disorder (ODD) A pattern of negative, defiant, disobedient, and hostile behavior toward parents and other authority figures, established prior to age 8.

organization The process of deriving generalizable schemes from specific experiences.

ossification The process of hardening by which soft tissue becomes bone.

otitis media (OM) An inflammation of the middle ear that is caused by a bacterial infection.

overextension The inappropriate use of a word to designate an entire category of objects, such as when a child uses the word *kitty* to refer to all animate objects.

overregularization Young children's applications of basic rules to irregular words.

overweight Describes a child whose BMI is at the 95th percentile.

ovum The cell released monthly from a woman's ovaries, which, if fertilized, forms the basis for the developing organism.

parallel play Form of play seen in toddlers, in which children play next to, but not with, one another.

perception The attribution of meaning to sensory information.

perceptual constancies A collection of mental rules that allow humans to perceive shape, size, and color as constant even when perceptual conditions (such as amount of light, angle of view, and the like) change.

perceptual reasoning index Tests on the WISC-IV, such as block design and picture completion, that tap nonverbal visual-processing abilities.

performance The behavior shown by a person under real-life rather than ideal circumstances. Even when researchers are interested in competence, all they can ever measure is performance.

permissive style One of the three parenting styles described by Baumrind, characterized by high levels of nurturance and low levels of control, maturity demands, and communication.

personality The collection of relatively enduring patterns of reacting to and interacting with others and the environment that distinguishes each child or adult.

pervasive developmental disorders (PDDs) A group of disorders in which children exhibit severe disturbances in social relationships.

phenotype The expression of a particular set of genetic information in a specific environment; the observable result of the joint operation of genetic and environmental influences.

phonological awareness Understanding of the rules governing the sounds of a language as well as knowledge of the connection between sounds and the way they are represented in written language.

phonology The sound patterns of a particular language and the rules for combining them.

pituitary gland Gland that provides the trigger for release of hormones from other glands.

placenta An organ that develops between the fetus and the wall of the uterus during gestation.

plasticity The ability of the brain to change in response to experience.

polygenic pattern of inheritance Any pattern of genetic transmission in which multiple genes contribute to the outcome, such as is presumed to occur for complex traits such as intelligence or temperament.

popular children Children who are described as well-liked by a majority of peers.

positive reinforcement The process of strengthening a behavior by the presentation of some pleasurable or positive stimulus.

practical intelligence One of three types of intelligence in Sternberg's triarchic theory of intelligence; often called "street smarts," this type of intelligence includes skill in applying information to the real world or solving practical problems.

pragmatics The rules for the use of language in communicative interaction, such as the rules for taking turns and the style of speech that is appropriate for different listeners.

preconventional morality The first level of moral development proposed by Kohlberg, in which moral judgments are dominated by consideration of what will be punished and what feels good.

prefrontal cortex (PFC) The part of the frontal lobe just behind the forehead that is responsible for executive processing.

prelinguistic phase The period before a child speaks his or her first words.

preoperational stage Piaget's term for the second major stage of cognitive development, from about 24 months to about age 6, marked by the ability to use symbols.

preterm infant An infant born before 38 weeks gestational age.

primary circular reactions Piaget's phrase to describe a baby's simple repetitive actions in substage 2 of the sensorimotor stage, organized around the baby's own body; the baby repeats some action in order to have some desired outcome occur again, such as putting his thumb in his mouth to repeat the good feeling of sucking.

primitive reflexes Collection of reflexes seen in young infants that gradually disappear during the first year of life, including the Moro and Babinski reflexes.

principle of contrast The assumption that every word has a different meaning, which leads a child to assume that two or more different words refer to different objects.

principled (postconventional) morality The third level of moral development proposed by Kohlberg, in which considerations of justice, individual rights, and social contracts dominate moral judgment.

processing speed index Timed tests on the WISC-IV, such as symbol search, that measure how rapidly an examinee processes information.

production deficiency A pattern whereby an individual can use some mental strategy if reminded to do so but fails to use the strategy spontaneously.

prosocial behavior Voluntary behavior intended to benefit another, such as giving away or sharing possessions, money, or time, with no obvious self-gain; altruism.

proximodistal One of two basic patterns of physical development in infancy (the other is cephalocaudal), in which development proceeds from the center outward—that is, from the trunk to the limbs.

pruning The process of eliminating unused synapses.

psychoanalytic theories Developmental theories based on the assumption that age-related change results from maturationally determined conflicts between internal drives and society's demands.

psychological disorder A pattern of behavior that is unusual in a person's culture and interferes with his or her psychological, social, and/or educational functioning.

psychosexual stages The stages of personality development suggested by Freud: the oral, anal, phallic, latency, and genital stages.

psychosocial stages The stages of personality development suggested by Erikson, involving tasks centered on trust, autonomy, initiative, industry, identity, intimacy, generativity, and ego integrity.

puberty The series of hormonal and physical changes at adolescence that bring about sexual maturity.

punishment The removal of a desirable stimulus or the administration of an unpleasant consequence after some undesired behavior in order to stop the behavior.

reaction range Term used by some psychologists for the range of possible outcomes (phenotypes) for some variable, given basic genetic patterning (the genotype). In the case of IQ scores, the reaction range is estimated at 20 to 25 points.

receptive language Comprehension of spoken language.

reciprocal determinism Bandura's model in which personal, behavioral, and environmental factors interact to influence personality development.

reciprocal friendship A friendship in which each partner identifies the other as a friend; also, a quality of friendship in school-aged children, when friendship is for the first time perceived as being based on reciprocal trust.

reflexes Automatic body reactions to specific stimulation, such as the knee jerk or the Moro reflex. Adults have many reflexes, but the newborn also has some primitive reflexes that disappear as the cortex develops.

rejected children Unpopular children who are explicitly avoided and not chosen as playmates or friends.

relational aggression Aggression aimed at damaging another person's self-esteem or peer relationships, such as by using ostracism or threats of ostracism, cruel gossiping, or facial expressions of disdain.

relational complexity The number of elements in a problem and the complexity of the relationships among the elements.

relative right-left orientation The ability to identify right and left from multiple perspectives.

reliability The stability of a test score over multiple testing sessions.

respiratory distress syndrome A problem frequently found in infants born more than 6 weeks before term, in which the infant's lungs lack a chemical (surfactant) needed to keep air sacs inflated.

response inhibition The ability to control responses to stimuli.

responsiveness An aspect of parent-child interaction; a responsive parent is sensitive to the child's cues and reacts appropriately, following the child's lead.

reticular formation The part of the brain that regulates attention.

reversibility One of the most critical of the operations Piaget identified as part of the concrete operations period: the understanding that actions and mental operations can be reversed.

role-taking The ability to look at a situation from another person's perspective.

rooting reflex The reflex that causes an infant to automatically turn toward a touch on the cheek, open the mouth, and make sucking movements.

scaffolding The term used by Bruner to describe the process by which a teacher (or parent, older child, or other person in the role of teacher) structures a learning encounter with a child, so as to lead the child from step to step—a process consistent with Vygotsky's theory of cognitive development.

schematic learning The development of expectancies concerning what actions lead to what results or what events tend to go together.

scheme Piaget's word for the basic actions of knowing, including both physical actions (sensorimotor schemes, such as looking or reaching) and mental actions (such as classifying, comparing, and reversing). An experience is assimilated into a scheme, and the scheme is created or modified through accommodation.

secondary circular reactions Repetitive actions in substage 3 of the sensorimotor period, oriented around external objects; the infant repeats some action in order to have some outside event recur, such as hitting a mobile repeatedly so that it moves.

secular trend A pattern of change in some characteristic over several cohorts, such as systematic changes in the average timing of menarche or in average height or weight.

secure attachment An internal working model of relationships in which the child uses the parent as a safe base and is readily consoled after separation, when fearful, or when otherwise stressed.

selective attention The ability to focus cognitive activity on the important elements of a problem or situation.

self-concept One's knowledge of and thoughts about the set of qualities attributed to the self.

self-efficacy Bandura's term for an individual's belief in his or her ability to accomplish tasks.

self-esteem A global evaluation of one's own worth; an aspect of self-concept.

semantics A particular language's system of meaning and the rules for conveying meaning.

sensation The process of taking in raw information through the senses.

sensation-seeking A strong desire to experience the emotional and physical arousal associated with risky behaviors such as fast driving and unprotected sex.

sensitive period A period during which particular experiences can best contribute to proper development. It is similar to a critical period, but the effects of deprivation during a sensitive period are not as severe as during a critical period.

sensorimotor stage Piaget's term for the first major stage of cognitive development, from birth to about 24 months, when the child uses sensory and motor skills to act on the environment.

sequential design A form of research study that combines cross-sectional and longitudinal designs in some way.

seriation The ability to use a rule to put an array of objects in order.

sex role The set of behaviors, attitudes, rights, duties, and obligations that are seen as appropriate for being male or female in any given culture.

sex-typed behavior Behavior that matches a culturally defined sex role.

sexually transmitted diseases (STDs) Category of disease spread by sexual contact, including chlamydia, genital warts, syphilis, gonorrhea, and HIV; also called *venereal diseases*.

shape constancy The ability to see an object's shape as remaining the same despite changes in the shape of the retinal image; a basic perceptual constancy.

shared environment Characteristics of a family that affect all children in the household.

short-term storage space (STSS) A neo-Piagetian term for working memory capacity.

size constancy The ability to see an object's size as remaining the same despite changes in size of the retinal image; a key element in size constancy is the ability to judge depth.

slow-to-warm-up child An infant who may seem unresponsive but who simply takes more time to respond than other infants do.

small-for-date infant An infant who weighs less than is normal for the number of weeks of gestation completed.

social cognition Thinking about and understanding the emotions of and interactions and relationships among people.

social referencing Using another person's emotional reaction to some situation as a basis for deciding one's own reaction. A baby does this when she checks her parent's facial expression or body language before responding positively or negatively to something new.

social status A term used by psychologists to refer to how well an individual child is liked by his or her peers.

socioeconomic status (SES) A collective term that includes the economic, occupational, and educational factors that influence a family's relative position in society.

spatial cognition The ability to infer rules from and make predictions about the movement of objects in space.

spatial perception The ability to identify and act on relationships of objects in space; in most people, this skill is lateralized to the right cerebral hemisphere.

sperm The cells produced in a man's testes that may fertilize an ovum following intercourse.

Stanford-Binet The best-known U.S. intelligence test. It was written by Lewis Terman and his associates at Stanford University and based on the first tests by Binet and Simon.

states of consciousness The periodic shifts in alertness, sleepiness, crankiness, and so on that characterize an infant's behavior.

Strange Situation A series of episodes used by Mary Ainsworth and others in studies of attachment. The child is observed with the mother, with a stranger, alone, when reunited with the stranger, and when reunited with the mother.

structured immersion An alternative to traditional bilingual education used in classrooms in which all children speak the same non-English native language. All basic instruction is in English, paced so that the children can comprehend, with the teacher translating only when absolutely necessary.

subjective self The component of the self-concept that involves awareness of the "I," the self that is separate from others.

submersion An approach to education of non–English-speaking students in which they are assigned to a classroom where instruction is given in English and are given no supplemental language assistance; also known as the *"sink or swim"* approach.

sudden infant death syndrome (SIDS) The unexpected death of an infant who otherwise appears healthy; also called *crib death*. The cause of SIDS is unknown.

superego In Freudian theory, the "conscience" part of personality, which contains parental and societal values and attitudes incorporated during childhood.

synapses Tiny spaces across which neural impulses flow from one neuron to the next.

synaptogenesis The process of synapse formation.

syntax The rules for forming sentences in a particular language.

systematic and explicit phonics Planned, specific instruction in sound-letter correspondences.

task goal A goal orientation associated with a desire for self-improvement.

telegraphic speech Term used by Roger Brown to describe the earliest sentences created by most children, which sound a bit like telegrams because they include key nouns and verbs but generally omit all other words and grammatical inflections.

temperament Inborn predispositions that form the foundations of personality.

teratogens Substances such as viruses and drugs or events that can cause birth defects.

tertiary circular reactions The deliberate experimentation with variations of previous actions, characteristic of substage 5 of the sensorimotor period, according to Piaget.

theory of mind Ideas that collectively explain other people's ideas, beliefs, desires, and behavior.

tracking Following a moving object with the eyes.

transitivity The ability to make inferences about logical relationships in an ordered set of stimuli.

triarchic theory of intelligence A theory advanced by Robert Sternberg, proposing the existence of three types of intelligence: analytical, creative, and practical.

umbilical cord The cord connecting the embryo/fetus to the placenta, containing two arteries and one vein.

underextension The use of words to apply only to specific objects, such as a child's use of the word *cup* to refer only to one particular cup.

undifferentiated One of four sex-role types suggested by the work of Bem and others; a type characterized by low scores on both masculinity and femininity measures.

uterus The female organ in which the embryo/fetus develops (popularly referred to as the *womb*).

utilization deficiency Using some specific mental strategy without deriving benefit from it.

validity The degree to which a test measures what it is intended to measure.

verbal comprehension index Tests on the WISC-IV that tap verbal skills such as knowledge of vocabulary and general information.

very low birth weight (VLBW) Term for any baby born with a weight below 1,500 grams (3.3 pounds).

viability The fetus's capacity for survival outside the womb.

visual acuity How well one can see.

warmth versus hostility The key dimension of emotional tone used to describe family interactions.

whole language approach An approach to reading instruction that places more emphasis on the meaning of written language than on its structure.

WISC-IV The most recent revision of the Wechsler Intelligence Scales for Children, a well-known IQ test developed in the United States that includes both verbal and performance (nonverbal) subtests.

working memory index Tests on the WISC-IV, such as digit span, that measure working memory efficiency.

WPPSI-III The third revision of the Wechsler Preschool and Primary Scale of Intelligence.

zone of proximal development In Vygotsky's theory, the range of tasks that are slightly too difficult for a child to do alone but that can be accomplished successfully with guidance from an adult or more experienced child.

zygote The single cell formed from separate sperm and egg cells at conception.

References

Abdel-Khalek, A., & Lynn, R. (2008). Intelligence, family size and birth order: Some data from Kuwait. *Personality and Individual Differences, 44*, 1032–1038.

Abdelrahman, A., Rodriguez, G., Ryan, J., French, J., & Weinbaum, D. (1998). The epidemiology of substance use among middle school students: The impact of school, familial, community and individual risk factors. *Journal of Child & Adolescent Substance Abuse, 8*, 55–75.

Abela, J., & Hankin, B. (2008). Cognitive vulnerability to depression in children and adolescents: A developmental psychopathology perspective. In J. Abela & B. Hankin (Eds.), *Handbook of depression in children and adolescents* (pp. 35–78). New York: Guilford Press.

Aboud, F. E., & Doyle, A. B. (1995). The development of in-group pride in black Canadians. *Journal of Cross-Cultural Psychology, 26*, 243–254.

Abramovitch, R., Pepler, D., & Corter, C. (1982). Patterns of sibling interaction among preschool-age children. In M. E. Lamb & B. Sutton-Smith (Eds.), *Sibling relationships: Their nature and significance across the life-span* (pp. 61–86). Hillsdale, NJ: Erlbaum.

Accardo, P., Tomazic, T., Fete, T., Heaney, M., Lindsay, R., & William, B. (1997). Maternally reported fetal activity levels and developmental diagnoses. *Clinical Pediatrics, 36*, 279–283.

Achenbach, T. M. (1974). *Developmental psychopathology.* New York: The Ronald Press Company.

Achenbach, T. M. (1982). *Developmental psychopathology* (2nd ed.). New York: Wiley.

Achenbach, T. M. (1993). Taxonomy and comorbidity of conduct problems: Evidence from empirically based approaches. *Development and Psychopathology, 5*, 51–64.

Achenbach, T. M. (1995). Developmental issues in assessment, taxonomy, and diagnosis of child and adolescent psychopathology. In D. Cicchetti & D. J. Cohen (Eds.), *Developmental psychopathology: Vol. 1. Theory and methods* (pp. 57–80). New York: Wiley.

Achenbach, T. M. (2008). Multicultural perspectives on developmental psychopathology. In J. Hudziak (Ed.), *Developmental psychopathology and wellness: Genetic and environmental influences* (pp. 23–47). Arlington, VA: American Psychiatric Publishing.

Achenbach, T. M., & Edelbrock, C. S. (1981). Behavioral problems and competencies reported by parents of normal and disturbed children aged 4 through 16. *Monographs of the Society for Research in Child Development, 46*(1, Serial No. 188).

Adab, N., Jacoby, A., Smith, D., & Chadwick, D. (2001). Additional educational needs in children born to mothers with epilepsy. *Journal of Neurology, Neurosurgery & Psychiatry, 70*, 15–21.

Adachi, M., Trehub, S., & Abe, J. (2004). Perceiving emotion in children's songs across age and culture. *Japanese Psychological Research, 46*, 322–336.

Adam, E., Gunnar, M., & Tanaka, A. (2004). Adult attachment, parent emotion, and observed parenting behavior: Mediator and moderator models. *Child Development, 75*, 110–122.

Adams, M., & Henry, M. (1997). Myths and realities about words and literacy. *School Psychology Review, 26*, 425–436.

Adams, M. J., Trieman, R., & Pressley, M. (1998). Reading, writing, and literacy. In W. Damon (Ed.), *Handbook of child psychology:*

Vol 4. Child psychology in practice (5th ed., pp. 275–355). New York: Wiley.

Adelman, W., & Ellen, J. (2002). *Adolescence.* In A. Rudolph, R. Kamei, & K. Overby (Eds.), *Rudolph's fundamentals of pediatrics* (3rd ed., pp. 70–109). New York: McGraw-Hill.

Adesman, A. R. (1996). Fragile X syndrome. In A. J. Capute & P. J. Accardo (Eds.), *Developmental disabilities in infancy and childhood: Vol. 2. The spectrum of developmental disabilities* (2nd ed., pp. 255–269). Baltimore: Brookes.

Adolph, K., & Berger, S. (2005). Physical and motor development. In M. Bornstein & M. Lamb (Eds.), *Developmental science: An advanced textbook* (5th ed., pp. 223–283). Hillsdale, NJ: Erlbaum.

Agnew, J., Dorn, C., & Eden, G. (2004). Effect of intensive training on auditory processing and reading skills. *Brain & Language, 88*, 21–25.

Ahmed, E., & Braithwaite, V. (2004). Bullying and victimization: Cause for concern for both families and schools. *Social Psychology of Education, 7*, 35–54.

Aiken, L. (1997). *Psychological testing and assessment* (9th ed.). Boston: Allyn & Bacon.

Ainsworth, M., & Bowlby, J. (1991). An ethological approach to personality development. *American Psychologist, 46*, 333–341.

Ainsworth, M. D. S. (1972). Attachment and dependency: A comparison. In J. L. Gewirtz (Ed.), *Attachment and dependency* (pp. 97–138). Washington, DC: Winston.

Ainsworth, M. D. S. (1982). Attachment: Retrospect and prospect. In C. M. Parkes & J. Stevenson-Hinde (Eds.), *The place of attachment in human behavior* (pp. 3–30). New York: Basic Books.

Ainsworth, M. D. S. (1989). Attachments beyond infancy. *American Psychologist, 44*, 709–716.

Ainsworth, M. D. S., Blehar, M., Waters, E., & Wall, S. (1978). *Patterns of attachment.* Hillsdale, NJ: Erlbaum.

Ainsworth, M. D. S., & Marvin, R. S. (1995). On the shaping of attachment theory and research: An interview with Mary D. S. Ainsworth (Fall 1994). *Monographs of the Society for Research in Child Development, 60*(244, Nos. 2–3), 3–21.

Akhtar, N. (2004). Nativist versus constructivist goals in studying child language. *Journal of Child Language, 31*, 459–462.

Aksan, N., & Kochanska, G. (2005). Conscience in childhood: Old questions, new answers. *Developmental Psychology, 41*, 506–516.

Aksu-Koc, A. A., & Slobin, D. I. (1985). The acquisition of Turkish. In D. I. Slobin (Ed.), *The crosslinguistic study of language acquisition: Vol. 1. The data* (pp. 839–878). Hillsdale, NJ: Erlbaum.

Alan Guttmacher Institute. (2004). *U.S. teenage pregnancy statistics with comparative statistics for women aged 20–24.* Retrieved May 6, 2005, from http://www.guttmacher.org/pubs/teen_stats.html

Albers, L. (1999). The duration of labor in healthy women. *Journal of Perinatology, 19*, 114–119.

Alexander, K. L., Entwisle, D. R., & Dauber, S. L. (1993). First-grade classroom behavior: Its short- and long-term consequences for school performance. *Child Development, 64*, 801–814.

Alford, K. (2007). African-American males and the rites of passage experience. In S. Logan, R. Denby, & P. Gibson (Eds.), *Mental health care in the African-American community* (pp. 305–319). New York: Haworth Press.

Alho, O., Laära, E., & Oja, H. (1996). How should relative risk estimates for acute otitis media in children aged less than 2 years be perceived? *Journal of Clinical Epidemiology, 49*, 9–14.

Allen, C., & Kisilevsky, B. (1999). Fetal behavior in diabetic and nondiabetic pregnant women: An exploratory study. *Developmental Psychobiology, 35*, 69–80.

Allen, J., Porter, M., McFarland, F., Marsh, P., & McElhaney, K. (2005). The two faces of adolescents' success with peers: Adolescent popularity, social adaptation, and deviant behavior. *Child Development, 76*, 747–760.

Allen, K., & Rainie, L. (2002). *Parents online.* Retrieved March 16, 2004, from http://www.pewinternet.org

Allen, M. (2004). Minority language school systems: A profile of students, schools and communities. *Education Quarterly Review, 9*, 9–29.

Al Otaiba, S., Connor, C., Lane, H., Kosanovich, M., Schatschneider, C., Dyrlund, A., Miller, M., & Wright, T. (2008). Reading First kindergarten classroom instruction and students' growth in phonological awareness and letter naming/decoding fluency. *Journal of School Psychology, 46*, 281–314.

Alsaker, F., & Olweus, D. (2002). Stability and change in global self-esteem and self-related affect. In T. Brinthaupt & R. Lipka (Eds.), *Understanding early adolescent self and identity: Applications and interventions* (pp. 193–223). Albany: State University of New York Press.

Alspaugh, J. (1998). Achievement loss associated with the transition to middle school and high school. *Journal of Educational Research, 92*, 20–25.

Alt, M., Plante, E., & Creusere, M. (2004). Semantic features in fast-mapping: Performance of preschoolers with specific language impairment versus preschoolers with normal language. *Journal of Speech, Language, & Hearing Research, 47*, 407–420.

Álvarez, J., Martín, A. F., Vergeles, M., & Martín, A. H. (2003). Substance use in adolescence: Importance of parental warmth and supervision. *Psicothema, 15*, 161–166.

Amato, P. R. (1993). Children's adjustment to divorce: Theories, hypotheses, and empirical support. *Journal of Marriage and the Family, 55*, 23–38.

Amato, S. (1998). Human genetics and dysmorphy. In R. Behrman & R. Kliegman (Eds.), *Nelson essentials of pediatrics* (3rd ed., pp. 129–146). Philadelphia: Saunders.

Ambert, A. (2001). *Families in the new millennium.* Boston, MA: Allyn & Bacon.

Ambuel, B. (1995). Adolescents, unintended pregnancy, and abortion: The struggle for a compassionate social policy. *Current Directions in Psychological Science, 4*, 1–5.

American Academy of Pediatrics (AAP). (2004). Clinical practice guideline: Diagnosis and management of acute otitis media. *Pediatrics, 113*, 1451–1465.

American Academy of Pediatrics (AAP). (2005). Breastfeeding and the use of human milk. *Pediatrics, 115*, 496–506.

American Academy of Pediatrics (AAP). (2008). *Recommended immunization schedule for persons aged 0–6 years: United States, 2008.* Retrieved August 7, 2008, from http://www.cispimmunize.org/IZSchedule_Childhood.pdf

American Academy of Pediatrics Committee on Infectious Diseases. (2000). Recommended childhood immunization schedule. *Pediatrics, 97*, 143–146.

American Academy of Pediatrics Committee on Psychosocial Aspects of Child and Family Health. (1998). Guidance for effective discipline. *Pediatrics, 101*, 723–728.

American College of Obstetricians and Gynecologists (ACOG). (2001, December 12). *ACOG addresses latest controversies in obstetrics.* Retrieved April 1, 2004, from http://www.acog.org

American College of Obstetricians and Gynecologists (ACOG). (2002, November 29). *Rubella vaccination recommendation changes for pregnant women.* Retrieved April 2, 2004, from http://www.acog.org

American College of Obstetricians and Gynecologists (ACOG). (2004a). *Ethics in obstetrics and gynecology.* Washington, DC: Author.

American College of Obstetricians and Gynecologists (ACOG). (2004b). *Pain relief during labor and delivery.* Retrieved August 6, 2008, from http://www.acog.org/publications/patient_education/bp086.cfm

American College of Obstetricians and Gynecologists (ACOG). (2007). *If your baby is breech.* Retrieved August 6, 2008, from http://www.acog.org/publications/patient_education/bp079.cfm

American College of Obstetricians and Gynecologists (ACOG). (2008a). *Cesarean birth.* Retrieved August 6, 2008, from http://www.acog.org/publications/patient_education/bp006.cfm

American College of Obstetricians and Gynecologists (ACOG). (2008b). *Surgery and patient choice.* Retrieved August 6, 2008, from http://www.acog.org/publications/patient_education/bp079.cfm

American Demographics. (2001). It's all homework. Retrieved June 23, 2004, from http://articles.findarticles.com/p/articles/mi_m4021/is_2001_Nov_1/ai_79501196

American Psychiatric Association. (2000). *Practice guidelines for eating disorders.* Retrieved June 9, 2005, from http://www.psych.org

American Psychological Association. (1993). *Violence and youth: Psychology's response: Vol. 1. Summary report of the American Psychological Association Commission on Violence and Youth.* Washington, DC: American Psychological Association.

Anderman, E. (1998). The middle school experience: Effects on the math and science achievement of adolescents with LD. *Journal of Learning Disabilities, 31*, 128–138.

Anderman, E., Maehr, M., & Midgley, C. (1999). Declining motivation after the transition to middle school: Schools can make a difference. *Journal of Research & Development in Education, 32*, 131–147.

Anderman, E., & Midgley, C. (1997). Changes in achievement goal orientations, perceived academic competence, and grades across the transition to middle-level schools. *Contemporary Educational Psychology, 22*, 269–298.

Anderman, L. (1999). Classroom goal orientation, school belonging and social goals as predictors of students' positive and negative affect following the transition to middle school. *Journal of Research & Development in Education, 32*, 89–103.

Anderman, L., & Anderman, E. (1999). Social predictors of changes in students' achievement goal orientations. *Contemporary Educational Psychology, 24*, 21–37.

Anderson, C., & Dill, K. (2000). Video games and aggressive thoughts, feelings, and behavior in the laboratory and in life. *Journal of Personality & Social Psychology, 78*, 772–790.

Anderson, M. (2005). Marrying intelligence and cognition: A developmental view. In J. Pretz & R. Sternberg (Eds.), *Cognition and intelligence: Identifying the mechanisms of mind* (pp. 268–287). New York: Cambridge University Press.

Anderson, R. (1998). Examining language loss in bilingual children. *Multicultural Electronic Journal of Communication Disorders, 1.*

Anderson, S., Dallal, G., & Must, A. (2003). Relative weight and race influence average age at menarche: Results from two nationally representative surveys of U.S. girls studied 25 years apart. *Pediatrics, 111*, 844–850.

Andersson, B. (1989). Effects of public day-care: A longitudinal study. *Child Development, 60*, 857–886.

Andersson, B. (1992). Effects of day-care on cognitive and socioemotional competence of thirteen-year-old Swedish school-children. *Child Development, 63*, 20–36.

Andreou, E., & Metallidou, P. (2004). The relationship of academic and social cognition to behaviour in bullying situations among Greek primary school children. *Educational Psychology, 24*, 27–41.

Andreucci, C. (2003). Comment l'idée d'instabilité du volume vient aux enfants. *Enfance, 55*, 139–158.

Andrews, G., & Halford, G. (1998). Children's ability to make transitive inferences: The importance of premise integration and structural complexity. *Cognitive Development, 13*, 479–513.

Andrews, G., & Halford, G. (2002). A cognitive complexity metric applied to cognitive development. *Cognitive Psychology, 45*, 153–219.

Anglin, J. M. (1993). Vocabulary development: A morphological analysis. *Monographs of the Society for Research in Child Development, 58*(Serial No. 238).

Anglin, J. M. (1995, April). *Word learning and the growth of potentially knowable vocabulary.* Paper presented at the biennial meetings of the Society for Research in Child Development, Indianapolis.

Anisfeld, M., Turkewitz, G., Rose, S., Rosenberg, F., Sheiber, F., Couturier-Fagan, D., Ger, J., & Sommer, I. (2001). No compelling evidence that newborns imitate oral gestures. *Infancy, 2*, 111–122.

Annett, M. (2003). Do the French and the English differ for hand skill asymmetry? Handedness subgroups in the sample of Doyen and Carlier (2002) and in English schools and universities. *Laterality: Asymmetries of Body, Brain, & Cognition, 8*, 233–245.

Anthony, J., & Lonigan, C. (2004). The nature of phonological awareness: Converging evidence from four studies of preschool and early grade school children. *Journal of Educational Psychology, 96*, 43–55.

Apgar, V. A. (1953). A proposal for a new method of evaluation of the newborn infant. *Current Research in Anesthesia and Analgesia, 32*, 260–267.

Aranha, M. (1997). Creativity in students and its relation to intelligence and peer perception. *Revista Interamericana de Psicologia, 31*, 309–313.

Armbruster, B., Lehr, F., & Osborn, J. (2003). *Put reading first: The research building blocks of reading instruction.* Retrieved June 20, 2008, from http://www.nifl.gov/partnershipforreading/publications/PFRbooklet.pdf

Armstrong, T. (2003). Effect of moral reconation therapy on the recidivism of youthful offenders: A randomized experiment. *Criminal Justice & Behavior, 30*, 668–687.

Arnold, G. (2007). *Phenylketonuria.* Retrieved August 7, 2008, from http://www.emedicine.com/ped/TOPIC1787.HTM

Asendorpf, J., Denissen, J., & van Aken, M. (2008). Inhibited and aggressive preschool children at 23 years of age: Personality and social transitions into adulthood. *Developmental Psychology, 44*, 997–1011.

Ashiabi, G., & O'Neal, K. (2007). Children's health status: Examining the associations among income poverty, material hardship, and parental factors. *PLoS ONE, 2*, e940.

Aslin, R. N. (1981). Experiential influences and sensitive periods in perceptual development: A unified model. In R. N. Aslin, J. R. Alberts, & M. R. Petersen (Eds.), *Development of perception. Psychobiological perspectives: Vol. 2. The visual system* (pp. 45–93). New York: Academic Press.

Aslin, R. N. (1987). Motor aspects of visual development in infancy. In P. Salapatek & L. Cohen (Eds.), *Handbook of infant perception: Vol. 1. From sensation to perception* (pp. 43–113). Orlando, FL: Academic Press.

Associated Press. (2005, February 8). "World's smallest baby goes home." Retrieved August 8, 2008, from http://www.cbsnews.com/stories/2005/02/08/health/main672488.shtml

Astington, J., & Jenkins, J. (1999). A longitudinal study of the relation between language and theory-of-mind development. *Developmental Psychology, 35*, 1311–1320.

Austin, M., Reiss, N., & Burgdord, L. (2007). *ADHD comorbidity.* Retrieved October 24, 2008, from http://www.mhmrcv.org/poc/view_doc.php?type=doc&id=13851&cn=3

Austin, S., Ziyadeh, N., Kahn, J., Camargo, C., Colditz, G., & Field, A. (2004). Sexual orientation, weight concerns, and eating-disordered behaviors in adolescent girls and boys. *Journal of the American Academy of Child & Adolescent Psychiatry, 43*, 1115–1123.

Austin, W. (2008). Relocation, research, and forensic evaluation, part I: Effects of residential mobility on children of divorce. *Family Court Review, 46*, 137–150.

Avis, J., & Harris, P. L. (1991). Belief-desire reasoning among Baka children: Evidence for a universal conception of mind. *Child Development, 62*, 460–467.

Bachman, J., Safron, D., Sy, S., & Schulenberg, J. (2003). Wishing to work: New perspectives on how adolescents' part-time work intensity is linked to educational disengagement, substance use, and other problem behaviours. *International Journal of Behavioral Development, 27*, 301–315.

Bachman, J. G., & Schulenberg, J. (1993). How part-time work intensity relates to drug use, problem behavior, time use, and satisfaction among high school seniors: Are these consequences or merely correlates? *Developmental Psychology, 29*, 220–235.

Baer, J., Sampson, P., Barr, H., Connor, P., & Streissguth, A. (2003). A 21-year longitudinal analysis of the effects of prenatal alcohol exposure on young adult drinking. *Archives of General Psychiatry, 60*, 377–385.

Bahrick, L., & Lickliter, R. (2000). Intersensory redundancy guides attentional selectivity and perceptual learning in infancy. *Developmental Psychology, 36*, 190–201.

Bailey, B., & Konstan, J. (2006). On the need for attention-aware systems: Measuring effects of interruption on task performance, error rate, and affective state. *Computers in Human Behavior, 22*, 685–708.

Bailey, J., Brobow, D., Wolfe, M., & Mikach, S. (1995). Sexual orientation of adult sons of gay fathers. *Developmental Psychology, 31*, 124–129.

Bailey, J., Pillard, R., Dawood, K., Miller, M., Farrer, L., Trivedi, S., & Murphy, R. (1999). A family history study of male sexual orientation using three independent samples. *Behavior Genetics, 29*, 79–86.

Bailey, J., & Zucker, K. (1995). Childhood sex-typed behavior and sexual orientation: A conceptual analysis and quantitative review. *Developmental Psychology, 31*, 43–55.

Bailey, S., & Zvonkovic, A. (2003). Parenting after divorce: Nonresidential parents' perceptions of social and institutional support. *Journal of Divorce & Remarriage, 39*, 59–80.

Baillargeon, R. (1994). How do infants learn about the physical world? *Current Directions in Psychological Science, 3*, 133–140.

Baillargeon, R. (2008). Innate ideas revisited: For a principle of persistence in infants' physical reasoning. *Perspectives on Psychological Science, 3*, 2–13.

Baker, S., Victor, J., Chambers, A., & Halverson, C. (2004). Adolescent personality: A five-factor model construct validation. *Assessment, 11*, 303–315.

Baker-Ward, L. (1995, April). *Children's reports of a minor medical emergency procedure.* Paper presented at the biennial meetings of the Society for Research in Child Development, Indianapolis.

Ball, E. (1997). Phonological awareness: Implications for whole language and emergent literacy programs. *Topics in Language Disorders, 17,* 14–26.

Bandura, A. (1973). *Aggression: A social learning analysis.* Englewood Cliffs, NJ: Prentice Hall.

Bandura, A. (1977). *Social learning theory.* Englewood Cliffs, NJ: Prentice Hall.

Bandura, A. (1982). Self-efficacy mechanism in human agency. *American Psychologist, 37,* 122–147.

Bandura, A. (1986). *Social foundations of thought and action: A social cognitive theory.* Englewood Cliffs, NJ: Prentice Hall.

Bandura, A. (1989). Social cognitive theory. *Annals of Child Development, 6,* 1–60.

Bandura, A. (1997). *Self-efficacy. The exercise of control.* New York: Freeman.

Bandura, A. (2004). Swimming against the mainstream: The early years from chilly tributary to transformative mainstream. *Behaviour Research & Therapy, 42,* 613–630.

Bandura, A. (2008). Reconstrual of "free will" from the agentic perspective of social cognitive theory. In J. Baer, J. Kaufman, & R. Baumeister (Eds.), *Are we free? Psychology and free will* (pp. 86–127). New York: Oxford University Press.

Bandura, A., & Bussey, K. (2004). On broadening the cognitive, motivational, and sociostructural scope of theorizing about gender development and functioning: Comment on Martin, Ruble, and Szkrybalo (2002). *Psychological Bulletin, 130,* 691–701.

Bandura, A., Caprara, G., Barbaranelli, C., Gerbino, M., & Pastorelli, C. (2003). Role of affective self-regulatory efficacy in diverse spheres of psychosocial functioning. *Child Development, 74,* 769–782.

Bandura, A., Ross, D., & Ross, S. (1961). Transmission of aggression through imitation of aggressive models. *Journal of Abnormal & Social Psychology, 63,* 575–582.

Barber, B., & Demo, D. (2006). The kids are alright (at least, most of them): Links between divorce and dissolution and child well-being. In M. Fine & J. Harvey (Eds.), *Handbook of divorce and relationship dissolution* (pp. 289–312). Mahwah, NJ: Erlbaum.

Barber, B., Eccles, J., & Stone, M. (2001). Whatever happened to the jock, the brain, and the princess? Young adult pathways linked to adolescent activity involvement and social identity. *Journal of Adolescent Research, 16,* 429–455.

Barenboim, C. (1977). Developmental changes in the interpersonal cognitive system from middle childhood to adolescence. *Child Development, 48,* 1467–1474.

Barenboim, C. (1981). The development of person perception in childhood and adolescence: From behavioral comparisons to psychological constructs to psychological comparisons. *Child Development, 52,* 129–144.

Barkley, R. A., Fischer, M., Edelbrock, C. S., & Smallish, L. (1990). The adolescent outcome of hyperactive children diagnosed by research criteria: I. An 8-year prospective follow-up study. *Journal of the American Academy of Child and Adolescent Psychiatry, 29,* 546–557.

Barnes, H. L., & Olson, D. H. (1985). Parent-adolescent communication and the circumplex model. *Child Development, 56,* 438–437.

Barnett, D., Manley, J., & Cicchetti, D. (1993). Defining child maltreatment: The interface between policy and research. In D. Cicchetti & S. Toth (Eds.), *Child abuse, child development, and social policy* (pp. 7–73). Norwood, NJ: Ablex.

Barnett, W. S. (1993). Benefit-cost analysis of preschool education: Findings from a 25-year follow-up. *American Journal of Orthopsychiatry, 63,* 500–508.

Baron-Cohen, S., Lutchmaya, S., & Knickmeyer, R. (2006). *Prenatal testosterone in mind.* Cambridge, MA: MIT Press.

Barrett, G. V., & Depinet, R. L. (1991). A reconsideration of testing for competence rather than for intelligence. *American Psychologist, 46,* 1012–1024.

Barrow, F., Armstrong, M., Vargo, A., & Boothroyd, R. (2007). Understanding the findings of resilience-related research for fostering the development of African American adolescents. *Child and Adolescent Psychiatric Clinics of North America, 16,* 393–413.

Barry, D., Bernard, M., & Beitel, M. (2008, in press). East Asian child-rearing attitudes: An exploration of cultural, demographic and self-disclosure factors among U.S. immigrants. *International Journal of Psychology.*

Bartels, M., Rietveld, M., Van Baal, G., & Boomsma, D. (2002). Genetic and environmental influences on the development of intelligence. *Behavior Genetics, 32,* 237–249.

Barth, R. (2001). Research outcomes of prenatal substance exposure and the need to review policies and procedures regarding child abuse reporting. *Child Welfare, 80,* 275–296.

Bartsch, K. (1993). Adolescents' theoretical thinking. In R. M. Lerner (Ed.), *Early adolescence: Perspectives on research, policy, and intervention* (pp. 143–157). Hillsdale, NJ: Erlbaum.

Basham, P. (2001). Home schooling: From the extreme to the mainstream. *Public Policy Sources/The Fraser Institute, 51.* Retrieved June 23, 2004, from http://www.fraserinstitute.ca/admin/books/files/homeschool.pdf

Bates, E. (1993). Commentary: Comprehension and production in early language development. *Monographs of the Society for Research in Child Development, 58*(3–4, Serial No. 233), 222–242.

Bates, E., Bretherton, I., Beeghly-Smith, M., & McNew, S. (1982). Social bases of language development: A reassessment. In H. W. Reese & L. P. Lipsitt (Eds.), *Advances in child development and behavior* (Vol. 16, pp. 8–68). New York: Academic Press.

Bates, E., Marchman, V., Thal, D., Fenson, L., Dale, P., Reznick, J. S., Reilly, J., & Hartung, J. (1994). Developmental and stylistic variation in the composition of early vocabulary. *Journal of Child Language, 21,* 85–123.

Bates, E., O'Connell, B., & Shore, C. (1987). Language and communication in infancy. In J. D. Osofsky (Ed.), *Handbook of infant development* (2nd ed., pp. 149–203). New York: Wiley.

Bates, J. E. (1989). Applications of temperament concepts. In G. A. Kohnstamm, J. E. Bates, & M. K. Rothbart (Eds.), *Temperament in childhood* (pp. 321–356). Chichester, England: Wiley.

Batterson, V., Rose, S., Yonas, A., Grant, K., & Sackett, G. (2008). The effect of experience on the development of tactual-visual transfer in pigtailed macaque monkeys. *Developmental Psychobiology, 50,* 88–96.

Baumeister, A. (2006). Mental retardation: Confusing sentiment with science. In H. Switzky & S. Greenspan (Eds.), *What is mental retardation?* (pp. 93–124). Washington, DC: American Association on Mental Retardation.

Baumeister, R., Bushman, B., & Campbell, W. (2000). Self-esteem, narcissism, and aggression: Does violence result from low self-esteem or from threatened egotism? *Current Directions in Psychological Science, 9,* 26–29.

Baumeister, R., Campbell, J., Krueger, J., & Vohs, K. (2003). Does high self-esteem cause better performance, interpersonal success, happiness, or healthier lifestyles? *Psychological Science in the Public Interest, 4*(1), 1–44.

Baumeister, R., Smart, L., & Boden, J. (1996). Relation of threatened egotism to violence and aggression: The dark side of high self-esteem. *Psychological Review, 103,* 5–33.

Bauminger, N., Finzi-Dottan, R., Chason, S., & Har-Even, D. (2008). Intimacy in adolescent friendship: The roles of attachment, coherence, and self-disclosure. *Journal of Social and Personal Relationships, 25*, 409–428.

Baumrind, D. (1971). Current patterns of parental authority. *Developmental Psychology Monograph, 4*(1, Part 2).

Baumrind, D. (1973). The development of instrumental competence through socialization. In A. D. Pick (Ed.), *Minnesota symposium on child psychology* (Vol. 7, pp. 3–46). Minneapolis: University of Minnesota Press.

Baumrind, D. (1991). The influence of parenting style on adolescent competence and substance use. *Journal of Early Adolescence, 11*, 56–95.

Bayley, N. (1969). *Bayley Scales of Infant Development.* New York: Psychological Corporation.

Bayley, N. (1993). *Bayley Scales of Infant Development: Birth to two years.* San Antonio, TX: Psychological Corporation.

Beauchaine, T., & Hinshaw, S. (2008). *Child and adolescent psychopathology.* New York: Wiley.

Beautrais, A., Joyce, P., & Mulder, R. (1999). Personality traits and cognitive styles as risk factors for serious suicide attempts among young people. *Suicide & Life-Threatening Behavior, 29*, 37–47.

Beaver, K., & Wright, J. (2005). Evaluating the effects of birth complications on low self-control in a sample of twins. *International Journal of Offender Therapy and Comparative Criminology, 49*, 450–471.

Bee, H. L., Barnard, K. E., Eyres, S. J., Gray, C. A., Hammond, M. A., Spietz, A. L., Snyder, C., & Clark, B. (1982). Prediction of IQ and language skill from perinatal status, child performance, family characteristics, and mother-infant interaction. *Child Development, 53*, 1135–1156.

Behrend, D., Scofield, J., & Kleinknecht, E. (2001). Beyond fast mapping: Young children's extensions of novel words and novel facts. *Developmental Psychology, 37*, 690–705.

Beilstein, C., & Wilson, J. (2000). Landmarks in route learning by girls and boys. *Perceptual & Motor Skills, 91*, 877–882.

Bell, L. G., & Bell, D. C. (1982). Family climate and the role of the female adolescent: Determinants of adolescent functioning. *Family Relations, 31*, 519–527.

Belsky, J. (1981). Early human experience: A family perspective. *Developmental Psychology, 17*, 3–23.

Belsky, J. (1985). Prepared statement on the effects of day care. In *Improving child care services: What can be done?* Select Committee on Children, Youth, and Families, House of Representatives, 98th Cong., 2d Sess. Washington, DC: U.S. Government Printing Office.

Belsky, J. (1992). Consequences of child care for children's development: A deconstructionist view. In A. Booth (Ed.), *Child care in the 1990s. Trends and consequences* (pp. 83–94). Hillsdale, NJ: Erlbaum.

Belsky, J. (2001). Developmental risks (still) associated with early child care. *Journal of Child Psychology & Psychiatry & Allied Disciplines, 42*, 845–859.

Belsky, J. (2002). Quantity counts: Amount of child care and children's socioemotional development. *Journal of Developmental and Behavioral Pediatrics, 23*, 167–170.

Belsky, J., Lang, M. E., & Rovine, M. (1985). Stability and change in marriage across the transition to parenthood: A second study. *Journal of Marriage and the Family, 47*, 855–865.

Belsky, J., & Rovine, M. (1988). Nonmaternal care in the first year of life and the security of infant-parent attachment. *Child Development, 59*, 157–167.

Bem, S. L. (1974). The measurement of psychological androgyny. *Journal of Consulting and Clinical Psychology, 42*, 155–162.

Bem, S. L. (1981). Gender schema theory: A cognitive account of sex-typing. *Psychological Review, 88*, 354–364.

Bem, S. L. (1989). Genital knowledge and gender constancy in preschool children. *Child Development, 60*, 649–662.

Benbow, C. P. (1988). Sex differences in mathematical reasoning ability in intellectually talented preadolescents: Their nature, effects, and possible causes. *Behavioral & Brain Sciences, 11*, 169–232.

Bender, S. L., Word, C. O., DiClemente, R. J., Crittenden, M. R., Persaud, N. A., & Ponton, L. E. (1995). The developmental implications of prenatal and/or postnatal crack cocaine exposure in preschool children: A preliminary report. *Journal of Developmental and Behavioral Pediatrics, 16*, 418–424.

Benenson, J. F. (1994). Ages four to six years: Changes in the structures of play networks of girls and boys. *Merrill-Palmer Quarterly, 40*, 478–487.

Bennett, M., & Sani, F. (2008a). Children's subjective identification with social groups: A self-stereotyping approach. *Developmental Science, 11*, 69–75.

Bennett, M., & Sani, F. (2008b). The effect of comparative context upon stereotype content: Children's judgments of ingroup behavior. *Scandinavian Journal of Psychology, 49*, 141–146.

Benoit, D., & Parker, K. C. H. (1994). Stability and transmission of attachment across three generations. *Child Development, 65*, 1444–1456.

Berch, D. B., & Bender, B. G. (1987, December). Margins of sexuality. *Psychology Today, 21*, 54–57.

Berger, L. (2004). Income, family structure, and child maltreatment risk. *Children and Youth Services Review, 26*, 725–748.

Bernardo, A., & Calleja, M. (2005). The effects of stating problems in bilingual students' first and second languages on solving mathematical word problems. *Journal of Genetic Psychology, 166*, 117–128.

Berndt, T. J. (1983). Social cognition, social behavior, and children's friendships. In E. T. Higgins, D. N. Ruble, & W. W. Hartup (Eds.), *Social cognition and social development: A sociocultural perspective* (pp. 158–192). Cambridge, England: Cambridge University Press.

Berndt, T. J. (1986). Children's comments about their friendships. In M. Perlmutter (Ed.), *Minnesota symposia on child psychology* (Vol. 18, pp. 189–212). Hillsdale, NJ: Erlbaum.

Berndt, T. J. (1992). Friendship and friends' influence in adolescence. *Current Directions in Psychological Science, 1*, 156–159.

Berndt, T. J. (2004). Children's friendships: Shifts over a half-century in perspectives on their development and their effects. *Merrill Palmer Quarterly Journal of Developmental Psychology, 50*, 206–223.

Berndt, T. J., & Hoyle, S. G. (1985). Stability and change in childhood and adolescent friendships. *Developmental Psychology, 21*, 1007–1015.

Berndt, T. J., & Keefe, K. (1995). Friends' influence on adolescents' adjustment to school. *Child Development, 66*, 1312–1329.

Berninger, V., Abbott, R., Zook, D., Ogier, S., et al. (1999). Early intervention for reading disabilities: Teaching the alphabet principle in a connectionist framework. *Journal of Learning Disabilities, 32*, 491–503.

Berninger, V., & Richards, T. (2002). *Brain literacy for educators and psychologists.* San Diego, CA: Academic Press.

Berthier, N., DeBlois, S., Poirier, C., Novak, M., & Clifton, R. (2000). Where's the ball? Two- and three-year-olds reason about unseen events. *Developmental Psychology, 36*, 394–401.

Best, C., Moffat, V., Power, M., Owens, D., & Johnstone, E. (2008). The boundaries of the cognitive phenotype of autism: Theory of mind, central coherence, and ambiguous figure perception in young people with autistic traits. *Journal of Autism and Developmental Disorders, 38*, 840–847.

Bettner, B. (2007). Recreating sibling relationships in marriage. *Journal of Individual Psychology, 63*, 339–344.

Bhatt, R. S., & Rovee-Collier, C. (1996). Infants' forgetting of correlated attributes and object recognition. *Child Development, 67*, 172–187.

Bialystok, E. (1997). Effects of bilingualism and biliteracy on children's emerging concepts of print. *Developmental Psychology, 33*.

Bialystok, E., Majumder, S., & Martin, M. (2003). Developing phonological awareness: Is there a bilingual advantage? *Applied Linguistics, 24*, 27–44.

Bialystok, E., Shenfield, T., & Codd, J. (2000). Languages, scripts, and the environment: Factors in developing concepts of print. *Developmental Psychology, 36*, 66–76.

Biederman, J., Faraone, S., Jetton, J., Kraus, I., Mick, E., Pert, J., Spencer, T., Weber, W., Wilens, T., Williamson, S., & Zallen, B. (1999). Clinical correlates of ADHD in females: Findings from a large group of girls ascertained from pediatric and psychiatric referral sources. *Journal of the American Academy of Child & Adolescent Psychiatry, 38*, 966–975.

Bigelow, B. J., & La Gaipa, J. J. (1975). Children's written descriptions of friendships: A multidimensional analysis. *Developmental Psychology, 11*, 857–858.

Bigler, R. S. (1995). The role of classification skill in moderating environmental influences on children's gender stereotyping: A study of the functional use of gender in the classroom. *Child Development, 66*, 1072–1087.

Bigler, R. S., & Liben, S. (1993). The role of attitudes and interventions in gender-schematic processing. *Child Development, 61*, 1440–1452.

Bilalic, M., McLeod, P., & Gobet, F. (2007). Personality profiles of young chess players. *Personality and Individual Differences, 42*, 901–910.

Billy, J. O. G., Brewster, K. L., & Grady, W. R. (1994). Contextual effects on the sexual behavior of adolescent women. *Journal of Marriage and the Family, 56*, 387–404.

Binet, A., & Simon, T. (1905). Méthodes nouvelles pour le diagnostic du niveau intellectuel des anormaux [New methods for diagnosing intellectual level in the abnormal]. *Année Psychologie, 11*, 191–244.

Birch, D. (1998). The adolescent parent: A fifteen year longitudinal study of school-age mothers and their children. *International Journal of Adolescent Medicine & Health, 10*, 141–153.

Biringen, A. (2000). Emotional availability: Conceptualization and research findings. *American Journal of Orthopsychiatry, 70*, 104–114.

Birney, D., Citron-Pousty, J., Lutz, D., & Sternberg, R. (2005). The development of cognitive and intellectual abilities. In M. Bornstein & M. Lamb (Eds.), *Developmental science: An advanced textbook* (5th ed., pp. 327–358). Hillsdale, NJ: Erlbaum.

Biswas, M. K., & Craigo, S. D. (1994). The course and conduct of normal labor and delivery. In A. H. DeCherney & M. L. Pernoll (Eds.), *Current obstetric and gynecologic diagnosis & treatment* (pp. 202–227). Norwalk, CT: Appleton & Lange.

Bivens, J. A., & Berk, L. E. (1990). A longitudinal study of the development of elementary school children's private speech. *Merrill-Palmer Quarterly, 36*, 443–463.

Bjorklund, D. F., Miller, P. H., Coyle, T. R., & Slawinski, J. L. (1997). Instructing children to use memory strategies: Evidence of utilization deficiencies in memory training studies. *Developmental Review, 17*, 411–441.

Bjorklund, D. F., & Muir, J. E. (1988). Remembering on their own: Children's development of free recall memory. In R. Vasta (Ed.), *Annals of child development* (Vol. 5, pp. 79–124). Greenwich, CT: JAI Press.

Blair, C. (2002). School readiness: Integrating cognition and emotion in a neurobiological conceptualization of children's functioning at school entry. *American Psychologist, 57*, 111–127.

Blair, C., Greenberg, M., & Crnic, K. (2001). Age-related increases in motivation among children with mental retardation and MA- and CA-matched controls. *American Journal on Mental Retardation, 106*, 511–524.

Blair, S. L., & Johnson, M. P. (1992). Wives' perceptions of the fairness of the division of household labor: The intersection of housework and ideology. *Journal of Marriage and the Family, 54*, 570–581.

Blake, I. K. (1994). Language development and socialization in young African-American children. In P. M. Greenfield & R. R. Cocking (Eds.), *Cross-cultural roots of minority child development* (pp. 167–195). Hillsdale, NJ: Erlbaum.

Blass, E. M., Ganchrow, J. R., & Steiner, J. E. (1984). Classical conditioning in newborn humans 2–48 hours of age. *Infant Behavior and Development, 7*, 223–235.

Blatt, S. (2008, in press). *Polarities of experience: Relatedness and self-definition in personality development, psychopathology, and the therapeutic process.* Washington, DC: American Psychological Association.

Block, J. (1971). *Lives through time.* Berkeley, CA: Bancroft.

Block, J., & Robins, R. W. (1993). A longitudinal study of consistency and change in self-esteem from early adolescence to early adulthood. *Child Development, 64*, 909–923.

Bloom, L. (1973). *One word at a time.* The Hague: Mouton.

Bloom, L. (1991). *Language development from two to three.* Cambridge, England: Cambridge University Press.

Bloom, L. (1993). *The transition from infancy to language: Acquiring the power of expression.* Cambridge, England: Cambridge University Press.

Bloom, L. (1997, April). *The child's action drives the interaction.* Paper presented at the biennial meetings of the Society for Research in Child Development, Washington, DC.

Bloom, L. (1998). Language acquisition in its developmental context. In W. Damon (Ed.), *Handbook of child psychology: Vol. 2. Cognition, perception, and language* (5th ed., pp. 309–370). New York: Wiley.

Blumberg, F., & Sokol, L. (2004). Boys' and girls' use of cognitive strategies when learning to play video games. *Journal of General Psychology, 131*, 151–158.

Boehnke, K., Silbereisen, R., Eisenberg, N., & Reykowski, J. (1989). Developmental pattern of prosocial motivation: A cross-national study. *Journal of Cross-Cultural Psychology, 20*, 219–243.

Bolger, K. (1997, April). *Children's adjustment as a function of timing of family economic hardship.* Paper presented at the biennial meetings of the Society for Research in Child Development, Washington, DC.

Bond, L., Braskamp, D., & Roeber, E. (1996). *The status report of the assessment programs in the United States.* Oakbrook, IL: North Central Regional Educational Laboratory. ERIC Document No. ED 401 333.

Bonde, E., Obel, C., Nedergard, N., & Thomsen, P. (2004). Social risk factors as predictors for parental report of deviant behaviour in 3-year-old children. *Nordic Journal of Psychiatry, 58*, 17–23.

Bong, M. (1998). Tests of the internal/external frames of reference model with subject-specific academic self-efficacy and frame-specific academic self-concepts. *Journal of Educational Psychology, 90*, 102–110.

Boom, J., Wouters, H., & Keller, M. (2007). A cross-cultural validation of stage development: A Rasch re-analysis of longitudinal socio-moral reasoning data. *Cognitive Development, 22*, 213–229.

Borkowski, M., Hunter, K., & Johnson, C. (2001). White noise and scheduled bedtime routines to reduce infant and childhood sleep disturbances. *Behavior Therapist, 24*, 29–37.

Born, A. (2007). Well-diffused? Identity diffusion and well-being in emerging adulthood. In M. Watzlawik & A. Born (Eds.), *Capturing identity: Quantitative and qualitative methods* (pp. 149–161). Lanham, MD: University Press of America.

Bornstein, M., Arterberry, M., & Nash, C. (2005). Perceptual development. In M. Bornstein & M. Lamb (Eds.), *Developmental science: An advanced textbook* (5th ed., pp. 283–326). Hillsdale, NJ: Erlbaum.

Bornstein, M., DiPietro, J., Hahn, C., Painter, K., Haynes, O., & Costigan, K. (2002). Prenatal cardiac function and postnatal cognitive development: An exploratory study. *Infancy, 3,* 475–494.

Bornstein, M. H. (Ed.). (1989). Maternal responsiveness: Characteristics and consequences. *New Directions for Child Development, 43.*

Bornstein, M. H. (1995). Parenting infants. In M. H. Bornstein (Ed.), *Handbook of parenting: Vol 1. Children and parenting* (pp. 3–39). Mahwah, NJ: Erlbaum.

Bornstein, M. H., Tamis-LeMonda, C. S., Tal, J., Ludemann, P., Toda, S., Rahn, C. W., Pecheux, M., Azuma, H., & Vardi, D. (1992). Maternal responsiveness to infants in three societies: The United States, France, and Japan. *Child Development, 63,* 808–821.

Boscardin, C., Muthén, B., Francis, D., & Baker, E. (2008). Early identification of reading difficulties using heterogeneous developmental trajectories. *Journal of Educational Psychology, 100,* 192–208.

Bostwick, J., & Martin, K. (2007). A man's brain in an ambiguous body: A case of mistaken gender identity. *American Journal of Psychiatry, 164,* 1499–1505.

Bosworth, R., & Birch, E. (2005). Motion detection in normal infants and young patients with infantile esotropia. *Vision Research, 45,* 1557–1567.

Bouchard, T. J., Jr., & McGue, M. (1981). Familial studies of intelligence: A review. *Science, 212,* 1055–1059.

Bougie, E., Wright, S., & Taylor, D. (2003). Early heritage language education and the abrupt shift to a dominant-language classroom: Impact on the persona and collective esteem of Inuit children in Arctic Québec. *International Journal of Bilingual Education and Bilingualism, 6,* 349–373.

Bowen, J., Gibson, F., & Hand, P. (2002). Educational outcome at 8 years for children who were born extremely prematurely: A controlled study. *Journal of Pediatrics & Child Health, 38,* 438–444.

Bower, B. (2005). Mental meeting of the sexes: Boys' spatial advantage fades in poor families. *Science News, 168,* 21.

Bower, T. G. R. (1966). The visual world of infants. *Scientific American, 215,* 80–92.

Bowerman, M. (1985). Beyond communicative adequacy: From piecemeal knowledge to an integrated system in the child's acquisition of language. In K. E. Nelson (Ed.), *Children's language* (Vol. 5, pp. 369–398). Hillsdale, NJ: Erlbaum.

Bowerman, M. (2007). Containment, support, and beyond: Constructing topological spatial categories in first language acquisition. In M. Aurnague, M. Hickmann, & L. Vieu (Eds.), *The categorization of spatial entities in language and cognition* (pp. 177–203). Amsterdam, Netherlands: John Benjamins Publishing Company.

Bowker, A. (2004). Predicting friendship stability during early adolescence. *Journal of Early Adolescence, 24,* 85–112.

Bowlby, J. (1969). *Attachment and loss: Vol. 1. Attachment.* New York: Basic Books.

Bowlby, J. (1988a). Developmental psychiatry comes of age. *American Journal of Psychiatry, 145,* 1–10.

Bowlby, J. (1988b). *A secure base.* New York: Basic Books.

Bowlby, R. (2007). Babies and toddlers in non-parental daycare can avoid stress and anxiety if they develop a lasting secondary attachment bond with one carer who is consistently accessible to them. *Attachment & Human Development, 9,* 307–319.

Bowler, D., Briskman, J., & Grice, S. (1999). Experimenter effects on children's understanding of false drawings and false beliefs. *Journal of Genetic Psychology, 160,* 443–460.

Bradbury, K., & Katz, J. (2002). Women's labor market involvement and family income mobility when marriages end. *New England Economic Review, Q4,* 41–74.

Bradley, R. H., Caldwell, B. M., Rock, S. L., Barnard, K. E., Gray, C., Hammond, M. A., Mitchell, S., Siegel, L., Ramey, C. D., Gottfried, A. W., & Johnson, D. L. (1989). Home environment and cognitive development in the first 3 years of life: A collaborative study involving six sites and three ethnic groups in North America. *Developmental Psychology, 25,* 217–235.

Bradley, R. H., Whiteside, L., Mundfrom, D. J., Casey, P. H., Kelleher, K. J., & Pope, S. K. (1994). Early indications of resilience and their relation to experiences in the home environments of low birthweight, premature children living in poverty. *Child Development, 65,* 346–360.

Bradmetz, J. (1999). Precursors of formal thought: A longitudinal study. *British Journal of Developmental Psychology, 17,* 61–81.

Brandenburg, N. A., Friedman, R. M., & Silver, S. E. (1990). The epidemiology of childhood psychiatric disorders: Prevalence findings from recent studies. *Journal of the American Academy of Child and Adolescent Psychiatry, 29,* 76–83.

Brandon, P. (1999). Determinants of self-care arrangements among school-age children. *Children & Youth Services Review, 21,* 497–520.

Brandon, P., & Hofferth, S. (2003). Determinants of out-of-school childcare arrangements among children in single-mother and two-parent families. *Social Science Research, 32,* 129–147.

Bray, N. W., Fletcher, K. L., & Turner, L. A. (1997). Cognitive competencies and strategy use in individuals with mental retardation. In W. E. MacLean, Jr. (Ed.), *Ellis' handbook of mental deficiency: Psychological theory and research* (3rd ed., pp. 197–217). Mahwah, NJ: Erlbaum.

Brazelton, T. D. (1984). *Neonatal Behavioral Assessment Scale.* Philadelphia: Lippincott.

Breitmayer, B. J., & Ramey, C. T. (1986). Biological nonoptimality and quality of postnatal environment as codeterminants of intellectual development. *Child Development, 57,* 1151–1165.

Breland, H. M. (1974). Birth order, family configuration, and verbal achievement. *Child Development, 45,* 1011–1019.

Brendgen, M., Boivin, M., Vitaro, F., Bukowski, W., Dionne, G., Tremblay, R., & Pérusse, D. (2008). Linkages between children's and their friends' social and physical aggression: Evidence for a gene-environment interaction? *Child Development, 79,* 13–29.

Brennan, F., & Ireson, J. (1997). Training phonological awareness: A study to evaluate the effects of a program of metalinguistic games in kindergarten. *Reading & Writing, 9,* 241–263.

Bretherton, I. (1991). Pouring new wine into old bottles: The social self as internal working model. In M. R. Gunnar & L. A. Sroufe (Eds.), *The Minnesota symposia on child development* (Vol. 23, pp. 1–42). Hillsdale, NJ: Erlbaum.

Bretherton, I. (1993). From dialogue to internal working models: The co-construction of self in relationships. In C. A. Nelson (Ed.), *The Minnesota symposia on child psychology* (Vol. 26, pp. 237–264). Hillsdale, NJ: Erlbaum.

Breyer, J., & Winters, K. (2005). *Adolescent brain development: Implications for drug use prevention.* Retrieved April 15, 2008, from http://www.mentorfoundation.org/pdfs/prevention_perspectives/19.pdf

Bridgeland, J., DiIulio, J., & Morison, K. (2006). *The silent epidemic: Perspectives of high school dropouts.* Retrieved September 9, 2008, from http://www.gatesfoundation.org/nr/downloads/ed/thesilentepidemic3-06final.pdf

Bright, S., McKillop, D., & Ryder, D. (2008). Cigarette smoking among young adults: Integrating adolescent cognitive egocentrism with the Trans-Theoretical Model. *Australian Journal of Psychology, 60,* 18–25.

Bright-Paul, A., Jarrold, C., & Wright, D. (2008). Theory-of-mind development influences suggestibility and source monitoring. *Developmental Psychology, 44,* 1055–1068.

Briones, T., Klintsova, A., & Greenough, W. (2004). Stability of synaptic plasticity in the adult rat visual cortex induced by complex environment exposure. *Brain Research, 1018,* 130–135.

British Columbia Ministry of Education. (2001). *English as a second language.* Retrieved October 6, 2001, from http://www.bced.gov.bc.ca/esl/policy/introduction.htm

Broberg, A. G., Wessels, H., Lamb, M. E., & Hwang, C. P. (1997). Effects of day care on the development of cognitive abilities in 8-year-olds: A longitudinal study. *Developmental Psychology, 33,* 62–69.

Brockington, I. (1996). *Motherhood and mental health.* Oxford, England: Oxford University Press.

Brody, G., Kim, S., Murry, V., & Brown, A. (2003). Longitudinal direct and indirect pathways linking older sibling competence to the development of younger sibling competence. *Developmental Psychology, 39,* 618–628.

Brody, G. H., Stoneman, Z., & Flor, D. (1995). Linking family processes and academic competence among rural African American youths. *Journal of Marriage and the Family, 47,* 567–579.

Brody, N. (1992). *Intelligence* (2nd ed.). San Diego, CA: Academic Press.

Brody, N. (1997). Intelligence, schooling, and society. *American Psychologist, 52,* 1046–1050.

Broman, C. L. (1993). Race differences in marital well-being. *Journal of Marriage and the Family, 55,* 724–732.

Broman, S. H., Nichols, P. L., & Kennedy, W. A. (1975). *Preschool IQ: Prenatal and early developmental correlates.* Hillsdale, NJ: Erlbaum.

Broman, S. H., Nichols, P. L., Shaughnessy, P., & Kennedy, W. (1987). *Retardation in young children.* Hillsdale, NJ: Erlbaum.

Bronfenbrenner, U. (1967, October 7). The split-level American family. *Saturday Review,* 60–66.

Bronfenbrenner, U. (1979). *The ecology of human development.* Cambridge, MA: Harvard University Press.

Bronfenbrenner, U. (1989). Ecological systems theory. *Annals of Child Development, 6,* 187–249.

Bronfenbrenner, U. (2001). The bioecological theory of human development. In N. Smelser & P. Baltes (Eds.), *International encyclopedia of the social and behavioral sciences* (pp. 6963–6970). New York: Elsevier.

Bronson, G. W. (1994). Infants' transitions toward adult-like scanning. *Child Development, 65,* 1253–1261.

Brook, J., Whiteman, M., Finch, S., & Cohen, P. (2000). Longitudinally foretelling drug use in the late twenties: Adolescent personality and social-environmental antecedents. *Journal of Genetic Psychology, 161,* 37–51.

Brook, U., & Boaz, M. (2005). Attention deficit and hyperactivity disorder/learning disabilities (ADHD/LD): Parental characterization and perception. *Patient Education & Counseling, 57,* 96–100.

Brooks-Gunn, J. (1987). Pubertal processes and girls' psychological adaptation. In R. M. Lerner & T. T. Foch (Eds.), *Biological-psychosocial interactions in early adolescence* (pp. 123–154). Hillsdale, NJ: Erlbaum.

Brooks-Gunn, J. (1988). Commentary: Developmental issues in the transition to early adolescence. In M. R. Gunnar & W. A. Collins (Eds.), *Minnesota symposia on child psychology* (Vol. 21, pp. 189–208). Hillsdale, NJ: Erlbaum.

Brooks-Gunn, J. (1995). Children in families in communities: Risk and intervention in the Bronfenbrenner tradition. In P. Moen, G. H. Elder Jr., & K. Lüscher (Eds.), *Examining lives in context: Perspectives on the ecology of human development* (pp. 467–519). Washington, DC: American Psychological Association.

Brooks-Gunn, J., & Duncan G. J. (1997). The effects of poverty on children. *The Future of Children, 7*(2), 55–71.

Brooks-Gunn, J., Duncan, G. J., & Aber, J. L. (Eds.). (1997). *Neighborhood poverty: Vol 1. Context and consequences for children.* New York: Russell Sage Foundation.

Brooks-Gunn, J., Guo, G., & Furstenberg, F. F., Jr. (1993). Who drops out of and who continues beyond high school? A 20-year follow-up of black urban youth. *Journal of Research on Adolescence, 3,* 271–294.

Brooks-Gunn, J., Han, W., & Waldfogel, J. (2002). Maternal employment and child cognitive outcomes in the first three years of life: The NICHD study of early child care. *Child Development, 73,* 1052–1072.

Brooks-Gunn, J., & Warren, M. P. (1985). The effects of delayed menarche in different contexts: Dance and nondance students. *Journal of Youth and Adolescence, 13,* 285–300.

Brosnan, M. (1998). Spatial ability in children's play with Lego blocks. *Perceptual & Motor Skills, 87,* 19–28.

Broverman, I. K., Broverman, D., Clarkson, F. E., Rosenkrantz, P. S., & Vogel, S. R. (1970). Sex-role stereotypes and clinical judgments of mental health. *Journal of Consulting and Clinical Psychology, 34,* 1–7.

Brown, A. (2000–2001). Prenatal infection and adult schizophrenia: A review and synthesis. *International Journal of Mental Health, 29,* 22–37.

Brown, A., & Day, J. (1983). Macrorules for summarizing text: The development of expertise. *Journal of Verbal Learning and Verbal Behavior, 22,* 1–14.

Brown, B. B. (1990). Peer groups and peer cultures. In S. S. Feldman & G. R. Elliott (Eds.), *At the threshold: The developing adolescent* (pp. 171–196). Cambridge, MA: Harvard University Press.

Brown, B. B., Dolcini, M. M., & Leventhal, A. (1995, April). *The emergence of peer crowds: Friend or foe to adolescent health?* Paper presented at the biennial meetings of the Society for Research in Child Development, Indianapolis.

Brown, B. B., Mory, M. S., & Kinney, D. (1994). Casting adolescent crowds in a relational perspective: Caricature, channel, and context. In R. Montemayor, G. R. Adams, & T. P. Gullotta (Eds.), *Personal relationships during adolescence* (pp. 123–167). Thousand Oaks, CA: Sage.

Brown, G., McBride, B., Shin, N., & Bost, K. (2007). Parenting predictors of father-child attachment security: Interactive effects of father involvement and fathering quality. *Fathering, 5,* 197–219.

Brown, L., Karrison, T., & Cibils, L. A. (1994). Mode of delivery and perinatal results in breech presentation. *American Journal of Obstetrics and Gynecology, 171,* 28–34.

Brown, N., & Amatea, E. (2000). *Love and intimate relationships.* New York: Psychology Press.

Brown, R. (1973). *A first language: The early stages.* Cambridge, MA: Harvard University Press.

Brown, R., & Bellugi, U. (1964). Three processes in the acquisition of syntax. *Harvard Educational Review, 334,* 133–151.

Brown, R., & Hanlon, C. (1970). Derivational complexity and order of acquisition. In J. R. Hayes (Ed.), *Cognition and the development of language* (pp. 155–207). New York: Wiley.

Brown, S., Estroff, J., & Barnewolf, C. (2004). Fetal MRI. *Applied Radiology, 33,* 9–25.

Brown, W., Kesler, S., Eliez, S., Warsofsky, I., Haberecht, M., Patwardhan, A., Ross, J., Neely, E., Zeng, S., Yankowitz, J., & Reiss, A. (2002). Brain development in Turner syndrome: A magnetic resonance imaging study. *Psychiatry Research: Neuroimaging, 116,* 187–196.

Brownell, C. A. (1990). Peer social skills in toddlers: Competencies and constraints illustrated by same-age and mixed-age interaction. *Child Development, 61,* 836–848.

Brownell, K. D., & Fairburn, C. G. (Eds.). (1995). *Eating disorders and obesity: A comprehensive handbook.* New York: Guilford Press.

Bruck, M., & Ceci, S. J. (1997). The suggestibility of young children. *Current Directions in Psychological Science, 6,* 75–79.

Bruck, M., Ceci, S. J., & Hembrooke, H. (1998). Reliability and credibility of young children's reports: From research to policy and practice. *American Psychologist, 53,* 136–151.

Bryant, P., MacLean, M., & Bradley, L. (1990). Rhyme, language, and children's reading. *Applied Psycholinguistics, 11,* 237–252.

Bryant, P. E., MacLean, M., Bradley, L. L., & Crossland, J. (1990). Rhyme and alliteration, phoneme detection, and learning to read. *Developmental Psychology, 26,* 429–438.

Buchanan, C. M., Maccoby, E. E., & Dornbusch, S. M. (1991). Caught between parents: Adolescents' experience in divorced homes. *Child Development, 62,* 1008–1029.

Buhrmester, D. (1992). The developmental courses of sibling and peer relationships. In F. Boer & J. Dunn (Eds.), *Children's sibling relationships: Developmental and clinical issues.* Hillsdale, NJ: Erlbaum.

Buhrmester, D. (1996). Need fulfillment, interpersonal competence, and the developmental contexts of early adolescent friendship. In W. M. Bukowski, A. F. Newcomb, & W. W. Hartup (Eds.), *The company they keep: Friendship in childhood and adolescence* (pp. 158–185). Cambridge, England: Cambridge University Press.

Buhrmester, D., & Furman, W. (1990). Perceptions of sibling relationships during middle childhood and adolescence. *Child Development, 61,* 1387–1398.

Bukowski, W., Sippola, L., & Hoza, B. (1999). Same and other: Interdependency between participation in same- and other-sex friendships. *Journal of Youth & Adolescence, 28,* 439–459.

Burchinal, M., Lee, M., & Ramey, C. (1989). Type of day-care and preschool intellectual development in disadvantaged children. *Child Development, 60,* 128–137.

Burgess, S. (1997). The role of shared reading in the development of phonological awareness: A longitudinal study of middle to upper class children. *Early Child Development & Care, 127–128,* 191–199.

Burgess, S. (2005). The preschool home literacy environment provided by teenage mothers. *Early Child Development & Care, 175,* 249–258.

Burgess, S., Propper, C., & Rigg, J. (2004). *The impact of low income on child health: Evidence from a birth cohort study.* CASE Paper 85. Center for Analysis of Social Exclusion. Retrieved March 20, 2008, from http://sticerd.lse.ac.uk/dps/case/cp/CASEpaper85.pdf

Burn, S., O'Neil, A., & Nederend, S. (1996). Childhood tomboyishness and adult androgyny. *Sex Roles, 34,* 419–428.

Burt, S., McGue, M., Krueger, R., & Iacono, W. (2005). How are parent-child conflict and childhood externalizing symptoms related over time? Results from a genetically informative cross-lagged study. *Journal of Child Psychology and Psychiatry, 46,* 263–274.

Burton, L. (1992). Black grandparents rearing children of drug-addicted parents: Stressors, outcomes, and the social service needs. *Gerontologist, 31,* 744–751.

Bus, A., & van IJzendoorn, M. (1999). Phonological awareness and early reading: A meta-analysis of experimental training studies. *Journal of Educational Psychology, 91,* 403–414.

Bushman, B., & Huesmann, R. (2006). Short-term and long-term effects of violent media on aggression in children and adults. *Archives of Pediatric Adolescent Medicine, 160,* 348–352.

Bushnell, I. (2001). Mother's face recognition in newborn infants: Learning and memory. *Infant and Child Development, 10,* 67–74.

Buss, A. H. (1989). Temperaments as personality traits. In G. A. Kohnstamm, J. E. Bates, & M. K. Rothbart (Eds.), *Temperament in childhood* (pp. 39–58). Chichester, England: Wiley.

Buss, A. H., & Plomin, R. (1984). *Temperament: Early developing personality traits.* Hillsdale, NJ: Erlbaum.

Buss, A. H., & Plomin, R. (1986). The EAS approach to temperament. In R. Plomin & J. Dunn (Eds.), *The study of temperament: Changes, continuities and challenges* (pp. 67–80). Hillsdale, NJ: Erlbaum.

Bussey, K., & Bandura, A. (2004). Social cognitive theory of gender development and functioning. In E. Eagly, A. Beall, & R. Sternberg (Eds.), *The psychology of gender* (2nd ed., pp. 92–119). New York: Guilford.

Butterfield, S., Lehnhard, R., Lee, J., & Coladarci, T. (2004). Growth rates in running speed and vertical jumping by boys and girls ages 11–13. *Perceptual & Motor Skills, 99,* 225–234.

Buzi, R., Roberts, R., Ross, M., Addy, R., & Markham, C. (2003). The impact of a history of sexual abuse on high-risk sexual behaviors among females attending alternative school. *Adolescence, 38,* 595–605.

Cairns, R. B. (1991). Multiple metaphors for a singular idea. *Developmental Psychology, 27,* 23–26.

Cairns, R. B., & Cairns, B. D. (1994). *Lifelines and risks: Pathways of youth in our time.* Cambridge, England: Cambridge University Press.

Caldera, Y. (2004). Paternal involvement and infant-father attachment: A Q-set study. *Fathering, 2,* 191–210.

Calhoun, S., & Dickerson Mayes, S. (2005). Processing speed in children with clinical disorders. *Psychology in the Schools, 42,* 333–343.

Calkins, S., Dedmon, S., Gill, K., Lomax, L., & Johnson, L. (2002). Frustration in infancy: Implications for emotion regulation, physiological processes, and temperament. *Infancy, 3,* 175–197.

Callaghan, T., Rochat, P., Lillard, A., Claux, M., Odden, H., Itakura, S., Tapanya, S., & Singh, S. (2005). Synchrony in the onset of mental-state reasoning: Evidence from five cultures. *Psychological Science, 16,* 378–384.

Callahan, K., Rademacher, J., Hildreth, B., & Hildreth, B. (1998). The effect of parent participation in strategies to improve the homework performance of students who are at risk. *Remedial & Special Education, 19,* 131–141.

Calvert, S., & Kotler, J. (2003). Lessons from children's television: The impact of the Children's Television Act on children's learning. *Applied Developmental Psychology, 24,* 275–335.

Camaioni, L., & Longobardi, E. (1995). Nature and stability of individual differences in early lexical development of Italian-speaking children. *First Language, 15,* 203–218.

Camarata, S., & Woodcock, R. (2006). Sex differences in processing speed: Developmental effects in males and females. *Intelligence, 34,* 231–252.

Cameron, L. (1998). *The music of light: The extraordinary story of Hikari and Kenzaburo Oe.* New York: Free Press.

Campbell, F., Pungello, E., Miler-Johnson, S., Burchinal, M., & Ramey, C. (2001). The development of cognitive and academic abilities: Growth curves from an early childhood educational experiment. *Developmental Psychology, 37,* 231–242.

Campbell, F. A., & Ramey, C. T. (1994). Effects of early intervention on intellectual and academic achievement: A follow-up study of children from low-income families. *Child Development, 65,* 684–698.

Campbell, R. L., & Bickhard, M. H. (1992). Types of constraints on development: An interactivist approach. *Developmental Review, 12,* 311–338.

Campbell, S. B., & Ewing, L. J. (1990). Follow-up of hard-to-manage preschoolers: Adjustment at age 9 and predictors of continuing symptoms. *Journal of Child Psychology and Psychiatry, 31,* 871–889.

Campbell, S. B., Pierce, E. W., March, C. L., & Ewing, L. J. (1991). Noncompliant behavior, overactivity, and family stress as predictors of negative maternal control with preschool children. *Development and Psychopathology, 3,* 175–190.

Campione, J. C., & Brown, A. L. (1984). Learning ability and transfer propensity as sources of individual differences in intelligence. In P. H. Brooks, C. McCauley, & R. Sperber (Eds.), *Learning and cognition in the mentally retarded.* Hillsdale, NJ: Erlbaum.

Campione, J. C., Brown, A. L., & Ferrara, R. A. (1982). Mental retardation and intelligence. In J. R. Sternberg (Ed.), *Handbook of human intelligence* (pp. 392–492). Cambridge, England: Cambridge University Press.

Campione, J. C., Brown, A. L., Ferrara, R. A., Jones, R. S., & Steinberg, E. (1985). Breakdowns in flexible use of information: Intelligence-related differences in transfer following equivalent learning performance. *Intelligence, 9,* 297–315.

Cantwell, D. P. (1990). Depression across the early life span. In M. Lewis & S. M. Miller (Eds.), *Handbook of developmental psychopathology* (pp. 293–310). New York: Plenum Press.

Cappella, E., & Weinstein, R. (2001). Turning around reading achievement: Predictors of high school students' academic resilience. *Journal of Educational Psychology, 93,* 758–771.

Capron, C., & Duyme, M. (1989). Assessment of effects of socioeconomic status on IQ in a full cross-fostering study. *Nature, 340,* 552–554.

Capute, A. J., Palmer, F. B., Shapiro, B. K., Wachtel, R. C., Ross, A., & Accardo, P. J. (1984). Primitive reflex profile: A quantification of primitive reflexes in infancy. *Developmental Medicine and Child Neurology, 26,* 375–383.

Caputo, R. (2004). Parent religiosity, family processes, and adolescent outcomes. *Families in Society, 85,* 495–510.

Carey, S., & Bartlett, E. (1978). Acquiring a single new word. *Papers & Reports on Child Language Development, 15,* 17–29.

Carlson, E., Sampson, M., & Sroufe, A. (2003). Implications of attachment theory and research for developmental-behavioral pediatrics. *Journal of Developmental and Behavioral Pediatrics, 24,* 364–379.

Carlson, E., & Sroufe, A. (1995). Contribution of attachment theory to developmental psychopathology. In D. Cicchetti & D. J. Cohen (Eds.), *Developmental psychopathology: Vol. 1. Theory and methods* (pp. 581–617). New York: Wiley.

Carlson, E., Sroufe, A., & Egeland, B. (2004). The construction of experience: A longitudinal study of representation and behavior. *Child Development, 75,* 66–83.

Carlson, S., & Meltzoff, A. (2008). Bilingual experience and executive functioning in young children. *Developmental Science, 11,* 282–298.

Carlson, V., & Harwood, R. (2003). Alternative pathways to competence: Culture and early attachment relationships. In S. Johnson & V. Whiffen (Eds.), *Attachment processes in couple and family therapy* (pp. 85–99). New York: Guilford Press.

Caron, A. J., & Caron, R. F. (1981). Processing of relational information as an index of infant risks. In S. Friedman & M. Sigman (Eds.), *Preterm birth and psychological development* (pp. 219–240). New York: Academic Press.

Caron, A. J., Caron R. F., Roberts, J., & Brooks, R. (1997). Infant sensitivity to deviations in dynamic facial-vocal displays: The role of eye regard. *Developmental Psychology, 33,* 802–813.

Carr, C. (2007). Where have all the tomboys gone? Women's accounts of gender in adolescence. *Sex Roles, 56,* 439–448.

Carson, D., Klee, T., & Perry, C. (1998). Comparisons of children with delayed and normal language at 24 months of age on measures of behavioral difficulties, social and cognitive development. *Infant Mental Health, 19,* 59–75.

Carter, A., Garrity-Rokous, F., Chazan-Cohen, R., Little, C., & Briggs-Gowan, M. (2001). Maternal depression and comorbidity: Predicting early parenting, attachment security, and toddler social-emotional problems and competencies. *Journal of the American Academy of Child and Adolescent Psychiatry, 40,* 18–26.

Carver, P., Egan, S., & Perry, D. (2004). Children who question their heterosexuality. *Developmental Psychology, 40,* 43–53.

Casasola, M., & Cohen, L. (2000). Infants' association of linguistic labels with causal actions. *Developmental Psychology, 36,* 155–168.

Case, A., Lee, D., & Paxson, C. (2007). *The income gradient in children's health: A comment on Currie, Shields and Wheatley Price.* NBER Working Paper No. W13495. Retrieved March 19, 2008, from http://ssrn.com/abstract=1021973

Case, A., Lubotsky, D., & Paxson, C. (2002). Economic status and health in childhood: The origins of the gradient. *American Economic Review, 92,* 1308–1334.

Case, R. (1985). *Intellectual development: Birth to adulthood.* New York: Academic Press.

Case, R. (1991). Stages in the development of the young child's first sense of self. *Developmental Review, 11,* 210–230.

Case, R. (1992). *The mind's staircase: Exploring thought and knowledge.* Hillsdale, NJ: Erlbaum.

Caselli, C., Casadio, P., & Bates, E. (1997). *A cross-linguistic study of the transition from first words to grammar* (Technical Report No. CND-9701). Center for Research in Language, University of California, San Diego.

Casey, B., McIntire, D., & Leveno, K. (2001). The continuing value of the Apgar score for the assessment of newborn infants. *New England Journal of Medicine, 344,* 467–471.

Cashmore, J., & Parkinson, P. (2008). Children's and parents' perceptions on children's participation in decision making after parental separation and divorce. *Family Court Review, 46,* 91–104.

Cashmore, J., Parkinson, P., & Taylor, A. (2008). Overnight stays and children's relationships with resident and nonresident parents after divorce. *Journal of Family Issues, 29,* 707–733.

Cashon, C., & Cohen, L. (2000). Eight-month-old infants' perceptions of possible and impossible events. *Infancy, 1,* 429–446.

Caslyn, C., Gonzales, P., & Frase, M. (1999). *Highlights from the third international Mathematics and Science Study.* Washington, DC: National Center for Educational Statistics.

Casper, L., & Smith, K. (2002). Dispelling the myths: Self-care, class, and race. *Journal of Family Issues, 23,* 716–727.

Caspi, A. (2000). The child is father of the man: Personality continuities from childhood to adulthood. *Journal of Personality & Social Psychology, 78,* 158–172.

Caspi, A., Harkness, A. R., Moffitt, T. E., & Silva, P. A. (1996). Intellectual performance: Continuity and change. In P. A. Silva & W. R. Stanton (Eds.), *From child to adult: The Dunedin Multidisciplinary Health and Development Study* (pp. 59–74). Aukland: Oxford University Press.

Caspi, A., Harrington, H., Milne, B., Amell, J., Theodore, R., & Moffitt, T. E. (2003). Children's behavioral styles at age 3 are linked to their adult personality traits at age 26. *Journal of Personality, 71,* 495–513.

Caspi, A., & Moffitt, T. E. (1991). Individual differences are accentuated during periods of social change: The sample case of girls at puberty. *Journal of Personality and Social Psychology, 61,* 157–168.

Caspi, A., & Moffitt, T. E. (2006). Gene-environment interactions in psychiatry: Joining forces with neuroscience. *Nature Reviews: Neuroscience, 7,* 583–590.

Caspi, A., & Shiner, R. (2006). Personality development. In N. Eisenberg, W. Damon, & R. Lerner (Eds.), *Handbook of child psychology: Vol. 3, Social, emotional, and personality development* (6th ed., pp. 300–365). Hoboken, NJ: Wiley.

Cassidy, J., & Berlin, L. J. (1994). The insecure/ambivalent pattern of attachment: Theory and research. *Child Development, 65,* 971–991.

Castellino, D., Lerner, J., Lerner, R., & von Eye, A. (1998). Maternal employment and education: Predictors of young adolescent career trajectories. *Applied Developmental Science, 2,* 114–126.

Cato, J., & Canetto, S. (2003). Attitudes and beliefs about suicidal behavior when coming out is the precipitant of the suicidal behavior. *Sex Roles, 49,* 497–505.

Cavill, S., & Bryden, P. (2003). Development of handedness: Comparison of questionnaire and performance-based measures of preference. *Brain & Cognition, 53,* 149–151.

Cecchini, M., Lai, C., & Langher, V. (2007). Communication and crying in newborns. *Infant Behavior & Development, 30,* 655–665.

Ceci, S. J., & Bruck, M. (1995). *Jeopardy in the courtroom: A scientific analysis of children's testimony.* Washington, DC: American Psychological Association.

Cederblad, M., Pruksachatkunakorn, P., Boripunkul, T., Intraprasert, S., & Hook, B. (2003). Sense of coherence in a Thai sample. *Transcultural Psychiatry, 40,* 585–600.

Centers for Disease Control. (1992). Pregnancy risks determined from birth certificate data—United States, 1989. *Morbidity & Mortality Weekly Report, 41*(30), 556–563.

Centers for Disease Control. (1995a). Chorionic villus sampling and amniocentesis: Recommendations for prenatal counseling. *Morbidity & Mortality Weekly Report, 44*(RR-9), 1–12.

Centers for Disease Control. (1995b). U.S. Public Health Service recommendations for human immunodeficiency virus counseling and voluntary testing for pregnant women. *Mortality & Morbidity Weekly Report, 44*(RR-7), 1–15.

Centers for Disease Control. (1996). Population-based prevalence of perinatal exposure to cocaine: Georgia, 1994. *Morbidity & Mortality Weekly Report, 45,* 887.

Centers for Disease Control. (2000). Youth risk behavior surveillance—United States, 1999. *Morbidity & Mortality Weekly Report, 49,* 1–96.

Centers for Disease Control (CDC). (2004a). Sexually transmitted disease surveillance 2001, supplement, chlamydia prevalence monitoring project. Retrieved May 4, 2005, from http://www.cdc.gov/std/Chlamydia2003/

Centers for Disease Control (CDC). (2004b). Surveillance summaries. *Morbidity & Mortality Weekly Report, 53,* 2–29.

Centers for Disease Control (CDC). (2006a). *Cytomegalovirus.* Retrieved August 4, 2008, from http://www.cdc.gov/cmv/facts.htm

Centers for Disease Control (CDC). (2006b). *HPV vaccine questions and answers.* Retrieved June 29, 2006, from http://www.cdc.gov/std/hpv/STDFact-HPV-vaccine.htm#vaccine

Centers for Disease Control (CDC). (2006c). Improved national prevalence estimates for 18 selected major birth defects: United States, 1999–2001. *Morbidity & Mortality Weekly Report, 54,* 1301–1305.

Centers for Disease Control (CDC). (2006d). *Sudden Infant Death Syndrome (SIDS): Risk factors.* Retrieved June 8, 2007, from http://www.cdc.gov/SIDS/riskfactors.htm

Centers for Disease Control (CDC). (2006e). *Understanding child maltreatment.* Retrieved June 14, 2007, from http://www.cdc.gov/ncipc/pub-res/CMFactsheet.pdf

Centers for Disease Control (CDC). (2006f). Youth risk behavior surveillance: United States, 2005. *Morbidity & Mortality Weekly Report, 55,* 1–112.

Centers for Disease Control (CDC). (2007a). *HIV/AIDS: Pregnancy and childbirth.* Retrieved August 4, 2008, from http://www.cdc.gov/hiv/topics/perinatal/index.htm

Centers for Disease Control (CDC). (2007b). *HIV/AIDS surveillance in adolescents and young adults (through 2005).* Retrieved April 11, 2008, from http://www.cdc.gov/hiv/topics/surveillance/resources/slides/adolescents/index.htm

Centers for Disease Control (CDC). (2007c). *Sexually transmitted disease surveillance 2006 supplement.* Retrieved April 9, 2008, from http://www.cdc.gov/std/Chlamydia2006/CTSurvSupp2006Short.pdf

Centers for Disease Control (CDC). (2007d). *Suicide: Fact sheet.* Retrieved June 22, 2007, from http://www.cdc.gov/ncipc/factsheets/suifacts.htm

Centers for Disease Control (CDC). (2007e). *Tips for parents: Ideas and tips to help prevent child overweight.* Retrieved June 19, 2007, from http://www.cdc.gov/nccdphp/dnpa/obesity/childhood/tips_for_parents.htm

Chalfant, J. C. (1989). Learning disabilities: Policy issues and promising approaches. *American Psychologist, 44,* 392–398.

Chambers, C., & Vaux, K. (2006). *Fetal alcohol syndrome.* Retrieved August 7, 2008, from http://www.emedicine.com/ped/TOPIC767.HTM

Chan, R., Raboy, B., & Patterson, C. (1998). Psychosocial adjustment among children conceived via donor insemination by lesbian and heterosexual mothers. *Child Development, 69,* 443–457.

Chang, F., & Burns, B. (2005). Attention in preschoolers: Associations with effortful control and motivation. *Child Development, 76,* 247–263.

Chang, L., & Murray, A. (1995, April). *Math performance of 5- and 6-year-olds in Taiwan and the U.S.: Maternal beliefs, expectations, and tutorial assistance.* Paper presented at the biennial meetings of the Society for Research in Child Development, Indianapolis.

Chang, L., Schwartz, D., Dodge, K., & McBride-Chang, C. (2003). Harsh parenting in relation to child emotion regulation and aggression. *Journal of Family Psychology, 17,* 598–606.

Chao, R., & Tseng, V. (2002). Parenting of Asians. In M. Bornstein (Ed.), *Handbook of parenting: Volume 4: Social conditions and applied parenting* (2nd ed., pp. 59–93). Mahwah, NJ: Erlbaum.

Chapa, J., & Valencia, R. R. (1993). Latino population growth, demographic characteristics, and educational stagnation: An examination of recent trends. *Hispanic Journal of Behavioral Sciences, 15,* 165–187.

Chapman, K., Nicholas, P., & Supramaniam, R. (2006). How much food advertising is there on Australian television? *Health Promotion International, 21,* 172–180.

Charman, T., Redfern, S., & Fonagy, P. (1995, April). *Individual differences in theory of mind acquisition: The role of attachment security.* Paper presented at the biennial meetings of the Society for Research in Child Development, Indianapolis.

Charman, T., Ruffman, T., & Clements, W. (2002). Is there a gender difference in false belief development? *Social Development, 11,* 1–10.

Charuvastra, A., & Cloitre, M. (2008). Social bonds and post traumatic stress disorder. *Annual Review of Psychology, 59,* 301–328.

Chase-Lansdale, P., Cherlin, A., & Kiernan, K. (1995). The long-term effects of parental divorce on the mental health of young adults: A developmental perspective. *Child Development, 66,* 1614–1634.

Chavajay, P., & Rogoff, B. (2002). Schooling and traditional collaborative social organization of problem solving by Mayan mothers and children. *Developmental Psychology, 38*, 55–66.

Chen, E. (2004). Why socioeconomic status affects the health of children: A psychosocial perspective. *Current Directions in Psychological Science, 13*, 112–115.

Chen, H. (2007). *Down syndrome.* Retrieved August 7, 2008, from http://www.emedicine.com/ped/TOPIC615.HTM

Chen, X., He, Y., Chang, L., & Liu, H. (2005). The peer group as a context: Moderating effects on relations between maternal parenting and social and school adjustment in Chinese children. *Child Development, 76*, 417–434.

Chen, X., Wang, L., & DeSouza, A. (2006). Temperament, socioemotional functioning, and peer relationships in Chinese and North American children. In X. Chen, D. French, & B. Schneider (Eds.), *Peer relationships in cultural context* (pp. 123–147). New York: Cambridge University Press.

Chen, Z. (1999). Ethnic similarities and differences in the association of emotional autonomy and adolescent outcomes: Comparing Euro-American and Asian-American adolescents. *Psychological Reports, 84*, 501–516.

Chen, Z., Dong, Q., & Zhou, H. (1997). Authoritative and authoritarian parenting practices and social and school performance in Chinese children. *International Journal of Behavioral Development, 21*, 855–873.

Cheng, A., McDonald, J., & Thielman, N. (2005). Infectious diarrhea in developed and developing countries. *Journal of Clinical Gastroenterology, 39*, 757–773.

Cherlin, A. (1992). *Marriage, divorce, remarriage.* Cambridge, MA: Harvard University Press.

Cherlin, A., Chase-Lansdale, P., & McRae, C. (1998). Effects of parental divorce on mental health throughout the life course. *American Sociological Review, 63*, 239–249.

Cherry, V., Belgrave, F., Jones, W., Kennon, D., Gray, F., & Phillips, F. (1998). NTU: An Africentric approach to substance abuse prevention among African American youth. *Journal of Primary Prevention, 18*, 319–339.

Chess, S., & Thomas, A. (1984). *Origins and evolution of behavior disorders: Infancy to early adult life.* New York: Brunner/Mazel.

Chi, M. T. (1978). Knowledge structure and memory development. In R. S. Siegler (Ed.), *Children's thinking: What develops?* (pp. 73–96). Hillsdale, NJ: Erlbaum.

Chiappe, P., Glaeser, B., & Ferko, D. (2007). Speech perception, vocabulary, and the development of reading skills in English among Korean- and English-speaking children. *Journal of Educational Psychology, 99*, 154–166.

Chiappe, P., & Siegel, L. (1999). Phonological awareness and reading acquisition in English- and Punjabi-speaking Canadian children. *Journal of Educational Psychology, 91*, 20–28.

Children's Hospital of Philadelphia. (2008, March 3). In early childhood, continuous care by one doctor best, study suggests. Retrieved March 18, 2008, from http://www.sciencedaily.com/releases/2008/03/080303072646.htm

"Children spend more time playing video games than watching TV, MSU survey shows." (2004, April 4). Retrieved July 23, 2005, from http://www.newsroom.msu.edu/site/indexer/1943/content.htm

Chisholm, J. S. (1989). Biology, culture, and the development of temperament: A Navaho example. In J. K. Nugent, B. M. Lester, & T. B. Brazelton (Eds.), *The cultural context of infancy: Vol. 1. Biology, culture, and infant development.* Norwood, NJ: Ablex.

Choi, S. (2000). Caregiver input in English and Korean: Use of nouns and verbs in book-reading and toy-play contexts. *Journal of Child Language, 27*, 69–96.

Chomsky, N. (1965). *Aspects of a theory of syntax.* Cambridge, MA: MIT Press.

Chomsky, N. (1975). *Reflections on language.* New York: Pantheon Books.

Chomsky, N. (1986). *Knowledge of language: Its nature, origin, and use.* New York: Praeger.

Chomsky, N. (1988). *Language and problems of knowledge.* Cambridge, MA: MIT Press.

Chong, B., Babcook, C., Salamat, M., Nemzek, W., Kroeker, D., & Ellis, W. (1996). A magnetic resonance template for normal neuronal migration in the fetus. *Neurosurgery, 39*, 110–116.

Chopak, J., Vicary, J., & Crockett, L. (1998). Predicting alcohol and tobacco use in a sample of rural adolescents. *American Journal of Health Behavior, 22*, 334–341.

Christakis, D., Zimmerman, F., Giuseppe, D., & McCarty, C. (2004). Early television exposure and subsequent attentional problems in children. *Pediatrics, 113*, 708–713.

Christensen, C. (1997). Onset, rhymes, and phonemes in learning to read. *Scientific Studies of Reading, 1*, 341–358.

Christie-Mizell, C., Pryor, E., & Grossman, E. (2008). Child depressive symptoms, spanking, and emotional support: Differences between African American and European American youth. *Family Relations, 57*, 335–350.

Chudley, A., Conry, J., Cook, J., Loock, C., Rosales, T., & LeBlanc, N. (2005). Fetal alcohol spectrum disorder: Canadian guidelines for diagnosis. *Canadian Medical Association Journal, 172*, S1–S21.

Chudzik, L. (2007). Moral judgment and conduct disorder intensity in adolescents involved in delinquency: Matching controls by school grade. *Psychological Reports, 101*, 221–236.

Cicchetti, D. (2008). A multiple-levels-of-analysis perspective on research in development and psychopathology. In T. Beauchaine & S. Hinshaw (Eds.), *Child and adolescent psychopathology* (pp. 27–57). Hoboken, NJ: Wiley.

Cicchetti, D., Rogosch, F., Maughan, A., Toth, S., & Bruce, J. (2003). False belief understanding in maltreated children. *Development & Psychopathology, 15*, 1067–1091.

Cicchetti, D., Rogosch, F., & Sturge-Apple, M. (2007). Interactions of child maltreatment and 5-HTT and monoamine oxidase A polymorphisms: Depressive symptomatology among adolescents from low-socioeconomic status backgrounds. *Development and Psychopathology, 19*, 1161–1180.

Cicchetti, D., & Toth, S. L. (1998). The development of depression in children and adolescents. *American Psychologist, 53*, 221–241.

Cillessen, A. H. N., van IJzendoorn, H. W., van Lieshout, C. F. M., & Hartup, W. W. (1992). Heterogeneity among peer-rejected boys: Subtypes and stabilities. *Child Development, 63*, 893–905.

Clark, E. V. (1975). Knowledge, context, and strategy in the acquisition of meaning. In D. P. Date (Ed.), *Georgetown University round table on language and linguistics.* Washington, DC: Georgetown University Press.

Clark, E. V. (1983). Meanings and concepts. In J. H. Flavell & E. M. Markman (Eds.), *Handbook of child psychology: Cognitive development* (Vol. 3, pp. 787–840). New York: Wiley.

Clark, E. V. (1990). On the pragmatics of contrast. *Journal of Child Language, 41*, 417–431.

Clarke, A. M., & Clarke, A. D. B. (1976). *Early experience: Myth and evidence.* New York: Free Press.

Clarke-Stewart, K. A., Gruber, C. P., & Fitzgerald, L. M. (1994). *Children at home and in day care.* Hillsdale, NJ: Erlbaum.

Clayton, V. (2004, September 8). *What's to blame for the rise in ADHD?* Retrieved November 22, 2004, from http://www.msnbc.msn.com/id/5933775/

Coatsworth, J., Maldonado-Molina, M., Pantin, H., & Szapocznik, J. (2005). A person-centered and ecological investigation of acculturation strategies in Hispanic immigrant youth. *Journal of Community Psychology, 33*, 157–174.

Cobb, K. (2000, September 3). Breaking in drivers: Texas could join states restricting teens in effort to lower rate of fatal accidents. *Houston Chronicle*, A1, A20.

Cocodia, E., Kim, J., Shin, H., Kim, J., Ee, J., Wee, M., & Howard, R. (2003). Evidence that rising population intelligence is impacting formal education. *Personality & Individual Differences, 35*, 797–810.

Coe, C., Hayashi, K. T., & Levine, S. (1988). Hormones and behavior at puberty: Activation or concatenation? In M. R. Gunnar & W. A. Collins (Eds.), *Development during the transition to adolescence: Minnesota symposia on child psychology* (Vol. 21, pp. 17–42). Hillsdale, NJ: Erlbaum.

Cohen, D., Pichard, N., Tordjman, S., Baumann, C., Burglen, L., Excoffier, E., Lazar, G., Mazet, P., Pinquier, C., Verloes, A., & Heron, D. (2005). Specific genetic disorders and autism: Clinical contribution towards their identification. *Journal of Autism & Developmental Disorders, 35*, 103–116.

Cohen-Kettenis, P., & van Goozen, S. (1997). Sex reassignment of adolescent transsexuals: A follow-up study. *Journal of the American Academy of Child & Adolescent Psychiatry, 36*, 263–271.

Coie, J. D. (1997a, April). *Initial outcome evaluation of the prevention trial.* Paper presented at the biennial meetings of the Society for Research in Child Development, Washington, DC.

Coie, J. D. (1997b, August). *Testing developmental theory of antisocial behavior with outcomes from the Fast Track Prevention Project.* Paper presented at the annual meeting of the American Psychological Association, Chicago.

Coie, J. D., & Cillessen, A. H. N. (1993). Peer rejection: Origins and effects on children's development. *Current Directions in Psychological Science, 2*, 89–92.

Coie, J. D., & Dodge, K. A. (1998). Aggression and antisocial behavior. In W. Damon (Ed.), *Handbook of child psychology: Vol. 3. Social, emotional, and personality development* (5th ed., pp. 779–862). New York: Wiley.

Coie, J. D., Terry, R., Lenox, K., Lochman, J., & Hyman, C. (1995). Childhood peer rejection and aggression as predictors of stable patterns of adolescent disorder. *Development and Psychopathology, 7*, 697–713.

Coiro, M. J. (1995, April). *Child behavior problems as a function of marital conflict and parenting.* Paper presented at the biennial meetings of the Society for Research in Child Development, Indianapolis.

Colby, A., & Damon, W. (1992). *Some do care: Contemporary lives of moral commitment.* New York: Free Press.

Colby, A., Kohlberg, L., Gibbs, J., & Lieberman, M. (1983). A longitudinal study of moral judgment. *Monographs of the Society for Research in Child Development, 48*(1–2, Serial No. 200).

Cole, M. (2005). Culture in development. In M. Bornstein & M. Lamb (Eds.), *Developmental science: An advanced textbook* (5th ed., pp. 45–102). Hillsdale, NJ: Erlbaum.

Cole, P., Martin, S., & Dennis, T. (2004). Emotion regulation as a scientific construct: Methodological challenges and directions for child development research. *Child Development, 75*, 317–333.

Coley, R., & Chase-Lansdale, L. (1998). Adolescent pregnancy and parenthood: Recent evidence and future directions. *American Psychologist, 53*, 152–166.

Collaer, M. L., & Hines, M. (1995). Human behavioral sex differences: A role for gonadal hormones during early development? *Psychological Bulletin, 118*, 55–107.

Collet, J. P., Burtin, P., Gillet, J., Bossard, N., Ducruet, T., & Durr, F. (1994). Risk of infectious diseases in children attending different types of day-care setting. Epicreche Research Group. *Respiration, 61*, 16–19.

Collins, R., Elliott, M., Berry, S., Kanouse, D., Kunkel, D., Hunter, S., & Miu, A. (2004). Watching sex on television predicts adolescent initiation of sexual behavior. *Pediatrics, 114*, 280–289.

Colombo, J. (1993). *Infant cognition: Predicting later intellectual functioning.* Newbury Park, CA: Sage.

Combrinck-Graham, L., & Fox, G. (2007). Development of school-age children. In A. Martin, F. Volkmar, & M. Lewis (Eds.), *Lewis's child and adolescent psychiatry* (pp. 267–278). Philadelphia: Lippincott, Williams, & Wilkins.

Compas, B. E., Ey, S., & Grant, K. E. (1993). Taxonomy, assessment, and diagnosis of depression during adolescence. *Psychological Bulletin, 114*, 323–344.

Condry, J., & Condry, S. (1976). Sex differences: A study in the eye of the beholder. *Child Development, 47*, 812–819.

Conduct Problems Prevention Research Group. (2007). Fast Track randomized controlled trial to prevent externalizing psychiatric disorders: Findings from grades 3 to 9. *Journal of the American Academy of Child & Adolescent Psychiatry, 46*, 1250–1262.

Conger, R. D., Conger, K. J., Elder, G. H., Jr., Lorenz, F. O., Simons, R. L., & Whitbeck, L. B. (1992). A family process model of economic hardship and adjustment of early adolescent boys. *Child Development, 63*, 526–541.

Conger, R. D., Ge, X., Elder, G. H., Jr., Lorenz, F. O., & Simons, R. L. (1994). Economic stress, coercive family process, and developmental problems of adolescence. *Child Development, 65*, 541–561.

Conger, R. D., Patterson, G. R., & Ge, X. (1995). It takes two to replicate: A mediational model for the impact of parents' stress on adolescent adjustment. *Child Development, 66*, 80–97.

Connolly, K., & Dalgleish, M. (1989). The emergence of a tool-using skill in infancy. *Developmental Psychology, 25*, 894–912.

Connor, P., Sampson, P., Bookstein, F., Barr, H., & Streissguth, A. (2001). Direct and indirect effects of prenatal alcohol damage on executive function. *Developmental Neuropsychology, 18*, 331–354.

Cooper, P. J. (1995). Eating disorders and their relationship to mood and anxiety disorders. In K. D. Brownell & C. G. Fairburn (Eds.), *Eating disorders and obesity: A comprehensive handbook* (pp. 159–164). New York: Guilford Press.

Cooper, R. P., & Aslin, R. N. (1994). Developmental differences in infant attention to the spectral properties of infant-directed speech. *Child Development, 65*, 1663–1677.

Cornelius, M., Goldschmidt, L., Day, N., & Larkby, C. (2002). Alcohol, tobacco and marijuana use among pregnant teenagers: 6-year follow-up of offspring growth effects. *Neurotoxicology & Teratology, 24*, 703–710.

Cornwell, A., & Feigenbaum, P. (2006). Sleep biological rhythms in normal infants and those at high risk for SIDS. *Chronobiology International, 23*, 935–961.

Corter, C. M., & Fleming, A. S. (1995). Psychobiology of maternal behavior in human beings. In M. H. Bornstein (Ed.), *Handbook of parenting: Vol. 2. Biology and ecology of parenting* (pp. 87–116). Mahwah, NJ: Erlbaum.

Costa, A., Torriero, S., Oliveri, M., & Caltagirone, C. (2008). Prefrontal and temporo-parietal involvement in taking others' perspective: TMS evidence. *Behavioural Neurology, 19*, 71–74.

Costa, P. T., Jr., & McCrae, R. R. (1984). Personality as a lifelong determinant of wellbeing. In C. Z. Malatesta & C. E. Izard (Eds.), *Emotion in adult development* (pp. 141–158). Beverly Hills, CA: Sage.

Costa, P. T., Jr., & McCrae, R. R. (1994). Set like plaster? Evidence for the stability of adult personality. In T. F. Hetherton & J. L. Weinberger (Eds.), *Can personality change?* (pp. 21–40). Washington, DC: American Psychological Association.

Costello, E., Sung, M., Worthman, C., & Angold, A. (2007). Pubertal maturation and the development of alcohol use and abuse. *Drug and Alcohol Dependence, 88*, S50–S59.

Coulton, C. J., Korbin, J. E., Su, M., & Chow, J. (1995). Community level factors and child maltreatment rates. *Child Development, 66*, 1262–1276.

Coury, D. (2002). Developmental and behavioral pediatrics. In A. Rudolph, R. Kamei, & K. Overby (Eds.), *Rudolph's fundamentals of pediatrics* (3rd ed., pp. 110–124). New York: McGraw-Hill.

Cowan, N., Nugent, L. D., Elliott, E., Ponomarev, I., & Saults, J. (1999). The role of attention in the development of short-term memory: Age differences in the verbal span of apprehension. *Child Development, 70*, 1082–1097.

Cox, T. (1983). Cumulative deficit in culturally disadvantaged children. *British Journal of Educational Psychology, 53*, 317–326.

Cramer, P. (2000). Defense mechanisms in psychology today. *American Psychologist, 55*, 637–646.

Cramond, B. (2004). Can we, should we, need we agree on a definition of giftedness? *Roeper Review, 27*, 15–16.

Crawford, A., & Manassis, K. (2001). Familial predictors of treatment outcome in childhood anxiety disorders. *Journal of the American Academy of Child and Adolescent Psychiatry, 40*, 1182–1189.

Crick, N., & Dodge, K. (1994). A review and reformulation of social information processing mechanisms in children's social adjustment. *Psychological Bulletin, 115*, 74–101.

Crick, N., & Dodge, K. (1996). Social information-processing mechanisms in reactive and proactive aggression. *Child Development, 67*, 993–1002.

Crick, N. R., & Grotpeter, J. K. (1995). Relational aggression, gender, and social-psychological adjustment. *Child Development, 66*, 710–722.

Crick, N. R., & Grotpeter, J. K. (1996). Children's treatment by peers: Victims of relational and overt aggression. *Development and Psychopathology, 8*, 367–380.

Crittenden, P. M. (1992). Quality of attachment in the preschool years. *Development and Psychopathology, 4*, 209–241.

Crnic, K. A., Greenberg, M. T., Ragozin, A. S., Robinson, N. M., & Basham, R. B. (1983). Effects of stress and social support on mothers and premature and full-term infants. *Child Development, 43*, 209–217.

Crocetti, E., Rubini, M., Luyckx, K., & Meeus, W. (2008). Identity formation in early and middle adolescents from various ethnic groups: From three dimensions to five statuses. *Journal of Youth and Adolescence, 37*, 983–996.

Crockenberg, S. B. (1981). Infant irritability, mother responsiveness, and social support influences on the security of infant-mother attachment. *Child Development, 52*, 857–865.

Crockenberg, S. B. (1987). Predictors and correlates of anger toward and punitive control of toddlers by adolescent mothers. *Child Development, 48*, 964–975.

Crockenberg, S. B. (2003). Rescuing the baby from the bath water: How gender and temperament (may) influence how child care affects child development. *Child Development, 74*, 1034–1038.

Crockenberg, S. B., & Leerkes, E. (2004). Infant and maternal behaviors regulate infant reactivity to novelty at 6 months. *Developmental Psychology, 40*, 1123–1132.

Crockenberg, S. B., & Litman, C. (1990). Autonomy as competence in 2-year-olds: Maternal correlates of child defiance, compliance, and self-assertion. *Development Psychology, 26*, 961–971.

Crockett, D. (2003). Critical issues children face in the 2000s. *School Psychology Quarterly, 18*, 446–453.

Crone, E., & van der Molen, M. (2004). Developmental changes in real life decision making: Performance on a gambling task previously shown to depend on the ventromedial prefrontal cortex. *Developmental Neuropsychology, 25*, 251–279.

Crook, C. (1987). Taste and olfaction. In P. Salapatek & L. Cohen (Eds.), *Handbook of infant perception, Vol. 1: From sensation to perception* (pp. 237–264). Orlando, FL: Academic Press.

Cross, W., & Cross, B. (2008). Theory, research, and models. In S. Quintana & C. McKown (Eds.), *Handbook of race, racism, and the developing child* (pp. 154–181). Hoboken, NJ: Wiley.

Crowell, J., & Hauser, S. (2008). AAIs in a high-risk sample: Stability and relation to functioning from adolescence to 39 years. In H. Steele & M. Steele (Eds.), *Clinical applications of the Adult Attachment Interview* (pp. 341–370). New York: Guilford Press.

Crowell, J. A., & Feldman, S. S. (1988). Mothers' internal models of relationships and children's behavioral and developmental status. A study of mother-child interaction. *Child Development, 50*, 1273–1285.

Crowell, J. A., & Feldman, S. S. (1991). Mothers' working models of attachment relationships and mother and child behavior during separation and reunion. *Developmental Psychology, 27*, 597–605.

Crystal, D. S., Chen, C., Fuligni, A. J., Stevenson, H. W., Hsu, C., Ko, H., Kitamura, S., & Kimura, S. (1994). Psychological maladjustment and academic achievement: A cross-cultural study of Japanese, Chinese, and American high school students. *Child Development, 65*, 738–753.

Cuffe, S., Moore, C., & McKeown, R. (2005). Prevalence and correlates of ADHD symptoms in the National Health Interview Survey. *Journal of Attention Disorders, 9*, 392–401.

Cunningham, M. (2001). The influence of parental attitudes and behaviors on children's attitudes toward gender and household labor in early adulthood. *Journal of Marriage and the Family, 63*, 111–122.

Cunningham, M., Swanson, D., Spencer, M., & Dupree, D. (2003). The association of physical maturation with family hassles among African American adolescent males. *Cultural Diversity and Ethnic Minority Psychology, 9*, 276–288.

Currie, A., Shields, M., & Wheatley Price, S. (2004). Is the child health/family income gradient universal? Evidence from England. *Journal of Health Economics, 26*, 213–232.

Currie, J., & Stabile, M. (2003). Socioeconomic status and child health: Why is the relationship stronger for older children? *American Economic Review, 93*, 1813–1823.

Curry, C. (2002). An approach to clinical genetics. In A. Rudolph, R. Kamei, & K. Overby (Eds.), *Rudolph's fundamentals of pediatrics* (3rd ed., pp. 184–220). New York: McGraw-Hill.

Cushner, K., McClelland, A., & Safford, P. (1992). *Human diversity in education.* New York: McGraw-Hill.

Cutrona, C. E., & Troutman, B. R. (1986). Social support, infant temperament, and parenting self-efficacy: A mediational model of post-partum depression. *Child Development, 57*, 1507–1518.

Cuvo, A. (1974). Incentive level influence on overt rehearsal and free recall as a function of age. *Journal of Experimental Child Psychology, 18*, 167–181.

Daley, T., Whaley, S., Sigman, M., Espinosa, M., & Neumann, C. (2003). IQ on the rise: The Flynn effect in rural Kenyan children. *Psychological Science, 14*, 215–219.

Dammeijer, P., Schlundt, B., Chenault, M., Manni, J., & Anteunis, I. (2002). Effects of early auditory deprivation and stimulation on auditory brain-stem responses in the rat. *Acta Oto-Laryngologica, 122*, 703–708.

Damon, W. (1977). *The social world of the child.* San Francisco: Jossey-Bass.

Damon, W. (1983). The nature of social-cognitive change in the developing child. In W. F. Overton (Ed.), *The relationship between social and cognitive development* (pp. 103–142). Hillsdale, NJ: Erlbaum.

Danby, S., & Baker, C. (1998). How to be masculine in the block area. *Childhood: A Global Journal of Child Research, 5*, 151–175.

Dark, V. J., & Benbow, C. P. (1993). Cognitive differences among the gifted: A review and new data. In D. K. Detterman (Ed.), *Current topics in human intelligence: Vol. 3. Individual differences and cognition* (pp. 85–120). Norwood, NJ: Ablex.

Darling, N., Cumsille, P., & Martínez, L. (2008). Individual differences in adolescents' beliefs about the legitimacy of parental authority and their own obligation to obey: A longitudinal investigation. *Child Development, 79,* 1103–1118.

Darlington, R. B. (1991). The long-term effects of model preschool programs. In L. Okagaki & R. J. Sternberg (Eds.), *Directors of development* (pp. 203–215). Hillsdale, NJ: Erlbaum.

Davidov, M., & Grusec, J. (2006). Untangling the links of parental responsiveness to distress and warmth to child outcomes. *Child Development, 77,* 44–58.

Davies, P., & Rose, J. (1999). Assessment of cognitive development in adolescents by means of neuropsychological tasks. *Developmental Neuropsychology, 15,* 227–248.

Dawood, K., Pillard, R., Horvath, C., Revelle, W., & Bailey, J. (2000). Familial aspects of male homosexuality. *Archives of Sexual Behavior, 29,* 155–163.

Dawson, G., Panagiotides, H., Klinger, L. G., & Spieker, S. (1997). Infants of depressed and nondepressed mothers exhibit differences in frontal brain electrical activity during the expression of negative emotions. *Developmental Psychology, 33,* 650–656.

Dawson, T. (2002). New tools, new insights: Kohlberg's moral judgement stages revisited. *International Journal of Behavioral Development, 26,* 154–166.

Deal, J., Halverson, C., Martin, R., Victor, J., & Baker, S. (2007). The Inventory of Children's Individual Differences: Development and validation of a short version. *Journal of Personality Assessment, 89,* 162–166.

de Angelis, T. (2004). Should we be giving psychotropics to children? *APA Monitor on Psychology, 35,* 42.

Deary, I., Thorpe, G., Wilson, V., Starr, J., & Whalley, L. (2003). Population sex differences in IQ at age 11: The Scottish mental survey 1932. *Intelligence, 31,* 533–542.

Deary, I., Whiteman, M., Starr, J., Whalley, L., & Fox, H. (2004). The impact of childhood intelligence on later life: Following up the Scottish mental surveys of 1932 and 1947. *Journal of Personality & Social Psychology, 86,* 139–147.

Deater-Deckard, K., & Plomin, R. (1997, April). *An adoption study of the etiology of teacher reports of externalizing problems in middle childhood.* Paper presented at the biennial meetings of the Society for Research in Child Development, Washington, DC.

DeBell, M., & Chapman, C. (2006). *Computer and Internet use by students in 2003.* Retrieved June 20, 2007, from http://nces.ed.gov/pubs2006/2006065.pdf

DeCasper, A. J., Lecaneut, J., Busnel, M., Granier-DeFerre, C., & Maugeais, R. (1994). Fetal reactions to recurrent maternal speech. *Infant Behavior and Development, 17,* 159–164.

DeCasper, A. J., & Spence, M. J. (1986). Prenatal maternal speech influences newborns' perception of speech sounds. *Infant Behavior and Development, 9,* 133–150.

Deci, E., Koestner, R., & Ryan, R. (1999). A meta-analytic review of experiments examining the effects of extrinsic rewards on intrinsic motivation. *Psychological Bulletin, 125,* 627–668.

DeFrancisco, B., & Rovee-Collier, C. (2008). The specificity of priming effects over the first year of life. *Developmental Psychobiology, 50,* 486–501.

Degnan, K., Henderson, H., Fox, N., & Rubin, K. (2008). Predicting social wariness in middle childhood: The moderating roles of childcare history, maternal personality and maternal behavior. *Social Development, 17,* 471–487.

de la Chica, R., Ribas, I., Giraldo, J., Egozcue, J., & Fuster, C. (2005). Chromosomal instability in amniocytes from fetuses of mothers who smoke. *JAMA: Journal of the American Medical Association, 293,* 1212–1222.

de Lacoste, M., Horvath, D., & Woodward, J. (1991). Possible sex differences in the developing human fetal brain. *Journal of Clinical and Experimental Neuropsychology, 13,* 831.

Delaney-Black, V., Covington, C., Templin, T., Kershaw, T., Nordstrom-Klee, B., Ager, J., Clark, N., Surendran, A., Martier, S., & Sokol, R. (2000). Expressive language development of children exposed to cocaine prenatally: Literature review and report of a prospective cohort study. *Journal of Communication Disorders, 33,* 463–481.

del Barrio, V., Moreno-Rosset, C., Lopez-Martinez, R., & Olmedo, M. (1997). Anxiety, depression and personality structure. *Personality & Individual Differences, 23,* 327–335.

DeLeire, T., & Kalil, A. (2002). Good things come in threes: Single-parent multigenerational family structure and adolescent adjustment. *Demography, 39,* 393–413.

Delgado-Gaitan, C. (1994). Socializing young children in Mexican-American families: An intergenerational perspective. In P. M. Greenfield & R. R. Cocking (Eds.), *Crosscultural roots of minority child development* (pp. 55–86). Hillsdale, NJ: Erlbaum.

Dellatolas, G., de Agostini, M., Curt, F., Kremin, H., Letierce, A., Maccario, J., & Lellouch, J. (2003). Manual skill, hand skill asymmetry, and cognitive performance in young children. *Laterality: Asymmetries of Body, Brain, & Cognition, 8,* 317–338.

DeLoache, J. S. (1989a). The development of representation in young children. In H. W. Reese (Ed.), *Advances in child development and behavior* (Vol. 22, pp. 2–37). San Diego, CA: Academic Press.

DeLoache, J. (1989b). Young children's understanding of the correspondence between a scale model and a larger space. *Cognitive Development, 4,* 121–139.

DeLoache, J. S. (1995). Early understanding and use of symbols: The model model. *Current Directions in Psychological Science, 4,* 109–113.

DeLoache, J. S., & Brown, A. L. (1987). Differences in the memory-based searching of delayed and normally developing young children. *Intelligence, 11,* 277–289.

DeLoache, J. S., Simcock, G., & Marzolf, D. (2004). Transfer by very young children in the symbolic retrieval task. *Child Development, 75,* 1708–1718.

de Medina, P., Visser, G., Huizink, A., Buitelaar, J., & Mulder, E. (2003). Fetal behavior does not differ between boys and girls. *Early Human Development, 73,* 17–26.

Dempster, F. (1981). Memory span: Sources of individual and developmental differences. *Psychological Bulletin, 89,* 63–100.

DeNavas-Walt, C., Proctor, B., & Smith, C. (2007). *Income, poverty, and health insurance coverage in the United States: 2006.* Retrieved June 20, 2008, from http://www.census.gov/prod/2007pubs/p60-233.pdf

Deneault, J., Ricard, M., Décarie, T., Morin, P., Quintal, G., Boilvin, M., Tremblay, R., & Pérusse, D. (2008). False belief and emotion understanding in monozygotic twins, dizygotic twins and non-twin children. *Cognition and Emotion, 22,* 697–708.

Denham, S., Blair, K., DeMulder, E., Levitas, J., Sawyer, K., Auerbach-Major, S., & Queenan, P. (2003). Preschool emotional competence: Pathway to social competence. *Child Development, 74,* 238–256.

Dennis, W. (1960). Causes of retardation among institutional children: Iran. *Journal of Genetic Psychology, 96,* 47–59.

Den Ouden, L., Rijken, M., Brand, R., Verloove-Vanhorick, S. P., & Ruys, J. H. (1991). Is it correct to correct? Developmental milestones in 555 "normal" preterm infants compared with term infants. *Journal of Pediatrics, 118,* 399–404.

DeRosier, M. E., Kupersmidt, J. B., & Patterson, C. J. (1994). Children's academic and behavioral adjustment as a function of the chronicity and proximity of peer rejection. *Child Development, 65,* 1799–1831.

DeRosier, M. E., & Marcus, S. (2005). Building friendships and combating bullying: Effectiveness of S.S.GRIN at one-year follow-up. *Journal of Clinical Child & Adolescent Psychology, 34,* 140–150.

Derryberry, D., & Rothbart, M. K. (1998). Reactive and effortful processes in the organization of temperament. *Development and Psychopathology, 9,* 633–652.

Derzon, J. (2001). Antisocial behavior and the prediction of violence: A meta-analysis. *Psychology in the Schools, 38,* 93–106.

De Schipper, J., Tavecchio, L., Van IJzendoorn, M., & Van Zeijl, J. (2004). Goodness-of-fit in center day care: Relations of temperament, stability, and quality of care with the child's adjustment. *Early Childhood Research Quarterly, 19,* 257–272.

de Villiers, P. A., & de Villiers, J. G. (1992). Language development. In M. H. Bornstein & M. E. Lamb (Eds.), *Developmental psychology: An advanced textbook* (3rd ed., pp. 337–418). Hillsdale, NJ: Erlbaum.

Dharan, V., Parviainen, E., Newcomb, P., & Poleshuck, V. (2006). *Psychosocial and environmental pregnancy risks.* Retrieved August 4, 2008, from http://www.emedicine.com/med/TOPIC3237.HTM

Diagnostic and statistical manual of mental disorders IV: Text revision (DSM-IV TR). (2000). Washington, DC: American Psychiatric Association.

Diamond, A., & Amso, D. (2008). Contributions of neuroscience to our understanding of cognitive development. *Current Directions in Psychological Science, 17,* 136–141.

Diamond, L. (2007). A dynamical systems approach to the development and expression of female same-sex sexuality. *Perspectives on Psychological Science, 2,* 142–161.

Dickens, W., & Flynn, J. (2001). Heritability estimates versus large environmental effects: The IQ paradox resolved. *Psychological Review, 108,* 346–369.

Diehl, L., Vicary, J., & Deike, R. (1997). Longitudinal trajectories of self-esteem from early to middle adolescence and related psychosocial variables among rural adolescents. *Journal of Research on Adolescence, 7,* 393–411.

Diener, M., Isabella, R., Behunin, M., & Wong, M. (2008). Attachment to mothers and fathers during middle childhood: Associations with child gender, grade, and competence. *Social Development, 17,* 84–101.

Diener, M., & Kim, D. (2004). Maternal and child predictors of preschool children's social competence. *Journal of Applied Developmental Psychology, 25,* 3–24.

Dieni, S., & Rees, S. (2003). Dendritic morphology is altered in hippocampal neurons following prenatal compromise. *Journal of Neurology, 55,* 41–52.

Dieter, J., Field, T., Hernandez-Reif, M., Emory, E., & Redzepi, M. (2003). Stable preterm infants gain more weight and sleep less after five days of massage therapy. *Journal of Pediatric Psychology, 28,* 403–411.

Dieterich, S., Hebert, H., Landry, S., Swank, P., & Smith, K. (2004). Maternal and child characteristics that influence the growth of daily living skills from infancy to school age in preterm and term children. *Early Education & Development, 15,* 283–303.

Dietrich, C., Swingley, D., & Werker, J. (2007). Native language governs interpretation of salient speech sound differences at 18 months. *Proceedings of the National Academy of Sciences, 104,* 16027–16031.

DiFranza, J., Aligne, C., & Weitzman, M. (2004). Prenatal and postnatal environmental tobacco smoke exposure and children's health. *Pediatrics, 113,* 1007–1015.

Digman, J. M. (1990). Personality structure: Emergence of the five-factor model. *Annual Review of Psychology, 41,* 417–440.

Dillingham, R., & Guerrant, R. (2004). Childhood stunting: Measuring and stemming the staggering costs of inadequate water and sanitation. *Lancet, 363,* 94–95.

Di Mario, S., Say, L., & Lincetto, O. (2007). Risk factors for stillbirth in developing countries: A systematic review of the literature. *Sexually Transmitted Diseases, 34,* S11–S21.

DiPietro, J. (2004). The role of prenatal maternal stress in child development. *Current Directions in Psychological Science, 13,* 71–74.

DiPietro, J., Bornstein, M., Costigan, K., Pressman, E., Hahn, C., Painter, K., Smith, B., & Yi, L. (2002). What does fetal movement predict about behavior during the first two years of life? *Psychobiology, 40,* 358–371.

DiPietro, J., Costigan, K., & Gurewitsch, E. (2003). Fetal response to induced maternal stress. *Early Human Development, 74,* 125–138.

DiPietro, J., Hilton, S., Hawkins, M., Costigan, K., & Pressman, E. (2002). Maternal stress and affect influence fetal neurobehavioral development. *Developmental Psychology, 38,* 659–668.

DiPietro, J., Hodgson, D., Costigan, K., Hilton, S., & Johnson, T. (1996). Fetal neurobehavioral development. *Child Development, 67,* 2553–2567.

DiPietro, J., Hodgson, D., Costigan, K., & Johnson, T. (1996). Fetal antecedents of infant temperament. *Child Development, 67,* 2568–2583.

Dishion, T. J. (1990). The family ecology of boys' peer relations in middle childhood. *Child Development, 61,* 874–892.

Dishion, T. J., French, D. C., & Patterson, G. R. (1995). The development and ecology of antisocial behavior. In D. Cicchetti & D. J. Cohen (Eds.), *Developmental psychopathology: Vol. 2. Risk, disorder, and adaptation* (pp. 421–471). New York: Wiley.

Distenfeld, A., & Woermann, U. (2007). *Sickle cell anemia.* Retrieved August 4, 2008, from http://www.emedicine.com/MED/topic2126.htm

Dixon, M., & Kaminska, Z. (2007). Does exposure to orthography affect children's spelling accuracy? *Journal of Research in Reading, 30,* 184–197.

Dockett, S., & Smith, I. (1995, April). *Children's theories of mind and their involvement in complex shared pretense.* Paper presented at the biennial meetings of the Society for Research in Child Development, Indianapolis.

Dodge, K. A. (1990). Developmental psychopathology in children of depressed mothers. *Developmental Psychology, 26,* 3–6.

Dodge, K. A. (1993). Social-cognitive mechanisms in the development of conduct disorder and depression. *Annual Review of Psychology, 44,* 559–584.

Dodge, K. A. (1997, April). *Testing developmental theory through prevention trials.* Paper presented at the biennial meetings of the Society for Research in Child Development, Washington, DC.

Dodge, K. A., Pettit, G. S., & Bates, J. E. (1994). Socialization mediators of the relation between socioeconomic status and child conduct problems. *Child Development, 65,* 649–665.

Doesum, K., Hosman, C., & Riksen-Walraven, J. (2005). A model-based intervention for depressed mothers and their infants. *Infant Mental Health Journal, 26,* 157–176.

Dogan-Até, A., & Carrión-Basham, C. (2007). Teenage pregnancy among Latinas. *Hispanic Journal of Behavioral Science, 29,* 554–579.

Domitrovich, C., & Bierman, K. (2001). Parenting practices and child social adjustment: Multiple pathways of influence. *Merrill-Palmer Quarterly, 47,* 235–263.

Donnellan, M., Trzesniewski, K., Robins, R., Moffitt, T., & Caspi, A. (2005). Low self-esteem is related to aggression, antisocial behavior, and delinquency. *Psychological Science, 16,* 328–335.

Donnerstein, E., Slaby, R. G., & Eron, L. D. (1994). The mass media and youth aggression. In L. D. Eron, J. H. Gentry, & P. Schlegel (Eds.), *Reason to hope: A psychosocial perspective on violence and youth* (pp. 219–250). Washington, DC: American Psychological Association.

Donohew, R., Hoyle, R., Clayton, R., Skinner, W., Colon, S., & Rice, R. (1999). Sensation seeking and drug use by adolescents and their friends: Models for marijuana and alcohol. *Journal of Studies on Alcohol, 60,* 622–631.

Dornbusch, S. M., Ritter, P. L., Liederman, P. H., Roberts, D. F., & Fraleigh, M. J. (1987). The relation of parenting style to adolescent school performance. *Child Development, 58,* 1244–1257.

Doty, R. (2003). *Handbook of olfaction and gustation.* New York: Informa Health Care.

Douglas-Hall, A., & Chau, M. (2007). *Basic facts abouty low-income children, birth to age 18.* New York: National Center for Children in Poverty, Mailman School of Public Health, Columbia University. Retrieved March 18, 2008, from http://nccp.org/publications/pub_762.html

Dowd, J. (2007). Early childhood origins of the income-health gradient: The role of maternal health behaviors. *Social Science and Medicine, 65,* 1202–1213.

Doyle, A. B., & Aboud, F. E. (1995). A longitudinal study of white children's racial prejudice as a social-cognitive development. *Merrill-Palmer Quarterly, 41,* 209–228.

Drum, P. (1985). Retention of text information by grade, ability and study. *Discourse Processes, 8,* 21–52.

DuBois, D., Burk-Braxton, C., Swenson, L., Tevendale, H., Lockerd, E., & Moran, B. (2002). Getting by with a little help from self and others: Self-esteem and social support as resources during early adolescence. *Developmental Psychology, 38,* 822–839.

DuBois, D. L., Felner, R. D., Brand, S., Phillips, R. S. C., & Lease, A. M. (1996). Early adolescent self-esteem: A developmental-ecological framework and assessment strategy. *Journal of Research on Adolescence, 6,* 543–579.

Duncan, G. J. (1993, April). *Economic deprivation and childhood development.* Paper presented at the biennial meetings of the Society for Research in Child Development, New Orleans.

Duncan, G. J., Brooks-Gunn, J., & Klebanov, P. K. (1994). Economic deprivation and early childhood development. *Child Development, 65,* 296–318.

Duncan, R. M. (1995). Piaget and Vygotsky revisited: Dialogue or assimilation? *Developmental Review, 15,* 458–472.

Dunn, J. (1992). Siblings and development. *Current Directions in Psychological Science, 1,* 6–9.

Dunn, J. (1993). *Young children's close relationships.* Newbury Park, CA: Sage.

Dunn, J. (1994). Experience and understanding of emotions, relationships, and membership in a particular culture. In P. Ekman & R. J. Davidson (Eds.), *The nature of emotion: Fundamental questions* (pp. 352–355). New York: Oxford University Press.

Dunn, J. (2007). Siblings and socialization. In J. Grusec & P. Hastings (Eds.), *Handbook of socialization: Theory and research* (pp. 309–327). New York: Guilford Press.

Dunn, J., Cutting, A., & Fisher, N. (2002). Old friends, new friends: Predictors of children's perspective on their friends at school. *Child Development, 73,* 621–635.

Dunn, J., & Kendrick, C. (1982). Siblings and their mothers: Developing relationships within the family. In M. E. Lamb & B. Sutton-Smith (Eds.), *Sibling relationships: Their nature and significance across the lifespan* (pp. 39–60). Hillsdale, NJ: Erlbaum.

Dunn, J., & McGuire, S. (1994). Young children's nonshared experiences: A summary of studies in Cambridge and Colorado. In E. M. Hetherington, D. Reiss, & R. Plomin (Eds.), *Separate social worlds of siblings: The impact of nonshared environment on development* (pp. 111–128). Hillsdale, NJ: Erlbaum.

Dunphy, D. C. (1963). The social structure of urban adolescent peer groups. *Sociometry, 26,* 230–246.

Dunsmore, J., Noguchi, R., Garner, P., Casey, E., & Bhullar, N. (2008). Gender-specific linkages of affective social competence with peer relations in preschool children. *Early Education and Development, 19,* 211–237.

Dupree, L., Watson, M., & Schneider, M. (2005). Preferences for mental health care: A comparison of older African Americans and older Caucasians. *Journal of Applied Gerontology, 24,* 196–210.

Duvall, S., Delquadri, J., & Ward, D. (2004). A preliminary investigation of the effectiveness of homeschool instructional environments for students with attention-deficit/hyperactivity disorder. *School Psychology Review, 33,* 140–158.

Dwairy, M. (2008). Parental inconsistency versus parental authoritarianism: Associations with symptoms of psychological disorders. *Journal of Youth and Adolescence, 37,* 616–626.

Dyl, J., Kittler, J., Phillips, K., & Hunt, J. (2006). Body dysmorphic disorder and other clinically significant body image concerns in adolescent psychiatric inpatients: Prevalence and clinical characteristics. *Child Psychiatry and Human Development, 36,* 369–382.

Easterbrooks, M. A., Davidson, C. E., & Chazan, R. (1993). Psychosocial risk, attachment, and behavior problems among school-aged children. *Development and Psychopathology, 5,* 389–402.

Eaton, W. (1994). Temperament, development, and the five-factor model: Lessons from activity level. In C. Halverson & G. Kohnstamm (Eds.), *The developing structure of temperament and personality from infancy to adulthood* (pp. 173–187). Hillsdale, NJ: Erlbaum.

EBC (1991). *Childhood: In the land of giants.* [Television series]. New York: Public Broadcasting System.

Ecalle, J., Magnan, A., & Gibert, F. (2006). Class size effects on literacy skills and literacy interest in first grade: A large-scale investigation. *Journal of School Psychology, 44,* 191–209.

Eccles, J., & Roeser, R. (2005). School and community influences on human development. In M. Bornstein & M. Lamb (Eds.), *Developmental science: An advanced textbook* (pp. 513–556). Mahwah, NJ: Erlbaum.

Edmonds, C., Isaacs, E., Visscher, P., Rogers, M., Lanigan, J., Singhal, A., Lucas, A., Gringras, P., Denton, J., & Deary, I. (2008). Inspection time and cognitive abilities in twins aged 7 to 17 years: Age-related changes, heritability and genetic covariance. *Intelligence, 36,* 210–255.

Egan, S., & Perry, D. (2001). Gender identity: A multidimensional analysis with implications for psychosocial adjustment. *Developmental Psychology, 37,* 451–463.

Egeland, B., & Sroufe, L. A. (1981). Attachment and early maltreatment. *Child Development, 52,* 44–52.

Eiden, R., Foote, A., & Schuetze, P. (2007). Maternal cocaine use and caregiving status: Group differences in caregiver and infant risk variables. *Addictive Behaviors, 32,* 465–476.

Eisenberg, N. (1986). *Altruistic emotion, cognition, and behavior.* Hillsdale, NJ: Erlbaum.

Eisenberg, N. (1988). The development of prosocial and aggressive behavior. In M. H. Bornstein & M. E. Lamb (Eds.), *Developmental psychology: An advanced textbook* (2nd ed., pp. 461–496). Hillsdale, NJ: Erlbaum.

Eisenberg, N. (1990). Prosocial development in early and mid-adolescence. In R. Montemayor, G. R. Adams, & T. P. Gullotta (Eds.), *From childhood to adolescence: A transitional period?* (pp. 240–268). Newbury Park, CA: Sage.

Eisenberg, N. (1992). *The caring child.* Cambridge, MA: Harvard University Press.

Eisenberg, N. (2000). Emotion, regulation, and moral development. *Annual Review of Psychology, 51,* 665–697.

Eisenberg, N. (2001). The core and correlates of affective social competence. *Social Development, 10,* 120–124.

Eisenberg, N., & Fabes, R. A. (1998). Prosocial behavior. In W. Damon (Ed.), *Handbook of child psychology: Vol 3. Social, emotional, and personality development* (5th ed., pp. 701–778). New York: Wiley.

Eisenberg, N., Fabes, R. A., Murphy, B., Karbon, M., Smith, M., & Maszk, P. (1996). The relations of children's dispositional empathy-related responding to their emotionality, regulation, and social functioning. *Developmental Psychology, 32,* 195–209.

Eisenberg, N., Fabes, R. A., Murphy, B., Maszk, P., Smith, M., & Karbon, M. (1995). The role of emotionality and regulation in children's social functioning: A longitudinal study. *Child Development, 66,* 1360–1384.

Eisenberg, N., Fabes, R., Murphy, B., Shepard, S., Guthrie, I., Mazsk, P., Paulin, R., & Jones, S. (1999). Prediction of elementary school children's socially appropriate and problem behavior from anger reactions at age 4–6 years. *Journal of Applied Developmental Psychology, 20,* 119–142.

Eisenberg, N., Fabes, R. A., Schaller, M., & Miller, P. A. (1989). Sympathy and personal distress: Development, gender differences, and interrelations of indexes. *New Directions for Child Development, 44,* 107–126.

Eisenberg, N., Gershoff, E., Fabes, R., Shepard, S., Cumberland, A., Losoya, S., Guthrie, I., & Murphy, B. (2001). Mother's emotional expressivity and children's behavior problems and social competence: Mediation through children's regulation. *Developmental Psychology, 37,* 475–490.

Eisenberg, N., Guthrie, I., Cumberland, A., Murphy, B., Shepard, S., Zhou, Q., & Carlo, G. (2007). Prosocial development in early adulthood: A longitudinal study. *Journal of Personality and Social Psychology, 82,* 993–1006.

Eisenberg, N., Hertz-Lazarowitz, R., & Fuchs, I. (1990). Prosocial moral judgment in Israeli kibbutz and city children: A longitudinal study. *Merrill-Palmer Quarterly, 36,* 273–285.

Eisenberg, N., Hofer, C., & Vaugh, J. (2007). Effortful control and its socioemotional consequences. In J. Gross (Ed.), *Handbook of emotion regulation* (pp. 287–306). New York: Guilford Press.

Eisenberg, N., Liew, J., & Pidada, S. (2001). The relations of parental emotional expressivity with quality of Indonesian children's social functioning. *Emotion, 1,* 116–136.

Eisenberg, N., & Murphy, B. (1995). Parenting and children's moral development. In M. H. Bornstein (Ed.), *Handbook of parenting: Vol. 4. Applied and practical parenting* (pp. 227–257). Mahwah, NJ: Erlbaum.

Eisenberg, N., Sadovsky, A., Spinrad, T., Fabes, R., Losoya, S., Valiente, C., Reiser, M., Cumberland, A., & Shepard, S. (2005). The relations of problem behavior status to children's negative emotionality, effortful control, and impulsivity: Concurrent relations and prediction of change. *Developmental Psychology, 41,* 193–211.

Eisenberger, N. (2003). Does rejection hurt? An fMRI study of social exclusion. *Science, 302,* 290–292.

Eisenberger, R., Pierce, W., & Cameron, J. (1999). Effects of reward on intrinsic motivation—negative, neutral, and positive: Comment on Deci, Koestner, and Ryan. *Psychological Bulletin, 125,* 677–691.

Ekman, P. (1972). Universals and cultural differences in facial expressions of emotion. In J. Cole (Ed.), *Nebraska symposium on motivation, 1971* (pp. 207–282). Lincoln: University of Nebraska Press.

Ekman, P. (1973). Cross-cultural studies of facial expression. In P. Ekman (Ed.), *Darwin and facial expression* (pp. 169–222). New York: Academic Press.

Ekman, P. (1989). The argument and evidence about universals in facial expressions of emotion. In H. Wagner & A. Manstead (Eds.), *Handbook of social psychophysiology* (pp. 143–164). Chichester, England: Wiley.

Ekman, P. (2007). The directed facial action task: Emotional responses without appraisal. In J. Coan & J. Allen (Eds.), *Handbook of emotion elicitation and assessment* (pp. 47–53). New York: Oxford University Press.

Eley, T., Liang, H., Plomin, R., Sham, P., Sterne, A., Williamson, R., & Purcell, S. (2004). Parental familial vulnerability, family environment, and their interactions as predictors of depressive symptoms in adolescents. *Journal of the American Academy of Child Psychiatry, 43,* 298–306.

Elkind, D. (1967). Egocentrism in adolescence. *Child Development, 38,* 1025–1034.

Ellenbogen, S., & Chamberland, C. (1997). The peer relations of dropouts: A comparative study of at-risk and not at-risk youths. *Journal of Adolescence, 20,* 355–367.

Elliot, A., & Hall, N. (1997). The impact of self-regulatory teaching strategies on "at-risk" preschoolers' mathematical learning in a computer-mediated environment. *Journal of Computing in Childhood Education, 8,* 187–198.

Elmas, C., Erdogan, D., & Özogul, C. (2003). Expression of growth factors in fetal human olfactory mucosa during development. *Growth, Development, and Aging, 67,* 11–25.

Englund, M., Luckner, A., Whaley, G., & Egeland, B. (2004). Children's achievement in early elementary school: Longitudinal effects of parental involvement, expectations, and quality of assistance. *Journal of Educational Psychology, 96,* 723–730.

Ensign, J. (1998). *Defying the stereotypes of special education: Homeschool students.* Paper presented at the annual meeting of the American Education Research Association, San Diego, CA.

Epstein, S. (1991). Cognitive-experiential self theory: Implications for developmental psychology. In M. R. Gunnar & L. A. Sroufe (Eds.), *The Minnesota symposia on child development* (Vol. 23, pp. 79–123). Hillsdale, NJ: Erlbaum.

Erel, O., & Burman, B. (1995). Interrelatedness of marital relations and parent-child relations: A meta-analytic review. *Psychological Bulletin, 118,* 108–312.

Ericsson, K. A., & Crutcher, R. J. (1990). The nature of exceptional performance. In P. B. Baltes, D. L. Featherman, & R. M. Lerner (Eds.), *Life-span development and behavior* (Vol. 10, pp. 188–218). Hillsdale, NJ: Erlbaum.

Escalona, K. S. (1981). The reciprocal role of social and emotional developmental advances and cognitive development during the second and third years of life. In E. K. Shapiro & E. Weber (Eds.), *Cognitive and affective growth: Developmental interaction* (pp. 87–108). Hillsdale, NJ: Erlbaum.

Escorihuela, R. M., Tobena, A., & Fernández-Teruel, A. (1994). Environmental enrichment reverses the detrimental action of early inconsistent stimulation and increases the beneficial effects of postnatal handling on shuttlebox learning in adult rats. *Behavioural Brain Research, 61,* 169–173.

Eslea, M., Menesini, E., Morita, Y., O'Moore, M., Mora-Merchan, J., Pereira, B., & Smith, P. (2004). Friendship and loneliness among bullies and victims: Data from seven countries. *Aggressive Behavior, 30,* 71–83.

Espy, K., Stalets, M., McDiarmid, M., Senn, T., Cwik, M., & Hamby, A. (2002). Executive functions in preschool children born preterm: Application of cognitive neuroscience paradigms. *Child Neuropsychology, 8,* 83–92.

Evans, G. (2004). The environment of childhood poverty. *American Psychologist, 59,* 77–92.

Ex, C., & Janssens, J. (1998). Maternal influences on daughters' gender role attitudes. *Sex Roles, 38,* 171–186.

Fabes, R., Eisenberg, N., Hanish, L., & Spinrad, T. (2001). Pre-schoolers' spontaneous emotion vocabulary: Relations to likability. *Early Education & Development, 12*, 11–27.

Faedda, G., Baldessarini, R., & Suppes, T. (1995). Pediatric-onset bipolar disorder: A neglected clinical and public health problem. *Harvard Review of Psychiatry, 3*, 171–195.

Fagan, J., & Holland, C. (2007). Racial equality in intelligence: Predictions from a theory of intelligence as processing. *Intelligence, 35*, 319–334.

Fagan, J. F., III, & Singer, L. T. (1983). Infant recognition memory as a measure of intelligence. In L. P. Lipsitt (Ed.), *Advances in infancy research* (Vol. 2, pp. 31–78). Norwood, NJ: Ablex.

Fagard, J., & Jacquet, A. (1989). Onset of bimanual coordination and symmetry versus asymmetry of movement. *Infant Behavior and Development, 12*, 229–235.

Fagot, B. I. (1995). Parenting boys and girls. In M. H. Bornstein (Ed.), *Handbook of parenting: Vol. 1. Children and parenting* (pp. 163–183). Mahwah, NJ: Erlbaum.

Fagot, B. I., & Hagan, R. (1991). Observations of parent reactions to sex-stereotyped behaviors: Age and sex effects. *Child Development, 62*, 617–628.

Fagot, B. I., & Leinbach, M. D. (1989). The young child's gender schema: Environmental input, internal organization. *Child Development, 60*, 663–672.

Fagot, B. I., Leinbach, M. D., & O'Boyle, C. (1992). Gender labeling, gender stereotyping, and parenting behaviors. *Developmental Psychology, 28*, 225–230.

Fallis, R., & Opotow, S. (2003). Are students failing school or are schools failing students? Class cutting in high school. *Journal of Social Issues, 59*, 103–119.

Fantuzzo, J., Sekino, Y., & Cohen, H. (2004). An examination of the contributions of interactive peer play to salient classroom competencies for urban Head Start children. *Psychology in the Schools, 41*, 323–336.

Fantz, R. L. (1956). A method for studying early visual development. *Perceptual & Motor Skills, 6*, 13–15.

Farmer, T., Estell, D., Leung, M., Trott, H., Bishop, J., & Cairns, B. (2003). Individual characteristics, early adolescent peer affiliations, and school dropout: An examination of aggressive and popular group types. *Journal of School Psychology, 41*, 217–232.

Farnham-Diggory, S. (1978). On the logic and pitfalls of logograph research. *Journal of Experimental Child Psychology, 25*, 366–370.

Farrar, M. J. (1992). Negative evidence and grammatical morpheme acquisition. *Developmental Psychology, 28*, 90–98.

Farver, J. (1996). Aggressive behavior in preschoolers' social networks: Do birds of a feather flock together? *Early Childhood Research Quarterly, 11*, 333–350.

Farver, J., Bhadha, B., & Narang, S. (2002). Acculturation and psychological functioning in Asian Indian adolescents. *Social Development, 11*, 11–29.

Featherman, D. L. (1980). Schooling and occupational careers: Constancy and change in worldly success. In O. G. Brim Jr. & J. Kagan (Eds.), *Constancy and change in human development* (pp. 675–738). Cambridge, MA: Harvard University Press.

Federal Interagency Forum on Child and Family Statistics (FIFCFS). (2008). *America's children in brief: Key national indicators of well-being, 2008.* Retrieved September 6, 2008, from http://www.childstats.gov/americaschildren/index.asp.

Federal Interagency Forum on Child and Family Statistics (FIFCFS). (2000). *America's children: Key national indicators of well-being 2000.* Washington, DC: Author.

Fein, J., Durbin, D., & Selbst, S. (2002). Injuries and emergencies. In A. Rudolph, R. Kamei, & K. Overby (Eds.), *Rudolph's fundamentals of pediatrics* (3rd ed., pp. 390–436). New York: McGraw-Hill.

Feinberg, M., Reiss, D., Neiderhiser, J., & Hetherington, E. (2005). Differential association of family subsystem negativity on siblings' maladjustment: Using behavior genetic methods to test process theory. *Journal of Family Psychology, 19*, 601–610.

Feinfield, K., Lee, P., Flavell, E., Green, F., & Flavell, J. (1999). Young children's understanding of intention. *Cognitive Development, 14*, 463–486.

Feiring, C. (1999). Other-sex friendship networks and the development of romantic relationships in adolescence. *Journal of Youth & Adolescence, 28*, 495–512.

Feldhusen, J. (2003). Lewis M. Terman: A pioneer in the development of ability tests. In B. Zimmerman & D. Schunk (Eds.), *Educational psychology: A century of contributions* (pp. 155–169). Mahwah, NJ: Erlbaum.

Feldman, D. (2004). Piaget's stages: The unfinished symphony of cognitive development. *New Ideas in Psychology, 22*, 175–131.

Feldman, R. (2003). Paternal socio-psychological factors and infant attachment: The mediating role of synchrony in father-infant interactions. *Infant Behavior and Development, 25*, 221–236.

Feldman, R. (2007). Parent-infant synchrony and the construction of shared timing: Physiological precursors, developmental outcomes, and risk conditions. *Journal of Child Psychology and Psychiatry, 48*, 329–354.

Feldman, R., & Eidelman, A. (2003). Skin-to-skin contact (Kangaroo Care) accelerates autonomic and neurobehavioural maturation in preterm infants. *Developmental Medicine & Child Neurology, 45*, 274–281.

Feldman, S. S. (1987). Predicting strain in mothers and fathers of 6-month-old infants. A short-term longitudinal study. In P. W. Berman & F. A. Pedersen (Eds.), *Men's transitions to parenthood* (pp. 13–36). Hillsdale, NJ: Erlbaum.

Feng, J., Spence, I., & Pratt, J. (2007). Playing an action video game reduces gender differences in spatial cognition. *Psychological Science, 18*, 850–855.

Fennig, S., Geva, K., Zalzman, G., Weitzman, A., Fennig, S., & Apter, A. (2005). Effect of gender on suicide attempters versus nonattempters in an adolescent inpatient unit. *Comprehensive Psychiatry, 46*, 90–97.

Fenson, L., Dale, P. S., Reznick, J. S., Bates, E., Thal, D. J., & Pethick, S. J. (1994). Variability in early communicative development. *Monographs of the Society for Research in Child Development, 59*(5, Serial No. 242).

Fernald, A. (1993). Approval and disapproval: Infant responsiveness to vocal affect in familiar and unfamiliar languages. *Child Development, 64*, 657–674.

Fernald, A., Taeschner, T., Dunn, J., Papousek, M., Boysson-Bardies, B., & Fukui, I. (1989). A cross-language study of prosodic modifications in mothers' and fathers' speech to preverbal infants. *Journal of Child Language, 16*, 477–501.

Fewell, R., & Deutscher, B. (2003). Contributions of early language and maternal facilitation variables to later language and reading abilities. *Journal of Early Intervention, 26*, 132–145.

Field, T., Hernandez-Reif, M., Feijo, L., & Freedman, J. (2006). Prenatal, perinatal and neonatal stimulation: A survey of neonatal nurseries. *Infant Behavior & Development, 29*, 24–31.

Field, T. M. (1977). Effects of early separation, interactive deficits, and experimental manipulations on infant-mother face-to-face interaction. *Child Development, 48*, 763–771.

Field, T. M. (1991). Quality infant day-care and grade school behavior and performance. *Child Development, 62*, 863–870.

Field, T. M., Healy, B., Goldstein, S., & Guthertz, M. (1990). Behavior-state matching and synchrony in mother-infant interactions of non-depressed versus depressed dyads. *Developmental Psychology, 26*, 7–14.

Field, T. M., Woodson, R., Greenberg, R., & Cohen, D. (1982). Discrimination and imitation of facial expressions by neonates. *Science, 218*, 179–181.

Figueiredo, B., Costa, R., Pacheco, A., & Pais, A. (2007). Mother-to-infant and father-to-infant initial emotional involvement. *Early Child Development and Care, 177*, 521–532.

Findling, R., Feeny, N., Stansbrey, R., Delporto-Bedoya, D., & Demeter, C. (2004). Special articles: Treatment of mood disorders in children and adolescents: Somatic treatment for depressive illnesses in children and adolescents. *Psychiatric Clinics of North America, 27*, 113–137.

Fine, L., Trentacosta, C., Izard, C., Mostow, A., & Campbell, J. (2004). Anger perception, caregivers' use of physical discipline, and aggression in children at risk. *Social Development, 13*, 213–228.

Fisch, H., Hyun, G., Goldern, R., Hensle, T., Olsson, C., & Liberson, G. (2003). The influence of paternal age on Down syndrome. *Journal of Urology, 169*, 2275–2278.

Fischer, K., & Rose, S. (1994). Dynamic development of coordination of components in brain and behavior: A framework for theory and research. In K. Fischer & G. Dawson (Eds.), *Human behavior and the developing brain* (pp. 3–66). New York: Guilford.

Fitzgerald, B. (1999). Children of lesbian and gay parents: A review of the literature. *Marriage & Family Review, 29*, 57–75.

Fitzgerald, D., & White, K. (2003). Linking children's social worlds: Perspective-taking in parent-child and peer contexts. *Social Behavior & Personality, 31*, 509–522.

Fitzgerald, M. (2004). The case of Robert Walser (1878–1956). *Irish Journal of Psychological Medicine, 21*, 138–142.

Flanagan, C. A., & Eccles, J. S. (1993). Changes in parents' work status and adolescents' adjustments at school. *Child Development, 64*, 246–257.

Flannery, D. J., Montemayor, R., & Eberly, M. B. (1994). The influence of parent negative emotional expression on adolescents' perceptions of their relationships with their parents. *Personal Relationships, 1*, 259–274.

Flavell, J. H. (1985). *Cognitive development* (2nd ed.). Englewood Cliffs, NJ: Prentice Hall.

Flavell, J. H. (1986). The development of children's knowledge about the appearance-reality distinction. *American Psychologist, 41*, 418–425.

Flavell, J. H. (1993). Young children's understanding of thinking and consciousness. *Current Directions in Psychological Science, 2*, 40–43.

Flavell, J. H. (1999). Cognitive development: Children's knowledge about the mind. *Annual Review of Psychology, 50*, 21–45.

Flavell, J. H. (2000). Development of children's knowledge about the mental world. *International Journal of Behavioral Development, 24*, 14–23.

Flavell, J. H. (2004). Theory-of-mind development: Retrospect and prospect. *Merrill-Palmer Quarterly, 50*, 274–290.

Flavell, J. H., & Green, F. L. (1999). Development of intuitions about the controllability of different mental states. *Cognitive Development, 14*, 133–146.

Flavell, J. H., Green, F. L., & Flavell, E. R. (1989). Young children's ability to differentiate appearance-reality and level 2 perspectives in the tactile modality. *Child Development, 60*, 201–213.

Flavell, J. H., Green, F. L., & Flavell, E. R. (1990). Developmental changes in young children's knowledge about the mind. *Cognitive Development, 5*, 1–27.

Flavell, J. H., Green, F. L., & Flavell, E. R. (1995). Young children's knowledge about thinking. *Monographs of the Society for Research in Child Development, 60*(1, Serial No. 243).

Flavell, J. H., Green, F. L., & Flavell, E. R. (1998). The mind has a mind of its own: Developing knowledge about mental uncontrollability. *Cognitive Development, 13*, 127–138.

Flavell, J. H., Green, F. L., & Flavell, E. R. (2000). Development of children's awareness of their own thoughts. *Journal of Cognition and Development, 1*, 97–112.

Flavell, J. H., Green, F. L., Flavell, E. R., & Lin, N. (1999). Development of children's knowledge about unconsciousness. *Child Development, 70*, 396–412.

Flavell, J. H., Green, F. L., Wahl, K. E., & Flavell, E. R. (1987). The effects of question clarification and memory aids on young children's performance on appearance-reality tasks. *Cognitive Development, 2*, 127–144.

Flavell, J. H., Miller, P. H., & Miller, S. A. (1993). *Cognitive development* (3rd ed.). Englewood Cliffs, NJ: Prentice Hall.

Flavell, J. H., Zhang, X., Zou, H., Dong, Q., & Qi, S. (1983). A comparison of the appearance-reality distinction in the People's Republic of China and the United States. *Cognitive Psychology, 15*, 459–466.

Flom, R., & Bahrick, L. (2007). The development of infant discrimination of affect in multimodal and unimodal stimulation: The role of intersensory redundancy. *Developmental Psychology, 43*, 238–252.

Floyd, F., & Bakeman, R. (2006). Coming-out across the life course: Implications of age and historical context. *Archives of Sexual Behavior, 35*, 287–297.

Flynn, J. (1999). Searching for justice: The discovery of IQ gains over time. *American Psychologist, 54*, 5–20.

Flynn, J. (2007). *What is intelligence? Beyond the Flynn Effect.* New York: Cambridge University Press.

Foehn, U. G. (2006). *Media multitasking among American youth: Prevalence, predictors and pairings—Key findings.* Retrieved September 6, 2008, from http://www.kff.org/entmedia/7593.cfm

Fombonne, E., Zakarian, R., Bennett, A., Meng, L., & McLean-Heywood, D. (2006). Pervasive developmental disorders in Montreal, Quebec, Canada: Prevalence and links with immunizations. *Pediatrics, 118*, e139–e150.

Fordham, K., & Stevenson-Hinde, J. (1999). Shyness, friendship quality, and adjustment during middle childhood. *Journal of Child Psychology & Psychiatry & Allied Disciplines, 40*, 757–768.

Foster, E., Jones, D., & Conduct Problems Prevention Research Group. (2007). The economic analysis of prevention: An illustration involving the Fast Track Project. *Journal of Mental Health Policy and Economics, 10*, 165–175.

Foulder-Hughes, L., & Cooke, R. (2003a). Do mainstream schoolchildren who were born preterm have motor problems? *British Journal of Occupational Therapy, 66*, 9–16.

Foulder-Hughes, L., & Cooke, R. (2003b). Motor, cognitive, and behavioural disorders in children born very preterm. *Developmental Medicine & Child Neurology, 45*, 97–103.

Fox, N., Henderson, H., Rubin, K., Calkins, S., & Schmidt, L. (2001). Continuity and discontinuity of behavioral inhibition and exuberance: Psychophysiological and behavioral influences across the first four years of life. *Child Development, 72*, 1–21.

Fox, N. A., Kimmerly, N. L., & Schafer, W. D. (1991). Attachment to mother/attachment to father: A meta-analysis. *Child Development, 62*, 210–225.

Francis, P. L., Self, P. A., & Horowitz, F. D. (1987). The behavioral assessment of the neonate: An overview. In J. D. Osofsky (Ed.), *Handbook of infant development* (2nd ed., pp. 723–779). New York: Wiley-Interscience.

Franco, N., & Levitt, M. (1998). The social ecology of middle childhood: Family support, friendship quality, and self-esteem. *Family Relations: Interdisciplinary Journal of Applied Family Studies, 47*, 315–321.

Franko, D., & Spurrell, E. (2000). Detection and management of eating disorders during pregnancy. *Obstetrics & Gynecology, 95*, 942–946.

Fraser, A. M., Brockert, J. E., & Ward, R. H. (1995). Association of young maternal age with adverse reproductive outcomes. *New England Journal of Medicine, 332,* 1113–1117.

Fredricks, J., & Eccles, J. (2002). Children's competence and value beliefs from childhood through adolescence: Growth trajectories in two male sex-typed domains. *Developmental Psychology, 38,* 519–533.

Fredricks, J., & Eccles, J. (2005). Family socialization, gender, and sport motivation and involvement. *Journal of Sport & Exercise Psychology, 27,* 3–31.

Fredriksen, K., Rhodes, J., Reddy, R., & Way, N. (2004). Sleepless in Chicago: Tracking the effects of adolescent sleep loss during the middle school years. *Child Development, 75,* 84–95.

Freedman, D. G. (1979). Ethnic differences in babies. *Human Nature, 2,* 36–43.

Freeman, C., & Fox, M. (2005). *Status and trends in the education of American Indians and Alaska Natives.* Retrieved June 27, 2008, from http://nces.ed.gov/pubs2005/2005108.pdf

French, S., Seidman, E., Allen, L., & Aber, J. (2006). The development of ethnic identity during adolescence. *Developmental Psychology, 42,* 1–10.

Freud, S. (1905). *The basic writings of Sigmund Freud* (A. A. Brill, Trans.). New York: Random House.

Freud, S. (1920). *A general introduction to psychoanalysis* (J. Riviere, Trans.). New York: Washington Square Press.

Frey, K. S., & Ruble, D. N. (1992). Gender constancy and the "cost" of sex-typed behavior: A test of the conflict hypothesis. *Developmental Psychology, 28,* 714–721.

Frichtel, M., & Lécuyer, R. (2006). The use of perspective as a depth cue with a 2D display in 4- and 5-month-old infants. *Infant Behavior and Development, 30,* 409–421.

Fried, P., & Smith, A. (2001). A literature review of the consequences of prenatal marihuana exposure: An emerging theme of a deficiency in aspects of executive function. *Neurotoxicology & Teratology, 23,* 1–11.

Friend, M., & Bursuck, W. (2006). *Including students with special needs: A practical guide for classroom teachers.* Boston: Allyn & Bacon.

Fujisawa, K., Kutsukake, N., & Hasegawa, T. (2008). Reciprocity of prosocial behavior in Japanese preschool children. *International Journal of Behavioral Development, 32,* 89–97.

Fuligni, A., Yip, T., & Tseng, V. (2002). The impact of family obligation on the daily activities and psychological well-being of Chinese American adolescents. *Child Development, 73,* 302–314.

Fuller, B. (2007). *Standardized childhood: The political and cultural struggle over early education.* Palo Alto, CA: Stanford University Press.

Funk, J., Bechtoldt-Baldacci, H., Pasold, T., & Baumgardner, J. (2004). Violence exposure in real-life, video games, television, movies, and the internet: Is there desensitization? *Journal of Adolescence, 27,* 23–39.

Funk, J., Buchman, D., Jenks, J., & Bechtoldt, H. (2003). Playing violent video games, desensitization, and moral evaluation in children. *Journal of Applied Developmental Psychology, 24,* 413–436.

Furlong, M., & Christenson, S. (2008). Engaging students at school and with learning: A relevant construct for all students. *Psychology in the Schools, 45,* 365–368.

Furman, E. (1995). Memories of a "qualified student." *Journal of Child Psychotherapy, 21,* 309–312.

Furnham, A. (2000). Parents' estimates of their own and their children's multiple intelligences. *British Journal of Developmental Psychology, 18,* 583–594.

Furnham, A., Petrides, K., Tsaousis, I., Pappas, K., & Garrod, D. (2005). A cross-cultural investigation into the relationships between personality traits and work values. *Journal of Psychology: Interdisciplinary & Applied, 139,* 5–32.

Furrow, D. (1984). Social and private speech at two years. *Child Development, 55,* 355–362.

Furrow, D., & Nelson, K. (1984). Environmental correlates of individual differences in language acquisition. *Journal of Child Language, 11,* 523–534.

Furstenberg, F., Brooks-Gunn, J., & Chase-Lansdale, L. (1989). Teenaged pregnancy and childbearing. *American Psychologist, 44,* 313–320.

Furstenberg, F. F., Jr., & Hughes, M. E. (1995). Social capital and successful development among at-risk youth. *Journal of Marriage and the Family, 57,* 580–592.

Fussell, J., & Burns, K. (2007). Attention deficit/hyperactivity disorder: A case study in differential diagnosis. *Clinical Pediatrics, 46,* 735–737.

Gabbard, C. (2008). *Lifelong motor development.* San Francisco: Benjamin Cummings.

Galambos, D. L., & Maggs, J. (1991). Out-of-school care of young adolescents and self-reported behavior. *Developmental Psychology, 27,* 644–655.

Galanaki, E. (2004). Teachers and loneliness: The children's perspective. *School Psychology International, 25,* 92–105.

Galassi, J., Gulledge, S., & Cox, N. (1997). Middle school advisories: Retrospect and prospect. *Review of Educational Research, 67,* 301–338.

Gale, C., O'Callaghan, F., Godfrey, K., Law, C., & Martyn, C. (2004). Critical periods of brain growth and cognitive function in children. *Brain, 127,* 321–329.

Gallagher, C., & Dobrin, A. (2005). The association between suicide screening practices and attempts requiring emergency care in juvenile justice facilities. *Journal of the American Academy of Child and Adolescent Psychiatry, 44,* 485–493.

Gallahue, D. L., & Ozmun, J. C. (1995). *Understanding motor development* (3rd ed.). Madison, WI: Brown & Benchmark.

Gallese, V. (2005). Embodied simulation: From neurons to phenomenal experience. *Phenomenology and the Cognitive Sciences, 4,* 23–48.

Galliher, R., Rostosky, S., & Hughes, H. (2004). School belonging, self-esteem, and depressive symptoms in adolescents: An examination of sex, sexual attraction status, and urbanicity. *Journal of Youth & Adolescence, 33,* 235–245.

Ganchrow, J. R., Steiner, J. E., & Daher, M. (1983). Neonatal facial expressions in response to different qualities and intensities of gustatory stimuli. *Infant Behavior and Development, 6,* 189–200.

Ganger, J., & Brent, M. (2001). Re-examining the vocabulary spurt and its implications: Is there really a sudden change in cognitive development? In A. Do, L. Domínguez, & A. Johansen (Eds.), *Proceedings of the 25th Annual Boston University Conference on Language Development* (pp. 296–306). Somerville, MA: Cascadilla Press.

Ganiban, J., Saudino, K., Ulbricht, J., Neiderhiser, J., & Reiss, D. (2008). Stability and change in temperament during adolescence. *Journal of Personality and Social Psychology, 95,* 222–236.

Garbarino, J. (2002). Foreword: Pathways from childhood traumas to adolescent violence and delinquency. *Journal of Aggression, Maltreatment, & Trauma, 6,* xxv–xxxi.

Garbarino, J., Dubrow, N., Kostelny, K., & Pardo, C. (1992). *Children in danger: Coping with the consequences of community violence.* San Francisco: Jossey-Bass.

Garbarino, J., & Kostelny, K. (1997). What children can tell us about living in a war zone. In J. D. Osofsky (Ed.), *Children in a violent society* (pp. 32–41). New York: Guilford Press.

Garbarino, J., Kostelny, K., & Dubrow, N. (1991). *No place to be a child: Growing up in a war zone.* Lexington, MA: Lexington Books.

Gardner, A. (2007). *Doctors' groups offer ADHD guide for parents.* Retrieved September 1, 2008, from http://health.usnews.com/usnews/health/healthday/071002/doctors-groups-offer-adhd-guide-for-parents.htm

Gardner, H. (1983). *Frames of mind: The theory of multiple intelligence.* New York: Basic Books.

Gardner, H. (2002). Learning from extraordinary minds. In M. Ferrari (Ed.), *The pursuit of excellence through education* (pp. 3–20). Mahwah, NJ: Erlbaum.

Gardner, J., Karmel, B., Freedland, R., Lennon, E., Flory, M., Miroschnichenko, I., Phan, H., Barone, A., & Harm, A. (2006). Arousal, attention, and neurobehavioral assessment in the neonatal period: Implications for intervention and policy. *Journal of Policy and Practice in Intellectual Disabilities, 3,* 22–32.

Garfinkel, P. E. (1995). Classification and diagnosis of eating disorders. In K. D. Brownell & C. G. Fairburn (Eds.), *Eating disorders and obesity: A comprehensive handbook* (pp. 125–134). New York: Guilford Press.

Garland, A. F., & Zigler, E. (1993). Adolescent suicide prevention: Current research and social policy implications. *American Psychologist, 48,* 169–182.

Garmezy, N. (1993). Vulnerability and resilience. In D. C. Funder, R. D. Parke, C. Tomlinson-Keasey, & K. Widaman (Eds.), *Studying lives through time: Personality and development* (pp. 377–398). Washington, DC: American Psychological Association.

Garmezy, N., & Masten, A. S. (1991). The protective role of competence indicators in children at risk. In E. M. Cummings, A. L. Green, & K. H. Karraker (Eds.), *Life-span developmental psychology: Perspectives on stress and coping* (pp. 151–174). Hillsdale, NJ: Erlbaum.

Garmezy, N., & Rutter, M. (Eds.). (1983). *Stress, coping, and development in children.* New York: McGraw-Hill.

Garnier, H., Stein, J., & Jacobs, J. (1997). The process of dropping out of high school: A 19-year perspective. *American Educational Research Journal, 34,* 395–419.

Gartstein, M., & Rothbart, M. (2003). Studying infant temperament via the revised infant behavior questionnaire. *Infant Behavior & Development, 26,* 64–86.

Gathercole, S., Pickering, S., Ambridge, B., & Wearing, H. (2004). The structure of working memory from 4 to 15 years of age. *Developmental Psychology, 40,* 177–190.

Gaultney, J., & Gingras, J. (2005). Fetal rate of behavioral inhibition and preference for novelty during infancy. *Early Human Development, 81,* 379–386.

Gauvain, M., Fagot, B., Leve, C., & Kavanagh, K. (2002). Instruction by mothers and fathers during problem solving with their young children. *Journal of Family Psychology, 16,* 81–90.

Ge, X., & Conger, R. (1999). Adjustment problems and emerging personality characteristics from early to late adolescence. *American Journal of Community Psychology, 27,* 429–459.

Geary, D. C. (1996). International differences in mathematical achievement: Their nature, causes, and consequences. *Current Directions in Psychological Science, 5,* 133–137.

Geary, D. C., Bow-Thomas, C. C., Liu, F., & Siegler, R. S. (1996). Development of arithmetical competencies in Chinese and American children: Influences of age, language, and schooling. *Child Development, 65,* 2022–2044.

Geary, D. C., Lin, F., Chen, G., Saults, S., et al. (1999). Contributions of computational fluency to cross-national differences in arithmetical reasoning abilities. *Journal of Educational Psychology, 91,* 716–719.

Gee, C., & Rhodes, J. (1999). Postpartum transitions in adolescent mothers' romantic and maternal relationships. *Merrill-Palmer Quarterly, 45,* 512–532.

Gee, C., & Rhodes, J. (2003). Adolescent mothers' relationship with their children's biological fathers: Social support, social strain and relationship continuity. *Journal of Family Psychology, 17,* 370–383.

Geissbuehler, V., & Eberhard, J. (2002). Fear of childbirth during pregnancy: A study of more than 8000 pregnant women. *Journal of Psychosomatic Obstetrics & Gynecology, 23,* 229–235.

Geltman, P., Grant-Knight, W., Mehta, S., Lloyd-Travaglini, C., Lustig, S., Landgraf, J., & Wise, P. (2005). The "Lost Boys of Sudan." *Archives of Pediatrics and Adolescent Medicine, 159,* 585–591.

Gentile, D., Lynch, P., Linder, J., & Walsh, D. (2004). The effects of violent video game habits on adolescent hostility, aggressive behaviors, and school performance. *Journal of Adolescence, 27,* 5–22.

Gentner, D. (1982). Why nouns are learned before verbs: Linguistic relativity versus natural partitioning. In S. A. Kuczaj, II (Ed.), *Language development: Vol. 2, Language, thought, and culture* (pp. 301–334). Hillsdale, NJ: Erlbaum.

Georgieff, M. K. (1994). Nutritional deficiencies as developmental risk factors: Commentary on Pollitt and Gorman. In C. A. Nelson (Ed.), *The Minnesota symposia on child development* (Vol. 27, pp. 145–159). Hillsdale, NJ: Erlbaum.

Gerhardstein, P., Adler, S., & Rovee-Collier, C. (2000). A dissociation in infants' memory for stimulus size: Evidence for the early development of multiple memory systems. *Developmental Psychobiology, 36,* 123–135.

Gershkoff-Stowe, L., & Hahn, E. (2007). Fast mapping skills in the developing lexicon. *Journal of Speech, Language, and Hearing Research, 50,* 682–696.

Gershoff, E. (2002). Corporal punishment by parents and associated child behaviors and experiences: A meta-analytic and theoretical review. *Psychological Bulletin, 128,* 539–579.

Gesell, A. (1925). *The mental growth of the preschool child.* New York: Macmillan.

Gesell, A. (1952). *Infant development: The embryology of early behavior.* New York: Harper & Brothers.

Ghetti, S., Papini, S., & Angelini, L. (2006). The development of the memorability-based strategy: Insight from a training study. *Journal of Experimental Child Psychology, 94,* 206–228.

Gibbs, J., Basinger, K., Grime, R., & Snarey, J. (2007). Moral judgment development across cultures: Revisiting Kohlberg's universality claims. *Developmental Review, 27,* 443–500.

Gibson, D. R. (1990). Relation of socioeconomic status to logical and sociomoral judgment of middle-aged men. *Psychology and Aging, 5,* 510–513.

Gibson, E. (2002). *Perceiving the affordances: A portrait of two psychologists.* Hillsdale, NJ: Erlbaum.

Gibson, E. J., & Walk, R. D. (1960). The "visual cliff." *Scientific American, 202,* 80–92.

Giedd, J. (2004). Structural magnetic resonance imaging of the adolescent brain. *Annals of the New York Academy of Sciences, 1021,* 77–85.

Giedd, J., Blumenthal, J., & Jeffries, N. (1999). Brain development during childhood and adolescence: A longitudinal MRI study. *Nature Neuroscience, 2,* 861–863.

Giedd, J., Blumenthal, J., Jeffries, N., Castellanos, F., Lui, H., & Paus, T. (1999). Brain development during childhood and adolescence: A longitudinal MRI study. *Nature Neuroscience, 2,* 861–863.

Gilbertson, M., & Bramlett, R. (1998). Phonological awareness screening to identify at-risk readers: Implications for practitioners. *Language, Speech, & Hearing Services in Schools, 29*, 109–116.

Giles, J., & Heyman, G. (2005). Young children's beliefs about the relationship between gender and aggressive behavior. *Child Development, 76*, 207–121.

Giles-Sims, J., & Lockhart, C. (2005). Culturally shaped patterns of disciplining children. *Journal of Family Issues, 26*, 196–218.

Gillespie, C., & Nemeroff, C. (2007). Corticotropin-releasing factor and the psychobiology of early-life stress. *Current Directions in Psychological Science, 16*, 85–89.

Gillies, V., & Lucey, H. (2006). 'It's a connection you can't get away from': Brothers, sisters and social capital. *Journal of Youth Studies, 9*, 479–493.

Gilligan, C. (1982). *In a different voice: Psychological theory and women's development.* Cambridge, MA: Harvard University Press.

Gilligan, C., & Wiggins, G. (1987). The origins of morality in early childhood relationships. In J. Kagan & S. Lamb (Eds.), *The emergence of morality in young children* (pp. 277–307). Chicago: University of Chicago Press.

Gilman, S., Abrams, D., & Buka, S. (2003). Socioeconomic status over the life course and stages of cigarette use: Initiation, regular use, and cessation. *Journal of Epidemiology and Community Health, 57*, 802–808.

Glasgow, K. L., Dornbusch, S. M., Troyer, L., Steinberg, L., & Ritter, P. L. (1997). Parenting styles, adolescents' attributions, and educational outcomes in nine heterogeneous high schools. *Child Development, 68*, 507–529.

Gleason, K., Jensen-Campbell, L., & Richardson, D. (2004). Agreeableness as a predictor of aggression in adolescence. *Aggressive Behavior, 30*, 43–61.

Gleitman, L. R., & Gleitman, H. (1992). A picture is worth a thousand words, but that's the problem: The role of syntax in vocabulary acquisition. *Current Directions in Psychological Science, 1*, 31–35.

Gleitman, L. R., & Wanner, E. (1988). Current issues in language learning. In M. H. Bornstein & M. E. Lamb (Eds.), *Developmental psychology: An advanced textbook* (2nd ed., pp. 297–358). Hillsdale, NJ: Erlbaum.

Glowinski, A., Bucholz, K., Nelson, E., Fu, Q., Madden, P., Reich, W., & Heath, A. (2001). Suicide attempts in an adolescent female twin sample. *Journal of the American Academy of Child and Adolescent Psychiatry, 40*, 1300–1307.

Glueck, S., & Glueck, E. (1972). *Identification of pre-delinquents: Validation studies and some suggested uses of Glueck table.* New York: Intercontinental Medical Book Corp.

Gnepp, J., & Chilamkurti, C. (1988). Children's use of personality attributions to predict other people's emotional and behavioral reactions. *Child Development, 50*, 743–754.

Gogtay, N., Giedd, J., Lusk, L., Hayashi, K., Greenstein, D., Vaituzis, A., Nugent, T., Herman, D., Clasen, L., Toga, A., Rapoport, J., & Thompson, P. (2004). Dynamic mapping of human cortical development during childhood through early adulthood. *Proceedings of the National Academy of Sciences, 17*, 17.

Goldberg, S. (1972). Infant care and growth in urban Zambia. *Human Development, 15*, 77–89.

Goldberg, W. A. (1990). Marital quality, parental personality, and spousal agreement about perceptions and expectations for children. *Merrill-Palmer Quarterly, 36*, 531–556.

Golden, M., & Birns, B. (1983). Social class and infant intelligence. In M. Lewis (Ed.), *Origins of intelligence: Infancy and early childhood* (2nd ed., pp. 347–398). New York: Plenum Press.

Goldfield, B. A. (1993). Noun bias in maternal speech to one-year-olds. *Journal of Child Language, 20*, 85–99.

Goldfield, B. A., & Reznick, J. S. (1990). Early lexical acquisition: Rate, content, and the vocabulary spurt. *Journal of Child Language, 17*, 171–183.

Goldin-Meadow, S. (2007a). Gesture with speech and without it. In S. Duncan, J. Cassell, & E. Levy (Eds.), *Gesture and the dynamic dimension of language: Essays in honor of David McNeill* (pp. 31–49). Amsterdam, Netherlands: John Benjamins Publishing Company.

Goldin-Meadow, S. (2007b). The challenge: Some properties of language can be learned without linguistic input. *Linguistic Review, 24*, 417–421.

Goldman, L. S., Genel, M., Bezman, R. J., & Slanetz, P. J. (1998). Diagnosis and treatment of attention-deficit/hyperactivity disorder in children and adolescents. *Journal of the American Medical Association, 279*, 1100–1107.

Goldsmith, H. H., & Alansky, J. (1987). Maternal and infant temperamental predictors of attachment: A meta-analytic review. *Journal of Consulting and Clinical Psychology, 55*, 805–806.

Goldsmith, H. H., Buss, K. A., & Lemery, K. S. (1997). Toddler and childhood temperament: Expanded content, stronger genetic evidence, new evidence for the importance of environment. *Developmental Psychology, 33*, 891–905.

Goldstein, R., & Volkow, N. (2002). Drug addiction and its underlying neurobiological basis: Neuroimaging evidence for the involvement of the frontal cortex. *American Journal of Psychiatry, 159*, 1642–1652.

Goldstein, S., Davis-Kean, P., & Eccles, J. (2005). Parents, peers, and problem behavior: A longitudinal investigation of the impact of relationship perceptions and characteristics on the development of adolescent problem behavior. *Developmental Psychology, 41*, 401–413.

Goleman, D. (1995a, October 4). Eating disorder rates surprise the experts. *The New York Times*, p. B7.

Goleman, D. (1995b). *Emotional intelligence.* New York: Bantam Books.

Golinkoff, R. M., Mervis, C. B., & Hirsh-Pasek, K. (1994). Early object labels: The case for lexical principles. *Journal of Child Language, 21*, 125–155.

Golombok, S., & Fivush, R. (1994). *Gender development.* Cambridge, England: Cambridge University Press.

Golombok, S., & Tasker, F. (1996). Do parents influence the sexual orientation of their children? Findings from a longitudinal study of lesbian families. *Developmental Psychology, 32*, 3–11.

Gonzales, P., Guzman, J., Partelow, L., Pahlke, E., Jocelyn, L., Kastberg, D., & Williams, T. (2004). *Highlights from the Trends in International Mathematics and Science Study: TIMSS 2003.* Retrieved August 14, 2008, from http://nces.ed.gov/pubsearch/pubsinfo.asp?pubid=2005005

Goossens, L., Beyers, W., Emmen, M., & van Aken, M. (2002). The imaginary audience and personal fable: Factor analyses and concurrent validity of the "New Look" measures. *Journal of Research on Adolescence, 12*, 193–215.

Goossens, R., & van IJzendoorn, M. (1990). Quality of infants' attachments to professional caregivers: Relation to infant-parent attachment and day-care characteristics. *Child Development, 61*, 832–837.

Gopnik, A., & Astington, J. W. (1988). Children's understanding of representational change and its relation to the understanding of false belief and the appearance-reality distinction. *Child Development, 59*, 26–37.

Gordon, N. (1995). Apoptosis (programmed cell death) and other reasons for elimination of neurons and axons. *Brain & Development, 17*, 73–77.

Gordon, R. (2001). Eating disorders East and West: A culture-bound syndrome unbound. In M. Nasser, M. Katzman, & R. Bordon (Eds.), *Eating disorders and cultures in transition* (pp. 1–23). New York: Taylor & Francis.

Gottesman, I. I., & Goldsmith, H. H. (1994). Developmental psychopathology of antisocial behavior: Inserting genes into its ontogenesis and epigenesis. In C. A. Nelson (Ed.), *The Minnesota symposia on child psychology* (Vol. 27, pp. 69–104). Hillsdale, NJ: Erlbaum.

Gottfried, A. E., Bathurst, K., & Gottfried, A. W. (1994). Role of maternal and dual-earner employment status in children's development: A longitudinal study from infancy through early adolescence. In A. E. Gottfried & A. W. Gottfried (Eds.), *Redefining families: Implications for children's development* (pp. 55–97). New York: Plenum Press.

Gottfried, A. W., Gottfried, A. E., Bathurst, K., & Guerin, D. W. (1994). *Gifted IQ: Early developmental aspects.* New York: Plenum Press.

Gottlieb, G. (1976a). Conceptions of prenatal development: Behavioral embryology. *Psychological Review, 83,* 215–234.

Gottlieb, G. (1976b). The roles of experience in the development of behavior and the nervous system. In G. Gottlieb (Ed.), *Neural and behavioral specificity.* New York: Academic Press.

Gottman, J. M. (1986). The world of coordinated play: Same- and cross-sex friendship in young children. In J. M. Gottman & J. G. Parker (Eds.), *Conversations of friends: Speculations on affective development* (pp. 139–191). Cambridge, England: Cambridge University Press.

Gould, M., Marrocco, F., Kleinman, M., Thomas, J., Mostkoff, K., Cote, J., & Davies, M. (2005). Evaluating iatrogenic risk of youth suicide screening programs: A randomized controlled trial. *Journal of the American Medical Association, 293,* 1635–1643.

Grabowski, L., Call, K., & Mortimer, J. (2001). Global and economic self-efficacy in the educational attainment process. *Social Psychology Quarterly, 64,* 164–197.

Graham, S., & Harris, K. (1997). It can be taught, but it does not develop naturally: Myths and realities in writing instruction. *School Psychology Review, 26,* 414–424.

Green, E., Deschamps, J., & Páez, D. (2005). Variation of individualism and collectivism within and between 20 countries: A typological analysis. *Journal of Cross-Cultural Psychology, 36,* 321–339.

Green, S. (2001). Systemic vs. individualistic approaches to bullying. *Journal of the American Medical Association, 286,* 787.

Green, S., Pring, L., & Swettenham, J. (2004). An investigation of first-order false belief understanding of children with congenital profound visual impairment. *British Journal of Developmental Psychology, 22,* 1–17.

Greenberger, E., & Steinberg, L. (1986). *When teenagers work: The psychological and social costs of adolescent employment.* New York: Basic Books.

Greene, K., Krcmar, M., Rubin, D., Walters, L., & Hale, J. (2002). Elaboration in processing adolescent health messages: The impact of egocentrism and sensation seeking on message processing. *Journal of Communication, 52,* 812–831.

Greenfield, P. (1995). Profile: On teaching. Culture, ethnicity, race, and development: Implications for teaching theory and research. *SRCD Newsletter* (Winter), 3–4, 12.

Greenfield, P., Brannon, C., & Lohr, D. (1994). Two-dimensional representation of movement through three-dimensional space: The role of video game expertise. *Journal of Applied Developmental Psychology, 15,* 87–104.

Greenough, W. T. (1991). Experience as a component of normal development: Evolutionary considerations. *Developmental Psychology, 27,* 11–27.

Greenough, W. T., Black, J. E., & Wallace, C. S. (1987). Experience and brain development. *Child Development, 58,* 539–559.

Gregg, V., Gibbs, J. C., & Basinger, K. S. (1994). Patterns of developmental delay in moral judgment by male and female delinquents. *Merrill-Palmer Quarterly, 40,* 538–553.

Grenier, G. (1985). Shifts to English as usual language by Americans of Spanish mother tongue. In R. O. De La Garza, F. D. Bean, C. M. Bonjean, R. Romo, & R. Alvarez (Eds.), *The Mexican American experience: An interdisciplinary anthology* (pp. 347–358). Austin: University of Texas Press.

Grolnick, W. S., & Slowiaczek, M. L. (1994). Parents' involvement in children's schooling: A multidimensional conceptualization and motivational model. *Child Development, 65,* 237–252.

Groome, L., Mooney, D., Holland, S., Smith, L., Atterbury, J., & Dykman, R. (1999). Behavioral state affects heart rate response to low-intensity sound in human fetuses. *Early Human Development, 54,* 39–54.

Grossmann, K., Grossmann, K. E., Spangler, G., Suess, G., & Unzner, L. (1985). Maternal sensitivity and newborns' orientation responses as related to quality of attachment in northern Germany. *Monographs of the Society of Research in Child Development, 50* (1–2, Serial No. 209), 233–256.

Grotevant, H. D., & Cooper, C. R. (1985). Patterns of interaction in family relationships and the development of identity exploration in adolescence. *Child Development, 56,* 415–428.

Grov, C., Bimbi, D., Nanin, J., & Parsons, J. (2006). Race, ethnicity, gender, and generational factors associated with the coming-out process among gay, lesbian, and bisexual individuals. *Journal of Sex Research, 43,* 115–121.

Grusec, J. E. (1992). Social learning theory and developmental psychology: The legacies of Robert Sears and Albert Bandura. *Developmental Psychology, 28,* 776–786.

Grusec, J. E., Saas-Kortsaak, P., & Simutis, Z. M. (1978). The role of example and moral exhortation in the training of altruism. *Child Development, 49,* 920–923.

Guerin, D. W., & Gottfried, A. W. (1994a). Developmental stability and change in parent reports of temperament: A ten-year longitudinal investigation from infancy through preadolescence. *Merrill-Palmer Quarterly, 40,* 334–355.

Guerin, D. W., & Gottfried, A. W. (1994b). Temperamental consequences of infant difficultness. *Infant Behavior and Development, 17,* 413–421.

Guertin, T., Lloyd-Richardson, E., Spirito, A., Donaldson, D., & Boergers, J. (2001). Self-mutilative behavior in adolescents who attempt suicide by overdose. *Journal of the American Academy of Child and Adolescent Psychiatry, 40,* 1062–1069.

Guglielmi, R. (2008). Native language proficiency, English literacy, academic achievement, and occupational attainment in limited-English-proficient students: A latent growth modeling perspective. *Journal of Educational Psychology, 100,* 322–342.

Guilford, J. (1967). *The nature of human intelligence.* New York: McGraw-Hill.

Gunnar, M., Sebanc, A., Tout, K., Donzella, B., & Van Dulmen, M. (2003). Peer rejection, temperament, and cortisol activity in preschoolers. *Developmental Psychobiology, 43,* 346–358.

Gunnar, M. R. (1994). Psychoendocrine studies of temperament and stress in early childhood: Expanding current models. In J. E. Bates & T. D. Wachs (Eds.), *Temperament: Individual differences at the interface of biology and behavior* (pp. 175–198). Washington, DC: American Psychological Association.

Gupta, R., Hasan, K., Trivedi, R., Pradhan, M., Das, V., Parikh, N., & Narayana, P. (2005). Diffusion tensor imaging of the developing human cerebrum. *Journal of Neuroscience Research, 81,* 172–178.

Guralnick, M. J., & Paul-Brown, D. (1984). Communicative adjustments during behavior-request episodes among children at different developmental levels. *Child Development, 55,* 911–919.

Gurnáková, J., & Kusá, D. (2004). Gender self-concept in personal theories of reality. *Studia Psychologica, 46,* 49–61.

Guthrie, R. (2004). *Even the rat was white.* Boston: Pearson Allyn & Bacon.

Guttentag, R. E., Ornstein, P. A., & Siemens, L. (1987). Children's spontaneous rehearsal: Transitions in strategy acquisition. *Cognitive Development, 2,* 307–326.

Guttman, A., & Dick, P. (2004). Infant hospitalization and maternal depression, poverty and single parenthood: A population-based study. *Child: Care, Health & Development, 30,* 67–75.

Gzesh, S. M., & Surber, C. F. (1985). Visual perspective-taking skills in children. *Child Development, 56,* 1204–1213.

Haan, N. (1981). Adolescents and young adults as producers of their own development. In R. M. Lerner & N. A. Busch-Rossnagel (Eds.), *Individuals as producers of their own development* (pp. 155–182). New York: Academic Press.

Hack, M., Taylor, C. B. H., Klein, N., Eiben, R., Schatschneider, C., & Mercuri-Minich, N. (1994). School-age outcomes in children with birth weights under 750 g. *New England Journal of Medicine, 331,* 753–759.

Hagan, J. (1997). Defiance and despair: Subcultural and structural linkages between delinquency and despair in the life course. *Social Forces, 76,* 119–134.

Hagerman, R. J. (1996). Growth and development. In W. W. Hay, Jr., J. R. Groothuis, A. R. Hayward, & M. J. Levin (Eds.), *Current pediatric diagnosis and treatment* (12th ed., pp. 65–84). Norwalk, CT: Appleton & Lange.

Haith, M. M. (1980). *Rules that babies look by.* Hillsdale, NJ: Erlbaum.

Hakansson, G., Salameh, E., & Nettelbladt, U. (2003). Measuring language development in bilingual children: Swedish-Arabic children with and without language impairment. *Linguistics, 41,* 255–288.

Hakimzadeh, S., & Cohn, D. (2007). *English usage among Hispanics in the United States.* Retrieved September 9, 2008, from http://pewhispanic.org/reports/report.php?ReportID=82

Halama, P., & Strízenec, M. (2004). Spiritual, existential or both? Theoretical considerations on the nature of "higher" intelligences. *Studia Psychologica, 46,* 239–253.

Hale, S., Fry, A. F., & Jessie, K. A. (1993). Effects of practice on speed of information processing in children and adults: Age sensitivity and age invariance. *Developmental Psychology, 29,* 880–892.

Halford, G., Bunch, K., & McCredden, J. (2007). Problem decomposability as a factor in complexity of the dimensional change card sort task. *Cognitive Development, 22,* 384–391.

Hall, G. (2003, September). Primary elective C-section up 20% from 1999 to 2001. *OB/GYN News.* Retrieved April 1, 2004, from http://www.imng.com

Hallowell, E. (2007). *Crazy busy: Overstretched, overbooked, and about to snap! Strategies for handling your fast-paced life.* New York: Ballantine Books.

Halmi, K. (2003). Classification, diagnosis and comorbidities of eating disorders. In M. Maj, K. Halmi, J. Lopez-Ibor, & N. Sartorius (Eds.), *Eating disorders* (pp. 1–33). New York: Wiley.

Halpern, C. T., Udry, J. R., Campbell, B., & Suchindran, C. (1993). Testosterone and pubertal development as predictors of sexual activity: A panel analysis of adolescent males. *Psychosomatic Medicine, 55,* 436–447.

Halpern, D., & Tan, U. (2001). Stereotypes and steroids: Using a psychobiosocial model to understand cognitive sex differences. *Brain & Cognition, 45,* 392–414.

Ham, B. (2004, October 29). *Hispanic children less likely to get ADHD diagnosis.* Retrieved June 20, 2008, from http://www.cfah.org/hbns/news/ADHD10-29-04.cfm

Hämäläinen, M., & Pulkkinen, L. (1996). Problem behavior as a precursor of male criminality. *Development and Psychopathology, 8,* 443–455.

Hamilton B., Martin J., & Ventura S. Births: preliminary data for 2006. *National Vital Statistics Reports, 56,* 1–18.

Hamm, J. (2000). Do birds of a feather flock together? The variable bases for African American, Asian American, and European American adolescents' selection of similar friends. *Developmental Psychology, 36,* 209–219.

Hamvas, A., Wise, P. H., Yang, R. K., Wampler, N. S., Noguchi, A., Maurer, M. M., Walentik, C. A., Schramm, W. F., & Cole, F. S. (1996). The influence of the wider use of surfactant therapy on neonatal mortality among blacks and whites. *New England Journal of Medicine, 334,* 1635–1640.

Han, W., Ruhm, C., Waldfogel, J., & Washbrook, E. (2008, June). The timing of mothers' employment after childbirth. *Monthly Labor Review,* 15–28.

Han, W., Waldfogel, J., & Brooks-Gunn, J. (2001). The effects of early maternal employment on later cognitive and behavioral outcomes. *Journal of Marriage and the Family, 63,* 336–354.

Hanish, L., Martin, C., Fabes, R., & Barcelo, H. (2008). The breadth of peer relationships among preschoolers: An application of the Q-connectivity method to externalizing behavior. *Child Development, 79,* 1119–1136.

Hanlon, H., Thatcher, R., & Cline, M. (1999). Gender differences in the development of EEG coherence in normal children. *Developmental Neuropsychology, 17,* 199–223.

Hanna, E., & Meltzoff, A. N. (1993). Peer imitation by toddlers in laboratory, home, and day-care contexts: Implications for social learning and memory. *Developmental Psychology, 29,* 701–710.

Hannigan, J., O'Leary-Moore, S., & Berman, R. (2007). Postnatal environmental or experiential amelioration of neurobehavioral effects of perinatal alcohol exposure in rats. *Neuroscience & Biobehavioral Reviews, 31,* 202–211.

Hannon, E., & Trehub, S. (2005). Metrical categories in infancy and adulthood. *Psychological Science, 16,* 48–55.

Hansen, J., & Bowey, J. A. (1994). Phonological analysis skills, verbal working memory, and reading ability in second-grade children. *Child Development, 65,* 938–950.

Hanshaw, J. B., Scheiner, A. P., Moxley, A. W., Gaeav, L., Abel, V., & Scheiner, B. (1976). School failure and deafness after "silent" congenital cytomegalovirus infection. *New England Journal of Medicine, 295,* 468–470.

Harden, K., Turkheimer, E., & Loehlin, J. (2007). Genotype by environment interaction in adolescents' cognitive aptitude. *Behavior Genetics, 37,* 273–283.

Hardy, C., & Van Leeuwen, S. (2004). Interviewing young children: Effects of probe structures and focus of rapport-building talk on the qualities of young children's eyewitness statements. *Canadian Journal of Behavioral Science, 36,* 155–165.

Harkness, S. (1998). Time for families. *Anthropology Newsletter, 39,* 1, 4.

Harkness, S., & Super, C. M. (1985). The cultural context of gender segregation in children's peer groups. *Child Development, 56,* 219–224.

Harkness, S., & Super, C. M. (1995). Culture and parenting. In M. H. Bornstein (Ed.), *Handbook of parenting: Vol. 2. Biology and ecology of parenting* (pp. 211–234). Mahwah, NJ: Erlbaum.

Harold, G. T., & Conger, R. D. (1997). Marital conflict and adolescent distress: The role of adolescent awareness. *Child Development, 68,* 333–350.

Harrington, R., Rutter, M., & Fombonne, E. (1996). Developmental pathways in depression: Multiple meanings, antecedents, and endpoints. *Development and Psychopathology, 8,* 601–616.

Harris, J. (1998). *The nurture assumption: Why kids turn out the way they do: Parents matter less than you think and peers matter more.* New York: Free Press.

Harris, J. (2005). The increased diagnosis of "Juvenile Bipolar Disorder": What are we treating? *Psychiatric Services, 56,* 529–531.

Harris, P. L. (1989). *Children and emotion: The development of psychological understanding.* Oxford: Basil Blackwell.

Harris, P. L., Olthof, T., & Terwogt, M. M. (1981). Children's knowledge of emotion. *Journal of Child Psychology and Psychiatry, 22,* 247–261.

Harrison, A. O., Wilson, M. N., Pine, C. J., Chan, S. Q., & Buriel, R. (1990). Family ecologies of ethnic minority children. *Child Development, 61,* 347–362.

Harrist, A., Zaia, A., Bates, J., Dodge, K., & Pettit, G. (1997). Subtypes of social withdrawal in early childhood: Sociometric status and social-cognitive differences across four years. *Child Development, 68,* 278–294.

Hart, B., & Risley, T. R. (1995). *Meaningful differences in the everyday experience of young American children.* Baltimore, MD: Brookes.

Hart, C., Olsen, S., Robinson, C., & Mandleco, B. (1997). The development of social and communicative competence in childhood: Review and a model of personal, familial, and extrafamilial processes. *Communication Yearbook, 20,* 305–373.

Hart, S., Boylan, L., Border, B., Carroll, S., McGunegle, D., & Lampe, R. (2004). Breast milk levels of cortisol and Secretory Immunoglobulin A (SIgA) differ with maternal mood and infant neuro-behavioral functioning. *Infant Behavior and Development, 27,* 101–106.

Harter, S. (1987). The determinants and mediational role of global self-worth in children. In N. Eisenberg (Ed.), *Contemporary topics in developmental psychology* (pp. 219–242). New York: Wiley-Interscience.

Harter, S. (1990). Processes underlying adolescent self-concept formation. In R. Montemayor, G. R. Adams, & T. P. Gullotta (Eds.), *From childhood to adolescence: A transitional period?* (pp. 205–239). Newbury Park, CA: Sage.

Harter, S. (1998). The development of self-representations. In W. Damon (Ed.), *Handbook of child psychology: Vol. 3. Social, emotional, and personality development* (5th ed., pp. 553–617). New York: Wiley.

Harter, S. (1999). *Developmental approaches to self processes.* New York: Guilford.

Harter, S. (2006a). The development of self-esteem. In M. Kernis (Ed.), *Self-esteem issues and answers: A sourcebook of current perspectives* (pp. 144–150). New York: Psychology Press.

Harter, S. (2006b). The self. In N. Eisenberg, W. Damon, & R. Lerner (Eds.), *Handbook of child psychology: Vol. 3, Social, emotional, and personality development* (6th ed., pp. 505–570). Hoboken, NJ: Wiley.

Harter, S., & Whitesell, N. R. (1996). Multiple pathways to self-reported depression and psychological adjustment among adolescents. *Development and Psychopathology, 8,* 761–777.

Harter, S., & Whitesell, N. R. (2003). Beyond the debate: Why some adolescents report stable self-worth over time and situation, whereas others report changes in self-worth. *Journal of Personality, 71,* 1027–1058.

Harton, H., & Latane, B. (1997). Social influence and adolescent lifestyle attitudes. *Journal of Research on Adolescence, 7,* 197–220.

Hartshorn, K., & Rovee-Collier, C. (1997). Infant learning and long-term memory at 6 months: A confirming analysis. *Developmental Psychobiology, 30,* 71–85.

Hartup, W. W. (1989). Social relationships and their developmental significance. *American Psychologist, 44,* 120–126.

Hartup, W. W. (1996). The company they keep: Friendships and their developmental significance. *Child Development, 67,* 1–13.

Hartup, W. W. (2006). Relationships in early and middle childhood. In A. Vangellisti & D. Perlman (Eds.), *The Cambridge handbook of personal relationships* (pp. 177–190). New York: Cambridge University Press.

Hartup, W. W., Laursen, B., Stewart, M. I., & Eastenson, A. (1988). Conflict and the friendship relations of young children. *Child Development, 59,* 1590–1600.

Hartup, W. W., & van Lieshout, C. F. M. (1995). Personality development in social context. *Annual Review of Psychology, 46,* 655–687.

Harvey, A., & Hill, R. (2004). Afrocentric youth and family rites of passage program: Promoting resilience among at-risk African American youths. *Social Work, 49,* 65–74.

Harvey, A., & Rauch, J. (1997). A comprehensive Afrocentric rites of passage program for black male adolescents. *Health & Social Work, 22,* 30–37.

Harwood, R. L. (1992). The influence of culturally derived values on Anglo and Puerto Rican mothers' perceptions of attachment behavior. *Child Development, 63,* 822–839.

Hashima, P. Y., & Amato, P. R. (1994). Poverty, social support, and parental behavior. *Child Development, 65,* 394–403.

Haskins, R. (1989). Beyond metaphor: The efficacy of early childhood education. *American Psychologist, 44,* 274–282.

Hatano, G., Siegler, R. S., Richards, D. D., Inagaki, K., Stavy, R., & Wax, N. (1993). The development of biological knowledge: A multi-national study. *Cognitive Development, 8,* 47–62.

Hatchett, S. J., & Jackson, J. S. (1993). African American extended kin systems: An assessment. In H. P. McAdoo (Ed.), *Family ethnicity: Strength in diversity* (pp. 90–108). Newbury Park, CA: Sage.

Haviland, J. M., & Lelwica, M. (1987). The induced affect response: 10-week-old infants' responses to three emotional expressions. *Developmental Psychology, 23,* 97–104.

Hay, D., Payne, A., & Chadwick, A. (2004). Peer relations in childhood. *Journal of Child Psychology and Psychiatry, 45,* 84–108.

Hayne, H., & Rovee-Collier, C. (1995). The organization of reactivated memory in infancy. *Child Development, 66,* 893–906.

Haynes, N. M., Ben-Avie, M., Squires, D. A., Howley, J. P., Negron, E. N., & Corbin, J. N. (1996). It takes a whole village: The SDP school. In J. P. Corner, N. M. Haynes, E. T. Joyner, & M. Ben-Avie (Eds.), *Rallying the whole village: The Comer process for reforming education* (pp. 42–71). New York: Teachers College Press.

Hedegaard, M., Henriksen, T. B., Secher, N. J., Hatch, M. C., & Sabroe, S. (1996). Do stressful life events affect duration of gestation and risk of preterm delivery? *Epidemiology, 7,* 339–345.

Heenan, J. (2005). *Character education transforms school.* Retrieved July 19, 2005, from http://www.cornerstonevalues.org/kew2.htm

Henneborn, W. J., & Cogan, R. (1975). The effect of husband participation on reported pain and the probability of medication during labour and birth. *Journal of Psychosomatic Research, 19,* 215–222.

Henry, B., Caspi, A., Moffitt, T., & Silva, P. (1996). Temperamental and familial predictors of violent and nonviolent criminal convictions: Age 3 to age 18. *Developmental Psychology, 32,* 614–623.

Hepworth, S., Rovet, J., & Taylor, M. (2001). Neurophysiological correlates of verbal and nonverbal short-term memory in children: Repetition of words and faces. *Psychophysiology, 38,* 594–600.

Herbert, J., Eckerman, C., Goldstein, R., & Stanton, M. (2004). Contrasts in infant classical eyeblink conditioning as a function of premature birth. *Infancy, 5,* 367–383.

Heron, M. (2007). Deaths: Leading causes for 2004. *National Vital Statistics Reports, 56*, 1–96.

Heron, M., Hoyert, D., Xu, J., Scott, C., & Tejada-Vera, B. (2008). Deaths: Preliminary data for 2006. *National Vital Statistics Reports, 56*, 1–52.

Herrenkohl, E., Herrenkohl, R., Egolf, B., & Russo, M. (1998). The relationship between early maltreatment and teenage parenthood. *Journal of Adolescence, 21*, 291–303.

Herrera, N., Zajonc, R., Wieczorkowska, G., & Cichomski, B. (2003). Beliefs about birth rank and their reflection in reality. *Journal of Personality & Social Psychology, 85*, 142–150.

Herring, W., McGrath, D., & Buckley, J. (2007). *Issue brief: Demographic and school characteristics of students receiving special education in the elementary grades.* Retrieved September 1, 2008, from http://nces.ed.gov/pubs2007/2007005.pdf

Hess, E. H. (1972). "Imprinting" in a natural laboratory. *Scientific American, 227*, 24–31.

Hetherington, E. (1989). Coping with family transitions: Winners, losers, and survivors. *Child Development, 60*, 1–14.

Hetherington, E. (1991a). Presidential address: Families, lies, and videotapes. *Journal of Research on Adolescence, 1*, 323–348.

Hetherington, E. (1991b). The role of individual differences and family relationships in children's coping with divorce and remarriage. In P. A. Cowen & M. Hetherington (Eds.), *Family transitions* (pp. 165–194). Hillsdale, NJ: Erlbaum.

Hetherington, E., Bridges, M., & Insabella, G. (1998). What matters? What does not? Five perspectives on the association between marital transitions and children's adjustment. *American Psychologist, 53*, 167–184.

Hetherington, E., Henderson, S., Reiss, D., Anderson, E., et al. (1999). Adolescent siblings in stepfamilies: Family functioning and adolescent adjustment. *Monographs of the Society for Research in Child Development, 64*, 222.

Hewitt, L., Hammer, C., Yount, K., & Tomblin, B. (2005). Language sampling for kindergarten children with and without SLI: Mean length of utterance, IPSYN, and NDW. *Journal of Communication Disorders, 38*, 197–213.

Heyman, G., (2001). Children's interpretation of ambiguous behavior: Evidence for a "boys are bad" bias. *Social Development, 10*, 230–247.

Hill, H. M., Soriano, F. I., Chen, S. A., & LaFromboise, T. D. (1994). Sociocultural factors in the etiology and prevention of violence among ethnic minority youth. In L. D. Eron, J. H. Gentry, & P. Schlegel (Eds.), *Reason to hope: A psychosocial perspective on violence and youth* (pp. 59–97). Washington, DC: American Psychological Association.

Hipwell, A., Keenan, K., Kasza, K., Loeber, R., Stouthamer-Loeber, M., & Bean, T. (2008). Reciprocal influences between girls' conduct problems and depression, and parental punishment and warmth. *Journal of Abnormal Child Psychology, 36*, 663–677.

Hirsh-Pasek, K., Trieman, R., & Schneiderman, M. (1984). Brown and Hanlon revisited: Mothers' sensitivity to ungrammatical forms. *Journal of Child Language, 11*, 81–88.

Ho, C., & Bryant, P. (1997). Learning to read Chinese beyond the logographic phase. *Reading Research Quarterly, 32*, 276–289.

Hodge, K. P., & Tod, D. A. (1993). Ethics of childhood sport. *Sports Medicine, 15*, 291–298.

Hoeksma, J., Oosterlaan, J., & Schipper, E. (2004). Emotion regulation and the dynamics of feelings: A conceptual and methodological framework. *Child Development, 75*, 354–360.

Hofferth, S. L., Boisjoly, J., & Duncan, G. (1995, April). *Does children's school attainment benefit from parental access to social capital?* Paper presented at the biennial meetings of the Society for Research in Child Development, Indianapolis.

Hoffman, H. J., & Hillman, L. S. (1992). Epidemiology of the sudden infant death syndrome: Maternal, neonatal, and postneonatal risk factors. *Clinics in Perinatology, 19*(4), 717–737.

Hoffman, M. L. (1982). Development of prosocial motivation: Empathy and guilt. In N. Eisenberg (Ed.), *The development of prosocial behavior* (pp. 281–314). New York: Academic Press.

Hoffman, M. L. (1988). Moral development. In M. H. Bornstein & M. E. Lamb (Eds.), *Developmental psychology: An advanced textbook* (2nd ed., pp. 497–548). Hillsdale, NJ: Erlbaum.

Hoffman, M. L. (2000). *Empathy and moral development: Implications for caring and justice.* Cambridge, England: Cambridge University Press.

Hoffman, M. L. (2007). The origins of empathic morality in toddlerhood. In C. Brownell & C. Kopp (Eds.), *Socioemotional development in the toddler years: Transitions and transformations.* New York: Guilford Press.

Holahan, C. K. (1988). Relation of life goals at age 70 to activity participation and health and psychological well-being among Terman's gifted men and women. *Psychology and Aging, 3*, 286–291.

Hollich, G., Golinkoff, R., & Hirsh-Pasek, K. (2007). Young children associate novel words with complex objects rather than salient parts. *Developmental Psychology, 43*, 1051–1061.

Holobow, N., Genesee, F., & Lambert, W. (1991). The effectiveness of a foreign language immersion program for children from different ethnic and social class backgrounds: Report 2. *Applied Psycholinguistics, 12*, 179–198.

Homer, B., & Hayward, E. (2008). Cognitive and representational development in children. In K. Cartwright (Ed.), *Literacy processes: Cognitive flexibility in learning and teaching* (pp. 19–41). New York: Guilford Press.

Honzik, M. P. (1986). The role of the family in the development of mental abilities: A 50-year study. In N. Datan, A. L. Greene, & H. W. Reese (Eds.), *Life-span developmental psychology: Intergenerational relations* (pp. 185–210). Hillsdale, NJ: Erlbaum.

Horowitz, F. D. (1987). *Exploring developmental theories: Toward a structural/behavioral model of development.* Hillsdale, NJ: Erlbaum.

Horowitz, F. D. (1990). Developmental models of individual differences. In J. Colombo & J. Fagen (Eds.), *Individual differences in infancy: Reliability, stability, prediction* (pp. 3–18). Hillsdale, NJ: Erlbaum.

Horowitz, F. D. (2003). Child development and the PITS: Simple questions, complex answers, and developmental theory. In M. Hertzig & E. Farber (Eds.), *Annual progress in child psychiatry and child development: 2000–2001* (pp. 3–19). New York: Brunner-Routledge.

Houck, G., & Lecuyer-Marcus, E. (2004). Maternal limit setting during toddlerhood, delay of gratification, and behavior problems at age five. *Infant Mental Health Journal, 25*, 28–46.

Hovell, M., Blumberg, E., Sipan, C., Hofstetter, C., Burkham, S., Atkins, C., & Felice, M. (1998). Skills training for pregnancy and AIDS prevention in Anglo and Latino youth. *Journal of Adolescent Health, 23*, 139–149.

Howes, C., Guerra, A., & Zucker, E. (2007). Cultural communities and parenting in Mexican-heritage families. *Parenting: Science and Practice, 7*, 235–270.

Hoyert, D., Kung, H., & Smith, B. (2005). Deaths: Preliminary data for 2003. *National Vital Statistics Reports, 53*(15), 1–48.

Hsu, V., & Rovee-Collier, C. (2006). Memory reactivation in the second year of life. *Infant Behavior and Human Development, 29*, 91–107.

Huang, H., & Hanley, J. (1997). A longitudinal study of phonological awareness, visual skills, and Chinese reading acquisition among first-graders in Taiwan. *International Journal of Behavioral Development, 20*, 249–268.

Hubel, D. H., & Weisel, T. N. (1963). Receptive fields of cells in striate cortex of very young, visually inexperienced kittens. *Journal of Neurophysiology, 26,* 994–1002.

Hudziak, J., van Beijsterveldt, C., Bartels, M., Rietveld, M., Rettew, D., Derks, E., & Boomsma, D. (2003). Individual differences in aggression: Genetic analyses by age, gender, and informant in 3-, 7-, and 10-year-old Dutch twins. *Behavior Genetics, 33,* 575–589.

Huebner, T., Vioet, T., Marx, I., Konrad, K., Fink, G., Herpetz, S., & Herpetz-Dahlmann, B. (2008). Morphometric brain abnormalities in boys with conduct disorder. *Journal of the American Academy of Child & Adolescent Psychiatry, 47,* 540–547.

Huesmann, L. R., Lagerspetz, K., & Eron, L. D. (1984). Intervening variables in the television violence-aggression relation: Evidence from two countries. *Developmental Psychology, 20,* 746–775.

Huesmann, L. R., Moise-Titus, J., Podolski, C., & Eron, L. D. (2003). Longitudinal relations between children's exposure to TV violence and their aggressive and violent behavior in young adulthood: 1977–1992. *Developmental Psychology, 39,* 201–221.

Hughes, C., Jaffee, S., Happé, F., Taylor, A., Caspi, A., & Moffitt, T. (2005). Origins of individual differences in theory of mind: From nature to nurture? *Child Development, 76,* 356–370.

Hulbert, A. (2003). *Raising America: Experts, parents, and a century of advice about children.* New York: Alfred A. Knopf.

Huntington, L., Hans, S. L., & Zeskind, P. S. (1990). The relations among cry characteristics, demographic variables, and developmental test scores in infants prenatally exposed to methadone. *Infant Behavior and Development, 13,* 533–538.

Hurry, J., & Sylva, K. (2007). Long-term outcomes of early reading intervention. *Journal of Research in Reading, 30,* 227–248.

Hurt, H., Malmus, D., Betancourt, L., Brodsky, N., & Giannetta, J. (2001). A prospective comparison of developmental outcomes of children with in utero cocaine exposure and controls using the Battelle Developmental Inventory. *Journal of Developmental and Behavioral Pediatrics, 22,* 27–34.

Hurwitz, E., Gunn, W. J., Pinsky, P. F., & Schonberger, L. B. (1991). Risk of respiratory illness associated with day-care attendance: A nationwide study. *Pediatrics, 87,* 62–69.

Huston, A., & Aronson, S. (2005). Mothers' time with infant and time in employment as predictors of mother-child relationships and children's early development. *Child Development, 76,* 467–482.

Huston, A. C. (1994). Children in poverty: Designing research to affect policy. *Social Policy Report, Society for Research in Child Development, 8*(2), 1–12.

Huston, A. C., & Wright, J. C. (1994). Educating children with television: The forms of the medium. In D. Zillmann, J. Bryant, & A. C. Huston (Eds.), *Media, children, and the family: Social scientific, psychodynamic, and clinical perspectives* (pp. 73–84). Hillsdale, NJ: Erlbaum.

Huston, A. C., & Wright, J. C. (1998). Mass media and children's development. In W. Damon (Ed.), *Handbook of child psychology: Vol. 4. Child psychology in practice* (5th ed., pp. 999–1058). New York: Wiley.

Hutt, S. J., Lenard, H. G., & Prechtl, H. E. R. (1969). Psychophysiological studies in newborn infants. In L. P. Lipsitt & H. W. Reese (Eds.), *Advances in child development and behavior* (Vol. 4, pp. 128–173). New York: Academic Press.

Huttenlocher, J. (1995, April). *Children's language in relation to input.* Paper presented at the biennial meetings of the Society for Research in Child Development, Indianapolis.

Huttenlocher, P. R. (1994). Synaptogenesis, synapse elimination, and neural plasticity in human cerebral cortex. In C. A. Nelson (Ed.), *The Minnesota symposia on child psychology* (Vol. 27, pp. 35–54). Hillsdale, NJ: Erlbaum.

Hyde, J. (2005). The gender similarities hypothesis. *American Psychologist, 60,* 581–592.

Hynd, G. W., Hern, K. L., Novey, E. S., Eliopulos, D., Marshall, R., Gonzalez, J. J., & Voeller, K. K. (1993). Attention deficit-hyperactivity disorder and asymmetry of the caudate nucleus. *Journal of Child Neurology, 8,* 339–347.

Iaquinta, A. (2006). Guided reading: A research-based response to the challenges of early reading instruction. *Early Childhood Education Journal, 33,* 1573–1707.

Iglowstein, I., Jenni, O., Molinari, L., & Largo, R. (2003). Sleep duration from infancy to adolescence: Reference values and generational trends. *Pediatrics, 111,* 302–307.

Inagaki, K., & Hatano, G. (2004). Vitalistic causality in young children's naive biology. *Trends in Cognitive Sciences, 8,* 356–362.

Ingoldsby, E., Shaw, D., Owens, E., & Winslow, E. (1999). A longitudinal study of interparental conflict, emotional and behavioral reactivity, and preschoolers' adjustment problems among low-income families. *Journal of Abnormal Child Psychology, 27,* 343–356.

Ingram, D. (1981). Early patterns of grammatical development. In R. E. Stark (Ed.), *Language behavior in infancy and early childhood* (pp. 327–358). New York: Elsevier/North-Holland.

Ingrassia, M. (1993, August 2). Daughters of Murphy Brown. *Newsweek,* 58–59.

Inhelder, B., & Piaget, J. (1958). *The growth of logical thinking from childhood to adolescence.* New York: Basic Books.

Interactive Digital Software Association. (1998). *Deep impact: How does the interactive entertainment industry affect the U.S. economy?* Retrieved from http://www.idsa.com

Isabella, R. A., Belsky, J., & von Eye, A. (1989). Origins of infant-mother attachment: An examination of interactional synchrony during the infant's first year. *Developmental Psychology, 25,* 12–21.

Issiaka, S., Cartoux, M., Zerbo, O., Tiendrebeogo, S., Meda, N., Dabis, F., & Van de Perre, P. (2001). Living with HIV: Women's experience in Burkina Faso, West Africa. *AIDS Care, 13,* 123–128.

Itier, R., & Taylor, M. (2004). Face inversion and contrast-reversal effects across development: In contrast to the expertise theory. *Developmental Science, 7,* 246–260.

Izard, C. E. (2007). Basic emotions, natural kinds, emotion schemas, and a new paradigm. *Perspectives on Psychological Science, 2,* 260–280.

Izard, C. E., & Abe, J. (2004). Developmental changes in facial expressions of emotions in the strange situation during the second year of life. *Emotion, 4,* 251–265.

Izard, C. E., Fantauzzo, C. A., Castle, J. M., Haynes, O. M., Rayias, M. F., & Putnam, P. H. (1995). The ontogeny and significance of infants' facial expressions in the first 9 months of life. *Developmental Psychology, 31,* 997–1013.

Izard, C. E., & Harris, P. (1995). Emotional development and developmental psychopathology. In D. Cicchetti & D. J. Cohen (Eds.), *Developmental psychopathology: Vol. 1. Theory and methods* (pp. 467–503). New York: Wiley.

Izard, C. E., & Malatesta, C. Z. (1987). Perspectives on emotional development I: Differential emotions theory of early emotional development. In J. D. Osofsky (Ed.), *Handbook of infant development* (2nd ed., pp. 494–554). New York: Wiley-Interscience.

Izard, C. E., Schultz, D., & Ackerman, B. P. (1997, April). *Emotion knowledge, social competence, and behavior problems in disadvantaged children.* Paper presented at the biennial meetings of the Society for Research in Child Development, Washington, DC.

Jackson, D., & Tein, J. (1998). Adolescents' conceptualization of adult roles: Relationships with age, gender, work goal, and maternal employment. *Sex Roles, 38,* 987–1008.

Jackson, E., Campos, J. J., & Fischer, K. W. (1978). The question of decalage between object permanence and person permanence. *Developmental Psychology, 14,* 1–10.

Jackson, L., & Bracken, B. (1998). Relationship between students' social status and global and domain-specific self-concepts. *Journal of School Psychology, 36*, 233–246.

Jackson, L., Pratt, M., Hunsberger, B., & Pancer, S. (2005). Optimism as a mediator of the relation between perceived parental authoritativeness and adjustment among adolescents: Finding the sunny side of the street. *Social Development, 14*, 273–304.

Jackson, L., von Eye, A., Biocca, F., Barbatsis, G., Zhao, Y., & Fitzgerald, H. (2006). Does home internet use influence the academic performance of low-income children? *Developmental Psychology, 42*, 429–435.

Jacobs, J., Lanza, S., Osgood, D., Eccles, J., & Wigfield, A. (2002). Changes in children's self-competence and values: Gender and domain differences across grades one through twelve. *Child Development, 73*, 509–527.

Jadack, R. A., Hyde, J. S., Moore, C. F., & Keller, M. L. (1995). Moral reasoning about sexually transmitted diseases. *Child Development, 66*, 167–177.

Jahnke, H. C., & Blanchard-Fields, F. (1993). A test of two models of adolescent egocentrism. *Journal of Youth & Adolescence, 22*, 313–326.

Jain, T., Harlow, B., & Hornstein, M. (2002). Insurance coverage and outcomes of in vitro fertilization. *New England Journal of Medicine, 347*, 661–666.

Jain, T., Missmer, S., & Hornstein, M. (2004). Trends in embryo-transfer practice and in outcomes of the use of assisted reproductive technology in the United States. *New England Journal of Medicine, 350*, 1639–1645.

Jambunathan, S., & Burts, D. (2003). Comparison of perception of self-competence among five ethnic groups of preschoolers in the US. *Early Childhood Education, 173*, 651–660.

James, W. (1890). *Principles of psychology.* Chicago: Encyclopaedia Britannica.

James, W. (1892). *Psychology: The briefer course.* New York: Holt.

Janosz, M., LeBlanc, M., Boulerice, B., & Tremblay, R. (2000). Predicting different types of school dropouts: A typological approach with two longitudinal samples. *Journal of Educational Psychology, 92*, 171–190.

Janssen, I., Heymsfield, S., Wang, Z., & Ross, R. (2000). Skeletal muscle mass and distribution in 468 men and women aged 18–88 yr. *Journal of Applied Physiology, 89*, 81–88.

Janssen, P. A., Holt, V. L., & Myers, S. J. (1994). Licensed midwife-attended, out-of-hospital births in Washington State: Are they safe? *Birth, 21*, 141–148.

Janssen, T., & Carton, J. (1999). The effects of locus of control and task difficulty on procrastination. *The Journal of Genetic Psychology, 160*, 436–442.

Jenkins, E. J., & Bell, C. C. (1997). Exposure and response to community violence among children and adolescents. In J. D. Osofsky (Ed.), *Children in a violent society* (pp. 9–31). New York: Guilford Press.

Jenkins, J., & Astington, J. (2000). Theory of mind and social behavior: Causal models tested in a longitudinal study. *Merrill-Palmer Quarterly, 46*, 203–220.

Jenkins, J., Simpson, A., Dunn, J., Rasbash, J., & O'Connor, T. (2005). Mutual influence of marital conflict and children's behavior problems: Shared and nonshared family risks. *Child Development, 76*, 24–39.

Jenkins, J. M., & Astington, J. W. (1996). Cognitive factors and family structure associated with theory of mind development in young children. *Developmental Psychology, 32*, 70–78.

Jenks, K., van Lieshout, E., & de Moor, J. (2008, in press). Arithmetic achievement in children with cerebral palsy or spina bifida meningomyelocele. *Remedial and Special Education.*

Jensen, A. R. (1980). *Bias in mental testing.* New York: Free Press.

Jessor, R. (1992). Risk behavior in adolescence: A psychosocial framework for understanding and action. *Developmental Review, 12*, 374–390.

Jirtle, R., & Weidman, J. (2007). Imprinted and more equal. *American Scientist, 95*, 143–149.

John, O. P., Caspi, A., Robins, R. W., Moffitt, T. E., & Stouthamer-Loeber, M. (1994). The "little five": Exploring the nomological network of the five-factor model of personality in adolescent boys. *Child Development, 65*, 160–178.

Johnson, A. (2007). The maternal experience of kangaroo holding. *Journal of Obstetric, Gynecologic, & Neonatal Nursing, 36*, 568–573.

Johnson, J. W. C., & Yancey, M. K. (1996). A critique of the new recommendations for weight gain in pregnancy. *American Journal of Obstetrics and Gynecology, 174*, 254–258.

Johnson, K., & Daviss, B. (2005). Outcomes of planned home births with certified professional midwives: Large prospective study in North America. *British Medical Journal, 330*, 1416.

Johnson, M. (2005). Developmental neuroscience, psychophysiology, and genetics. In M. Bornstein & M. Lamb (Eds.), *Developmental science: An advanced textbook* (5th ed., pp. 187–222). Hillsdale, NJ: Erlbaum.

Johnston, D., Nicholls, M., Shah, M., & Shields, M. (2008, in press). Nature's experiment? Handedness and early childhood development. *Demography.*

Johnston, J., Durieux-Smith, A., & Bloom, K. (2005). Teaching gestural signs to infants to advance child development: A review of the evidence. *First Language, 25*, 235–251.

Johnston, L., O'Malley, P. M., Bachman, J., & Schulenberg, J. (2007). *Monitoring the future: National results on adolescent drug use: Overview of key findings.* NIH Publication No. 07-6202. Retrieved June 22, 2007, from http://monitoringthefuture.org/pubs/monographs/overview2006.pdf

Jones, A. (2008). The AAI as clinical tool. In H. Steele & M. Steele (Eds.), *Clinical applications of the Adult Attachment Interview.* (pp. 175–194). New York: Guilford Press.

Jones, M. C. (1924). A laboratory study of fear: The case of Peter. *Pedagogical Seminary, 31*, 308–315.

Jones, S. (2003). *Let the games begin: Gaming technology and entertainment among college students.* Washington, DC: Pew Internet and American Life Project. Retrieved May 17, 2006, from http://www.pewinternet.org/PPF/r/93/report_display.asp

Jonsson, P. (2003). The new face of homeschooling. *Christian Science Monitor Online.* Retrieved June 23, 2004, from http://www.csmonitor.com/2003/0429/p01s01-ussc.html

Jordan, N. C., Huttenlocher, J., & Levine, S. C. (1992). Differential calculation abilities in young children from middle- and low-income families. *Developmental Psychology, 28*, 644–653.

Joseph, K., Young, D., Dodds, L., O'Connell, C., Allen, V., Chandra, S., & Allen, A. (2003). Changes in maternal characteristics and obstetric practice and recent increases in primary cesarean delivery. *Obstetrics and Gynecology, 102*, 791–800.

Joseph, R. (2000). Fetal brain behavior and cognitive development. *Developmental Review, 20*, 81–98.

Josephs, R., Newman, M., Brown, R., & Beer, J. (2003). Status, testosterone, and human intellectual performance. *Psychological Science, 14*, 158–163.

Jusczyk, P., & Hohne, E. (1997). Infants' memory for spoken words. *Science, 277*, n.p.

Justice, L., Invernizzi, M., Geller, K., Sullivan, A., & Welsch, J. (2005). Descriptive-developmental performance of at-risk preschoolers on early literacy tasks. *Reading Psychology, 26*, 1–25.

Kado, S., & Takagi, R. (1996). Biological aspects. In S. Sandberg (Ed.), *Hyperactivity disorders of childhood* (pp. 246–279). Cambridge, England: Cambridge University Press.

Kagan, J. (1971). *Change and continuity in infancy.* New York: Wiley.

Kagan, J. (1989). *Unstable ideas: Temperament, cognition, and self.* Cambridge, MA: Harvard University Press.

Kagan, J. (2007). A trio of concerns. *Perspectives on Psychological Science, 2,* 361–376.

Kagan, J., & Fox, N. (2006). Biology, culture, and temperamental biases. In N. Eisenberg, W. Damon, & R. Lerner (Eds.), *Handbook of child psychology: Vol. 3, Social, emotional, and personality development* (6th ed., pp. 167–225). Hoboken, NJ: Wiley.

Kagan, J., Arcus, D., Snidman, N., Feng, W. Y., Hendler, J., & Greene, S. (1994). Reactivity in infants: A cross-national comparison. *Developmental Psychology, 30,* 342–345.

Kagan, J., & Herschkowitz, N. (2005). *A young mind in a growing brain.* Mahwah, NJ: Erlbaum.

Kagan, J., Kearsley, R., & Zelazo, P. (1978). *Infancy: Its place in human development.* Cambridge, MA: Harvard University Press.

Kagan, J., Klein, R., Finley, G., Rogoff, B., Nolan, E., & Greenbaum, C. (1979). A cross-cultural study of cognitive development. *Monographs of the Society for Research in Child Development, 44,* 1–77.

Kagan, J., Reznick, J. S., & Snidman, N. (1990). The temperamental qualities of inhibition and lack of inhibition. In M. Lewis & S. M. Miller (Eds.), *Handbook of developmental psychopathology* (pp. 219–226). New York: Plenum Press.

Kagan, J., Snidman, N., & Arcus, D. (1993). On the temperamental categories of inhibited and uninhibited children. In K. H. Rubin & J. B. Asendorpf (Eds.), *Social withdrawal, inhibition, and shyness in childhood* (pp. 19–28). Hillsdale, NJ: Erlbaum.

Kahn, J., Slap, G., Bernstein, D., Kollar, L., Tissot, A., Hillard, P., & Rosenthal, S. (2005). Psychological, behavioral, and interpersonal impact of human papilloma virus and Pap test results. *Journal of Women's Health, 14,* 650–659.

Kail, R. (1990). *The development of memory in children* (3rd ed.). New York: Freeman.

Kail, R. (1997). Processing time, imagery, and spatial memory. *Journal of Experimental Child Psychology, 64,* 67–78.

Kail, R. (2004). Cognitive development includes global and domain-specific processes. *Merrill-Palmer Quarterly, 50,* 445–455.

Kail, R. (2007a). Cognitive development includes global and domain-specific processes. In G. Ladd (Ed.), *Appraising the human developmental sciences: Essays in honor of Merrill-Palmer Quarterly* (pp. 56–66). Detroit: Wayne State University Press.

Kail, R. (2007b). Longitudinal evidence that increases in processing speed and working memory enhance children's reasoning. *Psychological Science, 18,* 312–313.

Kail, R., & Hall, L. (1999). Sources of developmental change in children's word-problem performance. *Journal of Educational Psychology, 91,* 660–668.

Kaiser Family Foundation. (2004). *Children, the digital divide, and federal policy.* Retrieved September 9, 2008, from http://www.kff.org/entmedia/loader.cfm?url=/commonspot/security/getfile.cfm&PageID=46360

Kaiser Family Foundation. (2005). *Sex on TV.* Retrieved June 21, 2007, from http://www.kff.org/entmedia/entmedia110905pkg

Kaltiala-Heino, R., Kosunen, E., & Rimpela, M. (2003). Pubertal timing, sexual behavior and self-reported depression in middle adolescence. *Journal of Adolescence, 26,* 531–545.

Kamps, D., Tankersley, M., & Ellis, C. (2000). Social skills interventions for young at-risk students: A 2-year follow-up study. *Behavioral Disorders, 25,* 310–324.

Kandel, D., & Wu, P. (1995). The contributions of mothers and fathers to the intergenerational transmission of cigarette smoking in adolescence. *Journal of Research on Adolescence, 5,* 225–252.

Kanemura, H., Aihara, M., Aoki, S., Araki, T., & Nakazawa, S. (2004). Development of the prefrontal lobe in infants and children: A three-dimensional magnetic resonance volumetric study. *Brain and Development, 25,* 195–199.

Kann, L., Warren, C. W., Harris, W. A., Collins, J. L., Douglas, K. A., Collins, M. E., Williams, B. I., Ross, J. G., & Kolbe, L. J. (1995). Youth risk behavior surveillance—United States, 1993. *Morbidity & Mortality Weekly Reports, 44*(SS 1), 1–55.

Kaplan, P., Bachorowski, J., Smoski, M., & Zinser, M. (2001). Role of clinical diagnosis and medication use in effects of maternal depression on infant directed speech. *Infancy, 2,* 537–548.

Kashima, Y., Kashima, E., Chiu, C., Farsides, T., Gelfand, M., Hong, Y., Kim, U., Strack, F., Werth, L., Yuki, M., & Yzerbyt, V. (2005). Culture, essentialism, and agency: Are individuals universally believed to be more real entities than groups? *European Journal of Social Psychology, 35,* 147–169.

Katz, L., & Woodin, E. (2002). Hostility, hostile detachment, and conflict engagement in marriages: Effects on child and family functioning. *Child Development, 73,* 636–652.

Katz, P. A., & Ksansnak, K. R. (1994). Developmental aspects of gender role flexibility and traditionality in middle childhood and adolescence. *Developmental Psychology, 30,* 272–282.

Kauffman, J. (2005). *Characteristics of emotional and behavioral disorders of children and youth.* Upper Saddle River, NJ: Merrill.

Kaufman, A., & Kaufman, N. (2004). *Kaufman Assessment Battery for Children (KABC) II.* Bloomington, MN: Pearson AGS.

Kaufman, J., Kaufman, A., Kaufman-Singer, J., & Kaufman, N. (2005). The Kaufman Assessment Battery for Children–Second Edition and the Kaufman Adolescent and Adult Intelligence Test. In D. Flanagan & P. Harrison (Eds.), *Contemporary intellectual assessment: Theories, tests, and issues* (pp. 344–370). New York: Guilford Press.

Kavšek, M. (2002). The perception of static subjective contours in infancy. *Child Development, 73,* 331–344.

Kaye, K. (1982). *The mental and social life of babies: How parents create persons.* Chicago: University of Chicago Press.

Keating, D. P. (1980). Thinking processes in adolescence. In J. Adelson (Ed.), *Handbook of adolescent psychology* (pp. 211–246). New York: Wiley.

Keech, R. (2002). Ophthalmology. In A. Rudolph, R. Kamei, & K. Overby (Eds.), *Rudolph's fundamentals of pediatrics* (3rd ed., pp. 847–862). New York: McGraw-Hill.

Keefe, S. E., & Padilla, A. M. (1987). *Chicano ethnicity.* Albuquerque: University of New Mexico Press.

Keen, R. (2003). Representation of objects and events: Why do infants look so smart and toddlers look so dumb? *Current Directions in Psychological Science, 12,* 79–83.

Keeney, T. J., Cannizzo, S. R., & Flavell, J. H. (1967). Spontaneous and induced verbal rehearsal in a recall task. *Child Development, 38,* 935–966.

Kelley, M. L., Sanchez-Hucles, J., & Walker, R. R. (1993). Correlates of disciplinary practices in working- to middle-class African-American mothers. *Merrill-Palmer Quarterly, 39,* 252–264.

Kendler, K., Thornton, L., Gilman, S., & Kessler, R. (2000). Sexual orientation in a U.S. national sample of twin and nontwin sibling pairs. *American Journal of Psychiatry, 157,* 1843–1846.

Keniston, K. (1970). Youth: A "new" stage in life. *American Scholar, 8* (Autumn), 631–654.

Kennedy, D. M. (1995). Glimpses of a highly gifted child in a heterogeneous classroom. *Roeper Review, 17,* 164–168.

Kerns, K. A. (1996). Individual differences in friendship quality: Links to child-mother attachment. In W. M. Bukowski, A. F. Newcomb, & W. W. Hartup (Eds.), *The company they keep: Friendship in childhood and adolescence* (pp. 137–157). Cambridge, England: Cambridge University Press.

Kerr, C., McDowell, B., & McDonough, S. (2007). The relationship between gross motor function and participation restriction in children with cerebral palsy: An exploratory analysis. *Child: Care, Health and Development, 33,* 22–27.

Kiang, L., Harter, S., & Whitesell, N. (2007). Relational expression of ethnic identity in Chinese Americans. *Journal of Social and Personal Relationships, 24,* 277–296.

Kidger, J. (2004). 'You realise it could happen to you': The benefits to pupils of young mothers delivering school sex education. *Sex Education, 4,* 185–197.

Kilgore, P. E., Holman, R. C., Clarke, M. J., & Glass, R. I. (1995). Trends of diarrheal disease-associated mortality in US children, 1968 through 1991. *Journal of the American Medical Association, 274,* 1143–1148.

Killen, M., Pisacane, K., Lee-Kim, J., & Ardila-Rey, A. (2001). Fairness or stereotypes? Young children's priorities when evaluating group exclusion and inclusion. *Developmental Psychology, 37,* 587–596.

Kilpatrick, S. J., & Laros, R. K. (1989). Characteristics of normal labor. *Obstetrics and Gynecology, 74,* 85–87.

Kim, H., Baydar, N., & Greek, A. (2003). Testing conditions influence the race gap in cognition and achievement estimated by household survey data. *Journal of Applied Developmental Psychology, 23,* 567–582.

Kindermann, T. (2007). Effects of naturally existing peer groups on changes in academic engagement in a cohort of sixth graders. *Child Development, 78,* 1186–1203.

Kirk, K., Bailey, J., & Martin, N. (2000). Etiology of male sexual orientation in an Australian twin sample. *Psychology, Evolution, & Gender, 2,* 301–311.

Kirk, S., Gallagher, J., & Anastasiow, N. (1993). *Educating exceptional children* (7th ed.). Boston: Houghton Mifflin.

Kirkcaldy, B., Siefen, G., Surall, D., & Bischoff, R. (2004). Predictors of drug and alcohol abuse among children and adolescents. *Personality & Individual Differences, 36,* 247–265.

Kirsh, S., & Cassidy, J. (1997). Preschoolers' attention to and memory for attachment-relevant information. *Child Development, 68,* 1143–1153.

Klaczynski, P., Fauth, J., & Swanger, A. (1998). Adolescent identity: Rational vs. experiential processing, formal operations, and critical thinking beliefs. *Journal of Youth & Adolescence, 27,* 185–207.

Klahr, D. (1992). Information-processing approaches to cognitive development. In M. H. Bernstein & M. E. Lamb (Eds.), *Developmental psychology: An advanced textbook* (3rd ed., pp. 273–335). Hillsdale, NJ: Erlbaum.

Klar, A. (2003). Human handedness and scalp hair-whorl direction develop from a common genetic mechanism. *Genetics, 165,* 269–276.

Klass, P., & Costello, E. (2003). *Quirky kids: Understanding and helping your child who doesn't fit in—when to worry and when not to worry.* New York: Ballantine Books.

Klebanov, P. K., Brooks-Gunn, J., Hofferth, S., & Duncan, G. J. (1995, April). *Neighborhood resources, social support and maternal competence.* Paper presented at the biennial meetings of the Society for Research in Child Development, Indianapolis.

Klein, A., & Swartz, S. (1996). *Reading Recovery in California: Program overview.* San Francisco: San Francisco Unified School District.

Kliegman, R. (1998). Fetal and neonatal medicine. In R. Behrman & R. Kliegman (Eds.), *Nelson essentials of pediatrics* (3rd ed., pp. 167–225). Philadelphia: Saunders.

Kloos, H., Haddad, J., & Keen, R. (2006). Which cues are available to 24-month-olds? Evidence from point-of-gaze measures during search. *Infant Behavior and Development, 29,* 243–250.

Knafo, A., Daniel, D., & Khoury-Kassabri, M. (2008). Values as protective factors against violent behavior in Jewish and Arab high schools in Israel. *Child Development, 79,* 652–667.

Knight, G. P., Cota, M. K., & Bernal, M. E. (1993). The socialization of cooperative, competitive, and individualistic preferences among Mexican American children: The mediating role of ethnic identity. *Hispanic Journal of Behavioral Sciences, 15,* 291–309.

Kobayashi, M., Haynes, C., Macaruso, P., Hook, P., & Kato, J. (2005). Effects of mora deletion, nonword repetition, rapid naming, and visual search performance on beginning reading in Japanese. *Annals of Dyslexia, 55,* 105–128.

Kochanska, G. (1997). Mutually responsive orientation between mothers and their young children: Implications for early socialization. *Child Development, 68,* 94–112.

Kochanska, G., & Aksan, N. (2006). Children's conscience and self-regulation. *Journal of Personality, 74,* 1587–1617.

Kochanska, G., Gross, J., Lin, M., & Nichols, K. (2002). Guilt in young children: Development, determinants, and relations with a broader system of standards. *Child Development, 73,* 461–482.

Kochenderfer, B. J., & Ladd, G. W. (1996). Peer victimization: Cause or consequence of school maladjustment. *Child Development, 67,* 1305–1317.

Kodituwakku, P., May, P. A., Clericuzio, C., & Weers, D. (2001). Emotion-related learning in individuals prenatally exposed to alcohol: An investigation of the relation between set shifting, extinction of responses, and behavior. *Neuropsychologia, 39,* 699–708.

Koechlin, E., Basso, G., Pietrini, P., Panzer, S., & Grafman, J. (1999). Exploring the role of the anterior prefrontal cortex in human cognition. *Nature, 399,* 148–151.

Koenen, K. C., Moffitt, T. E., Poulton, R., Martin, J., & Caspi, A. (2007). Early childhood factors associated with the development of post-traumatic stress disorder: Results from a longitudinal birth cohort. *Psychological Medicine, 37,* 181–192.

Koenig, A., Cicchetti, D., & Rogosch, F. (2004). Moral development: The association between maltreatment and young children's prosocial behaviors and moral transgressions. *Social Development, 13,* 97–106.

Koeppe, R. (1996). Language differentiation in bilingual children: The development of grammatical and pragmatic competence. *Linguistics, 34,* 927–954.

Koesten, J. (2004). Family communication patterns, sex of subject, and communication competence. *Communication Monographs, 71,* 226–244.

Kohlberg, L. (1964). Development of moral character and moral ideology. In M. L. Hoffman & L. W. Hoffman (Eds.), *Review of child development research* (Vol. 1, pp. 283–332). New York: Russell Sage Foundation.

Kohlberg, L. (1966). A cognitive-developmental analysis of children's sex-role concept and attitudes. In E. E. Maccoby (Ed.), *The development of sex differences* (pp. 82–172). Stanford, CA: Stanford University Press.

Kohlberg, L. (1975). The cognitive-developmental approach to moral education. *Phi Delta Kappan,* 670–677.

Kohlberg, L. (1976). Moral stages and moralization: The cognitive-developmental approach. In T. Lickona (Ed.), *Moral development and behavior: Theory, research, and social issues* (pp. 31–53). New York: Holt.

Kohlberg, L. (1978). Revisions in the theory and practice of moral development. *New Directions for Child Development, 2,* 83–88.

Kohlberg, L. (1980). *The meaning and measurement of moral development.* Worcester, MA: Clark University Press.

Kohlberg, L. (1981). *Essays on moral development: Vol. 1. The philosophy of moral development.* New York: Harper & Row.

Kohlberg, L., Boyd, D. R., & Levine, C. (1990). The return of stage 6: Its principle and moral point of view. In T. E. Wren (Ed.), *The moral domain: Essays in the ongoing discussion between philosophy and the social sciences.* Cambridge: MIT Press.

Kohlberg, L., & Elfenbein, D. (1975). The development of moral judgments concerning capital punishment. *American Journal of Orthopsychiatry, 54,* 614–640.

Kohlberg, L., & Ullian, D. Z. (1974). Stages in the development of psychosexual concepts and attitudes. In R. C. Friedman, R. M. Richart, & R. L. Vande Wiele (Eds.), *Sex differences in behavior* (pp. 209–222). New York: Wiley.

Kopp, C. B., & Kaler, S. R. (1989). Risk in infancy: Origins and implications. *American Psychologist, 44,* 224–230.

Koppenhaver, D., Hendrix, M., & Williams, A. (2007). Toward evidence-based literacy interventions for children with severe and multiple disabilities. *Seminars in Speech & Language, 28,* 79–90.

Korner, A. F., Hutchinson, C. A., Koperski, J. A., Kraemer, H. C., & Schneider, P. A. (1981). Stability of individual differences of neonatal motor and crying patterns. *Child Development, 52,* 83–90.

Koskinen, P., Blum, I., Bisson, S., Phillips, S., et al. (2000). Book access, shared reading, and audio models: The effects of supporting the literacy learning of linguistically diverse students in school and at home. *Journal of Educational Psychology, 92,* 23–36.

Kost, K. (1997). The effects of support on the economic well-being of young fathers. *Families in Society, 78,* 370–382.

Kostanski, M., Fisher, A., & Gullone, E. (2004). Current conceptualisation of body image dissatisfaction: Have we got it wrong? *Journal of Child Psychology and Psychiatry, 45,* 1317–1325.

Kosterman, R., Graham, J., Hawkins, J., Catalano, R., & Herrenkohl, T. (2001). Childhood risk factors for persistence of violence in the transition to adulthood: A social development perspective. *Violence & Victims, 16,* 355–369.

Krcmar, M., & Vieira, E. (2005). Imitating life, imitating television: The effects of family and television models on children's moral reasoning. *Communication Research, 32,* 267–294.

Kroger, J. (2007). Why is identity achievement so elusive? *Identity, 7,* 331–348.

Kronlund, A., & Whittlesea, B. (2005). Seeing double: Levels of processing can cause false memory. *Canadian Journal of Experimental Psychology, 59,* 11–16.

Kron-Sperl, V., Schneider, W., & Hasselhorn, M. (2008). The development and effectiveness of memory strategies in kindergarten and elementary school: Findings from the Würzburg and Göttingen longitudinal memory studies. *Cognitive Development, 23,* 79–104.

Krueger, C., Holditch-Davis, D., Quint, S., & DeCasper, A. (2004). Recurring auditory experience in the 28- to 34-week-old fetus. *Infant Behavioral Development, 27,* 537–543.

Kuczaj, S. A., II. (1977). The acquisition of regular and irregular past tense forms. *Journal of Verbal Learning and Verbal Behavior, 49,* 319–326.

Kuczaj, S. A., II. (1978). Children's judgments of grammatical and ungrammatical irregular past tense verbs. *Child Development, 49,* 319–326.

Kuhn, D. (1992). Cognitive development. In M. H. Bornstein & M. E. Lamb (Eds.), *Developmental psychology: An advanced textbook* (3rd ed., pp. 211–272). Hillsdale, NJ: Erlbaum.

Kuhn, D. (2008). Formal operations from a twenty-first-century perspective. *Human Development, 51,* 48–55.

Kuhn, D., Garcia-Mila, M., Zohar, A., & Andersen, C. (1995). Strategies of knowledge acquisition. *Monographs of the Society for Research in Child Development, 60*(Serial No. 245).

Kuhn, D., Kohlberg, L., Languer, J., & Haan, N. (1977). The development of formal operations in logical and moral judgment. *Genetic Psychology Monographs, 95,* 97–188.

Kuperman, S., Schlosser, S., Kramer, J., Bucholz, K., Hesselbrock, V., Reich, T., & Reich, W. (2001). Developmental sequence from disruptive behavior diagnosis to adolescent alcohol dependence. *American Journal of Psychiatry, 158,* 2022–2026.

Kupersmidt, J. B., Griesler, P., DeRosier, M. E., Patterson, C. J., & Davis, P. W. (1995). Childhood aggression and peer relations in the context of family and neighborhood factors. *Child Development, 66,* 360–375.

Kurdek, L. (2003). Correlates of parents' perceptions of behavioral problems in their young children. *Journal of Applied Developmental Psychology, 24,* 457–473.

Kurdek, L. A., & Fine, M. A. (1994). Family acceptance and family control as predictors of adjustment in young adolescents: Linear, curvilinear, or interactive effects? *Child Development, 65,* 1137–1146.

Kusché, C. A., & Greenberg, M. T. (1994). *The PATHS Curriculum.* Seattle: Developmental Research and Programs.

Kuttler, A., LaGreca, A., & Prinstein, M. (1999). Friendship qualities and social-emotional functioning of adolescents with close, cross-sex friendships. *Journal of Research on Adolescence, 9,* 339–366.

Ladd, G., Herald-Brown, S., & Reiser, M. (2008). Does chronic classroom peer rejection predict the development of children's classroom participation during the grade school years? *Child Development, 79,* 1001–1015.

Ladd, G., & Troop-Gordon, W. (2003). The role of chronic peer difficulties in the development of children's psychological adjustment problems. *Child Development, 74,* 1344–1367.

La Freniere, P., Strayer, F. F., & Gauthier, R. (1984). The emergence of same-sex affiliative preferences among preschool peers: A developmental/ethological perspective. *Child Development, 55,* 1958–1965.

Lafuente, M., Grifol, R., Segarra, J., Soriano, J., Gorba, M., & Montesinos, A. (1997). Effects of the Firstart method of prenatal stimulation on psychomotor development: The first six months. *Pre- & Peri-Natal Psychology Journal, 11,* 151–162.

Lai, B., Tang, C., & Tse, W. (2005). Prevalence and psychosocial correlates of disordered eating among Chinese pregnant women in Hong Kong. *Eating Disorders: The Journal of Treatment & Prevention, 13,* 171–186.

Lai, K., & McBride-Chang, C. (2001). Suicidal ideation, parenting style, and family climate among Hong Kong adolescents. *International Journal of Psychology, 36,* 81–87.

Laible, D., Panfile, T., & Makariev, D. (2008). The quality and frequency of mother-toddler conflict: Links with attachment and temperament. *Child Development, 79,* 426–443.

Laidra, K., Pullmann, H., & Allik, J. (2007). Personality and intelligence as predictors of academic achievement: A cross-sectional study from elementary to secondary school. *Personality and Individual Differences, 42,* 441–451.

Lamb, M., Bornstein, M., & Teti, D. (2002). *Social development in infancy* (4th ed.). Mahwah, NJ: Erlbaum.

Lamb, M., & Lewis, C. (2005). The role of parent-child relationships in child development. In M. Bornstein & M. Lamb (Eds.), *Developmental science: An advanced textbook* (5th ed., pp. 429–468). Hillsdale, NJ: Erlbaum.

Lamb, M. E., Frodi, M., Hwang, C., & Frodi, A. M. (1983). Effects of paternal involvement on infant preferences for mothers and fathers. *Child Development, 54,* 450–458.

Lamb, M. E., Sternberg, K. J., & Prodromidis, M. (1992). Nonmaternal care and the security of infant-mother attachment: A reanalysis of the data. *Infant Behavior and Development, 15,* 71–83.

Lambert, S. (2005). Gay and lesbian families: What we know and where to go from here. *Family Journal: Counseling & Therapy, 13*, 43–51.

Lamborn, S. D., Dornbusch, S. M., & Steinberg, L. (1996). Ethnicity and community context as moderators of the relations between family decision making and adolescent adjustment. *Child Development, 67*, 283–301.

Lamborn, S. D., Mounts, N. S., Steinberg, L., & Dornbusch, S. M. (1991). Patterns of competence and adjustment among adolescents from authoritative, authoritarian, indulgent, and neglectful families. *Child Development, 62*, 1049–1065.

Lamke, L. K. (1982). Adjustment and sex-role orientation. *Journal of Youth & Adolescence, 11*, 247–259.

Landry, S., Smith, K., & Swank, P. (2006). Responsive parenting: Establishing early foundations for social, communication, and independent problem-solving skills. *Developmental Psychology, 42*, 627–642.

Laney, D. (2002). The gastrointestinal tract & liver. In A. Rudolph, R. Kamei, & K. Overby (Eds.), *Rudolph's fundamentals of pediatrics* (3rd ed., pp. 466–512).

Langer, G., Arndt, C., & Sussman, D. (2004). *Primetime Live poll: American sex survey analysis.* Retrieved June 22, 2007, from http://abcnews.go.com/Primetime/PollVault/story?id=156921&page=1

Langlois, J. H., Ritter, J. M., Roggman, L. A., & Vaughn, L. S. (1991). Facial diversity and infant preferences for attractive faces. *Developmental Psychology, 27*, 79–84.

Langlois, J. H., Roggman, L. A., Casey, R. J., Ritter, J. M., Rieser-Danner, L. A., & Jenkins, V. Y. (1987). Infant preferences for attractive faces: Rudiments of a stereotype? *Developmental Psychology, 23*, 363–369.

Langlois, J. H., Roggman, L. A., & Rieser-Danner, L. A. (1990). Infants' differential social responses to attractive and unattractive faces. *Developmental Psychology, 26*, 153–159.

La Paro, K., Justice, L., Skibbe, L., & Pianta, R. (2004). Relations among maternal, child, and demographic factors and the persistence of preschool language impairment. *American Journal of Speech-Language Pathology, 13*, 291–303.

Larson, R. (2000). Toward a psychology of positive youth development. *American Psychologist, 55*, 170–183.

Lau, A., Uba, A., & Lehman, D. (2002). Infectious diseases. In A. Rudolph, R. Kamei, & K. Overby (Eds.), *Rudolph's fundamentals of pediatrics* (3rd ed., pp. 289–389).

Lau, J., Riisdijk, F., Gregory, A., McGuffin, P., & Elev, T. (2007). Pathways to childhood depressive symptoms: The role of social, cognitive, and genetic risk factors. *Developmental Psychology, 43*, 1402–1414.

Laub, J. H., & Sampson, R. J. (1995). The long-term effect of punitive discipline. In J. McCord (Ed.), *Coercion and punishment in long-term perspectives* (pp. 247–258). Cambridge, England: Cambridge University Press.

Lauritsen, M., Pedersen, C., & Mortensen, P. (2004). The incidence and prevalence of pervasive developmental disorders: A Danish population-based study. *Psychological Medicine, 34*, 1339–1346.

Laursen, B. (1995). Conflict and social interaction in adolescent relationships. *Journal of Research on Adolescence, 5*, 55–70.

Laursen, B., & Mooney, K. (2007). Individual differences in adolescent dating and adjustment. In R. Engels, M. Kerr, & H. Stattin (Eds.), *Friends, lovers and groups: Key relationships in adolescence* (pp. 81–91). New York: Wiley.

Law, A., Logie, R., & Pearson, D. (2006). The impact of secondary tasks on multitasking in a virtual environment. *Acta Psychologica, 122*, 27–44.

Lawrence, V., Houghton, S., Douglas, G., Durkin, K., Whiting, K., & Tannock, R. (2004). Children with ADHD: Neuropsychological testing and real-world activities. *Journal of Attention Disorders, 7*, 137–149.

Layton, L., Deeny, K., Tall, G., & Upton, G. (1996). Researching and promoting phonological awareness in the nursery class. *Journal of Research in Reading, 19*, 1–13.

Leaper, C., Breed, L., Hoffman, L., & Perlman, C. (2002). Variations in the gender-stereotyped content of children's television cartoons across genres. *Journal of Applied Social Psychology, 32*, 1653–1662.

Learmonth, A., Lamberth, R., & Rovee-Collier, C. (2004). Generalization of deferred imitation during the first year of life. *Journal of Experimental Child Psychology, 88*, 297–318.

Learmonth, A., Lamberth, R., & Rovee-Collier, C. (2005). The social context of imitation in infancy. *Journal of Experimental Child Psychology, 91*, 297–314.

Lebra, T. S. (1994). Mother and child in Japanese socialization: A Japan-U.S. comparison. In P. M. Greenfield & R. R. Cocking (Eds.), *Cross-cultural roots of minority child development* (pp. 259–274). Hillsdale, NJ: Erlbaum.

Lee, C. C. (1985). Successful rural black adolescents: A psychological profile. *Adolescence, 20*, 129–142.

Lee, V. E., Burkham, D. T., Zimiles, H., & Ladewski, B. (1994). Family structure and its effect on behavioral and emotional problems in young adolescents. *Journal of Research on Adolescence, 4*, 405–437.

Leff, M., Moolchan, E., Cookus, B., Spurgeon, L., Evans, L., London, E., Kimes, A., Schroeder, J., & Ernst, M. (2003). Predictors of smoking initiation among at risk youth: A controlled study. *Journal of Child & Adolescent Substance Abuse, 13*, 59–76.

Leichtman, M. D., & Ceci, S. J. (1995). The effects of stereotypes and suggestions on preschoolers' reports. *Developmental Psychology, 31*, 568–578.

Lengua, L., & Kovacs, E. (2005). Bidirectional associations between temperament and parenting and the prediction of adjustment problems in middle childhood. *Journal of Applied Developmental Psychology, 26*, 21–38.

Leonard, L., Camarata, S., Pawtowska, M., Brown, B., & Camarata, M. (2008). The acquisition of tense and agreement morphemes by children with specific language impairment during intervention: Phase 3. *Journal of Speech, Language, and Hearing Research, 51*, 120–125.

Lerner, R., Theokas, C., & Bobek, C. (2005). Concepts and theories of human development: Historical and contemporary dimensions. In M. Bornstein & M. Lamb (Eds.), *Developmental science: An advanced textbook* (5th ed., pp. 3–44). Hillsdale, NJ: Erlbaum.

Lesaux, N., & Siegel, L. (2003). The development of reading in children who speak English as a second language. *Developmental Psychology, 39*, 1005–1019.

Leve, L. D., & Fagot, B. I. (1995, April). *The influence of attachment style and parenting behavior on children's prosocial behavior with peers.* Paper presented at the biennial meetings of the Society for Research in Child Development, Indianapolis.

Levine, D. (2002). MR imaging of fetal central nervous system abnormalities. *Brain & Cognition, 50*, 432–448.

Levine, J., Pollack, H., & Comfort, M. (2001). Academic and behavioral outcomes among the children of young mothers. *Journal of Marriage and the Family, 63*, 355–369.

Levine, S., Huttenlocher, J., Taylor A., & Langrock, A. (1999). Early sex differences in spatial skill. *Developmental Psychology, 35*, 940–949.

Levine, T., Liu, J., Das, A., Lester, B., Lagasse, L., Shankaran, S., Bada, H., Bauer, C., & Higgins, R. (2008). Effects of prenatal cocaine exposure on special education in school-aged children. *Pediatrics, 122*, e83–e91.

Levitt, M. J., Guacci-Franco, N., & Levitt, J. L. (1993). Convoys of social support in childhood and early adolescence: Structure and function. *Developmental Psychology, 29,* 811–818.

Levorato, M., & Donati, V. (1999). Conceptual and lexical knowledge of shame in Italian children and adolescents. *International Journal of Behavioral Development, 23,* 873–898.

Levy, G. D., & Fivush, R. (1993). Scripts and gender: A new approach for examining gender-role development. *Developmental Review, 13,* 126–146.

Levy-Shiff, R., Lerman, M., Har-Even, D., & Hod, M. (2002). Maternal adjustment and infant outcome in medically defined high-risk pregnancy. *Developmental Psychology, 38,* 93–103.

Levy-Shiff, R., Vakil, E., Dimitrovsky, L., Abramovitz, M., Shahar, N., Har-Even, D., Gross, S., Lerman, M., Levy, L., Sirota, L., & Fish, B. (1998). Medical, cognitive, emotional, and behavioral outcomes in school-age children conceived by in-vitro fertilization. *Journal of Clinical Child Psychology, 27,* 320–329.

Lewis, C., & Lamb, M. E. (2003). Fathers' influences on children's development: The evidence from two-parent families. *European Journal of Psychology of Education, 18,* 211–228.

Lewis, C. C. (1981). How adolescents approach decisions: Changes over grades seven to twelve and policy implications. *Child Development, 52,* 538–544.

Lewis, C. N., Freeman, N. H., & Maridaki-Kassotaki, K. (1995, April). *The social basis of theory of mind: Influences of siblings and, more importantly, interactions with adult kin.* Paper presented at the biennial meetings of the Society for Research in Child Development, Indianapolis.

Lewis, M. (1997). *Altering fate.* New York: Guilford Press.

Lewis, M., Allesandri, S. M., & Sullivan, M. W. (1992). Differences in shame and pride as a function of children's gender and task difficulty. *Child Development, 63,* 630–638.

Lewis, M., & Brooks, J. (1978). Self-knowledge and emotional development. In M. Lewis & L. A. Rosenblum (Eds.), *The development of affect* (pp. 205–226). New York: Plenum Press.

Lewis, M., & Ramsay, D. (2004). Development of self-recognition, personal pronoun use, and pretend play during the 2nd year. *Child Development, 75,* 1821–1831.

Lewis, M., Sullivan, M. W., Stanger, C., & Weiss, M. (1989). Self development and self-conscious emotions. *Child Development, 60,* 146–156.

Liben L., Bigler, R., & Krogh, H. (2001). Pink and blue collar jobs: Children's judgments of job status and job aspirations in relation to sex of worker. *Journal of Experimental Child Psychology, 79,* 346–363.

Lichter, D., & Eggebeen, D. (1994). The effect of parental employment on child poverty. *Journal of Marriage and the Family, 56,* 633–645.

Lickona, T. (1978). Moral development and moral education. In J. M. Gallagher & J. J. A. Easley (Eds.), *Knowledge and development* (Vol. 2, pp. 21–74). New York: Plenum.

Lickona, T. (1994). *Raising good children.* New York: Bantam Books.

Lickona, T. (2004). *Character matters: How to help our children develop good judgment, integrity, and other essential virtues.* New York: Simon & Schuster.

Lidz, C., & Macrine, S. (2001). An alternative approach to the identification of gifted culturally and linguistically diverse learners: The contribution of dynamic assessment. *School Psychology International, 22,* 74–96.

Liew, J., Eisenberg, N., & Reiser, M. (2004). Preschoolers' effortful control and negative emotionality, immediate reactions to disappointment, and quality of social functioning. *Journal of Experimental Child Psychology, 89,* 298–313.

Lillard, A. S., & Flavell, J. H. (1992). Young children's understanding of different mental states. *Developmental Psychology, 28,* 626–634.

Lindahl, L., & Haimann, M. (1997). Social proximity in early mother-infant interactions: Implications for gender differences? *Early Development & Parenting, 6,* 83–88.

Linnet, K., Dalsgaard, S., Obel, C., Wisborg, K., Henriksen, T., Rodriquez, A., Kotimaa, A., Moilanen, I., Thomsen, P., Olsen, J., & Jarvelin, M. (2003). Maternal lifestyle factors in pregnancy risk of attention deficit hyperactivity disorder and associated behaviors: Review of the current evidence. *American Journal of Psychiatry, 160,* 1028–1040.

Lippa, R. (2005). *Gender, nature, and nurture* (2nd ed.). Hillsdale, NJ: Erlbaum.

Lippé, R., Perchet, C., & Lassonde, M. (2007). Electrophysical markers of visuocortical development. *Cerebral Cortex, 17,* 100–107.

Litt, I. F. (1996). Special health problems during adolescence. In R. E. Behrman, R. M. Kliegman, & A. M. Arvin (Eds.), *Nelson textbook of pediatrics* (15th ed., pp. 541–565). Philadelphia: Saunders.

Liu, D., Wellman, H., Tardif, T., & Sabbagh, M. (2008). Theory of mind development in Chinese children: A meta-analysis of false-belief understanding across cultures and languages. *Developmental Psychology, 44,* 523–531.

Liu, J., Raine, A., Venables, P., & Mednick, S. (2004). Malnutrition at age 3 years and externalizing behavior problems at ages 8, 11, and 17 years. *American Journal of Psychiatry, 161,* 2005–2013.

Livesley, W. J., & Bromley, D. B. (1973). *Person perception in childhood and adolescence.* London: Wiley.

Livingstone, S., & Helsper, E. (2006). Does advertising literacy mediate the effects of advertising on children? A critical examination of two linked research literatures in relation to obesity and food choice. *Journal of Communication, 56,* 560–584.

Loeb, S., Fuller, B., Kagan, S., & Carrol, B. (2004). Child care in poor communities: Early learning effects of type, quality, and stability. *Child Development, 75,* 47–65.

Loeber, R., Tremblay, R. E., Gagnon, C., & Charlebois, P. (1989). Continuity and desistance in disruptive boys' early fighting at school. *Development and Psychopathology, 1,* 39–50.

Loehlin, J. C., Horn, J. M., & Willerman, L. (1994). Differential inheritance of mental abilities in the Texas Adoption Project. *Intelligence, 19,* 324–336.

Loftus, E. (1993). The reality of repressed memories. *American Psychologist, 48,* 518–537.

Lollis, S., Ross, H., & Leroux, L. (1996). An observational study of parents' socialization of moral orientation during sibling conflicts. *Merrill-Palmer Quarterly, 42,* 475–494.

Long, J. V. F., & Vaillant, G. E. (1984). Natural history of male psychological health: Escape from the underclass. *American Journal of Psychiatry, 141,* 341–346.

Loonsbury, J. (1992). Interdisciplinary instruction: A mandate for the nineties. In J. Loonsbury (Ed.), *Connecting the curriculum through interdisciplinary instruction.* Columbus, OH: National Middle School Association.

Louhiala, P. J., Jaakkola, N., Ruotsalainen, R., & Jaakkola, J. J. K. (1995). Form of day care and respiratory infections among Finnish children. *American Journal of Public Health, 85,* 1109–1112.

Love, J., Harrison, L., Sagi-Schwartz, A., van IJzendoorn, M., Ross, C., Ungerer, J., Raikes, H., Brady-Smith, C., Boller, K., Brooks-Gunn, J., Constantine, J., Kisker, E., Paulsell, D., & Chazan-Cohen, R. (2003). Child care quality matters: How conclusions may vary with context. *Child Development, 74,* 1021–1033.

Lubart, T. (2003). In search of creative intelligence. In R. Sternberg & T. Lubart (Eds.), *Models of intelligence: International perspective* (pp. 279–292). Washington, DC: American Psychological Association.

Lüdtke, O., Trautwein, N., & Köller, O. (2004). A validation of the NEO-FFI in a sample of young adults: Effects of the response format, factorial validity, and relations with indicators of academic achievement. *Diagnostica, 50,* 134–144.

Luna, B., Garver, K., Urban, T., Lazar, N., & Sweeney, J. (2004). Maturation of cognitive processes from late childhood to adulthood. *Child Development, 75,* 1357–1372.

Luster, T., & McAdoo, H. P. (1995). Factors related to self-esteem among African American youths: A secondary analysis of the High/Scope Perry Preschool data. *Journal of Research on Adolescence, 5,* 451–467.

Luster, T., & McAdoo, H. P. (1996). Family and child influences on educational attainment: A secondary analysis of the High/Scope Perry Preschool data. *Developmental Psychology, 32,* 26–39.

Luster, T., Lekskul, K., & Oh, S. (2004). Predictors of academic motivation in first grade among children born to low-income adolescent mothers. *Early Childhood Research Quarterly, 19,* 337–353.

Lynam, D. R. (1996). Early identification of chronic offenders: Who is the fledgling psychopath? *Psychological Bulletin, 120,* 209–234.

Lynn, R. (1991). Intelligence in China. *Social Behavior and Personality, 19,* 1–4.

Lynn, R., & Harvey, J. (2008). The decline of the world's IQ. *Intelligence, 36,* 112–120.

Lynn, R., & Song, M. (1992). General intelligence, visuospatial and verbal abilities in Korean children. *Journal of the Indian Academy of Applied Psychology, 18,* 1–3.

Lyon, T. D., & Flavell, J. H. (1994). Young children's understanding of "remember" and "forget." *Child Development, 65,* 1357–1371.

Lyons, N. P. (1983). Two perspectives: On self, relationships, and morality. *Harvard Educational Review, 53,* 125–145.

Lyons-Ruth, K., Easterbrooks, M. A., & Cibelli, C. D. (1997). Infant attachment strategies, infant mental lag, and maternal depressive symptoms: Predictors of internalizing and externalizing problems at age 7. *Developmental Psychology, 33,* 681–692.

Lytton, H., & Romney, D. M. (1991). Parents' differential socialization of boys and girls: A meta-analysis. *Psychological Bulletin, 109,* 267–296.

Ma, H. (2003). The relation of moral orientation and moral judgment to prosocial and antisocial behaviour of Chinese adolescents. *International Journal of Psychology, 38,* 101–111.

Maas, F. (2008). Children's understanding of promising, lying, and false belief. *Journal of General Psychology, 135,* 301–321.

Maccoby, E. E. (1980). *Social development: Psychological growth and the parent-child relationship.* New York: Harcourt Brace Jovanovich.

Maccoby, E. E. (1984). Middle childhood in the context of the family. In W. A. Collins (Ed.), *Development during middle childhood: The years from six to twelve* (pp. 184–239). Washington, DC: National Academy Press.

Maccoby, E. E. (1988). Gender as a social category. *Developmental Psychology, 24,* 755–765.

Maccoby, E. E. (1990). Gender and relationships: A developmental account. *American Psychologist, 45,* 513–520.

Maccoby, E. E. (1995). The two sexes and their social systems. In P. Moen, G. H. Elder, Jr., & K. Luscher (Eds.), *Examining lives in context: Perspectives on the ecology of human development* (pp. 347–364). Washington, DC: American Psychological Association.

Maccoby, E. E. (2002). Gender and group process: A developmental perspective. *Current Directions in Psychological Science, 11,* 54–58.

Maccoby, E. E., & Jacklin, C. N. (1987). Gender segregation in childhood. In H. W. Reese (Ed.), *Advances in child development and behavior* (Vol. 20, pp. 239–288). Orlando, FL: Academic Press.

Maccoby, E. E., & Lewis, C. (2003). Less day care or different day care? *Child Development, 74,* 1069–1075.

Maccoby, E. E., & Martin, J. A. (1983). Socialization in the context of the family: Parent-child interaction. In E. M. Hetherington (Ed.), *Handbook of child psychology: Socialization, personality, and social development* (Vol. 4, pp. 1–102). New York: Wiley.

MacDonald, K. (1992). Warmth as a developmental construct: An evolutionary analysis. *Child Development, 63,* 753–773.

MacDorman, M., & Atkinson, J. (1999). Infant mortality statistics from the 1997 period linked birth/infant death data set. *National Vital Statistics Reports, 47*(23). Hyattsville, MD: National Center for Health Statistics.

MacFarlane, A. (1977). *The psychology of child birth.* Cambridge, MA: Harvard University Press.

MacIver, D., Reuman, D., & Main, S. (1995). Social structuring of the school: Studying what is, illuminating what could be. *Annual Review of Psychology, 46,* 375–400.

MacLean, M., Bryant, P., & Bradley, L. (1987). Rhymes, nursery rhymes, and reading in early childhood. *Merrill-Palmer Quarterly, 33,* 255–281.

MacMillan, D. L., & Reschly, D. J. (1997). Issues of definition and classification. In W. E. MacLean, Jr. (Ed.), *Ellis' handbook of mental deficiency: Psychological theory and research* (pp. 47–74). Mahwah, NJ: Erlbaum.

MacWhinney, B. (2005). Language development. In M. Bornstein & M. Lamb (Eds.), *Developmental science: An advanced textbook* (5th ed., pp. 359–390). Hillsdale, NJ: Erlbaum.

Madsen, K., Hviid, A., Vestergaard, M., Schendel, D., Wohlfahrt, J., Thorsen, P., Olsen, J., & Melbye, M. (2002). A population-based study of measles, mumps, rubella vaccination and autism. *New England Journal of Medicine, 347,* 1477–1482.

Madsen, K., Lauritsen, M., Pederson, C., Thorsen, P., Plesner, A., Andersen, P., & Mortensen, P. (2003). Thimerosal and the occurrence of autism: Negative ecological evidence from Danish population-based data. *Pediatrics, 112,* 604–606.

Magarey, A., Daniels, I., Boulton, T., & Cockington, R. (2003). Predicting obesity in early adulthood from childhood and parental obesity. *International Journal of Obesity & Related Metabolic Disorders, 27,* 505–513.

Magiera, K., & Zigmond, N. (2005). Co-teaching in middle school classrooms under routine conditions: Does the instructional experience differ for students with disabilities in co-taught and solo-taught classes? *Learning Disabilities Research & Practice, 20,* 79–85.

Main, M., & Hesse, E. (1990). Parents' unresolved traumatic experiences are related to infant disorganized attachment status: Is frightened and/or frightening parental behavior the linking mechanism? In M. T. Greenberg, D. Cicchetti, & E. M. Cummings (Eds.), *Attachment in the preschool years: Theory, research, and intervention* (pp. 151–182). Chicago: University of Chicago Press.

Main, M., Hesse, E., & Goldwyn, R. (2008). Studying differences in language usage in recounting attachment history: An introduction to the AAI. In H. Steele & M. Steele (Eds.), *Clinical applications of the Adult Attachment Interview* (pp. 31–68). New York: Guilford Press.

Main, M., Kaplan, N., & Cassidy, J. (1985). Security in infancy, childhood, and adulthood: A move to the level of representation. *Monographs of the Society for Research in Child Development, 50*(Serial No. 209), 66–104.

Main, M., & Solomon, J. (1990). Procedures for identifying infants as disorganized/disoriented during the Ainsworth Strange Situation. In M. T. Greenberg, D. Cicchetti, & E. M. Cummings (Eds.), *Attachment in the preschool years: Theory, research, and intervention* (pp. 121–160). Chicago: University of Chicago Press.

Maitel, S., Dromi, E., Sagi, A., & Bornstein, M. (2000). The Hebrew Communicative Development Inventory: Language-specific properties and cross-linguistic generalizations. *Journal of Child Language, 27*, 43–67.

Makino, M., Tsuboi, K., & Dennerstein, L. (2004). Prevalence of eating disorders: A comparison of Western and non-Western countries. *Medscape General Medicine, 6*, 49.

Malamitsi-Puchner, A., Protonotariou, E., Boutsikou, T., Makrakis, E., Sarandakou, A., & Creatsas, G. (2005). The influence of the mode of delivery on circulating cytokine concentrations in the perinatal period. *Early Human Development, 81*, 387–392.

Malina, R. M. (1990). Physical growth and performance during the transitional years (9–16). In R. Montemayor, G. R. Adams, & T. P. Gullotta (Eds.), *From childhood to adolescence: A transitional period?* (pp. 41–62). Newbury Park, CA: Sage.

Malina, R. M. (2007). Physical fitness of children and adolescents in the United States: Status and secular change. In G. Tomkinson & T. Olds (Eds.), *Pediatric fitness: Secular trends and geographic variability.* Basel, Switzerland: Karger.

Maniadaki, K., Sonuga-Barke, E., & Kakouros, E. (2005). Parents' causal attributions about attention deficit/hyperactivity disorder: The effect of child and parent sex. *Child: Care, Health & Development, 31*, 331–340.

Manning, W., & Brower, S. (2006). Children's economic well-being in married and cohabiting parent families. *Journal of Marriage and the Family, 68*, 345–362.

Maratsos, M. (1983). Some current issues in the study of the acquisition of grammar. In J. H. Flavell & E. M. Markman (Eds.), *Handbook of child psychology: Cognitive development* (pp. 707–786). New York: Wiley.

Maratsos, M. (1998). The acquisition of grammar. In W. Damon (Ed.), *Handbook of child psychology, Vol. 2: Cognition, perception, and language* (5th ed., pp. 421–466). New York: Wiley.

Maratsos, M. (2000). More overregularizations after all: New data and discussion on Marcus, Pinker, Ullman, Hollander, Rosen, & Xu. *Journal of Child Language, 27*, 183–212.

March of Dimes. (2004). *Environmental risks and pregnancy.* Retrieved September 21, 2004, from http://www.marchofdimes.com/professionals/681_9146.asp

March of Dimes. (2008a). *Eating healthy.* Retrieved August 13, 2008, from http://www.marchofdimes.com/pnhec/159_823.asp

March of Dimes. (2008b). *Environmental risks and pregnancy.* Retrieved August 4, 2008, from http://www.marchofdimes.com/professionals/14332_9146.asp

Marcia, J. (2002). Identity and psychosocial development in adulthood. *Identity, 2*, 7–28.

Marcia, J. (2007). Theory and measure: The Identity Status Interview. In M. Watzlawik & A. Born (Eds.), *Capturing identity: Quantitative and qualitative methods* (pp. 1–14). Lanham, MD: University Press of America.

Marcia, J. E. (1966). Development and validation of ego identity status. *Journal of Personality & Social Psychology, 3*, 551–558.

Marcia, J. E. (1980). Identity in adolescence. In J. Adelson (Ed.), *Handbook of adolescent psychology* (pp. 159–187). New York: Wiley.

Marcia, J. E. (1993). The status of the statuses: Research review. In J. E. Marcia, A. S. Waterman, D. R. Matteson, S. L. Archer, & J. L. Orlofsky (Eds.), *Ego identity: A handbook for psychosocial research* (pp. 22–41). New York: Springer-Verlag.

Marcus, G. F., Pinker, S., Ullman, M., Hollander, M., Rosen, T. J., & Fei, X. (1992). Overregularization in language acquisition. *Monographs of the Society for Research in Child Development, 57*(4, Serial No. 228).

Markman, E., Wasow, J., & Hansen, C. (2003). Use of the mutual exclusivity assumption by young word learners. *Cognitive Psychology, 47*, 241–275.

Marschark, M. (1993). *Psychological development of deaf children.* New York: Oxford University Press.

Marsh, H., & Yeung, A. (1997). Coursework selection: Relations to academic self-concept and achievement. *American Educational Research Journal, 34*, 691–720.

Marshall, N. L., Coll, C. G., Marx, F., McCartney, K., Keefe, N., & Ruh, J. (1997). After-school time and children's behavioral adjustment. *Merrill-Palmer Quarterly, 43*, 497–514.

Martin, C. L. (1991). The role of cognition in understanding gender effects. In H. W. Reese (Ed.), *Advances in child development and behavior* (Vol. 23, pp. 113–150). San Diego, CA: Academic Press.

Martin, C. L. (1993). New directions for investigating children's gender knowledge. *Developmental Review, 13*, 184–204.

Martin, C. L., & Halverson, C. F., Jr. (1981). A schematic processing model of sex typing and stereotyping in children. *Child Development, 52*, 1119–1134.

Martin, C. L., & Halverson, C. F., Jr. (1983). Gender constancy: A methodological and theoretical analysis. *Sex Roles, 9*, 775–790.

Martin, C. L., & Ruble, D. (2004). Children's search for gender cues: Cognitive perspectives on gender development. *Current Directions in Psychological Science, 13*, 67–70.

Martin, E. P., & Martin, J. M. (1978). *The black extended family.* Chicago: University of Chicago Press.

Martin, E. W. (1995). Case studies on inclusion: Worst fears realized. *The Journal of Special Education, 29*, 192–199.

Martin, J., & D'Augelli, A. (2003). How lonely are gay and lesbian youth? *Psychological Reports, 93*, 486.

Martin, J., Hamilton, B., Sutton, P., Ventura, S., Menacker, F., & Kirmeyer, S. (2006). Births: Final data for 2004. *National Vital Statistics Reports, 55*, 1–102.

Martin, J., Hamilton, B., Sutton, P., Ventura, S., Menacker, F., Kirmeyer, S., & Munson, M. (2007). Births: Final data for 2005. *National Vital Statistics Reports, 56*, 1–104.

Martin, J., Hamilton, B., Sutton, P., Ventura, S., Menacker, F., & Munson, M. (2005). Births: Final data for 2003. *National Vital Statistics Reports, 54*, 1–116.

Martin, J., & Nguyen, D. (2004). Anthropometric analysis of homosexuals and heterosexuals: Implications for early hormone exposure. *Hormones & Behavior, 45*, 31–39.

Martin, R., Noyes, J., Wisenbaker, J., & Huttunen, M. (1999). Prediction of early childhood negative emotionality and inhibition from maternal distress during pregnancy. *Merrill-Palmer Quarterly, 45*, 370–391.

Martini, R., & Shore, B. (2008). Pointing to parallels in ability-related differences in the use of metacognition in academic and psychomotor tasks. *Learning and Individual Differences, 18*, 237–247.

Martorano, S. C. (1977). A developmental analysis of performance on Piaget's formal operations tasks. *Developmental Psychology, 13*, 666–672.

Mascolo, M. F., & Fischer, K. W. (1995). Developmental transformations in appraisals for pride, shame, and guilt. In J. P. Tangney & K. W. Fischer (Eds.), *Self-conscious emotions: The psychology of shame, guilt, embarrassment, and pride* (pp. 64–113). New York: Guilford Press.

Mash, C., Novak, E., Berthier, N., & Keen, R. (2006). What do two-year-olds understand about hidden-object events? *Developmental Psychology, 42*, 263–271.

Mason, C. A., Cauce, A. M., Gonzales, N., & Hiraga, Y. (1996). Neither too sweet nor too sour: Problem peers, maternal control, and problem behavior in African American adolescents. *Child Development, 67*, 2115–2130.

Mason, M., & Chuang, S. (2001). Culturally-based after-school arts programming for low-income urban children: Adaptive and preventive effects. *Journal of Primary Prevention, 22*, 45–54.

Massad, C. M. (1981). Sex role identity and adjustment during adolescence. *Child Development, 52*, 1290–1298.

Masten, A. S., Best, K. M., & Garmezy, N. (1990). Resilience and development: Contributions from the study of children who overcome adversity. *Development and Psychopathology, 2*, 425–444.

Masten, A. S., & Coatsworth, J. D. (1995). Competence, resilience, and psychopathology. In D. Cicchetti & D. J. Cohen (Eds.), *Developmental psychopathology: Vol. 2. Risk, disorder, and adaptation* (pp. 715–752). New York: Wiley-Interscience.

Masten, A. S., & Coatsworth, J. D. (1998). The development of competence in favorable and unfavorable environments: Lessons from research on successful children. *American Psychologist, 53*, 205–220.

Maszk, P., Eisenberg, N., & Guthrie, I. (1999). Relations of children's social status to their emotionality and regulation: A short-term longitudinal study. *Merrill-Palmer Quarterly, 454*, 468–492.

Matarazzo, J. D. (1972). *Wechsler's measurement and appraisal of adult intelligence* (5th enlarged ed.). New York: Oxford University Press.

Matarazzo, J. D. (1992). Biological and physiological correlates of intelligence. *Intelligence, 16*, 257–258.

Mather, P. L., & Black, K. N. (1984). Heredity and environmental influences on preschool twins' language skills. *Developmental Psychology, 20*, 303–308.

Matthews, R. (2006). The case for linguistic nativism. In R. Stainton (Ed.), *Contemporary debates in cognitive science* (pp. 81–96). Malden, MA: Blackwell Publishing.

Matthews, T. (2005). Racial/ethnic disparities in infant mortality— United States, 1995–2002. *Morbidity & Mortality Weekly Report, 54*, 553–556.

Maughan, B., Pickles, A., & Quinton, D. (1995). Parental hostility, childhood behavior, and adult social functioning. In J. McCord (Ed.), *Coercion and punishment in long-term perspectives* (pp. 34–58). Cambridge, England: Cambridge University Press.

Maye, J., Weiss, D., & Aslin, R. (2008). Statistical phonetic learning in infants: Facilitation and feature generalization. *Developmental Science, 11*, 122–134.

Mayeux, L., & Cillissen, A. (2003). Development of social problem solving in early childhood: Stability, change, and associations with social competence. *Journal of Genetic Psychology, 164*, 153–173.

McAllister, D., Kaplan, B., Edworthy, S., Martin, L., et al. (1997). The influence of systemic lupus erythematosus on fetal development: Cognitive, behavioral, and health trends. *Journal of the International Neurological Society, 3*, 370–376.

McBride-Chang, C., & Ho, C. (2000). Developmental issues in Chinese children's character acquisition. *Journal of Educational Psychology, 92*, 50–55.

McBride-Chang, C., Shu, H., Zhou, C., & Wagner, R. (2004). Morphological awareness uniquely predicts young children's Chinese character recognition. *Journal of Educational Psychology, 96*, 743–751.

McCabe, K., Hough, R., Wood, P., & Yeh, M. (2001). Childhood and adolescent onset conduct disorder: A test of the developmental taxonomy. *Journal of Abnormal Child Psychology, 29*, 305–316.

McClure, E. (2000). A meta-analytic review of sex differences in facial expression processing and their development in infants, children, and adolescents. *Psychological Bulletin, 126*, 242–453.

McCord, J. (1982). A longitudinal view of the relationship between parental absence and crime. In J. Gunn & D. P. Farrington (Eds.), *Abnormal offenders, delinquency, and the criminal justice system* (pp. 113–128). London: Wiley.

McCourt, C., Weaver, J., Statham, H., Beake, S., Gamble, J., & Creedy, D. (2007). Elective cesarean section and decision making: A critical review of the literature. *Birth, 34*, 65–79.

McCrae, R. R., & Costa, P. T., Jr. (1994). The stability of personality: Observations and evaluations. *Current Directions in Psychological Science, 3*, 173–175.

McCrae, R. R., & Terracciano, A. (2005). Universal features of personality traits from the observer's perspective: Data from 50 cultures. *Journal of Personality & Social Psychology, 88*, 547–561.

McCune, L. (1995). A normative study of representational play at the transition to language. *Developmental Psychology, 31*, 198–206.

McElhaney, K., Antonishak, J., & Allen, J. (2008). "They like me, they like me not": Popularity and adolescents' perceptions of acceptance predicting social functioning over time. *Child Development, 79*, 720–731.

McGee, B., Hewitt, P., Sherry, S., Parkin, M., & Flett, G. (2005). Perfectionistic self-presentation, body image, and eating disorder symptoms. *Body Image, 2*, 29–40.

McGrath, M., & Sullivan, M. (2002). Birth weight, neonatal morbidities, and school age outcomes in full-term and preterm infants. *Issues in Comprehensive Pediatric Nursing, 25*, 231–254.

McGue, M. (1994). Why developmental psychology should find room for behavior genetics. In C. A. Nelson (Ed.), *The Minnesota symposia on child development* (Vol. 27, pp. 105–119). Hillsdale, NJ: Erlbaum.

McGuire, S., McHale, S. M., & Updegraff, K. (1996). Children's perceptions of the sibling relationship in middle childhood: Connections within and between family relationships. *Personal Relationships, 3*, 229–239.

McIntosh, J., Wells, Y., Smyth, B., & Long, C. (2008). Child-focused and child-inclusive divorce mediation: Comparative outcomes from a prospective study of post-separation adjustment. *Family Court Review, 46*, 105–124.

McKown, C., & Weinstein, R. (2003). The development and consequences of stereotype consciousness in middle childhood. *Child Development, 74*, 498–515.

McLanahan, S. S., & Sandefur, G. (1994). *Growing up with a single parent: What hurts, what helps.* Cambridge, MA: Harvard University Press.

McLoyd, V. C. (1997, April). *Reducing stressors, increasing supports in the lives of ethnic minority children in America: Research and policy issues.* Paper presented at the biennial meetings of the Society for Research in Child Development, Washington, DC.

McLoyd, V. C. (1998). Socioeconomic disadvantage and child development. *American Psychologist, 53*, 185–204.

McLoyd, V. C., & Wilson, L. (1991). The strain of living poor: Parenting, social support, and child mental health. In A. C. Huston (Ed.), *Children in poverty: Child development and public policy* (pp. 105–135). Cambridge, England: Cambridge University Press.

McManis, M., Kagan, J., Snidman, N., & Woodward, S. (2002). EEG asymmetry, power, and temperament in children. *Developmental Psychobiology, 41*, 169–177.

McMaster, F., & Kusumakar, V. (2004). MRI study of the pituitary gland in adolescent depression. *Journal of Psychiatric Research, 38*, 231–236.

McRorie, M., & Cooper, C. (2004). Psychomotor movement and IQ. *Personality & Individual Differences, 37*, 523–531.

Measor, L. (2004). Young people's views of sex education: Gender, information and knowledge. *Sex Education, 4*, 153–166.

Mediascope Press. (1999). *Substance use in popular movies and music: Issue Brief Series.* Studio City, CA: Mediascope Inc.

Mediascope Press. (2000). *Teens, sex and the media.* Issue Brief Series. Studio City, CA: Mediascope Inc.

Medwell, J., & Wray, D. (2007). Handwriting: What do we know and what do we need to know? *Literacy, 41,* 10–15.

Mei, Z., Grummer-Strawn, L., Thompson, D., & Dietz, W. (2004). Shifts in percentiles of growth during early childhood: Analysis of longitudinal data from California Child Health and Development Study. *Pediatrics, 113,* 617–627.

Meighan, R. (1995). Home-based education effectiveness research and some of its implications. *Educational Review, 47,* 275–287.

Meijer, A., & Wittenboer, G. (2007). Contribution of infants' sleep and crying to marital relationship of first-time parent couples in the first year after childbirth. *Journal of Family Psychology, 21,* 49–57.

Meisinger, E., & Bradley, B. (2008). Classroom practices for supporting fluency development. In M. Kuhn & P. Schwanenflugel (Eds.), *Fluency in the classroom: Solving problems in the teaching of literacy* (pp. 36–54). New York: Guilford Press.

Melby, J. N., & Conger, R. D. (1996). Parental behaviors and adolescent academic performance: A longitudinal analysis. *Journal of Research on Adolescence, 6,* 113–137.

Melinder, A., Endestad, T., & Magnussen, S. (2006). Relations between episodic memory, suggestibility, theory of mind, and cognitive inhibition in the preschool child. *Scandinavian Journal of Psychology, 47,* 485–495.

Melot, A., & Houde, O. (1998). Categorization and theories of mind: The case of the appearance/reality distinction. *Cahiers de Psychologie Cognitive/Current Psychology of Cognition, 17,* 71–93.

Melson, G., Peet, S., & Sparks, C. (1991). Children's attachments to their pets: Links to socioemotional development. *Children's Environmental Quarterly, 8,* 55–65.

Meltzoff, A. N. (1988). Infant imitation and memory: Nine-month-olds in immediate and deferred tasks. *Child Development, 59,* 217–225.

Meltzoff, A. N. (1995). Understanding the intentions of others: Re-enactment of intended acts by 18-month-old children. *Developmental Psychology, 31,* 838–850.

Menesini, E., Sanchez, V., Fonzi, A., Ortega, R., Costabile, A., & Lo Feudo, G. (2003). Moral emotions and bullying: A cross-national comparison of differences between bullies, victims and outsiders. *Aggressive Behavior, 29,* 515–530.

Merrick, J., & Morad, M. (2002). Adolescent pregnancy in Israel. *International Journal of Adolescent Medicine, 14,* 161–164.

Mersereau, P., Kilker, K., Carter, H., Fassett, E., Williams, J., Flores, A., Prue, C., Williams, L., Mai, C., & Mulinare, J. (2004). Spina bifida and anencephaly before and after folic acid mandate: United States, 1995–1996 and 1999–2000. *Morbidity & Mortality Weekly Report, 53,* 362–365.

Mervis, C. B., & Bertrand, J. (1994). Acquisition of the novel name-nameless category (N3C) principle. *Child Development, 65,* 1646–1662.

Meyer-Bahlburg, H. F. L., Ehrhardt, A. A., Rosen, L. R., Gruen, R. S., Veridiano, N. P., Vann, F. H., & Neuwalder, H. F. (1995). Prenatal estrogens and the development of homosexual orientation. *Developmental Psychology, 31,* 12–21.

Mijuskovic, Z. (2006). *Phenylketonuria.* Retrieved August 4, 2008, from http://www.emedicine.com/derm/topic712.htm

Mikulincer, M., & Shaver, P. (2005). Attachment security, compassion, and altruism. *Current Directions in Psychological Science, 14,* 34–38.

Miller, B., Benson, B., & Galbraith, K. (2001). Family relationships and adolescent pregnancy risk: A research synthesis. *Developmental Review, 21,* 1–38.

Miller, C., Trautner, H., & Ruble, D. (2006). The role of gender stereotypes in children's preferences and behavior. In L. Balter &

C. Tamis-LeMonday (Eds.), *Child psychology: A handbook of contemporary issues* (2nd ed., pp. 293–323). New York: Psychology Press.

Miller, P. (2002). *Theories of development* (4th ed.). New York: Worth.

Miller, P., Eisenberg, N., Fabes, R., Shell, R., & Gular, S. (1989). Mothers' emotional arousal as a moderator in the socialization of children's empathy. *New Directions for Child Development, 44,* 65–83.

Milligan, K., Astington, J., & Dack, L. (2007). Language and theory of mind: Meta-analysis of the relation between language ability and false-belief understanding. *Child Development, 78,* 622–646.

Mills, D., Coffey-Corina, S., & Neville, H. (1994). Variability in cerebral organization during primary language acquisition. In G. Dawson & K. Fischer (Eds.), *Human behavior and the developing brain.* New York: Guilford.

Milos, G., Spindler, A., & Schnyder, U. (2004). Psychiatric comorbidity and Eating Disorder Inventory (EDI) profiles in eating disorder patients. *Canadian Journal of Psychiatry, 49,* 179–184.

Milos, G., Spindler, A., Ruggiero, G., Klaghofer, R., & Schnyder, U. (2002). Comorbidity of obsessive-compulsive disorders and duration of eating disorders. *International Journal of Eating Disorders, 31,* 284–289.

Mischel, W. (1966). A social learning view of sex differences in behavior. In E. E. Maccoby (Ed.), *The development of sex differences* (pp. 56–81). Stanford, CA: Stanford University Press.

Mischel, W. (1970). Sex typing and socialization. In P. H. Mussen (Ed.), *Carmichael's manual of child psychology* (Vol. 2, pp. 3–72). New York: Wiley.

Mischel, W. (2007). Toward a cognitive social learning reconceptualization of personality. In Y. Shoda, D. Cervone, & G. Downey (Eds.), *Persons in context: Building a science of the individual.* New York: Guilford Press.

Mishra, R. C. (2001). Cognition across cultures. In D. Matsumoto (Ed.), *Handbook of culture and psychology* (pp. 119–135). New York: Oxford University Press.

Misra, G. (1983). Deprivation and development: A review of Indian studies. *Indian Educational Review, 18,* 12–32.

Mitchell, A. (2002). Infertility treatment: More risks and challenges. *New England Journal of Medicine, 346,* 769–770.

Mitchell, J. E. (1995). Medical complications of bulimia nervosa. In K. D. Brownell & C. G. Fairburn (Eds.), *Eating disorders and obesity: A comprehensive handbook* (pp. 271–275). New York: Guilford Press.

Mitchell, K. (2002). Women's morality: A test of Carol Gilligan's theory. *Journal of Social Distress & the Homeless, 11,* 81–110.

Mitchell, P. R., & Kent, R. D. (1990). Phonetic variation in multisyllable babbling. *Journal of Child Language, 17,* 247–265.

Mofenson, L. (2002). U.S. Public Health Service Task Force recommendations for use of antiretroviral drugs in pregnant HIV-1 infected women for maternal health and interventions to reduce perinatal HIV-1 transmission in the United States. *Morbidity & Mortality Weekly Report, 51,* 1–38.

Moffitt, T. E. (1990). Juvenile delinquency and attention deficit disorder: Boys' developmental trajectories from age 3 to age 15. *Child Development, 61,* 893–910.

Moffitt, T. E. (1993). Adolescence-limited and life-course-persistent antisocial behavior: A developmental taxonomy. *Psychology Review, 100,* 674–701.

Moffitt, T. E., & Harrington, H. L. (1996). Delinquency: The natural history of antisocial behavior. In P. A. Silva & W. R. Stanton (Eds.), *From child to adult: The Dunedin multidisciplinary health and development study* (pp. 163–185). Aukland: Oxford University Press.

Mogro-Wilson, C. (2008). The influence of parental warmth and control on Latino adolescent alcohol use. *Hispanic Journal of Behavioral Sciences, 30*, 89–105.

Mohanty, A., & Perregaux, C. (1997). Language acquisition and bilingualism. In J. Berry, P. Dasen, & T. Saraswathi (Eds.), *Handbook of cross-cultural psychology: Vol. 2. Basic processes and human development.* Boston: Allyn & Bacon.

Mohsin, M., Wong, F., Bauman, A., & Bai, J. (2003). Maternal and neonatal factors influencing premature birth and low birth weight in Australia. *Journal of Biosocial Science, 35*, 161–174.

Moilanen, B. (2004). Vegan diets in infants, children, and adolescents. *Pediatrics in Review, 25*, 174–176.

Molfese, V. J., DiLalla, L. F., & Bunce, D. (1997). Prediction of the intelligence test scores of 3- to 8-year-old children by home environment, socioeconomic status, and biomedical risks. *Merrill-Palmer Quarterly, 43*, 219–234.

Money, J. (1975). Ablatio penis: Normal male infant sex-reassignment as a girl. *Archives of Sexual Behavior, 4*, 65–71.

Monga, M. (2007). Managers' moral reasoning: Evidence from large Indian manufacturing organisations. *Journal of Business Ethics, 71*, 179–194.

Montemayor, R., & Eisen, M. (1977). The development of self-conceptions from childhood to adolescence. *Developmental Psychology, 13*, 314–319.

Montgomery, M., & Sorell, G. (1998). Love and dating experience in early and middle adolescence: Grade and gender comparisons. *Journal of Adolescence, 21*, 677–689.

Moody, E. (1997). Lessons from pair counseling with incarcerated juvenile delinquents. *Journal of Addictions & Offender Counseling, 18*, 10–25.

Moon, C., & Fifer, W. P. (1990). Syllables as signals for 2-day-old infants. *Infant Behavior and Development, 13*, 377–390.

Moore, C., Barresi, J., & Thompson, C. (1998). The cognitive basis of future-oriented prosocial behavior. *Social Development, 7*, 198–218.

Moore, D. (2001). Reassessing emotion recognition performance in people with mental retardation: A review. *American Journal on Mental Retardation, 106*, 481–502.

Moore, E., & Rideout, V. (2007). The online marketing of food to children: Is it just fun and games? *Journal of Public Policy and Marketing, 26*, 202–220.

Moore, E. G. J. (1986). Family socialization and the IQ test performance of traditionally and transracially adopted black children. *Developmental Psychology, 22*, 317–326.

Moore, K. L., & Persaud, T. V. N. (1993). *The developing human: Clinically oriented embryology* (5th ed.). Philadelphia: Saunders.

Moore, R., Vadeyar, S., Fulford, J., Tyler, D., Gribben, C., Baker, P., James, D., & Gowland, P. (2001). Antenatal determination of fetal brain activity in response to an acoustic stimulus using functional magnetic resonance imaging. *Human Brain Mapping, 12*, 94–99.

Morgan, C., Finan, A., Yarnold, R., Petersen, S., Horsfield, M., Rickett, A., & Wailoo, M. (2002). Assessment of infant physiology and neuronal development using magnetic resonance imaging. *Child: Care, Health, & Development, 28*, 7–10.

Morgan, J. L. (1994). Converging measures of speech segmentation in preverbal infants. *Infant Behavior and Development, 17*, 389–403.

Morral, S., Gobbo, C., Marini, Z., & Sheese, R. (2008). *Cognitive development: Neo-Piagetian perspectives.* New York: Taylor & Francis Erlbaum.

Morrison, D. R., & Cherlin, A. J. (1995). The divorce process and young children's well-being: A prospective analysis. *Journal of Marriage and the Family, 57*, 800–812.

Morrison, F., Bachman, H., & Connor, C. (2005). *Improving literacy in America: Guidelines from research.* New Haven: Yale University Press.

Morrison, F. J., Smith, L., & Dow-Ehrensberger, M. (1995). Education and cognitive development: A natural experiment. *Developmental Psychology, 31*, 789–799.

Morrongiello, B. A. (1988). Infants' localization of sounds along the horizontal axis: Estimates of minimum audible angle. *Developmental Psychology, 24*, 8–13.

Morrongiello, B. A., Fenwick, K. D., & Chance, G. (1990). Sound localization acuity in very young infants: An observer-based testing procedure. *Developmental Psychology, 26*, 75–84.

Morrow, R. (2005). *Sesame Street and the reform of children's television.* Baltimore: Johns Hopkins University Press.

Morse, P. A., & Cowan, N. (1982). Infant auditory and speech perception. In T. M. Field, A. Houston, H. C. Quay, L. Troll, & G. E. Finley (Eds.), *Review of human development* (pp. 32–61). New York: Wiley.

Mortensen, E., Andresen, J., Kruuse, E., Sanders, S., & Reinisch, J. (2003). IQ stability: The relation between child and young adult intelligence test scores in low-birthweight samples. *Scandinavian Journal of Psychology, 44*, 395–398.

Mortimer, J., & Harley, C. (2002). The quality of work and youth mental health. *Work & Occupations, 29*, 166–197.

Mortimer, J., Zimmer-Gembeck, M., Holmes, M., & Shanahan, M. (2002). The process of occupational decision making: Patterns during the transition to adulthood. *Journal of Vocational Behavior, 61*, 439–465.

Moses, L., Baldwin, D., Rosicky, J., & Tidball, G. (2001). Evidence for referential understanding in the emotions domain at twelve and eighteen months. *Child Development, 72*, 718–735.

Moshman, D. (2005). *Rationality, morality, and identity.* Hillsdale, NJ: Erlbaum.

Mott, J., Crowe, P., Richardson, J., & Flay, B. (1999). After-school supervision and adolescent cigarette smoking: Contributions of the setting and intensity of after-school self-care. *Journal of Behavioral Medicine, 22*, 35–58.

Mounts, N., & Steinberg, L. (1995). An ecological analysis of peer influence on adolescent grade point average and drug use. *Developmental Psychology, 31*, 915–922.

Mueller, U., Overton, W., & Reene, K. (2001). Development of conditional reasoning: A longitudinal study. *Journal of Cognition & Development, 2*, 27–49.

Muhuri, P. K., Anker, M., & Bryce, J. (1996). Treatment patterns for childhood diarrhoea: Evidence from demographic and health surveys. *Bulletin of the World Health Organization, 74*, 135–146.

Muller, C. (1995). Maternal employment, parent involvement, and mathematics achievement among adolescents. *Journal of Marriage and the Family, 57*, 85–100.

Munir, K., & Beardslee, W. (2001). A developmental and psychobiological framework for understanding the role of culture in child and adolescent psychiatry. *Child & Adolescent Psychiatric Clinics of North America, 10*, 667–677.

Munro, G., & Adams, G. R. (1977). Ego-identity formation in college students and working youth. *Developmental Psychology, 13*, 523–524.

Munroe, R. H., Shimmin, H. S., & Munroe, R. L. (1984). Gender understanding and sex role preference in four cultures. *Developmental Psychology, 20*, 673–682.

Muraskas, J., & Hasson, A. (2004). A girl with a birth weight of 280 g, now 14 years old. *New England Journal of Medicine, 324*, 1598–1599.

Murphy, S. O. (1993, April). *The family context and the transition to siblinghood: Strategies parents use to influence sibling-infant relationships.* Paper presented at the biennial meetings of the Society for Research in Child Development, New Orleans.

Murray, B. (1998, June). Dipping math scores heat up debate over math teaching. *APA Monitor, 29,* 34–35.

Murray, J., Liotti, M., Ingmundson, P., Mayberg, H., Pu, U., Zamarripa, F., Liu, Y., Woldorff, M., Gao, J., & Fox, P. (2006). Children's brain activations while viewing televised violence revealed by MRO. *Media Psychology, 8,* 25–37.

Murray, J., & Youniss, J. (1968). Achievement of inferential transitivity and its relation to serial ordering. *Child Development, 39,* 1259–1268.

Murray, L., Woolgar, M., Martins, C., Christaki, A., Hipwell, A., & Cooper, P. (2006). Conversations around homework: Links to parental mental health, family characteristics and child psychological functioning. *British Journal of Developmental Psychology, 24,* 125–149.

Muscari, M. E. (1996). Primary care of adolescents with bulimia nervosa. *Journal of Pediatric Health Care, 10,* 17–25.

Must, O., Must, A., & Raudik, V. (2003). The secular rise in IQs: In Estonia, the Flynn effect is not a Jensen effect. *Intelligence, 31,* 461–471.

Nagy, E., & Molnar, P. (2004). Homo imitans or homo provocans? Human imprinting model of neonatal imitation. *Infant Behavior and Development, 27,* 54–63.

Nagy, W., Berninger, V., Abbott, R., Vaughan, K., & Vermeulen, K. (2004). Relationship of morphology and other language skills to literacy skills in at-risk second-grade readers and at-risk fourth-grade writers. *Journal of Educational Psychology, 96,* 730–742.

Narvaez, D. (1998). The influence of moral schemas on the reconstruction of moral narratives in eighth graders and college students. *Journal of Educational Psychology, 47,* 218–228.

National Abortion and Reproductive Rights Action League (NARAL). (1997). *Limitations on the rights of pregnant women* [NARAL Factsheet]. Retrieved March 5, 2001, from http://www.naral.org/publications/facts

National Association for the Education of Young Children (NAEYC). (2006). *Developmentally appropriate practice in early childhood programs serving children from birth through age 8.* Retrieved March 21, 2008, from http://www.naeyc.org/about/positions/dap1.asp

National Cancer Institute. (2006). *Breast cancer and the environment research centers chart new territory.* Retrieved June 21, 2007, from http://www.nci.nih.gov/ncicancerbulletin/NCI_Cancer_Bulletin_081506/page9

National Center for Chronic Disease Prevention and Health Promotion (NCCDPHP). (2000). *Obesity epidemic increases dramatically in the United States* [Online press release]. Retrieved August 23, 2000, from http://www.cdc.gov

National Center for Education Statistics (NCES). (2003). *Highlights from the TIMSS 1999 video study of eighth-grade mathematics teaching* (NCES Publication No. 2003011). Washington, DC: Author.

National Center for Education Statistics (NCES). (2005a). *The condition of education 2005, in brief.* Retrieved July 23, 2005, from http://nces.ed.gov/pubs2005/2005095.pdf

National Center for Education Statistics (NCES). (2005b). *The condition of education 2000–2005.* Retrieved July 23, 2005, from http://nces.ed.gov/programs/coe/

National Center for Education Statistics (NCES). (2006). *Fast facts: How many English language learners (ELL) students are receiving services in U.S. public schools?* Retrieved August 17, 2008, from http://nces.ed.gov/fastfacts/display.asp?id=96

National Center for Education Statistics (NCES). (2007). *Digest of education statistics.* Retrieved September 6, 2008, from http://nces.ed.gov/programs/digest/index.asp

National Center for Education Statistics (NCES). (2008). *The condition of education 2008.* Retrieved June 27, 2008, from http://nces.ed.gov/programs/coe/

National Center for Health Statistics (NCHS). (2007a). *Health, United States, 2007.* Hyattsville, MD: Author.

National Center for Health Statistics (NCHS). (2007b). *Prevalence of overweight among children and adolescents: United States 2003–2004.* Retrieved June 19, 2007, from http://www.cdc.gov/nchs/products/pubs/pubd/hestats/overweight/overwght_child_03.htm

National Council for Injury Prevention and Control (NCIPC). (2000). *Fact book for the year 2000.* Washington, DC: Author.

National Institute of Mental Health (NIMH). (2001a). NIMH research roundtable on prepubertal bipolar disorder. *Journal of the American Academy of Child & Adolescent Psychiatry, 40,* 871–878.

National Institute of Mental Health (NIMH). (2001b). *The numbers count: Mental disorders in America.* NIH Publication No. 01-4584. Retrieved June 10, 2005, from http://www.nimh.nih.gov

National Literacy Trust. (2003). *Mother tongues: What languages are spoken in the UK?* Retrieved July 9, 2005, from http://www.literacytrust.org.uk/Research/lostop3.html

Needlman, R., Frank, D. A., Augustyn, M., & Zuckerman, B. S. (1995). Neurophysiological effects of prenatal cocaine exposure: Comparison of human and animal investigations. In M. Lewis & M. Bendersky (Eds.), *Mothers, babies, and cocaine: The role of toxins in development* (pp. 229–250). Hillsdale, NJ: Erlbaum.

Needlman, R. D. (1996). Growth and development. In R. E. Behrman, R. M. Kliegman, & A. M. Arvin (Eds.), *Nelson textbook of pediatrics* (15th ed., pp. 30–72). Philadelphia: Saunders.

Neisser, U., Boodoo, G., Bouchard, T. J., Jr., Boykin, A. W., Brody, N., Ceci, S. J., Halpern, D. F., Loehlin, J. C., Perloff, R., Sternberg, R. J., & Urbina, S. (1996). Intelligence: Knowns and unknowns. *American Psychologist, 51,* 77–101.

Nelson, C., de Haan, M., & Thomas, K. (2006). *Neuroscience of cognitive development: The role of experience and the developing brain.* New York: Wiley.

Nelson, K. (1977). Facilitating children's syntax acquisition. *Developmental Psychology, 13,* 101–107.

Nelson, K. (1985). *Making sense: The acquisition of shared meaning.* New York: Academic Press.

Nelson, K. (1988). Constraints on word learning. *Cognitive Development, 3,* 221–246.

Nelson, S. (1980). Factors influencing young children's use of motives and outcomes as moral criteria. *Child Development, 51,* 823–829.

Nesdale, D., Durkin, K., Maass, A., & Griffiths, J. (2005). Threat, group identification, and children's ethnic prejudice. *Social Development, 14,* 189–205.

Nettelbeck, T., & Wilson, C. (2004). The Flynn effect: Smarter not faster. *Intelligence, 32,* 85–93.

Neufeld, G., & Maté, G. (2005). *Hold on to your kids: Why parents need to matter more than peers.* New York: Ballantine Books.

Neumark-Sztainer, D., Wall, M., Eisenberg, M., Story, M., & Hannan, P. (2006). Overweight status and weight control behaviors in adolescents: Longitudinal and secular trends from 1999 to 2004. *Preventive Medicine, 43,* 52–59.

Newcomb, A. F., & Bagwell, C. L. (1995). Children's friendship relations: A meta-analytic review. *Psychological Bulletin, 117,* 306–347.

Newcomb, A. F., Bukowski, W. M., & Pattee, L. (1993). Children's peer relations: A meta-analytic review of popular, rejected, neglected, controversial, and average sociometric status. *Psychological Bulletin, 113,* 99–128.

Newman, D., Caspi, A., Moffitt, T., & Silva, P. (1997). Antecedents of adult interpersonal functioning: Effects of individual differences in age 3 temperament. *Developmental Psychology, 33,* 206–217.

Newman, R. (2005). The cocktail party effect in infants revisited: Listening to one's name in noise. *Developmental Psychology, 41,* 352–362.

New Zealand Ministry of Education. (2003). *Homeschooling in 2003.* Retrieved June 23, 2004, from http://www.minedu.govt.nz/index.cfm?layout=document&documentid=6893&indexid=6852&indexparentid=5611

NICHD Early Child Care Research Network. (1997). Child care in the first year of life. *Merrill-Palmer Quarterly, 43,* 340–360.

NICHD Early Child Care Research Network. (1999). Chronicity of maternal depressive symptoms, maternal sensitivity, and child functioning at 36 months. *Developmental Psychology, 35,* 1297–1310.

NICHD Early Child Care Research Network. (2003). Does amount of time spent in child care predict socioemotional adjustment during the transition to kindergarten? *Child Development, 74,* 976–1005.

NICHD Early Child Care Research Network. (2004). Are child developmental outcomes related to before- and after-school care arrangements? Results from the NICHD Study of Early Child Care. *Child Development, 75,* 280–295.

NICHD Early Child Care Research Network. (2006). *The NICHD study of early child care and youth development.* Retrieved September 6, 2008, from http://www.nichd.nih.gov/publications/pubs/upload/seccyd_051206.pdf

Nicholls, C. (2005). Death by a thousand cuts: Indigenous language bilingual education programmes in the northern territory of Australia, 1972–1998. *International Journal of Bilingual Education & Bilingualism, 8,* 160–177.

Nicklaus, S., Boggio, V., & Issanchou, S. (2005). Gustatory perceptions in children. *Archives of Pediatrics, 12,* 579–584.

Nijhuis, J. (2003). Fetal behavior. *Neurobiology of Aging, 24,* S41–S46.

Nilsson, E., Gillberg, C., Gillberg, I., & Rastam, M. (1999). Ten-year follow-up of adolescent-onset anorexia nervosa: Personality disorders. *Journal of the American Academy of Child and Adolescent Psychiatry, 38,* 1389–1395.

Nisan, M., & Kohlberg, L. (1982). Universality and variation in moral judgment: A longitudinal and cross-sectional study in Turkey. *Child Development, 53,* 865–876.

Nolen-Hoeksema, S. (1994). An interactive model for the emergence of gender differences in depression in adolescence. *Journal of Research on Adolescence, 4,* 519–534.

Nomaguchi, K. (2006). Maternal employment, nonparental care, mother-child interactions, and child outcomes during preschool years. *Journal of Marriage and Family, 68,* 1341–1369.

Norboru, T. (1997). A developmental study of wordplay in preschool children: The Japanese game of "Shiritori." *Japanese Journal of Developmental Psychology, 8,* 42–52.

Norton, A., & D'Ambrosio, B. (2008). ZPC and ZPD: Zones of teaching and learning. *Journal for Research in Mathematics Education, 39,* 220–246.

Norwood, M. K. (1997, April). *Academic achievement in African-American adolescents as a function of family structure and child-rearing practices.* Paper presented at the biennial meetings of the Society for Research in Child Development, Washington, DC.

Nucci, L. P., & Nucci, M. S. (1982). Children's social interactions in the context of moral and conventional transgressions. *Child Development, 53,* 403–412.

Nunner-Winkler, G. (2007). Development of moral motivation from childhood to early adulthood. *Journal of Moral Education, 36,* 399–414.

Nussbaum, A., & Steele, C. (2007). Situational disengagement and persistence in the face of adversity. *Journal of Experimental Social Psychology, 43,* 127–134.

Oates, J. (1998). Risk factors for infant attrition and low engagement in experiments and free play. *Infant Behavior and Development, 21,* 555–569.

O'Beirne, H., & Moore, C. (1995, April). *Attachment and sexual behavior in adolescence.* Paper presented at the biennial meetings of the Society for Research in Child Development, Indianapolis.

Office of Juvenile Justice and Delinquency Prevention. (2006). *Juvenile offenders and victims: 2006 report.* Retrieved April 12, 2008, from http://ojjdp.ncjrs.gov/ojstatbb/nr2006/index.html

Offord, D. R., Boyle, M. H., & Racine, Y. A. (1991). The epidemiology of antisocial behavior in childhood and adolescence. In D. J. Pepler & K. H. Rubin (Eds.), *The development and treatment of childhood aggression* (pp. 31–54). Hillsdale, NJ: Erlbaum.

Ogbu, J. U. (1994). From cultural differences to differences in cultural frame of reference. In P. M. Greenfield & R. R. Cocking (Eds.), *Cross-cultural roots of minority child development* (pp. 365–391). Hillsdale, NJ: Erlbaum.

Ogbu, J. U. (2004). Collective identity and the burden of "acting white" in black history, community, and education. *Urban Review, 36,* 1–35.

Oldenburg, C., & Kerns, K. (1997). Associations between peer relationships and depressive symptoms: Testing moderator effects of gender and age. *Journal of Early Adolescence, 17,* 319–337.

O'Leary, S., Smith Slep, A., & Reid, M. (1999). A longitudinal study of mothers' overreactive discipline and toddlers' externalizing behavior. *Journal of Abnormal Child Psychology, 27,* 331–341.

Olfman, S. (2006). Introduction. In S. Olfman (Ed.), *No child left different* (pp. 1–14). Westport, CT: Greenwood Publishers.

Olivan, G. (2003). Catch-up growth assessment in long-term physically neglected and emotionally abused preschool age male children. *Child Abuse & Neglect, 27,* 103–108.

Oller, D., Cobo-Lewis, A., & Eilers, R. (1998). Phonological translation in bilingual and monolingual children. *Applied Psycholinguistics, 19,* 259–278.

Olshan, A. F., Baird, P. A., & Teschke, K. (1989). Paternal occupational exposures and the risk of Down syndrome. *American Journal of Human Genetics, 44,* 646–651.

Olthof, T., Ferguson, T., Bloemers, E., & Deij, M. (2004). Morality-and identity-related antecedents of children's guilt and shame attributions in events involving physical illness. *Cognition & Emotion, 18,* 383–404.

Olweus, D. (1995). Bullying or peer abuse at school: Facts and intervention. *Current Directions in Psychological Science, 4,* 196–200.

Ompad, D., Strathdee, S., Celentano, D., Latkin, C., Poduska, J., Kellam, S., & Ialongo, N. (2006). Predictors of early initiation of vaginal and oral sex among urban young adults in Baltimore, Maryland. *Archives of Sexual Behavior, 35,* 53–65.

O'Neill, D. K., Astington, J. W., & Flavell, J. H. (1992). Young children's understanding of the role that sensory experiences play in knowledge acquisition. *Child Development, 63,* 474–490.

Ontai, L., & Thompson, R. (2008). Attachment, parent-child discourse, and theory-of-mind development. *Social Development, 17,* 47–60.

Oosterlaan, J., Geurts, H., Knol, D., & Sergeant, J. (2005). Low basal salivary cortisol is associated with teacher-reported symptoms of conduct disorder. *Psychiatry Research, 134,* 1–10.

Organization of Teratology Information Specialists. (2005). *Acetaminophen and pregnancy.* Retrieved June 7, 2007, from http://www.otispregnancy.org/pdf/acetaminophen.pdf

O'Shea, T. M., Klinepeter, K. L., Goldstein, D. J., Jackson, B. W., & Dillard, R. G. (1997). Survival and developmental disability in infants with birth weights of 501 to 800 grams, born between 1979 and 1994. *Pediatrics, 100*, 982–986.

Osofsky, J. D. (1995). The effects of exposure to violence on young children. *American Psychologist, 50*, 782–788.

Osorio-O'Dea, P. (2001). *CRS report for Congress: Bilingual education.* Retrieved June 23, 2008, from http://www.policyalmanac. org/education/archive/bilingual.pdf

Overby, K. (2002). Pediatric health supervision. In A. Rudolph, R. Kamei, & K. Overby (Eds.), *Rudolph's fundamentals of pediatrics* (3rd ed., pp. 1–69). New York: McGraw-Hill.

Overton, W. F., & Reese, H. W. (1973). Models of development: Methodological implications. In J. R. Nesselroade & H. W. Reese (Eds.), *Life-span developmental psychology: Methodological issues* (pp. 65–86). New York: Academic Press.

Overton, W. F., Ward, S. L., Noveck, I. A., Black, J., & O'Brien, D. P. (1987). Form and content in the development of deductive reasoning. *Developmental Psychology, 23*, 22–30.

Owens, J., Spirito, A., McGuinn, M., & Nobile, C. (2000). Sleep habits and sleep disturbance in elementary school-aged children. *Journal of Developmental & Behavioral Pediatrics, 21*, 27–36.

Oyserman, D., Harrison, K., & Bybee, D. (2001). Can racial identity be promotive of academic efficacy? *International Journal of Behavioral Development, 25*, 379–385.

Pagani, L., Boulerice, B., Tremblay, R., & Vitaro, F. (1997). Behavioural development in children of divorce and remarriage. *Journal of Child Psychology & Psychiatry & Allied Disciplines, 38*, 769–781.

Paikoff, R. L., & Brooks-Gunn, J. (1990). Physiological processes: What role do they play during the transition to adolescence? In R. Montemayor, G. R. Adams, & T. P. Gullotta (Eds.), *From childhood to adolescence: A transitional period?* (pp. 63–81). Newbury Park, CA: Sage.

Painter, M., & Bergman, I. (1998). Neurology. In R. Behrman & R. Kliegman (Eds.), *Nelson essentials of pediatrics* (3rd ed., pp. 694–745). Philadelphia: Saunders.

Paiva, N. (2008). South Asian parents' constructions of praising their children. *Clinical Child Psychology and Psychiatry, 13*, 191–207.

Pajares, F., & Graham, L. (1999). Self-efficacy, motivation constructs, and mathematics performance of entering middle school students. *Contemporary Educational Psychology, 24*, 124–139.

Pajulo, M., Savonlahti, E., Sourander, A., Helenius, H., & Piha, J. (2001). Antenatal depression, substance dependency and social support. *Journal of Affective Disorders, 65*, 9–17.

Palkovitz, R. (1985). Fathers' birth attendance, early contact, and extended contact with their newborns: A critical review. *Child Development, 56*, 392–406.

Palmer, A. (2003). The street that changed everything. *APA Monitor on Psychology, 34*, 90.

Pan, B., Rowe, M., Singer, J., & Snow, C. (2005). Maternal correlates of growth in toddler vocabulary production in low-income families. *Child Development, 76*, 763–782.

Papousek, H., & Papousek, M. (1991). Innate and cultural guidance of infants' integrative competencies: China, the United States, and Germany. In M. H. Bornstein (Ed.), *Cultural approaches to parenting* (pp. 23–44). Hillsdale, NJ: Erlbaum.

Parault, S., & Schwanenflugel, P. (2000). The development of conceptual categories of attention during the elementary school years. *Journal of Experimental Child Psychology, 75*, 245–262.

Parent, S., Tillman, G., Jule, A., Skakkebaek, N., Toppari, J., & Bourguignon, J. (2003). The timing of normal puberty and the age limits of sexual precocity: Variations around the world, secular trends, and changes after migration. *Endocrine Review, 24*, 668–693.

Park, N. (2005). Life satisfaction among Korean children and youth: A developmental perspective. *School Psychology International, 26*, 209–223.

Parke, R. (2004). The Society for Research in Child Development at 70: Progress and promise. *Child Development, 75*, 1–24.

Parke, R. D. (1995). Fathers and families. In M. H. Bornstein (Ed.), *Handbook of parenting: Vol. 3. Status and social conditions of parenting* (pp. 27–63). Mahwah, NJ: Erlbaum.

Parke, R. D., & Buriel, R. (1998). Socialization in the family: Ethnic and ecological perspectives. In W. Damon (Ed.), *Handbook of child psychology: Vol 3. Social, emotional, and personality development* (5th ed., pp. 463–552). New York: Wiley.

Parmelee, A. H., Jr., Wenner, W. H., & Schulz, H. R. (1964). Infant sleep patterns from birth to 16 weeks of age. *Journal of Pediatrics, 65*, 576–582.

Parten, M. B. (1932). Social participation among preschool children. *Journal of Abnormal and Social Psychology, 27*, 243–269.

Pascalis, O., de Schonen, S., Morton, J., Derulle, C., & Fabre-Grenet, M. (1995). Mother's face recognition by neonates: A replication and extension. *Infant Behavior and Development, 18*, 79–85.

Passman, R. H., & Longeway, K. P. (1982). The role of vision in maternal attachment: Giving 2-year-olds a photograph of their mother during separation. *Developmental Psychology, 18*, 530–533.

Patterson, C. (1997). Children of lesbian and gay parents. *Advances in Clinical Child Psychology, 19*, 235–282.

Patterson, G. R. (1975). *Families: Applications of social learning to family life.* Champaign, IL: Research Press.

Patterson, G. R. (1996). Some characteristics of a developmental theory for early-onset delinquency. In M. F. Lenzenweger & J. J. Haugaard (Eds.), *Frontiers of developmental psychopathology* (pp. 81–124). New York: Oxford University Press.

Patterson, G. R., Capaldi, D., & Bank, L. (1991). An early starter model for predicting delinquency. In D. J. Pepler & K. H. Rubin (Eds.), *The development and treatment of childhood aggression* (pp. 139–168). Hillsdale, NJ: Erlbaum.

Patterson, G. R., Reid, J. B., & Dishion, T. J. (1992). *Antisocial boys.* Eugene, OR: Castalia Press.

Patterson, J. (1998). Expressive vocabulary of bilingual toddlers: Preliminary findings. *Electronic Multicultural Journal of Communication Disorders, 1.* Retrieved April 11, 2001, from http://www. asha.ucf.edu/patterson.html

Patterson, J. (2002). Relationships of expressive vocabulary to frequency of reading and television experience among bilingual toddlers. *Applied Psycholinguistics, 23*, 493–508.

Pedlow, R., Sanson, A., Prior, M., & Oberklaid, F. (1993). Stability of maternally reported temperament from infancy to 8 years. *Developmental Psychology, 29*, 998–1007.

Pegg, J. E., Werker, J. F., & McLeod, P. J. (1992). Preference for infant-directed over adult-directed speech: Evidence from 7-week-old infants. *Infant Behavior and Development, 15*, 325–345.

Peisner-Feinberg, E. S. (1995, April). *Developmental outcomes and the relationship to quality of child care experiences.* Paper presented at the biennial meetings of the Society for Research in Child Development, Indianapolis.

Peisner-Feinberg, E. S., & Burchinal, M. R. (1997). Relations between preschool children's child-care experiences and concurrent development: The Cost, Quality, and Outcomes Study. *Merrill-Palmer Quarterly, 43*, 451–477.

Pelham, W., Hoza, B., Pillow, D., Gnagy, E., Kipp, H., Greiner, A., Waschbusch, D., Trane, S., Greenhouse, J., Wolfson, L., & Fitzpatrick, E. (2002). Effects of methylphenidate and expectancy on children with ADHD: Behavior, academic performance, and attributions in a summer treatment program and regular classroom settings. *Journal of Consulting and Clinical Psychology, 70*, 320–335.

Pennington, B., Moon, J., Edgin, J., Stedron, J., & Nadel, L. (2003). The neuropsychology of Down syndrome: Evidence of hippocampal dysfunction. *Child Development, 74*, 75–93.

Pennington, D. (2000). *Social cognition.* Philadelphia: Taylor & Francis.

Peoples, C. E., Fagan, J. F., III, & Drotar, D. (1995). The influence of race on 3-year-old children's performance on the Stanford-Binet: Fourth edition. *Intelligence, 21*, 69–82.

Pereverzeva, M., Hui-Lin Chien, S., Palmer, J., & Teller, D. (2002). Infant photometry: Are mean adult isoluminance values a sufficient approximation to individual infant values? *Vision Research, 42*, 1639–1649.

Periasamy, S., & Ashby, J. (2002). Multidimensional perfectionism and locus of control: Adaptive vs. maladaptive perfectionism. *Journal of College Student Psychotherapy, 17*, 75–86.

Perkins, D. F., & Luster, T. (1997, April). *The relationship between sexual abuse and a bulimic behavior: Findings from community-wide surveys of female adolescents.* Paper presented at the biennial meetings of the Society for Research in Child Development, Washington, DC.

Perlman, M., Claris, O., Hao, Y., Pandid, P., Whyte, H., Chipman, M., & Liu, P. (1995). Secular changes in the outcomes to eighteen to twenty-four months of age of extremely low birth weight infants, with adjustment for changes in risk factors and severity of illness. *Journal of Pediatrics, 126*, 75–87.

Perry, D., Kusel, S. K., & Perry, L. C. (1988). Victims of peer aggression. *Developmental Psychology, 24*, 807–814.

Perry, T., Ohde, R., & Ashmead, D. (2001). The acoustic bases for gender identification from children's voices. *Journal of the Acoustical Society of America, 109*, 2988–2998.

Persson, A., & Musher-Eizenman, D. (2003). The impact of a prejudice-prevention television program on young children's ideas about race. *Early Childhood Research Quarterly, 18*, 530–546.

Petersen, A. C. (1987). The nature of biological-psychosocial interactions: The sample case of early adolescence. In R. M. Lerner & T. T. Foch (Eds.), *Biological-psychosocial interactions in early adolescence* (pp. 35–62). Hillsdale, NJ: Erlbaum.

Petersen, A. C., Compas, B. E., Brooks-Gunn, J., Stemmler, M., Ey, S., & Grant, K. E. (1993). Depression in adolescence. *American Psychologist, 48*, 155–168.

Petersen, A. C., Sarigiani, P. A., & Kennedy, R. E. (1991). Adolescent depression: Why more girls? *Journal of Youth & Adolescence, 20*, 247–272.

Petersen, A. C., & Taylor, B. (1980). The biological approach to adolescence. In J. Adelson (Ed.), *Handbook of adolescent psychology* (pp. 117–158). New York: Wiley.

Peterson, C., & Bell, M. (1996). Children's memory for traumatic injury. *Child Development, 67*, 3045–3070.

Peterson, C. C., & Siegal, M. (1995). Deafness, conversation and theory of mind. *Journal of Child Psychology and Psychiatry, 36*, 459–474.

Peterson, C. C., & Siegal, M. (1999). Representing inner worlds: Theory of mind in autistic, deaf, and normal hearing children. *Psychological Science, 10*, 126–129.

Peterson, C. C., Wellman, H., & Liu, D. (2005). Steps in theory-of-mind development for children with deafness or autism. *Child Development, 76*, 502–517.

Peterson, D., Marcia, J., & Carpendale, J. (2004). Identity: Does thinking make it so? In C. Lightfoot, C. Lalonde, & M. Chandler (Eds.), *Changing conceptions of psychological life* (pp. 113–126). Mahwah, NJ: Erlbaum.

Peterson, J., Pihl, R., Higgins, D., Seguin, J., & Tremblay, R. (2003). Neuropsychological performance, IQ, personality, and grades in a longitudinal grade-school male sample. *Individual Differences Research, 1*, 159–172.

Peterson, L., Ewigman, B., & Kivlahan, C. (1993). Judgments regarding appropriate child supervision to prevent injury: The role of environmental risk and child age. *Child Development, 64*, 934–950.

Pettit, G. S., Bates, J. E., & Dodge, K. A. (1997). Supportive parenting, ecological context, and children's adjustment: A seven-year longitudinal study. *Child Development, 68*, 908–923.

Pettit, G. S., Clawson, M. A., Dodge, K. A., & Bates, J. E. (1996). Stability and change in peer-rejected status: The role of child behavior, parenting, and family ecology. *Merrill-Palmer Quarterly, 42*, 295–318.

Pettit, G. S., Laird, R. D., Bates, J. E., & Dodge, K. A. (1997). Patterns of after-school care in middle childhood: Risk factors and developmental outcomes. *Merrill-Palmer Quarterly, 43*, 515–538.

Pezdek, K., Blandon-Gitlin, I., & Moore, C. (2003). Children's face recognition memory: More evidence for the cross-race effect. *Journal of Applied Psychology, 88*, 760–763.

Pezzella, F. (2006, November). *Authoritarian parenting: A race socializing protective factor that deters at risk African American males from delinquency and violence.* Paper presented at the annual meeting of the American Society of Criminology, Los Angeles.

Phares, V., & Compas, B. (1993). Fathers and developmental psychopathology. *Current Directions in Psychological Science, 2*, 162–165.

Phillips, D., Schwean, V., & Saklofske, D. (1997). Treatment effect of a school-based cognitive-behavioral program for aggressive children. *Canadian Journal of School Psychology, 13*, 60–67.

Phinney, J. S. (1990). Ethnic identity in adolescents and adults: Review of research. *Psychological Bulletin, 108*, 499–514.

Phinney, J. S., & Devich-Navarro, M. (1997). Variations in bicultural identification among African American and Mexican American adolescents. *Journal of Research on Adolescence, 7*, 3–32.

Phinney, J. S., Ferguson, D. L., & Tate, J. D. (1997). Intergroup attitudes among ethnic minority adolescents: A causal model. *Child Development, 68*, 955–969.

Phinney, J. S., Horenczyk, G., Liebkind, K., & Vedder, P. (2001). Ethnic identity, immigration, and well-being: An interactional perspective. *Journal of Social Issues, 57*, 493–510.

Phinney, J. S., Kim-Jo, T., Osorio, S., & Vilhjalmsdottir, P. (2005). Autonomy and relatedness in adolescent-parent disagreements: Ethnic and developmental factors. *Journal of Adolescent Research, 20*, 8–39.

Phinney, J. S., & Rosenthal, D. A. (1992). Ethnic identity in adolescence: Process, context, and outcome. In G. R. Adams, T. P. Gullotta, & R. Montemayor (Eds.), *Adolescent identity formation* (pp. 145–172). Newbury Park, CA: Sage.

Piaget, J. (1932). *The moral judgment of the child.* New York: Macmillan.

Piaget, J. (1952). *The origins of intelligence in children.* New York: International Universities Press.

Piaget, J. (1954). *The construction of reality in the child.* New York: Basic Books. (Originally published 1937)

Piaget, J. (1962). *Play, dreams, and imitation in childhood.* New York: W. W. Norton.

Piaget, J. (1965). *The moral judgment of the child.* New York: Free Press.

Piaget, J. (1970). Piaget's theory. In P. H. Mussen (Ed.), *Carmichael's manual of child psychology* (3rd ed., Vol. 1, pp. 703–732). New York: Wiley.

Piaget, J. (1977). *The development of thought: Equilibration of cognitive structures.* New York: Viking Press.

Piaget, J., & Inhelder, B. (1969). *The psychology of the child.* New York: Basic Books.

Pianta, R. C., & Egeland, B. (1994a). Predictors of instability in children's mental test performance at 24, 48, and 96 months. *Intelligence, 18,* 145–163.

Pianta, R. C., & Egeland, B. (1994b). Relation between depressive symptoms and stressful life events in a sample of disadvantaged mothers. *Journal of Consulting and Clinical Psychology, 62,* 1229–1234.

Pianta, R. C., Steinberg, M. S., & Rollins, K. B. (1995). Teacher-child relationships and deflections in children's classroom adjustment. *Development and Psychopathology, 7,* 295–312.

Pickens, J. (1994). Perception of auditory-visual distance relations by 5-month-old infants. *Developmental Psychology, 30,* 537–544.

Pickens, J., & Field, T. (1993). Facial expressivity in infants of depressed mothers. *Developmental Psychology, 29,* 986–988.

Pierce, M., & Leon, D. (2005). Age at menarche and adult BMI in the Aberdeen children of the 1950s cohort study. *American Journal of Clinical Nutrition, 82,* 733–739.

Pillow, B. (1999). Children's understanding of inferential knowledge. *Journal of Genetic Psychology, 160,* 419–428.

Pinker, S. (1994). *The language instinct: How the mind creates language.* New York: Morrow.

Pisecco, S., Wristers, K., Swank, P., Silva, P., & Baker, D. (2001). The effect of academic self-concept on ADHD and antisocial behaviors in early adolescence. *Journal of Learning Disabilities, 34,* 459–461.

Pittman, L., & Chase-Lansdale, P. (2001). African American adolescent girls in impoverished communities: Parenting style and adolescent outcomes. *Journal of Research on Adolescence, 11,* 199–224.

Planty, M., Hussar, W., Provasnik, S., Kena, G., Dinkes, R., Kewl-Ramani, A., Kemp, J., Kridl, B., & Livingston, A. (2008). *Condition of education 2007.* Retrieved August 17, 2008, from http://nces.ed.gov/pubsearch/pubsinfo.asp?pubid=2008031

Plomin, R. (1990). *Nature and nurture: An introduction to behavior genetics.* Pacific Grove, CA: Brooks/Cole.

Plomin, R. (1995). Genetics and children's experiences in the family. *Journal of Child Psychology and Psychiatry, 36,* 33–68.

Plomin, R. (2001). Genetics and behavior. *Psychologist, 14,* 134–139.

Plomin, R. (2004). Genetics and developmental psychology. *Merrill-Palmer Quarterly, 50,* 341–352.

Plomin, R., & DeFries, J. C. (1985). *Origins of individual differences in infancy: The Colorado Adoption Project.* Orlando, FL: Academic Press.

Plomin, R., Loehlin, J. C., & DeFries, J. C. (1985). Genetic and environmental components of "environmental" influences. *Developmental Psychology, 21,* 391–402.

Plomin, R., Reiss, D., Hetherington, E. M., & Howe, G. W. (1994). Nature and nurture: Genetic contributions to measures of the family environment. *Developmental Psychology, 30,* 32–43.

Plomin, R., & Rende, R. (1991). Human behavioral genetics. *Annual Review of Psychology, 42,* 161–190.

Plucker, J. (1999). Is the proof in the pudding? Reanalyses of Torrance's (1958 to present) longitudinal data. *Creativity Research Journal, 12,* 103–115.

Polanczyk, G., de Lima, M., Horta, B., Biederman, J., & Rohde, L. (2007). Worldwide prevalence of ADHD: A systematic review and metaregression analysis. *American Journal of Psychiatry, 164,* 942–948.

Polderman, T., Gosso, M., Posthuma, D., Van Beijsterveldt, T., Heutink, P., Verhulst, F., & Boomsma, D. (2006). A longitudinal twin study on IQ, executive functioning, and attention problems during childhood and early adolescence. *Acta Neurologica Belgica, 106,* 191–207.

Polivy, J., & Herman, C. P. (1995). Dieting and its relation to eating disorders. In K. D. Brownell & C. G. Fairburn (Eds.), *Eating disorders and obesity: A comprehensive handbook* (pp. 83–86). New York: Guilford Press.

Pomerantz, E., & Ruble, D. (1998). The role of maternal control in the development of sex differences in child self-evaluative factors. *Child Development, 69,* 458–478.

Pomerleau, A., Malcuit, G., Turgeon, L., & Cossette, L. (1997). Effects of labelled gender on vocal communication of young women with 4-month-old infants. *International Journal of Psychology, 32,* 65–72.

Pomerleau, A., Scuccimarri, C., & Malcuit, G. (2003). Mother-infant behavioral interactions in teenage and adult mothers during the first six months postpartum: Relations with infant development. *Infant Mental Health Journal, 24,* 495–509.

Pons, F., Harris, P., & de Rosnay, M. (2004). Emotion comprehension between 3 and 11 years: Developmental periods and hierarchical organization. *Journal of Developmental Psychology, 1,* 127–152.

Population Resource Center. (2004). *Latina teen pregnancy: Problems and prevention.* Retrieved May 6, 2005, from http://www.prcds.org/summaries/latinapreg04/latinapreg04/html

Porter, J., & Washington, R. (1993). Minority identity and self-esteem. *Annual Review of Sociology, 19,* 139–161.

Porter, M., Coltheart, M., & Langdon, R. (2008). Theory of mind in Williams syndrome assessed using a nonverbal task. *Journal of Autism and Developmental Disorders, 38,* 806–814.

Posada, G., Jacobs, A., Richmond, M., Carbonell, O., Alzate, G., Bustamante, M., & Quiceno, J. (2002). Maternal caregiving and infant security in two cultures. *Developmental Psychology, 38,* 67–78.

Posey, D., Puntney, J., Sasher, T., Kem, D., & McDougle, C. (2004). Guanfacine treatment of hyperactivity and inattention in pervasive developmental disorders: A retrospective analysis of 80 cases. *Journal of Child & Adolescent Psychopharmacology, 14,* 233–241.

Posner, J., & Vandell, D. (1994). Low-income children's after-school care: Are there beneficial effects of after-school programs? *Child Development, 65,* 440–456.

Posthuma, D., de Geus, E., & Boomsma, D. (2003). Genetic contributions to anatomical, behavioral, and neurophysiological indices of cognition. In R. Plomin, J. DeFries, I. Craig, & P. McGuffin (Eds.), *Behavioral genetics in the postgenomic era* (pp. 141–161). Washington, DC: American Psychological Association.

Poulin, F., & Boivin, M. (1999). Proactive and reactive aggression and boys' friendship quality in mainstream classrooms. *Journal of Emotional & Behavioral Disorders, 7,* 168–177.

Poulin, F., & Boivin, M. (2000). The role of proactive and reactive aggression in the formation and development of boys' friendships. *Developmental Psychology, 36,* 233–240.

Poulson, C. L., Nunes, L. R. D., & Warren, S. F. (1989). Imitation in infancy: A critical review. In H. W. Reese (Ed.), *Advances in child development and behavior* (Vol. 22, pp. 272–298). San Diego, CA: Academic Press.

Power, T. (2000). *Play and exploration in children and animals.* Hillsdale, NJ: Erlbaum.

Powlishta, K. K., Serbin, L. A., Doyle, A., & White, D. R. (1994). Gender, ethnic, and body type biases: The generality of prejudice in childhood. *Developmental Psychology, 30,* 526–536.

Pozzi, M. (2003). A three-year-old boy with ADHD and Asperger's syndrome treated with parent-child psychotherapy. *Journal of the British Association of Psychotherapists, 41,* 16–31.

Prat-Sala, M., Shillcock, R., & Sorace, A. (2000). Animacy effects on the production of object-dislocated description by Catalan-speaking children. *Journal of Child Language, 27*, 97–117.

Pratt, M., Arnold, M., & Pratt, A. (1999). Predicting adolescent moral reasoning from family climate: A longitudinal study. *Journal of Early Adolescence, 19*, 148–175.

Prechtl, H., & Beintema, D. (1964). *The neurological examination of the full-term newborn infant: Clinics in developmental medicine.* London: Heinemann.

Prentice, D., & Miller, D. (2002). The emergence of homegrown stereotypes. *American Psychologist, 57*, 352–359.

Pressley, M., & Dennis-Rounds, J. (1980). Transfer of a mnemonic keyword strategy at two age levels. *Journal of Educational Psychology, 72*, 575–582.

Pressley, M., & Wharton-McDonald, R. (1997). Skilled comprehension and its development through instruction. *School Psychology Review, 26*, 448–466.

Pressman, E., DiPietro, J., Costigan, K., Shupe, A., & Johnson, T. (1998). Fetal neurobehavioral development: Associations with socioeconomic class and fetal sex. *Developmental Psychobiology, 33*, 79–91.

Pretz, J., & Sternberg, R. (2005). Unifying the field: Cognition and intelligence. In J. Pretz & R. Sternberg (Eds.), *Cognition and intelligence: Identifying the mechanisms of mind* (pp. 306–318). New York: Cambridge University Press.

Price, C., & Kunz, J. (2003). Rethinking the paradigm of juvenile delinquency as related to divorce. *Journal of Divorce & Remarriage, 39*, 109–133.

Prinstein, M., & La Greca, A. (1999). Links between mothers' and children's social competence and associations with maternal adjustment. *Journal of Clinical Child Psychology, 28*, 197–210.

Public Health Policy Advisory Board. (2001). *Health and the American child: A focus on mortality among children.* Washington, DC: Author.

Pujol, J., Deus, J., Losilla, J., & Capdevila, A. (1999). Cerebral lateralization of language in normal left-handed people studied by functional MRI. *Neurology, 52*, 1038–1043.

Pulkkinen, L. (1982). Self-control and continuity from childhood to late adolescence. In P. Baltes & O. G. Brim, Jr. (Eds.), *Life span development and behavior* (Vol. 4, pp. 64–107). New York: Academic Press.

Purugganan, O., Stein, R., Johnson Silver, E., & Benenson, B. (2003). Exposure to violence and psychosocial adjustment among urban school-aged children. *Journal of Developmental and Behavioral Pediatrics, 24*, 424–430.

Putallaz, M., Grimes, C., Foster, K., Kupersmidt, J., Coie, J., & Dearing, K. (2007). Overt and relational aggression and victimization: Multiple perspectives within the school setting. *Journal of School Psychology, 45*, 523–547.

Putnam, J. W., Spiegel, A. N., & Bruininks, R. H. (1995). Future directions in education and inclusion of students with disabilities: A Delphi investigation. *Exceptional Children, 61*, 553–576.

Putnam, S., & Stifter, C. (2005). Behavioral approach-inhibition in toddlers: Prediction from infancy, positive and negative affective components, and relations with behavior problems. *Child Development, 76*, 212–226.

Putnins, A. (1997). Victim awareness programs for delinquent youths: Effects on moral reasoning maturity. *Adolescence, 32*, 709–714.

Qi, C., & Kaiser, A. (2003). Behavior problems of preschool children from low-income families: Review of the literature. *Early Childhood Special Education, 23*, 188–216.

Quick stats: Prevalence of HPV infection among sexually active females aged 14 to 59 years. (2007). *Morbidity and Mortality Weekly Report, 56*, 852.

Quintana, S. (2007). Racial and ethnic identity: Developmental perspectives and research. *Journal of Counseling Psychology, 54*, 259–270.

Raffaelli, M., & Ontai, L. (2004). Gender socialization in Latino/a families: Results from two retrospective studies. *Sex Roles, 50*, 287–299.

Ragnarsdottir, H., Simonsen, H., & Plunkett, K. (1999). The acquisition of past tense morphology in Icelandic and Norwegian children: An experimental study. *Journal of Child Language, 26*, 577–618.

Raja, S. N., McGee, R., & Stanton, W. R. (1992). Perceived attachments to parents and peers and psychological well-being in adolescence. *Journal of Youth & Adolescence, 21*, 471–485.

Ramey, C., & Ramey, S. (2004). Early learning and school readiness: Can early intervention make a difference? *Merrill-Palmer Quarterly, 50*, 471–491.

Ramey, C. T. (1993). A rejoinder to Spitz's critique of the Abecedarian experiment. *Intelligence, 17*, 25–30.

Ramey, C. T., & Campbell, F. A. (1987). The Carolina Abecedarian Project: An educational experiment concerning human malleability. In J. J. Gallagher & C. T. Ramey (Eds.), *The malleability of children* (pp. 127–140). Baltimore: Brookes.

Ramey, C. T., & Ramey, S. L. (1998). Early intervention and early experience. *American Psychologist, 53*, 109–120.

Ramey, S. L., Ramey, C. T., & Lanzi, R. (2007). Early intervention: Background, research findings, and future directions. In J. Jacobson, J. Mulick, & J. Rojahn (Eds.), *Issues in clinical child psychology* (pp. 445–463). New York: Springer.

Ranson, K., & Urichuk, L. (2008). The effect of parent-child attachment relationships on child biopsychosocial outcomes: A review. *Early Child Development and Care, 178*, 129–152.

Rattaz, C., Goubet, N., & Bullinger, A. (2005). The calming effect of a familiar odor on full-term newborns. *Journal of Developmental and Behavioral Pediatrics, 26*, 86–92.

Räty, H., Vänskä, J., Kasanen, K., & Kärkkäinen, R. (2002). Parents' explanations of their child's performance in mathematics and reading: A replication and extension of Yee and Eccles. *Sex Roles, 46*, 121–128.

Ray, B. (1999). *Home schooling on the threshold: A survey of research at the dawn of the new millennium.* Washington, DC: Home Education Research Institute.

Rees, J. M., Lederman, S. A., & Kiely, J. L. (1996). Birth weight associated with lowest neonatal mortality: Infants of adolescent and adult mothers. *Pediatrics, 98*, 1161–1166.

Rego, A. (2006). The alphabetic principle, phonics, and spelling: Teaching students the code. In J. Schumm (Ed.), *Reading assessment and instruction for all learners* (pp. 118–162). New York: Guilford Press.

Reiner, W., & Gearhardt, J. (2004). Discordant sexual identity in some genetic males with cloacal exstrophy assigned to female sex at birth. *New England Journal of Medicine, 350*, 333–341.

Reinherz, H. Z., Giaconia, R. M., Pakiz, B., Silverman, A. B., Frost, A. K., & Lefkowitz, E. S. (1993). Psychosocial risks for major depression in late adolescence: A longitudinal community study. *Journal of the American Academy of Child and Adolescent Psychiatry, 32*, 1155–1163.

Reis, S., & Park, S. (2001). Gender differences in high-achieving students in math and science. *Journal for the Education of the Gifted, 25*, 52–73.

Reisman, J. M., & Shorr, S. I. (1978). Friendship claims and expectations among children and adults. *Child Development, 49*, 913–916.

Reiss, D. (1998). Mechanisms linking genetic and social influences in adolescent development: Beginning a collaborative search. *Current Directions in Psychological Science, 6*, 100–105.

Remafedi, G., Resnick, M., Blum, R., & Harris, L. (1998). Demography of sexual orientation in adolescents. *Pediatrics, 89,* 714–721.

Renouf, A. G., & Harter, S. (1990). Low self-worth and anger as components of the depressive experience in young adolescents. *Development and Psychopathology, 2,* 293–310.

Resnick, M. D., Bearman, P. S., Blum, R. W., Bauman, K. E., Harris, K. M., Jones, J., Tabor, J., Beuhring, T., Sieving, R. E., Shew, M., Ireland, M., Bearinger, L. H., & Udry, J. R. (1997). Protecting adolescents from harm: Findings from the National Longitudinal Study on Adolescent Health. *Journal of the American Medical Association, 278,* 823–832.

Rest, J. R. (1983). Morality. In J. H. Flavell & E. M. Markman (Eds.), *Handbook of child psychology: Cognitive development* (Vol. 3, pp. 556–629). New York: Wiley.

Retz, W., Retz-Junginger, P., Hengesch, G., Schneider, M., Thome, J., Pajonk, F., Salahi-Disfan, A., Rees, O., Wender, P., & Rösler, M. (2004). Psychometric and psychopathological characterization of young male prison inmates with and without attention deficit/hyperactivity disorder. *European Archives of Psychiatry & Clinical Neuroscience, 254,* 201–208.

Rey, C. (2001). Empathy in children and adolescents with disocial conduct disorder, and the degree of rejection, affective marginalization and permissiveness tolerated by their fathers and mothers. *Avances en Psicologia Clinica Latinoamericana, 19,* 25–36.

Rey, J., Sawyer, M., Raphael, B., Patton, G., & Lynskey, M. (2002). Mental health of teenagers who use cannabis: Results of an Australian survey. *British Journal of Psychiatry, 180,* 216–221.

Reynolds, A. J. (1994). Effects of a preschool plus follow-on intervention for children at risk. *Developmental Psychology, 30,* 787–804.

Reynolds, A. J., & Bezruczko, N. (1993). School adjustment of children at risk through fourth grade. *Merrill-Palmer Quarterly, 39,* 457–480.

Rholes, W. S., & Ruble, D. N. (1984). Children's understanding of dispositional characteristics of others. *Child Development, 55,* 550–560.

Ricci, C. M., Beal, C. R., & Dekle, D. J. (1995, April). *The effect of parent versus unfamiliar interviewers on young witnesses' memory and identification accuracy.* Paper presented at the biennial meetings of the Society for Research in Child Development, Indianapolis.

Rice, M. L., Huston, A. C., Truglio, R., & Wright, J. (1990). Words from "Sesame Street": Learning vocabulary while viewing. *Developmental Psychology, 26,* 421–428.

Richards, H. C., Bear, G. G., Stewart, A. L., & Norman, A. D. (1992). Moral reasoning and classroom conduct: Evidence of a curvilinear relationship. *Merrill-Palmer Quarterly, 38,* 176–190.

Richards, M., Hardy, R., Kuh, D., & Wadsworth, M. (2001). Birth weight and cognitive function in the British 1946 birth cohort: Longitudinal population-based study. *BMJ: British Medical Journal, 322,* 199–203.

Richards, M. H., Crowe, P. A., Larson, R., & Swarr, A. (1998). Developmental patterns and gender differences in the experience of peer companionship during adolescence. *Child Development, 69,* 154–163.

Richters, J., & Pellegrini, D. (1989). Depressed mothers' judgments about their children: An examination of the depression-distortion hypothesis. *Child Development, 60,* 1068–1075.

Ridderinkhof, K., Scheres, A., Oosterlaan, J., & Sergeant, J. (2005). Delta plots in the study of individual differences: New tools reveal response inhibition deficits in AD/HD that are eliminated by methylphenidate treatment. *Journal of Abnormal Psychology, 114,* 197–215.

Riegel, K. F. (1975). Adult life crises: A dialectic interpretation of development. In N. Datan & L. H. Ginsberg (Eds.), *Lifespan developmental psychology: Normative life crises* (pp. 99–128). New York: Academic Press.

Rigby, K. (2005). Why do some children bully at school? The contributions of negative attitudes towards victims and the perceived expectations of friends, parents and teachers. *School Psychology International, 26,* 147–161.

Riggs, L. L. (1997, April). *Depressive affect and eating problems in adolescent females: An assessment of direction and influence using longitudinal data.* Paper presented at the biennial meetings of the Society for Research in Child Development, Washington, D.C.

Righetti, P. (1996). The emotional experience of the fetus: A preliminary report. *Pre- & Peri-Natal Psychology Journal, 11,* 55–65.

Rinderman, H., & Neubauer, A. (2004). Processing speed, intelligence, creativity, and school performance: Testing of causal hypotheses using structural equation models. *Intelligence, 32,* 573–589.

Ripple, C., & Zigler, E. (2003). Research, policy, and the federal role in prevention initiatives for children. *American Psychologist, 58,* 482–490.

Rizzolatti, G., Sinigaglia, C., & Anderson, F. (2008). *Mirrors in the brain: How our minds share actions and emotions.* New York: Oxford University Press.

Roberts, J., & Bell, M. (2000). Sex differences on a mental rotation task: Variations in electroencephalogram hemispheric activation between children and college students. *Developmental Neuropsychology, 17,* 199–223.

Robinson, H. B. (1981). The uncommonly bright child. In M. Lewis & L. A. Rosenblum (Eds.), *The uncommon child* (pp. 57–82). New York: Plenum Press.

Robinson, N., Lanzi, R., Weinberg, R., Ramey, S., & Ramey, C. (2002). Family factors associated with high academic competence in former Head Start children at third grade. *Gifted Child Quarterly, 46,* 278–290.

Robinson, N. M., & Janos, P. M. (1986). Psychological adjustment in a college-level program of marked academic acceleration. *Journal of Youth & Adolescence, 15,* 51–60.

Rochat, P., & Striano, T. (2002). Who's in the mirror? Self-other discrimination in specular images by four- and nine-month-old infants. *Child Development, 73,* 35–46.

Roche, A. F. (1979). Secular trends in human growth, maturation, and development. *Monographs of the Society for Research in Child Development, 44*(3–4, Serial No. 179).

Rock, A., Trainor, L., & Addison, T. (1999). Distinctive messages in infant-directed lullabies and play songs. *Developmental Psychology, 35,* 527–534.

Roderick, M., & Camburn, E. (1999). Risk and recovery from course failure in the early years of high school. *American Educational Research Journal, 36,* 303–343.

Rodkin, P., Farmer, T., Pearl, R., & Van Acker, R. (2000). Heterogeneity of popular boys: Antisocial and prosocial configurations. *Developmental Psychology, 36,* 14–24.

Rodrigo, M., Janssens, J., & Ceballos, E. (1999). Do children's perceptions and attributions mediate the effects of mothers' child rearing actions? *Journal of Family Psychology, 13,* 508–522.

Roeser, R., & Eccles J. (1998). Adolescents' perceptions of middle school: Relation to longitudinal changes in academic and psychological adjustment. *Journal of Research on Adolescence, 8,* 123–158.

Rogers, J. L., Rowe, D. C., & May, K. (1994). DF analysis of NLSY IQ/achievement data: Non-shared environmental influences. *Intelligence, 19,* 157–177.

Rogosch, F. A., Cicchetti, D., Shields, A., & Toth, S. L. (1995). Parenting dysfunction in child maltreatment. In M. H. Bornstein

(Ed.), *Handbook of parenting: Vol. 4. Applied and practical parenting* (pp. 127–159). Mahwah, NJ: Erlbaum.

Rohner, R. P., Kean, K. J., & Cournoyer, D. E. (1991). Effects of corporal punishment, perceived caretaker warmth, and cultural beliefs on the psychological adjustment of children in St. Kitts, West Indies. *Journal of Marriage and the Family, 53,* 681–693.

Rooks, J. P., Weatherby, N. L., Ernst, E. K. M., Stapleton, S., Rosen, D., & Rosenfield, A. (1989). Outcomes of care in birth centers: The National Birth Center Study. *New England Journal of Medicine, 321,* 1804–1811.

Rosario, M., Scrimshaw, E., & Hunter, J. (2004). Ethnic/racial differences in the coming-out process of lesbian, gay, and bisexual youths: A comparison of sexual identity development over time. *Cultural Diversity and Ethnic Minority Psychology, 10,* 215–228.

Rosario, M., Scrimshaw, E., Hunter, J., & Braun, L. (2006). Sexual identity development among lesbian, gay, and bisexual youths: Consistency and change over time. *Journal of Sex Research, 43,* 46–58.

Rose, A., & Asher, S. (2004). Children's strategies and goals in response to help-giving and help-seeking tasks within a friendship. *Child Development, 75,* 749–763.

Rose, A. J., & Montemayor, R. (1994). The relationship between gender role orientation and perceived self-competence in male and female adolescents. *Sex Roles, 31,* 579–595.

Rose, R. J. (1995). Genes and human behavior. *Annual Review of Psychology, 56,* 625–654.

Rose, S. A., & Feldman, J. F. (1995). Prediction of IQ and specific cognitive abilities at 11 years from infancy measures. *Developmental Psychology, 31,* 685–696.

Rose, S. A., & Feldman, J. F. (1997). Memory and speed: Their role in the relation of infant information processing to later IQ. *Child Development, 68,* 630–641.

Rose, S. A., & Ruff, H. A. (1987). Cross-modal abilities in human infants. In J. D. Osofsky (Ed.), *Handbook of infant development* (2nd ed., pp. 318–362). New York: Wiley-Interscience.

Rosenbaum, J. E. (1984). *Career mobility in a corporate hierarchy.* New York: Academic Press.

Rosenberg, M. (2003). Recognizing gay, lesbian, and transgender teens in a child and adolescent psychiatry practice. *Journal of the American Academy of Child & Adolescent Psychiatry, 42,* 1517–1521.

Rosenblatt, P., & Wallace, B. (2005). Narratives of grieving African Americans about racism in the lives of deceased family members. *Death Studies, 29,* 217–235.

Rosenthal, R. (1994). Interpersonal expectancy effects: A 30-year perspective. *Current Directions in Psychological Science, 3,* 176–179.

Rosenthal, S., & Gitelman, S. (2002). Endocrinology. In A. Rudolph, R. Kamei, & K. Overby (Eds.), *Rudolph's fundamentals of pediatrics* (3rd ed., pp. 747–795). New York: McGraw-Hill.

Rosenthal, S., Lewis, L., Succop, P., & Burklow, K. (1997). Adolescent girls' perceived prevalence of sexually transmitted diseases and condom use. *Journal of Developmental and Behavioral Pediatrics, 18,* 158–161.

Ross, G., Kagan, J., Zelazo, P., & Kotelchuk, M. (1975). Separation protest in infants in home and laboratory. *Developmental Psychology, 11,* 256–257.

Rostosky, S., Owens, G., Zimmerman, R., & Riggle, E. (2003). Associations among sexual attraction status, school belonging, and alcohol and marijuana use in rural high school students. *Journal of Adolescence, 26,* 741–751.

Rothbart, M. (2004). Temperament and the pursuit of an integrated developmental psychology. *Merrill-Palmer Quarterly, 50,* 492–505.

Rothbart, M. K. (2007). Temperament, development, and personality. *Current Directions in Psychological Science, 16,* 207–212.

Rothbart, M. K., Ahadi, S., & Evans, D. (2000). Temperament and personality: Origins and outcomes. *Journal of Personality & Social Psychology, 78,* 83–116.

Rothbart, M., Ahadi, S., Hersey, K., & Fisher, P. (2001). Investigations of temperament at three to seven years: The Children's Behavior Questionnaire. *Child Development, 72,* 1394–1408.

Rothbart, M. K., & Bates, J. E. (1998). Temperament. In W. Damon (Ed.), *Handbook of child psychology: Vol 3. Social, emotional, and personality development* (5th ed., pp. 105–176). New York: Wiley.

Rothbart, M. K., & Putnam, S. (2002). Temperament and socialization. In L. Pulkkinen & A. Caspi (Eds.), *Paths to successful development: Personality in the life course* (pp. 19–45). New York: Cambridge University Press.

Rothbaum, F., Pott, M., & Morelli, G. (1995, April). *Ties that bind: Cultural differences in the development of family closeness.* Paper presented at the biennial meetings of the Society for Research in Child Development, Indianapolis.

Rotter, J. (1990). Internal versus external control of reinforcement: A case history of a variable. *American Psychologist, 45,* 489–493.

Rovee-Collier, C. (1986). The rise and fall of infant classical conditioning research: Its promise for the study of early development. In L. P. Lipsitt & C. Rovee-Collier (Eds.), *Advances in infancy research* (Vol. 4, pp. 139–162). Norwood, NJ: Ablex.

Rovee-Collier, C. (1993). The capacity for long-term memory in infancy. *Current Directions in Psychological Science, 2,* 130–135.

Rovet, J., & Netley, C. (1983). The triple X chromosome syndrome in childhood: Recent empirical findings. *Child Development, 54,* 831–845.

Rowe, D. (2003). Assessing genotype-environment interactions and correlations in the postgenomic era. In R. Plomin, J. DeFries, I. Craig, & P. McGuffin (Eds.), *Behavioral genetics in the postgenomic era* (pp. 71–86). Washington, DC: American Psychological Association.

Rowe, I., & Marcia, J. E. (1980). Ego identity status, formal operations, and moral development. *Journal of Youth & Adolescence, 9,* 87–99.

Roy, E., Bryden, P., & Cavill, S. (2003). Hand differences in pegboard performance through development. *Brain & Cognition, 53,* 315–317.

Rubin, K. H., Burgess, K., Dwyer, K., & Hastings, P. D. (2003). Predicting preschoolers' externalizing behaviors from toddler temperament, conflict, and maternal negativity. *Developmental Psychology, 39,* 164–176.

Rubin, K. H., Burgess, K., & Hastings, P. D. (2002). Stability and social-behavioral consequences of toddlers' inhibited temperament and parenting behaviors. *Child Development, 73,* 483–495.

Rubin, K. H., Cheah, C., & Fox, N. (2001). Emotion regulation, parenting, and display of social reticence in preschoolers. *Early Education & Development, 12,* 97–115.

Rubin, K. H., & Coplan, R. (2004). Paying attention to and not neglecting social withdrawal and social isolation. *Merrill-Palmer Quarterly, 50,* 506–534.

Rubin, K. H., Coplan, R., Chen, X., Baskirk, A., & Wojslawowica, J. (2005). Peer relationships in childhood. In M. Bornstein & M. Lamb (Eds.), *Developmental science: An advanced textbook* (5th ed., pp. 469–512). Hillsdale, NJ: Erlbaum.

Rubin, K. H., Hastings, P. D., Stewart, S. L., Henderson, H. A., & Chen, X. (1997). The consistency and concomitants of inhibition: Some of the children, all of the time. *Child Development, 68,* 467–483.

Rubin, K. H., Hymel, S., Mills, R. S. L., & Rose-Krasnor, L. (1991). Conceptualizing different developmental pathways to and from social isolation in childhood. In D. Cicchetti & S. L. Toth (Eds.),

Internalizing and externalizing expressions of dysfunction: Rochester symposium on developmental psychopathology (Vol. 2, pp. 91–122). Hillsdale, NJ: Erlbaum.

Ruble, D. N. (1987). The acquisition of self-knowledge: A self-socialization perspective. In N. Eisenberg (Ed.), *Contemporary topics in developmental psychology* (pp. 243–270). New York: Wiley-Interscience.

Ruble, D. N., & Martin, C. L. (1998). Gender development. In W. Damon (Ed.), *Handbook of child psychology: Vol 3. Social, emotional, and personality development* (5th ed., pp. 933–1016). New York: Wiley.

Ruble, D., Martin, C., & Berenbaum, S. (2006). Gender development. In N. Eisenberg, W. Damon, & R. Lerner (Eds.), *Handbook of child psychology: Vol. 3. Social, emotional, and personality development* (6th ed., pp. 858–932). Hoboken, NJ: Wiley.

Rueter, M. A., & Conger, R. D. (1995). Antecedents of parent-adolescent disagreements. *Journal of Marriage and the Family, 57*, 435–448.

Runyan, D. K., Hunter, W. M., Socolar, R. R. S., Amaya-Jackson, L., English, D., Landsverk, J., Dubowitz, H., Browne, D. H., Bandiwala, S. I., & Mathew, R. M. (1998). Children who prosper in unfavorable environments: The relationship to social capital. *Pediatrics, 101*, 12–18.

Rushton, J., & Jensen, A. (2005). Thirty years of research on race differences in cognitive ability. *Psychology, Public Policy, & Law, 11*, 235–294.

Russell, J. A. (1989). Culture, scripts, and children's understanding of emotion. In C. Saarni & P. L. Harris (Eds.), *Children's understanding of emotion* (pp. 293–318). Cambridge, England: Cambridge University Press.

Rutter, D. R., & Durkin, K. (1987). Turn-taking in mother-infant interaction: An examination of vocalizations and gaze. *Developmental Psychology, 23*, 54–61.

Rutter, M. (1978). Early sources of security and competence. In J. S. Bruner & A. Garton (Eds.), *Human growth and development* (pp. 33–61). London: Oxford University Press.

Rutter, M. (1987). Continuities and discontinuities from infancy. In J. D. Osofsky (Ed.), *Handbook of infant development* (2nd ed., pp. 1256–1296). New York: Wiley-Interscience.

Rutter, M. (1989). Isle of Wight revisited: Twenty-five years of child psychiatric epidemiology. *Journal of the American Academy of Child and Adolescent Psychiatry, 28*, 633–653.

Rutter, M. (2002). Nature, nurture, and development: From evangelism through science toward policy and practice. *Child Development, 73*, 1–21.

Rutter, M. (2005a). Aetiology of autism: Findings and questions. *Journal of Intellectual Disability Research, 49*, 231–238.

Rutter, M. (2005b). Environmentally mediated risks for psychopathology: Research strategies and findings. *Journal of the American Academy of Child and Adolescent Psychiatry, 44*, 3–18.

Rutter, M., & Garmezy, N. (1983). Developmental psychopathology. In E. M. Hetherington (Ed.), *Handbook of child psychology: Vol 4. Socialization, personality, and social development* (pp. 775–912). New York: Wiley.

Rutter, M., Dunn, J., Plomin, R., Simonoff, E., Pickles, A., Maughan, B., Ormel, J., Meyer, J., & Eaves, L. (1997). Integrating nature and nurture: Implications of person-environment correlations and interactions for developmental psychopathology. *Development and Psychopathology, 9*, 335–364.

Rutter, M., & Sroufe, A. (2000). Developmental psychopathology: Concepts and challenges. *Development and Psychopathology, 12*, 265–296.

Rybakowski, J. (2001). Moclobemide in pregnancy. *Pharmacopsychiatry, 34*, 82–83.

Ryder, J., Tunmer, W., & Greaney, K. (2008). Explicit instruction in phonemic awareness and phonemically based decoding skills as an intervention strategy for struggling readers in whole language classrooms. *Reading and Writing, 21*, 349–369.

Sadeh, A., Gruber, R., & Raviv, A. (2002). Sleep, neurobehavioral functioning, and behavior problems in school-age children. *Child Development, 73*, 405–417.

Saewyc, E., Bearinger, L., Heinz, P., Blum, R., & Resnick, M. (1998). Gender differences in health and risk behaviors among bisexual and homosexual adolescents. *Journal of Adolescent Health, 23*, 181–188.

Safren, S., & Heimberg, R. (1999). Depression, hopelessness, suicidality, and related factors in sexual minority and heterosexual adolescents. *Journal of Consulting and Clinical Psychology, 67*, 859–866.

Sagi, A. (1990). Attachment theory and research from a cross-cultural perspective. *Human Development, 33*, 10–22.

Sagi, A., van IJzendoorn, M. H., & Koren-Karie, N. (1991). Primary appraisal of the Strange Situation: A cross-cultural analysis of preseparation episodes. *Developmental Psychology, 27*, 587–596.

Sai, F. (2005). The role of the mother's voice in developing mother's face preference: Evidence for intermodal perception at birth. *Infant & Child Development, 14*, 29–50.

Saigal, S., Szatmari, P., Rosenbaum, P., Campbell, D., & King, S. (1991). Cognitive abilities and school performance of extremely low birth weight children and matched term control children at age 8 years: A regional study. *Journal of Pediatrics, 118*, 751–760.

Sak, U., & Maker, C. (2006). Developmental variation in children's creative mathematical thinking as a function of schooling, age, and knowledge. *Creativity Research, 18*, 279–291.

Saluja, G., Iachan, R., Scheidt, P., Overpeck, M., Sun, W., & Giedd, J. (2004). Prevalence of and risk factors for depressive symptoms among young adolescents. *Archives of Pediatric & Adolescent Medicine, 158*, 760–765.

Sameroff, A. J., Seifer, R., Barocas, R., Zax, M., & Greenspan, S. (1987). Intelligence quotient scores of 4-year-old children: Social-environmental risk factors. *Pediatrics, 79*, 343–350.

Sampson, R. J. (1997, April). *Child and adolescent development in community context: New findings from a multilevel study of 80 Chicago neighborhoods.* Paper presented at the biennial meetings of the Society for Research in Child Development, Washington, DC.

Sampson, R. J., & Laub, J. H. (1994). Urban poverty and the family context of delinquency: A new look at structure and process in a classic study. *Child Development, 65*, 523–540.

Sanchez, R., Crismon, M., Barner, J., Bettinger, T., & Wilson, J. (2005). Assessment of adherence measures with different stimulants among children and adolescents. *Pharmacotherapy, 25*, 909–917.

Sandelowski, M. (1994). Separate, but less unequal: Fetal ultrasonography and the transformation of expectant mother/fatherhood. *Gender & Society, 8*, 230–245.

Sandler, I., Miles, J., Cookston, J., & Braver, S. (2008). Effects of father and mother parenting on children's mental health in high- and low-conflict divorces. *Family Court Review, 46*, 282–296.

Sandman, C., Wadhwa, P., Hetrick, W., Porto, M., & Peeke, H. (1997). Human fetal heart rate dishabituation between thirty and thirty-two weeks. *Child Development, 68*, 1031–1040.

Sandven, K., & Resnick, M. (1990). Informal adoption among Black adolescent mothers. *American Journal of Orthopsychiatry, 60*, 210–224.

Sandvig, C. (2006). The Internet at play: Child users of public Internet connections. *Journal of Computer-Mediated Communication, 11*, 932–956.

Sattler, J. (2008). *Assessment of children: Cognitive foundations* (5th ed.). San Diego, CA: Jerome M. Sattler, Publisher, Inc.

Saudino, K. J. (1998). Moving beyond the heritability question: New directions in behavioral genetic studies of personality. *Current Directions in Psychological Science, 6*, 86–90.

Saudino, K. J., & Plomin, R. (1997). Cognitive and temperamental mediators of genetic contributions to the home environment during infancy. *Merrill-Palmer Quarterly, 43*, 1–23.

Saudino, K. J., Wertz, A., Gagne, J., & Chawla, S. (2004). Night and day: Are siblings as different in temperament as parents say they are? *Journal of Personality & Social Psychology, 87*, 698–706.

Savage, J., Brodsky, N., Malmud, E., Giannetta, J., & Hurt, H. (2005). Attentional functioning and impulse control in cocaine-exposed and control children at age ten years. *Journal of Developmental and Behavioral Pediatrics, 26*, 42–47.

Savage, M., & Holcomb, D. (1999). Adolescent female athletes' sexual risk-taking behaviors. *Journal of Youth & Adolescence, 28*, 583–594.

Savage-Rumbaugh, E. S., Murphy, J., Sevcik, R. A., Brakke, K. E., Williams, S. L., & Rumbaugh, D. M. (1993). Language comprehension in ape and child. *Monographs of the Society for Research in Child Development, 58*(3–4, Serial No. 223).

Savin-Williams, R., & Ream, G. (2003). Suicide attempts among sexual-minority male youth. *Journal of Clinical Child & Adolescent Psychology, 32*, 509–522.

Scarr, S. (1997). Why child care has little impact on most children's development. *Current Directions in Psychological Science, 6*, 143–147.

Scarr, S., & Eisenberg, M. (1993). Child care research: Issues, perspectives, and results. *Annual Review of Psychology, 44*, 613–644.

Scarr, S., Weinberg, R. A., & Waldman, I. D. (1993). IQ correlations in transracial adoptive families. *Intelligence, 17*, 541–555.

Scerif, G., Karmiloff-Smith, A., Campos, R., Elsabbagh, M., Driver, J., & Cornish, K. (2005). To look or not to look? Typical and atypical development of oculomotor control. *Journal of Cognitive Neuroscience, 17*, 591–604.

Schaal, B., Marlier, L., & Soussignan, R. (1998). Olfactory function in the human fetus: Evidence from selective neonatal responsiveness to the odor of amniotic fluid. *Behavioral Neuroscience, 112*, 1438–1449.

Schank, R. C., & Abelson, R. (1977). *Scripts, plans, goals, and understanding.* Hillsdale, NJ: Erlbaum.

Schatschneider, C., Fletcher, J., Francis, D., Carlson, C., & Foorman, B. (2004). Kindergarten prediction of reading skills: A longitudinal comparative analysis. *Journal of Educational Psychology, 96*, 265–282.

Schatschneider, C., Francis, D., Foorman, B., Fletcher, J., & Mehta, P. (1999). The dimensionality of phonological awareness: An application of item response theory. *Journal of Educational Psychology, 91*, 439–449.

Schechter, R., & Grether, J. (2008). Continuing increases in autism reported to California's developmental services system: Mercury in retrograde. *Archives of General Psychiatry, 65*, 19.

Schermerhorn, A., Cummings, M., & Davies, P. (2008). Children's representations of multiple family relationships: Organizational structure and development in early childhood. *Journal of Family Psychology, 22*, 89–101.

Schlagmüller, M., & Schneider, W. (2002). The development of organizational strategies in children: Evidence from a microgenetic longitudinal study. *Journal of Experimental Child Psychology, 81*, 298–319.

Schmidt, L., Trainor, L., & Santesso, D. (2003). Development of frontal electroencephalogram (EEG) and heart rate (ECG) re-

sponses to affective musical stimuli during the first 12 months of post-natal life. *Brain & Cognition, 52*, 27–32.

Schmitz, S., Fulker, D., Plomin, R., Zahn-Waxler, C., Emde, R., & DeFries, J. (1999). Temperament and problem behavior during early childhood. *International Journal of Behavioral Development, 23*, 333–355.

Schneider, B., Hieshima, J. A., Lee, S., & Plank, S. (1994). East-Asian academic success in the United States: Family, school, and community explanations. In P. M. Greenfield & R. R. Cocking (Eds.), *Cross-cultural roots of minority child development* (pp. 323–350). Hillsdale, NJ: Erlbaum.

Schneider, M. L. (1992). The effect of mild stress during pregnancy on birthweight and neuromotor maturation in rhesus monkey infants *(Macaca mulatta). Infant Behavior and Development, 15*, 389–403.

Schneider, W., & Bjorklund, D. F. (1992). Expertise, aptitude, and strategic remembering. *Child Development, 63*, 461–473.

Schneider, W., & Bjorklund, D. F. (1998). Memory. In W. Damon (Ed.), *Handbook of child psychology: Vol. 2. Cognition, perception, and language* (5th ed., pp. 467–521). New York: Wiley.

Schneider, W., Gruber, H., Gold, A., & Opwis, K. (1993). Chess expertise and memory for chess positions in children and adults. *Journal of Experimental Child Psychology, 56*, 328–349.

Schneider, W., Reimers, P., Roth, E., & Visé, M. (1995, April). *Short- and long-term effects of training phonological awareness in kindergarten: Evidence from two German studies.* Paper presented at the biennial meetings of the Society for Research in Child Development, Indianapolis.

Schonert-Reichl, K. (1999). Relations of peer acceptance, friendship adjustment, and social behavior to moral reasoning during early adolescence. *Journal of Early Adolescence, 19*, 249–279.

Schoppe-Sullivan, S., Diener, M., Mangelsdorf, S., Brown, G., McHale, J., & Frosch, C. (2006). Attachment and sensitivity in family context: The roles of parent and infant gender. *Infant and Child Development, 15*, 367–385.

Schothorst, P., & van Engeland, H. (1996). Long-term behavioral sequelae of prematurity. *Journal of the American Academy of Child and Adolescent Psychiatry, 35*, 175–183.

Schott, J., & Rossor, M. (2003). The grasp and other primitive reflexes. *Journal of Neurology, Neurosurgery & Psychiatry, 74*, 558–560.

Schraf, M., & Hertz-Lazarowitz, R. (2003). Social networks in the school context: Effects of culture and gender. *Journal of Social & Personal Relationships, 20*, 843–858.

Schumm, J. S., & Vaughn, S. (1995). Getting ready for inclusion: Is the stage set? *Learning Disabilities Research and Practice, 10*, 169–179.

Schumm, W. (2004). What was really learned from Tasker and Golombok's (1995) study of lesbian and single parent mothers? *Psychological Reports, 94*, 422–424.

Schwartz, C. E., Snidman, N., & Kagan, J. (1996). Early childhood temperament as a determinant of externalizing behavior in adolescence. *Development and Psychopathology, 8*, 527–537.

Schwartz, C. E., Wright, C., Shin, L., Kagan, J., & Rauch, S. (2003). Inhibited and uninhibited infants "grown up": Adult amygdalar response to novelty. *Science, 300*, 1952–1953.

Schwartz, D., Dodge, K. A., & Coie, J. D. (1993). The emergence of chronic peer victimization in boys' play groups. *Child Development, 64*, 1755–1772.

Schwartz, R. M., Anastasia, M. L., Scanlon, J. W., & Kellogg, R. J. (1994). Effect of surfactant on morbidity, mortality, and resource use in newborn infants weighing 500 to 1500 g. *New England Journal of Medicine, 330*, 1476–1480.

Schwebel, D., Rosen, C., & Singer, J. (1999). Preschoolers' pretend play and theory of mind: The role of jointly constructed pretence. *British Journal of Developmental Psychology, 17,* 333–348.

Schweinle, A., & Wilcox, T. (2004). Intermodal perception and physical reasoning in young infants. *Infant Behavior and Development, 27,* 246–265.

Scialli, A. (2007). Maternal obesity and pregnancy. *Birth Defects Research Part A: Clinical and Molecular Teratology, 76,* 73–77.

Scollon, R. (1976). *Conversations with a one-year-old.* Honolulu: University of Hawaii Press.

Scott, J. (1998). Hematology. In R. Behrman & R. Kliegman (Eds.), *Nelson essentials of pediatrics* (3rd ed., pp. 545–582). Philadelphia: Saunders.

Scott, J. (2004). Family, gender, and educational attainment in Britain: A longitudinal study. *Journal of Comparative Family Studies, 35,* 565–589.

Sears, R. R., Maccoby, E. E., & Levin, H. (1977). *Patterns of child rearing.* Stanford, CA: Stanford University Press. (Originally published 1957 by Row, Peterson)

Sebanc, A. (2003). The friendship features of preschool children: Links with prosocial behavior and aggression. *Social Development, 12,* 249–268.

Sebanc, A., Kearns, K., Hernandez, M., & Galvin, K. (2007). Predicting having a best friend in young children: Individual characteristics and friendship features. *Journal of Genetic Psychology, 168,* 81–95.

Segal, N., McGuire, S., Havelena, J., Gill, P., & Hershberger, S. (2007). Intellectual similarity of virtual twin pairs: Developmental trends. *Personality and Individual Differences, 42,* 1209–1219.

Segers, E., & Verhoeven, L. (2004). Computer-supported phonological awareness intervention for kindergarten children with specific language impairment. *Language, Speech, & Hearing Services in Schools, 35,* 229–239.

Seibt, B., & Förster, J. (2004). Stereotype threat and performance: How self-stereotypes influence processing by inducing regulatory foci. *Journal of Personality & Social Psychology, 87,* 38–56.

Seidman, E., Allen, L., Aber, J. L., Mitchell, C., & Feinman, J. (1994). The impact of school transitions in early adolescence on the self-system and perceived social context of poor urban youth. *Child Development, 65,* 507–522.

Seidman, E., & French, S. (2004). Developmental trajectories and ecological transitions: A two-step procedure to aid in the choice of prevention and promotion interventions. *Development and Psychopathology, 16,* 1141–1159.

Seifer, R., Schiller, M., Sameroff, A., Resnick, S., & Riordan, K. (1996). Attachment, maternal sensitivity, and infant temperament during the first year of life. *Developmental Psychology, 32,* 12–25.

Seligman, S. (2005). Dynamic systems theories as a metaframework for psychoanalysis. *Psychoanalytic Dialogues, 15,* 285–319.

Selman, R. L. (1980). *The growth of interpersonal understanding.* New York: Academic Press.

Seo, S. (2006). A study of infant developmental outcome with a sample of Korean working mothers of infants in poverty: Implications for early intervention programs. *Early Childhood Education Journal, 33,* 253–260.

Serbin, L., & Karp, J. (2003). Intergenerational studies of parenting and the transfer of risk from parent to child. *Current Directions in Psychological Science, 12,* 138–142.

Serbin, L. A., Powlishta, K. K., & Gulko, J. (1993). The development of sex typing in middle childhood. *Monographs of the Society for Research in Child Development, 58*(2, Serial No. 232).

Serdula, M., Ivery, D., Coates, R., Freedman, D., Williamson, D., & Byers, T. (1993). Do obese children become obese adults? A review of the literature. *Preventive Medicine, 22,* 167–177.

Serpell, R., & Hatano, G. (1997). Education, schooling, and literacy. In J. Berry, P. Dasen, & T. Saraswathi (Eds.), *Handbook of cross-cultural psychology. Vol. 2: Basic processes and human development.* Boston: Allyn & Bacon.

Shaffer, D., Garland, A., Gould, M., Fisher, P., & Trautman, P. (1988). Preventing teenage suicide: A critical review. *Journal of the American Academy of Child and Adolescent Psychiatry, 27,* 675–687.

Shaffer, D., Garland, A., Vieland, V., Underwood, M., & Busner, C. (1991). The impact of curriculum-based suicide prevention programs for teenagers. *Journal of the American Academy of Child and Adolescent Psychiatry, 30,* 588–596.

Shakib, S. (2003). Female basketball participation. *American Behavioral Scientist, 46,* 1405–1422.

Shanahan, M., Sayer, A., Davey, A., & Brooks, J. (1997, April). *Pathways of poverty and children's trajectories of psychosocial adjustment.* Paper presented at the biennial meetings of the Society for Research in Child Development, Washington, DC.

Shantz, C. U. (1983). Social cognition. In J. H. Flavell & E. M. Markman (Eds.), *Handbook of child psychology: Vol. 3. Cognitive development* (pp. 495–555). New York: Wiley.

Sharma, V., & Sharma, A. (1997). Adolescent boys in Gujrat, India: Their sexual behavior and their knowledge of acquired immunodeficiency syndrome and other sexually transmitted diseases. *Journal of Developmental and Behavioral Pediatrics, 18,* 399–404.

Sharpe, P. (2002). Preparing for primary school in Singapore: Aspects of adjustment to the more formal demands of the primary one mathematics syllabus. *Early Child Development & Care, 172,* 329–335.

Shaw, D. S., Kennan, K., & Vondra, J. I. (1994). Developmental precursors of externalizing behavior: Ages 1 to 3. *Developmental Psychology, 30,* 355–364.

Shayer, M. (2008). Intelligence for education: As described by Piaget and measured by psychometrics. *British Journal of Educational Psychology, 78,* 1–29.

Shaywitz, S. (2008). Why some smart people can't read. In M. Immordino-Yang (Ed.), *The Jossey-Bass reader on the brain and learning* (pp. 242–250). San Francisco: Jossey-Bass.

Shaywitz, S. E., Mody, M., & Shaywitz, B. A. (2006). Neural mechanisms in dyslexia. *Current Directions in Psychological Science, 15,* 278–281.

Shaywitz, S. E., Shaywitz, B. A., Pugh, K. R., Fulbright, R. K., Constable, R. T., Mencl, W. E., Shankweiler, D. P., Liberman, A. M., Skudlarski, P., Fletcher, J. M., Katz, L., Marachione, K. E., Lacadie, C., Gatenby, C., & Gore, J. C. (1998). Functional disruption in the organization of the brain for reading in dyslexia. *Proceedings of the National Academy of Sciences, USA, 95,* 2636–2641.

Shearer, M. (2007). Malnutrition in middle-class pregnant women. *Birth, 7,* 27–35.

Sherblom, S. (2008). The legacy of the "care challenge": Re-envisioning the outcome of the justice-care debate. *Journal of Moral Education, 37,* 81–98.

Shirley, L., & Campbell, A. (2000). Same-sex preference in infancy. *Psychology, Evolution & Gender, 2,* 3–18.

Shochat, L. (2003). *Our Neighborhood:* Using entertaining children's television to promote interethnic understanding in Macedonia. *Conflict Resolution Quarterly, 21,* 79–93.

Shore, B., & Dover, A. (2004). Metacognition, intelligence, and giftedness. In R. Sternberg (Ed.), *Definitions and conceptions of giftedness* (pp. 39–45). Thousand Oaks, CA: Corwin Press.

Shore, C. (1986). Combinatorial play, conceptual development, and early multiword speech. *Developmental Psychology, 22,* 184–190.

Shore, C. M. (1995). *Individual differences in language development.* Thousand Oaks, CA: Sage.

Shum, D., Neulinger, K., O'Callaghan, M., & Mohay, H. (2008). Attentional problems in children born very preterm or with extremely low birth weight at 7–9 years. *Archives of Clinical Neuropsychology, 23,* 103–112.

Siegel, B. (1996). Is the emperor wearing clothes? Social policy and the empirical support for full inclusion of children with disabilities in the preschool and early elementary grades. *Social Policy Report, Society for Research in Child Development, 10*(2–3), 2–17.

Siegler, R. (1996). *Emerging minds: The process of change in children's thinking.* New York: Oxford University Press.

Siegler, R., & Chen, Z. (2002). Development of rules and strategies: Balancing the old and the new. *Journal of Experimental Child Psychology, 81,* 446–457.

Siegler, R., & Svetina, M. (2002). A microgenetic/cross-sectional study of matrix completion: Comparing short-term and long-term change. *Child Development, 73,* 793–809.

Siegler, R. S., & Ellis, S. (1996). Piaget on childhood. *Psychological Science, 7,* 211–215.

Sigman, M., & McGovern, C. (2005). Improvement in cognitive and language skills from preschool to adolescence in autism. *Journal of Autism & Developmental Disorders, 35,* 15–23.

Sigman, M., Neumann, C., Carter, E., Cattle, D. J., D'Souza, S., & Bwibo, N. (1988). Home interactions and the development of Embu toddlers in Kenya. *Child Development, 59,* 1251–1261.

Silverberg, S. B., & Gondoli, D. M. (1996). Autonomy in adolescence: A contextualized perspective. In G. R. Adams, R. Montemayor, & T. P. Gullotta (Eds.), *Psychosocial development during adolescence: Progress in developmental contextualism* (pp. 12–61). Thousand Oaks, CA: Sage.

Silvia, P., Winterstein, B., Willse, J., Barona, C., Cram, J., Hess, K., Martinez, J., & Richard, C. (2008). Assessing creativity with divergent thinking tasks: Exploring the reliability and validity of new subjective scoring methods. *Psychology of Aesthetics, Creativity, and the Arts, 2,* 68–85.

Simmons, R. G., Burgeson, R., & Reef, M. J. (1988). Cumulative change at entry to adolescence. In M. R. Gunnar & W. A. Collins (Eds.), *The Minnesota symposia on child psychology* (Vol. 21, pp. 123–150). Hillsdale, NJ: Erlbaum.

Simonoff, E., Pickles, A., Meyer, J. M., Silberg, J. L., Maes, H. H., Loeber, R., Rutter, M., Hewitt, J. K., & Eaves, L. J. (1997). The Virginia twin study of adolescent behavioral development. *Archives of General Psychiatry, 54,* 801–808.

Simons, R. L., Robertson, J. F., & Downs, W. R. (1989). The nature of the association between parental rejection and delinquent behavior. *Journal of Youth & Adolescence, 18,* 297–309.

Simpkins, S., Davis-Kean, P., & Eccles, J. (2005). Parents' socializing behavior and children's participation in math, science, and computer out-of-school activities. *Applied Development Science, 9,* 14–30.

Singer, L., Arendt, R., & Minnes, S. (1993). Neurodevelopmental effects of cocaine. *Clinics in Perinatology, 20,* 245–262.

Singh, A., Mulder, J., Twisk, W., van Mechelen, M., & Chinapaw, M. (2008). Tracking of childhood overweight into adulthood: A systematic review of the literature. *Obesity Reviews, 9,* in press.

Singh, G. K., & Yu, S. M. (1996). US childhood mortality, 1950 through 1993: Trends and socioeconomic differentials. *American Journal of Public Health, 86,* 505–512.

Singh, S., & Darroch, J. (2000). Adolescent pregnancy and childbearing: Levels and trends in industrialized countries. *Family Planning Perspectives, 32,* 14–23.

Skinner, B. F. (1957). *Verbal behavior.* New York: Prentice Hall.

Skwarchuk, S., & Anglin, J. (2002). Children's acquisition of the English cardinal number words: A special case of vocabulary development. *Journal of Educational Psychology, 94,* 107–125.

Slaby, R. G., & Frey, K. S. (1975). Development of gender constancy and selective attention to same-sex models. *Child Development, 46,* 849–856.

Slaughter-Defoe, D., & Rubin, H. (2001). A longitudinal case study of Head Start eligible children: Implications for urban education. *Educational Psychologist, 36,* 31–44.

Slobin, D. I. (1985a). Crosslinguistic evidence for the language-making capacity. In D. I. Slobin (Ed.), *The crosslinguistic study of language acquisition, Vol. 2: Theoretical issues* (pp. 1157–1256). Hillsdale, NJ: Erlbaum.

Slobin, D. I. (1985b). Introduction: Why study acquisition crosslinguistically? In D. I. Slobin (Ed.), *The crosslinguistic study of language acquisition, Vol. 1: The data* (pp. 3–24). Hillsdale, NJ: Erlbaum.

Smetana, J. G. (1990). Morality and conduct disorders. In M. Lewis & S. M. Miller (Eds.), *Handbook of developmental psychopathology* (pp. 157–180). New York: Plenum Press.

Smetana, J. G., Killen, M., & Turiel, E. (1991). Children's reasoning about interpersonal and moral conflicts. *Child Development, 62,* 629–644.

Smith, A., Lalonde, R., & Johnson, S. (2004). Serial migration and its implications for the parent-child relationship: A retrospective analysis of the experiences of the children of Caribbean immigrants. *Cultural Diversity & Ethnic Minority Psychology, 10,* 107–122.

Smith, C., & Farrington, D. (2004). Continuities in antisocial behavior and parenting across three generations. *Journal of Child Psychology and Psychiatry, 45,* 230–247.

Smith, J. R., Brooks-Gunn, J., & Klebanov, P. K. (1997). Consequences of living in poverty for young children's cognitive and verbal ability and early school achievement. In G. J. Duncan & J. Brooks-Gunn (Eds.), *Consequences of growing up poor* (pp. 132–179). New York: Russell Sage Foundation.

Smith, S., Howard, J., & Monroe, A. (1998). An analysis of child behavior problems in adoptions in difficulty. *Journal of Social Service Research, 24,* 61–84.

Smolak, L., Levine, M. P., & Streigel-Moore, R. (Eds.). (1996). *The developmental psychopathology of eating disorders.* Mahwah, NJ: Erlbaum.

Smoll, F. L., & Schutz, R. W. (1990). Quantifying gender differences in physical performance: A developmental perspective. *Developmental Psychology, 26,* 360–369.

Snarey, J. R. (1985). Cross-cultural universality of social-moral development: A critical review of Kohlbergian research. *Psychological Bulletin, 97,* 202–232.

Snarey, J. R., Reimer, J., & Kohlberg, L. (1985). Development of social-moral reasoning among kibbutz adolescents: A longitudinal cross-sectional study. *Developmental Psychology, 21,* 3–17.

Snow, C. E. (1997, April). *Cross-domain connections and social class differences: Two challenges to nonenvironmentalist views of language development.* Paper presented at the biennial meetings of the Society for Research in Child Development, Washington, DC.

Society for Assisted Reproductive Technology (SART). (2004). *Guidelines on number of embryos transferred: Committee report.* Retrieved August 18, 2004, from http://www.sart.org

Society for Assisted Reproductive Technology (SART). (2008). *All SART member clinics: Clinic summary report.* Retrieved March 5, 2008, from https://www.sartcorsonline.com/rptCSR_PublicMultYear.aspx?ClinicPKID=0

Soderstrom, M. (2007). Beyond babytalk: Re-evaluating the nature and content of speech input to preverbal infants. *Developmental Review, 27,* 501–532.

Soderstrom, M., & Morgan, J. (2007). Twenty-two-month-olds discriminate fluent from disfluent adult-directed speech. *Developmental Science, 10,* 641–653.

Sola, A., Rogido, M., & Partridge, J. (2002). The perinatal period. In A. Rudolph, R. Kamei, & K. Overby (Eds.), *Rudolph's fundamentals of pediatrics* (3rd ed., pp. 125–183). New York: McGraw-Hill.

Soltis, J. (2004). The signal functions of early infant crying. *Brain and Behavior Sciences, 27,* 443–458.

Somers, C., & Surmann, A. (2004). Adolescents' preferences for source of sex education. *Child Study Journal, 34,* 47–59.

Sonnenschein, S. (1986). Development of referential communication skills: How familiarity with a listener affects a speaker's production of redundant messages. *Developmental Psychology, 22,* 549–552.

Sotelo, M., & Sangrador, J. (1997). Psychological aspects of political tolerance among adolescents. *Psychological Reports, 81,* 1279–1288.

Soto, C., John, O., Gosling, S., & Potter, J. (2008). The developmental psychometrics of Big Five self-reports: Acquiescence, factor structure, coherence, and differentiation from ages 10 to 20. *Journal of Personality and Social Psychology, 94,* 718–737.

Sowell, E., Peterson, B., Thompson, P., Welcome, S., Henkenius, A., & Toga, A. (2003). Mapping cortical change across the human life span. *Nature Neuroscience, 6,* 309–315.

Spelke, E., & Kinzler, K. (2007). Core knowledge. *Developmental Science, 10,* 89–96.

Spelke, E. S. (1979). Exploring audible and visible events in infancy. In A. D. Pick (Ed.), *Perception and its development: A tribute to Eleanor J. Gibson* (pp. 221–236). Hillsdale, NJ: Erlbaum.

Spelke, E. S. (1982). Perceptual knowledge of objects in infancy. In J. Mehler, E. C. T. Walker, & M. Garrett (Eds.), *Perspectives on mental representation* (pp. 409–430). Hillsdale, NJ: Erlbaum.

Spelke, E. S. (1985). Perception of unity, persistence, and identity: Thoughts on infants' conceptions of objects. In J. Mehler & R. Fox (Eds.), *Neonate cognition* (pp. 89–113). Hillsdale, NJ: Erlbaum.

Spelke, E. S. (1991). Physical knowledge in infancy: Reflections on Piaget's theory. In S. Carey & R. Gelman (Eds.), *The epigenesis of mind: Essays on biology and cognition* (pp. 133–169). Hillsdale, NJ: Erlbaum.

Spelke, E. S., von Hofsten, C., & Kestenbaum, R. (1989). Object perception in infancy: Interaction of spatial and kinetic information for object boundaries. *Developmental Psychology, 25,* 185–196.

Spence, J. T., & Helmreich, R. L. (1978). *Masculinity and femininity.* Austin: University of Texas Press.

Spencer, N. (2003). Social, economic, and political determinants of child health. *Pediatrics, 112,* 704–706.

Spiker, D. (1990). Early intervention from a developmental perspective. In D. Cicchetti & M. Beeghly (Eds.), *Children with Down syndrome: A developmental perspective* (pp. 424–448). Cambridge, England: Cambridge University Press.

Spreen, O., Risser, A., & Edgell, D. (1995). *Developmental neuropsychology.* New York: Oxford University Press.

Sroufe, A., Egeland, B., Carlson, E., & Collins, W. (2005). *The development of the person: The Minnesota study of risk and adaptation from birth to adulthood.* New York: Guilford Publications.

Sroufe, A., Egeland, B., & Kreutzer, T. (1990). The fate of early experience following developmental change: Longitudinal approaches to individual adaptation in childhood. *Child Development, 61,* 1363–1373.

Sroufe, L., Bennett, C., England, M., Urban, J., & Shulman, S. (1993). The significance of gender boundaries in preadolescence: Contemporary correlates and antecedants of boundary violations and maintenance. *Child Development, 64,* 455–466.

Sroufe, L. A. (1983). Infant-caregiver attachment and patterns of adaptation in preschool: The roots of maladaption and competence. In M. Perlmutter (Ed.), *The Minnesota symposia on child psychology* (Vol. 16, pp. 41–84). Hillsdale, NJ: Erlbaum.

Sroufe, L. A. (1988). The role of infant-caregiver attachment in development. In J. Belsky & T. Nezworski (Eds.), *Clinical implications of attachment* (pp. 18–40). Hillsdale, NJ: Erlbaum.

Sroufe, L. A. (1989). Pathways to adaptation and maladaptation: Psychopathology as developmental deviation. In D. Cicchetti (Ed.), *The emergence of a discipline: Rochester symposium on developmental psychopathology* (pp. 13–40). Hillsdale, NJ: Erlbaum.

Sroufe, L. A. (1990). A developmental perspective on day care. In N. Fox & G. G. Fein (Eds.), *Infant day care: The current debate* (pp. 51–60). Norwood, NJ: Ablex.

Sroufe, L. A. (1996). *Emotional development: The organization of emotional life in the early years.* Cambridge, England: Cambridge University Press.

Sroufe, L. A. (1997). Psychopathology as an outcome of development. *Development and Psychopathology, 9,* 251–268.

Sroufe, L. A., & Rutter, M. (1984). The domain of developmental psychopathology. *Child Development, 55,* 17–29.

Stainback, S., & Stainback, W. (1985). The merger of special and regular education: Can it be done? A response to Lieberman and Mesinger. *Exceptional Children, 51,* 517–521.

Stansfield, S., Head, J., Bartley, M., & Fonagy, P. (2008). Social position, early deprivation, and the development of attachment. *Social Psychiatry and Psychiatric Epidemiology, 43,* 516–526.

Starfield, B. (1991). Childhood morbidity: Comparisons, clusters, and trends. *Pediatrics, 88,* 519–526.

Stattin, H., & Klackenberg-Larsson, I. (1993). Early language and intelligence development and their relationship to future criminal behavior. *Journal of Abnormal Psychology, 102,* 369–378.

Steele, C., & Aronson, J. (1995). Stereotype threat and the intellectual test performance of African Americans. *Journal of Personality & Social Psychology, 69,* 797–811.

Steele, C., & Aronson, J. (2004). Stereotype threat does not live by Steele and Aronson (1995) alone. *American Psychologist, 59,* 47–48.

Steele, H., Holder, J., & Fonagy, P. (1995, April). *Quality of attachment to mother at one year predicts belief-desire reasoning at five years.* Paper presented at the biennial meetings of the Society for Research in Child Development, Indianapolis.

Steele, J., & Mayes, S. (1995). Handedness and directional asymmetry in the long bones of the human upper limb. *International Journal of Osteoarchaeology, 5,* 39–49.

Steele, M., Hodges, J., Kaniuk, J., Hillman, S., & Henderson, K. (2003). Attachment representations and adoption: Associations between maternal states of mind and emotion narratives in previously maltreated children. *Journal of Child Psychotherapy, 29,* 187–205.

Stein, K., Roeser, R., & Markus, H. (1998). Self-schemas and possible selves as predictors and outcomes of risky behaviors in adolescents. *Nursing Research, 47,* 96–106.

Steinberg, E., Tanofsky-Kraff, M., Cohen, M., Elberg, J., Freedman, R., Semega-Janneh, M., Yanovski, S., & Yanovski, J. (2004). Comparison of the child and parent forms of the Questionnaire on Eating and Weight Patterns in the assessment of children's eating-disordered behaviors. *International Journal of Eating Disorders, 36,* 183–194.

Steinberg, L. (1986). Latchkey children and susceptibility to peer pressure: An ecological analysis. *Developmental Psychology, 22,* 433–439.

Steinberg, L. (1996). *Beyond the classroom: Why school reform has failed and what parents need to do.* New York: Simon & Schuster.

Steinberg, L. (2008). A social neuroscience perspective on adolescent risk-taking. *Developmental Review, 28,* 78–106.

Steinberg, L., Blatt-Eisengart, I., & Cauffman, E. (2006). Patterns of competence and adjustment among adolescents from authoritative, authoritarian, indulgent, and neglectful homes: A replication in a sample of serious juvenile offenders. *Journal of Research on Adolescence, 16*, 47–58.

Steinberg, L., Darling, N. E., Fletcher, A. C., Brown, B. B., & Dornbusch, S. M. (1995). Authoritative parenting and adolescent adjustment: An ecological journey. In P. Moen, G. H. Elder, Jr., & K. Lüscher (Eds.), *Examining lives in context: Perspectives on the ecology of human development* (pp. 423–466). Washington, DC: American Psychological Association.

Steinberg, L., & Dornbusch, S. M. (1991). Negative correlates of part-time employment during adolescence: Replication and elaboration. *Developmental Psychology, 27*, 304–313.

Steinberg, L., Dornbusch, S. M., & Brown, B. B. (1992). Ethnic differences in adolescent achievement: An ecological perspective. *American Psychologist, 47*, 723–729.

Steinberg, L., Elmen, J. D., & Mounts, N. S. (1989). Authoritative parenting, psychosocial maturity, and academic success among adolescents. *Child Development, 60*, 1424–1436.

Steinberg, L., Lamborn, S. D., Darling, N., Mounts, N. S., & Dornbusch, S. M. (1994). Over-time changes in adjustment and competence among adolescents from authoritative, authoritarian, indulgent, and neglectful families. *Child Development, 65*, 754–770.

Steinberg, L., Lamborn, S. D., Dornbusch, S. M., & Darling, N. (1992). Impact of parenting practices on adolescent achievement: Authoritative parenting, school involvement, and encouragement to succeed. *Child Development, 63*, 1266–1281.

Steinberg, L., Mounts, N. S., Lamborn, S. D., & Dornbusch, S. D. (1991). Authoritative parenting and adolescent adjustment across varied ecological niches. *Journal of Research on Adolescence, 1*, 19–36.

Steinberg, L., & Silk, J. (2002). Parenting adolescents. In M. Bornstein, (Ed.), *Handbook of parenting: Volume 1: Children and parenting* (2nd ed.), (pp. 103–133). Mahwah, NJ: Erlbaum.

Steiner, J. E. (1979). Human facial expressions in response to taste and smell stimulation. In H. W. Reese & L. P. Lipsitt (Eds.), *Advances in child development and behavior* (Vol. 13, pp. 257–296). New York: Academic Press.

Stelzl, I., Merz, F., Ehlers, T., & Remer, H. (1995). The effect of schooling on the development of fluid and crystallized intelligence: A quasi-experimental study. *Intelligence, 21*, 279–296.

Sternberg, R. (2001). What is the common thread of creativity? Its dialectical relation to intelligence and wisdom. *American Psychologist, 56*, 360–362.

Sternberg, R. (2003). Construct validity of the theory of successful intelligence. In R. Sternberg, J. Lautrey, & T. Lubart (Eds.), *Models of intelligence: International perspectives* (pp. 55–80). Washington, DC: American Psychological Association.

Sternberg, R., Castejon, J., Prieto, M., Hautamaeki, J., & Grigorenko, E. (2001). Confirmatory factor analysis of the Sternberg Triarchic Abilities Test in three international samples: An empirical test of the triarchic theory of intelligence. *European Journal of Psychological Assessment, 17*, 1–16.

Sternberg, R., & Grigorenko, E. (2006). Cultural intelligence and successful intelligence. *Group & Organization Management, 31*, 37–39.

Sternberg, R., Grigorenko, E., & Bundy, D. (2001). The predictive value of IQ. *Merrill-Palmer Quarterly, 47*, 1–41.

Sternberg, R. J. (1985). *Beyond IQ: A triarchic theory of human intelligence.* New York: Cambridge University Press.

Sternberg, R. J., & Davidson, J. E. (1985). Cognitive development in the gifted and talented. In F. D. Horowitz & M. O'Brien (Eds.), *The gifted and talented: Developmental perspectives*

(pp. 37–74). Washington, DC: American Psychological Association.

Sternberg, R. J., & Wagner, R. K. (1993). The g-ocentric view of intelligence and job performance is wrong. *Current Directions in Psychological Science, 2*, 1–5.

Sternberg, R. J., Wagner, R. K., Williams, W. M., & Horvath, J. A. (1995). Testing common sense. *American Psychologist, 50*, 912–927.

Stevenson, H. W. (1988). Culture and schooling: Influences on cognitive development. In E. M. Hetherington, R. M. Lerner, & M. Perlmutter (Eds.), *Child development in life span perspective* (pp. 241–258). Hillsdale, NJ: Erlbaum.

Stevenson, H. W., & Lee, S. (1990). Contexts of achievement: A study of American, Chinese, and Japanese children. *Monographs of the Society for Research in Child Development, 55*(1–2, Serial No. 221).

Stevenson, H. W., Lee, S., Chen, C., Lummis, M., Stigler, J., Fan, L., & Ge, F. (1990). Mathematics achievement of children in China and the United States. *Child Development, 61*, 1053–1066.

Stewart, P. (2007). Who is kin? Family definition and African American families. *Journal of Human Behavior in the Social Environment, 15*, 163–181.

Stewart, R. B., Beilfuss, M. L., & Verbrugge, K. M. (1995, April). *That was then, this is now: An empirical typology of adult sibling relationships.* Paper presented at the biennial meetings of the Society for Research in Child Development, Indianapolis.

Stigler, J. W., Lee, S., & Stevenson, H. W. (1987). Mathematics classrooms in Japan, Taiwan, and the United States. *Child Development, 58*, 1272–1285.

Stigler, J. W., & Stevenson, H. W. (1991, Spring). How Asian teachers polish each lesson to perfection. *American Educator 12–20*, 43–47.

St. James-Roberts, I., Bowyer, J., Varghese, S., & Sawdon, J. (1994). Infant crying patterns in Manila and London. *Child: Care, Health and Development, 20*, 323–337.

Stolarova, M., Whitney, H., Webb, S., deRegnier, R., Georgieff, M., & Nelson, C. (2003). Electrophysiological brain responses of six-month-old low risk premature infants. *Infancy, 4*, 437–450.

Stoutjesdyk, D., & Jevne, R. (1993). Eating disorders among high performance athletes. *Journal of Youth & Adolescence, 22*, 271–282.

Straus, M. A. (1995). Corporal punishment of children and adult depression and suicidal ideation. In J. McCord (Ed.), *Coercion and punishment in long-term perspectives* (pp. 59–77). Cambridge, England: Cambridge University Press.

Strauss, S., & Altwerger, B. (2007). The logographic nature of English alphabetics and the fallacy of direct intensive phonics instruction. *Journal of Early Childhood Literacy, 7*, 299–319.

Strayer, J., & Roberts, W. (2004). Empathy and observed anger and aggression in five-year-olds. *Social Development, 13*, 1–13.

Streissguth, A. P., Barr, H. M., & Sampson, P. D. (1990). Moderate prenatal alcohol exposure: Effects on child IQ and learning problems at age 7½ years. *Alcoholism: Clinical and Experimental Research, 14*, 662–669.

Streissguth, A. P., Barr, H. M., Sampson, P. D., Darby, B. L., & Martin, D. C. (1989). IQ at age 4 in relation to maternal alcohol use and smoking during pregnancy. *Developmental Psychology, 25*, 3–11.

Streissguth, A. P., Bookstein, F. L., Barr, H. M., Sampson, P. D., O'Malley, K., & Young, J. (2004). Risk factors for adverse life outcomes in fetal alcohol syndrome and fetal alcohol effects. *Journal of Developmental and Behavioral Pediatrics, 25*, 228–238.

Streissguth, A. P., Bookstein, F. L., Sampson, P. D., & Barr, H. M. (1995). Attention: Prenatal alcohol and continuities of vigilance and attentional problems from 4 through 14 years. *Development and Psychopathology, 7,* 419–446.

Streissguth A. P., Landesman-Dwyer, S., Martin, J. C., & Smith, D. W. (1980). Teratogenic effects of alcohol in humans and laboratory animals. *Science, 209,* 353–361.

Streissguth, A. P., Martin, D. C., Barr, H. M., Sandman, B. M., Kirchner, G. L., & Darby, B. L. (1984). Intrauterine alcohol and nicotine exposure: Attention and reaction time in 4-year-old children. *Developmental Psychology, 20,* 533–541.

Streissguth, A. P., Martin, D. C., Martin, J. C., & Barr, H. M. (1981). The Seattle longitudinal prospective study on alcohol and pregnancy. *Neurobehavioral Toxicology and Teratology, 3,* 223–233.

Stroganova, T., Posikera, I., Pushina, N., & Orekhova, E. (2003). Lateralization of motor functions in early human ontogeny. *Human Physiology, 29,* 48–58.

Stunkard, A. J., Harris, J. R., Pedersen, N. L., & McClearn, G. E. (1990). The body-mass index of twins who have been reared apart. *New England Journal of Medicine, 322,* 1483–1487.

Styne, D., & Glaser, N. (2002). Endocrinology. In R. Behrman & R. Klingman (Eds.), *Nelson essentials of pediatrics* (4th ed., pp. 711–766). Philadelphia: Saunders.

Sudarkasa, N. (1993). Female-headed African American households: Some neglected dimensions. In H. P. McAdoo (Ed.), *Family ethnicity* (pp. 81–89). Newbury Park, CA: Sage.

Suizzo, M., & Stapleton, L. (2007). Home-based parental involvement in young children's education: Examining the effects of maternal education across U.S. ethnic groups. *Educational Psychology, 27,* 1–24.

Sulkes, S. (1998). Developmental and behavioral pediatrics. In R. Behrman & R. Kliegman (Eds.), *Nelson essentials of pediatrics* (3rd ed.). Philadelphia: Saunders.

Sullivan, K., Zaitchik, D., & Tager-Flusberg, H. (1994). Preschoolers can attribute second-order beliefs. *Developmental Psychology, 30,* 395–402.

Sulloway, F. (1996). *Born to rebel.* New York: Pantheon Books.

Susman, E. J., Inoff-Germain, G., Nottelmann, E. D., Loriaux, D. L., Cutler, G. B., Jr., & Chrousos, G. P. (1987). Hormones, emotional dispositions, and aggressive attributes in young adolescents. *Child Development, 58,* 1114–1134.

Suzuki, L., & Aronson, J. (2005). The cultural malleability of intelligence and its impact on the racial/ethnic hierarchy. *Psychology, Public Policy, & Law, 11,* 320–327.

Swain, I. U., Zelazo, P. R., & Clifton, R. K. (1993). Newborn infants' memory for speech sounds retained over 24 hours. *Developmental Psychology, 29,* 312–323.

Swanson, L., & Kim, K. (2007). Working memory, short-term memory, and naming speed as predictors of children's mathematical performance. *Intelligence, 35,* 151–168.

Swedo, S. E., Rettew, D. C., Kuppenheimer, M., Lum, D., Dolan, S., & Goldberger, E. (1991). Can adolescent suicide attempters be distinguished from at-risk adolescents? *Pediatrics, 88,* 620–629.

Sweeting, H., & West, P. (2002). Gender differences in weight related concerns in early to late adolescence. *Journal of Family Issues, 23,* 728–747.

Taga, K., Markey, C., & Friedman, H. (2006). A longitudinal investigation of associations between boys' pubertal timing and adult behavioral health and well-being. *Journal of Youth and Adolescence, 35,* 401–411.

Takei, W. (2001). How do deaf infants attain first signs? *Developmental Science, 4,* 71–78.

Takimoto, H. (2006). Malnutrition during pregnancy in Japan and proposals for improvement. *Acta Obstetrica et Gynaecologica Japonica, 58,* 1514–1518.

Talmor, R., Reiter, S., & Feigin, N. (2005). Factors relating to regular education teacher burnout in inclusive education. *European Journal of Special Needs Education, 20,* 215–229.

Tamis-LeMonda, C., Shannon, J., Cabrera, N., & Lamb, M. (2004). Fathers and mothers at play with their 2- and 3-year-olds: Contributions to language and cognitive development. *Child Development, 76,* 1806–1820.

Tani, F., Greenman, P., Schneider, B., & Fregoso, M. (2003). Bullying and the Big Five: A study of childhood personality and participant roles in bullying incidents. *School Psychology International, 24,* 131–146.

Tani, F., Rossi, S., & Smorti, M. (2005). Friendship choice criteria in children and adolescents: A study on personality characteristics. *Eta Evolutiva, 81,* 33–43.

Tanner, J. M. (1990). *Foetus into man* (revised and enlarged ed.). Cambridge, MA: Harvard University Press.

Tan-Niam, C., Wood, D., & O'Malley, C. (1998). A cross-cultural perspective on children's theories of mind and social interaction. *Early Child Development & Care, 144,* 55–67.

Tare, M., Shatz, M., & Gilbertson, L. (2008). Maternal uses of non-object terms in child-directed speech: Color, number and time. *First Language, 28,* 87–100.

Tasbihsazan, R., Nettelbeck, T., & Kirby, N. (2003). Predictive validity of the Fagan Test of Infant Intelligence. *British Journal of Developmental Psychology, 21,* 585–597.

Task Force on Sudden Infant Death Syndrome. (2005). The changing concept of Sudden Infant Death Syndrome: Diagnostic coding shifts, controversies regarding the sleeping environment, and new variables to consider in reducing risk. *Pediatrics, 116,* 1245–1255.

Taylor, M. G. (1996). The development of children's beliefs about social and biological aspects of gender differences. *Child Development, 67,* 1555–1571.

Taylor, N., Donovan, W., & Leavitt, L. (2008). Consistency in infant sleeping arrangements and mother-infant interaction. *Infant Mental Health Journal, 29,* 77–94.

Taylor, R. D., Casten, R., & Flickinger, S. M. (1993). Influence of kinship social support on the parenting experiences and psychosocial adjustment of African-American adolescents. *Developmental Psychology, 29,* 382–388.

Taylor, R. D., Casten, R., Flickinger, S. M., Roberts, D., & Fulmore, C. D. (1994). Explaining the school performance of African-American adolescents. *Journal of Research on Adolescence, 4,* 21–44.

Taylor, R. D., & Roberts, D. (1995). Kinship support and maternal and adolescent well-being in economically disadvantaged African-American families. *Child Development, 66,* 1585–1597.

Taylor, W., Ayars, C., Gladney, A., Peters, R., Roy, J., Prokhorov, A., Chamberlain, R., & Gritz, E. (1999). Beliefs about smoking among adolescents: Gender and ethnic differences. *Journal of Child & Adolescent Substance Abuse, 8,* 37–54.

Teasdale, T., & Owen, D. (2005). A long-term rise and recent decline in intelligence test performance: The Flynn Effect in reverse. *Personality and Individual Differences, 39,* 837–843.

Teasdale, T., & Owen, D. (2008). Secular declines in cognitive test scores: A reversal of the Flynn Effect. *Intelligence, 36,* 121–126.

Teitelman, A., Ratcliffe, S., & Cederbaum, J. (2008). Parent-adolescent communication about sexual pressure, maternal norms about relationship power, and STI/HIV protective behaviors of minority urban girls. *Journal of the American Psychiatric Nurses Association, 14,* 50–60.

ter Laak, J., de Goede, M., Alevan, L., Brugman, G., van Leuven, M., & Hussmann, J. (2003). Incarcerated adolescent girls: Personality, social competence and delinquency. *Adolescence, 38,* 251–265.

Terman, L. (1916). *The measurement of intelligence.* Boston: Houghton Mifflin.

Terman, L. (1925). *Genetic studies of genius: Vol. 1. Mental and physical traits of a thousand gifted children.* Stanford: CA: Stanford University Press.

Terman, L., & Merrill, M. A. (1937). *Measuring intelligence: A guide to the administration of the new revised Stanford-Binet tests.* Boston: Houghton Mifflin.

Terman, L., & Oden, M. (1959). *Genetic studies of genius: Vol. 5. The gifted group at mid-life.* Stanford, CA: Stanford University Press.

Tershakovec, A., & Stallings, V. (1998). Pediatric nutrition and nutritional disorders. In R. Behrman & R. Kliegman (Eds.), *Nelson essentials of pediatrics* (3rd ed.). Philadelphia: Saunders.

Tessier, R., Cristo, M., Velez, S., Giron, M., Line, N., Figueroa de Calume, Z., Ruiz-Palaez, J., & Charpak, N. (2003). Kangaroo Mother Care: A method for protecting high-risk low-birth-weight and premature infants against developmental delay. *Infant Behavior and Development, 26,* 384–397.

Thal, D., Tobias, S., & Morrison, D. (1991). Language and gesture in late talkers: A 1-year follow-up. *Journal of Speech & Hearing Research, 34,* 604–612.

Thapar, A. (2003). Attention deficit hyperactivity disorder: New genetic findings, new directions. In R. Plomin, J. DeFries, I. Craig, & P. McGuffin (Eds.), *Behavioral genetics in the postgenomic era* (pp. 445–462). Washington, DC: American Psychological Association.

Thapar, A., Fowler, T., Rice, F., Scourfield, J., van den Bree, M., Thomas, H., Harold, G., & Hay, G. (2003). Maternal smoking during pregnancy and attention deficit hyperactivity disorder symptoms in offspring. *American Journal of Psychiatry, 160,* 1985–1989.

Tharenou, P. (1999). Is there a link between family structures and women's and men's managerial career advancement? *Journal of Organizational Behavior, 20,* 837–863.

Tharpe, A. (2006). *The impact of minimal and mild hearing loss on children.* Retrieved March 19, 2008, from http://www.medicalhomeinfo.org/screening/EHDI/June_26_2006_FINAL_MildHearingLoss.pdf

Thelen, E. (1983). Learning to walk is still an "old" problem: A reply to Zelazo. *Journal of Motor Behavior, 15,* 139–161.

Thelen, E. (1995). Motor development: A new synthesis. *American Psychologist, 50,* 79–95.

Thelen, E., & Adolph, K. E. (1992). Arnold L. Gesell: The paradox of nature and nurture. *Developmental Psychology, 28,* 368–380.

Theriault, J. (1998). Assessing intimacy with the best friend and the sexual partner during adolescence: The PAIR-M inventory. *Journal of Psychology, 132,* 493–506.

Thomas, A., Bulevich, J., & Loftus, E. (2003). Exploring the role of repetition and sensory elaboration in the imagination inflation effect. *Memory & Cognition, 31,* 630–640.

Thomas, A., & Chess, S. (1977). *Temperament and development.* New York: Brunner/Mazel.

Thomas, M. (2000). *Comparing theories of child development* (5th ed.). Pacific Grove, CA: Brooks/Cole.

Thomas, M., & Karmiloff-Smith, A. (2003). Connectionist models of development, developmental disorders, and individual differences. In R. Sternberg, J. Lautrey, & T. Lubart (Eds.), *Models of intelligence: International perspectives* (pp. 133–150). Washington, DC: American Psychological Association.

Thomas, R. (2005). *Comparing theories of child development* (6th ed.). Pacific Grove, CA: Brooks/Cole.

Thomas, R. M. (1990). Motor development. In R. M. Thomas (Ed.), *The encyclopedia of human development and education: Theory, research, and studies* (pp. 326–330). Oxford: Pergamon Press.

Thompson, J., & Halberstadt, A. (2008). Children's accounts of sibling jealousy and their implicit theories about relationships. *Social Development, 17,* 488–511.

Thompson, P., Cannon, T., Narr, K., van Erp, T., Poutanen, V., Huttunen, M., Lovist, J., Nordenstam, C., Kaprio, J., Khaledy, M., Dail, R., Zoumalan, C., & Toga, A. (2001). Genetic influences on brain structure. *Nature Neuroscience, 4,* 1253–1258.

Thompson, P., Giedd, J., Woods, R., MacDonald, D., Evans, A., & Toga, A. (2000). Growth patterns in the developing brain detected by using continuum mechanical tensor maps. *Nature, 404,* 190–193.

Thompson, R., & Goodvin, R. (2005). The individual child: Temperament, emotion, self, and personality. In M. Bornstein & M. Lamb (Eds.), *Developmental science: An advanced textbook* (5th ed., pp. 391–428). Hillsdale, NJ: Erlbaum.

Thompson, R. A. (1998). Early sociopersonality development. In W. Damon (Ed.), *Handbook of child psychology: Vol. 3. Social, emotional, and personality development* (5th ed., pp. 25–104). New York: Wiley.

Thompson, S. K. (1975). Gender labels and early sex role development. *Child Development, 46,* 339–347.

Thorn, A., & Gathercole, S. (1999). Language-specific knowledge and short-term memory in bilingual and non-bilingual children. *Quarterly Journal of Experimental Psychology: Human Experimental Psychology, 52A,* 303–324.

Tideman, E., Nilsson, A., Smith, G., & Stjernqvist, K. (2002). Longitudinal follow-up of children born preterm: The mother-child relationship in a 19-year perspective. *Journal of Reproductive & Infant Psychology, 20,* 43–56.

Tiedemann, J. (2000). Parents' gender stereotypes and teachers' beliefs as predictors of children's concept of their mathematical ability in elementary school. *Journal of Educational Psychology, 92,* 144–151.

Timimi, S., & Leo, J. (2009). *Rethinking ADHD.* London, UK: Palgrave Macmillan.

Todd, R. D., Swarzenski, B., Rossi, P. G., & Visconti, P. (1995). Structural and functional development of the human brain. In D. Cicchetti & D. J. Cohen (Eds.), *Developmental psychopathology: Vol. 1. Theory and methods* (pp. 161–194). New York: Wiley.

Tomasello, M., & Mannle, S. (1985). Pragmatics of sibling speech to one-year-olds. *Child Development, 56,* 911–917.

Tomlinson-Keasey, C., Eisert, D. C., Kahle, L. R., Hardy-Brown, K., & Keasey, B. (1979). The structure of concrete operational thought. *Child Development, 50,* 1153–1163.

Toomela, A. (1999). Drawing development: Stages in the representation of a cube and a cylinder. *Child Development, 70,* 1141–1150.

Toronto District School Board (2001). *Facts and figures about the TDSB.* Retrieved October 6, 2001, from http://www.tdsb.on.ca/communications/TDSBFacts.html

Torrance, P. (1998). *Torrance Tests of Creative Thinking.* Bensenville, IL: Scholastic Testing Service.

Tortora, G., & Derrickson, B. (2005). *Principles of anatomy and physiology* (11th ed.). New York: Wiley.

Tortora, G., & Grabowski, S. (1993). *Principles of anatomy and physiology.* New York: HarperCollins.

Townsend, G., & Belgrave, F. (2003). The influence of cultural and racial identification on the psychosocial adjustment of inner-city African American children in school. *American Journal of Community Psychology, 32,* 217–228.

Trainor, L., Anonymous, & Tsang, C. (2004). Long-term memory for music: Infants remember tempo and timbre. *Developmental Science, 7,* 289–296.

Trainor, L., Tsang, C., & Cheung, V. (2002). Preference for sensory consonance in 2- and 4-month-old infants. *Music Perception, 20,* 187–194.

Trautner, H., Gervai, J., & Nemeth, R. (2003). Appearance-reality distinction and development of gender constancy understanding in children. *International Journal of Behavioral Development, 27,* 275–283.

Trehub, S. (2003). The developmental origins of musicality. *Nature Neuroscience, 6,* 669–673.

Trehub, S. E., Bull, D., & Thorpe, L. A. (1984). Infants' perception of melodies: The role of melodic contour. *Child Development, 55,* 821–830.

Trehub, S. E., & Rabinovitch, M. S. (1972). Auditory-linguistic sensitivity in early infancy. *Developmental Psychology, 6,* 74–77.

Trehub, S., Hill, D., & Kamenetsky, S. (1997). Parents' sung performances for infants. *Canadian Journal of Experimental Psychology, 51,* 385–396.

Trehub, S. E., Thorpe, L. A., & Morrongiello, B. A. (1985). Infants' perception of melodies: Changes in a single tone. *Infant Behavior and Development, 8,* 213–223.

Treiman, R. (2004). Spelling and dialect: Comparisons between speakers of African American vernacular English and White speakers. *Psychonomic Bulletin & Review, 11,* 338–342.

Tremblay, R. E., Mêsse, L. C., Vitaro, F., & Dobkin, P. L. (1995). The impact of friends' deviant behavior on early onset of delinquency: Longitudinal data from 6 to 13 years of age. *Development and Psychopathology, 7,* 649–667.

Tronick, E. Z. (2007). *The neurobehavioral and social-emotional development of infants and children.* New York: Norton & Co.

Tronick, E. Z., Morelli, G. A., & Ivey, P. K. (1992). The Efe forager infant and toddler's pattern of social relationships: Multiple and simultaneous. *Developmental Psychology, 28,* 568–577.

Tsujimoto, S., Yamamoto, T., Kawaguchi, H., Koizumi, H., & Sawaguchi, T. (2004). Children: An event-related optical topography study. *Cerebral Cortex, 14,* 703–712.

Tuna, J. M. (1989). Mental health services for children: The state of the art. *American Psychologist, 44,* 188–199.

Turecki, S. (2000). *The difficult child.* New York: Bantam Books.

Turiel, E. (1983). *The development of social knowledge: Morality and convention.* New York: Cambridge University Press.

Turiel, E. (1998). The development of morality. In W. Damon (Ed.), *Handbook of child psychology: Vol. 3. Social, emotional, and personality development* (5th ed., pp. 863–932). New York: Wiley.

Turkheimer, E., & Gottesman, I. I. (1991). Individual differences and the canalization of human behavior. *Developmental Psychology, 27,* 18–22.

Turkheimer, E., Haley, A., Waldron, M., D'Onofrio, B., & Gottesman, I. (2003). Socioeconomic status modifies heritability of IQ in young children. *Psychological Science, 14,* 623–628.

Turnage, B. (2004). African American mother-daughter relationships mediating daughter's self-esteem. *Child & Adolescent Social Work Journal, 21,* 155–173.

Tynan, D. (2008). *Oppositional defiant disorder.* Retrieved October 24, 2008, from http://www.emedicine.com/ped/TOPIC2791

Udry, J. R., & Campbell, B. C. (1994). Getting started on sexual behavior. In A. S. Rossi (Ed.), *Sexuality across the life course* (pp. 187–208). Chicago: University of Chicago Press.

Ukeje, I., Bendersky, M., & Lewis, M. (2001). Mother-infant interaction at 12 months in prenatally cocaine-exposed children. *American Journal of Drug & Alcohol Abuse, 27,* 203–224.

Umberson, D., & Gove, W. R. (1989). Parenthood and psychological well-being. Theory, measurement, and stage in the family life course. *Journal of Family Issues, 10,* 440–462.

Umetsu, D. (1998). Immunology and allergy. In R. Behrman & R. Kliegman (Eds.), *Nelson essentials of pediatrics* (3rd ed.). Philadelphia: Saunders.

Underwood, M. (1997). Peer social status and children's understanding of the expression and control of positive and negative emotions. *Merrill-Palmer Quarterly, 43,* 610–634.

Underwood, M. K., Coie, J. D., & Herbsman, C. R. (1992). Display rules for anger and aggression in school-age children. *Child Development, 63,* 366–380.

Underwood, M. K., Kupersmidt, J. B., & Coie, J. D. (1996). Childhood peer sociometric status and aggression as predictors of adolescent childbearing. *Journal of Research on Adolescence, 6,* 201–224.

Uno, D., Florsheim, P., & Uchino, B. (1998). Psychosocial mechanisms underlying quality of parenting among Mexican-American and white adolescent mothers. *Journal of Youth & Adolescence, 27,* 585–605.

Urberg, K., Degirmencioglu, S., & Pilgrim, C. (1997). Close friend and group influence on adolescent cigarette smoking and alcohol use. *Developmental Psychology, 33,* 834–844.

U.S. Census Bureau. (1998). *Statistical abstract of the United States: 1998* (118th ed.). Washington, DC: U.S. Government Printing Office.

U.S. Census Bureau. (2001). *Statistical abstract of the United States: 2000.* Washington, DC: U.S. Government Printing Office.

U.S. Census Bureau. (2003). *2002, American Community Survey.* Retrieved June 18, 2004, from http://www.census.gov/acs/www/index.html

U.S. Census Bureau. (2008a). *Community population survey, 2007.* Retrieved September 7, 2008, from http://pubdb3.census.gov/macro/032008/pov/toc.htm/

U.S. Census Bureau. (2008b). *Statistical abstract of the United States.* Retrieved September 7, 2008, from http://www.census.gov/compendia/statab/index.html

U.S. Department of Energy. (2001). *The Human Genome Program* [Online report]. Retrieved July 6, 2001, from http://www.ornl.gov/TechResources/Human_Genome/home.html

U.S. Department of Health and Human Services. (2008). *Annual update of the HHS poverty guidelines.* Retrieved March 12, 2008, from http://aspe.hhs.gov/poverty/08fedreg.htm

U.S. Department of the Treasury. (2008). *Income mobility in the U.S. from 1996 to 2005.* Retrieved March 13, 2008, from http://www.treas.gov/offices/tax-policy/library/incomemobilitystudy03-08revise.pdf

U.S. Food and Drug Administration. (2004, October 15). *Suicidality in children and adolescents being treated with antidepressant medication.* Retrieved May 12, 2005, from http://www.fda.gov/cder/drug/antidepressants/SSRIPHA200410.htm

U.S. National Library of Medicine Genetics Home Reference. (2008). *Color vision deficiency.* Retrieved August 14, 2008, from http://ghr.nlm.nih.gov/condition=colorvisiondeficiency

Valentine, J., DuBois, D., & Cooper, H. (2004). The relation between self-beliefs and academic achievement: A meta-analytic review. *Educational Psychologist, 39,* 111–133.

Valiente, C., Eisenberg, N., Fabes, R., Shepard, S., Cumberland, A., & Losoya, S. (2004). Prediction of children's empathy-related responding from their effortful control and parents' expressivity. *Developmental Psychology, 40,* 911–926.

Valleroy, L., MacKellar, D., Karon, J., Rosen, D., McFarland, W., Shehan, D., Stoyanoff, S., LaLota, M., Celentano, D., Koblin, B., Thieded, H., Katz, M., Torian, L., & Janssen, R. (2000). HIV prevalence and associated risks in young men who have sex with men. *Journal of the American Medical Association, 284,* 198–204.

van Balen, F. (1998). Development of IVF children. *Developmental Review, 18,* 30–46.

van Beijsterveldt, C., Bartels, M., Hudziak, J., & Boomsma, D. (2003). Causes of stability of aggression from early childhood to adolescence: A longitudinal genetic analysis in Dutch twins. *Behavior Genetics, 33,* 591–605.

van Brakel, A., Muris, P., Bögels, S., & Thomassen, C. (2006). A multifactorial model for the etiology of anxiety in non-clinical adolescents: Main and interactive effects of behavioral inhibition, attachment, and parental rearing. *Journal of Child and Family Studies, 15,* 569–579.

van den Boom, D. C. (1994). The influence of temperament and mothering on attachment and exploration: An experimental manipulation of sensitive responsiveness among lower-class mothers with irritable infants. *Child Development, 65,* 1457–1477.

van den Boom, D. C. (1995). Do first-year intervention effects endure? Follow-up during toddlerhood of a sample of Dutch irritable infants. *Child Development, 66,* 1798–1816.

Van den Broek, P., Lynch, J., Naslund, J., Ievers-Landis, C., & Verduin, K. (2004). The development of comprehension of main ideas in narratives: Evidence from the selection of titles. *Journal of Educational Psychology, 96,* 707–718.

van der Molen, M., & Molenaar, P. (1994). Cognitive psychophysiology: A window to cognitive development and brain maturation. In G. Dawson & K. Fischer (Eds.), *Human behavior and the developing brain.* New York: Guilford.

van Doesum, K., Riksen-Walraven, J., Hosman, C., & Hoefnagels, C. (2008). A randomized controlled trial of a home-visiting intervention aimed at preventing relationship problems in depressed mothers and their infants. *Child Development, 79,* 547–561.

van IJzendoorn, M. H. (1995). Adult attachment representations, parental responsiveness, and infant attachment: A meta-analysis on the predictive validity of the Adult Attachment Interview. *Psychological Bulletin, 117,* 387–403.

van IJzendoorn, M. H. (1997, April). *Attachment, morality, and aggression: Toward a developmental socioemotional model of antisocial behavior.* Paper presented at the biennial meetings of the Society for Research in Child Development, Washington, DC.

van IJzendoorn, M. H., Goldberg, S., Kroonenberg, P. M., & Frenkel, O. J. (1992). The relative effects of maternal and child problems on the quality of attachment: A meta-analysis of attachment in clinical samples. *Child Development, 63,* 840–858.

van IJzendoorn, M. H., Juffer, F., & Poelhuis, C. (2005). Adoption and cognitive development: A meta-analytic comparison of adopted and nonadopted children's IQ and school performance. *Psychological Bulletin, 131,* 301–316.

van IJzendoorn, M. H., & Kroonenberg, P. M. (1988). Cross-cultural patterns of attachment: A meta-analysis of the Strange Situation. *Child Development, 59,* 147–156.

van Leeuwen, M., van den Berg, S., & Boomsma, D. (2008). A twin-family study of general IQ. *Learning and Individual Differences, 18,* 76–88.

van Lieshout, C. F. M., & Haselager, G. J. T. (1994). The Big Five personality factors in Q-sort descriptions of children and adolescents. In C. F. Halverson, Jr., G. A. Kohnstamm, & R. P. Martin (Eds.), *The developing structure of temperament and personality from infancy to adulthood* (pp. 293–318). Hillsdale, NJ: Erlbaum.

Van Mierlo, J., & Van den Bulck, J. (2004). Benchmarking the cultivation approach to video game effects: A comparison of the correlates of TV viewing and game play. *Journal of Adolescence, 27,* 97–111.

van Wormer, K., & McKinney, R. (2003). What schools can do to help gay/lesbian/bisexual youth: A harm reduction approach. *Adolescence, 38,* 409–420.

Vartanian, L. (2001). Adolescents' reactions to hypothetical peer group conversations: Evidence for an imaginary audience? *Adolescence, 36,* 347–380.

Vaughn, B., Stevenson-Hinde, J., Waters, E., Kotsaftis, A., Lefever, G., Shouldice, A., Trudel, M., & Belsky, J. (1992). Attachment security and temperament in infancy and early childhood: Some conceptual clarification. *Developmental Psychology, 28,* 463–473.

Venerosi, A., Valanzano, A., Cirulli, F., Alleva, E., & Calamandrei, G. (2004). Acute global anoxia during C-section birth affects dopamine-mediated behavioural responses and reactivity to stress. *Behavioural Brain Research, 154,* 155–164.

Vernon, P. A. (1993). Intelligence and neural efficiency. In D. K. Detterman (Ed.), *Current topics in human intelligence: Vol. 3. Individual differences and cognition* (pp. 171–187). Norwood, NJ: Ablex.

Vernon, P. A., & Mori, M. (1992). Intelligence, reaction times, and peripheral nerve conduction velocity. *Intelligence, 16,* 273–288.

Véronneau, M., Vitaro, F., Pedersen, S., & Tremblay, R. (2008). Do peers contribute to the likelihood of secondary school graduation among disadvantaged boys? *Journal of Educational Psychology, 100,* 429–442.

Victorian Infant Collaborative Study Group. (1991). Eight-year outcome in infants with birth weight of 500–999 grams: Continuing regional study of 1979 and 1980 births. *Journal of Pediatrics, 118,* 761–767.

Vida, J. (2005). Treating the "wise baby." *American Journal of Psychoanalysis, 65,* 3–12.

Vikat, A., Rimpela, A., Kosunen, E., & Rimpela, M. (2002). Sociodemographic differences in the occurrence of teenage pregnancies in Finland in 1987–1998: A follow up study. *Journal of Epidemiology & Community Health, 56,* 659–670.

Viner, R. (2002). Is puberty getting earlier in girls? *Archives of Disease in Childhood, 86,* 8–10.

Visser, S., & Lesesne, C. (2005). Mental health in the United States: Prevalence of diagnosis and medication treatment for attention-deficit/hyperactivity disorder: United States, 2003. *Morbidity and Mortality Weekly Report, 54,* 842–847.

Vitaro, F., Barker, E., Boivin, M., Brendgen, M., & Tremblay, R. (2006). Do early difficult temperament and harsh parenting differentially predict reactive and proactive aggression? *Journal of Abnormal Child Psychology, 34,* 681–691.

Vitaro, F., Tremblay, R. E., Kerr, M., Pagani, L., & Bukowski, W. M. (1997). Disruptiveness, friends' characteristics, and delinquency in early adolescence: A test of two competing models of development. *Child Development, 68,* 676–689.

Vogin, J. (2005). *Taking medication while pregnant.* Retrieved June 7, 2007, from http://www.medicinenet.com/script/main/art.asp?articlekey=51639

Volbrecht, M., Lemery-Chalfant, K., Aksan, N., Zahn-Waxler, C., & Goldsmith, H. (2007). Examining the familial link between positive affect and empathy development in the second year. *Journal of Genetic Psychology, 168,* 105–129.

Volling, B., McElwain, N., & Miller, A. (2002). Emotion regulation in context: The jealousy complex between young siblings and its relations with child and family characteristics. *Child Development, 73,* 581–600.

von Károlyi, C., & Winner, E. (2005). Extreme giftedness. In R. Sternberg (Ed.), *Conceptions of giftedness* (2nd ed., pp. 377–394). New York: Cambridge University Press.

Votruba-Drzal, E., Li-Grining, C., & Maldonado-Carreño, C. (2008). A developmental perspective on full- versus part-day kindergarten and children's academic trajectories through fifth grade. *Child Development, 79,* 957–978.

Vuorenkoski, L., Kuure, O., Moilanen, I., & Peninkilampi, V. (2000). Bilingualism, school achievement, and mental wellbeing: A follow-up study of return migrant children. *Journal of Child Psychology & Psychiatry & Allied Disciplines, 41,* 261–266.

Vygotsky, L. S. (1978). *Mind and society: The development of higher mental processes.* Cambridge, MA: Harvard University Press. (Original works published 1930, 1933, and 1935)

Waddington, C. H. (1957). *The strategy of the genes.* London: Allen.

Waddington, C. H. (1974). A catastrophe theory of evolution. *Annals of the New York Academy of Sciences, 231,* 32–41.

Wade, T., Bulik, C., & Kendler, K. (2001). Investigation of quality of the parental relationship as a risk factor for subclinical bulimia nervosa. *International Journal of Eating Disorders, 30,* 389–400.

Wagner, R. K., Torgesen, J. K., Rashotte, C. A., Hecht, S. A., Barker, T. A., Burgess, S. R., Donahue, J., & Garon, T. (1997). Changing relations between phonological processing abilities and word-level reading as children develop from beginning to skilled readers: A 5-year longitudinal study. *Developmental Psychology, 33,* 468–479.

Waldrop, M., & Halverson, C. (1975). Intensive and extensive peer behavior: Longitudinal and cross-sectional analyses. *Child Development, 46,* 19–26.

Walker, E. (2002). Adolescent neurodevelopment and psychopathology. *Current Directions in Psychological Science, 11,* 24–28.

Walker, H., Messinger, D., Fogel, A., & Karns, J. (1992). Social and communicative development in infancy. In V. B. Van Hasselt & M. Hersen (Eds.), *Handbook of social development: A lifespan perspective* (pp. 157–181). New York: Plenum Press.

Walker, L. J. (1980). Cognitive and perspective-taking prerequisites for moral development. *Child Development, 51,* 131–139.

Walker, L. J. (1989). A longitudinal study of moral reasoning. *Child Development, 60,* 157–160.

Walker, L. J. (1991). Sex differences in moral reasoning. In W. M. Kurtines & J. L. Gewirtz (Eds.), *Handbook of moral behavior and development: Vol. 2. Research* (pp. 333–364). Hillsdale, NJ: Erlbaum.

Walker, L. J., de Vries, B., & Trevethan, S. D. (1987). Moral stages and moral orientations in real-life and hypothetical dilemmas. *Child Development, 58,* 842–858.

Walker-Andrews, A. S. (1997). Infants' perception of expressive behaviors: Differentiation of multimodal information. *Psychological Bulletin, 121,* 437–456.

Walker-Barnes, C., & Mason, C. (2004). Delinquency and substance use among gang-involved youth: The moderating role of parenting practices. *American Journal of Community Psychology, 34,* 235–250.

Wallerstein, J., & Lewis, J. (1998). The long-term impact of divorce on children: A first report from a 25-year study. *Family & Conciliation Courts Review, 36,* 368–383.

Walters, R. H., & Brown, M. (1963). Studies of reinforcement of aggression: III. Transfer of responses to an interpersonal situation. *Child Development, 34,* 563–571.

Walusinski, O., Kurjak, A., Andonotopo, W., & Azumendi, G. (2005). Fetal yawning: A behavior's birth with 4D US revealed. *The Ultrasound Review of Obstetrics & Gynecology, 5,* 210–217.

Wang, Y. (2002). Is obesity associated with early sexual maturation? A comparison of the association in American boys versus girls. *Pediatrics, 110,* 903–910.

Wang, Y., & Lobstein, T. (2006). Worldwide trends in childhood overweight and obesity. *International Journal of Pediatric Obesity, 1,* 11–25.

Ward, S. L., & Overton, W. F. (1990). Semantic familiarity, relevance, and the development of deductive reasoning. *Developmental Psychology, 26,* 488–493.

Wardle, J., Carnell, S., Haworth, C., & Plomin, R. (2008). Evidence for a strong genetic influence on childhood adiposity despite the force of the obesogenic environment. *American Journal of Clinical Nutrition, 87,* 398–404.

Warfield-Coppock, N. (1997). The balance and connection of manhood and womanhood training. *Journal of Prevention & Intervention in the Community, 16,* 121–145.

Warren, S., & Simmens, S. (2005). Predicting toddler anxiety/depressive symptoms: Effects of caregiver sensitivity on temperamentally vulnerable children. *Infant Mental Health Journal, 26,* 40–55.

Waseem, M. (2007). *Otitis media.* Retrieved March 18, 2008, from http://www.emedicine.com/ped/TOPIC1689.HTM

Watamura, S., Donzella, B., Alwin, J., & Gunnar, M. (2003). Morning-to-afternoon increases in cortisol concentrations for infants and toddlers at child care: Age differences and behavioral correlates. *Child Development, 74,* 1006–1020.

Waterman, A. S. (1985). Identity in the context of adolescent psychology. *New Directions for Child Development, 30,* 5–24.

Waterman, A. S. (1988). Identity status theory and Erikson's theory: Communalities and differences. *Developmental Review, 8,* 185–208.

Waterman, A. S. (1992). Identity as an aspect of optimal psychological functioning. In G. R. Adams, T. P. Gullotta, & R. Montemayor (Eds.), *Adolescent identity formation* (pp. 50–72). Newbury Park, CA: Sage.

Watson, A., Nixon, C., Wilson, A., & Capage, L. (1999). Social interaction skills and theory of mind in young children. *Developmental Psychology, 35,* 386–391.

Watson, J. B. (1913). Psychology as the behaviorist views it. *Psychological Review, 20,* 158–177.

Watson, J. B. (1928). *Psychological care of the infant and child.* New York: Norton.

Watson, J. B. (1930). *Behaviorism.* New York: Norton.

Watson, J. B., & Rayner, R. (1920). Conditioned emotional reactions. *Journal of Experimental Psychology, 3,* 1–14.

Watson, M. W., & Getz, K. (1990a). Developmental shifts in Oedipal behaviors related to family role understanding. *New Directions for Child Development, 48,* 29–48.

Watson, M. W., & Getz, K. (1990b). The relationship between Oedipal behaviors and children's family role concepts. *Merrill-Palmer Quarterly, 36,* 487–506.

Waxman, S. R., & Kosowski, T. D. (1990). Nouns mark category relations: Toddlers' and preschoolers' word-learning biases. *Child Development, 61,* 1461–1473.

Webb, R., Lubinski, D., & Benbow, C. (2002). Mathematically facile adolescents with math-science aspirations: New perspectives on their educational and vocational development. *Journal of Educational Psychology, 94,* 785–794.

Webster-Stratton, C., & Hammond, M. (1988). Maternal depression and its relationship to life stress, perceptions of child behavior problems, parenting behaviors and child conduct problems. *Journal of Abnormal Child Psychology, 16,* 299–315.

Webster-Stratton, C., & Reid, M. (2003). Treating conduct problems and strengthening social and emotional competence in young children: The dina dinosaur treatment program. *Journal of Emotional & Behavioral Disorders, 11,* 130–143.

Wechsler, D. (1974). *Manual for the Wechsler Intelligence Scale for Children–Revised.* New York: Psychological Corp.

Weimer, B., Kerns, K., & Oldenburg, C. (2004). Adolescents' interactions with a best friend: Associations with attachment style. *Journal of Experimental Psychology, 88,* 102–120.

Weinberg, R. A. (1989). Intelligence and IQ: Landmark issues and great debates. *American Psychologist, 44,* 98–104.

Weinfield, N., & Egeland, B. (2004). Continuity, discontinuity, and coherence in attachment from infancy to late adolescence: Sequelae of organization and disorganization. *Attachment & Human Development, 6,* 73–97.

Weisner, T. S. (1984). Ecocultural niches of middle childhood: A cross-cultural perspective. In W. A. Collins (Ed.), *Development during middle childhood: The years from six to twelve* (pp. 335–369). Washington, DC: National Academy Press.

Weiss, L. H., & Schwarz, J. C. (1996). The relationship between parenting types and older adolescents' personality, academic achievement, adjustment, and substance use. *Child Development, 67,* 2101–2114.

Welch-Ross, M. (1997). Mother-child participation in conversation about the past: Relationships to preschoolers' theory of mind. *Developmental Psychology, 33*, 618–629.

Wellman, H. M., & Hickling, A. K. (1994). The mind's "I": Children's conception of the mind as an active agent. *Child Development, 65*, 1564–1580.

Wentzel, K. R., & Asher, S. R. (1995). The academic lives of neglected, rejected, popular, and controversial children. *Child Development, 66*, 754–763.

Wenz-Gross, M., Siperstein, G., Untch, A., & Widaman, K. (1997). Stress, social support, and adjustment of adolescents in middle school. *Journal of Early Adolescence, 17*, 129–151.

Werker, J. F., & Desjardins, R. N. (1995). Listening to speech in the first year of life: Experiential influences on phoneme perception. *Current Directions in Psychological Science, 4*, 76–81.

Werker, J. F., Pegg, J. E., & McLeod, P. J. (1994). A cross-language investigation of infant preference for infant-directed communication. *Infant Behavior and Development, 17*, 323–333.

Werker, J. F., & Tees, R. C. (1984). Cross-language speech perception: Evidence for perceptual reorganization during the first year of life. *Infant Behavior and Development, 7*, 49–63.

Werker, J. F., & Tees, R. C. (2005). Speech perception as a window for understanding plasticity and commitment in language systems of the brain. *Developmental Psychobiology, 46*, 233–234.

Werner, E. E. (1986). A longitudinal study of perinatal risk. In D. C. Farran & J. D. McKinney (Eds.), *Risk in intellectual and psychosocial development* (pp. 3–28). Orlando, FL: Academic Press.

Werner, E. E. (1993). Risk, resilience, and recovery: Perspectives from the Kauai Longitudinal Study. *Development and Psychopathology, 5*, 503–515.

Werner, E. E. (1995). Resilience in development. *Current Directions in Psychological Science, 4*, 81–85.

Werner, E. E., & Smith, R. (2001). *Journeys from childhood to midlife: Risk, resilience, and recovery.* Ithaca, NY: Cornell University Press.

Werner, L. A., & Gillenwater, J. M. (1990). Pure-tone sensitivity of 2- to 5-week-old infants. *Infant Behavior and Development, 13*, 355–375.

West, P., Sweeting, H., & Ecob, R. (1999). Family and friends' influences on the uptake of regular smoking from mid-adolescence to early adulthood. *Addiction, 97*, 1397–1411.

Wetzel, N., Widmann, A., Berti, S., & Schröger, E. (2006). The development of involuntary and voluntary attention from childhood to adulthood: A combined behavioral and event-related potential study. *Clinical Neurophysiology, 117*, 2191–2203.

White, K. S., Bruce, S. E., Farrell, A. D., & Kliewer, W. L. (1997, April). *Impact of exposure to community violence on anxiety among urban adolescents: Family social support as a protective factor.* Paper presented at the biennial meetings of the Society for Research in Child Development, Washington, DC.

White, M., & Glick, J. (2000). Generation status, social capital, and the routes out of high school. *Sociological Forum, 15*, 671–691.

Whitehurst, G. J. (1995, April). *Levels of reading readiness and predictors of reading success among children from low-income families.* Paper presented at the biennial meetings of the Society for Research in Child Development, Indianapolis.

White-Traut, R., Nelson, M., Silvestri, J., Vasan, U., Littau, S., Meleedy-Rey, P., Gu, G., & Patel, M. (2002). Effect of auditory, tactile, visual, and vestibular intervention on length of stay, alertness, and feeding progression in preterm infants. *Developmental Medicine and Child Neurology, 44*, 91–97.

Whitfield, J. (2007). Semi-identical twins discovered. *Nature, 13*, 520–521.

Wicks-Nelson, R., & Israel, A. (1997). *Behavior disorders of childhood.* Upper Saddle River, NJ: Prentice-Hall.

Wiehe, V. (2003). Empathy and narcissism in a sample of child abuse perpetrators and a comparison sample of foster parents. *Child Abuse & Neglect, 27*, 541–555.

Wiesner, M., Kim, H., & Capaldi, D. (2005). Developmental trajectories of offending: Validation and prediction to young adult alcohol use, drug use, and depressive symptoms. *Development and Psychopathology, 17*, 251–270.

Wigfield, A., Eccles, J. S., MacIver, D., Reuman, D. A., & Midgley, C. (1991). Transitions during early adolescence: Changes in children's domain-specific self-perceptions and general self-esteem across the transition to junior high school. *Developmental Psychology, 27*, 552–565.

Williams, J E.., & Best, D. L.. (1994). Cross-cultural views of women and men. In W. Lonner & R. Malpass (Eds.), *Psychology and culture* (pp. 191–201). Boston: Allyn & Bacon.

Williams, J. E., & Best, D. L. (1990). *Measuring sex stereotypes: A multination study* (rev. ed.). Newbury Park, CA: Sage.

Williams, W. (1998). Are we raising smarter children today? School and home related influences on IQ. In U. Neisser (Ed.), *The rising curve: Long-term gains in IQ and related measures* (pp. 125–154). Washington, DC: American Psychological Association.

Williams, W. M., & Ceci, S. J. (1997). Are Americans becoming more or less alike? Trends in race, class, and ability differences in intelligence. *American Psychologist, 52*, 1226–1235.

Willinger, M., Hoffman, H. J., & Hartford, R. B. (1994). Infant sleep position and risk for sudden infant death syndrome: Report of meeting held January 13 and 14, 1994, National Institutes of Health, Bethesda, MD. *Pediatrics, 93*, 814–819.

Wilson, M. N. (1986). The black extended family: An analytical consideration. *Developmental Psychology, 22*, 246–258.

Wilson, M. N. (1989). Child development in the context of the black extended family. *American Psychologist, 44*, 380–385.

Wilson, W. J. (1995). Jobless ghettos and the social outcome of youngsters. In P. Moen, G. H. Elder, Jr., & K. Lüscher (Eds.), *Examining lives in context: Perspectives on the ecology of human development* (pp. 527–543). Washington, DC: American Psychological Association.

Winfield, L. F. (1995). The knowledge base on resilience in African-American adolescents. In L. J. Crockett & A. C. Crouter (Eds.), *Pathways through adolescence* (pp. 87–118). Mahwah, NJ: Erlbaum.

Wolpe, J. (1958). *Psychotherapy by reciprocal intuition.* Stanford, CA: Stanford University Press.

Wonderlich, S., Crosby, R., Mitchell, J., Thompson, K., Redlin, J., Demuth, G., Smith, J., & Haseltine, B. (2001). Eating disturbance and sexual trauma in childhood and adulthood. *International Journal of Eating Disorders, 30*, 401–412.

Wong, C., & Tang, C. (2004). Coming out experiences and psychological distress of Chinese homosexual men in Hong Kong. *Archives of Sexual Behavior, 33*, 149–157.

Wong, D. (1993). *Whaley & Wong's essentials of pediatric nursing.* St. Louis, MO: Mosby-Yearbook, Inc.

Wood, C., & Terrell, C. (1998). Pre-school phonological awareness and subsequent literacy development. *Educational Psychology, 18*, 253–274.

Wood, D. J., Bruner, J. S., & Ross, G. (1976). The role of tutoring in problem solving. *Journal of Child Psychology and Psychiatry, 17*, 89–100.

Woodward, A. L., & Markman, E. M. (1998). Early word learning. In W. Damon (Ed.), *Handbook of child psychology: Vol. 2. Cognition, perception, and language* (5th ed., pp. 371–420). New York: Wiley.

Woodward, S., McManis, M., Kagan, J., Deldin, P., Snidman, N., Lewis, M., & Kahn, V. (2001). Infant temperament and the brainstem auditory evoked response in later childhood. *Developmental Psychology, 37*, 533–538.

Worrell, F. (1997). Predicting successful or non-successful at-risk status using demographic risk factors. *High School Journal, 81,* 46–53.

Wozniak, J., Biederman, J., Kwon, A., Mick, E., Faraone, S., Orlovsky, K., Schnare, L., Cargol, C., & van Grondelle, A. (2005). How cardinal are cardinal symptoms in pediatric bipolar disorder? An examination of clinical correlates. *Biological Psychiatry, 58,* 583–588.

Wright, J., Huston, A., Murphy, K., St. Peters, M., Pinon, M., Scantlin, R., & Kotler, J. (2001). The relations of early television viewing to school readiness and vocabulary of children from low-income families: The early window project. *Child Development, 72,* 1347–1366.

Wright, K., Fineberg, D., Brown, K., & Perkins, A. (2005). Theory of mind may be contagious, but you don't catch it from your twin. *Child Development, 76,* 97–106.

Wright, V., Schieve, L., Reynolds, M., & Jeng, G. (2005). Assisted reproductive technology surveillance—United States, 2002. *Morbidity & Mortality Weekly Report, 54,* 1–24.

Wyatt, J., & Carlo, G. (2002). What will my parents think? Relations among adolescents' expected parental reactions, prosocial moral reasoning and prosocial and antisocial behaviors. *Journal of Adolescent Research, 17,* 646–666.

Xia, G., & Qian, M. (2001). The relationship of parenting style to self-reported mental health among two subcultures of Chinese. *Journal of Adolescence, 24,* 251–260.

Xie, H., Cairns, R., & Cairns, B. (1999). Social networks and configurations in inner-city schools: Aggression, popularity, and implications for students with EBD. *Journal of Emotional & Behavioral Disorders, 7,* 147–155.

Yamada, A., & Singelis, T. (1999). Biculturalism and self-construal. *International Journal of Intercultural Relations, 23,* 697–709.

Yirmiya, N., & Shulman, C. (1996). Seriation, conservation, and theory of mind abilities in individuals with autism, individuals with mental retardation, and normally developing children. *Child Development, 67,* 2045–2059.

Yonas, A. (1981). Infants' responses to optical information for collision. In R. Aslin, J. R. Alberts, & M. R. Peterson (Eds.), *Development of perception: Vol. 2. From perception to cognition* (pp. 80–122). Orlando, FL: Academic Press.

Young, A. (1997). I think, therefore I'm motivated: The relations among cognitive strategy use, motivational orientation and classroom perceptions over time. *Learning & Individual Differences, 9,* 249–283.

Young, M., & Bradley, M. (1998). Social withdrawal: Self-efficacy, happiness, and popularity in introverted and extroverted adolescents. *Canadian Journal of School Psychology, 14,* 21–35.

Young, T., Turner, J., Denny, G., & Young, M. (2004). Examining external and internal poverty as antecedents of teen pregnancy. *American Journal of Health Behavior, 28,* 361–373.

Zahn-Waxler, C., & Radke-Yarrow, M. (1982). The development of altruism: Alternative research strategies. In N. Eisenberg (Ed.), *The development of prosocial behavior* (pp. 109–138). New York: Academic Press.

Zahn-Waxler, C., Radke-Yarrow, M., & King, R. (1979). Child rearing and children's prosocial initiations toward victims of distress. *Child Development, 50,* 319–330.

Zahn-Waxler, C., Radke-Yarrow, M., Wagner, E., & Chapman, M. (1992). Development of concern for others. *Developmental Psychology, 28,* 125–136.

Zajonc, R., & Sulloway, F. (2007). The confluence model: Birth order as a within-family or between-family dynamic? *Personality and Social Psychology Bulletin, 33,* 1187–1194.

Zakriski, A., & Coie, J. (1996). A comparison of aggressive-rejected and nonaggressive-rejected children's interpretation of self-directed and other-directed rejection. *Child Development, 67,* 1948–2070.

Zamboni, B. (2006). Therapeutic considerations in working with the family, friends, and partners of transgendered individuals. *The Family Journal, 14,* 174–179.

Zametkin, A. J., Nordahl, T. E., Gross, M., King, A. C., Semple, W. E., Rumsey, J., Hamburger, S., & Cohen, R. M. (1990). Cerebral glucose metabolism in adults with hyperactivity of childhood onset. *New England Journal of Medicine, 323,* 1361–1366.

Zani, B. (1993). Dating and interpersonal relationships in adolescence. In S. Jackson & H. Rodrigues-Tomé (Eds.), *Adolescence and its social worlds* (pp. 95–119). Hove, England: Erlbaum.

Zaslow, M. J., & Hayes, C. D. (1986). Sex differences in children's responses to psychosocial stress: Toward a cross-context analysis. In M. E. Lamb, A. L. Brown, & B. Rogoff (Eds.), *Advances in developmental psychology* (Vol. 4, pp. 285–338). Hillsdale, NJ: Erlbaum.

Zeanah, C., & Fox, N. (2004). Temperament and attachment disorders. *Journal of Clinical Child & Adolescent Psychology, 33,* 32–41.

Zelazo, N. A., Zelazo, P. R., Cohen, K., & Zelazo, P. N. (1993). Specificity of practice effects on elementary neuromotor patterns. *Developmental Psychology, 29,* 686–691.

Zelazo, P. D., Helwig, C. C., & Lau, A. (1996). Intention, act, and outcome in behavioral prediction and moral judgment. *Child Development, 67,* 2478–2492.

Zelazo, P. R., Zelazo, N. A., & Kolb, S. (1972). "Walking" in the newborn. *Science, 176,* 314–315.

Zeskind, P. S., & Barr, R. G. (1997). Acoustic characteristics of naturally occurring cries of infants with "colic." *Child Development, 68,* 394–403.

Zeskind, P. S., & Ramey, C. T. (1981). Preventing intellectual and interactional sequelae of fetal malnutrition: A longitudinal, transactional, and synergistic approach to development. *Child Development, 52,* 213–218.

Zhang, R., & Yu, Y. (2002). A study of children's coordinational ability for outcome and intention information. *Psychological Science (China), 25,* 527–530.

Zigler, E., & Finn-Stevenson, M. (1993). *Children in a changing world: Developmental and social issues.* Pacific Grove, CA: Brooks/Cole.

Zigler, E. F., & Hodapp, R. M. (1991). Behavioral functioning in individuals with mental retardation. *Annual Review of Psychology, 42,* 29–50.

Zigler, E. F., & Styfco, S. J. (1993). Using research and theory to justify and inform Head Start expansion. *Social Policy Report, Society for Research in Child Development, 7*(2), 1–21.

Zill, N., Moore, K. A., Smith, E. W., Stief, T., & Coiro, M. J. (1995). The life circumstances and development of children in welfare families: A profile based on national survey data. In P. L. Chase-Lansdale & J. Brooks-Gunn (Eds.), *Escape from poverty: What makes a difference for children?* (pp. 39–59). Cambridge, England: Cambridge University Press.

Zill, N., & Nord, C. W. (1994). *Running in place: How American families are faring in a changing economy and an individualistic society.* Washington, DC: Child Trends.

Zimmerman, M., Copeland, L., Shope, J., & Dielman, T. (1997). A longitudinal study of self-esteem: Implications for adolescent development. *Journal of Youth & Adolescence, 26,* 117–141.

Zimmermann, P. (2004). Attachment representations and characteristics of friendship relations during adolescence. *Journal of Experimental Child Psychology, 88,* 83–101.

Zoccolillo, M. (1993). Gender and the development of conduct disorder. *Development and Psychopathology, 5*, 65–78.

Zoghbi, H. (2003). Postnatal neurodevelopmental disorders. *Science, 302*, 826–830.

Zola, S., & Squire, L. (2003). Genetics of childhood disorders: Learning and memory: Multiple memory systems. *Journal of the American Academy of Child & Adolescent Psychiatry, 42*, 504–506.

Zuloaga, D., Puts, D., Jordan, C., & Breedlove, S. (2008). The role of androgen receptors in the masculinization of brain and behavior: What we've learned from the testicular feminization mutation. *Hormones and Behavior, 53*, 613–626.

Photo Credits

1: © Andersen Ross/Getty Images/Blend Images
3: Archives of the History of American History, Akron, OH
4: (left) © Pablo Paul/Alamy; (right) © David Young-Wolff/PhotoEdit
6: © David Young-Wolff/PhotoEdit
9: © Robert Nickelsberg/Getty Images
11: (top left) © Michael Krasowitz/Taxi/Getty Images; (top right) © Mel Yates/Taxi/Getty Images; (bottom) © Liane/ Superstock
13: © Wayne Ford
16: © Ken Hayman/Stockphoto.com
17: © Andersen Ross/Getty Images/Blend Images
22: © Laura Dwight Photography
26: © Jeremy Horner/Corbis
30: © Saturn Stills/SPL/Photo Researchers, Inc.
32: (top) Courtesy of Lisa McClellan; (bottom) © Leroy Francis/SPL/Photo Researchers, Inc.
38: (clockwise from top) © Motta & Van Blerkon/Photo Researchers, Inc.; © Lennart Nilsson/A Child is Born/Bonnierforlagen AB; © Claude Edelmann/Photo Researchers, Inc.; © Petit Format/Photo Researchers, Inc.; © James Stevenson/Photo Researchers, Inc.; © Petit Format/Photo Researchers, Inc.
41: (top) Courtesy of Dr. Oliver Walusinski, www.yawning.info; (bottom) Reprinted with permission of Anderson Publishing Ltd. From Brown, S.D., Estroff, J.A., & Barnewolt, C.E. (2004). Fetal MRI. *Applied Radiology*, 33(2), pp. 9–25, Fig. 2, Copyright © Anderson Publishing Ltd.
46: © Saturn Stills/SPL/Photo Researchers, Inc.
47: © moodboard/Alamy
51: (left) © George Steinmetz Photography; (right) © George Steinmetz Photography
59: © Elizabeth Crews/The Image Works
60: AP Images/Loyola University Health System, HO
61: © RIA Novosti /Topham /The Image Works
62: (top) © David Young-Wolff/Alamy; (bottom) © Suzanne Arms/ The Image Works
67: © ERproductions Ltd/Getty Images/Blend Images
68: (top) © Elizabeth Crews/The Image Works; (bottom) © Laura Dwight Photography
73: © Elizabeth Crews/The Image Works
76: (left) © Laura Dwight Photography; (right) © Laura Dwight Photography
77: © Lynne J. Weinstein/Woodfin Camp & Associates
79: © Richard Meats/Getty Images/Stone
85: © Jack Hollingsworth/Getty Images/Photodisc
86: © Zena Holloway/Getty Images/Taxi
96: (left to right) © Laura Dwight Photography; © Jack Hollingsworth Getty Images/Photodisc; © Jose Luis Pelaez/Getty Images/Iconica
98: © Journal-Courier/Steve Warmowski /The Image Works
103: © V.C.L./Taxi/Getty Images
107: © Ed Quinn/Corbis
109: © Jose Luis Pelaez, Inc./Blend Images/Corbis
111: © Digital Vision/Alamy
121: © Michael Newman/PhotoEdit
123: © Ellen Senisi /The Image Works

125: © Michael Newman/PhotoEdit
127: Steiner, J.E., "Human Facial Expressions in Response to Taste and Smell Stimulation," in *Advances in Child Development and Behavior*, Vol. 13, H.W. Reese and L.P. Lipsitt, eds. © 1979 by Academic Press. By permission.
128: © Elizabeth Crews Photography
129: © Mark Richards/PhotoEdit
132: © Ariel Skelley/Blend/photolibrary
133: © David Young-Wolff/PhotoEdit
136: © Ruth Jenkinson/Getty Images/Dorling Kindersley
137: © Jorgen Schytte/Peter Arnold Inc.
139: Courtesy Paul Ekman
142: © Bob Daemmrich/The Image Works
144: © Ellen B. Senisi/The Image Works
148: © Elizabeth Crews/The Image Works
149: © Carolyn Rovee-Collier
150: © Ericka McConnell/Taxi/Getty Images
155: (top) © Sean Sprague/The Image Works; (bottom) © David Young-Wolff/PhotoEdit
159: © Derke/O'Hara/Stone/Getty Images
162: © Elizabeth Crews/The Image Works
173: © Bob Daemmrich/The Image Works
176: © Albert Fanning/The Image Works
181: © Laura Dwight/PhotoEdit
182: © Ellen Senisi/The Image Works
183: © Peter Hvizdak/The Image Works
187: © Albert Fanning/The Image Works
189: © Paul Conklin/PhotoEdit
194: © Cindy Charles/PhotoEdit
200: © Mike Greenlar/Syracuse Newspapers/The Image Works
203: © Creatas/Photolibrary
204: © H.S. Terrace/Anthro-Photo File
205: © Larry Williams/Corbis
209: (top) © Creatas/Photolibrary; (bottom) © F. Hache/Explorer/ Photo Researchers, Inc.
211: © David Young-Wolff/PhotoEdit
215: © S. Villager/Explorer/Photo Researchers, Inc.
221: © Larry Mangino/The Image Works
222: © Ellen B. Senisi
225: © Michael Newman/PhotoEdit
229: © Laura Dwight/PhotoEdit
232: © Don Mason/Corbis
234: © Laura Dwight/PhotoEdit
236: © Joshua Zuckerman/Workbook Stock/Jupiter Images
238: © Geri Enberg/The Image Works
240: © SW Productions/Photodisc/Getty Images
242: © Peter Beck/Corbis
246: © Ellen B. Senisi/The Image Works
248: © Eric Fowke/PhotoEdit
255: AP Images/Paul Battaglia
257: © Camille Tokerud/Getty Images/Stone
261: © Bob Daemmrich/PhotoEdit

262: © Jeff Greenberg/The Image Works
265: (top) © Bananastock/Superstock; (bottom) © Bob Daemmrich/
PhotoEdit
266: © Mark Richards/PhotoEdit
268: © Michael Newman/PhotoEdit
270: © Myrleen Ferguson Cate/PhotoEdit
272: © Laura Dwight Photography
275: © Robert W. Ginn/Index Stock/Jupiter Images
276: AP Images/Paul Battaglia
282: © Gary Conner/Jupiter Images
283: © James Marshall/The Image Works
286: © UpperCut Images/Alamy
287: © Laura Dwight/Creative Eye/MIRA.com
288: © Myrleen Ferguson Cate/PhotoEdit
289: © Lisette Le Bon/Superstock
293: © Gary Conner/Jupiter Images
294: © age fotostock/Superstock
297: © Ellen B. Senisi/The Image Works
299: © Whitaker, Ross/Image Bank/Getty Images
300: © Mark Hall/Getty Images/Taxi
302: (top) © Spencer Grant/PhotoEdit; (bottom) © Image Source/
Superstock
306: © Bob Daemmrich/The Image Works
312: © Tom Prettyman/PhotoEdit
315: © David Young-Wolff/PhotoEdit
318: © David Young-Wolff/PhotoEdit
320: (left) ©Tom Prettyman/PhotoEdit; (right) © David Grossman/
The Image Works
327: © Kuttig-People/Alamy
328: © Kapoor Baldev/Sygma/Corbis
332: © Esbin-Anderson/The Image Works
336: © Asia Images Group/photolibrary
338: AP Images
339: © Asia Images Group/photolibrary
344: © Bonnie Kamin/PhotoEdit
349: © Will & Deni McIntyre/Photo Researchers, Inc.
351: © Yvan Dubé/Alamy
352: © Bill Bachmann/PhotoEdit
353: © GoGo Images Corporation/Alamy

355: (top) © Michael Newman/PhotoEdit ; (bottom) © Cindy Charles/
PhotoEdit
357: (left) © David Young-Wolff/PhotoEdit; (right) © Bob Daemmrich/
The Image Works
358: © Robert Giroux/Getty Images
361: © Bob Daemmrich/The Image Works
363: © Dennis MacDonald/PhotoEdit
371: © Chris Ware/The Image Works
375: © Barros & Barros/Image Bank/Getty Images
376: © David Young-Wolffe/PhotoEdit
377: © Bob Daemmrich/The Image Works
378: © Will Hart/PhotoEdit
380: © Corbis/SuperStock
382: © Bob Daemmrich/The Image Works
386: © Mark Ludak/The Image Works
388: © Reuters/Chip East/Landov
389: © The Record/MCT/Landov
390: © Tony Freeman/PhotoEdit
392: © JUPITERIMAGES/Creatas/Alamy
396: © Laura Dwight Photography
398: © Esbin Anderson/The Image Works
400: © David Young-Wolffe/PhotoEdit
404: © David Young-Wolff/PhotoEdit
407: © Thinkstock/Superstock
409: © Jocelyn Lee
410: © keith morris/Alamy
416: © Ellen B. Senisis/The Image Works
417: © Dal Bayles/The New York Times/Redux
419: © age fotostock/Superstock
422: © Laura Dwight Photography
426: © Lisette Le Bon/Superstock
428: © Laura Dwight Photography
432: © Ben Blankenburg/Corbis
435: © Lisette Le Bon/Superstock
439: © Spencer Grant/PhotoEdit
440: © David Young-Wolff/PhotoEdit
442: © Elizabeth Crews/The Image Works
444: © Ellen B. Senisi
447: © Bruce Robertson/Photo Researchers, Inc.

Name Index

Abbott, R., 223
Abdel-Khalek, A., 188
Abdelrahman, A., 117
Abe, J., 132, 259
Abela, J., 401
Abelson, R., 314
Aber, J. L., 385
Aboud, F. E., 265, 273, 315
Abramovitch, R., 304
Abrams, D., 114
Accardo, P., 44
Achenbach, T., 400
Adab, N., 49
Adachi, M., 132
Adam, E., 296
Adams, G. R., 264
Adams, M. J., 222, 223
Addison, T., 132
Addy, R., 104
Adelman, W., 100, 101
Adesman, A. R., 46
Adler, S., 148
Adolph, K., 73
Adolph, K. E., 5
Agnew, J., 224
Ahadi, S., 231, 237
Ahmed, E., 308
Aihara, M., 88
Aiken, L., 200
Ainsworth, M., 283, 284, 287, 291, 292, 309
Ainsworth, M. D. S., 292, 343
Akhtar, N., 218
Aksan, N., 259, 319, 323
Aksu-Koc, A. A., 221
Alan Guttmacher Institute, 106
Alansky, J., 294
Albers, L., 63
Alexander, K., 372
Alford, K., 266
Aligne, C., 51
Allen, C., 50
Allen, J., 291, 299
Allen, M., 225
Allesandri, S. M., 258
Alleva, E., 63
Allik, J., 234
Al Otaiba, S., 222
Alsaker, F., 269
Alspaugh, J., 373, 374

Alt, M., 220
Altwerger, B., 223
Álvarez, J., 347
Alwin, J., 365
Amatea, E., 351
Amato, P. R., 44, 45, 47, 355, 385
Amato, S., 36, 53
Ambert, A., 354
Ambridge, B., 172
Ambuel, B., 105
American Academy of Pedi-atrics (AAP), 78, 79, 80
American College of Obstetri-cians and Gynecologists (ACOG), 49, 61, 63, 65
American Demographics, 379
American Psychiatric Associa-tion, 410
American Psychological Associ-ation, 391
Amso, D., 67, 68
Anastasia, M. L., 67
Anderman, E., 373, 374
Anderman, L., 374
Anderson, C., 381
Anderson, F., 343
Anderson, M., 197
Anderson, R., 225
Anderson, S., 101
Andersson, B., 365
Andonotopo, W., 40, 41, 43
Andreou, E., 308
Andresen, J., 183
Andreucci, C., 151
Andrews, G., 161
Angelini, L., 170
Anglin, J., 210, 214
Angold, A., 102
Anisfeld, M., 150
Anker, M., 80
Annett, M., 93
Anteunis, I., 124
Anthony, J., 222
Antonishak, J., 299
Aoki, S., 88
Apgar, V., 65
Araki, T., 88
Aranha, M., 299
Arcus, D., 232
Ardila-Rey, A., 274

Arendt, R., 52
Armbruster, B., 223
Armstrong, M., 115
Armstrong, T., 319, 331
Arnedt, C., 106
Arnold, G., 45
Arnold, M., 330
Aronson, J., 192
Aronson, S., 358
Arterberry, M., 122, 129
Asendorpf, J., 234
Ashby, J., 243
Asher, S., 320
Asher, S. R., 299
Ashiabi, G., 114
Ashmead, D., 270
Aslin, R., 7, 126
Aslin, R. N., 217
Associated Press, 59
Astington, J., 154, 433
Astington, J. W., 153, 171
Atkinson, J., 82, 83
Augustyn, M., 52
Austin, M., 405
Austin, S., 106
Austin, W., 356
Avis, J., 155
Azumendi, G., 40, 41, 43

Bachman, H., 370
Bachman, J., 115, 117, 376
Bachorowski, J., 138
Baer, J., 51, 52
Bagwell, C. L., 297, 298
Bahrick, L., 132, 138
Bai, J., 50
Bailey, B., 383
Bailey, J., 106, 107, 353
Bailey, S., 354
Baillargeon, R., 135, 148
Bakeman, R., 303
Baker, C., 274
Baker, D., 262
Baker, E., 222
Baker, S., 234
Baldessarini, R., 411
Baldwin, D., 139
Ball, E., 222
Bandura, A., 17, 239, 240, 241, 257, 275, 324, 380

Bank, L., 433
Barbaranelli, C., 241
Barber, B., 302, 355
Barcelo, H., 307
Barenboim, C., 316
Barker, E., 76
Barkley, R., 401
Barner, J., 405
Barnes, H., 345
Barnett, D., 110
Barnett, W. S., 189
Barnewolf, C., 41
Baron-Cohen, S., 42
Barr, H., 51, 52
Barresi, J., 48
Barrett, G. V., 378
Barrow, F., 115
Barry, D., 392
Bartels, M., 182, 309
Barth, R., 50
Bartlett, E., 209, 210
Bartley, M., 342
Basham, P., 378, 379
Basham, R. B., 358
Basinger, K., 329
Baskirk, A., 313
Bass, E., 74
Basso, G., 382
Bates, E., 205, 206, 207, 208, 209, 211, 220, 221, 429
Bates, J., 231, 299, 365
Bates, J. E., 239, 299, 342, 367, 384
Bathurst, K., 357, 418
Batterson, V., 124
Bauman, A., 50
Baumeister, A., 415
Baumeister, R., 407
Baumgardner, J., 380
Bauminger, N., 295
Baumrind, D., 344, 346
Baydar, N., 193
Bayley, N., 180, 181
Bear, G. C., 330
Beardslee, W., 400
Beauchaine, T., 400
Bearinger, L., 108
Beautrais, A., 441
Beaver, K., 63
Bechtoldt, H., 380, 381

Schaal, B., 43
Schaller, M., 317
Schank, R. C., 314
Schatschneider, C., 168, 222
Schechter, R., 420
Scheres, A., 404
Schermerhorn, A., 285
Schieve, L., 32
Schiller, M., 294
Schipper, E., 259
Schlagmuller, M., 170
Schlundt, B., 124
Schmidt, L., 132, 237
Schmitz, S., 260
Schneider, B., 194, 308
Schneider, M., 389
Schneider, M. L., 55
Schneider, P. A., 72
Schneider, W., 148, 170, 173, 198
Schneiderman, M., 216
Schnyder, U., 410
Schonert-Reichl, K., 330
Schoppe-Sullivan, S., 294
Schothorst, P., 260
Schott, J., 70
Schraf, M., 298, 320
Schrimshaw, E., 303
Schroger, E., 90
Schuetze, P., 110
Schulenberg, J., 115, 117, 376
Schultz, R. W., 95, 96
Schulz, H. R., 70
Schumm, W., 353
Schwanenflugel, P., 172
Schwartz, C. E., 236, 237
Schwartz, D., 308, 309
Schwartz, R. M., 67
Schwarz, J. C., 347
Schwean, V., 307
Schwebel, D., 154
Schweinle, A., 132
Scialli, A., 54
Scofield, J., 209
Scollon, R., 207
Scott, C., 81
Scott, J., 46, 344, 356
Scuccimarri, C., 106
Sears, R. R., 240
Sebanc, A., 297
Segal, N., 185
Segers, E., 222
Seguin, J., 183
Seidman, E., 269
Seifer, R., 294
Sekino, Y., 260
Selbst, S., 81, 110
Self, P. A., 65
Seligman, S., 249
Selman, R. L., 313, 320, 330
Serbin, L., 400
Serbin, L. A., 272, 273
Serdula, M., 112
Sergeant, J., 404, 406
Serpell, R., 194, 222

Shaffer, D., 412, 413
Shah, M., 93
Shanahan, M., 376, 385
Shantz, C. U., 316
Sharma, A., 104
Sharma, V., 104
Sharpe, P., 194
Shatz, M., 217
Shaver, P., 295
Shaw, D., 354
Shaw, D. S., 406
Shayer, M., 143, 196
Shaywitz, B. A., 416
Shaywitz, S., 416
Shaywitz, S. E., 416
Shearer, M., 54
Sheese, R., 156
Shell, R., 319
Shenfield, T., 225
Sherblom, S., 333
Sherry, S., 409
Shields, A., 110
Shields, M., 93, 114, 383
Shillcock, R., 214
Shimmin, H. S., 271
Shin, L., 236
Shin, N., 286
Shiner, R., 232, 237
Shirley, L., 270
Shochat, L., 380
Shope, J., 269
Shore, B., 172, 417
Shore, C., 205, 218, 221
Shorr, S. I., 298
Shu, H., 223
Shulman, C., 154
Shulman, S., 252
Shum, D., 67
Shupe, A., 43
Siefen, G., 116, 117
Siegel, L., 222
Siegler, R., 157, 160
Siemens, L., 170
Sigman, M., 179, 187, 420
Silbereisen, R., 332
Silk, J., 289, 290
Silva, P., 262, 309
Silva, P. A., 183
Silverberg, S. B., 290
Silvia, P., 200
Simcock, G., 169
Simmens, S., 42
Simmons, R. G., 438
Simon, T., 177
Simons, R. L., 342, 358
Simonsen, H., 214
Simpkins, S., 275
Simutis, Z. M., 241
Singelis, T., 266
Singer, J., 217
Singer, L., 52
Singer, L. T., 191
Singh, A., 112
Singh, G. K., 117
Singh, S., 105

Sinigaglia, C., 343
Siperstein, G., 374
Sippola, L., 303
Skibbe, L., 187
Skinner, B. F., 16, 216, 323
Skwarchuk, S., 210
Slaby, R. G., 271, 380
Slanetz, P. J., 404
Slaughter-Defoe, D., 189
Slawinski, J. L., 170
Slobin, D., 217, 218, 221
Slobin, D. I., 221
Slowiaczek, M. L., 372
Smart, L., 407
Smetana, J. G., 330, 333
Smith, A., 52, 289
Smith, B., 117
Smith, C., 383, 384, 407
Smith, D., 49
Smith, E. W., 385
Smith, G., 295
Smith, I., 154
Smith, J. R., 385
Smith, K., 68, 367
Smith, L., 373
Smith, R., 9, 387
Smolak, L., 408
Smoll, F. L., 95, 96
Smorti, M., 300
Smoski, M., 138
Smyth, B., 356
Snarey, J. R., 328, 329
Snidman, N., 232, 237
Snow, C., 216
Society for Assisted Reproductive Technology (SART), 32
Soderstrom, M., 217
Sola, A., 61, 67, 70
Solomon, J., 291, 292
Soltis, J., 72
Somers, C., 105
Song, M., 193
Sonnenschein, S., 215
Sonuga-Barke, E., 341
Sorace, A., 214
Sorell, G., 303
Soriano, F. I., 388
Sotelo, M., 330
Soto, C., 234, 235
Sourander, A., 50
Soussignan, R., 43
Sowell, E., 90
Spangler, G., 293
Sparks, C., 271
Spelke, E., 5, 133, 134, 148
Spence, I., 381
Spence, J., 277
Spence, J. T., 44
Spence, M. J., 44
Spencer, M., 289
Spencer, N., 56
Spiegel, A. N., 422
Spieker, S., 138
Spindler, A., 410

Spinrad, T., 317
Spirito, A., 109, 412
Spock, B., 2
Spreen, O., 87, 88, 90, 91
Spurrell, E., 54
Squire, L., 91
Sroufe, A., 292, 294, 295, 445, 446
Sroufe, L., 252
Sroufe, L. A., 77, 259, 343, 389, 441, 444
Stabile, M., 114, 383
Stainback, S., 420
Stainback, W., 420
Stallings, V., 78, 79, 112
Stansfield, S., 342
Stanton, M., 74
Stanton, W. R., 290
Stapleton, L., 369
Starr, J., 182, 196
Stattin, H., 184
Stedron, J., 414
Steele, C., 192
Steele, H., 433
Steele, J., 93
Steele, M., 296
Stein, J., 377
Stein, R., 385
Steinberg, E., 197
Steinberg, L., 115, 289, 290, 346, 347, 348, 349, 367, 372, 375, 376, 377, 407, 439
Steinberg, M. S., 372
Steiner, J. E., 127
Stelzl, I., 373
Sternberg, K. J., 364
Sternberg, R., 14, 181, 198, 199
Sternberg, R. J., 198
Stevenson, H. W., 194, 392
Stevenson-Hinde, J., 299
Stewart, A. L., 330
Stewart, M. I., 297
Stewart, P., 389
Stewart, R. B., 304
Stewart, S. L., 237
Stief, T., 385
Stifter, C., 404
Stigler, J. W., 194
St. James-Roberts, I., 72
Stjernqvist, K., 295
Stone, M., 302
Stoneman, Z., 372
Story, M., 113
Strange, C., 258
Straus, M. A., 345
Strauss, S., 223
Strayer, F. F., 274
Strayer, J., 319
Streigel-Moore, R., 408
Streissguth, A., 51, 52
Striano, T., 257
Strizenec, M., 200
Stroganova, T., 93
Stunkard, A. J., 112
Sturge-Apple, M., 400

Subject Index

Cues
  binocular/monocular, 128, 129
  emotional, 137–139
  interposition, 128
  kinetic, 128–129
  social, 137–139
Culture, 8, 393. *See also* Ethnicity; *specific cultures*
  ADHD and, 402
  attachment quality and, 292–293
  elementary school experiences and, 373, 436
  facial expressions and, 139
  false belief tasks and, 155–156
  formal operational thinking and, 166
  infant caretaking and, 288
  IQ scores and, 191–195
  language development and, 220–221
  moral reasoning and, 329
  object permanence and, 137
  parent-child bond and, 286
  prosocial reasoning and, 331–332
  sex-role stereotypes and, 273–274
  temperament and, 232–233
  vocabulary growth and, 208
Cumulative deficit, 187
CVS, 46
Cytomegalovirus (CMV), 49, 447

Day-care centers, 362, 363–366
Deafness, 92, 206
Decalage, horizontal, 159–160
Decentration, 151, 431
Decomposition strategy, 160
Deductive logic, 158, 162–164
Defense mechanisms, 12
Deferred imitation, 150
Deficiency
  production, 169
  utilization, 170
Deficit, cumulative, 187
Delinquency, 235, 407–408
Dendrites, 40, 88, 89
Denver Developmental Screening Test, 181
Deoxyribonucleic acid (DNA), 32
Dependent variable, 24
Depression, 410–413
  parental, 55, 138, 341–342, 358
  self-esteem and, 270
Depth perception, 124, 128–129
Derived words, 210
DES, 107
Descriptions of others, 314–316

Descriptive methods, of research, 22–23, 27
Desensitization, systematic, 16
Designs, research, 21–22, 27
Detached attachment, 296
Detached/avoidant pattern, 291–293
Developmental approaches, to education, 368
Developmental disability, 413–415
Developmental leaps, 426. *See also* Dilemmas
Developmental psychopathology, 400–401
Developmental science, 2, 20–21
Developmental stages, 446
Developmental theories, 11–20
Developmentally appropriate practices, 369
Dialogic reading, 222
Diarrhea, in infants, 79–80
Diet. *See* Nutrition
Diethylstilbestrol (DES), 107
Difficult child, 76–77, 231, 232, 237, 238, 260, 294
Dilation, 62
Dilemmas, 247–248, 426, 445–446
Disabilities
  developmental, 413–415
  theory of mind and, 154
Discontinuity-continuity issue, 418
Dishabituation, 75–76
Dismissing attachment, 296
Disorganized/disoriented pattern, 291–292
Disruptive behavior disorders, 398, 405–408
Divergent thinking, 200
Divorce, parental, 251, 354–356, 359
Dizygotic twins, 36. *See also* Twin studies
DNA, 32
Dominance
  left-/right-brain, 91–92
  mixed, 91
Dominant/recessive pattern of inheritance, 34, 45–46
Dopamine, 88
Down syndrome, 46, 70
Dropouts, 376–378
Drugs
  adolescent use of, 102, 104, 115–117, 377
  maternal use of, 32, 50–53, 61
Dynamic systems theory, 69

Ear infections, 80–81
Early childhood education, 368–371

Easy child, 76, 231, 294
Eating disorders, 113, 408–410
Eclecticism, 20
Ecological perspective, 8–9
Education. *See* School(s)
Education for All Handicapped Children Act, 419
Education of the Handicapped Act of 1986, 419
Effacement, 62
Efficiency, operational, 156
Effortful control, 232, 233, 319, 404
Ego, 12
Ego ideal, 323
Ego integrity vs. despair, 247
Egocentric empathy, 318
Egocentric speech, 157, 215
Egocentrism, 151–153, 154
8-4 system, 373
Elaboration, 169
ELBW, 66
Electronic multitasking, 382–383
Elementary school years, 433–436
  attachment in, 289
  education in, 233–235, 251
  health in, 108–115, 117–118
  peer relationships in, 297–298
  Piaget's view of, 158–160. *See also* Concrete operations stage
  Siegler's view of, 160–161
ELLs, 224–226
Embryonic stage, 37–39, 40
Emotion
  expression of, 77–78, 137–139
  knowledge of, 317–319
  moral, 322–323
  regulation of, 259–260, 298
  sex-role, 274
Emotional availability, of caretaker, 291
Emotional cues, 137–139
Emotional disturbances, 398, 408–413
Emotional intelligence, 184
Emotional Intelligence (Goleman), 317
Emotional self, 259–260
Emotional stability, 233–235, 251
Emotionality, 232, 233
Empathy, 317–319
Empiricism, 2–4, 122, 124–125. *See also* Nature-nurture debate
Employment
  parental, 356–358
  teenaged, 376
Encoding, 14

Endocrine system, 97–102
Endomorphic body type, 101
Endorphins, 88
Engagement, student, 375–378
English-as-a-second-language (ESL) programs, 226
English-language learners (ELLs), 224–226
Enmeshed attachment, 296
Entertainment media, and aggression, 380, 381
Environment, 443–445
  electronic multitasking, 382–383
  empathy and, 319
  family, in infancy, 430
  heredity and, 2–4, 6, 18, 190–191, 442–443
  intelligence and, 185–191, 196
  linguistic, 216–217
  models of influence of, 7
  nonshared, 187–188
  personality/temperament and, 230, 237–238, 250–252
  prenatal development and, 50
  shared, 186
Environmental influence, model of (Aslin), 7
Environmental theories, of language development, 216–217, 443
Epidural blocks, 61
Episiotemy, 61
Equilibration, 13, 145, 146
ESL programs, 226
Estradiol, 98, 99
Ethics, and research, 26–27
Ethnic group, 315, 388
Ethnic identity, 264–267
Ethnicity. *See also* Culture
  achievement/IQ scores and, 191–195
  ADHD and, 403–404
  family structure and, 352, 353–354
  genetic disorders and, 45
  identity and, 264–267
  infant mortality and, 82–83
  parenting styles and, 348–350
  poverty rates and, 384
  race and, 388–392
  sexual activity and, 103
  teenage pregnancy and, 105–106
Ethnography, 26
Evidence, anecdotal, 25
Excessive weight gain, 111–113
Executive processing, 88, 171–173
Existential intelligence, 199–200
Exosystems, 338–339

Expansion pattern, of speech, 217
Expectancies. See Schemas
Experience
  internal models of, 6–7
  in sensorimotor stage, 146–147
  timing of, 5
Experiential intelligence, 198–199
Experimental group, 24
Experiments, 23–25, 27
Expertise, and memory, 172–173
Expressive language, 205
Expressive style, of language acquisition, 221
Expressivity, of genes, 34
Extended family, 352, 389
Extensive relationships, 298
External locus of control, 243
Externalizing problems, 398, 405–408
Extinction, of response, 17, 240
Extraversion, 233–235
Extremely low birth weight (ELBW), 66
Eye color, 35

Fable, personal, 166
Facial expressions, 139, 150, 287
Facilitation, 443
Facilitation effect, 124
Facilitative environment, 7, 9–10
Fallopian tube, 31
False belief principle, 153, 154, 155–156
Family. See also Family interaction; Family structure; Family systems theory
  African American culture and, 389–390
  Asian American culture and, 391–392
  blended, 351
  Hispanic American culture and, 391
  infancy and, 430
  IQ scores and, 186–188
  poverty and, 384–385
  preschool years and, 433
Family interaction
  dimensions of, 339–345
  model of (Belsky), 338
Family structure, 350–354
Family systems theory, 337–338. See also Family interaction; Family structure
FAS, 51
Fast-mapping, 209–210
Fast Track Project, 319
Fat, body, 95–96

Father
  at delivery, 62
  relationship of with child, 62
Fear of strangers, 287–288
Femininity, 278
Feminization, 42
Fertility drugs, 32
Fetal alcohol syndrome (FAS), 51
Fetal-maternal medicine, 50
Fetal stage, 38, 39
Fetoscopy, 46
Fetus, 38–44. See also Prenatal development
Fictive kin, 391
Figurative schemes, 144–145
Fine motor skills, 96–97
5-3-4 system, 373
Fixation, 245, 248
Fluency, computational, 194
Flynn effect, 178, 179
Focus on one or more figures phase, 287
Folic acid, 53
Follicle-stimulating hormone (FSH), 98
Fontanels, 95
Foreclosure, identity, 263, 264
Formal operations stage (Piaget), 146, 161–166
Fragile-X syndrome, 46, 419
Fraternal twins, 36. See also Twin studies
Friendships
  describing, 319–321
  reciprocal, 297–298
Frontal lobes, 87, 88, 90, 440
FSH, 98
Full scale IQ, 179
Fusion, binocular, 129

Gametes, 32–33. See also Ovum; Sperm
Gay families, 353
Gender, 255, 270–272. See also Gender role; Sex differences
Gender constancy, 271–272
Gender identity, 271
Gender role, 270, 272–279, 433
Gender schema theory, 276–278, 433
Gender stability, 271
General anesthesia, 61
Generativity vs. stagnation, 247
Genes, 32–33. See also Genetics
  disorders of, 44–46
  dominant/recessive, 34, 45–46
  environment and, 2–4, 6
  lateralization and, 91
Genetics
  behavior, 6, 400

heredity and, 34–36
  personality and, 236–239
Genital stage, 12, 245, 246
Genomic imprinting, 35–36
Genotype, 34
Germ cells. See Gametes; Ovum; Sperm
German measles, 48–49
Germinal stage, 37, 38
Gestational age, 67
Gestures, and language development, 205–206, 218
GH, 98
Giftedness, 417–418
Glial cells, 40, 88
Global empathy, 317–318
Glutamate, 127–128
Goal-corrected partnership, 289, 340–341
Goals, ability/task, 374
Gonadotrophic hormones, 98
Gonorrhea, 49
Good boy/nice girl stage, 327, 328, 329
Goodness-of-fit, 231, 294
Grammar development, 211–214
Grandparents, 352, 362
Grasp reflex, 68, 69
Gross motor skills, 96–97
Group differences
  in intelligence, 191–196
  in language development, 219–221
Growth
  of body, 93–102, 109
  of brain, 87–93
  of vocabulary, 207–211
Growth curve, 94, 109
Growth hormone (GH), 98, 99
Growth spurts, 87–88, 94–95, 101

Habituation, 75
  IQ and, 197
  memory and, 148
  perception and, 123, 130
Hair type, 34
Handedness, 92–93
Health
  in childhood/adolescence, 108–118
  in early infancy, 78–83
Hearing, 126–127
Hedonism, naïve, 326–327, 328, 329
Hedonistic reasoning, 331
Height, and heredity, 35
Heinz dilemma (Kohlberg), 325, 326–327, 328, 333
Hemispheres, of brain, 91–93
Hemophilia, 46

Heredity. See also Twin studies
  environment and, 2–4, 6, 18, 190–191, 442–443
  patterns of, 34–36
Heroin, 52–53
Herpes virus, 49
Heterosexuality, 106–107, 108, 302–303
Heterozygous genetic pattern, 34
Heuristic value, 19
HGP, 33
High-risk behavior, 115
Hippocampus, 91
Hispanic American culture, 390–391
History-graded changes, normative, 10–11
HIV/AIDS, 49, 105
Holophrases, 211–212
Homegrown stereotypes, 265
Homeschooling, 378–379
Homicide rate, 118
Homosexuality, 106–108, 303
Homozygous genetic pattern, 34
Horizontal decalage, 159–160
Hormones, 98–102, 439–440. See also Androgens
  adolescent sexual behavior and, 102–104
  sex-role development and, 278–279
  spatial abilities and, 195–196
Hostile aggression, 306
HPV, 104–105
Human Genome Project (HGP), 33
Human papilloma virus (HPV), 104–105
Huntington's disease, 45
Hyperplasia, congenital adrenal, 42
Hypotheses, 20–21
Hypothetico-deductive reasoning, 162–164, 165, 166

Id, 12
Ideal, ego, 323
Idealism, 3, 163, 164
Identical twins, 36. See also Twin studies
Identification process, 246
Identity
  in adolescence, 261–267, 274–275
  alternating bicultural, 265
  blended bicultural, 265, 266
  gender, 271
  occupational, 248
  vs. role confusion, 247, 248, 263–264
  sexual, 248
  statuses of (Marcia), 263–264
Identity prototype, 302

Mental retardation (MR), 413–415
Mental rotation task, 195
Mercury, and prenatal development, 50
Mesomorphic body type, 101
Metacognition, 171–173
Metalinguistic ability, 225
Metamemory, 170, 171–173
Methadone, 52–53
Methylphenidate, 404–405
Microsystems, 338–339
Midbrain, 87
Middle childhood. *See* Elementary school years
Min strategy, 160
Mind, theory of, 153–156, 432
Mirror neurons, 343
Mitochondria, 36
Mitochondrial inheritance, 36
Mitosis, 32
Mixed dominance, 91
MLU, 219–220
Modeling. *See* Observational learning
Monoamine, 404
Monocular cues, 128, 129
Monozygotic twins, 36. *See also* Twin studies
Montessori method, 368
Moral behavior, 323–324, 330–331
Moral development, 322–333
Moral emotions, 322–323
Moral realism stage, 324–325
Moral reasoning, 324–325
  age and, 328
  cognitive development and, 329–330
  across cultures, 329
  moral behavior and, 330–331
  prosocial reasoning and, 332
Moral relativism stage, 325
Moral rules, 321–322
Morality, conventional, 326–329
Moratorium, identity, 263
Moro reflex, 68, 69, 70, 75
Mortality
  in adolescence, 117–118, 412–413
  in childhood, 117–118
  in infancy, 81–82
Mother
  attachment and, 296
  language development and, 217
  prenatal development and, 47–56
Motherese, 217
Motion parallax, 128
Motion perception, 128
Motor skills, 73–74, 96–97
MR, 413–415
Multifactorial pattern of inheritance, 35

Multiple births, 32, 36, 55
Multiple intelligences (Gardner), 199–200
Multitasking, electronic, 382–383
Muscle development, 95
Musical intelligence, 199
Mutual exclusivity constraint, 210
Mutual interpersonal expectations, relationships, and interpersonal conformity stage, 327, 328, 329
Mutuality, 285, 291–292
Myelin, 90–91
Myelination, 82, 90–91

Naïve hedonism, 326–327, 328, 329
Naïve idealism, 163, 164
Naïve psychology stage (Vygotsky), 157
Narcissism, 407–408
National Longitudinal Survey of Labor Market Experience of Youth (NLSY), 216
Nativism, 2–4, 122, 123–125, 217–218. *See also* Nature-nurture debate
Natural childbirth, 61
Naturalistic intelligence, 199
Naturalistic observation, 23, 27
Nature-nurture debate, 2–4, 6, 18, 190–191, 442–443
Needs-oriented reasoning, 331
Negative correlation, 23
Negative emotionality, 232, 233
Negative reinforcement, 16
Negatives, in grammar explosion, 213
Neglecting parenting style, 110, 299, 346, 347
Neglected children, 298–299
Neo-Piagetian theories, 156–157
Nervous system, 39–41, 87–92
Neuronal migration, 39–41
Neuronal proliferation, 39
Neurons, 39–41, 88–89, 90–91
Neuroticism, 233–235, 251
Neurotransmitters, 88
Nicotine, 50–51
NLSY, 216
No Child Left Behind, 422
Nonfocused orienting and signaling, 287
Nonnormative changes, 11, 184–191, 446–447
Nonparental care, 362–367
Nonshared environment, 187–188
Normative age-graded changes, 10, 21–26
Normative history-graded changes, 10–11

Norms, 3, 10–11, 21–26
Nutrition
  in childhood, 110–111
  in early infancy, 78
  maternal, 53–54
  plasticity and, 89–90

Oakland Growth Study, 21
Obesity, 111–113
Object constancy, 133–134, 136
Object perception, 134–137
Object permanence, 134, 137, 148, 287
Objective self, 256, 257–259
Observation
  blind, 23
  naturalistic, 23
Observational learning, 17–18, 240–242, 275–276
Observer bias, 23
Obsessive-compulsive disorder, 410
Occupational identity, 248
ODD, 405–406
Oedipus conflict, 245–246, 248–249
OM, 80–81
Open receptivity, 328
Openness/intellect, 233–235. *See also* Effortful control
Operant conditioning (Skinner), 16, 19, 20, 75
  IQ and, 194–195
  moral behavior and, 323–324
  perception and, 123
Operational efficiency, 156
Operative schemes, 145, 150
Oppositional defiant disorder (ODD), 405–406
Oral rehydration salts (ORS), 80
Oral stage, 12, 13, 245
Ordinal position, 188, 340
Organization (Piaget), 144
Organizing relationships, 316
Organogenesis, 38, 39
Original sin, 3
Ossification, 95
Otitis media (OM), 80–81
Outcome variable, 24
Over-the-counter drugs
  adolescent use of, 115–116
  prenatal development and, 53
Overextension, 209
Overregularization, 213–214
Overweight children, 112, 113
Ovum, 31–33, 37, 38

Parallax, motion, 129
Parallel play, 297
Parent-child relationship, 283–291. *See also* Attachment; Parenting styles

age and, 117, 289–291, 340–341
  communication in, 343–345
  in elementary school, 372
Parenting styles, 345–350, 359, 406, 407
Partial reinforcement, 17, 240
PATHS program, 317, 319
PBD, 411
PCBs, 50
PDDs, 418–420
Peabody Picture Vocabulary Test (PPVT), 180–181, 216
Pediatric bipolar disorder (PBD), 411
Pediatrics, 25
Peers, 296–309. *See also* Friendships
  dropping out and, 377
  in elementary school years, 297–298, 435–436
  substance abuse and, 116–117
Percentile rank, 94
Perception, 73, 74
  depth, 124, 128–129
  development of, 122–128
  habituation and, 123, 130
  intermodal, 132–133
  motion, 128
  object, 134–137
  of social signals, 137–139
  spatial, 92
  speech, 131–132
Perceptual constancies, 133–134
Perceptual reasoning index, 179
Perceptual skills, 122–123, 128–134
Performance measures, 181–182
Permissive parenting style, 346
Perry Preschool Project, 189
Personal fable, 165
Personality, 230–235. *See also* Temperament
  genetics and, 236–239
  interactive model of, 250–252
  learning and, 239–243
  nonparental care and, 365–366
Pervasive developmental disorders (PDDs), 418–420
PFC, 88, 115
Phallic stage, 12, 245–246
Phenotype, 34
Phenylalanine, 45
Phenylketonuria (PKU), 45
Phonological awareness, 222–223
Phonology, 204
Physical abuse, 110
Physical neglect, 110
Pictorial cues, 128, 129
Pituitary gland, 98
PKU, 45

gender, 276–278, 433
operative, 145, 150
Schematic learning, 75
Schemes (Piaget), 144–150
School(s)
care before/after, 362, 363–367
early childhood, 368–371
elementary, 371–373
home-, 378–379
secondary, 373–378
School refusal, 16
Scripts, social, 258–259, 314
Secondary circular reactions, 147–148
Secondary school
engagement/disengagement in, 375–378
transition to, 373–378
Secondary sex characteristics, 99, 100
Secular trend, 100, 178, 180
Secure attachment, 238, 251, 291–293, 294–295, 342–343, 441
Secure/autonomous/balanced attachment, 295–296
Secure base behavior, 287, 288–289
Selective attention, 90
Self-awareness, 257–258
Self-care children, 367
Self-concept, 7, 242, 250, 251, 256–267
Self-definitions, 258–259
of adolescent, 261–264
of school-aged child, 260–261
Self-directing speech, 215
Self-efficacy, 241, 251
Self-esteem, 267–270
delinquency and, 407
sex role and, 278
Self-scheme. See Self-concept
Semantics, 204
Semi-identical twins, 30–31
Sensation, 73, 122. See also Sensory skills
Sensation-seeking, 115, 116, 383
Sensitive period, 5
Sensorimotor stage (Piaget), 146, 147–150
Sensory deprivation, 89
Sensory memory, 14
Sensory skills, 74, 125–128
Sentences
complex, 214
early, 211–213
Separation anxiety, 287–288
Sequential designs, 21, 27
Seriation, 161
Serotonin, 88
SES, 114
Sesame Street, 361–362
Settling activities, 109

Sex, vs. gender, 255
Sex characteristics, 99, 100
Sex chromosomes, 33
Sex-determining region of the Y chromosome (SRY), 33
Sex differences
in ADHD, 403
in aggression, 307–308
in friendship quality, 298
in IQ, 195–196
parental demands and, 341
prenatal development and, 41–42
in spatial abilities, 195–196
in temperament, 271
Sex education, 105
Sex hormones, 42, 98, 99, 102–104, 278–279
Sex role, 270, 272–279
Sex-role orientation, 276–277, 433
Sex-typed behavior, 270, 274
Sexual abuse, 110
Sexual behavior, in adolescence, 102–108
Sexual identity, 248
Sexual orientation, 106–108
Sexually transmitted diseases (STDs), 49, 104–105
Shape constancy, 133–134
Shaping, 216
Shared environment, 186
Shared pretending, 156
Shared reading, 222
Shiritori, 222
Short-term memory, 14–15, 156, 167–168, 223
Short-term storage space (STSS), 156. See also Short-term memory
Shyness. See Inhibition, behavioral
Sibling relationships, 304–305
Sickle-cell disease, 45
SIDS, 81–82
Sign language, 206
Simulation theory, 343
Single-parent families, 351–352
6-3-3 system, 373
Size constancy, 133
Skin color, 35
Sleep/wakefulness cycle, 70–73, 109
Slow-to-warm-up child, 76, 231, 294
SLT, 220
Small-for-date infant, 66
Smelling, 127
Smoking
in adolescence, 117
prenatal development and, 50–51
SIDS and, 81
Sociability, 232, 233
Social clock, 10

Social cognition, 313–322
Social cognitive theory (Bandura), 17–18, 19
Social contract orientation, 327, 328, 329
Social convoy, 290
Social cues, 137–139
Social learning, and sex-role behavior, 275–276
Social referencing, 138–139, 287
Social scripts, 258–259, 314
Social skills
in early infancy, 76–78
in gifted children, 417–418
PDDs and, 418–420
in preschool years, 432–433
Social smile, 259
Social status, 298–300
Social support, 250, 251, 268–269, 358–359
Social system and conscience stage, 327, 328, 329
Social transmission, 146, 147
Socio-cultural theory (Vygotsky), 13–14, 19, 157–158
Socioeconomic status (SES), 114. See also Poverty
development and, 383–388
IQ and, 186–187, 386–387
parenting styles and, 349–350
Sound(s)
correspondence of to letters, 223, 224
location of, 126–127
speech, and infants, 131–132
Source monitoring skills, 167
Spanking, 344, 345
Spatial abilities, 195–196
Spatial cognition, 92, 199
Spatial orientation task, 195
Spatial perception, 92
Spatial visualization task, 195
Speech
infants' sounds of, 131–132
patterns of, 217
private, 215
telegraphic, 212
Speech-language therapy (SLT), 220
Speech perception, 131–132
Spelling, invented, 223
Sperm, 31–33, 37
Spina bifida, 53
Sponge/rock task (Flavell), 153, 155, 171, 271
SRY, 33
Stability, gender, 271
Stability-change issue, 4, 18
Stage 1 grammar, 211–212
Stage 2 grammar, 212–214
Stamina, 96
Stanford-Binet V, 178–180, 182
Startle reflex, 68, 69, 70, 75
States of consciousness, 70–73, 109

STDs, 49, 104–105
Stereopsis, 129. See also Depth perception
Stereotype(s)
homegrown, 265
sex-role, 272–277
temperamental, 341
Stereotype threat, 192
Sternberg Triarchic Abilities Test, 198–199
Stimulus, conditional, 15
Storage, 14
Strange Situation, 291–293
Strangers, fear of, 287–288
Stress
depression and, 412–413
maternal, 55–56
poverty and, 387–388
Stressed syllables, 131, 218
Structured immersion, 225
STSS, 156
Subjective self, 256–257
Submersion, 226
Sudden infant death syndrome (SIDS), 81–82
Suicide, 118, 411–413
Superego, 12, 323
Supernutrition, 90
Surfactant, 67
Surgency, 231
Syllables, stressed, 131, 218
Symbol use
in infancy, 147–148
in preschool years, 150–151, 432
Synapses, 40, 88–90
Synaptogenesis, 88–89, 90
Synchrony, 285, 291–292
Syntax, 204
Syphilis, 49
Systematic and explicit phonics, 223
Systematic desensitization, 16
Systematic searching, 169
Systemic analgesics, 61
Systems perspective, 337

Task goals, 374
Task persistence, 232
Tasting, 127–128
Tay-Sachs disease, 45
Teacher/child ratio, in child-care center, 366
Teenage pregnancy, 105–106
Telegraphic speech, 212
Television, impact of, 379–381
Temperament, 76–77, 231–233, 250–252
attachment and, 293–294
environment and, 230, 237–238, 250–252
family system and, 340
gender differences in, 271
stereotypes and, 341
twin studies of, 236